VINE'S DICTIONARY OF BIBLE WORDS

W. E. VINE

THOMAS NELSON PUBLISHERS
Nashville • Atlanta • London • Vancouver

Published in Nashville, Tennessee, by Thomas Nelson, Inc. Distributed in Canada by Nelson/Word Inc.

The publisher wishes to acknowledge the editorial and composition services of James A. Swanson, John R. Kohlenberger III, and Multnomah Graphics.

Library of Congress Cataloging-in-Publication Data

Vine, W. E. (William Edwy), 1873–1949.
  [Dictionary of Bible words]
  Vine's dictionary of Bible words / W. E. Vine.
    p. cm.—(Nelson's Quick reference)
  ISBN 0-7852-1169-1 (pbk.)
  1. Bible—Dictionaries. 2. Bible—Concordances, English.
 3. Greek language, Biblical—Glossaries, vocabularies, etc.
 4. Hebrew language—Glossaries, vocabularies, etc. I. Title.
II. Series.
BS440.V747 1997
220.3—dc21   96–46032
                                                      CIP

Printed in the United States of America
1 2 3 4 5 6 7 8 9 10 — 01 00 99 98 97

Publisher's Preface

The *Nelson's Quick Reference*® edition of *Vine's Dictionary of Bible Words* combines in one handy volume condensed versions of W. E. Vine's *Expository Dictionary of New Testament Words* and *Nelson's Expository Dictionary of the Old Testament* by Merrill Unger and William White, Jr. For the first time these popular works are blended into one continuous presentation.

The book is organized alphabetically by English words. These words represent the key vocabulary of biblical theology as well as other terms of interpretive importance, colorful in background, rich in cultural significance, or obscure to modern readers. Articles that treat both Hebrew-Aramaic and Greek terms are subdivided by Testament and are further subdivided by part of speech: Verb, Noun, Adjective, etc.

The key Hebrew, Aramaic, and Greek words that underlie the English words are spelled in a simplified system of transliteration, according to the tables that follow. Each word is also keyed to the widely-used numbering system of James Strong's *Exhaustive Concordance*. This cross-indexing is ideal for readers who wish to study every biblical reference to any Hebrew, Aramaic, or Greek word treated in this volume or who wish to see the word spelled in the original language or in a more exacting system of transliteration.

Each entry exposits or explains the meaning of the terms represented by the English words. The insights applied to specific biblical passages allow this book to function as an alphabetical commentary on the Bible.

This handy edition of two popular reference books is a valuable resource, making available to those with no training in biblical languages rich and interesting insights from God's Word.

The Publisher

Hebrew–Aramaic Transliteration

Consonant	Name	Transliteration	Vowel	Name	Transliteration
א	Alep	ʾ	ָ	patah	a
ב	Bet	b	ָ	qamets	a
ג	Gimel	g	ֶ	segol	e
ד	Dalet	d	ֵ	sere	e
ה	He	h	ִ	hireq	i
ו	Waw	w	ֻ	qibbuts	u
ז	Zayin	z	ֹ	holem	o
ח	Het	h	וּ	shureq	u
ט	Tet	t	ְ	shewa (vocal)	e
י	Yod	y	ֲ	hatep-patah	a
כ, ך	Kap	k	ֳ	hatep-qamets	o
ל	Lamed	l	ֱ	hatep-segol	e
מ, ם	Mem	m			
נ, ן	Nun	n			
ס	Samek	s			
ע	Ayin	ʿ			
פ, ף	Pe	p			
צ, ץ	Sade	s			
ק	Qop	q			
ר	Resh	r			
שׂ	Sin	s			
שׁ	Shin	s			
ת	Taw	t			

Greek Transliteration

Letter	Name	Transliteration	Letter	Name	Transliteration
α	alpha	a	ξ	xi	x
β	beta	b	ο	omicron	o
γ	gamma	g	π	pi	p
δ	delta	d	ρ	rho	r
ε	epsilon	e	σ, ς	sigma	s
ζ	zeta	z	τ	tau	t
η	eta	e	υ	upsilon	u or y
θ	theta	th	φ	phi	ph
ι	iota	i	χ	chi	ch
κ	kappa	k	ψ	pso	ps
λ	lambda	l	ω	omega	o
μ	mu	m		rough	h
ν	nu	n		breathing	

A

ABASE

tapeinoo (*5013*) signifies "to make low, bring low," (a) of bringing to the ground, making level, reducing to a plain, as in Luke 3:5; (b) metaphorically in the active voice, to bring to a humble condition, "to abase," 2 Cor. 11:7, and in the passive, "to be abased," Phil. 4:12; in Matt. 23:12; Luke 14:11; 18:14, the KJV has "shall be abased." It is translated "humble yourselves" in the middle voice sense in Jas. 4:10; 1 Pet. 5:6; "humble," in Matt. 18:4; 2 Cor. 12:21 and Phil. 2:8.

ABBA

abba (5) is an Aramaic word, found in Mark 14:36; Rom. 8:15 and Gal. 4:6. In the Gemara (a Rabbinical commentary on the Mishna, the traditional teaching of the Jews) it is stated that slaves were forbidden to address the head of the family by this title. It approximates to a personal name, in contrast to "Father," with which it is always joined in the NT. This is probably due to the fact that, ***abba*** having practically become a proper name, Greek-speaking Jews added the Greek word ***pater***, "father," from the language they used. ***abba*** is the word framed by the lips of infants, and betokens unreasoning trust; "father" expresses an intelligent apprehension of the relationship. The two together express the love and intelligent confidence of the child.

ABIDE, ABODE

A. Verbs.

1. ***meno*** (*3306*), used (a) of place, e.g., Matt. 10:11, metaphorically 1 John 2:19, is said of God, 1 John 4:15; Christ, John 6:56; 15:4, etc.; the Holy Spirit, John 1:32-33; 14:17; believers, John 6:56; 15:4; 1 John 4:15, etc.; the Word of God, 1 John 2:14; the truth, 2 John 2, etc.; (b) of time; it is said of believers, John 21:22-23; Phil. 1:25; 1 John 2:17; Christ, John 12:34; Heb. 7:24; the Word of God, 1 Pet. 1:23; sin, John 9:41; cities, Matt. 11:23; Heb. 13:14; bonds and afflictions, Acts 20:23; (c) of qualities; faith, hope, love, 1 Cor. 13:13; Christ's love, John 15:10; afflictions, Acts 20:23; brotherly love, Heb. 13:1; the love of God, 1 John 3:17; the truth, 2 John 2.

2. ***epimeno*** (*1961*), "to abide in, continue in, tarry," is a strengthened form of ***meno*** (***epi***, "intensive"), sometimes indicating perse-

verance in continuing, whether in evil, Rom. 6:1; 11:23, or good, Rom. 11:22; 1 Tim. 4:16.

3. *katameno* (2650), *kata*, "down" (intensive), and No. 1, is used in Acts 1:13. The word may signify "constant residence," but more probably indicates "frequent resort." In 1 Cor. 16:6, it denotes "to wait."

4. *parameno* (3887), "to remain beside," "to continue near," came to signify simply "to continue," e.g., negatively, of the Levitical priests, Heb. 7:23. In Phil. 1:25, the apostle uses both the simple verb *meno* and the compound *parameno* (some mss. have *sumparameno*), to express his confidence that he will "abide," and "continue to abide," with the saints. In 1 Cor. 16:6 some mss. have this word. In Jas. 1:25, of steadfast continuance in the law of liberty.

5. *hupomeno* (5278), lit., "to abide under," signifies "to remain in a place instead of leaving it, to stay behind," e.g., Luke 2:43; Acts 17:14; or "to persevere," Matt. 10:22; 24:13; Mark 13:13; in each of which latter it is used with the phrase "unto the end"; or "to endure bravely and trustfully," e.g., Heb. 12:2-3, 7, suggesting endurance under what would be burdensome. See also Jas. 1:12; 5:11; 1 Pet. 2:20.

6. *prosmeno* (4357), "to abide still longer, continue with" is used (a) of place, Matt. 15:32; Mark 8:2; Acts 18:18; 1 Tim. 1:3; (b) metaphorically, "of cleaving unto a person," Acts 11:23, indicating persistent loyalty; of continuing in a thing, Acts 13:43; 1 Tim. 5:5.

B. Noun.

mone (3438), "an abode" (akin to No. 1), is found in John 14:2, "mansions," and 14:23, "abode."

ABOLISH

katargeo (2673), lit., "to reduce to inactivity" (*kata*, "down," *argos*, "inactive"), is translated "abolish" in Eph. 2:15 and 2 Tim. 1:10. It is rendered "is abolished" in the KJV of 2 Cor. 3:13. In this and similar words not loss of being is implied, but loss of well being.

The barren tree was cumbering the ground, making it useless for the purpose of its existence, Luke 13:7; the unbelief of the Jews could not "make of none effect" the faithfulness of God, Rom. 3:3; the preaching of the gospel could not "make of none effect" the moral enactments of the Law, 3:31; the Law could not make the promise of "none effect," 4:14; Gal. 3:17; the effect of the identification of the believer with Christ in His death is to render inactive his body in regard to sin, Rom. 6:6; the death of a woman's first husband discharges her from the law of the husband, that is, it makes void her status as his wife in the eyes of the law, 7:2; in that sense the believer has been discharged from the Law, 7:6; God has

A

chosen things that are not "to bring to nought things that are," i.e., to render them useless for practical purposes, 1 Cor. 1:28; the princes of this world are "brought to nought," i.e., their wisdom becomes ineffective, 2:6; the use for which the human stomach exists ceases with man's death, 6:13; knowledge, prophesyings, and that which was in part were to be "done away," 1 Cor. 13:8, 10, i.e., they were to be rendered of no effect after their temporary use was fulfilled; when the apostle became a man he did away with the ways of a child, v. 11; God is going to abolish all rule and authority and power, i.e., He is going to render them inactive, 1 Cor. 15:24; the last enemy that shall be abolished, or reduced to inactivity, is death, v. 26; the glory shining in the face of Moses, "was passing away," 2 Cor. 3:7, the transitoriness of its character being of a special significance; so in vv. 11, 13; the veil upon the heart of Israel is "done away" in Christ, v. 14; those who seek justification by the Law are "severed" from Christ, they are rendered inactive in relation to Him, Gal. 5:4; the essential effect of the preaching of the Cross would become inoperative by the preaching of circumcision, 5:11; by the death of Christ the barrier between Jew and Gentile is rendered inoperative as such, Eph. 2:15; the Man of Sin is to be reduced to inactivity by the manifestation of the Lord's *parousia* with His people, 2 Thess. 2:8; Christ has rendered death inactive for the believer, 2 Tim. 1:10, death becoming the means of a more glorious life, with Christ; the Devil is to be reduced to inactivity through the death of Christ, Heb. 2:14.

ABOMINABLE, ABOMINATION
Old Testament

A. Noun.

to'ebah (8441), "abomination; loathsome, detestable thing."

First, *to'ebah* defines something or someone as essentially unique in the sense of being "dangerous," "sinister," and "repulsive" to another individual, Gen. 43:32. To the Egyptians, eating bread with foreigners was repulsive because of their cultural or social differences, cf. Gen. 46:34; Ps. 88:8. Another clear illustration of this essential clash of disposition appears in Prov. 29:27. When used with reference to God, this nuance of the word describes people, things, acts, relationships, and characteristics that are "detestable" to Him because they are contrary to His nature. Things related to death and idolatry are loathsome to God, Deut. 14:3. People with habits loathsome to God are themselves detestable to Him, Deut. 22:5. Directly opposed to *to'ebah* are such reactions as "delight" and "loveth," Prov. 15:8-9.

Second, *to'ebah* is used in some contexts to describe pagan practices and objects, Deut. 7:25-26. In other contexts, *to'ebah* describes the repeated failures to observe divine regulations, Ezek.

5:7, 9. *to'ebah* may represent the pagan cultic practices themselves, as in Deut. 12:31, or the people who perpetrate such practices, Deut. 18:12. If Israelites are guilty of such idolatry, however, their fate will be worse than exile: death by stoning, Deut. 17:2-5.

Third, *to'ebah* is used in the sphere of jurisprudence and of family or tribal relationships. Certain acts or characteristics are destructive of societal and familial harmony; both such things and the people who do them are described by *to'ebah*, Prov. 6:16-19. God says, "The scorner is an abomination to men," Prov. 24:9 because he spreads his bitterness among God's people, disrupting unity and harmony.

B. Verb.

ta'ab (8581), "to abhor, treat as abhorrent, cause to be an abomination, act abominably." This verb occurs 21 times, and the first occurrence is in Deut. 7:26.

New Testament

A. Adjectives.

1. *athemitos* (*111*) occurs in Acts 10:28, "unlawful," and 1 Pet. 4:3, "abominable" (*a*, negative, *themitos*, an adjective from *themis*, "law").

2. *bdeluktos* (*947*), Titus 1:16, is said of deceivers who profess to know God, but deny Him by their works.

B. Noun.

bdelugma (*946*), akin to A, No. 2 denotes an "object of disgust, an abomination." This is said of the image to be set up by Antichrist, Matt. 24:15; Mark 13:14; of that which is highly esteemed amongst men, in contrast to its real character in the sight of God, Luke 16:15. The constant association with idolatry suggests that what is highly esteemed among men constitutes an idol in the human heart. In Rev. 21:27, entrance is forbidden into the Holy City on the part of the unclean, or one who "maketh an abomination and a lie." It is also used of the contents of the golden cup in the hand of the evil woman described in Rev. 17:4, and of the name ascribed to her in the following verse.

ABSTAIN, ABSTINENCE

apecho (*568*), "to hold oneself from," in the NT, invariably refers to evil practices, moral and ceremonial, Acts 15:20, 29; 1 Thess. 4:3; 5:22; 1 Tim. 4:3; 1 Pet. 2:11.

ABUNDANCE, ABUNDANT, ABUNDANTLY, ABOUND

A. Nouns.

1. *hadrotes* (*100*), which, in 2 Cor. 8:20, in reference to the gifts

from the church at Corinth for poor saints in Judea, is derived from *hadros*, "thick, fat, full-grown, rich." In regard, therefore, to the offering in 2 Cor. 8:20 the thought is that of bountiful giving, a fat offering, not mere "abundance."

2. *perisseia* (4050), "an exceeding measure, something above the ordinary," is used four times; Rom. 5:17, "of abundance of grace"; 2 Cor. 8:2, "of abundance of joy"; 2 Cor. 10:15, of the extension of the apostle's sphere of service through the practical fellowship of the saints at Corinth; in Jas. 1:21 it is rendered, metaphorically, "overflowing," KJV "superfluity," with reference to wickedness. Some would render it "residuum," or "what remains."

3. *perisseuma* (4051) denotes "abundance" in a slightly more concrete form, 2 Cor. 8:13-14, where it stands for the gifts in kind supplied by the saints. In Matt. 12:34 and Luke 6:45 it is used of the "abundance" of the heart; in Mark 8:8, of the broken pieces left after feeding the multitude "that remained over."

4. *huperbole* (5236), lit., "a throwing beyond," denotes "excellence, exceeding greatness," of the power of God in His servants, 2 Cor. 4:7; of the revelations given to Paul, 12:7; with the preposition *kata*, the phrase signifies "exceeding," Rom. 7:13; "still more excellent," 1 Cor. 12:31; "exceedingly," 2 Cor. 1:8; "beyond measure," Gal. 1:13; and, in a more extended phrase, "more and more exceedingly," 2 Cor. 4:17.

B. Verbs.

1. *perisseuo* (4052), akin to A, Nos. 2 and 3, is used intransitively (a) "of exceeding a certain number, or measure, to be over, to remain," of the fragments after feeding the multitude, Luke 9:17; John 6:12-13; "to exist in abundance"; as of wealth, Luke 12:15; 21:4; of food, 15:17. In this sense it is used also of consolation, 2 Cor. 1:5; of the effect of a gift sent to meet the need of saints, 2 Cor. 9:12; of rejoicing, Phil. 1:26; of what comes or falls to the lot of a person in large measure, as of the grace of God and the gift by the grace of Christ, Rom. 5:15, of the sufferings of Christ, 2 Cor. 1:5.

(b) "to redound to, or to turn out abundantly for something," as of the liberal effects of poverty, 2 Cor. 8:2; in Rom. 3:7, argumentatively of the effects of the truth of God, as to whether God's truthfulness becomes more conspicuous and His glory is increased through man's untruthfulness; of numerical increase, Acts 16:5.

(c) "to be abundantly furnished, to abound in a thing," as of material benefits, Luke 12:15; Phil. 4:18 of spiritual gifts, 1 Cor. 14:12, or "to be pre-eminent, to excel, to be morally better off," as regards partaking of certain meats; 1 Cor. 8:8, "are we the better," "to abound" in hope, Rom. 15:13; the work of the Lord, 1 Cor. 15:58; faith and grace, 2 Cor. 8:7; thanksgiving, Col. 2:7; walking so as to please God, Phil. 1:9; 1 Thess. 4:1, 10; of righteousness, Matt. 5:20;

of the Gospel, as the ministration of righteousness, 2 Cor. 3:9, "exceed."

It is used transitively, in the sense of "to make to abound," e.g., to provide a person richly so that he has "abundance," as of spiritual truth, Matt. 13:12; the right use of what God has entrusted to us, 25:29; the power of God in conferring grace, 2 Cor. 9:8; Eph. 1:8; to "make abundant" or to cause to excel, as of the effect of grace in regard to thanksgiving, 2 Cor. 4:15; His power to make us "to abound" in love, 1 Thess. 3:12.

2. *huperperisseuo* (5248), a strengthened form of No. 1, signifies "to abound exceedingly," Rom. 5:20, of the operation of grace; 2 Cor. 7:4, in the middle voice, of the apostle's joy in the saints.

3. *pleonazo* (4121), from *pleion*, or *pleon*, "more" (greater in quantity), akin to *pleo*, "to fill," signifies (a) intransitively, "to superabound," of a trespass or sin, Rom. 5:20; of grace, Rom. 6:1; 2 Cor. 4:15; of spiritual fruit, Phil. 4:17; of love, 2 Thess. 1:3; of various fruits, 2 Pet. 1:8; of the gathering of the manna, 2 Cor. 8:15, "had...over"; (b) transitively, "to make to increase," 1 Thess. 3:12.

4. *huperpleonazo* (5250), a strengthened form of No. 3, signifying "to abound exceedingly," is used in 1 Tim. 1:14, of the grace of God.

5. *plethuno* (4129), a lengthened form of *pletho*, "to fill," akin to No. 3, and to *plethos*, "a multitude," signifies "to increase, to multiply," and, in the passive voice, "to be multiplied."

ACCEPT, ACCEPTED, ACCEPTABLE

A. Verbs.

1. *dechomai* (1209) signifies "to accept," by a deliberate and ready reception of what is offered (cf. No. 4), e.g., 1 Thess. 2:13; 2 Cor. 8:17; 11:4.

2. *apodechomai* (588), consisting of *apo*, "from," intensive, and No. 1, expresses *dechomai* more strongly, signifying "to receive heartily, to welcome," Luke 8:40 (KJV, "gladly received"); Acts 2:41; 18:27; 24:3; 28:30.

3. *prosdechomai* (4327), *pros*, "to," and No. 1, "to accept favorably, or receive to oneself," is used of things future, in the sense of expecting; with the meaning of "accepting," it is used negatively in Heb. 11:35, "not accepting their deliverance"; of receiving, e.g., Luke 15:2; Rom. 16:2; Phil. 2:29.

B. Adjectives.

The following adjectives are translated "acceptable," or in some cases "accepted."

1. *dektos* (1184), akin to No. 1, denotes "a person or thing who has been regarded favorably," Luke 4:19, 24; Acts 10:35; 2 Cor. 6:2 (in this verse No. 3 is used in the second place); Phil. 4:18.

2. *apodektos* (587), a strengthened form of No. 1 (*apo*, "from,"

used intensively), signifies "acceptable," in the sense of what is pleasing and welcome, 1 Tim. 2:3; 5:4.

3. *euprosdektos* (*2144*), a still stronger form of No. 1, signifies a "very favorable acceptance" (*eu*, "well," *pros*, "towards," No. 1), Rom. 15:16, 31; 2 Cor. 6:2; 8:12; 1 Pet. 2:5.

4. *euarestos* (*2101*), *eu*, "well," *arestos*, "pleasing," is rendered "acceptable," in the KJV of Rom. 12:1-2; 14:18; in 2 Cor. 5:9, "accepted"; Eph. 5:10. The RV usually has "well-pleasing"; so KJV and RV in Phil. 4:18; Col. 3:20; in Titus 2:9, "please well," KJV, Heb. 13:21.

D. Nouns.

1. *apodoche* (*594*), akin to B, No. 2, signifies "worthy to be received with approbation, acceptation," 1 Tim. 1:15; 4:9. The phrase in 1:15 is found in a writing in the 1st century expressing appreciation of a gift from a princess.

2. *charis* (*5485*), "grace," indicating favor on the part of the giver, "thanks" on the part of the receiver, is rendered "acceptable" in 1 Pet. 2:19-20.

ACCESS

prosagoge (*4318*), lit., "a leading or bringing into the presence of," denotes "access," with which is associated the thought of freedom to enter through the assistance or favor of another. It is used three times, Rom. 5:2; Eph. 2:18; 3:12.

ACCOMPANY

propempo (*4311*), translated "accompanied," in Acts 20:38, KJV, lit. means "to send forward"; hence of assisting a person on a journey either (a) in the sense of fitting him out with the requisites for it, or (b) actually "accompanying" him for part of the way. The former seems to be indicated in Rom. 15:24 and 1 Cor. 16:6, and v. 11, where the RV has "set him forward." So in 2 Cor. 1:16 and Titus 3:13, and of John's exhortation to Gaius concerning traveling evangelists, "whom thou wilt do well to set forward on their journey worthily of God," 3 John 6, RV. While personal "accompaniment" is not excluded, practical assistance seems to be generally in view, as indicated by Paul's word to Titus to set forward Zenas and Apollos on their journey and to see "that nothing be wanting unto them." In regard to the parting of Paul from the elders of Ephesus at Miletus, personal "accompaniment" is especially in view, perhaps not without the suggestion of assistance, Acts 20:38, RV "brought him on his way"; "accompaniment" is also indicated in 21:5; "they all with wives and children brought us on our way, till we were out of the city." In Acts 15:3, both ideas perhaps are suggested.

ACCOMPLISH, ACCOMPLISHMENT

A. Verbs.

1. *exartizo* (*1822*), "to fit out," (from *ek*, "out," and a verb derived from *artos*, "a joint"), means "to furnish completely," 2 Tim. 3:17, or "to accomplish," Acts 21:5, there said of a number of days, as if to render the days complete by what was appointed for them.

2. *pleroo* (*4137*), "to fulfill, to complete, carry out to the full" (as well as to fill), is translated "perfect" in Rev. 3:2, KJV; RV, "I have found no works of thine fulfilled before My God"; "accomplish" in Luke 9:31.

3. *teleo* (*5055*), "to finish, to bring to an end," frequently signifies, not merely to terminate a thing, but to carry out a thing to the full. It is used especially in the Apocalypse, where it occurs eight times, and is rendered "finish" in 10:7; 11:7, and in the RV of 15:1, which rightly translates it "(in them) is finished (the wrath of God)." So in v. 8; in 17:17, RV, "accomplish," and "finish" in 20:3, 5, 7; in Luke 2:39, RV, "accomplish," for KJV, performed.

4. *epiteleo* (*2005*), *epi*, "up," intensive, and No. 3, is a strengthened form of that verb, in the sense of "accomplishing." The fuller meaning is "to accomplish perfectly"; in Rom. 15:28, RV, "accomplish"; "perfecting" in 2 Cor. 7:1; "complete" in 8:6 and 11; "completion" in the latter part of this 11th verse, which is better than "performance"; "perfected" in Gal. 3:3; "perfect" in Phil. 1:6. In Heb. 8:5 the margin rightly has "complete" instead of "make," with regard to the tabernacle. In Heb. 9:6 it is translated "accomplish" and in 1 Pet. 5:9.

5. *teleioo* (*5048*), though distinct grammatically from *teleo*, has much the same meaning. The main distinction is that *teleo* more frequently signifies "to fulfill." *teleioo*, more frequently signifies "to make perfect," one of the chief features of the Epistle to the Hebrews, where it occurs nine times. It is rendered "accomplish" in the RV of John 4:34; 5:36; 17:4, and Acts 20:24.

6. *pletho* (*4130*), "to fulfill," is translated "accomplished" in the KJV of Luke 1:23; 2:6, 21-22 (RV, "fulfilled").

ACCORD

A. Adverb.

homothumadon (*3661*), "of one mind," occurs eleven times, ten in the Acts, 1:14; 2:46; 4:24; 5:12; 7:57; 8:6; 12:20; 15:25; 18:12, 19:29, and the other in Rom. 15:6, where, for KJV, "with one mind," the RV has "with one accord," as throughout the Acts.

B. Adjectives.

"Of one's own accord."

1. *authairetos* (*830*), from *autos*, "self," and *haireomai*, "to choose, self-chosen, voluntary, of one's own accord," occurs in

2 Cor. 8:3 and 17, of the churches of Macedonia as to their gifts for the poor saints in Judea, and of Titus in his willingness to go and exhort the church in Corinth concerning the matter. In 8:3 the RV translates it "(gave) of their own accord," consistently with the rendering in v. 17.

2. *sumpsuchos* (4861), lit., "fellow-souled or minded," occurs in Phil. 2:2, "of one accord."

ACCURATELY

akribos (199) is correctly translated in the RV of Luke 1:3, "having traced the course of all things accurately" (KJV, "having had perfect understanding"). It is used in Matt. 2:8, of Herod's command to the wise men as to searching for the young Child (RV, "carefully"; KJV, "diligently"); in Acts 18:25, of Apollos' teaching of "the things concerning Jesus" (RV, "carefully"; KJV, "diligently"); in Eph. 5:15, of the way in which believers are to walk (RV, "carefully"; KJV, "circumspectly"); in 1 Thess. 5:2, of the knowledge gained by the saints through the apostle's teaching concerning the Day of the Lord (RV and KJV, "perfectly"). The word expresses that "accuracy" which is the outcome of carefulness. It is connected with *akros*, "pointed."

ACCUSATION, ACCUSE

A. Nouns.

1. *aitia* (156) probably has the primary meaning of "a cause, especially an occasion of something evil, hence a charge, an accusation." It is used in a forensic sense, of (a) an accusation, Acts 25:18 (RV, "charge"), 27; (b) a crime, Matt. 27:37; Mark 15:26, John 18:38; 19:4, 6; Acts 13:28; 23:28; 28:18.

2. *aitioma* (157), "an accusation," expressing No. 1 more concretely, is found in Acts 25:7, RV, "charges," for KJV, "complaints."

3. *enklema* (1462) is "an accusation made in public," but not necessarily before a tribunal. That is the case in Acts 23:29, "laid to his charge." In 25:16 it signifies a matter of complaint; hence, the RV has "the matter laid against him" (KJV, "crime").

4. *kategoria* (2724), "an accusation," is found in John 18:29; 1 Tim. 5:19 and Titus 1:6, lit., "not under accusation." This and the verb *kategoreo*, "to accuse," and the noun *kategoros*, "an accuser" (see below), all have chiefly to do with judicial procedure, as distinct from *diaballo*, "to slander." It is derived from *agora*, "a place of public speaking," prefixed by *kata*, "against"; hence, it signifies a speaking against a person before a public tribunal. It is the opposite to *apologia*, "a defense."

B. Verbs.

1. *diaballo* (1225), used in Luke 16:1, in the passive voice, lit. signifies "to hurl across," and suggests a verbal assault. It stresses

the act rather than the author, as in the case of *aitia* and *kategoria*. *diabolos* is connected.

2. *enkaleo* (*1458*), "to bring a charge against, or to come forward as an accuser against," lit. denotes "to call in," i.e., "to call (something) in or against (someone)"; hence, "to call to account, to accuse," Acts 19:38, RV (KJV, "implead"); in v. 40, "accused" (KJV, "call in question"). It is used in four other places in the Acts, 23:28-29; 26:2, 7, and elsewhere in Rom. 8:33, "shall lay to the charge."

3. *epereazo* (*1908*), besides its more ordinary meaning, "to insult, treat abusively, despitefully," Luke 6:28, has the forensic significance "to accuse falsely," and is used with this meaning in 1 Pet. 3:16, RV, "revile."

4. *kategoreo* (*2723*), "to speak against, accuse" (cf. A, No. 4), is used (a) in a general way, "to accuse," e.g., Luke 6:7, RV, "how to accuse"; Rom. 2:15; Rev. 12:10; (b) before a judge, e.g., Matt. 12:10; Mark 15:4 (RV, "witness against"); Acts 22:30; 25:16. In Acts 24:19, RV renders it "make accusation," for the KJV, "object."

5. *sukophanteo* (*4811*), (Eng., "sycophant") means (a) "to accuse wrongfully"; Luke 3:14 (KJV and RV, margin); RV, "exact wrongfully"; (b) "to exact money wrongfully, to take anything by false accusation," Luke 19:8, and the RV text of 3:14.

ACCUSER

1. *diabolos* (*1228*), "an accuser," is used 34 times as a title of Satan, the Devil (the English word is derived from the Greek); once of Judas, John 6:70, who, in his opposition to God, acted the part of the Devil. Apart from John 6:70, men are never spoken of as devils. It is always to be distinguished from *daimon*, "a demon." It is found three times, 1 Tim. 3:11; 2 Tim. 3:3; Titus 2:3, of false accusers, slanderers.

2. *kategoros* (*2725*), "an accuser," is used in John 8:10; Acts 23:30, 35; 24:8; 25:16, 18. In Rev. 12:10, it is used of Satan.

ACKNOWLEDGE (-MENT)

A. Verb.

epiginosko (*1921*) signifies (a) "to know thoroughly"; (b) "to acknowledge," 1 Cor. 14:37 (RV, "take knowledge of"); 16:18; 2 Cor. 1:13-14.

B. Noun.

epignosis (*1922*), akin to A, "full, or thorough knowledge, discernment, recognition," is translated "acknowledging" in the KJV of 2 Tim. 2:25; Titus 1:1 and Philem. 6 (in all three, RV, "knowledge," properly, "thorough knowledge"). In Col. 2:2, KJV, "acknowledgement," RV, "that they may know" (i.e., "unto the full knowledge).

ACQUAINTANCE

1. *gnostos* (1110), signifies "known, or knowable"; hence, "one's acquaintance"; it is used in this sense, in the plural, in Luke 2:44 and 23:49.

2. *idios* (2398), "one's own," is translated "acquaintance" in the KJV of Acts 24:23, "friends" (RV).

ADD

1. *prostithemi* (4369), "to put to," "to add, or to place beside." In Gal. 3:19, "What then is the law? It was "added" because of transgressions." There is no contradiction of what is said in v. 15, the meaning is not that something had been 'added' to the promise with a view to complete it, which the apostle denies, but that something had been given "in addition" to the promise, as in Rom. 5:20, "The law came in beside."

2. *epidiatasso* (1928), lit., "to arrange in addition," is used in Gal. 3:15 ("addeth," or rather, "ordains something in addition"). If no one does such a thing in the matter of a human covenant, how much more is a covenant made by God inviolable! The Judaizers by their "addition" violated this principle, and, by proclaiming the divine authority for what they did, they virtually charged God with a breach of promise. He gave the Law, indeed, but neither in place of the promise nor to supplement it.

ADJURE

1. *horkizo* (3726), "to cause to swear, to lay under the obligation of an oath" (*horkos*, Mark 5:7; Acts 19:13), is connected with the Heb. word for a thigh, cf. Gen. 24:2, 9; 47:29. Some mss. have this word in 1 Thess. 5:27. The most authentic have No. 3 (below).

2. *exorkizo* (1844), an intensive form of No. 1, signifies "to appeal by an oath, to adjure," Matt. 26:63.

3. *enorkizo* (1722 and 3726), "to put under (or bind by) an oath," is translated "adjure" in the RV of 1 Thess. 5:27 (KJV, "charge").

ADMONITION, ADMONISH

A. Noun.

nouthesia (3559), lit., "a putting in mind," is used in 1 Cor. 10:11, of the purpose of the Scriptures; in Eph. 6:4, of that which is ministered by the Lord; and in Titus 3:10, of that which is to be administered for the correction of one who creates trouble in the church. *nouthesia* is "the training by word," whether of encouragement, or, if necessary, by reproof or remonstrance. In contrast to this, the synonymous word *paideia* stresses training by act, though both words are used in each respect.

B. Verbs.

1. *noutheteo* (3560), cf. the noun above, means "to put in mind, admonish," Acts 20:31 (KJV, "warn"); Rom. 15:14; 1 Cor. 4:14 (KJV, "warn"); Col. 1:28 (KJV, "warning"); Col. 3:16; 1 Thess. 5:12, 14 (KJV, "warn"); 2 Thess. 3:15.

It is used, (a) of instruction, (b) of warning. It is thus distinguished from *paideuo*, "to correct by discipline, to train by act," Heb. 12:6; cf. Eph. 6:4.

2. *chrematizo* (5537), primarily, "to transact business," then, "to give advice to enquirers" (especially of official pronouncements of magistrates), or "a response to those consulting an oracle," came to signify the giving of a divine "admonition" or instruction or warning, in a general way; "admonished" in Heb. 8:5, KJV (RV, "warned"). Elsewhere it is translated by the verb "to warn."

ADOPTION

huiothesia (5206), from *huios*, "a son," and *thesis*, "a placing," signifies the place and condition of a son given to one to whom it does not naturally belong. The word is used by the apostle Paul only.

In Rom. 8:15, believers are said to have received "the Spirit of adoption," that is, the Holy Spirit who, given as the Firstfruits of all that is to be theirs, produces in them the realization of sonship and the attitude belonging to sons. In Gal. 4:5 they are said to receive "the adoption of sons," i.e., sonship bestowed in distinction from a relationship consequent merely upon birth; here two contrasts are presented, (1) between the sonship of the believer and the unoriginated sonship of Christ, (2) between the freedom enjoyed by the believer and bondage, whether of Gentile natural condition, or of Israel under the Law. In Eph. 1:5 they are said to have been foreordained unto "adoption as sons" through Jesus Christ. In Rom. 8:23 the "adoption" of the believer is set forth as still future, as it there includes the redemption of the body, when the living will be changed and those who have fallen asleep will be raised. In Rom. 9:4 "adoption" is spoken of as belonging to Israel, in accordance with the statement in Exod. 4:12, "Israel is My Son," cf. Hos. 11:1. Israel was brought into a special relation with God, a collective relationship, not enjoyed by other nations, Deut. 14:1; Jer. 31:9, etc.

ADULTERER (-ESS), ADULTEROUS, ADULTERY

A. Nouns.

1. *moichos* (3432) denotes one "who has unlawful intercourse with the spouse of another," Luke 18:11; 1 Cor. 6:9; Heb. 13:4. As to Jas. 4:4, see below.

A

2. *moichalis* (*3428*), "an adulteress," is used (a) in the natural sense, 2 Pet. 2:14; Rom. 7:3; (b) in the spiritual sense, Jas. 4:4; here the RV rightly omits the word "adulterers." It was added by a copyist. As in Israel the breach of their relationship with God through their idolatry, was described as "adultery" or "harlotry" (e.g., Ezek. 16:15, etc.; 23:43), so believers who cultivate friendship with the world, thus breaking their spiritual union with Christ, are spiritual "adulteresses," having been spiritually united to Him as wife to husband, Rom. 7:4. It is used adjectively to describe the Jewish people in transferring their affections from God, Matt. 12:39; 16:4; Mark 8:38.

3. *moicheia* (*3430*), "adultery," is found in Matt. 15:19; Mark 7:21; John 8:3 (KJV only).

B. Verbs.

1. *moichao* (*3429*), used in the middle voice in the NT, is said of men in Matt. 5:32; 19:9; Mark 10:11; of women in Mark 10:12.

2. *moicheuo* (*3431*) is used in Matt. 5:27-28, 32 (in v. 32 some texts have No. 1); 19:18; Mark 10:19; Luke 16:18; 18:20; John 8:4; Rom. 2:22; 13:9; Jas. 2:11; in Rev. 2:22, metaphorically, of those who are by a Jezebel's solicitations drawn away to idolatry.

ADVANTAGE

1. *opheleo* (*5623*) signifies "to be useful, do good, profit," Rom. 2:25; with a negative, "to be of no use, to effect nothing," Matt. 27:24; John 6:63, "profiteth"; 12:19, "prevail"; in Luke 9:25, KJV, "(what is a man) advantaged?" RV, "profited."

2. *pleonekteo* (*4122*), lit., "to seek to get more" (*pleon*, "more," *echo*, "to have"); hence, "to get an advantage of, to take advantage of." In 2 Cor. 7:2 the KJV has "defrauded," the RV, "took advantage of"; in 1 Thess. 4:6, KJV, "defraud," RV, "wrong." In the other three places the RV consistently translates it by the verb "to take advantage of," 2 Cor. 2:11, of Satan's effort to gain an "advantage" over the church, through their neglect to restore the backslider; in 2 Cor. 12:17-18, KJV, "make a gain of."

ADVERSARY

A. Noun.

antidikos (*476*), firstly, "an opponent in a lawsuit," Matt. 5:25 (twice); Luke 12:58; 18:3, is also used to denote "an adversary or an enemy," without reference to legal affairs, and this is perhaps its meaning in 1 Pet. 5:8, where it is used of the Devil. Some would regard the word as there used in a legal sense, since the Devil accuses men before God.

B. Verb.

antikeimai (*480*) is, lit., "to lie opposite to, to be set over against."

In addition to its legal sense it signifies "to withstand"; the present participle of the verb with the article, which is equivalent to a noun, signifies "an adversary," e.g., Luke 13:17; 21:15; 1 Cor. 16:9; Phil. 1:28; 1 Tim. 5:14. This construction is used of the Man of Sin, in 2 Thess. 2:4, and is translated "He that opposeth," where, adopting the noun form, we might render by "the opponent and self-exalter against...." In Gal. 5:17 it is used of the antagonism between the Holy Spirit and the flesh in the believer; in 1 Tim. 1:10, of anything, in addition to persons, that is opposed to the doctrine of Christ. In these two places the word is rendered "contrary to."

ADVICE, ADVISE

1. *gnome* (1106), "to know, perceive," firstly means "the faculty or knowledge, reason"; then, "that which is thought or known, one's mind." Under this heading there are various meanings: (1) a view, judgment, opinion, 1 Cor. 1:10; Philem. 14; Rev. 17:13, 17; (2) an opinion as to what ought to be done, either (a) by oneself, and so a resolve, or purpose, Acts 20:3; or (b) by others, and so, judgment, advice, 1 Cor. 7:25, 40; 2 Cor. 8:10.

2. *boule* (1012), from a root meaning "a will," hence "a counsel, a piece of advice," is to be distinguished from *gnome*; *boule* is the result of determination, *gnome* is the result of knowledge; (a) counsel of God, in Luke 7:30; Acts 2:23; 4:28; 13:36; 20:27; Eph. 1:11; Heb. 6:17; (b) counsel of men, Luke 23:51; Acts 27:12, 42; 1 Cor. 4:5.

AFFECTION (-S), AFFECTED

A. Nouns.

1. *pathos* (3806), from *pascho*, "to suffer," primarily denotes whatever one suffers or experiences in any way; hence, "an affection of the mind, a passionate desire." Used by the Greeks of either good or bad desires, it is always used in the NT of the latter, Rom. 1:26 (KJV, "affections," RV, "passions"); Col. 3:5 (KJV, "inordinate affection," RV, "passion"); 1 Thess. 4:5 (KJV, "lust," RV, "passion").

2. *splanchna* (4698), lit., "the bowels," which were regarded by the Greeks as the seat of the more violent passions, by the Hebrews as the seat of the tender "affections"; hence the word denotes "tender mercies" and is rendered "affections" in 2 Cor. 6:12 (KJV, "bowels"); "inward affection," 2 Cor. 7:15. Cf. *epithumia*, "desire."

3. *pathema* (3804), Gal. 5:24.

B. Adjectives.

1. *astorgos* (794) signifies "without natural affection" especially of parents for children and children for parents, Rom. 1:31; 2 Tim. 3:3.

2. *philostorgos* (5387), "tenderly loving" (from *philos*, "friendly,"

storge, see No. 1), is used in Rom. 12:10, RV, "tenderly affectioned" (KJV, "kindly affectioned").

AFFLICT (-ED), AFFLICTION

A. Verbs.

1. *kakopatheo* (2553), from *kakos*, "evil," *pathos*, "suffering," signifies "to suffer hardship." So the RV in 2 Tim. 2:9; and 4:5; in Jas. 5:13, "suffer" (KJV, "afflicted").

2. *thlibo* (2346), "to suffer affliction, to be troubled," has reference to sufferings due to the pressure of circumstances, or the antagonism of persons, 1 Thess. 3:4; 2 Thess. 1:6-7; "straitened," in Matt. 7:14 (RV); "throng," Mark 3:9; "afflicted," 2 Cor. 1:6; 7:5 (RV); 1 Tim. 5:10; Heb. 11:37; "pressed," 2 Cor. 4:8. Both the verb and the noun (see B, No. 4), when used of the present experience of believers, refer almost invariably to that which comes upon them from without.

3. *talaiporeo* (5003), "to be afflicted," is used in Jas. 4:9, in the middle voice ("afflict yourselves").

B. Nouns.

1. *kakopatheia* (2552), from *kakos*, "evil," and *pascho*, "to suffer" is rendered "suffering" in Jas. 5:10, RV (KJV, "suffering affliction").

2. *kakosis* (2561), "affliction, ill treatment," is used in Acts 7:34.

3. *pathema* (3804), "affliction." The word is frequent in Paul's epistles and is found three times in Hebrews, four in 1 Peter; it is used (a) of "afflictions," Rom. 8:18, etc.; of Christ's "sufferings," 1 Pet. 1:11; 5:1; Heb. 2:9; of those as shared by believers, 2 Cor. 1:5; Phil. 3:10; 1 Pet. 4:13; 5:1; (b) of "an evil emotion, passion," Rom. 7:5; Gal. 5:24.

4. *thlipsis* (2347) primarily means "a pressing, pressure," (see A, No. 4), anything which burdens the spirit. In two passages in Paul's Epistles it is used of future retribution, in the way of "affliction," Rom. 2:9; 2 Thess. 1:6. In Matt. 24:9.

AFOREPROMISED

proepangellomai (4279), "to promise before," is translated by the one word "aforepromised," in the RV of 2 Cor. 9:5; in Rom. 1:2, "promised afore."

AGE

1. *aion* (165), "an age, era," signifies a period of indefinite duration, or time viewed in relation to what takes place in the period.

The phrases containing this word should not be rendered literally, but consistently with its sense of indefinite duration. Thus *eis ton aiona* does not mean "unto the age" but "for ever" (see, e.g., Heb. 5:6). The Greeks contrasted that which came to an end with that which was expressed by this phrase, which shows that they conceived of it as expressing interminable duration.

The word occurs most frequently in the Gospel of John, the Hebrews and Revelation. It is sometimes wrongly rendered "world." It is a characteristic word of John's gospel.

2. *genea* (*1074*), In some contexts, the meaning focuses from people to the time in which they lived, the word means "an age," i.e., a period ordinarily occupied by each successive generation, say, of thirty or forty years, Acts 14:16; 15:21; Eph. 3:5; Col. 1:26; see also, e.g., Gen. 15:16. In Eph. 3:21 *genea* is combined with *aion* in a remarkable phrase in a doxology.

3. *helikia* (*2244*), primarily "an age," as a certain length of life, John 9:21, 23, or beyond a certain stage of life, Heb. 11:11.

AGED

1. *presbutes* (*4246*), "an elderly man," is a longer form of *presbus*, the comparative degree of which is *presbuteros*, "a senior, elder," both of which, as also the verb *presbeuo*, "to be elder, to be an ambassador," are derived from *proeisbaino*, "to be far advanced." The noun is found in Luke 1:18, "an old man"; Titus 2:2, "aged men," and Philem. 9, where the RV marg., "Paul an ambassador," is to be accepted, the original almost certainly being *presbeutes* (not *presbutes*), "an ambassador." So he describes himself in Eph. 6:20. As Lightfoot points out, he is hardly likely to have made his age a ground of appeal to Philemon, who, if he was the father of Archippus, cannot have been much younger than Paul himself.

2. *presbutis* (*4247*), "an aged woman," Titus 23.

AGREE, AGREEMENT

A. Verbs.

1. *sumphoneo* (*4856*), lit., "to sound together," in the NT of the "agreement" (a) of persons concerning a matter, Matt. 18:19; 20:2, 13; Acts 5:9; (b) of the writers of Scripture, Acts 15:15; (c) of things that are said to be congruous in their nature, Luke 5:36.

2. *suntithemi* (*4934*), lit., "to put together," in the middle voice, means "to make an agreement, or to assent to"; translated "covenanted" in Luke 22:5; "agreed" in John 9:22, and Acts 23:20; "assented" in Acts 24:9.

B. Nouns.

1. *gnome* (*1106*), "mind, will," is used with *poieo*, "to make," in the sense of "to agree," Rev. 17:17 (twice), lit., "to do His mind, and to make one mind"; RV, "to come to one mind," KJV, "to agree.

2. *sunkatathesis* (*4783*), 2 Cor. 6:16.

A

ALIEN

allotrios (245), primarily, "belonging to another" (the opposite to *idios*, "one's own"), came to mean "foreign, strange, not of one's own family, alien, an enemy"; "aliens" in, Heb. 11:34, elsewhere "strange," etc.

ALIENATE

apallotrioo (526) consists of *apo*, "from," and the above; it signifies "to be rendered an alien, to be alienated." In Eph. 2:12 the RV corrects to the verbal form "alienated," for the noun "aliens"; elsewhere in Eph. 4:18 and Col. 1:21; the condition of the unbeliever is presented in a threefold state of "alienation," (a) from the commonwealth of Israel, (b) from the life of God, (c) from God Himself.

ALLEGORY

allegoreo (238), translated in Gal. 4:24 "contain an allegory," came to signify "to speak," not according to the primary sense of the word, but so that the facts stated are applied to illustrate principles.

ALMIGHTY

pantokrator (3841), "almighty, or ruler of all," is used of God only, and is found, in the Epistles, only in 2 Cor. 6:18, where the title is suggestive in connection with the context; elsewhere only in the Apocalypse, nine times. In one place, 19:6, the KJV has "omnipotent"; RV, "(the Lord our God,) the Almighty."

ALMS, ALMSDEEDS

eleemosune (1654), connected with *eleemon*, "merciful," signifies (a) "mercy, pity, particularly in giving alms," Matt. 6:1 (see below), 2-4; Acts 10:2; 24:17; (b) the benefaction itself, the "alms" (the effect for the cause), Luke 11:41; 12:33; Acts 3:2-3, 10; 9:36, "almsdeeds"; 10:2, 4, 31.

ALTAR

Old Testament

mizbeach (4196), "altar." This word signifies a raised place where a sacrifice was made, as in Gen. 8:20 (its first biblical appearance). In later references, this word may refer to a table upon which incense was burned, Exod. 30:1.

At Sinai, God directed Israel to fashion altars of valuable woods and metals. This taught them that true worship required man's best and that it was to conform exactly to God's directives; God, not man, initiated and controlled worship. The altar that stood before the holy place, Exod. 27:1-8, and the altar of incense within the holy place, Exod. 30:1-10, had "horns." These horns had a vital function in some offerings, Lev. 4:30; 16:18,. For example, the sacrificial animal may have been bound to these horns in order to allow its blood to drain away completely, Ps. 118:27.

mizbeach is also used of pagan altars, Exod. 34:13.

New Testament

1. *thusiasterion* (2379), derived from *thusiazo*, "to sacrifice." Accordingly it denotes an "altar" for the sacrifice of victims, though it was also used for the "altar" of incense, e.g., Luke 1:11. In the NT this word is reserved for the "altar" of the true God, Matt. 5:23-24; 23:18-20, 35; Luke 11:51; 1 Cor. 9:13; 10:18, in contrast to *bomos*, No. 2, below.

2. *bomos* (1041), properly, "an elevated place," always denotes either a pagan "altar" or an "altar" reared without divine appointment. In the NT the only place where this is found is Acts 17:23, as this is the only mention of such.

AMAZE, AMAZEMENT

A. Nouns.

1. *ekstasis* (1611) is, lit., "a standing out." Eng. "ecstasy" is a transliteration. It is translated "amazement" in Acts 3:10. It was said of any displacement, and especially, with reference to the mind, of that alteration of the normal condition by which the person is thrown into a state of surprise or fear, or both; Acts 10:10; 11:5; 22:17.

2. *thambos* (2285), "amazement, wonder," is probably connected with a root signifying "to render immovable"; it is frequently associated with terror as well as astonishment, as with the verb in Acts 9:6. It occurs in Luke 4:36; 5:9; Acts 3:10.

B. Verbs.

1. *existemi* (1839), akin to A, No. 1, lit. means "to stand out from." Like the noun, this is used with two distinct meanings: (a) in the sense of amazement, the word should be invariably rendered "amazed," as in the RV, e.g., in the case of Simon Magus (for KJV, "bewitched"), Acts 8:9 and 11. It is used, in the passive voice, of Simon himself in the 13th v., RV, "he was amazed," for KJV, "wondered." "Amaze" is preferable to "astonish" throughout; (b) in Mark 3:21 and 2 Cor. 5:13 it is used with its other meaning of being beside oneself.

2. *ekplesso* (1605), lit., "to strike out," signifies "to be exceedingly struck in mind, to be astonished" (*ek*, intensive). The English "astonish" should be used for this verb, and "amaze" for *existemi*, as in the RV; see Matt. 19:25; Luke 2:48; 9:43.

AMBASSADOR, AMBASSAGE

A. Verb.

presbeuo (4243) denotes (a) "to be elder or eldest, prior in birth or age"; (b) "to be an ambassador," 2 Cor. 5:20, and Eph. 6:20. There is a suggestion that to be an "ambassador" for Christ involves the experience suggested by the word "elder." Elder men were chosen as "ambassadors."

B. Noun.

presbeia (4242), primarily, "age, eldership, rank," hence, "an embassy or ambassage," is used in Luke 14:32; in 19:14, RV, "ambassage," for KJV, "message."

AMEN

amen (281) is transliterated from Hebrew into both Greek and English. Its meanings may be seen in such passages as Deut. 7:9, 'the faithful (the Amen) God,' Isa. 49:7, 'Jehovah that is faithful.' 65:16, 'the God of truth,' marg., 'the God of Amen.' And if God is faithful His testimonies and precepts are "sure (*amen*)," Ps. 19:7; 111:7, as are also His warnings, Hos. 5:9, and promises, Isa. 33:16; 55:3. 'Amen' is used of men also, e.g., Prov. 25:13.

Once in the NT 'Amen' is a title of Christ, Rev. 3:14, because through Him the purposes of God are established, 2 Cor. 1:20.

The early Christian churches followed the example of Israel in associating themselves audibly with the prayers and thanksgivings offered on their behalf, 1 Cor. 14:16, where the article 'the' points to a common practice. Moreover this custom conforms to the pattern of things in the Heavens, see Rev. 5:14, etc.

The Lord Jesus often used 'Amen,' translated 'verily,' to introduce new revelations of the mind of God. Matt. 16:28; Mark 9:1; Luke 18:29.

ANEW

anothen (509), lit., "from above," in the phrase rendered "anew" in the RV (KJV, "again") of John 3:3, 7.

ANGEL

Old Testament

mal'ak (4397), "messenger; angel." The word *mal'ak* denotes someone sent over a great distance by an individual, Gen. 32:3, or by a community, Num. 21:21, in order to communicate a message. Often several messengers are sent together, 2 Kings 1:2. The introductory formula of the message borne by the *mal'ak* often contains the phrase "Thus says...," or "This is what...says," signifying the authority of the messenger in giving the message of his master, Judg. 11:15.

As a representative of a king, the **mal'ak** might have performed the function of a diplomat. In 1 Kings 20:1ff., we read that Benhadad sent messengers with the terms of surrender.

These passages confirm the important place of the **mal'ak**. Honor to the messenger signified honor to the sender, and the opposite was also true. David took personally the insult of Nabal, 1 Sam. 25:14ff.; and when Hanun, king of Ammon, humiliated David's servants, 2 Sam. 10:4ff., David was quick to dispatch his forces against the Ammonites.

God also sent messengers. First, there are the prophetic messengers, 2 Chron. 36:15-16. Haggai called himself "the messenger of the Lord," **mal'ak Yahweh**.

There were also angelic messengers. The English word *angel* is etymologically related to the Greek word **angelos,** whose translation is similar to the Hebrew: "messenger" or "angel." The angel is a supernatural messenger of the Lord sent with a particular message. Two angels came to Lot at Sodom, Gen. 19:1. The angels were also commissioned to protect God's people, Ps. 91:11.

Third, and most significant, are the phrases **mal'ak Yahweh,** "the angel of the Lord," and **mal'ak 'elohim,** "the angel of God." The phrase is always used in the singular. It denotes an angel who had mainly a saving and protective function, Exod. 23:23. He might also bring about destruction, 1 Chron. 21:16.

The relation between the Lord and the "angel of the Lord" is often so close that it is difficult to separate the two, Gen. 16:7ff.; 21:17ff.; 22:11ff.; 31:11ff.; Exod. 3:2ff.; Judg. 6:11ff.; 13:21ff. This identification has led some interpreters to conclude that the "angel of the Lord" was the pre-incarnate Christ.

New Testament

angelos (32), "a messenger," sent whether by God or by man or by Satan, is also used of a guardian or representative in Rev. 1:20, cf. Matt. 18:10; Acts 12:15 (where it is better understood as 'ghost'), but most frequently of an order of created beings, superior to man, Heb. 2:7; Ps. 8:5, belonging to Heaven, Matt. 24:36; Mark 12:25, and to God, Luke 12:8, and engaged in His service, Ps. 103:20. "Angels" are spirits, Heb. 1:14, i.e., they have not material bodies as men have; they are either human in form, or can assume the human form when necessary, cf. Luke 24:4, with v. 23, Acts 10:3 with v. 30.

ANGER, ANGRY
Old Testament
A. Verb.

charah (2734), "to get angry, be angry." In the causative stem, *charah* means "to become heated with work" or "with zeal for work," Neh. 3:20.

B. Noun.

charon (2740), "burning anger." This word refers exclusively to divine anger as that which is "burning." *charon* first appears in Exod. 32:12: "Turn from thy fierce wrath [*charon*], and repent of this evil against thy people."

New Testament
A. Noun.

orge (3709), originally any "natural impulse, or desire, or disposition," came to signify "anger," as the strongest of all passions. It is used of the wrath of man, Eph. 4:31; Col. 3:8; 1 Tim. 2:8; Jas. 1:19-20; the displeasure of human governments, Rom. 13:4-5; the sufferings of the Jews at the hands of the Gentiles, Luke 21:23; the terrors of the Law, Rom. 4:15; "the anger" of the Lord Jesus, Mark 3:5; God's "anger" with Israel in the wilderness, in a quotation from the OT, Heb. 3:11; 4:3; God's present "anger" with the Jews nationally, Rom. 9:22; 1 Thess. 2:16; His present "anger" with those who disobey the Lord Jesus in His gospel, John 3:36; God's purposes in judgment, Matt. 3:7; Luke 3:7; Rom. 1:18; 2:5, 8; 3:5; 5:9; 12:19; Eph. 2:3; 5:6; Col. 3:6; 1 Thess. 1:10; 5:9.

Notes: (1) *thumos*, "wrath" (not translated "anger"), is to be distinguished from *orge*, in this respect, that *thumos* indicates a more agitated condition of the feelings, an outburst of wrath from inward indignation, while *orge* suggests a more settled or abiding condition of mind, frequently with a view to taking revenge. *orge* is less sudden in its rise than *thumos*, but more lasting in its nature. *thumos* expresses more the inward feeling, *orge* the more active emotion. *thumos* may issue in revenge, though it does not necessarily include it. It is characteristic that it quickly blazes up and quickly subsides, though that is not necessarily implied in each case.

(2) *parorgismos*, a strengthened form of *orge*, and used in Eph. 4:26, RV margin, "provocation," points especially to that which provokes the wrath, and suggests a less continued state than No. (1). "The first keenness of the sense of provocation must not be cherished, though righteous resentment may remain" (Westcott). The preceding verb, *orgizo*, in this verse implies a just occasion for the feeling. This is confirmed by the fact that it is a quotation

from Ps. 4:4 (Sept.), where the Hebrew word signifies to quiver with strong emotion.

thumos is found eighteen times in the NT, ten of which are in the Apocalypse, in seven of which the reference is to the wrath of God; so in Rom. 2:8, RV, "wrath (*thumos*) and indignation" (*orge*); the order in the KJV is inaccurate. Everywhere else the word *thumos* is used in a bad sense. In Gal. 5:20, it follows the word "jealousies," which when smoldering in the heart break out in wrath. *thumos* and *orge* are coupled in two places in the Apocalypse, 16:19, "the fierceness (*thumos*) of His wrath" (*orge*); and 19:15, "the fierceness of the wrath of Almighty God."

(3) *aganaktesis* originally signified "physical pain or irritation" (probably from *agan*, "very much," and *achomai*, "to grieve"), hence, "annoyance, vexation," and is used in 2 Cor. 7:11, "indignation."

B. Verbs.

1. *orgizo* (3710), "to provoke, to arouse to anger," is used in the middle voice in the eight places where it is found, and signifies "to be angry, wroth"; of individuals, in Matt. 5:22; of nations, Rev. 11:18; of Satan as the Dragon, 12:17.

2. *parorgizo* (3949) is "to arouse to wrath, provoke"; Rom. 10:19, "will I anger"; Eph. 6:4, "provoke to wrath."

3. *cholao* (5520), connected with *chole*, "gall, bile," which became used metaphorically to signify bitter anger, means "to be enraged," John 7:23.

ANGUISH

A. Nouns.

1. *stenochoria* (4730), lit., "narrowness of place," metaphorically came to mean the "distress arising from that condition, anguish." It is used in the plural, of various forms of distress, 2 Cor. 6:4 and 12:10, and of "anguish" or distress in general, Rom. 2:9; 8:35, RV, "anguish" for KJV, "distress." The opposite state, of being in a large place, and so metaphorically in a state of joy, is represented by the word *platusmos* in certain Psalms as, e.g., Ps. 118:5; see also 2 Sam. 22:20.

2. *sunoche* (4928), lit., "a holding together, or compressing," was used of the narrowing of a way. It is found only in its metaphorical sense, of "straits, distress, anguish," Luke 21:25, "distress of nations," and 2 Cor. 2:4, "anguish of heart."

B. Verbs.

1. *stenochoreo* (4729), akin to A, No. 1, lit., "to crowd into a narrow space," or, in the passive voice "to be pressed for room," hence, metaphorically, "to be straitened," 2 Cor. 4:8 and 6:12.

2. *sunecho* (4912), akin to A, No. 2, lit., "to hold together," is used

physically of being held, or thronged, Luke 8:45; 19:43; 22:63; of being taken with a malady, Matt. 4:24; Acts 28:8; with fear, Luke 8:37; of being straitened or pressed in spirit with desire, Luke 12:50; Acts 18:5; Phil. 1:23; with the love of Christ, 2 Cor. 5:14. In one place it is used of the stopping of their ears by those who killed Stephen.

3. *odunao* (*3600*), in the middle and passive voices, signifies "to suffer pain, be in anguish, be greatly distressed" (akin to *odune*, "pain, distress"); it is rendered "sorrowing" in Luke 2:48; in 16:24-25, RV, "in anguish," for KJV, "tormented"; in Acts 20:38, "sorrowing."

ANOINT, ANOINTING
Old Testament

A. Verb.

mashach (*4886*), "to anoint, smear, consecrate." Gen. 31:13 illustrates the idea of anointing something or someone as an act of consecration. The basic meaning of the word, however, is simply to "smear" an oily or viscous substance on an object, Exod. 29:2; Isa. 21:5; Jer. 22:14.

The Old Testament most commonly uses *mashach* to indicate "anointing" in the sense of a special setting apart for an office or function. Thus, Elisha was "anointed" to be a prophet, 1 Kings 19:16. More typically, kings were "anointed" for their office, 1 Sam. 16:12; 1 Kings 1:39.

B. Noun.

mashiach (*4899*), "anointed one." A word that is important both to Old Testament and New Testament understandings is the noun *mashiach*, which gives us the term *messiah*. As is true of the verb, *mashiach* implies an anointing for a special office or function. Thus, David refused to harm Saul because Saul was "the Lord's anointed," 1 Sam. 24:6. The Psalms often express the messianic ideals attached to the Davidic line by using the phrase "the Lord's anointed," Ps. 2:2; 18:50; 89:38, 51.

The New Testament title of *Christ* is derived from the Greek *christos* which is exactly equivalent to the Hebrew *mashiach,* for it is also rooted in the idea of "to smear with oil." So the term *Christ* emphasizes the special anointing of Jesus of Nazareth for His role as God's chosen one.

New Testament

A. Verbs.

1 *aleipho* (*218*) is a general term used for "an anointing" of any kind, whether of physical refreshment after washing, e.g., in the NT, Matt. 6:17; Luke 7:38, 46; John 11:2; 12:3; or of the sick, Mark

6:13; Jas. 5:14; or a dead body, Mark 16:1. The material used was either oil, or ointment, as in Luke 7:38, 46.

2. *chrio* (5548) is more limited in its use than No. 1; it is confined to "sacred and symbolical anointings"; Luke 4:18; Acts 4:27; 10:38; Heb. 1:9. The title Christ signifies "The Anointed One," The word (*christos*) is rendered "(His) Anointed" in Acts 4:26, RV. Once it is said of believers, 2 Cor. 1:21. Among the Greeks it was used in other senses than the ceremonial, but in the Scriptures it is not found in connection with secular matters.

B. Noun.

chrisma (5545), the corresponding noun to No. 2, above, signifies "an unguent, or an anointing." It was prepared from oil and aromatic herbs. It is used only metaphorically in the NT; by metonymy, of the Holy Spirit, 1 John 2:20, 27, twice. The RV translates it "anointing" in all three places, instead of the KJV "unction" and "anointing."

That believers have "an anointing from the Holy One" indicates that this anointing renders them holy, separating them to God. The passage teaches that the gift of the Holy Spirit is the all-efficient means of enabling believers to possess a knowledge of the truth.

ANOTHER

allos (243) and *heteros* (2087) have a difference in meaning, which is to be observed in numerous passages. *allos* expresses a numerical difference and denotes "another of the same sort"; *heteros* expresses a qualitative difference and denotes "another of a different sort." Christ promised to send "another Comforter" (*allos*, "another like Himself," not *heteros*), John 14:16. Paul speaks of "a different gospel (*heteros*), which is not another" (*allos*, another like the one he preached), Gal. 1:6-7.

ANSWER

A. Nouns.

apologia (627), a "verbal defense, a speech in defense," is sometimes translated "answer," in the KJV, Acts 25:16; 1 Cor. 9:3; 2 Tim. 4:16, all which the RV corrects to "defense." See Acts 22:1; Phil. 1:7, 16; 2 Cor. 7:11, "clearing." Once it signifies an "answer," 1 Pet. 3:15. Cf. B, No. 4.

B. Verb.

apologeomai (626), cf. above, lit., "to talk oneself off from" (*apo*, "from," *lego*, "to speak"), "to answer by way of making a defense for oneself" (besides its meaning "to excuse," Rom. 2:15; 2 Cor. 12:19), is translated "answer" in Luke 12:11; 21:14; in Acts 19:33, KJV and RV both have "made defense"; in Acts 24:10; 25:8; 26:1-2, the RV has the verb to make a defense, for the KJV, "to answer," and in 26:24 for the KJV, "spake for himself."

ANTICHRIST

antichristos (500) can mean either "against Christ" or "instead of Christ," or perhaps, combining the two, "one who, assuming the guise of Christ, opposes Christ" (Westcott). The word is found only in John's epistles, (a) of the many "antichrists" who are forerunners of the "Antichrist" himself, 1 John 2:18, 22; 2 John 7; (b) of the evil power which already operates anticipatively of the "Antichrist," 1 John 4:3; cf. 2 Thess. 2; Rev. 13.

APOSTLE, APOSTLESHIP

1. *apostolos* (652) is, lit., "one sent forth." The word is used of the Lord Jesus to describe His relation to God, Heb. 3:1; see John 17:3. The twelve disciples chosen by the Lord for special training were so called, Luke 6:13; 9:10. Paul, though he had seen the Lord Jesus, 1 Cor. 9:1; 15:8, had not 'companied with' the Twelve 'all the time' of His earthly ministry, and hence was not eligible for a place among them, according to Peter's description of the necessary qualifications, Acts 1:22. Paul was commissioned directly, by the Lord Himself, after His Ascension, to carry the gospel to the Gentiles.

It also can refer to those who are not the Twelve, or Paul; Barnabas and others; Acts 14:4, 14; in Rom. 16:7; 2 Cor. 8:23; Phil. 2:25; 1 Thess. 2:6.

2. *apostole* (651), "a sending, a mission," signifies an apostleship, Acts 1:25; Rom. 1:5; 1 Cor. 9:2; Gal. 2:8.

APPEAR, APPEARING

A. Verbs.

1. *phaino* (5316) signifies, in the active voice, "to shine"; in the passive, "to be brought forth into light, to become evident, to appear." In Rom. 7:13, concerning sin, the RV has "might be shewn to be," for KJV, "appear."

It is used of the "appearance" of Christ to the disciples, Mark 16:9; of His future "appearing" in glory as the Son of Man, spoken of as a sign to the world, Matt. 24:30; there the genitive is subjective, the sign being the "appearing" of Christ Himself; of Christ as the light, John 1:5; of John the Baptist, 5:35; of the "appearing" of an angel of the Lord, either visibly, Matt. 1:20, or in a dream, 2:13; of a star, 2:7; of men who make an outward show, Matt. 6:5; 6:18 (see the RV); 23:27-28; 2 Cor. 13:7; of tares, Matt. 13:26; of a vapor, Jas. 4:14; of things physical in general, Heb. 11:3; used impersonally in Matt. 9:33, "it was never so seen"; also of what appears to the mind, and so in the sense of to think, Mark 14:64, or to seem, Luke 24:11 (RV, appeared).

2. *epiphaino* (*2014*), a strengthened form of No. 1 but differing in meaning, *epi* signifying "upon," is used in the active voice with the meaning "to give light," Luke 1:79; in the passive voice, "to appear, become visible." It is said of heavenly bodies, e.g., the stars, Acts 27:20 (RV, "shone"); metaphorically, of things spiritual, the grace of God, Titus 2:11; the kindness and the love of God, 3:4.

3. *anaphaino* (*398*), *ana*, "forth, or up," perhaps originally a nautical term, "to come up into view," hence, in general, "to appear suddenly," is used in the passive voice, in Luke 19:11, of the Kingdom of God; active voice, in Acts 21:3, "to come in sight of," RV; "having sighted" would be a suitable rendering (KJV, "having discovered").

4. *phaneroo* (*5319*), akin to No. 1, signifies, in the active voice, "to manifest"; in the passive voice, "to be manifested"; so, regularly, in the RV, instead of "to appear." See 2 Cor. 7:12; Col. 3:4; Heb. 9:26; 1 Pet. 5:4; 1 John 2:28; 3:2; Rev. 3:18. To be manifested, in the Scriptural sense of the word, is more than to "appear." A person may "appear" in a false guise or without a disclosure of what he truly is; to be manifested is to be revealed in one's true character; this is especially the meaning of *phaneroo*, see, e.g., John 3:21; 1 Cor. 4:5; 2 Cor. 5:10-11; Eph. 5:13.

5. *emphanizo* (*1718*), from *en*, "in," intensive, and *phaino*, "to shine," is used, either of "physical manifestation," Matt. 27:53; Heb. 9:24; cf. John 14:22, or, metaphorically, of "the manifestation of Christ" by the Holy Spirit in the spiritual experience of believers who abide in His love, John 14:21. It has another, secondary meaning, "to make known, signify, inform." This is confined to the Acts, where it is used five times, 23:15, 22; 24:1; 25:2, 15. There is perhaps a combination of the two meanings in Heb. 11:14, i.e., to declare by oral testimony and to "manifest" by the witness of the life.

B. Nouns.

1. *apokalupsis* (*602*), lit., "an uncovering, unveiling," denotes "a revelation, or appearing" (Eng., apocalypse). It is translated "the appearing" in 1 Pet. 1:7, KJV (RV, "revelation").

2. *epiphaneia* (*2015*), "epiphany," lit., "a shining forth," was used of the "appearance" of a god to men, and of an enemy to an army in the field, etc. In the NT it occurs of (a) the advent of the Savior when the Word became flesh, 2 Tim. 1:10; (b) the coming of the Lord Jesus into the air to the meeting with His saints, 1 Tim. 6:14; 2 Tim. 4:1, 8; (c) the shining forth of the glory of the Lord Jesus, Matt. 24:27.

APPEARANCE

A. Noun.

eidos (*1491*), properly "that which strikes the eye, that which is exposed to view," signifies the "external appearance, form, or shape," and in this sense is used of the Holy Spirit in taking bodily form, as a dove, Luke 3:22; of Christ, 9:29, "the fashion of His countenance." Christ used it, negatively, of God the Father, when He said "Ye have neither heard His voice at any time, nor seen His form," John 5:37. Thus it is used with reference to each person of the Trinity. Probably the same meaning attaches to the word in the apostle's statement, "We walk by faith, not by sight (*eidos*)," 2 Cor. 5:7. It has a somewhat different significance in 1 Thess. 5:22, in the exhortation, "Abstain from every form of evil," i.e., every sort or kind of evil.

B. Verb.

phantazo (*5324*), "to make visible," is used in its participial form (middle voice), with the neuter article, as equivalent to a noun, and is translated "appearance," RV, for KJV, "sight," Heb. 12:21.

APPOINT, APPOINTED

1. *histemi* (*2476*), "to make to stand," means "to appoint," in Acts 17:31, of the day in which God will judge the world by Christ. In Acts 1:23, with reference to Joseph and Barnabas, the RV has "put forward"; for these were not both "appointed" in the accepted sense of the term, but simply singled out, in order that it might be made known which of them the Lord had chosen.

2. *kathistemi* (*2525*), a strengthened form of No. 1, usually signifies "to appoint a person to a position." In this sense the verb is often translated "to make" or "to set," in appointing a person to a place of authority, e.g., a servant over a household, Matt. 24:45, 47; 25:21, 23; Luke 12:42, 44; a judge, Luke 12:14; Acts 7:27, 35; a governor, Acts 7:10; man by God over the work of His hands, Heb. 2:7. It is rendered "appoint," with reference to the so-called seven deacons in Acts 6:3. The RV translates it by "appoint" in Titus 1:5, instead of "ordain," of the elders whom Titus was to "appoint" in every city in Crete. Not a formal ecclesiastical ordination is in view, but the "appointment," for the recognition of the churches, of those who had already been raised up and qualified by the Holy Spirit, and had given evidence of this in their life and service (see No.9). It is used of the priests of old, Heb. 5:1; 7:28; 8:3 (RV, "appointed").

3. *tithemi* (*5087*), "to put," is used of "appointment" to any form of service. Christ used it of His followers, John 15:16 (RV, "appointed" for KJV, "ordained"). "I set you" would be more in keeping with the metaphor of grafting. The verb is used by Paul of his

service in the ministry of the gospel, 1 Tim. 1:12 (RV, "appointing" for "putting"); 2:7 (RV, "appointed" for "ordained"); and 2 Tim. 1:11 (RV, "appointing" for "putting"); of the overseers, or bishops, in the local church at Ephesus.

4. *diatithemi* (*1303*), a strengthened form of No. 3, is used in the middle voice only. The Lord used it of His disciples with reference to the kingdom which is to be theirs hereafter, and of Himself in the same respect, as that which has been "appointed" for Him by His Father, Luke 22:29.

5. *tasso* (*5021*), "to place in order, arrange," signifies "to appoint," e.g., of the place where Christ had "appointed" a meeting with His disciples after His resurrection, Matt. 28:16; of positions of military and civil authority over others, whether "appointed" by men, Luke 7:8, or by God, Rom. 13:1, "ordained." It is said of those who, having believed the gospel, "were ordained to eternal life," Acts 13:48. The house of Stephanas at Corinth had "set themselves" to the ministry of the saints (KJV, "addicted"), 1 Cor. 16:15. Other instances of the arranging of special details occur in Acts 15:2; 22:10; 28:23.

6. *diatasso* (*1299*), a strengthened form of No. 5, frequently denotes "to arrange, appoint, prescribe," e.g., of what was "appointed" for tax collectors to collect, Luke 3:13; of the tabernacle, as "appointed" by God for Moses to make, Acts 7:44; of the arrangements "appointed" by Paul with regard to himself and his travelling companions, Acts 20:13; of what the apostle "ordained" in all the churches in regard to marital conditions, 1 Cor. 7:17; of what the Lord "ordained" in regard to the support of those who proclaimed the gospel, 1 Cor. 9:14; of the Law as divinely "ordained," or administered, through angels, by Moses, Gal. 3:19.

7. *suntasso* (*4929*), *sun*, "with," and No. 5, lit., "to arrange together with," hence "to appoint, prescribe," is used twice, in Matt. 26:19 of what the Lord "appointed" for His disciples, and in 27:10, in a quotation concerning the price of the potter's field.

8. *protasso* (*4384*), *pro*, "before," and No. 5, "to appoint before," is used in Acts 17:26 (RV, "appointed"), of the seasons arranged by God for nations, and the bounds of their habitation.

9. *cheirotoneo* (*5500*), primarily used of voting in the Athenian legislative assembly and meaning "to stretch forth the hands," is not to be taken in its literal sense; it could not be so taken in its compound *procheirotoneo*, "to choose before, appoint" since it is said of God, Acts 10:41.

10. *procheirizo* (*4400*), "at hand," signifies (a) "to deliver up, appoint," Acts 3:20 (RV, "appointed"); (b) in the middle voice, "to take into one's hand, to determine, appoint beforehand," translated "appointed" in Acts 22:14, RV (for KJV, "hath chosen"), and "to appoint" in 26:16 (for KJV, "to make").

11. *horizo* (*3724*), (Eng., "horizon"), lit., "to mark by a limit,"

hence, "to determine, ordain," is used of Christ as ordained of God to be a judge of the living and the dead, Acts 17:31; of His being "marked out" as the Son of God, Rom. 1:4; of divinely appointed seasons, Acts 17:26, "having determined."

APPREHEND

katalambano (2638) properly signifies "to lay hold of"; then, "to lay hold of so as to possess as one's own, to appropriate." Hence it has the same twofold meaning as the Eng. "to apprehend"; (a), "to seize upon, take possession of," (1) with a beneficial effect, of "laying hold" of the righteousness which is of faith, Rom. 9:30 (not there a matter of attainment, as in the Eng. versions, but of appropriation); of the obtaining of a prize, 1 Cor. 9:24 (RV, "attain"); of the apostle's desire "to apprehend," or "lay hold of," that for which he was apprehended by Christ, Phil. 3:12-13; (2) with a detrimental effect, e.g., of demon power, Mark 9:18; of human action in seizing upon a person, John 8:3-4; metaphorically, with the added idea of overtaking, of spiritual darkness in coming upon people, John 12:35; of the Day of the Lord, in suddenly coming upon unbelievers as a thief, 1 Thess. 5:4; (b), "to lay hold of" with the mind, to understand, perceive, e.g., metaphorically, of darkness with regard to light, John 1:5, though possibly here the sense is that of (a) as in 12:35; of mental perception, Acts 4:13; 10:34; 25:25; Eph. 3:18.

APPROACH

A. Verb.

engizo (1448), "to draw near, to approach," from *engus*, "near," is used (a) of place and position, literally and physically, Matt. 21:1; Mark 11:1; Luke 12:33; 15:25; figuratively, of drawing near to God, Matt. 15:8; Heb. 7:19; Jas. 4:8; (b) of time, with reference to things that are imminent, as the kingdom of heaven, Matt. 3:2; 4:17; 10:7.

B. Adjective.

aprositos (676), "unapproachable, inaccessible," in 1 Tim. 6:16, of the light in which God dwells (KJV, "which no man can approach unto"; RV, "unapproachable").

APPROVE, APPROVED

A. Verbs.

1. *dokimazo* (1381), primarily, of metals; signifies "to prove," e.g., 1 John 4:1, more frequently to prove with a view to approval, e.g., Rom. 1:28, KJV, "they did not like to retain God in their knowledge"; RV, "they refused"; marg., "did not approve," the true meaning. Their refusal was not the outcome of ignorance; they had the power to make a deliberate choice; they willfully disap-

proved of having God in their knowledge; Rom. 2:18; 14:22; 1 Cor. 16:3; 2 Cor. 8:22; Phil. 1:10; 1 Thess. 2:4.

2. *sunistemi* (4921), lit., "to set together," hence signifies "to set one person or thing with another by way of presenting and commending." This meaning is confined to Romans and 2 Corinthians. The saints at Corinth had "approved themselves in everything to be pure," in the matter referred to, 2 Cor. 7:11. The word often denotes "to commend," so as to meet with approval, Rom. 3:5; 5:8; 16:1; 2 Cor. 4:2; 6:4 (RV); 10:18; 12:11, etc.

3. *apodeiknumi* (584), lit., "to point out, to exhibit," "to show," is used once in the sense of proving by demonstration, and so bringing about an "approval." The Lord Jesus was "a Man approved of God by mighty works and wonders and signs," Acts 2:22.

B. Adjective.

dokimos (1384), akin to *dechomai*, "to receive," always signifies "approved"; so the RV everywhere, e.g., in Jas. 1:12 for KJV, "when he is tried."

ARCHANGEL

archangelos (743) A being of exalted rank, named Michael, 1 Thess. 4:16 and Jude 9; cf. also Rev. 12:7; cf. also Rom. 8:38; Eph. 1:21; Col. 1:16. In 1 Thess. 4:16 the meaning seems to be that the voice of the Lord Jesus will be of the character of an "archangelic" shout.

ARISE, AROSE, AROUSE, RAISE, RISE, ROUSE

1. *anistemi* (450), "to stand up or to make to stand up," is used (a) of a physical change of position, Mark 1:35; Luke 4:29; Matt. 26:62. (b) metaphorically, of "rising" up antagonistically against persons, e.g. of officials against people, Acts 5:17; of a seditious leader, 5:36, of the "rising" up of Satan, Mark 3:26; of false teachers, Acts 20:30; (c) of "rising" to a position of preeminence or power; e.g., of Christ as a prophet, Acts 3:22; 7:37. (d) of a spiritual awakening from lethargy, Eph. 5:14; (e) of resurrection from the dead: (1) of Christ, Mark 8:31; 9:9-10, 31; 10:34; (2) of believers, John 6:39-40; 1 Thess. 4:16; of unbelievers, Matt. 12:41.

2. *exanistemi* (1817), a strengthened form of No. 1, signifies "to raise up," Mark 12:19; Luke 20:28; intransitively, "to rise up, Acts 15:5.

3. *egeiro* (1453) is frequently used in the NT in the sense of "raising" (active voice), or "rising" (middle and passive voices): (a) from sitting, lying, sickness, e.g., Matt. 2:14; 9:5, 7, 19; Jas. 5:15; Rev. 11:1; (b) of causing to appear, or, in the passive, appearing, or raising up so as to occupy a place in the midst of people, Matt. 3:9; 11:11; Mark 13:22; Acts 13:22. It is thus said of Christ in Acts 13:23; cf. No.

A

1, (c); (c) of rousing, stirring up, or "rising" against, Matt. 24:7; Mark 13:8; (d) of "raising buildings," John 2:19-20; (e) of "raising or rising" from the dead; (1) of Christ, Matt. 16:21; and frequently elsewhere (but not in Phil., 2 Thess., 1 Tim., Titus, Jas., 2 Pet., 1, 2, 3 John, and Jude); (2) of Christ's "raising" the dead, Matt. 11:5; Mark 5:41; Luke 7:14; John 12:1, 9, 17; (3) of the act of the disciples, Matt. 10:8; (4) of the resurrection of believers, Matt. 27:52; John 5:21; 1 Cor. 15:15-16, 29, 32, 35, 42-44 52; 2 Cor. 1:9; 4:14; of unbelievers, Matt. 12:42 (cf. v. 41, No. 1).

4. *diegeiro* (1326), a strengthened form of No. 3, signifies "to rouse, to awaken from sleep." The active voice is not used intransitively. In Matt. 1:24, RV, "Joseph arose from his sleep," the passive participle is, lit., "being aroused." In Mark 4:39 (KJV, "he arose," RV, "he awoke"), the lit. rendering is "he being awakened." In John 6:18 the imperfect tense of the passive voice is used, and the rendering should be, "the sea was being aroused."

5. *anatello* (393), "to arise," is used especially of things in the natural creation, Matt. 4:16; in Heb. 7:14 metaphorically, of the Incarnation of Christ.

ARK

Old Testament

'aron (727), "ark; coffin; chest; box." In Gen. 50:26, this word represents a coffin or sarcophagus, In 2 Kings 12:9, this is a chest with a hole in its lid. In most occurrences, *'aron* refers to the "ark of the covenant." This piece of furniture functioned primarily as a container. As such the word is often modified by divine names or attributes. The divine name first modifies *'aron* in 1 Sam. 3:3. *'aron* is first modified by God's covenant name, **Yahweh,** in Josh. 4:5. Judg. 20:27 is the first appearance of the "ark" as the ark of the covenant of *'elohim*. First Samuel 5:11 uses the phrase "the ark of the God [*'elohim*] of Israel," and 1 Chron. 15:12 employs "the ark of the Lord [**Yahweh**] God [*'elohim*] of Israel."

As such, the ark contained the memorials of God's great redemptive acts—the tablets upon which were inscribed the Ten Commandments, an omer or two quarts of manna, and Aaron's rod. By Solomon's day, only the stone tablets remained in the ark, 1 Kings 8:9. This chest was also called "the ark of the testimony," Exod. 25:22, which indicates that the two tablets were evidence of divine redemption, for description, see Exodus 25:10-22.

In addition to containing memorials of divine redemption, the ark represented the presence of God. To be before it was to be in God's presence, Num. 10:35, although His presence was not limited to the ark (cf. 1 Sam. 4:3-11; 7:2, 6). The ark ceased to have this sacramental function when Israel began to regard it as a magical box with sacred power (a *palladium*).

God promised to meet Moses at the ark, Exod. 25:22. Thus, the ark functioned as a place where divine revelation was received, Lev. 1:1; 16:2; Num. 7:89. The ark served as an instrument through which God guided and defended Israel during the wilderness wandering, Num. 10:11. Finally, it was upon this ark that the highest of Israel's sacraments, the blood of atonement, was presented and received, Lev. 16:2ff..

New Testament

kibotos (2787), "a wooden box, a chest," is used of (a) Noah's vessel, Matt. 24:38; Luke 17:27; Heb. 11:7; 1 Pet. 3:20; (b) the "ark" of the covenant in the tabernacle, Heb. 9:4; (c) the "ark" seen in vision in the heavenly temple, Rev. 11:19.

ARM

zeroa' (2220) means "arm," a part of the body, Deut. 33:20. The word refers to arms in Gen. 49:24, In some passages, *zeroa'* refers especially to the forearm, Isa. 17:5. Elsewhere, "shoulder," 2 Kings 9:24. In Num. 6:19 *zeroa'* is used of an animal's shoulder, cf. Deut. 18:3.

zeroa' connotes the "seat of strength," Ps. 18:34. In Job 26:2, the poor are described as the arm that has no strength. God's strength is figured by anthropomorphisms (attributing to Him human bodily parts), such as His "stretched out arm," Deut. 4:34, or His "strong arm," Jer. 21:5. In Isa. 30:30, the word seems to represent lightning bolts, cf. Job 40:9.

The arm is frequently a symbol of strength, both of man, 1 Sam. 2:31, and of God, Ps. 71:18. In Ezek. 22:6 *zeroa'* may be translated "power." A third nuance is "help," Ps. 83:8. The word can also represent political or military forces, Dan. 11:15; cf. Ezek. 17:9.

ARMS (weapons), ARMOR, TO ARM

A. Nouns.

1. *hoplon* (3696), originally any tool or implement for preparing a thing, became used in the plural for "weapons of warfare." Once in the NT it is used of actual weapons, John 18:3; elsewhere, metaphorically, of (a) the members of the body as instruments of unrighteousness and as instruments of righteousness, Rom. 6:13; (b) the "armor" of light, Rom. 13:12; the "armor" of righteousness, 2 Cor. 6:7; the weapons of the Christian's warfare, 2 Cor. 10:4.

2. *panoplia* (3833), (Eng., "panoply"), lit., "all armor, full armor,," is used (a) of literal "armor," Luke 11:22; (b) of the spiritual helps supplied by God for overcoming the temptations of the Devil, Eph. 6:11, 13.

B. Verbs.

1. *hoplizo* (3695), "to arm oneself," is used in 1 Pet. 4:1, in an ex-

A

hortation "to arm" ourselves with the same mind as that of Christ in regard to His sufferings.

2. *kathoplizo* (2528) is an intensive form, "to furnish fully with arms," Luke 11:21, lit., "a strong man fully armed."

ASHAMED (to be), SHAME

A. Verbs.

1. *aischuno* (153), always used in the passive voice, signifies (a) "to have a feeling of fear or shame which prevents a person from doing a thing," e.g., Luke 16:3; (b) "the feeling of shame arising from something that has been done," e.g., 2 Cor. 10:8; Phil. 1:20; 1 John 2:28, of the possibility of being "ashamed" before the Lord Jesus at His judgment seat in His Parousia with His saints; in 1 Pet. 4:16, of being ashamed of suffering as a Christian.

2. *epaischunomai* (1870), a strengthened form of No. 1, is used only in the sense (b) in the preceding paragraph. It is said of being "ashamed" of persons, Mark 8:38; Luke 9:26; the gospel, Rom. 1:16; former evil doing, Rom. 6:21; "the testimony of our Lord," 2 Tim. 1:8; suffering for the gospel, v. 12; rendering assistance and comfort to one who is suffering for the gospel's sake, v. 16. It is used in Heb., of Christ in calling those who are sanctified His brethren, 2:11, and of God in His not being "ashamed" to be called the God of believers, 11:16.

3. *kataischuno* (2617), another strengthened form, is used (a) in the active voice, "to put to shame," e.g., Rom. 5:5; 1 Cor. 1:27 (KJV, "confound"); 11:4-5 ("dishonoreth"), and v. 22; (b) in the passive voice, Rom. 9:33; 10:11; 2 Cor. 7:14; 1 Pet. 2:6; 3:16.

B. Noun.

1. *aischune* (152), "shame," akin to A, No. 1, signifies (a) subjectively, the confusion of one who is "ashamed" of anything, a sense of "shame," Luke 14:9; those things which "shame" conceals, 2 Cor. 4:2; (b) objectively, ignominy, that which is visited on a person by the wicked, Heb. 12:2; that which should arise from guilt, Phil. 3:19; (c) concretely, a thing to be "ashamed" of, Rev. 3:18; Jude 13, where the word is in the plural, lit., "basenesses," "disgraces."

ASHERAH

'asherah (842) refers to a cultic object representing the presence of the Canaanite goddess Asherah. When the people of Israel entered Palestine, they were to have nothing to do with the idolatrous religions of its inhabitants, but destroy the *'asherim*, Exod. 34:13. This cult object was manufactured from wood, Judg. 6:26; 1 Kings 14:15, and it could be burned, Deut. 12:3. Some scholars conclude that it was a sacred pole set up near an altar to Baal. Since there was only one goddess with this name, the plural (*'asherim*) probably represents her several "poles."

'asherah signifies the name of the goddess herself: "Now therefore send, and gather to me all Israel unto mount Carmel, and the prophets of Baal four hundred and fifty, and the prophets of the groves [*'asherah*] four hundred, which eat at Jezebel's table," 1 Kings 18:19. The Canaanites believed that *'asherah* ruled the sea, was the mother of all the gods including Baal, and sometimes was his deadly enemy.

ASK

Old Testament

A. Verb.

sha'al (7592), "to ask, inquire, consult." Since prayer often includes petition, *sha'al* is sometimes used in the sense of "praying for" something: "Pray for the peace of Jerusalem," Ps. 122:6. In the idiomatic phrase, "to ask another of his welfare," it carries the sense of a greeting, cf. Exod. 18:7; Judg. 18:15; 1 Sam. 10:4. Frequently, it is used to indicate someone's asking for God's direction or counsel, Josh. 9:14; Isa. 30:2. In Ps. 109:10 it is used to indicate a begging.

B. Noun.

she'ol (7585), "place of the dead." Often incorrectly translated "hell" in the KJV, *she'ol* was not understood to be a place of punishment, but simply the ultimate resting place of all mankind, Gen. 37:35. Thus, it was thought to be the land of no return, Job 16:22; 17:14-16. It was a place to be dreaded, not only because it meant the end of physical life on earth, but also because there was no praise of God there, Ps. 6:5. Deliverance from it was a blessing, Ps. 30:3.

she'ol is translated variously in the English versions· "hell, pit, grave" (KJV); "netherworld" (NAB). Some versions simply give the transliteration, Sheol" (RSV, JB, NASB).

New Testament

A. Verbs.

1. *aiteo* (154), "to ask," is to be distinguished from No. 2. *aiteo* more frequently suggests the attitude of a suppliant, the petition of one who is lesser in position than he to whom the petition is made; e.g., in the case of men in asking something from God, Matt. 7:7; a child from a parent, Matt. 7:9-10; a subject from a king, Acts 12:20.

2. *erotao* (2065) more frequently suggests that the petitioner is on a footing of equality or familiarity with the person whom he requests. It is used of a king in making request from another king, Luke 14:32; of the Pharisee who "desired" Christ that He would

eat with him, an indication of the inferior conception he had of Christ, Luke 7:36; cf. 11:37; John 9:15; 18:19.

In this respect it is significant that the Lord Jesus never used *aiteo* in the matter of making request to the Father. "The consciousness of His equal dignity, of His potent and prevailing intercession, speaks out in this, that as often as He asks, or declares that He will ask anything of the Father, it is always *erotao*, an asking, that is, upon equal terms, John 14:16; 16:26; 17:9, 15, 20, never *aiteo*, that He uses. Martha, on the contrary, plainly reveals her poor unworthy conception of His person, that...she ascribes that *aiteo* to Him which He never ascribes to Himself, John 11:22" (Trench, *Syn.* Sec. xl).

3. *eperotao* (*1905*), a strengthened form of No. 2, is frequently used in the synoptic Gospels, but only twice in the Gospel of John, 18:7, 21. In Rom. 10:20 it is rendered "asked of" (KJV, "asked after"). The more intensive character of the "asking" may be observed in Luke 2:46; 3:14; 6:9; 17:20; 20:21, 27, 40; 22:64, 23:3, 6, 9. In Matt. 16:1, it virtually signifies to demand (its meaning in later Greek).

B. Noun.

aitema (*155*), akin to No. 1, lit., "that which has been asked for," is used in Luke 23:24, RV, "what they asked for" (KJV, "required"); Phil. 4:6, "requests"; 1 John 5:15, petitions.

ASLEEP, SLEEP

A. Verbs.

1. *katheudo* (*2518*), "to go to sleep," is chiefly used of natural "sleep," and is found most frequently in the Gospels, especially Matthew and Luke. With reference to death it is found in the Lord's remark concerning Jairus' daughter, Matt. 9:24; Mark 5:39; Luke 8:52. In the epistles of Paul it is used as follows: (a) of natural "sleep," e.g., 1 Thess. 5:7; (b) of carnal indifference to spiritual things on the part of believers, Eph. 5:14; 1 Thess. 5:6, 10 (as in Mark 13:36), a condition of insensibility to divine things involving conformity to the world.

2. *koimaomai* (*2837*) is used of natural "sleep," Matt. 28:13; Luke 22:45; John 11:12; Acts 12:6; of the death of the body, but only of such as are Christ's; yet never of Christ Himself, though He is "the firstfruits of them that have fallen asleep," 1 Cor. 15:20, of saints who departed before Christ came, Matt. 27:52; Acts 13:36; of Lazarus, while Christ was yet upon the earth, John 11:11; of believers since the Ascension, 1 Thess. 4:13-15, and Acts 7:60; 1 Cor. 7:39; 11:30; 15:6, 18, 51; 2 Pet. 3:4.

In Paul's writings, it is evident the word 'sleep,' where applied to the departed Christians, is not intended to convey the idea that the spirit is unconscious, but the physical frame is dissolved and returns to the dust.

B. Noun.

hupnos (*5278*) is never used of death. In five places in the NT it is used of physical "sleep"; in Rom. 13:11, metaphorically, of a slumbering state of soul, i.e., of spiritual conformity to the world, out of which believers are warned to awake.

ASSEMBLE

1. *sunago* (*4863*), "to assemble," is used of the "gathering together" of people or things; in Luke 12:17-18.

2. *sunalizo* (*4871*), "to gather together, to assemble," with the suggestion of a crowded meeting. The corresponding adjective is *hales*, "thronged," is used in Acts 1:4.

3. *sunerchomai* (*4905*), "to come together," is once rendered "assemble," Mark 14:53, KJV. It is frequently used of "coming together," especially of the "gathering" of a local church, 1 Cor. 11:17-18, 20, 33-34; 14:23, 26; it is rendered "resorted" in Acts 16:13, KJV, where the RV adheres to the lit. rendering, "came together."

ASSEMBLY

Old Testament

A. Noun.

qahal (*6951*), "assembly; company." In many contexts, the word means an assembly gathered to plan or execute war. One of the first of these is Gen. 49:6. In 1 Kings 12:3 (RSV), "all the assembly of Israel" asked Rehoboam to ease the tax burden imposed by Solomon. When Rehoboam refused, they withdrew from him and rejected their feudal (military) allegiance to him. For the application of *qahal* to an army, see Ezek. 17:17.

Quite often, *qahal* is used to denote a gathering to judge or deliberate. This emphasis first appears in Ezek. 23:45-47, where the "company" judges and executes judgment. In many passages, the word signifies an assembly representing a larger group, 1 Chron. 13:1-2, RSV. Here, "the whole assembly" of Israel refers to the assembled leaders, cf. 2 Chron. 1:2. Thus, in Lev. 4:13 we find that the sin of the whole congregation of Israel can escape the notice of the "assembly" (the judges or elders who represent the congregation).

Sometimes *qahal* represents all the males of Israel who were eligible to bring sacrifices to the Lord, Deut. 23:1, RSV. The only eligible members of the assembly were men who were religiously bound together under the covenant, who were neither strangers (living in Israel temporarily) nor sojourners (permanent non-Hebrew residents), Num. 15:15. In Num. 16:3 and 33, it is clear that the "assembly" was the worshiping, voting community, cf. 18:4.

Elsewhere, the word *qahal* is used to signify all the people of Israel. The whole congregation of the sons of Israel complained that Moses had brought them forth into the wilderness to kill the whole assembly with hunger, Exod. 16:31. The first occurrence of the word also bears the connotation of a large group, Gen. 28:3.

B. Verb.

qahal (6950), "to gather." It means "to gather" as a *qahal* for conflict or war, for religious purposes, and for judgment, 1 Kings 8:1.

New Testament

1. *ekklesia* (1577), "a calling out of," was used among the Greeks of a body of citizens "gathered" to discuss the affairs of state, Acts 19:39. In Acts 7:38 it is used of Israel; in 19:32, 41, of a riotous mob. It has two applications to companies of Christians, (a) to the whole company of the redeemed throughout the present era, the company of which Christ said, "I will build My Church," Matt. 16:18, and which is further described as "the Church which is His Body," Eph. 1:22; 5:23, (b) in the singular number (e.g., Matt. 18:17, RV marg., "congregation"), to a company consisting of professed believers, e.g., Acts 20:28; 1 Cor. 1:2; Gal. 1:13; 1 Thess. 1:1; 2 Thess. 1:1; 1 Tim. 3:5, and in the plural, with reference to churches in a district.

2. *paneguris* (3831), "any kind of assembly," denoted, among the Greeks, an assembly of the people in contrast to the council of national leaders, or a "gathering" of the people in honor of a god, or for some public festival, such as the Olympic games. The word is used in Heb. 12:23, coupled with the word "church," as applied to all believers who form the body of Christ.

ASSURANCE, ASSURE, ASSUREDLY

A. Nouns.

1. *pistis* (4102), "faith," has the secondary meaning of "an assurance or guarantee," e.g., Acts 17:31; by raising Christ from the dead, God has given "assurance" that the world will be judged by Him (the KJV margin, "offered faith" does not express the meaning). Cf. 1 Tim. 5:12, where "faith" means "pledge."

2. *plerophoria* (4136), "a fullness, abundance," also means "full assurance, entire confidence;" lit., a "full-carrying." Some explain it as full fruitfulness (cf. RV, "fullness" in Heb. 6:11). In 1 Thess. 1:5 it describes the willingness and freedom of spirit enjoyed by those who brought the gospel to Thessalonica; in Col. 2:2, the freedom of mind and confidence resulting from an understanding in Christ; in Heb. 6:11 (KJV, "full assurance," RV, "fullness"), the engrossing effect of the expectation of the fulfillment of God's prom-

ises; in Heb. 10:22, the character of the faith by which we are to draw near to God.

3. *hupostasis* (5287), lit., "a standing under, support," hence, an "assurance," is so rendered in Heb. 11:1, RV, for KJV, "substance." It here may signify a title-deed, as giving a guarantee, or reality.

B. Verbs.

1. *pistoo* (4104), "to trust or give assurance to" (cf. A, No. 1), has a secondary meaning, in the passive voice, "to be assured of," 2 Tim. 3:14.

2. *plerophoreo* (4135), akin to A, No. 2, "to bring in full measure, to fulfill," also signifies "to be fully assured," Rom. 4:21, RV, of Abraham's faith. In 14:5 it is said of the apprehension of the will of God. So in Col. 4:12 in the best mss. In these three places it is used subjectively, with reference to an effect upon the mind. For its other and objective use, referring to things external.

3. *peitho* (3782), "to persuade," is rendered "assure" in 1 John 3:19 (marg., "persuade"), where the meaning is that of confidence toward God consequent upon loving in deed and in truth.

ATONE, ATONEMENT
Old Testament

A. Verb.

kapar (3722), "to cover over, atone, propitiate, pacify." This root is found in the Hebrew language at all periods of its history, and perhaps is best known from the term *Yom Kippur*, "Day of Atonement."

Most uses of the word, however, involve the theological meaning of "covering over," often with the blood of a sacrifice, in order to atone for some sin. It is not clear whether this means that the "covering over" hides the sin from God's sight or implies that the sin is wiped away in this process.

As might be expected, this word occurs more frequently in the Book of Leviticus than in any other book, since Leviticus deals with the ritual sacrifices that were made to atone for sin. For example, Lev. 4:13-21 gives instructions for bringing a young bull to the tent of meeting for a sin offering. After the elders laid their hands on the bull (to transfer the people's sin to the bull), the bull was killed. The priest then brought some of the blood of the bull into the tent of meeting and sprinkled it seven times before the veil. Some of the blood was put on the horns of the altar and the rest of the blood was poured at the base of the altar of burnt offering. The fat of the bull was then burned on the altar. The bull itself was to be burned outside the camp. By means of this ritual, "the priest shall make an atonement [*kapar*] for them, and it shall be forgiven them," Lev. 4:20.

Sometimes atonement for sin was made apart from or without blood offerings. During his vision-call experience, Isaiah's lips were touched with a coal of fire taken from the altar by one of the seraphim. With that, he was told, "Thy sin is purged [*kapar*]" Isa. 6:7. The English versions translate the word variously as "purged" (KJV, JB); "forgiven" (RSV, NASB, TEV); and "wiped away" (NEB). In another passage, Scripture says that the guilt or iniquity of Israel would be "purged" (KJV, NEB) by the destruction of the implements of idolatrous worship, Isa. 27:9. In this case, the RSV renders *kapar* as "expiated," while the NASB and TEV translate it as "forgiven."

B. Noun.

kapporet (3727), "mercy seat; throne of mercy." This noun form of *kapar* has been variously interpreted by the English versions as "mercy seat" (KJV, RSV); "cover" (NEB); "lid" (TEV); "throne of mercy" (JB); and "throne" (Knox). It refers to a slab of gold that rested on top of the ark of the covenant. Images of two cherubims stood on this slab, facing each other. This slab of gold represented the throne of God and symbolized His real presence in the worship shrine.

New Testament

katallage (2643), translated "atonement" in the KJV of Rom. 5:11, signifies, not "atonement," but "reconciliation," as in the RV. See also Rom. 11:15; 2 Cor. 5:18-19. The corresponding NT words are *hilasmos*, "propitiation," 1 John 2:2; 4:10, and *hilasterion*, Rom. 3:25; Heb. 9:5, "mercy-seat," the covering of the ark of the covenant. These describe the means (in and through the person and work of the Lord Jesus Christ, in His death on the cross by the shedding of His blood in His vicarious sacrifice for sin) by which God shows mercy to sinners.

ATTAIN

1. *katantao* (2658), a strengthened form of *antao*, "to come opposite to," signifies "to reach, to arrive at." It is used in its local significance several times in the Acts, e.g. 27:12.

In its metaphorical sense of "attaining" to something it is used in three places: Acts 26:7, of the fulfillment of the promise of God made to the ancestors of Israel, to which promise the twelve tribes "hope to attain" (RV); in Eph. 4:13, of "attaining" to the unity of the faith and of the knowledge of the Son of God; in Phil. 3:11, of the paramount aims of the apostle's life, "if by any means," he says, "I might attain unto the resurrection from the dead," not the physical resurrection, which is assured to all believers hereafter, but to the present life of identification with Christ in His resurrection. For the metaphorical sense in 1 Cor. 10:11 and 14:36.

2. *katalambano* (2638), "to seize, to apprehend," whether physically or mentally, is rendered "attain" in the sense of making something one's own, appropriating a thing, Rom. 9:30, said of the Gentiles, who through the gospel have "attained" to, or laid hold of, the righteousness which is of faith, in contrast to the present condition of Israel; in 1 Cor. 9:24, of securing a prize.

3. *phthano* (5348), "to anticipate," also means "to reach, attain to a thing"; negatively of Israel. The only other passage where it has this significance is Phil. 3:16, "we have attained."

4. *tunchano* (5177), "to reach, meet with," signifies "to attain to," in Luke 20:35, RV (for KJV, obtain).

AUSTERE

austeros (840), akin to *auo*, "to dry up" (Eng., "austere"), primarily denotes "stringent to the taste," like new wine not matured by age, unripe fruit, etc., hence, "harsh, severe," Luke 19:21-22.

AUTHOR

1. *aitios* (159), an adjective, denotes "that which causes something." This and No. 2 are both translated "author" in Hebrews. *aitios*, in Heb. 5:9, describes Christ as the "Author of eternal salvation unto all them that obey Him." He is the concrete and active cause of our salvation. He has not merely caused or effected it, He is, as His name, "Jesus," implies, our salvation itself, Luke 2:30; 3:6.

2. *archegos* (747), translated "Prince" in Acts 3:15 and 5:31, but "Author" in Heb. 2:10, RV, "Captain," RV marg., and KJV, and "Author" in 12:2, primarily signifies "one who takes a lead in, or provides the first occasion of, anything." That Christ is the Prince of life signifies, as Chrysostom says, that "the life He had was not from another; the Prince or Author of life must be He who has life from Himself." But the word does not necessarily combine the idea of the source or originating cause with that of leader. In Heb. 12:2 where Christ is called the "Author and Perfecter of faith," He is represented as the one who takes precedence in faith and is thus the perfect exemplar of it. The pronoun "our" does not correspond to anything in the original, and may well be omitted. Christ in the days of His flesh trod undeviatingly the path of faith, and as the Perfecter has brought it to a perfect end in His own person. Thus He is the leader of all others who tread that path.

AUTHORITY

A. Noun.

1. *exousia* (1849) denotes "authority" (from the impersonal verb *exesti*, "it is lawful"). From the meaning of "leave or permission," or liberty of doing as one pleases, it passed to that of "the ability or strength with which one is endued," then to that of the "power

of authority," the right to exercise power, e.g., Matt. 9:6; 21:23; 2 Cor. 10:8; or "the power of rule or government," the power of one whose will and commands must be obeyed by others, e.g., Matt. 28:18; John 17:2; Jude 25; Rev. 12:10; 17:13; more specifically of apostolic "authority," 2 Cor. 10:8; 13:10; the "power" of judicial decision, John 19:10; of "managing domestic affairs," Mark 13:34. By metonymy, or name-change (the substitution of a suggestive word for the name of the thing meant), it stands for "that which is subject to authority or rule," Luke 4:6 (RV, "authority," for the KJV "power"); or, as with the English "authority," "one who possesses authority, a ruler, magistrate," Rom. 13:1-3; Luke 12:11; Titus 3:1; or "a spiritual potentate," e.g., Eph. 3:10; 6:12; Col. 1:16; 2:10, 15; 1 Pet. 3:22. The RV usually translates it "authority."

B. Verbs.

1. *exousiazo* (1850), akin to A, signifies "to exercise power," Luke 22:25; 1 Cor. 6:12; 7:4 (twice).

2. *katexousiazo* (2175), "to exercise authority upon," is used in Matt. 20:25, and Mark 10:42.

AVENGE, AVENGER
Old Testament

A. Verb.

naqam (5358), "to avenge, take vengeance, punish." Lamech's sword song is a scornful challenge to his fellows and a blatant attack on the justice of God, Gen. 4:23-24.

The Lord reserves vengeance as the sphere of His own action: "To me belongeth vengeance, and recompense...for he will avenge the blood of his servants, and will render vengeance to his adversaries," Deut. 32:35, 43. The law therefore forbade personal vengeance, Lev. 19:18. Hence the Lord's people commit their case to Him, as David, 1 Sam. 24:12.

The Lord uses men to take vengeance, Num. 31:2-3. Vengeance for Israel is the Lord's vengeance.

The law stated, "And if a man smite his servant, or his maid, with a rod, and he die under his hand; he shall be surely punished," Exod. 21:20. In Israel, this responsibility was given to the "avenger of blood," Deut. 19:6. He was responsible to preserve the life and personal integrity of his nearest relative.

When a man was attacked because he was God's servant, he could rightly call for vengeance on his enemies, Judg. 16:28.

In the covenant, God warned that His vengeance may fall on His own people, Lev. 26:25; Isa. 1:24.

B. Noun.

naqam (5359), "vengeance." The noun is first used in the Lord's promise to Cain, Gen. 4:15.

In some instances a man may call for "vengeance" on his enemies, such as when another man has committed adultery with his wife, Prov. 6:34.

The prophets frequently speak of God's "vengeance" on His enemies: Isa. 59:17; Mic. 5:15; Nah. 1:2. It will come at a set time, Isa. 34:8.

Isaiah brings God's "vengeance" and redemption together in the promise of messianic salvation, Isa. 61:1-2. When Jesus announced that this was fulfilled in Himself, He stopped short of reading the last clause; but His sermon clearly anticipated that "vengeance" would come on Israel for rejecting Him, Isa. 63:4.

New Testament

A. Verb.

ekdikeo (1556), *ek*, "from," *dike*, "justice," i.e., that which proceeds from justice, means (a) "to vindicate a person's right," (b) "to avenge a thing." With the meaning (a), it is used in the parable of the unjust judge, Luke 18:3, 5, of the "vindication" of the rights of the widow; with the meaning (b) it is used in Rev. 6:10 and 19:2, of the act of God in "avenging" the blood of the saints; in 2 Cor. 10:6, of the apostle's readiness to use his apostolic authority in punishing disobedience on the part of his readers; here the RV substitutes "avenge" for the KJV, "revenge"; in Rom. 12:19 of "avenging" oneself, against which the believer is warned.

B. Nouns.

1. *ekdikos* (1558), primarily, "without law," then, "one who exacts a penalty from a person, an avenger, a punisher," is used in Rom. 13:4 of a civil authority in the discharge of his function of executing wrath on the evildoer (KJV, wrongly, "revenger"); in 1 Thess. 4:6, of God as the avenger of the one who wrongs his brother, here particularly in the matter of adultery.

2. *ekdikesis* (1557), vengeance," is used with the verb *poieo*, "to make," i.e., to avenge, in Luke 18:7-8; Acts 7:24; twice it is used in statements that "vengeance" belongs to God, Rom. 12:19; Heb. 10:30. In 2 Thess. 1:8 it is said of the act of divine justice which will be meted out to those who know not God and obey not the gospel, when the Lord comes in flaming fire at His second advent, though with no element of vindictiveness.

AVOID

1. *ekklino* (1578), "to turn away from, to turn aside," lit., "to bend out of" (*ek*, "out," *klino*, "to bend"), is used in Rom. 3:12, of the sinful condition of mankind, KJV, "gone out of the way," RV, "turned aside"; in Rom. 16:17, of turning away from those who cause offenses and occasions of stumbling (KJV, "avoid"); in 1 Pet. 3:11 of turning away from evil (KJV, "eschew").

A

2. *ektrepo* (*1624*), lit., "to turn or twist out," is used in the passive voice in Heb. 12:13, "that which is lame be not turned out of the way" (or rather, "put out of joint"); in the sense of the middle voice (though passive in form) of turning aside, or turning away from, 2 Tim. 4:4 (KJV, "shall be turned unto fables," RV, "shall turn aside"); in 1 Tim. 1:6, of those who, having swerved from the faith, have turned aside unto vain talking; in 5:15, of those who have turned aside after Satan; in 6:20, RV, of "turning away from (KJV, 'avoiding') profane babblings and oppositions of the knowledge which is falsely so called."

3. *paraiteomai* (*3868*), lit., "to ask aside," signifies (a) "to beg of (or from) another," Mark 15:6, in the most authentic mss.; (b) "to deprecate," (1) "to entreat (that) not," Heb. 12:19; (2) "to refuse, decline, avoid," 1 Tim. 4:7; 5:11; 2 Tim. 2:23; Titus 3:10 (see No. 4 for v. 9); Heb. 12:25; (c) "to beg off, ask to be excused," Luke 14:18-19 (some would put Heb. 12:25 here).

4. *periistemi* (*4026*), in the active voice, means "to stand around," John 11:42; Acts 25:7; in the middle voice, "to turn oneself about," for the purpose of avoiding something, "to avoid, shun," said of profane babblings, 2 Tim. 2:16; of foolish questions, genealogies, strife, etc., Titus 3:9 (KJV, "avoid").

5. *stello* (*4724*), "to place," sometimes signifies, in the middle voice, "to take care against a thing, to avoid," 2 Cor. 8:20; in 2 Thess. 3:6, "of withdrawing from a person."

AWAKE

1. *egeiro* (*1453*) is used, (a) in the active voice, of "arousing a person from sleep" in Matt. 8:25 of the act of the disciples in awaking the Lord; in Acts 12:7, of the awaking of Peter, RV, "awake him"; (b) in the passive voice, with a middle significance, of the virgins, in "arousing themselves" from their slumber, Matt. 25:7; in Rom. 13:11, and Eph. 5:14, metaphorically, "of awaking from a state of moral sloth.

2. *diegeiro* (*1326*), is used of "awaking from natural sleep," Matt. 1:24; Mark 4:38; of the act of the disciples in "awaking" the Lord, Luke 8:24.

3. *eknepho* (*1594*), primarily, "to return to one's sense from drunkenness, to become sober," in the NT in 1 Cor. 15:34, "Awake up righteously and sin not" (RV), suggesting a return to soberness of mind from the stupor consequent upon the influence of evil doctrine.

4. *exupnizo* (*1852*), "to rouse a person out of sleep," is used metaphorically, in John 11:11.

5. *diagregoreo* (*1235*), "to watch intensely" is used in Luke 9:32, RV, "were fully awake." KJV "were awake."

B

BAAL, MASTER

ba'al (1167), "master; baal." The word *ba'al* occurs 84 times in the Hebrew Old Testament, 15 times with the meaning of "husband" and 50 times as a reference to a deity.

The primary meaning of *ba'al* is "possessor." Isaiah's use of *ba'al* in parallel with *qanah* clarifies this basic significance of *ba'al*, Isa. 1:3. Man may be the owner [ba'al] of an animal, Exod. 22:10, a house, Exod. 22:7, a cistern, Exod. 21:34, or even a wife, Exod. 21:3.

A secondary meaning, "husband," is clearly indicated by the phrase *ba'al ha-ishshah*, literally, "owner of the woman," Exod. 21:22. The meaning of *ba'al* is closely related to *ish* "man," as is seen in 2 Sam. 11:26.

The word *ba'al* with another noun may signify a peculiar characteristic or quality, Gen. 37:19; the KJV offers a literal translation of the Hebrew—"master of dreams"—as an alternative.

Thirdly, the word *ba'al* may denote any deity other than the God of Israel. Baal was a common name given to the god of fertility in Canaan. In the Canaanite city of Ugarit, Baal was especially recognized as the god of fertility. The Old Testament records that Baal was "the god" of the Canaanites. The Israelites worshiped Baal during the time of the judges, Judg. 6:25-32, and of King Ahab. Elijah stood as the opponent of the Baal priests at Mount Carmel, 1 Kings 18:21ff. Many cities made Baal a local god and honored him with special acts of worship: Baal-peor, Num. 25:5, Baal-berith at Shechem, Judg. 8:33, Baal-zebub, 2 Kings 1:2-16, at Ekron, Baal-zephon, Num. 33:7, and Baal-hermon, Judg. 3:3.

BABBLER, BABBLINGS

1. *spermologos* (4691), "a babbler," is used in Acts 17:18. Primarily an adjective, it came to be used as a noun signifying a crow, or some other bird, picking up seeds (*sperma*, "a seed," *lego*, "to collect"). Then it seems to have been used of a man accustomed to hang about the streets and markets, picking up scraps which fall from loads; hence a parasite, who lives at the expense of others, a hanger on.

Metaphorically it became used of a man who picks up scraps of information and retails them secondhand, a plagiarist, or of those who make a show, in unscientific style, of knowledge obtained from misunderstanding lectures.

2. *kenophonia* (2757), "babbling" (from *kenos*, "empty," and *phone*, "a sound"), signifies empty discussion, discussion on useless subjects, 1 Tim. 6:20 and 2 Tim. 2:16.

BABY

1. *brephos* (1025) denotes (a) "an unborn child," as in Luke 1:41, 44; (b) "a newborn child, or an infant still older," Luke 2:12, 16; 18:15; Acts 7:19; 2 Tim. 3:15; 1 Pet. 2:2.

2. *nepios* (3516), lit., "without the power of speech," denotes "a little child," the literal meaning having been lost in the general use of the word. It is used (a) of "infants," Matt. 21:16; (b) metaphorically, of the unsophisticated in mind and trustful in disposition, Matt. 11:25 and Luke 10:21, where it stands in contrast to the wise; of those who are possessed merely of natural knowledge, Rom. 2:20; 1 Cor. 3:1; Heb. 5:13; Gal. 4:3; Eph. 4:14. "Immaturity" is always associated with this word.

BACKBITER, BACKBITING

katalalos (2637), a "backbiter," and *katalalia* (2636), "backbiting." *katalalos* is used in Rom. 1:30. *katalalia* is translated "evil speaking" in 1 Pet. 2:1, "backbiting" in 2 Cor. 12:20.

BAD

1. *kakos* (2556) indicates the lack in a person or thing of those qualities which should be possessed; it means "bad in character" (a) morally, by way of thinking, feeling or acting, e.g., Mark 7:21, "thoughts"; 1 Cor. 15:33, "company"; Col. 3:5, "desire"; 1 Tim. 6:10, "all kinds of evil"; 1 Pet. 3:9, "evil for evil"; (b) in the sense of what is injurious or baneful, e.g., the tongue as "a restless evil," Jas. 3:8; "evil beasts," Titus 1:12; "harm," Acts 16:28; once it is translated "bad," 2 Cor. 5:10. It is the opposite of *agathos*, "good."

2. *poneros* (4190), connected with *ponos*, "labor," expresses especially the "active form of evil," and is practically the same in meaning as (b), under No. 1. It is used, e.g., of thoughts, Matt. 15:19 (cf. *kakos*, in Mark 7:21); of speech, Matt. 5:11 (cf. *kakos*, in 1 Pet. 3:10); and of acts, 2 Tim. 4:18. Where *kakos* and *poneros* are put together, *kakos* is always put first and signifies "bad in character, base," *poneros*, "bad in effect, malignant": see 1 Cor. 5:8, and Rev. 16:2. *kakos* has a wider meaning, *poneros* a stronger meaning. *poneros* alone is used of Satan and might well be translated "the malignant one," e.g., Matt. 5:37 and five times in 1 John (2:13-14; 3:12; 5:18-19, RV); of demons, e.g., Luke 7:21. Once it is translated bad, Matt. 22:10.

3. *sapros* (4550), "corrupt, rotten" (akin to *sepo*, "to rot"), of trees

and fruit; Luke 6:43; of certain fish, Matt. 13:48; of defiling speech, Eph. 4:29.

BAPTISM, BAPTIST, BAPTIZE

A. Nouns.

1. ***baptisma*** (*908*), "baptism," consisting of the processes of immersion, submersion and emergence (from ***bapto***, "to dip"), is used (a) of John's "baptism," (b) of Christian "baptism"; (c) of the overwhelming afflictions and judgments to which the Lord voluntarily submitted on the cross, e.g., Luke 12:50; (d) of the sufferings His followers would experience, not of a vicarious character, but in fellowship with the sufferings of their Master. Some mss. have the word in Matt. 20:22-23; it is used in Mark 10:38-39, with this meaning.

2. ***baptismos*** (*909*), as distinct from ***baptisma*** (the ordinance), is used of the "ceremonial washing of articles," Mark 7:4, 8, in some texts; Heb. 9:10; once in a general sense, Heb. 6:2.

3. ***baptistes*** (*910*), "a baptist," is used only of John the Baptist, and only in the Synoptists, 14 times.

B. Verb.

baptizo (*907*), "to baptize," primarily a frequentative form of ***bapto***, "to dip," was used among the Greeks to signify the dyeing of a garment, or the drawing of water by dipping a vessel into another, etc. Plutarchus uses it of the drawing of wine by dipping the cup into the bowl (*Alexis*, 67) and Plato, metaphorically, of being overwhelmed with questions (*Euthydemus*, 277 D).

It is used in the NT in Luke 11:38 of washing oneself. In the early chapters of the four Gospels and in Acts 1:5; 11:16; 19:4, it is used of the rite performed by John the Baptist who called upon the people to repent that they might receive remission of sins. Those who obeyed came "confessing their sins," thus acknowledging their unfitness to be in the Messiah's coming kingdom. Distinct from this is the "baptism" enjoined by Christ, Matt. 28:19, a "baptism" to be undergone by believers, thus witnessing to their identification with Him in death, burial and resurrection, e.g., Acts 19:5; Rom. 6:3-4; 1 Cor. 1:13-17; 12:13; Gal. 3:27; Col. 2:12. The phrase in Matt. 28:19, "baptizing them into the Name" (RV; cf. Acts 8:16, RV), would indicate that the "baptized" person was closely bound to, or became the property of, the one into whose name he was "baptized."

In Acts 22:16 it is used in the middle voice, in the command given to Saul of Tarsus, "arise and be baptized," the significance of the middle voice form being "get thyself baptized." The experience of those who were in the ark at the time of the Flood was a figure or type of the facts of spiritual death, burial, and resurrection, Christian "baptism" being an ***antitupos***, "a corresponding type," a "like figure," 1 Pet. 3:21. Likewise the nation of Israel was figuratively baptized when made to pass through the Red Sea under the cloud, 1 Cor. 10:2. The verb is used metaphorically also in two distinct senses: firstly, of "baptism" by the Holy Spirit, which took place on the Day of Pentecost; secondly, of the calamity which would come upon the nation of the Jews, a "baptism" of the fire of divine judgment for rejection of the will and word of God, Matt. 3:11; Luke 3:16.

BARBARIAN, BARBAROUS

barbaros (915) properly meant "one whose speech is rude, or harsh"; the word is onomatopoeic, indicating in the sound the un-couth character represented by the repeated syllable "bar-bar." Hence it signified one who speaks a strange or foreign language. See 1 Cor. 14:11. It then came to denote any foreigner ignorant of the Greek language and culture. After the Persian war it ac-quired the sense of rudeness and brutality. In Acts 28:2, 4, it is used unreproachfully of the inhabitants of Malta, who were of Phoenician origin. So in Rom. 1:14, where it stands in distinction from Greeks, and in implied contrast to both Greeks and Jews. Cf. the contrasts in Col. 3:11, where all such distinctions are shown to be null and void in Christ. "Berber" stood similarly in the language of the Egyptians for all non-Egyptian peoples.

BARREN

steiros (4723), from a root *ster*— meaning "hard, firm" (hence Eng., "sterile"), signifies "barren, not bearing children," of natural state, Luke, 1:7, 36; 23:29; and of spiritual state, Gal. 4:27.

BASE, BASER

1. *agenes* (36), "of low birth," hence denoted "that which is of no reputation, of no account," 1 Cor. 1:28, "the base things of the world," i.e., those which are of no account or fame in the world's esteem. That the neuter plural of the adjective bears reference to persons is clear from verse 26.

2. *tapeinos* (5011), primarily "that which is low, and does not rise far from the ground," metaphorically, signifies "lowly, of no de-gree." So the RV in 2 Cor. 10:1. Cf. Luke 1:52 and Jas. 1:9, "of low degree."

3. *agoraios* (60), translated in the KJV of Acts 17:5 "of the baser sort," RV, "of the rabble," signifies, lit., "relating to the market place"; hence, frequenting markets, and so sauntering about idly. It is also used of affairs usually transacted in the market-place, and hence of judicial assemblies, Acts 19:38.

BASTARD

nothos (3541) denotes "an illegitimate child, one born out of lawful wedlock," Heb. 12:8.

BEAR

(*in the sense of "carrying, supporting"*)

1. *bastazo* (941) signifies "to support as a burden." It is used with the meaning (a) "to take up," John 10:31; (b) "to carry" something, Matt. 3:11; (c) "to bear" a burden, whether physically, as of the cross, John 19:17, or metaphorically in respect of sufferings endured in the cause of Christ, Luke 14:27; (d) to "bear" by way of carrying off, John 12:6.

2. *phero* (5342), "to bring or bear," is translated in the RV by the latter verb in Luke 23:26; John 2:8 (twice); 12:24; 15:2 (twice); Heb. 13:13.

3. *anaphero* (399), No. 2, with *ana*, up, is used of "leading persons up to a higher place," and, in this respect, of the Lord's ascension, Luke 24:51. It is used twice of the Lord's propitiatory sacrifice, in His bearing sins on the cross, Heb. 9:28 and 1 Pet. 2:24.

4. *ekphero* (1627), No. 2, with *ek*, "out," is used, literally, "of carrying something forth, or out," e.g., a garment, Luke 15:22; sick folk, Acts 5:15; a corpse, Acts 5:6; 9-10; of the impossibility of "carrying" anything out from this world at death, 1 Tim. 6:7.

5. *periphero* (4064), No. 2, with *peri*, "about," signifies "to carry about, or bear about," and is used literally, of carrying the sick Mark 6:55, or of physical sufferings endured in fellowship with Christ, 2 Cor. 4:10; metaphorically, of being "carried" about by different evil doctrines, Eph. 4:14; Heb. 13:9; Jude 12.

6. *hupophero* (5297), lit., "to bear up under," is best rendered by "endure," as 1 Cor. 10:13, RV, of enduring temptations; of "enduring" persecutions, 2 Tim. 3; grief, 1 Pet. 2:19.

7. *phoreo* (5409), a frequentative form of *phero*, is to be distinguished from it as denoting, not a simple act of bearing, but a continuous or habitual condition, e.g., of the civil authority in "bearing" the sword as symbolic of execution, Rom. 13:4; of a natural state of bodily existence in this life, spoken of as "the image of the earthy," and the spiritual body of the believer hereafter, "the image of the heavenly," 1 Cor. 15:49, the word "image" denoting the actual form and not a mere similitude.

8. *tropophoreo* (5159), from *tropos*, "a manner," and *phoreo*, "to endure," is found in Acts 13:18, where some ancient authorities have the verb *trophophoreo*, "He bare them as a nursing father," (from *trophos*, "a feeder, a nurse," and *phoreo*, "to carry").

9. *airo* (142) signifies here (a) "to suspend, to keep in suspense," John 10:24; (b) "to take away what is attached to anything, to re-

move," as of Christ, in taking (or "bearing," marg.) away the sin of the world, John 1:29

10. *anechomai* (430) signifies "to hold up against a thing and so to bear with," e.g., Matt. 17:7; 1 Cor. 4:12; 2 Cor. 11:1, 4, 19-20; Heb. 13:22, etc.

11. *makrothumeo* (3114), "to be long-tempered," is translated "is longsuffering over" in Luke 18:7, RV (KJV, "bear long with").

BEAST

1. *zoon* (2226) primarily denotes "a living being" (*zoe*, "life"). The Eng., "animal," is the equivalent, stressing the fact of life as the characteristic feature. In Heb. 13:11 the KJV and the RV translate it "beasts" ("animals" would be quite suitable). In 2 Pet. 2:12 and Jude 10, the KJV has "beasts," the RV "creatures." In the Apocalypse, where the word is found some 20 times, and always of those beings which stand before the throne of God, who give glory and honor and thanks to Him, 4:6, and act in perfect harmony with His counsels, 5:14; 6:1-7, e.g., the word "beasts" is most unsuitable; the RV, "living creatures," should always be used; it gives to *zoon* its appropriate significance.

2. *therion* (2342), to be distinguished from *zoon*, almost invariably denotes "a wild beast." In Acts 28:4, "venomous beast" is used of the viper which fastened on Paul's hand. *zoon* stresses the vital element, *therion* the bestial. The idea of a "beast" of prey is not always present. Once, in Heb. 12:20, it is used of the animals in the camp of Israel, such, e.g., as were appointed for sacrifice.

therion, in the sense of wild "beast," is used in the Apocalypse for the two antichristian potentates who are destined to control the affairs of the nations with Satanic power in the closing period of the present era, 11:7; 13:1-18; 14:9, 11; 15:2; 16:2, 10, 13; 17:3-17; 19:19-20; 20:4, 10.

BEAUTIFUL

1. *horaios* (5611) describes "that which is seasonable, produced at the right time," as of the prime of life, or the time when anything is at its loveliest and best (from *hora*, "a season," a period fixed by natural laws and revolutions, and so the best season of the year). It is used of the outward appearance of whited sepulchres in contrast to the corruption within Matt. 23:27; of the Jerusalem gate called "Beautiful," Acts 3:2, 10; of the feet of those that bring glad tidings, Rom. 10:15.

2. *asteios* (791), connected with *astu*, "a city," was used primarily "of that which befitted the town, town-bred" (corresponding Eng. words are "polite," "polished," connected with *polis*, "a town"; cf. "urbane," from Lat., *urbs*, "a city"). Among Greek writers it is set in contrast to *agroikos*, "rustic," and *aischros*, "base," and was used, e.g., of clothing. It is found in the NT only of Moses, Acts 7:20,

"(exceeding) fair," lit., "fair (to God)," and Heb. 11:23, "goodly"
(KJV, "proper").

BECKON

1. **neuo** (*3506*), lit., "to give a nod, to signify by a nod," is used in
John 13:24, of Peter's beckoning to John to ask the Lord of whom
He had been speaking; in Acts 24:10, of the intimation given by
Felix to Paul to speak.

2. **dianeuo** (*1269*), "to express one's meaning by a sign" (No. 1,
with **dia**, "through," used intensively), is said of the act of
Zacharias, Luke 1:22.

3. **kataneuo** (*2656*), No. 1, with **kata**, "down," intensive, is used of
the fishermen-partners in Luke 5:7, "beckoned."

BECOME (to be fitting)

A. Verb.

prepo (*4241*) means "to be conspicuous among a number, to be
eminent, distinguished by a thing," hence, "to be becoming, seemly, fit"; 1 Tim. 2:10; Titus 2:1; Heb. 7:26.

B. Adjective.

hieroprepes (*2412*), from **hieros**, "sacred," with the adjectival
form of **prepo**, denotes "suited to a sacred character, that which is
befitting in persons, actions or things consecrated to God," Titus
2:3.

BEFIT, BEFITTING

1. **prepo** (*4241*) is translated "befit" in Titus 2:1, RV (KJV, "become").

2. **aneko** (*433*), primarily, "to have arrived at, reached to, pertained to," came to denote "what is due to a person, one's duty,
what is befitting." It is used ethically in the NT; Eph. 5:4, RV, "are
(not) befitting," for KJV, "are (not) convenient"; Col. 3:18, concerning the duty of wives towards husbands, RV, "as is fitting," for KJV,
"as it is fit." In Philem. 8, the participle is used with the article, signifying "that which is befitting," RV (KJV, "that which is convenient").

BEG, BEGGAR, BEGGARLY

A. Verbs.

1. **epaiteo** (*1871*), a strengthened form of **aiteo**, is used in Luke
16:3.

2. **prosaiteo** (*4319*), lit., "to ask besides," "to ask earnestly, to im-
portune, continue asking," is said of the blind beggar in John 9:8.
In Mark 10:46 and Luke 18:35 certain mss. have this verb; the most
authentic have **prosaites**, "a beggar," a word used in John 9:8.

B. Adjective.

ptochos (*4434*), an adjective describing "one who crouches and cowers," is used as a noun, "a beggar," Luke 14:13, 21 ("poor"); 16:20, 22; as an adjective, "beggarly" in Gal. 4:9, i.e., poverty-stricken (condition), powerless to enrich, metaphorically descriptive of the religion of the Jews.

BEGET, BEAR (of begetting), BORN

A. Verbs.

1. *gennao* (*1080*), "to beget," in the passive voice, "to be born," is chiefly used of men or women "begetting" children, Matt. 1:2-16; Luke 1:13, 57. In Gal. 4:24, it is used allegorically, to contrast Jews under bondage to the Law, and spiritual Israel, KJV, "gendereth," RV, "bearing children," to contrast the natural birth of Ishmael and the supernatural birth of Isaac. In Matt. 1:20 it is used of conception. It is used of the act of God in the birth of Christ, Acts 13:33; Heb. 1:5; 5:5, quoted from Psalm 2:7, none of which indicate that Christ became the Son of God at His birth.

It is used metaphorically (a) of the gracious act of God in conferring upon those who believe the nature and disposition of "children," imparting to them spiritual life, John 3:3, 5, 7; 1 John 2:29; 3:9; 4:7; 5:1, 4, 18; (b) of one who by means of preaching the gospel becomes the human instrument in the impartation of spiritual life, 1 Cor. 4:15; Philem. 10; (c) in 2 Pet. 2:12, with reference to the evil men whom the apostle is describing, the RV rightly has "born mere animals"; (d) in the sense of gendering strife, 2 Tim. 2:23.

2. *anagennao* (*313*), *ana*, "again, or from above," with No. 1, is found in 1 Pet. 1:3, 23.

3. *apokueo* (*616*), "to give birth to," Jas. 1:18.

4. *tikto* (*5088*), "to bring forth," (a) lit. Luke 1:57; John 16:21; Heb. 11:11; Rev. 12:2, 4, or, (b) metaphorically in Jas. 1:15.

B. Noun.

genos (*1085*), "a generation, kind, stock," is used in the dative case, with the article, to signify "by race," in Acts 18:2 and 24, RV, for the KJV, "born."

C. Adjectives.

1. *gennetos* (*1084*), "born" (related to *gennao*, verb No. 1), is used in Matt. 11:11 and Luke 7:28 in the phrase "born of women," a periphrasis for "men," and suggestive of frailty.

2. *artigennetos* (*738*), "newborn" (*arti*, "newly, recently," and No. 1), is used in 1 Pet. 2:2.

BEGUILE

1. *apatao* (538), "to deceive," is rendered "beguiled" in the RV of 1 Tim. 2:14.

2. *exapatao* (1818), a strengthened form of No. 1, is rendered "beguile," 2 Cor. 11:3; the more adequate rendering would be "as the serpent thoroughly beguiled Eve." So in 1 Tim. 2:14, in the best mss., this stronger form is used of Satan's deception of Eve, lit., "thoroughly beguiled"; the simpler verb, No. 1, is used of Adam. In each of these passages the strengthened form is used. So of the influence of sin, Rom. 7:11 (RV, "beguile"); of self-deception, 1 Cor. 3:18 (RV, "deceive"); of evil men who cause divisions, Rom. 16:18 (RV, "beguile"); of deceitful teachers, 2 Thess. 2:3 (RV, "beguile").

3. *paralogizomai* (3884), lit. and primarily, "to reckon wrong," hence means "to reason falsely." Col. 2:4; Jas. 1:22.

4. *deleazo* (1185) originally meant "to catch by a bait" (from *delear*, "a bait"); hence "to beguile, entice by blandishments": in Jas. 1:14, "entice"; in 2 Pet. 2:14, KJV, "beguile"; in v. 18, KJV, "allure"; RV, "entice" in both.

BEHAVE, BEHAVIOR

A. Verb.

anastrepho (390), "to turn back, return" (*ana*, "back," *strepho*, "to turn"), hence, "to move about in a place, to sojourn," and, in the middle and passive voices, "to conduct oneself," indicating one's manner of life and character; 1 Tim. 3:15; Eph. 2:3; 2 Cor. 1:12.

B. Noun.

anastrophe (391), lit., "a turning back" (cf. Verb, above), is translated "manner of life," "living," etc. in the RV, for KJV, "conversation," Gal. 1:13; Eph. 4:22; 1 Tim. 4:12; Heb. 13:7; Jas. 3:13; 1 Pet. 1:15, 18; 2:1 ("behavior"); 3:1, 2, 16 (ditto); 2 Pet. 2:7; 3:11.

C. Adjective.

kosmios (2887), "orderly, modest," is translated "orderly" in 1 Tim. 3:2, RV, for KJV, "of good behavior." Both have "modest" in 1 Tim. 2:9.

BEHOLD, BEHELD

1. *horao* (3708), with its aorist form *eidon*, "to see" (in a few places the KJV uses the verb "to behold"), is said (a) of bodily vision, e.g., Mark 6:38; John 1:18, 46; (b) of mental perception, e.g., Rom. 15:21; Col. 2:18; (c) of taking heed, e.g., Matt. 8:4; 1 Thess. 5:15; (d) of experience, as of death, Luke 2:26; Heb. 11:5; life, John 3:36; corruption, Acts 2:27; (e) of caring for, Matt. 27:4; Acts 18:15 (here the form *opsomai* is used).

2. *blepo* (991) is also used of (a) bodily and (b) mental vision, (a)

"to perceive," e.g., Matt. 13:13; (b) "to take heed," e.g., Mark 13:23, 33; it indicates greater vividness than *horao*, expressing a more intent, earnest contemplation; in Luke 6:41, of "beholding" the mote in a brother's eye; Luke 24:12, of "beholding" the linen clothes in the empty tomb; Acts 1:9, of the gaze of the disciples when the Lord ascended. The greater earnestness is sometimes brought out by the rendering "regardest," Matt. 22:16.

3. *emblepo* (*1689*), from *en*, "in" (intensive), and No. 2, (not to be rendered literally), expresses "earnest looking," e.g., in the Lord's command to "behold" the birds of the heaven, with the object of learning lessons of faith from them, Matt. 6:26. See also 19:26; Mark 8:25; 10:21, 27; 14:67; Luke 20:17; 22:61; John 1:36; of the Lord's looking upon Peter, John 1:42; Acts 1:11; 22:11.

4. *ide* and *idou* (*2396* and *2400*) are imperative moods, active and middle voices, respectively, of *eidon*, "to see," calling attention to what may be seen or heard or mentally apprehended in any way. These are regularly rendered "behold." See especially the Gospels, Acts and the Apocalypse.

5. *epide* (*1896***), a strengthened form of No. 4 (with *epi*, "upon," prefixed), is used in Acts 4:29 of the entreaty made to the Lord to "behold" the threatenings of persecutors.

6. *theoreo* (*2334*), from *theoros*, "a spectator," is used of one who looks at a thing with interest and for a purpose, usually indicating the careful observation of details; this marks the distinction from No. 2; see, e.g., Mark 15:47; Luke 10:18; 23:35; John 20:6 (RV, "beholdeth," for KJV, "seeth"); so in verses 12 and 14; "consider," in Heb. 7:4. It is used of experience, in the sense of partaking of, in John 8:51; 17:24.

7. *anatheoreo* (*333*), *ana*, "up" (intensive), and No. 6, "to view with interest, consider contemplatively," is translated "beheld," in Acts 17:23, RV, "observed"; "considering" in Heb. 13:7.

8. *theaomai* (*2300*), "to behold, view attentively, contemplate," had, in earlier Greek usage, the sense of a wondering regard. This idea was gradually lost. It signifies a more earnest contemplation than the ordinary verbs for "to see," "a careful and deliberate vision which interprets its object," and is more frequently rendered "behold" in the RV than the KJV. Both translate it by "behold" in Luke 23:55 (of the sepulchre); "we beheld," in John 1:14, of the glory of the Son of God; "beheld," RV, in John 1:32; Acts 1:11; 1 John 1:1 (more than merely seeing); 4:12, 14.

9. *atenizo* (*816*) from *atenes*, "strained, intent," denotes "to gaze upon," "beholding earnestly," or "steadfastly" in Acts 14:9; 23:1.

10. *katanoeo* (*2657*), a strengthened form of *noeo*, "to perceive," (*kata*, intensive), denotes "the action of the mind in apprehending certain facts about a thing"; hence, "to consider"; "behold," Acts 7:31-32; Jas. 1:23-24.

11. *katoptrizo* (*2734*), from *katoptron*, "a mirror," in the active

voice, signifies "to make to reflect, to mirror"; in the middle voice "to reflect as a mirror"; so the RV in 2 Cor. 3:18, for KJV, "beholding as in a glass."

BELIAL

belial (955) came to be a proper name for Satan. There may be an indication of this in Nahum 1:15, where the word translated "the wicked one" is *Belial*.

The oldest form of the word is "Beliar," possibly from a phrase signifying "Lord of the forest," or perhaps simply a corruption of the form "Belial," due to harsh Syriac pronunciation. In the NT, in 2 Cor. 6:15, it is set in contrast to Christ and represents a personification of the system of impure worship connected especially with the cult of Aphrodite.

BELIEF, BELIEVE, BELIEVERS
Old Testament

A. Verb.

'aman (539), "to be firm, endure, be faithful, be true, stand fast, trust, have belief, believe." In the passive stem, *'aman* has several emphases. First, it indicates that a subject is "lasting" or "enduring," which is its meaning in Deut. 28:59. It also signifies the element of being "firm" or "trustworthy." In Isa. 22:23, *'aman* refers to a "firm" place, a place into which a peg will be driven so that it will be immovable. The peg will remain firmly anchored, even though it is pushed so hard that it breaks off at the point of entry, Isa. 22:25. The Bible also speaks of "faithful" people who fulfill their obligations, cf. 1 Sam. 22:14; Prov. 25:13.

The meaning "trustworthy" also occurs, Prov. 11:13; cf. Isa. 8:2. An office-bearer may be conceived as an "entrusted one," Job 12:20

In Gen. 42:20 Joseph requests that his brothers bring Benjamin to him; "so shall your words be verified," cf. 1 Kings 8:26; Hos. 5:9. In Hos. 11:12, *'aman* contrasts Judah's actions ("faithful") with those of Ephraim and Israel ("deceit"). So here *'aman* represents both "truthfulness" and "faithfulness," cf. Ps. 78:37; Jer. 15:18. The word may be rendered "true" in several passages, 1 Kings 8:26; 2 Chron. 1:9; 6:17.

'aman refers to what God has done ("faithfulness"), rather than what He will do ("trustworthy"), because He has already proved Himself faithful by keeping the covenant, Deut. 7:9.

Even more often, this stem connotes a psychological or mental certainty, as in Job 29:24. Considering something to be trustworthy is an act of full trusting or believing. This is the emphasis in the first biblical occurrence of *'aman*, Gen. 15:6. The meaning here is that Abram was full of trust and confidence in God, and that he did not fear Him (v. 1). It was not primarily in God's words that he believed, but in God Himself. Nor does the text tell us that Abram believed God so as to accept what He said as "true" and "trustworthy," cf. Gen. 45:26, but simply that he believed in God. In other words, Abram came to experience a personal relationship to God rather than an impersonal relationship with His promises, Exod. 4:9.

A more precise sense of *'aman* does appear sometimes: "That they may believe that the Lord..hath appeared unto thee," Exod. 4:5; cf. 1 Kings 10:7.

In other instances, *'aman* has a cultic use, by which the worshiping community affirms its identity with what the worship leader says, 1 Chron. 16:32. The "God of the *'amen*," 2 Chron. 20:20; Isa. 65:16, is the God who always accomplishes what He says; He is a "God who is faithful."

B. Noun.

'emunah (530), "firmness; faithfulness; truth; honesty; official obligation," Exod. 17:12; Isa. 33:6: 1 Chron. 9:22. The most frequent sense of *'emunah* is "faithfulness," 1 Sam. 26:23.

The essential meaning of *'emunah* is "established" or "lasting," "continuing," "certain," cf. 2 Sam. 7:16; Isa. 16:5. Thus, the phrase frequently rendered "with lovingkindness and truth" should be rendered "with perpetual (faithful) lovingkindness," cf. Josh. 2:14. He who sows righteousness earns a "true" or "lasting" reward, Prov. 11:18, a reward on which he can rely.

Quite often, this word means "truthfulness," as when it is contrasted to false swearing, lying, Jer. 5:1; cf. Jer. 5:2. Here *'emunah* signifies the condition of being faithful to God's covenant, practicing truth, or doing righteousness. On the other hand, the word can represent the abstract idea of "truth," Jer. 7:28. *'emunah* means "true"—the personal sense, which identifies a subject as honest, trustworthy, faithful, truthful (Prov. 12:22); and the factual sense, which identifies a subject as being factually true (cf. Prov. 12:27), as opposed to that which is false.

In other contexts, *'emunah* embraces other aspects of the concept of truth, Ps. 98:3. Here the emphasis is on truth as a subjective quality, defined personally. In a similar sense, one can both practice, Gen. 47:29, and speak the "truth," 2 Sam. 7:28.

C. Adverb.

'amen (543), "truly; genuinely; amen; so be it." The term *'amen* is used 30 times as an adverb. This Hebrew word usually appears as a response to a curse that has been pronounced upon someone, as the one accursed accepts the curse upon himself. By so doing, he binds himself to fulfill certain conditions or else be subject to the terms of the curse, cf. Deut. 29:15-26.

Although signifying a voluntary acceptance of the conditions of a covenant, the *'amen* was sometimes pronounced with coercion. Even in these circumstances, the one who did not pronounce it received the punishment embodied in the curse, Num. 5:22; Neh. 5:1-13; Jer. 18:6.

In 1 Kings 1:36, *'amen* is noncovenantal. It functions as an assertion of a person's agreement with the intent of a speech just delivered.

New Testament

A. Verb.

pisteuo (4100), "to believe," also "to be persuaded of," and hence, "to place confidence in, to trust," signifies, in this sense of the word, reliance upon, not mere credence. It is most frequent in the writings of the apostle John, especially the Gospel. He does not use the noun form (see below). For the Lord's first use of the verb, see 1:50. Of the writers of the Gospels, Matthew uses the verb ten times, Mark ten, Luke nine, John ninety-nine. In Acts 5:14 the present participle of the verb is translated "believers."

B. Noun.

pistis (4102), "faith," is translated "belief" in Rom. 10:17; 2 Thess. 2:13. Its chief significance is a conviction respecting God and His Word and the believer's relationship to Him.

C. Adjective.

pistos (4103), (a) in the active sense means "believing, trusting"; (b) in the passive sense, "trusty, faithful, trustworthy." It is translated "believer" in 2 Cor. 6:15; "them that believe" in 1 Tim. 4:12, RV (KJV, "believers "); in 1 Tim. 5:16, "if any woman that believeth," lit. "if any believing woman." So in 6:2, "believing masters." In 1 Pet. 1:21 the RV, following the most authentic mss., gives the noun form, "are believers in God" (KJV, "do believe in God"). In John 20:27 it is translated "believing." It is best understood with significance (a), above, e.g., in Gal. 3:9; Acts 16:1; 2 Cor. 6:15; Titus 1:6; it has significance (b), e.g., in 1 Thess. 5:24; 2 Thess. 3:3.

Notes: (1) The corresponding negative verb is *apisteo*, 2 Tim. 2:13, KJV, "believe not" RV, "are faithless," in contrast to the statement "He abideth faithful."

(2) The negative noun *apistia*, "unbelief," is used twice in Matthew (13:58); 17:20), three times in Mark (6:6; 9:24; 16:14), four times in Romans (3:3; 4:20; 11:20, 23); elsewhere in 1 Tim. 1:13 and Heb. 3:12, 19.

(3) The adjective *apistos* is translated "unbelievers" in 1 Cor. 6:6, and 2 Cor. 6:14; in v. 15, RV, "unbeliever" (KJV, "infidel"); so in 1 Tim. 5:8; "unbelieving" in 1 Cor. 7:12-15; 14:22-24; 2 Cor. 4:4; Titus 1:15; Rev. 21:8; "that believe not" in 1 Cor. 10:27. In the Gospels it

is translated "faithless" in Matt. 17:17; Mark 9:19; Luke 9:41; John 20:27, but in Luke 12:46, RV, "unfaithful," KJV, "unbelievers." Once it is translated "incredible," Acts 26:8.

(4) *plerophoreo*, in Luke 1:1 (KJV, "are most surely believed," lit., "have had full course"), the RV renders "have been fulfilled."

BELLY

1. *koilia* (2836), from *koilos*, "hollow" (Lat., *coelum*, "heaven," is connected), denotes the entire physical cavity, but most frequently was used to denote "the womb." In John 7:38 it stands metaphorically for the innermost part of man, the soul, the heart.

2. *gaster* (1064), (cf. Eng., "gastritis"), is used much as No. 1, but in Titus 1:12, by synecdoche (a figure of speech in which the part is put for the whole, or vice versa), it is used to denote "gluttons," RV, for KJV, "bellies."

BELOVED

A. Adjective.

agapetos (27), from *agapao*, "to love," is used of Christ as loved by God, e.g., Matt. 3:17; of believers (ditto), e.g., Rom. 1:7; of believers, one of another, 1 Cor. 4:14; often, as a form of address, e.g., 1 Cor. 10:14. Whenever the KJV has "dearly beloved," the RV has "beloved"; so, "well beloved" in 3 John 1; in 1 John 2:7, KJV, "brethren" (*adelphos*), the RV has "beloved," according to the mss. which have *agapetos*.

B. Verb.

agapao (25), in its perfect participle passive form, is translated "beloved" in Rom. 9:25; Eph. 1:6; Col. 3:12; 1 Thess. 1:4; 2 Thess. 2:13. In Jude 1 the best texts have this verb (RV); the KJV, "sanctified" follows those which have *hagiazo*.

BENEFIT, BENEFACTOR

1. *euergesia* (2108), lit., "good work" (*eu*, "well," *ergon*, "work"), is found in Acts 4:9, "good deed," and 1 Tim. 6:2, "benefit."

2. *euergetes* (2110), "a benefactor," expresses the agent, Luke 22:25.

3. *charis* (5485), "grace," is once rendered "benefit," 2 Cor. 1:15; it stresses the character of the "benefit," as the effect of the gracious disposition of the benefactor.

4. *agathon* (18), the neuter of *agathos*, used as a noun in Philem. 14, is translated "benefit," KJV; RV, "goodness."

BENEVOLENCE

eunoia (2133), "good will" (*eu*, "well," *nous*, "the mind"), is rendered "benevolence" in 1 Cor. 7:3, KJV. The RV, following the texts which have *opheilen* ("due"), has "her due," a more comprehensive expression; in Eph. 6:7, "good will."

BEREAVED, BEREFT

1. *aporphanizomai* (642), lit., "to be rendered an orphan" (*apo*, "from," with the thought of separation, and *orphanos*, "an orphan"), is used metaphorically in 1 Thess. 2:17 (KJV, "taken from"; RV, "bereaved"), in the sense of being "bereft" of the company of the saints through being compelled to leave them (cf. the similes in 7 and 11). The word has a wider meaning than that of being an orphan.

2. *apostereo* (650), "to rob, defraud, deprive," is used in 1 Tim. 6:5, in the passive voice, of being deprived or "bereft" (of the truth), with reference to false teachers (KJV, destitute).

BESET

euperistatos (2139), used in Heb. 12:1, and translated "which doth so easily beset," lit. signifies "standing well (i.e., easily) around," "standing," i.e., easily encompassing. It describes sin as having advantage in favor of its prevailing.

BESIDE ONESELF (to be)

1. *existemi* (1839), primarily and lit. means "to put out of position, displace": hence, (a) "to amaze," Luke 24:22 (for KJV, "make..astonished"); Acts 8:9, 11 (KJV, "bewitched "); or "to be amazed, astounded," Matt. 12:23; Mark 6:51; (b) "to be out of one's mind, to be beside oneself," Mark 3:21; 2 Cor. 5:13, in the latter of which it is contrasted with *sophroneo*, "to be of a sound mind, sober."

2. *mainomai* (3105), "to be mad, to rave," is said of one who so speaks that he appears to be out of his mind, Acts 26:24, translated "thou art beside thyself," KJV; RV, "thou art mad." In v. 25; John 10:20; Acts 12:15; 1 Cor. 14:23, both versions use the verb to be mad.

BEST

1. *protos* (4413) is one of two words translated "best" in the KJV, but the only one so rendered in the RV. In Luke 15:22 "the best (robe)" is, lit., "the first (robe)," i.e., chief, principal, first in rank or quality.

2. *meizon* (3187), "greater," is translated "best" in 1 Cor. 12:31, "the best gifts," greater, not in quality, but in importance and value. It is the comparative degree of *megas*, "great"; the superlative, *megistos*, is used only in 2 Pet. 1:4.

BETRAY, BETRAYER

A. Verb.

paradidomi (*3860*), "to betray," lit., "to give over," is used either **B** (a) in the sense of delivering a person or thing to be kept by another, to commend, e.g., Acts 28:16; (b) to deliver to prison or judgment, e.g., Matt. 4:12; 1 Tim. 1:20; (c) to deliver over treacherously by way of "betrayal," Matt. 17:22 (RV, "delivered"); 26:16; John 6:64 etc.; (d) to hand on, deliver, e.g., 1 Cor. 11:23; (e) to allow of something being done, said of the ripening of fruit, Mark 4:29, RV, "is ripe" (marg., "alloweth").

B. Noun.

prodotes (*4273*), "a betrayer" (akin to A), is translated "betrayers" in Acts 7:52; "traitor," "traitors," in Luke 6:16 and 2 Tim. 3:4.

BETTER

1. *kreisson* (*2909*), from *kratos*, "strong" (which denotes power in activity and effect), serves as the comparative degree of *agathos*, "good" (good or fair, intrinsically). *kreisson* is especially characteristic of the Epistle to the Hebrews, where it is used 12 times; it indicates what is (a) advantageous or useful, 1 Cor. 7:9, 38; 11:17; Heb. 11:40; 12:24; 2 Pet. 2:21; Phil. 1:23, where it is coupled with *mallon*, "more," and *pollo*, "much, by far," "very far better" (RV); (b) excellent, Heb. 1:4; 6:9; 7:7, 19, 22; 8:6; 9:23; 10:34; 11:16, 35.

2. *kalon..mallon*, the neuter of *kalos*, with *mallon*, "more," is used in Mark 9:42, "it were better (lit., 'much better') for him if a great millstone were hanged about his neck." In verses 43, 45, 47, *kalos* is used alone (RV, "good," for KJV, "better").

BEWAIL

1. *klaio* (*2799*), "to wail," whether with tears or any external expression of grief, is regularly translated "weep" in the RV; once in the KJV it is rendered "bewail," Rev. 18:9.

2. *kopto* (*2875*), primarily, "to beat, smite"; then, "to cut off," Matt. 21:8; Mark 11:8, is used in the middle voice, of beating oneself, beating the breast, as a token of grief; hence, "to bewail," Matt. 11:17 (RV, "mourn," for KJV, "lament"); 24:30, "mourn"; Rev. 1:7 (RV, "mourn"; KJV, "wail"); in Luke 8:52; 23:27 "bewail"; in Rev. 18:9, "wail" (for KJV, "lament").

3. *pentheo* (*3996*) denotes "to lament, mourn," especially for the dead; in 2 Cor. 12:21, RV, "mourn" (KJV, "bewail"). See also Rev. 18:11, 15, 19.

BEWARE

1. *blepo* (*991*), "to see," is applied to mental vision, and is sometimes used by way of warning "to take heed" against an object,

Mark 8:15; 12:38; Acts 13:40; Phil. 3:2 (three times); in Col. 2:8, RV, "take heed."

2. *prosecho* (4337), lit., "to hold to" (*pros*, "to," *echo*, "to have, to hold"), hence, "to turn one's mind or attention to a thing by being on one's guard against it," is translated "beware" in Matt. 7:15; 10:17; 16:6, 11-12; Luke 12:1; 20:46.

3. *phulasso* (5442), "to guard, watch, keep," is used, in the middle voice, of being "on one's guard against" (the middle v. stressing personal interest in the action), Luke 12:15, "beware of," RV, "keep yourselves from," as in Acts 21:25; in 2 Tim. 4:15, "be thou ware"; in 2 Pet. 3:17, "beware."

BEWITCH

1. *baskaino* (940), primarily, "to slander, to prate about anyone"; then "to bring evil on a person by feigned praise, or mislead by an evil eye, and so to charm, bewitch" (Eng., "fascinate" is connected), is used figuratively in Gal. 3:1, of leading into evil doctrine.

2. *existemi* (1839) is rendered "bewitch" in Acts 8:9, 11, KJV, concerning Simon the sorcerer; it does not mean "to bewitch," as in the case of the preceding verb, but "to confuse, amaze" (RV).

BILL

1. *biblion* (975), primarily "a small book, a scroll, or any sheet on which something has been written"; hence, in connection with *apostasion*, "divorce," signifies "a bill of divorcement," Matt. 19:7 (KJV, "writing"); Mark 10:4.

2. *gramma* (1121), from *grapho*, "to write" (Eng., "graph, graphic," etc.), in Luke 16:6, KJV, is translated "bill." It lit. signifies that which is drawn, a picture; hence, a written document; hence, a "bill," or bond, or note of hand, showing the amount of indebtedness.

BIND, BINDING

Old Testament

'asar (631), "to bind, imprison, tie, gird, to harness," Gen. 39:20. The common word for "tying up" for security and safety, *'asar* is often used to indicate the tying up of horses and donkeys, 2 Kings 7:10. Similarly, oxen are "harnessed" to carts, 1 Sam. 6:7, 10. Frequently, *'asar* is used to describe the "binding" of prisoners with cords and various fetters, Gen. 42:24; Judg. 15:10, 12-13. Samson misled Delilah as she probed for the secret of his strength, telling her to "bind" him with bowstrings, Judg. 16:7, and new ropes, Judg. 16:11, none of which could hold him.

Used in an abstract sense, *'asar* refers to those who are spiritually "bound," Ps. 146:7; Isa. 49:9; 61:1 or a man who is emotionally "captivated" by a woman's hair, Song of Sol. 7:5. Only in Num. 30 does it refer to the binding of an oath.

New Testament

1. *deo* (*1210*), "to bind," is used (a) literally, of any sort of "binding," Acts 22:5; 24:27; (b) figuratively, of the Word of God, as not being "bound," 2 Tim. 2:9; Paul speaks of himself, in Acts 20:22, as being "bound in the spirit," i.e. compelled by his convictions, under the constraining power of the Spirit of God, to go to Jerusalem. A wife is said to be "bound" to her husband, Rom. 7:2; 1 Cor. 7:39; and the husband to the wife, 1 Cor. 7:27. The Lord's words to the apostle Peter in Matt. 16:19, as to "binding," and to all the disciples in 18:18.

2. *perideo* (*4019*), *peri*, "around," with No. 1, "to bind around," is used in John 11:44 of the napkin around the face of Lazarus.

3. *hupodeo* (*5265*), *hupo*, "under," with No. 1, "to bind underneath," is used of binding of sandals, Acts 12:8; rendered "shod" in Mark 6:9 and Eph. 6:15.

4. *katadeo* (*2611*), *kata*, "down," with No. 1, "to bind or tie down, or bind up," is used in Luke 10:34 of the act of the good Samaritan.

5. *sundeo* (*4887*), *sun*, "together," and No. 1, "to bind together," implying association, is used in Heb. 13:3 of those bound together in confinement.

6. *desmeuo* or *desmeo* (*1195*) signifies "to put in fetters or any kind of bond," Luke 8:29; Acts 22:4, or "to bind a burden upon a person," Matt. 23:4. The verb is connected with No. 1.

BIRTHRIGHT

prototokia (*4415*), a birthright" (from *protos*, "first," *tikto*, "to beget"), is found in Heb. 12:16, with reference to Esau. The "birthright" involved preeminence and authority, Gen. 27:29; 49:3. Another right was that of the double portion, Deut. 21:17; 1 Chron. 5:1-2. Connected with the "birthright" was the progenitorship of the Messiah. Esau transferred his "birthright" to Jacob for a paltry mess of pottage, profanely despising this last spiritual privilege, Gen. 25 and 27. In the history of the nation God occasionally set aside the "birthright," to show that the objects of His choice depended not on the will of the flesh, but on His own authority. Thus Isaac was preferred to Ishmael, Jacob to Esau, Joseph to Reuben, David to his elder brethren, Solomon to Adonijah.

BISHOP (Overseer)

1. *episkopos* (*1985*), lit., "an overseer," whence Eng. "bishop," which has precisely the same meaning, is found in Acts 20:28; Phil. 1:1; 1 Tim. 3:2; Titus 1:7; 1 Pet. 2:25.

2. *episkope* (*1984*), besides its meaning, "visitation," e.g., 1 Pet. 2:12, is rendered "office," in Acts 1:20, RV (KJV, "bishoprick"); in

1 Tim. 3:1 "the office of a bishop," lit., "(if any one seeketh) over-seership," there is no word representing office.

BITTER, BITTERLY, BITTERNESS

A. Adjective.

pikros (*4089*), from a root *pik*—, meaning "to cut, to prick," hence, lit., "pointed, sharp, keen, pungent to the sense of taste, smell, etc.," is found in Jas. 3:11, 14. In v. 11 it has its natural sense, with reference to water; in v. 14 it is used metaphorically of jealousy, RV.

B. Verb.

pikraino (*4087*), related to A, signifies, in the active voice, "to be bitter," Col. 3:19, or "to embitter, irritate, or to make bitter," Rev. 10:9; the passive voice, "to be made bitter," is used in Rev. 8:11; 10:10.

C. Noun.

pikria (*4088*) denotes "bitterness." It is used in Acts 8:23, metaphorically, of a condition of extreme wickedness, "gall of bitterness" or "bitter gall"; in Rom. 3:14, of evil speaking; in Eph. 4:31, of "bitter" hatred; in Heb. 12:15, in the same sense, metaphorically, of a root of "bitterness," producing "bitter" fruit.

D. Adverb.

pikros (*4090*), "bitterly," is used of the poignant grief of Peter's weeping for his denial of Christ, Matt. 26:75; Luke 22:62.

BLACK, BLACKNESS

1. *gnophos* (*1105*), Heb. 12:18, "blackness, gloom," seems to have been associated with the idea of a tempest. It is related to *skotos*, "darkness."

2. *zophos* (*2217*), akin to No. 1, especially "the gloom of the regions of the lost," is used four times; 2 Pet. 2:4, "darkness" (RV); 2:17, RV, "blackness," for KJV, "mist"; Jude 6, "darkness"; v. 13, "blackness," suggesting a kind of emanation.

BLAME, BLAMELESS

A. Verb.

momaomai (*3469*), "to find fault with, to blame, or calumniate," is used in 2 Cor. 6:3, of the ministry of the gospel; in 8:20, of the ministration of financial help.

B. Adjectives.

1. *amomos* (*299*): See BLEMISH, B.

2. *amometos* (*298*), translated in Phil. 2:15 "without blemish"

(KJV, "without rebuke"), is rendered "blameless" in 2 Pet. 3:14 (KJV and RV).

3. *amemptos* (273), is translated "unblameable" in 1 Thess. 3:13; "blameless," in Luke 1:6; Phil. 2:15; 3:6; "faultless" in Heb. 8:7.

B

C. Adverb.

amemptos (274), in 1 Thess. 2:10, "unblameably"; in 5:23, "without blame," KJV, "blameless," is said of believers at the judgment-seat of Christ in His Parousia (His presence after His coming), as the outcome of present witness and steadfastness.

BLASPHEME, BLASPHEMY, BLASPHEMER, BLASPHEMOUS

A. Noun.

blasphemia (988), either from *blax*, "sluggish, stupid," or, probably, from *blapto*, "to injure," and *pheme*, "speech," (Eng. "blasphemy") is so translated thirteen times in the RV, but "railing" in Matt. 15:19; Mark 7:22; Eph. 4:31; Col. 3:8; 1 Tim. 6:4; Jude 9. The word "blasphemy" is practically confined to speech defamatory of the Divine Majesty.

B. Verb.

blasphemeo (987), "to blaspheme, rail at or revile," is used (a) in a general way, of any contumelious speech, reviling, calumniating, railing at, etc., as of those who railed at Christ, e.g., Matt. 27:39; Mark 15:29; Luke 22:65 (RV, "reviling"); 23:39; (b) of those who speak contemptuously of God or of sacred things, e.g., Matt. 9:3; Mark 3:28; Rom. 2:24; 1 Tim. 1:20; 6:1; Rev. 13:6; 16:9, 11, 21; "hath spoken blasphemy," Matt. 26:65; "rail at," 2 Pet. 2:10; Jude 8, 10; "railing," 2 Pet. 2:12; "slanderously reported," Rom. 3:8; "be evil spoken of," Rom. 14:16; 1 Cor. 10:30; 2 Pet. 2:2; "speak evil of," Titus 3:2; 1 Pet. 4:4; "being defamed," 1 Cor. 4:13. The verb (in the present participial form) is translated "blasphemers" in Acts 19:37; in Mark 2:7, "blasphemeth," RV, for KJV, "speaketh blasphemies."

There is no noun in the original representing the English "blasphemer." This is expressed either by the verb, or by the adjective *blasphemos*.

C. Adjective.

blasphemos (989), "abusive, speaking evil," is translated "blasphemous," in Acts 6:11, 13; "a blasphemer," 1 Tim. 1:13; "railers," 2 Tim. 3:2, RV; "railing," 2 Pet. 2:11.

BLEMISH

A. Noun.

momos (*3470*), akin to *momaomai*, signifies "a shame, a moral disgrace," metaphorical of the licentious, 2 Pet. 2:13.

B. Adjective.

amomos (*299*), "without blemish"; is always so rendered in the RV, Eph. 1:4; 5:27; Phil. 2:15; Col. 1:22; Heb. 9:14; 1 Pet. 1:19; Jude 24; Rev. 14:5.

BLESS, BLESSED, BLESSEDNESS, BLESSING

Old Testament

A. Verb.

barak (1288), "to kneel, bless, be blessed, curse." *barak* occurs about 330 times in the Bible, first in Gen. 1:22, when God blesses creation. *barak* is used again of man, Gen. 5:2; Gen. 9:1; Gen. 12:2-3. The covenant promise called the nations to seek the "blessing," cf. Isa. 2:2-4, but made it plain that the initiative in blessing rests with God, and that Abraham and his seed were the instruments of it, Num. 6:23-27. The passive form of *barak* is used in pronouncing God's "blessing on men," Gen. 14:19; 9:26; 14:20. *barak* was also a common form of greeting, 1 Sam. 13:10.

B. Nouns.

berakah (1293), "blessing," used in conjunction with the verb *barak*, Gen. 12:2. When expressed by men, a "blessing" was a wish or prayer for favorable circumstance, Gen. 28:4. Patriarchs customarily extended this wish or prayer upon their children before they died: Jacob's, Gen. 49; Moses', Deut. 33:1ff. Blessing was the opposite of a cursing (*qelalah*), Gen. 27:12; 33:11; Neh. 9:5.

The Lord's "blessing" rests on those who are faithful to Him, Deut. 11:27. His blessing brings righteousness, Ps. 24:5, life, Ps. 133:3, prosperity, 2 Sam. 7:29, and salvation, Ps. 3:8. The "blessing" is portrayed as a rain or dew, Ezek. 34:26; cf. Ps. 84:6. In the fellowship of the saints, the Lord commands His "blessing," Ps. 133:3. In a few cases, the Lord made people to be a "blessing" to others. Abraham is a blessing to the nations, Gen. 12:2. His descendants are expected to become a blessing to the nations, Isa. 19:24; Zech. 8:13.

'asher (835), "blessed; happy," mostly in Psalms and Proverbs. Basically, this word connotes the state of "prosperity" or "happiness" that comes when a superior bestows his favor (blessing) on one. In most passages, the one bestowing favor is God Himself, Deut. 33:29; Job 5:17-18; 5:22. A human can call another blessed, 1 Kings 10:8.

New Testament

A. Verbs.

1. *eulogeo* (2127), lit., "to speak well of," signifies, (a) "to praise, to celebrate with praises," of that which is addressed to God, acknowledging His goodness, with desire for His glory, Luke 1:64; 2:28; 24:51, 53; Jas. 3:9; (b) "to invoke blessings upon a person;" e.g., Luke 6:28; Rom. 12:14. The present participle passive, "blessed, praised," is especially used of Christ in Matt. 21:9; 23:39, and the parallel passages; also in John 12:13; (c) "to consecrate a thing with solemn prayers, to ask God's blessing on a thing," e.g., Luke 9:16; 1 Cor. 10:16; (d) "to cause to prosper, to make happy, to bestow blessings on," said of God, e.g., in Acts 3:26; Gal. 3:9; Eph. 1:3.

2. *eneulogeomai* (1757), "to bless," is used in the passive voice, Acts 3:25, and Gal. 3:8. The prefix *en* apparently indicates the person on whom the blessing is conferred.

3. *makarizo* (3106), from a root *mak—*, meaning "large, lengthy," found also in *makros*, "long," *mekos*, "length," hence denotes "to pronounce happy, blessed," Luke 1:48 and Jas. 5:11.

B. Adjectives.

1. *eulogetos* (2128), akin to A, 1, means "blessed, praised"; it is applied only to God, Mark 14:61; Luke 1:68; Rom. 1:25; 9:5; 2 Cor. 1:3; 11:31; Eph. 1:3; 1 Pet. 1:3.

2. *makarios* (3107), akin to A, No. 3, is used in the beatitudes in Matt. 5 and Luke 6, is especially frequent in the Gospel of Luke, and is found seven times in Revelation, 1:3; 14:13; 16:15; 19:9; 20:6; 22:7, 14. It is said of God twice, 1 Tim. 1:11; 6:15. In the beatitudes the Lord indicates not only the characters that are "blessed," but the nature of that which is the highest good.

C. Nouns.

1. *eulogia* (2129), akin to A, 1, lit., "good speaking, praise," is used of (a) God and Christ, Rev. 5:12-13; 7:12; (b) the invocation of blessings, benediction, Heb. 12:17; Jas. 3:10; (c) the giving of thanks, 1 Cor. 10:16; (d) a blessing, a benefit bestowed, Rom. 15:29; Gal. 3:14; Eph. 1:3; Heb. 6:7; of a monetary gift sent to needy believers, 2 Cor. 9:5-6; (e) in a bad sense, of fair speech, Rom. 16:18, RV, where it is joined with *chrestologia*, "smooth speech," the latter relating to the substance, *eulogia* to the expression.

2. *makarismos* (3109), akin to A, 3, "blessedness," indicates an ascription of blessing rather than a state; hence in Rom. 4:6, where the KJV renders it as a noun, "(describeth) the blessedness"; the RV rightly puts "(pronounceth) blessing." So v. 9. In Gal. 4:15 the KJV has "blessedness," RV, "gratulation." The Galatian believers had counted themselves happy when they heard and received the gospel. Had they lost that opinion?

BLIND, BLINDNESS

A. Verbs.

1. *tuphloo* (*5186*), "to blind," from a root *tuph*—, "to burn, smoke"; is used metaphorically, of the dulling of the intellect, John 12:40; 2 Cor. 4:4; 1 John 2:11.

2. *poroo* (*4456*) signifies "to harden" (from *poros*, "a thick skin, a hardening"); rendered "blinded," KJV, in Rom. 11:7 and 2 Cor. 3:14 (RV, "hardened"); cf. 4:4.

B. Adjective.

tuphlos (*5185*), "blind," is used both physically and metaphorically, chiefly in the Gospels; elsewhere four times; physically, Acts 13:11; metaphorically, Rom. 2:19; 2 Pet. 1:9; Rev. 3:17. The word is frequently used as a noun, signifying "a blind man."

C. Noun.

porosis (*4457*), akin to A. No. 2, primarily means "a covering with a callus," a "hardening," Rom. 11:25 and Eph. 4:18, RV for KJV, "blindness"; Mark 3:5, RV, for KJV, "hardness." It is metaphorical of a dulled spiritual perception.

BLOOD

Old Testament

dam (*1818*), "blood," is used to denote the "blood" of animals, birds, and men, never of fish, . In Gen. 9:4, "blood" is synonymous with "life," also Lev. 3:17. Only infrequently does this word mean "blood-red," a color, 2 Kings 3:22. In two passages, *dam* represents "wine," Gen. 49:11; cf. Deut. 32:14. *dam* can mean "blood shed by violence," Num. 35:33. "Blood" can also mean "death," Ezek. 5:17. Next, *dam* may connote an act by which a human life is taken, Deut. 17:8; . Gen. 9:6; Lev. 17:3-4.

In judicial language, "to stand against one's blood" means to stand before a court and against the accused as a plaintiff, witness, or judge, Lev. 19:16. The phrase, "his blood be on his head," signifies that the guilt and punishment for a violent act shall be on the perpetrator, Lev. 20:9.

Animal blood could take the place of a sinner's blood in atoning (covering) for sin, Lev. 17:11. Adam's sin merited death and brought death on all his posterity, Rom. 5:12; so the offering of an animal in substitution not only typified the payment of that penalty, but it symbolized that the perfect offering would bring life for Adam and all others represented by the sacrifice, Heb. 10:4. The animal sacrifice prefigured and typologically represented the blood of Christ, who made the great and only effective substitutionary atonement, and whose offering was the only offering that gained life for those whom He represented. The shedding of His "blood" seals the covenant of life between God and man, Matt. 26:28.

New Testament

B.

A. Nouns.

1. **haima** (*129*), (hence Eng., prefix **hem**—), besides its natural meaning, stands, (a) in conjunction with **sarx**, "flesh," "flesh and blood," Matt. 16:17; 1 Cor. 15:50; Gal. 1:16; the original has the opposite order, blood and flesh, in Eph. 6:12 and Heb. 2:14; this phrase signifies, by **synecdoche**, "man, human beings." It stresses the limitations of humanity; the two are essential elements in man's physical being; "the life of the flesh is in the blood," Lev. 17:11; (b) for human generation, John 1:13; (c) for "blood" shed by violence, e.g., Matt. 23:35; Rev. 17:6; (d) for the "blood" of sacrificial victims, e.g., Heb. 9:7; of the "blood" of Christ, which betokens His death by the shedding of His "blood" in expiatory sacrifice; to drink His "blood" is to appropriate the saving effects of His expiatory death, John 6:53. As "the life of the flesh is in the blood," Lev. 17:11, and was forfeited by sin, life eternal can be imparted only by the expiation made, in the giving up of the life by the sinless Savior.

2. **haimatekchusia** (*130*) denotes "shedding of blood," Heb. 9:22.

B. Verb.

haimorrhoeo (*131*), from **haima**, "blood," **rheo**, "to flow" (Eng., "hemorrhage"), signifies "to suffer from a flow of blood," Matt. 9:20.

BLOT OUT

exaleipho (*1813*), from **ek**, "out," used intensively, and **aleipho**, "to wipe," signifies "to wash, or to smear completely." Hence, metaphorically, in the sense of removal, "to wipe away, wipe off, obliterate"; Acts 3:19, of sins; Col. 2:14, of writing; Rev. 3:5, of a name in a book; Rev. 7:17; 21:4, of tears.

BOAST, BOASTER, BOASTFUL

A. Verbs.

1. **kauchaomai** (*2744*), and its related words **katakauchaomai**, "to glory or boast" and the nouns **kauchesis** and **kauchema**, translated "boast," and "boasting," in the KJV, are always translated "glory," and "glorying" in the RV, e.g., 2 Cor. 10:15; 11:10, 17; Eph. 2:9.

2. **megalaucheo** (*3166*), from **megala**, "great things," and **aucheo**, "to lift up the neck," hence, "to boast," is found in some texts of Jas. 3:5. The most authentic mss. have the two words separated. It

indicates any kind of haughty speech which stirs up strife or provokes others.

B. Nouns.

1. *alazon* (*213*), "a boaster," Rom. 1:30 and 2 Tim. 3:2, KJV, "boasters," RV, "boastful," primarily signifies "a wanderer about the country" (from *ale*, "wandering"), "a vagabond," hence, "an impostor."

2. *alazoneia* (*212*), the practice of an *alazon*, denotes quackery; hence, "arrogant display, or boastings," Jas. 4:16, RV, "vauntings"; in 1 John 2:16, RV, "vainglory"; KJV, "pride."

BODY, BODILY

A. Nouns.

soma (*4983*) is "the body as a whole, the instrument of life," whether of man living, e.g., Matt. 6:22, or dead, Matt. 27:52; or in resurrection, 1 Cor. 15:44; or of beasts, Heb. 13:11; of grain, 1 Cor. 15:37-38; of the heavenly hosts, 1 Cor. 15:40. In Rev. 18:13 it is translated "slaves." In its figurative uses the essential idea is preserved.

Sometimes the word stands, by *synecdoche*, for "the complete man," Matt. 5:29; 6:22; Rom. 12:1; Jas. 3:6; Rev. 18:13. Sometimes the person is identified with his or her "body," Acts 9:37; 13:36, and this is so even of the Lord Jesus, John 19:40 with 42.

The word is also used for physical nature, as distinct from *pneuma*, "the spiritual nature," e.g., 1 Cor. 5:3, and from *psuche*, "the soul," e.g., 1 Thess. 5:23.

It is also used metaphorically, of the mystic body of Christ, with reference to the whole church, e.g., Eph. 1:23; Col. 1:18, 22, 24; also of a local church, 1 Cor. 12:27.

B. Adjectives.

1. *sussomos* (*4954*), *sun*, "with," and A, No. 1., means "united in the same body," Eph. 3:6, of the church.

2. *somatikos* (*4984*), "bodily," is used in Luke 3:22, of the Holy Spirit in taking a bodily shape; in 1 Tim. 4:8 of bodily exercise.

C. Adverb.

somatikos (*4985*), "bodily, corporeally," is used in Col. 2:9.

BOLD, BOLDNESS, BOLDLY

A. Verbs.

1. *tharreo* (*2292*), a later form of *tharseo*, is connected with *thero*, "to be warm" (warmth of temperament being associated with confidence); hence, "to be confident, bold, courageous"; RV, invariably, "to be of good courage"; 2 Cor. 5:6, 8 (KJV, "to be confident"); 7:16 (KJV, "to have confidence"); 10:1-2 (KJV, "to be bold");

Heb. 13:6, KJV, "boldly"; RV, "with good courage" (lit., "being courageous").

2. *parrhesiazomai* (3955), "to speak boldly, or freely," primarily had reference to speech, but acquired the meaning of "being bold, or waxing bold," 1 Thess. 2:2; in Acts 13:46, RV, "spake out boldly" (the aorist participle here signifies "waxing bold"); Acts 9:27, 29, "preached boldly" (see also 18:26; 19:8); in 26:26, "speak freely."

3. *tolmao* (5111) signifies "to dare to do, or to bear, something terrible or difficult"; hence, "to be bold, to bear oneself boldly, deal boldly"; it is translated "be bold" in 2 Cor. 10:2, as contrasted with *tharreo* in verse 1, and the first line of verse 2, "shew courage"; in 10:12, RV, "are not bold to," for KJV, "dare not make ourselves of." *tharreo* denotes confidence in one's own powers, and has reference to character; *tolmao* denotes boldness in undertaking and has reference to manifestation.

4. *apotolmao* (662), *apo* (intensive), with No. 3, means "to be very bold, to speak out boldly," and is used in Rom. 10:20.

B. Noun.

parrhesia (3954), from *pas*, "all," *rhesis*, "speech," denotes (a), primarily, "freedom of speech, unreservedness of utterance," Acts 4:29, 31; 2 Cor. 3:12; 7:4; Philem. 8; or "to speak without ambiguity, plainly," John 10:24; or "without figures of speech," John 16:25; (b) "the absence of fear in speaking boldly; hence, confidence, cheerful courage, boldness, without any connection necessarily with speech"; the RV has "boldness" in the following; Acts 4:13; Eph. 3:12; 1 Tim. 3:13; Heb. 3:6; 4:16; 10:19, 35; 1 John 2:28; 3:21; 4:17; 5:14; (c) the deportment by which one becomes conspicuous, acts openly, or secures publicity, Col. 2:15.

C. Adverb.

tolmeroteros (5112), the comparative degree of *tolmeros*, means "the more boldly," Rom. 15:15; in some texts, *tolmeroteron*.

BOND

1. *desmos* (1199), from *deo*, "to bind"; (a) "bonds" of a prisoner, Luke 8:29; (b) a figurative sense for "a condition of imprisonment," Phil. 1:7, 13.

2. *desmios* (1198), "a binding," denotes "a prisoner," e.g., Acts 25:14, RV, for the KJV, "in bonds"; Heb. 13:3, "them that are in bonds." Paul speaks of himself as a prisoner of Christ, Eph. 3:1; 2 Tim. 1:8; Philem. 1, 9; "in the Lord," Eph. 4:1.

3. *sundesmos* (4886), "that which binds together" (*sun*, "with," and No. 1), is said of "the bond of iniquity," Acts 8:23; "the bond of peace," Eph. 4:3; "the bond of perfectness," Col. 3:14 (figurative of the ligaments of the body); elsewhere; Col. 2:19, "bands," figuratively of the bands which unite the church, the body of Christ.

BONDAGE

A. Noun.

douleia (*1397*), akin to *deo*, "to bind," primarily "the condition of being a slave," came to denote any kind of bondage, as, e.g., of the condition of creation, Rom. 8:21; of that fallen condition of man himself which makes him dread God, v. 15, and fear death, Heb. 2:15; of the condition imposed by the Mosaic Law, Gal. 4:24.

B. Verbs.

1. *douleuo* (*1398*), "to serve as a slave, to be a slave, to be in bondage," is frequently used without any association of slavery, e.g., Acts 20:19; Rom. 6:6; 7:6; 12:11; Gal. 5:13.

2. *douloo* (*1402*), different from No. 1, in being transitive instead of intransitive, signifies "to make a slave of, to bring into bondage," Acts 7:6; 1 Cor. 9:19, RV; in the passive voice, "to be brought under bondage," 2 Pet. 2:19; "to be held in bondage," Gal. 4:3 (lit., "were reduced to bondage"); Titus 2:3, "of being enslaved to wine"; Rom. 6:18, "of service to righteousness" (lit., "were made bondservants"). As with the purchased slave there were no limitations either in the kind or the time of service, so the life of the believer is to be lived in continuous obedience to God.

3. *doulagogeo* (*1396*), "to bring into bondage" (from A, above, and *ago*, "to bring"), is used in 1 Cor. 9:27, concerning the body, RV, "bondage," for KJV, "subjection."

4. *katadouloo* (*2615*), "to bring into bondage," occurs in 2 Cor. 11:20; Gal. 2:4.

BONDMAN, BONDMAID

doulos (*1401*), from *deo*, "to bind," "a slave," originally the lowest term in the scale of servitude, came also to mean "one who gives himself up to the will of another," e.g., 1 Cor. 7:23; Rom. 6:17, 20, and became the most common and general word for "servant," as in Matt. 8:9, without any idea of bondage. In calling himself, however, a "bondslave of Jesus Christ," e.g., Rom. 1:1, the apostle Paul intimates (1) that he had been formerly a "bondslave" of Satan, and (2) that, having been bought by Christ, he was now a willing slave, bound to his new Master.

The feminine, *doule*, signifies "a handmaid," Luke 1:38, 48; Acts 2:18.

BOOK

Old Testament

sepher (*5612*), "book; document; writing." The most common translation of *sepher* is "book." A manuscript was written, Exod. 32:32; Deut. 17:18, and sealed, Isa. 29:11, to be read by the addressee, 2 Kings 22:16. The sense of *sepher* is similar to "scroll" (*megillah*): "Therefore go thou, and read in the roll [*sepher*] which thou hast written from my mouth, the words of the Lord in the ears of the people in the Lord's house upon the fasting day: and also thou shalt read them in the ears of all Judah that come out of their cities" (Jer. 36:6). *sepher* is also closely related to "book" (*siphra*) (Ps. 56:8).

Many "books" are named in the Old Testament: of remembrance, Mal. 3:16; of life, Ps. 69:28, of Jasher, Josh. 10:13, of generations, Gen. 5:1, of the Lord, of chronicles, 2 Chron. 24:27. Prophets wrote "books" in their lifetime, Nah. 1:1. Jeremiah had several "books" written in addition to his letters to the exiles, Jer. 36. In this context, we learn about the nature of writing a "book," Jer. 36:32. Ezekiel was commanded to eat a "book," Ezek. 2:8-3:1 as a symbolic act of God's judgment on and restoration of Judah.

sepher can also signify "a letter," Jer. 29:1. The contents of the *sepher* varied. It might contain a written order, a commission, a request, or a decree, Esth. 8:10; Deut. 24:1; Jer. 32:14.

New Testament

1. **biblos** (976) (Eng. "Bible") was the inner part, or rather the cellular substance, of the stem of the papyrus (Eng. "paper"). It came to denote the paper made from this plant in Egypt, and then a written "book," roll, or volume. It is used in referring to "books" of Scripture, the "book," or scroll, of Matthew's Gospel, Matt. 1:1; the Pentateuch, as the "book" of Moses, Mark 12:26; Isaiah, as "the book of the words of Isaiah," Luke 3:4; the Psalms, Luke 20:42 and Acts 1:20; "the prophets," Acts 7:42; to "the Book of Life," Phil. 4:3; Rev. 3:5; 20:15. Once only it is used of secular writings, Acts 19:19.

2. **biblion** (975), "a scroll or a small book." It is used in Luke 4:17, 20, of the "book" of Isaiah; in John 20:30, of the Gospel of John; in Gal. 3:10 and Heb. 10:7, of the whole of the OT; in Heb. 9:19, of the "book" of Exodus; in Rev. 1:11; 22:7, 9-10, 18 (twice), 19, of the Apocalypse; in John 21:25 and 2 Tim. 4:13, of "books" in general; in Rev. 13:8; 17:8; 20:12; 21:27, of the "Book" of Life; in Rev. 20:12, of other "books" to be opened in the Day of Judgment, containing, it would seem, the record of human deeds. In Matt. 19:7 and Mark 10:4 the word is used of a bill of divorcement.

3. **biblaridion** (974), another diminutive of No. 1, is always rendered "little book," in Rev. 10:2, 9-10. Some texts have it also in verse 8, instead of **biblion**.

BOSOM

Old Testament

cheq (2436), "bosom; lap; base." The word represents the "outer front of one's body" where beloved ones, infants, and animals are pressed closely, Num. 11:12; Gen. 16:5; Deut. 28:56. In a figurative inward sense, Ps. 35:13; cf. Job 19:27; 1 Kings 22:35. *cheq* represents a fold of one's garment above the belt, often rendered "lap" in the modern versions Exod. 4:6; Prov. 16:33; 2 Sam. 12:3. Finally, *cheq* means the "base of the altar," as described in Ezek. 43:13-17.

New Testament

kolpos (*2859*) signifies (a) "the front of the body between the arms"; hence, to recline in the "bosom" was said of one who so reclined at table that his head covered, as it were, the "bosom" of the one next to him, John 13:23. Hence, figuratively, it is used of a place of blessedness with another, as with Abraham in paradise, Luke 16:22-23 (plural in v. 23), from the custom of reclining at table in the "bosom," a place of honor; of the Lord's eternal and essential relation with the Father, in all its blessedness and affection as intimated in the phrase, "The Only-begotten Son, which is in the bosom of the Father" (John 1:18); (b) "of the bosom of a garment, the hollow formed by the upper forepart of a loose garment, bound by a girdle and used for carrying or keeping things"; thus figuratively of repaying one liberally, Luke 6:38; cf. Isa. 65:6; Jer. 39:18; (c) "of an inlet of the sea," because of its shape, like a bosom, Acts 27:39.

BOTTOM, BOTTOMLESS

A. Adverb.

kato (*2736*). From *kata*, it signifies to be "down," or "below," another spacial object, Matt. 4:6; 27:51; Mark 14:66; 15:38; Luke 4:9; John 8:3; Acts 2:19; 20:9.

B. Adjective.

abussos (*12*), "bottomless"; Eng., "bath," is used as a noun denoting the abyss (KJV, "bottomless pit"). It describes an immeasurable depth, the underworld, the lower regions, the abyss of Sheol. In Rom. 10:7, quoted from Deut. 30:13, the abyss (the abode of the lost dead) is substituted for the sea (the change in the quotation is due to the facts of the death and resurrection of Christ); the KJV has "deep" here and in Luke 8:31; the reference is to the lower regions as the abode of demons, out of which they can be let loose, Rev. 11:7; 17:8, it is found seven times in the Apocalypse, 9:1-2, 11; 11:7; 17:8; 20:1, 3; in 9:1, 2.

BOUND (to be)

(a) *of obligation:*
opheilo (*3784*), "to owe, whether a debt or any obligation," is translated "we are bound," in 2 Thess. 1:3 and 2:13 (the apostle expressing his obligation to give thanks for his readers).

(b) *of binding:*
perikeimai (*4029*), lit., "to lie around," "to be compassed," is used of binding fetters around a person, Acts 28:20; in Mark 9:42, and

Luke 17:2, to hang about a person's neck; in Heb. 5:2, to compass about, metaphorically of infirmities; in 12:1, of those who have witness borne to their faith.

B

BOUNTY, BOUNTIFULLY

1. *eulogia* (2129), "a blessing," has the meaning of "bounty" in 2 Cor. 9:5, of the offering sent by the church at Corinth to their needy brethren in Judea.

2. *haplotes* (572), from *haplous*, "simple, single," is translated "bountifulness" in 2 Cor. 9:11, KJV; RV, "liberality" (marg., "singleness"); cf. 8:2; 9:13; from sincerity of mind springs "liberality." The thought of sincerity is present in Rom. 12:8; 2 Cor. 11:3; Eph. 6:5; Col. 3:22.

3. *charis* (5485), "grace," is rendered, "bounty" in 1 Cor. 16:3, RV, (KJV, "liberality"), by metonymy for a material gift.

4. *hadrotes* (100), lit. "fatness," is used of a monetary gift, in 2 Cor. 8:20, KJV, "abundance," RV, "bounty."

BOW, BOWED (Verb)

Old Testament

kara' (3766), "to bow, bow down, bend the knee," Gen. 49:9. "Bow" could be a common stance of body, Judg. 7:5-6; or worship to deity, 1 Kings 8:54; Ezra 9:5; Isa. 45:23; cf. Phil. 2:10. To "bow down upon" a woman was an euphemism for sexual intercourse, Job 31:10; for birthing, 1 Sam. 4:19; in old age, Job 4:4.

New Testament

1. *kampto* (2578), "to bend," is used especially of bending the knees in religious veneration, Rom. 11:4; 14:11; Eph. 3:14; Phil. 2:10.

2. *sunkampto* (4781) signifies "to bend completely together, to bend down by compulsory force," Rom. 11:10.

3. *sunkupto* (4794), "to bow together," is said, in Luke 13:11, of the woman crippled with a physical infirmity.

4. *klino* (2827), "to incline, to bow down," is used of the women who in their fright "bowed" their faces to the earth at the Lord's empty tomb, Luke 24:5; of the act of the Lord on the cross immediately before giving up His Spirit. What is indicated in the statement "He bowed His head," is not the helpless dropping of the head after death, but the deliberate putting of His head into a position of rest, John 19:30. The verb is deeply significant here. The Lord reversed the natural order. The same verb is used in His statement in Matt. 8:20 and Luke 9:58, "the Son of Man hath not where to lay His head." It is used, too, of the decline of day, Luke 9:12; 24:29; of turning enemies to flight, Heb. 11:34.

BOWELS

splanchnon (*4698*), always in the plural, properly denotes "the physical organs of the intestines," and is once used in this respect, Acts 1:18. The RV substitutes the following for the word "bowels": "affections," 2 Cor. 6:12; "affection," 2 Cor. 7:15; "tender mercies," Phil. 1:8; 2:1; "a heart (of compassion)," Col. 3:12; "heart," Philem. 12, 20; "hearts," Philem. 7; "compassion," 1 John 3:17. The word is rendered "tender" in the KJV and RV of Luke 1:78, in connection with the word "mercy."

BOY

pais (*3816*) denotes "a boy" (in contrast to *paidion*, a diminutive of *pais*, and to *teknon*, "a child"). With reference to Christ, instead of the KJV "child," the RV suitably translates otherwise as follows: Luke 2:43, "the boy Jesus"; Acts 4:27, 30, "Thy Holy Servant, Jesus." So in the case of others, Matt. 17:18 and Luke 9:42 ("boy").

BRAIDED (KJV, BROIDED)

plegma (*4117*) signifies "what is woven" (from *pleko*, "to weave, plait"), whether a net or basket (Josephus uses it of the ark of bulrushes in which the infant Moses was laid), or of a web, plait, braid. It is used in 1 Tim. 2:9, of "braided hair," which the Vulgate signifies as "ringlets, curls."

BRANDED

kausteriazo (*2743*), "to burn in with a branding iron" (cf. Eng., "caustic"), is found, in the best mss., in 1 Tim. 4:2, RV "branded." Others have *kauteriazo* (from *kauterion*, "a branding-iron," Eng., "cauterize"), to mark by "branding," an act not quite so severe as that indicated by the former. The reference is to apostates whose consciences are "branded" with the effects of their sin.

BRASS, BRAZEN

1. *chalkos* (*5475*), primarily, "copper," became used for metals in general, later was applied to bronze, a mixture of copper and tin, then, by metonymy, to any article made of these metals, e.g., money, Matt. 10:9; Mark 6:8; 12:41, or a sounding instrument, 1 Cor. 13:1, figurative of a person destitute of love. See Rev. 18:12.

2. *chalkeos* (*5470*), "made of brass or bronze," is used of idols, Rev. 9:20.

3. *chalkion* (*5473*) is used in Mark 7:4 of "brazen vessels."

4. *chalkolibanon* (*5474*) is used of "white or shining copper or bronze," and describes the feet of the Lord, in Rev. 1:15 and 2:18.

5. *chalkeus* (*5471*) denotes "a coppersmith," 2 Tim. 4:14.

BRAWLER

1. *paroinos* (*3943*), an adjective, lit., "tarrying at wine" (*para*, "at," *oinos*, "wine"), "given to wine," 1 Tim. 3:3 and Titus 1:7, KJV, probably has the secondary sense, of the effects of wine-bibbing, viz., abusive brawling. Hence RV, "brawler."

2. *amachos* (*269*), an adjective, lit. "not fighting" (*a*, negative, *mache*, "a fight"), came to denote, metaphorically, "not contentious," 1 Tim. 3:3, and Titus 3:2, RV, for KJV, "not a brawler," "not brawlers."

BREAK, BREAKER, BREAKING, BRAKE

A. Verbs.

1. *klao* or *klazo* (*2806*), "to break, to break off pieces," is used of "breaking bread," (a) of the Lord's act in providing bread for people, Matt. 14:19; 15:36; Mark 8:6, 19; (b) of the "breaking of bread" in the Lord's Supper, Matt. 26:26; Mark 14:22; Luke 22:19; Acts 20:7; 1 Cor. 10:16; 11:24; (c) of an ordinary meal, Acts 2:46; 20:11; 27:35; (d) of the Lord's act in giving evidence of His resurrection, Luke 24:30.

2. *ekklao* (*1575*), *ek*, "off," and No. 1, "to break off" is used metaphorically of branches, Rom. 11:17, 19-20.

3. *kataklao* (*2622*), *kata*, "down," and No. 1, is used in Mark 6:41 and Luke 9:16, of Christ's "breaking" loaves for the multitudes.

4. *luo* (*3089*), "to loosen," especially by way of deliverance, sometimes has the meaning of "breaking, destructively," e.g., of "breaking" commandments, not only infringing them, but loosing the force of them, rendering them not binding, Matt. 5:19; John 5:18; of "breaking" the Law of Moses, John 7:23; Scripture, John 10:35; of the "breaking up" of a ship, Acts 27:41; the "breaking down" of the middle wall of partition, Eph. 2:14; of the marriage tie, 1 Cor. 7:27.

5. *rhegnumi* (*4486*), "to tear, rend, as of garments, etc.," is translated "break" in the KJV, of Matt. 9:17, of wine-skins (RV, "burst"); as in Mark 2:22 and Luke 5:37.; "break forth" in Gal. 4:27.

6. *diarrhegnumi* (*1284*), *dia*, "through" (intensive), and No. 5, "to burst asunder, to rend, cleave," is said of the rending of garments, Matt. 26:65; Mark 14:63; Acts 14:14; of the "breaking" of a net, Luke 5:6; of fetters, 8:29.

7. *katagnumi* (*2608*), *kata*, "down" (intensive), and No. 5, is used of the "breaking" of a bruised reed, Matt. 12:20, and of the "breaking" of the legs of those who were crucified, John 19:31, 32, 33.

8. *diorusso* (*1358*), lit., "to dig through" (*dia*, "through," *orusso*, "to dig"), is used of the act of thieves in "breaking" into a house, Matt. 6:19, 20; 24:43; Luke 12:39.

9. *exorusso* (*1846*), lit., "to dig out" (cf. No. 8), is used of the "breaking up" of part of a roof, Mark 2:4, and, in a vivid expression, of plucking out the eyes, Gal. 4:15.

B. Nouns.

1. *parabasis* (3847), "a transgression" (*para*, "across," *baino*, "to go"), is translated "breaking" in Rom. 2:23, KJV; RV, "transgression"; KJV and RV ditto in 4:15; 5:14; Gal. 3:19; 1 Tim. 2:14; Heb. 2:2; 9:15.

2. *parabates* (3848), "a transgressor" (cf. No. 1), is translated "breaker," Rom. 2:25, KJV; RV, "transgressor." In v. 27 the KJV turns it into a verb, "dost transgress." See Gal. 2:18; Jas. 2:9, 11.

BREASTPLATE

thorax (2382), primarily, "the breast," denotes "a breastplate or corselet," consisting of two parts and protecting the body on both sides, from the neck to the middle. It is used metaphorically of righteousness, Eph. 6:14; of faith and love, 1 Thess. 5:8, with perhaps a suggestion of the two parts, front and back, which formed the coat of mail (an alternative term for the word in the NT sense); elsewhere in Rev. 9:9, 17.

BREATH, BREATHE

Old Testament

hebel (1892), "breath; vanity; idol."

First, the word represents human "breath" as a transitory thing, Job 7:16. Second, *hebel* means something meaningless and purposeless, Eccl. 1:2. Third, this word signifies a worthless "idol," Deut. 32:21.

New Testament

A. Nouns.

1. *pnoe* (4157), akin to *pneo*, "to blow," lit., "a blowing," signifies (a) "breath, the breath of life," Acts 17:25; (b) "wind," Acts 2:2.

2. *pneuma* (4151), "spirit," also denotes "breath," Rev. 11:11 and 13:15, RV. In 2 Thess. 2:8, the KJV has "spirit" for RV, breath.

B. Verbs.

1. *empneo* (1709), lit., "to breathe in, or on," is used in Acts 9:1, indicating that threatening and slaughter were, so to speak, the elements from which Saul drew and expelled his breath.

2. *emphusao* (1720), "to breathe upon," is used of the symbolic act of the Lord Jesus in breathing upon His apostles the communication of the Holy Spirit, John 20:22.

BRIDE, BRIDECHAMBER, BRIDEGROOM

numphe (3565) (Eng. "nymph") "a bride, or young wife," John 3:29; Rev. 18:23; 21:2, 9; 22:17, is probably connected with the Latin *nubo*, "to veil"; the "bride" was often adorned with embroidery and jewels (see Rev. 21:2), and was led veiled from her home to the "bridegroom." Hence the secondary meaning of "daughter-in-law," Matt. 10:35; Luke 12:53. For the relationship between Christ and a local church, under this figure, see 2 Cor. 11:2; regarding the whole church, Eph. 5:23-32; Rev. 22:17.

numphios (3566), "a bridegroom," occurs fourteen times in the gospels, and in Rev. 18:23. "The friend of the bridegroom," John 3:29, is distinct from "the sons of the bridechamber" who were numerous. When John the Baptist speaks of "the friend of the Bridegroom," he uses language according to the customs of the Jews.

numphon (3567), signifies (a) "the room or dining hall in which the marriage ceremonies were held," Matt. 22:10; some mss. have *gamos*, "a wedding," here; (b) "the chamber containing the bridal bed," "the sons of the bridechamber" being the friends of the bridegroom, who had the charge of providing what was necessary for the nuptials, Matt. 9:15; Mark 2:19; Luke 5:34.

BRIGHT, BRIGHTNESS

A. Adjective.

lampros (2986), "shining, brilliant, bright," is used of the clothing of an angel, Acts 10:30 and Rev. 15:6; symbolically, of the clothing of the saints in glory, Rev. 19:8, RV, in the best texts (KJV, "white"); of Christ as the Morning Star, 22:16; of the water of life, 22:1, KJV, "clear."

B. Noun.

lamprotes (2987), "brightness," akin to A, above is found in Acts 26:13.

BRIMSTONE

1. *theion* (2303) originally denoted "fire from heaven." It is connected with sulphur. Places touched by lightning were called *theia*, and, as lightning leaves a sulphurous smell, and sulphur was used in pagan purifications, it received the name of *theion* Luke 17:29; Rev. 9:17-18; 14:10; 19:20; 20:10; 21:8.

2. *theiodes* (2306), akin to No. 1, signifies "brimstone-like, or consisting of brimstone," Rev. 9:17.

BROTHER, BRETHREN, BROTHERHOOD, BROTHERLY

Old Testament

'ach (251), "brother." *'ach* means "male sibling," i.e., a "brother," Gen. 4:2; ; a full brother or a half-brother, Gen. 37:14. *'ach* means a "blood relative," such as a nephew or grandson, Gen. 9:25; 14:16; 29:12. *'achim* (plural) means "tribe," Judg. 1:3. The word *'ach* is used of a fellow tribesman, Gen. 31:32. Elsewhere it describes a fellow countryman, Exod. 2:11, or simply a fellow human being,

Gen. 9:5-6. *'ach* connotes "companion" or "colleague"—that is, a brother by choice, 2 Kings 9:2; cf. Isa. 41:6; Num. 8:26, or by circumstance, Gen. 9:5-6. Somewhat along this line is the covenantal use of the word as a synonym for "ally," Num. 20:14 and 1 Kings 9:13. *'ach* can also be a term of polite address, Gen. 29:4

New Testament

adelphos (80) denotes "a brother, or near kinsman"; in the plural, "a community based on identity of origin or life." It is used of:—

(1) male children of the same parents, Matt. 1:2; 14:3; (2) male descendants of the same parents, Acts 7:23, 26; Heb. 7:5; (3) male children of the same mother, Matt. 13:55; 1 Cor. 9:5; Gal. 1:19; (4) people of the same nationality, Acts 3:17, 22; Rom. 9:3. With "men" (*aner*, "male"), prefixed, it is used in addresses only, Acts 2:29, 37, etc.; (5) any man, a neighbor, Luke 10:29; Matt. 5:22; 7:3; (6) persons united by a common interest, Matt. 5:47; (7) persons united by a common calling, Rev. 22:9; (8) mankind, Matt. 25:40; Heb. 2:17; (9) the disciples, and so, by implication, all believers, Matt. 28:10; John 20:17; (10) believers, apart from sex, Matt. 23:8; Acts 1:15; Rom. 1:13; 1 Thess. 1:4; Rev. 19:10 (the word "sisters" is used of believers, only in 1 Tim. 5:2); (11) believers, with *aner*, "male," prefixed, and with "or sister" added, 1 Cor. 7:14 (RV), 15; Jas. 2:15, male as distinct from female, Acts 1:16; 15:7, 13, but not 6:3.

BRUISE

thrauo (2352), "to smite through, shatter," is used in Luke 4:18, "them that are bruised," i.e., broken by calamity.

BRUTE

alogos (249), translated "brute" in the KJV of 2 Pet. 2:12 and Jude 10, signifies "without reason," RV, though, as J. Hastings points out, "brute beasts" is not at all unsuitable, as "brute" is from Latin *brutus*, which means "dull, irrational"; in Acts 25:27 it is rendered "unreasonable."

BUFFET

1. *kolaphizo* (2852) signifies "to strike with clenched hands, to buffet with the fist" (*kolaphos*, "a fist"), Matt. 26:67; Mark 14:65; 1 Cor. 4:11; 2 Cor. 12:7; 1 Pet. 2:20.

2. *hupopiazo* (5299), lit., "to strike under the eye," hence, to beat the face black and blue (to give a black eye), is used metaphorically, and translated "buffet" in 1 Cor. 9:27 (KJV, "keep under"), of Paul's suppressive treatment of his body, in order to keep himself spiritually fit (RV marg., "bruise"); so RV marg. in Luke 18:5, of the persistent widow, text, "wear out" (KJV, "weary").

BUILD, BUILDER, BUILDING
Old Testament

A. Verb.

banah (1129), "to build, establish, construct, rebuild." *banah* means to construct, fashion, or manufacture a new object, Gen. 2:22; 4:17; 8:20; Ezek. 27:5; 1 Kings 15:22; *banah* can also refer to "rebuilding"; Josh. 6:26; *banah* also means "having children," Gen. 16:2; Deut. 25:9; or "to found a dynasty," 2 Sam. 7:27.

B. Nouns.

ben (1121), "son." *bat* (1323), "daughter, " derived from the verb, see above. *ben* and *bat* means a "male or female offspring," Gen. 3:16; 5:4; 49:11. The words *ben* and *bat* can signify "descendants" in general—daughters, sons, granddaughters, and grandsons, Gen. 31:28; cf. v. 43. The phrase, "my son," may be used by a superior to a subordinate as a term of familiar address, Josh. 7:19. A special use of "my son" is a teacher's speaking to a disciple, referring to intellectual or spiritual sonship, Prov. 1:10. *ben* can also be used in an adoption formula, Ps. 2:7; Hos. 11:1.

The Bible also refers to the heavenly court as the "sons of God," Job 1:6. God called the elders of Israel the "sons [KJV, "children"] of the Most High," Ps. 82:6. In Gen. 6:2, the phrase "sons of God" is variously understood as members of the heavenly court, the spiritual disciples of God (the sons of Seth), and the boastful among mankind.

ben may signify "young men" in general, Prov. 7:7. A city may be termed a "mother" and its inhabitants its "sons," Ps. 147:13. *ben* is sometimes used to mean a single individual, Gen. 18:7. The phrase "son of man" is used in this sense—God is asked to save the poor individuals, not the children of the poor, Ps. 72:4. *ben* may also denote a member of a group, 1 Kings 20:35; cf. Amos 7:14, or someone worthy of a certain fate, Deut. 21:18. Used figuratively, "son of" can mean "something belonging to"—e.g., "the arrow [literally, "the son of a bow"] cannot make him flee," Job 41:28.

New Testament

A. Verbs.

1. *oikodomeo* (3618), lit., "to build a house," hence, to build anything, e.g., Matt. 7:24; Luke 4:29; 6:48, RV, "well builded" (last clause of verse); John 2:20; is frequently used figuratively, e.g., Acts 20:32 (some mss. have No. 3 here); Gal. 2:18; especially of edifying, Acts 9:31; Rom. 15:20; 1 Cor. 10:23; 14:4; 1 Thess. 5:11 (RV). In 1 Cor. 8:10 it is translated "emboldened" (marg., "builded up"). The participle with the article (equivalent to a noun) is rendered "builder," Matt. 21:42; Acts 4:11; 1 Pet. 2:7.

2. *anoikodomeo* (456) signifies "to build again," Acts 15:16.

3. *epoikodomeo* (2026) signifies "to build upon," 1 Cor. 3:10, 12, 14; Eph. 2:20; Jude 20; or up, Acts 20:32; Col. 2:7.

4. *sunoikodomeo* (4925), "to build together," is used in Eph. 2:22, metaphorically, of the church, as a spiritual dwelling-place for God.

B. Nouns.

1. *oikodome* (3619), "a building, or edification," is used (a) literally, e.g., Matt. 24:1; Mark 13:1-2; (b) figuratively, e.g., Rom. 14:19 (lit., "the things of building up"); 15:2 of a local church as a spiritual building, 1 Cor. 3:9, or the whole church, the body of Christ, Eph. 2:21. It expresses the strengthening effect of teaching, 1 Cor. 14:3, 5, 12, 26; 2 Cor. 10:8; 12:19; 13:10, or other ministry, Eph. 4:12, 16, 29 (the idea conveyed is progress resulting from patient effort). It is also used of the believer's resurrection body, 2 Cor. 5:1.

2. *endomesis* (1739), "a thing built, structure," is used of the wall of the heavenly city, Rev. 21:18 (some suggest that the word means "a fabric"; others, "a roofing or coping"; these interpretations are questionable; the probable significance is "a building").

BURDEN, BURDENED, BURDENSOME

A. Nouns.

1. *baros* (922) denotes "a weight, anything pressing on one physically," Matt. 20:12, or "that makes a demand on one's resources," whether material, 1 Thess. 2:6 (to be burdensome), or spiritual, Gal. 6:2; Rev. 2:24, or religious, Acts 15:28. In one place it metaphorically describes the future state of believers as "an eternal weight of glory," 2 Cor. 4:17.

2. *phortion* (5413), lit., "something carried" (from *phero*, "to bear"), is always used metaphorically (except in Acts 27:10, of the lading of a ship); of that which, though "light," is involved in discipleship of Christ, Matt. 11:30; of tasks imposed by the scribes, Pharisees and lawyers, Matt. 23:4; Luke 11:46; of that which will be the result, at the judgment-seat of Christ, of each believer's work, Gal. 6:5.

B. Verbs.

1. *bareo* (916), akin to A, No. 1, is used of the effect of drowsiness, "were heavy," Matt. 26:43; Mark 14:40; Luke 9:32; of the effects of gluttony, Luke 21:34 ("overcharged"); of the believer's present physical state in the body, 2 Cor. 5:4; of persecution, 2 Cor. 1:8; of a charge upon material resources, 1 Tim. 5:16 (RV).

2. *epibareo* (1912), "to burden heavily," is said of material resources, 1 Thess. 2:9 (RV); 2 Thess. 3:8, RV, "burden," KJV, "be chargeable to," of the effect of spiritual admonition and discipline, 2 Cor. 2:5, RV, "press heavily," KJV, "overcharge."

3. *katabareo* (2599), "to weigh down," "overload," is used of material charges, in 2 Cor. 12:16.

C. Adjective.

B

abares (4), "without weight" (*a*,) negative, and *baros*, "see" A, No. 1), is used in 2 Cor. 11:9, lit. "I kept myself burdensomeless."

BURN, BURNING
Old Testament

A. Verb.

saraph (8313), "to burn." Since burning is the main characteristic of fire, the term *saraph* is usually used to describe the destroying of objects of all kinds, Josh. 6:24; Judg. 9:52; 1 Sam. 30:1; Jer. 36:25, 27-28; Amos 2:1.

Interestingly, *saraph* is never used for the "burning" of a sacrifice on the altar, although a few times it designates the disposal of refuse, unused sacrificial parts, and some diseased parts. The "burning" of a red heifer was for the purpose of producing ashes for purification, Lev. 19:5, 8.

B. Nouns.

saraph (8314), "burning one; fiery being." In Num. 21:6, 8, the term *saraph* describes the serpents that attacked the Israelites in the wilderness. They are referred to as "fiery" serpents. A "fiery" flying serpent appears in Isa. 14:29, as well as in Isa. 30:6.

seraphim (8314), "burning, noble." *seraphim* refers to the ministering beings in Isa. 6:2, 6, and may imply either a serpentine form (albeit with wings, human hands, and voices) or beings that have a "glowing" quality about them. One of the *seraphim* ministered to Isaiah by bringing a glowing coal from the altar.

New Testament

A. Verbs.

1. *kaio* (2545), "to set fire to, to light"; in the passive voice, "to be lighted, to burn," Matt. 5:15; John 15:6; Heb. 12:18; Rev. 4:5; 8:8, 10; 19:20; 21:8; 1 Cor. 13:3, is used metaphorically of the heart, Luke 24:32; of spiritual light, Luke 12:35; John 5:35.

2. *katakaio* (2618), from *kata*, "down" (intensive), and No. 1, signifies "to burn up, burn utterly," as of chaff, Matt. 3:12; Luke 3:17; tares, Matt. 13:30, 40; the earth and its works, 2 Pet. 3:10; trees and grass, Rev. 8:7. This form should be noted in Acts 19:19; 1 Cor. 3:15; Heb. 13:11, Rev. 17:16. In each place the full rendering "burn utterly" might be used, as in Rev. 18:8.

3. *ekkaio* (1572), from *ek*, out (intensive), and No. 1, lit., "to burn out," in the passive voice, "to be kindled, burn up," is used of the lustful passions of men, Rom. 1:27.

4. *puroomai* (*4448*), from *pur*, "fire, to glow with heat," is said of the feet of the Lord, in the vision in Rev. 1:15; it is translated "fiery" in Eph. 6:16 (of the darts of the evil one); used metaphorically of the emotions, in 1 Cor. 7:9; 2 Cor. 11:29; elsewhere literally, of the heavens, 2 Pet. 3:12; of gold, Rev. 3:18 (RV, "refined").

B. Nouns.

1. *kausis* (*2740*), akin to A, No. 1 (Eng., "caustic"), is found in Heb. 6:8, lit. "whose end is unto burning."

2. *kauson* (*2742*) is rendered "burning heat" in Jas. 1:11, KJV (RV, "scorching").

3. *purosis* (*4451*), akin to A. No. 4, is used literally in Rev. 18:9, 18; metaphorically in 1 Pet. 4:12, "fiery trial."

TO BURN INCENSE

A. Verb.

qatar (*6999*), "to burn incense, cause to rise up in smoke." *qatar* means "offering true offerings" every time it appears in the causative stem, cf. Hos. 4:13; 11:2; 2 Chron. 13:11. Offerings are burned in order to change the thing offered into smoke (the ethereal essence of the offering), which would ascend to God as a pleasing or placating savor.

Such offerings represent both the giving of the thing offered and a vicarious substitution of the offering for the offerer, cf. John 17:19; Eph. 5:2. Because of man's sinfulness, Gen. 8:21; Rom. 5:12, he was unable to initiate a relationship with God. Therefore, God Himself told man what was necessary in order to worship and serve Him. God specified that only the choicest of one's possessions could be offered, and the best of the offering belonged to Him, Lev. 4:10. Only His priests were to offer sacrifices, 2 Kings 16:13. All offerings were to be made at the designated place; after the conquest, this was the central sanctuary, Lev. 17:6.

B. Nouns.

qetorel (*7004*), "incense." The word represents "perfume" in Prov. 27:9.

qitter means "incense." This word appears once in the Old Testament, in Jer. 44:21. Another noun, *qetorah*, also means "incense." This word's only appearance is in Deut. 33:10. *qitor* refers to "smoke; vapor." This word does not refer to the smoke of an offering, but to other kinds of smoke or vapor. The reference in Ps. 148:8 ("vapor") is one of its four biblical occurrences. *muqtar* means "the kindling of incense." The word is used only once, Mal. 1:11.

miqteret means "censer; incense." The word occurs twice. *miqteret* represents a "censer"—a utensil in which coals are carried—in 2 Chron. 26:19. The word refers to "incense" in Ezek. 8:11.

B

meqatterah refers to "incense altar." The word occurs once, 2 Chron. 26:19. *miqtar* means a "place of sacrificial smoke; altar." The word appears once, Exod. 30:1.

BURNT (offering)

holokautoma (3646) denotes "a whole burnt offering" (*holos*, "whole," *kautos*, for *kaustos*, a verbal adjective from *kaio*, "to burn"), i.e., "a victim," the whole of which is burned, as in Ex. 30:20; Lev. 5:12; 23:8, 25, 27. It is used in Mark 12:33, by the scribe who questioned the Lord as to the first commandment in the Law and in Heb. 10:6, 8, RV "whole burnt offerings."

BURST (asunder)

lakeo or *lasko* (2997), primarily, "to crack, or crash," denotes "to burst asunder with a crack, crack open" (always of making a noise), is used in Acts 1:18.

BUSINESS

A. Nouns.

1. *chreia* (5532), translated "business" in Acts 6:3, of the distribution of funds, signifies "a necessity, a need," and is used in this place concerning duty or business.

2. *ergasia* (2039) denotes "a business," Acts 19:24, 25, RV, KJV, "gain" and "craft" (from *ergon*, "work").

B. Adjective.

idios (2398) expresses "what is one's own" (hence, Eng. "idiot," in a changed sense, lit., "a person with his own opinions"); the neuter plural with the article (*ta idia*) signifies "one's own things." In 1 Thess. 4:11, the noun is not expressed in the original but is supplied in the English versions by "business," "your own business." For the same phrase, otherwise expressed, see John 1:11, "His own (things)"; 16:32 and 19:27, "his own (home)"; Acts 21:6, "home." In Luke 2:49, the phrase "in My Father's house" (RV), "about My Father's business" (KJV), is, lit., "in the (things, the neuter plural of the article) of My Father."

BUSYBODY

A. Verb.

periergazomai (4020), lit., "to be working round about, instead of at one's own business," signifies to take more pains than enough about a thing, to waste one's labor, to be meddling with, or bustling about, other people's matters. This is found in 2 Thess. 3:11, where, following the verb *ergazomai*, "to work," it forms a *paronomasia*. This may be produced in a free rendering: "some who are not busied in their own business, but are overbusied in that of others."

B. Adjective.

periergos (*4021*), akin to A, denoting "taken up with trifles," is used of magic arts in Acts 19:19; "busybodies" in 1 Tim. 5:13, i.e., meddling in other persons' affairs.

C. Noun.

allotrioepiskopos (*244*), from *allotrios*, "belonging to another person," and *episkopos*, "an overseer," translated "busybody" in the KJV of 1 Pet. 4:15, "meddler," RV, was a legal term for a charge brought against Christians as being hostile to civilized society, their purpose being to make Gentiles conform to Christian standards. Some explain it as a pryer into others' affairs.

BUY, BOUGHT

Old Testament

qanah (*7069*), "to get, acquire, create, buy." *qanah* expresses a basic meaning of God's "creating" or "bringing into being," Gen. 4:1; 14:19,22. In Deut. 32:6, God is called the "father" who "created" Israel; a father begets or "creates," rather than "acquires" children. In the Wisdom version of the Creation story, Ps 139:13; Prov. 8:22-36. *qanah* is used several times to express God's redeeming activity in behalf of Israel, again reflecting "creativity" rather than "purchase," Exod. 15:16; See also Ps. 74:2; 78:54. *qanah* also means frequently "make a purchase agreement with another," Gen. 47:20; Exod. 21:2.

New Testament

agorazo (*59*), primarily, "to frequent the market-place," the *agora*, hence "to do business there, to buy or sell," is used lit., e.g., in Matt. 14:15. Figuratively Christ is spoken of as having bought His redeemed, making them His property at the price of His blood (i.e., His death through the shedding of His blood in expiation for their sins), 1 Cor. 6:20; 7:23; 2 Pet. 2:1; see also Rev. 5:9; 14:3-4 (not as KJV, "redeemed"). *agorazo* does not mean "to redeem."

C

CALL, CALLED, CALLING
Old Testament

A. Verb.

qara' (7121), "to call, call out, recite."

qara' may signify the "specification of a name." Naming a thing is frequently an assertion of sovereignty over it, which is the case in the first use of *qara'*, Gen. 1:5. God's act of creating, "naming," and numbering includes the stars, Ps. 147:4, and all other things, Isa. 40:26. He allowed Adam to "name" the animals as a concrete demonstration of man's relative sovereignty over them, Gen. 2:19. Divine sovereignty and election are extended over all generations, for God "called" them all from the beginning, Isa. 41:4; cf. Amos 5:8. "Calling" or "naming" an individual may specify the individual's primary characteristic, Gen. 27:36; it may consist of a confession or evaluation, Isa. 58:13; 60:14; and it may recognize an eternal truth, Isa. 7:14.

This verb also is used to indicate "calling to a specific task," Exod. 2:7.

To "call" on God's name is to summon His aid, Gen. 4:26. The "calling" on God's name is clearly not the beginning of prayer, Gen. 4:7ff. The sense of "summoning" God to one's aid was surely in Abraham's mind when he "called upon" God's name, Gen. 12:8. "Calling" in this sense constitutes a prayer prompted by recognized need and directed to One who is able and willing to respond, Ps. 145:18; Isa. 55:6.

Basically, *qara'* means "to call out loudly" in order to get someone's attention so that contact can be initiated, Job 5:11. Often this verb represents sustained communication, paralleling "to say" (*'amar*), as in Gen. 3:9. *qara'* can also mean "to call out a warning," Lev. 13:45.

qara' may mean "to shout" or "to call out loudly." Goliath "shouted," 1 Sam. 17:8.

qara' may also mean "to proclaim" or "to announce," Judg. 21:13; Esth. 6:9. In prophetic literature, *qara'* is a technical term for "declaring" a prophetic message: "For the saying which he *cried* by the word of the Lord…shall surely come to pass," 1 Kings 13:32.

Another major emphasis of *qara'* is "to summon," Gen. 12:18. Often the summons is in the form of a friendly invitation, Exod. 2:20. The participial form of *qara'* is used to denote "invited guests," 1 Sam. 9:13, NASB. This verb is also used in judicial contexts, to mean being "summoned to court," Deut. 25:8. *qara'* is used of mustering an army, Judg. 8:1.

qara' means "to dictate," Jer. 36:18.

B. Noun.

miqra' (4744), "public worship service; convocation." The word implies the product of an official summons to worship ("convocation"). In one of its 23 appearances, *miqra'* refers to Sabbaths as "convocation days" (Lev. 23:2).

New Testament

A. Verbs.

1. *kaleo* (2564), derived from the root *kal—*, whence Eng. "call" and "clamor," is used (a) with a personal object, "to call anyone, invite, summon," e.g., Matt. 20:8; 25:14; it is used particularly of the divine call to partake of the blessings of redemption, e.g., Rom. 8:30; 1 Cor. 1:9; 1 Thess. 2:12; Heb. 9:15; cf. B and C, below; (b) of nomenclature or vocation, "to call by a name, to name"; in the passive voice, "to be called by a name, to bear a name." Thus it suggests either vocation or destination; the context determines which, e.g., Rom. 9:25-26.

2. *eiskaleo* (1528), lit., "to call in," hence, "to invite" (*eis*, "in," and No. 1), is found in Acts 10:23.

3. *epikaleo* (1941), *epi*, "upon," and No. 1., denotes (a) "to surname"; (b) "to be called by a person's name"; hence it is used of being declared to be dedicated to a person, as to the Lord, Acts 15:17 (from Amos 9:12); Jas. 2:7; (c) "to call a person by a name by charging him with an offense," as the Pharisees charged Christ with doing His works by the help of Beelzebub, Matt. 10:25 (the most authentic reading has *epikaleo*, for *kaleo*); (d) "to call upon, invoke"; in the middle voice, "to call upon for oneself" (i.e., on one's behalf), Acts 7:59, or "to call upon a person as a witness," 2 Cor. 1:23, or to appeal to an authority, Acts 25:11, etc.; (e)"to call upon by way of adoration, making use of the Name of the Lord," Acts 2:21; Rom. 10:12-14; 2 Tim. 2:22.

4. *metakaleo* (3333), *meta*, implying "change," and No. 1, "to call from one place to another, to summon," is used in the middle voice only, "to call for oneself, to send for, call hither," Acts 7:14; 10:32; 20:17; 24:25.

5. *proskaleo* (4341), *pros*, "to," and No. 1, signifies (a) "to call to oneself, to bid to come"; it is used only in the middle voice, e.g., Matt. 10:1; Acts 5:40; Jas. 5:14; (b) "God's call to Gentiles through

the gospel," Acts 2:39; (c) the divine call in entrusting men with the preaching of the gospel," Acts 13:2; 16:10.

6. **sunkaleo** (*4779*) signifies "to call together," Mark 15:16; Luke 9:1; 15:6, 9; 23:13; Acts 5:21; 10:24; 28:17.

7. **aiteo** (*154*), "to ask," is translated "called for" in Acts 16:29 ("he called for lights").

8. **phoneo** (*5455*), "to sound" (Eng., "phone"), is used of the crowing of a cock, e.g., Matt. 26:34; John 13:38; of "calling" out with a clear or loud voice, to cry out, e.g. Mark 1:26 (some mss. have **krazo** here); Acts 16:28; of "calling" to come to oneself, e.g., Matt. 20:32; Luke 19:15; of "calling" forth, as of Christ's call to Lazarus to come forth from the tomb, John 12:17; of inviting, e.g. Luke 14:12; of "calling" by name, with the implication of the pleasure taken in the possession of those "called," e.g., John 10:3; 13:13.

9. **lego** (*3004*), "to speak," is used of all kinds of oral communication, e.g. "to call, to call by name," to surname, Matt. 1:16; 26:36; John 4:5; 11:54; 15:15; Rev. 2:2, RV, "call themselves," etc.

10. **epilego** (*1951*), **epi** "upon," and No. 9, signifies "to call in addition," i.e., by another name besides that already intimated, John 5:2; for its other meaning in Acts 15:40, see CHOOSE.

11. **chrematizo** (*5337*), occasionally means "to be called or named," Acts 11:26 (of the name "Christians") and Rom. 7:3, the only places where it has this meaning. Its primary significance, "to have business dealings with," led to this. They "were (publicly) called" Christians, because this was their chief business.

12. **eipon** (*3004*), "to say, speak," akin to 9 above, means "to call by a certain appellation," John 10:35.

13. **krino** (*2919*), "to judge," is translated "to call in question," in Acts 23:6; 24:21.

B. Noun.

klesis (*2821*), "a calling" (akin to A, No. 1), is always used in the NT of that "calling" the origin, nature and destiny of which are heavenly (the idea of invitation being implied); it is used especially of God's invitation to man to accept the benefits of salvation, Rom. 11:29; 1 Cor. 1:26; 7:20 (said there of the condition in which the "calling" finds one); Eph. 1:18, "His calling"; Phil. 3:14, the "high calling"; 2 Thess. 1:11 and 2 Pet. 1:10, "your calling"; 2 Tim. 1:9, a "holy calling"; Heb. 3:1, a "heavenly calling"; Eph. 4:1, "the calling wherewith ye were called"; 4:4, "in one hope of your calling."

C. Adjective.

kletos (*2822*), "called, invited," is used, (a) "of the call of the gospel," Matt. 20:16; 22:14, not there "an effectual call," as in the Epistles, Rom. 1:1, 6-7; 8:28; 1 Cor. 1:2, 24; Jude 1; Rev. 17:14; in Rom. 1:7 and 1 Cor. 1:2 the meaning is "saints by calling"; (b) of "an appointment to apostleship," Rom. 1:1; 1 Cor. 1:1.

CAMP

machaneh (*4264*), "camp; encampment; host." Those who travel were called "campers," or in most versions (KJV, RSV, NASB) a "company" or "group" (NIV), as in Gen. 32:8. Naaman stood before Elisha "with all his company," 2 Kings 5:15 NASB, NEB, "retinue." Jacob "encamped" by the Jabbok with his retinue, Gen. 32:10. The name *Mahanaim*, Gen. 32:2, "camps," owes its origin to Jacob's experience with the angels, calling it God's camp, Gen. 32:2.

Usage of *machaneh* varies according to context. First, it signifies a nation set over against another, Exod. 14:20. Second, the word refers to a division concerning the Israelites; each of the tribes had a special "encampment" in relation to the tent of meeting, Num. 1:52. Third, the word "camp" is used to describe the whole people of Israel, Exod. 19:16.

CANAAN; CANAANITE

kena'an (*3667*), "Canaan"; *kena'ani* (*3669*), "Canaanite; merchant." "Canaan" is first used of a person in Gen. 9:18; later it referenced an area, from Sidon to Gaza, to Sodom, west of the Jordan, Gen. 15:18-20; cf. Exod. 3:8, 17; Josh. 3:10. "Canaanite" is a general term for all the descendants of "Canaan," Deut. 7:1. It is interchanged with Amorite in Gen. 15:16. "Canaanite" also refers to one specific people in Canaan, Num. 13:29; cf. Josh. 5:1; 2 Sam. 24:7. These peoples were traders, Prov. 31:24; Job 41:6.

Gen. 9:25-27 stamps a theological significance on "Canaan" from the beginning. Noah prophetically placed this curse on "Canaan" because his father had stared at Noah's nakedness and reported it grossly to his brothers. Ham's sin, deeply rooted in his youngest son, is observable in the Canaanites, Lev. 18:3. The command to destroy the "Canaanites" was very specific, Deut. 7:2-6. But, too often the house of David and Judah "built them high places, 1 Kings 14:23-24; cf. 2 Kings 16:3-4; 21:1-15. "Canaanite" became synonymous with religious and moral perversions of every kind, Zech. 14:21, cf. Rev. 21:27.

CAPTAIN

1. *chiliarchos* (*5506*), denoting "a commander of 1000 soldiers," was the Greek word for the Persian vizier, and for the Roman military tribune, the commander of a Roman cohort, e.g., John 18:12; Acts 21:31-33, 37. One such commander was constantly in charge of the Roman garrison in Jerusalem. The word became used also for any military commander, e.g., a "captain" or "chief captain," Mark 6:21; Rev. 6:15; 19:18.

2. *strategos* (*4755*), originally the commander of an army (from *stratos*, "an army," and *ago*, "to lead"), came to denote "a civil commander, a governor" (Latin, *duumvir*), the highest magistrate,

or any civil officer in chief command, Acts 16:20, 22, 35-36, 38; also the "chief captain" cf the Temple, himself Levite, having command of the Levites who kept guard in and around the Temple, Luke 22:4, 52; Acts 4:1; 5:24, 26. Cf. Jer. 20:1.

3. *archegos* (747): Acts 3:15; 5:31; Heb. 2:10; 12:2.

CAPTIVE, CAPTIVITY

A. Nouns.

1. *aichmalotos* (164), lit., "one taken by the spear," a verbal adjective, from *halonai*, "to be captured," hence denotes "a captive," Luke 4:18.

2. *aichmalosia* (161), "captivity," the abstract noun in contrast to No. 1, the concrete, is found in Rev. 13:10 and Eph. 4:8, where "He led captivity captive," seems to be an allusion to the triumphal procession by which a victory was celebrated, the "captives" taken forming part of the procession. See Judg. 5:12. The quotation is from Ps. 68:18, and probably is a forceful expression for Christ's victory, through His death, over the hostile powers of darkness. An alternative suggestion is that at His ascension Christ transferred the redeemed Old Testament saints from Sheol to His own presence in glory.

B. Verbs.

1. *aichmaloteuo* (162) signifies (a) "to be a prisoner of war," (b) "to make a prisoner of war." The latter meaning is the only one used in the NT, Eph. 4:8.

2. *aichmalotizo* (163), practically synonymous with No. 1, denotes either "to lead away captive," Luke 21:24, or "to subjugate, to bring under control," said of the effect of the Law in one's members in bringing the person into captivity under the law of sin, Rom. 7:23; or of subjugating the thoughts to the obedience of Christ, 2 Cor. 10:5; or of those who took captive "silly women laden with sins," 2 Tim. 3:6.

3. *zogreo* (2221), lit. signifies "to take men alive," Luke 5:10, there of the effects of the work of the gospel; in 2 Tim. 2:26 it is said of the power of Satan to lead men astray. The verse should read "and that they may recover themselves out of the snare of the Devil (having been taken captive by him), unto the will of God." This is the probable meaning rather than "to take alive or for life."

CARE (noun and verb), CAREFUL, CAREFULLY, CAREFULNESS

A. Nouns.

1. *merimna* (3308), probably connected with *merizo*, "to draw in different directions, distract," hence signifies "that which causes this, a care, especially an anxious care," Matt. 13:22; Mark 4:19;

Luke 8:14; 21:34; 2 Cor. 11:28 (RV, "anxiety for"), 1 Pet. 5:7 (RV, "anxiety").

2. *spoude* (*4710*), primarily "haste, zeal, diligence," hence means "earnest care, carefulness," 2 Cor. 7:11-12; 8:16 (RV, "earnest care," in each place). *merimna* conveys the thought of anxiety, *spoude*, of watchful interest and earnestness.

B. Verbs.

1. *merimnao* (*3309*), akin to A No. 1, signifies "to be anxious about, to have a distracting care," e.g., Matt. 6:25, 28, RV, "be anxious," for KJV, "take thought"; 10:19; Luke 10:41 (RV, "anxious," for KJV, "careful"); 12:11 (RV, "anxious"); to be careful for, 1 Cor. 7:32-34; to have a care for, 1 Cor. 12:25; to care for, Phil. 2:20; "be anxious," Phil. 4:6, RV.

2. *melei* (*3199*), the third person sing. of *melo*, used impersonally, signifies that "something is an object of care," especially the care of forethought and interest, rather than anxiety, Matt. 22:16; Mark 4:38; 12:14; Luke 10:40; John 10:13; 12:6; Acts 18:17; 1 Cor. 9:9 (RV, "Is it for the oxen that God careth?" The KJV seriously misses the point. God does "care" for oxen, but there was a divinely designed significance in the OT passage, relating to the service of preachers of the gospel); 7:21; 1 Pet. 5:7.

3. *epimeleomai* (*1959*) signifies "to take care of," involving forethought and provision (*epi* indicating "the direction of the mind toward the object cared for"), Luke 10:34-35, of the Good Samaritan's care for the wounded man, and in 1 Tim. 3:5, of a bishop's (or overseer's) care of a church—a significant association of ideas.

4. *phrontizo* (*5431*), "to think, consider, be thoughtful" (from *phren*, "the mind"), is translated "be careful" in Titus 3:8.

5. *phroneo* (*5426*), translated "be careful," in Phil. 4:10, KJV [RV, "(ye did) take thought"], has a much wider range of meaning than No. 5, and denotes to be minded, in whatever way.

C. Adverb.

spoudaioteros, (*4708*), the comparative adverb corresponding to A, No. 2, signifies "the more diligently," Phil. 2:28.

CARNAL, CARNALLY

1. *sarkikos* (*4559*), from *sarx*, "flesh," signifies (a) "having the nature of flesh," i.e., sensual, controlled by animal appetites, governed by human nature, instead of by the Spirit of God, 1 Cor. 3:3 (for v. 1, see below; same mss. have it in v. 4); having its seat in the animal nature, or excited by it, 1 Pet. 2:11, "fleshly"; or as the equivalent of "human," with the added idea of weakness, figuratively of the weapons of spiritual warfare, "of the flesh" (KJV, "carnal"), 2 Cor. 10:4; or with the idea of unspirituality, of human wisdom, "fleshly," 2 Cor. 1:12; (b) "pertaining to the flesh" (i.e., the

body), Rom. 15:27; 1 Cor. 9:11.

2. *sarkinos* (*4560*), (a) "consisting of flesh," 2 Cor. 3:3; (b) "pertaining to the natural, transient life of the body," Heb. 7:16; (c) given up to the flesh, Rom. 7:14. It is hard to distinguish 1 & 2 in 1 Cor. 3:1 and some other passages.

CARPENTER

tekton (*5405*) denotes any craftsman, but especially a worker in wood, a carpenter, Matt. 13:55; Mark 6:3.

CATCH

1. *harpazo* (*726*), "to snatch or catch away," is said of the act of the Spirit of the Lord in regard to Philip in Acts 8:39; of Paul in being "caught" up to paradise, 2 Cor. 12:2, 4; of the rapture of the saints at the return of the Lord, 1 Thess. 4:17; of the rapture of the man child in the vision of Rev. 12:5. This verb conveys the idea of force suddenly exercised, as in Matt. 11:12, "take (it) by force"; 12:29, "spoil" (some mss. have *diarpazo* here), in 13:19, RV, "snatcheth"; for forceful seizure, see also John 6:15; 10:12 28-29; Acts 23:10; in Jude 23, RV, "snatching."

2. *lambano* (*2983*), "to receive," is once used of "catching" by fraud, circumventing, 2 Cor. 12:16. In Matt. 21:39 and Mark 12:3, RV "took," for KJV "caught."

3. *agreuo* (*4*), "to take by hunting" (from *agra*, "a hunt, a catch"), is used metaphorically, of the Pharisees and Herodians in seeking to catch Christ in His talk, Mark 12:13.

4. *sunarpazo* (*4884*), *sun*, used intensively, and No. 1, "to snatch, to seize, to keep a firm grip of," is used only by Luke, and translated "caught" in the KJV of Luke 8:29, of demon-possession; in Acts 6:12, of the act of the elders and scribes in seizing Stephen, RV, more suitably, "seized." So in Acts 19:29. In 27:15, it is used of the effects of wind upon a ship.

5. *sullambano* (*4815*), *sun*, and No. 2, "to seize," is used, similarly to No. 6, in Acts 26:21, of the act of the Jews in seizing Paul in the temple.

6. *epilambano* (*1949*), "to lay hold" (*epi*, intensive, and No. 2), Acts 16:19.

CEASE

Old Testament

A. Verbs.

chadal (*2308*), "to cease, come to an end, desist, forbear, lack." *chadal* means "coming to an end." Thus, Sarah's capacity for childbearing had long since "ceased" before an angel informed her that she was to have a son, Gen. 18:11. The Mosaic law made provision for the poor, since they would "never cease out of the land," Deut. 15:11; Matt. 26:11. In Exod. 14:12, this verb is better translated "let us alone" for the literal "cease from us."

shabat (7673), "to rest, cease." The basic and most frequent meaning of *shabat* is shown in Gen. 8:22; Jer. 31:36. We find a variety of senses: "put away," Exod. 12:15; "be lacking," Lev. 2:13; "put down," 2 Kings 23:5; "eliminate," Lev. 26:6.

B. Noun.

shabbat (7676), "the sabbath," the seventh day of rest, Exod. 23:12. A man's "rest" was to include his animals and servants, Exod. 23:12; 31:17; 34:21. There is also a sabbath year, Lev. 25:2,4. The "sabbath" was a "day of worship," Lev. 23:3, as well as a "day of rest and refreshment" for man, Exod. 23:12. God "rested and was refreshed," Exod. 31:17. The "sabbath" was the covenant sign of God's lordship over the creation. By observing the "sabbath," Israel confessed that they were God's redeemed people, subject to His lordship to obey the whole of His law. They were His stewards to show mercy with kindness and liberality to all, Exod. 23:12; Lev. 25.

The prophets rebuked Israel for their neglect of the sabbath, Isa. 1:13; Jer. 17:21-27; Ezek. 20:12-24; Amos 8:5. They also proclaimed "sabbath" observance as a blessing in the messianic age and a sign of its fullness, Isa. 56:2-4; 58:13; 66:23; Ezek. 44:24; 45:17; 46:1, 3-4, 12. The length of the Babylonian Captivity was determined by the extent of Israel's abuse of the sabbatical year, 2 Chron. 36:21; cf. Lev. 26:34-35.

New Testament

A. Verbs.

1. *pauo* (3973), "to stop, to make an end," is used chiefly in the middle voice in the NT, signifying "to come to an end, to take one's rest, a willing cessation" (in contrast to the passive voice which denotes a forced cessation); Luke 5:4, of a discourse; 8:24, of a storm, 11:1, of Christ's prayer; Acts 5:42, of teaching and preaching; 6:13, of speaking against; 13:10, of evil doing; 20:1, of an uproar; 20:31, of admonition; 21:32, of a scourging; 1 Cor. 13:8, of tongues; Eph. 1:16, of giving thanks; Col. 1:9, of prayer; Heb. 10:2, of sacrifices; 1 Pet. 4:1, of "ceasing" from sin. It is used in the active voice in 1 Pet. 3:10, "let him cause his tongue to cease from evil."

2. *dialeipo* (1257), lit., "to leave between," i.e., "to leave an interval, whether of space or time," *leipo*, "to leave"); hence, "to intermit, desist, cease," in Luke 7:45 is used of the kissing of the Lord's feet.

3. *hesuchazo* (2270), "to be quiet, still, at rest," is said of Paul's friends in Caesarea, in "ceasing" to persuade him not to go to

Jerusalem, Acts 21:14; it is used of silence (save in Luke 23:56 and 1 Thess. 4:11) in Luke 14:4 and Acts 11:18.

4. *kopazo* (*2869*), "to cease through being spent with toil, to cease raging" (from *kopos*, "labor, toil," *kopiao*, "to labor"), is said of the wind only, Matt. 14:32; Mark 4:39; 6:51.

5. *aphiemi* (*863*), "to let go," is translated "let us cease to" in Heb. 6:1.

6. *katapauo* (*2664*), "to rest" (*kata*, "down," intensive, and No. 1), is so translated in Heb. 4:10, for the KJV "hath ceased."

B. Adjective.

adialeiptos (*88*), "unceasing" (from *a*, negative, *dia*, "through," *leipo*, "to leave"), is used of "incessant" heart pain, Rom. 9:2, KJV, "continual," RV, "unceasing," and in 2 Tim. 1:3, of remembrance in prayer; the meaning in each place is not that of unbroken continuity, but without the omission of any occasion.

C. Adverb.

adialeiptos (*89*), "unceasingly, without ceasing," is used with the same significance as the adjective, not of what is not interrupted, but of that which is constantly recurring; in Rom. 1:9 and 1 Thess. 5:17, of prayer; in 1 Thess. 1:3, of the remembrance of the work, labor and patience of saints; in 1 Thess. 2:13, of thanksgiving.

CENSER

1. *thumiaterion* (*2369*), "a vessel for burning incense," 2 Chron. 26:19; Ezek. 8:11, is found in Heb. 9:4.

2. *libanotos* (*3031*) denotes "frankincense," the gum of the *libanos*, "the frankincense tree"; in a secondary sense, "a vessel in which to burn incense," Rev. 8:3, 5.

CENTURION

1. *hekatontarchos* (*1543*), "a centurion," denotes a military officer commanding from 50 to 100 men, according to the size of the legion of which it was a part (*hekaton*, "a hundred," *archo*, "to rule"), e.g., Matt. 8:5, 8., cf. Acts 10:1, 22.

2. *kenturion* (*2760*) is a Greek transliteration of the Latin *centurio*, signifying practically the same as No. 1, Mark 15:39, 44-45.

CERTAIN, CERTAINTY, CERTAINLY, CERTIFY

A. Noun.

asphaleia (*803*), primarily, "not liable to fall, steadfast, firm," hence denoting "safety," Acts 5:23, and 1 Thess. 5:3, has the further meaning, "certainty," Luke 1:4.

B. Adjective.

asphales (*804*), safe, is translated "certainty," Acts 21:34; 22:30; "certain," Acts 25:26; "safe," Phil. 3:1; "sure," Heb. 6:19.

CHAMBERING

koite (*2845*), primarily a place in which to lie down, hence, "a bed, especially the marriage bed"; denotes, in Rom. 13:13, "illicit intercourse."

CHAMBERLAIN

ho epi tou koitonos, lit., "the (one) over the bedchamber," denotes "a chamberlain," an officer who had various duties in the houses of kings and nobles. The importance of the position is indicated by the fact that the people of Tyre and Sidon sought the favor of Herod Agrippa through the mediation of Blastus, Acts 12:20.

CHARGE (Nouns, Adjective and Verbs), CHARGEABLE

A. Nouns.

(a) *With the meaning of* "*an accusation.*"

1. *aitia* (*156*), "a cause, accusation," is rendered "charges" in Acts 25:27 (KJV, crimes); cf. v. 18.

2. *aitioma* (*157*), in some texts *aitiama*, denotes "a charge," Acts 25:7.

3. *enklema* (*1462*), Acts 23:29; 25:16.

(b) *With the meaning of* "*something committed or bestowed.*"

4. *kleros* (*2819*), "a lot, allotment, heritage" (whence Eng. "clergy"), is translated in 1 Pet. 5:3.

5. *opsonion* (*3800*), (from *opson*, "meat," and *oneomai*, "to buy"), primarily signified whatever is brought to be eaten with bread provisions, supplies for an army, soldier's pay, "charges," 1 Cor. 9:7, of the service of a soldier. It is rendered "wages" in Luke 3:14; Rom. 6:23; 2 Cor. 11:8.

6. *parangelia* (*3852*), "a proclamation, a command or commandment," is strictly used of commands received from a superior and transmitted to others, Acts 5:28; 16:24; 1 Thess. 4:2; 1 Tim. 1:5,18.

B. Adjective.

adapanos (*77*), lit., "without expense," is used in 1 Cor. 9:18, "without charge" (of service in the gospel).

C. Verbs.

1. *diamarturomai* (*1263*), a strengthened form of *marturomai* (*dia*, "through," intensive), is used in the middle voice; primarily it

signifies to testify through and through, bear a solemn witness; hence, "to charge earnestly," 1 Tim. 5:21; 2 Tim. 2:14; 4:1.

2. *diastellomai* (*1291*), lit., "to draw asunder," signifies "to admonish, order, charge," Matt. 16:20; Mark 5:43; 7:36 (twice); 8:15; 9:9. In Acts 15:24 it is translated "gave commandment"; in Heb. 12:20, KJV, "commanded," RV, "enjoined."

3. *embrimaomai* (*1690*), (from *en*, "in," intensive, and *brime*, "strength"), primarily signifies "to snort with anger, as of horses." Used of men it signifies "to fret, to be painfully moved"; then, "to express indignation against"; hence, "to rebuke sternly, to charge strictly," Matt. 9:30; Mark 1:43, it is rendered "murmured against" in Mark 14:5; "groaned" in John 11:33; "groaning" in v. 38.

4. *entellomai* (*1781*), to order, command, enjoin (from *en*, in, used intensively, and *teleo*, to fulfill), is translated by the verb to give charge, Matt. 4:6; 17:9 (AV); Luke 4:10.

5. *epitimao* (*2008*), signifies (a) to put honour upon; (b) to adjudge, to find fault with, rebuke; hence to charge, or rather, to charge strictly (*epi*, intensive), e.g., Matt. 12:16; Mark 3:12, "charged much"; Mark 8:30.

6. *parangello* (*3853*), lit., "to announce beside," "to hand on an announcement from one to another," usually denotes "to command, to charge," Luke 5:14; 8:56; 1 Cor. 7:10 (KJV, "command"), "give charge," RV; 11:17, "in giving you this charge," RV; 1 Tim. 1:3; 6:13, RV, and 6:17. It is rendered by the verb "to charge" in the RV of Acts 1:4; 4:18; 5:28; 15:5; 1 Thess. 4:11. See Acts 5:28 under A, No. 6.

7. *proaitiaomai* (*4256*), "to accuse beforehand, to have already brought a charge," is used in Rom. 3:9, "we before laid to the charge."

CHASTE

hagnos (*53*) signifies (a) "pure from every fault, immaculate," 2 Cor. 7:11 (KJV, "clear"); Phil. 4:8; 1 Tim. 5:22; Jas. 3:17; 1 John 3:3 (in all which the RV rendering is "pure"), and 1 Pet. 3:2, "chaste"; (b) "pure from carnality, modest," 2 Cor. 11:2, RV, "pure"; Titus 2:5, "chaste."

CHASTEN, CHASTENING, CHASTISE, CHASTISEMENT

A. Verb.

paideuo (*3811*) primarily denotes "to train children," suggesting the broad idea of education (*pais*, "a child"), Acts 7:22; 22:3; see also Titus 2:12, "instructing" (RV), here of a training gracious and firm; grace, which brings salvation, employs means to give us full possession of it, hence, "to chastise," this being part of the training, whether (a) by correcting with words, reproving, and admonishing, 1 Tim. 1:20 (RV, "be taught"); 2 Tim. 2:25, or (b) by "chastening" by the infliction of evils and calamities, 1 Cor. 11:32; 2 Cor. 6:9; Heb. 12:6-7, 10; Rev. 3:19. The verb also has the meaning "to chastise with blows, to scourge," said of the command of a judge, Luke 23:16, 22.

B. Noun.

paideia (3809) denotes "the training of a child, including instruction"; hence, "discipline, correction," "chastening," Eph. 6:4, RV (KJV, "nurture"), suggesting the Christian discipline that regulates character; so in Heb. 12:5, 7, 8 (in v. 8, KJV, "chastisement," the RV corrects to "chastening"); in 2 Tim. 3:16, "instruction."

CHEER, CHEERFUL, CHEERFULLY, CHEERFULNESS

A. Verbs.

1. **euthumeo** (2114) signifies, in the active voice, "to put in good spirits, to make cheerful," "mind or passion"; or, intransitively, "to be cheerful," Acts 27:22, 25; Jas. 5:13 (RV, "cheerful," for KJV, "merry").

2. **tharseo** (2293), "to be of good courage, of good cheer," is used only in the imperative mood, in the NT; "be of good cheer," Matt. 9:2, 22; 14:27; Mark 6:50; 10:49; Luke 8:48; John 16:33; Acts 23:11.

B. Adjectives.

1. **euthumos** (2115) means "of good cheer" (see A, No. 1), Acts 27:36.

2. **hilaros** (2431), from **hileos**, "propitious," signifies that readiness of mind, that joyousness, which is prompt to do anything; hence, "cheerful" (cf. Eng., "hilarious"), 2 Cor. 9:7.

C. Adverb.

euthumos (2115), cheerfully (see A, No. 1), Acts 24:10.

D. Noun.

hilarotes (2432), "cheerfulness" (akin to B, No. 2), is used in Rom. 12:8, in connection with showing mercy.

CHERISH

thalpo (2282) primarily means "to heat, to soften by heat"; then, "to keep warm;" metaphorically, "to cherish with tender love, to foster with tender care"; in Eph. 5:29 of Christ and the church; in 1 Thess. 2:7 of saints care.

CHERUBIM

cheroubim (3742) are regarded by some as the ideal representatives of redeemed animate creation. In the tabernacle and Temple they were represented by the two golden figures of two-winged living creatures. The first reference to the "cherubim" is in Gen. 3:24. The presence of the "cherubim" suggests that redeemed men, restored to God on God's conditions, would have access to the Tree of Life, see Rev. 22:14. Certain other references in the OT give clear indication that angelic beings are upon occasion in view, e.g., Ps. 18:10; Ezek. 28:4. So with the vision of the cherubim in Ezek. 10:1-20; 11:22. In the NT the word is found in Heb. 9:5, where the reference is to the ark in the tabernacle, and the thought is suggested of those who minister to the manifestation of the glory of God.

CHIEF, CHIEFEST, CHIEFLY

A. Adjective.

protos (4413) denotes "the first," whether in time or place. It is translated "chief" in Mark 6:21, RV, of men of Galilee, in Acts 13:50, of men in a city; in 28:7, of the "chief" man in the island of Melita; in 17:4, of "chief" women in a city; in 28:17, of Jews; in 1 Tim. 1:15-16, of a sinner. In the following, where the KJV has "chief," or "chiefest," the RV renderings are different: Matt. 20:27 and Mark 10:44, "first"; Luke 19:47 and Acts 25:2, "principal men"; Acts 16:12, said of Philippi, "the first (city) of the district," RV, for incorrect KJV, "the chief city of that part of Macedonia." Amphipolis was the "chief" city of that part. *protos* here must mean the first in the direction in which the apostle came.

B. Nouns.

1. *kephalaion* (2774), denotes the chief point or principal thing in a subject, Heb. 8:1, "the chief point is this" (KJV, "the sum"); elsewhere in Acts 22:28 (of principal, as to money), "(a great) sum."

2. *archiereus* (749), "a chief priest, high priest," is frequent in the gospels, Acts and Hebrews, but there only in the NT. It is used of Christ, e.g., in Heb. 2:17; 3:1; of "chief" priests, including ex-high-priests and members of their families, e.g., Matt. 2:4; Mark 8:31.

3. *archipoimen* (750), "a chief shepherd," is said of Christ only, 1 Pet. 5:4. Modern Greeks use it of tribal chiefs.

4. *architelones* (754) denotes "a chief tax-collector, or publican," Luke 19:2.

5. *akrogoniaios* (204) denotes "a chief corner-stone" (from *akros*, "highest, extreme," *gonia*, "a corner, angle"), Eph. 2:20 and 1 Pet. 2:6.

6. *protokathedria* (4410), "a sitting in the first or chief seat," is found in Matt. 23:6; Mark 12:39; Luke 11:43; 20:46.

7. *protoklisia* (4411), "the first reclining place, the chief place at table," Matt. 23:6; Mark 12:39 (as with No. 6); Luke 14:7-8; 20:46.

8. *chiliarchos* (5506) denotes "a chief captain," Mark 6:21.

9. *asiarches* (775), "an Asiarch," was one of certain officers elect-

ed by various cities in the province of Asia, whose function consisted in celebrating, partly at their own expense, the public games and festivals; in Acts 19:31, RV, the word is translated "chief officers of Asia" (KJV, "chief of Asia").

10. *archon* (758), "a ruler," is rendered "chief" in the KJV of Luke 14:1 (RV, "ruler"); "chief rulers," in John 12:42, RV, "rulers (of the people)," i.e., of members of the Sanhedrin; "chief," in Luke 11:15 (RV, "prince"), in reference to Beelzebub, the prince of demons.

11. *archisunagogos* (752), "a ruler of a synagogue," translated "chief ruler of the synagogue," in Acts 18:8, 17, KJV, was the administrative officer supervising the worship.

C. Verb.

hegeomai (2233), "to lead the way, to preside, rule, be the chief," is used of the ambition "to be chief" among the disciples of Christ, Luke 22:26; of Paul as the "chief" speaker in gospel testimony at Lystra, Acts 14:12; of Judas and Silas, as chief (or rather, "leading") men among the brethren at Jerusalem, Acts 15:22.

CHILD, CHILDREN, CHILDBEARING, CHILDISH, CHILDLESS

1. *teknon* (5043), "a child" (akin to *tikto*, "to beget, bear"), is used in both the natural and the figurative senses. In contrast to *huios*, "son" (see below), it gives prominence to the fact of birth, whereas *huios* stresses the dignity and character of the relationship. Figuratively, *teknon* is used of "children" of (a) God, John 1:12; (b) light, Eph. 5:8; (c) obedience, 1 Pet. 1:14; (d) a promise, Rom. 9:8; Gal. 4:28; (e) the Devil, 1 John 3:10; (f) wrath, Eph. 2:3; (g) cursing, 2 Pet. 2:14; (h) spiritual relationship, 2 Tim. 2:1; Philem. 10.

2. *teknion* (5040), "a little child," a diminutive of No. 1, is used only figuratively in the NT, and always in the plural. It is found frequently in 1 John, see 2:1, 12, 28; 3:7, 18; 4:4; 5:21; elsewhere, once in John's Gospel, 13:33, once in Paul's epistles, Gal. 4:19. It is a term of affection by a teacher to his disciples.

3. *huios* (5207), "a son," is always so translated in the RV, except in the phrase "children of Israel," e.g., Matt. 27:9; and with reference to a foal, Matt. 21:5.

4. *pais* (3816) signifies (a) "a child in relation to descent," (b) "a boy or girl in relation to age," (c) "a servant, attendant, maid, in relation to condition." As an instance of (a) see Matt. 21:15, "children," and Acts 20:12 (RV, "lad"). In regard to (b) the RV has "boy" in Matt. 17:18 and Luke 9:42. In Luke 2:43 it is used of the Lord Jesus. In regard to (c), see Matt. 8:6, 8, 13, etc. As to (a) note Matt. 2:16, RV, male children.

5. *paidion* (3813), a diminutive of 4. above, signifies "a little or young child"; it is used of an infant just born, John 16:21, of a male child recently born, e.g., Matt. 2:8; Heb. 11:23; of a more advanced

child, Mark 9:24; of a son, John 4:49; of a girl, Mark 5:39, 40, 41; in the plural, of "children," e.g., Matt. 14:21. It is used metaphorically of believers who are deficient in spiritual understanding, 1 Cor. 14:20, and in affectionate and familiar address by the Lord to His disciples, almost like the Eng., "lads," John 21:5.

6. *paidarion* (*3808*), another diminutive of 4. above, is used of "boys and girls," in Matt. 11:16 (the best texts have *paidiois* here), and a "lad," John 6:9; the tendency in colloquial Greek was to lose the diminutive character of the word.

7. *nepios* (*3516*), lit., "not-speaking" (from *ne*, a negative, and *epos*, a word) is rendered "childish" in 1 Cor. 13:11.

8. *monogenes* (*3439*), lit., "only-begotten," is translated "only child" in Luke 9:38.

9. *teknogonia* (*5042*), "to beget," denotes "bearing children," implying the duties of motherhood, 1 Tim. 2:15.

B. Verbs.

1. *nepiazo* (*3515*), "to be a baby," is used in 1 Cor. 14:20, "(in malice) be ye babes" (akin to No. 7, above).

2. *teknotropheo* (*5044*), "to rear young," (*teknon*, and *trepho*, "to rear"), signifies "to bring up children," 1 Tim. 5:10.

3. *teknogoneo* (*5041*), "to bear children" (*teknon*, and *gennao*, "to beget"), see No. 9 above, is found in 1 Tim. 5:14.

C. Adjectives.

1. *enkuos* (*1471*) denotes "great with child" (*en*, "in," and *kuo*, "to conceive"), Luke 2:5.

2. *philoteknos* (*5388*), (from *phileo*, "to love," and *teknon*), signifies "loving one's children," Titus 2:4.

3. *ateknos* (*815*), (from *a*, negative, and *teknon*), signifies "childless," Luke 20:28-30.

CHOICE, CHOOSE, CHOSEN
Old Testament

A. Verb.

bachar (*977*), "to choose." *bachar* is often used with a man as the subject, Gen. 13:11. In more than half of the occurrences, God is the subject of *bachar*, Num. 16:5. Neh. 9:7-8 describes God's "choosing" (election) of persons as far back as Abram. *bachar* is used 30 times in Deuteronomy, all but twice referring to God's "choice" of Israel or something in Israel's life, Deut. 4:37; 14:1-2. God's choices shaped the history of Israel; His "choice" led to their redemption from Egypt, Deut. 7:7-8, sent Moses and Aaron to work miracles in Egypt, Ps. 105:26-27, and gave them the Levites "to bless in the name of the Lord," Deut. 21:5, and many more examples, Deut. 12:5; 2 Chron. 6:5, 21. Men and women are called to respond to God's election, Deut. 30:19; cf. Josh. 24:22.

B. Noun.

bachir (972), "chosen ones." Another noun, *bachir*, is used 13 times, always of the Lord's "chosen ones": "Saul, whom the Lord did choose," 2 Sam. 21:6; "ye children of Jacob, his chosen ones," 1 Chron. 16:13.

New Testament

A. Verbs.

1. *eklego* (1586), "to pick out, select," means, in the middle voice, "to choose for oneself," not necessarily implying the rejection of what is not chosen, but "choosing" with the subsidiary ideas of kindness or favor or love, Mark 13:20; Luke 6:13; 9:35 (RV); 10:42; 14:7; John 6:70; 13:18; 15:16, 19; Acts 1:2, 24; 6:5; 13:17; 15:22, 25; in 15:7 it is rendered "made choice"; 1 Cor. 1:27-28; Eph. 1:4; Jas. 2:5.

2. *epilego* (1951), in the middle voice, signifies "to choose," either in addition or in succession to another. It has this meaning in Acts 15:40, of Paul's choice of Silas.

3. *cheirotoneo* (5500), Acts 14:23; 2 Cor. 8:19.

4. *procheirotoneo* (4401) signifies "to choose before," Acts 10:41, where it is used of a choice made before by God.

B. Adjective.

eklektos (1588), akin to A, No. 1, signifies "chosen out, select," e.g., Matt. 22:14; Luke 23:35; Rom. 16:13 (perhaps in the sense of "eminent"), Rev. 17:14. In 1 Pet. 2:4, 9, the RV translates it "elect."

C. Noun.

ekloge (1589), akin to A, No. 1 and B, "a picking out, choosing" (Eng., "eclogue"), is translated "chosen" in Acts 9:15, lit., "he is a vessel of choice unto Me." In the six other places where this word is found it is translated "election."

CHRIST

christos (5547), "anointed," translates, in the Sept., the word "Messiah," a term applied to mere humans with a special office, Lev. 4:3, 5, 16; Ps. 105:15. A king of Israel was "the anointed of the Lord," 1 Sam. 2:10, 35; 2 Sam. 1:14; Ps. 2:2; 18:50; Hab. 3:13; Isa. 45:1.

The title *ho Christos*, in the NT is frequently used with the article, of the Lord Jesus, as an appellative rather than a title, e.g., Matt. 2:4; Acts 2:31; without the article, Luke 2:11; 23:2; John 1:41.

It is added as an appellative to the proper name "Jesus," e.g., John 17:3, the only time when the Lord so spoke of Himself; Acts 9:34; 1 Cor. 3:11; 1 John 5:6. It is distinctly a proper name in many passages, whether with the article, e.g., Matt. 1:17; 11:2; Rom. 7:4; 9:5; 15:19; 1 Cor. 1:6, or without the article, Mark 9:41; Rom. 6:4; 8:9, 17; 1 Cor. 1:12; Gal. 2:16. The single title *Christos* is sometimes used without the article to signify the One who by His Holy Spirit and power indwells believers and molds their character in conformity to His likeness, Rom. 8:10; Gal. 2:20; 4:19; Eph. 3:17. As to the use or absence of the article, the title with the article specifies the Lord Jesus as "the Christ"; the title without the article stresses His character and His relationship with believers. Again, speaking generally, when the title is the subject of a sentence it has the article; when it forms part of the predicate the article is absent.

CHRISTS (FALSE)

pseudochristos (5580) denotes "one who falsely lays claim to the name and office of the Messiah," Matt. 24:24; Mark 13:22.

CHRISTIAN

christianos (5546), "Christian," a word formed after the Roman style, signifying an adherent of Jesus, was first applied to such by the Gentiles and is found in Acts 11:26; 26:28; 1 Pet. 4:16.

Though the word rendered "were called" in Acts 11:26 might be used of a name adopted by oneself or given by others, the "Christians" do not seem to have adopted it for themselves in the times of the apostles. In 1 Pet. 4:16, the apostle is speaking from the point of view of the persecutor, cf. "as a thief," "as a murderer." Nor is it likely that the appellation was given by Jews. As applied by Gentiles there was no doubt an implication of scorn, as in Agrippa's statement in Acts 26:28, though after Bible times, a title of honor.

CIRCUMCISION, UNCIRCUMCISION, CIRCUMCISE

Old Testament

mul (4135), "to circumcise, cut off." The physical act of circumcision was introduced by God as a sign of the Abrahamic covenant, Gen. 17:10-11, NIV. It was a permanent "cutting off" of the foreskin of the male organ, and as such was a reminder of the perpetuity of the covenantal relationship. Israel was enjoined to be faithful in "circumcising" all males; each male baby was to be "circumcised" on the eighth day, Gen. 17:12; Lev. 12:3.

To be figuratively circumcised in the "heart" (or inner self), was to not be obstinate, but to respond to God's will, and be obedient, Deut. 10:16, NIV; cf. 30:6; Jer. 4:4. Few occurrences of the verb differ from the physical and the spiritual usage of "to circumcise." *mul* in the Book of Psalms has the meaning of "to cut off, destroy," Ps. 118:10, NIV; cf. vv. 11-12. In the English versions, the verb is rendered "to circumcise," "to destroy" (KJV), as well as "to cut off" and "to wither" (RSV, NASB, NIV).

New Testament

A. Nouns.

1. *peritome* (*4061*), lit., "a cutting round, circumcision" (the verb is *peritemno*), was a rite enjoined by God upon Abraham and his male descendants and dependents, as a sign of the covenant made with him, Gen. 17; Acts 7:8; Rom. 4:11. Hence Israelites termed Gentiles "the uncircumcised," Judg. 15:18; 2 Sam. 1:20. So in the NT, but without the suggestion of contempt, e.g., Rom. 2:26; Eph. 2:11.

The rite had a moral significance, Ex. 6:12, 30, where it is metaphorically applied to the lips; so to the ear, Jer. 6:10, and the heart, Deut. 30:6; Jer. 4:4. Cf. Jer. 9:25-26. It refers to the state of "circumcision," in Rom. 2:25-28; 3:1; 4:10; 1 Cor. 7:19; Gal. 5:6; 6:15; Col. 3:11.

In the economy of grace no account is taken of any ordinance performed on the flesh; the old racial distinction is ignored in the preaching of the gospel, and faith is the sole condition upon which the favor of God in salvation is to be obtained, Rom. 10:11-13; 1 Cor. 7:19. See also Rom. 4:9-12.

Upon the preaching of the gospel to, and the conversion of, Gentiles, a sect of Jewish believers arose who argued that the gospel, without the fulfillment of "circumcision," would make void the Law and make salvation impossible, Acts 15:1. Hence this party was known as "the circumcision," Acts 10:45; 11:2; Gal. 2:12; Col. 4:11; Titus 1:10 (the term being used by metonymy, the abstract being put for the concrete, as with the application of the word to Jews generally, Rom. 3:30; 4:9, 12; 15:8; Gal. 2:7-9; Eph. 2:11). It is used metaphorically and spiritually of believers with reference to the act, Col. 2:11 and Rom. 2:29; to the condition, Phil. 3:3.

2. *akrobustia* (*203*), "uncircumcision," is used (a) of the physical state, in contrast to the act of "circumcision," Acts 11:3 (lit., "having uncircumcision"); Rom. 2:25-26; 4:10-11 ("though they be in uncircumcision," RV), 12; 1 Cor. 7:18-19; Gal. 5:6; 6:15; Col. 3:11; (b) by metonymy, for Gentiles, e.g., Rom. 2:26-27; 3:30; 4:9; Gal. 2:7; Eph. 2:11; (c) in a metaphorical or transferred sense, of the moral condition in which the corrupt desires of the flesh still operate, Col. 2:13.

B. Adjective.

aperitmetos (*564*), "uncircumcised" (*a*, negative, *peri*, "around," *temno*, "to cut"), is used in Acts 7:51, metaphorically, of "heart and ears."

C. Verb.

peritemno (*4059*), "to circumcise," is used (a) lit., e.g., Luke 1:59;

2:21; of receiving circumcision, Gal. 5:2-3; 6:13, RV; (b) metaphorically, of spiritual circumcision, Col. 2:11.

CITIZEN, CITIZENSHIP

1. *polites* (4177), "a member of a city or state, or the inhabitant of a country or district," Luke 15:15, is used elsewhere in Luke 19:14; Acts 21:39, and, in the most authentic mss., in Heb. 8:11 (where some texts have *plesion*, "a neighbor"). Apart from Heb. 8:11, the word occurs only in the writings of Luke (himself a Greek).

2. *sumpolites* (4847), *sun*, "with," and No. 1, denotes "a fellow-citizen," i.e., possessing the same "citizenship," Eph. 2:19, used metaphorically in a spiritual sense.

3. *politeia* (4174) signifies (a) "the relation in which a citizen stands to the state, the condition of a citizen, citizenship," Acts 22:28, "with a great sum obtained I this citizenship" (KJV, "freedom"). While Paul's "citizenship" of Tarsus was not of advantage outside that city, yet his Roman "citizenship" availed throughout the Roman Empire and, besides private rights, included (1) exemption from all degrading punishments; (2) a right of appeal to the emperor after a sentence; (3) a right to be sent to Rome for trial before the emperor if charged with a capital offense. Paul's father might have obtained "citizenship" (1) by manumission; (2) as a reward of merit; (3) by purchase; the contrast implied in Acts 22:28 is perhaps against the last mentioned; (b) "a civil polity, the condition of a state, a commonwealth," said of Israel, Eph. 2:12.

4. *politeuma* (4175) signifies "the condition, or life, of a citizen, citizenship"; it is said of the heavenly status of believers, Phil. 3:20.

CITY

Old Testament

'ir (5892), "city; town; village; quarter [of a city]." The word suggests a "village." An unwalled village is represented by the Hebrew word *chatser. qiryat*, a synonym of *'ir*, is an Aramaic loanword.

But *'ir* and its synonym do not necessarily suggest a walled city. This usage is seen in Deut. 3:5, where *'ir* may be a city standing in the open country (perhaps surrounded by dirt or stone ramparts for protection): "All these cities were fenced with high walls, gates, and bars; beside unwalled towns a great many." A comparison of Lev. 25:29 and Lev. 25:31 shows that *'ir* can be used as synonym of *chatser:* "And if a man sell a dwelling house in a walled city, then he may redeem it within a whole year after it is sold;.but the houses of the villages [*chatser*] which have no wall round about them shall be counted as the fields of the country..."

'ir can signify not only a "village consisting of permanent houses" but also one in a permanent place, even though the

dwellings are tents, 1 Sam. 15:5. As a rule, there are no political overtones to the word; *'ir* simply represents the "place where people dwell on a permanent basis." At some points, however, *'ir* represents a political entity, 1 Sam. 15:5; 30:29. This word can also represent "those who live in a given town," 1 Sam. 4:13. *'ir* can also signify only "a part of a city," such as a stronghold, 2 Sam. 5:7. Ancient cities (especially larger ones) were sometimes divided into sections (quarters) by walls, in order to make it more difficult to capture them. This suggests that, by the time of the statement just cited, *'ir* normally implied a "walled city."

New Testament

polis (*4172*), primarily "a town enclosed with a wall"; of the heavenly Jerusalem, the abode and community of the redeemed, Heb. 11:10, 16; 12:22; 13:14; Rev. 3:12; 21:2, 14, 19; its inhabitants, Matt. 8:34; 12:25; 21:10; Mark 1:33; Acts 13:44.

CLANGING

alalazo (*214*), in the NT, in Mark 5:38, of wailing mourners; in 1 Cor. 13:1, of the "clanging" of cymbals.

CLEAN, CLEANNESS, CLEANSE, CLEANSING

Old Testament

A. Verb.

taher (*2891*), "to be clean, pure." Since the fall of Adam and Eve, none of their offspring is clean in the sight of the holy God, Prov. 20:9; Job 4:17. There is hope, however, because God promised penitent Israel: "And I will cleanse them from all their iniquity, whereby they have sinned against me..." Jer. 33:8; Ezek. 37:23.

God required that His people observe purification rites when they came into His presence for worship. On the Day of Atonement, for example, prescribed ceremonies were performed to "cleanse" the altar from "the uncleanness of the children of Israel" and to "hallow it," Lev. 16:17-19; cf. Exod. 29:36ff. The priests were to be purified before they performed their sacred tasks. Moses was directed to "take the Levites...and cleanse them," Num. 8:6; cf. Lev. 8:5-13. After they had been held captive in the unclean land of Babylon, "...the priests and the Levites purified themselves, and purified the people, and the gates, and the wall [of the rebuilt city of Jerusalem]," Neh. 12:30. Some cleansing rites required blood as the purifying agent, Lev. 16:19. Sacrifices were offered to make atonement for a mother after childbirth, Lev. 12:8.

B. Adjective.

tahor (*2889*), "clean; pure." The word denotes the absence of impurity, filthiness, defilement, or imperfection. It is applied concretely to substances that are genuine or unadulterated as well as describing an unstained condition of a spiritual or ceremonial nature. Gold is a material frequently said to be free of baser ingredients. Thus the ark of the covenant, the incense altar, and the porch of the temple and many other items were "overlaid with pure gold," Exod. 25:11; 37:11, 26; 2 Chron. 3:4.

C

God demands that His people have spiritual and moral purity, unsullied by sin, Job 14:4; Ps. 51:10. In sharp contrast with mankind's polluted nature and actions, "the words of the Lord are pure words..." Ps. 12:6. The Lord is "of purer eyes than to behold evil," Hab. 1:13.

The people of the old covenant were told that "he that toucheth the dead body of any man shall be unclean seven days," Num. 19:11. A priest was not to defile himself "for the dead among his people" except "for his kin, that is near unto him," Lev. 21:1-2. This relaxation of the rule was even denied the high priest and a Nazarite during "all the days that he separateth himself unto the Lord," Num. 6:6ff. Also cleansing was necessary for childbirth and menstrual period, Lev. 15:1-18. To be ceremonially "clean," the Israelite also had to abstain from eating certain animals and even from touching them, Lev. 11; Deut. 14:3-21. After the Israelites settled in the Promised Land, some modifications were made in the regulations, Deut. 12:15, 22; 15:22.

Purification rites frequently involved the use of water in washing his body, and many things that were around him, including clothing, Lev. 15:27; Num. 19:18. However, the rites were not meritorious deeds, earning God's favor and forgiveness. Nor did the ceremonies serve their intended purpose if performed mechanically. Unless the rites expressed a person's contrite and sincere desire to be cleansed from the defilement of sin, they were an abomination to God and only aggravated a person's guilt. Anyone who appeared before Him in ritual and ceremony with "hands...full of blood," Isa. 1:15, and did not plead for cleansing of his crimes was judged to be as wicked as the people of Sodom and Gomorrah. Zion's hope lay in this cleansing by means of an offering: "And they shall bring all your brethren for an offering unto the Lord out of all nations upon horses...as the children of Israel bring an offering in a clean vessel into the house of the Lord," Isa. 66:20.

New Testament

A. Adjective.

katharos (*2513*), "free from impure admixture, without blemish, spotless," is used (a) physically, e.g., Matt. 23:26; 27:59; John 13:10 (where the Lord, speaking figuratively, teaches that one who has been entirely "cleansed," needs not radical renewal, but only to be "cleansed" from every sin into which he may fall); 15:3; Heb.

10:22; Rev. 15:6; 19:8, 14; 21:18, 21; (b) in a Levitical sense, Rom. 14:20; Titus 1:15, "pure"; (c) ethically, with the significance free from corrupt desire, from guilt, Matt. 5:8; John 13:10-11; Acts 20:26; 1 Tim. 1:5; 3:9; 2 Tim. 1:3; 2:22; Titus 1:15; Jas. 1:27; blameless, innocent (a rare meaning for this word), Acts 18:6; (d) in a combined Levitical and ethical sense ceremonially, Luke 11:41, "all things are clean unto you."

B. Verbs.

1. *katharizo* (2511), akin to A, signifies (1) "to make clean, to cleanse" (a) from physical stains and dirt, as in the case of utensils, Matt. 23:25 (figuratively in verse 26); from disease, as of leprosy, Matt. 8:2; (b) in a moral sense, from the defilement of sin, Acts 15:9; 2 Cor. 7:1; Heb. 9:14; Jas. 4:8, "cleanse" from the guilt of sin, Eph. 5:26; 1 John 1:7; (2) "to pronounce clean in a Levitical sense," Mark 7:19, RV; Acts 10:15; 11:9; "to consecrate by cleansings," Heb. 9:22, 23; 10:2.

2. *diakatharizo* (1245), "to cleanse thoroughly," is used in Matt. 3:12, RV.

C. Nouns.

1. *katharismos* (2512), akin to A, denotes "cleansing," (a) both the action and its results, in the Levitical sense, Mark 1:44; Luke 2:22, "purification"; 5:14, "cleansing"; John 2:6; 3:25, "purifying"; (b) in the moral sense, from sins, Heb. 1:3; 2 Pet. 1:9.

2. *katharotes* (2514), akin to B, "cleanness, purity," is used in the Levitical sense in Heb. 9:13, RV, "cleanness."

CLEAR, CLEARING, CLEARLY

A. Verb.

krustallizo (2929), "to shine like crystal, to be of crystalline brightness, or transparency," is found in Rev. 21:11, "clear as crystal," or transitive, so speaking of Christ.

B. Adjective.

lampros (2986) is said of crystal, Rev. 22:1.

CLEAVE, CLAVE

Old Testament

dabaq (1692), "to cling, cleave, keep close"; used of a man and wife, Gen. 2:24, of a sword, 2 Sam. 23:10; of clothing, Jer. 13:11; of a tongue, Job 29:10; of a body prone in the dirt, Ps. 119:25.

The figurative use of *dabaq* in the sense of "loyalty" and "affection" is based on the physical closeness of the persons involved, such as a husband's closeness to his wife, Gen. 2:24, Shechem's affection for Dinah, Gen. 34:3, or Ruth's staying with Naomi, Ruth 1:14. "Cleaving" to God is equivalent to "loving" God, Deut. 30:20.

New Testament

1. **kollao** (2853), "to join fast together, to glue, cement," is primarily said of metals and other materials (from **kolla**, "glue"). In the NT it is used only in the passive voice, with reflexive force, in the sense of "cleaving unto," as of cleaving to one's wife, Matt. 19:5; some mss. have the intensive verb No. 2, here; 1 Cor. 6:16-17, "joined." In the corresponding passage in Mark 10:7, the most authentic mss. omit the sentence. In Luke 10:11 it is used of the "cleaving" of dust to the feet; in Acts 5:13; 8:29; 9:26; 10:28; 17:34, in the sense of becoming associated with a person so as to company with him, or be on his side, said, in the last passage, of those in Athens who believed: in Rom. 12:9, ethically, of "cleaving" to that which is good.

2. **proskollao** (4347), in the passive voice, used reflexively, "to cleave unto," is found in Eph. 5:31 (KJV "joined to").

CLEMENCY

epieikeia (1932), "mildness, gentleness, kindness" (what Matthew Arnold has called "sweet reasonableness"), is translated "clemency" in Acts 24:4; elsewhere, in 2 Cor. 10:1, of the gentleness of Christ.

CLOKE (Pretense)

1. **epikalumma** (1942) is "a covering, a means of hiding"; hence, "a pretext, a cloke, for wickedness," 1 Pet. 2:16.

2. **prophasis** (4392), probably from **pro**, and **phemi**, "to say," is rendered "cloke" (of covetousness) in 1 Thess. 2:5; "excuse" in John 15:22 (KJV "cloke"); "pretense" in Matt. 23:14; Mark 12: 40; Luke 20:47 (KJV "show"); Phil. 1:18; "color" in Acts 27:30. It signifies the assuming of something so as to disguise one's real motives.

CLOSE (Verb)

kammuo (2576), denotes "to close down"; hence, "to shut the eyes," in stubbornness Matt. 13:15 and Acts 28:27.

COLLECTION

logia (3048), akin to **lego**, "to collect," is used in 1 Cor. 16:1, 2.

COLT

polos (4454), "a foal," whether "colt or filly," had the general significance of "a young creature"; in Matt. 21:2, and parallel passages, "an ass's colt."

TO COME NEAR, APPROACH

nagash (5066), "to approach, draw near, bring," Gen. 18:23. The word is often used to describe ordinary "contact" of one person with another, Gen. 27:22; 43:19. Sometimes *nagash* describes "contact" for the purpose of sexual intercourse, Exod. 19:15. More frequently, it is used to speak of the priests "coming into the presence of" God, Ezek. 44:13, or of the priests' "approach" to the altar, Exod. 30:20. Opposing armies are said "to draw near" to battle each other, Judg. 20:23. Inanimate objects, such as the close-fitting scales of the crocodile, are said to be so "near" to each other that no air can come between them, Job 41:16. Sometimes the word is used to speak of "bringing" an offering to the altar, Mal. 1:7.

TO COME UP, ASCEND

A. Verb.

'alah (5927), "to go up, ascend, offer up." Basically, *'alah* suggests movement from a lower to a higher place, Gen. 2:6; Isa. 14:13. This word may mean "to take a journey," Gen. 13:1. "To extend, reach," is another meaning, Josh. 18:12. It can also mean general linear movement with no particular focus on ascending, Gen. 44:17; Ezra 2:1. The verb became a technical term for "making a pilgrimage," Exod. 34:24 or "going up" before the Lord; in a secular context, compare Joseph's "going up" before Pharaoh, Gen. 46:31.

Another special use of *'alah* is "to overpower" (literally, "to go up from"). For example, the Pharaoh feared the Israelites lest in a war they join the enemy, fight against Egypt, and "overpower" the land, Exod. 1:10. "To go up" may also be used of "increasing in strength," as the lion that becomes strong from his prey: The lion "goes up from his prey," Gen. 49:9; cf. Deut. 28:43.

'alah can be used also of the "increasing" of wrath, 2 Sam. 11:20, the "ascent" of an outcry before God, Exod. 2:23. Sometimes "go up" means "placed," even when the direction is downward, as when placing a yoke upon an ox, Num. 19:2, or going to one's grave, Job 5:26. This may be an illustration of how Hebrew verbs can sometimes mean their opposite. The verb is also used of "recording" a census, 1 Chron. 27:24.

'alah signifies "presenting an offering" to God, especially the whole burnt offering, Lev. 14:20; Isa. 57:6.

B. Nouns.

'elyon (5945), "the upper; the highest." The use of *'elyon* in Gen. 40:17 means "the upper" as opposed to "the lower." Where referring to or naming God, *'elyon* means "the highest," Gen. 14:18.

ma'alah (4699), "step; procession; pilgrimage." *ma'alah* signifies a "step" or "stair," cf. Exod. 20:26. The word can also mean "procession," Ps. 84:6.

COMELINESS, COMELY

A. Noun.

euschemosune (2157), "elegance of figure, gracefulness, comeliness" (*eu*, "well," *schema*, "a form"), is found in this sense in 1 Cor. 12:23.

B. Adjective.

euschemon (2158), akin to A, "elegant in figure, well formed, graceful," is used in 1 Cor. 12:24, of parts of the body (see above); in 1 Cor. 7:35 RV, "(that which is) seemly," KJV, "comely"; "honourable," Mark 15:43; Acts 13:50; 17:12.

COMFORT, COMFORTER, COMFORTLESS

A. Nouns.

1. *paraklesis* (3874), means "a calling to one's side"; hence, either "an exhortation, or consolation, comfort," e.g., Luke 2:25 (here "looking for the consolation of Israel" is equivalent to waiting for the coming of the Messiah); 6:24; Acts 9:31; Rom. 15:4-5; 1 Cor. 14:3, "exhortation"; 2 Cor. 1:3, 4-7; 7:4, 7, 13; 2 Thess. 2:16; Philem. 7. In 2 Thess. 2:16 it combines encouragement with alleviation of grief. The RV changes "consolation" into "comfort," except in Luke 2:25; 6:24; Acts 15:31; in Heb. 6:18, "encouragement"; in Acts 4:36, "exhortation." RV (KJV, consolation).

2. *paramuthia* (3889), primarily "a speaking closely to anyone"; hence denotes "consolation, comfort," with a greater degree of tenderness than No. 1, 1 Cor. 14:3.

3. *paramuthion* (3890) has the same meaning as No. 2, the difference being that *paramuthia* stresses the process or progress of the act, *paramuthion* the instrument as used by the agent, Phil. 2:1.

4. *parakletos* (3875), lit., "called to one's side," i.e., to one's aid, is primarily a verbal adjective, and suggests the capability or adaptability for giving aid. It was used in a court of justice to denote a legal assistant, counsel for the defense, an advocate; then, generally, one who pleads another's cause, an intercessor, advocate, as in 1 John 2:1, of the Lord Jesus. In the widest sense, it signifies a "succorer, comforter," John 14:16. In 14:26; 15:26; 16:7.

B. Verbs.

1. *parakaleo* (3870) has the same variety of meanings as Noun, No. 1, above, e.g., Matt. 2:18; 1 Thess. 3:2, 7; 4:18. In 2 Cor. 13:11, it signifies "to be comforted" (so the RV).

2. *sumparakaleo* (4837), *sun*, "with," and No. 1, signifies "to comfort together," Rom. 1:12.

3. *paramutheomai* (3888), akin to Noun No. 2, "to soothe, console, encourage," is translated, in John 11:31, "comforted", in v. 19,

RV, "console." In 1 Thess. 2:11 and 5:14, RV, "encourage," as the sense there is that of stimulating to the earnest discharge of duties.

COMING (Noun)

parousia (3952), lit., "a presence," *para*, "with," and *ousia*, "being" (from *eimi*, "to be"), denotes both an "arrival" and a consequent "presence with." For instance, in a papyrus letter a lady speaks of the necessity of her parousia in a place in order to attend to matters relating to her property there. Paul speaks of his *parousia* in Philippi, Phil. 2:12 (in contrast to his *apousia*, "his absence"). *parousia* is used to describe the presence of Christ with His disciples on the Mount of Transfiguration, 2 Pet. 1:16. When used of the return of Christ, at the rapture of the church, it signifies, not merely His momentary "coming" for His saints, but His presence with them from that moment until His revelation and manifestation to the world. In some passages the word gives prominence to the beginning of that period, the course of the period being implied, 1 Cor. 15:23; 1 Thess. 4:15; 5:23; 2 Thess. 2:1; Jas. 5:7-8; 2 Pet. 3:4. In some, the course is prominent, Matt. 24:3, 37; 1 Thess. 3:13; 1 John 2:28; in others the conclusion of the period, Matt. 24:27; 2 Thess. 2:8.

The word is also used of the Lawless One, the Man of Sin, his access to power and his doings in the world during his *parousia*, 2 Thess. 2:9. In addition to Phil. 2:12 (above), it is used in the same way of the apostle, or his companions, in 1 Cor. 16:17; 2 Cor. 7:6-7; 10:10; Phil. 1:26; of the Day of God, 2 Pet. 3:12.

COMMAND (Verbs)

Old Testament

tsawah (6680), "to command," refers to verbal communication by which a superior "orders" or "commands" a subordinate. The word implies the content of what was said, Gen. 12:20. This order defines an action relevant to a specific situation. *tsawah* can also connote "command" in the sense of the establishment of a rule by which a subordinate is to act in every recurring similar situation, Gen. 2:16. In this case, the word does not contain the content of the action but focuses on the action itself.

The verb *tsawah* can be used of a commission or charge, such as the act of "commanding," "telling," or "sending" someone to do a particular task, Gen. 32:4; 49:30. One of the recurring formulas in the Bible is "X did all that Y commanded him," Ruth 3:6. This means that she carried out Naomi's "orders."

The most frequent subject of this verb is God. However, He is not to be questioned or "commanded" to explain the work of His hands, Isa. 45:11. He tells Israel that His "commands" are unique, requiring an inner commitment and not just external obedience, as the commands of men do, Gen. 29:13; Exod. 25:22; Lev. 7:38; cf. 17:1ff.; Ps. 33:9. He also issues "orders" through and to the prophets, Jer. 27:4, who explain, apply, and speak His "commands," Jer. 1:17.

New Testament

1. **diatasso** (1299) signifies "to set in order, appoint, command," Matt. 11:1; Luke 8:55; 17:9-10; Acts 18:2; 23:31; "gave order," 1 Cor. 16:1, RV. So in Acts 24:23, where it is in the middle voice.

2. **epo** (2036) denotes "to speak" (connected with **eipon**, "to say"); hence, among various renderings, "to bid, command," Matt. 4:3; Mark 5:43; 8:7; Luke 4:3; 19:15.

3. **entello** (1781) signifies "to enjoin upon, to charge with"; it is used in the middle voice in the sense of commanding, Matt. 19:7; 28:20; Mark 10:3; 13:34; John 8:5; 15:14, 17; Acts 13:47; Heb. 9:20; 11:22, "gave commandment."

4. **epitasso** (2004) signifies to appoint over, put in charge (**epi**, "over," **tasso**, "to appoint"); then, "to put upon one as a duty, to enjoin," Mark 1:27; 6:27, 39; 9:25; Luke 4:36; 8:25, 31; 14:22; Acts 23:2; Philem. 8.

5. **keleuo** (2753), "to urge, incite, order," suggests a stronger injunction than No. 6, Matt. 14:9, 19; 15:35; 18:25; 27:58, 64; Luke 18:40; Acts 4:15 (frequently in Acts, not subsequently in the NT).

6. **parangello** (3853), "to announce beside," "to pass on an announcement," hence denotes "to give the word, order, give a charge, command," e.g., Mark 6:8; Luke 8:29; 9:21; Acts 5:28; 2 Thess. 3:4, 6, 10, 12.

7. **prostasso** (4367) denotes "to arrange or set in order towards"; hence "to prescribe, give command," Matt. 1:24; 8:4; Mark 1:44; Luke 5:14; Acts 10:33, 48.

COMMANDMENT

Old Testament

mitswah (4687), "commandment." This noun occurs 181 times in the Old Testament. Its first occurrence is in Gen. 26:5, where **mitswah** is synonymous with **choq** ("statute") and **torah** ("law"): "Because that Abraham obeyed my voice, and kept my charge, my *commandments,* my statutes, and my laws."

In the Pentateuch, God is always the Giver of the **mitswah**," Deut. 8:1-2. The "commandment" was to be heard and kept, Exod. 15:26; Deut. 4:2; 11:13 Any failure to do so signified a covenantal breach, Num. 15:31, transgression, 2 Chron. 24:20, and apostasy, 1 Kings 18:18. Outside the Pentateuch, "commandments" are given by kings, 1 Kings 2:43, fathers, Jer. 35:14, people, Isa. 29:13, and teachers of wisdom, Prov. 6:20; cf. 5:13. The plural of **mitswah** often denotes a "body of laws" given by divine revelation, Ps. 119:9.

New Testament

1. **diatagma** (*1297*) signifies "that which is imposed by decree or law," Heb. 11:23. It stresses the concrete character of the "commandment" more than *epitage* (No. 4).

2. **entole** (*1785*), akin to No. 3, above, denotes, in general, "an injunction, charge, precept, commandment." It is the most frequent term, and is used of moral and religious precepts, e.g., Matt. 5:19; it is frequent in the Gospels, especially that of John, and in his Epistles. See also, e.g., Acts 17:15; Rom. 7:8-13; 13:9; 1 Cor. 7:19; Eph. 2:15; Col. 4:10.

3. **entalma** (*1778*), akin to No. 2, marks more especially "the thing commanded, a commission"; in Matt. 15:9; Mark 7:7; Col. 2:22, RV, "precepts," KJV, "commandments."

4. **epitage** (*2003*), akin to No. 4, above, stresses "the authoritativeness of the command"; it is used in Rom. 16:26; 1 Cor. 7:6, 25; 2 Cor. 8:8; 1 Tim. 1:1; Tit. 1:3; 2:15.

COMMEND, COMMENDATION

A. Verbs.

1. **epaineo** (*1867*), "to praise," is an intensive form of *aineo*, Luke 16:8. It is elsewhere translated by the verb "to praise," in the RV, Rom. 15:11; 1 Cor. 11:2, 17, 22.

2. **paradidomi** (*3860*), lit., to give or deliver over," is said of "commending," or "committing," servants of God to Him (KJV, "recommend), Acts 14:26; 15:40.

3. **paratithemi** (*3908*), lit., "to put near," denotes "to place with someone, entrust, commit." In the sense of commending, it is said (a) of the Lord Jesus in "commending" His spirit into the Father's hands, Luke 23:46; (b) of "commending" disciples to God, Acts 14:23; (c) of "commending" elders to God, Acts 20:32. Cf. No. 2.

4. **paristemi** (*3936*), lit., "to place near, set before," is used of "self-commendation," 1 Cor. 8:8.

5. **sunistemi** (*4921*), or **sunistano** (*4921*), lit., "to place together," denotes "to introduce one person to another, represent as worthy," e.g., Rom. 3:5; 5:8; 16:1; 2 Cor. 4:2; 6:4; 10:18; 12:11. In 2 Cor. 3:1; 5:12 and 10:12, the verb **sunistano** is used.

B. Adjective.

sustatikos (*4956*), akin to A, No. 5, lit., "placing together," hence, "commendatory," is used of letters of "commendation," 2 Cor. 3:1, lit., "commendatory letters."

COMMIT, COMMISSION

A. Verbs.

1. **paradidomi** (*3860*), "to give over," is often rendered by the

verb "to commit," e.g., to prison, Acts 8:3; to the grace of God, Acts 14:26; to God, 1 Pet. 2:23; by God to pits of darkness, 2 Pet. 2:4.

2. *pisteuo* (4100) signifies "to entrust, commit to," Luke 16:11; 1 Tim. 1:11, "committed to (my) trust."

3. *tithemi* (5087), "to put, place," signifies, in the middle voice, "to put for oneself, assign, place in," 2 Cor. 5:19, "having committed (unto us)."

4. *paratithemi* (3908), signifies "to entrust, commit to one's charge," e.g., in Luke 12:48; 1 Tim. 1:18; 2 Tim. 2:2; 1 Pet. 4:19 (KJV, "commit the keeping").

B. Nouns.

paratheke (3866) (akin to 4. above), "a putting with, a deposit," 2 Tim. 1:12, "that which He hath committed unto me," RV, marg., lit., "my deposit" (perhaps "my deposit with Him"), the latter in 1 Tim. 6:20, where "guard that which is committed unto thee" is, lit., "guard the deposit," and 2 Tim. 1:14, "that good thing which was committed unto thee," i.e., the good deposit; RV, marg., "the good deposit."

COMMON, COMMONLY

A. Adjective.

koinos (2834) denotes (a) "common, belonging to several" (Lat., *communis*), said of things had in common, Acts 2:44; 4:32; of faith, Titus 1:4; of salvation, Jude 3; it stands in contrast to *idios*, "one's own"; (b) "ordinary, belonging to the generality, as distinct from what is peculiar to the few", hence the application to religious practices of Gentiles in contrast with those of Jews; or of the ordinary people in contrast with those of the Pharisees; hence the meaning "unhallowed, profane," Levitically unclean (Lat., *profanus*), said of hands, Mark 7:2 (KJV, "defiled,") RV marg., "common"; of animals, ceremonially unclean, Acts 10:14; 11:8; of a man, 10:28; of meats, Rom. 14:14, "unclean"; of the blood of the covenant, as viewed by an apostate, Heb. 10:29, "unholy" (RV, marg., "common"); of everything unfit for the holy city, Rev. 21:27, RV, "unclean" (marg., "common"). Some mss. have the verb here.

B. Verb.

koinoo (2840), "to make, or count, common," has this meaning in Acts 10:15; 11:9.

COMMUNICATE, COMMUNICATION

A. Verbs.

1. *koinoneo* (2841) is used in two senses, (a) "to have a share in," Rom. 15:27; 1 Tim. 5:22; Heb. 2:14; 1 Pet. 4:13; 2 John 11; (b) "to give a share to, go shares with," Rom. 12:13, RV, "communicating," for

KJV, "distributing"; Gal. 6:6, "communicate"; Phil. 4:15, KJV, "did communicate," RV, "had fellowship with."

2. *sunkoinoneo* (*4790*), "to share together with" (*sun* "and" No. 1), is translated "communicated with" in Phil. 4:14; "have fellowship with," Eph. 5:11; "be...partakers of," Rev. 18:4 (RV, "have fellowship"). The thought is that of sharing with others what one has, in order to meet their needs.

B. Nouns.

1. *koinonia* (*2842*), akin to A (which see), is translated in Heb. 13:16 "to communicate," lit., "be not forgetful of good deed and of fellowship"; "fellowship" (KJV, "communication") in Philem. 6, RV.

2. *logos* (*3056*), "a word, that which is spoken" (*lego*, "to speak"), is used in the plural with reference to a conversation; "communication," Luke 24:17. Elsewhere with this significance the RV renders it "speech," Matt. 5:37; Eph. 4:29.

C. Adjective.

koinonikos (*2843*), akin to A, No. 1 and B, No. 1, means "apt, or ready, to communicate," 1 Tim. 6:18.

COMMUNION

A. Noun.

koinonia (*2842*), "a having in common (*koinos*), partnership, fellowship," denotes (a) the share which one has in anything, a participation, fellowship recognized and enjoyed; thus it is used of the common experiences and interests of Christian men, Acts 2:42; Gal. 2:9; of participation in the knowledge of the Son of God, 1 Cor. 1:9; of sharing in the realization of the effects of the blood (i.e., the death) of Christ and the body of Christ, as set forth by the emblems in the Lord's Supper, 1 Cor. 10:16; of participation in what is derived from the Holy Spirit, 2 Cor. 13:14 (RV, "communion"); Phil. 2:1; of participation in the sufferings of Christ, Phil. 3:10; of sharing in the resurrection life possessed in Christ, and so of fellowship with the Father and the Son, 1 John 1:3, 6-7; negatively, of the impossibility of "communion" between light and darkness, 2 Cor. 6:14; (b) fellowship manifested in acts, the practical effects of fellowship with God, wrought by the Holy Spirit in the lives of believers as the outcome of faith, Philem. 6, and finding expression in joint ministration to the needy, Rom. 15:26; 2 Cor. 8:4; 9:13; Heb. 13:16, and in the furtherance of the Gospel by gifts, Phil. 1:5.

B. Adjective.

koinonos (*2844*), "having in common," is rendered "have communion with (the altar),"—the altar standing by metonymy for that which is associated with it—in 1 Cor. 10:18, RV (for KJV, "are partakers of"), and in v. 20, for KJV, "have fellowship with (demons)."

COMPANION

Old Testament

A. Nouns.

rea' (7453), "friend; companion." A *rea'* is a "personal friend" with whom one shares confidences and to whom one feels very close, Exod. 33:11. In this sense, the word is a synonym of *'ah*, "brother," and of *qarob*, "kin," Exod. 32:27. *rea'* also means "marriage partner," Song of Sol. 5:16; or paramour, Jer. 3:1, cf. Hosea's wife.

rea' is also a *neighbor*, the person with whom one associates regularly or casually without establishing close relations, Exod. 20:16. The prophets charged Israel with breaking the commandment regarding respect for one's neighbor, Isa. 3:5; Jer. 5:8; 22:13; Ezek. 18:6. *rea'* can also mean "friend," Prov. 19:4. Here the "friend" is a person whose association is not long-lasting, whose friendship is superficial.

re'eh also means "friend," Judg. 11:27; 1 Kings 4:5. The noun *ra'yah* means "beloved companion; bride." *ra'yah* occurs many times in the Song of Solomon: 1:9, 15; 2:2, 10, 13; 4:1, 7; 5:2; 6:4. *re'ut* refers to a "fellow woman."

B. Verb.

ra'ah (7462), "to associate with." This word appears in Prov. 22:24: "Make no friendship with an angry man; and with a furious man thou shalt not go..."

New Testament

koinonos (2844) is rendered "companions" in the KJV of Heb. 10:33 (RV "partakers"). So *sunkoinonos* in Rev. 1:9, KJV, "companion"; RV, "partaker with you."

COMPASS

1. *kukleuo* (2944v) denotes "to encircle, surround," and is found in the best texts in John 10:24, "came round about," and Rev. 20:9, of a camp surrounded by foes; some mss. have No. 2 in each place.

2. *kukloo* (2944), (cf. Eng., cycle), signifies "to move in a circle, to compass about," as of a city "encompassed" by armies, Luke 21:20; Heb. 11:30; in Acts 14:20, "stood round about.

3. *perikukloo* (4033), *peri*, "about," with No. 2, is used in Luke 19:43, "shall compass...round.

COMPASSION, COMPASSIONATE

Old Testament

A. Verb.

racham (7355), "to have compassion, be merciful, pity." *racham* is used in God's promise to declare His name to Moses, with a special focus on His love, Exod. 33:19; Ps. 25:6; Isa. 54:7-8.

B. Nouns.

rechem (7358), "bowels; womb; mercy." The first use of *rechem* is in its primary meaning of "womb": "The Lord had fast closed up all the wombs of the house of Abimelech," Gen. 20:18. The word is personified in Judg. 5:30: "Have they not divided the prey; to every man a damsel or two...?" In another figurative sense, the KJV reads in 1 Kings 3:26: "Her bowels yearned upon her son," which the NIV translates more idiomatically: "[She] was filled with compassion for her son." The greatest frequency is in this figurative sense of "tender love," such as a mother has for the child she has borne.

rachamim (7356), "bowels; mercies; compassion." This noun, always used in the plural intensive, occurs in Gen. 43:14: "And God Almighty give you mercy [NASB, "compassion"]." In Gen. 43:30, it is used of Joseph's feelings toward Benjamin: "His bowels did yearn upon his brother." (NIV, "He was deeply moved at the sight of his brother.") *rachamim* is most often used of God, as by David in 2 Sam. 24:14: "Let us fall now into the hand of the Lord; for his mercies are great..." We have the equivalent Aramaic word in Daniel's request to his friends: "That they would desire mercies of the God of heaven concerning this secret..." Dan. 2:18.

C. Adjective.

rachum (7349), "compassionate; merciful," Exod. 34:6.

New Testament

A. Verbs.

1. *oikteiro* (3627), "to have pity, a feeling of distress through the ills of others," is used of God's compassion, Rom. 9:15.

2. *splanchnizomai* (4697), "to be moved as to one's inwards (*splanchna*), to be moved with compassion, to yearn with compassion," is frequently recorded of Christ towards the multitude and towards individual sufferers, Matt. 9:36; 14:14; 15:32; 18:27; 20:34; Mark 1:41; 6:34; 8:2; 9:22 (of the appeal of a father for a demon-possessed son); Luke 7:13; 10:33; of the father in the parable of the Prodigal Son, 15:20.

3. *sumpatheo* (4834), "to suffer with another, to be affected similarly" (Eng., "sympathy"), to have "compassion" upon, Heb. 10:34, of "compassionating" those in prison, is translated "be touched with" in Heb. 4:15, of Christ as the High Priest.

4. *eleeo* (1653), "to have mercy (*eleos*, "mercy"), to show kindness, by beneficence, or assistance," is translated "have compassion" in Matt. 18:33 (KJV); Mark 5:19 and Jude 22.

5. *metriopatheo* (*3356*) is rendered "have compassion," in Heb. 5:2, KJV.

B. Nouns.

1. *oiktirmos* (*3628*), akin to A, No. 1, is used with *splanchna* (see below), "the viscera, the inward parts," as the seat of emotion, the "heart," Phil. 2:1; Col. 3:12, "a heart of compassion" (KJV, "bowels of mercies"). In Heb. 10:28 it is used with *choris*, "without," (lit., "without compassions"). It is translated "mercies" in Rom. 12:1 and 2 Cor. 1:3.

2. *splanchnon* (*4698*), always used in the plural, is suitably rendered "compassion" in the RV of Col. 3:12 and 1 John 3:17; "compassions" in Phil. 2:1, Cf. A, No. 2.

C. Adjective.

sumpathes (*4835*) denotes suffering with, "compassionate," 1 Pet. 3:8.

COMPEL

1. *anankazo* (*315*) denotes "to put constraint upon (from *ananke*, 'necessity'), to constrain, whether by threat, entreaty, force or persuasion"; Christ "constrained" the disciples to get into a boat, Matt. 14:22; Mark 6:45; the servants of the man who made a great supper were to constrain people to come in, Luke 14:23 (RV, "constrain"); Saul of Tarsus "strove" to make saints blaspheme, Acts 26:11, RV (KJV, "compelled"); Titus, though a Greek, was not "compelled" to be circumcised, Gal. 2:3, as Galatian converts were, 6:12, RV; Peter was "compelling" Gentiles to live as Jews, Gal. 2:14; Paul was "constrained" to appeal to Caesar, Acts 28:19, and was "compelled" by the church at Corinth to become foolish in speaking of himself, 2 Cor. 12:11.

2. *angareuo* (*29*), "to dispatch as an *angaros*" (a Persian courier kept at regular stages with power of impressing men into service), and hence, in general, "to impress into service," is used of "compelling" a person to go a mile, Matt. 5:41; of the impressing of Simon to bear Christ's cross, Matt. 27:32; Mark 15:21.

COMPLAINER, COMPLAINT

1. *mempsimoiros* (*3202*) denotes "one who complains," lit., "complaining of one's lot," Jude 16.

2. *momphe* (*3437*), denotes "blame," "an occasion of complaint," Col. 3:13.

3. *aitioma* (*157v*), "a charge," is translated "complaints" in Acts 25:7, KJV.

COMPLETE, COMPLETION, COMPLETELY

1. *epiteleo* (*2005*), "to complete," Rom. 15:28.

2. *exartizo* (*1822*), "to fit out," lit., "exactly right,", is said of the equipment of the man of God, 2 Tim. 3:17, "furnished completely" (KJV, "thoroughly furnished"); elsewhere in Acts 21:5, "accomplished.

3. *sunteleo* (*4931*), "to end together, bring quite to an end," is said (a) of the "completion" of a period of days, Luke 4:2; Acts 21:27; (b) of "completing" something; some mss. have it in Matt. 7:28, of the Lord, in ending His discourse (the best mss. have *teleo*, "to finish"); of God, in finishing a work, Rom. 9:28, in making a new covenant, Heb. 8:8, marg., "accomplish"; of the fulfillment of things foretold, Mark 13:4; of the Devil's temptation of the Lord, Luke 4:13.

4. *pleroo* (*4137*), "to fill" (in the passive voice, "to be made full"), is translated "complete" in the KJV of Col. 2:10 (RV, "made full"; cf v. 9).

5. *plerophoreo* (*4135*), "to be fully assured," is translated "complete" in Col. 4:12.

CONCEITS

1. *en heautois*, lit., "in yourselves," is used with *phronimos*, "wise," in Rom. 11:25, "(wise) in your own conceits (i.e., opinions)."

2. *par' heautois*, (*para*, "with, in the estimation of"), in Rom. 12:16 has the same rendering as No. 1.

CONCEIVE

1. *gennao* (*1080*), "to conceive, beget," Matt. 1:20.

2. *sullambano* (*4815*), lit., "to take together," is used (a) of a woman, to "conceive," Luke 1:24, 31, 36; in the passive voice. Luke 2:21; (b) metaphorically, of the impulse of lust in the human heart, enticing to sin, Jas. 1:15.

CONCISION

katatome (*2699*), lit., "a cutting off," "a mutilation," is a term found in Phil. 3:2.

CONCLUDE

sumbibazo (*4822*), lit., "to make to come together," is translated "concluding" in Acts 16:10.

CONCORD

sumphonesis (*4857*), lit., "a sounding together"; cf. Eng., "symphony," is found in 2 Cor. 6:15.

CONDEMN, CONDEMNATION

A. Verbs.

1. *kataginosko* (*2607*), "to know something against," hence, "to

think ill of, to condemn," is said, in Gal. 2:11, of Peter's conduct (RV, "stood condemned"), he being "self-condemned" as the result of an exercised and enlightened conscience, and "condemned" in the sight of others; so of "self-condemnation" due to an exercise of heart, 1 John 3:20-21.

2. *katadikazo* (*2613*) signifies "to exercise right or law against anyone"; hence, "to pronounce judgment, to condemn," Matt. 12:7, 37; Luke 6:37; Jas. 5:6.

3. *krino* (*2919*), "to distinguish, choose, give an opinion upon, judge," sometimes denotes "to condemn," e.g., Acts 13:27; Rom. 2:27; Jas. 5:9 (in the best mss.). Cf. No. 1, below.

4. *katakrino* (*2632*), a strengthened form of No. 3, signifies "to give judgment against, pass sentence upon"; hence, "to condemn," implying (a) the fact of a crime, e.g., Rom. 2:1; 14:23; 2 Pet. 2:6; some mss. have it in Jas. 5:9; (b) the imputation of a crime, as in the "condemnation" of Christ by the Jews, Matt. 20:18; Mark 14:64. It is used metaphorically of "condemning" by a good example, Matt. 12:41-42; Luke 11:31-32; Heb. 11:7.

B. Nouns.

1. *krima* (*2917*) denotes (a) "the sentence pronounced, a verdict, a condemnation, the decision resulting from an investigation," e.g., Mark 12:40; Luke 23:40; 1 Tim. 3:6; Jude 4; (b) "the process of judgment leading to a decision," 1 Pet. 4:17 ("judgment"), where *krisis* (see No. 3, below) might be expected. In Luke 24:20, "to be condemned" translates the phrase *eis krima*, "unto condemnation" (i.e., unto the pronouncement of the sentence of "condemnation"). For the rendering "judgment," see, e.g., Rom. 11:33; 1 Cor. 11:34; Gal. 5:10; Jas. 3:1. In these (a) the process leading to a decision and (b) the pronouncement of the decision, the verdict, are to be distinguished. In 1 Cor. 6:7 the word means a matter for judgment, a lawsuit.

2. *katakrima* (*2631*), cf. No. 4, above, is "the sentence pronounced, the condemnation" with a suggestion of the punishment following; it is found in Rom. 5:16, 18; 8:1.

3. *krisis* (*2920*) (a) denotes "the process of investigation, the act of distinguishing and separating" (as distinct from *krima*, see No. 1 above); hence "a judging, a passing of judgment upon a person or thing"; it has a variety of meanings, such as judicial authority, John 5:22, 27; justice, Acts 8:33; Jas. 2:13; a tribunal, Matt. 5:21-22; a trial, John 5:24; 2 Pet. 2:4; a judgment, 2 Pet. 2:11; Jude 9; by metonymy, the standard of judgment, just dealing, Matt. 12:18, 20; 23:23; Luke 11:42; divine judgment executed, 2 Thess. 1:5; Rev. 16:7; (b) sometimes it has the meaning "condemnation."

4. *katakrisis* (*2633*), a strengthened form of No. 3, denotes "a judgment against, condemnation," with the suggestion of the process leading to it, as of "the ministration of condemnation,"

2 Cor. 3:9; in 7:3, "to condemn," more lit., "with a view to condemnation."

C. Adjective.

autokatakritos (843), "self-condemned," i.e., on account of doing himself what he condemns in others, is used in Titus 3:11.

CONDUCT

A. Noun.

agoge (72), from *ago*, "to lead," properly denotes "a teaching"; then, figuratively, "a training, discipline," and so, the life led, a way or course of life, conduct, 2 Tim. 3:10, RV, "conduct"; KJV, "manner of life."

B. Verbs.

1. *kathistemi* (2525), lit., "to stand down or set down," has, among its various meanings, "the significance of bringing to a certain place, conducting," Acts 17:15 (so the Sept. in Josh. 6:23; 1 Sam. 5:3; 2 Chron. 28:15).

2. *propempo* (4311) signifies "to set forward, conduct," 1 Cor. 16:11.

CONFER, CONFERENCE

1. *prosanatithemi* (4323), lit., "to put before," i.e., "to lay a matter before others so as to obtain counsel or instruction," is used of Paul's refraining from consulting human beings, Gal. 1:16.

2. *sullaleo* (4814), "to speak together with," is translated "conferred" in Acts 25:12; elsewhere of talking with Matt. 17:3; Mark 9:4; Luke 4:36; 9:30; "communed" in Luke 22:4.

3. *sumballo* (4820), lit., "to throw together," is used of "conversation, to discourse or consult together, confer," Acts 4:15.

CONFESS, CONFESSION

Old Testament

yadah (3034), "to confess, praise, give thanks." *yadah* overlaps in meaning with a number of other Hebrew words implying public "praise," and "thanksgiving," such as *halal* (whence *halleluyah*). Humans are occasionally the object of *yadah*; but usually God is the object. Praise inevitably entails confession of sin, but also a pronouncement of forgiveness by God.

Often the direct object of *yadah* is the "name" of Yahweh, e.g., Ps. 105:1; Isa. 12:4; 1 Chron. 16:8. In one sense, this idiom is simply synonymous with praising Yahweh. In another sense, however, it introduces the entire dimension evoked by the "name" in biblical usage. It reminds us that the holy God cannot be directly approached by fallen man, but only through His "name"—i.e., His

Word and reputation, an anticipation of the incarnation. God reveals Himself only in His "name," especially in the sanctuary where He "causes His name to dwell" (a phrase especially frequent in Deuteronomy).

The vista of *yadah* expands both vertically and horizontally—vertically to include all creation, and horizontally stretching forward to that day when praise and thanksgiving shall be eternal, e.g., Ps. 29; 95:10; 96:7-9; 103:19-22.

New Testament

A. Verbs.

1. *homologeo* (3670), lit., "to speak the same thing," "to assent, accord, agree with," denotes, (a) "to confess, declare, admit," John 1:20; e.g., Acts 24:14; Heb. 11:13; (b) "to confess by way of admitting oneself guilty of what one is accused of, the result of inward conviction," 1 John 1:9; (c) "to declare openly by way of speaking out freely, such confession being the effect of deep conviction of facts," Matt. 7:23; 10:32 (twice) and Luke 12:8; John 9:22; 12:42; Acts 23:8; Rom. 10:9-10 ("confession is made"); 1 Tim. 6:12 (RV); Titus 1:16; 1 John 2:23; 4:2, 15; 2 John 7 (in John's epistle it is the necessary antithesis to Gnostic docetism); Rev. 3:5, in the best mss. (some have No. 2 here); (d) "to confess by way of celebrating with praise," Heb. 13:15; (e) "to promise," Matt. 14:7.

2. *exomologeo* (1843), (*ek*, "out," intensive, and No. 1), and accordingly stronger than No. 1, "to confess forth," i.e., "freely, openly," is used (a) "of a public acknowledgment or confession of sins," Matt. 3:6; Mark 1:5; Acts 19:18; Jas. 5:16; (b) "to profess or acknowledge openly," Matt. 11:25 (translated "thank," but indicating the fuller idea); Phil. 2:11 (some mss. have it in Rev. 3:5: see No. 1); (c) "to confess by way of celebrating, giving praise," Rom. 14:11; 15:9. In Luke 10:21, it is translated "I thank," the true meaning being "I gladly acknowledge." In Luke 22:6 it signifies to consent (RV), for KJV, "promised."

B. Noun.

homologia (3671), akin to A, No. 1, denotes "confession, by acknowledgment of the truth," 2 Cor. 9:13; 1 Tim. 6:12-13; Heb. 3:1; 4:14; 10:23 (KJV, incorrectly, "profession," except in 1 Tim. 6:13).

CONFIDENCE (Noun, or Verb with "have"), CONFIDENT (-LY)

A. Nouns.

1. *pepoithesis* (4006), akin to *peitho*, B, No. 1 below, denotes "persuasion, assurance, confidence," 2 Cor. 1:15; 3:4, KJV, "trust"; 8:22; 10:2; Eph. 3:12; Phil. 3:4.

2. *hupostasis* (5287), lit., "a standing under" (*hupo*, "under,"

stasis, "a standing"), "that which stands, or is set, under, a foundation, beginning"; hence, the quality of confidence which leads one to stand under, endure, or undertake anything, 2 Cor. 9:4; 11:17; Heb. 3:14. Twice in Heb. it signifies "substance," 1:3 (KJV, "Person") and 11:1.

3. *parrhesia* (3954), often rendered "confidence" in the KJV, is in all such instances rendered "boldness" in the RV, Acts 28:31; Heb. 3:6; 1 John 2:28; 3:21; 5:14.

B. Verbs.

peitho (3982), "to persuade," or, intransitively, "to have confidence, to be confident" (cf. A, No. 1), has this meaning in the following, Rom. 2:19; 2 Cor. 2:3; Gal. 5:10; Phil. 1:6, 14 (RV, "being confident," for KJV, "waxing confident"), 25; 3:3-4; 2 Thess. 3:4; Philem. 21.

CONFIRM, CONFIRMATION

A. Verbs.

1. *bebaioo* (950), "to make firm, establish, make secure" (the connected adjective *bebaios* signifies "stable, fast, firm"), is used of "confirming" a word, Mark 16:20; promises, Rom. 15:8; the testimony of Christ, 1 Cor. 1:6; the saints by the Lord Jesus Christ, 1 Cor. 1:8; the saints by God, 2 Cor. 1:21 ("stablisheth"); in faith, Col. 2:7; the salvation spoken through the Lord and "confirmed" by the apostles, Heb. 2:3; the heart by grace, Heb. 13:9 ("stablished").

2. *episterizo* (1991), "to make to lean upon, strengthen" (*epi*, "upon," *sterix*, "a prop, support"), is used of "confirming" souls Acts 14:22, brethren, 15:32; churches, 15:41; disciples, 18:23, in some mss. ("stablishing," RV, "strengthening," KJV); the most authentic mss. have *sterizo* in 18:23.

3. *kuroo* (2964), "to make valid, ratify, impart authority or influence" (from *kuros*, "might," *kurios*, "mighty, a head, as supreme in authority"), is used of spiritual love, 2 Cor. 2:8; a human covenant, Gal. 3:15.

4. *prokuroo* (4300), (*pro*, "before," and No. 3), "to confirm or ratify before," is said of the divine confirmation of a promise given originally to Abraham, Gen. 12, and "confirmed" by the vision of the furnace and torch, Gen. 15, by the birth of Isaac, Gen. 21, and by the oath of God, Gen. 22, all before the giving of the Law, Gal. 3:17.

B. Noun.

bebaiosis (951), akin to A, No. 1, is used in two senses (a) "of firmness, establishment," said of the "confirmation" of the gospel, Phil. 1:7; (b) "of authoritative validity imparted," said of the settlement of a dispute by an oath to produce confidence, Heb. 6:16. The word is found frequently in the papyri of the settlement of a business transaction.

CONFLICT (Noun)

1. *agon* (73), from *ago*, "to lead," signifies (a) "a place of assembly," especially the place where the Greeks assembled for the Olympic and Pythian games; (b) "a contest of athletes," metaphorically, 1 Tim. 6:12; 2 Tim. 4:7, "fight"; Heb. 12:1, "race"; hence, (c) "the inward conflict of the soul"; inward "conflict" is often the result, or the accompaniment, of outward "conflict," Phil. 1:30; 1 Thess. 2:2, implying a contest against spiritual foes, as well as human adversaries; so Col. 2:1.

2. *athlesis* (119) denotes "a combat, contest of athletes"; hence, "a struggle, fight," Heb. 10:32, with reference to affliction.

CONFORMED, CONFORMABLE

A. Verb.

summorphizo (4833v), "to make of like form with another person or thing, to render like" (*sun*, "with," *morphe*, "a form"), is found in Phil. 3:10, focusing on death of the carnal self.

B. Adjective.

summorphos (4832), akin to A, signifies "having the same form as another, conformed to"; (a) of the "conformity" of children of God "to the image of His Son," Rom. 8:29; (b), of their future physical "conformity" to His body of glory, Phil. 3:21.

CONFOUND, CONFUSE, CONFUSION

A. Nouns.

1. *akatastasia* (181), "instability," (*a*, negative, *kata*, "down," *stasis*, "a standing"), denotes "a state of disorder, confusion, tumult," 1 Cor. 14:33; Jas. 3:16, "revolution or anarchy"; translated "tumults" in Luke 21:9 (KJV, "commotions"); 2 Cor. 6:5; 12:20.

2. *sunchusis* (4799), "a pouring or mixing together," hence "a disturbance, confusion, a tumultuous disorder, as of riotous persons," is found in Acts 19:29.

B. Verb.

suncheo (4797), or *sunchunno* or *sunchuno* (the verb form of A., No. 2), lit., "to pour together, commingle," hence (said of persons), means "to trouble or confuse, to stir up," Acts 19:32 (said of the mind); "to be in confusion," 21:31, RV (KJV, "was in an uproar")· 21:27, "stirred up"; Acts 2:6; 9:22, "confounded.

CONFUTE

diakatelenchomai (*1246*), "to confute powerfully," with a focus on ascribing moral blame, Acts 18:28.

CONGREGATION

Old Testament

'edah (5712), "congregation," it is similar to the Greek words *sunagoge* and *ekklesia*. The most general meaning of *'edah* is "group," whether of animals, Judg. 14:8; Ps. 68:30; Hos. 7:12—or of people, such as the righteous, Ps. 1:5, the evildoers, Ps. 22:16, and the nations, Ps. 7:7.

mo'ed (4150), "appointed place of meeting; meeting." The word *mo'ed* keeps its basic meaning of "appointed," but varies as to what is agreed upon or appointed according to the context: the time, the place, or the meeting itself. The usage of the verb in Amos 3:3 is illuminating: "Can two walk together, except they be agreed?"

The meaning of *mo'ed* is fixed within the context of Israel's religion. First, the prescribed festivals came to be known as the "appointed times" or the set feasts, Lev. 23:15ff.

The word *mo'ed* also signifies a "fixed place," though not frequent, Job 30:23; Isa. 14:13.

'ohel mo'ed means "tent of meeting," it signifies that the Lord has an "appointed, fixed place," Exod. 28:43; cf. Rev. 15:5.

New Testament

1. *ekklesia* (1577) is translated "congregation" in Heb. 2:12, RV, instead of the usual rendering "church."

2. *sunagoge* (4864) is translated "congregation" in Acts 13:43, KJV (RV, "synagogue).

CONQUER, CONQUEROR

1. *nikao* (3528), "to overcome" (its usual meaning), is translated "conquering" and "to conquer" in Rev. 6:2.

2. *hupernikao* (5245), "to be more than conqueror" (*huper*, "over," and No. 1), "to gain a surpassing victory," is found in Rom. 8:37, lit., "we are hyper-conquerors," i.e., we are pre-eminently victorious.

CONSCIENCE

suneidesis (4893), lit., "a knowing with," i.e., "a co-knowledge (with oneself), the witness borne to one's conduct by conscience, that faculty by which we apprehend the will of God, as that which is designed to govern our lives"; hence (a) the sense of guiltiness before God; Heb. 10:2; (b) that process of thought which distinguishes what it considers morally good or bad, commending the good, condemning the bad, and so prompting to do the former, and avoid the latter; Rom. 2:15 (bearing witness with God's law); 9:1; 2 Cor. 1:12; acting in a certain way because "conscience" requires it, Rom. 13:5; so as not to cause scruples of "conscience" in another, 1 Cor. 10:28-29; not calling a thing in question unnecessarily, as if conscience demanded it, 1 Cor. 10:25, 27; "commending oneself to every man's conscience," 2 Cor. 4:2; cf. 5:11. There may be a "conscience" not strong enough to distinguish clearly between the lawful and the unlawful, 1 Cor. 8:7, 10, 12 (some regard consciousness as the meaning here). The phrase "conscience toward God," in 1 Pet. 2:19, signifies a "conscience" (or perhaps here, a consciousness) so controlled by the apprehension of God's presence, that the person realizes that griefs are to be borne in accordance with His will. Heb. 9:9 teaches that sacrifices under the Law could not so perfect a person that he could regard himself as free from guilt.

For various descriptions of "conscience" see Acts 23:1; 24:16; 1 Cor. 8:7; 1 Tim. 1:5, 19; 3:9; 4:2; 2 Tim. 1:3; Titus 1:15; Heb. 9:14; 10:22; 13:18; 1 Pet. 3:16, 21.

CONSENT

A. Verbs.

1. *exomologeo* (1843), "to agree openly, to acknowledge outwardly, or fully," is translated "consented" in the RV of Luke 22:6 (KJV, promised).

2. *sumphemi* (4852), lit., "to speak with," hence, "to express agreement with," is used of "consenting" to the Law, agreeing that it is good, Rom. 7:16.

3. *suneudokeo* (4909), lit., "to think well with," to take pleasure with others in anything, to approve of, to assent, is used in Luke 11:48, of "consenting" to the evil deeds of predecessors (KJV, "allow"); in Rom. 1:32, of "consenting" in doing evil; in Acts 8:1; 22:20, of "consenting" to the death of another. All these are cases of "consenting" to evil things. In 1 Cor. 7:12-13, it is used of an unbelieving wife's "consent" to dwell with her converted husband, and of an unbelieving husband's "consent" to dwell with a believing wife (KJV, "be pleased"; RV, "be content").

B. Phrases.

1. *apo mias*, lit., "from one," is found in Luke 14:18, some word like "consent" being implied; e.g., "with one consent."

2. *ek sumphonou*, lit., "from (or by) agreement" (*sun*, "with," *phone*, "a sound"), i.e., "by consent," is found in 1 Cor. 7:5.

CONSIDER

1. *eidon* (Aor. of 3708), used as the aorist tense of *horao*, "to see," is translated "to consider" in Acts 15:6, of the gathering of the

apostles and elders regarding the question of circumcision in relation to the gospel.

2. *suneidon* (*4894*), *sun*, with, and No. 1, used as the aorist tense of *sunorao*, to see with one view, to be aware, conscious, as the result of mental perception, is translated "considered" in Acts 12:12, of Peter's consideration of the circumstances of his deliverance from.

3. *katamanthano* (*2648*), lit., "to learn thoroughly," hence, "to note accurately, consider well," is used in the Lord's exhortation to "consider" the lilies. Matt. 6:28.

4. *noeo* (*3539*), "to perceive with the mind" (*nous*), "think about, ponder," is translated "consider," only in Paul's exhortation to Timothy in 2 Tim. 2:7.

5. *katanoeo* (*2657*), "to perceive clearly" (*kata*, intensive, and No. 4), "to understand fully, consider closely," is used of not "considering" thoroughly the beam in one's own eye, Matt. 7:3 and Luke 6:41 (KJV, "perceivest"); of carefully "considering" the ravens, Luke 12:24; the lilies, v. 27; of Peter's full "consideration" of his vision, Acts 11:6; of Abraham's careful "consideration" of his own body, and Sarah's womb, as dead, and yet accepting by faith God's promise, Rom. 4:19 (RV); of "considering" fully the Apostle and High Priest of our confession, Heb. 3:1; of thoughtfully "considering" one another to provoke unto love and good works, Heb. 10:24. It is translated by the verbs "behold," Acts 7:31-32; Jas. 1:23-24; "perceive," Luke 20:23; "discover," Acts 27:39.

6. *logizomai* (*3049*) signifies "to take account of," 2 Cor. 10:7 (RV, "consider," KJV, "think"), the only place where the RV translates it "consider."

7. *theoreo* (*2334*), Heb 7:4.

8. *anatheoreo* (*333*), "to consider carefully," Heb 13:7.

9. *analogizomai* (*357*), "to consider," occurs in Heb. 12:3.

CONSIST

sunistemi (*4921*), (*sun*, "with," *histemi* "to stand"), denotes, in its intransitive sense, "to stand with or fall together, to be constituted, to be compact"; it is said of the universe as upheld by the Lord, Col. 1:17, lit., "by Him all things stand together," i.e., "consist."

CONSOLATION, CONSOLE

A. Nouns.

1. *paraklesis* (*3874*) is translated "consolation," in both KJV and RV, in Luke 2:25; 6:24; Acts 15:31; in 1 Cor. 14:3, KJV, "exhortation," RV, "comfort"; in the following the KJV has "consolation," the RV, "comfort," Rom. 15:5; 2 Cor. 1:6-7; 7:7; Phil. 2:1; 2 Thess. 2:16; Philem. 7; in Acts 4:36, RV, "exhortation"; in Heb. 6:18, RV, "encouragement."

2. *paramuthia* (*3889*), "a comfort, consolation," 1 Cor. 14:3.

3. *paramuthion* (*3890*), "an encouragement, consolation," Phil. 2:1, RV, in the phrase "consolation of love."

B. Verb.

paramutheomai (*3888*), "to speak soothingly to," is translated "console," John 11:19, RV; in v. 31 "were comforting"; in 1 Thess. 2:11 and 5:14, KJV, "comforted" and "comfort," RV, "encouraged" and "encourage."

CONSTRAIN, CONSTRAINT

A. Verbs.

1. *anankazo* (*315*), Gal. 6:12.

2. *sunecho* (*4912*), "to hold together, confine, secure, to hold fast" (*echo*, "to have or hold"), "to constrain," is said (a) of the effect of the word of the Lord upon Paul, Acts 18:5 (KJV, "was pressed in spirit," RV, "was constrained by the word"); of the effect of the love of Christ, 2 Cor. 5:14; (b) of being taken with a disease, Matt. 4:24; Luke 4:38; Acts 28:8; with fear, Luke 8:37; (c) of thronging or holding in a person, Luke 8:45; being straitened, Luke 12:50; being in a strait betwixt two, Phil. 1:23; keeping a city in on every side, Luke 19:43; keeping a tight hold on a person, as the men who seized the Lord Jesus did, after bringing Him into the High Priest's house, Luke 22:63; (d) of stopping the ears in refusal to listen, Acts 7:57. Luke uses the word nine times out of its twelve occurrences in the NT.

B. Adverb.

anankastos (*317*), akin to A, No. 1, "by force, unwillingly, by constraint," is used in 1 Pet. 5:2.

CONSULT, CONSULTATION

A. Verbs.

1. *bouleuo* (*1011*), used in the middle voice, means (a) "to consult," Luke 14:31; (b) "to resolve," John 12:10, KJV, "consulted"; RV, took counsel."

2. *sumbouleuo* (*4823*), "to take counsel together," is translated "consulted together," in Matt. 26:4.

B. Noun.

sumboulion (*4824*), a word of the Graeco-Roman period (akin to A, No. 2), "counsel, advice," is translated "consultation" in Mark 15:1.

CONSUME

1. *analisko* (*355*), "to use up, spend up, especially in a bad sense, to destroy," is said of the destruction of persons, (a) literally, Luke

9:54 and the RV marg. of 2 Thess. 2:8 (text, "shall slay"); (b) metaphorically, Gal. 5:15 "(that) ye be not consumed (one of another)."

2. *katanalisko* (2654), "to consume utterly, wholly" (*kata*, intensive), is said, in Heb. 12:29, of God as "a consuming fire."

3. *aphanizo* (853), lit., "to cause to disappear, put out of sight," came to mean "to do away with" (*a*, negative, *phaino*, "to cause to appear"), said of the destructive work of moth and rust, Matt. 6:19-20.

CONTEND (-ING)

1. *athleo* (118), "to engage in a contest" (cf. Eng., "athlete"), "to contend in public games," is used in 2 Tim. 2:5.

2. *epagonizomai* (1864) signifies "to contend about a thing, as a combatant" (*epi*, "upon or about," intensive, *agon*, "a contest"), "to contend earnestly," Jude 3. The word "earnestly" is added to convey the intensive force of the preposition.

CONTENT (to be), CONTENTMENT

A. Verb.

arkeo (174) primarily signifies "to be sufficient, to be possessed of sufficient strength, to be strong, to be enough for a thing"; hence, "to defend, ward off"; in the middle voice, "to be satisfied, contented with," Luke 3:14, with wages; 1 Tim. 6:8, with food and raiment; Heb. 13:5, with "such things as ye have"; negatively of Diotrephes, in 3 John 10, "not content therewith."

B. Adjective.

autarkes (842), as found in the papyri writings, means "sufficient in oneself" (*autos*, "self," *arkeo*, "see" A), "self-sufficient, adequate, needing no assistance"; hence, "content," Phil. 4:11.

C. Noun.

autarkeia (841), "contentment, satisfaction with what one has," is found in 1 Tim. 6:6. For its other meaning "sufficiency," in 2 Cor. 9:8.

CONTENTION, CONTENTIOUS

A. Nouns.

1. *eris* (2054), "strife, quarrel, especially rivalry, contention, wrangling," as in the church in Corinth, 1 Cor. 1:11, is translated "contentions" in Titus 3:9, KJV.

2. *paroxusmos* (3948), (Eng., "paroxysm"), lit., "a sharpening," hence "a sharpening of the feeling, or action," denotes an incitement, a sharp contention, Acts 15:39, the effect of irritation; elsewhere in Heb. 10:24, "provoke," unto love.

3. *philoneikia* (5379), lit., "love of strife," signifies "eagerness to contend"; hence, a "contention," said of the disciples, Luke 22:24. Cf. B, 2.

B. Adjectives.

1. *amachos* (269), lit., "not fighting," primarily signifying "invincible," came to mean "not contentious," 1 Tim. 3:3, RV; Titus 3:2 (KJV, "not a brawler," "no brawlers").

2. *philoneikos* (5380), akin to A, No. 3, is used in 1 Cor. 11:16.

CONTRADICT, CONTRADICTION

A. Verb.

antilego (483), lit., "to speak against," is translated "contradict" in Acts 13:45.

B. Noun.

antilogia (485), akin to A, is translated "contradiction" in the KJV of Heb. 7:7; 12:3, "dispute," and "gainsaying."

CONTRARY

A. Verb.

antikeimai (480), "to be contrary," (*anti*, "against," *keimai*, "to lie"), Gal. 5:17; 1 Tim. 1:10.

B. Adjectives.

1. *enantios* (1727), "over against," place, Mark 15:39; metaphorically, opposed as an adversary, antagonistic, Acts 26:9; 1 Thess. 2:15; Titus 2:8; Acts 28:17.

2. *hupenantios* (5227), (*hupo*, "under," and No. 1), opposite to, is used of "that which is contrary to persons," Col. 2:14, and as a noun, "adversaries," Heb. 10:27.

CONTRIBUTION

koinonia (2842) is twice rendered "contribution," Rom. 15:26, and 2 Cor. 9:13, RV, (KJV, "distribution).

CONVENIENT, CONVENIENTLY

A. Adjective.

eukairos (2121), lit., "well-timed," hence signifies "timely, opportune, convenient"; it is said of a certain day, Mark 6:21; elsewhere, Heb. 4:16, "in time of need."

B. Adverb.

eukairos (2122), "conveniently," Mark 14:11, is used elsewhere in 2 Tim. 4:2, "in season."

C. Verbs.

1. *aneko* (433) is rendered "befitting" in Eph. 5:4, for KJV, "convenient"; so in Philem. 8.

2. *katheko* (2520), "to be fitting," is so translated in Rom. 1:28, RV; KJV, "(not) convenient"; in Acts 22:22, "it is (not) fit."

CONVERT, CONVERSION

A. Verbs.

1. *strepho* (4762), "to turn," is translated "be converted" in Matt. 18:3, KJV.

2. *epistrepho* (1994), "to turn about, turn towards" (*epi*, "towards" and No. 1), is used transitively, and so rendered "convert" (of causing a person to turn) in Jas. 5:19-20. Elsewhere, where the KJV translates this verb, either in the middle voice and intransitive use, or the passive, the RV adheres to the middle voice significance, and translates by "turn again," Matt. 13:15; Mark 4:12; Luke 22:32; Acts 3:19; 28:27.

B. Noun.

epistrophe (1995), akin to A, No. 2, "a turning about, or round, conversion," is found in Acts 15:3. The word implies "a turning from and a turning to"; corresponding to these are repentance and faith; cf. "turned to God from idols," 1 Thess. 1:9. Divine grace is the efficient cause, human agency the responding effect.

CONVICT (including the KJV, "convince")

1. *elencho* (1651) signifies (a) "to convict, confute, refute," usually with the suggestion of putting the convicted person to shame; see Matt. 18:15, where more than telling the offender his fault is in view; it is used of "convicting" of sin, John 8:46; 16:8; gainsayers in regard to the faith, Titus 1:9; transgressors of the Law, Jas. 2:9; some texts have the verb in John 8:9; (b) "to reprove," 1 Cor. 14:24, RV (for KJV, "convince"), for the unbeliever is there viewed as being reproved for, or "convicted" of, his sinful state; so in Luke 3:19; it is used of reproving works, John 3:20; Eph. 5:11, 13; 1 Tim. 5:20; 2 Tim. 4:2; Titus 1:13; 2:15; all these speak of reproof by word of mouth. In Heb. 12:5 and Rev. 3:19, the word is used of reproving by action.

2. *exelencho* (1827), an intensive form of No. 1, "to convict thoroughly," is used of the Lord's future "conviction" of the ungodly, Jude 15.

COPY

hupodeigma (5262), (from *hupo*, "under," *deiknumi*, "to show"), properly denotes "what is shown below or privately"; it is translated "example," Heb. 8:5, KJV (RV, "copy"). It signifies (a) a sign suggestive of anything, the delineation or representation of a thing, and so, a figure, "copy"; in Heb. 9:23 the RV has "copies," for the KJV, "patterns"; (b) an example for imitation, John 13:15; Jas. 5:10; for warning, Heb. 4:11; 2 Pet. 2:6 (KJV "ensample").

CORBAN

korban (2878) signifies (a) "an offering," and was a Hebrew term for any sacrifice, whether by the shedding of blood or otherwise; (b) "a gift offered to God," Mark 7:11. Jews were much addicted to rash vows; a saying of the rabbis was, "It is hard for the parents, but the law is clear, vows must be kept."

CORNER, CORNERSTONE

1. *gonia* (1137), "an angle" (Eng., "*coin*"), signifies (a) "an external angle," as of the "corner" of a street, Matt. 6:5; or of a building, 21:42; Mark 12:10; Luke 20:17; Acts 4:11; 1 Pet. 2:7, "the corner stone or head-stone of the corner"; or the four extreme limits of the earth, Rev. 7:1; 20:8; (b) "an internal corner," a secret place, Acts 26:26.

2. *arche* (746), "a beginning" (its usual meaning), "first in time, order, or place," is used to denote the extremities or "corners" of a sheet, Acts 10:11; 11:5.

CORRECT, CORRECTION, CORRECTOR, CORRECTING

A. Nouns.

1. *diorthoma* (1357v) signifies "a reform, amendment, correction," lit., "a making straight." In Acts 24:2, lit., "reformations come about (or take place, lit., `become')," the RV has "evils are corrected," KJV, "worthy deeds are done"; there is no word for "worthy" or for "deeds" in the original. Some texts have *katorthoma*, which has the same meaning.

2. *epanorthosis* (1882), lit., "a restoration to an upright or right state" (*epi*, "to," *ana*, "up, or again," and *orthoo*, see No. 1), hence, "correction," is used of the Scripture in 2 Tim. 3:16, referring to improvement of life and character.

3. *paideutes* (3810) has two meanings, corresponding to the two meanings of the verb *paideuo* (see below) from which it is derived, (a) "a teacher, preceptor, corrector," Rom. 2:20 (KJV, "instructor"), (b) "a chastiser," Heb. 12:9, rendered "to chasten" (KJV, "which corrected"; lit., "chastisers").

B. Verb.

paideuo (381), "to train up a child" (*pais*), is rendered "correcting in 2 Tim. 2:25, RV, KJV, "instructing.

CORRUPT, verb and adjective. CORRUPTION, CORRUPTIBLE, INCORRUPTION, INCORRUPTIBLE

A. Verbs.

1. *kapeleuo* (2585) primarily signifies "to be a retailer, to peddle, to hucksterize" (from *kapelos*, "an inn-keeper, a petty retailer, especially of wine, a huckster, peddler," in contrast to *emporos*, "a merchant"); hence, "to get base gain by dealing in anything," and so, more generally, "to do anything for sordid personal advantage." It is found in 2 Cor. 2:17, with reference to the ministry of the gospel. The significance can be best ascertained by comparison and contrast with the verb *doloo* (likewise there only in the NT), "to handle deceitfully." The meanings are not identical. While both involve the deceitful dealing of adulterating the word of truth, *kapeleuo* has the broader significance of doing so in order to make dishonest gain. Those to whom the apostle refers in 2:17 are such as make merchandise of souls through covetousness, cf. Titus 1:11; 2 Pet. 2:3, 14-15; Jude 11, 16; Ezek. 13:19; accordingly "hucksterizing" would be the most appropriate rendering in this passage, while "handling deceitfully" is the right meaning in 4:2.

2. *phtheiro* (5351) signifies "to destroy by means of corrupting," and so "bringing into a worse state"; (a) with this significance it is used of the effect of evil company upon the manners of believers, and so of the effect of association with those who deny the truth and hold false doctrine, 1 Cor. 15:33 (this was a saying of the pagan poet Menander, which became a well known proverb); in 2 Cor. 7:2, of the effects of dishonorable dealing by bringing people to want (a charge made against the apostle); in 11:3, of the effects upon the minds (or thoughts) of believers by "corrupting" them "from the simplicity and the purity that is toward Christ"; in Eph. 4:22, intransitively, of the old nature in waxing "corrupt," "morally decaying, on the way to final ruin" (Moule), "after the lusts of deceit"; in Rev. 19:2, metaphorically, of the Babylonian harlot, in "corrupting" the inhabitants of the earth by her false religion.

(b) With the significance of destroying, it is used of marring a local church by leading it away from that condition of holiness of life and purity of doctrine in which it should abide, 1 Cor. 3:17 (KJV, "defile"), and of God's retributive destruction of the offender who is guilty of this sin (id.); of the effects of the work of false and abominable teachers upon themselves, 2 Pet. 2:12 (some texts have *kataphtheiro*; KJV, "shall utterly perish"), and Jude 10.

3. *diaphtheiro* (1311), (*dia*, "through," intensive, and No. 2), "to corrupt utterly, through and through," is said of men "corrupted in mind," whose wranglings result from the doctrines of false teachers, 1 Tim. 6:5 (the KJV wrongly renders it as an adjective,

"corrupt"). It is translated "destroyeth" instead of "corrupteth," in the RV of Luke 12:33, of the work of a moth, in Rev. 8:9, of the effect of divine judgments hereafter upon navigation, in 11:18, of the divine retribution of destruction upon those who have destroyed the earth; in 2 Cor. 4:16 it is translated "is decaying," said of the human body.

4. *kataphtheiro* (2704), (*kata*, "down," intensive, and No. 2), is said of men who are reprobate concerning the faith, "corrupted in mind" (KJV, "corrupt"), 2 Tim. 3:8. For 2 Pet. 2:12, RV, "shall be destroyed," see No. 2.

B. Nouns.

1. *phthora* (5356), connected with *phtheiro*, No. 2, above, signifies "a bringing or being brought into an inferior or worse condition, a destruction or corruption." It is used (a) physically, (1) of the condition of creation, as under bondage, Rom. 8:21; (2) of the effect of the withdrawal of life, and so of the condition of the human body in burial, 1 Cor. 15:42; (3) by metonymy, of anything which is liable to "corruption," 1 Cor. 15:50; (4) of the physical effects of merely gratifying the natural desires and ministering to one's own needs or lusts, Gal. 6:8, to the flesh in contrast to the Spirit, "corruption" being antithetic to "eternal life"; (5) of that which is naturally short-lived and transient, Col. 2:22, "perish"; (b) of the death and decay of beasts, 2 Pet. 2:12, RV, "destroyed" (first part of verse; lit., "unto...destruction"); (c) ethically, with a moral significance, (1) of the effect of lusts, 2 Pet. 1:4; (2) of the effect upon themselves of the work of false and immoral teachers, 2 Pet. 2:12, RV, "destroying"; KJV, "corruption," and verse 19.

2. *diaphthora* (1312), an intensified form of No. 1, "utter or thorough corruption," referring in the NT to physical decomposition and decay, is used six times, five of which refer, negatively, to the body of God's "Holy One," after His death, which body, by reason of His absolute holiness, could not see "corruption," Acts 2:27, 31; 13:34-35, 37; once it is used of a human body, that of David, which, by contrast, saw "corruption," Acts 13:36.

3. *aphtharsia* (861), "incorruption," (*a*, negative, with A, No. 2) is used (a) of the resurrection body, 1 Cor. 15:42, 50, 53-54; (b) of a condition associated with glory and honor and life, including perhaps a moral significance, Rom. 2:7; 2 Tim. 1:10; this is wrongly translated "immortality" in the KJV; (c) of love to Christ, that which is sincere and undiminishing, Eph. 6:24 (translated "uncorruptness").

4. *aphthoria* (5356d), similar to No. 3, "uncorruptness, free from (moral) taint," is said of doctrine, Titus 2:7 (some texts have *adiaphthoria*, the negative form of No. 2, above).

C. Adjectives.

1. *phthartos* (5349), "corruptible," akin to A, No. 2, is used (a) of man as being mortal, liable to decay (in contrast to God), Rom. 1:23; (b) of man's body as death-doomed, 1 Cor. 15:53-54; (c) of a crown of reward at the Greek games, 1 Cor. 9:25; (d) of silver and gold, as specimens or "corruptible" things, 1 Pet. 1:18; (e) of natural seed, 1 Pet. 1:23.

2. *aphthartos* (862), "not liable to corruption or decay, incorruptible" (*a*, negative, and A, No. 2), is used of (a) God, Rom. 1:23; 1 Tim. 1:17 (KJV, "immortal"); (b) the raised dead, 1 Cor. 15:52; (c) rewards given to the saints hereafter, metaphorically described as a "crown," 1 Cor. 9:25; (d) the eternal inheritance of the saints, 1 Pet. 1:4; (e) the Word of God, as incorruptible" seed, 1 Pet. 1:23; (f) a meek and quiet spirit, metaphorically spoken of as "incorruptible" apparel, 1 Pet. 3:4.

COST, COSTLINESS, COSTLY

A. Nouns.

1. *dapane* (1160), "expense, cost" (from *dapto*, "to tear"; from a root *dap*—meaning "to divide"), is found in Luke 14:28, in the Lord's illustration of counting the "cost" of becoming His disciple.

2. *timiotes* (5094), "costliness" (from *timios*, "valued at great price, precious"; see No. 3, below), is connected with *time*, "honor, price," and used in Rev. 18:19, in reference to Babylon.

B. Adjectives.

1. *timios* (5093), akin to A, No. 2, is translated "costly" in 1 Cor. 3:12, of "costly" stones, in a metaphorical sense (KJV, "precious"). Cf. Rev. 17:4; 18:12, 16; 21:19.

2. *poluteles* (4185), primarily, "the very end or limit" (from *polus*, "much," *telos*, "revenue"), with reference to price, of highest "cost," very expensive, is said of spikenard, Mark 14:3; raiment, 1 Tim. 2:9; metaphorically, of a meek and quiet spirit, 1 Pet. 3:4, "of great price"; cf. No. 1 and A, No. 2, above.

3. *polutimos* (4186), lit., "of great value" (see A, No. 2 and B, No. 1), is used of a pearl, Matt. 13:46; of spikenard, John 12:3 (RV, "very precious," KJV "very costly"). The comparative *polutimo* (v.l. *io) teros*, "much more precious," is used in 1 Pet. 1:7.

COUNCIL

1. *sumboulion* (4824), "a uniting in counsel," denotes (a) "counsel" which is given, taken and acted upon, e.g., Matt. 12:14, RV, "took counsel," for KJV, "held a council"; 22:15; hence (b) "a council," an assembly of counsellors or persons in consultation, Acts 25:12, of the "council" with which Festus conferred concerning Paul. The governors and procurators of provinces had a board of

advisers or assessors, with whom they took "counsel," before pronouncing judgment.

2. *sunedrion* (*4892*), properly, "a settling together" (*sun*, "together," *hedra*, "a seat"), hence, (a) "any assembly or session of persons deliberating or adjusting"; Prov. 22:10; Jer. 15:17, etc.; in the NT, e.g., Matt. 10:17; Mark 13:9; John 11:47, in particular, it denoted (b) "the Sanhedrin," the Great Council at Jerusalem, consisting of 71 members, namely, prominent members of the families of the high priest, elders and scribes. The Jews trace the origin of this to Num. 11:16. The more important causes came up before this tribunal. The Roman rulers of Judea permitted the Sanhedrin to try such cases, and even to pronounce sentence of death, with the condition that such a sentence should be valid only if confirmed by the Roman procurator. In John 11:47, it is used of a meeting of the Sanhedrin; in Acts 4:15, of the place of meeting.

COUNSEL

Old Testament

A. Verb.

ya'as (*3289*), "to advise, counsel, consult." While *ya'as* most often describes the "giving of good advice," Num. 24:14, the opposite is sometimes true, 2 Chron. 22:3. The idea of "decision" is expressed in Isa. 23:9.

B. Noun.

yo'es (*3289*), "counselor," means one who gives counsel; as messiah, Isa. 9:6; or as counsel for political and military leaders, 2 Sam. 15:12; 1 Chron. 13:1.

New Testament

A. Nouns.

1. *boule* (*1012*), Luke 23:51.
2. *sumboulos* (*4825*), "a councillor with," occurs in Rom. 11:34.

B. Verbs.

1. *bouleuo* (*1011*), "to take counsel, to resolve," is used in the middle voice in the NT, "took counsel" in Acts 5:33, KJV (RV translates *boulomai*); both in 27:39; in Luke 14:31, RV "take counsel" (KJV, "consulteth"); in John 11:53, KJV and RV (so the best mss.); 12:10, RV, "took counsel," for KJV, "consulted"; in 2 Cor. 1:17 (twice), "purpose."

2. *sumbouleuo* (*4823*), in the active voice, "to advise, to counsel," John 18:14, "gave counsel"; in Rev. 3:18, "I counsel"; in the middle voice, "to take counsel, consult," Matt. 26:4, RV, "took counsel together," for KJV, "consulted"; Acts 9:23, "took counsel" (RV adds "together"); in some mss. John 11:53.

COUNTENANCE

1. *opsis* (*3799*): only Rev. 1:16 has "countenance."

2. *prosopon* (*4383*), is translated "countenance" in Luke 9:29; Acts 2:28, and in the KJV of 2 Cor. 3:7 (RV, "face").

3. *eidea* (*2397*), Matt. 28:3.

COURAGE

A. Noun.

tharsos (*2294*), akin to *tharseo*, "to be of good cheer," is found in Acts 28:15.

B. Verb.

tharreo (*2292*) is translated by some form of the verb "to be of good courage," in the RV in five of the six places where it is used: 2 Cor. 5:6, "being of good courage" (KJV, "we are...confident"); 5:8, "we are of good courage" (KJV, "we are confident"); 7:16, "I am of good courage" (KJV, "I have confidence"); 10:1, "I am of good courage" (KJV, "I am bold"); 10:2, "show courage" (KJV, "be bold"); Heb. 13:6, "with good courage," lit., "being of good courage" (KJV, "boldly").

COURT

Old Testament

chatser (*2691*), "court; enclosure, settlement." The *chatser* ("settlement") was a place where people lived without an enclosure to protect them, Lev. 25:31. *chatser* also denotes a "settlement" of people outside the city wall, as a new quarter of the city, 2 Kings 22:14. The Book of Joshua includes Israel's victories in Canaan's major cities as well as the suburbs: "Ain, Remmon, and Ether, and Ashan; four cities and their villages..." Josh. 19:7; cf. 15:45, 47; 21:12.

The predominant usage of *chatser* is "court," whether of a house, a palace, or the temple. Each house generally had a courtyard surrounded by a wall or else one adjoined several homes, 2 Sam. 17:18; Ps. 84:3,10; 116:19.

New Testament

aule (*833*), primarily, "an uncovered space around a house, enclosed by a wall, where the stables were," hence was used to describe (a) "the courtyard of a house"; in the OT it is used of the "courts" of the tabernacle and Temple; in this sense it is found in the NT in Rev. 11:2; (b) "the courts in the dwellings of well-to-do folk," which usually had two, one exterior, between the door and the street (called the *proaulion*, or "porch," Mark 14:68.), the other, interior, surrounded by the buildings of the dwellings, as in Matt. 26:69 (in contrast to the room where the judges were sitting);

Mark 14:66; Luke 22:55; KJV, "hall"; RV "court" gives the proper significance, Matt. 26:3, 58; Mark 14:54; 15:16 (RV, "Praetorium"); Luke 11:21; John 18:15. It is here to be distinguished from the Praetorium, translated "palace."

COURTEOUS, COURTEOUSLY

1. *philophronos* (5390), lit., "friendly," or, more fully, "with friendly thoughtfulness" (*philos*, "friend," *phren*, "the mind"), is found in Acts 28:7, of the hospitality showed by Publius to Paul and his fellow-shipwrecked travelers.

2. *philanthropos* (5364), Acts 27:3, (cf. Eng., "philanthropically").

COUSIN

anepsios (431), in Col. 4:10 denotes a "cousin," not "nephew."

COVENANT (Noun and Verb)

Old Testament

berit (1285), "covenant; league; confederacy." *berit* refers to a political agreement; within Israel, 2 Sam. 3:12-13, 21; 5:3, or between nations, 1 Kings 15:19.

berit means "covenant," as a binding agreement between two parties, either individuals or nations, Gen. 21:32; 1 Sam. 18:3; 20:8, 16-18, 42; Ezek. 17:13.

In Israel, the kingship was based on "covenant": "...David made a covenant [KJV, "league"] with them [the elders of Israel] in Hebron before the Lord..." 2 Sam. 5:3. The "covenant" was based on their knowledge that God had appointed him, 2 Sam. 5:2; thus they became David's subjects, cf. 2 Kings 11:4, 17.

The great majority of occurrences of *berit* are of God's "covenants" with men, as in Gen. 6:18 above. The verbs used are important: "I will *establish* my covenant," Gen. 6:18—literally, "cause to stand" or "confirm." "I will *make* my covenant," Gen. 17:2, RSV. "He *declared* to you his covenant," Deut. 4:13. "My covenant which I *commanded* them..." Josh. 7:11. "I have *remembered* my covenant. Wherefore...I will bring you out from under the burdens of the Egyptians," Exod. 6:5-6. God will not reject Israel for their disobedience so as "to destroy them utterly, and to *break* my covenant with them..." Lev. 26:44. "He will not... forget the covenant...which he *sware* unto them," Deut. 4:31.

"Covenant" is parallel or equivalent to the Hebrew words *dabar* ("word"), *hoq* ("statute"), *piqqud*, "precepts"—Ps. 103:18, NASB, *'edah*, "testimony"—Ps. 25:10, *torah*, "law"—Ps. 78:10, and *hesed*, "lovingkindness"—Deut. 7:9, NASB. These words emphasize the authority and grace of God in making and keeping the "covenant," and the specific responsibility of man under the covenant.

The words of the "covenant" were written in a book, Exod. 24:4, 7; Deut. 31:24-26, and on stone tablets, Exod. 34:28.

Men "enter into," Deut. 29:12, or "join," Jer. 50:5, God's "covenant." They are to obey, Gen. 12:4, and "observe carefully" all the commandments of the "covenant," Deut. 4:6. But above all, the "covenant" calls Israel to "love the Lord thy God with all thine heart, and with all thy soul, and with all thy might," Deut. 6:5. God's "covenant" is a relationship of love and loyalty between the Lord and His chosen people.

The use of "Old Testament" and "New Testament" as the names for the two sections of the Bible indicates that God's "covenant" is central to the entire book. The Bible relates God's "covenant" purpose, that man be joined to Him in loving service and know eternal fellowship with Him through the redemption that is in Jesus Christ.

New Testament

diatheke (1242) primarily signifies "a disposition of property by will or otherwise." In its use in the Sept., it is the rendering of a Hebrew word meaning a "covenant" or agreement, from a verb signifying "to cut or divide," in allusion to a sacrificial custom in connection with "covenant-making," e.g., Gen. 15:10, "divided" Jer. 34:18-19. In contradistinction to the English word "covenant" (lit., "a coming together"), which signifies a mutual undertaking between two parties or more, each binding himself to fulfill obligations, it does not in itself contain the idea of joint obligation, it mostly signifies an obligation undertaken by a single person. For instance, in Gal. 3:17 it is used as an alternative to a "promise" (vv. 16-18). God enjoined upon Abraham the rite of circumcision, but His promise to Abraham, here called a "covenant," was not conditional upon the observance of circumcision, though a penalty attached to its nonobservance.

"The NT uses of the word may be analyzed as follows: (a) a promise or undertaking, human or divine, Gal. 3:15; (b) a promise or undertaking on the part of God, Luke 1:72; Acts 3:25; Rom. 9:4; 11:27; Gal. 3:17 Eph. 2:12; Heb. 7:22; 8:6, 8, 10; 10:16; (c) an agreement, a mutual undertaking, between God and Israel, see Deut. 29-30 (described as a 'commandment,' Heb. 7:18, cf. v. 22); Heb. 8:9; 9:20; (d) by metonymy, the token of the covenant, or promise, made to Abraham, Acts 7:8, (e) by metonymy, the record of the covenant, 2 Cor. 3:14; Heb. 9:4; cf. Rev. 11:19; (f) the basis, established by the death of Christ, on which the salvation of men is secured, Matt. 26:28; Mark 14:24; Luke 22:20; 1 Cor. 11:25; 2 Cor. 3:6; Heb. 10:29; 12:24; 13:20.

"This covenant is called the 'new,' Heb. 9:15, the 'second,' 8:7, the 'better,' 7:22. In Heb. 9:16-17, the translation is much disputed. There does not seem to be any sufficient reason for departing in these verses from the word used everywhere else.

COVENANT-BREAKERS

asunthetos (802), signifies "not covenant-keeping," i.e., refusing to abide by "covenants" made, "covenant-breaking," faithless, Rom. 1:31.

COVET, COVETOUS, COVETOUSNESS

A. Verbs.

1. *epithumeo* (1937), "to fix the desire upon," whether things good or bad; hence, "to long for, lust after, covet," is used with the meaning "to covet evilly" in Acts 20:33, of "coveting money and apparel"; so in Rom. 7:7; 13:9.

2. *zeloo* (2206) is rendered "covet earnestly," in 1 Cor. 12:31, KJV; RV, "desire earnestly," as in 14:39 (KJV "covet").

3. *orego* (3713), "to stretch after," is rendered "covet after" in 1 Tim. 6:10, KJV; RV, "reaching after."

B. Nouns.

1. *epithumetes* (1938), "a luster after" (akin to A, No. 1), is translated in 1 Cor. 10:6, in verbal form, "should not lust after."

2. *epithumia* (1939) denotes "coveting," Rom. 7:7-8, RV; KJV, "lust" and "concupiscence"; the commandment here referred to convicted him of sinfulness in his desires for unlawful objects besides that of gain.

3. *pleonexia* (4124), "covetousness," lit., "a desire to have more," always in a bad sense, is used in a general way in Mark 7:22 (plural, lit., "covetings," i.e., various ways in which "covetousness" shows itself); Rom. 1:29; Eph. 5:3; 1 Thess. 2:5. Elsewhere it is used, (a) of material possessions, Luke 12:15; 2 Pet. 2:3; 2 Cor. 9:5 (RV, "extortion"), lit., "as (a matter of) extortion" i.e., a gift which betrays the giver's unwillingness to bestow what is due; (b) of sensuality, Eph. 4:19, "greediness"; Col. 3:5 (where it is called "idolatry"); 2 Pet. 2:14 (KJV, "covetous practices").

C. Adjectives.

1. *pleonektes* (4123), lit., "(eager) to have more" (see B, No. 3), i.e., to have what belongs to others; hence, "greedy of gain, covetous," 1 Cor. 5:10-11; 6:10; Eph. 5:5 ("covetous man").

2. *philarguros* (5366), lit., "money-loving," is rendered "covetous" in the KJV of Luke 16:14 and 2 Tim. 3:2; RV, "lovers of money," the wider and due significance.

3. *aphilarguros* (866), No. 2, with negative prefix, is translated "without covetousness" in Heb. 13:5, KJV; RV, "free from the love of money." In 1 Tim. 3:3, the KJV has "not covetous," the RV, "no lover of money."

CRAFTINESS, CRAFTY

A. Noun.

panourgia (*3834*), lit., "all-working," i.e., doing everything (*pan*, "all," *ergon*, "work"), hence, "unscrupulous conduct, craftiness," is always used in a bad sense in the NT, Luke 20:23; 1 Cor. 3:19; 2 Cor. 4:2; 11:3; Eph. 4:14, KJV, "cunning craftiness."

B. Adjective.

panourgos (*3835*), "cunning, crafty," is found in 2 Cor. 12:16, where the apostle is really quoting an accusation made against him by his detractors.

C. Noun.

dolos (*1388*), primarily, "a bait," hence, "fraud, guile, deceit," Mark 14:1.

CREATE, CREATION, CREATOR, CREATURE
Old Testament

bara' (1254), "to create, make," The verb expresses creation out of nothing, Gen. 1:1; cf. Gen. 2:3; Isa. 40:26; 42:5. All other verbs for "creating" allow a much broader range of meaning, including forming an existing thing, or establishing an existing thing; they have both divine and human subjects, and are used in contexts where bringing something or someone into existence is not the issue.

Objects of the verb include the heavens and earth, Gen. 1:1; Isa. 40:26; 42:5; 45:18; 65:17; man, Gen. 1:27; 5:2; 6:7; Deut. 4:32; Ps. 89:47; Isa. 43:7; 45:12; Israel Isa. 43:1; Mal. 2:10; a new thing, Jer. 31:22; cloud and smoke, Isa. 4:5; north and south, Ps. 89:12; salvation and righteousness, Isa. 45:8; speech, Isa. 57:19; darkness, Isa. 45:7; wind, Amos 4:13; and a new heart, Ps. 51:10. A careful study of the passages where *bara'* occurs shows that in the few nonpoetic uses (primarily in Genesis), the writer uses scientifically precise language to demonstrate that God brought the object or concept into being from previously nonexistent material. Isa 45-65 has a special focus on Yahweh as Creator, and so powerful and able to deliver, Isa. 43:16-21; 44:12-20; 45:12; 46:1-7; 65:17-25.

Though a precisely correct technical term to suggest cosmic, material creation from nothing, *bara'* is a rich theological vehicle for communicating the sovereign power of God, who originates and regulates all things to His glory.

qanah (7069), "to get, acquire, earn," and so as a figurative extension, this verb means "create," Gen. 14:19, 22.

'asah (6213), "to create, do, make," Only when *'asah* is parallel to *bara'* that we can be sure that it implies creation, Gen. 2:3, and then *'asah* may have a focus of manipulating existing material.

But one must exhibit caution, it is unwarranted to overly refine the meaning of *'asah* to suggest that it means creation from something, as opposed to creation from nothing. Only context can determine its special nuance. It can mean either, depending upon the situation.

New Testament

C

A. Verb.

ktizo (2936), used among the Greeks to mean the founding of a place, a city or colony, signifies, in Scripture, "to create," always of the act of God, whether (a) in the natural creation, Mark 13:19; Rom. 1:25 (where the title "The Creator" translates the article with the aorist participle of the verb); 1 Cor. 11:9; Eph. 3:9; Col. 1:16; 1 Tim. 4:3; Rev. 4:11; 10:6, or (b) in the spiritual creation, Eph. 2:10, 15; 4:24; Col. 3:10.

B. Nouns.

1. *ktisis* (2937), primarily "the act of creating," or "the creative act in process," has this meaning in Rom. 1:20 and Gal. 6:15. Like the English word "creation," it also signifies the product of the "creative" act, the "creature," as in Mark 16:15, RV; Rom. 1:25; 8:19; Col. 1:15 etc.; in Heb. 9:11, KJV, "building." In Mark 16:15 and Col. 1:23 its significance has special reference to mankind in general. As to its use in Gal. 6:15 and 2 Cor. 5:17, in the former, apparently, the reference is to the creative act of God, whereby a man is introduced into the blessing of salvation, in contrast to circumcision done by human hands, which the Judaizers claimed was necessary to that end. In 2 Cor. 5:17 the reference is to what the believer is in Christ; in consequence of the creative act he has become a new creature.

2. *ktisma* (2938) has the concrete sense, "the created thing, the creature, the product of the creative act," 1 Tim. 4:4; Jas. 1:18; Rev. 5:13; 8:9.

3. *ktistes* (2939), among the Greeks, the founder of a city, etc., denotes in Scripture "the Creator," 1 Pet. 4:19 (cf. Rom. 1:20, under B, No. 1, above).

CROSS, CRUCIFY

A. Noun.

stauros (4716) denotes, primarily, "an upright pale or stake." On such malefactors were nailed for execution. Both the noun and the verb *stauroo*, "to fasten to a stake or pale," are originally to be distinguished from the ecclesiastical form of a two beamed "cross." The shape of the latter had its origin in ancient Chaldea, and was used as the symbol of the god Tammuz (being in the shape of the mystic Tau, the initial of his name) in that country and in adjacent lands, including Egypt. By the middle of the 3rd

cent. A.D. the churches had either departed from, or had traves-
tied, certain doctrines of the Christian faith. In order to increase
the prestige of the apostate ecclesiastical system pagans were received into the churches apart from regeneration by faith, and
were permitted largely to retain their pagan signs and symbols.
Hence the Tau or T, in its most frequent form, with the cross-piece
lowered, was adopted to stand for the "cross" of Christ.

The method of execution was borrowed by the Greeks and Romans from the Phoenicians. The *stauros* denotes (a) "the cross, or
stake itself," e.g., Matt. 27:32; (b) "the crucifixion suffered," e.g.,
1 Cor. 1:17-18, where "the word of the cross," RV, stands for the
gospel; Gal. 5:11, where crucifixion is metaphorically used of the
renunciation of the world, that characterizes the true Christian
life; 6:12, 14; Eph. 2:16; Phil. 3:18.

The judicial custom by which the condemned person carried his
stake to the place of execution, was applied by the Lord to those
sufferings by which His faithful followers were to express their fellowship with Him, e.g., Matt. 10:38.

B. Verbs.

1. *stauroo* (*4717*) signifies (a) "the act of crucifixion," e.g., Matt.
20:19; (b) metaphorically, "the putting off of the flesh with its passions and lusts," a condition fulfilled in the case of those who are
"of Christ Jesus," Gal. 5:24, RV; so of the relationship between the
believer and the world, 6:14.

2. *sustauroo* (*4957*), "to crucify with," is used (a) of actual "crucifixion" in company with another, Matt. 27:44; Mark 15:32; John
19:32; (b) metaphorically, of spiritual identification with Christ in
His death, Rom. 6:6, and Gal. 2:20.

3. *anastauroo* (*388*) (*ana*, again) is used in Heb. 6:6 of Hebrew
apostates, who as merely nominal Christians, in turning back to
Judaism, were thereby virtually guilty of "crucifying" Christ
again.

4. *prospegnumi* (*4362*), "to fix or fasten to anything" (*pros*, "to,"
pegnumi, "to fix"), is used of the "crucifixion" of Christ, Acts 2:23.

CROWN (Noun and Verb)

A. Nouns.

1. *stephanos* (*4735*), primarily, "that which surrounds, as a wall
or crowd" (from *stepho*, "to encircle"), denotes (a) "the victor's
crown," the symbol of triumph in the games or some such contest;
hence, by metonymy, a reward or prize; (b) "a token of public
honor" for distinguished service, military prowess, etc., or of nup-
tial joy, or festal gladness, especially at the parousia of kings. It
was woven as a garland of oak, ivy, parsley, myrtle, or olive, or in
imitation of these in gold. In some passages the reference to the
games is clear, 1 Cor. 9:25; 2 Tim. 4:8 ("crown of righteousness"); it

may be so in 1 Pet. 5:4, where the fadeless character of "the crown of glory" is set in contrast to the garlands of earth. In other passages it stands as an emblem of life, joy, reward and glory, Phil. 4:1; 1 Thess. 2:19; Jas. 1:12 ("crown of life "); Rev. 2:10 (ditto); 3:11; 4:4, 10: of triumph, 6:2; 9:7; 12:1; 14:14.

It is used of "the crown of thorns" which the soldiers plaited and put on Christ's head, Matt. 27:29; Mark 15:17; John 19:2, 5. At first sight this might be taken as an alternative for *diadema*, "a kingly crown."

2. *diadema* (*1238*) is never used as *stephanos* is; it is always the symbol of kingly or imperial dignity, and is translated "diadem" instead of "crown" in the RV, of the claims of the Dragon, Rev. 12:3; 13:1; 19:12.

B. Verb.

stephanoo (*4737*), "to crown," conforms in meaning to *stephanos;* it is used of the reward of victory in the games, in 2 Tim. 2:5; of the glory and honor bestowed by God upon man in regard to his position in creation, Heb. 2:7; of the glory and honor bestowed upon the Lord Jesus in His exaltation, v. 9.

CRY (Noun and Verb), CRYING

Old Testament

tsa'aq (*6817*), "to cry, cry out, call." This word is often used in the sense of "crying out" for help, Gen. 41:55; Exod. 14:10; Isa. 46:7.

za'aq (*2199*), "to cry, cry out, call." *za'aq* is perhaps most frequently used to indicate the "crying out" for aid in time of emergency, especially "crying out" for divine aid, Judg. 3:9, 15; 6:7; 10:10; Jer. 11:12; Jonah 1:5. That *za'aq* means more than a normal speaking volume is indicated in appeals to the king, 2 Sam. 19:28.

The word may imply a "crying out" in distress, 1 Sam. 4:13, a "cry" of horror, 1 Sam. 5:10, or a "cry" of sorrow, 2 Sam. 13:19. Used figuratively, it is said that "the stone shall cry out of the wall," Hab. 2:11 of a house that is built by means of evil gain.

New Testament

A. Nouns.

1. *krauge* (*2906*), an onomatopoeic word, is used in Matt. 25:6; Luke 1:42 (some mss. have *phone*); Acts 23:9, RV, "clamor"; Eph. 4:31, "clamor"; Heb. 5:7; Rev. 21:4, "crying." Some mss. have it in Rev. 14:18 (the most authentic have *phone*).

2. *boe* (*995*), especially "a cry for help," an onomatopoeic word (cf. Eng., "boo"), connected with *boao* (see B, No. 1), is found in Jas. 5:4.

B. Verbs.

1. *boao* (*994*), akin to A, No. 2, signifies (a) "to raise a cry,"

whether of joy, Gal. 4:27, or vexation, Acts 8:7; (b) "to speak with a strong voice," Matt. 3:3; Mark 1:3; 15:34; Luke 3:4; 9:38 (some mss. have **anaboao** here: see No. 2); John 1:23; Acts 17:6; 25:24 (some mss. have **epiboao**, No. 3, here); (c) "to cry out for help," Luke 18:7, 38.

2. **anaboao** (310), **ana,** "up," intensive, and No. 1, "to lift up the voice, cry out," is said of Christ at the moment of His death, a testimony to His supernatural power in giving up His life, Matt. 27:46; in some mss. in Mark 15:8, of the shouting of a multitude; in some mss. in Luke 9:38, of the "crying" out of a man in a company (see No. 1).

3. **epiboao** (1916), **epi,** "upon," intensive, and No. 1, "to cry out, exclaim vehemently," is used in some mss. in Acts 25:24 (see No. 1.)

4. **krazo** (2896), akin to A, No. 1, "to cry out," an onomatopoeic word, used especially of the "cry" of the raven; then, of any inarticulate cries, from fear, pain etc.; of the "cry" of a Canaanitish woman, Matt. 15:22 (so the best mss., instead of **kraugazo**); of the shouts of the children in the Temple, Matt. 21:15; of the people who shouted for Christ to be crucified, 27:23; Mark 15:13-14; of the "cry" of Christ on the Cross at the close of His sufferings, Matt. 27:50; Mark 15:39 (see No. 2, above).

5. **anakrazo** (349), **ana,** "up," intensive, and No. 4, signifies "to cry out loudly," Mark 1:23; 6:49; Luke 4:33; 8:28; 23:18.

6. **kraugazo** (2905), a stronger form of No. 4, "to make a clamor or outcry" (A, No. 1), is used in Matt. 12:19, in a prophecy from Isaiah of Christ; in Luke 4:41 (in the best mss., instead of **krazo**); John 11:43; 12:13 (in the best mss.); 18:40; 19:6, 12, 15; Acts 22:23.

CRYSTAL

A. Noun.

krustallos (2930), from **kruos,** "ice," and hence properly anything congealed and transparent, denotes "crystal," a kind of precious stone, Rev. 4:6; 22:1. Rock crystal is pure quartz; it crystallizes in hexagonal prisms, each with a pyramidical apex.

B. Verb.

krustallizo (2929), "to be of crystalline brightness and transparency, to shine like crystal," is found in Rev. 21:11, where it is said of Christ as the "Light-giver" (**phoster**) of the heavenly city (not **phos,** "light," RV and KJV). Possibly there the verb has a transitive force, "to transform into crystal splendor," as of the effect of Christ upon His saints.

CUBIT

Old Testament

'ammah (520), "cubit," a primary unit of linear measurement in the Old Testament, possibly based on the Egyptian system. A "cubit" ordinarily was the distance from one's elbow to the tip of the middle finger.

There was an official "cubit" in Egypt. In fact, there were both a shorter "cubit" (17.6 inches) and a longer "cubit" (20.65 inches). The Siloam inscription states that the Siloam tunnel was 1,200 "cubits" long. This divided by its measurement in feet (1,749) demonstrates that as late as Hezekiah's day, cf. 2 Chron. 32:4, the "cubit" was about 17.5 inches or the shorter Egyptian cubit. Ezekiel probably used the Babylonian "cubit" in describing the temple. The Egyptian shorter cubit is only about three inches shorter than the longer cubit; on the other hand, the Babylonian shorter cubit was about four-fifths the length of the official royal "cubit," about a handbreadth shorter: "And behold a wall on the outside of the house round about, and in the man's hand a measuring reed of six cubits long by the cubit and a handbreadth..." Ezek. 40:5. In other words, it was the width of seven palms rather than six.

New Testament

pechus (*4083*), Matt. 6:27; Luke 12:25; John 21:8; Rev. 21:17; see also above.

CUP

poterion (*4221*), a diminutive of *poter*, denotes, primarily, a "drinking vessel"; hence, "a cup" (a) literal, as, e.g., in Matt. 10:42. The "cup" of blessing, 1 Cor. 10:16, is so named from the third (the fourth according to Edersheim) "cup" in the Jewish Passover feast, over which thanks and praise were given to God. This connection is not to be rejected on the ground that the church at Corinth was unfamiliar with Jewish customs. That the contrary was the case, see 5:7; (b) figurative, of one's lot or experience, joyous or sorrowful (frequent in the Psalms; cf. Ps. 116:18, "cup of salvation"); in the NT it is used most frequently of the sufferings of Christ, Matt. 20:22-23; 26:39; Mark 10:38-39; 14:36; Luke 22:42; John 18:11; also of the evil deeds of Babylon, Rev. 17:4; 18:6; of divine punishments to be inflicted, Rev. 14:10; 16:19. Cf. Ps. 11:6; 75:8; Isa. 51:17; Jer. 25:15; Ezek. 23:32-34; Zech. 12:2.

CURSE, CURSING (Noun and Verb), CURSED, ACCURSED

Old Testament

A. Verbs.

qalal (*7043*), "to be trifling, light, swift; to curse." The idea of "to be swifter" is expressed in 2 Sam. 1:23; 1 Sam. 18:23.

qalal frequently includes the idea of "cursing" or "scorning or mocking, Exod. 21:17; 1 Sam. 17:43; Job 24:18; Isa 65:20.

The causative form of the verb sometimes expressed the idea of "lightening, lifting a weight," and so being in an easier circumstance, 1 Sam. 6:5; Exod. 18:22.

'arar (779), "to curse," usually parallel with "bless." The two "curses" in Gen. 3 are in bold contrast to the two blessings ("And God blessed them...") in Gen. 1. The covenant with Abraham includes: "I will bless them that bless thee, and curse [different root] him that curseth thee..." Gen. 12:3. Compare Jeremiah's "Cursed be the man that trusteth in man" and "Blessed is the man that trusteth in the Lord," Jer. 17:5, 7.

God alone truly "curses." It is a revelation of His justice, in support of His claim to absolute obedience. Men may claim God's "curses" by committing their grievances to God and trusting in His righteous judgment, cf. Ps. 109:26-31; Christ alone redeems from the curse of the law, Gal. 3:13.

B. Noun.

'alah (423), "curse; oath." *'alah* basically refers to "the execution of a proper oath to legalize a covenant or agreement." As a noun, *'alah* refers to the "oath" itself, Gen. 24:41; Lev. 5:1. So *'alah* functions as a "curse" sanctioning a pledge or commission, and it can close an agreement or covenant. On the other hand, the word sometimes represents a "curse" against someone else, whether his identity is known or not.

New Testament

A. Nouns.

1. *ara* (685), in its most usual meaning, "a malediction, cursing" (its other meaning is "a prayer"), is used in Rom. 3:14.

2. *katara* (2671), *kata*, "down," intensive, and No. 1, denotes an "execration, imprecation, curse," uttered out of malevolence, Jas. 3:10; 2 Pet. 2:14; or pronounced by God in His righteous judgment, as upon a land doomed to barrenness, Heb. 6:8; upon those who seek for justification by obedience, in part or completely, to the Law, Gal. 3:10, 13; in this 13th verse it is used concretely of Christ, as having "become a curse" for us, i.e., by voluntarily undergoing on the cross the appointed penalty of the "curse." He thus was identified, on our behalf, with the doom of sin.

3. *anathema* (33), transliterated from the Greek, is frequently used in the Sept., where it translates the Heb. *cherem*, "a thing devoted to God," whether (a) for His service, as the sacrifices, Lev. 27:28 (cf. *anathema*, a votive offering, gift), or (b) for its destruction, as an idol, Deut. 7:26, or a city, Josh. 6:17. Later it acquired the more general meaning of "the disfavor of Jehovah," e.g., Zech. 14:11. This is the meaning in the NT. It is used of (a) the sentence pronounced, Acts 23:14 (lit., "cursed themselves with a curse"); (b) of the object on which the "curse" is laid, "accursed"; in the following, the RV keeps to the word "anathema," Rom. 9:3; 1 Cor.

12:3; 16:22; Gal. 1:8-9, all of which the KJV renders by "accursed" except 1 Cor. 16:22, where it has "Anathema." In Gal. 1:8-9, the apostle declares in the strongest manner that the gospel he preached was the one and only way of salvation, and that to preach another was to nullify the death of Christ.

4. *katathema* (*2652*), or, as in some mss., the longer form *katanathema*, is stronger than No. 3 (*kata*, intensive), and denotes, by metonymy, "an accursed thing" (the object "cursed" being put for the "curse" pronounced), Rev. 22:3.

B. Verbs.

1. *anathematizo* (*332*), akin to No. 3, signifies "to declare anathema," i.e., "devoted to destruction, accursed, to curse," Mark 14:71, or "to bind by a curse," Acts 23:12, 14, 21.

2. *katanathematizo* (*2653*), a strengthened form of No. 1, denotes "to utter curses against," Matt. 26:74; cf. Mark's word concerning the same occasion (No. 1).

3. *kataraomai* (*2672*), akin to A, No. 2, primarily signifies "to pray against, to wish evil against a person or thing"; hence "to curse," Matt. 25:41; Mark 11:21; Luke 6:28; Rom. 12:14; Jas. 3:9. Some mss. have it in Matt. 5:44.

C. Adjectives.

1. *epikataratos* (*1944*), "cursed, accursed" (*epi* "upon," and A, No. 2), is used in Gal. 3:10, 13.

2. *eparatos* (*1883a*), "accursed," is found, in the best mss., in John 7:49, RV, "accursed," instead of No. 1.

CUSTOM (Usage), ACCUSTOM (Verb)

A. Nouns.

1. *ethos* (*1485*) denotes (a) "a custom, usage, prescribed by law," Acts 6:14; 15:1; 25:16; "a rite or ceremony," Luke 2:42; (b) a "custom, habit, manner," Luke 22:39; John 19:40; Heb. 10:25 (KJV, "manner").

2. *sunetheia* (*4914*), (*sun*, "with," *ethos*, see No. 1), denotes (a) "an intercourse, intimacy," a meaning not found in the NT; (b) "a custom, customary usage," John 18:39; 1 Cor. 11:16; "or force of habit," 1 Cor. 8:7, RV, "being used to" (some mss. here have *suneidis*, "conscience"; whence KJV, "with conscience of").

B. Verbs.

1. *ethizo* (*1480*), akin to A, No. 1, signifies "to accustom," or in the passive voice, "to be accustomed." In the participial form it is equivalent to a noun, "custom, Luke 2:27.

2. *etho* (*1486*), "to be accustomed," as in the case of No. 1, is used in the passive participle as a noun, signifying "a custom," Luke 4:16; Acts 17:2 (KJV, "manner"; RV, "custom"); in Matt. 17:15 and Mark 10:1, "was wont."

D

DAILY (Adjective)

1. *epiousios* (*1967*) is found in Matt. 6:11 and Luke 11:3. Its derivation likely is from *epi*, and *eimi*, "to go," so then, (bread) for going on, i.e., for the morrow and after, or (bread) coming (for us).

2. *ephemeros* (*2184*) signifies "for the day," cf. Eng., "ephemeral," Jas. 2:15.

3. *kathemerinos* (*2522*) means, lit., "according to the day," so, "day by day, daily," Acts 6:1.

DAINTY

liparos (*3045*) properly signifies "oily, or anointed with oil" (from *lipos*, "grease," connected with *aleipho*, "to anoint"); it is said of things which pertain to delicate and sumptuous living; hence, "dainty," Rev. 18:14.

DAMSEL

1. *korasion* (*2877*), a diminutive of *kore*, "a girl," denotes "a little girl" (properly a colloquial word, often used disparagingly, but not so in later writers); in the NT it is used only in familiar conversation, Matt. 9:24-25 (KJV, "maid"); 14:11; Mark 5:41-42; 6:22, 28.

2. *paidion* (*3813*), a diminutive of *pais*, denotes "a young child (male or female)" in the KJV of Mark 5:39-41.

3. *paidiske* (*3814*) denotes "a young girl, or a female slave"; "damsel," KJV, in John 18:17; Acts 12:13; 16:16; RV "maid" in each case.

DANCE

orcheo (*3738*), (cf. Eng., "orchestra"), probably originally signified "to lift up," as of the feet; hence, "to leap with regularity of motion." It is always used in the middle voice, Matt. 11:17; 14:6; Mark 6:22; Luke 7:32. The performance by the daughter of Herodias is the only clear instance of artistic dancing, a form introduced from Greek customs.

DANGER, DANGEROUS

A. Verb.

kinduneuo (*2793*) properly signifies "to run a risk, face danger," but is used in the NT in the sense of "being in danger, jeopardy," Acts 19:27, 40. It is translated "were in jeopardy" in Luke 8:23, and "stand we in jeopardy," 1 Cor. 15:30.

B. Adjectives.

1. *enochos* (*1777*), lit., "held in, contained in," hence, "bound under obligation to, liable to, subject to," is used in the sense of being in "danger" of the penal effect of a misdeed, i.e.. in a forensic sense, signifying the connection of a person with (a) his crime, "guilty of an eternal sin," Mark 3:29, RV; (b) the trial or tribunal, as a result of which sentence is passed, Matt. 5:21-22, "the judgment," "the council"; *enochos* here has the obsolete sense of control; (c) the penalty itself, 5:22, "the hell of fire," and, with the translation "worthy" (KJV, "guilty"), of the punishment determined to be inflicted on Christ, Matt. 26:66 and Mark 14:64, "death"; (d) the person or thing against whom or which the offense is committed 1 Cor. 11:27, "guilty," the crime being against "the body and blood of the Lord"; Jas. 2:10, "guilty" of an offense against all the Law, because of a breach of one commandment.

2. *episphales* (*2000*), lit., "prone to fall," hence, "insecure, dangerous," is used in Acts 27:9.

DARE, DARING, DURST

A. Verb.

tolmao (*5111*) signifies "to dare," (a) in the sense of not dreading or shunning through fear, Matt. 22:46; Mark 12:34; Mark 15:43, "boldly," lit., "having dared, went in"; Luke 20:40; John 21:12; Acts 5:13; 7:32; Rom. 15:18; 2 Cor. 10:2, RV, "show courage," (KJV, "be bold"); 10:12, RV, "are (not) bold," 11:21; Phil. 1:14, "are bold"; Jude 9; (b) in the sense of bearing, enduring, bringing oneself to do a thing, Rom. 5:7; 1 Cor. 6:1. Cf. *apotolmao*, "to be very bold," Rom. 10:20.

B. Adjective.

tolmetes (*5113*), akin to A, "daring," is used in 2 Pet. 2:10, RV, "daring" (KJV "presumptuous"), "shameless and irreverent daring."

DARK, DARKEN, DARKLY, DARKNESS

A. Adjectives.

1. *skoteinos* (*4652*), "full of darkness, or covered with darkness," is translated "dark" in Luke 11:36; "full of darkness," in Matt. 6:23 and Luke 11:34, where the physical condition is figurative of the moral. The group of *skot*— words is derived from a root *ska*—, meaning "to cover." The same root is to be found in *skene*, "a tent."

2. *auchmeros* (*850*), from *auchmos*, "drought produced by excessive heat," hence signifies "dry, murky, dark," 2 Pet. 1:19.

B. Nouns.

1. *skotia* (4653) is used (a) of physical darkness, "dark," John 6:17, lit., "darkness had come on," and 20:1, lit., "darkness still being"; (b) of secrecy, in general, whether what is done therein is good or evil, Matt. 10:27; Luke 12:3; (c) of spiritual or moral "darkness," emblematic of sin, as a condition of moral or spiritual depravity, Matt. 4:16; John 1:5; 8:12; 12:35, 46; 1 John 1:5; 2:8-9, 11.

2. *skotos* (4655), an older form than No. 1, grammatically masculine, is found in some mss. in Heb. 12:18.

3. *skotos* (4655), the equivalent of No. 1; (a) of "physical darkness," Matt. 27:45; 2 Cor. 4:6; (b) of "intellectual darkness," Rom. 2:19 (cf. C, No. 1); (c) of "blindness," Acts 13:11; (d) by metonymy, of the "place of punishment," e.g., Matt. 8:12; 2 Pet. 2:17; Jude 13; (e) metaphorically, of "moral and spiritual darkness," e.g., Matt. 6:23; Luke 1:79; 11:35; John 3:19; Acts 26:18; 2 Cor. 6:14; Eph. 6:12; Col. 1:13; 1 Thess. 5:4-5; 1 Pet. 2:9; 1 John 1:6; (f) by metonymy, of "those who are in moral or spiritual darkness," Eph. 5:8; (g) of "evil works," Rom. 13:12; Eph. 5:11, (h) of the "evil powers that dominate the world," Luke 22:53; (i) "of secrecy" [as in No. 1, (b)].

4. *zophos* (2217) denotes "the gloom of the nether world," hence, "thick darkness, darkness that may be felt"; it is rendered "darkness" in Heb. 12:18; 2 Pet. 2:4 and Jude 6; in 2 Pet. 2:17, RV, "blackness," KJV, "mists"; in Jude 13, RV and KJV, blackness.

C. Verbs.

1. *skotizo* (4654), "to deprive of light, to make dark," is used in the NT in the passive voice only, (a) of the heavenly bodies Matt. 24:29; Mark 13:24; Rev. 8:12; (b) metaphorically, of the mind, Rom. 1:21; 11:10; (some mss. have it in Luke 23:45).

2. *skotoo* (4656), "to darken," is used (a) of the heavenly bodies, Rev. 9:2; 16:10; (b) metaphorically, of the mind, Eph. 4:18.

DAUGHTER, DAUGHTER-IN-LAW

1. *thugater* (2364), "a daughter," (etymologically, Eng., "daughter" is connected), is used of (a) the natural relationship (frequent in the gospels); (b) spiritual relationship to God, 2 Cor. 6:18; (c) the inhabitants of a city or region, Matt. 21:5; John 12:15 ("of Zion"); (d) the women who followed Christ to Calvary, Luke 23:28; (e) women of Aaron's posterity, Luke 1:5.

2. *thugatrion* (2365), a diminutive of No. 1, denotes "a little daughter," Mark 5:23; 7:25.

3. *parthenos* (3933), "a maiden, virgin," e.g., Matt. 1:23, signifies a virgin-daughter in 1 Cor. 7:36-38 (RV); in Rev. 14:4, it is used of chaste persons.

4. *numphe* (3565), (Eng., "nymph"), denotes "a bride," John 3:29; also "a daughter-in-law," Matt. 10:35; Luke 12:53.

DAY

Old Testament

yom (3117), "daylight; day; time; moment; year." *yom* has several meanings. The word represents the period of "daylight," Gen. 8:22. The word denotes a period of twenty-four hours, Gen. 39:10. *yom* can also signify a period of time of unspecified duration, Gen. 2:3. Another nuance appears in Gen. 2:17, where the word represents a "point of time" or "a moment." Finally, when used in the plural, the word may represent "year," Exod. 13:10.

yom can mean "first," as in a series, Gen. 25:31. It may also mean "one day," or "about this day," Gen. 39:11. When used with the definite article *ha*, the noun may mean "today," as it does in Gen. 4:14, or refer to some particular "day," 1 Sam. 1:4, and the "daytime," Neh. 4:16.

The "day of the Lord" is used to denote both the end of the age (eschatologically) or some occurrence during the present age (non-eschatologically). It may be a day of either judgment or blessing, or both, cf. Isa. 2.

It is noteworthy that Hebrew people did not divide the period of daylight into regular hourly periods, whereas nighttime was divided into three watches, Exod. 14:24; Judg. 7:19. The beginning of a "day" is sometimes said to be dusk, Esth. 4:16, and sometimes dawn, Deut. 28:66-67.

New Testament

A. Nouns.

1. *hemera* (2250), "a day," is used of (a) the period of natural light, Gen. 1:5; Prov. 4:18; Mark 4:35; (b) the same, but figuratively, for a period of opportunity for service, John 9:4; Rom. 13:13; (c) one period of alternate light and darkness, Gen. 1:5; Mark 1:13; (d) a period of undefined length marked by certain characteristics, Rom. 2:5; (e) an appointed time, Ecc. 8:6; Eph. 4:30; (f) of a time of life, Luke 1:17-18 ("years").

As the "day" throws light upon things that have been in darkness, the word is often associated with the passing of judgment upon circumstances, 1 Cor. 4:3; Rev. 1:10.

The phrases "the day of Christ," Phil. 1:10; 2:16; "the day of Jesus Christ," 1:6; "the day of the Lord Jesus," 1 Cor. 5:5; 2 Cor. 1:14; "the day of our Lord Jesus Christ," 1 Cor. 1:8, denote the time of the Parousia of Christ with His saints, subsequent to the Rapture, 1 Thess. 4:16-17. In 2 Pet. 1:19 this is spoken of simply as the day.

In the NT "the day of the Lord" is mentioned in 1 Thess. 5:2 and 2 Thess. 2:2, RV, where the apostle's warning is that the church at Thessalonica should not be deceived by thinking that "the Day of the Lord is now present." This period will not begin till the circumstances mentioned in verses 3 and 4 take place.

2. *auge* (*827*), "brightness, bright, shining, as of the sun"; hence, "the beginning of daylight," is translated "break of day" in Acts 20:11.

B. Adverb.

ennucha (*1773***), lit., "in night," signifies "very early, yet in the night," "a great while before day," Mark 1:35.

DAYSPRING

anatole (*395*), lit., "a rising up," is used of the rising of the sun and stars; it chiefly means the east, as in Matt. 2:1, etc.; rendered "dayspring" in Luke 1:78.

DAY-STAR

phosphoros (*5459*), (Eng., "phosphorus," lit., "light-bearing," is used of the morning star, as the light-bringer, 2 Pet. 1:19, where it indicates the arising of the light of Christ as the personal fulfillment, in the hearts of believers, of the prophetic Scriptures concerning His coming to receive them to Himself.

DEACON

diakonos (*1249*), (Eng., "deacon"), primarily denotes a "servant," whether as doing servile work, or as an attendant rendering free service, without particular reference to its character. It occurs in the NT of domestic servants, John 2:5, 9; the civil ruler, Rom. 13:4; Christ, Rom. 15:8; Gal. 2:17; the followers of Christ in relation to their Lord, John 12:26; Eph. 6:21; Col. 1:7; 4:7; the followers of Christ in relation to one another, Matt. 20:26; 23:11, Mark 9:35; 10:43; the servants of Christ in the work of preaching and teaching, 1 Cor. 3:5; 2 Cor. 3:6; 6:4; 11:23; Eph. 3:7; Col. 1:23, 25; 1 Thess. 3:2; 1 Tim. 4:6; those who serve in the churches, Rom. 16:1 (used of a woman here only in NT); Phil. 1:1; 1 Tim. 3:8, 12; false apostles, servants of Satan, 2 Cor. 11:15.

diakonos is, generally speaking, to be distinguished from *doulos*, "a bondservant, slave"; *diakonos* views a servant in relationship to his work, *doulos* views him in relationship to his master. See, e.g., Matt. 22:2-14; those who bring in the guests (vv. 3-4, 6, 8, 10) are *douloi*; those who carry out the king's sentence (v. 13) are *diakonoi*.

DEAD

A. Noun and Adjective.

nekros (*3498*) is used of (a) the death of the body, cf. Jas. 2:26, its most frequent sense: (b) the actual spiritual condition of unsaved men, Matt. 8:22; John 5:25; Eph. 2:1, 5; 5:14; Phil. 3:11; Col. 2:13; cf. Luke 15:24: (c) the ideal spiritual condition of believers in regard to sin, Rom. 6:11: (d) a church in declension, inasmuch as in that

state it is inactive and barren, Rev. 3:1: (e) sin, which apart from
law cannot produce a sense of guilt, Rom. 7:8: (f) the body of the
believer in contrast to his spirit, Rom. 8:10: (g) the works of the
Law, inasmuch as, however good in themselves, Rom. 7:13, they
cannot produce life, Heb. 6:1; 9:14: (h) the faith that does not produce works, Jas. 2:17, 26; cf. v. 20.

B. Verbs.

1. *nekroo* (3499), "to put to death," is used in the active voice in
the sense of destroying the strength of, depriving of power, with
reference to the evil desires which work in the body, Col. 3:5. In
the passive voice it is used of Abraham's body as being "as good as
dead," Rom. 4:19 with Heb. 11:12.

2. *thanatoo* (2289), "to put to death," Matt. 10:21.

DEADLY

1. *thanatephoros* (2287), lit., "death-bearing, deadly," is used in
Jas. 3:8.

2. *thanasimos* (2286), from *thanatos* (akin to No. 1), "belonging to
death, or partaking of the nature of death," is used in Mark 16:18.

HALF DEAD

hemithanes (2253), from *hemi*, "half," and *thnesko*, "to die," is
used in Luke 10:30.

DEADNESS

nekrosis (3500), "a putting to death," is rendered "dying" in
2 Cor. 4:10; "deadness" in Rom. 4:19, i.e., the state of being virtually "dead."

DEAR

1. *timios* (5093), from *time*, "honor, price," signifies (a), primarily, "accounted as of great price, precious, costly," 1 Cor. 3:12; Rev.
17:4; 18:12, 16; 21:19, and in the superlative degree, 18:12; 21:11; the
comparative degree is found in 1 Pet. 1:7 (*polutimoteros*, in the
most authentic mss., "much more precious"); (b) in the metaphorical sense, "held in honor, esteemed, very dear," Acts 5:34, "had in
honor," RV (KJV, "had in reputation"); so in Heb. 13:4, RV, "let marriage be had in honor"; KJV, "is honorable"; Acts 20:24, "dear,"
negatively of Paul's estimate of his life; Jas. 5:7, "precious" (of
fruit); 1 Pet. 1:19, "precious" (of the blood of Christ); 2 Pet. 1:4 (of
God's promises).

2. *entimos* (1784), "held in honor" (*time*, see above), "precious,
dear," is found in Luke 7:2, of the centurion's servant; 14:8, "more
honorable"; Phil. 2:29, "honor" (KJV, "reputation"), of devoted servants of Christ, in 1 Pet. 2:4, 6, "precious," of stones, metaphorically.

3. *agapetos* (27), from *agape*, "love," signifies "beloved"; it is rendered "very dear" in 1 Thess. 2:8 (KJV, "dear"), of the affection of Paul and his fellow workers for the saints at Thessalonica; in Eph. 5:1 and Col. 1:7, KJV, "dear"; RV, "beloved."

DEATH, DEATH-STROKE (See also DIE)

Old Testament

mawet (4194), "death," the opposite of "life," Deut. 30:19. "Death" is the natural end of human life on this earth; it is an aspect of God's judgment on man, Gen. 2:17. Hence all men die, Num. 16:29. The Old Testament uses "death" in phrases such as "the day of death," Gen. 27:2, and "the year of death," Isa. 6:1, or to mark an event as occurring before, Gen. 27:7, 10, or after, Gen. 26:18, someone's passing away.

"Death" may also come upon someone in a violent manner, as an execution of justice, Deut. 21:22-23. Saul declared David to be a "son of death" because he intended to have David killed, 1 Sam. 20:31; cf. Prov. 16:14. In one of his experiences, David composed a psalm expressing how close an encounter he had had with death, 2 Sam. 22:5-6; cf. Ps. 18:5-6. Isaiah predicted the Suffering Servant was to die a violent death, Isa. 53:9.

Finally, the word *mawet* denotes the "realm of the dead" or *she'ol*. This place of death has gates, Ps. 9:13; 107:18, and chambers, Prov. 7:27; the path of the wicked leads to this abode, Prov. 5:5.

Isaiah expected "death" to be ended when the Lord's full kingship would be established, Isa. 25:8. Paul argued on the basis of Jesus' resurrection that this event had already taken place, 1 Cor. 15:54, but John looked forward to the hope of the resurrection when God would wipe away our tears, Rev. 21:4.

New Testament

A. Nouns

1. *thanatos* (2288), "death," is used in Scripture of:

(a) the separation of the soul (the spiritual part of man) from the body (the material part), the latter ceasing to function and turning to dust, e.g., John 11:13; Heb. 2:15; 5:7; 7:23. In Heb. 9:15, the KJV, "by means of death" is inadequate; the RV, "a death having taken place" is in keeping with the subject. In Rev. 13:3, 12, the RV, "death-stroke" (KJV, "deadly wound") is, lit., "the stroke of death."

(b) the separation of man from God; Adam died on the day he disobeyed God, Gen. 2:17, and hence all mankind are born in the same spiritual condition, Rom. 5:12, 14, 17, 21, from which, however, those who believe in Christ are delivered, John 5:24; 1 John 3:14. "Death" is the opposite of life; it never denotes nonexistence. As spiritual life is "conscious existence in communion with God," so spiritual "death" is "conscious existence in separation from God."

2. *anairesis* (*336*), another word for "death," lit. signifies "a taking up or off," as of the taking of a life, or "putting to death"; it is found in Acts 8:1, of the murder of Stephen. Some mss. have it in 22:20.

3. *teleute* (*5054*), "an end, limit," hence, "the end of life, death," is used of the "death" of Herod, Matt. 2:15.

B. Adjective.

epithanatios (*1935*), "doomed to death" (*epi*, "upon," *thanatos*, A, No. 1), is said of the apostles, in 1 Cor. 4:9.

C. Verbs.

1. *thanatoo* (*2289*), "to put to death" (akin to A, No. 1), in Matt. 10:21; Mark 13:12; Luke 21:16, is translated "shall...cause (them) to be put to death." It is used of the death of Christ in Matt. 26:59; 27:1; Mark 14:55 and 1 Pet. 3:18. In Rom. 7:4 (passive voice) it is translated "ye...were made dead," RV (for KJV, "are become"), with reference to the change from bondage to the Law to union with Christ; in 8:13, "mortify," of the act of the believer in regard to the deeds of the body; in 8:36, "are killed"; so in 2 Cor. 6:9.

2. *anaireo* (*337*), lit., "to take or lift up or away" (see A, No. 2), hence, "to put to death," is usually translated "to kill or slay"; in two places "put to death," Luke 23:32; Acts 26:10. It is used 17 times, with this meaning, in Acts.

3. *apago* (*520*), lit., "to lead away" (*apo*, "away," *ago*, "to lead"), is used especially in a judicial sense, "to put to death," e.g., Acts 12:19.

4. *apokteino* (*615*), to kill, is so translated in the RV, for the KJV, "put to death," in Mark 14:1; Luke 18:33; in John 11:53; 12:10 and 18:31, RV, "put to death."

DEBT

1. *opheile* (*3782*), "that which is owed," is translated "debt" in Matt. 18:32; in the plural, "dues," Rom. 13:7; "(her) due," 1 Cor. 7:3, of conjugal duty: some texts here have *opheilomenen* (*eunoian*) "due (benevolence)," KJV; the context confirms the RV.

2. *opheilema* (*3783*), a longer form of No. 1, expressing a "debt" more concretely, is used (a) literally, of that which is legally due, Rom. 4:4; (b) metaphorically, of sin as a "debt," because it demands expiation, and thus payment by way of punishment, Matt. 6:12.

3. *daneion* (*1156*), "a loan," is translated "debt" in Matt. 18:27.

DEBTOR

1. *opheiletes* (*3781*), "one who owes anything to another," primarily in regard to money; in Matt. 18:24, "who owed" (lit., "one

was brought, a debtor to him of ten thousand talents"). The slave could own property, and so become a "debtor" to his master, who might seize him for payment. It is used metaphorically, (a) of a person who is under an obligation, Rom. 1:14, of Paul, in the matter of preaching the gospel; in Rom. 8:12, of believers, to mortify the deeds of the body; in Rom. 15:27, of gentile believers, to assist afflicted Jewish believers; in Gal. 5:3, of those who would be justified by circumcision, to do the whole Law: (b) of those who have not yet made amends to those whom they have injured, Matt. 6:12, "our debtors"; of some whose disaster was liable to be regarded as a due punishment, Luke 13:4.

2. *chreopheiletes* (*5533*), lit., "a debt-ower" (*chreos*, "a loan, a debt," and No. 1), is found in Luke 7:41, of the two "debtors" mentioned in the Lord's parable addressed to Simon the Pharisee, and in 16:5, of the "debtors" in the parable of the unrighteous steward. This parable indicates a system of credit in the matter of agriculture.

DECAY

1. *palaioo* (*3822*), "to make old" (*palaios*), is translated in Heb. 8:13, firstly, "hath made...old," secondly (passive voice), RV "is becoming old" (KJV, "decayeth"); "wax old," Luke 12:33 and Heb. 1:11.

2. *diaphtheiro* (*1311*), "to destroy utterly," as used in 2 Cor. 4:16 (here in the passive voice, lit., "is being destroyed"), is rendered "is decaying" (RV, for KJV, "perish").

DECEASE

A. Noun.

exodos (*1841*), (Eng., "exodus"), lit. signifies "a way out"; hence, "a departure," especially from life, "a decease"; in Luke 9:31, of the Lord's death, "which He was about to accomplish"; in 2 Pet. 1:15, of Peter's death; "departure" in Heb. 11:22, RV.

B. Verb.

teleutao (*5053*), lit., "to end," is used intransitively and translated "deceased" in Matt. 22:25.

DECEIT, DECEITFUL, DECEITFULLY, DECEITFULNESS, DECEIVE, DECEIVABLENESS

Old Testament

shaw' (*7723*), "deceit; deception; malice; falsity; vanity; emptiness," often used in a legal context, Exod. 23:1; Ps. 31:6; Job 15:31.

New Testament

A. Nouns.

1. *apate* (*539*), "deceit or deceitfulness" (akin to *apatao*, "to cheat, deceive, beguile"), that which gives a false impression, whether by appearance, statement or influence, is said of riches, Matt. 13:22; Mark 4:19; of sin, Heb. 3:13. The phrase in Eph. 4:22, "deceitful lusts," KJV, "lusts of deceit," RV, signifies lusts excited by "deceit," of which "deceit" is the source of strength, not lusts "deceitful" in themselves. In 2 Thess. 2:10, "all deceit of unrighteousness," RV, signifies all manner of unscrupulous words and deeds designed to "deceive" (see Rev. 13:13-15). In Col. 2:8, "vain deceit" suggests that "deceit" is void of anything profitable.

2. *dolos* (*1388*), primarily "a bait, snare"; hence, "craft, deceit, guile," is translated "deceit" in Mark 7:22; Rom. 1:29.

B. Adjective.

dolios (*1386*), "deceitful," is used in 2 Cor. 11:13, of false apostles as "deceitful workers"; cf. A, No. 2.

C. Verbs.

1. *apatao* (*538*), "to beguile, deceive" (see A, No. 1), is used (a) of those who "deceive" "with empty words," belittling the true character of the sins mentioned, Eph. 5:6; (b) of the fact that Adam was "not beguiled," 1 Tim. 2:14, RV.

2. *exapatao* (*1818*), *ek* (*ex*), intensive, and No. 1, signifies "to beguile thoroughly, to deceive wholly," 1 Tim. 2:14, RV.

3. *phrenapatao* (*5422*), lit., "to deceive in one's mind" (*phren*, "the mind," and No. 1), "to deceive by fancies," is used in Gal. 6:3, with reference to self-conceit, which is "self-deceit," a sin against common sense.

4. *dolioo* (*1387*), "to lure," as by a bait (see A, No. 2), is translated "have used deceit" in Rom. 3:13.

5. *doloo* (*1389*), a short form of No. 4, primarily signifies "to ensnare"; hence, "to corrupt," especially by mingling the truths of the Word of God with false doctrines or notions, and so handling it "deceitfully," 2 Cor. 4:2.

6. *planao* (*4105*), in the passive form sometimes means "to go astray, wander," Matt. 18:12; 1 Pet. 2:25; Heb. 11:38; frequently active, "to deceive, by leading into error, to seduce," e.g., Matt. 24:4, 5, 11, 24; John 7:12, "leadeth astray," RV (cf. 1 John 3:7). In Rev. 12:9 the present participle is used with the definite article, as a title of the Devil, "the Deceiver," lit., "the deceiving one." Often it has the sense of "deceiving oneself," e.g., 1 Cor. 6:9; 15:33; Gal. 6:7; Jas. 1:16, "be not deceived," RV, "do not err," KJV.

7. *paralogizomai* (*3884*), lit., "to reason amiss," Col. 2:4; Jas. 1:22.

DECEIVER

1. *planos* (*4108*) is, properly, an adjective, signifying "wandering, or leading astray, seducing," 1 Tim. 4:1, "seducing (spirits)," used as a noun, it denotes an impostor of the vagabond type, and so any kind of "deceiver" or corrupter, Matt. 27:63; 2 Cor. 6:8; 2 John 7 (twice), in the last of which the accompanying definite article necessitates the translation "the deceiver," RV.

2. *phrenapates* (*5423*), akin to C, No. 3, under DECEIVE, lit., "a mind-deceiver," is used in Titus 1:10.

DECENTLY

euschemonos (*2156*) denotes "gracefully, becomingly, in a seemly manner" (*eu*, "well," *schema*, "a form, figure"); "honestly," in Rom. 13:13, in contrast to the shamefulness of gentile social life; in 1 Thess. 4:12, the contrast is to idleness and its concomitant evils and the resulting bad testimony to unbelievers; in 1 Cor. 14:40, "decently," where the contrast is to disorder in oral testimony in the churches.

DECIDE, DECISION

A. Verb.

diakrino (*1252*) primarily signifies "to make a distinction," hence, "to decide, especially judicially, to decide a dispute, to give judgment," 1 Cor. 6:5, KJV, "judge"; RV, "decide," where church members are warned against procuring decisions by litigation in the world's law courts.

B. Nouns.

1. *diagnosis* (*1233*), transliterated in English, primarily denotes "a discrimination" (*dia*, "apart," *ginosko*, "to know"), hence, "a judicial decision," which is its meaning in Acts 25:21, RV, "for the decision of the Emperor" (KJV, "hearing").

2. *diakrisis* (*1253*), "a distinguishing," and so "a decision" (see A), signifies "discerning" in 1 Cor. 12:10; Heb. 5:14, lit., "unto a discerning of good and evil" (translated "to discern"); in Rom. 14:1.

DECLARE, DECLARATION

A. Verbs.

1. *anangello* (*312*) signifies "to announce, report, bring back tidings." Possibly the *ana* carries the significance of upward, i.e., heavenly, as characteristic of the nature of the tidings. In the following, either the KJV or the RV translates the word by the verb "to declare"; in John 4:25, RV, "declare," KJV, "tell"; in 16:13-15, RV, "declare," KJV, "shew"; in Acts 15:4, RV, "rehearsed," KJV, "declared"; in 19:18, RV, "declaring," KJV, "shewed" (a reference, per-

haps, to the destruction of their idols, in consequence of their new faith); in 20:20, RV, "declaring," KJV, "have shewed"; in 1 John 1:5, RV, "announce," KJV, "declare."

2. *apangello* (518) signifies "to announce or report from a person or place"; hence, "to declare, publish"; it is rendered "declare" in Luke 8:47; Heb. 2:12; 1 John 1:3. It is very frequent in the Gospels and Acts; elsewhere, other than the last two places mentioned, only in 1 Thess. 1:9 and 1 John 1:2.

3. *diangello* (1229), lit., "to announce through," hence, "to declare fully, or far and wide," Acts 21:26, RV (KJV, "to signify"); in Luke 9:60, RV, "publish abroad" (for KJV, "preach"), giving the verb its fuller significance; so in Rom. 9:17, for KJV, "declared."

4. *katangello* (2605), lit., "to report down," is ordinarily translated "to preach"; "declare" in Acts 17:23, KJV (RV, "set forth"); in 1 Cor. 2:1, RV, "proclaiming," for KJV, "declaring." It is nowhere translated by "declare" in the RV.

5. *parangello* (3853) lit., "to announce beside," Acts 10:42.

B. Noun.

endeixis (1732), "a showing, pointing out," is said of the "showing forth" of God's righteousness, in Rom. 3:25-26, KJV, "to declare"; RV, "to show," and "(for) the showing." In 2 Cor. 8:24, "proof"; Phil. 1:28, "an evident token."

DECREASE (Verb)

elattoo (1642) signifies "to make less or inferior, in quality, position or dignity"; "madest...lower" and "hast made...lower," in Heb. 2:7, 9. In John 3:30, it is used in the middle voice, in John the Baptist's "I must decrease," indicating the special interest he had in his own "decrease," i.e., in authority and popularity.

DECREE (Noun and Verb)

dogma (1378), transliterated in English, primarily denoted "an opinion or judgment" (from *dokeo*, "to be of opinion"), hence, an "opinion expressed with authority, a doctrine, ordinance, decree"; "decree," Luke 2:1; Acts 16:4; 17:7; in the sense of ordinances, Eph. 2:15; Col. 2:14.

DEDICATE, DEDICATION

A. Verb.

enkainizo (1457) primarily means "to make new, to renew," so then, to initiate or "dedicate," Heb. 9:18, with reference to the first covenant, as not "dedicated" without blood; in 10:20, of Christ's "dedication" of the new and living way (KJV, "consecrated"; RV, "dedicated").

B. Noun.

enkainia (*1456*), akin to A, "dedication," became used particularly for the annual eight days' feast beginning on the 25th of Chisleu (mid. of Dec.), instituted by Judas Maccabaeus, 164 B.C., to commemorate the cleansing of the Temple from the pollutions of Antiochus Epiphanes; hence it was called the Feast of the Dedication, John 10:22.

DEED, DEEDS

1. *ergon* (*2041*) denotes "a work" (Eng., "work" is etymologically akin), "deed, act." When used in the sense of a "deed or act," the idea of "working" is stressed, e.g., Rom. 15:18; it frequently occurs in an ethical sense of human actions, good or bad, e.g., Matt. 23:3; 26:10; John 3:20-21; Rom. 2:7, 15; 1 Thess. 1:3; 2 Thess. 1:11, etc.; sometimes in a less concrete sense, e.g., Titus 1:16; Jas. 1:25 (RV that worketh, lit., of work).

2. *praxis* (*4234*) denotes "a doing, transaction, a deed the action of which is looked upon as incomplete and in progress"; in Matt. 16:27, RV, "deeds," for KJV, "works"; in Luke 23:51, "deed"; in v. 41, the verb is used; Acts 19:18; Rom. 8:13; Col. 3:9. In Rom. 12:4 it denotes an "action," business, or function, translated "office."

DEEP (Noun and Adjective), DEEPNESS, DEEPLY, DEPTH

A. Nouns.

1. *bathos* (*899*) is used (a) naturally, in Matt. 13:5, "deepness"; Mark 4:5, KJV, "depth," RV, "deepness"; Luke 5:4, of "deep" water; Rom. 8:39 (contrasted with *hupsoma*, "height"); (b) metaphorically, in Rom. 11:33, of God's wisdom and knowledge; in 1 Cor. 2:10, of God's counsels; in Eph. 3:18, of the dimensions of the sphere of the activities of God's counsels, and of the love of Christ which occupies that sphere; in 2 Cor. 8:2, of "deep" poverty; some mss. have it in Rev. 2:24.

2. *buthos* (*1037*), "a depth," is used in the NT only in the natural sense, of the sea 2 Cor. 11:25.

B. Adjective and Adverb.

bathus (*901*), akin to A, No. 1, "deep," is said in John 4:11, of a well; in Acts 20:9, of sleep; in Rev. 2:24 the plural is used, of the "deep things," the evil designs and workings of Satan.

C. Verb.

bathuno (*900*), "to deepen, make deep," is used in Luke 6:48.

DEFAME

dusphemeo (*1418* and *5346*), lit., "to speak injuriously" (from *dus—*, an inseparable prefix signifying "opposition, injury, etc.," and *phemi*, "to speak"), is translated "defamed," 1 Cor. 4:13.

DEFENSE

A. Noun.

apologia (*627*), a speech made in defense, Acts 22:1.

B. Verb.

apologeomai (*626*), lit., "to talk oneself off," Luke 12:11.

D

DEFILE, DEFILEMENT

A. Verbs.

1. *koinoo* (*2840*) denotes (a) "to make common"; hence, in a ceremonial sense, "to render unholy, unclean, to defile," Matt. 15:11, 18, 20; Mark 7:15, 18, 20, 23; Acts 21:28 (RV, "defiled"; KJV, "polluted"); Heb. 9:13 (RV, "them that have been defiled," KJV, "the unclean"); (b) "to count unclean," Acts 10:15; 11:9.

2. *miaino* (*3392*), primarily, "to stain, to tinge or dye with another color," as in the staining of a glass, hence, "to pollute, contaminate, soil, defile," is used (a) of "ceremonial defilement," John 18:28; (b) of "moral defilement," Titus 1:15 (twice); Heb. 12:15; "of moral and physical defilement," Jude 8.

3. *moluno* (*3435*) properly denotes "to besmear," as with mud or filth, "to befoul." It is used in the figurative sense, of a conscience "defiled" by sin, 1 Cor. 8:7; of believers who have kept themselves (their "garments") from "defilement," Rev. 3:4.

4. *spiloo* (*4695*), "to make a stain or spot," and so "to defile," is used in Jas. 3:6 of the "defiling" effects of an evil use of the tongue; in Jude 23, "spotted," with reference to moral "defilement."

B. Nouns.

1. *miasma* (*3393*), whence the Eng. word, denotes "defilement" (akin to A, No. 2), and is found in 2 Pet. 2:20, AV, "pollutions," RV, "defilements," the vices of the ungodly which contaminate a person in his intercourse with the world.

2. *miasmos* (*3394*), also akin to A, No. 2, primarily denotes "the act of defiling," the process, in contrast to the "defiling" thing (No. 1). It is found in 2 Pet. 2:10 (KJV, "uncleanness," RV, "defilement").

3. *molusmos* (*3436*), akin to A, No. 3, denotes "defilement," in the sense of an action by which anything is "defiled," 2 Cor. 7:1.

C. Adjective.

koinos (*2839*), akin to A, No. 1, common, and, from the idea of coming into contact with everything, "defiled," is used in the ceremonial sense in Mark 7:2.

DEFRAUD

1. *apostereo* (*650*) signifies "to rob, despoil, defraud," Mark 10:19; 1 Cor. 6:8; 7:5 (of that which is due to the condition of natural relationship of husband and wife); in the middle voice, "to allow oneself to be defrauded," 1 Cor. 6:7; in the passive voice, "bereft," 1 Tim. 6:5.

2. *pleonekteo* (*4122*), translated "defraud" in 1 Thess. 4:6.

DELAY

A. Verbs.

1. *okneo* (*3635*), akin to *oknos*, "a shrinking, to be loath or slow to do a thing, to hesitate, delay," is used in Acts 9:38.

2. *chronizo* (*5549*), from *chronos*, "time," lit. means "to while away time," i.e., by way of lingering, tarrying, "delaying"; "delayeth," Matt. 24:48; Luke 12:45, "tarried" Matt. 25:5; "tarried so long," Luke 1:21; "will (not) tarry," Heb. 10:37.

B. Noun.

anabole (*311*) lit. signifies "that which is thrown up" (*ana*, "up," *ballo*, "to throw"); hence "a delay," Acts 25:17.

DELICATELY (live)

A. Verbs.

truphao (*5171*), from *thrupto*, "to enervate," signifies "to lead a voluptuous life, to give oneself up to pleasure," Jas. 5:5, RV, "ye have lived delicately"; KJV, "ye have lived in pleasure."

B. Noun.

truphe (*5172*), akin to A, "luxuriously," "delicately," Luke 7:25, and denotes effeminacy, softness; "to revel" in 2 Pet. 2:13.

DELIGHT IN

sunedomai (*4913*), lit., "to rejoice with (anyone), to delight in (a thing) with (others)," signifies "to delight with oneself inwardly in a thing," in Rom. 7:22.

DELIVER, DELIVERANCE, DELIVERER

Old Testament

A. Verbs.

nathan (*5414*), "to deliver, give, place, set up, lay, make, do"; first, *nathan* represents the action by which something is set going or actuated. Achsah asked her father Caleb to "give" her a blessing, such as a tract of land with abundant water, as her dowry; she wanted him to "transfer" it from his possession to hers, Josh. 15:19. There is a technical use of this verb without an object: Moses instructs Israel to "give" generously to the man in desperate need, Deut. 15:10. In some instances, **nathan** can mean to "send forth," as in "sending forth" a fragrance, Song of Sol. 1:12.

nathan also has a technical meaning in the area of jurisprudence, meaning to hand something over to someone—for example, "to pay," Gen. 23:9, or "to loan," Deut. 15:10. A girl's parent or someone else in a responsible position may "give" her to a man to be his wife, Gen. 16:3, as well as presenting a bride price, Gen. 34:12, and dowry, 1 Kings 9:16. The verb also is used of "giving" or "granting" a request, Gen. 15:2.

Sometimes, **nathan** can be used to signify "putting" ("placing") someone into custody, 2 Sam. 14:7; Jer. 37:4. This same basic sense may be applied to "dedicating" ("handing over") something or someone to God, such as the first-born son, Exod. 22:29. Levites are those who have been "handed over" in this way, Num. 3:9. "To give something into someone's hand" is to "commit" it to his care, Gen. 9:2; 2 Sam. 16:8; or transfer control Deut. 7:24. "To give one's heart" to something or someone is "to be concerned about it"; Pharaoh was not "concerned" about ("did not set his heart to") Moses' message from God, Exod. 7:23. "To put [give] something into one's heart" is to give one ability and concern to do something; thus God "put" it in the heart of the Hebrew craftsmen to teach others, Exod. 36:2.

nathan can be used of "giving" or "ascribing" glory and praise to God, Josh. 7:19. **nathan** can focus on a result or effect, so "yield" fruit, Deut. 25:19. In some passages, this verb means "to procure" ("to set up"), as when God "gave" ("procured, set up") favor for Joseph, Gen. 39:21. The word can be used of sexual activity, too, Lev. 18:23.

"To give one's face to" is to focus one's attention on something, as when Jehoshaphat was afraid of the alliance of the Transjordanian kings and "set [his face] to seek the Lord," 2 Chron. 20:3. This same phrase can merely mean "to be facing someone or something," cf. Gen. 30:40. "To give one's face against" is a hostile action, Lev. 17:10.

yasha' (3467), "to deliver, help," with a special focus of being delivered from danger, Isa. 30:15.

B. Nouns.

yeshu'ah (3444), "deliverance." "Salvation" in the Old Testament is not understood as a salvation from sin, since the word denotes broadly anything from which "deliverance" must be sought: distress, war, servitude, or enemies. There are both human and divine deliverers, but the word **yeshu'ah** rarely refers to human "deliverance." A couple of exceptions are when Jonathan brought respite to the Israelites from the Philistine pressure, 1 Sam. 14:45, and when Joab and his men were to help one another in battle, 2 Sam. 10:11. "Deliverance" is generally used with God as the subject, Deut. 32:15; cf. Isa. 12:2. He worked many wonders on behalf of His people, Ps. 98:1. *yeshu'ah* occurs either in the context of rejoicing, Ps. 9:14, or prayer for "deliverance," Ps. 69:29.

Many personal names contain a form of the root, such as *Joshua* ("the Lord is help"), *Isaiah* ("the Lord is help"), and *Jesus* (a Greek form of *yeshu'ah*).

yesha' (3468), "deliverance," Ps. 50:23.

teshu'ah (8668), "deliverance," Isa. 45:17.

New Testament

A. Verbs.

1. *didomi* (1325), "to give," is translated "delivered" in Luke 7:15; RV, "gave"; so 19:13.

2. *anadidomi* (325), "to deliver over, give up," is used of "delivering" the letter mentioned in Acts 23:33.

3. *apodidomi* (591), "to give away," hence, "to give back or up," is used in Pilate's command for the Lord's body to be "given up," Matt. 27:58; in the sense of "giving back," of the Lord's act in giving a healed boy back to his father, Luke 9:42.

4. *epididomi* (1929), lit., "to give upon or in addition," as from oneself to another, hence, "to deliver over," is used of the "delivering" of the scroll of Isaiah to Christ in the synagogue, Luke 4:17; of the "delivering" of the epistle from the elders at Jerusalem to the church at Antioch, Acts 15:30.

5. *paradidomi* (3860), "to deliver over," in Rom. 6:17, RV, "that form of teaching whereunto ye were delivered," the figure being that of a mold which gives its shape to what is cast in it (not as the KJV). In Rom. 8:32 it is used of God in "delivering" His Son to expiatory death; so 4:25; see Mark 9:31; of Christ in "delivering" Himself up, Gal. 2:20; Eph. 5:2, 25. In Mark 1:14, RV, it is used of "delivering" John the Baptist to prison.

6. *rhuomai* (4506), "to rescue from, to preserve from," and so, "to deliver," the word by which it is regularly translated, is largely synonymous with *sozo*, "to save," though the idea of "rescue from" is predominant in *rhuomai* (see Matt. 27:43), that of "preservation from," in *sozo*. In Rom. 11:26 the present participle is used with the article, as a noun, "the Deliverer." This is the construction in 1 Thess. 1:10, where Christ is similarly spoken of. Here the KJV wrongly has "which delivered" (the tense is not past); RV, "which delivereth"; the translation might well be (as in Rom. 11:26), "our Deliverer," that is, from the retributive calamities with which God will visit men at the end of the present age. From that wrath believers are to be "delivered." The verb is used with *apo*, "away from," in Matt. 6:13; Luke 11:4 (in some mss.); so also in 11:4; Rom. 15:31; 2 Thess. 3:2; 2 Tim. 4:18; and with *ek*, "from, out of," in Luke 1:74; Rom. 7:24; 2 Cor. 1:10; Col. 1:13, from bondage; in 2 Pet. 2:9, from temptation, in 2 Tim. 3:11, from persecution; but *ek* is used of ills impending, in 2 Cor. 1:10; in 2 Tim. 4:17, *ek* indicates that the

danger was more imminent than in v. 18, where *apo* is used. Accordingly the meaning "out of the midst of" cannot be pressed in 1 Thess. 1:10.

B. Nouns.

1. *apolutrosis* (*629*) denotes "redemption" (*apo*, "from," *lutron*, "a price of release"). In Heb. 11:35 it is translated "deliverance"; usually the release is effected by the payment of a ransom, or the required price, the *lutron* (ransom).

D

2. *aphesis* (*859*) denotes "a release, from bondage, imprisonment, etc." (the corresponding verb is *aphiemi*, "to send away, let go"); in Luke 4:18 it is used of "liberation" from captivity (KJV, "deliverance," RV, "release").

3. *lutrotes* (*3086*), "a redeemer, one who releases" (see No. 1), is translated "deliverer" in Acts 7:35.

C. Verbal Adjective.

ekdotos (*1560*), lit., "given up," so "delivered up" (to enemies, or to the power or will of someone), is used of Christ in Acts 2:23.

DELUDE, DELUSION

A. Verb.

paralogizomai (*3884*) lit., "to reason amiss," Col. 2:4; Jas. 1:22.

B. Noun.

plane (*4106*), lit., "a wandering," whereby those who are led astray roam hither and thither, is always used in the NT, of mental straying, wrong opinion, error in morals or religion, 2 Thess. 2:11.

DEMON, DEMONIAC

A. Nouns.

1. *daimon* (*1142*), "a demon," signified, among pagan Greeks, an inferior deity, whether good or bad. In the NT it denotes "an evil spirit." It is used in Matt. 8:31, mistranslated "devils."

2. *daimonion* (*1140*), not a diminutive of *daimon*, No. 1, but the neuter of the adjective *daimonios*, pertaining to a demon, is also mistranslated "devil," "devils." In Acts 17:18, it denotes an inferior pagan deity. "Demons" are the spiritual agents acting in all idolatry. The idol itself is nothing, but every idol has a "demon" associated with it who induces idolatry, with its worship and sacrifices, 1 Cor. 10:20-21; Rev. 9:20; cf. Deut. 32:17; Isa. 13:21; 34:14; 65:3, 11. They disseminate errors among men, and seek to seduce believers, 1 Tim. 4:1.

Acting under Satan (cf. Rev. 16:13-14), "demons" are permitted to afflict with bodily disease, Luke 13:16. Being unclean they tempt human beings with unclean thoughts, Matt. 10:1; Mark 5:2; 7:25;

Luke 8:27-29; Rev. 16:13; 18:2, e.g. They differ in degrees of wickedness, Matt. 12:45. They will instigate the rulers of the nations at the end of this age to make war against God and His Christ, Rev. 16:14.

B. Verb.

daimonizomai (*1139*) signifies "to be possessed of a demon, to act under the control of a demon." Those who were thus afflicted expressed the mind and consciousness of the "demon" or "demons" indwelling them, e.g., Luke 8:28. The verb is found chiefly in Matt. and Mark; Matt. 4:24; 8:16, 28, 33; 9:32; 12:22; 15:22; Mark 1:32; 5:15-16, 18; elsewhere in Luke 8:36 and John 10:21, "him that hath a devil (demon)."

C. Adjective.

daimoniodes (*1141*) signifies "proceeding from, or resembling, a demon, Jas. 3:15.

DENY

1. **arneomai** (*720*) signifies (a) "to say...not, to contradict," e.g., Mark 14:70; John 1:20; 18:25, 27; 1 John 2:22; (b) "to deny" by way of disowning a person, as, e.g., the Lord Jesus as master, e.g., Matt. 10:33; Luke 12:9; John 13:38 (in the best mss.); 2 Tim. 2:12; or, on the other hand, of Christ Himself, "denying" that a person is His follower, Matt. 10:33; 2 Tim. 2:12; or to "deny" the Father and the Son, by apostatizing and by disseminating pernicious teachings, to "deny" Jesus Christ as master and Lord by immorality under a cloak of religion, 2 Pet. 2:1; Jude 4; (c) "to deny oneself," either in a good sense, by disregarding one's own interests, Luke 9:23, or in a bad sense, to prove false to oneself, to act quite unlike oneself, 2 Tim. 2:13; (d) to "abrogate, forsake, or renounce a thing," whether evil, Titus 2:12, or good, 1 Tim. 5:8; 2 Tim. 3:5; Rev. 2:13; 3:8; (e)"not to accept, to reject" something offered, Acts 3:14; 7:35, "refused"; Heb. 11:24 "refused."

2. **aparneomai** (*533*), a strengthened form of No. 1, with **apo**, "from," prefixed (Lat., **abnego**), means (a) "to deny utterly," to abjure, to affirm that one has no connection with a person, as in Peter's denial of Christ, Matt. 26:34-35, 75; Mark 14:30-31, 72; Luke 22:34, 61 (some mss. have it in John 13:38). This stronger form is used in the Lord's statements foretelling Peter's "denial," and in Peter's assurance of fidelity; the simple verb (No. 1) is used in all the records of his actual denial.

DESERT (Noun and Adjective)

A. Noun.

eremia (*2047*), primarily "a solitude, an uninhabited place," in contrast to a town or village, is translated "deserts" in Heb. 11:38;

"the wilderness" in Matt. 15:33, KJV, "a desert place," RV; so in Mark 8:4; "wilderness" in 2 Cor. 11:26. It does not always denote a barren region, void of vegetation; it is often used of a place uncultivated, but fit for pasturage.

B. Adjective.

eremos (*2048*), used as a noun, has the same meaning as *eremia*, in Luke 5:16 and 8:29, RV, "deserts," for KJV, "wilderness"; in Matt. 24:26 and John 6:31, RV, "wilderness," for KJV, "desert." As an adjective, it denotes (a), with reference to persons, "deserted," "desolate, deprived of the friends and kindred, e.g. of a woman deserted by a husband, Gal 4:21; (b) so of a city, as Jerusalem, Matt. 23:38; or uninhabited places, "desert," e.g., Matt. 14:13, 15; Acts 8:26; in Mark 1:35.

DESIRE (Noun and Verb), DESIROUS

A. Nouns.

1. *epithumia* (*1939*), "a desire, craving, longing, mostly of evil desires," frequently translated "lust," is used in the following, of good "desires": of the Lord's "wish" concerning the last Passover, Luke 22:15, of Paul's "desire" to be with Christ, Phil. 1:23; of his "desire" to see the saints at Thessalonica again, 1 Thess. 2:17.

With regard to evil "desires," in Col. 3:5 the RV has "desire," for the KJV, "concupiscence"; in 1 Thess. 4:5, RV, "lust," for KJV, "concupiscence"; there the preceding word *pathos* is translated "passion," RV, for KJV, "lust"; also in Col. 3:5 *pathos* and *epithumia* are associated, RV, "passion," for KJV, "inordinate affection." *epithumia* is combined with *pathema*, in Gal. 5:24; for the KJV, "affections and lusts," the RV has "passions, and the lusts thereof." *epithumia* is the more comprehensive term, including all manner of "lusts and desires"; *pathema* denotes suffering; in the passage in Gal. 5:24 the sufferings are those produced by yielding to the flesh; *pathos* points more to the evil state from which "lusts" spring.

2. *eudokia* (*2107*), lit., "good pleasure" (*eu*, "well," *dokeo*, "to seem"), implies a gracious purpose, a good object being in view, with the idea of a resolve, showing the willingness with which the resolve is made. It is often translated "good pleasure," e.g., Eph. 1:5, 9; Phil. 2:13; in Phil. 1:15, "good will"; in Rom. 10:1, "desire."

3. *epipothesis* (*1972*), "an earnest desire, a longing for" (*epi*, "upon," intensive, *potheo*, "to desire"), is found in 2 Cor. 7:7, 11, KJV, "earnest desire," and "vehement desire"; RV, "longing" in both places.

4. *epipothia* (*1974*), with the same meaning as No. 3, is used in Rom. 15:23, RV, "longing," KJV, "great desire."

5. *thelema* (*2307*) denotes "a will, that which is willed" (akin to B, No. 4). It is rendered "desires" in Eph. 2:3.

B. Verbs.

1. *epithumeo* (*1937*), "to desire earnestly" (as with A, No. 1), stresses the inward impulse rather than the object desired. It is translated "to desire" in Luke 16:21; 17:22; 22:15; 1 Tim. 3:1; Heb. 6:11; 1 Pet. 1:12; Rev. 9:6.

2. *homeiromai* or *himeiromai* (2442), "to have a strong affection for, a yearning after," is found in 1 Thess. 2:8, "being affectionately desirous of you." It is probably derived from a root indicating remembrance.

3. *orego* (3713), "to reach or stretch out," is used only in the middle voice, signifying the mental effort of stretching oneself out for a thing, of longing after it, with stress upon the object desired; it is translated "desire" in Heb. 11:16; in 1 Tim. 3:1, RV, "seeketh," for KJV, "desireth"; in 1 Tim. 6:10, RV, "reached after," for KJV, "coveted after." In Heb. 11:16, a suitable rendering would be "reach after."

4. *thelo* (2309), "to will, to wish," implying volition and purpose, frequently a determination, is most usually rendered "to will." It is translated "to desire" in the RV of the following: Matt. 9:13; 12:7; Mark 6:19; Luke 10:29; 14:28; 23:20; Acts 24:27; 25:9; Gal. 4:17; 1 Tim. 5:11; Heb. 12:17; 13:18.

5. *boulomai* (1014), "to wish, to will deliberately," expresses more strongly than *thelo* (No. 6) the deliberate exercise of the will; it is translated "to desire" in the RV of the following: Acts 22:30; 23:38; 27:43; 28:18; 1 Tim. 2:8; 5:14; 6:9 and Jude 5.

6. *zeloo* (2206), "to have a zeal for, to be zealous towards," whether in a good or evil sense, the former in 1 Cor. 14:1, concerning spiritual gifts RV, "desire earnestly," KJV, "desire"; in an evil sense, in Jas. 4:2, RV, "covet," for KJV, "desire to have."

DESOLATE (Verb and Adjective), DESOLATION

Old Testament

shamem (8074), "to be desolate, astonished, appalled, devastated, ravaged." *shamem* often expresses the idea of to "devastate" or "ravage": "I will destroy her vines," Hos. 2:12. What one sees sometimes is so horrible that it "horrifies" or "appalls," Job 21:5.

New Testament

A. Verbs.

1. *eremoo* (2049) signifies "to make desolate, lay waste." From the primary sense of "making quiet" comes that of "making lonely." It is used only in the passive voice in the NT; in Rev. 17:16, "shall make desolate" is, lit., "shall make her desolated"; in 18:17, 19, "is made desolate"; in Matt. 12:25 and Luke 11:17, "is brought to desolation."

B. Adjectives.

1. *eremos* (2048) is translated "desolate" in the Lord's words against Jerusalem, Matt. 23:38; some mss. have it in Luke 13:35; in reference to the habitation of Judas, Acts 1:20, and to Sarah, from whom, being barren, her husband had turned, Gal. 4:27.

2. *orphanos* (3737) (Eng., "orphan"; Lat., "*orbus*"), signifies "bereft of parents or of a father." In Jas. 1:27 it is translated "fatherless." It was also used in the general sense of being "friendless or desolate," John 14:18.

C. Noun.

eremosis (2050), akin to A, No. 1, denotes "desolation," (a) in the sense of "making desolate," e.g., in the phrase "the abomination of desolation," Matt. 24:15; Mark 13:14; the genitive is objective, "the abomination that makes desolate"; (b) with stress upon the effect of the process, Luke 21:20, with reference to the "desolation" of Jerusalem.

DESPAIR

1. *exaporeo* (1820) "to be utterly without a way," so "to be quite at a loss, without resource, in despair." It is used in 2 Cor. 1:8, with reference to life; in 4:8, in the sentence "perplexed, yet not unto (KJV, 'in') despair," the word "perplexed" translates the verb *aporeo*, and the phrase "unto despair" translates the intensive form *exaporeo*, a play on the words.

2. *apelpizo* (560), lit., "to hope away," i.e., "to give up in despair, to despair," is used in Luke 6:35.

DESPISE, DESPISER

Old Testament

ma'as (3988), "to reject, refuse, despise." God will not force man to do His will, so He sometimes must "reject" him, Hos. 4:6. Although God had chosen Saul to be king, Saul's response caused a change in God's attitude, 1 Sam. 15:23; likewise, as a creature of free choice, man may "reject" God, Isa. 7:15-16. When the things that God requires are done with the wrong motives or attitudes, God "despises" such actions, Amos 5:21.

New Testament

A. Verbs.

1. *exoutheneo* (1848), "to make of no account" (*ex*, "out," *oudeis*, "nobody," alternatively written, *outheis*), "to regard as nothing, to despise utterly, to treat with contempt." This is usually translated to "set at nought," Luke 18:9, RV, KJV, "despised." So in Rom. 14:3. Both have "set at nought" in Luke 23:11; Acts 4:11; Rom. 14:10. Both have "despise" in 1 Cor. 16:11; Gal. 4:14, and 1 Thess. 5:20; in 2 Cor.

10:10, RV, "of no account," for KJV, "contemptible"; in 1 Cor. 1:28, KJV and RV, "despised."

2. *kataphroneo* (*2706*), lit., "to think down upon or against anyone," hence signifies "to think slightly of, to despise," Matt. 6:24; 18:10; Luke 16:13; Rom. 2:4; 1 Cor. 11:22; 1 Tim. 4:12; 6:2; Heb. 12:2; 2 Pet. 2:10.

3. *periphroneo* (*4065*) lit. denotes "to think round a thing, to turn over in the mind"; hence, "to have thoughts beyond, to despise," Titus 2:15.

B. Adjective.

atimos (*820*), "without honor," is translated as a verb in 1 Cor. 4:10, KJV, "are despised"; RV, "have dishonor," lit., "(we are) without honor"; "without honor" in Matt. 13:57; Mark 6:4.

C. Noun.

kataphronetes (*2707*), lit., "one who thinks down against," hence, "a despiser" (see A, No. 2), is found in Acts 13:41.

DESPITE, DESPITEFUL, DESPITEFULLY (use)

1. *enubrizo* (*1796*), "to treat insultingly, with contumely" (*en*, intensive, *hubrizo*, "to insult"; some connect it with *huper*, "above, over," Lat. *super*, which suggests the insulting disdain of one who considers himself superior), is translated "hath done despite" in Heb. 10:29.

2. *epereazo* (*1908*), A text variant in Matt. 5:44, and found in Luke 6:28, where the KJV and RV have "despitefully use"; in 1 Pet. 3:16, KJV, "falsely accuse," RV, "revile."

DESTITUTE (be, etc.)

1. *apostereo* (*650*), signifies to "rob or steal," Jas. 5:4.

2. *hustereo* (*5302*), primarily, "to be behind, to be last," hence, "to lack, fail of, come short of," is translated "being destitute" in Heb. 11:37.

3. *leipo* (*3007*) signifies "to leave, forsake"; in the passive voice, "to be left, forsaken, destitute"; in Jas. 2:15, KJV, "destitute," RV, "be in lack."

DESTROY, DESTROYER, DESTRUCTION, DESTRUCTIVE

Old Testament

shamad (*8045*), "to destroy, annihilate, exterminate." This word always expresses complete "destruction" or "annihilation." While the word is often used to express literal "destruction" of people, Deut. 2:12; Judg. 21:16, *shamad* frequently is part of an open threat or warning given to the people of Israel, promising "destruction" if they forsake God for idols, cf. Deut. 4:25-26. This word also expresses the complete "destruction" of the pagan high places, Hos. 10:8, of Baal and his images, 2 Kings 10:28.

shachat (7843), "to corrupt, spoil, ruin, mar, destroy," Gen. 6:11-12, 17. Anything that is good can be "corrupted" or "spoiled," such as Jeremiah's loincloth, Jer. 13:7, a vineyard, Jer. 12:10, cities, Gen. 13:10, and a temple, Lam. 2:6. *shachat* has the meaning of "to waste" when used of words that are inappropriately spoken, Prov. 23:8. *shachat* is used frequently by the prophets in the sense of "to corrupt morally," Isa. 1:4; Ezek. 23:11; Zeph. 3:7.

D

New Testament

A. Verbs.

1. *apollumi* (622), a strengthened form of *ollumi*, signifies "to destroy utterly"; in middle voice, "to perish." The idea is not extinction but ruin, loss, not of being, but of well-being. This is clear from its use, as, e.g., of the marring of wine skins, Luke 5:37; of lost sheep, i.e., lost to the shepherd, metaphorical of spiritual destitution, Luke 15:4, 6, etc.; the lost son, 15:24; of the perishing of food, John 6:27; of gold, 1 Pet. 1:7. So of persons, Matt. 2:13, "destroy"; 8:25, "perish"; 22:7; 27:20; of the loss of well-being in the case of the unsaved hereafter, Matt. 10:28; Luke 13:3, 5; John 3:16 (v. 15 in some mss.); 10:28; 17:12; Rom. 2:12; 1 Cor. 15:18; 2 Cor. 2:15, "are perishing"; 4:3; 2 Thess. 2:10; Jas. 4:12; 2 Pet. 3:9.

2. *katargeo* (2673) lit., "to reduce to inactivity," 1 Cor. 6:13.

3. *kathaireo* (2507), "to cast down, pull down by force, etc.," is translated "to destroy" in Acts 13:19. In Acts 19:27, KJV, "should be destroyed," the RV suitably has "should be deposed."

4. *luo* (3089), "to loose, dissolve, sever, break, demolish," is translated "destroy," in 1 John 3:8, of the works of the Devil.

5. *kataluo* (2647), *kata*, "down," intensive, and No. 4, "to destroy utterly, to overthrow completely," is rendered "destroy," in Matt. 5:17, twice, of the Law; Matt. 24:2; 26:61; 27:40; Mark 13:2; 14:58; 15:29; Luke 21:6, of the Temple; in Acts 6:14, of Jerusalem; in Gal. 2:18, of the Law as a means of justification; in Rom. 14:20 (KJV, "destroy," RV, "overthrow"), of the marring of a person's spiritual well-being (in v. 15 *apollumi*, No. 1, is used in the same sense); in Acts 5:38 and 39 (RV, "overthrow") of the failure of purposes; in 2 Cor. 5:1, of the death of the body ("dissolved").

6. *olothreuo* (3645), "to destroy," especially in the sense of slaying, is found in Heb. 11:28, where the RV translates the present participle with the article by the noun "destroyer." See B, below.

7. *exolothreuo* (1842), *ek*, "out of" (intensive), and No. 6, "to destroy utterly to slay wholly," is found in Acts 3:23, RV, "utterly destroyed," referring to the "destruction" of one who would refuse to hearken to the voice of God through Christ.

B. Nouns.

(I) *(Personal: DESTROYER)*

olothreutes *(3644)*, akin to A, No. 6, "a destroyer," is found in 1 Cor. 10:10.

(II) *(Abstract: DESTRUCTION)*

1. **apoleia** *(684)*, akin to A, No. 1, and likewise indicating "loss of well-being, not of being," is used (a) of things, signifying their waste, or ruin; of ointment, Matt. 26:8; Mark 14:4; of money, Acts 8:20 ("perish"); (b) of persons, signifying their spiritual and eternal perdition, Matt. 7:13; John 17:12; 2 Thess. 2:3, where "son of perdition" signifies the proper destiny of the person mentioned; metaphorically of men persistent in evil, Rom. 9:22, where "fitted" is in the middle voice, indicating that the vessels of wrath fitted themselves for "destruction," of the adversaries of the Lord's people, Phil. 1:28 ("perdition"); of professing Christians, really enemies of the cross of Christ, Phil. 3:19 (RV, "perdition"); of those who are subjects of foolish and hurtful lusts, 1 Tim. 6:9.

2. **kathairesis** *(2506)*, akin to A, No. 3, "a taking down, a pulling down," is used three times in 2 Cor., "casting down" in the RV in each place; in 10:4 (KJV, "pulling down"); in 10:8 and 13:10 (KJV, "destruction").

3. **olethros** *(3639)*, "ruin, destruction," akin to A, No. 6, always translated "destruction," is used in 1 Cor. 5:5, of the effect upon the physical condition of an erring believer for the purpose of his spiritual profit; in 1 Thess. 5:3 and 2 Thess. 1:9, of the effect of the divine judgments upon men at the ushering in of the Day of the Lord and the revelation of the Lord Jesus; in 1 Tim. 6:9, of the consequences of the indulgence of the flesh, referring to physical "ruin" and possibly that of the whole being, the following word **apoleia** (see No. 1) stressing the final, eternal and irrevocable character of the ruin.

4. **suntrimma** *(4938)*, "a breaking in pieces, shattering," Rom. 3:16, from Isa. 59:7.

DETERMINE, DETERMINATE

1. **krino** *(2919)*, primarily "to separate," hence, "to be of opinion, approve, esteem," Rom. 14:5, also "to determine, resolve, decree," is used in this sense in Acts 3:13; 20:16; 25:25; 27:1; 1 Cor. 2:2; 2 Cor. 2:1; Titus 3:12.

2. **horizo** *(3724)* denotes "to bound, to set a boundary" (Eng., "horizon"); hence, "to mark out definitely, determine"; it is translated "to determine" in Luke 22:22, of the foreordained pathway of Christ; Acts 11:29, of a "determination" to send relief; 17:26, where it is used of fixing the bounds of seasons. In Acts 2:23 the verb is translated "determinate," with reference to counsel. Here the

verbal form might have been adhered to by the translation "determined"; that is to say, in the sense of "settled."

In Rom. 1:4 it is translated "declared," where the meaning is that Christ was marked out as the Son of God by His resurrection and that of others. In Acts 10:42 and 17:31 it has its other meaning of "ordain," that is, "to appoint by determined counsel."

3. *proorizo* (4309), *pro*, "beforehand," and No. 2, denotes "to mark out beforehand, to determine before, foreordain"; in Acts 4:28, KJV, "determined before," RV, "foreordained"; so the RV in 1 Cor. 2:7, KJV, "ordained," in Rom. 8:29-30 and Eph. 1:5, 11, KJV, "predestinate," RV, "foreordain."

D

DEVICE

1. *enthumesis* (1761), "a cogitation, an inward reasoning" (generally, evil surmising or supposition), is formed from *en*, "in," and *thumos*, "strong feeling, passion"; Eng., "fume" is akin; the root, *thu*, signifies "to rush, rage."

2. *noema* (3540) denotes "thought, that which is thought out"; hence, "a purpose, device"; translated "devices" in 2 Cor. 2:11; "minds" in 2 Cor. 3:14; 4:4; 11:3; in 2 Cor. 10:5, "thought"; in Phil. 4:7, KJV, "minds," RV, "thoughts."

DEVIL, DEVILISH

diabolos (1228), "an accuser, a slanderer" (from *diaballo*, "to accuse, to malign"), is one of the names of Satan. From it the English word "Devil" is derived, and should be applied only to Satan, as a proper name. *daimon*, "a demon," is frequently, but wrongly, translated "devil"; it should always be translated "demon," as in the RV margin. There is one "Devil," there are many demons. Being the malignant enemy of God and man, he accuses man to God, Job 1:6-11; 2:1-5; Rev. 12:9, 10, and God to man, Gen. 3. He afflicts men with physical sufferings, Acts 10:38. Being himself sinful, 1 John 3:8, he instigated man to sin, Gen. 3, and tempts man to do evil, Eph. 4:27; 6:11, encouraging him thereto by deception, Eph. 2:2. Death having been brought into the world by sin, the "Devil" had the power of death, but Christ through His own death, has triumphed over him, and will bring him to nought, Heb. 2:14; his power over death is intimated in his struggle with Michael over the body of Moses, Jude 9. Judas, who gave himself over to the "Devil," was so identified with him, that the Lord described him as such, John 6:70 (see 13:2). As the "Devil" raised himself in pride against God and fell under condemnation, so believers are warned against similar sin, 1 Tim. 3:6; for them he lays snares, v. 7, seeking to devour them as a roaring lion, 1 Pet. 5:8; those who fall into his snare may be recovered therefrom unto the will of God, 2 Tim. 2:26, "having been taken captive by him (i.e., by the 'Devil')"; "by the Lord's servant" is an alternative, which some regard as confirmed by the use of *zogreo* ("to catch alive") in Luke 5:10; but the general use is that of taking captive in the usual way. If believers resist he will flee from them, Jas. 4:7. His fury and malignity will be especially exercised at the end of the present age, Rev. 12:12. His doom is the lake of fire, Matt. 25:41; Rev. 20:10. The noun is applied to slanderers, false accusers, 1 Tim. 3:11; 2 Tim. 3:3; Titus 2:3.

DEVISED (cunningly)

sophizo (4679), from *sophos*, "wise" (connected etymologically with *sophes*, "tasty"), in the active voice signifies "to make wise," 2 Tim. 3:15. In the New Testament it means, "to play the sophist, to devise cleverly," it is used with this meaning in the passive voice in 2 Pet. 1:16, "cunningly devised fables."

DEVOUT

1. *eulabes* (2126), lit., "taking hold well" (*eu*, "well," *lambano*, "to take hold"), primarily, "cautious," signifies in the NT, "careful as to the realization of the presence and claims of God, reverencing God, pious, devout"; in Luke 2:25 it is said of Simeon; in Acts 2:5, of certain Jews; in 8:2, of those who bore Stephen's body to burial; of Ananias, 22:12 (see No. 2).

2. *eusebes* (2152), from *eu*, "well," *sebomai*, "to reverence," the root *seb*— signifying "sacred awe," describes "reverence" exhibited especially in actions, reverence or awe well directed. Among the Greeks it was used, e.g., of practical piety towards parents. In the NT it is used of a pious attitude towards God, Acts 10:2, 7; (in some mss. in 22:12); "godly," in 2 Pet. 2:9.

DIADEM

diadema (1238) is derived from *diadeo*, "to bind round." It was the kingly ornament for the head; among the Greeks and Romans it was the distinctive badge of royalty. The word is found in Rev. 12:3; 13:1; 19:12, where it symbolizes the rule respectively of the Dragon, the Beast, and Christ.

DIE, DEAD (to be, become), DYING

Old Testament

mot (4191), "to die, kill," i.e., "lose one's life," with special reference to animate, physical death, Gen. 33:13; Job 14:8. Occasionally, *mot* is used figuratively of land, Gen. 47:19, or wisdom, Job 12:2. Then, too, there is the unique hyperbolic expression that Nabal's heart had "died" within him, indicating that he was overcome with great fear, 1 Sam. 25:37.

In the usual causative stem, this verb can mean "to cause to die" or "to kill"; God is the one who "puts to death" and gives life, Deut. 32:39.

God is clearly the ultimate Ruler of life and death, cf. Deut. 32:39. This idea is especially clear in the Creation account, in which God tells man that he will surely die if he eats of the forbidden fruit, Gen. 2:17. Apparently there was no death before this time. When Adam and Eve ate of the fruit, both spiritual and physical death came upon Adam and Eve and their descendants, cf. Rom. 5:12.

New Testament

1. *thnesko* (2348), "to die" (in the perf. tense, "to be dead"), in the NT is always used of physical "death," except in 1 Tim. 5:6, where it is metaphorically used of the loss of spiritual life.

2. *apothnesko* (599), lit., "to die off or out," is used (a) of the separation of the soul from the body, i.e., the natural "death" of human beings, e.g., Matt. 9:24; Rom. 7:2; by reason of descent from Adam, 1 Cor. 15:22; or of violent "death," whether of men or animals; with regard to the latter it is once translated "perished," Matt. 8:32; of vegetation, Jude 12; of seeds, John 12:24; 1 Cor. 15:36; it is used of "death" as a punishment in Israel under the Law, in Heb. 10:28; (b) of the separation of man from God, all who are descended from Adam not only "die" physically, owing to sin, see (a) above, but are naturally in the state of separation from God, 2 Cor. 5:14. From this believers are freed both now and eternally, John 6:50; 11:26, through the "death" of Christ, Rom. 5:8, e.g.; unbelievers, who "die" physically as such, remain in eternal separation from God, John 8:24. Believers have spiritually "died" to the Law as a means of life, Gal. 2:19; Col. 2:20; to sin, Rom. 6:2, and in general to all spiritual association with the world and with that which pertained to their unregenerate state, Col. 3:3, because of their identification with the "death" of Christ, Rom. 6:8 (see No. 3, below). As life never means mere existence, so "death," the opposite of life, never means nonexistence.

3. *sunapothnesko* (4880), "to die with, to die together," is used of association in physical "death," Mark 14:31; in 2 Cor. 7:3, the apostle declares that his love to the saints makes separation impossible, whether in life or in "death." It is used once of association spiritually with Christ in His "death," 2 Tim. 2:11. See No. 2 (b).

4. *teleutao* (5053), "to end," hence, "to end one's life," is used (a) of the "death" of the body, Matt. 2:19; 9:18; 15:4, where "die the death" means "surely die," RV, marg., lit., "let him end by death"; Mark 7:10; Matt. 22:25, "deceased"; Luke 7:2; John 11:39, some mss. have verb No. 1 here; Acts 2:29; 7:15; Heb. 11:22 (RV, "his end was nigh"); (b) of the gnawings of conscience in self reproach, under the symbol of a worm, Mark 9:48 (vv. 44 and 46, KJV).

DIGNITY, DIGNITIES

doxa (*1391*) primarily denotes "an opinion, estimation, repute"; in the NT, always "good opinion, praise, honor, glory, an appearance commanding respect, magnificence, excellence, manifestation of glory"; hence, of angelic powers, in respect of their state as commanding recognition, "dignities," 2 Pet. 2:10; Jude 8.

DILIGENCE, DILIGENT, DILIGENTLY

A. Nouns.

1. *ergasia* (*2039*), (a) lit., "a working" (akin to *ergon*, "work"), is indicative of a process, in contrast to the concrete, *ergon*, e.g., Eph. 4:19, lit., "unto a working" (RV marg., "to make a trade of"); contrast *ergon* in v. 12; (b) "business," Acts 19:25, RV (for KJV, "craft"); or gain got by "work," Acts 16:16, 19; 19:24; (c) endeavor, pains, "diligence," Luke 12:58.

2. *spoude* (*4710*), "earnestness, zeal," or sometimes "the haste accompanying this," Mark 6:25; Luke 1:39.

B. Verb.

spoudazo (*4704*) has meanings corresponding to A, No. 2; it signifies "to hasten to do a thing, to exert oneself, endeavor, give diligence"; in Gal. 2:10, of remembering the poor, KJV, "was forward," RV, "was zealous"; in Eph. 4:3, of keeping the unity of the Spirit, KJV "endeavoring," RV, "giving diligence"; in 1 Thess. 2:17, of going to see friends, "endeavored"; in 2 Tim. 4:9; 4:21, "do thy diligence"; in the following the RV uses the verb "to give diligence": 2 Tim. 2:15, KJV, "study"; Titus 3:12, KJV, "be diligent"; Heb. 4:11, of keeping continuous Sabbath rest, KJV, "let us labor"; in 2 Pet. 1:10, of making our calling and election sure; in 2 Pet. 1:15, of enabling believers to call Scripture truth to remembrance, KJV, "endeavour"; in 2 Pet. 3:14, of being found in peace without fault and blameless, when the Lord comes, KJV, be diligent.

C. Adjectives.

1. *spoudaios* (*4705*), akin to A, No. 2 and B, No. 1, primarily signifies "in haste"; hence, diligent, earnest, zealous, 2 Cor. 8:22, KJV, "diligent," RV, "earnest."

2. *spoudaioteros* (*4707*), the comparative degree of No. 1, 2 Cor. 8:22.

D. Adverbs.

1. *spoudaios* (*4709*), "speedily, earnestly, diligently," is translated "earnestly" in the RV of Luke 7:4 (KJV, "instantly"); "diligently" in Titus 3:13.

2. *spoudaioteros* (*4708*), the comparative degree of No. 1, "more diligently," is used in Phil. 2:28.

DINE, DINNER

A. Verb.

aristao (709), primarily, "to breakfast" (see B), was later used also with the meaning "to dine," e.g., Luke 11:37; in John 21:12, 15, RV, "break your fast," and "had broken their fast," for KJV, "dine"; obviously there it was the first meal in the day.

B. Noun.

ariston (712), primarily, "the first food," taken early in the morning before work; the meal in the Pharisee's house, in Luke 11:37, was a breakfast or early meal; the dinner was called *deipnon*. Later the breakfast was called *akratisma* (not in NT), and dinner, *ariston*, as in Matt. 22:4; Luke 11:38; 14:12.

DIP, DIPPED, DIPPETH

1. *bapto* (911), "to immerse, dip" (derived from a root signifying "deep"), also signified "to dye," which is suggested in Rev. 19:13, of the Lord's garment "dipped (i.e. dyed) in blood," also Luke 16:24; John 13:26.

2. *embapto* (1686), *en*, "in," and No. 1, "to dip into," is used of the act of Judas in "dipping" his hand with that of Christ in the dish, Matt. 26:23; Mark 14:20.

DISANNUL, DISANNULLING

A. Verbs.

1. *atheteo* (114) signifies "to put as of no value" (*a*, negative and *theton*, "what is placed," from *tithemi*, "to put, place"); hence, (a) "to act towards anything as though it were annulled"; e.g., to deprive a law of its force by opinions or acts contrary to it, Gal. 3:15, KJV, "disannulleth," RV, "maketh void"; (b) "to thwart the efficacy of anything, to nullify, to frustrate it," Luke 7:30, "rejected"; 1 Cor. 1:19, "will I reject"; to make void, Gal. 2:21; to set at nought, Jude 8, RV (KJV, "despised"); the parallel passage, in 2 Pet. 2:10, has *kataphroneo*. In Mark 6:26, the thought is that of breaking faith with.

2. *akuroo* (208), "to deprive of authority," hence, "to make of none effect," Matt. 15:6; Mark 7:13, with reference to the commandment or word of God, RV, "to make void," is translated "disannul" in Gal. 3:17, of the inability of the Law to deprive of force God's covenant with Abraham. This verb stresses the effect of the act, while No. 1 stresses the attitude of the rejecter.

B. Noun.

athetesis (115), akin to A, No. 1, "a setting aside, abolition," is translated "disannulling" in Heb. 7:18, with reference to a commandment; in 9:26 "to put away," with reference to sin, lit., "for a putting away."

DISBELIEVE

apisteo (*569*), "to be unbelieving" (*a*, negative, *pistis*, "faith"); is translated "believed not," etc., in the KJV (except in 1 Pet. 2:7, "be disobedient"); "disbelieve" (or "disbelieved") in the RV, in Mark 16:11, 16; Luke 24:11, 41; Acts 28:24; "disbelieve" is the best rendering, implying that the unbeliever has had a full opportunity of believing and has rejected it.

DISCERN, DISCERNER, DISCERNMENT

Old Testament

nakar (*5234*), "to discern, regard, recognize, pay attention to, be acquainted with." The basic meaning of the term is a "physical apprehension," whether through sight, touch, or hearing. Darkness sometimes makes "recognition" impossible, Ruth 3:14. People are often "recognized" by their voices, Judg. 18:3. *nakar* sometimes has the meaning of "pay attention to," a special kind of "recognition," Ruth 2:19. The sense of "to distinguish" is seen in Ezra 3:13.

New Testament

A. Verbs.

1. *anakrino* (*350*), "to distinguish, or separate out so as to investigate (*krino*) by looking throughout (*ana*, intensive) objects or particulars," hence signifies "to examine, scrutinize, question, to hold a preliminary judicial examination preceding the trial proper" (this first examination, implying more to follow, is often present in the non-legal uses of the word), e.g. Luke 23:14; figuratively, in 1 Cor. 4:3; it is said of searching the Scriptures in Acts 17:11; of "discerning" or determining the excellence or defects of a person or thing, e.g., 1 Cor. 2:14, KJV, "discerned"; RV, "judged"; in 1 Cor. 10:27, "asking (no) question" (i.e., not raising the question as to whether the meat is the residue from an idolatrous sacrifice). Except in Luke 23:14, this word is found only in Acts and 1 Cor.

2. *diakrino* (*1252*) signifies "to separate, discriminate"; then, "to learn by discriminating, to determine, decide." It is translated "discern" in Matt. 16:3, of discriminating between the varying conditions of the sky (see No. 3, below, in Luke 12:56), and in 1 Cor. 11:29, with reference to partaking of the bread and the cup of the Lord's Supper unworthily, by not "discerning" or discriminating what they represent; in v. 31, the RV has "discerned," for the KJV, "would judge," of trying oneself, "discerning" one's condition, and so judging any evil before the Lord; in 14:29, regarding oral testimony in a gathering of believers, it is used of "discerning" what is of the Holy Spirit, RV, "discern" (KJV, "judge").

3. *dokimazo* (*1381*) signifies "to test, prove, scrutinize," so as "to decide." It is translated "discern" in the KJV of Luke 12:56.

B. Noun.

diakrisis (*1253*), cf. A, No. 2, "a distinguishing, a clear discrimination, discerning, judging," is translated "discernings" in 1 Cor. 12:10, of "discerning" spirits, judging by evidence whether they are evil or of God. In Heb. 5:14 the phrase consisting of pros, with this noun, lit., "towards a discerning," is translated "to discern," said of those who are capable of discriminating between good and evil. In Rom. 14:1 the word has its other sense of decision or judgment, and the phrase "doubtful disputations" is, lit., "judgments of reasonings."

C. Adjective.

kritikos (*2924*) signifies "that which relates to judging (*krino*, "to judge"), fit for, or skilled in, judging" (Eng., "critical"), found in Heb. 4:12, of the Word of God as "quick to discern the thoughts and intents of the heart," (lit., "critical of, etc."), i.e., discriminating and passing judgment on the thoughts and feelings.

DISCIPLE

A. Nouns.

1. *mathetes* (*3101*), lit., "a learner" (from *manthano*, "to learn," from a root *math*—, indicating thought accompanied by endeavor), in contrast to *didaskalos*, "a teacher"; hence it denotes "one who follows one's teaching," as the "disciples" of John, Matt. 9:14; of the Pharisees, Matt. 22:16; of Moses, John 9:28; it is used of the "disciples" of Jesus (a) in a wide sense, of Jews who became His adherents, John 6:66; Luke 6:17, some being secretly so, John 19:38; (b) especially of the twelve apostles, Matt. 10:1; Luke 22:11, e.g.; (c) of all who manifest that they are His "disciples" by abiding in His Word, and so be an adherent, John 8:31.

2. *mathetria* (*3102*), "a female disciple," is said of Tabitha, Acts 9:36.

3. *summathetes* (*4827*) means "a fellow disciple" (*sun*, with, and No. 1), John 11:16.

B. Verb.

matheteuo (*3100*) is used in the active voice, intransitively, in some mss., in Matt. 27:57, in the sense of being the "disciple" of a person; here, however, the best mss. have the passive voice, lit., "had been made a disciple," as in Matt. 13:52, RV, "who hath been made a disciple." It is used in this transitive sense in the active voice in 28:19 and Acts 14:21.

DISCIPLINE

sophronismos (*4995*), from *sophron*, lit., "saving the mind," primarily, "an admonishing or calling to soundness of mind, or to self-control," is used in 2 Tim. 1:7, KJV, "a sound mind"; RV, "discipline."

DISCREET, DISCREETLY

A. Adjective.

sophron (*4998*), "of sound mind self-controlled," is translated "sober-minded," in its four occurrences in the RV, 1 Tim. 3:2 (KJV, "sober"); Titus 1:8 (KJV, "sober"); 2:2 (KJV, "temperate"); 2:5 (KJV, "discreet").

B. Adverb.

nounechos (*3562*), lit., "mind-possessing" (*nous*, "mind, understanding," *echo*, "to have"), hence denotes "discreetly, sensibly prudently." Mark 12:34.

DISEASE, DISEASED (BE)

A. Nouns.

1. *astheneia* (*769*), lit., "lacking strength" (*a*, negative, *sthenos*, "strength"), "weakness, infirmity," is translated "diseases" in Matt. 8:17, RV, for KJV, "sicknesses," and in Acts 28:9. Its usual rendering is "infirmity" or "infirmities"; "sickness," in John 11:4.

2. *malakia* (*3119*) primarily denotes "softness"; hence, "debility, disease." It is found in Matthew only, 4:23; 9:35; 10:1.

3. *nosos* (*3554*), akin to Lat. *nocere*, "to injure" (Eng., "noxious"), is the regular word for "disease, sickness," Matt. 4:23; 8:17; 9:35; 10:1, RV, "disease," KJV, "sickness"; in Matt. 4:24; Mark 1:34; Luke 4:40; 6:17; 9:1; Acts 19:12, KJV and RV render it "diseases." In Luke 7:21, KJV has "infirmities." The most authentic mss. omit the word in Mark 3:15.

4. *nosema* (*3553*), an alternative form of No. 3, is found in some mss. in John 5:4.

B. Verbs.

1. *astheneo* (*770*), akin to A, No. 1, "to lack strength, to be weak, sick," is translated "were diseased" in John 6:2, KJV (RV, "were sick").

2. *echo kakos* lit., "to have badly," i.e., "to be ill or in an evil case," is used in Matt. 14:35 (KJV, "were diseased," RV, "were sick"); so in Mark 1:32; Luke 7:2.

DISHONESTY

aischune (*152*), "shame," so the RV in 2 Cor. 4:2 (for KJV, "dishonesty"), is elsewhere rendered "shame," Luke 14:9; Phil. 3:19; Heb. 12:2; Jude 13; Rev. 3:18.

DISHONOR

A. Noun.

atimia (*819*), from *a*, negative, *time*, "honor," denotes "dishonor, ignominy, disgrace," in Rom. 1:26, "vile passions" (RV), lit., 'passions of dishonor;' in Rom. 9:21, "dishonor," of vessels designed for meaner household purposes (in contrast to *time*, "honor," as in 2 Tim. 2:20); in 1 Cor. 11:14, said of long hair, if worn by men, RV, "dishonor," for KJV, "shame," in contrast to *doxa*, glory, v. 15; so in 1 Cor. 15:43, of the "sowing" of the natural body, and in 2 Cor. 6:8, of the apostle Paul's ministry.

B. Verb.

1. *atimazo* (*818*) akin to A, signifies "to dishonour, treat shamefully, insult," whether in word, John 8:49, or deed, Mark 12:4; Luke 20:11, RV "handled (him) shamefully," (RV "entreated...shamefully"); Rom. 1:24; 2:23, "dishonorest"; Jas. 2:6, RV, "ye have dishonored (the poor)," (KJV, "despised"); in the passive voice, to suffer dishonor, Acts 5:41 (KJV, "suffer shame").

TO BE DISMAYED

chatat (*2865*), "to be dismayed, shattered, broken, terrified." *chatat* is often used in parallelism with the Hebrew term for "fear," cf. Deut. 31:8; Josh. 8:1; 1 Sam. 17:11. Similarly, *chatat* is frequently used in parallelism with "to be ashamed," Isa. 20:5; Jer. 8:9.

DISOBEDIENCE, DISOBEDIENT

A. Nouns.

1. *apeitheia* (*543*), lit., "the condition of being unpersuadable," denotes "obstinacy, obstinate rejection of the will of God"; hence, "disobedience"; Eph. 2:2; 5:6; Col. 3:6, and in the RV of Rom. 11:30, 32 and Heb. 4:6, 11 (for KJV, "unbelief"), speaking of Israel, past and present.

2. *parakoe* (*3876*), primarily, "hearing amiss," hence signifies "a refusal to hear"; hence, "an act of disobedience," Rom. 5:19; 2 Cor. 10:6; Heb. 2:2. It is broadly to be distinguished from No. 1, as an act from a condition, though *parakoe* itself is the effect, in transgression, of the condition of failing or refusing to hear. Carelessness in attitude is the precursor of actual "disobedience." In the OT "disobedience" is frequently described as "a refusing to hear," e.g., Jer. 11:10; 35:17; cf. Acts 7:57.

B. Adjective.

apeithes (*545*), akin to A, No. 1, signifies "unwilling to be persuaded, spurning belief, disobedient," Luke 1:17; Acts 26:19; Rom. 1:30; 2 Tim. 3:2; Titus 1:16; 3:3.

C. Verb.

apeitheo (544), akin to A, No. 1, and B, "to refuse to be persuaded, to refuse belief, to be disobedient," is translated "disobedient," or by the verb "to be disobedient," in the RV of Acts 14:2 (KJV, "unbelieving"), and 19:9 (KJV, "believed not"); it is absent from the most authentic mss. in Acts 17:5; in John 3:36 "obeyeth not," RV (KJV, "believeth not"); in Rom. 2:8 "obey not"; in 10:21, "disobedient"; in 11:30, 31, "were disobedient" (KJV, "have not believed"); so in 15:31; Heb. 3:18; 11:31; in 1 Pet. 2:8, "disobedient"; so in 3:20; in 3:1 and 4:17, "obey not."

DISORDERLY

A. Adjective.

ataktos (813) signifies "not keeping order"; it was especially a military term, denoting "not keeping rank, insubordinate"; it is used in 1 Thess. 5:14, describing certain church members who manifested an insubordinate spirit, whether by excitability or officiousness or idleness.

B. Adverb.

ataktos (814) signifies "disorderly, with slackness" (like soldiers not keeping rank) 2 Thess. 3:6; in v. 11 it is said of those in the church who refused to work, and became busybodies (cf. 1 Tim. 5:13).

C. Verb.

atakteo (812) signifies "to be out of rank, out of one's place, undisciplined, to behave disorderly": in the military sense, "to break rank"; negatively in 2 Thess. 3:7, of the example set by the apostle and his fellow missionaries, in working for their bread while they were at Thessalonica so as not to burden the saints.

DISPENSATION

oikonomia (3622) primarily signifies "the management of a household or of household affairs" (*oikos*, "a house," *nomos*, "a law"); then the management or administration of the property of others, and so "a stewardship," Luke 16:2-4; elsewhere only in the epistles of Paul, who applies it (a) to the responsibility entrusted to him of preaching the gospel, 1 Cor. 9:17 (RV, "stewardship," KJV, "dispensation"); (b) to the stewardship committed to him "to fulfill the Word of God," the fulfillment being the unfolding of the completion of the divinely arranged and imparted cycle of truths which are consummated in the truth relating to the church as the body of Christ, Col. 1:25 (RV and KJV, "dispensation"); so in Eph. 3:2, of the grace of God given him as a stewardship ("dispensation") in regard to the same "mystery"; (c) in Eph. 1:10 and 3:9, it is used of the arrangement or administration by God, by which in "the fullness of the times" (or seasons) God will sum up all things in the heavens and on earth in Christ.

DISPERSE, DISPERSION

A. Verbs.

1. *dialuo* (1262), "to dissolve," is used in Acts 5:36 of the breaking up and dispersion of a company of men.

2. *skorpizo* (4650), "to scatter," is used in Matt. 12:30; Luke 11:23; John 10:12; 16:32; in the RV of 2 Cor. 9:9, "scattered abroad" (KJV, "he hath dispersed abroad"), of one who liberally dispenses benefits.

3. *diaskorpizo* (1287), *dia*, "through," and No. 2, signifies "to scatter abroad," in Matt. 26:31; Mark 14:27, metaphorically of sheep, in Luke 1:51, of the proud; in John 11:52, of the "scattering" of the children of God; in Acts 5:37, of the followers of Judas of Galilee.

4. *diaspeiro* (1289), "to scatter abroad" (*dia*, "through," *speiro*, "to sow"), is used in Acts 8:1, 4; 11:19.

B. Noun.

diaspora (1290), akin to A, No. 4, "a scattering, a dispersion," was used of the Jews who from time to time had been scattered among the Gentiles, John 7:35; later with reference to Jews, so "scattered," who had professed, or actually embraced, the Christian faith, "the Dispersion," Jas. 1:1, RV; especially of believers who were converts from Judaism and "scattered" throughout certain districts, "sojourners of the Dispersion," 1 Pet. 1:1, RV.

DISPLEASED

1. *aganakteo* (23), from *agan*, "much," and *achomai*, "to grieve," primarily meant "to feel a violent irritation, physically"; it was used, too, of the fermenting of wine hence, metaphorically, "to show signs of grief, to be displeased, to be grieved, vexed"; it is translated "sore displeased" in Matt. 21:15, KJV; "much displeased," in Mark 10:14, 41; the RV always renders it "to be moved with, or to have, indignation," as the KJV elsewhere, Matt. 20:24; 26:8; Mark 14:4; Luke 13:14.

2. *prosochthizo* (4360), "to be wroth or displeased with" (*pros*, "toward," or "with," *ochtheo*, "to be sorely vexed"), is used in Heb. 3:10, 17 (KJV, "grieved"; RV, "displeased"). "Grieved" does not adequately express the righteous anger of God intimated in the passage.

3. *thumomacheo* (2371), lit., "to fight with great animosity," hence, "to be very angry, to be highly displeased," is said of Herod's "displeasure" with the Tyrians and Sidonians, Acts 12:20.

DISPOSITION

diatage (1296), an ordinance, e.g., Rom. 13:2 (cf. *diatasso*, "to appoint, ordain"), is rendered "disposition" in Acts 7:53; cf. Deut. 33:2. In Acts 7:53 Stephen mentions the angels to stress the majesty of the Law.

DISPUTATION

1. *zetesis* (2214) denotes, firstly, "a seeking" (*zeteo*, "to seek"), then, "a debate, dispute, questioning," Acts 15:2, 7.

2. *dialogismos* (1261) is translated "disputations" in Rom. 14:1.

DISPUTE, DISPUTER, DISPUTING

A. Nouns.

1. *dialogismos* (1261) denotes, primarily, "an inward reasoning, an opinion" (*dia*, "through," suggesting separation, *logismos*, "a reasoning"), e.g., Luke 2:35; 5:22; 6:8; then, "a deliberating, questioning," Luke 24:38; (more strongly) "a disputing," Phil. 2:14; 1 Tim. 2:8 (KJV, "doubtings"); in Rom. 14:1, "disputations"; marg., "(not for decisions) of doubts" (lit., "not unto discussions or doubts," which is perhaps a suitable rendering).

2. *logomachia* (3055) denotes "a dispute about words" (*logos*, "a word," *mache*, "a fight"), or about trivial things, 1 Tim. 6:4, RV, "disputes," KJV, "strifes."

3. *antilogia* (485) denotes "a gainsaying, contradiction" (*anti*, "against," *lego*, "to speak"), Heb. 6:16; 7:7; 12:3; Jude 11.

4. *suzetetes* (4804), from *sun*, "with," *zeteo*, "to seek," denotes "a disputer," 1 Cor. 1:20, where the reference is especially to a learned "disputant," a sophist.

B. Verbs.

1. *dialegomai* (1256), akin to A No. 1, primarily signifies "to think different things with oneself, to ponder"; then, with other persons, "to converse, argue, dispute"; it is translated "to dispute" in Mark 9:34 (for v. 33, see No. 2), the RV and KJV "had disputed" is somewhat unsuitable here, for the delinquency was not that they had wrangled, but that they had reasoned upon the subject at all; in Acts 17:17, KJV (RV, "reasoned," as in the KJV of 18:4, 19); in 19:8-9 (RV, "reasoning"); in 24:12, "disputing"; in Jude 9, "disputed."

2. *dialogizomai* (1260), akin to A, No. 1, "to bring together different reasons, to reckon them up, to reason, discuss," in Mark 9:33 is translated "ye disputed among yourselves," KJV; RV, "were reasoning."

3. *suzeteo* (4802), akin to A, No. 4, lit., "to seek or examine together," signifies "to discuss," but is translated "to dispute" in Acts 6:9, and 9:29; elsewhere only in Mark and Luke.

DISSENSION

stasis (4714), akin to *histemi*, "to stand," denotes (a) "a standing, stability," Heb. 9:8, "(while as the first tabernacle) is yet standing"; (b) "an insurrection, uproar," Mark 15:7; Luke 23:19, 25; Acts 19:40; 24:5; (c) "a dissension," Acts 15:2; 23:7, 10.

DISSIMULATION, DISSEMBLE

A. Noun.

hupokrisis (5272), primarily, "a reply," came to mean "the acting of a stageplayer," because such answered one another in dialogue; hence the meaning "dissembling or pretense." It is translated "dissimulation" in Gal. 2:13 (see B).

B. Verb.

sunupokrinomai (4942), lit., "to join in acting the hypocrite," in pretending to act from one motive, whereas another motive really inspires the act. So in Gal. 2:13, Peter with other believing Jews, in separating from believing Gentiles at Antioch, pretended that the motive was loyalty to the Law of Moses, whereas really it was fear of the Judaizers.

C. Adjective.

anupokritos (505), from *a*, negative, *n*, euphonic, and an adjectival form corresponding to A, signifies "unfeigned"; it is said of love, 2 Cor. 6:6; 1 Pet. 1:22; Rom. 12:9, KJV, "without dissimulation," RV, "without hypocrisy"; of faith, 1 Tim. 1:5; 2 Tim. 1:5, "unfeigned"; of the wisdom that is from above, Jas. 3:17, "without hypocrisy."

DISTRESS, DISTRESSED

Old Testament

A. Nouns.

tsarah (6869), "distress; straits," in a psychological or spiritual sense, which is its meaning in Gen. 42:21.

tsar (6862), "distress." This word also occurs mostly in poetry. In Prov. 24:10, *tsar* means "scarcity" or the "distress" caused by scarcity. The emphasis of the noun is sometimes on the feeling of "dismay" arising from a distressful situation, Job 7:11. In this usage the word *tsar* represents a psychological or spiritual status. In Isa. 5:30, the word describes conditions that cause distress, cf. Isa. 30:20.

B. Verb.

tsarar (6887), "to wrap, tie up, be narrow, be distressed, be in pangs of birth," Judg. 11:7.

C. Adjective.

tsar (6862), "narrow," Num. 22:26.

New Testament

A. Noun.

ananke (*318*) denotes (a) "a necessity," imposed whether by external circumstances, e.g., Luke 23:17, or inward pressure, e.g., 1 Cor. 9:16; (b) "straits, distress," Luke 21:23; 1 Cor. 7:26; 1 Thess. 3:7; the last two refer to the lack of material things.

B. Verbs.

1. *basanizo* (*928*), properly signifies "to test by rubbing on the touchstone" (*basanos*, "a touchstone"), then, "to question by applying torture"; hence "to vex, torment"; in the passive voice, "to be harassed, distressed"; it is said of men struggling in a boat against wind and waves, Matt. 14:24, RV, "distressed" (KJV, "tossed"); Mark 6:48, RV, "distressed" (KJV, toiling).

2. *kataponeo* (*2669*), primarily, "to tire down with toil, exhaust with labor" (*kata*, "down," *ponos*, "labor"), hence signifies "to afflict, oppress"; in the passive voice, "to be oppressed, much distressed"; it is translated "oppressed" in Acts 7:24, and "sore distressed" in 2 Pet. 2:7, RV, (KJV, "vexed").

DISTRIBUTE, DISTRIBUTION

A. Verb.

diadidomi (*1239*), lit., "to give through," (*dia*, "through," *didomi*, "to give"), as from one to another, "to deal out," is said of "distributing" to the poor, Luke 18:22; Acts 4:35.

B. Adjective.

eumetadotos (*2130*), "ready to impart" (*eu*, "well," *meta*, "with," *didomi*, "to give": see A, is used in 1 Tim. 6:18, "ready to distribute."

DIVERS

A. Adjectives.

1. *diaphoros* (*1313*) is rendered divers in Heb. 9:10.

2. *poikilos* (*4164*) denotes "parti-colored, variegated" (*poikillo* means "to make bright, various colors," hence "divers"), Matt. 4:24; Mark 1:34; Luke 4:40; 2 Tim. 3:6; Titus 3:3; Heb. 2:4 (RV, "manifold"), 13:9; Jas. 1:2 (RV, "manifold"); in 1 Pet. 1:6 and 4:10, "manifold," both KJV and RV.

B. Adverb.

polutropos (*4187*) means "in many ways," Heb. 1:1.

DIVIDE, DIVIDER, DIVIDING
Old Testament
A. Verb.

chalaq (2505), "to divide, share, plunder, assign, distribute." The sense of "dividing" or "allotting" is found in Deut. 4:19, where the sun, moon, and stars are said to have been "allotted" to all peoples by God. A similar use is seen in Deut. 29:26, where God is said not to have "allotted" false gods to His people.

chalaq is used in the legal sense of "sharing" an inheritance in Prov. 17:2. The word is used three times in reference to "sharing" the spoils of war in 1 Sam. 30:24.

This verb describes the "division" of the people of Israel, as one half followed Tibni and the other half followed Omri, 1 Kings 16:21.

B. Noun.

cheleq (2506), "portion; territory." It has a variety of meanings, such as "booty" of war, Gen. 14:24, a "portion" of food, Lev. 6:17, a "tract" of land, Josh. 18:5, a spiritual "possession" or blessing, Ps. 73:26, and a chosen "pattern" or "life-style," Ps. 50:18.

New Testament
A. Verbs.

1. *aphorizo* (873), lit., "to mark off by boundaries or limits" (*apo*, "from," *horizo*, "to determine, mark out"), denotes "to separate"; "divideth," Matt. 25:32.

2. *diaireo* (1244), lit., "to take asunder," "to divide into parts, to distribute," is found in Luke 15:12 and 1 Cor. 12:11.

3. *diakrino* (1252), "to separate," discriminate, hence, "to be at variance with oneself, to be divided in one's mind," is rendered "divided" in Jas. 2:4, RV; KJV, "partial."

4. *merizo* (3307), akin to *meros*, "a part, to part, divide into," in the middle voice means "to divide anything with another, to share with." The usual meaning is "to divide," Matt. 12:25, 26; Mark 3:24-26; 6:41; Luke 12:13 (middle voice); Rom. 12:3, "hath dealt"; 1 Cor. 1:13; Heb. 7:2, RV (KJV, "gave a part"). Elsewhere with other meanings, 1 Cor. 7:17, 34; 2 Cor. 10:13.

5. *diamerizo* (1266), *dia*, "through," and No. 4, "to divide through," i.e., "completely, to divide up," is translated "to divide" in Luke 11:17-18; 12:52-53; 22:17; "parted" in Matt. 27:35; Mark 15:24; Luke 23:34; John 19:24; Acts 2:45; in Acts 2:3, KJV, "cloven," RV, "parting asunder."

6. *orthotomeo* (3718), lit., "to cut straight" (*orthos*, "straight," *temno*, "to cut"), is found in 2 Tim. 2:15, KJV, "rightly dividing," RV, "handling aright," used figuratively, means teaching Scripture accurately.

B. Nouns.

1. *meristes* (*3312*), "a divider," is found in Luke 12:14.

2. *merismos* (*3311*), akin to No. 1, primarily denotes "a division, partition" (*meros*, "a part"); hence, (a) "a distribution," Heb. 2:4, "gifts"; (b) likely means, "an active dividing or separation," Heb. 4:12.

DIVINATION, (TO) DIVINE

Old Testament

qasam (*7080*), "to divine, practice divination." Divination was a pagan parallel to prophesying, and so forbidden, Deut. 18:10, 14-15. It is a seeking after the will of the gods, in an effort to learn their future action or divine blessing on some proposed future action, Josh. 13:22, likely demons, 1 Cor. 10:20. The pagan practice of divination might involve: sacrifice, Num. 23:1ff.; speaking to the spirits of the dead, 1 Sam. 28:8; shaking of arrows; or studying the livers of sacrificed animals, Ezek. 21:21.

New Testament

puthon (*4436*), (Eng., "python"), in Greek mythology was the name of the Pythian serpent or dragon, Acts 16:16; which here refers to being possessed by a demon instigating the cult of Apollo.

DIVINE

A. Adjective.

theios (*2304*), "divine" (from *theos*, "God"), is used of the power of God, 2 Pet. 1:3, and of His nature, v. 4, in each place, as that which proceeds from Himself. In Acts 17:29 it is used as a noun with the definite article, to denote "the Godhead," the Deity (i.e., the one true God). This word, instead of *theos*, was purposely used by the apostle in speaking to Greeks on Mars Hill, as in accordance with Greek usage.

B. Noun.

latreia (*2999*), akin to *latreuo*, "to serve," primarily, any service for hire denotes in Scripture the service of God according to the requirements of the Levitical Law, Rom. 9:4; Heb. 9:1, 6, "divine service." It is used in the more general sense of service to God, in John 16:2; Rom. 12:1.

DIVINITY

theiotes (*2305*), divinity, the RV rendering in Rom. 1:20 (KJV, "Godhead"), is derived from *theios*, and is to be distinguished from *theotes*, in Col. 2:9, "Godhead." In Rom. 1:20 the apostle "is declaring how much of God may be known from the revelation of Himself which He has made in nature, from those vestiges of Himself which men may everywhere trace in the world around them. Yet it is not the personal God whom any man may learn to know by these aids; He can be known only by the revelation of Himself in His Son;...But in the second passage, Col. 2:9, Paul is declaring that in the Son there dwells all the fullness of absolute Godhead."

DIVORCE, DIVORCEMENT

A. Verb.

apoluo (*630*), "to let loose from, let go free" (*apo*, "from," *luo*, "to loose"), is translated "is divorced" in the KJV of Matt. 5:32 (RV, "is put away"); it is further used of "divorce" in Matt. 1:19; 19:3, 7-9; Mark 10:2, 4 11; Luke 16:18. The Lord also used it of the case of a wife putting away her husband, Mark 10:12, a usage among Greeks and Romans, not among Jews.

B. Noun.

apostasion (*647*), primarily, "a defection," lit., "a standing off," denotes in the NT, "a writing or bill of divorcement," Matt. 5:31; 19:7; Mark 10:4.

DOCTRINE

1. *didache* (*1322*), denotes "teaching," either (a) that which is taught, e.g., Matt. 7:28, KJV, "doctrine," RV, "teaching"; Titus 1:9, RV; Rev. 2:14-15, 24, or (b) the act of teaching, instruction, e.g., Mark 4:2, KJV, "doctrine," RV, "teaching" the RV has "the doctrine" in Rom. 16:17.

2. *didaskalia* (*1319*) denotes, as No. 1 (from which, however, it is to be distinguished), (a) "that which is taught, doctrine," Matt. 15:9; Mark 7:7; Eph. 4:14; Col. 2:22; 1 Tim. 1:10; 4:1, 6; 6:1, 3; 2 Tim. 3:16; Titus 1:9 ("doctrine," in last part of verse: see also No. 1); 2:1, 10; (b) "teaching, instruction," Rom. 12:7, "teaching"; 15:4, "learning," 1 Tim. 4:13, KJV, "doctrine," RV, "teaching"; v. 16, KJV, "the doctrine," RV, (correctly) "thy teaching; 5:17, KJV, "doctrine," RV "teaching"; 2 Tim. 3:10, 16 ("doctrine"); Titus 2:7, "thy doctrine."

DOG

1. *kuon* (*2965*) is used in two senses, (a) natural, Matt. 7:6; Luke 16:21; 2 Pet. 2:22; (b) metaphorical, Phil. 3:2; Rev. 22:15, of those whose moral impurity will exclude them from the New Jerusalem.

2. *kunarion* (*2952*), a diminutive of No. 1, "a little dog, a puppy," is used in Matt. 15:26-27; Mark 7:27, 28.

DOMINION (have...over)

A. Nouns.

1. *kratos* (*2904*), "force, strength, might," more especially "man-

ifested power," is derived from a root *kra*—, "to perfect, to complete": "creator" is probably connected. It also signifies "dominion," and is so rendered frequently in doxologies, 1 Pet. 4:11; 5:11; Jude 25; Rev. 1:6; 5:13 (RV); in 1 Tim. 6:16, and Heb. 2:14 it is translated "power."

2. *kuriotes* (2963) denotes "lordship" (*kurios*, "a lord"), "power, dominion," whether angelic or human, Eph. 1:21; Col. 1:16; 2 Pet. 2:10 (RV, for KJV, "government"); Jude 8. In Eph. and Col. it indicates a grade in the angelic orders, in which·it stands second.

B. Verbs.

1. *kurieuo* (2961), "to be lord over, rule over, have dominion over" (akin to A, No. 2), is used of (a) divine authority over men, Rom. 14:9, "might be Lord"; (b) human authority over men, Luke 22:25, "lordship," 1 Tim. 6:15, "lords"; (c) the permanent immunity of Christ from the "dominion" of death, Rom. 6:9; (d) the deliverance of the believer from the "dominion" of sin, Rom. 6:14; (e) the "dominion" of law over men, Rom. 7:1; (f) the "dominion" of a person over the faith of other believers, 2 Cor. 1:24 (RV, "lordship").

2. *katakurieuo* (2634), *kata*, "down" (intensive), and No. 1, "to exercise, or gain, dominion over, to lord it over," is used of (a) the "lordship" of gentile rulers, Matt. 20:25, KJV, "exercise dominion," RV, "lord it," Mark 10:42, KJV, "exercise lordship," RV, "lord it"; (b) the power of demons over men, Acts 19:16, KJV, "overcame," RV, "mastered"; (c) of the evil of elders in "lording" it over the saints under their spiritual care, 1 Pet. 5:3.

DOOR

thura (2374), "a door, gate" (Eng., "door" is connected), is used (a) literally, e.g., Matt. 6:6; 27:60; (b) metaphorically, of Christ, John 10:7, 9; of faith, by acceptance of the gospel, Acts 14:27; of "openings" for preaching and teaching the Word of God, 1 Cor. 16:9; 2 Cor. 2:12; Col. 4:3; Rev. 3:8; of "entrance" into the Kingdom of God, Matt. 25:10; Luke 13:24-25; of Christ's "entrance" into a repentant believer's heart, Rev. 3:20; of the nearness of Christ's second advent, Matt. 24:33; Mark 13:29; cf. Jas. 5:9; of "access" to behold visions relative to the purposes of God, Rev. 4:1.

DOTE

noseo (3552) signifies "to be ill, to be ailing," whether in body or mind; hence, "to be taken with such a morbid interest in a thing as is tantamount to a disease, to dote," 1 Tim. 6:4.

DOUBLE-MINDED

dipsuchos (1374) lit. means "two-souled," hence, "double-minded," Jas. 1:8; 4:8.

DOUBLE-TONGUED

dilogos (1351) primarily means "saying the same thing twice, or given to repetition"; hence, "saying a thing to one person and giving a different view of it to another, double-tongued," 1 Tim. 3:8.

DOUBT (be in, make to), DOUBTFUL, DOUBTING

D

A. Verbs.

1. *aporeo* (639), always used in the middle voice, lit. means "to be without a way" (*a*, negative, *poros*, "a way, transit"), "to be without resources, embarrassed, in doubt, perplexity, at a loss," as was Herod regarding John the Baptist, Mark 6:20 (RV, following the most authentic mss., "was much perplexed"); as the disciples were, regarding the Lord's betrayal, John 13:22, "doubting"; and regarding the absence of His body from the tomb, Luke 24:4, "were perplexed"; as was Festus, about the nature of the accusations brought against Paul, Acts 25:20, KJV "doubted," RV, "being perplexed"; as Paul was, in his experiences of trial 2 Cor. 4:8, "perplexed," and, as to the attitude of the believers of the churches in Galatia towards Judaistic errors, Gal. 4:20, KJV, "I stand in doubt," RV, "I am perplexed." Perplexity is the main idea.

2. *diaporeo* (1280), *dia*, "asunder" (intensive), and No. 1, signifies "to be thoroughly perplexed," with a perplexity amounting to despair, Acts 2:12; 5:24 and 10:17, KJV, "were in doubt," "doubted," RV, "were (was) perplexed." See also Luke 9:7 (some mss. have it in Luke 24:4, where the most authentic have No. 1).

3. *diakrino* (1252): in Acts 11:12, KJV, "nothing doubting," RV, "making no distinction"; in Jude 22, RV, "who are in doubt"; in Jas. 1:6, KJV, "wavereth," RV, "doubteth." This verb suggests, not so much weakness of faith, as lack of it (contrast, Nos. 4 and 5).

4. *distazo* (1365), "to stand in two ways," implying "uncertainty which way to take," is used in Matt. 14:31 and 28:17; said of believers whose faith is small.

5. *meteorizo* (3349), (Eng., "meteor"), signifying "in mid air, raised on high," was primarily used of putting a ship out to sea, or of "raising" fortifications, in the NT used metaphorically, of "being anxious," through a "distracted" state of mind, of "wavering" between hope and fear, Luke 12:29.

6. *psuchen airo*, lit., "to raise the breath, or to lift the soul," signifies "to hold in suspense," RV of John 10:24 (KJV, "make us to doubt"), suggestive of "an objective suspense due to lack of light," through a failure of their expectations, rather than, subjectively, through unbelief. The meaning may thus be, "How long dost Thou raise our expectations without satisfying them?"

B. Noun.

dialogismos (1261) expresses reasoning or questioning hesitation, 1 Tim. 2:8.

DOVE, TURTLE-DOVE

1. *peristera* (4058) denotes "a dove or pigeon," Matt. 3:16; 10:16 (indicating its proverbial harmlessness); 21:12; Mark 1:10; 11:15; Luke 2:24 ("pigeons"); 3:22; John 1:32; 2:14, 16.

2. *trugon* (5167) denotes "a turtledove" (from *truzo*, "to murmur, to coo"), Luke 2:24.

DRAGON

drakon (1404) denoted "a mythical monster, a dragon"; also a large serpent, so called because of its keen power of sight (from a root *derk—*, signifying "to see"). Twelve times in the Apocalypse it is used of the Devil 12:3-4, 7, 9, 13, 16-17; 13:2, 4, 11; 16:13; 20:2.

DRAW (Away, Back, Nigh, On, Out, Up)

(A) *In the sense of "dragging, pulling, or attracting"*:

1. *spao* (4685), "to draw or pull," is used, in the middle voice of "drawing" a sword from its sheath, Mark 11:47; Acts 16:27.

2. *anaspao* (385), *ana*, "up," and No. 1, "to draw up," is used of "drawing" up an animal out of a pit, Luke 14:5 (RV, "draw up"; KJV, "pull out"), and of the "drawing" up of the sheet into heaven, in the vision in Acts 11:10.

3. *apospao* (645), *apo*, "from," and No. 1, "to draw away," lit., "to wrench away from," is used of a sword, Matt. 26:51, of "drawing" away disciples into error, Acts 20:30; of Christ's "withdrawal" from the disciples, in Gethsemane, Luke 22:41, KJV, "was withdrawn," RV, "was parted" (or "was reft away from them"); of "parting" from a company, Acts 21:1 (KJV, "were gotten," RV, "were parted").

4. *antleo* (501) signified, primarily, "to draw out a ship's bilgewater, to bale or pump out" (from *antlos*, "bilge-water"), hence, "to draw water" in any way (*ana*, "up" and a root, *tel—*, "to lift, bear"), John 2:8-9; 4:7, 15.

5. *exelko* (1828), "to draw away, or lure forth," is used metaphorically in Jas. 1:14, of being "drawn away" by lust. As in hunting or fishing the game is "lured" from its haunt, so man's lust "allures" him from the safety of his self-restraint.

9. *anatassomai* (392), "to arrange in order," is used in Luke 1:1, RV, "to draw up."

(B) *In the sense of "approaching or withdrawing"*:

1. *engizo* (1448), "to come near, draw nigh" (akin to *engus*, "near"), is translated by the verb "draw near or nigh," in the RV, Luke 12:33, KJV, "approacheth"; Heb. 10:25, KJV, "approaching";

Luke 18:35; 19:29, 37; Acts 22:6, KJV, "was come nigh"; Luke 7:12 "came nigh"; Acts 9:3, "came near."

2. *proserchomai* (*4334*) is translated "draw near" in Heb. 4:16; 7:25, RV, and 10:22, KJV and RV; in Acts 7:31, "drew near."

3. *prosago* (*4317*), used transitively, "to bring to"; intransitively, "to draw near," is so rendered in Acts 27:27.

4. *hupostello* (*5288*), "to draw back, withdraw," perhaps a metaphor from lowering a sail and so slackening the course, and hence of being remiss in holding the truth; in the active voice, rendered "drew back" in Gal. 2:12, RV (KJV, "withdrew"); in the middle, in Heb. 10:38, "shrink back" RV (KJV, "draw back"); the prefix *hupo*, "underneath," is here suggestive of stealth. In v. 39 the corresponding noun, *hupostole*, is translated "of them that shrink back," RV; KJV, "draw back" (lit., "of shrinking back"). In Acts 20:20, 27, "shrank," RV.

5. *epiphosko* (*2020*), "to dawn" (lit., "to make to shine upon"), is said of the approach of the Sabbath, Luke 23:54; cf. Matt. 28:1.

DREAM (noun and verb), DREAMER

Old Testament

A. Noun.

chalom (2472), "dream." It is used of the ordinary dreams of sleep, Job 7:14. The most significant use of this word, however, is with reference to prophetic "dreams" and/or "visions," Deut. 13:1ff.

B. Verb.

chalam (2492), "to become healthy or strong; to dream." The meaning, "to become healthy," applies only to animals though "to dream" is used of human dreams, Gen. 28:12.

New Testament

A. Nouns.

1. *onar* (*3677*) is "a vision in sleep," in distinction from a waking vision, Matt. 1:20; 2:12-13, 19, 22; 27:19.

2. *enupnion* (*1798*), is, lit., "what appears in sleep," an ordinary "dream," Acts 2:17.

B. Verb.

enupniazo (*1797*), akin to A, No. 2, is used in Acts 2:17, in the passive voice in a phrase (according to the most authentic mss.) which means "shall be given up to dream by dreams," translated "shall dream dreams" metaphorically in Jude 8, of being given over to sensuous "dreamings."

DRIFT

pararheo *(3901)*, lit., "to flow past, glide by," is used in Heb. 2:1, where the significance is to find oneself "flowing" or "passing by," without giving due heed to a thing, here "the things that were heard," or perhaps the salvation of which they spoke; hence the RV, "lest haply we drift away from them," for KJV, "let them slip."

DRUNK, (-EN, be), DRUNKARD, DRUNKENNESS

Old Testament

shatah *(8354)* means "to drink," related to both creatures and things Gen. 9:21; 24:19; Ps. 50:13. Priests were commanded to practice a partial fast when they served before God—they were not to drink wine or strong drink, Lev. 10:9. They and all Israel were to eat no unclean thing. These conditions were stricter for Nazirites, who lived constantly before God, Num. 6:3; cf. Judg. 13:4; 1 Sam. 1:15. The phrase, "eating and drinking," may also signify life in general; 1 Kings 4:20; cf. Eccl. 2:24; 5:18; Jer. 22:15.

New Testament

A. Verbs.

1. ***methuo*** *(3184)* signifies "to be drunk with wine" (from ***methu***, "mulled wine"; hence Eng., "mead, honey-wine"); originally it denoted simply "a pleasant drink." The verb is used of "being intoxicated" in Matt. 24:49; Acts 2:15; 1 Cor. 11:21; 1 Thess. 5:7*b*; metaphorically, of the effect upon men of partaking of the abominations of the Babylonish system, Rev. 17:2; of being in a state of mental "intoxication," through the shedding of men's blood profusely, v. 6.

2. ***methusko*** *(3182)* signifies "to make drunk, or to grow drunk" (an inceptive verb, marking the process or the state expressed in No. 1), "to become intoxicated," Luke 12:45; Eph. 5:18; 1 Thess. 5:7*a*.

B. Adjective.

methusos *(3183)*, "drunken," is used as noun, in the singular, in 1 Cor. 5:11, and in the plural, in 6:10, "drunkard," "drunkards."

C. Noun.

methe *(3178)*, "strong drink" (akin to ***methu***, "wine," see under A. 1, above), denotes "drunkenness, habitual intoxication," Luke 21:34; Rom. 13:13; Gal. 5:21.

DULL

A. Adjective.

nothros *(3576)*, "slow, sluggish, indolent, dull" (the etymology is uncertain), is translated "dull" in Heb. 5:11 (in connection with *akoe*, "hearing"; lit., "in hearings"); "sluggish," in 6:12.

B. Adverb.

bareos (*917*), "heavily, with difficulty" (*barus*, "heavy"), is used with *akouo*, "to hear," in Matt. 13:15, and Acts 28:27, from Isa. 6:10, lit., "to hear heavily, to be dull of hearing."

DUMB

A. Adjectives.

1. *alalos* (*216*), lit., "speechless," is found in Mark 7:37; 9:17, 25.

2. *aphonos* (*880*), lit., "voiceless, or soundless," has reference to voice, Acts 8:32; 1 Cor. 12:2; 2 Pet. 2:16, while *alalos* has reference to words. In 1 Cor. 14:10 it is used metaphorically of the significance of voices or sounds, "without signification."

B. Verb.

siopao (*4623*), from *siope*, "silence, to be silent," is used of Zacharias' "dumbness," Luke 1:20.

DUNG

1. *skubalon* (*4657*) denotes "refuse," whether (a) "excrement," that which is cast out from the body, or (b) "the leavings of a feast," that which is thrown away from the table, Phil. 3:8.

2. *koprion* (*2874d*), "manure," Luke 13:8, used in the plural with *ballo*, "to throw," is translated by the verb "to dung." Some mss. have the accusative case of the noun *kopria*, "a dunghill."

DWELL, DWELLERS, DWELLING (place)
Old Testament

A. Verbs.

yashab (3427), "to dwell, sit, abide, inhabit, remain." *yashab* is first used in Gen. 4:16, in its most common connotation of "to dwell." The word has the sense of "to remain"; Gen. 38:11; and it is used of God in a similar sense, Lam. 5:19.

yashab is sometimes combined with other words to form expressions in common usage. For example, Deut. 17:18; cf. 1 Kings 1:13, 17, 24 carries the meaning "begins to reign"; or "to decide a case," Ruth 4:1-2. "Sit thou at my right hand," Ps. 110:1, means to assume a ruling position as deputy. "There will I sit to judge all the heathen," Joel 3:12, was a promise of eschatological judgment. "To sit in the dust" or "to sit on the ground," Isa. 47:1, was a sign of humiliation and grief.

yashab is often used figuratively of God. The sentences, "I saw the Lord sitting on his throne," 1 Kings 22:19; "He that sitteth in the heavens shall laugh," Ps. 2:4; and "God sitteth upon the throne of his holiness," Ps. 47:8, all describe God as the exalted Ruler over the universe.

The word is also used to describe man's being in God's presence, Ps. 27:4; cf. Ps. 23:6; Exod. 15:17.

shakan (7931), "to dwell, inhabit, settle down, abide." *shakan* is first used in the sense of "to dwell" in Gen. 9:27; and of God, Exod. 25:8. *shakan* is a word from nomadic life, meaning "to live in a tent.," Num. 24:2, where it refers to temporary "camping," but it can also refer to being permanently "settled," Ps. 102:28. God promised to give Israel security, 2 Sam. 7:10.

B. Noun.

mishkan (4908), "dwelling place; tent." This word occurs nearly 140 times, and often refers to the wilderness "tabernacle," Exod. 25:9. *mishkan* was also used later to refer to the "temple." This usage probably prepared the way for the familiar term *shekinah*.

C. Participle.

yashab (3427), "remaining; inhabitant." This participle is sometimes used as a simple adjective: "...Jacob was a plain man, *dwelling* in tents," Gen. 25:27. But the word is more often used as in Gen. 19:25: "...All the *inhabitants* of the cities."

New Testament

A. Verbs.

1. *oikeo* (*3611*), "to dwell" (from *oikos*, "a house"), "to inhabit as one's abode," is derived from the Sanskrit, *vic*, "a dwelling place" (the Eng. termination "—wick" is connected). It is used (a) of God as "dwelling" in light, 1 Tim. 6:16; (b) of the "indwelling" of the Spirit of God in the believer, Rom. 8:9, 11, or in a church, 1 Cor. 3:16; (c) of the "indwelling" of sin, Rom. 7:20; (d) of the absence of any good thing in the flesh of the believer, Rom. 7:18; (e) of the "dwelling" together of those who are married, 1 Cor. 7:12-13.

2. *katoikeo* (*2730*), *kata*, "down," and No. 1, the most frequent verb with this meaning, properly signifies "to settle down in a dwelling, to dwell fixedly in a place." Besides its literal sense, it is used of (a) the "indwelling" of the totality of the attributes and powers of the Godhead in Christ, Col. 1:19; 2:9; (b) the "indwelling" of Christ in the hearts of believers ("may make a home in your hearts"), Eph. 3:17; (c) the "dwelling" of Satan in a locality, Rev. 2:13; (d) the future "indwelling" of righteousness in the new heavens and earth, 2 Pet. 3:13. It is translated "dwellers" in Acts 1:19; 2:9; "inhabitants" in Rev. 17:2, KJV (RV, "they that dwell"), "inhabiters" in Rev. 8:13 and 12:12, KJV (RV, "them that dwell").

3. *katoikizo* (*2730*), "to cause to dwell," is said of the act of God concerning the Holy Spirit in Jas. 4:5, RV (some mss. have No. 2).

4. *enoikeo* (*1774*), lit., "to dwell in" (*en*, "in," and No. 1), is used,

with a spiritual significance only, of (a) the "indwelling" of God in believers, 2 Cor. 6:16; (b) the "indwelling" of the Holy Spirit, Rom. 8:11; 2 Tim. 1:14; (c) the "indwelling" of the Word of Christ, Col. 3:16; (d) the "indwelling" of faith, 2 Tim. 1:5; (e) the "indwelling" of sin in the believer, Rom. 7:17.

5. *perioikeo* (*4039*), *peri*, "around," and No. 1, "to dwell around, be a neighbor," is used in Luke 1:65.

6. *sunoikeo* (*4924*), *sun*, "with," and No. 1, "to dwell with," is used in 1 Pet. 3:7.

7. *enkatoikeo* (*1460*), *en*, "in," and No. 2, "to dwell among," is used in 2 Pet. 2:8.

8. *meno* (*3306*), "to abide, remain," is translated "to dwell," in the KJV of John 1:38-39; 6:56; 14:10, 17; Acts 28:16. The RV adheres throughout to the verb "to abide."

9. *skenoo* (*4637*), "to pitch a tent" (*skene*), "to tabernacle," John 1:14; Rev. 7:15; 12:12; 13:6; 21:3.

10. *kataskenoo* (*2681*), "to pitch one's tent" (*kata*, "down," *skene*, "a tent"), is translated "lodge" in Matt. 13:32; Mark 4:32; Luke 13:19; in Acts 2:26, RV, "dwell," KJV, "rest."

B. Nouns.

1. *paroikia* (*3940*) denotes "a sojourning," Acts 13:17, lit., "in the sojourning," translated "when they sojourned," RV (KJV, "dwelt as strangers"); in 1 Pet. 1:17, "sojourning."

2. *katoikesis* (*2731*), akin to A, No. 2, "a dwelling, a habitation," is used in Mark 5:3.

E

EACH OTHER

allelon (*240*), a reciprocal pronoun, preceded by the preposition *meta*, "with," signifies "with each other," Luke 23:12, RV, for KJV, "together." Similarly in 24:14 *pros allelous*, where *pros* suggests greater intimacy.

EAGLE

aetos (*105*), "an eagle" (also a vulture), is perhaps connected with *aemi*, "to blow," as of the wind, on account of its wind-like flight. In Matt. 24:28 and Luke 17:37 the vultures are probably intended. The "eagle" is mentioned elsewhere in the NT in Rev. 4:7; 8:13 (RV); 12:14. There are eight species in Palestine.

EAR (of the body)

1. *ous* (*3775*), Latin *auris*, Hebrew *'ozen* (*241*), is used (a) of the physical organ, e.g., Luke 4:21; Acts 7:57; in Acts 11:22, in the plural with *akouo*, "to hear," lit., "was heard into the ears of someone," i.e., came to the knowledge of; similarly, in the singular, Matt. 10:27, in familiar private conversation; in Jas. 5:4 the phrase is used with *eiserchomai*, "to enter into"; in Luke 1:44, with *ginomai*, "to become, to come"; in Luke 12:3, with *lalein*, "to speak" and *pros*, "to"; (b) metaphorically, of the faculty of perceiving with the mind, understanding and knowing, Matt. 13:16; frequently with *akouo*, "to hear," e.g., Matt. 11:15; 13:9, 43; Rev. 2 and 3, at the close of each of the messages to the churches, in Matt. 13:15 and Acts 28:27, with *bareos*, "heavily," of being slow to understand and obey; with a negative in Mark 8:18; Rom. 11:8; in Luke 9:44 the lit. meaning is "put those words into your ears," i.e., take them into your mind and keep them there; in Acts 7:51 it is used with *aperitmetos*, "uncircumcised." As seeing is metaphorically associated with conviction, so hearing is with obedience (*hupakoe*, lit., "hearing under"; the Eng., "obedience" is etymologically "hearing over against," i.e., with response in the hearer).

2. *otion* (*5621*), a diminutive of No. 1, but without the diminutive force, it being a common tendency in everyday speech to apply a diminutive form to most parts of the body, is used in Matt. 26:51; Mark 14:47 (in some mss.); Luke 22:51; John 18:10 (in some mss.) and v. 26, all with reference to the "ear" of Malchus.

3. *akoe* (*189*), "hearing," denotes (a) the sense of "hearing," e.g., 1 Cor. 12:17; 2 Pet. 2:8; (b) that which is "heard," a report, e.g., Matt. 4:24; (c) the physical organ, Mark 7:35, standing for the sense of "hearing"; so in Luke 7:1, RV, for KJV, "audience"; Acts 17:20; 2 Tim. 4:3-4 (in v. 3, lit., "being tickled as to the ears"); (d) a message or teaching, John 12:38; Rom. 10:16-17; Gal. 3:2, 5; 1 Thess. 2:13; Heb. 4:2, RV, "(the word) of hearing," for KJV, "(the word) preached."

EARNEST (Noun)

arrabon (*728*), originally, "earnest-money" deposited by the purchaser and forfeited if the purchase was not completed, was probably a Phoenician word, introduced into Greece. In general usage it came to denote "a pledge" or "earnest" of any sort; in the NT it is used only of that which is assured by God to believers; it is said of the Holy Spirit as the divine "pledge" of all their future blessedness, 2 Cor. 1:22; 5:5; in Eph. 1:14, particularly of their eternal inheritance.

EARNEST, EARNESTNESS, EARNESTLY

A. Noun.

spoude (*4710*), "to hasten," denotes "haste," Mark 6:25; Luke 1:39; hence, "earnestness," 2 Cor. 8:7, RV, for KJV, "diligence," and v. 8, for KJV, "forwardness"; in 7:12, "earnest care," for KJV, "care"; in 8:16, earnest care.

B. Adjective.

spoudaios (*4705*), akin to A, denotes "active, diligent, earnest," 2 Cor. 8:22 RV, "earnest," for KJV, "diligent"; in the latter part of the verse the comparative degree, *spoudaioteros*, is used, RV, "more earnest," for KJV, "more diligent"; in v. 17, RV, in the superlative sense, "very earnest," for KJV, "more forward."

C. Adverbs.

1. *ektenos* (*1619*), "earnestly" (*ek*, "out," *teino*, "to stretch"; Eng., "tension," etc.), is used in Acts 12:5, "earnestly," RV, for KJV, "without ceasing" (some mss. have the adjective *ektenes*, "earnest"); in 1 Pet. 1:22, "fervently." The idea suggested is that of not relaxing in effort, or acting in a right spirit.

2. *ektenesteron* (*1617*), the comparative degree of No. 1, used as an adverb in this neuter form, denotes "more earnestly, fervently," Luke 22:44.

3. *spoudaios* (*4709*), akin to B, signifies "with haste," or "with zeal, earnestly," Luke 7:4, RV, "earnestly," for KJV, "instantly"; in 2 Tim. 1:17, RV, and Titus 3:13, "diligently"; in Phil. 2:28, the comparative *spoudaioteros*, RV, "the more diligently," KJV, "the more carefully."

D. Adverbial Phrase.

en ekteneia, lit., "in earnestness," cf. C, No. 1, is translated "earnestly" in Acts 26:7, RV, for KJV, "instantly."

EARTH

Old Testament

'erets (776), "earth; land." *'erets* may be translated "earth," the temporal scene of human activity, experience, and history. The material world had a beginning when God "made the earth by His power," "formed it," and "spread it out," Isa. 40:28; 42:5; 45:12, 18; Jer. 27:5; 51:15. Because He did so, it follows that "the earth is the Lord's," Ps. 24:1; Deut. 10:1; Exod. 9:29; Neh. 9:6.

God formed the earth to be inhabited, Isa. 45:18. Having "authority over the earth" by virtue of being its Maker, He decreed to "let the earth sprout vegetation: of every kind," Job 34:13; Gen. 1:11. It was never to stop its productivity, for "while the earth stands, seedtime and harvest, and cold and heat, and summer and winter, and day and night shall not cease," Gen. 8:22. "The earth is full of God's riches" and mankind can "multiply and fill the earth and subdue it," Ps. 104:24; Gen. 1:28; 9:1. Let no one think that the earth is an independent, self-contained mechanism, for "the Lord reigns" as He "sits on the vault of the earth" from where "He sends rain on the earth," Ps. 97:1; Isa. 40:22; 1 Kings 17:14; Ps. 104:4. What the Creator formed "in the beginning" is also to have an end, for He will "create a new heaven and a new earth," Isa. 65:17; 66:22.

The Hebrew word *'erets* also occurs frequently in the phrase "heaven and earth" or "earth and heaven." In other words, the Scriptures teach that our terrestrial planet is a part of an all-embracing cosmological framework which we call the universe, Ps. 121:2; 124:8; 134:3. *'erets* also means a smaller part of the whole earth, translated by words like *land*, *country*, *ground*, and *soil*, which transfer its meanings into our language. Quite frequently, it refers to an area occupied by a nation or tribe, Gen. 47:13; Zech. 2:5; 2 Kings 5:2, 4; Judg. 21:21.

The Hebrew noun may also be translated "the ground," Job 2:13; Amos 3:5; Gen. 24:52; Ezek. 43:14. When God executes judgment, "He brings down the wicked to the ground," Ps. 147:6, NASB.

New Testament

1. *ge* (1093) denotes (a) "earth as arable land," e.g., Matt. 13:5, 8, 23; in 1 Cor. 15:47 it is said of the "earthly" material of which "the first man" was made, suggestive of frailty; (b) "the earth as a whole, the world," in contrast, whether to the heavens, e.g., Matt. 5:18, 35, or to heaven, the abode of God, e.g., Matt. 6:19, where the context suggests the "earth" as a place characterized by mutabil-

ity and weakness; in Col. 3:2 the same contrast is presented by the word "above"; in John 3:31 (RV, "of the earth," for KJV, "earthly") it describes one whose origin and nature are "earthly" and whose speech is characterized thereby, in contrast with Christ as the One from heaven; in Col. 3:5 the physical members are said to be "upon the earth," as a sphere where, as potential instruments of moral evils, they are, by metonymy, spoken of as the evils themselves; (c) "the inhabited earth," e.g., Luke 21:35; Acts 1:8; 8:33; 10:12; 11:6; 17:26; 22:22; Heb. 11:13; Rev. 13:8. In the following the phrase "on the earth" signifies "among men," Luke 12:49; 18:8; John 17:4, (d) "a country, territory," e.g. Luke 4:25; John 3:22; (e) "the ground," e.g., Matt. 10:29; Mark 4:26, RV, "(upon the) earth," for KJV, "(into the) ground"; (f) "land," e.g., Mark 4:1; John 21:8-9, 11. Cf. Eng. words beginning with *ge—*, e.g., "geodetic," "geodesy," "geology," "geometry," "geography."

2. *oikoumene* (3625), the present participle, passive voice, of *oikeo*, "to dwell, inhabit," denotes the "inhabited earth." It is translated "world" in every place where it has this significance, except in Luke 21:26, KJV, where it is translated "earth."

EARTHEN, EARTHLY, EARTHY

1. *ostrakinos* (3749) signifies "made of earthenware or clay," 2 Tim. 2:20, "of earth"; 2 Cor. 4:7, "earthen."

2. *epigeios* (1919), "on earth," is rendered "earthly" in John 3:12; 2 Cor. 5:1; Phil. 3:19; Jas. 3:15; in Phil. 2:10, "on earth," RV; "terrestrial" in 1 Cor. 15:40 (twice).

3. *choikos* (5517) denotes "earthy," made of earth, from *chous*, "soil, earth thrown down or heaped up," 1 Cor. 15:47-49.

4. *katachthonios* (2709), "under the earth, subterranean" (*kata*, "down," *chthon*, "the ground," from a root signifying that which is deep), is used in Phil. 2:10.

EASE, EASED

A. Verb.

anapauo (373) signifies "to cause or permit one to cease from any labor or movement" so as to recover strength. It implies previous toil and care. Its chief significance is that of taking, or causing to take, rest; it is used in the middle voice in Luke 12:19, "take (thine) ease," indicative of unnecessary, self-indulgent relaxation. In the papyri it is used technically, as an agricultural term.

B. Noun.

anesis (425) denotes "a letting loose, relaxation, easing"; it is connected with *aniemi*, "to loosen, relax" (*ana*, "back," and *hiemi*, "to send"). It signifies "rest," not from toil, but from endurance and suffering. Thus it is said (a) of a "less vigorous" condition in imprisonment, Acts 24:23, "indulgence," AV, "liberty"; (b) "relief" from anxiety, 2 Cor. 2:13; 7:5, "relief" (KJV, "rest"), (c) "relief" from persecutions, 2 Thess. 1:7, "rest"; (d) of "relief" from the sufferings of poverty, 2 Cor. 8:13, "be eased," lit., "(that there should be) easing for others (trouble to you)."

EAST

anatole (395), primarily "a rising," as of the sun and stars, corresponds to *anatello*, "to make to rise," or, intransitively, "to arise," which is also used of the sunlight, as well as of other objects in nature. In Luke 1:78 it is used metaphorically of Christ as "the Dayspring," the One through whom light came into the world, shining immediately into Israel, to dispel the darkness which was upon all nations. Cf. Mal. 4:2. Elsewhere it denotes the "east," as the quarter of the sun's rising, Matt. 2:1-2, 9; 8:11; 24:27; Luke 13:29; Rev. 7:2; 16:12; 21:13. The "east" in general stands for that side of things upon which the rising of the sun gives light. In the heavenly city itself, Rev. 21:13, the reference to the "east" gate points to the outgoing of the influence of the city "eastward."

EASTER

pascha (3957), mistranslated "Easter" in Acts 12:4, KJV, denotes the Passover (RV). The phrase "after the Passover" signifies after the whole festival was at an end. The term "Easter" is not of Christian origin. It is another form of *Astarte*, one of the titles of the Chaldean goddess, the queen of heaven. The festival of Pasch held by Christians in post-apostolic times was a continuation of the Jewish feast, but was not instituted by Christ, nor was it connected with Lent. From this Pasch the pagan festival of "Easter" was quite distinct and was introduced into the apostate Western religion, as part of the attempt to adapt pagan festivals to Christianity.

EASY, EASIER, EASILY

1. *chrestos* (5543) primarily signifies "fit for use, able to be used" (akin to *chraomai*, "to use"), hence, "good, virtuous, mild, pleasant" (in contrast to what is hard, harsh, sharp, bitter). It is said (a) of the character of God as "kind, gracious," Luke 6:35; 1 Pet. 2:3; "good," Rom. 2:4, where the neuter of the adjective is used as a noun, "the goodness," of the yoke of Christ, Matt. 11:30, "easy" (a suitable rendering would be "kindly"); (c) of believers, Eph. 4:32; (d) of things, as wine, Luke 5:39.

2. *eukopoteros* (2123), the comparative degree of *eukopos*, "easy, with easy labor," hence, of that which is "easier to do," is found in the Synoptics only, Matt. 9:5; 19:24; Mark 2:9; 10:25; Luke 5:23; 16:17; 18:25.

EAT, EAT WITH, EATING

Old Testament

A. Verb.

'akal (398), "to eat, feed, consume, devour." Essentially, this root refers to the "consumption of food by man or animals," Gen. 3:6. The function of eating is presented along with seeing, hearing, and smelling as one of the basic functions of living, Deut. 4:28. Before Christ, certain foods could not be eaten, Gen. 1:29; 9:3; Lev. 11; Deut. 14. This verb is often used figuratively, "to destroy," Gen. 3:17; Isa. 1:7; Deut. 18:1; Isa. 3:10.

E

The word can refer not only to "eating" but to the entire concept "room and board," 2 Sam. 9:11, 13, the special act of "feasting," Eccl. 10:16, or the entire activity of "earning a living," Amos 7:12; cf. Gen. 3:19. "To eat another's flesh," used figuratively, means "killing him," Ps. 27:2.

Unlike the pagan deities, Deut. 32:37-38, God "eats" no food, Ps. 50:13; although as a "consuming" fire, Deut. 4:24, He is ready to defend His own honor and glory. He "consumes" evil and the sinner.

B. Noun.

'okel (400), "food," as that which is physically consumed, Gen. 41:35; Ps. 104:21; 145:15. A related noun, *'aklah*, also means "food."

New Testament

A. Verbs.

1. *esthio* (2068) signifies "to eat" (as distinct from **pino**, "to drink"); cf. Eng., "edible"; in Heb. 10:27, metaphorically, "devour"; it is said of the ordinary use of food and drink, 1 Cor. 9:7; 11:22; of partaking of food at table, e.g., Mark 2:16; of reveling, Matt. 24:49; Luke 12:45.

2. *phago* (5315), "to eat, devour, consume," is obsolete in the present and other tenses, but supplies certain tenses which are wanting in No. 1, above. In Luke 8:55 the KJV has "(to give her) meat," the RV "(that something be given her) to eat." The idea that this verb combines both "eating" and "drinking," while No. 1 differentiates the one from the other, is not borne out in the NT. The word is very frequent in the Gospels and is used eleven times in 1 Cor. See also No. 3.

3. *trogo* (5176), primarily, "to gnaw, to chew," stresses the slow process; it is used metaphorically of the habit of spiritually feeding upon Christ, John 6:54, 56-58 (the aorists here do not indicate a definite act, but view a series of acts seen in perspective); of the constant custom of "eating" in certain company, John 13:18; of a practice unduly engrossing the world, Matt. 24:38.

4. *geuo* (1089), primarily, "to cause to taste, to give one a taste of," is used in the middle voice and denotes (a) "to taste," its usual

meaning; (b) "to take food, to eat," Acts 10:10; 20:11; 23:14; the meaning to taste must not be pressed in these passages, the verb having acquired the more general meaning. As to whether Acts 20:11 refers to the Lord's Supper or to an ordinary meal, the addition of the words "and eaten" is perhaps a sufficient indication that the latter is referred to here, whereas v. 7, where the single phrase "to break bread" is used, refers to the Lord's Supper. A parallel instance is found in Acts 2:43, 46. In the former verse the phrase "the breaking of bread," unaccompanied by any word about taking food, clearly stands for the Lord's Supper; whereas in v. 46 the phrase "breaking bread at home" is immediately explained by "they did take their food," indicating their ordinary meals.

5. *bibrosko* (977), "to eat," is derived from a root, *bor—*, "to devour" (likewise seen in the noun *broma*, "food, meat"; cf. Eng., "carnivorous," "voracious," from Lat. *vorax*). This verb is found in John 6:13. The difference between this and *phago*, No. 2, above, may be seen perhaps in the fact that whereas in the Lord's question to Philip in v. 5, *phago* intimates nothing about a full supply, the verb *bibrosko*, in v. 13, indicates that the people had been provided with a big meal, of which they had partaken eagerly.

6. *sunesthio* (4906), "to eat with," is found in Luke 15:2; Acts 10:41; 11:3; 1 Cor. 5:11; Gal. 2:12.

B. Nouns.

1. *brosis* (1035), akin to A, No. 5, denotes (a) "the act of eating," e.g., Rom. 14:17; said of rust, Matt. 6:19-20; or, more usually (b) "that which is eaten, food" (like *broma*, "food"), "meat," John 4:32; 6:27, 55; Col. 2:16; Heb. 12:16 ("morsel of meat"); "food," 2 Cor. 9:10; "eating," 1 Cor. 8:4.

2. *prosphagion* (4371), primarily "a dainty or relish" (especially cooked fish), to be eaten with bread (*pros*, "to," and A, No. 2), then, "fish" in general, is used in John 21:5.

C. Adjective.

brosimos (1034), akin to A, No. 5, and B., signifying "eatable," is found in Luke 24:41, RV, appropriately, "to eat," for the KJV, "meat."

EDIFICATION, EDIFY, EDIFYING

A. Noun.

oikodome (3619) denotes (a) "the act of building" (*oikos*, "a home," and *demo*, "to build"); this is used only figuratively in the NT, in the sense of edification, the promotion of spiritual growth (lit., "the things of building up"), Rom. 14:19; 15:2; 1 Cor. 14:3, 5, 12, 26, e.g.; (b) "a building, edifice," whether material, Matt. 24:1, e.g., or figurative, of the future body of the believer, 2 Cor. 5:1, or of a local church, 1 Cor. 3:9, or the whole church, "the body of Christ," Eph. 2:21.

B. Verb.

oikodomeo (*3618*), lit., "to build a house" (see above), (a) usually signifies "to build," whether literally, or figuratively; the present participle, lit., "the (ones) building," is used as a noun, "the builders," in Matt. 21:42; Mark 12:10; Luke 20:17; Acts 4:11 (in some mss.; the most authentic have the noun *oikodomos*;) 1 Pet. 2:7; (b) is used metaphorically, in the sense of "edifying," promoting the spiritual growth and development of character of believers, by teaching or by example, suggesting such spiritual progress as the result of patient labor. It is said (1) of the effect of this upon local churches, Acts 9:31; 1 Cor. 14:4; (2) of the individual action of believers towards each other, 1 Cor. 8:1; 10:23; 14:17; 1 Thess. 5:11; (3) of an individual in regard to himself, 1 Cor. 14:4. In 1 Cor. 8:10, where it is translated "emboldened," the apostle uses it with pathetic irony, of the action of a brother in "building up" his brother who had a weak conscience, causing him to compromise his scruples; "strengthened," or "confirmed," would be suitable renderings.

EFFECT (of none)

1. *akuroo* (*208*) signifies "to render void, deprive of force and authority." It is used of making "void" the Word of God, Matt. 15:6; Mark 7:13 (KJV, "making of none effect"), and of the promise of God to Abraham as not being deprived of authority by the Law 430 years after, Gal. 3:17.

2. *katargeo* (*2673*), "to reduce to inactivity, to render useless," is translated "to make of none effect," in Rom. 3:3, 31; 4:14; Gal. 3:17.

3. *kenoo* (*2758*), "to make empty, to empty," is translated "should be made of none effect" in 1 Cor. 1:17, KJV (RV "made void"); it is used (a) of the Cross of Christ, there; (b) of Christ, in emptying Himself, Phil. 2:7; (c) of faith, Rom. 4:14; (d) of the apostle Paul's glorying in the gospel ministry, 1 Cor. 9:15; (e) of his glorying on behalf of the church at Corinth, 2 Cor. 9:3.

EFFECTUAL

A. Adjective.

energes (*1756*) denotes "active, powerful in action" (*en*, "in," *ergon*, "work"; Eng. "energy"; the word "work" is derived from the same root). It is translated "effectual" in 1 Cor. 16:9, of the door opened for the gospel in Ephesus, and made "effectual" in the results of entering it; and in Philem. 6, of the fellowship of Philemon's faith "in the knowledge of every good thing" (RV). In Heb. 4:12 it describes the Word of God as "active," RV (KJV, "powerful"), i.e., full of power to achieve results.

B. Verb.

energeo (*1754*), "to put forth power, be operative, to work" (its usual meaning), is rendered by the verb "to work effectually," or "to be effectual," in the KJV of 2 Cor. 1:6; Gal. 2:8 and 1 Thess. 2:13; in each case the RV translates it by the simple verb "to work" (past tense, "wrought"). In Jas. 5:16 the RV omits the superfluous word "effectual," and translates the sentence "the supplication of a righteous man availeth much in its working," the verb being in the present participial form. Here the meaning may be "in its inworking," i.e., in the effect produced in the praying man, bringing him into line with the will of God, as in the case of Elijah.

EFFEMINATE

malakos (*3120*), "soft, soft to the touch" (Lat., ***mollis***, Eng., "mollify," "emollient," etc.), is used (a) of clothing, Matt. 11:8 (twice); Luke 7:25; (b) metaphorically, in a bad sense, 1 Cor. 6:9, "effeminate," not simply of a male who practices forms of lewdness, but persons in general, who are guilty of addiction to sins of the flesh, voluptuous.

EFFULGENCE

apaugasma (*541*), "radiance, effulgence," is used of light shining from a luminous body (*apo*, "from," and *auge*, "brightness"). The word is found in Heb. 1:3, where it is used of the Son of God as "being the effulgence of His glory."

ELDER, ELDEST

Old Testament

zaqen (*2204, 2205*), "old man; old woman; elder; old," can refer to a person of old age, one in the very latter stage of life, opposite of being "young," Gen. 18:11; 19:4; Josh. 6:21; 1 Kings 12:8; Jer. 31:13.

The word *zaqen* has a more specialized use with the sense of "elder," a man, with gifts of leadership, wisdom, and justice; his duties varied to include religious, civic, and judicial activities, Josh. 23:2; 1 Kings 12:8; Ezek. 8:1.

zaqan means "beard," i.e., the uncut, untrimmed hair on the face of a Hebrew man, Ps. 133:2.

New Testament

A. Adjectives.

1. *presbuteros* (*4245*), an adjective, the comparative degree of *presbus*, "an old man, an elder," is used (a) of age, whether of the "elder" of two persons, Luke 15:25, or more, John 8:9, "the eldest," or of a person advanced in life, a senior, Acts 2:17; in Heb. 11:2, the "elders" are the forefathers in Israel so in Matt. 15:2; Mark 7:3, 5 the feminine of the adjective is used of "elder" women in the churches, 1 Tim. 5:2, not in respect of position but in seniority of age; (b) of rank or positions of responsibility, (1) among Gentiles, as in the Sept. of Gen. 50:7; Num. 22:7, (2) in the Jewish nation, firstly,

those who were the heads or leaders of the tribes and families, as of the seventy who assisted Moses, Num. 11:16; Deut. 27:1, and those assembled by Solomon; secondly, members of the Sanhedrin, consisting of the chief priests, "elders" and scribes, learned in Jewish law, e.g., Matt. 16:21; 26:47; thirdly, those who managed public affairs in the various cities, Luke 7:3; (3) in the Christian churches those who, being raised up and qualified by the work of the Holy Spirit, were appointed to have the spiritual care of, and to exercise oversight over, the churches. To these the term "bishops," *episkopoi*, or "overseers," is applied (see Acts 20, v. 17 with v. 28, and Titus 1:5 and 7), the latter term indicating the nature of their work, *presbuteroi* their maturity of spiritual experience. The divine arrangement seen throughout the NT was for a plurality of these to be appointed in each church, Acts 14:23; 20:17; Phil. 1:1; 1 Tim. 5:17; Titus 1:5. The duty of "elders" is described by the verb *episkopeo*. They were appointed according as they had given evidence of fulfilling the divine qualifications, Titus 1:6 to 9; cf. 1 Tim. 3:1-7 and 1 Pet. 5:2; (4) the twenty-four "elders" enthroned in heaven around the throne of God, Rev. 4:4, 10; 5:5-14; 7:11, 13; 11:16; 14:3; 19:4. The number twenty-four is representative of earthly conditions. The word "elder" is nowhere applied to angels.

2. **sumpresbuteros** (*4850*) "a fellow-elder" (*sun*, "with"), is used in 1 Pet. 5:1.

B. Noun.

presbuterion (*4244*) "an assembly of aged men," denotes (a) the Council or Senate among the Jews, Luke 22:66; Acts 22:5; (b) the "elders" or bishops in a local church, 1 Tim. 4:14, "the presbytery." For their functions see A, No. 1, (3).

ELECT, ELECTED, ELECTION

A. Adjectives.

1. **eklektos** (*1588*) lit. signifies "picked out, chosen," and is used of (a) Christ, the "chosen" of God, as the Messiah, Luke 23:35, and metaphorically as a "living Stone," "a chief corner Stone," 1 Pet. 2:4, 6; some mss. have it in John 1:34, instead of *huios*, "Son"; (b) angels, 1 Tim. 5:21, as "chosen" to be of especially high rank in administrative association with God, or as His messengers to human beings, doubtless in contrast to fallen angels (see 2 Pet. 2:4 and Jude 6); (c) believers (Jews or Gentiles), Matt. 24:22, 24, 31; Mark 13:20, 22, 27; Luke 18:7; Rom. 8:33; Col. 3:12; 2 Tim. 2:10; Titus 1:1; 1 Pet. 1:1; 2:9 (as a spiritual race); Matt. 20:16; 22:14 and Rev. 17:14, "chosen"; individual believers are so mentioned in Rom. 16:13; 2 John 1, 13.

Believers were "chosen" "before the foundation of the world" (cf. "before times eternal," 2 Tim. 1:9), in Christ, Eph. 1:4, to adoption, Eph. 1:5; good works, 2:10; conformity to Christ, Rom. 8:29; salvation from the delusions of the Antichrist and the doom of the deluded, 2 Thess. 2:13; eternal glory, Rom. 9:23.

The source of their "election" is God's grace, not human will, Eph. 1:4, 5; Rom. 9:11; 11:5. They are given by God the Father to Christ as the fruit of His death, all being foreknown and foreseen by God, John 17:6 and Rom. 8:29. While Christ's death was sufficient for all men, and is effective in the case of the "elect," yet men are treated as responsible, being capable of the will and power to choose. For the rendering "being chosen as firstfruits," an alternative reading in 2 Thess. 2:13.

2. *suneklektos* (4899) means "elect together with," 1 Pet. 5:13.

B. Noun.

ekloge (1589) denotes "a picking out, selection" (Eng., "eclogue"), then, "that which is chosen"; in Acts 9:15, said of the "choice" of God of Saul of Tarsus, the phrase is, lit., "a vessel of choice." It is used four times in Romans; in 9:11, of Esau and Jacob, where the phrase "the purpose...according to election" is virtually equivalent to "the electing purpose"; in 11:5, the "remnant according to the election of grace" refers to believing Jews, saved from among the unbelieving nation; so in v. 7; in v. 28, "the election" may mean either the "act of choosing" or the "chosen" ones; the context, speaking of the fathers, points to the former, the choice of the nation according to the covenant of promise. In 1 Thess. 1:4, "your election" refers not to the church collectively, but to the individuals constituting it; the apostle's assurance of their "election" gives the reason for his thanksgiving. Believers are to give "the more diligence to make their calling and election sure," by the exercise of the qualities and graces which make them fruitful in the knowledge of God, 2 Pet. 1:10.

ELOQUENT

logios (3052), an adjective, from *logos*, "a word," primarily meant "learned, a man skilled in literature and the arts," and could communicate the learning effectively, Acts 18:24.

EMBRACE

1. *aspazomai* (782) lit. signifies "to draw to oneself"; hence, "to greet, salute, welcome," the ordinary meaning, e.g., in Rom. 16, where it is used 21 times. It also signifies "to bid farewell," e.g., Acts 20:1, RV, "took leave of" (KJV, "embraced"). A "salutation or farewell" was generally made by embracing and kissing.

2. *sumperilambano* (4843), lit., "to take around with," (*sun*, "with" *peri* "around," *lambano*, "to take"), "to embrace," is used in Acts 20:10, in connection with Paul's recovery of Eutychus.

EMPEROR

sebastos (4575), "august, reverent," the masculine gender of an adjective (from *sebas*, "reverential awe"), became used as the title of the Roman emperor, Acts 25:21, 25, RV, for KJV, "Augustus"; then, taking its name from the emperor, it became a title of honor applied to certain legions or cohorts or battalions, marked for their valor, Acts 27:1.

EMPTY

A. Verb.

kenoo (2758), "to empty," is so translated in Phil. 2:7, RV, for KJV, "made...of no reputation." The clauses which follow the verb are exegetical of its meaning, especially the phrases "the form of a servant," and "the likeness of men." Christ did not "empty" Himself of Godhood. For other occurrences of the word, see Rom. 4:14; 1 Cor. 1:17; 9:15; 2 Cor. 9:3.

B. Adjective.

kenos (2756) expresses the "hollowness" of anything, the "absence," especially of quality, of that which otherwise might be possessed. It is used (a) literally, Mark 12:3; Luke 1:53; 20:10-11; (b) metaphorically, of imaginations, Acts 4:25; of words which convey erroneous teachings, Eph. 5:6; of deceit, Col. 2:8; of a person whose professed faith is not accompanied by works, Jas. 2:20; negatively, concerning the grace of God, 1 Cor. 15:10; of refusal to receive it, 2 Cor. 6:1; of faith, 1 Cor. 15:14; of preaching (id.); and other forms of Christian activity and labor, 1 Cor. 15:58; Gal. 2:2; Phil. 2:16; 1 Thess. 2:1; 3:5.

ENCHANTER

'ashap (825), "enchanter, " the *ashipu* offered incantations to deliver a person from evil magical forces (demons). The sick often underwent actual surgery while the incantations were spoken, Dan. 1:20.

ENCOURAGE, ENCOURAGEMENT

A. Verbs.

1. *protrepo* (4389), "to urge forward, persuade," is used in Acts 18:27 in the middle voice, RV, "encouraged," indicating their particular interest in giving Apollos the "encouragement" mentioned; the KJV, "exhorting," wrongly connects the verb.

2. *paramutheomai* (3888), from *para*, "with," and *muthos*, "counsel, advice," is translated "encouraging" in 1 Thess. 2:11, RV, and "encourage" in 5:14, RV, there signifying to stimulate to the discharge of the ordinary duties of life. In John 11:19, 31, it means "to comfort."

B. Noun.

paraklesis (3874), "a calling to one's aid" (*para*, "by the side," *kaleo*, "to call"), then, "an exhortation, encouragement," is translated "encouragement" in Heb. 6:18, RV, for KJV, "consolation"; it is akin to *parakaleo*, "to beseech or exhort, encourage, comfort," and *parakletos*, "a paraclete or advocate."

END, ENDING

Old Testament

A. Nouns.

'ephes (657), "end; not; nothing; only," often referring to the outer, end part of a space or limit, Prov. 30:4; cf. Ps. 72:8. In other contexts, *'ephes* means the "territory" of the nations other than Israel, as an "outer region, from the writer's point of view, " Deut. 33:17; Ps. 2:8; 22:27.

'epec also is used to express "non-existence," as a state or condition, or refer to non-person, translated "not" or "no," 2 Sam. 9:3; "none" or "no one," Isa 45:6. This word can also mean "nothing" in the sense of "powerlessness" and "worthlessness," Isa. 40:17, or "nothing other than" or "only," Num. 22:35.

qets (7093), "end," denotes the "end of a person" or "death," Gen. 6:13; Ps. 39:4; "end" as the state of "being annihilated," Job 28:3; "end," of a period of time, 2 Chron. 18:2; cf. Gen. 4:3; "end" of a boundary or limit of a space, Ps. 119:96.

qatseh (7097), "end; border; extremity," in the sense of the limit or boundary of a space, Exod. 13:20; Deut. 30:4. *qatseh* can also signify an "end," of a time or sequence, Gen. 8:3.

qatsah (7098), "end; border; edge; extremity," refers primarily to concrete objects, Job 26:14, so translate, "fringe."

'acharit (319), "hind-part; end; issue; outcome; posterity," used spatially, the word identifies the "remotest and most distant part of something," Ps. 139:9. The most frequent emphasis of the word is "outcome," Deut. 11:12. A slight shift of meaning occurs in Dan. 8:23, where *'acharit* is applied to time in a relative or comparative sense. In some passages, *'acharit* represents the "ultimate outcome" of a person's life, Num. 23:10, In other passages, *'acharit* refers to "all that comes afterwards," Jer. 31:17. In Amos 9:1, *'acharit* is used of the "rest" (remainder) of one's fellows. Both conclusion and result are apparent in passages such as Isa. 41:22, where the word represents the "end" or "result" of a matter.

Another nuance of *'acharit* indicates the "last" or the "least in importance," Jer. 50:12. The fact that *'acharit* used with "day" or "years" may signify either "a point at the end of time" or "a period of the end time," referring to a near or possibly far time, an issue much debated, but unfortunately the meaning of this word does not definitively answer this debate, but rather involves other theological issues, Isa. 2:2; Dan. 10:14.

B. Adverb.

'ephes (657), "howbeit; notwithstanding; however; without cause." This word's first occurrence is in Num. 13:28: "*Nevertheless* the people be strong that dwell in the land...."

New Testament

A. Nouns.

1. *telos* (5056) signifies (a) "the limit," either at which a person or thing ceases to be what he or it was up to that point, or at which previous activities were ceased, 2 Cor. 3:13; 1 Pet. 4:7; (b) "the final issue or result" of a state or process, e.g., Luke 1:33; in Rom. 10:4, Christ is described as "the end of the Law unto righteousness to everyone that believeth"; this is best explained by Gal. 3:23-26; cf. Jas. 5:11; the following more especially point to the issue or fate of a thing, Matt. 26:58; Rom. 6:21; 2 Cor. 11:15; Phil. 3:19; Heb. 6:8; 1 Pet. 1:9; (c) "a fulfillment," Luke 22:37, KJV, "(have) an end"; (d) "the utmost degree" of an act, as of the love of Christ towards His disciples, John 13:1; (e) "the aim or purpose" of a thing, 1 Tim. 1:5; (f) "the last" in a succession or series Rev. 1:8 (KJV, only, "ending"); 21:6; 22:13.

2. *sunteleia* (4930) signifies "a bringing to completion together" (*sun* "with," *teleo*, "to complete," akin to No. 1), marking the "completion" or consummation of the various parts of a scheme, Matt. 13:39-40, 49; 24:3; 28:20. The word does not denote a termination, but the heading up of events to the appointed climax. *aion* is not the world, but a period or epoch or era in which events take place. In Heb. 9:26, the word translated "world" (KJV) is in the plural, and the phrase is "the consummation of the ages." It was at the heading up of all the various epochs appointed by divine counsels that Christ was manifested (i.e., in His Incarnation) "to put away sin by the sacrifice of Himself."

B. Verbs.

1. *teleo* (5055), "to complete, finish, bring to an end," is translated "had made an end," in Matt. 11:1.

2. *sunteleo* (4931), cf. A, No. 2, signifies (a) "to bring to an end, finish completely" (*sun*, "together," imparting a perfective significance to *teleo*), Matt. 7:28 (in some mss.); Luke 4:2, 13; Acts 21:27, RV, "completed"; (b) "to bring to fulfillment," Mark 13:4; Rom. 9:28; (c) "to effect, make," Heb. 8:8.

C. Adjective.

eschatos (2078), "last, utmost, extreme," is used as a noun (a) of time, rendered "end" in Heb. 1:2, RV, "at the 'end' of these days," i.e., at the "end" of the period under the Law, for KJV, "in these last days"; so in 1 Pet. 1:20, "at the end of the times." In 2 Pet. 2:20, the plural, *ta eschata*, lit., "the last things," is rendered "the latter end," KJV, (RV, "the last state"); the same phrase is used in Matt. 12:45; Luke 11:26; (b) of place, Acts 13:47, KJV, "ends (of the earth)," RV, "uttermost part."

ENDURE, ENDURING

A. Verbs.

1. *meno* (3306), "to abide," is rendered "to endure" in the KJV of John 6:27 and 1 Pet. 1:25 (RV, "abideth"); Heb. 10:34, KJV, "enduring (substance)," RV, "abiding."

2. *hupomeno* (5278), a strengthened form of No. 1, denotes "to abide under, to bear up courageously" (under suffering), Matt. 10:22; 24:13; Mark 13:13; Rom. 12:12, translated "patient"; 1 Cor. 13:7; 2 Tim. 2:10, 12 (KJV, "suffer"); Heb. 10:32; 12:2-3, 7; Jas. 1:12; 5:11; 1 Pet. 2:20, "ye shall take it patiently." It has its other significance, "to tarry, wait for, await," in Luke 2:43; Acts 17:14 (in some mss., Rom. 8:24).

3. *phero* (5342), "to bear," is translated "endured" in Rom. 9:22 and Heb. 12:20.

4. *hupophero* (5297), a strengthened form of No. 3, "to bear or carry," by being under, is said metaphorically of "enduring" temptation, 1 Cor. 10:13, KJV, "bear"; persecutions, 2 Tim. 3:11; griefs, 1 Pet. 2:19.

5. *anecho* (430), "to hold up" (*ana*, "up," *echo*, "to hold or have"), always in the middle voice in the NT, is rendered "endure" in 2 Thess. 1:4, of persecutions and tribulations; in 2 Tim. 4:3, of sound doctrine.

6. *kartereo* (2594), "to be steadfast, patient," is used in Heb. 11:27, "endured," of Moses in relation to Egypt.

7. *makrothumeo* (3114), "to be long-tempered" (*makros*, "long," *thumos*, "mind"), is rendered "patiently endured" in Heb. 6:15, said of Abraham. See B, below.

B. Noun.

hupomone (5281), "patience," lit., "a remaining under" (akin to A, No. 2), is translated "patient enduring" in 2 Cor. 1:6, RV, for KJV, "enduring."

ENEMY

Old Testament

'oyeb (341), "enemy." *'oyeb* refers to both individuals and nations, Gen. 22:17; Exod. 23:4; Ps. 38:19; or, one might be an "enemy" of God, Nah. 1:2.

tsar (6862), "adversary; enemy; foe," a general designation for "enemy": a nation, 2 Sam. 24:13, or, more rarely, an individual, cf.

Gen. 14:20; Ps. 3:1. The Lord may also be the "enemy" of His sinful people as His judgment comes upon them, cf. Deut. 32:41-43; Lam. 2:4.

The word *tsar* has several synonyms: *'oyeb*, "enemy," cf. Lam. 2:5; *sone'*, "hater," Ps. 44:7; *rodep*, "persecutor," Ps. 119:157; *'arits*, "tyrant; oppressor," Job 6:23.

New Testament

echthros (*2190*), an adjective, primarily denoting "hated" or "hateful" (akin to *echthos*, "hate"; perhaps associated with *ekos*, "outside"), hence, in the active sense, denotes "hating, hostile"; it is used as a noun signifying an "enemy," adversary, and is said (a) of the Devil, Matt. 13:39; Luke 10:19; (b) of death, 1 Cor. 15:26; (c) of the professing believer who would be a friend of the world, thus making himself an enemy of God, Jas. 4:4; (d) of men who are opposed to Christ, Matt. 13:25, 28; 22:44; Mark 12:36; Luke 19:27; 20:43; Acts 2:35; Rom. 11:28; Phil. 3:18; Heb. 1:13; 10:13; or to His servants, Rev. 11:5, 12; to the nation of Israel, Luke 1:71, 74; 19:43; (e) of one who is opposed to righteousness, Acts 13:10; (f) of Israel in its alienation from God, Rom. 11:28; (g) of the unregenerate in their attitude toward God, Rom. 5:10; Col. 1:21; (h) of believers in their former state, 2 Thess. 3:15; (i) of foes, Matt. 5:43-44; 10:36; Luke 6:27, 35; Rom. 12:20; 1 Cor. 15:25; of the apostle Paul because he told converts "the truth," Gal. 4:16.

ENGRAVE

entupoo (*1795*), "to imprint, engrave," is used of the "engraving" of the Law on the two stones, or tablets, 2 Cor. 3:7.

ENLIGHTEN

photizo (*5461*), from *phos*, "light," (a), used intransitively, signifies "to give light, shine," Rev. 22:5; (b), used transitively, "to enlighten, illumine," is rendered "enlighten" in Eph. 1:18, metaphorically of spiritual "enlightenment"; so John 1:9, i.e., "lighting every man" (by reason of His coming); Eph. 3:9, "to make (all men) see"; Heb. 6:4, "were enlightened"; 10:32, RV, "enlightened," KJV, "illuminated."

ENOUGH

A. Adjectives.

1. *arketos* (*713*), "sufficient," akin to *arkeo* (see B, No. 1), is rendered "enough" in Matt. 10:25; "sufficient" in Matt. 6:34; "suffice" in 1 Pet. 4:3, lit., "(is) sufficient."

2. *hikanos* (*2425*), "sufficient, competent, fit" (akin to *hikano* and *hiko*, "to reach, attain" and *hikanoo*, "to make sufficient"), is translated "enough" in Luke 22:38, of the Lord's reply to Peter concerning the swords.

B. Verbs.

1. *arkeo* (714), "to ward off"; hence, "to aid, assist"; then, "to be strong enough," i.e., "to suffice, to be enough" (cf. A, No. 1), is translated "be enough" in Matt. 25:9.

2. *apecho* (568), lit., "to hold off from, to have off or out" (*apo*, "from," *echo*, "to have"), i.e., "to have in full, to have received," is used impersonally in Mark 14:41, "it is enough," in the Lord's words to His slumbering disciples in Gethsemane.

ENROLL, ENROLLMENT

A. Verb.

apographo (583) primarily signifies "to write out, to copy"; then, "to enroll, to inscribe," as in a register. It is used of a census, Luke 2:1, RV, "be enrolled," for KJV, "be taxed"; in the middle voice, vv. 3, 5, to enroll oneself, KJV, "be taxed." Confirmation that this census (not taxation) was taken in the dominions of the Roman Empire is given by the historians Tacitus and Suetonius. Augustus himself drew up a sort of Roman Doomsday Book, a Rationarium, afterwards epitomized into a Breviarium, to include the allied kingdoms, appointing twenty commissioners to draw up the lists. In Heb. 12:23 the members of the church of the firstborn are said to be "enrolled," RV.

B. Noun.

apographe (582) primarily denotes "a written copy," or, as a law term, "a deposition"; then, "a register, census, enrollment," Luke 2:2; Acts 5:37.

ENSAMPLE

1. *tupos* (5179) primarily denoted "a blow" (from a root *tup—*, seen also in *tupto*, "to strike"), hence, (a) an impression, the mark of a "blow," John 20:25; (b) the "impress" of a seal, the stamp made by a die, a figure, image, Acts 7:43; (c) a "form" or mold, Rom. 6:17 (see RV); (d) the sense or substance of a letter, Acts 23:25; (e) "an ensample," pattern, Acts 7:44; Heb. 8:5, "pattern"; in an ethical sense, 1 Cor. 10:6; Phil. 3:17; 1 Thess. 1:7; 2 Thess. 3:9; 1 Tim. 4:12, RV, "ensample"; Titus 2:7, RV, "ensample," for KJV, "pattern"; 1 Pet. 5:3; in a doctrinal sense, a type, Rom. 5:14.

2. *hupotuposis* (5296), "an outline, sketch," akin to *hupotupoo*, "to delineate," is used metaphorically to denote a "pattern," an "ensample," 1 Tim. 1:16, RV, "ensample," for KJV, "pattern"; 2 Tim. 1:13, RV, "pattern," for KJV, "form."

3. *hupodeigma* (5262), lit., "that which is shown" (from *hupo*, "under," and *deiknumi*, "to show"), hence, (a) "a figure, copy," Heb. 8:5, RV, "copy," for KJV, "example"; 9:23; (b) "an example," whether

for imitation, John 13:15; Jas. 5:10, or for warning, Heb. 4:11; 2 Pet. 2:6, RV, "example."

ENSLAVED

douloo (*1402*), "to make a slave of," is rendered "enslaved" (to much wine) in Titus 2:3, RV, for KJV, "given to."

ENTANGLE

1. *empleko* (*1707*), "to weave in," hence, metaphorically, to be involved, entangled in, is used in the passive voice in 2 Tim. 2:4, "entangleth himself"; 2 Pet. 2:20, "are entangled."

2. *enecho* (*1758*), "to hold in," is said (a) of being "entangled" in a yoke of bondage, such as Judaism, Gal. 5:1. Some mss. have the word in 2 Thess. 1:4, the most authentic have *anecho*, "to endure"; (b) with the meaning to set oneself against, be urgent against, said of the plotting of Herodias against John the Baptist, Mark 6:19, RV, "set herself against," KJV, "had a quarrel against"; of the effort of the scribes and Pharisees to provoke the Lord to say something which would provide them with a ground of accusation against Him, Luke 11:53.

ENTERTAIN

xenizo (*3579*) signifies (a) "to receive as a guest" (*xenos*, "a guest") rendered "entertained" in Acts 28:7, RV, for KJV, "lodged"; in Heb. 13:2, "have entertained"; (b) "to be astonished by the strangeness of a thing," Acts 17:20; 1 Pet. 4:4, 12.

ENTICE, ENTICING

A. Verb.

deleazo (*1185*), primarily, "to lure by a bait" (from *delear*, "a bait"), is used metaphorically in Jas. 1:14, of the "enticement" of lust; in 2 Pet. 2:14, of seducers, RV, "enticing," for KJV, "beguiling"; in v. 18, RV, "entice (in)," for AV, "allure (through)."

B. Adjective.

peithos (*3981*), "apt to persuade" (from *peitho*, "to persuade"), is used in 1 Cor. 2:4, KJV, "enticing," RV, "persuasive."

ENVY, ENVYING

A. Noun.

phthonos (*5355*), "envy," is the feeling of displeasure produced by witnessing or hearing of the advantage or prosperity of others; this evil sense always attaches to this word, Matt. 27:18; Mark 15:10; Rom. 1:29; Gal. 5:21; Phil. 1:15; 1 Tim. 6:4; Titus 3:3; 1 Pet. 2:1; so in Jas. 4:5, where the question is rhetorical and strongly remonstrative, signifying that the Spirit (or spirit) which God made to dwell in us was certainly not so bestowed that we should be guilty of "envy."

B. Verbs.

1. *phthoneo* (5354), "to envy" (akin to A.), is used in Gal. 5:26.

2. *zeloo* (2206) denotes "to be zealous, moved with jealousy," Acts 7:9 and 17:5, RV, "moved with jealousy" (KJV, "moved with envy"); both have "envieth" in 1 Cor. 13:4.

EPILEPTIC

seleniazo (4583), lit., "to be moon struck" (from *selene*, "the moon"), is used in the passive voice with active significance, RV, "epileptic," for KJV, "lunatick," Matt. 4:24; 17:15; the corresponding English word is "lunatic." Epilepsy was supposed to be influenced by the moon.

EPISTLE

epistole (1992), primarily "a message" (from *epistello*, "to send to"), hence, "a letter, an epistle," is used in the singular, e.g., Acts 15:30; in the plural, e.g., Acts 9:2; 2 Cor. 10:10. Epistle is a less common word for a letter. A letter affords a writer more freedom, both in subject and expression, than does a formal treatise. A letter is usually occasional, that is, it is written in consequence of some circumstance which requires to be dealt with promptly. The style of a letter depends largely on the occasion that calls it forth. "A broad line is to be drawn between the letter and the epistle. The one is essentially a spontaneous product dominated throughout by the image of the reader, his sympathies and interests, instinct also with the writer's own soul: it is virtually one half of an imaginary dialogue, the suppressed responses of the other party shaping the course of what is actually written....the other has a general aim, addressing all and sundry whom it may concern: it is like a public speech and looks towards publication" (J. V. Bartlet).

EQUAL, EQUALITY

A. Adjective.

isos (2470), "the same in size, number, quality," etc., is translated "equal" in John 5:18; Phil. 2:6; in the latter the word is in the neuter plural, lit., "equalities"; in the RV the words are translated 'on an equality with God,' instead of 'equal with God,' as in the KJV. The change is of great importance to the right interpretation of the whole passage.

B. Nouns.

1. *isotes* (2471), "equality" (akin to A.), is translated "equality" in 2 Cor. 8:14, twice; in Col. 4:1, with the article, "that which is...equal," i.e. equity, fairness.

2. *sunelikiotes* (4915) denotes "one of the same age, an equal in age" (*sun*, "with," *helikia*, "an age"), "a contemporary," Gal. 1:14, RV, "of mine own age," for KJV "mine equals," the reference being to the apostle's good standing among his fellow students in the rabbinical schools; cf. Acts 22:3.

ERR

1. *planao* (4105), in the active voice, signifies "to cause to wander, lead astray, deceive" (*plane*, "a wandering"; cf. Eng., "planet"); in the passive voice, "to be led astray, to err." It is translated "err," in Matt. 22:29; Mark 12:24, 27; Heb. 3:10; Jas. 1:16 (KJV, "do not err," RV, "be not deceived"); 5:19.

2. *apoplanao* (635), "to cause to wander away from, to lead astray from" (*apo*, "from," and No. 1), is used metaphorically of leading into error, Mark 13:22, KJV, "seduce," RV "lead astray"; 1 Tim. 6:10, in the passive voice, KJV, "have erred," RV, "have been led astray."

3. *astocheo* (795), "to miss the mark, fail," is used only in the Pastoral Epistles, 1 Tim. 1:6, "having swerved"; 6:21 and 2 Tim. 2:18, "have erred."

ERROR

1. *plane* (4106), akin to *planao*, "a wandering, a forsaking of the right path, see Jas. 5:20, whether in doctrine, 2 Pet. 3:17; 1 John 4:6, or in morals, Rom. 1:27; 2 Pet. 2:18; Jude 11, though, in Scripture, doctrine and morals are never divided by any sharp line. See also Matt. 27:64, where it is equivalent to fraud." "Errors" in doctrine are not infrequently the effect of relaxed morality, and vice versa.

2. *agnoema* (51), "a sin of ignorance," is used in the plural in Heb. 9:7.

ESCAPE

Old Testament

malat (4422), "to escape, slip away, deliver, give birth," its most common use of this word is to express the "escaping" from any kind of danger, such as an enemy, Isa. 20:6, a trap, 2 Kings 10:24, or a temptress, Eccl. 7:26. It may also mean to "save, deliver from destruction," 2 Kings 23:18. *malat* is used once in the sense of "delivering (birthing) a child," Isa. 66:7.

New Testament

A. Verbs.

1. *pheugo* (5343), "to flee" (Lat., *fuga*, "flight," etc.; cf. Eng., "fugitive, subterfuge"), is rendered "escape" in Matt. 23:33; Heb. 11:34.

2. *apopheugo* (668), "to flee away from" (*apo*, "from," and No. 1), is used in 2 Pet. 1:4; 2:18, 20.

3. *diapheugo* (1309), lit., "to flee through," is used of the "escaping" of prisoners from a ship, Acts 27:42. For the word in v. 44, see No. 5.

4. *ekpheugo* (1628), "to flee out of a place" (*ek*, "out of," and No. 1), is said of the "escape" of prisoners, Acts 16:27; of Sceva's sons, "fleeing" from the demoniac, 19:16; of Paul's escape from Damascus, 2 Cor. 11:33; elsewhere with reference to the judgments of God, Luke 21:36; Rom. 2:3; Heb. 2:3; 12:25; 1 Thess. 5:3.

5. *diasozo* (1295), in the active voice, "to bring safely through a danger" (*dia*, "through," intensive, *sozo*, "to save"), to make completely whole, to heal, Luke 7:3; to bring "safe," Acts 23:24; "to save," 27:43; in the passive voice, Matt. 14:36, "were made whole"; 1 Pet. 3:20. It is also used in the passive voice, signifying "to escape," said of shipwrecked mariners, Acts 27:44; 28:1, 4.

B. Noun.

ekbasis (1545), "a way out," denotes (a) "an escape," 1 Cor. 10:13, used with the definite article and translated "the way of escape," as afforded by God in case of temptation; (b) "an issue or result," Heb. 13:7.

ESPOUSED

1. *harmozo* (718), "to fit, join" (from *hamnos*, "a joint, joining"; the root *ar*—, signifying "to fit," is in evidence in various languages; cf. *arthron*, "a joint," *arithmos*, "a number," etc.), is used in the middle voice, of marrying or giving in marriage; in 2 Cor. 11:2 it is rendered "espoused," metaphorically of the relationship established between Christ and the local church, through the apostle's instrumentality. The thought may be that of "fitting" or "joining" to one husband, the middle voice expressing the apostle's interest or desire in doing so.

2. *mnesteuo* (3423), "to woo and win, to espouse or promise in marriage," is used in the passive voice in Matt. 1:18; Luke 1:27; 2:5, all with reference to the Virgin Mary, RV, "betrothed," for KJV, "espoused," in each case.

ESTABLISH

1. *sterizo* (4741), "to fix, make fast, to set" (from *sterix*, "a prop"), is used of "establishing" or "stablishing" (i.e., the confirmation) of persons; the apostle Peter was called by the Lord to "establish" his brethren, Luke 22:32, translated "strengthen"; Paul desired to visit Rome that the saints might be "established," Rom. 1:11; cf. Acts 8:23; so with Timothy at Thessalonica, 1 Thess. 3:2; the "confirmation" of the saints is the work of God, Rom. 16:25, "to stablish (you)"; 1 Thess. 3:13, "stablish (your hearts)"; 2 Thess. 2:17, "stablish them (in every good work and word)"; 1 Pet. 5:10, "stablish"; the means used to effect the "confirmation" is the ministry of the

Word of God, 2 Pet. 1:12, "are established (in the truth which is with you)"; James exhorts Christians to "stablish" their hearts, Jas. 5:8; cf. Rev. 3:2, RV.

2. *stereoo* (*4732*), "to make firm, or solid" (akin to *stereos*, "hard, firm, solid"; cf. Eng., "stereotype"), is used only in Acts, (a) physically, 3:7, "received strength"; 3:16, "hath made strong"; (b) metaphorically, of establishment in the faith, 16:5, RV, "strengthened," for KJV established.

3. *histemi* (*2476*), "to cause to stand," is translated "establish" in Rom. 3:31; 10:3; Heb. 10:9.

4. *bebaioo* (*950*), "to confirm," is rendered "stablish," 2 Cor. 1:21; "stablished," Col. 2:7; "be established," Heb. 13:9.

ESTATE, STATE

1. *euschemon* (*2158*), signifying "elegant, graceful, comely" (*eu*, "well," *schema*, "figure, fashion"), is used (a) in a moral sense, seemly, becoming, 1 Cor. 7:35; (b) in a physical sense, comely, 1 Cor. 12:24; (c) with reference to social degree, influential, a meaning developed in later Greek, and rendered of "honorable estate" in the RV of Mark 15:43; Acts 13:50; 17:12 (for KJV, "honorable").

2. *tapeinosis* (*5014*) denotes "abasement, humiliation, low estate" (from *tapeinos*, "lowly"), Luke 1:48, "low estate"; Acts 8:33, "humiliation"; Phil. 3:21, RV, "of humiliation," for KJV, "vile"; Jas. 1:10, "is made low," lit., "in his low estate."

3. *hupsos* (*5311*), signifying "height," is rendered "(in his) high estate," Jas. 1:9, RV, for KJV, "in that he is exalted"; "on high," Luke 1:78; 24:49; Eph. 4:8; "height," Eph. 3:18; Rev. 21:16.

ESTEEM

1. *hegeomai* (*2233*) signifies "to lead"; then, "to lead before the mind, to suppose, consider, esteem"; translated "esteem" in Phil. 2:3, KJV, RV, "counting"; in 1 Thess. 5:13, "esteem"; in Heb. 11:26, KJV, "esteeming," RV, "accounting."

2. *krino* (*2919*) signifies "to separate, choose"; then, "to approve, esteem"; translated "esteemeth" in Rom. 14:5 (twice), said of days; here the word "alike" (KJV) is rightly omitted in the RV, the meaning being that every day is especially regarded as sacred.

3. *logizomai* (*3049*), "to reckon," is translated "esteemeth" in Rom. 14:14 (RV, "accounteth").

ETERNAL

1. *aion* (*165*), "an age," is translated "eternal" in Eph. 3:11, lit., "(purpose) of the ages," and 1 Tim. 1:17, lit. "(king) of the ages."

2. *aionios* (*166*) describes "duration," either undefined but not endless, as in Rom. 16:25; 2 Tim. 1:9; Titus 1:2; or undefined because it is endless as in Rom. 16:26, and the other sixty-six places in the NT.

The predominant meaning of *aionios*, that with which it is used everywhere in the NT, save the places noted above, may be seen in 2 Cor. 4:18, where it is set in contrast with *proskairos*, lit., "for a season," and in Philem. 15, where only in the NT it is used without a noun. Moreover it is used of persons and things which are in their nature endless, as, e.g., of God, Rom. 16:26; of His power, 1 Tim. 6:16, and of His glory, 1 Pet. 5:10; of the Holy Spirit, Heb. 9:14; of the redemption effected by Christ, Heb. 9:12, and of the consequent salvation of men, 5:9, as well as of His future rule, 2 Pet. 1:11, which is elsewhere declared to be without end, Luke 1:33; of the life received by those who believe in Christ, John 3:16, concerning whom He said, "they shall never perish," 10:28, and of the resurrection body, 2 Cor. 5:1, elsewhere said to be "immortal," 1 Cor. 15:53, in which that life will be finally realized, Matt. 25:46; Titus 1:2.

EUNUCH

A. Noun.

eunouchos (*2135*) denotes (a) "an emasculated man, a eunuch," Matt. 19:12; (b) in the 3rd instance in that verse, "one naturally incapacitated for, or voluntarily abstaining from, wedlock"; (c) one such, in a position of high authority in a court, "a chamberlain," Acts 8:27-39.

B. Verb.

eunouchizo (*2134*), "to make a eunuch" (from A), is used in Matt. 19:12, as under (b) in A; and in the passive voice, "were made eunuchs," probably an allusion by the Lord to the fact that there were eunuchs in the courts of the Herods, as would be well known to His hearers.

EVANGELIST

euangelistes (*2099*), lit., "a messenger of good," denotes a "preacher of the gospel," Acts 21:8; Eph. 4:11, which makes clear the distinctiveness of the function in the churches; 2 Tim. 4:5.

EVER, FOREVER, EVERMORE

Old Testament

'*olam* (*5769*), "eternity; remotest time; perpetuity," usually signifies "remotest time" or "remote time." In 1 Chron. 16:36, God is described as blessed "from everlasting to everlasting" (KJV, "for ever and ever"), or from the most distant past time to the most distant future time. In passages where God is viewed as the One who existed before the creation was brought into existence, '*olam* may mean: (1) "at the very beginning," Isa. 46:9; or (2) "from eternity, from the pre-creation, till now," Ps. 25:6. In other passages. the word means "from (in) olden times," Gen. 6:4. In Isa. 42:14, the word is used hyperbolically meaning "for a long time." In Josh. 24:2, the word means "formerly; in ancient times." When used with the negative, *'olam* can mean "never," Isa. 63:19.

With the preposition *'ad*, the word can mean "into the indefinite future," Deut. 23:3. The same construction can signify "as long as one lives," 1 Sam. 1:22. This construction then sets forth an extension into the indefinite future, beginning from the time of the speaker.

In the largest number of its occurrences, *'olam* appears with the preposition *le*. This construction is weaker and less dynamic in emphasis than the previous phrase, insofar as it envisions a "simple duration." This difference emerges in 1 Kings 2:33, where both phrases occur. *le'olam* is applied to the curse set upon the dead Joab and his descendants. The other more dynamic phrase (*'ad 'olam*), applied to David and his descendants, emphasizes the ever-continued, ever-acting presence of the blessing extended into the "indefinite future." In Exod. 21:6 the phrase *le 'olam* means "as long as one lives," Gen. 3:22.

The same emphasis on "simple duration" pertains when *'olam* is used in passages such as Ps. 61:8, where it appears by itself. In Gen. 9:16, the word (used absolutely) means the "most distant future." In other places, the word means "without beginning, without end, and ever-continuing," Isa. 26:4.

New Testament

A. Adverbs.

1. *pantote* (3842), "at all times, always" (from *pas*, "all"), is translated "ever" in Luke 15:31; John 18:20; 1 Thess. 4:17; 5:15; 2 Tim. 3:7; Heb. 7:25; "evermore" in John 6:34; in 1 Thess. 5:16, RV, "alway," for KJV, "evermore." It there means "on all occasions," as, e.g., in 1 Thess. 1:2; 3:6; 5:15; 2 Thess. 1:3, 11; 2:13.

2. *aei* (104), "ever," is used (a) of continuous time, signifying "unceasingly, perpetually," Acts 7:51; 2 Cor. 4:11; 6:10; Titus 1:12; Heb. 3:10; (b) of successive occurrences, signifying "on every occasion," 1 Pet. 3:15; 2 Pet. 1:12. Some texts have the word in Mark 15:8.

B. Phrases.

The following phrases are formed in connection with *aion*, "an age": they are idiomatic expressions betokening undefined periods and are not to be translated literally: (a) *eis aiona*, lit., "unto an age," Jude 13, "for ever"; (b) *eis ton aiona*, lit., "unto the age," "for ever" (or, with a negative, "never"), Matt. 21:19; Mark 3:29; 11:14; Luke 1:55; John 4:14; 6:51, 58; 8:35 (twice), 51-52; 10:28; 11:26; 12:34; 13:8; 14:16; 1 Cor. 8:13; 2 Cor. 9:9; Heb. 5:6; 6:20; 7:17, 21, 24, 28; 1 Pet. 1:25; 1 John 2:17; 2 John 2; (c) *eis tous aionas*, lit., "unto the ages," "for ever," Matt. 6:13 (KJV only); Luke 1:33; Rom. 1:25; 9:5; 11:36; 16:27 (some mss. have the next phrase here); 2 Cor. 11:31;

Heb. 13:8; (d) *eis tous aionas ton aionon*, lit. "unto the ages of the ages," "for ever and ever," or "for evermore," Gal. 1:5; Phil. 4:20; 1 Tim. 1:17; 2 Tim. 4:18; Heb. 13:21; 1 Pet. 4:11; 5:11 [(c) in some mss.]; Rev. 1:6 [(c) in some mss.]; 1:18, "for evermore"; 4:9-10; 5:13; 7:12; 10:6; 11:15; 15:7; 19:3; 20:10; 22:5; (e) *eis aionas aionon*, lit., "unto ages of ages," "for ever and ever," Rev. 14:11; (f) *eis ton aiona tou aionos*, lit., "unto the age of the age," "for ever and ever," Heb. 1:8; (g) *tou aionos ton aionon*, lit., "of the age of the ages," "for ever and ever," Eph. 3:21; (h) *eis pantas tous aionas*, lit., "unto all the ages," Jude 25 ("for evermore," RV; "ever," KJV); (i) *eis hemeran aionos*, lit., "unto a day of an age," "for ever," 2 Pet. 3:18.

EVERLASTING

1. *aidios* (126) denotes "everlasting" (from *aei*, "ever"), Rom. 1:20, RV, "everlasting," for KJV, "eternal"; Jude 6, KJV and RV "everlasting." *aionios* should always be translated "eternal," and *aidios*, "everlasting."

EVIDENT, EVIDENTLY

A. Adjectives.

1. *delos* (1212), properly signifying "visible, clear to the mind, evident," is translated "evident" in Gal. 3:11 and 1 Cor. 15:27, RV (KJV, "manifest"); "bewrayeth," Matt. 26:73; "certain," 1 Tim. 6:7, KJV.

2. *katadelos* (2612), a strengthened form of No. 1, "quite manifest, evident," is used in Heb. 7:15 (KJV, "more evident"). For the preceding verse see No. 3.

3. *prodelos* (4271), "manifest beforehand" (*pro*, "before," and No. 1), is used in Heb. 7:14 in the sense of "clearly evident." So in 1 Tim. 5:24-25, RV, "evident," for KJV, "open beforehand," and "manifest beforehand." The *pro* is somewhat intensive.

B. Adverb.

phaneros (5320), manifestly, is rendered "openly" in Mark 1:45; "publicly" in John 7:10, RV (opposite to "in secret"); in Acts 10:3, RV, "openly," for KJV, evidently.

EVIL, EVIL-DOER

A. Adjectives.

1. *kakos* (2556) stands for "whatever is evil in character, base," in distinction (wherever the distinction is observable) from *poneros* (see No. 2), which indicates "what is evil in influence and effect, malignant." *kakos* is the wider term and often covers the meaning of *poneros*. *kakos* is antithetic to *kalos*, "fair, advisable, good in character," and to *agathos*, "beneficial, useful, good in act"; hence it denotes what is useless, incapable, bad; *poneros* is essentially antithetic to *chrestos*, "kind, gracious, serviceable";

hence it denotes what is destructive, injurious, evil. As evidence that *poneros* and *kakos* have much in common, though still not interchangeable, each is used of thoughts, cf. Matt. 15:19 with Mark 7:21; of speech, Matt. 5:11 with 1 Pet. 3:10; of actions, 2 Tim. 4:18 with 1 Thess. 5:15; of man, Matt. 18:32 with 24:48.

The use of *kakos* may be broadly divided as follows: (a) of what is morally or ethically "evil," whether of persons, e.g., Matt. 21:41; 24:48; Phil. 3:2; Rev. 2:2, or qualities, emotions, passions, deeds, e.g., Mark 7:21; John 18:23, 30; Rom. 1:30; 3:8; 7:19, 21; 13:4; 14:20; 16:19; 1 Cor. 13:5; 2 Cor. 13:7; 1 Thess. 5:15; 1 Tim. 6:10; 2 Tim. 4:14; 1 Pet. 3:9, 12; (b) of what is injurious, destructive, baneful, pernicious, e.g., Luke 16:25; Acts 16:28; 28:5; Titus 1:12; Jas. 3:8; Rev. 16:2, where *kakos* and *poneros* come in that order, "noisome and grievous." See B, No. 3.

2. *poneros* (4190), akin to *ponos*, "labor, toil," denotes "evil that causes labor, pain, sorrow, malignant evil" (see No. 1); it is used (a) with the meaning bad, worthless, in the physical sense, Matt. 7:17-18; in the moral or ethical sense, "evil," wicked; of persons, e.g., Matt. 7:11; Luke 6:45; Acts 17:5; 2 Thess. 3:2; 2 Tim. 3:13; of "evil" spirits, e.g., Matt. 12:45; Luke 7:21; Acts 19:12-13, 15-16; of a generation, Matt. 12:39, 45; 16:4; Luke 11:29; of things, e.g., Matt. 5:11; 6:23; 20:15; Mark 7:22; Luke 11:34; John 3:19; 7:7; Acts 18:14; Gal. 1:4; Col. 1:21; 1 Tim. 6:4; 2 Tim. 4:18; Heb. 3:12; 10:22; Jas. 2:4; 4:16; 1 John 3:12; 3 John 10; (b) with the meaning toilsome, painful, Eph. 5:16; 6:13; Rev. 16:2.

3. *phaulos* (5337) primarily denotes "slight, trivial, blown about by every wind"; then, "mean, common, bad," in the sense of being worthless, paltry or contemptible, belonging to a low order of things; in John 5:29, those who have practiced "evil" things, RV, "ill" (*phaula*), are set in contrast to those who have done good things (*agatha*); the same contrast is presented in Rom. 9:11 and 2 Cor. 5:10, in each of which the most authentic mss. have *phaulos* for *kakos*; he who practices "evil" things (RV, "ill") hates the light, John 3:20; jealousy and strife are accompanied by "every vile deed," Jas. 3:16. It is used as a noun in Titus 2:8 (see B, No. 4).

B. Nouns.

1. *kakia* (2549), primarily, "badness" in quality (akin to A, No. 1), denotes (a) "wickedness, depravity, malignity," e.g., Acts 8:22, "wickedness"; Rom. 1:29, "maliciousness"; in Jas. 1:21, KJV, "naughtiness"; (b) "the evil of trouble, affliction," Matt. 6:34, only, and here alone translated "evil."

2. *poneros* (4190), the adjective (A, No. 2), is used as a noun, (a) of Satan as the "evil" one, Matt. 5:37; 6:13; 13:19, 38; Luke 11:4 (in some texts); John 17:15; Eph. 6:16; 2 Thess. 3:3; 1 John 2:13-14; 3:12; 5:18-19; (b) of human beings, Matt. 5:45; (probably v. 39); 13:49; 22:10; Luke 6:35; 1 Cor. 5:13; (c) neuter, "evil (things)," Matt. 9:4;

12:35; Mark 7:23; Luke 3:19; "that which is evil," Luke 6:45; Rom. 12:9; Acts 28:21, "harm."

3. *kakon* (2556), the neuter of A, No. 1, is used with the article, as a noun, e.g., Acts 23:9; Rom. 7:21; Heb. 5:14; in the plural, "evil things," e.g., 1 Cor. 10:6; 1 Tim. 6:10, "all kinds of evil," RV.

4. *phaulon* (5337), the neuter of A, No. 3, is used as a noun in Titus 2:8.

5. *kakopoios* (2555), properly the masculine gender of the adjective, denotes an "evil-doer" (*kakon*, "evil," *poieo*, "to do"), 1 Pet. 2:12, 14; 4:15; in some mss. in 3:16 and John 18:30 (so the KJV).

C. Verbs.

1. *kakoo* (2559), "to ill-treat" (akin to A, No. 1), is rendered "to entreat evil" in Acts 7:6, 19; "made (them) evil affected," 14:2.

2. *kakopoieo* (2554) signifies "to do evil" (cf. B, No. 5), Mark 3:4 (RV, "to do harm"); so, Luke 6:9; in 3 John 11, "doeth evil"; in 1 Pet. 3:17, "evil doing."

D. Adverb.

kakos (2560), "badly, evilly," akin to A, No. 1, is used in the physical sense, "to be sick," e.g., Matt. 4:24; Mark 1:32, 34; Luke 5:31. In Matt. 21:41 this adverb is used with the adjective, "He will miserably destroy those miserable men," more lit., "He will evilly destroy those men (evil as they are)," with stress on the adjective; (b) in the moral sense, "to speak evilly," John 18:23; Acts 23:5; to ask evilly, Jas. 4:3.

EVIL SPEAKING

1. *blasphemia* (988) is translated "evil speaking" in Eph. 4:31, KJV (RV, railing).

2. *katalalia* (2636), "evil speaking," 1 Pet. 2:1.

EXALT, EXALTED

Old Testament

A. Verb.

rum (7311), "to be high, exalted," means either the "state of being on a higher plane," Gen. 7:17, or "movement in an upward direction," Gen. 14:22. Used of men, this verb may refer to their "physical stature," Deut. 1:28. *rum* also means to give great honor and status to another, Ps. 12:8; Isa. 52:13. Another meaning is found in Ezek. 31:4, this verb is used of "making a plant grow larger," or raising a child, so rear a child, Isa. 1:2. The word sometimes means "to take up away from, remove," Lev 2:9; Isa. 57:14. *rum* also means to "be haughty," and so have improper "raised opinion" about oneself, and thus have a moral flaw of arrogance,

2 Sam. 22:28. When referring to the voice, **rum** means to "cry aloud," Deut. 27:14.

The raising of the hand serves as a symbol of power and strength and signifies being "mighty" or "triumphant," Deut. 32:27. To raise one's hand against someone is to rebel against him, 1 Kings 11:26. The raising of one's horn suggests the picture of a wild ox standing in all its strength. This is a picture of "triumph" over one's enemies, 1 Sam. 2:1. Raising one's head may be a public gesture of "triumph and supremacy," Ps. 110:7. Raising the head also came to signify "to mark with distinction," "to give honor to," Ps. 3:3. To raise one's eyes or heart is to be "proud" and "arrogant," Deut. 8:14.

B. Nouns.

rum (7312), "height; haughtiness." Physical height, Prov. 25:3; improper pride, Isa. 2:11.

marom (4791), "higher plane; height; high social position." Job 16:19 and Isa. 33:5 contain the word with the meaning of "the height" as the abode of God. Job 5:11 uses the word to refer to "a high social position." **marom** can also signify improper pride, or "self-exaltation," 2 Kings 19:22; Ps. 73:8.

New Testament

A. Verbs.

1. **hupsoo** (5312), "to lift up" (akin to **hupsos**, "height"), is used (a) literally of the "lifting" up of Christ in His crucifixion, John 3:14; 8:28; 12:32, 34; illustratively, of the serpent of brass, John 3:14; (b) figuratively, of spiritual privileges bestowed on a city, Matt. 11:23; Luke 10:15; of "raising" to dignity and happiness, Luke 1:52; Acts 13:17; of haughty self-exaltation, and, contrastingly, of being "raised" to honor, as a result of self-humbling, Matt. 23:12; Luke 14:11; 18:14; of spiritual "uplifting" and revival, Jas. 4:10; 1 Pet. 5:6; of bringing into the blessings of salvation through the gospel, 2 Cor. 11:7; (c) with a combination of the literal and metaphorical, of the "exaltation" of Christ by God the Father, Acts 2:33; 5:31.

2. **huperupsoo** (5251), "to exalt highly" (**huper**, "over," and No. 1), is used of Christ, as in No. 1, (c), in Phil. 2:9.

3. **epairo** (1869), "to lift up" (**epi**, "up," **airo**, "to raise"), is said (a) literally, of a sail, Acts 27:40; hands, Luke 24:50; 1 Tim. 2:8; heads, Luke 21:28; eyes, Matt. 17:8, etc.; (b) metaphorically, of "exalting" oneself, being "lifted up" with pride, 2 Cor. 10:5; 11:20.

4. **huperairo** (5229), "to raise over" (**huper**, "above," and **airo**, see No. 3), is used in the middle voice, of "exalting" oneself exceedingly, 2 Cor. 12:7; 2 Thess. 2:4.

B. Adjective.

hupselos (5308), "high, lofty," is used metaphorically in Luke

16:15, as a noun with the article, RV, "that which is exalted," KJV, "that which is highly esteemed."

EXAMINATION, EXAMINE

A. Noun.

anakrisis (351), from *ana*, "up or through," and *krino*, "to distinguish," was a legal term among the Greeks, denoting the preliminary investigation for gathering evidence for the information of the judges, Acts 25:26.

B. Verbs.

1. *anakrino* (350), "to examine, investigate," is used (a) of searching or enquiry, Acts 17:11; 1 Cor. 9:3; 10:25, 27; (b) of reaching a result of the enquiry, judging, 1 Cor. 2:14-15; 4:3-4; 14:24; (c) forensically, of examining by torture, Luke 23:14; Acts 4:9; 12:19; 24:8; 28:18.

2. *anetazo* (426), "to examine judicially," is used in Acts 22:24, 29.

3. *dokimazo* (1381), "to prove, test, approve," is rendered "examine" in 1 Cor. 11:28, KJV (RV, prove).

4. *peirazo* (3985), "to tempt, try," is rendered "examine" in 2 Cor. 13:5, KJV (RV, try).

EXAMPLE

A. Nouns.

1. *deigma* (1164), primarily "a thing shown, a specimen" (akin to *deiknumi*, "to show"), denotes an "example" given as a warning, Jude 7.

2. *hupogrammos* (5261), lit., "an under-writing" (from *hupographo*, "to write under, to trace letters" for copying by scholars); hence, "a writing-copy, an example," 1 Pet. 2:21, said of what Christ left for believers, by His sufferings (not expiatory, but exemplary), that they might "follow His steps."

B. Verbs.

1. *deigmatizo* (1165), "to make a show of, to expose" (akin to A, No. 1), is translated "to make a public example," in Matt. 1:19 (some mss. have the strengthened form *paradeigmatizo* here; "put...to an open shame," Heb. 6:6,); in Col. 2:15, "made a show of."

2. *hupodeiknumi* (5263), primarily, "to show secretly" (*hupo*, "under," *deiknumi*, "to show"), "to show by tracing out" (akin to A, No. 1); hence, "to teach, to show by example," Acts 20:35, RV, "I gave you an example," for KJV, "I showed you." Elsewhere, "to warn," Matt. 3:7; Luke 3:7; 12:5, RV, for KJV, "forewarn"; "to show," Luke 6:47; Acts 9:16.

EXCEED, EXCEEDING, EXCEEDINGLY

A. Verbs.

1. *huperballo* (5235), "to throw over or beyond" (*huper*, "over," *ballo*, "to throw"), is translated "exceeding" in 2 Cor. 9:14; Eph. 1:19; 2:7; "excelleth" (RV, "surpasseth") in 2 Cor. 3:10; "passeth" in Eph. 3:19 ("surpasseth" might be the meaning here).

2. *perisseuo* (4052), "to be over and above, over a certain number or measure, to abound, exceed," is translated "exceed" in Matt. 5:20; 2 Cor. 3:9.

B. Adverbs and Adverbial Phrases.

1. *sphodra* (4970), properly the neuter plural of *sphodros*, "excessive, violent" (from a root indicating restlessness), signifies "very, very much, exceedingly," Matt. 2:10; 17:6, "sore"; 17:23; 18:31, RV, "exceeding," for KJV, "very"; 19:25; 26:22; 27:54, RV, "exceedingly" for KJV, "greatly"; Mark 16:4, "very"; Luke 18:23 (ditto); Acts 6:7, RV, "exceedingly," for KJV, greatly; Rev. 16:21.

2. *sphodros* (4971), "exceedingly," is used in Acts 27:18.

3. *perissos* (4057), akin to A. 2., is used in Matt. 27:23, RV, "exceedingly," for KJV, "the more"; Mark 10:26, RV, "exceedingly," for KJV, "out of measure"; in Acts 26:11, "exceedingly." In Mark 15:14, the most authentic mss. have this word (RV, "exceedingly") for No. 4 (KJV, "the more exceedingly").

4. *perissoteros* (4056), akin to A. 2., "abundantly, exceedingly," Gal. 1:14, "more exceedingly"; 1 Thess. 2:17.

5. *huperekperissou* (5528 and 1537 and 4053) denotes "superabundantly" (*huper*, "over," *ek*, "from," *perissos*, "abundant"); in 1 Thess. 3:10, "exceedingly"; Eph. 3:20, "exceeding abundantly." Another form, *huperekperissos* (*huper*, "and" *ek* and No. 3), is used in 1 Thess. 5:13 (in the best mss.), "exceeding highly." Cf. the verb *huperperisseuo*, "to abound more exceedingly," Rom. 5:21; in 2 Cor. 7:4, "I overflow (with joy)," RV, for KJV, "I am exceeding (joyful)."

EXCEL, EXCELLENCY, EXCELLENT

A. Verbs.

1. *perisseuo* (4052), "to be over and above," is rendered "abound" in 1 Cor. 14:12, RV, for KJV, "excel."

2. *huperecho* (5242), lit., "to have over" (*huper*, "over," *echo*, "to have"), is translated "excellency" in Phil. 3:8, "the surpassingness" (Moule); the phrase could be translated "the surpassing thing, which consists in the knowledge of Christ Jesus," and this is the probable meaning. This verb is used three times in Philippians, here and in 2:3; 4:7. See also Rom. 13:1; 1 Pet. 2:13.

3. *diaphero* (1308), "to differ," is used in the neuter plural of the

present participle with the article, in Phil. 1:10, "the things that
are excellent."

B. Nouns.

1. *huperbole* (5236), lit., "a throwing beyond," hence, "a surpassing, an excellence," is translated "excellency" in 2 Cor. 4:7, KJV;
RV, "exceeding greatness." It always betokens preeminence.

2. *huperoche* (5247), akin to A, No. 2, strictly speaking, "the act
of overhanging" (*huper*, and *echo*, "to hold") or "the thing which
overhangs," hence, "superiority, preeminence," is translated "excellency (of speech)" in 1 Cor. 2:1; elsewhere, in 1 Tim. 2:2, RV,
"high place," for KJV, "authority."

C. Adjectives.

1. *megaloprepes* (3169) signifies "magnificent, majestic, that
which is becoming to a great man" (from *megas*, "great," and
prepo, "to be fitting or becoming"), in 2 Pet. 1:17, "excellent."

2. *diaphoroteros* (1313*), comparative degree of *diaphoros*, "excellent," akin to A, No. 3, is used twice, in Heb. 1:4, "more excellent (name)," and 8:6, "more excellent (ministry)." For the positive
degree see Rom. 12:6; Heb. 9:10.

3. *pleion* (4119), "more, greater," the comparative degree of
polus, "much," is translated "more excellent" in Heb. 11:4, of
Abel's sacrifice; *pleion* is used sometimes of that which is superi-
or by reason of inward worth, cf. 3:3, "more (honor)"; in Matt. 6:25,
of the life in comparison with meat.

4. *kratistos* (2903), "mightiest, noblest, best," the superlative degree of *kratus*, "strong" (cf. *kratos*, "strength"), is used as a title of
honor and respect, "most excellent," Luke 1:3 (Theophilus was
quite possibly a man of high rank); Acts 23:26; 24:3 and 26:25, RV,
for KJV, "most noble."

EXCESS

1. *akrasia* (192) lit. denotes "want of strength," hence, "want of
self-control, incontinence," Matt. 23:25, "excess"; 1 Cor. 7:5, "in-
continency."

2. *anachusis* (401), lit., "a pouring out, overflowing" (akin to
anacheo, "to pour out"), is used metaphorically in 1 Pet. 4:4, "excess," said of the riotous conduct described in v. 3.

EXCHANGE

A. Noun.

antallagma (465), "the price received as an equivalent of, or in
exchange for, an article, an exchange" (*anti*, "instead of," *allasso*,
"to change," akin to *allos*, "another"), hence denotes the price at
which the "exchange" is effected, Matt. 16:26; Mark 8:37. Connect-

ed with this is the conception of atonement, as in the word *lutron*, "a ransom."

B. Verb.

metallasso (*3337*) denotes (a) "to exchange," *meta*, "with," implying change, and *allasso* (see A), Rom. 1:25, of "exchanging" the truth for a lie, RV, for KJV, "changed"; (b) "to change," v. 26, a different meaning from that in the preceding verse.

EXCUSE

A. Adjective (negative).

anapologetos (*379*), "without excuse, inexcusable" (*a*, negative, *n*, euphonic, and *apologeomai*, see B, No. 1, below), is used, Rom. 1:20, "without excuse," of those who reject the revelation of God in creation; 2:1, RV, for KJV, "inexcusable," of the Jew who judges the Gentile.

B. Verbs.

1. *apologeomai* (*626*), lit., "to speak oneself off," hence "to plead for oneself," and so, in general, (a) "to defend," as before a tribunal; in Rom. 2:15, RV, "excusing them," means one "excusing" others (not themselves); the preceding phrase "one with another" signifies one person with another, not one thought with another; it may be paraphrased, "their thoughts with one another, condemning or else excusing one another"; conscience provides a moral standard by which men judge one another; (b) "to excuse" oneself, 2 Cor. 12:19.

2. *paraiteomai* (*3868*) is used in the sense of "begging off, asking to be excused or making an excuse," in Luke 14:18 (twice) and v. 19. In the first part of v. 18 the verb is used in the middle voice, "to make excuse" (acting in imagined self-interest); in the latter part and in v. 19 it is in the passive voice, "have me excused."

EXERCISE

A. Verb.

gumnazo (*1128*) primarily signifies "to exercise naked" (from *gumnos*, "naked"); then, generally, "to exercise, to train the body or mind" (Eng., "gymnastic"), 1 Tim. 4:7, with a view to godliness; Heb. 5:14, of the senses, so as to discern good and evil; 12:11, of the effect of chastening, the spiritual "exercise producing the fruit of righteousness"; 2 Pet. 2:14, of certain evil teachers with hearts "exercised in covetousness," RV.

B. Noun.

gumnasia (*1129*) primarily denotes "gymnastic exercise" (akin to A), 1 Tim. 4:8, where the immediate reference is probably not to mere physical training for games but to discipline of the body such as that to which the apostle refers in 1 Cor. 9:27, though there may be an allusion to the practices of asceticism.

EXHORT, EXHORTATION

A. Verbs.

1. *parakaleo* (*3870*), primarily, "to call to a person" (*para*, "to the side," *kaleo*, "to call"), denotes (a) "to call on, entreat"; (b) to admonish, exhort, to urge one to pursue some course of conduct (always prospective, looking to the future, in contrast to the meaning to comfort, which is retrospective, having to do with trial experienced), translated "exhort" in the RV of Phil. 4:2; 1 Thess. 4:10; Heb. 13:19, 22, for KJV, "beseech"; in 1 Tim. 5:1, for KJV, "intreat"; in 1 Thess. 5:11, for KJV, "comfort"; "exhorted" in 2 Cor. 8:6 and 12:18, for KJV, "desired"; in 1 Tim. 1:3, for KJV, "besought."

2. *paraineo* (*3867*), primarily, "to speak of near" (*para*, "near," and *aineo*, "to tell of, speak of," then, "to recommend"), hence, "to advise, exhort, warn," is used in Acts 27:9, "admonished," and v. 22, "I exhort."

3. *protrepo* (*4389*), lit., "to turn forward, propel" (*pro*, "before," *trepo*, "to turn"); hence, "to impel morally, to urge forward, encourage," is used in Acts 18:27, RV, "encouraged him" (Apollos), with reference to his going into Achaia; KJV, "exhorting the disciples"; while the encouragement was given to Apollos, a letter was written to the disciples in Achaia to receive him.

B. Noun.

paraklesis (*3874*), akin to A, No. 1, primarily "a calling to one's side," and so "to one's aid," hence denotes (a) an appeal, "entreaty," 2 Cor. 8:4; (b) encouragement, "exhortation," e.g., Rom. 12·8; in Acts 4:36, RV, "exhortation," for KJV, "consolation"; (c) "consolation and comfort," e.g., Rom. 15:4.

EXORCIST

exorkistes (*1845*) denotes (a) "one who administers an oath"; (b) "an exorcist" (akin to *exorkizo*, "to adjure," from *orkos*, "an oath"), "one who employs a formula of conjuration for the expulsion of demons," Acts 19:13. The practice of "exorcism" was carried on by strolling Jews, who used their power in the recitation of particular names.

EXPECT, EXPECTATION

A. Verbs.

1. *ekdechomai* (*1551*), lit. and primarily, "to take or receive from" (*ek*, "from," *dechomai*, "to receive"), hence denotes "to await, expect," the only sense of the word in the NT; it suggests a reaching out in readiness to receive something; "expecting," Heb.

10:13; "expect," 1 Cor. 16:11, RV (KJV, "look for"); to wait for, John 5:3 (KJV only); Acts 17:16; 1 Cor. 11:33, RV (KJV, "tarry for"); Jas. 5:7; to wait, 1 Pet. 3:20 in some mss.; "looked for," Heb. 11:10.

2. **prosdokao** (4328), "to watch toward, to look for, expect" (**pros**, "toward," **dokeo**, "to think": **dokao** "does not exist"), is translated "expecting" in Matt. 24:50 and Luke 12:46, RV (KJV," "looketh for"); Luke 3:15, "were in expectation"; Acts 3:5, "expecting" (KJV and RV); 28:6 (twice), "expected that," RV (KJV, "looked when") and "when they were long in expectation" (KJV, "after they had looked a great while").

B. Nouns.

1. **apokaradokia** (603), primarily "a watching with outstretched head" (**apo**, "from," **kara**, "the head," and **dokeo**, "to look, to watch"), signifies "strained expectancy, eager longing," the stretching forth of the head indicating an "expectation" of something from a certain place, Rom. 8:19 and Phil. 1:20. The prefix **apo** suggests "abstraction and absorption" (Lightfoot), i.e., abstraction from anything else that might engage the attention, and absorption in the object expected "till the fulfillment is realized" (Alford). The intensive character of the noun, in comparison with No. 2 (below), is clear from the contexts; in Rom. 8:19 it is said figuratively of the creation as waiting for the revealing of the sons of God ("waiting" translates the verb **apekdechomai**, a strengthened form of A, No. 1. In Phil. 1:20 the apostle states it as his "earnest expectation" and hope, that, instead of being put to shame, Christ shall be magnified in his body, "whether by life, or by death," suggesting absorption in the person of Christ, abstraction from aught that hinders.

2. **prosdokia** (4329), "a watching for, expectation" (akin to A, No. 2, which see), is used in the NT only of the "expectation" of evil, Luke 21:26, RV, "expectation," KJV, "looking for," regarding impending calamities; Acts 12:11, "the expectation" of the execution of Peter. 3. **ekdoche** (1561), primarily "a receiving from," hence, "expectation" (akin to A, No. 1), is used in Heb. 10:27 (RV, "expectation"; KJV, "looking for"), of judgment.

EXPERIENCE (without), EXPERIMENT

1. **apeiros** (552), "without experience" (**a**, negative, **peira**, "a trial, experiment") is used in Heb. 5:13, RV, "without experience," KJV, "unskillful," with reference to "the word of righteousness."

2. **dokime** (1382) means (a) "the process of proving"; it is rendered "experiment" in 2 Cor. 9:13, KJV, RV, "the proving (of you)"; in 8:2, KJV, "trial," RV "proof"; (b) "the effect of proving, approval, approvedness," RV, "probation," Rom. 5:4 (twice), for KJV, "experience"; KJV and RV, "proof" in 2 Cor. 2:9; 13:3 and Phil. 2:22.

EXPLAIN

diasapheo (*1285*), "to make clear, explain fully" (*dia* "through," intensive, and *saphes*, "clear"), is translated "explain" in Matt. 13:36 RV (KJV, "declare") translates *phrazo*; in 18:31, "told."

EXPOUND

1. *ektithemi* (*1620*), "to set out expose" (*ek*, "out," *tithemi*, "to place"), is used (a) literally, Acts 7:21; (b) metaphorically, in the middle voice, "expound," of circumstances, Acts 11:4; of the way of God, 18:26; of the kingdom of God, 28:23.

2. *epiluo* (*1956*), primarily, "to loose, release," a strengthened form of *luo*, "to loose," signifies "to solve, explain, expound," Mark 4:34, "expounded"; in Acts 19:39, of settling a controversy, RV, "it shall be settled," for KJV, "it shall be determined."

3. *diermeneuo* (*1329*), "to interpret fully" (*dia* "through," intensive, *hermeneuo*, "to interpret"); (Eng., "hermeneutics"), is translated, "He expounded" in Luke 24:27, KJV, RV, "interpreted"; in Acts 9:36, "by interpretation," lit., "being interpreted"; see also 1 Cor. 12:30; 14:5, 13, 27.

EXTORT, EXTORTION, EXTORTIONER

A. Verb.

prasso (*4238*), "to practice," has the special meaning "extort" in Luke 3:13, RV (KJV, "exact"). In Luke 19:23 it is translated "required"; it may be that the master, in addressing the slothful servant, uses the word "extort" or "exact" (as in 3:13), in accordance with the character attributed to him by the servant.

B. Nouns.

1. *harpage* (*724*) denotes "pillage, plundering, robbery, extortion" (akin to *harpazo*, "to seize, carry off by force," and *harpagmos*, "a thing seized, or the act of seizing"; from the root *arp*, seen in Eng., "rapacious"; an associated noun, with the same spelling, denoted a rake, or hook for drawing up a bucket); it is translated "extortion" in Matt. 23:25; Luke 11:39, RV, KJV, "ravening"; Heb. 10:34, "spoiling."

2. *pleonexia* (*4124*), "covetousness, desire for advantage," is rendered "extortion" in 2 Cor. 9:5.

C. Adjective.

harpax (*727*), "rapacious" (akin to No. 1), is translated as a noun, "extortioners," in Luke 18:11; 1 Cor. 5:10-11; 6:10; in Matt. 7:15 "ravening" (of wolves).

EYE

Old Testament

'ayin (*5869*), "eye; well; surface; appearance; spring of water."

First, the word represents the bodily part, "eye," Gen. 13:10. The expression "between the eyes" means "on the forehead," as a part of the body, Exod. 13:9.

'ayin is often used in connection with expressions of "seeing," Gen. 45:12. The expression "to lift up one's eyes," means to look up and see an object in front of one's view, Gen. 13:10. "Lifting up one's eyes" may also be an act expressing "desire," "longing," Gen. 39:7. The "eyes" may be used in gaining or seeking a judgment, in the sense of "seeing intellectually," "making an evaluation," or "seeking an evaluation or proof of faithfulness," Gen. 44:21.

"Eyes" are used figuratively of mental and spiritual abilities, acts and states. So the "opening of the eyes" in Gen. 3:5 (the first occurrence) means to become autonomous by setting standards of good and evil for oneself. In passages such as Prov. 4:25, "eye" represents a moral faculty. The phrase, "in the eye of," means "in one's view or opinion," Gen. 16:4. Another phrase, "from the eyes of," may signify that a thing or matter is "hidden" from one's knowledge, Num. 5:13. In Exod. 10:5, the word represents the "visible surface of the earth." Lev. 13:5 uses *'ayin* to represent "one's appearance." A "gleam or sparkle" is described in the phrase, "to give its eyes," KJV "giveth his colour," Prov. 23:31.

ma'yan (4599), "spring," means a body of water that naturally comes from the ground as compared to a stored body of water in a well or cistern, Gen. 7:11. This spring may occasionally refer to the life-giving elements which water of course has, Ps 87:7; Lev. 11:36.

New Testament

1. *ophthalmos* (3788), akin to *opsis*, "sight," probably from a root signifying "penetration, sharpness" (Curtius, *Gk. Etym.*) (cf. Eng., "ophthalmia," etc.). is used (a) of the physical organ, e.g., Matt. 5:38; of restoring sight, e.g., Matt. 20:33; of God's power of vision, Heb. 4:13; 1 Pet. 3:12; of Christ in vision, Rev. 1:14; 2:18; 19:12; of the Holy Spirit in the unity of Godhood with Christ, Rev. 5:6; (b) metaphorically, of ethical qualities, evil, Matt. 6:23; Mark 7:22 (by metonymy, for envy); singleness of motive, Matt. 6:22; Luke 11:34; as the instrument of evil desire, "the principal avenue of temptation," 1 John 2:16; of adultery, 2 Pet. 2:14; (c) metaphorically, of mental vision, Matt. 13:15; John 12:40; Rom. 11:8; Gal. 3:1, where the metaphor of the "evil eye" is altered to a different sense from that of bewitching (the posting up or placarding of an "eye" was used as a charm, to prevent mischief); by gospel-preaching Christ had been, so to speak, placarded before their "eyes"; the question may be paraphrased, "What evil teachers have been malignly fascinating you?"; Eph. 1:18, of the "eyes of the heart," as a means of knowledge.

2. *trumalia* (*5168*) is used of the "eye" of a needle, Mark 10:25 (from *trume*, "a hole," *truo*, "to wear away").

EYE-SERVICE

ophthalmodoulia (*3787*) denotes "service performed only under the master's eye," diligently performed when he is looking, but neglected in his absence, Eph. 6:6 and Col. 3:22.

EYEWITNESS

1. *autoptes* (*845*) signifies "seeing with one's own eyes," Luke 1:2.

2. *epoptes* (*2030*), primarily "an overseer" (*epi*, "over"), then, a "spectator, an eyewitness" of anything, is used in 2 Pet. 1:16 of those who were present at the transfiguration of Christ, with a possible focus that this is sight which observes a revelation not given to all.

F

FABLE

muthos (3454) primarily signifies "speech, conversation." The first syllable comes from a root *mu*—, signifying "to close, keep secret, be dumb"; whence, *muo*, "to close" (eyes, mouth) and *musterion*, "a secret, a mystery"; hence, "a story, narrative, fable, fiction" (Eng., "myth"). The word is used of Gnostic errors and of Jewish and profane fables and genealogies, in 1 Tim. 1:4; 4:7; 2 Tim. 4:4; Titus 1:14; of fiction, in 2 Pet. 1:16.

muthos is to be contrasted with *aletheia*, "truth," and with *logos*, "a story, a narrative purporting to set forth facts," e.g., Matt. 28:15, a "saying" (i.e., an account, story, in which actually there is a falsification of facts); Luke 5:15, RV, "report."

FACE

Old Testament

panim (6440), "face." In its most basic meaning, this noun refers to the "face," on the head of a person, Gen. 17:3. Also *panim* means "the look on one's face," or one's "countenance," often with a focus on the person himself, Gen. 4:5; Deut. 7:10. *panim* can also be used of the surface or visible side of a thing, Gen. 1:2; Exod. 26:9.

This noun is sometimes used anthropomorphically of God; the Bible speaks of God as though He had a "face": "...For therefore I have seen thy face, as though I had seen the face of God," Gen. 33:10. The Bible clearly teaches that God is a spiritual being and ought not to be depicted by an image or any likeness whatever, Exod. 20:4.

New Testament

1. *prosopon* (4383) denotes "the countenance," lit., "the part towards the eyes" (from *pros*, "towards," *ops*, "the eye"), and is used (a) of the "face," Matt. 6:16-17; 2 Cor. 3:7, 2nd part (KJV, "countenance"); in 2 Cor. 10:7, in the RV, "things that are before your face" (KJV, "outward appearance"), the phrase is figurative of superficial judgment; (b) of the look i.e., the "face," which by its various movements affords an index of inward thoughts and feelings, e g., Luke 9:51, 53; 1 Pet. 3:12; (c) the presence of a person, the "face" being the noblest part, e.g., Acts 3:13, RV, "before the face of," KJV, "in the presence of"; 5:41, "presence"; 2 Cor. 2:10, "person"; 1 Thess. 2:17 (first part), "presence"; 2 Thess. 1:9, RV, "face," KJV,

"presence"; Rev. 12:14, "face"; (d) the person himself, e.g., Gal. 1:22; 1 Thess. 2:17 (second part); (e) the appearance one presents by his wealth or poverty, his position or state, Matt. 22:16; Mark 12:14; Gal. 2:6; Jude 16; (f) the outward appearance of inanimate things, Matt. 16:3; Luke 12:56; 21:35; Acts 17:26.

2. *opsis* (*3799*) is primarily "the act of seeing"; then, (a) "the face"; of the body of Lazarus, John 11:44; of the "countenance" of Christ in a vision, Rev. 1:16; (b) the "outward appearance" of a person or thing, John 7:24.

FACTION, FACTIOUS

erithia (or —*eia*) (*2052*) denotes "ambition, self-seeking, rivalry," self-will being an underlying idea in the word; hence it denotes "party-making." It is derived, not from *eris*, "strife," but from *erithos*, "a hireling"; hence the meaning of "seeking to win followers," "factions," so rendered in the RV of 2 Cor. 12:20, KJV, "strifes"; not improbably the meaning here is rivalries, or base ambitions (all the other words in the list express abstract ideas rather than factions); Gal. 5:20; Phil. 1:17 (RV; KJV, v. 16, "contention"); 2:3 (KJV, "strife"); Jas. 3:14, 16; in Rom. 2:8 it is translated as an adjective, "factious" (KJV, "contentious"). The order "strife, jealousy, wrath, faction," is the same in 2 Cor. 12:20 and Gal. 5:20. "Faction" is the fruit of jealousy. Cf. the synonymous adjective *hairetikos*, Titus 3:10, causing division (marg., "factious"), not necessarily "heretical," in the sense of holding false doctrine.

FADE (away)

A. Verb.

maraino (*3133*) was used (a) to signify "to quench a fire," and in the passive voice, of the "dying out of a fire"; hence (b) in various relations, in the active voice, "to quench, waste, wear out"; in the passive, "to waste away"; Jas. 1:11, of the "fading" away of a rich man, as illustrated by the flower of the field.

B. Adjectives (negative).

1. *amarantos* (*263*), "unfading" (*a*, negative, and A, above), whence the "amaranth," an unfading flower, a symbol of perpetuity, is used in 1 Pet. 1:4 of the believer's inheritance, "that fadeth not away."

2. *amarantinos* (*262*) primarily signifies "composed of amaranth" (see No. 1); hence, "unfading," 1 Pet. 5:4, of the crown of glory promised to faithful elders.

FAIL

A. Verbs.

1. *ekleipo* (*1587*), "to leave out" (*ek*, "out," *leipo*, "to leave"), used

intransitively, means "to leave off, cease, fail"; it is said of the cessation of earthly life, Luke 16:9; of faith, 22:32; of the light of the sun, 23:45 (in the best mss.); of the years of Christ, Heb. 1:12.

2. *epileipo* (1952), "not to suffice for a purpose" (*epi*, over), is said of insufficient time, in Heb. 11:32.

3. *pipto* (4098), "to fall," is used of the law of God in its smallest detail, in the sense of losing its authority or ceasing to have force, Luke 16:17. In 1 Cor. 13:8 it is used of love (some mss. have *ekpipto*, "to fall off").

B. Adjective.

anekleiptos (413), "unfailing" (*a*, negative, and A, No. 1), is rendered "that faileth not," in Luke 12:33. In a Greek document dated A.D. 42, some contractors undertake to provide "unfailing" heat for a bath during the current year.

FAIN

1. *boulomai* (1014), "to will deliberately, wish, desire, be minded," implying the deliberate exercise of volition (contrast No. 3), is translated "would fain" in Philem. 13 (in the best mss.).

2. *epithumeo* (1937), "to set one's heart upon, desire," is translated "would fain" in Luke 15:16, of the Prodigal Son.

3. *thelo* (2309), "to wish, to design to do anything," expresses the impulse of the will rather than the intention (see No. 1); the RV translates it "would fain" in Luke 13:31, of Herod's desire to kill Christ, KJV, "will (kill)"; in 1 Thess. 2:18, of the desire of the missionaries to return to the church in Thessalonica.

FAINT

1. *ekluo* (1590) denotes (a) "to loose, release" (*ek*, "out," *luo*, "to loose"); (b) "to unloose," as a bow-string, "to relax," and so, "to enfeeble," and is used in the passive voice with the significance "to be faint, grow weary," (1) of the body, Matt. 15:32; (some mss. have it in 9:36); Mark 8:3; (2) of the soul, Gal. 6:9 (last clause), in discharging responsibilities in obedience to the Lord; in Heb. 12:3, of becoming weary in the strife against sin; in v. 5, under the chastening hand of God.

2. *enkakeo* or *ekkakeo* (1573), "to lack courage, lose heart, be fainthearted" (*en*, "in," *kakos*, "base"), is said of prayer, Luke 18:1; of gospel ministry, 2 Cor. 4:1, 16; of the effect of tribulation, Eph. 3:13; as to well doing, 2 Thess. 3:13, "be not weary" (KJV marg., "faint not"). Some mss. have this word in Gal. 6:9 (No. 1).

3. *kamno* (2577) primarily signified "to work"; then, as the effect of continued labor, "to be weary"; it is used in Heb. 12:3, of becoming "weary" (see also No. 1), RV, "wax not weary"; in Jas. 5:15, of sickness; some mss. have it in Rev. 2:3, KJV, "hast (not) fainted," RV, "grown weary."

FAINTHEARTED

oligopsuchos (3642), lit., "small-souled," denotes "despondent"; then, "fainthearted," 1 Thess. 5:14, RV, for the incorrect KJV, "feeble-minded."

FAIR

1. *asteios* (791), lit., "of the city" (from *astu*, "a city"; like Lat. *urbanus*, from *urbs*, "a city"; Eng., "urbane"; similarly, "polite," from *polis*, "a town"), hence, "fair, elegant" (used in the papyrus writings of clothing), is said of the external form of a child, Acts 7:20, of Moses "(exceeding) fair," lit., "fair to God"; Heb. 11:23 (RV, "goodly," KJV, "proper").

2. *eudia* (2105) denotes "fair weather," Matt. 16:2, (from *eudios*, "calm"; from *eu*, "good," and *dios*, "divine"), among the pagan Greeks, akin to the name for the god Zeus, or Jupiter. Some would derive *dios* and the Latin *deus* (god) and *dies* (day) from a root meaning "bright."

FAITH, FAITHFULNESS

Old Testament

'emunah (530), The basic meaning of *'emunah* is "certainty" and "faithfulness," 1 Sam. 26:23. But generally, the Person to whom one is "faithful" is the Lord Himself, 2 Chron. 19:9. The Lord has manifested His "faithfulness" to His people, Deut. 32:4. All his works reveal his "faithfulness," Ps. 33:4. His commandments are an expression of his "faithfulness," Ps. 119:86; those who seek them are found on the road of "faithfulness," Ps. 119:30. The Lord looks for those who seek to do His will with all their hearts. Their ways are established and His blessing rests on them, Prov. 28:20.

Man's acts, Prov. 12:22, and speech, 12:17, must reflect his favored status with God. As in the marriage relationship, "faithfulness" is not optional. For the relation to be established, the two parties are required to respond to each other in "faithfulness," Jer. 5:1; cf. Isa. 59:4; Jer. 7:28; 9:3. Hosea portrays God's relation to Israel as a marriage and states God's promise of "faithfulness" to Israel (where several Hebrew words describe faithfulness), Hos. 2:19-20.

New Testament

pistis (4102), primarily, "firm persuasion," a conviction based upon hearing (akin to *peitho*, "to persuade"), is used in the NT always of "faith in God or Christ, or things spiritual."

The word is used of (a) trust, e.g., Rom. 3:25; 1 Cor. 2:5; 15:14, 17; 2 Cor. 1:24; Gal. 3:23; Phil. 1:25; 2:17; 1 Thess. 3:2; 2 Thess. 1:3; 3:2; (b) trust-worthiness, e.g., Matt. 23:23; Rom. 3:3, RV, "the faithfulness of God"; Gal. 5:22 (RV, "faithfulness"); Titus 2:10, "fidelity";

(c) by metonymy, what is believed, the contents of belief, the "faith," Acts 6:7; 14:22; Gal. 1:23; 3:25 [contrast 3:23, under (a)]; 6:10; Phil. 1:27; 1 Thess. 3:10; Jude 3, 20 (and perhaps 2 Thess. 3:2); (d) a ground for "faith," an assurance, Acts 17:31 (not as in KJV, marg., "offered faith"); (e) a pledge of fidelity, plighted "faith," 1 Tim. 5:12.

The main elements in "faith" in its relation to the invisible God, as distinct from "faith" in man, are especially brought out in the use of this noun and the corresponding verb, *pisteuo*; they are (1) a firm conviction, producing a full acknowledgement of God's revelation or truth, e.g., 2 Thess. 2:11-12; (2) a personal surrender to Him, John 1:12; (3) a conduct inspired by such surrender, 2 Cor. 5:7. Prominence is given to one or other of these elements according to the context. All this stands in contrast to belief in its purely natural exercise, which consists of an opinion held in good "faith" without necessary reference to its proof. The object of Abraham's "faith" was not God's promise (that was the occasion of its exercise); his "faith" rested on God Himself, Rom. 4:17, 20-21.

FAITH (of little)

oligopistos (3640), lit., "little of faith" (*oligos*, "little," *pistis*, "faith"), is used only by the Lord, and as a tender rebuke, for anxiety, Matt. 6:30 and Luke 12:28; for fear, Matt. 8:26; 14:31; 16:8.

FAITHFUL, FAITHFULLY, FAITHLESS

1. *pistos* (4103), a verbal adjective, akin to *peitho*, is used in two senses, (a) passive, "faithful, to be trusted, reliable," said of God, e.g., 1 Cor. 1:9; 10:13; 2 Cor. 1:18 (KJV, "true"); 2 Tim. 2:13; Heb. 10:23; 11:11; 1 Pet. 4:19; 1 John 1:9; of Christ, e.g., 2 Thess. 3:3; Heb. 2:17; 3:2; Rev. 1:5; 3:14; 19:11; of the words of God, e.g., Acts 13:34, "sure"; 1 Tim. 1:15; 3:1 (KJV, "true"); 4:9; 2 Tim. 2:11; Titus 1:9; 3:8; Rev. 21:5; 22:6; of servants of the Lord, Matt. 24:45; 25:21, 23; Acts 16:15; 1 Cor. 4:2, 17; 7:25; Eph. 6:21; Col. 1:7; 4:7, 9; 1 Tim. 1:12; 3:11; 2 Tim. 2:2; Heb. 3:5; 1 Pet. 5:12; 3 John 5; Rev. 2:13; 17:14; of believers, Eph. 1:1; Col. 1:2; (b) active, signifying "believing, trusting, relying," e.g., Acts 16:1 (feminine); 2 Cor. 6:15; Gal. 3:9 seems best taken in this respect, as the context lays stress upon Abraham's "faith" in God, rather than upon his "faithfulness." In John 20:27 the context requires the active sense, as the Lord is reproaching Thomas for his want of "faith." See No. 2.

2. *apistos* (571) is used with meanings somewhat parallel to No. 1; (a) "untrustworthy" (*a*, negative, and No. 1), not worthy of confidence or belief, is said of things "incredible," Acts 26:8 (b) "unbelieving, distrustful," used as a noun, "unbeliever," Luke 12:46; 1 Tim. 5:8 (RV, for KJV, "infidel"); in Titus 1:15 and Rev. 21:8, "unbelieving"; "faithless" in Matt. 17:17; Mark 9:19; Luke 9:41; John 20:27. The word is most frequent in 1 and 2 Corinthians.

FALL, FALLEN, FALLING, FELL

A. Nouns.

1. **ptosis** (*4431*); "a fall" (akin to B, No. 1), is used (a) literally, of the "overthrow of a building," Matt. 7:27; (b) metaphorically, Luke 2:34, of the spiritual "fall" of those in Israel who would reject Christ; the word "again" in the KJV of the next clause is misleading; the "rising up" (RV) refers to those who would acknowledge and receive Him, a distinct class from those to whom the "fall" applies. The "fall" would be irretrievable, cf. (a); such a lapse as Peter's is not in view.

2. **paraptoma** (*3900*), primarily "a false step, a blunder" (*para*, "aside," *pipto*, "to fall"), then "a lapse from uprightness, a sin, a moral trespass, misdeed," is translated "fall" in Rom. 11:11-12, of the sin and "downfall" of Israel in their refusal to acknowledge God's claims and His Christ; by reason of this the offer of salvation was made to Gentiles.

3. **apostasia** (*646*), "a defection, revolt, apostasy," is used in the NT of religious apostasy; in Acts 21:21, it is translated "to forsake," lit., "thou teachest apostasy from Moses." In 2 Thess. 2:3 "the falling away" signifies apostasy from the faith. In papyri documents it is used politically of rebels.

B. Verbs.

1. **pipto** (*4098*), "to fall," is used (a) of descent, to "fall" down from, e.g., Matt. 10:29; 13:4; (b) of a lot, Acts 1:26; (c) of "falling" under judgment, Jas. 5:12 (cf. Rev. 18:2, RV); (d) of persons in the act of prostration, to prostrate oneself, e.g., Matt. 17:6; John 18:6; Rev. 1:17; in homage and worship, e.g., Matt. 2:11; Mark 5:22; Rev. 5:14; 19:4; (e) of things, "falling" into ruin, or failing, e.g., Matt. 7:25; Luke 16:17, RV, "fall," for KJV, "fail"; Heb. 1:30; (f), of "falling" in judgment upon persons, as of the sun's heat, Rev. 7:16, RV, "strike," KJV, "light"; of a mist and darkness, Acts 13:11.

2. **apopipto** (*634*), "to fall from" (*apo*, "from"), is used in Acts 9:18, of the scales which "fell" from the eyes of Saul of Tarsus.

3. **ekpipto** (*1601*), to fall out of (*ek*, "out," and No. 1), is used in the NT, literally, of flowers that wither in the course of nature, Jas. 1:11; 1 Pet. 1:24; of a ship not under control, Acts 27:17, 26, 29, 32; of shackles loosed from a prisoner's wrist, 12:7; figuratively, of the Word of God (the expression of His purpose), which cannot "fall" away from the end to which it is set, Rom. 9:6; of the believer who is warned lest he "fall" away from the course in which he has been confirmed by the Word of God, 2 Pet. 3:17. So of those who seek to be justified by law, Gal. 5:4, "ye are fallen away from grace." Some mss. have this verb in Mark 13:25, for No. 1; so in Rev. 2:5.

4. **empipto** (*1706*), "to fall into, or among" (*en*, "in," and No. 1), is used (a) literally, Matt. 12:11; Luke 6:39 (some mss. have No. 1 here); 10:36; some mss. have it in 14:5; (b) metaphorically, into con-

demnation, 1 Tim. 3:6; reproach, 3:7; temptation and snare, 6:9; the hands of God in judgment, Heb. 10:13.

5. *epipipto* (1968), "to fall upon" (*epi*, "upon," and No. 1), is used (a) literally, Mark 3:10, "pressed upon"; Acts 20:10, 37; (b) metaphorically, of fear, Luke 1:12; Acts 19:17; Rev. 11:11 (No. 1, in some mss.); reproaches, Rom. 15:3; of the Holy Spirit, Acts 8:16; 10:44; 11:15.

6. *katapipto* (2667), "to fall down" (*kata*, "down," and No. 1), is used in Luke 8:6 (in the best mss.); Acts 26:14; 28:6.

7. *parapipto* (3895), akin to A, No. 2, properly, "to fall in one's way" (*para*, "by"), signifies "to fall away" (from adherence to the realities and facts of the faith), Heb. 6:6.

8. *peripipto* (4045), "to fall around" (*peri*, "around"), hence signifies to "fall" in with, or among, to light upon, come across, Luke 10:30, "among (robbers)"; Acts 27:41.

F

FALSE, FALSEHOOD, FALSELY

Old Testament

sheqer (8267), "falsehood; lie." In about thirty-five passages, *sheqer* describes the nature of "deceptive speech": "to speak," Isa. 59:3, "to teach," Isa. 9:15, "to prophesy," Jer. 14:14, and "to lie," Mic. 2:11. It may also indicate a "deceptive character," as expressed in one's acts: "to deal treacherously," 2 Sam. 18:13, and "to deal falsely," Hos. 7:1. Thus *sheqer* defines a way of life that goes contrary to the law of God, Ps. 119:29-30; cf. vv. 104, 118, 128. The Old Testament saint was instructed to avoid "deception" and the liar, Exod. 23:7; cf. Prov. 13:5.

New Testament

A. Adjectives.

1. *pseudes* (5571), is used of "false witnesses," Acts 6:13; "false apostles," Rev. 2:2, RV, "false," KJV, "liars"; Rev. 21:8, "liars."

2. *pseudonumos* (5581), "under a false name" (No. 1, and *onoma*, "a name"; Eng., "pseudonym"), is said of the knowledge professed by the propagandists of various heretical cults, 1 Tim. 6:20.

B. Noun.

pseudos (5579), "a falsehood" (akin to A, No. 1), is so translated in Eph. 4:25, RV (KJV, "lying"); in 2 Thess. 2:9, "lying wonders" is lit. "wonders of falsehood," i.e., wonders calculated to deceive; it is elsewhere rendered "lie," John 8:44; Rom. 1:25; 2 Thess. 2:11; 1 John 2:21, 27; Rev. 14:5, RV; 21:27; 22:15.

C. Verb.

pseudo (5574), "to deceive by lies," is used in the middle voice, translated "to say... falsely," in Matt. 5:11; it is elsewhere rendered "to lie," Acts 5:3-4; Rom. 9:1; 2 Cor. 11:31; Gal. 1:20; Col. 3:9; 1 Tim. 2:7.

FAME

A. Noun.

pheme (*5345*) originally denoted "a divine voice, an oracle"; hence, "a saying or report" (akin to **phemi**, "to say," from a root meaning "to shine, to be clear"; hence, Lat., **fama**, Eng., "fame"), is rendered "fame" in Matt. 9:26 and Luke 4:14.

B. Verb.

diaphemizo (*1310*) signifies "to spread abroad a matter," Matt. 28:15, RV; Mark 1:45, RV (from **dia**, "throughout," and **phemi**, "to say"); hence, "to spread abroad one's fame," Matt. 9:31. All the passages under this heading relate to the testimony concerning Christ in the days of His flesh.

FAMILY

Old Testament

mishpachah (4940), "family; clan, kind." **mishpachah** basically means persons or creatures that are associated with each other, so refer to "kinds," of animals, Gen. 8:19; or all members of a group who were related by blood and who still felt a sense of consanguinity belonged to the "clan" or "the extended family," or "immediate family," 1 Sam. 9:21; Lev. 25:48-49; Josh. 6:23; or a "major tribal division, Num. 1-4; 26; or the "families" of the nations, Ps. 22:28; 96:7; cf. Gen. 10:5; 12:3.

New Testament

1. **oikos** (*3624*) signifies (a) "a dwelling, a house" (akin to **oikeo**, to dwell); (b) "a household, family," translated "family" in 1 Tim. 5:4, RV, for KJV, "at home."

2. **patria** (*3965*), primarily "an ancestry, lineage," signifies in the NT "a family or tribe"; it is used of the "family" of David, Luke 2:4, RV, for KJV, "lineage"; in the wider sense of "nationalities, races," Acts 3:25, RV, "families," for KJV, "kindreds"; in Eph. 3:15, RV, "every family," for KJV, "the whole family," the reference being to all those who are spiritually related to God the Father, He being the Author of their spiritual relationship to Him as His children.

FARE, FAREWELL

1. **euphraino** (*2165*), in the active voice, signifies "to cheer, gladden," 2 Cor. 2:2; in the passive, "to rejoice, make merry"; translated "faring sumptuously" in Luke 16:19, especially of food (RV, marg., "living in mirth and splendor").

2. **rhonnumi** (*4517*), "to strengthen, to be strong," is used in the imperative mood as a formula at the end of letters, signifying "Farewell," Acts 15:29.

3. **chairo** (*5463*), "to joy, rejoice, be glad," is used in the impera-

tive mood in salutations, (a) on meeting, "Hail," e.g., Matt. 26:49; or with *lego*, "to say, to give a greeting," 2 John 11; in letters, "greeting," e.g., Acts 15:23; (b) at parting, the underlying thought being joy, 2 Cor. 13:11.

FASHION

A. Nouns.

1. *eidos* (1491), "that which is seen, an appearance," is translated "fashion" in Luke 9:29, of the Lord's countenance at the Transfiguration.

2. *prosopon* (4383), "the face, countenance," is translated "fashion" in Jas. 1:11, of the flower of grass.

3. *schema* (4976), "a figure, fashion" (akin to *echo*, "to have"), is translated "fashion" in 1 Cor. 7:31, of the world, signifying that which comprises the manner of life, actions, etc. of humanity in general; in Phil. 2:8 it is used of the Lord in His being found "in fashion" as a man.

4. *tupos* (5179), "a type, figure, example," is translated "fashion" in the KJV of Acts 7:44, RV, "figure," said of the tabernacle.

B. Verbs.

1. *metaschematizo* (3345), "to change in fashion or appearance" (*meta*, "after," here implying change, *schema*, see A, No. 3), is rendered "shall fashion anew" in Phil. 3:21, RV; KJV, "shall change," of the bodies of believers as changed or raised at the Lord's return; in 2 Cor. 11:13, 14, 15, the RV uses the verb "to fashion oneself," for KJV, to transform, of Satan and his human ministers, false apostles; in 1 Cor. 4:6 it is used by way of a rhetorical device, with the significance of transferring by a figure.

2. *suschematizo* (4964), "to give the same figure or appearance as, to conform to" (*sun*, "with," *schema*, cf. No. 1), used in the passive voice, signifies "to fashion oneself, to be fashioned," Rom. 12:2, RV, "be not fashioned according to," for KJV, "be not conformed to"; 1 Pet. 1:14, "(not) fashioning yourselves."

C. Adjective.

summorphos (4832), "having like form with" (*sun*, "with," *morphe*, "form"), is used in Rom. 8:29 and Phil. 3:21 (KJV, "fashioned," RV, "conformed").

FAST, FASTING

A. Nouns.

1. *nesteia* (3521), "a fasting, fast" (from *ne*, a negative prefix, and *esthio*, "to eat"), is used (a) of voluntary abstinence from food, Luke 2:37; Acts 14:23 (some mss. have it in Matt. 17:21 and Mark 9:29); "fasting" had become a common practice among Jews, and

was continued among Christians; in Acts 27:9, "the Fast" refers to the Day of Atonement, Lev. 16:29; that time of the year would be one of dangerous sailing; (b) of involuntary abstinence (perhaps voluntary is included), consequent upon trying circumstances, 2 Cor. 6:5; 11 27.

2. *nestis* (3523), "not eating" (see No. 1), "fasting," is used of lack of food, Matt. 15:32; Mark 8:3.

B. Verb.

nesteuo (3522), "to fast, to abstain from eating" (akin to A, Nos. 1 and 2), is used of voluntary "fasting," Matt. 4:2; 6:16, 17, 18; 9:14, 15; Mark 2:18, 19, 20; Luke 5:33, 34, 35; 18:12; Acts 13:2, 3. Some of these passages show that teachers to whom scholars or disciples were attached gave them special instructions as to "fasting." Christ taught the need of purity and simplicity of motive.

C. Adjectives.

asitos (777), "without food" (*a*, negative, *sitos*, "corn, food"), is used in Acts 27:33, "fasting."

asphalizo (805), "to make secure, safe, firm" (akin to *asphales*, "safe"), (*a*, negative, and *sphallo*, "to trip up"), is translated "make...fast," in Acts 16:24, of prisoners' feet in the stocks. In Matt. 27:64, 65, 66, it is rendered "to make sure."

FATHER

Old Testament

'ab (1), "father; grandfather; forefather; ancestor." Basically, *'ab* relates to the familial relationship represented by the word "father," Gen. 2:24. *'ab* also means "grandfather" and/or "great-grandfather," as in Gen. 28:2,13; 1 Kings 19:4; "forefather," Jer. 35:6. *'ab* can also mean "founder of a class or station," such as a trade, Gen. 4:20, and a title of respect, usually applied to an older person, like, "sir," with a focus on relationship 1 Sam. 24:11; 2 Kings 2:12; 6:21; Jer. 3:4. In Gen. 45:8, the noun is used of an "advisor." In conjunction with *bayit* ("house"), the word *'ab* may mean "family," Exod. 6:25; 12:3.

God is described as the "father" of Israel, Deut. 32:6. Mal. 2:10 tells us that God is the "father" of all people. He is especially the "protector" or "father" of the fatherless, Ps. 68:5. As the "father" of a king, God especially aligns Himself to that man and his kingdom, 2 Sam. 7:14; Ps. 2:7. One of the Messiah's enthronement names is "Eternal Father," Isa. 9:6.

New Testament

A. Noun.

pater (3962), from a root signifying "a nourisher, protector, upholder" (Lat., *pater*, Eng., "father," are akin), is used (a) of the nearest ancestor, e.g., Matt. 2:22; (b) of a more remote ancestor, the progenitor of the people, a "forefather," e.g., Matt. 3:9; 23:30; 1 Cor. 10:1; the patriarchs, 2 Pet. 3:4; (c) one advanced in the knowledge of Christ, 1 John 2:13; (d) metaphorically, of the originator of a family or company of persons animated by the same spirit as himself, as of Abraham, Rom. 4:11, 12, 16, 17, 18, or of Satan, John 8:38, 41, 44; (e) of one who, as a preacher of the gospel and a teacher, stands in a "father's" place, caring for his spiritual children, 1 Cor. 4:15 (not the same as a mere title of honor, which the Lord prohibited, Matt. 23:9); (f) of the members of the Sanhedrin, as of those who exercised religious authority over others, Acts 7:2; 22:1; (g) of God in relation to those who have been born anew (John 1:12, 13), and so are believers, Eph 2:18; 4:6 (cf. 2 Cor. 6:18), and imitators of their "Father," Matt. 5:45, 48; 6:1, 4, 6, 8, 9, etc. Christ never associated Himself with them by using the personal pronoun "our"; He always used the singular, "My Father"; His relationship being unoriginated and essential, whereas theirs is by grace and regeneration, e.g., Matt. 11:27; 25:34; John 20:17; Rev. 2:27; 3:5, 21; so the apostles spoke of God as the "Father" of the Lord Jesus Christ, e.g., Rom. 15:6; 2 Cor. 1:3; 11:31; Eph. 1:3; Heb. 1:5; 1 Pet. 1:3; Rev. 1:6; (h) of God, as the "Father" of lights, i.e., the Source or Giver of whatsoever provides illumination, physical and spiritual, Jas. 1:17; of mercies, 2 Cor. 1:3; of glory, Eph. 1:17; (i) of God, as Creator, Heb. 12:9, cf. Zech. 12:1.

B. Adjectives.

1. *patroos* (3971) signifies "of one's fathers," or "received from one's fathers" (akin to A), Acts 22:3; 24:14; 28:17.

2. *patrikos* (3967), "from one's fathers, or ancestors," is said of that which is handed down from one's "forefathers," Gal. 1:14.

3. *apator* (540), "without father," signifies, in Heb. 7:3, i.e., with no recorded genealogy.

4. *patroparadotos* (3970), "handed down from one's fathers," is used in 1 Pet. 1:18.

FATHERLESS

orphanos (3737), properly, "an orphan," is rendered "fatherless" in Jas. 1:27; "desolate" in John 14:18, for KJV, "comfortless."

FAULT, FAULTLESS

A. Noun.

aition (158), properly the neuter of *aitios*, causative of, responsible for, is used as a noun, "a crime, a legal ground for punishment," translated "fault" in Luke 23:4, 14; in v. 22, cause.

B. Adjective.

amemptos (273), "without blame," is rendered "faultless," in Heb. 8:7.

C. Verbs.

1. *memphomai* (3201), "to blame," is translated "to find fault" in Rom. 9:19 and Heb. 8:8. Some mss. have the verb in Mark 7:2.

2. *elencho* (1651), "to convict, reprove, rebuke," is translated "shew (him) his fault" in Matt. 18:15.

FAVOR, FAVORED

Old Testament

A. Noun.

ratson (7522), "favor; goodwill; acceptance; will; desire; pleasure." *ratson* represents a concrete reaction of the superior to an inferior. When used of God, *ratson* may represent that which is shown in His blessings, Deut. 33:16. Thus Isaiah speaks of the day, year, or time of divine "favor"—in other words, the day of the Lord when all the blessings of the covenant shall be heaped upon God's people, Isa. 49:8; 58:5; 61:2. This word represents the position one enjoys before a superior who is favorably disposed toward him, Exod. 28:38.

ratson also signifies a voluntary or arbitrary decision, Ezra 10:11. When a man does according to his own "will," he does "what he desires," Dan. 8:4. In Ps. 145:16, the word *ratson* means "one's desire" or "what one wants," cf. Esth. 1:8.

B. Verb.

ratsah (7521), "to be pleased with," Gen. 33:10, (see A. above).

New Testament

A. Noun.

charis (5485) denotes (a) objectively, "grace in a person, graciousness," (b) subjectively, (1) "grace on the part of a giver, favor, kindness," (2) "a sense of favor received, thanks." It is rendered "favor" in Luke 1:30; 2:52; Acts 2:47; 7:10, 46; 24:27 and 25:9, RV (for KJV, "pleasure"); 25:3.

B. Verb.

charitoo (5487), akin to A, to endow with *charis*, primarily signified "to make graceful or gracious," and came to denote, in Hellenistic Greek, "to cause to find favor," Luke 1:28, "highly favored"; in Eph. 1:6, it is translated "made...accepted," KJV, "freely bestowed," RV (lit., "graced"); it does not here mean to endue with grace. Grace implies more than favor; grace is a free gift, favor may be deserved or gained.

FEAR, FEARFUL, FEARFULNESS
Old Testament
A. Verb.

yare' (3372), "to be afraid, stand in awe, fear." Basically, this verb connotes the psychological reaction of "fear, dread, anxiety." *yare'* may indicate being afraid of something or someone, or simply in the state of fear, Gen. 32:11; cf. 19:30. Used of a person in an exalted position, *yare'* connotes "standing in awe," Gen. 22:12, 17; Exod. 14:31; 20:20.

B. Nouns.

mora' (4172), "fear." The noun *mora'*, is used exclusively of the fear of being before a superior kind of being. Usually it is used to describe the reaction evoked in men by God's mighty works of destruction and sovereignty, Deut. 4:24. Hence, the word represents a very strong "fear" or "terror." In the singular, this word emphasizes the divine acts themselves. *mora'* may suggest the reaction of animals to men, Gen. 9:2, and of the nations to conquering Israel, Deut. 11:25.

yir'ah (3374), "fear; reverence," of men, Deut. 2:25; of things, Isa. 7:25; of situations, Jonah 1:10; and of God, Jonah 1:12; it may also mean "reverence" of God, Gen. 20:11.

New Testament
A. Nouns.

1. *phobos* (5401) first had the meaning of "flight," that which is caused by being scared; then, "that which may cause flight," (a) "fear, dread, terror," always with this significance in the four Gospels; also e.g., in Acts 2:43; 19:17; 1 Cor. 2:3; 1 Tim. 5:20 (lit., "may have fear"); Heb. 2:15; 1 John 4:18; Rev. 11:11; 18:10, 15; by metonymy, that which causes "fear," Rom. 13:3; 1 Pet. 3:14, RV, "(their) fear," KJV "(their) terror," an adaptation of the Sept. of Isa. 8:12, "fear not their fear"; hence some take it to mean, as there, "what they fear," but in view of Matt. 10:28, e.g., it seems best to understand it as that which is caused by the intimidation of adversaries; (b) "reverential fear," (1) of God, as a controlling motive of the life, in matters spiritual and moral, not a mere "fear" of His power and righteous retribution, but a wholesome dread of displeasing Him, a "fear" which banishes the terror that shrinks from His presence, Rom. 8:15, and which influences the disposition and attitude of one whose circumstances are guided by trust in God, through the indwelling Spirit of God, Acts 9:31; Rom. 3:18; 2 Cor. 7:1; Eph. 5:21 (RV, "the fear of Christ"); Phil. 2:12; 1 Pet. 1:17 (a comprehensive phrase: the reverential "fear" of God will inspire a constant carefulness in dealing with others in His "fear"); 3:2, 15; the association of "fear and trembling," as, e.g., in Phil. 2:12, has in

the Sept. a much sterner import, e.g., Gen. 9:2; Exod. 15:16; Deut. 2:25; 11:25; Ps. 55:5; Isa. 19:16; (2) of superiors, e.g., Rom. 13:7; 1 Pet. 2:18.

2. *deilia* (*1167*), "fearfulness" (from *deos*, "fright"), is rightly rendered "fearfulness" in 2 Tim. 1:7, RV (for KJV, "fear "). That spirit is not given us of God. The word denotes "cowardice and timidity" and is never used in a good sense, as No. 1 is.

3. *eulabeia* (*2124*) signifies, firstly, "caution"; then, "reverence, godly fear," Heb. 5:7; 12:28.

B. Adjectives.

1. *phoberos* (*5398*), "fearful" (akin to A, No. 1), is used only in the active sense in the NT, i.e., causing "fear," terrible, Heb. 10:27, 31; 12:21, RV, "fearful," for KJV, "terrible."

2. *deilos* (*1169*), "cowardly" (see A, No. 2), "timid," is used in Matt. 8:26; Mark 4:40; Rev. 21:8 (here "the fearful" are first in the list of the transgressors).

3. *ekphobos* (*1630*), signifies "frightened outright" (*ek*, "out," intensive, and A, No. 1), Heb. 12:21 (with *eimi*, "I am"), "I exceedingly fear" (see No. 4); Mark 9:6, "sore afraid."

4. *entromos* (*1790*), "trembling with fear" (*en*, "in," intensive, and *tremo*, "to tremble, quake"; Eng., "tremor," etc.), is used with *ginomai*, "to become," in Acts 7:32, "trembled"; 16:29, RV, "trembling for fear"; with *eimi*, "to be," in Heb. 12:21, "quake" (some mss. have *ektromos* here). The distinction between No. 3 and No. 4, as in Heb. 12:21, would seem to be that *ekphobos* stresses the intensity of the "fear," *entromos* the inward effect, "I inwardly tremble (or quake)."

C. Adverb.

aphobos (*880*) denotes "without fear" (*a*, negative, and A, No. 1), and is said of serving the Lord, Luke 1:74; of being among the Lord's people as His servant, 1 Cor. 16:10; of ministering the Word of God, Phil. 1:14; of the evil of false spiritual shepherds, Jude 12.

D. Verbs.

1. *phobeo* (*5399*), in earlier Greek, "to put to flight" (see A, No. 1), in the NT is always in the passive voice, with the meanings either (a) "to fear, be afraid," its most frequent use, e.g., Acts 23:10, according to the best mss. (see No. 2); or (b) "to show reverential fear" [see A, No. 1, (b)], (1) of men, Mark 6:20; Eph. 5:33, RV, "fear," for KJV, "reverence"; (2) of God, e.g., Acts 10:2, 22; 13:16, 26; Col. 3:22 (RV, "the Lord "); 1 Pet. 2:17; Rev. 14:7; 15:4; 19:5; (a) and (b) are combined in Luke 12:4, 5, where Christ warns His followers not to be afraid of men, but to "fear" God.

2. *eulabeomai* (*2125*), "to be cautious, to beware" (see A, No. 3), signifies to act with the reverence produced by holy "fear," Heb. 11:7, "moved with godly fear."

FEAST

Old Testament

chag (2282), "feast; festal sacrifice." This word refers especially to a "feast observed by a pilgrimage," Exod. 10:9; three are referred to in Ezek. 45:17; Hos. 2:11.

There are two unique uses of *chag*. First, Aaron proclaimed a "feast to the Lord" at the foot of Mt. Sinai. This "feast" involved no pilgrimage but was celebrated with burnt offerings, communal meals, singing, and dancing. The whole matter was displeasing to God, Exod. 32:5-7.

In two passages, *chag* represents the "sacrificial animal," Ps. 118:27; cf. Exod. 23:18.

New Testament

A. Nouns.

1. *heorte* (*1859*), "a feast or festival," is used (a) especially of those of the Jews, and particularly of the Passover; the word is found mostly in John's gospel (seventeen times); apart from the Gospels it is used in this way only in Acts 18:21; (b) in a more general way, in Col. 2:16, KJV, "holy day," RV, "a feast day."

2. *deipnon* (*1173*) denotes (a) "the chief meal of the day," dinner or supper, taken at or towards evening; in the plural "feasts," Matt. 23:6; Mark 6:21; 12:39; Luke 20:46; otherwise translated "supper," Luke 14:12, 16, 17, 24; John 12:2; 13:2, 4; 21:20; 1 Cor. 11:21 (of a social meal); (b) "the Lord's Supper," 1 Cor. 11:20; (c) "the supper or feast" which will celebrate the marriage of Christ with His spiritual Bride, at the inauguration of His Kingdom, Rev. 19:9; (d) figuratively, of that to which the birds of prey will be summoned after the overthrow of the enemies of the Lord at the termination of the war of Armageddon, 19:17, cf. Ezek. 39:4, 17-20.

3. *doche* (*1403*), "a reception feast, a banquet" (from *dechomai*, "to receive"), Luke 5:29; 14:13 (not the same as No 2; see v. 12).

4. *gamos* (*1062*), "a wedding," especially a wedding "feast" (akin to *gameo*, "to marry"); it is used in the plural in the following passages (the RV rightly has "marriage feast" for the KJV, "marriage," or "wedding," Matt. 22:2, 3, 4, 9 (in verses 11, 12, it is used in the singular, in connection with the wedding garment); 25:10; Luke 12:36; 14:8; in the following it signifies a wedding itself, John 2:1, 2; Heb. 13:4; and figuratively in Rev. 19:7, of the marriage of the Lamb; in v. 9 it is used in connection with the supper, the wedding supper (or what in English is termed "breakfast"), not the wedding itself, as in v. 7.

5. *agape* (*26*), "love," is used in the plural in Jude 12, signifying "love feasts," RV (KJV, "feasts of charity"); in the corresponding passage, 2 Pet. 2:13, the most authentic mss. have the word *apate*, in the plural, "deceivings."

B. Verb.

heortizo (*1858*), "to keep festival" (akin to A, No. 1) is translated "let us keep the feast," in 1 Cor. 5:8. This is not the Lord's Supper, nor the Passover, but has reference to the continuous life of the believer as a festival or holy-day, in freedom from "the leaven of malice and wickedness, but with the unleavened bread of sincerity and truth."

FEEBLE

asthenes (*772*), "without strength," is translated "feeble" in 1 Cor. 12:22, of members of the body.

FEEL, FEELING, FELT

1. *ginosko* (*1097*), "to know, perceive," is translated "she felt (in her body)," of the woman with the issue of blood, Mark 5.29, i.e., she became aware of the fact.

2. *phroneo* (*5426*), "to think, to be minded," is translated "I felt" in the RV of 1 Cor. 13:11 (for KJV, I understood).

3. *pselaphao* (*5584*), "to feel or grope about" (from *psao*, "to touch"), expressing the motion of the hands over a surface, so as to "feel" it, is used (a) metaphorically, of seeking after God, Acts 17:27; (b) literally, of physical handling or touching, Luke 24:39 with 1 John 1:1; Heb. 12:18.

4. *sumpatheo* (*4834*), "to have a fellow-feeling for or with," is rendered "touched with the feeling of" in Heb. 4:15; "have compassion" in 10:34.

5. *apalgeo* (*524*) signifies "to cease to feel pain for" (*apo*, "from," *algeo*, "to feel pain"; cf. Eng., "neuralgia"); hence, to be callous, "past feeling," insensible to honor and shame, Eph. 4:19.

FEIGN, FEIGNED

A. Verb.

hupokrinomai (*5271*) primarily denotes "to answer"; then, "to answer on the stage, play a part," and so, metaphorically, "to feign, pretend," Luke 20:20.

B. Adjective.

plastos (*4112*) primarily denotes "formed, molded" (from *plasso*, to mold; Eng., "plastic"); then, metaphorically, "made up, fabricated, feigned," 2 Pet. 2:3.

FELLOWSHIP

A. Nouns.

1. *koinonia* (*2842*), (a) "communion, fellowship, sharing in common" (from *koinos*, "common"), is translated "communion" in 1 Cor. 10:16; Philem. 6, RV, "fellowship," for KJV, "communication";

it is most frequently translated "fellowship"; (b) "that which is the outcome of fellowship, a contribution," e.g., Rom. 15:26; 2 Cor. 8:4.

2. *metoche* (3352), "partnership," is translated "fellowship" in 2 Cor. 6:4.

3. *koinonos* (2844) denotes "a partaker" or "partner" (akin to No. 1); in 1 Cor. 10:20 it is used with *ginomai*, "to become," "that ye should have communion with," RV (KJV, fellowship with).

B. Verbs.

1. *koinoneo* (2841), "to have fellowship," is so translated in Phil. 4:15, RV, for KJV, "did communicate."

2. *sunkoinoneo* (4790), "to have fellowship with or in" (*sun*, "with," and No. 1), is used in Eph. 5:11; Phil. 4:14, RV, "ye had fellowship," for KJV, "ye did communicate"; Rev. 18:4, RV, "have (no) fellowship with," for KJV, "be (not) partakers of."

FERVENT, FERVENTLY

A. Adjective.

ektenes (1618) denotes "strained, stretched" (*ek*, "out," *teino*, "to stretch"); hence, metaphorically, "fervent," 1 Pet. 4:8. Some mss. have it in Acts 12:5, for the adverb (see B).

B. Adverb.

ektenos (1619), "fervently" (akin to A), is said of love, in 1 Pet. 1:22; of prayer, in some mss., Acts 12:5; for the comparative degree in Luke 22:44.

C. Verb.

zeo (2204), "to be hot, to boil" (Eng. "zeal" is akin), is metaphorically used of "fervency" of spirit, Acts 18:25; Rom. 12:11.

FIGHT

Old Testament

A. Verb.

lacham (3898), "to fight, do battle, engage in combat," commonly used in the context of "armies engaged in pitched battle" against each other, Num. 21:23; Josh. 10:5; Judg. 11:5, or "hand-to-hand combat," 1 Sam. 17:32-33. Frequently, God "fights" the battle for Israel, Deut. 20:4. Instead of swords, words spoken by a lying tongue are often used "to fight" against God's servants, Ps. 109:2.

B. Noun.

milchamah (4421), "battle; war," so referring to either a pitched attack by two opposing armies as a single event, or many battles over a period of time, "war," Gen. 14:8.

New Testament

A. Nouns.

1. *agon* (73), akin to *ago*, "to lead," primarily "a gathering," then, "a place of assembly," and hence, "a contest, conflict," is translated "fight" in 1 Tim. 6:12; 2 Tim. 4:7.

2. *athlesis* (119) is translated "fight" in Heb. 10:32, KJV.

B. Verbs.

1. *agonizomai* (75), from A, No. 1, denotes (a) "to contend" in the public games, 1 Cor. 9:25 ("striveth in the games," RV); (b) "to fight, engage in conflict," John 18:36; (c) metaphorically, "to contend" perseveringly against opposition and temptation, 1 Tim. 6:12; 2 Tim. 4:7 (cf. A, No. 1; in regard to the meaning there, the evidence of *Koine* inscriptions is against the idea of games-contests); to strive as in a contest for a prize, straining every nerve to attain to the object Luke 13:24; to put forth every effort, involving toil, Col. 1:29; 1 Tim. 4:10 (some mss. have *oneidizomai* here, "to suffer reproach"); to wrestle earnestly in prayer, Col. 4:12.

2. *pukteuo* (4438), "to box" (from *puktes*, "a pugilist"), one of the events in the Olympic games, is translated "fight" in 1 Cor. 9:26.

3. *machomai* (3164), "to fight," is so rendered in Jas. 4:2 (cf. "fightings," v. 1, see below), and translated "strive" in 2 Tim. 2:24; "strove" in John 6:52; Acts 7:26.

4. *theriomacheo* (2341) signifies "to fight with wild beasts" (*therion*, "a beast," and No. 3), 1 Cor. 15:32. Some think that the apostle was condemned to fight with wild beasts; if so, he would scarcely have omitted it from 2 Cor. 11:23-end.

FIGHTING

A. Noun.

mache (3163), "a fight, strife" (akin to B, No. 3, under FIGHT, *New Testament*), is always used in the plural in the NT, and translated "fightings" in 2 Cor. 7:5; Jas. 4:1; and Titus 3:9, RV (for KJV, "strivings"); "strifes in 2 Tim. 2:23.

B. Adjective.

theomachos (2314), "fighting against God" (*theos*, "God," and A, occurs in Acts 5:39 (KJV, "to fight"), lit., "God-fighters."

FIGURE

1. *tupos* (5179), "a type, figure, pattern," is translated "figures" (i.e., representations of gods) in Acts 7:43; in the RV of v. 44 (for KJV, "fashion") and in Rom. 5:14, of Adam as a "figure of Christ."

2. *antitupos* (499), an adjective, used as a noun, denotes, lit., "a striking back"; metaphorically, "resisting, adverse"; then, in a passive sense, "struck back"; in the NT metaphorically, "correspond-

ing to," (a) a copy of an archetype (*anti*, "corresponding to, and No. 1), i.e., the event or person or circumstance corresponding to the type, Heb. 9:24, RV, "like in pattern" (KJV, "the figure of"), of the tabernacle which, with its structure and appurtenances, was a pattern of that "holy place," "Heaven itself," "the true," into which Christ entered, "to appear before the face of God for us." The earthly tabernacle anticipatively represented what is now made good in Christ; it was a "figure" or "parable" (9:9), "for the time now present," RV, i.e., pointing to the present time, not "then present," KJV (see below); (b) "a corresponding type," 1 Pet. 3:21, said of baptism; the circumstances of the flood, the ark and its occupants, formed a type, and baptism forms "a corresponding type" (not an antitype), each setting forth the spiritual realities of the death, burial, and resurrection of believers in their identification with Christ. It is not a case of type and antitype, but of two types, that in Genesis, the type, and baptism, the corresponding type.

3. *parabole* (*3850*), "a casting or placing side by side" (*para*, "beside," *ballo*, "to throw") with a view to comparison or resemblance, a parable, is translated "figure" in the KJV of Heb. 9:9 (RV, "a parable for the time now present") and 11:19, where the return of Isaac was (parabolically, in the lit. sense of the term) figurative of resurrection (RV, "parable"). See No. 2 (a).

FILL, FILL UP
Old Testament

A. Verb.

male' (4390), "to fill, fulfill, overflow, ordain, endow." *male'* means "to be full" in the sense of having something done to one, Gen. 6:13; 2 Kings 4:6. Used transitively, this verb means the act or state of "filling something," Gen. 1:22; Exod. 40:34. *male'* is sometimes used in the sense "coming to an end," 1 Kings 2:27. In a different but related nuance, the verb signifies "to confirm," someone's word, 1 Kings 1:14. This verb is used to signify filling something to the full extent of what is necessary, in the sense of being "successfully completed," Isa. 40:2.

male' is used of "filling to overflowing," Josh. 3:15. A special nuance appears when the verb is used with "heart"; in such cases, it means "to presume," Esth. 7:5; Jer. 4:5. The word often has a special meaning in conjunction with "hand." *male'* can connote "endow," (often with an office, or a power), Exod. 28:3; Judg. 17:5; Ezek. 43:26. In military contexts, "to fill one's hand" is to prepare for battle, or prepare to wield a weapon, 2 Sam. 23:7; 2 Kings 9:24; Jer. 51:11.

B. Adjective.

male' (4390), "full," Deut. 6:11; Ruth 1:21.

New Testament

A. Verbs.

1. *pleroo* (4137) denotes (1) "to make full, to fill to the full"; in the passive voice, "to be filled, made full"; it is used (I) of things: a net, Matt. 13:48; a building, John 12:3; Acts 2:2; a city, Acts 5:28; needs, Phil. 4:19, KJV "supply," RV, "fulfill"; metaphorically, of valleys, Luke 3:5; figuratively, of a measure of iniquity, Matt. 23:32; (2) of persons: (a) of the members of the church, the body of Christ, as filled by Him, Eph. 1:23 ("all things in all the members"); 4:10; in 3:19, of their being filled "into" (*eis*), RV, "unto," KJV, "with" (all the fullness of God); of their being "made full" in Him, Col. 2:10 (RV, for KJV, "complete"); (b) of Christ Himself: with wisdom, in the days of His flesh, Luke 2:40; with joy, in His return to the Father, Acts 2:28; (c) of believers: with the Spirit, Eph. 5:18; with joy, Acts 13:52; 2 Tim. 1:4; with joy and peace, Rom. 15:13, [from these are to be distinguished those passages which speak of joy as being fulfilled or completed, which come under FULFILL, John 3:29; 15:11 (RV); 16:24 (RV); Phil. 2:2; 1 John 1:4 (RV); 2 John 12 (RV)]; with knowledge, Rom. 15:14; with comfort, 2 Cor. 7:4; with the fruits of righteousness, Phil. 1:11 (Gk. "fruit"); with the knowledge of God's will, Col. 1:9; with abundance through material supplies by fellow believers, Phil. 4:18; (d) of the hearts of believers as the seat of emotion and volition, John 16:6 (sorrow); Acts 5:3 (deceitfulness); (e) of the unregenerate who refuse recognition of God, Rom. 1:29; (II), "to accomplish, complete, fulfill."

2. *anapleroo* (378), "to fill up adequately, completely" (*ana*, "up," and No. 1), is twice translated by the verbs "to fill, to fill up," in 1 Cor. 14:16, RV (for KJV, "occupieth"), of a believer as a member of an assembly, who "fills" the position or condition (not one who "fills" it by assuming it) of being unable to understand the language of him who had the gift of tongues; in 1 Thess. 2:16, "to fill up their sins," of the Jews who persisted in their course of antagonism and unbelief.

3. *antanapleroo* (466), "to fill up in turn" (or "on one's part"; *anti*, "corresponding to," and No. 2), is used in Col. 1:24, of the apostle's responsive devotion to Christ in "filling" up, or undertaking on his part a full share of, the sufferings which follow after the sufferings of Christ, and are experienced by the members of His Body, the church. "The point of the apostle's boast is that Christ, the sinless Master, should have left something for Paul, the unworthy servant, to suffer" (Lightfoot, on Col., p. 165).

4. *sumpleroo* (4845), "to fill completely" (*sun*, "with," and No. 1), is used in the passive voice (a) of a boat filling with water, and, by metonymy, of the occupants themselves, Luke 8:23 (RV, "were filling"); (b) of "fulfilling," with regard to time, "when the days were

well-nigh come," RV, for KJV, "when the time was come," Luke 9:51; Acts 2:1.

5. *pimplemi* (*4130*) and *pletho* (*4130*), lengthened forms of *pleo*, "to fill" (*pletho* supplies certain tenses of *pimplemi*), is used (1) of things; boats, with fish, Luke 5:7; a sponge, with vinegar, Matt. 27:48 (some mss. have this verb in John 19:29); a city, with confusion, Acts 19:29; a wedding, with guests, Matt. 22:10; (2) of persons (only in Luke's writings): (a) with the Holy Spirit, Luke 1:15, 41, 67; Acts 2:4; 4:8, 31; 9:17; 13:9; (b) with emotions: wrath, Luke 4:28; fear, 5:26; madness, 6:11; wonder, amazement, Acts 3:10; jealousy, 5:17, RV for KJV, "indignation," and 13:45 (KJV, "envy"). For its other significance, "to complete."

6. *empiplemi* (*1705*) or *empletho* (as in No. 5), "to fill full, to satisfy," is used (a) of "filling" the hungry, Luke 1:53; John 6:12; of the abundance of the rich, Luke 6:25; (b) metaphorically, of a company of friends, Rom. 15:24, RV, "satisfied," for KJV, "filled."

7. *empiplao* (*1705v*), an alternative form of No. 6, is found in Acts 14:17, "filling (your hearts)," of God's provision for mankind.

B. Noun.

pleroma (*4138*), fullness, has two meanings, (a) in the active sense, "that which fills up," a piece of undressed cloth on an old garment, Matt. 9:16; Mark 2:21, lit., "the filling" (RV, "that which should fill it up"), i.e., "the patch," which is probably the significance; (b) "that which has been completed, the fullness," e.g., Mark 8:20.

FILTH

1. *perikatharma* (*4027*) denotes "offscouring, refuse" (lit., "cleanings," i.e., that which is thrown away in cleansing; from *perikathairo*, "to purify all around." It is used in 1 Cor. 4:13 much in this sense (not of sacrificial victims), "the filth of the world" representing "the most abject and despicable men," i.e., the scum or rubbish of humanity.

2. *rhupos* (*4509*) denotes "dirt, filth," 1 Pet. 3:21.

FILTHINESS, FILTHY (to make)

A. Nouns.

1. *aischrotes* (*151*), "baseness" (from *aischos*, "shame, disgrace"), is used in Eph. 5:4, of obscenity, all that is contrary to purity.

2. *rhuparia* (*4507*) denotes "dirt, filth," and is used metaphorically of moral "defilement" in Jas. 1:21.

3. *molusmos* (*3436*), "a soiling, defilement," is used in 2 Cor. 7:1.

4. *aselgeia* (*766*), "wantonness, licentiousness, lasciviousness," is translated "filthy (conversation)," in 2 Pet. 2:7, KJV; RV, lascivious (life).

B. Adjectives.

1. *aischros* (150), "base, shameful" (akin to A, No. 1), is used of "base gain," "filthy (lucre)," Titus 1:11, and translated "shame" in 1 Cor. 11:6, with reference to a woman with shorn hair; in 14:35, of oral utterances of women in a church gathering (RV, "shameful"); in Eph. 5:12, of mentioning the base and bestial practices of those who live lascivious lives.

2. *aischrokerdes* (146), "greedy of base gain" (No. 1, and *kerdos*, "gain"), is used in 1 Tim. 3:8 and Titus 1:7, "greedy of filthy lucre"; some mss. have it also in 1 Tim. 3:3.

3. *rhuparos* (4508), akin to A, No. 2, is said of shabby clothing, Jas. 2:2: metaphorically, of moral "defilement," Rev. 22:11 (in the best mss.).

C. Adverb.

aischrokerdos (147), "eagerness for base gain" (akin to B, No. 2), is used in 1 Pet. 5:2, "for filthy lucre."

D. Verb.

rhupaino (4510v), "to make filthy, defile" (from A, No. 2), is used in the passive voice, in an ethical sense, in Rev. 22:11 (cf. B, No. 3, in the same verse), "let him be made filthy," RV. The tense (the aorist) marks the decisiveness of that which is decreed. Some texts have *rhupareuomai*, here, with the same meaning; some have *rhupoo*, in the middle voice, "to make oneself filthy."

FINISH

1. *teleo* (5055), "to bring to an end" (*telos*, "an end"), in the passive voice, "to be finished," is translated by the verb "to finish" in Matt. 13:53; 19:1; 26:1; John 19:28, where the RV "are...finished" brings out the force of the perfect tense (the same word as in v. 30, "It is finished"), which is missed in the KJV; the word was in His heart before He uttered it, 2 Tim. 4:7; Rev. 10:7; 11:7; 20:3, RV, "should be finished" (KJV, "fulfilled"), 5, 7, RV, "finished" (KJV, "expired"). In Rev. 15:1 the verb is rightly translated "is finished." In 15:8 the RV, "should be finished" corrects the KJV, "were fulfilled."

2. *teleioo* (5048), akin to the adjective *teleios*, "complete, perfect," and to No. 1, denotes "to bring to an end" in the sense of completing or perfecting, and is translated by the verb "to finish" in John 4:34; 5:36; 17:4; Acts 20:24.

3. *ekteleo* (1615), lit., "to finish out," i.e., "completely" (*ek*, "out," intensive, and No. 1) is used in Luke 14:29, 30.

4. *epiteleo* (2005), "to bring through to an end," is rendered "finish" in 2 Cor. 8:6, KJV (RV, "complete").

5. *sunteleo* (4931), "to bring to fulfillment, to effect," is translated "finishing" (KJV, "will finish") in Rom. 9:28.

FIRM

1. *bebaios* (949), "firm, steadfast, secure" (from *baino*, "to go"), is translated "firm" in Heb. 3:6, of the maintenance of the boldness of the believer's hope, and in 3:14, RV, of "the beginning of our confidence" (KJV, "steadfast").

2. *stereos* (4731), "solid, hard, stiff," is translated "firm" in 2 Tim. 2:19; 1 Pet. 5:9.

FIRST-BEGOTTEN, FIRSTBORN

Old Testament

bekor (1060), "firstborn." The word represents the "firstborn" individual in a family, Gen. 25:13; or fig. Num. 3:46; or quality animal, Exod. 11:5; Lev. 27:26. The "oldest" or "firstborn" son, Exod. 6:14, had special privileges within the family. He received the family blessing, which meant spiritual and social leadership and a double portion of the father's possessions—or twice what all the other sons received, Deut. 21:17. Israel was God's "firstborn," enjoying a privileged position and blessings over other nations, Exod. 4:22; Jer. 31:9.

bikkurim (1061), "first fruits," produce offered to God, Num. 28:26; at festivals, Lev. 23:20; Num. 28:26.

New Testament

prototokos (4416), "firstborn" (from *protos*, "first," and *tikto*, "to beget"), is used of Christ as born of the Virgin Mary, Luke 2:7; further, in His relationship to the Father, expressing His priority to, and preeminence over, creation, not in the sense of being the "first" to be born. It is used occasionally of superiority of position in the OT, see Exod. 4:22; Deut. 21:16, 17, the prohibition being against the evil of assigning the privileged position of the "firstborn" to one born subsequently to the "first" child.

The five passages in the NT relating to Christ may be set forth chronologically thus: (a) Col. 1:15, where His eternal relationship with the Father is in view, and the clause means both that He was the "Firstborn" before all creation and that He Himself produced creation (the genitive case being objective, as v. 16 makes clear); (b) Col. 1:18 and Rev. 1:5, in reference to His resurrection; (c) Rom. 8:29, His position in relationship to the church; (d) Heb. 1:6, RV, His second advent (the RV "when He again bringeth in," puts "again" in the right place, the contrast to His first advent, at His birth, being implied); cf. Ps. 89:27. The word is used in the plural, in Heb. 11:28, of the firstborn sons in the families of the Egyptians, and in 12:23, of the members of the Church.

FIRSTFRUIT(S)

aparche (536) denotes, primarily, "an offering of firstfruits"; in sacrifices, "to offer firstfruits." "Though the English word is plural in each of its occurrences save Rom. 11:16, the Greek word is always singular. Two Hebrew words are thus translated, one meaning the "chief" or "principal part," e.g., Num. 18:12; Prov 3:9; the other, "the earliest ripe of the crop or of the tree," e.g., Exod. 23:16; Neh. 10:35; they are found together, e.g., in Exod. 23:19, "the first of the firstfruits."

The term is applied in things spiritual, (a) to the presence of the Holy Spirit with the believer as the firstfruits of the full harvest of the Cross, Rom. 8:23; (b) to Christ Himself in resurrection in relation to all believers who have fallen asleep, 1 Cor. 15:20, 23; (c) to the earliest believers in a country in relation to those of their countrymen subsequently converted, Rom. 16:5; 1 Cor. 16:15; (d) to the believers of this age in relation to the whole of the redeemed, 2 Thess. 2:13.

FISH

1. *ichthus* (2486) denotes "a fish," Matt. 7:10; Mark 6:38, etc.; apart from the Gospels, only in 1 Cor. 15:39.

2. *ichthudion* (2485) is a diminutive of No. 1, "a little fish," Matt. 15:34; Mark 8:7.

3. *opsarion* (3795) is a diminutive of *opson*, "cooked meat," or "a relish, a dainty dish, especially of fish"; it denotes "a little fish," John 6:9, 11; 21:9, 10, 13.

FIT (Adjective and Verb), FITLY, FITTING

A. Adjectives.

1. *euthetos* (2111), "ready for use, fit, well adapted," lit., "well placed" (*eu*, "well," *tithemi*, "to place"), is used (a) of persons, Luke 9:62, negatively, of one who is not fit for the kingdom of God; (b) of things, Luke 14:35, of salt that has lost its savor; rendered "meet" in Heb. 6:7, of herbs.

2. *arestos* (701), "pleasing" (akin to *aresko*, "to please"), is translated "(it is not) fit," RV (KJV, "reason"), in Acts 6:2.

B. Verbs.

1. *aneko* (433), properly, "to have come up to" (*ana*, "up," and *heko*, "to arrive"), is translated "is fitting," in Col. 3:18, RV.

2. *katheko* (2520), "to come or reach down to" (*kata*, "down"), hence, "to befit, be proper," is translated "is (not fit)" in Acts 22:22; in Rom. 1:28, RV, "fitting" (KJV, "convenient").

3. *katartizo* (2675), "to make fit, to equip, prepare" (*kata*, "down," *artos*, "a joint"), is rendered "fitted" in Rom. 9:22, of vessels of wrath; here the middle voice signifies that those referred to "fitted" themselves for destruction (as illustrated in the case of Pharaoh, the self-hardening of whose heart is accurately presented in the RV in the first part of the series of incidents in the Exodus narrative, which records Pharaoh's doings; only after repeated and

persistent obstinacy on his part is it recorded that God hardened his heart.

4. *sunarmologeo* (*4883*), "to fit or frame together" (*sun*, "with," *harmos*, "a joint, in building," and *lego*, "to choose"), is used metaphorically of the various parts of the church as a building, Eph. 2:21, "fitly framed together"; also of the members of the church as the body of Christ, 4:16, RV, "fitly framed... together."

FLATTERY (-ING)

kolakia (or -*eia*) (*2850*), akin to *kolakeuo*, "to flatter," is used in 1 Thess. 2:5 of "words of flattery" (RV), adopted as "a cloke of covetousness," i.e., words which "flattery" uses, not simply as an effort to give pleasure, but with motives of self-interest.

FLEE, FLED

Old Testament

barach (1272), "to flee, pass through," means to move from one place to another, often to escape danger or unfavorable circumstance, Gen. 16:6; 1 Sam. 20:1; Job 20:24. In its figurative use, the word describes days "fleeing" away, Job 9:25, or frail man "fleeing" like a shadow, Job 14:2. A rather paradoxical use is found in Song of Sol. 8:14, in which "flee" must mean "come quickly."

nus (5127), "to flee, escape, take flight, depart." *nus* is the common word for "fleeing" from an enemy or danger, Gen. 39:12; Num. 16:34; Josh. 10:6. The word is also used to describe "escape," as in Jer. 46:6 and Amos 9:1. In a figurative use, the word describes the "disappearance" of physical strength, Deut. 34:7, the "fleeing" of evening shadows, Song of Sol. 2:17, and the "fleeing away" of sorrow, Isa. 35:10.

New Testament

1. *pheugo* (*5343*), "to flee from or away" (Lat., *fugio*; Eng., "fugitive," etc.), besides its literal significance, is used metaphorically, (a) transitively, of "fleeing" fornication, 1 Cor. 6:18; idolatry, 10:14; evil doctrine, questionings, disputes of words, envy, strife, railings, evil surmisings, wranglings, and the love of money, 1 Tim. 6:11; youthful lusts, 2 Tim. 2:22; (b) intransitively, of the "flight" of physical matter, Rev. 16:20; 20:11; of death, 9:6; cf. also Acts 14:6; 16:27; Heb. 6:18; 12:25.

FLESH

Old Testament

basar (1320), "flesh; meat; male sex organ." The word means the "meaty part plus the skin" of men or animal, often referring to the entire organ of the body called "the skin," Num. 11:33; Deut. 14:8; Job 10:11, or the "edible part," of animals, cooked or raw, 1 Sam.

2:13,15; Dan. 10:3. *basar* can also be a specific organ of the body, the "male sex organ," Lev 15:2.

Flesh represents the "physical aspect" of man or animals as contrasted with the spirit, soul, or heart (the nonphysical aspect), Num. 16:22. It means collectively "all mankind"; Deut. 5:26, or "all creatures," Gen. 6:17. Flesh also means "blood relative," Gen. 29:14; 37:27; Lev. 18:6.

New Testament

sarx (4561) has a wider range of meaning in the NT than *basar* in the OT. Its uses in the NT may be analyzed as follows: (a) "the substance of the body," whether of beasts or of men, 1 Cor. 15:39; (b) "the human body," 2 Cor. 10:3a; Gal. 2:20; Phil. 1:22; (c) by synecdoche, of "mankind," in the totality of all that is essential to manhood, i.e., spirit, soul, and body, Matt. 24:22; John 1:13; Rom. 3:20; (d) by synecdoche, of "the holy humanity" of the Lord Jesus, in the totality of all that is essential to manhood, i.e., spirit, soul, and body John 1:14; 1 Tim. 3:16; 1 John 4:2; 2 John 7, in Heb. 5:7, "the days of His flesh," i.e., His past life on earth in distinction from His present life in resurrection; (e) by synecdoche, for "the complete person," John 6:51-57; 2 Cor. 7:5; Jas. 5:3; (f) "the weaker element in human nature," Matt. 26:41; Rom. 6:19; 8:3a; (g) "the unregenerate state of men," Rom. 7:5; 8:8, 9; (h) "the seat of sin in man" (but this is not the same thing as in the body), 2 Pet. 2:18; 1 John 2:16; (i) "the lower and temporary element in the Christian," Gal. 3:3; 6:8, and in religious ordinances, Heb. 9:10; (j) "the natural attainments of men," 1 Cor. 1:26; 2 Cor. 10:2, 3b; (k) "circumstances," 1 Cor. 7:28; the externals of life, 2 Cor. 7:1; Eph. 6:5; Heb. 9:13; (l) by metonymy, "the outward and seeming," as contrasted with the spirit, the inward and real, John 6:63; 2 Cor. 5:16; (m) "natural relationship, consanguine," 1 Cor. 10:18; Gal. 4:23, or marital, Matt. 19:5.

In Matt. 26:41; Rom. 8:4, 13; 1 Cor. 5:5; Gal. 6:8 (not the Holy Spirit, here), "flesh" is contrasted with spirit, in Rom. 2:28, 29, with heart and spirit; in Rom. 7:25, with the mind; cf. Col. 2:1, 5. It is coupled with the mind in Eph. 2:3, and with the spirit in 2 Cor. 7:1.

FLESHLY, FLESHY

1. *sarkikos* (4559), akin to *sarx*, under FLESH, signifies (a) associated with or pertaining to, "the flesh, carnal," Rom. 15:27; 1 Cor. 9:11; (b) of "the nature of the flesh, sensual," translated "fleshly" in 2 Cor. 1:12, of wisdom, in 1 Pet. 2:11, of lusts; in 2 Cor. 10:4, negatively, of the weapons of the Christian's warfare, RV, "of the flesh" (KJV, "carnal").

2. *sarkinos* (4560) denotes "of the flesh, fleshly" (the termination —*inos* signifying the substance or material of a thing); in 2 Cor. 3:3, RV, "(tables that are hearts) of flesh," KJV, fleshly (tables), etc.

FLOCK

Old Testament

tso'n (6629), "flock; small cattle; sheep; goats." The primary meaning of **tso'n** is "small cattle" (so, "sheep, goats, flocks") to be distinguished from **baqar** ("herd, large four-footed mammals"); sheep only, 1 Sam. 25:2; or to both sheep and goats, Gen. 30:33. In the metaphorical usage of **tso'n**, the imagery of a "multitude" may apply to people, Ps. 100:3; cf. Ps. 23; 79:13; Isa 53:6; Ezek. 36:38; Mic. 7:14.

New Testament

1. **poimne** (4167), akin to **poimen**, "a shepherd," denotes "a flock" (properly, of sheep), Matt. 26:31; Luke 2:8; 1 Cor. 9:7; metaphorically, of Christ's followers, John 10:16.

2. **poimnion** (4168), possibly a diminutive of No. 1, is used in the NT only metaphorically, of a group of Christ's disciples, Luke 12:32; of local churches cared for by elders, Acts 20:28, 29; 1 Pet. 5:2, 3.

FLOOD

A. Noun.

kataklusmos (2627), "a deluge" (Eng., "cataclysm"), akin to **katakluzo**, "to inundate," 2 Pet. 3:6, is used of the "flood" in Noah's time, Matt. 24:38, 39; Luke 17:27; 2 Pet. 2:5; cf. also Luke 6:4; Matt. 7:25, 27; in Rev. 12:15, 16.

B. Adjective.

potamophoretos (4216) signifies "carried away by a stream or river," Rev. 12:15, RV, "carried away by the stream" (KJV, "of the flood").

FOLLOW, FOLLOW AFTER

1. **akoloutheo** (190), to be an **akolouthos**, "a follower," or "companion" (from the prefix **a**, here expressing "union, likeness," and **keleuthos**, "a way"; hence, "one going in the same way"), is used (a) frequently in the literal sense, e.g., Matt. 4:25; (b) metaphorically, of "discipleship," e.g., Mark 8:34; 9:38; 10:21. It is used 77 times in the Gospels, of "following" Christ, and only once otherwise, Mark 14:13.

2. **exakoloutheo** (1811), "to follow up, or out to the end" (**ek**, "out," used intensively, and No. 1), is used metaphorically, and only by the apostle Peter in his second epistle: in 1:16, of cunningly devised fables; 2:2 of lascivious doings; 2:15, of the way of Balaam.

3. **epakoloutheo** (1872), "to follow after, close upon" (**epi**, "upon," and No. 1). is used of signs "following" the preaching of the gospel, Mark 16:20; of "following" good works, 1 Tim. 5:10; of sins "follow-

ing" after those who are guilty of them, 5:24; of "following" the steps of Christ, 1 Pet. 2:21.

4. *katakoloutheo* (2628), "to follow behind or intently after" (*kata*, "after," used intensively, and No. 1), is used of the women on their way to Christ's tomb, Luke 23:55; of the demon-possessed maid in Philippi in "following" the missionaries, Acts 16:17.

5. *parakoloutheo* (3877) lit. signifying "to follow close up, or side by side," hence, "to accompany, to conform to" (*para*, "beside," and No. 1), is used of signs accompanying "them that believe," Mark 16:17; of tracing the course of facts, Luke 1:3, RV, of "following" the good doctrine, 1 Tim. 4:6, RV (KJV, "attained"); similarly of "following" teaching so as to practice it, 2 Tim. 3:10, RV, "didst follow" (KJV, "hast fully known").

6. *sunakoloutheo* (4870), "to follow along with, to accompany a leader" (*sun*, "with," and No. 1), is given its true rendering in the RV of Mark 5:37, "He suffered no man to follow with Him"; in 14:51, of the young man who "followed with" Christ (inferior mss. have No. 1 here); Luke 23:49, of the women who "followed with" Christ from Galilee.

7. *dioko* (1377) denotes (a) "to drive away," Matt. 23:34; (b) "to pursue without hostility, to follow, follow after," said of righteousness, Rom. 9:30; the Law, 9:31; 12:13, hospitality ("given to") lit., "pursuing" (as one would a calling), the things which make for peace, 14:19; love, 1 Cor. 14:1; that which is good, 1 Thess. 5:15; righteousness, godliness, faith, love, patience, meekness, 1 Tim. 6:11; righteousness, faith, love, peace, 2 Tim. 2:22; peace and sanctification, Heb. 12:14; peace, 1 Pet. 3:11; (c) "to follow on" (used intransitively), Phil. 3:12, 14, RV, "I press on"; "follow after," is an inadequate meaning.

8. *katadioko* (2614), "to follow up or closely," with the determination to find (*kata*, "down," intensive, giving the idea of a hard, persistent search, and No. 7), Mark 1:36, "followed after (Him)," is said of the disciples in going to find the Lord who had gone into a desert place to pray. The verb is found, e.g., in 1 Sam. 30:22; Ps. 23:6, and with hostile intent in Gen. 31:36.

FOLLY

anoia (454) lit. signifies "without understanding" (*a*, negative, *nous*, "mind"); hence, "folly," or, rather, "senselessness," 2 Tim. 3:9; in Luke 6:11 it denotes violent or mad rage, "madness."

FOOL, FOOLISH, FOOLISHLY, FOOLISHNESS
Old Testament

'*ewil* (191), "fool," This word describes a person who lacks wisdom; indeed, wisdom is beyond his grasp, Prov. 24:7. In another nuance, "fool" is a morally undesirable individual who despises wisdom and discipline, Prov. 1:7; 15:5. He mocks guilt, Prov. 14:9, and is quarrelsome, Prov. 20:3, and licentious, Prov. 7:22. Trying to give him instruction is futile, Prov. 16:22.

'iwwelet (200), "foolishness; stupidity." This noun can mean "foolishness" in the sense of violating God's law, or "sin," Ps. 38:5. The word also describes the activities and life-style of the man who ignores the instructions of wisdom, Prov. 5:23. In another nuance, the noun means "thoughtless." Hence *'iwwelet* describes the way a young person is prone to act, Prov. 22:15 and the way any fool or stupid person chatters, Prov. 15:2.

nebalah (5039), "foolishness; senselessness; impropriety; stupidity." This abstract noun is most often used as a word for a serious sin, Gen. 34:7, which is of course a disregard for God's will.

F

New Testament

A. Adjectives.

1. *aphron* (878) signifies "without reason" (*a*, negative, *phren*, "the mind"), "want of mental sanity and sobriety, a reckless and inconsiderate habit of mind" (Hort), or "the lack of commonsense perception of the reality of things natural and spiritual...or the imprudent ordering of one's life in regard to salvation"; it is mostly translated "foolish" or "foolish ones" in the RV; Luke 11:40; 12:20; Rom. 2:20; 1 Cor. 15:36; 2 Cor. 11:16 (twice), 19 (contrasted with *phronimos*, "prudent"); 12:6, 11; Eph. 5:17; 1 Pet. 2:15.

2. *anoetos* (453) signifies "not understanding" (*a*, negative, *noeo*, "to perceive, understand"), not applying *nous*, "the mind," Luke 24:25; in Rom. 1:14 and Gal. 3:1, 3 it signifies "senseless," an unworthy lack of understanding; sometimes it carries a moral reproach (in contrast with *sophron*, "sober-minded, self-controlled") and describes one who does not govern his lusts, Titus 3:3; in 1 Tim. 6:9 it is associated with evil desires, lusts.

3. *moros* (3474) primarily denotes "dull, sluggish"; hence, "stupid, foolish"; it is used (a) of persons, Matt. 5:22, "Thou fool"; here the word means morally worthless, a scoundrel, a more serious reproach than "Raca"; the latter scorns a man's mind and calls him stupid; *moros* scorns his heart and character; hence the Lord's more severe condemnation; in 7:26, "a foolish man"; 23:17, 19, "fools"; 25:2, 3, 8, "foolish"; in 1 Cor. 3:18, "a fool"; the apostle Paul uses it of himself and his fellow-workers, in 4:10, "fools" (i.e., in the eyes of opponents); (b) of things, 2 Tim. 2:23, "foolish and ignorant questionings"; so Titus 3:9; in 1 Cor. 1:25, "the foolishness of God," not *moria*, "foolishness" as a personal quality (see C, No. 1), but adjectively, that which is considered by the ignorant as a "foolish" policy or mode of dealing, lit., "the foolish (thing)"; so in v. 27, the foolish (things) of the world."

4. *asunetos* (801) denotes "without discernment," or "understanding" (*a*, negative, *suniemi*, "to understand"); hence "sense-

less," as in the RV of Rom. 1:21 (KJV, "foolish"), of the heart; in 10:19, KJV, "foolish," RV, "void of understanding."

B. Verb.

moraino (3471) is used (a) in the causal sense, "to make foolish," 1 Cor. 1:20; (b) in the passive sense, "to become foolish," Rom. 1:22; in Matt. 5:13 and Luke 14:34 it is said of salt that has lost its flavor, becoming tasteless.

C. Nouns.

1. *moria* (3472) denotes "foolishness" (akin to A, No. 3 and B, No. 1), and is used in 1 Cor. 1:18, 21, 23; 2:14; 3:19.

2. *aphrosune* (877), "senselessness," is translated "foolishness" in Mark 7:22; 2 Cor. 11:1, 17, 21, "foolishness," RV (KJV "folly" and "foolishly").

FOOTSTOOL

hupopodion (5286), from *hupo*, "under," and *pous*, "a foot," is used (a) literally in Jas. 2:3, (b) metaphorically, of the earth as God's "footstool," Matt. 5:35.

FORBEAR, FORBEARANCE

A. Verbs.

1. *anecho* (430), "to hold up" (*ana*, "up," *echo*, "to have or hold"), is used in the middle voice in the NT, signifying "to bear with, endure"; it is rendered "forbearing (one another)" in Eph. 4:2 and Col. 3:13.

2. *aniemi* (447), lit., "to send up or back" (*ana*, "up," *hiemi*, "to send"), hence, "to relax, loosen," or, metaphorically, "to desist from," is translated "forbearing" (threatening) in Eph. 6:9 ("giving up your threatening," T. K. Abbott).

3. *pheidomai* (5339), "to spare" (its usual meaning), "to refrain from doing something," is rendered "I forbear" in 2 Cor. 12:6.

4. *stego* (4722) properly denotes "to protect by covering"; then, "to conceal"; then, by covering, "to bear up under"; it is translated "forbear" in 1 Thess. 3:1, 5.

B. Noun.

anoche (463), "a holding back" (akin to A, No. 1), denotes "forbearance," a delay of punishment, Rom. 2:4; 3:25, in both places of God's "forbearance" with men, in the latter passage His "forbearance" is the ground, not of His forgiveness, but of His praetermission of sins, His withholding punishment. In 2:4 it represents a suspense of wrath which must eventually be exercised unless the sinner accepts God's conditions; in 3:25 it is connected with the passing over of sins in times past, previous to the atoning work of Christ.

C. Adjectives.

1. *anexikakos* (420) denotes "patiently forbearing evil," lit., "patient of wrong," (from *anecho*, A, No. 1 and *kakos*, "evil"), "enduring"; it is rendered "forbearing" in 2 Tim. 2:24.

2. *epieikes* (1933), an adjective (from *epi*, used intensively, and *eikos*, "reasonable"), is used as a noun with the article in Phil. 4:5, and translated "forbearance" in the RV.

FORBID, FORBADE

koluo (2967), "to hinder, restrain, withhold, forbid" (akin to *kolos*, "docked, lopped, clipped"), is most usually translated "to forbid," often an inferior rendering to that of hindering or restraining, e.g., 1 Thess. 2:16; Luke 23:2; 2 Pet. 2:16, where the RV has "stayed"; in Acts 10:47 "forbid." In Luke 6:29, the RV has "withhold not (thy coat also)."

FORCE

harpazo (726), "to snatch away, carry off by force," Matt. 11:12, "men of violence (KJV 'the violent') take it by force," the meaning being, as determined by the preceding clause, that those who are possessed of eagerness and zeal, instead of yielding to the opposition of religious foes, such as the scribes and Pharisees, press their way into the kingdom, so as to possess themselves of it. It is elsewhere similarly rendered in John 6:15, of those who attempted to seize the Lord, and in Acts 23:10, of the chief captain's command to the soldiers to rescue Paul.

FOREFATHER

1. *progonos* (4269), an adjective, primarily denoting "born before" (*pro*, "before," and *ginomai*, "to become"), is used as a noun in the plural, 2 Tim. 1:3, "forefathers" (in 1 Tim. 5:4, "parents").

2. *propator* (4253 and 3962), "a forefather" (*pro*, "before," *pater*, "a father"), is used of Abraham in Rom. 4:1.

FOREKNOW, FOREKNOWLEDGE

A. Verb.

proginosko (4267), "to know before" (*pro*, "before," *ginosko*, "to know"), is used (a) of divine knowledge, concerning (1) Christ, 1 Pet. 1:20, RV, "foreknown" (KJV, "foreordained"); (2) Israel as God's earthly people, Rom. 11:2; (3) believers, Rom. 8:29; "the foreknowledge" of God is the basis of His foreordaining counsels; (b) of human knowledge, (1) of persons, Acts 26:5; (2) of facts, 2 Pet. 3:17.

B. Noun.

prognosis (4268), "a foreknowledge" (akin to A.), is used only of divine "foreknowledge," Acts 2:23; 1 Pet. 1:2. "Foreknowledge" is one aspect of omniscience; it is implied in God's warnings, promises and predictions. See Acts 15:18. God's "foreknowledge" involves His electing grace, but this does not preclude human will. He "foreknows" the exercise of faith which brings salvation. The apostle Paul stresses especially the actual purposes of God rather than the ground of the purposes, see, e.g., Gal. 1:16; Eph. 1:5, 11. The divine counsels will ever be unthwartable.

FORERUNNER

prodromos (*4274*), an adjective signifying "running forward, going in advance," is used as a noun, of "those who were sent before to take observations," acting as scouts, especially in military matters; or of "one sent before a king" to see that the way was prepared, Isa. 40:3; (cf. Luke 9:52; and, of John the Baptist, Matt. 11:10, etc.). In the NT it is said of Christ in Heb. 6:20, as going in advance of His followers who are to be where He is, when He comes to receive them to Himself.

FORESEE, FORESEEN

1. *proorao* (*4308*), with the aorist form *proeidon* (used to supply tenses lacking in *proorao*), "to see before" (*pro*, "before," *horao*, "to see"), is used with reference (a) to the past, of seeing a person before, Acts 21:29; (b) to the future, in the sense of "foreseeing" a person or thing, Acts 2:25, with reference to Christ and the Father, RV, "beheld" (here the middle voice is used).

2. *proeidon* (*4275*), an aorist tense form without a present, "to foresee," is used of David, as foreseeing Christ, in Acts 2:31, RV, "foreseeing" (KJV, "seeing before"); in Gal. 3:8 it is said of the Scripture, personified, personal activity being attributed to it by reason of its divine source (cf. v. 22). "What saith the Scripture?" was a common formula among the Rabbis.

3. *problepo* (*4265*), from *pro*, "before," and *blepo*, "to see, perceive," is translated "having provided" in Heb. 11:40 (middle voice), marg., "foreseen," which is the lit. meaning of the verb, as with Eng. "provide."

FORETELL

prolego (*4302*), with the aorist form *proeipon*, and a perfect form *proeireka* (from *proereo*), signifies (1) "to declare openly" or "plainly," or "to say" or "tell beforehand" (*pro*, "before," *lego*, "to say"), translated in 2 Cor. 13:2 (in the first sentence), RV, "I have said beforehand," KJV, "I told...before," in the next sentence, KJV, "I foretell," RV, "I do say beforehand" (marg., "plainly"); not prophecy is here in view, but a warning given before and repeated; (2) "to speak before, of prophecy," as "foretelling" the future, Mark 13:23, KJV, "have foretold," RV, "have told...beforehand"; Acts 1:16

(of the prophecy concerning Judas); Rom. 9:29; 2 Pet. 3:2; Jude 17; some inferior mss. have it in Heb. 10:15.

FOREWARN

prolego (4302), with verbal forms as mentioned above, is translated "I forewarn" and "I did forewarn," in the RV of Gal. 5:21, KJV, "I tell (you) before" and "I have told (you) in time past"; here, however, as in 2 Cor. 13:2 and 1 Thess. 3:4 (see below), the RV marg., "plainly" is to be preferred to "beforehand" or "before"; the meaning in Gal. 5:21 is not so much that Paul prophesied the result of the practice of the evils mentioned but that he had told them before of the consequence and was now repeating his warning, as leaving no possible room for doubt or misunderstanding; in 1 Thess. 3:4, the subject told before was the affliction consequent upon the preaching of the Gospel; in 1 Thess. 4:6, "we forewarned," the warning was as to the consequences of whatsoever violates chastity.

FORFEIT

zemioo (2210), in the active voice signifies "to damage"; in the passive, "to suffer loss, forfeit," Matt. 16:26 and Mark 8:36, of the "life," RV; KJV, and RV marg., "soul"; in each place the RV has "forfeit," for A.V., "lose"; Luke 9:25, "his own self" (RV, "forfeit," KJV, "be cast away"; here the preceding word "lose" translates *apollumi*, "to destroy"). What is in view here is the act of "forfeiting" what is of the greatest value, not the casting away by divine judgment, though that is involved, but losing or penalizing one's own self, with spiritual and eternal loss. The word is also used in 1 Cor. 3:15; 2 Cor. 7:9; Phil. 3:8.

FORGET, FORGETFUL

Old Testament

shakach (7911), "to forget," can mean simply to forget information or feelings related to that information, Gen. 27:45. But "to forget," can also mean, "to not take action, implying a lack of relationship, Lam. 5:20; Hos. 4:6.

New Testament

A. Verbs.

1. *lanthano* (2990), "to escape notice," is translated "they (wilfully) forget" in 2 Pet. 3:5, RV, lit., "this escapes them (i.e., their notice, wilfully on their part)," KJV, "they willingly are ignorant of"; in v. 8, RV, "forget not," lit., "let not this one thing escape you" (your notice), KJV, "be not ignorant of."

2. *epilanthanomai* (1950), "to forget, or neglect" (*epi*, "upon," used intensively, and No. 1), is said (a) negatively of God, indicat-

ing His remembrance of sparrows, Luke 12:6, and of the work and labor of love of His saints, Heb. 6:10; (b) of the disciples regarding taking bread, Matt. 16:5: Mark 8:14; (c) of Paul regarding "the things which are behind," Phil. 3:13; (d) of believers, as to showing love to strangers, Heb. 13:2, RV, and as to doing good and communicating, v. 16; (e) of a person who after looking at himself in a mirror, forgets what kind of person he is, Jas. 1:24; cf. also Heb. 12:5.

B. Nouns.

1. *lethe* (3024), "forgetfulness" (from *letho*, "to forget," an old form of *lanthano*, see A, No. 1; cf. Eng. "lethal," "lethargy," and the mythical river "Lethe," which was supposed to cause forgetfulness of the past to those who drank of it), is used with *lambano*, "to take," in 2 Pet. 1:9, "having forgotten," lit., "having taken forgetfulness" (cf. 2 Tim. 1:5, lit., "having taken reminder"), a periphrastic expression for a single verb.

2. *epilesmone* (1953), "forgetfulness" (akin to A, No. 2), is used in Jas. 1:25, "a forgetful hearer," RV, "a hearer that forgetteth," lit., "a hearer of forgetfulness," i.e., a hearer characterized by "forgetfulness."

FORGIVE, FORGAVE, FORGIVENESS

Old Testament

calach (5545), "to forgive." The basic meaning undergoes no change throughout the Old Testament. God is always the subject of "forgiveness." No other Old Testament verb means "to forgive," although several verbs include "forgiveness" in the range of meanings given in a particular context, e.g., *naca'* and *'awon* in Exod. 32:32; *kapar* in Ezek. 16:63.

The verb occurs throughout the Old Testament. Most occurrences of *calach* are in the sacrificial laws of Leviticus and Numbers. In the typology of the Old Testament, sacrifices foreshadowed the accomplished work of Jesus Christ, and the Old Testament believer was assured of "forgiveness" based on sacrifice:, Num. 15:25, 28; Lev. 4:26; cf. vv. 20, 31, 35; 5:10, 13, 16, 18. The mediators of the atonement were the priests who offered the sacrifice. The sacrifice was ordained by God to promise ultimate "forgiveness" in God's sacrifice of His own Son. Moreover, sacrifice was appropriately connected to atonement, as there is no forgiveness without the shedding of blood, Lev. 4:20; cf. Heb. 9:22. When the temple was destroyed and sacrifices ceased, God sent the prophetic word that He graciously would restore Israel out of exile and "forgive" its sins, Jer. 31:34.

New Testament

A. Verbs.

1. *aphiemi* (863), primarily, "to send forth, send away" (*apo*,

"from," *hiemi*, "to send"), denotes, besides its other meanings, "to remit or forgive" (a) debts, Matt. 6:12; 18:27, 32, these being completely cancelled; (b) sins, e.g., Matt. 9:2, 5, 6; 12:31, 32; Acts 8:22 ("the thought of thine heart"); Rom. 4:7; Jas. 5:15; 1 John 1:9; 2:12. In this latter respect the verb, like its corresponding noun (below), firstly signifies the remission of the punishment due to sinful conduct, the deliverance of the sinner from the penalty divinely, and therefore righteously, imposed; secondly, it involves the complete removal of the cause of offense; such remission is based upon the vicarious and propitiatory sacrifice of Christ. In the OT atoning sacrifice and "forgiveness" are often associated, e.g., Lev. 4:20, 26.

Human "forgiveness" is to be strictly analogous to divine "forgiveness," e.g., Matt. 6:12. If certain conditions are fulfilled, there is no limitation to Christ's law of "forgiveness," Matt. 18:21, 22. The conditions are repentance and confession, Matt. 18:15-17; Luke 17:3.

As to limits to the possibility of divine "forgiveness," see Matt. 12:32; 1 John 5:16.

2. *charizomai* (5483), "to bestow a favor unconditionally," is used of the act of "forgiveness," whether divine, Eph. 4:32; Col. 2:13; 3:13; or human, Luke 7:42, 43 (debt); 2 Cor. 2:7, 10; 12:13; Eph. 4:32 (1st mention). Paul uses this word frequently, but No. 1 only, in Rom. 4:7, in this sense of the word.

B. Noun.

aphesis (859) denotes "a dismissal, release" (akin to A, No. 1); it is used of the remission of sins, and translated "forgiveness" in Mark 3:29; Eph. 1:7; Col. 1:14, and in the KJV of Acts 5:31; 13:38; 26:18, in each of which the RV has "remission." Eleven times it is followed by "of sins," and once by "of trespasses." It is never used of the remission of sins in the Sept., but is especially connected with the Year of Jubilee (Lev. 25:10, etc.). Cf. the RV of Luke 4:18, "release" (KJV, "liberty"). For the significance in connection with remission of sins and the propitiatory sacrifice of Christ, see A, No. 1.

FORM (Noun)

1. *morphe* (3444) denotes "the special or characteristic form or feature" of a person or thing; it is used with particular significance in the NT, only of Christ, in Phil. 2:6, 7, in the phrases "being in the form of God," and "taking the form of a servant." *morphe* is therefore properly the nature or essence, not in the abstract, but as actually subsisting in the individual, and retained as long as the individual itself exists....Thus in the passage before us *morphe theou* is the Divine nature actually and inseparably subsisting in the Person of Christ....For the interpretation of 'the form of

God' it is sufficient to say that (1) it includes the whole nature and essence of Deity, and is inseparable from them, since they could have no actual existence without it; and (2) that it does not include in itself anything 'accidental' or separable, such as particular modes of manifestation, or conditions of glory and majesty, which may at one time be attached to the 'form,' at another separated from it..." (Gifford).

The definition above mentioned applies to its use in Mark 16:12, as to the particular ways in which the Lord manifested Himself.

2. *morphosis* (3446), "a form or outline," denotes, in the NT, "an image or impress, an outward semblance," Rom. 2:20, of knowledge of the truth; 2 Tim. 3:5, of godliness. It is thus to be distinguished from *morphe* (No. 1).

3. *tupos* (5179), "the representation or pattern" of anything, is rendered "form" in Rom. 6:17, "that form (or mold) of teaching whereunto ye were delivered," RV. The metaphor is that of a cast or frame into which molten material is poured so as to take its shape. The Gospel is the mould; those who are obedient to its teachings become conformed to Christ, whom it presents. In Acts 23:25, it is used of a letter, RV, "form" (KJV, "manner"), with reference to the nature of the contents.

4. *eidos* (1491), lit., "that which is seen," "an appearance or external form," is rendered "form" in the RV of Luke 3:22, of the Holy Spirit's appearance at the baptism of Christ; in John 5:37, in the Lord's testimony concerning the Father; in Luke 9:29 it is said of Christ Himself; it is translated "sight" in 2 Cor. 5:7, the Christian being guided by what he knows to be true, though unseen; in 1 Thess. 5:22 Christians are exhorted to abstain from "every form of evil," RV (the KJV, "appearance" is inadequate), i.e., from every kind of evil.

FORM (Verb)

Old Testament

yatsar (3335), "to form, mold, fashion." *yatsar* is a technical potter's word, and it is often used in connection with the potter at work, Isa. 29:16; Jer. 18:4, 6. The word is sometimes used as a general term of "craftsmanship or handiwork," whether molding, carving, or casting, Isa. 44:9-10, 12. The word may be used to express the "forming of plans in one's mind," Ps. 94:20. *yatsar* is frequently used to describe God's creative activity, whether literally or figuratively. Thus, God "formed" not only man, Gen. 2:7-8, but the animals, Gen. 2:19. God also "formed" the nation of Israel, Isa. 27:11; 45:9, 11; Israel was "formed" as God's special servant even from the womb, Isa. 44:2, 24; 49:5. While yet in the womb, Jeremiah was "formed" to be a prophet, Jer. 1:5. God "formed" locusts as a special visual lesson for Amos, Amos 7:1; the great sea monster, Leviathan, was "formed" to play in the seas, Ps. 104:26.

New Testament

A. Verbs.

1. *morphoo* (3445), like the noun *morphe* , refers, not to the external and transient, but to the inward and real; it is used in Gal. 4:19, expressing the necessity of a change in character and conduct to correspond with inward spiritual condition, so that there may be moral conformity to Christ.

2. *plasso* (4111), "to mold, to shape," was used of the artist who wrought in clay or wax (Eng., "plastic," "plasticity"), and occurs in Rom. 9:20; 1 Tim. 2:13.

B. Noun.

plasma (4110) denotes "anything molded or shaped into a form" (akin to A, No. 2), Rom. 9:20, "the thing formed."

FORNICATION, FORNICATOR

A. Nouns.

1. *porneia* (4202) is used (a) of "illicit sexual intercourse," in John 8:41; Acts 15:20, 29; 21:25; 1 Cor. 5:1; 6:13, 18; 2 Cor. 12:21; Gal. 5:19; Eph. 5:3; Col. 3:5; 1 Thess. 4:3; Rev. 2:21; 9:21; in the plural in 1 Cor. 7:2; in Matt. 5:32 and 19:9 it stands for, or includes, adultery; it is distinguished from it in 15:19 and Mark 7:21; (b) metaphorically, of "the association of pagan idolatry with doctrines of, and professed adherence to, the Christian faith," Rev. 14:8; 17:2, 4; 18:3; 19:2; some suggest this as the sense in 2:21.

2. *pornos* (4205) denotes "a man who indulges in fornication, a fornicator," 1 Cor. 5:9, 10, 11; 6:9; Eph. 5:5, RV; 1 Tim. 1:10, RV; Heb. 12:16; 13:4, RV; Rev. 21:8 and 22:15, RV (KJV, " whoremonger").

B. Verbs.

1. *porneuo* (4203) "to commit fornication," is used (a) literally, Mark 10:19; 1 Cor. 6:18; 10:8; Rev. 2:14, 20, see Nouns A. 1. (a) and (b) above; (b) metaphorically, Rev. 17:2; 18:3, 9.

2. *ekporneuo* (1608), a strengthened form of No. 1 (*ek*, used intensively), "to give oneself up to fornication," implying excessive indulgence, Jude 7.

FORSAKE

Old Testament

'*azab* (5800), "to leave, forsake, abandon, leave behind, be left over, let go." Basically '*azab* means "to depart from something," or "to leave," Gen. 2:24. A special nuance of the word is "to leave in the lurch," Num. 10:31. The word also carries the meaning "forsake," implying the severing or straining of a relationship, Isa. 7:16; 54:6-7; 62:4. A second emphasis of *'azab* is "to leave behind," meaning to allow something to remain while one leaves the scene, Gen. 39:6,12.

In a somewhat different nuance, the word means to "let someone or something alone with a problem," Exod. 23:5. Used figuratively, *'azab* means to "put distance between" in a spiritual or intellectual sense: "Cease from anger, and forsake wrath...," Ps. 37:8. The third emphasis of the word is "to be left over, a remainder," of physical collection or mass, Lev. 19:10.

Finally, *'azab* can mean "to let go" or "allow to leave," Ps. 49:10. A different nuance occurs in Ruth 2:16, where the verb means "to let something lie" on the ground. *'azab* can also mean "to give up," Prov. 28:13, "to set free," as in 2 Chron. 28:14, to "allow someone to do something," as in 2 Chron. 32:31; Neh. 5:10. *'azab* is sometimes used in a judicial technical sense of "being free," Deut. 32:36.

New Testament

A. Verbs.

1. *kataleipo* (2641), a strengthened form of *leipo*, "to leave," signifies (a) "to leave, to leave behind," e.g., Matt. 4:13; (b) "to leave remaining, reserve," e.g., Luke 10:40; (c) "to forsake," in the sense of abandoning, translated "to forsake" in the RV of Luke 5:28 and Acts 6:2; in Heb. 11:27 and 2 Pet. 2:15, KJV and RV. In this sense it is translated "to leave," in Mark 10:7; 14:52; Luke 15:4; Eph. 5:31.

2. *enkataleipo* (1459), from *en*, "in," and No. 1, denotes (a) "to leave behind, among, leave surviving," Rom. 9:29; (b) "to forsake, abandon, leave in straits, or helpless," said by, or of, Christ, Matt. 27:46; Mark 15:34; Acts 2:27, 31 (No. 1 in some mss.); of men, 2 Cor. 4:9; 2 Tim. 4:10, 16; by God, Heb. 13:5; of things, by Christians (negatively), Heb. 10:25.

3. *aphiemi* (863) sometimes has the significance of "forsaking," Mark 1:18; 14:50 (RV, "left"); so Luke 5:11.

4. *apotasso* (657), primarily, "to set apart" (*apo*, off, "from," *tasso*, "to arrange"), is used in the middle voice, meaning (a) "to take leave of," e.g., Mark 6:46, (b) "to renounce, forsake," Luke 14:33, KJV, "forsaketh," RV, "renounceth" ("all that he hath").

B. Noun.

apostasia (646), "an apostasy, defection, revolt," always in NT of religious defection, is translated "to forsake" in Acts 21:2 lit., "(thou teachest) apostasy (from Moses)"; in 2 Thess. 2:3, "falling away."

FORSWEAR

epiorkeo (1964) signifies "to swear falsely, to undo one's swearing, forswear oneself" (*epi*, "against," *orkos*, "an oath"), Matt. 5:33.

FOUNDATION (to lay), FOUNDED

A. Nouns.

1. *themelios*, or *themelion* (2310) is properly an adjective denoting "belonging to a foundation" (connected with *tithemi*, "to place"). It is used (1) as a noun, with *lithos*, "a stone," understood, in Luke 6:48, 49; 14:29; Heb. 11:10; Rev. 21:14, 19; (2) as a neuter noun in Acts 16:26, and metaphorically, (a) of "the ministry of the gospel and the doctrines of the faith," Rom. 15:20; 1 Cor. 3:10, 11, 12; Eph. 2:20, where the "of" is not subjective (i.e., consisting of the apostles and prophets), but objective, (i.e., laid by the apostles, etc.); so in 2 Tim. 2:19, where "the foundation of God" is "the foundation laid by God,"—not the Church (which is not a "foundation"), but Christ Himself, upon whom the saints are built; Heb. 6:1; (b) "of good works," 1 Tim. 6:19.

2. *katabole* (2602), lit., "a casting down," is used (a) of "conceiving seed," Heb. 11:11; (b) of "a foundation," as that which is laid down, or in the sense of founding; metaphorically, of "the foundation of the world"; in this respect two phrases are used, (1) "from the foundation of the world," Matt. 25:34 (in the most authentic mss. in 13:35 there is no phrase representing "of the world"); Luke 11:50; Heb. 4:3; 9:26; Rev. 13:8; 17:8; (2) "before the foundation of the world," John 17:24; Eph. 1:4; 1 Pet. 1:20. The latter phrase looks back to the past eternity.

B. Verb.

themelioo (2311), "to lay a foundation, to found" (akin to A, No. 1), is used (a) literally, Matt. 7:25; Luke 6:48; Heb. 1:10; (b) metaphorically, Eph. 3:17, "grounded (in love)"; Col. 1:23 (ditto, "in the faith"); 1 Pet. 5:10, KJV, "settle."

FOUNTAIN

pege (4077), "a spring or fountain," is used of (a) "an artificial well," fed by a spring, John 4:6; (b) metaphorically (in contrast to such a well), "the indwelling Spirit of God," 4:14; (c) "springs," metaphorically in 2 Pet. 2:17, RV, for KJV, "wells"; (d) "natural fountains or springs," Jas. 3:11, 12; Rev. 8:10; 14:7; 16:4; (e) metaphorically, "eternal life and the future blessings accruing from it," Rev. 7:17; 21:6; (f) "a flow of blood," Mark 5:29.

FRAME (Verb)

1. *katartizo* (2675), "to fit, to render complete," is translated "have been framed" in Heb. 11:3, of the worlds or ages.

2. *sunarmologeo* (4883), "to fit or frame together" (*sun*, "with," *harmos*, "a joint," *lego*, "to choose"), is used metaphorically of the church as a spiritual temple, the parts being "fitly framed

together," Eph. 2:21; as a body, 4:16, RV, "fitly framed," (for KJV, "fitly joined").

FRANKINCENSE

libanos (2030), Matt. 2:11; Rev. 18:13, from a Semitic verb signifying "to be white," is a vegetable resin, bitter and glittering, obtained by incisions in the bark of the *arbor thuris*, "the incense tree." The Indian variety is called *looban*.

FRAUD

aphustereo (575 and 5302), "to keep back, deprive" (*apo*, "from," *hustereo*, "to be lacking"), is used in Jas. 5:4, "is kept back by fraud" (some mss. have *apostereo*, "to defraud"). The word is found in a papyrus writing of A.D. 42, of a bath insufficiently warmed.

FREE, FREEDOM, FREELY, FREEMAN, FREEDMAN, FREEWOMAN

A. Adjective.

eleutheros (1658), primarily of "freedom to go wherever one likes," is used (a) of "freedom from restraint and obligation" in general, Matt. 17:26; Rom. 6:20 (i.e., righteousness laid no sort of bond upon them, they had no relation to it); (b) in a civil sense, "free" from bondage or slavery, John 8:33; 1 Cor. 7:21, 22, 2nd part (for v. 22, 1st part, see C, No. 2); 12:13; Gal. 3:28; Eph. 6:8; Rev. 13:16; 19:18; as a noun, "freeman," Col. 3:11, RV; Rev. 6:15; "freewoman," Gal. 4:22, 23, 30, and v. 31, RV.

B. Verb.

eleutheroo (1659), "to make free" (akin to A), is used of deliverance from (a) sin, John 8:32, 36; Rom. 6:18, 22; (b) the Law, Rom. 8:2; Gal. 5:1 (see, however under C); (c) the bondage of corruption, Rom. 8:21.

C. Nouns.

1. *eleutheria* (1657), "liberty" (akin to A and B), is rendered "freedom" in Gal. 5:1, "with freedom did Christ set us free." The combination of the noun with the verb stresses the completeness of the act, the aorist (or point) tense indicating both its momentary and comprehensive character; it was done once for all. The RV margin "for freedom" gives perhaps the preferable meaning, i.e., "not to bring us into another form of bondage did Christ liberate us from that in which we were born, but in order to make us free from bondage."

The word is twice rendered "freedom" in the RV of Gal. 5:13

(KJV, "liberty"). The phraseology is that of manumission from slavery, which among the Greeks was effected by a legal fiction, according to which the manumitted slave was purchased by a god; as the slave could not provide the money, the master paid it into the temple treasury in the presence of the slave, a document being drawn up containing the words "for freedom." No one could enslave him again, as he was the property of the god. Hence the word *apeleutheros*, No. 2. The word is also translated "freedom" in 1 Pet. 2:16, RV. In 2 Cor. 3:17 the word denotes "freedom" of access to the presence of God.

2. *apeleutheros* (558), "a freed man" (*apo*, "from," and A), is used in 1 Cor. 7:22, "the Lord's freedman."

D. Adverb.

dorean (1432), from *dorea*, "a gift" is used as an adverb in the sense "freely," in Matt. 10:8; Rom. 3:24; 2 Cor. 11:7 (RV, "for nought"); Rev. 21:6; 22:17. Here the prominent thought is the grace of the Giver.

FRIEND (make one's)

Old Testament

rea' (7453), "friend; companion; fellow." The word refers to a "friend" in 2 Sam. 13:3: "But Amnon had a friend, whose name was Jonadab." The word may be used of a husband, Jer. 3:20, or a beloved one, Song of Sol. 5:16.

In another sense, *rea'* may be used of any person with whom one has reciprocal relations: "And they said every one to his fellow, Come, and let us cast lots...," Jonah 1:7. The word also appears in such phrases as "one another," found in Gen. 11:3: "And they said *one to another*...," cf. Gen. 31:49.

Other related nouns that appear less frequently are *re'eh*, which means "friend" about 5 times, e.g., 1 Kings 4:5; and *re'ah*, which means "companion or attendant," Judg. 11:38; Ps. 45:14.

New Testament

A. Nouns.

1. *philos* (5384), primarily an adjective, denoting "loved, dear, or friendly," became used as a noun, (a) masculine, Matt. 11:19; fourteen times in Luke (once feminine, 15:9); six in John; three in Acts; two in James, 2:23, "the friend of God"; 4:4, "a friend of the world"; 3 John 14 (twice); (b) feminine, Luke 15:9, "her friends."

2. *hetairos* (2083), "a comrade, companion, partner," is used as a term of kindly address in Matt. 20:13; 22:12; 26:50. This, as expressing comradeship, is to be distinguished from No. 1, which is a term of endearment.

B. Verb.

peitho (3982), "to persuade, influence," is rendered "having made...their friend" in Acts 12:20, of the folks of Tyre and Sidon in winning the good will of Blastus, Herod's chamberlain, possibly with bribes.

FRIENDSHIP

philia (5373), akin to *philos*, "a friend" (see above), is rendered in Jas. 4:4, "the friendship (of the world)." It involves "the idea of loving as well as being loved" (Mayor); cf. the verb in John 15:19.

FRUIT (bear), FRUITFUL, UNFRUITFUL

Old Testament

A. Noun.

peri (6529), "fruit; reward; price; earnings; product; result." First, *peri* represents the mature edible product of a plant, Gen. 1:11; Ps. 107:34. Second, *peri* means "offspring," or the "fruit of a womb," of any creature, Gen. 1:22; Deut. 7:13. Third, the "product" or "result," of an action Ps. 58:11; Prov. 31:16,31.

B. Verb.

parah (6504), "to be fruitful, bear fruit," Gen. 1:22.

New Testament

A. Noun.

karpos (2590), "fruit," is used (I) of the fruit of trees, fields, the earth, that which is produced by the inherent energy of a living organism, e.g., Matt. 7:17; Jas. 5:7, 18; plural, e.g., in Luke 12:17 and 2 Tim. 2:6; of the human body, Luke 1:42; Acts 2:30; (II), metaphorically, (a) of works or deeds, "fruit" being the visible expression of power working inwardly and invisibly, the character of the "fruit" being evidence of the character of the power producing it, Matt. 7:16. The invisible power of the Holy Spirit in those who are brought into living union with Christ (John 15:2-8, 16) produces "the fruit of the Spirit," Gal. 5:22. So in Phil. 1:11, marg., "fruit of righteousness." In Heb. 12:11, "the fruit of righteousness" is described as "peaceable fruit," the outward effect of divine chastening; "the fruit of righteousness is sown in peace," Jas. 3:18, i.e., the seed contains the fruit; those who make peace, produce a harvest of righteousness; in Eph. 5:9, "the fruit of the light" (RV, and see context) is seen in "goodness and righteousness and truth," as the expression of the union of the Christian with God; for God is good, Mark 10:18, the Son is "the righteous One," Acts 7:52, the Spirit is "the Spirit of truth," John 16:13; (b) of advantage, profit, consisting (1) of converts as the result of evangelistic ministry, John 4:36; Rom. 1:13; Phil. 1:22; (2) of sanctification, through deliverance from a life of sin and through service to God, Rom. 6:22, in contrast to (3) the absence of anything regarded as advantageous as the result of former sins, v. 21; (4) of the reward for ministration to servants of God, Phil. 4:17; (5) of the effect of making confession to God's Name by the sacrifice of praise, Heb. 13:15.

B. Adjective.

akarpos (175), "unfruitful" (*a*, negative, and *karpos* above), is used figuratively (a) of "the word of the Kingdom," rendered "unfruitful" in the case of those influenced by the cares of the world and the deceitfulness of riches, Matt. 13:22; Mark 4:19; (b) of the understanding of one praying with a "tongue," which effected no profit to the church without an interpretation of it, 1 Cor. 14:14; (c) of the works of darkness, Eph. 5:11; (d) of believers who fail "to maintain good works," indicating the earning of one's living so as to do good works to others, Titus 3:14; of the effects of failing to supply in one's faith the qualities of virtue, knowledge, temperance, patience, godliness, love of the brethren, and love, 2 Pet. 1:8. In Jude 12 it is rendered "without fruit," of ungodly men, who oppose the gospel while pretending to uphold it, depicted as "autumn trees."

C. Verb.

karpophoreo (2592), "to bear or bring forth fruit," is used (a) in the natural sense, of the "fruit of the earth," Mark 4:28; (b) metaphorically, of conduct, or that which takes effect in conduct, Matt. 13:23; Mark 4:20; Luke 8:15; Rom. 7:4, 5 (the latter, of evil "fruit," borne "unto death," of activities resulting from a state of alienation from God); Col. 1:6 in the middle voice; Col. 1:10.

FULFILL, FULFILLING, FULFILLMENT

A. Verbs.

1. *pleroo* (4137) signifies (1) "to fill"; (2) "to fulfill, complete," (a) of time, e.g., Mark 1:15; Luke 21:24; John 7:8 (KJV, "full come"); Acts 7:23, RV, "he was well-nigh forty years old" (KJV, "was full" etc.), lit., "the time of forty years was fulfilled to him"; v. 30, RV, "were expired"; 9:23; 24:27 (KJV, "after two years"; RV, "when two years were fulfilled"); (b) of number, Rev. 6:11; (c) of good pleasure, 2 Thess. 1:11; (d) of joy, Phil. 2:2; in the passive voice, "to be fulfilled," John 3:29 and 17:13; in the following the verb is rendered "fulfilled" in the RV, for the KJV, "full," John 15:11; 16:24; 1 John 1:4; 2 John 12; (e) of obedience, 2 Cor. 10:6; (f) of works, Rev. 3:2; (g) of the future Passover, Luke 22:16; (h) of sayings, prophecies, etc., e.g., Matt. 1:22 (twelve times in Matt., two in Mark, four in Luke, eight in John, two in Acts); Jas. 2:23; in Col. 1:25 the word signifies to preach "fully," to complete the ministry of the Gospel appointed.

2. *anapleroo* (*378*), "to fill up fill completely" (*ana*, "up, up to," and No. 1), is used (a) of Isaiah's prophecy of Israel's rejection of God, fulfilled in the rejection of His Son, Matt. 13:14; (b) of the status of a person in a church, RV, "filleth the place," for KJV, "occupieth the room," 1 Cor. 14:16; (c) of an adequate supply of service, 1 Cor. 16:17, "supplied"; Phil. 2:30, "to supply"; (d) of sins, 1 Thess. 2:16; (e) of the law of Christ; Gal. 6:2.

3. *teleo* (*5055*), "to end" (akin to *telos*, "an end"), signifies, among its various meanings, "to give effect to," and is translated "fulfill," of the Law, intentionally, Jas. 2:8, or unconsciously, Rom. 2:27; of the prophetic Scriptures concerning the death of Christ, Acts 13:29; prohibitively, of the lust of the flesh, Gal. 5:16.

4. *sunteleo* (*4931*), "to complete," is translated "fulfilled" in the KJV of Mark 13:4 (RV, "accomplished").

5. *teleioo* (*5048*), "to bring to an end, fulfill," is rendered "to fulfill," of days. Luke 2:43; of the Scripture, John 19:28.

6. *plerophoreo* (*4135*), "to bring in full measure," from *pleroo* (see No. 1), and *phoreo*, "to bring"; hence, "to fulfill," of circumstances relating to Christ, Luke 1:1, RV, "have been fulfilled" (KJV "are most surely believed"); of evangelical ministry, 2 Tim. 4:5, "fulfill" (KJV, "make full proof"); so in v. 17, RV, "fully proclaimed" (KJV, "fully known").

7. *ekpleroo* (*1603*), a strengthened form of No. 1, occurs in Acts 13:33.

B. Nouns.

1. *pleroma* (*4138*) stands for the result of the action expressed in *pleroo*, "to fill." It is used to signify (a) "that which has been completed, the complement, fullness," e.g., John 1:16; Eph. 1:23; some suggest that the "fullness" here points to the body as the filled receptacle of the power of Christ (words terminating in —*ma* are frequently concrete in character.

2. *teleiosis* (*5058*), a fulfillment, is so rendered in Luke 1:45, akin to A. 3.

FULL

A. Adjectives.

1. *pleres* (*4134*) denotes "full," (a) in the sense of "being filled," materially, Matt. 14:20; 15:37; Mark 8:19 (said of baskets "full" of bread crumbs); of leprosy, Luke 5:12; spiritually, of the Holy Spirit, Luke 4:1; Acts 6:3; 7:55; 11:24; grace and truth, John 1:14; faith, Acts 6:5; grace and power, 6:8; of the effects of spiritual life and qualities, seen in good works, Acts 9:36; in an evil sense, of guile and villany, Acts 13:10; wrath, 19:28; (b) in the sense of "being complete," "full corn in the ear," Mark 4:28; of a reward hereafter, 2 John 8.

2. *mestos* (*3324*) probably akin to a root signifying "to measure,"

hence conveys the sense of "having full measure," (a) of material things, a vessel, John 19:29; a net, 21:11; (b) metaphorically, of thoughts and feelings, exercised (1) in evil things, hypocrisy, Matt. 23:28; envy, murder, strife, deceit, malignity, Rom. 1:29; the utterances of the tongue, Jas. 3:8; adultery, 2 Pet. 2:14; (2) in virtues, goodness, Rom. 15:14; mercy, etc., Jas. 3:17.

B. Verb.

gemo (1073), "to be full, to be heavily laden with," was primarily used of a ship; it is chiefly used in the NT of evil contents, such as extortion and excess, Matt. 23:25; dead men's bones, v. 27; extortion and wickedness, Luke 11:39; cursing, Rom. 3:14; blasphemy, Rev. 17:3; abominations, v. 4; of divine judgments 15:17; 21:9; (RV, "laden," KJV, "full"); of good things, 4:6, 8; 5:8.

FULLER

gnapheus (102), akin to *knapto*, "to card wool," denotes "a cloth-carder, or dresser" (*gnaphos*, "the prickly teasel-cloth"; hence, "a carding comb"); it is used of the raiment of the Lord in Mark 9:3.

FULLNESS

pleroma (4138) denotes "fullness," that of which a thing is "full"; it is thus used of the grace and truth manifested in Christ, John 1:16; of all His virtues and excellencies, Eph. 4:13; "the blessing of Christ," Rom. 15:29, RV (not as KJV); the conversion and restoration of Israel, Rom. 11:12; the completion of the number of Gentiles who receive blessing through the gospel, v. 25; the complete products of the earth, 1 Cor. 10:26; the end of an appointed period, Gal. 4:4; Eph. 1:10; God, in the completeness of His Being, Eph. 3:19; Col. 1:19; 2:9; the church as the complement of Christ, Eph. 1:23. In Mark 6:43, "basketfuls," RV, is, lit., "fullnesses of baskets."

FURNISH

exartizo (1822), "to fit out, to prepare perfectly, to complete for a special purpose" (*ex*, "out," used intensively, and *artios*, "joined," *artos*, "a joint"), is used of "accomplishing" days, Acts 21:5, i.e., of "terminating" a space of time; of being "completely furnished," by means of the Scriptures, for spiritual service, 2 Tim. 3:17.

G

GAIN (Noun and Verb)

A. Nouns.

1. *ergasia* (*2039*) signifies (a) "work, working, performance" (from *ergon*, "work"), Eph. 4:19; in Luke 12:58, "diligence"; (b) "business or gain got by work," Acts 16:16, 19; in 19:24, 25, the RV adheres to the meaning "business" (KJV, "gain" and "craft").

2. *porismos* (*4200*) primarily denotes "a providing" (akin to *porizo*, "to procure"), then, "a means of gain," 1 Tim. 6:5 (RV, "a way of gain"); 6:6.

3. *kerdos* (*2771*), "gain" (akin to *kerdaino*, see below), occurs in Phil. 1:21; 3:7; Titus 1:11.

B. Verbs.

1. *kerdaino* (*2770*), akin to A, No. 3, signifies (I), literally, (a) "to gain something," Matt. 16:26; 25:16 (in the best mss.), 17, 20, 22; Mark 8:36; Luke 9:25; (b) "to get gain, make a profit," Jas. 4:13; (II), metaphorically, (a) "to win persons," said (1) of "gaining" an offending brother who by being told privately of his offense, and by accepting the representations, is won from alienation and from the consequences of his fault, Matt. 18:15; (2) of winning souls into the kingdom of God by the gospel, 1 Cor. 9:19, 20 (twice), 21, 22, or by godly conduct, 1 Pet. 3:1 (RV, "gained"); (3) of so practically appropriating Christ to oneself that He becomes the dominating power in and over one's whole being and circumstances, Phil. 3:8 (RV, "gain"); (b) "to gain things," said of getting injury and loss, Acts 27:21, RV, "gotten."

2. *diapragmateuomai* (*1281*) signifies "to gain by trading," Luke 19:15 (from *dia*, "through," used intensively, and *pragmateuomai*, "to busy oneself, to be engaged in business").

3. *peripoieo* (*4046*), "to save for oneself, gain," is in the middle voice in the best mss. in Luke 17:33, RV, gain.

GAINSAY, GAINSAYER, GAINSAYING

A. Verbs.

1. *antilego* (*483*), "to contradict, oppose," lit., "say against," is translated "gainsaying" in Rom. 10:21 and Titus 2:9, RV (KJV, "answering again"), of servants in regard to masters; in Titus 1:9 "gainsayers."

2. *anteipon* (483), which serves as an aorist tense of No. 1, is rendered "gainsay" in Luke 21:15; "say against" in Acts 4:14.

B. Noun.

antilogia (485), akin to A, No. 1, is rendered "gainsaying," in Heb. 12:3, RV, and Jude 11. Opposition in act seems to be implied in these two places; though this sense has been questioned by some, it is confirmed by instances from the papyri.

C. Adjective.

anantirrhetos (368), lit., "not to be spoken against" (*a*, negative, *n*, euphonic, *anti*, "against," *rhetos*, "spoken"), is rendered "cannot be gainsaid" in Acts 19:36, RV.

D. Adverb.

anantirrhetos (369), corresponding to C, is translated "without gainsaying" in Acts 10:29; it might be rendered "unquestioningly."

GARNER

apotheke (596), "a storehouse, granary" (from *apo*, "away," and *tithemi*, "to put"), is translated "garner" in Matt. 3:12 and Luke 3:17.

GARNISH

kosmeo (2885) is translated by the verb "to garnish" in Matt. 12:44; 23:29; Luke 11:25; and in the KJV of Rev. 21:19.

GAZINGSTOCK

theatrizo (2301) signifies "to make a spectacle" (from *theatron*, "a theater, spectacle, show"); it is used in the passive voice in Heb. 10:33, "being made a gazingstock."

GENEALOGY

A. Noun.

genealogia (1076) is used in 1 Tim. 1:4 and Titus 3:9, with reference to such "genealogies" as are found in Philo, Josephus and the book of Jubilees, by which Jews traced their descent from the patriarchs and their families, and perhaps also to Gnostic "genealogies" and orders of aeons and spirits. Amongst the Greeks, as well as other nations, mythological stories gathered round the birth and "genealogy" of their heroes. Probably Jewish "genealogical" tales crept into Christian communities. Hence the warnings to Timothy and Titus.

B. Verb.

genealogeo (1075), "to reckon or trace a genealogy" (from *genea*, "a race," and *lego*, "to choose, pick out"), is used, in the passive voice, of Melchizedek in Heb. 7:6.

C. Adjective (negative).

agenealogetos (35), denoting "without recorded pedigree" (*a*, negative, and an adjectival form from B), is rendered "without genealogy" in Heb. 7:3. The narrative in Gen. 14 is so framed in facts and omissions as to foreshadow the person of Christ.

GENERATION

Old Testament

dor (1755), "generation." First the concrete meaning of "generation" is the "period during which people live," Gen. 7:1. A *dor* is roughly the period of time from one's birth to one's maturity, which in the Old Testament corresponds to a period of about 40 years, Num. 14:33 cf. also Exod. 20:5; Deut. 7:9. The psalmist recognized the obligation of one "generation" to the "generations" to come," Ps. 71:17-18; 145:4.

New Testament

1. *genea* (1074), "generation," Acts 8:33.

2. *genesis* (1078) denotes "an origin, a lineage, or birth," translated "generation" in Matt. 1:1.

GENTILES

A. Nouns.

1. *ethnos* (1484), whence Eng., "heathen," denotes, firstly, "a multitude or company"; then, "a multitude of people of the same nature or genus, a nation, people"; it is used in the singular, of the Jews, e.g., Luke 7:5; 23:2; John 11:48, 50-52; in the plural, of nations (Heb., *goiim*) other than Israel, e.g., Matt. 4:15; Rom. 3:29; 11:11; 15:10; Gal. 2:8; occasionally it is used of gentile converts in distinction from Jews, e.g., Rom. 11:13; 16:4; Gal. 2:12, 14; Eph. 3:1.

2. *hellen* (1672) originally denoted the early descendants of Thessalian Hellas; then, Greeks as opposed to barbarians, Rom. 1:14. It became applied to such Gentiles as spoke the Greek language, e.g., Gal. 2:3; 3:28. Since that was the common medium of intercourse in the Roman Empire, Greek and Gentile became more or less interchangeable terms. For this term the RV always adheres to the word "Greeks," e.g., John 7:35; Rom. 2:9, 10; 3:9; 1 Cor. 10:32, where the local church is distinguished from Jews and Gentiles; 12:13.

B. Adjective.

ethnikos (1482) is used as noun, and translated "Gentiles" in the RV of Matt. 5:47; 6:7; "the Gentile" in 18:17 (KJV, "an heathen man"); "the Gentiles" in 3 John 7, KJV and RV.

C. Adverb.

ethnikos (*1483*), "in Gentile fashion, in the manner of Gentiles," is used in Gal. 2:14, "as do the Gentiles," RV.

GENTLE, GENTLENESS, GENTLY

A. Adjectives.

1. *epieikes* (*1933*), from *epi*, "unto," and *eikos*, "likely," denotes "seemly, fitting"; hence, "equitable, fair, moderate, forbearing, not insisting on the letter of the law"; it expresses that considerateness that looks "humanely and reasonably at the facts of a case"; it is rendered "gentle" in 1 Tim. 3:3, RV (KJV, "patient"), in contrast to contentiousness; in Titus 3:2, "gentle," in association with meekness, in Jas. 3:17, as a quality of the wisdom from above, in 1 Pet. 2:18, in association with the good; for the RV rendering "forbearance" in Phil. 4:5.

2. *epios* (*2261*), "mild, gentle," was frequently used by Greek writers as characterizing a nurse with trying children or a teacher with refractory scholars, or of parents toward their children. In 1 Thess. 2:7, the apostle uses it of the conduct of himself and his fellow missionaries towards the converts at Thessalonica (cf. 2 Cor. 11:13, 20); in 2 Tim. 2:24, of the conduct requisite for a servant of the Lord.

B. Noun.

epieikeia (*1932*), or *epieikia*, denotes "fairness, moderation, gentleness," "sweet reasonableness" (Matthew Arnold); it is said of Christ, 2 Cor. 10:1, where it is coupled with *prautes*, "meekness"; for its meaning in Acts 24:4.

GHOST (give up the)

1. *ekpneo* (*1606*), lit., "to breathe out," "to expire," is used in the NT, without an object, "soul" or "life" being understood, Mark 15:37, 39, and Luke 23:46, of the death of Christ. In Matt. 27:50 and John 19:30, where different verbs are used, the act is expressed in a way which stresses it as of His own volition: in the former, "Jesus...yielded up His spirit (*pneuma*)"; in the latter, "He gave up His spirit."

2. *ekpsucho* (*1634*), "to expire," lit., "to breathe out the soul (or life), to give up the ghost" (*ek*, "out," *psuche*, "the soul"), is used in Acts 5:5, 10; 12:23.

GIFT, GIVING

1. *doron* (*1435*), akin to *didomi*, "to give," is used (a) of "gifts" presented as an expression of honor, Matt. 2:11; (b) of "gifts" for the support of the temple and the needs of the poor, Matt. 15:5; Mark 7:11; Luke 21:1, 4; (c) of "gifts" offered to God, Matt. 5:23, 24; 8:4;

23:18, 19; Heb. 5:1; 8:3, 4; 9:9; 11:4; (d) of salvation by grace as the "gift" of God, Eph. 2:8; (e) of "presents" for mutual celebration of an occasion, Rev. 11:10.

2. *dorea* (*1431*) denotes "a free gift," stressing its gratuitous character; it is always used in the NT of a spiritual or supernatural gift, John 4:10; Acts 8:20; 11:17; Rom. 5:15; 2 Cor. 9:15; Eph. 3:7; Heb. 6:4; in Eph. 4:7, "according to the measure of the gift of Christ," the "gift" is that given by Christ; in Acts 2:28, "the gift of the Holy Ghost," the clause is epexegetical, the "gift" being the Holy Ghost Himself; cf. 10:45; 11:17, and the phrase, "the gift of righteousness," Rom. 5:17.

3. *dorema* (*1434*): "gift," Rom. 5:16; Jas. 1:17.

4. *doma* (*1390*) lends greater stress to the concrete character of the "gift," than to its beneficent nature, Matt. 7:11; Luke 11:13; Eph. 4:8; Phil. 4:17.

5. *dosis* (*1394*) denotes, properly, "the act of giving," Phil. 4:15, euphemistically referring to "gifts" as a matter of debt and credit accounts; then, objectively, "a gift," Jas. 1:17.

6. *charisma* (*5486*), "a gift of grace, a gift involving grace" (*charis*) on the part of God as the donor, is used (a) of His free bestowments upon sinners, Rom. 5:15, 16; 6:23; 11:29; (b) of His endowments upon believers by the operation of the Holy Spirit in the churches, Rom. 12:6; 1 Cor. 1:7; 12:4, 9, 28, 30, 31; 1 Tim. 4:14; 2 Tim. 1:6; 1 Pet. 4:10; (c) of that which is imparted through human instruction, Rom. 1:11; (d) of the natural "gift" of continence, consequent upon the grace of God as Creator, 1 Cor. 7:7; (e) of gracious deliverances granted in answer to the prayers of fellow believers, 2 Cor. 1:11.

7. *merismos* (*3311*), "a dividing" (from *meros*, "a part"), is translated "gifts" in Heb. 2:4, "gifts of the Holy Ghost" (marg., "distributions"); in 4:12, "dividing."

GIRD, GIRDED, GIRT (about, up)

1. *zonnumi* (*2224*), or *zonnuo*, "to gird" in the middle voice, "to gird oneself," is used of the long garments worn in the east, John 21:18; Acts 12:8 (*perizonnumi* in some mss.).

2. *anazonnumi* (*328*), "to gird up" (*ana*, "up," and No. 1), is used metaphorically of the loins of the mind, 1 Pet. 1:13; cf. Luke 12:35 (see No. 4). The figure is taken from the circumstances of the Israelites as they ate the Passover in readiness for their journey, Exod. 12:11; the Christian is to have his mental powers alert in expectation of Christ's coming. The verb is in the middle voice, indicating the special interest the believer is to take in so doing.

3. *diazonnumi* (*1241*), "to gird round," i.e., firmly (*dia*, "throughout," used intensively), is used of the Lord's act in "girding" Himself with a towel, John 13:4, 5, and of Peter's girding himself with his coat, 21:7.

4. *perizonnumi* (*4024*), "to gird around or about," is used (a) lit-

erally, of "girding" oneself for service, Luke 12:37; 17:8; for rapidity of movement, Acts 12:8; (b) figuratively, of the condition for service on the part of the followers of Christ, Luke 12:35; Eph. 6:14; (c) emblematically, of Christ's priesthood, Rev. 1:13, indicative of majesty of attitude and action, the middle voice suggesting the particular interest taken by Christ in "girding" Himself thus; so of the action of the angels mentioned in 15:6.

GIRDLE

zone (2223), Eng., "zone," denotes "a belt or girdle," Matt. 3:4; Mark 1:6; Acts 21:11; Rev. 1:13; 15:6; it was often hollow, and hence served as a purse, Matt. 10:9; Mark 6:8.

GIVE

1. *didomi* (1325), "to give," is used with various meanings according to the context; it is said, e.g., of seed "yielding fruit," Mark 4:7, 8; of "giving" (i.e., exercising) diligence, Luke 12:58; of giving lots, Acts 1:26, RV (KJV, "gave forth"); of "rendering" vengeance, 2 Thess. 1:8; of "striking or smiting" Christ, John 18:22 (lit., "gave a blow") and 19:3 (lit., "they gave Him blows"); of "putting" a ring on the hand, Luke 15:22; of Paul's "adventuring" himself into a place, Acts 19:31. (In Rev. 17:13 some mss. have *diadidomi*, "to divide").

2. *apodidomi* (591) signifies "to give up or back, to restore, return, render what is due, to pay, give an account" (*apo*, "back," and No. 1), e.g., of an account. Matt. 5:26; 12:36; Luke 16:2; Acts 19:40; Heb. 13:17; 1 Pet. 4:5; of wages, etc., e.g., Matt. 18:25-34; 20:8; of conjugal duty, 1 Cor. 7:3; of a witness, Acts 4:33; frequently of recompensing or rewarding, 1 Tim. 5:4; 2 Tim. 4:8, 14; 1 Pet. 3:9; Rev. 18:6; 22:12. In the middle voice it is used of "giving" up what is one's own; hence, "to sell," Acts 5:8; 7:9; Heb. 12:16.

3. *epididomi* (1929) signifies (a) "to give by handing, to hand" (*epi*, "over"), e.g., Matt. 7:9, 10; Luke 4:17; 24:30, here of the Lord's act in "handing" the broken loaf to the two at Emmaus, an act which was the means of the revelation of Himself as the crucified and risen Lord; the simple verb, No. 1, is used of His "handing" the bread at the institution of the Lord's Supper, Matt. 26:26; Mark 14:22; Luke 22:19; this meaning of the verb *epididomi* is found also in Acts 15:30, "they delivered"; (b) "to give in, give way," Acts 27:15, RV, "we gave way to it."

4. *metadidomi* (3330), "to give a share of, impart" (*meta*, "with"), as distinct from "giving." The apostle Paul speaks of "sharing" some spiritual gift with Christians at Rome, Rom. 1:11, "that I may impart," and exhorts those who minister in things temporal, to do so as "sharing," and that generously, 12:8, "he that giveth"; so in Eph. 4:28; Luke 3:11; in 1 Thess. 2:8 he speaks of himself and his fellow missionaries as having been well pleased to impart to the converts both God's gospel and their own souls (i.e., so "sharing"

those with them as to spend themselves and spend out their lives for them).

5. *paradidomi* (3860), "to give or hand over," is said of "giving" up the ghost, John 19:30; of "giving" persons up to evil, Acts 7:42; Rom. 1:24, 26; of "giving" one's body to be burned, 1 Cor. 13:3; of Christ's "giving" Himself up to death, Gal. 2:20; Eph. 5:2, 25.

6. *prodidomi* (4272), "to give before, or first" (*pro*, "before"), is found in Rom. 11:35.

7. *charizomai* (5483) primarily denotes "to show favor or kindness," as in Gal. 3:18, RV, "hath granted" (KJV, "gave"); then, to "give" freely, bestow; in this sense it is used almost entirely of that which is "given" by God, Acts 27:24, "God hath granted thee all them that sail with thee" (RV); in Rom. 8:32, "shall...freely give"; 1 Cor. 2:12, "are freely given"; Phil. 1:29, "it hath been granted" (said of believing on Christ and suffering for Him); 2:9, "hath given" (said of the name of Jesus as "given" by God); Philem. 22, "I shall be granted unto you" (RV). In Luke 7:21, it is said in regard to the blind, upon whom Christ "bestowed" sight (RV). The only exceptions, in this sense of the word, as to divinely imparted "gifts," are Acts 3:14, of the "granting" of Barabbas by Pilate to the Jews, and Acts 25:11, 16, of the "giving" up of a prisoner to his accusers or to execution.

8. *parecho* (3930), in the active voice, signifies "to afford, furnish, provide, supply" (lit., "to hold out or towards"; *para*, "near," *echo*, "to hold"); it is translated "hath given" in Acts 17:31; "giveth" in 1 Tim. 6:17 (in the sense of affording); in Col. 4:1, RV, "render" (KJV, "give").

9. *doreo* (143), akin to No. 1, and used in the middle voice, "to bestow, make a gift of," is translated in the RV by the verb "to grant," instead of the KJV, "to give," Mark 15:45; 2 Pet. 1:3, 4.

GLAD (be, make), GLADLY

A. Verbs.

1. *chairo* (5463) is the usual word for "rejoicing, being glad"; it is rendered by the verb "to be glad" in Mark 14:11; Luke 15:32; 22:5; 23:8; John 8:56; 11:15; 20:20; Acts 11:23; 13:48; in the following the RV has "to rejoice" for KJV, "to be glad," Rom. 16:19; 1 Cor. 16:17; 2 Cor. 13:9; 1 Pet. 4:13; Rev. 19:7.

2. *agalliao* (21), "to exult, rejoice greatly," is chiefly used in the middle voice (active in Luke 1:47; some mss. have the passive in John 5:35, "to be made glad"). It conveys the idea of jubilant exultation, spiritual "gladness," Matt. 5:12, "be exceeding glad," the Lord's command to His disciples; Luke 1:47, in Mary's song; 10:21, of Christ's exultation ("rejoiced"); cf. Acts 2:26, "(My tongue) was glad," KJV (RV, "rejoiced"); John 8:56, of Abraham; Acts 16:34, RV, "rejoiced greatly" (of the Philippian jailor); 1 Pet. 1:6, 8; 4:13 ("with

exceeding joy"), of believers in general; in Rev. 19:7, RV, "be exceeding glad" (KJV, "rejoice").

3. *euphraino* (*2165*), "to cheer, gladden," is rendered "maketh...glad" in 2 Cor. 2:2.

B. Adverbs.

1. *hedeos* (*2234*), "gladly" (from *hedus*, "sweet"), is used in Mark 6:20; 12:37; 2 Cor. 11:19.

2. *hedista* (*2236*), the superlative degree of No. 1, "most gladly, most delightedly, with great relish," is rendered "most gladly" in 2 Cor. 12:9, and in v. 15 (RV; KJV, "very gladly").

3. *asmenos* (*780*), "with delight, delightedly, gladly," is found in Acts 21:17.

GLADNESS

1. *chara* (*5479*), "joy, delight" (akin to A, No. 1 above), is rendered "gladness" in the KJV of Mark 4:16; Acts 12:14 and Phil. 2:29 (RV "joy," in both versions).

2. *agalliasis* (*20*), "exultation, exuberant joy" (akin to A, No. 2), is translated "gladness" in Luke 1:14; Acts 2:6; Heb. 1:9; "joy" in Luke 1:44; "exceeding joy" in Jude 24. It indicates a more exultant "joy" than No. 1.

3. *euphrosune* (*2167*), "good cheer, joy, mirth, gladness of heart" (akin to A, No. 3), from *eu*, "well," and *phren*, "the mind," is rendered "gladness" in Acts 2:28, RV (KJV, "joy") and 14:17.

GLORIFY

1. *doxazo* (*1392*) primarily denotes "to suppose" (from *doxa*, "an opinion"); in the NT (a) "to magnify, extol, praise," especially of "glorifying"; God, i.e., ascribing honor to Him, acknowledging Him as to His being, attributes and acts, i.e., His glory, e.g., Matt. 5:16; 9:8; 15:31; Rom. 15:6, 9; Gal. 1:24; 1 Pet. 4:16; the Word of the Lord, Acts 13:48; the Name of the Lord, Rev. 15:4; also of "glorifying" oneself, John 8:54; Rev. 18:7; (b) "to do honor to, to make glorious," e.g., Rom. 8:30; 2 Cor. 3:10; 1 Pet. 1:8, "full of glory," passive voice (lit., "glorified"); said of Christ, e.g., John 7:39; 8:54, RV, "glorifieth," for KJV, "honor" and "honoreth" (which would translate *timao*, "to honor"); of the Father, e.g., John 13:31, 32; 21:19; 1 Pet. 4:11; of "glorifying" one's ministry, Rom. 11:13, RV, "glorify" (KJV, "magnify"); of a member of the body, 1 Cor. 12:26, "be honored" (RV marg., "be glorified").

God manifests all His goodness in the Son by glorifying Him, John 12:28, Christ so glorifies the Father, John 17:1, 4; or the Father is glorified in Him, 13:31; 14:13; 15:8. When *doxazo* is predicated of Christ, it means simply that His innate glory is brought to light, cf. John 11:4; so 7:39; 12:16, 23; 13:31; 17:1, 5.

2. *endoxazo* (*1740*), No. 1 prefixed by *en*, "in," signifies, in the passive voice, "to be glorified," i.e., to exhibit one's glory; it is said

of God, regarding His saints in the future, 2 Thess. 1:10, and of the name of the Lord Jesus as "glorified" in them in the present, v. 12.

3. *sundoxazo* (*4888*), "to glorify together" (*sun*, "with"), is used in Rom. 8:17.

GLORY, GLORIOUS

Old Testament

tip'eret (8597), "glory; beauty; ornament; distinction; pride." The word represents "beauty," Exod. 28:2; or "adornment," Isa. 4:2. *tip'eret* (or *tip'arah*) means "glory" in several instances. The word is used of one's rank. A crown of "glory" is a crown which, by its richness, indicates high rank, Prov. 4:9; 16:31; Isa. 62:3. In another related nuance, the noun is used of God, to emphasize His rank, renown, and inherent "beauty," 1 Chron. 29:11; used of a nation, Lam. 2:1. In Isa. 10:12, the word represents a raising of oneself to a high rank in one's own eyes, and so be improper pride.

kabod is another common word for "glory." which often means to be in a state of high status, Josh. 7:19; or speaking honor toward another of high status, whether God or mankind, Prov. 11:16. *kabod* also can mean, "great wealth," or related "reward," Gen. 31:1; Num. 24:11. It can also mean a "ruler," with a special focus on a person of high regard and possibly wealth, Esth. 1:4, or a display of power as in a miracle, with a special focus that this act of power produces awe in those who see it, Exod. 16:7. *kabod* is a title of God, as one who is "totally awesome," and so glorious, filling a space with divine light whenever he is present, Ps 106:20; cf. Exod. 29:43.

New Testament

A. Nouns.

1. *doxa* (*1391*), "glory" (from *dokeo*, "to seem"), primarily signifies an opinion, estimate, and hence, the honor resulting from a good opinion. It is used (I) (a) of the nature and acts of God in self-manifestation, i.e., what He essentially is and does, as exhibited in whatever way He reveals Himself in these respects, and particularly in the person of Christ, in whom essentially His "glory" has ever shone forth and ever will do, John 17:5, 24; Heb. 1:3; it was exhibited in the character and acts of Christ in the days of His flesh, John 1:14; John 2:11; at Cana both His grace and His power were manifested, and these constituted His "glory," so also in the resurrection of Lazarus 11:4, 40; the "glory" of God was exhibited in the resurrection of Christ, Rom. 6:4, and in His ascension and exaltation, 1 Pet. 1:21, likewise on the Mount of Transfiguration, 2 Pet. 1:17. In Rom. 1:23 His "everlasting power and Divinity" are spoken of as His "glory," i.e., His attributes and power as revealed through creation; in Rom. 3:23 the word denotes the manifested perfection of His character, especially His righteousness, of which

all men fall short; in Col. 1:11 "the might of His glory" signifies the might which is characteristic of His "glory"; in Eph. 1:6, 12, 14, "the praise of the glory of His grace" and "the praise of His glory" signify the due acknowledgement of the exhibition of His attributes and ways; in Eph. 1:17, "the Father of glory" describes Him as the source from whom all divine splendor and perfection proceed in their manifestation, and to whom they belong; (b) of the character and ways of God as exhibited through Christ to and through believers, 2 Cor. 3:18 and 4:6; (c) of the state of blessedness into which believers are to enter hereafter through being brought into the likeness of Christ, e.g., Rom. 8:18, 21; Phil. 3:21 (RV, "the body of His glory"); 1 Pet. 5:1, 10; Rev. 21:11; (d) brightness or splendor, (1) supernatural, emanating from God (as in the *shekinah* "glory," in the pillar of cloud and in the Holy of Holies, e.g., Exod. 16:10; 25:22), Luke 2:9; Acts 22:11; Rom. 9:4; 2 Cor. 3:7; Jas. 2:1; in Titus 2:13 it is used of Christ's return, "the appearing of the glory of our great God and Savior Jesus Christ" (RV); cf. Phil. 3:21, above; (2) natural, as of the heavenly bodies, 1 Cor. 15:40, 41; (II) of good reputation, praise, honor, Luke 14:10 (RV, "glory," for KJV, "worship"); John 5:41 (RV, "glory," for KJV, "honor"); 7:18; 8:50; 12:43 (RV, "glory," for KJV, "praise"); 2 Cor. 6:8 (RV, "glory," for KJV "honor"); Phil. 3:19; Heb. 3:3; in 1 Cor. 11:7, of man as representing the authority of God, and of woman as rendering conspicuous the authority of man; in 1 Thess. 2:6, "glory" probably stands, by metonymy, for material gifts, an honorarium, since in human estimation "glory" is usually expressed in things material.

　　2. *kleos* (*2811*), "good report, fame, renown," is used in 1 Pet. 2:20. The word is derived from a root signifying "hearing"; hence, the meaning "reputation."

B. Adjective.

　　endoxos (*1741*) signifies (a) "held in honor," "of high repute," 1 Cor. 4:10, RV "have glory" (KJV, "are honorable"); (b) "splendid, glorious," said of apparel, Luke 7:25, "gorgeously"; of the works of Christ, 13:17; of the church, Eph. 5:27.

GLORY (to boast), GLORYING

A. Verbs.

　　1. *kauchaomai* (*2744*), "to boast or glory," is always translated in the RV by the verb "to glory," where the KJV uses the verb "to boast" (see, e.g., Rom. 2:17, 23; 2 Cor. 7:14; 9:2; 10:8, 13, 15, 16); it is used (a) of "vainglorying," e.g., 1 Cor. 1:29; 3:21; 4:7; 2 Cor. 5:12; 11:12, 18; Eph. 2:9; (b) of "valid glorying," e.g., Rom. 5:2, "rejoice"; 5:3, 11 (RV, "rejoice"); 1 Cor. 1:31; 2 Cor. 9:2; 10:8, 12:9; Gal. 6:14; Phil. 3:3 and Jas. 1:9, RV, "glory" (KJV, "rejoice").

　　2. *katakauchaomai* (*2620*), a strengthened form of No. 1 (*kata*, intensive), signifies "to boast against, exult over," Rom. 11:18, RV,

"glory" (KJV, "boast"); Jas. 2:13, RV, "glorieth" (KJV, "rejoiceth"); 3:14, "glory (not).

3. *enkauchaomai*, *en*, "in," and No. 1, "to glory in," is found, in the most authentic mss., in 2 Thess. 1:4.

B. Nouns.

1. *kauchema* (2745), akin to A, No. 1, denotes "that in which one glories, a matter or ground of glorying," Rom. 4:2 and Phil. 2:16, RV, "whereof to glory" (for Rom. 3:27, see No. 2); in the following the meaning is likewise "a ground of glorying": 1 Cor. 5:6; 9:15, "glorying," 16, "to glory of"; 2 Cor. 1:14 RV; 9:3, RV; Gal. 6:4, RV (KJV, "rejoicing"); Phil. 1:26 (ditto); Heb. 3:6 (ditto). In 2 Cor. 5:12 and 9:3 the word denotes the boast itself, yet as distinct from the act (see No. 2).

2. *kauchesis* (2746) denotes "the act of boasting," Rom. 3:27; 15:17, RV, "(my) glorying" (KJV, "whereof I may glory"); 1 Cor. 15:31, RV, "glorying"; 2 Cor. 1:12 (ditto); 7:4, 14 (KJV, "boasting"); 8:24; 11:10, and 17 (ditto); 1 Thess. 2:19 (KJV, "rejoicing"); Jas. 4:16 (ditto). The distinction between this and No. 1 is to be observed in 2 Cor. 8:24, speaking of the apostle's act of "glorying" in the liberality of the Corinthians, while in 9:3 he exhorts them not to rob him of the ground of his "glorying" (No. 1). Some take the word in 2 Cor. 1:12 (see above) as identical with No. 1, a boast, but there seems to be no reason for regarding it as different from its usual sense, No. 2.

GOAL

skopos (4649), primarily, "a watcher" (from *skopeo*, "to look at"; Eng., "scope"), denotes "a mark on which to fix the eye," and is used metaphorically of an aim or object in Phil. 3:14, RV, "goal" (KJV, "mark").

GOAT

1. *eriphos* (2056) denotes "a kid or goat," Matt. 25:32 (RV, marg., "kids"); Luke 15:29, "a kid"; some mss. have No. 2 here, indicating a sneer on the part of the elder son, that his father had never given him even a tiny kid.

2. *eriphion* (2055), a diminutive of No. 1, is used in Matt. 25:33. In v. 32 *eriphos* is purely figurative; in v. 33, where the application is made, though metaphorically, the change to the diminutive is suggestive of the contempt which those so described bring upon themselves by their refusal to assist the needy.

3. *tragos* (5131) denotes "a he-goat," Heb. 9:12, 13, 19; 10:4, the male prefiguring the strength by which Christ laid down His own life in expiatory sacrifice.

GOAT-DEMONS

sa'ir (8163), "goat-demons; goat-idols." This word occurs 4 times in biblical Hebrew. In its first biblical appearance, the word represents "goat-demons" (some scholars translate it "goat-idols"): "And they shall no more offer their sacrifices unto devils [NASB, "goat demons"], after whom they have gone a whoring," Lev. 17:7. This passage demonstrates that the word represents beings that were objects of pagan worship.

GOD

Old Testament

'el (410), "God, god," A term of supreme power and divinity, which can refer to the true God, Gen. 33:20; or to false gods, such as "*El*," the chief Canaanite god. Names with *'el* as one of their components were common in the Near East in the second millennium B.C. The names Methusael, Gen. 4:18, and Ishmael, Gen. 16:11, come from a very early period. When the true God is called "El," he reveals himself in power and enters into a covenant relationship with His people, Ps. 7:11; 85:8; Isa. 43:12; 46:9. The name of *'el* was commonly used by the Israelites to denote supernatural provision or power; or negatively, punishment.

'elah (426), "god." This Aramaic word is the equivalent of the Hebrew *'eloah.* It is a general term for "God" in the Aramaic passages of the Old Testament, and it is a cognate form of the word *'allah,* the designation of deity used by the Arabs, Ezra 4:24—7:26; Jer. 10:11; Dan. 2:11.

'eloah (433), "god," (singular version of the common plural form *'elohim*), The word *'eloah* is predominant in poetry rather than prose literature, and this is especially true of the Book of Job. Some scholars have suggested that the author of Job deliberately chose a description for godhead that avoided the historical associations found in a phrase such as "the God of Bethel," Gen. 31:13, or "God of Israel," Exod. 24:10. But even the Book of Job is by no means historically neutral, since places and peoples are mentioned in introducing the narrative, cf. Job 1:1, 15, 17. Perhaps the author considered *'eloah* a suitable term for poetry and used it accordingly with consistency. This is also apparently the case in Ps. 18:31, where *'eloah* is found instead of *'el,* as in the parallel passage of 2 Sam. 22:32. *'eloah* also appears as a term for God in Ps. 50:22; 139:19; and Prov. 30:5. Although *'eloah* as a divine name is rarely used outside Job, its literary history extends from at least the second millennium B.C., as in Deut. 32:15, to the fifth century B.C., as in Neh. 9:17.

'el shadday (410, 7706), "God Almighty," A title of the true God, which has a focus on the power, and all-surpassing provision of God, Gen. 17:1; *'el shadday,* is the God who will keep His promises, and the power to see His will be done, Gen. 49:26; see also Exod. 3:15, 6:3. In the early Mosaic era, the new redemptive name of "God" and the formulation of the Sinai covenant made *'el shad-*

day largely obsolete as a designation of deity. Subsequently, the name occurs about 35 times in the Old Testament, most of which are in the Book of Job. Occasionally, the name is used synonymously with the name of God, Yahweh, Ruth 1:21; Ps. 91:1-2, to emphasize the power and might of "God."

'el 'olam (410, 5769), "God of eternity; God the everlasting; God for ever," Ps. 90:2. The name *'el 'olam* was associated predominantly with Beer-sheba, Gen. 21:25-34. Abraham planted a commemorative tree in Beer-sheba and invoked the name of the Lord as *'el 'olam*.

New Testament

theos (2316), (I) in the polytheism of the Greeks, denoted "a god or deity," e.g., Acts 14:11; 19:26; 28:6; 1 Cor. 8:5; Gal. 4:8.

(II) (a) Hence the word was appropriated by Jews and retained by Christians to denote "the one true God."

In the NT, these and all the other divine attributes are predicated of Him. To Him are ascribed, e.g., His unity, or monism, e.g., Mark 12:29; 1 Tim. 2:5; self-existence, John 5:26; immutability, Jas. 1:17; eternity, Rom. 1:20; universality, Matt. 10:29; Acts 17:26-28; almighty power Matt. 19:26; infinite knowledge, Acts 2:23; 15:18; Rom. 11:33, creative power, Rom. 11:36; 1 Cor. 8:6; Eph. 3:9; Rev. 4:11; 10:6; absolute holiness, 1 Pet. 1:15; 1 John 1:5; righteousness, John 17:25; faithfulness, 1 Cor. 1:9; 10:13; 1 Thess. 5:24; 2 Thess. 3:3; 1 John 1:9; love, 1 John 4:8, 16; mercy, Rom. 9:15, 18; truthfulness, Titus 1:2; Heb. 6:18.

(b) The divine attributes are likewise indicated or definitely predicated of Christ, e.g., Matt. 20:18-19; John 1:1-3; 1:18, RV, marg.; 5:22-29; 8:58; 14:6; 17:22-24; 20:28; Rom. 1:4; 9:5; Phil. 3:21; Col. 1:15; 2:3; Titus 2:13, RV; Heb. 1:3; 13:8; 1 John 5:20; Rev. 22:12, 13.

(c) Also of the Holy Spirit, e.g., Matt. 28:19; Luke 1:35; John 14:16; 15:26; 16:7-14; Rom. 8:9, 26; 1 Cor. 12:11; 2 Cor. 13:14.

(d) *theos* is used with and without the definite article, but that point cuts no figure in the Greek idiom. As to this latter it is usual to employ the article with a proper name, when mentioned a second time. There are, of course, exceptions to this, as when the absence of the article serves to lay stress upon, or give precision to, the character or nature of what is expressed in the noun. A notable instance of this is in John 1:1, "and the Word was God"; here a double stress is on *theos*, by the absence of the article and by the emphatic position. To translate it literally, "a god was the Word," is entirely misleading. Where two or more epithets are applied to the same person or thing, one article usually serves for both (the exceptions being when a second article lays stress upon different aspects of the same person or subject, e.g., Rev. 1:17). In Titus 2:13

the RV correctly has "our great God and Savior Jesus Christ"; so in 2 Pet. 1:1 (cf. 1:11; 3:18).

In the following titles God is described by certain of His attributes; the God of glory, Acts 7:2; of peace, Rom. 15:33; 16:20; Phil. 4:9; 1 Thess. 5:23; Heb. 13:20; of love and peace, 2 Cor. 13:11; of patience and comfort, Rom. 15:5; of all comfort, 2 Cor. 1:3; of hope, Rom. 15:13; of all grace, 1 Pet. 5:10. These describe Him, not as in distinction from other persons, but as the source of all these blessings; hence the employment of the definite article. In such phrases as "the God of a person," e.g., Matt. 22:32, the expression marks the relationship in which the person stands to God and God to him.

(e) The phrase "the things of God" (translated literally or otherwise) stands for (1) His interests, Matt. 16:23; Mark 8:33; (2) His counsels, 1 Cor. 2:11; (3) things which are due to Him, Matt. 22:21; Mark 12:17; Luke 20:25. The phrase "things pertaining to God," Rom. 15:17; Heb. 2:17; 5:1, describes, in the Heb. passages, the sacrificial service of the priest; in the Rom. passage the gospel ministry as an offering to God.

(III) The word is used of divinely appointed judges in Israel, as representing God in His authority, John 10:34, quoted from Ps. 82:6, which indicates that God Himself sits in judgment on those whom He has appointed. The application of the term to the Devil, 2 Cor. 4:4, and the belly, Phil. 3:19, virtually places these instances under (I).

GOD (without)

atheos (112), cf. Eng., "atheist," primarily signifies "godless" (*a*, negative), i.e., destitute of God; in Eph. 2:12 the phrase indicates, not only that the Gentiles were void of any true recognition of God, and hence became morally "godless," Rom. 1:19-32, but that being given up by God, they were excluded from communion with God and from the privileges granted to Israel (see the context and cf. Gal. 4:8).

GODDESS

thea (2299) is found in Acts 19:27 (in some mss. in vv. 35, 37).

GODLINESS, GODLY

A. Nouns.

1. *eusebeia* (2150), from *eu*, "well," and *sebomai*, "to be devout," denotes that piety which, characterized by a Godward attitude, does that which is well-pleasing to Him. This and the corresponding adjective and adverb (see below) are frequent in the Pastoral Epistles, but do not occur in previous epistles of Paul. The apostle Peter has the noun four times in his 2nd Epistle, 1:3, 6, 7; 3:11. Else-

where it occurs in Acts 3:12; 1 Tim. 2:2; 3:16; 4:7, 8; 6:3, 5, 6, 11; 2 Tim. 3:5; Titus 1:1. In 1 Tim. 6:3 "the doctrine which is according to godliness" signifies that which is consistent with "godliness," in contrast to false teachings; in Titus 1:1, "the truth which is according to godliness" is that which is productive of "godliness"; in 1 Tim. 3:16, "the mystery of godliness" is "godliness" as embodied in, and communicated through, the truths of the faith concerning Christ; in 2 Pet. 3:11, the word is in the plural, signifying acts of "godliness."

2. *theosebeia* (2317) denotes "the fear or reverence of God," from *theos*, "god," and *sebomai* (see No. 1), 1 Tim. 2:10.

B. Adjective.

eusebes (2152), akin to A, No. 1, denotes "pious, devout, godly," indicating reverence manifested in actions; it is rendered "godly" in 2 Pet. 2:9.

C. Adverb.

eusebos (2153) denotes "piously, godly"; it is used with the verb "to live" (of manner of life) in 2 Tim. 3:12; Titus 2:12.

GOLD, GOLDEN

Old Testament

zahab (2091), "gold," a precious metal, often used to make ornaments, or as units of money. *zahab* can refer to "gold ore," or "gold in its raw state," Gen. 2:11; Exod. 25:11; Job 23:10; or in bars, pieces, or lumps, Gen. 13:2; Job 28:17; Ezek. 27:22. *zahab* is also used for the color "gold," Zech. 4:12.

New Testament

A. Nouns.

1. *chrusos* (5557) is used (a) of "coin," Matt. 10:9; Jas. 5:3; (b) of "ornaments," Matt. 23:16, 17; Jas. 5:3 (perhaps both coin and ornaments); Rev. 18:12; some mss. have it instead of No. 2 in 1 Cor. 3:12; (c) of "images," Acts 17:29; (d) of "the metal in general," Matt. 2:11; Rev. 9:7 (some mss. have it in Rev. 18:16).

2. *chrusion* (5553), a diminutive of No. 1, is used (a) of "coin," primarily smaller than those in No. 1 (a), Acts 3:6; 20:33; 1 Pet. 1:18; (b) of "ornaments," 1 Pet. 3:3, and the following (in which some mss. have No. 1), 1 Tim. 2:9; Rev. 17:4; 18:16; (c) of "the metal in general," Heb. 9:4; 1 Pet. 1:7; Rev. 21:18, 21; metaphorically, (d) of "sound doctrine and its effects," 1 Cor. 3:12; (e) of "righteousness of life and conduct," Rev. 3:18.

B. Adjective.

chruseos (5552) denotes "golden," i.e., made of, or overlaid with, gold, 2 Tim. 2:20; Heb. 9:4, and fifteen times in the Apocalypse.

GOOD, GOODLY, GOODNESS
Old Testament

A. Adjective.

tob (2896), "good; favorable; festive; pleasing; pleasant; well; better; right; best." This adjective denotes "good" in every sense of that word. For example, *tob* is used in the sense "pleasant" or "delightful," Gen. 49:15; or as in Gen. 40:16, "favorable" or "in one's favor." God is described as One who is "good," or One who gives "delight" and "pleasure," Ps. 73:28. *tob* often qualifies a common object or activity. When the word is used in this sense, no ethical overtones are intended, 1 Sam. 19:4; 25:15; 1 Kings 12:7; Gen. 2:18. Elsewhere *tob* is applied to an evaluation of one's well-being or of the well-being of a situation or thing, Gen. 1:4.

tob is used to describe land and agriculture, Exod. 3:8; 1 Sam. 8:14. *tob* is used to describe men or women. Sometimes it is used of an "elite corps" of people, 1 Sam. 8:16, 27. In other passages, *tob* describes physical appearance, Gen. 24:16. Dying "at a good old age" describes "advanced age," rather than moral accomplishment, but a time when due to divine blessings one is fulfilled and satisfied, Gen. 15:15. *tob* indicates that a given word, act, or circumstance contributes positively to the condition of a situation, Gen. 40:16; The judgment may be ethical, Neh. 5:9. The word may also represent "agreement" or "concurrence," Gen. 24:50.

B. Verbs.

yatab (3190), "to be good, do well, be glad, please, do good," This word means to do an activity which is favorable to a circumstance, of quality deemed of value, or of what is right according to a standard: Gen. 4:7; "to deal well," Exod. 1:20; "to play [a musical instrument] well," 1 Sam. 16:17; "to adorn, make beautiful," 2 Kings 9:30; and "to inquire diligently," Deut. 17:4.

tob (2896), "good." This word in Hebrew has about the same very broad range of meanings as it does in English. It means generally, "that which is valuable according to a standard, be it things, or events, Gen. 1:4,31. As a positive term, with a basic meaning of "good," with a focus on the emotional attitude which one responds to a favorable circumstance; the word is used to express many nuances of that which is "good," such as a "glad" heart, Judg. 18:20, "pleasing," words Gen. 34:18, and a "cheerful" face, Prov. 15:13.

New Testament

A. Adjectives.

1. *agathos* (18) describes that which, being "good" in its character or constitution, is beneficial in its effect; it is used (a) of things physical, e.g., a tree, Matt. 7:17; ground, Luke 8:8; (b) in a moral

sense, frequently of persons and things. God is essentially, absolutely and consummately "good," Matt. 19:17; Mark 10:18; Luke 18:19. To certain persons the word is applied in Matt. 20:15; 25:21, 23; Luke 19:17; 23:50; John 7:12; Acts 11:24; Titus 2:5; in a general application, Matt. 5:45; 12:35; Luke 6:45; Rom. 5:7; 1 Pet. 2:18.

The neuter of the adjective with the definite article signifies that which is "good," lit., "the good," as being morally honorable, pleasing to God, and therefore beneficial. Christians are to prove it, Rom. 12:2; to cleave to it, 12:9; to do it, 13:3; Gal. 6:10; 1 Pet. 3:11 (here, and here only, the article is absent); John 5:29 (here, the neuter plural is used, "the good things"); to work it, Rom. 2:10; Eph. 4:28; 6:8; to follow after it, 1 Thess. 5:15; to be zealous of it, 1 Pet. 3:13; to imitate it, 3 John 11; to overcome evil with it, Rom. 12:21. Governmental authorities are ministers of "good," i.e., that which is salutary, suited to the course of human affairs, Rom. 13:4. In Philem. 14, "thy goodness," RV (lit., "thy good"), means "thy benefit." As to Matt. 19:17, "why askest thou Me concerning that which is good?" the RV follows the most ancient mss.

The neuter plural is also used of material "goods," riches, etc., Luke 1:53; 12:18, 19; 16:25; Gal. 6:6 (of temporal supplies); in Rom. 10:15; Heb. 9:11; 10:1, the "good" things are the benefits provided through the sacrifice of Christ, in regard both to those conferred through the gospel and to those of the coming messianic kingdom.

2. *kalos* (2570) denotes that which is intrinsically "good," and so, "goodly, fair, beautiful," as (a) of that which is well adapted to its circumstances or ends, e.g., fruit, Matt. 3:10; a tree, 12:33; ground, 13:8, 23; fish, 13:48; the Law, Rom. 7:16; 1 Tim. 1:8; every creature of God, 1 Tim. 4:4; a faithful minister of Christ and the doctrine he teaches, 4:6; (b) of that which is ethically good, right, noble, honorable e.g., Gal. 4:18; 1 Tim. 5:10, 25; 6:18; Titus 2:7, 14; 3:8, 14. The word does not occur in the Apocalypse, nor indeed after 1 Peter.

Christians are to "take thought for things honorable" (*kalos*), 2 Cor. 8:21, RV; to do that which is honorable, 13:7; not to be weary in well doing, Gal. 6:9; to hold fast "that which is good," 1 Thess. 5:21; to be zealous of good works, Titus 2:14; to maintain them, 3:8; to provoke to them, Heb. 10:24; to bear testimony by them, 1 Pet. 2:12. *kalos* and *agathos* occur together in Luke 8:15; Rom. 7:18; 1 Thess. 5:15.

3. *chrestos* (5543), said of things, "that which is pleasant," said of persons, "kindly, gracious," is rendered "good" in 1 Cor. 15:33, "goodness" in Rom 2:4.

B. Nouns.

1. *chrestotes* (5544), akin to A, No. 3, denotes "goodness" (a) in the sense of what is upright, righteous, Rom. 3:12 (translated "good"); (b) in the sense of kindness of heart or act, said of God,

Rom. 2:4; 11:22 (thrice); Eph. 2:7 ("kindness"); Titus 3:4 ("kindness"); said of believers and rendered "kindness," 2 Cor. 6:6; Col. 3:12; Gal. 5:22 (RV; KJV, "gentleness"). It signifies "not merely goodness as a quality, rather it is goodness in action, goodness expressing itself in deeds; yet not goodness expressing itself in indignation against sin, for it is contrasted with severity in Rom. 11:22, but in grace and tenderness and compassion."

2. *agathosune* (19), "goodness," signifies that moral quality which is described by the adjective *agathos* (see A, No. 1). It is used, in the NT, of regenerate persons, Rom. 15:14; Gal. 5:22; Eph. 5:9; 2 Thess. 1:11; in the last, the phrase "every desire of goodness" (RV; the addition of "His" in the KJV is an interpolation; there is no pronoun in the original) may be either subjective, i.e., desire characterized by "goodness," "good" desire, or objective, i.e., desire after "goodness," to be and do good.

Trench, following Jerome, distinguishes between **chrestotes** and **agathosune** in that the former describes the kindlier aspects of "goodness," Luke 7:37-50, the latter includes also the sterner qualities by which doing "good" to others is not necessarily by gentle means, Matt. 21:12, 13; 23:13-29.

3. *eupoiia* (2140), "beneficence, doing good," is translated as a verb in Heb. 13:16, "to do good."

C. Adverbs.

1. *kalos* (2573), "well, finely," is used in some mss. in Matt. 5:44, with *poieo*, "to do," and translated "do good." In Jas. 2:3 it is rendered "in a good place" (KJV marg., "well" or "seemly").

2. *eu* (2095), "well," used with *poieo*, is translated "do...good" in Mark 14:7.

D. Verbs (to do, or be, good).

1. *agathopoieo* (15), from A, No. 1, and *poieo*, "to do," is used (a) in a general way, "to do well," 1 Pet. 2:15, 20; 3:6, 17; 3 John 11; (b) with pointed reference "to the benefit of another," Luke 6:9, 33, 35; in Mark 3:4 the parts of the word are separated in some mss. Some mss. have it in Acts 14:17, for No. 2.

2. *agathourgeo* (14), for *agathoergeo*, "to do good" (from A, No. 1, and *ergon*, "a work"), is used in Acts 14:17 (in the best mss.; see No. 1), where it is said of God's beneficence towards man, and 1 Tim. 6:18, where it is enjoined upon the rich.

3. *euergeteo* (2109), "to bestow a benefit, to do good" (*eu*, "well," and a verbal form akin to *ergon*), is used in Acts 10:38.

GOODMAN

oikodespotes (3617) denotes "the master of a house," "a householder." It occurs only in the Synoptics, and there 12 times. It is rendered "goodman" in Luke 22:11, where "of the house" is put separately; in Matt. 20:11, where the KJV has "the goodman of the house" for the one word; in 24:43; Mark 14:14; Luke 12:39.

GOODS

1. For the neuter plural of *agathos*, used as a noun, "goods," see Luke 12:18, 19, where alone this word is so rendered.

2. *huparxis* (5223), primarily, "subsistence," then, "substance, property, goods" (akin to *huparcho*, "to exist, be, belong to"), is translated "goods" in Acts 2:45; "possession." RV (KJV, "substance") in Heb. 10:34.

3. *bios* (979), which denotes (a) "life, lifetime," (b) "livelihood, living, means of living," is translated "goods" in 1 John 3:17, RV (KJV, "good").

4. *skeuos* (4632), "a vessel," denotes "goods" in Matt. 12:29; Mark 3:27; Luke 17:31, RV (KJV, stuff).

GORGEOUS, GORGEOUSLY

lampros (2986), "bright, splendid," is rendered "gorgeous" in Luke 23:11 of the apparel in which Herod and his soldiers arrayed Christ.

GOSPEL (Noun and Verb: to preach)

A. Noun.

euangelion (2098) originally denoted a reward for good tidings; later, the idea of reward dropped, and the word stood for "the good news" itself. The Eng. word "gospel," i.e. "good message," is the equivalent of *euangelion* (Eng., "evangel"). In the NT it denotes the "good tidings" of the kingdom of God and of salvation through Christ, to be received by faith, on the basis of His expiatory death, His burial, resurrection, and ascension, e.g., Acts 15:7; 20:24; 1 Pet. 4:17. Apart from those references and those in the gospels of Matthew and Mark, and Rev. 14:6, the noun is confined to Paul's epistles. The apostle uses it of two associated yet distinct things, (a) of the basic facts of the death, burial and resurrection of Christ, e.g., 1 Cor. 15:1-3; (b) of the interpretation of these facts, e.g., Rom. 2:16; Gal. 1:7, 11; 2:2; in (i.) the "gospel" is viewed historically, in (ii.) doctrinally, with reference to the interpretation of the facts, as is sometimes indicated by the context.

The following phrases describe the subjects or nature or purport of the message; it is the "gospel" of God, Mark 1:14; Rom. 1:1; 15:16; 2 Cor. 11:7; 1 Thess. 2:2, 9; 1 Pet. 4:17; God, concerning His Son, Rom. 1:1-3; His Son, Rom. 1:9; Jesus Christ, the Son of God, Mark 1:1; our Lord Jesus, 2 Thess. 1:8; Christ, Rom. 15:19, etc.; the glory of Christ, 2 Cor. 4:4; the grace of God, Acts 20:24; the glory of the blessed God, 1 Tim. 1:11; your salvation, Eph. 1:13; peace, Eph. 6:15. Cf. also "the gospel of the Kingdom," Matt. 4:23; 9:35; 24:14;

"an eternal gospel," Rev. 14:6.

In Gal. 2:14, "the truth of the gospel" denotes, not the true "gospel," but the true teaching of it, in contrast to perversions of it.

The following expressions are used in connection with the "gospel": (a) with regard to its testimony: (1) *kerusso*, "to preach it as a herald," e.g., Matt. 4:23; Gal. 2:2; (2) *laleo*, "to speak," 1 Thess. 2:2; (3) *diamarturomai*, "to testify (thoroughly)," Acts 20:24; (4) *eu-angelizo*, "to preach," e.g., 1 Cor. 15:1; 2 Cor. 11:7; Gal. 1:11 (see B, No. 1 below); (5) *katangello*, "to proclaim," 1 Cor. 9:14; (6) *douleuo eis*, "to serve unto" ("in furtherance of"), Phil. 2:22; (7) *sunathleo en*, "to labor with in," Phil. 4:3; (8) *hierourgeo*, "to minister," Rom. 15:16; (9) *pleroo*, "to preach fully," Rom. 15:19; (10) *sunkakopatheo*, "to suffer hardship with," 2 Tim. 1:8; (b) with regard to its reception or otherwise: *dechomai*, "to receive," 2 Cor. 11:4; *hupakouo*, "to hearken to, or obey," Rom. 10:16; 2 Thess. 1:8; *pisteuo en*, "to believe in," Mark 1:15; *metastrepho*, "to pervert," Gal. 1:7.

B. Verbs.

1. *euangelizo* (*2097*), "to bring or announce glad tidings" (Eng., "evangelize"), is used (a) in the active voice in Rev. 10:7 ("declared") and 14:6 ("to proclaim," RV, KJV, "to preach"); (b) in the passive voice, of matters to be proclaimed as "glad tidings," Luke 16:16; Gal. 1:11; 1 Pet. 1:25; of persons to whom the proclamation is made, Matt. 11:5; Luke 7:22; Heb. 4:2, 6; 1 Pet. 4:6; (c) in the middle voice, especially of the message of salvation, with a personal object, either of the person preached, e.g., Acts 5:42; 11:20; Gal. 1:16, or, with a preposition, of the persons evangelized, e.g., Acts 13:32, "declare glad tidings"; Rom. 1:15; Gal. 1:8; with an impersonal object, e.g., "the word," Acts 8:4; "good tidings," 8:12; "the word of the Lord," 15:35; "the gospel," 1 Cor. 15:1; 2 Cor. 11:7; "the faith," Gal. 1:23; "peace," Eph. 2:17; "the unsearchable riches of Christ," 3:8.

2. *proeuangelizomai* (*4283*), "to announce glad tidings beforehand," is used in Gal. 3:8.

GOVERNMENT

kubernesis (*2941*), from *kubernao*, "to guide" (whence Eng., "govern"), denotes (a) "steering, pilotage"; (b) metaphorically, "governments or governings," said of those who act as guides in a local church, 1 Cor. 12:28.

GOVERNOR

A. Nouns.

1. *hegemon* (*2232*) is a term used (a) for "rulers" generally, Mark 13:9; 1 Pet. 2:14; translated "princes" (i.e., leaders) in Matt. 2:6; (b) for the Roman procurators, referring in the gospels to Pontius Pilate, e.g., Matt. 27:2; Luke 20:20 (so designated by Tacitus, *Annals,*

xv. 44); to Felix, Acts 23:26. Technically the procurator was a financial official under a proconsul or propraetor, for collecting the imperial revenues, but entrusted also with magisterial powers for decisions of questions relative to the revenues. In certain provinces, of which Judea was one (the procurator of which was dependent on the legate of Syria), he was the general administrator and supreme judge, with sole power of life and death. Such a governor was a person of high social standing. Felix, however, was an ex-slave, a freedman, and his appointment to Judea could not but be regarded by the Jews as an insult to the nation. The headquarters of the governor of Judea was Caesarea, which was made a garrison town.

2. *ethnarches* (*1481*), "an ethnarch," lit. "a ruler of a nation" (*ethnos*, "a people," *arche*, "rule"), is translated "governor" in 2 Cor. 11:32; it describes normally the ruler of a nation possessed of separate laws and customs among those of a different race. Eventually it denoted a ruler of a province, superior to a tetrarch, but inferior to a king (e.g., Aretas).

3. *oikonomos* (*3623*), lit., "one who rules a house" (*oikos*, "a house," *nomos*, "a law"), Gal. 4:2, denotes a superior servant responsible for the family housekeeping, the direction of other servants, and the care of the children under age.

4. *architriklinos* (*755*), from *arche*, "rule," and *triklinos*, "a room with three couches," denotes "the ruler of a feast," John 2:8, RV (KJV, "the governor of the feast"), a man appointed to see that the table and couches were duly placed and the courses arranged, and to taste the food and wine.

B. Verbs.

1. *hegeomai* (*2233*), akin to A, No. 1, is used in the present participle to denote "a governor," lit., "(one) governing," Matt. 2:6; Acts 7:10.

2. *hegemoneuo* (*2230*), to be a *hegemon*, "to lead the way," came to signify to be "a governor of a province"; it is used of Quirinius, governor of Syria, Luke 2:2.

GRACE

1. *charis* (*5485*) has various uses, (a) objective, that which bestows or occasions pleasure, delight, or causes favorable regard; it is applied, e.g., to beauty, or gracefulness of person, Luke 2:40; act, 2 Cor. 8:6, or speech, Luke 4:22, RV, "words of grace" (KJV, "gracious words"); Col. 4:6; (b) subjective, (1) on the part of the bestower, the friendly disposition from which the kindly act proceeds, graciousness, loving-kindness, goodwill generally, e.g., Acts 7:10; especially with reference to the divine favor or "grace," e.g., Acts 14:26; in this respect there is stress on its freeness and universality, its spontaneous character, as in the case of God's re-

demptive mercy, and the pleasure or joy He designs for the recipient; thus it is set in contrast with debt, Rom. 4:4, 16, with works, 11:6, and with law, John 1:17; see also, e.g., Rom. 6:14, 15; Gal. 5:4; (2) on the part of the receiver, a sense of the favor bestowed, a feeling of gratitude, e.g., Rom. 6:17 ("thanks"); in this respect it sometimes signifies "to be thankful," e.g., Luke 17:9 ("doth he thank the servant?" lit., "hath he thanks to"); 1 Tim. 1:12; (c) in another objective sense, the effect of "grace," the spiritual state of those who have experienced its exercise, whether (1) a state of "grace," e.g., Rom. 5:2; 1 Pet. 5:12; 2 Pet. 3:18, or (2) a proof thereof in practical effects, deeds of "grace," e.g., 1 Cor. 16:3, RV, "bounty" (KJV, "liberality"); 2 Cor. 8:6, 19 (in 2 Cor. 9:8 it means the sum of earthly blessings); the power and equipment for ministry, e.g., Rom. 1:5; 12:6; 15:15; 1 Cor. 3:10; Gal. 2:9; Eph. 3:2, 7.

To be in favor with is to find "grace" with, e.g., Acts 2:47; hence it appears in this sense at the beginning and the end of several epistles, where the writer desires "grace" from God for the readers, e.g., Rom. 1:7; 1 Cor. 1:3; in this respect it is connected with the imperative mood of the word *chairo*, "to rejoice," a mode of greeting among Greeks, e.g., Acts 15:23; Jas. 1:1 (marg.); 2 John 10, 11, RV, "greeting" (KJV, "God speed").

The fact that "grace" is received both from God the Father, 2 Cor. 1:12, and from Christ, Gal. 1:6; Rom. 5:15 (where both are mentioned), is a testimony to the deity of Christ. See also 2 Thess. 1:12, where the phrase "according to the grace of our God and the Lord Jesus Christ" is to be taken with each of the preceding clauses, "in you," and ye in Him."

In Jas. 4:6, "But He giveth more grace" (Greek, "a greater grace," RV, marg.), the statement is to be taken in connection with the preceding verse, which contains two remonstrating, rhetorical questions, "Think ye that the Scripture speaketh in vain?" and "Doth the Spirit (the Holy Spirit) which He made to dwell in us long unto envying?" (see the RV). The implied answer to each is "it cannot be so." Accordingly, if those who are acting so flagrantly, as if it were so, will listen to the Scripture instead of letting it speak in vain, and will act so that the Holy Spirit may have His way within, God will give even "a greater grace," namely, all that follows from humbleness and from turning away from the world.

2. *euprepeia* (*2143*), "comeliness, goodly appearance," is said of the outward appearance of the flower of the grass, Jas. 1:11.

GRACIOUS, TO BE GRACIOUS, SHOW FAVOR

Old Testament

A. Verb.

chanan (2603), "to be gracious, considerate; to show favor," Gen. 33:5. *chanan* may express "generosity," a gift from the heart, Ps.

37:21. God especially is the source of undeserved "favor," Gen. 33:11, and He is asked repeatedly for such "gracious" acts as only He can do, Num. 6:25; Gen. 43:29. God's "favor" is especially seen in His deliverance from one's enemies or surrounding evils, Ps. 77:9; Amos 5:15. However, God extends His "graciousness" in His own sovereign way and will, to whomever He chooses, Exod. 33:19.

B. Noun.

chen (2580), "favor; grace." The basic meaning of *chen* is "favor." Whatever is "pleasant and agreeable" can be described by this word. When a woman is said to have *chen*, she is a "gracious" woman, Prov. 11:16; or the word may have the negative association of being "beautiful without sense," Prov. 31:30. A person's speech may be characterized by "graciousness," Prov. 22:11; cf. Ps. 45:2. *chen* also denotes the response to whatever is "agreeable," Gen. 39:21; Exod. 3:21; Ruth 2:10.

C. Adjective.

channun (2587), "gracious," Exod. 34:6.

New Testament

chrestos (5543) is rendered "gracious" in 1 Pet. 2:3, as an attribute of the Lord.

GRAVE (Noun)

1. *mnemeion* (3419) primarily denotes "a memorial" (akin to *mnaomai*, "to remember"), then, "a monument" (the significance of the word rendered "tombs," KJV, "sepulchres," in Luke 11:47), anything done to preserve the memory of things and persons; it usually denotes a tomb, and is translated either "tomb" or "sepulchre" or "grave." Apart from the Gospels, it is found only in Acts 13:29. Among the Hebrews it was generally a cavern, closed by a door or stone, often decorated. Cf. Matt. 23:29.

2. *mnema* (3418), akin to No. 1, like which it signified "a memorial" or "record of a thing or a dead person," then "a sepulchral monument," and hence "a tomb"; it is rendered "graves" in the KJV of Rev. 11:9 (RV, "a tomb"); "tomb" or "tombs," Mark 5:3, 5 (some mss. have No. 1, as in 15:46, KJV, "sepulchre") and 16:2 (KJV, "sepulchre"); Luke 8:27; Acts 2:29 and 7:16 (KJV, "sepulchre").

GRAVE (Adjective)

semnos (4518) first denoted "reverend, august, venerable" (akin to *sebomai*, "to reverence"); then, "serious, grave," whether of persons, 1 Tim. 3:8, 11 (deacons and their wives); Titus 2:2 (aged men); or things, Phil. 4:8, RV, "honorable" (marg., "reverend"), KJV, "honest."

GRAVEN

charagma (5480), from *charasso*, "to engrave" (akin to *charakter*, "an impress," RV, marg., of Heb. 1:3), denotes (a) "a mark" or "stamp," e.g., Rev. 13:16, 17; 14:9, 11; 16:2; 19:20; 20:4; 15:2 in some mss.; (b) "a thing graven," Acts 17:29.

GREAT

Old Testament

A. Verbs.

kabed (3515), "to be heavy, weighty, burdensome, dull, honored, glorious." *kabed* basically means to be "heavy," or "weighty," so "rich," Gen. 13:2; then, by figurative extension, "being honored" or "glorious." The word includes negative as well as positive aspects. Thus, calamity is "heavier than the sand of the sea," Job 6:3, and the hand of God is "very heavy" in punishing the Philistines, 1 Sam. 5:11. "To honor" or "glorify" anything is to add something which it does not have in itself, or that which others can give. Children are commanded to "honor" their parents, Exod. 20:12; Deut. 5:16; Balak promised "honor" to Balaam, Num. 22:17.

kabed is also the Hebrew word for "liver," Exod. 29:13, an organ of the body.

rabab (7231), "to be numerous, great, large, powerful." *rabab* can also mean "to be great" in size, prestige, or power, or number, cf. Gen. 18:20; Job 33:12; Ps. 49:16. With a subject indicating time, this verb implies "lengthening," Gen. 38:12, and with special subjects the word may imply "extension of space," Deut. 14:24.

B. Nouns.

rob (7230), "multitude; abundance." This noun has numerical implications apparent in its first biblical appearance, Gen. 16:10. When applied to time or distance, *rob* indicates a "large amount" or "long," Josh. 9:13. In several passages, *rob* means "great" or "greatness," Isa. 63:1.

rab (7227), "chief." This word is a transliteration of the Akkadian *rab*, an indication of "military rank" similar to our word *general*, Jeremiah 39:9-13.

C. Adjective.

rab (7227), "many; great; large; prestigious; powerful." First, this word represents plurality in number or amount, whether applied to people or to things. *rab* is applied to people in Gen. 26:14; or things, 13:6; or groups, Exod. 5:5; or collections or masses, Num. 20:11; or land, 1 Sam. 26:13. The phrase "many waters" is a fixed phrase meaning the "sea," Isa. 23:2-3. Used in conjunction with "days" or "years," *rab* means "long," Gen. 21:34.

New Testament

1. **megas** (*3173*) is used (a) of external form, size, measure, e.g., of a stone, Matt. 27:60; fish, John 21:11; (b) of degree and intensity, e.g., of fear, Mark 4:41; wind, John 6:18; Rev. 6:13, RV, "great" (KJV, "mighty"); of a circumstance, 1 Cor. 9:11; 2 Cor. 11:15; in Rev. 5:2, 12, the RV has "great" (KJV, "loud"), of a voice; (c) of rank, whether of persons, e.g., God, Titus 2:13; Christ as a "great Priest," Heb. 10:21, RV; Diana, Acts 19:27, Simon Magus, Acts 8:9 "(some) great one"; in the plural "great ones," Matt. 20:25; Mark 10:42, those who hold positions of authority in gentile nations; or of things, e.g., a mystery, Eph. 5:32.

2. **polus** (*4183*), "much, many, great," is used of number, e.g., Luke 5:6; Acts 11:21; degree, e.g., of harvest, Matt. 9:37; mercy, 1 Pet. 1:3, RV "great" (KJV, "abundant"); glory, Matt. 24:30; joy, Philem. 7, RV, "much" (KJV, "great"); peace, Acts 24:2. The best mss. have it in Acts 8:8 (RV, "much"), of joy.

3. **hikanos** (*2425*), lit., "reaching to" (from **hikano**, "to reach"), denotes "sufficient, competent, fit," and is sometimes rendered "great," e.g., of number (of people), Mark 10:46; of degree (of light), Acts 22:6.

4. **helikos** (*2245*) primarily denotes "as big as, as old as" (akin to **helikia**, "an age"); then, as an indirect interrogation, "what, what size, how great, how small" (the context determines the meaning), said of a spiritual conflict, Col. 2:1, KJV, "what great (conflict) I have"; RV, "how greatly (I strive)"; of much wood as kindled by a little fire, Jas. 3:5 (twice in the best mss.), "how much (wood is kindled by) how small (a fire)," RV, said metaphorically of the use of the tongue. Some mss. have No. 4 in Gal. 6:11; the most authentic have No. 5.

5. **pelikos** (*4080*), primarily a direct interrogative, "how large? how great?" is used in exclamations, indicating magnitude, like No. 4 (No. 6 indicates quantity), in Gal. 6:11, of letter characters; in Heb. 7:4, metaphorically, of the distinguished character of Melchizedek.

6. **posos** (*4214*), an adjective of number, magnitude, degree etc., is rendered "how great" in Matt. 6:23.

7. **hosos** (*3745*), "how much, how many," is used in the neuter plural to signify how great things, Mark 5:19, 20; Luke 8:39 (twice); Acts 9:16, KJV, "how many things"); in Rev. 21:16 (in the best mss.), "as great as," RV (KJV, "as large as," said of length).

8. **tosoutos** (*5118*), "so great, so many, so much," of quantity, size, etc., is rendered "so great," in Matt. 8:10, and Luke 7:9, of faith; Matt. 15:33, of a multitude; Heb. 12:1, of a cloud of witnesses; Rev. 18:17, of riches.

9. **telikoutos** (*5082*), "so great," is used in the NT of things only, a death, 2 Cor. 1:10; salvation, Heb. 2:3; ships, Jas. 3:4; an earth-

quake, Rev. 16:18, KJV, "so mighty," corrected in the RV to "so great."

GREATER

1. *meizon* (3187) is the comparative degree of *megas*, e.g., Matt. 11:11; in Matt. 13:32, the RV rightly has "greater than" (KJV, "the greatest among"); 23:17; in Luke 22:26, RV, "the greater (among you)"·(KJV, "greatest"); in Jas. 3:1, RV, "the heavier (marg., greater) judgment" (KJV, "the greater condemnation"); it is used in the neuter plural in John 1:50, "greater things"; in 14:12, "greater works" (lit., "greater things"); in 1 Cor. 12:31, RV, "the greater," KJV, "the best."

2. *meizoteros* (3186), a double comparative of *megas* (cf. No. 1, above), is used in 3 John 4, of joy.

3. *pleion* (4119), the comparative of *polus*, is used (a) as an adjective, "greater, more," e.g., Acts 15:28; (b) as a noun, e.g., Matt. 12:41, "a greater (than Jonah)"; v. 42, "a greater (than Solomon)"; in these instances the neuter *pleion*, "something greater," is "a fixed or stereotyped form" of the word; in 1 Cor. 15:6, "the greater part" (masculine plural); (c) as an adverb, e.g., Matt. 5:20, lit., "(except your righteousness abound) more greatly (than of scribes and Pharisees)"; so 26:53, "more"; Luke 9:13.

4. *perissoteros* (4055), the comparative of *perissos*, "over and above, abundant," signifies "more abundant, greater," e.g., of condemnation, Mark 12:40; Luke 20:47.

GREATEST

1. *megas* (3173), "the greatest," in Acts 8:10 and Heb. 8:11. The whole phrase, lit., "from small to great," is equivalent to the Eng. idiom "one and all."

2. *meizon* (3187), the comparative of No. 1, is sometimes translated "greatest"; besides the two cases given under GREATER, No. 1, where the RV corrects the KJV, "greatest" to "greater" (Matt 13:32 and Luke 22:26), the RV itself has "greatest" for this comparative in the following, and relegates "greater" to the margin Matt. 18:1, 4; 23:11; Mark 9:34; Luke 9:46; 22:24.

GREEN

1. *chloros* (5515), akin to *chloe*, "tender foliage" (cf. the name "Chloe," 1 Cor. 1:11, and Eng., "chlorine"), denotes (a) "pale green," the color of young grass, Mark 6:39; Rev. 8:7; 9:4, "green thing"; hence, (b) "pale," Rev. 6:8, the color of the horse whose rider's name is Death.

2. *hugros* (5200) denotes "wet, moist" (the opposite of *xeros*, "dry"); said of wood, sappy, "green," Luke 23:31, i.e., if they thus by the fire of their wrath treated Christ, the guiltless, holy, the fruit-

ful, what would be the fate of the perpetrators, who were like the dry wood, exposed to the fire of divine wrath.

GREET, GREETING

A. Verbs.

1. *aspazomai* (782) signifies "to greet welcome," or "salute." In the KJV it is chiefly rendered by either of the verbs "to greet" or "to salute." In two passages the renderings vary otherwise; in Acts 20:1, of bidding farewell, KJV, "embraced them"; in Heb. 11:13, of welcoming promises, KJV, "embraced," RV, "greeted." The verb is used as a technical term for conveying "greetings" at the close of a letter, often by an amanuensis, e.g., Rom. 16:22, the only instance of the use of the first person in this respect in the NT; see also 1 Cor. 16:19, 20; 2 Cor. 13:13; Phil. 4:22; Col. 4:10-15; 1 Thess. 5:26; 2 Tim. 4:21; Titus 3:15; Philem. 23; Heb. 13:24; 1 Pet. 5:13, 14; 2 John 13. This special use is largely illustrated in the papyri, one example of this showing how keenly the absence of the greeting was felt.

2. *chairo* (5463), "to rejoice," is thrice used as a formula of salutation in the NT; in Acts 15:23, KJV, "send greeting," RV, "greeting"; so 23:26; Jas. 1:1. In 2 John 10, 11, the RV substitutes the phrase (to give) "greeting," for the KJV (to bid) "God speed."

B. Noun.

aspamos (783), a salutation, is always so rendered in the RV; KJV, "greetings" in Matt. 23:7; Luke 11:43; 20:46, it is used (a) orally in those instances and in Mark 12:38; Luke 1:29, 41, 44; (b) in written salutations, 1 Cor. 16:21 (cf. A, No. 1, in v. 20); Col. 4:18; 2 Thess. 3:17.

GRIEF, GRIEVE

A. Noun.

lupe (3077) signifies "pain," of body or mind; it is used in the plural in 1 Pet. 2:19 only, RV, "griefs" (KJV, "grief"); here, however, it stands, by metonymy, for "things that cause sorrow, grievances"; hence Tyndale's rendering, "grief," for Wycliffe's "sorews"; everywhere else it is rendered "sorrow," except in Heb. 12:11, where it is translated "grievous" (lit., "of grief").

B. Verbs.

1. *lupeo* (3076), akin to A, denotes (a), in the active voice, "to cause pain, or grief, to distress, grieve," e.g., 2 Cor. 2:2 (twice, active and passive voices); v. 5 (twice), RV, "hath caused sorrow" (KJV, "have caused grief," and "grieved"); 7:8, "made (you) sorry"; Eph. 4:30, of grieving the Holy Spirit of God (as indwelling the believer); (b) in the passive voice, "to be grieved, to be made sorry, to

be sorry, sorrowful," e.g., Matt. 14:9, RV, "(the king) was grieved" (KJV, "was sorry"); Mark 10:22, RV, "(went away) sorrowful" (KJV, "grieved"); John 21:17, "(Peter) was grieved," Rom. 14:15, "(if...thy brother) is grieved"; 2 Cor. 2:4, "(not that) ye should be made sorry," RV, KJV, "ye should be grieved."

2. *sunlupeo* (*4818*), or *sullupeo*, is used in the passive voice in Mark 3:5, "to be grieved" or afflicted together with a person, said of Christ's "grief" at the hardness of heart of those who criticized His healing on the Sabbath day; it here seems to suggest the sympathetic nature of His grief because of their self-injury. Some suggest that the *sun* indicates the mingling of "grief" with His anger.

3. *stenazo* (*4727*), "to groan" (of an inward, unexpressed feeling of sorrow), is translated "with grief" in Heb. 13:17 (marg. "groaning"). It is rendered "sighed" in Mark 7:34; "groan," in Rom. 8:23; 2 Cor. 5:2, 4; "murmur," in Jas. 5:9, RV (KJV, "grudge").

GRIEVOUS, GRIEVOUSLY

A. Adjectives.

1. *barus* (*926*) denotes "heavy, burdensome"; it is always used metaphorically in the NT, and is translated "heavy" in Matt. 23:4, of Pharisaical ordinances; in the comparative degree "weightier," 23:23, of the law of God; "grievous," metaphorically of wolves, in Acts 20:29; of charges, 25:7; negatively of God's commandments, 1 John 5:3 (causing a burden on him who fulfills them); in 2 Cor. 10:10, "weighty," of Paul's letters.

2. *poneros* (*4190*), "painful, bad," is translated "grievous" in Rev. 16:2, of a sore inflicted retributively.

3. *dusbastaktos* (*1419*), "hard to be borne" (from *dus*, an inseparable prefix, like Eng. "mis-," and "un-," indicating "difficulty, injuriousness, opposition," etc., and *bastazo*, "to bear"), is used in Luke 11:46 and, in some mss., in Matt. 23:4, "grievous to be borne"; in the latter the RV marg. has "many ancient authorities omit."

4. *chalepos* (*5467*), "hard," signifies (a) "hard to deal with," Matt. 8:28; (b) "hard to bear, grievous," 2 Tim. 3:1, RV, "grievous" (KJV, "perilous"), said of a characteristic of the last days of this age.

B. Adverbs.

1. *deinos* (*1171*), akin to *deos*, "fear," signifies (a) "terribly," Matt. 8:6, "grievously (tormented)"; (b) "vehemently," Luke 11:53.

2. *kakos* (*2560*), "badly, ill," is translated "grievously (vexed)," in Matt. 15:22.

GROAN, GROANING

A. Verbs.

1. *embrimaomai* (*1690*), from *en*, "in," and *brime*, "strength," is rendered "groaned" in John 11:33 (preferable to the RV marg.,

"He had indignation"); so in v. 38. The Lord was deeply moved doubtless with the combination of circumstances, present and in the immediate future. Indignation does not here seem to express His feelings.

2. *stenazo* (4727), "groan," Mark 7:34.

3. *sustenazo* (4959), "to groan together" (*sun*, "with," and No. 2) is used of the Creation in Rom. 8:22. In v. 23, No. 2 is used..

B. Noun.

stenagmos (4726), akin to A No. 2, is used in Acts 7:34.

GROSS (to wax)

pachuno (3975), from *pachus*, "thick," signifies "to thicken, fatten"; in the passive voice, "to grow fat"; metaphorically said of the heart, to wax gross or dull, Matt. 13:15; Acts 28:27.

GROUND, GROUNDED

A. Nouns.

1. *ge* (1093), "the earth, land," etc., often denotes "the ground," e.g., Matt. 10:29; Mark 8:6.

2. *edaphos* (1475), "a bottom, base," is used of the "ground" in Acts 22:7, suggestive of that which is level and hard. Cf. B, No. 1, below.

3. *chora* (5561), "land, country," is used of property, "ground," in Luke 12:16, "the ground (of a certain rich man)."

4. *chorion* (5564), a diminutive of No. 3, "a piece of land, a place, estate," is translated "parcel of ground" in John 4:5.

5. *hedraioma* (1477), "a support, bulwark, stay" (from *hedraios*, "steadfast, firm"; from *hedra*, "a seat"), is translated "ground" in 1 Tim. 3:15 (said of a local church); the RV marg., "stay" is preferable.

B. Verbs.

1. *edaphizo* (1474), akin to A, No. 2.

2. *themelioo* (2311) signifies "to lay the foundation of, to found" (akin to *themelios*, "a foundation"; from *tithemi*, "to put"), and is rendered "grounded" in Eph. 3:17, said of the condition of believers with reference to the love of Christ; in Col. 1:23, of their continuance in the faith.

GROW

1. *auxano* (837), "to grow or increase," of the growth of that which lives, naturally or spiritually, is used (a) transitively, signifying to make to increase, said of giving the increase, 1 Cor. 3:6, 7; 2 Cor. 9:10, the effect of the work of God, according to the analogy of His operations in nature; "to grow, become greater," e.g. of plants and fruit, Matt. 6:28; used in the passive voice in 13:32 and

Mark 4:8, "increase"; in the active in Luke 12:27; 13:19; of the body, Luke 1:80; 2:40; of Christ, John 3:30, "increase"; of the work of the gospel of God, Acts 6:7, "increased"; 12:24; 19:20; of people, Acts 7:17; of faith, 2 Cor. 10:15 (passive voice), RV, "groweth" (KJV, "is increased"); of believers individually, Eph. 4:15; Col. 1:6, RV, 10 (passive voice), "increasing"; 1 Pet. 2:2; 2 Pet. 3:18; of the church, Col. 2:19; of churches, Eph. 2:21.

2. *mekunomai* (3373), "to grow long, lengthen, extend" (from *mekos*, "length"), is used of the "growth" of plants, in Mark 4:27.

3. *huperauxano* (5232), "to increase beyond measure," is used of faith and love, in their living and practical effects, 2 Thess. 1:3. Lightfoot compares this verb and the next in the verse (*pleonazo*, "to abound") in that the former implies "an internal, organic growth, as of a tree," the latter "a diffusive or expansive character, as of a flood irrigating the land."

4. *sunauxano* (4885), "to grow together," is in Matt. 13:30.

5. *phuo* (5453), "to produce," is rendered "grew" (passive voice) in Luke 8:6.

6. *sumphuo* (4855) is used in Luke 8:7, RV, "grow with."

GUARD (Noun and Verb)

A. Nouns.

1. *koustodia* (2892); "a guard," (Latin, *custodia*, Eng., "custodian"), is used of the soldiers who "guarded" Christ's sepulchre, Matt. 27:65, 66 and 28:11, and is translated "(ye have) a guard," "the guard (being with them)," and "(some of) the guard," RV, KJV, "...a watch," "(setting a) watch," and "...the watch." This was the Temple guard, stationed under a Roman officer in the tower of Antonia, and having charge of the high priestly vestments. Hence the significance of Pilate's words "Ye have a guard."

2. *spekoulator* (4688), Latin, *speculator*, primarily denotes "a lookout officer," or "scout," but, under the emperors, "a member of the bodyguard"; these were employed as messengers, watchers and executioners; ten such officers were attached to each legion; such a guard was employed by Herod Antipas, Mark 6:27, RV, "a soldier of his guard" (KJV, "executioner").

3. *phulax* (5441), "a guard, keeper" (akin to *phulasso*, "to guard, keep"), is translated "keepers" in Acts 5:23; in 12:6, 19, RV, "guards" (KJV, "keepers").

B. Verbs.

1. *phulasso* (5442), "to guard, watch, keep" (akin to A, No. 3), is rendered by the verb "to guard" in the RV (KJV, "to keep") of Luke 11:21; John 17:12; Acts 12:4; 28:16; 2 Thess. 3:3; 1 Tim. 6:20; 2 Tim. 1:12, 14; 1 John 5:21; Jude 24. In Luke 8:29, "was kept under guard, RV (KJV, kept).

2. *diaphulasso* (1314), a strengthened form of No. 1 (*dia*,

"through," used intensively), "to guard carefully, defend," is found in Luke 4:10, RV, "to guard" (KJV, "to keep").

3. *phroureo* (5432), a military term, "to keep by guarding, to keep under guard," as with a garrison (*phrouros*, "a guard, or garrison"), is used, (a) of blocking up every way of escape, as in a siege; (b) of providing protection against the enemy, as a garrison does; see 2 Cor. 11:32, "guarded." KJV, "kept," i.e., kept the city, "with a garrison." It is used of the security of the Christian until the end, 1 Pet. 1:5, RV, "are guarded," and of the sense of that security that is his when he puts all his matters into the hand of God, Phil. 4:7, RV, "shall guard." In these passages the idea is not merely that of protection, but of inward garrisoning as by the Holy Spirit; in Gal. 3:23 ("were kept in ward"), it means rather a benevolent custody and watchful guardianship in view of worldwide idolatry (cf. Isa. 5:2).

GUARDIAN

epitropos (2012), lit., "one to whose care something is committed," is rendered "guardians" in Gal. 4:2, RV, KJV, "tutors" (in Matt. 20:8 and Luke 8:3, "steward"). The corresponding verb, *epitrepo*, is translated "permit, give leave, suffer"; see 1 Cor. 14:34; 16:7; 1 Tim. 2:12. An allied noun, *epitrope*, is translated "commission" in Acts 26:12, and refers to delegated authority over persons. This usage of cognate words suggests that the *epitropos* was a superior servant responsible for the persons composing the household, whether children or slaves.

GUEST

anakeimai (345), "to recline at table," frequently rendered "to sit at meat," is used in its present participial form (lit., "reclining ones") as a noun denoting "guests," in Matt. 22:10, 11.

GUEST-CHAMBER

kataluma (2646), akin to *kataluo*, signifies (a) "an inn, lodging-place," Luke 2:7; (b) "a guest-room," Mark 14:14; Luke 22:11. The word is used of the place where travelers and their beasts untied their packages, girdles and sandals. The two passages in the NT concern a room in a private house, which the owner readily placed at the disposal of Jesus and His disciples for the celebration of the Passover.

GUILE

dolos (1388), "a bait, snare, deceit," is rendered "guile" in John 1:47, negatively of Nathanael; Acts 13:10, RV, KJV, "subtlety" (of Bar-Jesus); 2 Cor. 12:16, in a charge made against Paul by his detractors, of catching the Corinthian converts by "guile" (the apostle is apparently quoting the language of his critics); 1 Thess. 2:3, negatively, of the teaching of the apostle and his fellow missionaries; 1 Pet. 2:1, of that from which Christians are to be free; 2:22, of the guileless speech of Christ; 3:10, of the necessity that the speech of Christians should be guileless. See also Matt. 26:4; Mark 7:22; 14:1.

GUILELESS (WITHOUT GUILE)

1. *adolos* (97), "without guile," "pure, unadulterated," is used metaphorically of the teaching of the Word of God, 1 Pet. 2:2, RV. It is used in the papyri writings of seed, corn, wheat, oil, wine, etc.

2. *akakos* (172), lit., "without evil," signifies "simple, guileless," Rom. 16:18, "simple," of believers (perhaps = unsuspecting, or rather, innocent, free from admixture of evil); in Heb. 7:26, RV, "guileless" (KJV, "harmless"), the character of Christ (more lit., "free from evil").

GUILTLESS

Old Testament

A. Verb.

naqah (5352), "to be pure, innocent." The verb is most often used to mean being "free" (with the preposition *min* [from]) an obligation, Gen. 24:8, 41; Num. 5:31; from punishment, Exod. 21:19; Num. 5:28. The verb also appears with the legal connotation of "innocence," Ps. 19:13. The punishment of the person who is not "acquitted" is also expressed by a negation of the verb *naqah*: "The Lord will not hold anyone guiltless who misuses his name," Exod. 20:7.

B. Adjective.

naqi (5355), "innocent," Ps. 15:5.

New Testament

anaitios (338), "innocent, guiltless" (*a*, negative, *n*, euphonic, *aitia*, "a charge of crime"), is translated "blameless" in Matt. 12:5, KJV, "guiltless" in v. 7; RV, "guiltless" in each place.

GUILTY (Adjective)

enochos (1777), lit., "held in, bound by, liable to a charge or action at law," Mark 3:29.

GULF

chasma (5490), akin to *chasko*, "to yawn" (Eng., "chasm"), is found in Luke 16:26.

H

HADES

hades (*86*), "the region of departed spirits of the lost" (but including the blessed dead in periods preceding the ascension of Christ). It has been thought by some that the word etymologically meant "the unseen" (from *a*, negative, and *eido*, "to see"), but this derivation is questionable; a more probable derivation is from *hado*, signifying "all-receiving." It corresponds to "Sheol" in the OT. In the KJV of the OT and NT, it has been unhappily rendered "hell," e.g., Ps. 16:10; or "the grave," e.g., Gen. 37:35; or "the pit," Num. 16:30, 33; in the NT the revisers have always used the rendering "hades"; in the OT, they have not been uniform in the translation, e.g. in Isa. 14:15 "hell" (marg., "Sheol"); usually they have "Sheol" in the text and "the grave" in the margin. It never denotes the grave, nor is it the permanent region of the lost; in point of time it is, for such, intermediate between decease and the doom of Gehenna. For the condition, see Luke 16:23-31.

HAIR

thrix (*2359*) denotes the "hair," whether of beast, as of the camel's "hair" which formed the raiment of John the Baptist, Matt. 3:4; Mark 1:6; or of man. Regarding the latter (a) it is used to signify the minutest detail, as that which illustrates the exceeding care and protection bestowed by God upon His children, Matt. 10:30; Luke 12:7; 21:18; Acts 27:34; (b) as the Jews swore by the "hair," the Lord used the natural inability to make one "hair" white or black, as one of the reasons for abstinence from oaths, Matt. 5:36; (c) while long "hair" is a glory to a woman, and to wear it loose or dishevelled is a dishonor, yet the woman who wiped Christ's feet with her "hair" (in place of the towel which Simon the Pharisee omitted to provide), despised the shame in her penitent devotion to the Lord (slaves were accustomed to wipe their masters' feet), Luke 7:38, 44 (RV, "hair"); see also John 11:2; 12:3; (d) the dazzling whiteness of the head and "hair" of the Son of Man in the vision of Rev. 1 (v. 14) is suggestive of the holiness and wisdom of "the Ancient of Days"; (e) the long "hair" of the spirit-beings described as locusts in Rev. 9:8 is perhaps indicative of their subjection to their satanic master (cf. 1 Cor. 11:10, RV); (f) Christian women are exhorted to refrain from adorning their "hair" for outward show, 1 Pet. 3:3.

HALLELUJAH

hallelouia (239) signifies "Praise ye Jah." In the NT it is found in Rev. 19:1, 3, 4, 6, as the keynote in the song of the great multitude in heaven. See PRAISE.

HALLOW

hagiazo (37), "to make holy" (from *hagios*, "holy"), signifies to set apart for God, to sanctify, to make a person or thing the opposite of *koinos*, "common"; it is translated "hallowed," with reference to the name of God the Father in the Lord's Prayer, Matt. 6:9; Luke 11:2.

HAND

Old Testament

H

yad (3027), "hand; side; border; alongside; hand-measure; portion; arm (rest); monument; manhood (male sex organ); power; rule." The primary sense of this word is "hand," as a part of the body which can grasp, extend, do things, etc. Gen. 3:22; Num. 35:17. *yad* also means "human," Dan. 8:25; cf. Job 34:20, and is used of God as a figure of speech, Jer. 16:21. In several passages, *yad* is used in the sense of "power" or "rule," 1 Sam. 23:7; cf. Prov. 18:21.

yad is employed in several other noteworthy phrases. The "lifting of the hand" may be involved in "taking an oath," Gen. 14:22; Prov. 11:21. "Putting one's hand on one's mouth" is a gesture of silence, Prov. 30:32; or submission, 1 Chron. 29:24; or entrusting, Gen. 42:37.

yad represents the location, *beside*, 2 Sam. 15:2; or "border," of a land, 2 Chron. 21:16; or "bank," of a river, Dan. 10:4. *yad* also means a part or fraction of something, Gen. 43:34. Other meanings include "support," 1 Kings 7:35ff., an "arm rest," 1 Kings 10:19, and a "monument" or "stele," 1 Sam. 15:12. *yad* sometimes represents the "male sex organ," Isa. 57:8; cf. v. 10; 6:2; 7:20.

New Testament

cheir (5495), "the hand," is used, besides its ordinary significance, (a) in the idiomatic phrases, "by the hand of," "at the hand of," etc., to signify "by the agency of," Acts 5:12; 7:35; 17:25; 14:3; Gal. 3:19 (cf. Lev. 26:46); Rev. 19:2; (b) metaphorically, for the power of God, e.g., Luke 1:66; 23:46; John 10:28, 29; Acts 11:21; 13:11; Heb. 1:10; 2:7; 10:31; (c) by metonymy, for power, e.g., Matt. 17:22; Luke 24:7; John 10:39; Acts 12:11.

HANDED DOWN

patroparadotos (3970), an adjective, denoting "handed down from one's fathers," 1 Pet. 1:18.

HANDS (made by, not made with)

1. *cheiropoietos* (5499), "made by hand," of human handiwork, is said of the temple in Jerusalem, Mark 14:58; temples in general, Acts 7:48 (RV, "houses"); 17:24; negatively, of the heavenly and spiritual tabernacle, Heb. 9:11; of the holy place in the earthly tabernacle, v. 24; of circumcision, Eph. 2:11.

2. *acheiropoietos* (886), "not made by hands" (*a*, negative, and No. 1), is said of an earthly temple, Mark 14:58; of the resurrection body of believers, metaphorically as a house, 2 Cor. 5:1; metaphorically, of spiritual circumcision, Col. 2:11.

HANDLE

1. *pselaphao* (5584), "to feel, touch, handle," is rendered by the latter verb in Luke 24:39, in the Lord's invitation to the disciples to accept the evidence of His resurrection in His being bodily in their midst; in 1 John 1:1, in the apostle's testimony (against the Gnostic error that Christ had been merely a phantom) that he and his fellow apostles had handled Him.

2. *thingano* (2345) signifies (a) "to touch, to handle" (though "to handle" is rather stronger than the actual significance compared with No 1). In Col. 2:21 the RV renders it "touch," and the first verb (*hapto*, "to lay hold of") "handle," i.e., "handle not, nor taste, nor touch"; "touch" is the appropriate rendering; in Heb. 12:20 it is said of a beast's touching Mount Sinai; (b) "to touch by way of injuring," Heb. 11:28.

3. *orthotomeo* (3718), "to cut straight," as in road-making, is used metaphorically in 2 Tim. 2:15, of "handling aright (the word of truth)," RV (KJV, "rightly dividing"). The stress is on *orthos*; the Word of God is to be "handled" strictly along the lines of its teaching. If the metaphor is taken from plowing, cutting a straight furrow, the word would express a careful cultivation, the Word of God viewed as ground designed to give the best results from its ministry and in the life.

HARD, HARDEN, HARDENING, HARDNESS

A. Adjectives.

1. *skleros* (4642), from *skello*, "to dry," signifies "trying, exacting."

2. *duskolos* (1422) primarily means "hard to satisfy with food" (*dus*, a prefix like Eng., *un—* or *mis—*, indicating "difficulty, opposition, injuriousness," etc., the opposite of, *eu*, "well," and *kolon*,

"food"); hence, "difficult," Mark 10:24, of the "difficulty," for those who trust in riches, to enter into the Kingdom of God.

B. Nouns.

1. *sklerotes* (*4643*), akin to A, No. 1, is rendered "hardness" in Rom. 2:5.

2. *porosis* (*4457*) denotes "a hardening," a covering with a *poros*, a kind of stone, indicating "a process" (from *poroo*, C, No. 1), and is used metaphorically of dulled spiritual perception, Mark 3:5, RV, "at the hardening of their hearts"; Rom. 11:25, RV, "a hardening" (KJV, "blindness"), said of the state of Israel; Eph. 4:8, RV, "hardening," of the heart of Gentiles.

C. Verbs.

1. *poroo* (*4456*), "to make hard, callous, to petrify" (akin to B, No. 2), is used metaphorically, of the heart, Mark 6:52; 8:17; John 12:40; of the mind (or thoughts), 2 Cor. 3:14, of those in Israel who refused the revealed will and ways of God in the gospel, as also in Rom. 11:7, RV, "hardened" (KJV, "blinded"), in both places.

2. *skleruno* (*4645*), "to make dry or hard" (akin to A, No. 1 and B, No. 1), is used in Acts 19:9; in Rom. 9:18, illustrated by the case of Pharaoh; in Heb. 3:8, 13, 15; 4:7, warnings against the "hardening" of the heart.

HARDSHIP (to suffer)

1. *kakopatheo* (*2553*), "to suffer evil," is translated "suffer hardship" in three places in the RV, 2 Tim. 2:3 (in some mss.; see No. 2), KJV, "endure hardness"; 2:9, KJV, "suffer trouble"; 4:5, KJV, "endure affliction"; in Jas. 5:13, RV, "suffering" (KJV, "afflicted").

2. *sunkakopatheo* (*4777*), "to suffer hardship with," is so rendered in 2 Tim. 1:8, RV, KJV, "be thou partaker of the afflictions" (of the gospel), and, in the best mss., in 2:3, "suffer hardship with me."

HARLOT

Old Testament

zanah (*2181*), "to go a whoring, commit fornication, be a harlot, serve other gods." This word describes sexual misconduct on the part of a female in the Old Testament (occasionally a male), Deut. 31:16. *zanah* became, then, the common term for spiritual backsliding. The act of harloting after strange gods was more than changing gods, however. This was especially true when Israel went after the Canaanite gods, for the worship of these pagan deities involved actual prostitution with cult prostitutes connected with the Canaanite shrines. In the Old Testament sometimes the use of the phrase "go a whoring after" gods implies an individual's involvement with cult prostitutes, Exod. 34:15-16.

H

The Book of Hosea, in which Hosea's wife Gomer became unfaithful and most likely was involved in such cult prostitution, again illustrates not only Hosea's heartbreak but also God's own heartbreak because of the unfaithfulness of his wife, Israel. Israel's unfaithfulness appears in Hos. 9:1: "Rejoice not, O Israel, for joy, as other people: for thou hast gone a whoring from thy God, thou hast loved a reward upon every cornfloor."

New Testament

porne (*4204*), "a prostitute, harlot" (from *pernemi*, "to sell"), is used (a) literally, in Matt. 21:31, 32, of those who were the objects of the mercy shown by Christ; in Luke 15:30, of the life of the Prodigal; in 1 Cor. 6:15, 16, in a warning to the Corinthian church against the prevailing licentiousness which had made Corinth a byword; in Heb. 11:31 and Jas. 2:25, of Rahab; (b) metaphorically, of mystic Babylon, Rev. 17:1, 5 (KJV, "harlots"), 15, 16; 19:2, RV, for KJV, "whore."

HARM

A. Nouns.

1. *kakos* (*2556*), "evil," is rendered "harm" in Acts 16:28; 28:5.

2. *poneros* (*4190*), "evil," generally of a more malignant sort than No. 1, is translated "harm" in Acts 28:21.

B. Verb.

1. *kakoo* (*2559*), "to do evil to a person" (akin to A, No. 1), is rendered "harm" in 1 Pet. 3:13, and in the RV of Acts 18:10 (KJV, "hurt").

2. *kakopoieo* (*2554*), "to do harm" (A, No. 1, and *poieo*, "to do"), is so rendered in the RV of Mark 3:4 and Luke 6:9 (KJV, "to do evil"), with reference to the moral character of what is done; in 1 Pet. 3:17, "evil doing"; 3 John 11, "doeth evil."

HARMLESS

1. *akeraios* (*185*), lit., "unmixed, with absence of foreign mixture" (from *a*, negative, and *kerannumi*, "to mix"), "pure," is used metaphorically in the NT of what is guileless, sincere, Matt. 10:16, "harmless" (marg., "simple"), i.e., with the simplicity of a single eye, discerning what is evil, and choosing only what glorifies God; Rom. 16:19, "simple (unto that which is evil)," KJV marg., "harmless"; Phil. 2:15, "harmless," KJV marg., "sincere."

2. *akakos* (*172*), the negative of *kakos*, is rendered "harmless" in Heb. 7:26 (RV, "guileless"), of the character of Christ as a High Priest; in Rom. 16:18, RV, "innocent," KJV, "simple."

HARVEST

therismos (*2326*), akin to *therizo*, "to reap," is used (a) of "the act of harvesting," John 4:35; (b) "the time of harvest," figuratively, Matt. 13:30, 39; Mark 4:29; (c) "the crop," figuratively, Matt. 9:37, 38; Luke 10:2; Rev. 14:15. The beginning of "harvest" varied according to natural conditions, but took place on the average about the middle of April in the eastern lowlands of Palestine, in the latter part of the month in the coast plains and a little later in high districts. Barley "harvest" usually came first and then wheat. "Harvesting" lasted about seven weeks, and was the occasion of festivities.

HATE, HATEFUL, HATER, HATRED
Old Testament

A. Verb.

sane' (8130), "to hate, come to hate" (or weakened sense) "set against." The strong sense of the word typifies the emotion of intense jealousy, or bitter disdain, which could plot murder and torture, Gen. 37:18ff. In a weaker sense, *sane'* signifies "being set against," Exod. 18:21; or unloved, or lesser loved, Deut. 22:16.

B. Noun.

sin'ah (8135), "hatred," Num. 35:20.

New Testament

A. Verb.

miseo (3404), "to hate," is used especially (a) of malicious and unjustifiable feelings towards others, whether towards the innocent or by mutual animosity, e.g., Matt. 10:22; 24:10; Luke 6:22, 27; 19:14; John 3:20, of "hating" the light (metaphorically); 7:7; 15:18, 19, 23-25; Titus 3:3; 1 John 2:9, 11; 3:13, 15; 4:20; Rev. 18:2, where "hateful" translates the perfect participle passive voice of the verb, lit., "hated," or "having been hated"; (b) of a right feeling of aversion from what is evil; said of wrongdoing, Rom. 7:15; iniquity, Heb. 1:9; "the garment (figurative) spotted by the flesh," Jude 23; "the works of the Nicolaitans," Rev. 2:6 (and v. 15, in some mss.; see the KJV); (c) of relative preference for one thing over another, by way of expressing either aversion from, or disregard for, the claims of one person or thing relatively to those of another, Matt. 6:24, and Luke 16:13, as to the impossibility of serving two masters; Luke 14:26, as to the claims of parents relatively to those of Christ; John 12:25, of disregard for one's life relatively to the claims of Christ; Eph. 5:29, negatively, of one's flesh, i.e. of one's own, and therefore a man's wife as one with him.

B. Adjective.

stugetos (4767), "hateful" (from *stugeo*, "to hate," not found in the NT), is used in Titus 3:3.

C. Nouns.

1. *echthra* (*2189*), "hatred," Rom. 8:7.

2. *theostuges* (*2319*), from *theos*, "God," and *stugeo* (see B), is used in Rom. 1:30, KJV, and RV, marg., "haters of God," RV, "hateful to God"; the former rendering is appropriate to what is expressed by the next words, "insolent," "haughty," but the RV text seems to give the true meaning. Lightfoot quotes from the Epistle of Clement of Rome, in confirmation of this, "those who practice these things are hateful to God."

HAUGHTY

huperephanos (*5244*), "showing oneself above others" (*huper*, "over," *phainomai*, "to appear"), though often denoting preeminent, is always used in the NT in the evil sense of "arrogant, disdainful, haughty"; it is rendered "haughty" in Rom. 1:30 and 2 Tim. 3:2, RV, KJV, "proud," but "proud" in both versions in Luke 1:51; Jas. 4:6, and 1 Pet. 5:5; in the last two it is set in opposition to *tapeinos*, "humble, lowly."

HEAD

Old Testament

A. Nouns.

ro'sh (*7218*), "head; top; first; sum." This word often represents a "head," a bodily part, Gen. 40:20; Dan. 2:32; 7:9. To "lift up one's own head" may be a sign of declaring one's innocence, Job 10:15. This same figure of speech may indicate an intention to begin a war, the most violent form of self-assertion, Ps. 83:2. Used transitively (i.e., to lift up someone else's "head"), this word may connote restoring someone to a previous position: "Yet within three days shall Pharaoh lift up thine head, and restore thee unto thy place...," Gen. 40:13. It can also denote the release of someone from prison, 2 Kings 25:27.

The word can connote unity, representing every individual in a given group, Judg. 5:30; or a total in a group, Num. 1:2.

ro'sh sometimes means "leader," Exod. 18:25; 2 Kings 25:18. When used of things, *ro'sh* means "point" or "beginning of a space," Gen. 11:4;. In Gen. 47:31, the word denotes the "head" of a bed, or where one lays his "head." In 1 Kings 8:8, *ro'sh* refers to the ends of poles, Ezek. 16:25; cf. Dan. 7:1; headwaters, Gen. 2:10; the "head" of the stars is a star located at the zenith of the sky, Job 22:12. The "head" cornerstone occupies a place of primary importance. It is the stone by which all the other stones are measured; it is the chief cornerstone, Ps. 118:22.

This word may have a temporal significance, meaning "beginning" or "first of a series," 1 Chron. 16:7.

re'shit (*7225*), "beginning; first; choicest." The abstract word *re'shit* corresponds to the temporal and estimative sense of *ro'sh*. *re'shit* connotes the "beginning" of a fixed period of time, Deut. 11:12; of one's life, Job 42:12; of creation, Gen. 1:1. Estimatively, this word can mean the "first" or "choicest," Exod. 23:19; Dan. 11:41.

Used substantively, the word can mean "first fruits," as the first of a harvest time, Lev. 2:12; of an offering, Num. 15:20.

B. Adjective.

ri'shon (7223), "first; foremost; preceding; former." It denotes the "first" in a temporal sequence, Gen. 8:13; or first of rank, Ezra 9:2.

A second meaning of this adjective is "preceding" or "former," Gen. 13:4; used locally in Gen. 33:2.

New Testament

kephale (2776), besides its natural significance, is used (a) figuratively in Rom. 12:20, of heaping coals of fire on a "head"; in Acts 18:6, "Your blood be upon your own heads," i.e., "your blood-guiltiness rest upon your own persons," a mode of expression frequent in the OT, and perhaps here directly connected with Ezek. 3:18, 20; 33:6, 8; see also Lev. 20:16; 2 Sam. 1:16; 1 Kings 2:37; (b) metaphorically, of the authority or direction of God in relation to Christ, of Christ in relation to believing men, of the husband in relation to the wife, 1 Cor. 11:3; of Christ in relation to the Church, Eph. 1:22; 4:15; 5:23; Col. 1:18; 2:19; of Christ in relation to principalities and powers, Col. 2:10. As to 1 Cor. 11:10, taken in connection with the context, the word "authority" probably stands, by metonymy, for a sign of authority (RV), the angels being witnesses of the preeminent relationship as established by God in the creation of man as just mentioned, with the spiritual significance regarding the position of Christ in relation to the Church; cf. Eph. 3:10; it is used of Christ as the foundation of the spiritual building set forth by the Temple, with its "corner stone," Matt. 21:42; symbolically also of the imperial rulers of the Roman power, as seen in the apocalyptic visions, Rev. 13:1, 3; 17:3, 7, 9.

HEAL, HEALING

Old Testament

rapa' (7495), "to heal," i.e., "restoring to normal," an act which God typically performs, Ps. 6:2; Jer. 17:14; or restoring food or drink, 2 Kings 2:22; Ezek. 47:8; even pottery is "healed" or restored, Jer. 19:11.

A large number of the uses of *rapa'* express the "healing," as a figure of the act of God's grace and forgiveness, as well as the nation's repentance, Jer. 51:8-9.

New Testament

A. Verbs.

1. *therapeuo* (2323) primarily signifies "to serve as a *therapon*, an attendant"; then, "to care for the sick, to treat, cure, heal" (Eng., "therapeutics"). It is chiefly used in Matthew and Luke, once in John (5:10), and, after the Acts, only Rev. 13:3 and 12.

2. *iaomai* (4390), "to heal," is used (a) of physical treatment 22 times; in Matt. 5:28, KJV, "made whole," RV, "healed"; so in Acts 9:34; (b) figuratively, of spiritual "healing," Matt. 13:15; John 12:40; Acts 28:27; Heb. 12:13; 1 Pet. 2:24; possibly, Jas. 5:16 includes both (a) and (b); some mss. have the word, with sense (b), in Luke 4:18. Apart from this last, Luke, the physician, uses the word fifteen times.

3. *sozo* (4982), "to save," is translated by the verb "to heal" in the KJV of Mark 5:23 and Luke 8:36 (RV, "to make whole"; so KJV frequently); the idea is that of saving from disease and its effects.

4. *diasozo* (1295), "to save thoroughly" (*dia*, "through," and No. 3), is translated "heal" in Luke 7:3, KJV (RV, "save").

B. Nouns.

1. *therapeia* (2322), akin to A, No. 1, primarily denotes "care, attention," Luke 12:42; then, "medical service, healing" (Eng., "therapy"), Luke 9:11; Rev. 22:2, of the effects of the leaves of the tree of life, perhaps here with the meaning "health."

2. *iama* (2386), akin to A, No. 2, formerly signified "a means of healing"; in the NT, "a healing" (the result of the act), used in the plural, in 1 Cor. 12:9, 28, 30, RV, "healings"; of divinely imparted gifts in the churches in apostolic times.

3. *iasis* (2392), akin to A, No. 2, stresses the process as reaching completion, Luke 13:32, "cures," of the acts of Christ in the days of His flesh; Acts 4:22, 30, "to heal," lit. 'unto healing.'

HEAR, HEARING

Old Testament

A. Verb.

shama' (8085), "to hear, hearken, listen, obey, publish." Basically, this verb means to "hear" something with one's ears, Gen. 37:17; or eavesdropping, Gen. 18:10; or "listening," Gen. 37:6; 1 Chron. 28:2. *shama'* may also imply to "gain knowledge" or to "get knowledge," Jer. 37:5; or "come into knowledge about," Num. 9:8.

"Hearing," often means to listen and respond to a message or information: spiritually, Num. 24:4; or obey outright, Gen. 22:18.

To have a "hearing heart" is to have "discernment" or "understanding," 1 Kings 3:9. Certainly when Moses told Israel's judges to "hear" cases, he meant more than listening with one's ear. He meant for them to examine the merits of a case, so as to render a just decision, Deut. 1:16.

B. Nouns.

shema' (8088), "report," Gen. 29:13. *shemu'ah* (8052), "revelation; something heard," Isa. 28:9.

New Testament

A. Verbs.

1. *akouo* (191), the usual word denoting "to hear," is used (a) intransitively, e.g., Matt. 11:15; Mark 4:23; (b) transitively when the object is expressed, sometimes in the accusative case, sometimes in the genitive.

2. *eisakouo* (1522), "to listen to" (*eis*, to, and No. 1), has two meanings, (a) "to hear and to obey," 1 Cor. 14:21, "they will not hear"; (b) "to hear so as to answer," of God's answer to prayer, Matt. 6:7; Luke 1:13; Acts 10:31; Heb. 5:7.

3. *diakouo* (1251), "to hear through, hear fully" (*dia*, "through," and No. 1), is used technically, of "hearing" judicially, in Acts 23:35, of Felix in regard to the charges against Paul.

4. *epakouo* (1873), "to listen to, hear with favor, at or upon an occasion" (*epi*, "upon," and No. 1), is used in 2 Cor. 6:2 (RV, "hearken").

5. *epakroaomai* (1874), "to listen attentively to" (*epi*, used intensively, and a verb akin to No. 1), is used in Acts 16:25, "(the prisoners) were listening to (them)," RV, expressive of rapt attention.

6. *proakouo* (4257) signifies "to hear before" (*pro*), Col. 1:5, where Lightfoot suggests that the preposition contrasts what they heard before, the true gospel, with the false gospel of their recent teachers.

7. *parakouo* (3878) primarily signifies "to overhear, hear amiss or imperfectly" (*para*, "beside, amiss," and No. 1); then (in the NT) "to hear without taking heed, to neglect to hear," Matt. 18:17 (twice); in Mark 5:36 the best mss. have this verb, which the RV renders "not heeding" (marg., "overhearing"); some mss. have No. 1, KJV, "hearing." It seems obvious that the Lord paid no attention to those from the ruler's house and their message that his daughter was dead.

B. Nouns.

1. *akoe* (189), akin to A, No. 1, denotes (a) "the sense of hearing," 1 Cor. 12:17; 2 Pet. 2:8; a combination of verb and noun is used in phrases which have been termed Hebraic as they express somewhat literally an OT phraseology, e.g., "By hearing ye shall hear," Matt. 13:14; Acts 28:26, RV, a mode of expression conveying emphasis; (b) "the organ of hearing," Mark 7:35, "ears"; Luke 7:1, RV, "ears," for KJV, "audience"; Acts 17:20; 2 Tim. 4:3, 4; Heb. 5:11, "dull

of hearing," lit., "dull as to ears"; (c) "a thing heard, a message or teaching," John 12:38, "report"; Rom. 10:16; 1 Thess. 2:13, "the word of the message," lit. "the word of hearing" (KJV, "which ye heard"); Heb. 4:2, "the word of hearing," RV, for KJV, "the word preached"; in a somewhat similar sense, "a rumor, report," Matt. 4:24; 14:1; Mark 1:28, KJV, "fame," RV, "report"; Matt. 24:6; Mark 13:7, "rumors (of wars)"; (d) "the receiving of a message," Rom. 10:17, something more than the mere sense of "hearing" [see (a)]; so with the phrase "the hearing of faith," Gal. 3:2, 5, which it seems better to understand so than under (c).

HEART, HEARTILY

Old Testament

leb (3820), "heart; mind; midst." *leb* and its synonym *lebab*, often means the inner person, with a focus on the psychological aspects of the mind and heart, which also includes decision making ability, Gen. 6:5,6. "Heart" may refer to the organ of the body, 2 Sam. 18:14, and can be used of the inner man, i.e., that part of man which thinks, lives, has a personality, and most of all responds to God, Deut. 30:14; cf. Prov. 23:7; Joel 2:13.

The "heart" is regarded as the seat of emotions, Deut. 6:5; for joy, Judg. 16:25; or fear and sorrow, 1 Sam. 4:13, and also as the seat of conscience and moral character, 2 Sam. 24:10. The "heart" is the fountain of man's deeds, 1 Kings 3:6; Isa. 38:3. A "pure heart," Ps. 24:4, can stand in God's presence. God controls the "heart." Because of his natural "heart," man's only hope is in the promise of God, Ezek. 36:26; it can be cleaned, Ps. 51:10; the heart can be tested, Ps. 86:11; yet a man cannot understand his own "heart," Jer. 17:9; it can become hard, Deut. 30:6.

leb may also refer to the inner part or middle of a space, Exod. 15:8; or heaven, Deut. 4:11.

New Testament

kardia (2588), "the heart" (Eng., "cardiac," etc.), the chief organ of physical life ("for the life of the flesh is in the blood," Lev. 17:11), occupies the most important place in the human system. By an easy transition the word came to stand for man's entire mental and moral activity, both the rational and the emotional elements. In other words, the heart is used figuratively for the hidden springs of the personal life. The Bible describes human depravity as in the 'heart,' because sin is a principle which has its seat in the center of man's inward life, and then 'defiles' the whole circuit of his action, Matt. 15:19, 20. On the other hand, Scripture regards the heart as the sphere of Divine influence, Rom. 2:15; Acts 15:9.... The heart, as lying deep within, contains 'the hidden man,' 1 Pet. 3:4, the real man. It represents the true character but conceals it.

As to its usage in the NT it denotes (a) the seat of physical life,

Acts 14:17; Jas. 5:5; (b) the seat of moral nature and spiritual life, the seat of grief, John 14:1; Rom. 9:2; 2 Cor. 2:4; joy, John 16:22; Eph. 5:19; the desires, Matt. 5:28; 2 Pet. 2:14; the affections, Luke 24:32; Acts 21:13; the perceptions, John 12:40; Eph. 4:18; the thoughts, Matt. 9:4; Heb. 4:12; the understanding, Matt. 13:15; Rom. 1:21; the reasoning powers, Mark 2:6; Luke 24:38; the imagination, Luke 1:51; conscience, Acts 2:37; 1 John 3:20; the intentions, Heb. 4:12, cf. 1 Pet. 4:1; purpose, Acts 11:23; 2 Cor. 9:7; the will, Rom. 6:17; Col. 3:15; faith, Mark 11:23; Rom. 10:10; Heb. 3:12.

2. *psuche* (5590), the soul, or life, is rendered "heart" in Eph. 6:6 (marg., "soul"), "doing the will of God from the heart." In Col. 3:23, a form of the word *psuche* preceded by *ek*, from, lit., "from (the) soul," is rendered "heartily."

HEART (hardness of)

sklerokardia (4641), "hardness of heart" (*skleros*, "hard," and *kardia*), is used in Matt. 19:8; Mark 10:5; 16:14.

HEART (knowing the)

kardiognostes (2589), "a knower of hearts" (*kardia* and *ginosko*, "to know"), is used in Acts 1:24; 15:8.

HEAVEN, HEAVENLY (-IES)

Old Testament

shamayim (8064), "heavens; heaven; sky." First, *shamayim* is the usual Hebrew word for the "sky" and the "realm of the sky," where birds fly, Deut. 4:17; or just above the surface of earth, 2 Sam. 18:9; or very high, near God's realm, heaven, 1 Chron. 21:16. Second, this word represents an area farther removed from the earth's surface, the place of the windows of heaven from which precipitation comes, Gen. 8:2; Deut. 28:12. Third, *shamayim* also represents the realm in which the sun, moon, and stars are located, Gen. 1:14; Ps. 104:2; Isa. 34:4. Fourth, the phrase "heaven and earth," may denote the entire creation, the totality of the whole, Gen. 1:1. Fifth, "heaven" is the dwelling place of God, Ps. 2:4; cf. Deut. 4:39; 10:14.

New Testament

A. Noun.

ouranos (3772), probably akin to *ornumi*, "to lift, to heave," is used in the NT (a) of "the aerial heavens," e.g., Matt. 6:26; 8:20; Acts 10:12; 11:6 (RV, "heaven," in each place, KJV, "air"); Jas. 5:18; (b) "the sidereal," e.g., Matt. 24:29, 35; Mark 13:25, 31; Heb. 11:12, RV, "heaven," KJV, "sky"; Rev. 6:14; 20:11; they, (a) and (b), were created by the Son of God, Heb. 1:10, as also by God the Father, Rev. 10:6; (c) "the eternal dwelling place of God," Matt. 5:16; 12:50; Rev.

3:12; 11:13; 16:11; 20:9. From thence the Son of God descended to become incarnate, John 3:13, 31; 6:38, 42. In His ascension Christ "passed through the heavens," Heb. 4:14, RV; He "ascended far above all the heavens," Eph. 4:10, and was "made higher than the heavens," Heb. 7:26; He "sat down on the right hand of the throne of the Majesty in the heavens," Heb. 8:1; He is "on the right hand of God," having gone into heaven, 1 Pet. 3:22. Since His ascension it is the scene of His present life and activity, e.g., Rom. 8:34; Heb. 9:24. From thence the Holy Spirit descended at Pentecost, 1 Pet. 1:12. It is the abode of the angels, e.g., Matt. 18:10; 22:30; cf. Rev. 3:5. Thither Paul was "caught up," whether in the body or out of the body, he knew not, 2 Cor. 12:2. It is to be the eternal dwelling place of the saints in resurrection glory, 2 Cor. 5:1. From thence Christ will descend to the air to receive His saints at the Rapture, 1 Thess. 4:16; Phil. 3:20, 21, and will subsequently come with His saints and with His holy angels at His second advent, Matt. 24:30; 2 Thess. 1:7. In the present life "heaven" is the region of the spiritual citizenship of believers, Phil. 3:20. The present "heavens," with the earth, are to pass away, 2 Pet. 3:10, "being on fire," v. 12 (see v. 7); Rev. 20:11, and new "heavens" and earth are to be created, 2 Pet. 3:13; Rev. 21:1, with Isa. 65:17.

B. Adjectives.

1. *ouranios* (3770), signifying "of heaven, heavenly," corresponding to *ouranos* above, is used (a) as an appellation of God the Father, Matt. 6:14, 26, 32, "your heavenly Father"; 15:13, "My heavenly Father"; (b) as descriptive of the holy angels, Luke 2:13; (c) of the vision seen by Paul, Acts 26:19.

2. *epouranios* (2032), "heavenly," what pertains to, or is in, heaven (*epi*, in the sense of "pertaining to," not here, "above"), has meanings corresponding to some of the meanings of *ouranos* above. It is used (a) of God the Father, Matt. 18:35; (b) of the place where Christ "sitteth at the right hand of God" (i.e., in a position of divine authority), Eph. 1:20; and of the present position of believers in relationship to Christ, 2:6; where they possess "every spiritual blessing," 1:3; (c) of Christ as "the Second Man," and all those who are related to Him spiritually, 1 Cor. 15:48; (d) of those whose sphere of activity or existence is above, or in contrast to that of earth, of "principalities and powers," Eph. 3:10; of "spiritual hosts of wickedness," 6:12, RV, "in heavenly places," for KJV, "in high places"; (e) of the Holy Spirit, Heb. 6:4; (f) of "heavenly things," as the subjects of the teaching of Christ, John 3:12, and as consisting of the spiritual and "heavenly" sanctuary and "true tabernacle" and all that appertains thereto in relation to Christ and His sacrifice as antitypical of the earthly tabernacle and sacrifices under the Law, Heb. 8:5; 9:23; (g) of the "calling" of believers, Heb. 3:1; (h) of heaven as the abode of the saints, "a better country" than

that of earth, Heb. 11:16, and of the spiritual Jerusalem, 12:22; (i) of the kingdom of Christ in its future manifestation, 2 Tim. 4:18; (j) of all beings and things, animate and inanimate, that are "above the earth," Phil. 2:10; (k) of the resurrection and glorified bodies of believers, 1 Cor. 15:49; (l) of the "heavenly orbs," 1 Cor. 15:40 ("celestial," twice, and so rendered here only).

C. Adverb.

ouranothen (3771), formed from *ouranos* above, and denoting "from heaven," is used of (a) the aerial heaven, Acts 14:17; (b) heaven, as the uncreated sphere of God's abode, 26:13.

HEAVY, HEAVINESS

A. Noun.

lupe (3077), "grief, sorrow," is rendered "heaviness" in the KJV of Rom. 9:2; 2 Cor. 2:1 (RV, "sorrow," in both places).

B. Verb.

1. *lupeo* (3076), "to distress, grieve" (akin to *lupe* above), is rendered "are in heaviness" in 1 Pet. 1:6, KJV (RV, "have been put to grief"); here, as frequently, it is in the passive voice.

2. *bareo* (916), always in the passive voice in the NT, is rendered "were heavy" in Matt. 26:43; Mark 14:40; Luke 9:32.

C. Adjective.

barus (926), "heavy" (akin to B, No. 2), is so rendered in Matt. 23:4.

HEED (to give, to take)

1. *blepo* (991), "to look," see, usually implying more especially an intent, earnest contemplation, is rendered "take heed" in Matt. 24:4; Mark 4:24; 13:5, 9, 23, 33; Luke 8:18; 21:8; 1 Cor. 3:10; 8:9; 10:12; Gal. 5:15; Col. 2:8 (KJV, "beware"); 4:17; Heb. 3:12.

2. *horao* (3708), "to see," usually expressing the sense of vision, is rendered "take heed" in Matt. 16:6; 18:10, KJV (RV, "see"); Mark 8:15; Luke 12:15; Acts 22:26 (KJV only).

3. *prosecho* (4337), lit., "to hold to," signifies "to turn to, turn one's attention to"; hence, "to give heed"; it is rendered "take heed" in Matt. 6:1; Luke 17:3; 21:34; Acts 5:35; 20:28; 2 Pet. 1:19; to give heed to, in Acts 8:6, 10; in v. 11 (KJV, "had regard to"); 16:14 (KJV, "attended unto"); 1 Tim. 1:4; 4:1, 13 (KJV, "give attendance to"); Titus 1:14; Heb. 2:1, lit., "to give heed more earnestly."

4. *epecho* (1907), lit., "to hold upon," then, "to direct towards, to give attention to," is rendered "gave heed," in Acts 3:5; "take heed," in 1 Tim. 4:16.

HEIR

A. Noun.

1. *kleronomos* (*2818*) lit. denotes "one who obtains a lot or portion (*kleros*, "a lot," *nemomai*, "to possess"), especially of an inheritance. The NT usage may be analyzed as under: (a) the person to whom property is to pass on the death of the owner, Matt. 21:38; Mark 12:7; Luke 20:14; Gal. 4:1; (b) one to whom something has been assigned by God, on possession of which, however, he has not yet entered, as Abraham, Rom. 4:13, 14; Heb. 6:17; Christ, Heb. 1:2; the poor saints, Jas. 2:5; (c) believers, inasmuch as they share in the new order of things to be ushered in at the return of Christ, Rom. 8:17; Gal. 3:29; 4:7; Titus 3:7; (d) one who receives something other than merit, as Noah, Heb. 11:7.

2. *sunkleronomos* (*4789*), "a joint-heir, co-inheritor" (*sun*, "with," and No. 1), is used of Isaac and Jacob as participants with Abraham in the promises of God, Heb. 11:9; of husband and wife who are also united in Christ, 1 Pet. 3:7; of Gentiles who believe, as participants in the gospel with Jews who believe, Eph. 3:6; and of all believers as prospective participants with Christ in His glory, as recompense for their participation in His sufferings, Rom. 8:17.

B. Verb.

kleronomeo (*2816*), "to be an heir to, to inherit" (see A, No. 1), is rendered "shall (not) inherit with" in Gal. 4:30, RV, KJV, "shall (not) be heir with"; in Heb. 1:14, RV, "shall inherit," KJV, "shall be heirs of."

HELL

1. *geenna* (*1067*) represents the Hebrew *ge-hinnom* (the valley of Tophet) and a corresponding Aramaic word; it is found twelve times in the NT, eleven of which are in the Synoptists, in every instance as uttered by the Lord Himself, Matt. 5:22; 18:8, 9; Mark 9:43-47.

HELMET

perikephalaia (*4030*), from *peri*, "around," and *kephale*, "a head," is used figuratively in Eph. 6:17, with reference to salvation, and 1 Thess. 5:8, where it is described as "the hope of salvation."

HELP, HOLPEN

Old Testament

'azar (*5826*), "to help, assist, aid." Help or aid comes from a variety of sources: Thirty-two kings "helped" Ben-hadad, 1 Kings 20:6; one city "helps" another, Josh. 10:33; even false gods are believed to be of "help," 2 Chron. 28:23. Of course, the greatest source of

help is God Himself; He is "the helper of the fatherless," Ps. 10:14. God promises: "I will help thee," Isa. 41:10; "and the Lord shall help them, and deliver them...," Ps. 37:40.

New Testament

A. Nouns.

1. *antilepsis* or *antilempsis* (484) properly signifies "a laying hold of, an exchange" (*anti*, "in exchange," or, in its local sense, "in front," and *lambano*, "to take, lay hold of," so as to support); then, "a help" (akin to B, No. 1); it is mentioned in 1 Cor. 12:28, as one of the ministrations in the local church, by way of rendering assistance, perhaps especially of "help" ministered to the weak and needy. So Theophylact defines the injunction in 1 Thess. 5:14, "support the weak"; cf. Acts 20:35.

2. *boetheia* (996), from *boe*, "a shout," and *theo*, "to run," denotes "help, succour," Heb. 4:16, lit., "(grace) unto (timely) help"; in Acts 27:17, where the plural is used, the term is nautical, "frapping."

3. *epikouria* (1947) strictly denotes such aid as is rendered by an *epikouros*, "an ally, an auxiliary"; Paul uses it in his testimony to Agrippa, "having therefore obtained the help that is from God," Acts 26:22, RV.

B. Verbs.

1. *antilambano* (482), lit., "to take instead of, or in turn" (akin to A, No. 1), is used in the middle voice, and rendered "He hath holpen" in Luke 1:54; "to help," RV, "to support," KJV, in Acts 20:35; its other meaning, "to partake of," is used of partaking of things, 1 Tim. 6:2, "that partake of," for KJV, "partakers of."

2. *sullambano* (4815), "to assist, take part with" (*sun*, "with," and *lambano*), is used, in the middle voice, of rendering help in what others are doing, Luke 5:7, of bringing in a catch of fish; in Phil. 4:3, in an appeal to Synzygus ("yokefellow") to help Euodia and Syntyche (v. 2).

3. *sunantizambano* (4878) signifies "to lake hold with at the side for assistance" (*sun*, "with," and No. 1); hence, "to take a share in, help in bearing, to help in general." It is used, in the middle voice in Martha's request to the Lord to bid her sister help her, Luke 10:40; and of the ministry of the Holy Spirit in helping our infirmities, Rom. 8:26.

4. *boetheo* (997), "to come to the aid of anyone, to succour" (akin to A, No. 2), is used in Matt. 15:25; Mark 9:22, 24; Acts 16:9; 21:28; 2 Cor. 6:2, "did I succour"; Heb. 2:18, "to succour"; Rev. 12:16.

5. *sumballo* (4820), lit., "to throw together" (*sun*, "with," *ballo*, "to throw"), is used in the middle voice in Acts 18:27, of helping or benefiting believers by discussion or ministry of the Word of God.

6. *sunupourgeo* (4943) denotes "to help together," 2 Cor. 1:11.

7. *sunergeo* (*4903*), "to help in work, to co-operate, be a co-worker," is rendered "that helpeth with" in 1 Cor. 16:16.

HELPER, FELLOW-HELPER

1. *boethos* (*998*), an adjective, akin to A, No. 2, and B, No. 4, under HELP, signifying "helping," is used as a noun in Heb. 13:6, of God as the helper of His saints.

2. *sunergos* (*4904*), an adjective, akin to B, No. 7, under HELP, "a fellow worker," is translated "helper" in the KJV of Rom. 16:3, 9; 2 Cor. 1:24, "helpers"; in 2 Cor. 8:23, KJV, "fellow helper; so the plural in 3 John 8.

HERESY

hairesis (*139*) denotes "a choosing, choice" (from *haireomai*, "to choose"); then came to mean in NT, "a sect" that leads to divisions, Acts 5:17; 15:5; 24:5, 14; 26:5; 28:22; "heresies" in 1 Cor. 11:19.

HERETICAL

hairetikos (*141*), akin to the above, primarily denotes "capable of choosing" (*haireomai*); hence, "causing division by a party spirit, factious," Titus 3:10, RV, "heretical."

HERITAGE

kleroo (*2820*), primarily, "to cast lots" or "to choose by lot," then, "to assign a portion," is used in the passive voice in Eph. 1:11, "we were made a heritage."

HERO

A. Nouns.

gibbor (*1368*), "mighty one." In the context of battle, the word is better understood to refer to the category of proven, effective, warriors, Josh. 1:14; 2 Sam. 23. The phrase *gibbor chayil* may also refer to a man of a high social class, the landed man who had military responsibilities, such as Saul, 1 Sam. 9:1.

The king symbolized the strength of his kingdom. He had to lead his troops in battle, and as commander he was expected to be a "hero." Early in David's life, he was recognized as a "hero," 1 Sam. 18:7; so also of God, Ps. 45:3; or Messiah, Isa. 9:6.

Israel's God was a mighty God, Isa. 10:21. He had the power to deliver, Zeph. 3:17.

geber (*181*), "man," i.e., an adult male, 1 Chron. 23:3.

B. Verb.

gabar (*1396*), "to be strong," Job 21:7.

C. Adjective.

gibbor (1368), "strong," often referring to physical strength or prowess, 1 Sam. 14:52; lion, Prov. 30:30; hunter, Gen. 10:9; unique race, Gen. 6:1-4.

HIDE, HID, HIDDEN

Old Testament

satar (5641), "to conceal, hide, shelter." *satar* has the sense of "separation," in some passages, Gen. 31:49; or take refuge, 1 Sam. 23:19; or shelter from danger, Jer. 36:26.

New Testament

A. Verbs.

1. *krupto* (2928), "to cover, conceal, keep secret" (Eng., "crypt," "cryptic," etc.), is used (a) in its physical significance, e.g., Matt. 5:14; 13:44; 25:18 (some mss. have No. 2); (b) metaphorically, e.g., Matt. 11:25 (some mss. have No. 2 here); 13:35, RV, "(things) hidden"; KJV, "(things) which have been kept secret"; Luke 18:34; 19:42; John 19:38, "secretly."

2. *apokrupto* (613), "to conceal from, to keep secret" (*apo*, "from," and No. 1), is used metaphorically, in Luke 10:21, of truths "hidden" from the wise and prudent and revealed to babes; 1 Cor. 2:7, of God's wisdom; Eph. 3:9, of the mystery of the unsearchable riches of Christ, revealed through the gospel;Col. 1:26, of the mystery associated with the preceding.

3. *enkrupto* (1470), "to hide in anything" (*en*, "in," and No. 1), is used in Matt. 13:33, of leaven "hidden" in meal.

4. *perikrupto* (4032) signifies "to hide by placing something around, to conceal entirely, to keep hidden" (*peri*, "around," used intensively, and No. 1), Luke 1:24.

B. Adjectives.

1. *kruptos* (2927), akin to A, No. 1, "hidden, secret," is translated "hid" in Matt. 10:26; Mark 4:22; Luke 8:17, RV, for KJV, "secret"; 12:2 (last part); in 1 Cor. 4:5, "hidden (things of darkness)"; 2 Cor. 4:2, "hidden (things of shame)"; 1 Pet. 3:4, "hidden (man of the heart)."

2. *apokruphos* (614), "hidden away from" (corresponding to A, No. 2; cf. Eng., "apocryphal"), is translated, "made (KJV, kept) secret," in Mark 4:22; in Luke 8:17, RV, "secret," for KJV, "hid"; in Col. 2:3, RV, "hidden," KJV, "hid."

HIGH (from on, most), HIGHLY

Old Testament

A. Adjective.

gaboah (1364), "high; exalted." This word means "lofty, tall in dimension," Gen. 7:19; of a man's height, 1 Sam. 9:2; cf. 16:7; of horns, Dan. 8:2. The word also means "high or exalted in station," and so have much recognition or status, Ezek. 21:26; Eccl. 5:8. *gaboah* may be used self-exaltation, or "haughtiness," 1 Sam. 2:3.

'elyon (5945), "high; top; uppermost; highest; upper; height." This word indicates the "uppermost" (as opposed to the lower) of a spacial position, an elevation, Gen. 40:16-17; Ezek. 42:5. A figurative use of the word appears in 2 Chron. 7:21, where it modifies the dynasty (house) of Solomon. The messianic Davidic king will be God's firstborn, "higher than the kings of the earth," Ps. 89:27. This word is frequently used in a name *el 'elyon* of God; it describes Him as the Most High, the "highest" and only Supreme Being. The emphasis here is on divine supremacy, Gen. 14:18.

Also the figurative use of *'elyon* to describe the "house" or dynasty of Israel takes an unusual turn in 1 Kings 9:8, where the kingdom is said to be the "height" of astonishment.

B. Verb.

gabah (1362), "to be high, exalted, lofty." This verb, which occurs 38 times in the Bible, has cognates in Akkadian, Aramaic, and Arabic. Its meanings parallel those of the adjective. It may mean "to be high, lofty." In this sense, it is used of trees, Ezek. 19:11, the heavens, Job 35:5, and a man, 1 Sam. 10:23. It may mean "to be exalted" in dignity and honor, Job 36:7. Or it may simply mean "to be lofty," used in the positive sense of "being encouraged," 2 Chron. 17:6, or in the negative sense of "being haughty or proud," 2 Chron. 26:16.

C. Noun.

gobah (1363), "height; exaltation; grandeur; haughtiness; pride." This noun, which occurs 17 times in biblical Hebrew, refers to the "height" of things, 2 Chron. 3:4; exaltation, Job 40:10; haughtiness or pride, 2 Chron. 32:26.

New Testament

A. Adjectives.

1. *hupselos* (5308), "high, lofty," is used (a) naturally, of mountains, Matt. 4:8; 17:1; Mark 9:2; Rev. 21:10; of a wall, Rev. 21:12; (b) figuratively, of the arm of God, Acts 13:17; of heaven, "on high," plural, lit., "in high (places)," Heb. 1:3; (c) metaphorically, Luke 16:15, RV, "exalted" (KJV, "highly esteemed"); Rom. 11:20, in the best texts, "high-minded" [lit., "mind (not) high things"]; 12:16.

2. *hupsistos* (5310), "most high," is a superlative degree, the positive not being in use; it is used of God in Luke 1:32, 35, 76; 6:35, in each of which the RV has "the most High," for KJV, "the highest," KJV and RV in Mark 5:7; Luke 8:28; Acts 7:48; 16:17; Heb. 7:1.

B. Nouns.

1. *hupsos* (5311), "height," is used with *ex* (*ek*) "from," in the phrase "on high," Luke 1:78; 24:49; with *eis*, "in" or "into," Eph. 4:8.

2. *hupsoma* (5313), "high thing," 2 Cor. 10:5; in Rom. 8:39, "height."

HIGH PLACE

bamah (1116), "high place." *bamah* is a pagan worship center, often in a geographically elevated spot, an evil place to be destroyed, Lev. 26:30. Not every literal *bamah* was a cultic high place; the word may simply refer to a geographically elevated place, with no denotation of a worship center, Amos 4:13; Mic. 3:12. Before the temple was built, Solomon worshiped the Lord at the great *bamah* of Gideon, 1 Kings 3:4. This was permissible until the temple was constructed; however, history demonstrates that Israel soon adopted these "high places" for pagan customs. The *bamah* was found in the cities of Samaria, 2 Kings 23:19, in the cities of Judah, 2 Chron. 21:11, and even in Jerusalem, 2 Kings 23:13. The *bamah* was a place of cult prostitution, Amos 2:7-8.

HIGH-MINDED

1. *tuphoo* (5187) properly means "to wrap in smoke" (from *tuphos*, "smoke"; metaphorically, for "conceit"); it is used in the passive voice, metaphorically in 1 Tim. 3:6, "puffed up," RV (KJV, "lifted up with pride"); so 6:4, KJV, "proud," and 2 Tim. 3:4, KJV, "high-minded."

2. *hupselophroneo* (5309), "to be highminded," is used in 1 Tim. 6:17.

HINDER, HINDRANCE

Verbs.

1. *enkopto* (1465), lit., "to cut into" (*en*, "in," *kopto*, "to cut"), was used of "impeding" persons by breaking up the road, or by placing an obstacle sharply in the path; hence, metaphorically of "detaining" a person unnecessarily, Acts 24:4, of "hindrances" in the way of reaching others, Rom. 15:22; or returning to them, 1 Thess. 2:18; of "hindering" progress in the Christian life, Gal. 5:7.

2. *koluo* (2967), "to hinder, forbid, restrain," is translated "to hinder" in Luke 11:52; Acts 8:36; Rom. 1:13, RV (KJV, "was let"); Heb. 7:23, RV (KJV, "were not suffered").

3. *diakoluo* (1254), a strengthened form of No. 2, "to hinder thoroughly," is used in Matt. 3:14, of John the Baptist's endeavor to "hinder" Christ from being baptized, KJV, "forbad," RV, "would have hindered," lit., "was hindering."

HIRED SERVANT, HIRELING

1. *misthotos* (*3411*), an adjective denoting "hired," is used as a noun, signifying "one who is hired," "hired servants," Mark 1:20; "hireling," John 10:12, 13; here, it expresses, not only one who has no real interest in his duty (that may or may not be present in its use in Mark 1:20, and in *misthios*, No. 2), but one who is unfaithful in the discharge of it; that sense attaches always to the word rendered "hireling."

2. *misthios* (*3407*), an adjective, akin to No. 1, and similarly signifying "a hired servant," is used in Luke 15:17, 19 (in some texts, v. 21).

HOLINESS, HOLY, HOLILY

Old Testament

A. Adjective.

qadosh (6918), "holy." In the Old Testament *qadosh* has a strongly religious connotation. In one sense the word describes an object or place or day to be "holy" with the meaning of "devoted" or "dedicated" to a particular purpose, Num. 5:17. Particularly the sabbath day is "devoted" as a day of rest, Isa. 58:13-14.

God has dedicated Israel as His people. They are "holy" by their relationship to the "holy" God. All of the people are in a sense "holy," as members of the covenant community, irrespective of their faith and obedience, Num. 16:3. God's intent was to use this "holy" nation as a "holy," royal priesthood amongst the nations, Exod. 19:6. The priests were chosen to officiate at the Holy Place of the tabernacle/temple. Because of their function as intermediaries between God and Israel and because of their proximity to the temple, they were dedicated by God to the office of priest, with instructions for a holy life, Lev. 21:6-8; Ps. 106:16.

The Old Testament clearly and emphatically teaches that God is "holy." He is "the Holy One of Israel," Isa. 1:4, the "holy God," Isa. 5:16, and "the Holy One," Isa. 40:25. His name is "Holy," 1 Sam. 2:2; Zech. 14:5, cf. Isa. 6:3.

B. Verb.

qadesh (6942), or *qadash* (6942), "to be holy; to sanctify," Exod. 29:37; Lev. 6:18; 2 Chron. 29:5.

C. Nouns.

qodesh (6944), "holiness; holy thing; sanctuary"; "holiness," Exod. 15:11; "holy thing," Num. 4:15; and "sanctuary," Exod. 36:4.

Another noun, *qadesh*, means "temple-prostitute" or "sodomite," with a focus on one set apart (here negatively) for a special purpose, Deut. 23:17.

New Testament

A. Nouns.

1. *hagiasmos* (38), translated "holiness" in the KJV of Rom. 6:19, 22; 1 Thess. 4:7; 1 Tim. 2:15; Heb. 12:14, is always rendered "sanctification" in the RV. It signifies (a) separation to God, 1 Cor. 1:30; 2 Thess. 2:13; 1 Pet. 1:2; (b) the resultant state, the conduct befitting those so separated, 1 Thess. 4:3, 4, 7, and the four other places mentioned above.

2. *hagiosune* (42) denotes the manifestation of the quality of "holiness" in personal conduct; (a) it is used in Rom. 1:4, of the absolute "holiness" of Christ in the days of His flesh, which distinguished Him from all merely human beings; this (which is indicated in the phrase "the spirit of holiness") and (in vindication of it) His resurrection from the dead, marked Him out as (He was "declared to be") the Son of God; (b) believers are to be "perfecting holiness in the fear of God," 2 Cor. 7:1, i.e., bringing "holiness" to its predestined end, whereby (c) they may be found "unblameable in holiness" in the Parousia of Christ, 1 Thess. 3:13.

3. *hagiotes* (41), "sanctity," the abstract quality of "holiness," is used (a) of God, Heb. 12:10; (b) of the manifestation of it in the conduct of the apostle Paul and his fellowlaborers, 2 Cor. 1:12.

4. *hosiotes* (3742) is to be distinguished from No. 3, as denoting that quality of "holiness" which is manifested in those who have regard equally to grace and truth; it involves a right relation to God; it is used in Luke 1:75 and Eph. 4:24, and in each place is associated with righteousness.

B. Adjectives.

1. *hagios* (40), akin to A, Nos. 1 and 2, which are from the same root as *hagnos* (found in *hazo*, "to venerate"), fundamentally signifies "separated" (among the Greeks, dedicated to the gods), and hence, in Scripture in its moral and spiritual significance, separated from sin and therefore consecrated to God, sacred.

(a) It is predicated of God (as the absolutely "Holy" One, in His purity, majesty and glory): of the Father, e.g., Luke 1:49; John 17:11; 1 Pet. 1:15, 16; Rev. 4:8; 6:10; of the Son, e.g., Luke 1:35; Acts 3:14; 4:27, 30; 1 John 2:20; of the Spirit, e.g., Matt. 1:18 and frequently in all the Gospels, Acts, Romans, 1 and 2 Cor., Eph., 1 Thess.; also in 2 Tim. 1:14; Titus 3:5; 1 Pet. 1:12; 2 Pet. 1:21; Jude 20.

(b) It is used of men and things (see below) in so far as they are devoted to God. Indeed the quality, as attributed to God, is often presented in a way which involves divine demands upon the conduct of believers. These are called *hagioi*, "saints," i.e., "sanctified" or "holy" ones.

This sainthood is not an attainment, it is a state into which God in grace calls men; yet believers are called to sanctify themselves

H

(consistently with their calling, 2 Tim. 1:9), cleansing themselves from all defilement, forsaking sin, living a "holy" manner of life, 1 Pet. 1:15; 2 Pet. 3:11, and experiencing fellowship with God in His holiness. The saints are thus figuratively spoken of as "a holy temple," 1 Cor. 3:17 (a local church); Eph. 2:21 (the whole Church), cf. 5:27; "a holy priesthood," 1 Pet. 2:5; "a holy nation," 2:9.

The adjective is also used of the outer part of the tabernacle, Heb. 9:2 (RV, "the holy place"); of the inner sanctuary, 9:3, RV, "the Holy of Holies"; 9:4, "a holy place," RV; v. 25 (plural), of the presence of God in heaven, where there are not two compartments as in the tabernacle, all being "the holy place"; 9:8, 12 (neuter plural); 10:19, "the holy place," RV (KJV, "the holiest," neut. plural); of the city of Jerusalem, Rev. 11:2; its temple, Acts 6:13; of the faith, Jude 20; of the greetings of saints, 1 Cor. 16:20; of angels, e.g., Mark 8:38; of apostles and prophets, Eph. 3:5; of the future heavenly Jerusalem, Rev. 21:2, 10; 22:19.

2. *hosios* (3741), akin to A, No. 4, signifies "religiously right, holy," as opposed to what is unrighteous or polluted. It is commonly associated with righteousness (see A, No. 4). It is used of God, Rev. 15:4; 16:5; and of the body of the Lord Jesus, Acts 2:27; 13:35, citations from Ps. 16:10.

C. Adverb.

hosios (3743), akin to A, No. 4, and B, No. 2, "holily," i.e., pure from evil conduct, and observant of God's will, is used in 1 Thess. 2:10, of the conduct of the apostle and his fellow missionaries.

D. Verb.

hagiazo (37), "to hallow, sanctify," in the passive voice, "to be made holy, be sanctified," is translated "let him be made holy" in Rev. 22:11, the aorist or point tense expressing the definiteness and completeness of the divine act; elsewhere it is rendered by the verb "to sanctify."

HONEST, HONESTLY, HONESTY

A. Adjective.

kalos (2570), "good, admirable, becoming," has also the ethical meaning of what is "fair, right, honorable, of such conduct as deserves esteem"; it is translated "honest" [cf. Latin *honestus* (from *honos*, "honor")], which has the same double meaning as "honest" in the KJV, namely, regarded with honor, honorable, and bringing honor, becoming; in Luke 8:15 (KJV, and RV), "an honest and good (*agathos*) heart"; Rom. 12:17; 2 Cor. 8:21 and 13:7, RV, "honorable" (KJV, "honest"), of things which are regarded with esteem; in 1 Pet. 2:12, of behavior, RV, "seemly," KJV, "honest" (i.e., becoming).

B. Adverbs.

1. *kalos* (2573), corresponding to A, *kalos* above, is used in Heb. 13:18, "honestly," i.e., honorably.

2. *euschemonos* (2156), "becomingly, decently," is rendered "honestly" in Rom. 13:13, where it is set in contrast with the confusion of gentile social life, and in 1 Thess. 4:12, of the manner of life of believers as a witness to "them that are without"; in 1 Cor. 14:40, "decently," in contrast with confusion in the churches.

C. Noun.

semnotes (4587) denotes "gravity, dignified seriousness"; it is rendered "honesty" in the KJV of 1 Tim. 2:2, RV, "gravity."

HONOR (Noun and Verb)
Old Testament

A. Verbs.

kabed (3513), "to honor," i.e., give high praise and status to another, in word and deed, Deut. 5:16.

hadar (1921), "to honor, prefer, exalt oneself, behave arrogantly"; honor, Exod. 23:3; to behave arrogantly, Prov. 25:6.

B. Nouns.

kabod (3519), "honor; glory; great quantity; multitude; wealth; reputation [majesty]; splendor." *kabod* refers to the great physical weight or "quantity" of a thing, Nah. 2:9. *kabod* often refers to both "wealth" and significant and positive "reputation"; wealth, Gen. 31:1; majesty, 45:13. So also in Ps. 85:9 is the idea of richness or abundance.

kabod can also have an abstract emphasis of "glory." When used in the sense of "honor" or "importance," cf. Gen. 45:13, there are two nuances of the word. First, *kabod* can emphasize the position of an individual within the sphere in which he lives, Prov. 11:16. This "honor" can be lost through wrong actions or attitudes, Prov. 26:1, 8 and evidenced in proper actions, Prov. 20:3; 25:2. This emphasis then is on a relationship between personalities. Second, there is a suggestion of nobility in many uses of the word, such as "honor" that belongs to a royal family, 1 Kings 3:13. Thus, *kabod* can be used of the social distinction and position of respect enjoyed by nobility.

When applied to God, the word represents a quality corresponding to Him and by which He is recognized. Joshua commanded Achan to give glory to God, to recognize His importance, worth, and significance, Josh. 7:19. In this and similar instances "giving honor" refers to saying something; what Achan was to do was to tell the truth. In other passages giving honor to God is a cultic recognition and confession of God as God, Ps. 29:1.

hadar (1926), "honor; splendor." First, *hadar* refers to "splendor" in nature," Lev. 23:40. Second, this word is a counterpart to Hebrew words for "glory" and "dignity." Thus *hadar* means not so much overwhelming beauty as a combination of physical attractiveness and social position. The Messiah is said to have "no form nor [majesty]; and when we shall see him, there is no beauty that we should desire him," Isa. 53:2. Mankind is crowned with "glory and honor" in the sense of superior desirability (for God) and rank, Ps. 8:5. In the case of earthly kings their beauty or brilliance usually arises from their surroundings, Ezek. 27:10-11.

The noun *hadarah* means "majesty; splendor; exaltation; adornment," Ps. 29:2.

C. Adjective.

kabed (3515), "heavy; numerous; severe; rich." The adjective *kabed* occurs about 40 times. Basically this adjective connotes "heavy." In Exod. 17:12 the word is used of physical weight: "But Moses' hands were heavy; and they took a stone, and put it under him, and he sat thereon; and Aaron and Hur stayed up his hands...." This adjective bears the connotation of heaviness as an enduring, ever-present quality, a lasting thing, Ps. 38:4. A task can be described as "heavy," Exod. 18:18. Moses argued his inability to lead God's people out of Egypt because he was "slow of speech, and of a slow tongue"; his speech or tongue was not smooth-flowing but halting, Exod. 4:10. Another nuance of this word appears in Exod. 7:14, where it is applied to Pharaoh's refusing heart.

A second series of passages uses this word of something that falls upon or overcomes one. So God sent upon Egypt a "heavy" hail, Exod. 9:18, a "great" swarm of insects, 8:24, "numerous" locusts, and a "severe" pestilence, 9:3. The first appearance of the word belongs to this category: "the famine was [severe] in the land" of Egypt, Gen. 12:10.

Used with a positive connotation, *kabed* can describe the amount of "riches," Gen. 13:2; or a collection of persons, Gen. 50:9.

New Testament

A. Noun.

time (5092), primarily "a valuing," hence, objectively, (a) "a price paid or received," e.g., Matt. 27:6, 9; Acts 4:34; 5:2, 3; 7:16, RV, "price" (KJV, "sum"); 19:19; 1 Cor. 6:20; 7:23; (b) of "the preciousness of Christ" unto believers, 1 Pet. 2:7, RV, i.e., the honor and inestimable value of Christ as appropriated by believers, who are joined, as living stones, to Him the cornerstone; (c) in the sense of value, of human ordinances, valueless against the indulgence of the flesh, or, perhaps of no value in attempts at asceticism, Col. 2:23; (d) "honor, esteem," (1) used in ascriptions of worship to God, 1 Tim. 1:17; 6:16; Rev. 4:9, 11; 5:13; 7:12; to Christ, 5:12, 13; (2) bestowed upon Christ by the Father, Heb. 2:9; 2 Pet. 1:17; (3) bestowed upon man, Heb. 2:7; (4) bestowed upon Aaronic priests, Heb. 5:4; (5) to be the reward hereafter of "the proof of faith" on the part of tried saints, 1 Pet. 1:7, RV; (6) used of the believer who as a vessel is "meet for the Master's use," 2 Tim. 2:21; (7) to be the reward of patience in well-doing, Rom. 2:7, and of working good (a perfect life to which man cannot attain, so as to be justified before God thereby), 2:10; (8) to be given to all to whom it is due, Rom. 13:7 (see 1 Pet. 2:17, under B, below); (9) as an advantage to be given by believers one to another instead of claiming it for self, Rom. 12:10; (10) to be given to elders that rule well ("double honor"), 1 Tim. 5:17 (here the meaning may be an honorarium); (11) to be given by servants to their master, 1 Tim. 6:1; (12) to be given to wives by husbands, 1 Pet. 3:7; (13) said of the husband's use of the wife, in contrast to the exercise of the passion of lust, 1 Thess. 4:4 (some regard the "vessel" here as the believer's body); (14) of that bestowed upon; parts of the body, 1 Cor. 12:23, 24; (15) of that which belongs to the builder of a house in contrast to the house itself, Heb. 3:3; (16) of that which is not enjoyed by a prophet in his own country, John 4:44; (17) of that bestowed by the inhabitants of Melita upon Paul and his fellow-passengers, in gratitude for his benefits of healing, Acts 28:10; (18) of the festive honor to be possessed by nations, and brought into the Holy City, the heavenly Jerusalem, Rev. 21:26 (in some mss., v. 24); (19) of honor bestowed upon things inanimate, a potter's vessel, Rom. 9:21; 2 Tim. 2:20.

B. Verb.

timao (*5091*), "to honor" (akin to A, above), is used of (a) valuing Christ at a price, Matt. 27:9, cf. A, above, (a); (b) "honoring" a person: (1) the "honor" done by Christ to the Father, John 8:49; (2) "honor" bestowed by the Father upon him who serves Christ, John 12:26; (3) the duty of all to "honor" the Son equally with the Father, 5:23; (4) the duty of children to "honor" their parents, Matt. 15:4; 19:19; Mark 7:10; 10:19; Luke 18:20; Eph. 6:2; (5) the duty of Christians to "honor" the king, and all men, 1 Pet. 2:17; (6) the respect and material assistance to be given to widows "that are widows indeed," 1 Tim. 5:3; (7) the "honor" done to Paul and his companions by the inhabitants of Melita, Acts 28:10; (8) mere lip profession of "honor" to God, Matt. 15:8; Mark 7:6.

HONORABLE, WITHOUT HONOR

1. *endoxos* (*1741*) denotes (a) "held in honor," "of high repute," 1 Cor. 4:10, KJV "(are) honorable," RV, "(have) glory," in contrast to *atimos*, "without honor."

2. *entimos* (*1784*), lit., "in honor," is used of the centurion's servant in Luke 7:2. "dear" (RV marg., "precious...or honorable"): of self-sacrificing servants of the Lord, said of Epaphroditus, Phil.

2:29, RV "(hold such) in honor" (KJV, "in reputation"; marg., "honor such"); of Christ, as a precious stone, 1 Pet. 2:4, 6 (RV marg., "honorable").

3. *euschemon* (2158) signifies "elegant, comely, of honorable position," KJV, "honorable," RV, "of honorable estate," Mark 15:43; Acts 13:50; 17:12; for other renderings in 1 Cor. 7:35 and 12:24.

4. *timios* (5093), "precious, valuable, honorable" (akin to *time*, "honor"; see No. 2), is used of marriage in Heb. 13:4, KJV, as a statement, "(marriage) is honorable (in all)," RV, as an exhortation, "let (marriage) be had in honor (among all)."

5. *kalos* (2570), "good, fair," is translated "honorable" in Rom. 12:17; 2 Cor. 8:21; 13:7, RV (KJV, "honest").

HOPE (Noun and Verb), HOPE (for)

A. Noun.

elpis (1680), in the NT, "favorable and confident expectation." It has to do with the unseen and the future, Rom. 8:24, 25. "Hope" describes (a) the happy anticipation of good (the most frequent significance), e.g., Titus 1:2; 1 Pet. 1:21; (b) the ground upon which "hope" is based, Acts 16:19; Col. 1:27, "Christ in you the hope of glory"; (c) the object upon which the "hope" is fixed, e.g., 1 Tim. 1:1.

Various phrases are used with the word "hope," in Paul's epistles and speeches: (1) Acts 23:6, "the hope and resurrection of the dead"; this has been regarded as a hendiadys (one by means of two), i.e., the "hope" of the resurrection; but the *kai*, "and," is epexegetic, defining the "hope," namely, the resurrection; (2) Acts 26:6, 7, "the hope of the promise (i.e., the fulfillment of the promise) made unto the fathers"; (3) Gal. 5:5, "the hope of righteousness"; i.e., the believer's complete conformity to God's will, at the coming of Christ; (4) Col. 1:23, "the hope of the Gospel," i.e., the "hope" of the fulfillment of all the promises presented in the gospel; cf. 1:5; (5) Rom. 5:2, "(the) hope of the glory of God," i.e., as in Titus 2:13, "the blessed hope and appearing of the glory of our great God and Savior Jesus Christ"; cf. Col. 1:27; (6) 1 Thess. 5:8, "the hope of salvation," i.e., of the rapture of believers, to take place at the opening of the Parousia of Christ; (7) Eph. 1:18, "the hope of His (God's) calling," i.e., the prospect before those who respond to His call in the gospel; (8) Eph. 4:4, "the hope of your calling," the same as (7), but regarded from the point of view of the called; (9) Titus 1:2, and 3:7, "the hope of eternal life," i.e., the full manifestation and realization of that life which is already the believer's possession; (10) Acts 28:20, "the hope of Israel," i.e., the expectation of the coming of the Messiah.

In Rom. 15:13 God is spoken of as "the God of hope," i.e., He is the author, not the subject, of it. "Hope" is a factor in salvation, Rom. 8:24; it finds its expression in endurance under trial, which is the effect of waiting for the coming of Christ, 1 Thess. 1:3; it is "an anchor of the soul," staying it amidst the storms of this life, Heb. 6:18, 19; it is a purifying power, "every one that hath this hope set on Him (Christ) purifieth himself, even as He is pure," 1 John 3:3, RV (the apostle John's one mention of "hope").

B. Verbs.

1. *elpizo* (*1679*), "to hope," is not infrequently translated in the KJV, by the verb "to trust"; the RV adheres to some form of the verb "to hope," e.g., John 5:45, "Moses, on whom ye have set your hope"; 2 Cor. 1:10, "on whom we have set our hope"; so in 1 Tim. 4:10; 5:5; 6:17; see also, e.g., Matt. 12:21; Luke 24:21; Rom. 15:12, 24.

The verb is followed by three prepositions: (1) *eis*, rendered "on" in John 5:45 (as above); the meaning is really "in" as in 1 Pet. 3:5, "who hoped in God"; the "hope" is thus said to be directed to, and to center in, a person; (2) *epi*, "on," Rom. 15:12, "On Him shall the Gentiles hope," RV; so 1 Tim. 4:10; 5:5 (in the best mss.); 6:17, RV; this expresses the ground upon which "hope" rests; (3) *en*, "in," 1 Cor. 15:19, "we have hoped in Christ," RV, more lit., "we are (men) that have hoped in Christ," the preposition expresses that Christ is not simply the ground upon whom, but the sphere and element in whom, the "hope" is placed. The form of the verb (the perfect participle with the verb to be, lit., "are having hoped") stresses the character of those who "hope," more than the action; "hope" characterizes them, showing what sort of persons they are.

2. *proelpizo* (*4276*), "to hope before" (*pro*, "before," and No. 1), is found in Eph. 1:12.

3. *apelpizo* (*560*), lit., "to hope from," Luke 6:35.

HORN

keras (*2768*), "a horn," is used in the plural, as the symbol of strength, (a) in the apocalyptic visions; (1) on the head of the Lamb as symbolic of Christ, Rev. 5:6; (2) on the heads of beasts as symbolic of national potentates, Rev. 12:3; 13:1, 11; 17:3, 7, 12, 16 (cf. Dan. 7:8; 8:9; Zech. 1:18, etc.); (3) at the corners of the golden altar, Rev. 9:13 (cf. Exod. 30:2; the horns were of one piece with the altar, as in the case of the brazen altar, 27:2, and were emblematic of the efficacy of the ministry connected with it); (b) metaphorically, in the singular, "a horn of salvation," Luke 1:69.

HORSE

hippos (*2462*), apart from the fifteen occurrences in the Apocalypse, occurs only in Jas. 3:3; in the Apocalypse "horses" are seen in visions in 6:2, 4, 5, 8; 9:7, 9, 17 (twice); 14:20; 19:11, 14, 19, 21; otherwise in 18:13; 19:18.

HOSANNA

hosanna (5614), in the Hebrew, means "save, we pray." The word seems to have become an utterance of praise rather than of prayer, though originally, probably, a cry for help. The people's cry at the Lord's triumphal entry into Jerusalem (Matt. 21:9, 15; Mark 11:9, 10; John 12:13) was taken from Ps. 118, which was recited at the Feast of Tabernacles in the great Hallel (Psalms 113 to 118).

HOSPITALITY

A. Noun.

philoxenia (5381), "love of strangers" (*philos*, "loving," *xenos*, "a stranger"), is used in Rom. 12:13; Heb. 13:2, lit. "(be not forgetful of) hospitality.

B. Adjective.

philoxenos (5382), "hospitable," occurs in 1 Tim. 3:2; Titus 1:8; 1 Pet. 4:9.

HOST (of angels, etc.)
Old Testament

A. Noun.

tsaba' (6633), "host; military service; war; army; service; labor; forced labor; conflict." This word involves several interrelated ideas: a group; impetus; difficulty; and force. These ideas undergird the general concept of "service" which one does for or under a superior rather than for himself. *tsaba'* is usually applied to "military service" but is sometimes used of "work" in general (under or for a superior). In Num. 1:2-3 the word means "military service." Num. 31:14 uses *tsaba'* of the actual battling itself. The word can also represent an "army," Num. 31:48. In Num. 1, 2, and 10, where *tsaba'* occurs with regard to a census of Israel, it is possibly suggested that this was a military census by which God organized His "army" to march through the wilderness.

That *tsaba'* can refer to a "group" for any purpose, Ps. 68:11; of stars, Zeph. 1:5; Deut. 4:19; or angels, 1 Kings 22:19; Dan. 8:10-11. Another meaning of the phrase "the host(s) of heaven" is simply "the numberless stars," Jer. 33:22; including all heavenly bodies, Ps. 33:6. The meaning "nonmilitary service in behalf of a superior" emerges in Num. 4:2-3. In Job 7:1 the word represents the burdensome everyday "toil" of mankind. In Job 14:14 *tsaba'* seems to represent "forced labor." In Dan. 10:1 the word is used for "conflict."

B. Verb.

tsaba' (6633), "to wage war, to muster an army, to serve in worship," Num. 31:7; or muster an army, 2 Kings 25:19; or serving in worship, Num. 4:23.

New Testament

stratia (4756), "an army," is used of angels, Luke 2:13; of stars, Acts 7:42.

HOT

zestos (2200), "boiling hot" (from *zeo*, "to boil, be hot, fervent"; cf. Eng., "zest"), is used, metaphorically, in Rev. 3:15, 16.

HOUR

hora (5610), whence Lat., *hora*, Eng., "hour," primarily denoted any time or period, especially a season. In the NT it is used to denote (a) "a part of the day," especially a twelfth part of day or night, an "hour," e.g., Matt. 8:13; Acts 10:3, 9; 23:23; Rev. 9:15; in 1 Cor. 15:30, "every hour" stands for "all the time"; in some passages it expresses duration, e.g., Matt. 20:12; 26:40; Luke 22:59; inexactly, in such phrases as "for a season," John 5:35; 2 Cor. 7:8; "for an hour," Gal. 2:5; "for a short season," 1 Thess. 2:17, RV (KJV, "for a short time," lit., "for the time of an hour"); (b) "a period more or less extended," e.g., 1 John 2:18, "it is the last hour," RV; (C) "a definite point of time," e.g., Matt. 26:45, "the hour is at hand"; Luke 1:10; 10:21; 14:17, lit., "at the hour of supper"; Acts 16:18; 22:13; Rev. 3:3; 11:13; 14:7; a point of time when an appointed action is to begin, Rev. 14:15; in Rom. 13:11, "it is high time," lit., "it is already an hour," indicating that a point of time has come later than would have been the case had responsibility been realized. In 1 Cor. 4:11, it indicates a point of time previous to which certain circumstances have existed.

HOUSE

oikos (3624) denotes (a) "a house, a dwelling," e.g., Matt. 9:6, 7; 11:8; it is used of the Tabernacle, as the House of God, Matt. 12:4, and the Temple similarly, e.g., Matt. 21:13; Luke 11:51, KJV, "temple," RV, "sanctuary"; John 2:16, 17; called by the Lord "your house" in Matt. 23:38 and Luke 13:35 (some take this as the city of Jerusalem); metaphorically of Israel as God's house, Heb. 3:2, 5, where "his house" is not Moses', but God's; of believers, similarly, v. 6, where Christ is spoken of as "over God's House" (the word "own" is rightly omitted in the RV); Heb. 10:21; 1 Pet. 2:5; 4:17; of the body, Matt. 12:44; Luke 11:24; (b) by metonymy, of the members of a household or family, e.g., Luke 10:5; Acts 7:10; 11:14; 1 Tim. 3:4, 5, 12; 2 Tim. 1:16; 4:19, RV (KJV, "household"); Titus 1:11 (plural); of a local church, 1 Tim. 3:15; of the descendants of Jacob (Israel) and David, e.g., Matt. 10:6; Luke 1:27, 33; Acts 2:36; 7:42.

HOUSEHOLD

A. Nouns.

1. *oikos* (3624) is translated "household" in Acts 16:15; 1 Cor. 1:16; in the KJV of 2 Tim. 4:19 (RV, "house").

2. *oikia* (3614) is translated "household" in Phil. 4:22.

3. *oiketeia* (3610d) denotes "a household of servants," Matt. 24:45 (some mss. have No. 4 here).

4. *therapeia* (2322), "service, care, attention," is also used in the collective sense of "a household," in Luke 12:42 (see No. 3).

B. Adjectives.

1. *oikeios* (3609), akin to A, No. 1, primarily signifies "of, or belonging to, a house," hence, "of persons, one's household, or kindred," as in 1 Tim. 5:8, RV, "household," KJV "house," marg., "kindred"; in Eph. 2:19, "the household of God" denotes the company of the redeemed; in Gal. 6:10, it is called "the household of the faith," RV.

2. *oikiakos* (3615), from A, No. 2, denotes "belonging to one's household, one's own"; it is used in Matt. 10:25, 36.

HOUSEHOLDER

A. Noun.

oikodespotes (3617), "a master of a house" appears in Matt. 10:25; Luke 13:25, and 14:21, where the context shows that the authority of the "householder" is stressed; "goodman of the house," is used in Matt. 24:43; Mark 14:14; and Luke 12:39; "householder" is the rendering in Matt. 13:27, 52; 20:1; 21:33.

B. Verb.

oikodespoteo (3616), corresponding to A, "to rule a house," is used in 1 Tim. 5:14.

HOWL

ololuzo (3649), an onomatopoeic verb (expressing its significance in its sound), "to cry aloud"; it is found in Jas. 5:1 in an exhortation to the godless rich.

HUMBLE (Adjective and Verb)

Old Testament

A. Verbs.

kana' (3665), "to be humble, to humble, subdue," used in subduing enemies, 2 Sam. 8:1; 1 Chron. 17:10; Ps. 81:14. "To humble oneself" before God in repentance is a common theme and need in the life of ancient Israel, Lev. 26:41; 2 Chron. 7:14; 12:6-7, 12.

shapel (8213), "to be low, become low; sink down; be humiliated;

be abased," generally used in a figurative sense. *shapel* rarely denotes a literal lowness. Even in passages where the meaning may be taken literally, the prophet communicates a spiritual truth, Isa. 10:33; 40:4. Isaiah particularly presented Judah's sin as one of rebellion, self-exaltation, and pride, 2:17; 3:16-17. Pride and self-exaltation have no place in the life of the godly, as the Lord "brings low" a person, a city, and a nation, 1 Sam. 2:7.

B. Nouns.

Some nouns related to this verb occur infrequently. *shepel* refers to a "low condition, low estate." This word appears twice, Ps. 136:23; Eccl. 10:6. The noun *shiplah* means a "humiliated state." This noun occurs once: "When it shall hail, coming down on the forest; and the city shall be low in a low place," Isa. 32:19; the city is leveled completely. *shepelah* means "lowland." This word is used most often as a technical designation for the low-lying hills of the Judean hill country, cf. Deut. 1:7; Josh. 9:1. *shiplut* refers to a "sinking." This noun's single appearance is in Eccl. 10:18.

C. Adjective.

shapal (8217), means "low; humble." This word means "low" in Ezek. 17:24: "And all the trees of the field shall know that I the Lord have brought down the high tree, have exalted the low tree...." In Isa. 57:15 *shapal* refers to "humble": "...I dwell in the high and holy place, with him also that is of a contrite and humble spirit, to revive the spirit of the humble, and to revive the heart of the contrite ones."

New Testament

A. Adjectives.

1. *tapeinos* (5011) primarily signifies "low-lying." It is used always in a good sense in the NT, metaphorically, to denote (a) "of low degree, brought low," Luke 1:52; Rom. 12:16, KJV, "(men) of low estate," RV, "(things that are) lowly" (i.e., of low degree); 2 Cor. 7:6, KJV, "cast down," RV, "lowly"; the preceding context shows that this occurrence belongs to (a); Jas. 1:9, "of low degree"; (b) humble in spirit, Matt. 11:29; 2 Cor. 10:1, RV, "lowly," KJV "base"; Jas. 4:6; 1 Pet. 5:5.

2. *tapeinophron*, "humble-minded" (*phren*, "the mind"), 1 Pet. 3:8.

B. Verb.

tapeinoo (5013), akin to A, signifies "to make low," (a) literally, "of mountains and hills," Luke 3:5 (passive voice); (b) metaphorically, in the active voice, Matt. 18:4; 23:12 (2nd part); Luke 14:11 (2nd part); 18:14 (2nd part); 2 Cor. 11:7 ("abasing"); 12:21; Phil. 2:8; in the passive voice, Matt. 23:12 (1st part), RV, "shall be humbled," KJV, "shall be abased"; Luke 14:11; 18:14; Phil. 4:12, "to be abased";

in the passive, with middle voice sense, Jas. 4:10, "humble yourselves"; 1 Pet. 5:6.

TO BE HUMBLED, AFFLICTED

A. Verb.

'anah (6031), "to be afflicted, be bowed down, be humbled, be meek." 'anah often expresses harsh and painful treatment. Sarai "dealt hardly" with Hagar, Gen. 16:6. When Joseph was sold as a slave, his feet were hurt with fetters, Ps. 105:18. Frequently the verb expresses the idea that God sends affliction for disciplinary purposes, 1 Kings 11:39; Ps. 90:15.

B. Noun.

'ani (6041), "poor; humble; meek." Especially in later Israelite history, just before the Exile and following, this noun came to have a special connection with those faithful ones who were being abused, taken advantage of, by the rich, Isa. 29:19; 32:7; Amos 2:7. The prophet Zephaniah's reference to them as the "meek of the earth," Zeph. 2:3 set the stage for Jesus' concern and ministry to the "poor" and the "meek," Matt. 5:3, 5; Luke 4:18; cf. Isa. 61:1.

HUMBLENESS OF MIND, HUMILITY

tapeinophrosune (5012), "lowliness of mind," is rendered "humility of mind" in Acts 20:19, KJV (RV, "lowliness of mind"); in Eph. 4:2, "lowliness"; in Phil. 2:3, "lowliness of mind"; in Col. 2:18, 23, of a false "humility"; in Col. 3:12, KJV, "humbleness of mind," RV, "humility"; 1 Pet. 5:5, "humility."

HUMILIATION

tapeinosis (5014), akin to tapeinos, is rendered "low estate" in Luke 1:48; "humiliation," Acts 8:33; Phil. 3:21, RV "(the body of our) humiliation," KJV, "(our) vile (body)"; Jas. 1:10, where "in that he is made low " is, lit., "in his humiliation."

HUNGER (Noun and Verb), HUNGERED, HUNGRY

A. Noun.

limos (3042) has the meanings "famine" and "hunger"; "hunger" in Luke 15:17; 2 Cor. 11:27; in Rev. 6:8, RV "famine" (KJV, "hunger").

B. Verb.

peinao (3983), "to hunger, be hungry, hungered," is used (a) literally, e.g., Matt. 4:2; 12:1; 21:18; Rom. 12:20; 1 Cor. 11:21, 34; Phil. 4:12; Rev. 7:16; Christ identifies Himself with His saints in speaking of Himself as suffering in their sufferings in this and other respects, Matt. 25:35, 42; (b) metaphorically, Matt. 5:6; Luke 6:21, 25; John 6:35.

C. Adjective.

prospeinos (*4361*) signifies "hungry" (*pros*, "intensive," *peina*, "hunger"), Acts 10:10, KJV, "very hungry," RV, "hungry."

HURT (Noun and Verb), HURTFUL

A. Verbs

1. *adikeo* (*91*) signifies, intransitively, "to do wrong, do hurt, act unjustly" (*a*, negative, and *dike*, "justice"), transitively, "to wrong, hurt or injure a person." It is translated "to hurt" in the following: (a), intransitively, Rev. 9:19; (b) transitively, Luke 10:19; Rev 2:11 (passive); 6:6; 7:2, 3; 9:4, 10; 11:5.

2. *blapto* (*984*) signifies "to injure, mar, do damage to," Mark 16:18, "shall (in no wise) hurt (them)"; Luke 4:35, "having done (him no) hurt," RV. *adikeo* stresses the unrighteousness of the act, *blapto* stresses the injury done.

3. *kakoo* (*2559*), "to do evil to anyone," Acts 7:6.

B. Adjective.

blaberos (*983*), akin to A, No. 2, signifies "hurtful," 1 Tim. 6:9, said of lusts.

HUSBANDMAN

georgos (*1092*), from *ge*, "land, ground," and *ergo* (or *erdo*), "to do" (Eng., "George"), denotes (a) "a husbandman," a tiller of the ground, 2 Tim. 2:6; Jas. 5:7; (b) "a vinedresser," Matt. 21:33-35, 38, 40, 41; Mark 12:1, 2, 7, 9; Luke 20:9, 10, 14, 16; John 15:1, where Christ speaks of the Father as the "Husbandman," Himself as the Vine, His disciples as the branches, the object being to bear much fruit, life in Christ producing the fruit of the Spirit, i.e., character and ways in conformity to Christ.

HYMN (Noun and Verb)

A. Noun.

humnos (*5215*) denotes "a song of praise addressed to God" (Eng., "hymn"), Eph. 5:19; Col. 3:16, in each of which the punctuation should probably be changed; in the former "speaking to one another" goes with the end of v. 18, and should be followed by a semicolon; similarly in Col. 3:16, the first part of the verse should end with the words "admonishing one another," where a semicolon should be placed.

B. Verb.

humneo (*5214*), akin to A, is used (a) transitively, Matt. 26:30; Mark 14:26, where the "hymn" was that part of the Hallel consisting of

Psalms 113-118; (b) intransitively, where the verb itself is rendered "to sing praises" or "praise," Acts 16:25; Heb. 2:12. The Psalms are called, in general, "hymns," by Philo; Josephus calls them "songs and hymns."

HYPOCRISY

hupokrisis (5272) primarily denotes "a reply, an answer" (akin to *hupokrinomai*, "to answer"); then, "play-acting," as the actors spoke in dialogue; hence, "pretence, hypocrisy"; it is translated "hypocrisy" in Matt. 23:28; Mark 12:15; Luke 12:1; 1 Tim. 4:2; the plural in 1 Pet. 2:1. For Gal. 2:13 and *anupokritos*, "without hypocrisy," in Jas. 3:17.

HYPOCRITE

hupokrites (5273), corresponding to the above, primarily denotes "one who answers"; then, "a stage-actor"; it was a custom for Greek and Roman actors to speak in large masks with mechanical devices for augmenting the force of the voice; hence the word became used metaphorically of "a dissembler, a hypocrite." It is found only in the Synoptists, and always used by the Lord, fifteen times in Matthew; elsewhere, Mark 7:6; Luke 6:42; 11:44 (in some mss.); 12:56; 13:15.

HYSSOP

hussopos (5301), a bunch of which was used in ritual sprinklings, is found in Heb. 9:19; in John 19:29 the reference is apparently to a branch or rod of "hyssop," upon which a sponge was put and offered to the Lord on the cross.

I

IDLE

argos (*692*) denotes "inactive, idle, unfruitful, barren" (**a**, negative, and **ergon**, "work"); it is used (a) literally, Matt. 20:3, 6; 1 Tim. 5:13 (twice); Titus 1:12, RV, "idle (gluttons); 2 Pet. 1:8, RV, "idle," KJV, "barren"; (b) metaphorically in the sense of "ineffective, worthless," as of a word, Matt. 12:36; of faith unaccompanied by works, Jas. 2:20 (some mss. have **nekra**, "dead").

IDOL

Old Testament

terapim (*8655*), "idol; household idol; cultic mask; divine symbol." *terapim* first appears in Gen. 31:19. Hurrian law of this period recognized "household idols" as deeds to the family's succession and goods. To understand the *terapim* [here a plural of "majesty"] of 1 Sam. 19:13 as a "household idol" is difficult, in view of verse 11, where it is said to be in David's private quarters. In Judg. 18:14-17 *terapim* appears to be distinguished from idols: "...there is in these houses an ephod, and *terapim*, and a graven image, and a molten image?" *terapim* may signify an "idol," a "cultic mask," or perhaps a "symbol of the divine presence," Judg. 18:31.

'elil (*457*), "idol; gods; nought; vain." This disdainful word signifies an "idol" or "false god," Lev. 19:4; 26:1; Ps. 96:5. Second, *'elil* can mean "nought" or "vain." 1 Chron. 16:26 might well be rendered: "For all the gods of the people are nought." This nuance appears clearly in Job 13:4.

gillulim (*1544*), "idols." Of the 48 occurrences of this word, all but 9 appear in Ezekiel. This word for "idols" is a disdainful word and may originally have meant "dung pellets," Lev. 26:30. This word and others for "idol" exhibit the horror and scorn that biblical writers felt toward them. In passages such as Isa. 66:3 the word for "idol," *'awen*, means "uncanny or wickedness." Jer. 50:38 evidences the word *'emim*, which means "fright or horror." The word *'elil* appears for "idol" in Lev. 19:4; it means "nothingness or feeble." 1 Kings 15:13 uses the Hebrew word, *mipletset*, meaning a "horrible thing, a cause of trembling.

New Testament

eidolon (*1497*), primarily "a phantom or likeness" (from **eidos**, "an appearance," lit., "that which is seen"), or "an idea, fancy," denotes in the NT (a) "an idol," an image to represent a false god, Acts 7:41; 1 Cor. 12:2; Rev. 9:20; (b) "the false god" worshipped in an image, Acts 15:20; Rom. 2:22; 1 Cor. 8:4, 7; 10:19; 2 Cor. 6:16; 1 Thess. 1:9; 1 John 5:21.

The corresponding Heb. word denotes "vanity," Jer. 14:22; 18:15; "thing of nought," Lev. 19:4, marg., cf. Eph. 4:17. Hence what represented a deity to the Gentiles, was to Paul a "vain thing," Acts 14:15; "nothing in the world," 1 Cor. 8:4; 10:19. Jeremiah calls the idol a "scarecrow" ("pillar in a garden," 10:5, marg.), and Isaiah, 44:9-20, etc., and Habakkuk, 2:18, 19 and the Psalmist, 115:4-8, etc., are all equally scathing. It is important to notice, however, that in each case the people of God are addressed. When he speaks to idolaters, Paul, knowing that no man is won by ridicule, adopts a different line, Acts 14:15-18; 17:16, 21-31.

IDOLS (full of)

kateidolos (2712), an adjective denoting "full of idols" (*kata*, "throughout," and *eidolon*), is said of Athens in Acts 17:16, RV, and KJV, marg. (KJV, "wholly given to idolatry").

IDOLS (offered to, sacrificed to)

1. *eidolothutos* (1494) is an adjective signifying "sacrificed to idols" (*eidolon*, as above, and *thuo*, "to sacrifice"), Acts 15:29; 21:25; 1 Cor. 8:1, 4, 7, 10; 10:19 (in all these the RV substitutes "sacrificed" for the KJV); Rev. 2:14, 20 (in these the RV and KJV both have "sacrificed"). Some inferior mss. have this adjective in 1 Cor. 10:28; see No. 2. The flesh of the victims, after sacrifice, was eaten or sold.

2. *nierothutos*, "offered in sacrifice" (*hieros*, "sacred," and *thuo*, "to sacrifice"), is found in the best mss. in 1 Cor. 10:28 (see No. 1).

IDOLATER

eidololatres (1496), an "idolater" (from *eidolon*, and *latris*, "a hireling"), is found in 1 Cor. 5:10, 11; 6:9; 10:7; the warning is to believers against turning away from God to idolatry, whether "openly or secretly, consciously or unconsciously"; Eph. 5:5; Rev. 21:8; 22:15.

IDOLATRY

eidololatria (or -*eia*) (1495), whence Eng., "idolatry," (from *eidolon*, and *latreia*, "service"), is found in 1 Cor. 10:14; Gal. 5:20; Col. 3:5; and, in the plural, in 1 Pet. 4:3.

Heathen sacrifices were sacrificed to demons, 1 Cor. 10:19; there was a dire reality in the cup and table of demons and in the involved communion with demons. In Rom. 1:22-25, "idolatry," the sin of the mind against God (Eph. 2:3), and immorality, sins of the flesh, are associated, and are traced to lack of the acknowledgment of God and of gratitude to Him. An "idolater" is a slave to the depraved ideas his idols represent, Gal. 4:8, 9; and thereby, to divers lusts, Titus 3:3.

IGNORANCE, IGNORANT, IGNORANTLY

A. Nouns.

1. *agnoia* (52), lit., "want of knowledge or perception" (akin to *agnoeo*, "to be ignorant"), denotes "ignorance" on the part of the Jews regarding Christ, Acts 3:17; of Gentiles in regard to God, 17:30; Eph. 4:18 (here including the idea of willful blindness: see Rom. 1:28, not the "ignorance" which mitigates guilt); 1 Pet. 1:14, of the former unregenerate condition of those who became believers (RV, "in *the time of* your ignorance").

2. *agnosia* (56) denotes "ignorance" as directly opposed to *gnosis*, which signifies "knowledge" as a result of observation and experience (*a*, negative, *ginosko*, "to know"; cf. Eng., "agnostic"); 1 Cor. 15:34 ("no knowledge"); 1 Pet. 2:15. In both these passages reprehensible "ignorance" is suggested.

3. *agnoema* (51), "a sin of ignorance," occurs in Heb. 9:7, "errors" (RV marg., "ignorances"). For the corresponding verb in Heb. 5:2 see B, No. 1. What is especially in view in these passages is unwitting error. For Israel a sacrifice was appointed, greater in proportion to the culpability of the guilty, greater, for instance, for a priest or ruler than for a private person. Sins of "ignorance," being sins, must be expiated. A believer guilty of a sin of "ignorance" needs the efficacy of the expiatory sacrifice of Christ, and finds "grace to help." Yet, as the conscience of the believer receives enlightenment, what formerly may have been done in "ignorance" becomes a sin against the light and demands a special confession, to receive forgiveness, 1 John 1:8, 9.

B. Verbs.

1. *agnoeo* (50), signifies (a) "to be ignorant, not to know," either intransitively, 1 Cor. 14:38 (in the 2nd occurrence in this verse, the RV text translates the active voice, the margin the passive); 1 Tim. 1:13, lit., "being ignorant (I did it)"; Heb. 5:2, "ignorant"; or transitively, 2 Pet. 2:12, KJV, "understand not," RV, "are ignorant (of)"; Acts 13:27, "knew (Him) not"; 17:23, RV, "(what ye worship) in ignorance," for KJV, "(whom ye) ignorantly (worship)," lit., "(what) not knowing (ye worship"; also rendered by the verb "to be ignorant that," or "to be ignorant of," Rom. 1:13; 10:3; 11:25; 1 Cor. 10:1; 12:1; 2 Cor. 1:8; 2:11; 1 Thess. 4:13; to know not, Rom. 2:4; 6:3; 7:1; to be unknown (passive voice), 2 Cor. 6:9; Gal. 1:22; (b) "not to understand," Mark 9:32; Luke 9:45.

IMAGE

1. *eikon* (1504) denotes "an image"; the word involves the two

ideas of representation and manifestation. "The idea of perfection does not lie in the word itself, but must be sought from the context" (Lightfoot); the following instances clearly show any distinction between the imperfect and the perfect likeness.

The word is used (1) of an "image" or a coin (not a mere likeness), Matt. 22:20; Mark 12:16; Luke 20:24; so of a statue or similar representation (more than a resemblance), Rom. 1:23; Rev. 13:14, 15 (thrice); 14:9, 11; 15:2; 16:2; 19:20; 20:4; of the descendants of Adam as bearing his image, 1 Cor. 15:49, each a representation derived from the prototype; (2) of subjects relative to things spiritual, Heb. 10:1, negatively of the Law as having "a shadow of the good things to come, not the very image of the things," i.e., not the essential and substantial form of them; the contrast has been likened to the difference between a statue and the shadow cast by it; (3) of the relations between God the Father, Christ, and man, (a) of man as he was created as being a visible representation of God, 1 Cor. 11:7, a being corresponding to the original; the condition of man as a fallen creature has not entirely effaced the "image"; he is still suitable to bear responsibility, he still has Godlike qualities, such as love of goodness and beauty, none of which are found in a mere animal; in the Fall man ceased to be a perfect vehicle for the representation of God; God's grace in Christ will yet accomplish more than what Adam lost; (b) of regenerate persons, in being moral representations of what God is, Col. 3:10; cf. Eph. 4:24; (c) of believers, in their glorified state, not merely as resembling Christ but representing Him, Rom. 8:29; 1 Cor. 15:49; here the perfection is the work of divine grace; believers are yet to represent, not something like Him, but what He is in Himself, both in His spiritual body and in His moral character; (d) of Christ in relation to God, 2 Cor. 4:4, "the image of God," i.e., essentially and absolutely the perfect expression and representation of the Archetype, God the Father; in Col. 1:15, "the image of the invisible God" gives the additional thought suggested by the word "invisible," that Christ is the visible representation and manifestation of God to created beings; the likeness expressed in this manifestation is involved in the essential relations in the Godhead, and is therefore unique and perfect; "he that hath seen Me hath seen the Father," John 14:9. "The epithet 'invisible'…must not be confined to the apprehension of the bodily senses, but will include the cognizance of the inward eye also" (Lightfoot).

2. *charakter* (5481) denotes, firstly, "a tool for graving" (from *charasso*, "to cut into, to engross"; cf. Eng., "character," "characteristic"); then, "a stamp" or "impress," as on a coin or a seal, in which case the seal or die which makes an impression bears the "image" produced by it, and, *vice versa*, all the features of the "image" correspond respectively with those of the instrument producing it. In the NT it is used metaphorically in Heb. 1:3, of the Son of God as "the very image (marg., 'the impress') of His substance."

IMAGINATION

1. *logismos* (3053), "a reasoning, a thought" (akin to *logizomai*, "to count, reckon"), is translated "thoughts" in Rom. 2:15, suggestive of evil intent, not of mere reasonings; "imaginations" in 2 Cor. 10:5. The word suggests the contemplation of actions as a result of the verdict of conscience.

2. *dialogismos* (1261), *dia*, and No. 1, is rendered "imaginations" in Rom. 1:21, carrying with it the idea of evil purposes.

3. *dianoia* (1271), strictly, "a thinking over," denotes "the faculty of thinking"; then, "of knowing"; hence, "the understanding," and in general, "the mind," and so, "the faculty of moral reflection"; it is rendered "imagination" in Luke 1:51, "the imagination of their heart" signifying their thoughts and ideas.

IMITATE, IMITATOR

A. Verb.

mimeomai (3401), "a mimic, an actor" (Eng., "mime," etc.), is always translated "to imitate" in the RV, for KJV, "to follow," (a) of imitating the conduct of missionaries, 2 Thess. 3:7, 9; the faith of spiritual guides, Heb. 13:7; (b) that which is good, 3 John 11. The verb is always used in exhortations, and always in the continuous tense, suggesting a constant habit or practice.

B. Nouns.

1. *mimetes* (3402), akin to A, "an imitator," so the RV for KJV, "follower," is always used in a good sense in the NT. In 1 Cor. 4:16; 11:1; Eph. 5:1; Heb. 6:12, it is used in exhortations, accompanied by the verb *ginomai*, "to be, become," and in the continuous tense (see A) except in Heb. 6:12, where the aorist or momentary tense indicates a decisive act with permanent results; in 1 Thess. 1:6; 2:14, the accompanying verb is in the aorist tense, referring to the definite act of conversion in the past. These instances, coupled with the continuous tenses referred to, teach that what we became at conversion we must diligently continue to be thereafter.

2. *summimetes* (4831) denotes "a fellow imitator" (*sun*, "with," and No. 1), Phil. 3:17, RV, "imitators together" (KJV, "followers together").

IMMORTAL, IMMORTALITY

athanasia (110), lit., "deathlessness," is rendered "immortality" in 1 Cor. 15:53, 54, of the glorified body of the believer; 1 Tim. 6:16, of the nature of God. In the NT *athanasia* expresses more than deathlessness, it suggests the quality of the life enjoyed, as is clear from 2 Cor. 5:4; for the believer what is mortal is to be "swallowed up of life."

˙IMMUTABLE, IMMUTABILITY

ametathetos (276), an adjective signifying "immutable" (*a*, negative, *metatithemi*, "to change"), Heb. 6:18, where the "two immutable things" are the promise and the oath. In v. 17 the word is used in the neuter with the article, as a noun, denoting "the immutability," with reference to God's counsel. Examples from the papyri show that the word was used as a technical term in connection with wills. The connotation adds considerably to the force of Heb. 6:17ff.

IMPEDIMENT

mogilalos (3424) denotes "speaking with difficulty," "stammering," Mark 7:32.

IMPENITENT

ametanoetos (279), lit., "without change of mind," is used in Rom. 2:5, "impenitent" (or "unrepentant"). Moulton and Milligan show from the papyri writings that the word is also used "in a passive sense, not affected by change of mind,' like *ametameletos* in Rom. 11:29," "without repentance."

IMPLANTED

emphutos (1721), "implanted," or "rooted" (from *emphuo*, "to implant"), is used in Jas. 1:21, RV, "implanted," for KJV, "engrafted," of the Word of God, as the "rooted word," i.e., a word whose property it is to root itself like a seed in the heart. "The KJV seems to identify it with *emphuteuton*, which however would be out of place here, since the word is sown, not grafted, in the heart" (Mayor).

IMPORTUNITY

anaidia (or *anaideia*) (335), denotes "shamelessness, importunity" (*a*, negative, *n*, euphonic, and *aidos*, "shame, modesty"), and is used in the Lord s illustration concerning the need of earnestness and perseverance in prayer, Luke 11:8. If shameless persistence can obtain a boon from a neighbor, then certainly earnest prayer will receive our Father's answer.

IMPOSED

epikeimai (1945) denotes "to be placed on, to lie on," (a) literally, as of the stone on the sepulchre of Lazarus, John 11:38; of the fish on the fire of coals, 21:9; (b) figuratively, of a tempest (to press upon), Acts 27:20; of a necessity laid upon the apostle Paul, 1 Cor. 9:16; of the pressure of the multitude upon Christ to hear Him, Luke 5:1, "pressed upon"; of the insistence of the chief priests, rulers and people that Christ should be crucified, Luke 23:23, "were instant"; of carnal ordinances "imposed" under the Law until a time of reformation, brought in through the High Priest-hood of Christ, Heb. 9:10.

IMPOSSIBLE

A. Adjective.

adunatos (102), from *a*, negative, and *dunatos*, "able, strong," is used (a) of persons, Acts 14:8, "impotent"; figuratively, Rom. 15:1, "weak"; (b) of things, "impossible," Matt. 19:26; Mark 10:27; Luke 18:27; Heb. 6:4, 18; 10:4; 11:6; in Rom. 8:3, "for what the Law could not do," is, more lit., "the inability of the law"; the meaning may be either "the weakness of the Law," or "that which was impossible for the Law"; the latter is perhaps preferable; literalism is ruled out here, but the sense is that the Law could neither justify nor impart life.

B. Verb.

adunateo (101) signifies "to be impossible" (corresponding to A, No. 1), "unable"; in the NT it is used only of things, Matt. 17:20.

IMPOSTORS

I

goes (1114) primarily denotes "a wailer" (*goao*, "to wail"); hence, from the howl in which spells were chanted, "a wizard, sorcerer, enchanter," and hence, "a juggler, cheat, impostor," rendered "im-postors" in 2 Tim. 3:13.

IMPUTE

1. *logizomai* (3049), "to reckon, take into account," or, metaphor-ically, "to put down to a person's account," is never rendered in the RV by the verb "to impute." In the following, where the KJV has that rendering, the RV uses the verb "to reckon," which is far more suitable, Rom. 4:6, 8, 11, 22, 23, 24; 2 Cor. 5:19; Jas. 2:23.

2. *ellogao*, or *-eo* (1677) (the *-ao* termination is the one found in the *Koine*, the language covering the NT period), denotes "to charge to one's account, to lay to one's charge," and is translated "imputed" in Rom. 5:13. In Philem. 18 the verb is rendered "put (that) to (mine) account."

INCENSE (burn)

A. Noun.

thumiama (2368) denotes "fragrant stuff for burning, incense" (from *thuo*, "to offer in sacrifice"), Luke 1:10, 11; in the plural, Rev. 5:8 and 18:13, RV (KJV, "odors"); 8:3, 4, signifying "frankincense" here. In connection with the tabernacle, the "incense" was to be prepared from stacte, onycha, and galbanum, with pure frankin-cense, an equal weight of each; imitation for private use was for-bidden, Exod. 30:34-38.

B. Verb.

thumiao (2370), "to burn incense" (see A), is found in Luke 1:9.

INCREASE (Verb)

1. *perisseo* (4052), "to be over and above, to abound," is translated "increased" in Acts 16:5, of churches; "increase" in the KJV of 1 Thess. 4:10 (RV, abound).

2. *pleonazo* (4121), "to make to abound," is translated "make (you) to increase" in 1 Thess. 3:12.

3. *prokopto* (4278) is translated by the verb "to increase" in Luke 2:52 and in the KJV of 2 Tim. 2:16 (RV, "will proceed further").

4. *prostithemi* (4369), "to put to, add to," is translated "increase" in Luke 17:5.

INDEBTED (to be)

opheilo (3784), "to owe, to be a debtor," is translated "is indebted" in Luke 11:4. Luke does not draw a parallel between our forgiving and God's; he speaks of God's forgiving sins, of our forgiving "debts," moral debts, probably not excluding material debts.

INDIGNATION

A. Noun.

aganaktesis (24) is rendered "indignation" in 2 Cor. 7:11.

B. Verb.

aganakteo (23), "to be indignant, to be moved with indignation" (from *agan*, "much," *achomai*, "to grieve"), is translated "were moved with indignation" of the ten disciples against James and John, Matt. 20:24; in Mark 10:41, RV (KJV, "they began to be much displeased"); in Matt. 21:15, of the chief priests and scribes, against Christ and the children, RV, "they were moved with indignation" (KJV, "they were sore displeased"); in 26:8, of the disciples against the woman who anointed Christ's feet, "they had indignation"; so Mark 14:4; in Mark 10:14, of Christ, against the disciples, for rebuking the children, "He was moved with indignation," RV (KJV, "he was much displeased"); in Luke 13:14, of the ruler of the synagogue against Christ for healing on the Sabbath, "being moved with indignation," RV, KJV, "(answered) with indignation."

INDULGENCE

1. *anesis* (425), "a loosening, relaxation of strain" (akin to *aniemi*, "to relax, loosen"), is translated "indulgence" in Acts 24:23, RV (KJV, "liberty"), in the command of Felix to the centurion, to moderate restrictions upon Paul. In the NT it always carries the thought of relief from tribulation or persecution; so 2 Thess. 1:7, "rest"; in 2 Cor. 2:13 and 7:5 it is rendered "relief," RV (KJV, "rest"); in 8:13, "eased."

2. *plesmone* (*4140*), "a filling up, satiety" (akin to *pimplemi*, "to fill"), is translated "indulgence (of the flesh)" in Col. 2:23, RV (KJV, "satisfying").

INFERIOR

hettaomai, or *hessaomai* (*2274*), "to be less or inferior," is used in the passive voice, and translated "ye were made inferior," in 2 Cor. 12:13, RV, for KJV, "ye were inferior," i.e., were treated with less consideration than other churches, through his independence in not receiving gifts from them. In 2 Pet. 2:19, 20 it signifies to be overcome, in the sense of being subdued and enslaved.

INFIRMITY

1. *ostheneia* (*769*), lit., "want of strength" (*a*, negative, *sthenos*, "strength"), "weakness," indicating inability to produce results, is most frequently translated "infirmity," or "infirmities"; in Rom. 8:26, the RV has "infirmity" (KJV, "infirmities"); in 2 Cor. 12:5, 9, 10, "weaknesses" and in 11:30, "weakness" (KJV, "infirmities"); in Luke 13:11 the phrase "a spirit of infirmity" attributes her curvature directly to satanic agency. The connected phraseology is indicative of trained medical knowledge on the part of the writer.

2. *asthenema* (*771*), akin to No. 1, is found in the plural in Rom. 15:1, "infirmities," i.e., those scruples which arise through weakness of faith. The strong must support the infirmities of the weak (*adunatos*) by submitting to self-restraint.

INFORM

1. *emphanizo* (*1718*), "to manifest, exhibit," in the middle and passive voices, "to appear, also signifies to declare, make known," and is translated "informed" in Acts 24:1; 25:2, 15.

2. *katecheo* (*2727*) primarily denotes "to resound" (*kata*, "down," *echos* "a sound"); then, "to sound down the ears, to teach by word of mouth, instruct, inform" (Eng., "catechize, catechumen"); it is rendered, in the passive voice, by the verb "to inform," in Acts 21:21, 24.

INHERIT, INHERITANCE

Old Testament

A. Verb.

nachal (*5157*), "to inherit, get possession of, take as a possession." Usually this term means to take a possession, and not inherit, Deut. 21:16; Prov. 28:10.

B. Noun.

nachalah (*5159*), "possession; property; inheritance." The basic translation of *nachalah* is "inheritance," 1 Kings 21:3. The word more appropriately refers to a "possession" to which one has received the legal claim, Num. 26:56; Josh. 11:23; 1 Kings 21:3-4; Ruth 4:10.

Metaphorically, Israel is said to be God's "possession," Deut. 4:20. Within the special covenantal status Israel experienced the blessing that its children were a special gift from the Lord, Ps. 127:3. However, the Lord abandoned Israel as His "possession" to the nations, cf. Isa. 47:6, and permitted a remnant of the "possession" to return, Mic. 7:18.

New Testament

A. Verbs.

1. **kleronomeo** (*2816*) strictly means "to receive by lot" (**kleros**, "a lot," **nemomai**, "to possess"); then, in a more general sense, "to possess oneself of, to receive as one's own, to obtain." The following list shows how in the NT the idea of inheriting broadens out to include all spiritual good provided through and in Christ, and particularly all that is contained in the hope grounded on the promises of God.

The verb is used of the following objects:

(a) birthright, that into the possession of which one enters in virtue of sonship, not because of a price paid or of a task accomplished, Gal. 4:30; Heb. 1:4; 12:17:

(b) that which is received as a gift, in contrast with that which is received as the reward of law-keeping, Heb. 1:14; 6:12 ("through," i.e., "through experiences that called for the exercise of faith and patience," but not "on the ground of the exercise of faith and patience").

(c) the reward of that condition of soul which forbears retaliation and self-vindication, and expresses itself in gentleness of behavior.... Matt. 5:5.

(d) the reward (in the coming age, Mark 10:30) of the acknowledgment of the paramountcy of the claims of Christ, Matt. 19:29. In the three accounts given of this incident, see Mark 10:17-31; Luke 18:18-30, the words of the question put to the Lord are, in Matthew, "that I may have," in Mark and Luke, "that I may inherit." In the report of the Lord's word to Peter in reply to his subsequent question, Matthew has "inherit eternal life," while Mark and Luke have "receive eternal life." It seems to follow that the meaning of the word "inherit" is here ruled by the words "receive" and "have," with which it is interchanged in each of the three Gospels, i.e., the less common word "inherit" is to be regarded as equivalent to the more common words "receive" and "have." Cf. Luke 10:25:

(e) the reward of those who have shown kindness to the "brethren" of the Lord in their distress, Matt. 25:34:

2. **kleroo** (*2820*) is used in the passive voice in Eph. 1:11, KJV, "we have obtained an inheritance"; RV, "we were made a heritage."

B. Nouns.

1. *kleronomia* (*2817*), "a lot" (see A), properly "an inherited property, an inheritance." It is always rendered inheritance in NT, but only in a few cases in the Gospels has it the meaning ordinarily attached to that word in English, i.e., that into possession of which the heir enters only on the death of an ancestor. The NT usage may be set out as follows: (a) that property in real estate which in ordinary course passes from father to son on the death of the former, Matt. 21:38; Mark 12:7; Luke 12:13; 20:14; (b) a portion of an estate made the substance of a gift, Acts 7:5; Gal. 3:18, which also is to be included under (c); (c) the prospective condition and possessions of the believer in the new order of things to be ushered in at the return of Christ, Acts 20:32; Eph. 1:14; 5:5; Col. 3:24; Heb. 9:15; 1 Pet. 1:4; (d) what the believer will be to God in that age, Eph. 1:18.

2. *kleros* (*2819*), (whence Eng., "clergy"), denotes (a) "a lot," given or cast (the latter as a means of obtaining divine direction), Matt. 27:35; Mark 15:24; Luke 23:24; John 19:24; Acts 1:26; (b) "a person's share" in anything, Acts 1:17, RV, "portion" (KJV, "part"); 8:21, "lot"; (c) "a charge" (lit., "charges") "allotted," to elders, 1 Pet. 5:3, RV [KJV, "(God's) heritage"]; the figure is from portions of lands allotted to be cultivated; (d) "an inheritance," as in No. 1 (c); Acts 26:18; Col. 1:12.

INIQUITY

Old Testament

A. Verb.

'awah (*5753*), "to do iniquity," *'awah* is often used as a synonym of *chata'*, "to sin," as in Ps. 106:6.

B. Nouns.

'awon (*5771*), "iniquity; guilt; punishment." The most basic meaning of *'awon* is "iniquity." The word signifies an offense, intentional or not, against God's law. This meaning is also most basic to the word *chatta't*, "sin," Isa. 6:7.

"Iniquity" as an offense to God's law is punishable. The individual is warned that the Lord punishes man's transgression, Jer. 31:30. There is also a collective sense in that the one is responsible for the many, Exod. 20:5. No generation, however, was to think that it bore God's judgment for the "iniquity" of another generation, Ezek. 18:19-20.

Israel went into captivity for the sin of their fathers and for their own sins, Ezek. 39:23.

Serious as "iniquity" is in the covenantal relationship between the Lord and His people, the people are reminded that He is a living God who willingly forgives "iniquity," Exod. 34:7; Ps. 32:5; 51:2.

The usage of *'awon* includes the whole area of sin, judgment, and "punishment" for sin. The Old Testament teaches that God's forgiveness of "iniquity" extends to the actual sin, the guilt of sin, God's judgment upon that sin, and God's punishment of the sin, Ps. 32:2.

'awen (205), "iniquity; misfortune." The meaning of "misfortune" comes to expression in the devices of the wicked against the righteous. The psalmist expected "misfortune" to come upon him, Ps. 41:6. *'awen* in this sense is synonymous with *'ed*, "disaster," Job 18:12. In a real sense *'awen* is part of human existence, and as such the word is identical with *'amal*, "toil," as in Ps. 90:10.

'awen in a deeper sense characterizes the way of life of those who are without God, Isa. 32:6. The being of man is corrupted by "iniquity." Though all of mankind is subject to *'awen* ("toil"), there are those who delight in causing difficulties and "misfortunes" for others by scheming, lying, and acting deceptively, Ps. 7:14; cf. Job 15:35.

Those who are involved in the ways of darkness are the "workers of iniquity," the doers of evil or the creators of "misfortune" and disaster. Synonyms for *'awen* with this sense are *ra'*, "evil," and *rasha'*, "wicked," opposed to "righteousness" and "justice." They seek the downfall of the just, Ps. 141:9. The qualitative aspect of the word comes to the best expression in the verbs with *'awen*. The wicked work, speak, beget, think, devise, gather, reap, and plow *'awen*, and it is revealed ("comes forth") by the misfortune that comes upon the righteous. Ultimately when Israel's religious festivals, Isa. 1:13, and legislation, Isa. 10:1, were affected by their apostate way of life, they had reduced themselves to the Gentile practices and way of life. The prophetic hope lay in the period after the purification of Israel, when the messianic king would introduce a period of justice and righteousness, Isa. 32, and the evil men would be shown up for their folly and ungodliness.

New Testament

1. *anomia* (458), lit., "lawlessness" (*a*, negative, *nomos*, "law"), is used in a way which indicates the meaning as being lawlessness or wickedness. Its usual rendering in the NT is "iniquity," which lit. means unrighteousness. It is used (a) of iniquity in general, Matt. 7:23; 13:41; 23:28; 24:12; Rom. 6:19 (twice); 2 Cor. 6:14, RV, "iniquity" (KJV, "unrighteousness"); 2 Thess. 2:3, in some mss.; the KJV and RV follow those which have *hamartia*, "(man of) sin"; 2:7, RV, "lawlessness" (KJV, "iniquity"); Titus 2:14; Heb. 1:9; 1 John 3:4 (twice), RV, "(doeth)...lawlessness" and "lawlessness" (KJV, "transgresseth the law" and "transgression of the law"); (b) in the plural, of acts or manifestations of lawlessness, Rom. 4:7; Heb. 10:17 (some inferior mss. have it in 8:12, for the word *hamartia*).

2. *adikia* (93) denotes "unrighteousness," lit., "unrightness" (*a*, negative, *dike*, "right"), a condition of not being right, whether with God, according to the standard of His holiness and righteousness, or with man, according to the standard of what man

knows to be right by his conscience. In Luke 16:8 and 18:6, the phrases lit. are, "the steward of unrighteousness" and "the judge of injustice," the subjective genitive describing their character; in 18:6 the meaning is "injustice" and so perhaps in Rom. 9:14. The word is usually translated "unrighteousness," but is rendered "iniquity" in Luke 13:27; Acts 1:18; 8:23; 1 Cor. 13:6, KJV (RV, "unrighteousness"); so in 2 Tim. 2:19; Jas. 3:6.

3. *adikema* (92) denotes "a wrong, injury, misdeed" (akin to No. 2; from *adikeo*, "to do wrong"), the concrete act, in contrast to the general meaning of No. 2, and translated "a matter of wrong," in Acts 18:14; "wrongdoing," 24:20 (KJV, "evil-doing"); "iniquities," Rev. 18:5.

4. *poneria* (4189), akin to *poneo*, "to toil," denotes "wickedness," and is so translated in Matt. 22:18; Mark 7:22 (plural); Luke 11:39; Rom. 1:29; 1 Cor. 5:8; Eph. 6:12; in Acts 3:26, "iniquities."

5. *paranomia* (3892), "lawbreaking" (*para*, "against," *nomos*, "law"), denotes "transgression," so rendered in 2 Pet. 2:16, for KJV, "iniquity."

INJURE, INJURIOUS

A. Verb.

adikeo (91) is usually translated either "to hurt," or by some form of the verb "to do wrong." In the KJV of Gal. 4:12, it is rendered "ye have (not) injured me."

B. Adjective.

hubristes (5197), "a violent, insolent man," is translated "insolent" in Rom. 1:30, RV, for KJV, "despiteful"; in 1 Tim. 1:13, "injurious."

INNOCENT

1. *athoos* (121) primarily denotes "unpunished" (*a*, negative, *thoe*, "a penalty"); then, "innocent," Matt. 27:4, "innocent blood," i.e., the blood of an "innocent" person, the word "blood" being used both by synecdoche (a part standing for the whole), and by metonymy (one thing standing for another), i.e., for death by execution (some mss. have *dikaion*, "righteous"); v. 24, where Pilate speaks of himself as "innocent."

2. *akakos* (172), lit., "not bad," denotes "guileless, innocent," Rom. 16:18, RV, "innocent" (KJV, "simple"); "harmless" in Heb. 7:26.

INQUIRE, INQUIRY (make)

A. Verbs.

1. *punthanomai* (4441), "to inquire," is translated "inquired" in Matt. 2:4, and Acts 21:33, RV (KJV, "demanded"); in Luke 15:26; 18:36 and Acts 4:7 (KJV, "asked"); "inquired" (KJV, "inquired") in John 4:52; "inquire" (KJV, "inquire") in Acts 23:20; in Acts 23:34 it

denotes "to learn by inquiry," KJV, and RV, "when (he) understood"; elsewhere it is rendered by the verb "to ask," Acts 10:18, 29; 23:19.

2. *zeteo* (*2212*), "to seek," is rendered "inquire" in John 16:19; "inquire...for" in Acts 9:11.

3. *dierotao* (*1331*), "to find by inquiry, to inquire through to the end" (*dia*, intensive, *erotao*, "to ask") is used in Acts 10:17.

4. *exetazo* (*1833*), "to examine, seek out, inquire thoroughly," is translated "inquire" in Matt. 10:11, KJV (RV, "search out"); in John 21:12, "durst inquire," RV [KJV, "(durst) ask"]; in Matt. 2:8, RV, "search out" (KJV, "search").

B. Noun.

zetesis (*2214*) primarily denotes "a search"; then, "an inquiry, a questioning, debate"; it forms part of a phrase translated by the verb "to inquire," in Acts 25:20, RV, "how to inquire," lit. "(being perplexed as to) the inquiry."

INSPIRATION OF GOD, INSPIRED OF GOD

theopneustos (*2315*), "inspired by God" (*theos*, "God," *pneo*, "to breathe"), is used in 2 Tim. 3:16, of the Scriptures as distinct from non-inspired writings.

INSTRUCT, INSTRUCTION, INSTRUCTOR
Old Testament

A. Noun.

musar (*4148*), "instruction; chastisement; warning." One of the major purposes of the wisdom literature was to teach wisdom and *musar*, Prov. 1:2. *musar* is discipline, but more; it teaches how to live correctly in the fear of the Lord, so that the wise man learns his lesson before temptation and testing, Prov. 24:32. When *musar* as "instruction" has been given, but was not observed, the *musar* as "chastisement" or "discipline" may be the next step, Prov. 22:15.

Careful attention to "instruction" brings honor, Prov. 1:9, life, Prov. 4:13, and wisdom, Prov. 8:33, and above all it pleases God, Prov. 8:35. Discipline from parents and leaders are an example of God's discipline, Jer. 5:3; 35:13; Isa. 53:5.

B. Verb.

yasar (*3256*), "to discipline," cf. Prov. 19:18.

New Testament

A. Verbs.

1. *katecheo* (*2727*), "to teach orally, inform, instruct," is translated by the verb "to instruct" in Luke 1:4; Acts 18:25 (RV marg., "taught by word of mouth"); Rom. 2:18; 1 Cor. 14:19, RV (KJV, "teach").

2. *paideuo* (*3811*), "to train children, teach," is rendered "was instructed," in Acts 7:22, RV (KJV, "learned"); "instructing" in 2 Tim. 2:25, KJV (RV, "correcting"); Titus 2:12, RV, "instructing" (KJV, "teaching"). The verb is used of the family discipline, as in Heb. 12:6, 7, 10; cf. 1 Cor. 11:32; 2 Cor. 6:9; Rev. 3:19. In 1 Tim. 1:20 (passive voice) it is translated "might be taught," RV (KJV, "may learn"), but, however the passage is to be understood, it is clear that not the impartation of knowledge but severe discipline is intended. In Luke 23:16, 22, Pilate, since he had declared the Lord guiltless of the charge brought against Him, and hence could not punish Him, weakly offered, as a concession to the Jews, to 'chastise, *paideuo*, Him, and let Him go.'

3. *matheteuo* (*3100*), used transitively, "to make a disciple," is translated "which is instructed" in Matt. 13:52, KJV (RV, "who hath been made a disciple").

4. *probibazo* (*4264*), "to lead forward, lead on" (the causal of *probaino*, "to go forward"; *pro*, "forward," *bibazo*, "to lift up"), is used in the passive voice in Matt. 14:8, and translated, KJV, "being before instructed," RV, "being put forward." Some mss. have it in Acts 19:33, instead of No. 5.

5. *sumbibazo* (*4822*), to join, knit, unite (*sun*, "with"), then, "to compare," and so, "to prove," hence, "to teach, instruct," is so rendered in 1 Cor. 2:16; it is found in the best mss. in Acts 19:33 (RV marg., "instructed").

B. Nouns.

(INSTRUCTION)

paideia (*3809*), "training, instruction," is translated "instruction" in 2 Tim. 3:16.

(INSTRUCTOR)

1. *paidagogos* (*3807*), "a guide," or "guardian" or "trainer of boys," lit., "a child-leader" (*pais*, "a boy, or child," *ago*, "to lead"), "a tutor," is translated "instructors" in 1 Cor. 4:15, KJV (RV, "tutors"); here the thought is that of pastors rather than teachers; in Gal. 3:24, 25, KJV, "schoolmaster" (RV, "tutor,"), but here the idea of instruction is absent.

2. *paideutes* (*3810*), akin to A, No. 2, denotes (a) "an instructor, a teacher," Rom. 2:20, KJV, "an instructor" (RV, "a corrector"); (b) "one who disciplines, corrects, chastens," Heb. 12:9, RV, "to chasten" [KJV, "which corrected" (lit., "correctors")]. In (a) the discipline of the school is in view; in (b) that of the family.

INSTRUMENTS

hoplon (*3696*), "a tool, instrument, weapon," is used metaphorically in Rom. 6:13 of the members of the body as "instruments" (marg., "weapons"), negatively, of unrighteousness, positively, of righteousness.

INSURRECTION

A. Nouns.

1. *stasis* (*4714*), akin to *histemi*, "to make to stand," denotes (a) primarily, "a standing or place," Heb. 9:8; (b) "an insurrection, sedition," translated "insurrection" in Mark 15:7; "insurrections" in Acts 24:5, RV (KJV, "sedition"); in Luke 23:19, 25 (KJV "sedition"), "riot," Acts 19:40, RV (KJV, "uproar"); (c) "a dissension," Acts 15:2; in Acts 23:7, 10, "dissension."

2. *stasiastes* (*4955v*) denotes "a rebel, revolutionist, one who stirs up sedition" (from *stasiazo*, "to stir up sedition"), Mark 15:7, "had made insurrection."

B. Verb.

katephistemi (*2721*) signifies "to rise up against"; lit., "to cause to stand forth against," Acts 18:12.

INTEND

1. *boulomai* (*1014*), "to will, wish, desire, purpose" (expressing a fixed resolve, the deliberate exercise of volition), is translated "intend" in Acts 5:28, and "intending" in 12:4.

2. *thelo* (*2309*), "to will, be willing, desire" (less strong, and more frequent than No. 1), is translated "intending" in Luke 14:28, KJV (RV, "desiring").

INTENT

1. *ennoia* (*1771*), primarily "a thinking, idea, consideration," denotes "purpose, intention, design" (*en*, in, *nous*, mind); it is rendered "intents" in Heb. 4:12; "mind," in 1 Pet. 4:1.

2. *logos* (*3056*), "a word, account, etc.," sometimes denotes "a reason, cause; intent," e.g., Matt. 5:32, "cause"; it is rendered "intent" in Acts 10:29.

INTERCESSIONS

A. Noun.

enteuxis (*1783*) primarily denotes "a lighting upon, meeting with" (akin to B); then, "a conversation"; hence, "a petition," a meaning frequent in the papyri; it is a technical term for approaching a king, and so for approaching God in "intercession"; it is rendered "prayer" in 1 Tim. 4:5; in the plural in 2:1 (i.e., seeking the presence and hearing of God on behalf of others).

B. Verbs.

1. *entunchano* (*1793*), primarily "to fall in with, meet with in order to converse"; then, "to make petition," especially "to make intercession, plead with a person," either for or against others; (a) against, Acts 25:24, "made suit to (me)," RV [KJV, "have dealt with

(me)"l, i.e., against Paul; in Rom. 11:2, of Elijah in "pleading" with God, RV (KJV, "maketh intercession to"), against Israel; (b) for, in Rom. 8:27, of the intercessory work of the Holy Spirit for the saints; v. 34, of the similar intercessory work of Christ; so Heb. 7:25.

2. *huperentunchano* (5241), "to make a petition" or "intercede on behalf of another" (*huper*, "on behalf of," and No. 1), is used in Rom. 8:26 of the work of the Holy Spirit in making "intercession."

INTEREST

tokos (5110), primarily "a bringing forth, birth" (from *tikto*, "to beget"), then, "an offspring," is used metaphorically of the produce of money lent out, "interest," usury, Matt. 25:27; Luke 19:23.

INTERPRET, INTERPRETATION, INTERPRETER

A. Verbs.

1. *hermeneuo* (2059), (cf. Eng., "hermeneutics"), and is used of explaining the meaning of words in a different language, John 1:38.

2. *diermeneuo* (1329), a strengthened form of No. 1 (*dia*, "through," used intensively), signifies "to interpret fully, to explain." In Luke 24:27, it is used of Christ in interpreting to the two on the way to Emmaus "in all the Scriptures the things concerning Himself," RV, "interpreted" (KJV, "expounded"); in Acts 9:36, it is rendered "is by interpretation," lit., "being interpreted" (of Tabitha, as meaning Dorcas); in 1 Cor. 12:30 and 14:5, 13, 27, it is used with reference to the temporary gift of tongues in the churches; this gift was inferior in character to that of prophesying unless he who spoke in a "tongue" interpreted his words, 14:5; he was, indeed, to pray that he might interpret, v. 13; only two, or at the most three, were to use the gift in a gathering, and that "in turn" (RV); one was to interpret; in the absence of an interpreter, the gift was not to be exercised, v. 27.

3. *methermeneuo* (3177), "to change or translate from one language to another (*meta*, implying change, and No. 1), to interpret," is always used in the passive voice in the NT, "being interpreted," of interpreting the names, Immanuel, Matt. 1:23; Golgotha, Mark 15:22; Barnabas, Acts 4:36; in Acts 13:8, of Elymas, the verb is rendered "is...by interpretation," lit., "is interpreted"; it is used of interpreting or translating sentences in Mark 5:41; 15:34; in the best mss., John 1:38 (Rabbi, interpreted as "Master"); v. 41 (Messiah, interpreted as "Christ"); see No. 1.

B. Nouns.

(INTERPRETATION)

1. *hermeneia* (or -*ia*) (2058), akin to A, No. 1, is used in 1 Cor. 12:10; 14:26 (see A, No. 2).

2. *epilusis* (1955), from *epiluo*, "to loose, solve, explain," denotes "a solution, explanation," lit., "a release" (*epi*, "up," *luo*, "to loose"),

2 Pet. 1:20, "(of private) interpretation"; i.e., the writers of Scripture did not put their own construction upon the "God-breathed" words they wrote.

(INTERPRETER)

diermeneutes (*1328*), lit., "a thorough interpreter" (cf. A, No. 2), is used in 1 Cor. 14:28 (some mss. have *hermeneutes*).

INTERROGATION

eperotema (*1906*), primarily a question or inquiry, denotes "a demand or appeal," 1 Pet. 3:21, RV (KJV, "answer"). Some take the word to indicate that baptism affords a good conscience, an appeal against the accuser.

INTRUST

pisteuo (*4100*), "to believe," also means "to entrust," and in the active voice is translated "to commit," in Luke 16:11; John 2:24; in the passive voice, "to be intrusted with," Rom. 3:2, RV, "they were intrusted with" (KJV, "unto them were committed"), of Israel and the oracles of God; 1 Cor. 9:17, RV, "I have...intrusted to me" (KJV, "is committed unto me"), of Paul and the stewardship of the gospel; so Gal. 2:7; Titus 1:3; in 1 Thess. 2:4, where he associates with himself his fellow missionaries, RV, "to be intrusted with" (KJV, "to be put in trust with").

INVISIBLE

aoratos (*517*), lit., "unseen" (*a*, negative, *horao*, "to see"), is translated "invisible" in Rom. 1:20, of the power and divinity of God; of God Himself, Col. 1:15; 1 Tim. 1:17; Heb. 11:27; of things unseen, Col. 1:16.

INWARD (man, part), INWARDLY

1. *eso* (*2080*), "within, inward," is used adjectivally in Rom. 7:22, "(the) inward (man)"; 2 Cor. 4:16, with "man" expressed in the preceding clause, but not repeated in the original, "(our) inward (man)" (some mss. have *esothen*, "from within"); Eph. 3:16, RV, "(the) inward (man)" (KJV, "inner").

2. *esothen* (*2081*) is used in Luke 11:39, as a noun with the article, "part" being understood, "(your) inward part"; in Matt. 7:15 it has its normal use as an adverb, "inwardly."

ITCHING

knetho (*2833*), "to scratch, tickle," is used in the passive voice, metaphorically, of an eagerness to hear, in 2 Tim. 4:3, lit., "itched (as to the hearing)," of those who, not enduring sound doctrine, heap to themselves teachers.

J

JEALOUS, JEALOUSY
Old Testament

A. Verb.

qana' (7065), "to be jealous; to be zealous." At the inter-human level *qana'* has a strongly competitive sense. In its most positive sense the word means "to be filled with righteous zeal or jealousy." The law provides that a husband who suspects his wife of adultery can bring her to a priest, who will administer a test of adultery, Num. 5:12-31. *qana'*, then, in its most basic sense is the act of advancing one's rights to the exclusion of the rights of others: "...Ephraim shall not envy Judah, and Judah shall not vex Ephraim," Isa. 11:13. Saul sought to murder the Gibeonite enclave "in his zeal to the children of Israel and Judah," 2 Sam. 21:2. Next, the word signifies the attitude of envy toward an opponent. Rachel in her barren state "envied her sister," Gen. 30:1, and in the state of envy approached Jacob, Gen. 26:14. The Bible contains a strong warning against being envious of sinners, who might prosper and be powerful today, but will be no more tomorrow, Prov. 3:31, NIV; cf. Ps. 37:1.

In man's relation to God, the act of zeal is more positively viewed as the act of the advancement of God and His glory over against substitutes. The tribe of Levi received the right to service because "he was zealous for his God," Num. 25:13; 1 Kings 19:10. However, the sense of *qana'* is "to make jealous," that is, "to provoke to anger," Deut. 32:16.

B. Noun.

qin'ah (7068), "ardor; zeal; jealousy," Deut. 29:20.

C. Adjective.

qanna' (7067), "jealous." This adjective occurs 6 times in the Old Testament. The word refers directly to the attributes of God's justice and holiness, as He is the sole object of human worship and does not tolerate man's sin, Exod. 20:5. The adjective *qanno'* also means "jealous," Josh. 24:19; Nah. 1:2.

New Testament

A. Noun.

zelos (2205), "zeal, jealousy," is rendered "jealousy" in the RV

(KJV, "envying") in Rom. 13:13; 1 Cor. 3:3; Jas. 3:14, 16; in 2 Cor. 12:20 (KJV, "envyings"); in Gal. 5:20, KJV, ("emulations"); in Acts 5:17 (KJV, "indignation"); in 13:45 (KJV, "envy"); in 2 Cor. 11:2 it is used in the phrase "with a godly jealousy."

B. Verbs.

1. *zeloo* (2206), akin to A, "to be jealous, to burn with jealousy" (otherwise, to seek or desire eagerly), is rendered "moved with jealousy," in Acts 7:9 and 17:5 (KJV, "moved with envy"); in 1 Cor. 13:4, "envieth (not)"; in Jas. 4:2, RV marg. (KJV, "desire to have").

2. *parazeloo* (3863), "to provoke to jealousy" (*para*, "beside," used intensively, and No. 1), is found in Rom. 10:19 and 11:11, of God's dealings with Israel through his merciful dealings with Gentiles; in 11:14, RV, "I may provoke to jealousy" (KJV, "...emulation"), of the apostle's evangelical ministry to Gentiles with a view to stirring his fellow nationals to a sense of their need and responsibilities regarding the gospel; in 1 Cor. 10:22, of the provocation of God on the part of believers who compromise their divine relationship by partaking of the table of demons; in Gal. 5:20, of the works of the flesh.

JESTING

eutrapelia (2160) properly denotes "wit, facetiousness, versatility" (lit., "easily turning," from *eu*, "well," *trepo*, "to turn"); by New Testament times it certainly deteriorated, and it came to denote "coarse jesting, ribaldry," as in Eph. 5:4.

JESUS

Iesous (2424) is a transliteration of the Heb. "Joshua," meaning "Jehovah is salvation," i.e., "is the Savior," "a common name among the Jews, e.g., Ex. 17:9; Luke 3:29 (RV); Col. 4:11. It was given to the Son of God in Incarnation as His personal name, in obedience to the command of an angel to Joseph, the husband of His Mother, Mary, shortly before He was born, Matt. 1:21. By it He is spoken of throughout the Gospel narratives generally, but not without exception, as in Mark 16:19, 20; Luke 7:13, and a dozen other places in that Gospel, and a few in John.

"Jesus Christ" occurs only in Matt. 1:1, 18; 16:21, marg.; Mark 1:1; John 1:17; 17:3. In Acts the name "Jesus" is found frequently. "Lord Jesus" is the normal usage, as in Acts 8:16; 19:5, 17; see also the reports of the words of Stephen, 7:59, of Ananias, 9:17, and of Paul, 16:31; though both Peter, 10:36, and Paul, 16:18, also used "Jesus Christ."

In the Epistles of James, Peter, John and Jude, the personal name is not once found alone, but in Rev. eight times (RV), 1:9; 12:17; 14:12; 17:6; 19:10 (twice); 20:4; 22:16.

In the Epistles of Paul "Jesus" appears alone just thirteen times, and in the Hebrews eight times; in the latter the title "Lord" is added once only, at 13:20. In the Epistles of James, Peter, John, and Jude, who had companied with the Lord in the days of His flesh, "Jesus Christ" is the invariable order (RV) of the Name and Title, for this was the order of their experience; as "Jesus" they knew Him first, that He was Messiah they learned in His resurrection. But Paul came to know Him first in the glory of heaven, Acts 9:1-6, and his experience being thus the reverse of theirs, the reverse order, "Christ Jesus," is frequent in his letters, but, with the exception of Acts 24:24, does not occur elsewhere in the RV.

JEW(-S) (live as do the), JEWESS, JEWISH, JEWRY, JEWS' RELIGION

A. Adjectives.

1. *ioudaios* (2453), is used (a) adjectivally, with the lit. meaning, "Jewish," sometimes with the addition of *aner*, "a man," Acts 10:28; 22:3; in 21:39 with *anthropos*, in some mss. (a man in the generic sense); the best mss. omit the phrase here; in 13:6, lit., "a Jewish false-prophet"; in John 3:22, with the word *chora*, "land" or "country," signifying "Judean," lit., "Judean country"; used by metonymy for the people of the country; (b) as a noun, "a Jew, Jews," e.g., Matt. 2:2; Mark 7:3. The name "Jew" is primarily tribal (from Judah). It is first found in 2 Kings 16:6, as distinct from Israel, of the northern kingdom. After the Captivity it was chiefly used to distinguish the race from Gentiles, e.g., John 2:6; Acts 14:1; Gal. 2:15, where it denotes Christians of "Jewish" race; it distinguishes Jews from Samaritans, in John 4:9; from proselytes, in Acts 2:10. The word is most frequent in John's gospel and the Acts, John 3:25; 5:10; 7:13; 9:22; Rom. 2:28, 29.

It also denotes Judea, e.g., Matt. 2:1; Luke 1:5; John 4:3, the word "country" being understood [cf. (a) above]. In Luke 23:5 and John 7:1, where the KJV has "Jewry," the RV translates it as usual, "Judea."

2. *ioudaikos* (2451) denotes "Jewish," Titus 1:14.

B. Noun.

ioudaismos (2454), "Judaism," denotes "the Jews' religion," Gal. 1:13, 14, and stands, not for their religious beliefs, but for their religious practices, not as instituted by God, but as developed and extended from these by the traditions of the Pharisees and scribes. In the Apocrypha it denotes comprehensively "the Government, laws, institutions and religion of the Jews."

C. Verb.

ioudaizo (2450), lit., "to Judaize," i.e., to conform to "Jewish" religious practices and manners, is translated "to live as do the Jews," in Gal. 2:14.

D. Adverb.

ioudaikos (2452), "in Jewish fashion," is translated "as do the Jews," in Gal. 2:14.

JOIN

1. *kollao* (2853), primarily, "to glue or cement together," then, generally, "to unite, to join firmly," is used in the passive voice signifying "to join oneself to, to be joined to," Luke 15:15; Acts 5:13; 8:29; 9:26; 10:28, RV (KJV, "to keep company with"); 1 Cor. 6:16, 17; elsewhere, "to cleave to," Luke 10:11; Acts 17:34; Rom. 12:9.

2. *proskollao* (4347), "to stick to," a strengthened form of No. 1, with *pros*, "to," intensive, is used in the passive voice, reflexively, in a metaphorical sense, with the meanings (a) "to join oneself to," in Acts 5:36; (b) "to cleave to," of the husband with regard to the wife, Matt. 19:5; Mark 10:7; in Eph. 5:31.

3. *su(n)zeugnumi* (4801), "to yoke together," is used metaphorically of union in wedlock, in Matt. 19:6; Mark 10:9.

JOINT

1. *harmos* (719), "a joining, joint" (akin to *harmozo*, "to fit, join"), is found in Heb. 4:12, figuratively (with the word "marrow") of the inward moral and spiritual being of man, as just previously expressed literally in the phrase "soul and spirit."

2. *haphe* (860), "a ligature, joint" (akin to *hapto*, "to fit, to fasten"), occurs in Eph. 4:16 and Col. 2:19.

JOT

iota (2503), from the Heb. *yodh*, the smallest Hebrew letter, mentioned to express the fact that not a single item of the Law will pass away or remain unfulfilled.

JOURNEY (Noun and Verb), JOURNEYINGS

A. Nouns.

1. *hodos* (3598), "a way, path, road," used of a traveler's way, a "journey," is rendered "journey" in Matt. 10:13; Mark 6:8; Luke 2:44, "a day's journey" (probably to Beeroth, six miles north of Jerusalem); 9:3; 11:6; Acts 1:12, "a Sabbath day's journey," i.e., the journey which a Jew was allowed to take on the Sabbath, viz., about 2,000 yards or cubits (estimates vary). The regulation was not a Mosaic enactment, but a rabbinical tradition, based upon an exposition of Exod. 16:29, and a comparison of the width of the suburb of a Levitical city as enjoined in Num. 35:4, 5, and the distance between the ark and the people at the crossing of the Jordan, Josh. 3:4. In regard to Acts 1:12, there is no discrepancy between this and Luke 24:50, where the RV rightly translates by "over against Bethany," which does not fix the exact spot of the Ascension.

2. *hodoiporia* (3597), "a wayfaring, journeying" (No. 1, and *poros*, "a way, a passage"), is used of the Lord's journey to Samaria, John 4:6, and of Paul's "journeyings," 2 Cor. 11:26. Cf. B, No. 1.

B. Verbs.

1. *hodoiporeo* (3596), "to travel, journey" (akin to A, No. 2), is found in Acts 10:9.

2. *hodeuo* (3593), "to be on the way, journey" (from *hodos*, "a way"), the simplest form of the verbs denoting "to journey," is used in the parable of the good Samaritan, Luke 10:33.

3. *sunodeuo* (4922), *sun*, "with," and No. 2, "to journey with," occurs in Acts 9:7.

4. *euodoo* (2137), "to help on one's way" (*eu*, "well," and *hodos*), is used in the passive voice with the meaning "to have a prosperous journey"; so the KJV of Rom. 1:10; the RV. "I may be prospered" rightly expresses the metaphorical use which the verb acquired, without reference to a "journey"; see 1 Cor. 16:2; 3 John 2.

JOY (Noun and Verb), JOYFULNESS, JOYFULLY, JOYOUS

A. Nouns.

1. *chara* (5479), "joy, delight" (akin to *chairo*, "to rejoice"), is found frequently in Matthew and Luke, and especially in John, once in Mark (4:16, KJV, "gladness"); it is absent from 1 Cor. (though the verb is used three times), but is frequent in 2 Cor., where the noun is used five times, and the verb eight times, suggestive of the apostle's relief in comparison with the circumstances of the First Epistle; in Col. 1:11, KJV, "joyfulness." The word is sometimes used, by metonymy, of the occasion or cause of "joy," Luke 2:10; in 2 Cor. 1:15, in some mss., for *charis*, "benefit"; Phil. 4:1, where the readers are called the apostle's "joy"; so 1 Thess. 2:19, 20; Heb. 12:2, of the object of Christ's "joy"; Jas. 1:2, where it is connected with falling into trials; perhaps also in Matt. 25:21, 23, where some regard it as signifying, concretely, the circumstances attending cooperation in the authority of the Lord.

2. *agalliasis* (20), "exultation, exuberant joy." Cf. B, No. 3, below.

3. *euphrosune* (2167) is rendered "joy" in the KJV of Acts 2:28, RV. "gladness," as in 14:17.

B. Verbs.

1. *chairo* (5463), "to rejoice, be glad," is translated "joyfully" in Luke 19:6, lit., "rejoicing"; "we joyed," 2 Cor. 7:13; "I joy," Phil. 2:17; "do ye joy," 2:18; "joying," Col. 2:5; "we joy," 1 Thess. 3:9. It is contrasted with weeping and sorrow, e.g., in John 16:20, 22; Rom. 12:15; 1 Cor. 7:30 (cf. Ps. 30:5).

2. *kauchaomai* (2744), "to boast, glory, exult," is rendered "we

joy," in Rom. 5:11, KJV. It would have been an advantage to translate this word distinctively by the verbs "to glory" or "to exult."

3. *agalliao* (21), "to exult, rejoice greatly," is translated "with exceeding joy" in 1 Pet. 4:13 (middle voice), lit., "(ye rejoice, *chairo*) exulting." Cf. A, No. 2.

JUDGE (Noun and Verb)

Old Testament

A. Verb.

shapat (8199), "to judge, deliver, rule." In many contexts this root has a judicial sense. *shapat* refers to the activity of a third party who sits over two parties at odds with one another. This third party hears their cases against one another and decides where the right is and what to do about it (he functions as both judge and jury), Gen. 16:5, 6, Here, Abram acts according to Nuzu law.

shapat also speaks of the accomplishing of a sentence. Both this concept and those of hearing the case and rendering a decision are seen in Gen. 18:25; 1 Sam. 3:13. In some cases "judging" really means delivering from injustice or oppression, 1 Sam. 24:15, or the process of maintaining order and law within a group, Judg. 4:4. The military deliverer was the head over a volunteer army summoned when danger threatened (militia), so Saul became a judge and king, 1 Sam. 8:6-18.

mishpat (4941), "judgment; rights." This word has two main senses; 1) the act of sitting as a judge, hearing a case, and rendering a proper verdict, Eccl. 12:14; 2) *mishpat* can also refer to the "rights" belonging to someone, Exod. 23:6. The noun *shepatim* refers to "acts of judgment," Num. 33:4.

New Testament

A. Nouns.

1. *krites* (2923), "a judge," is used (a) of God, Heb. 12:23, where the order in the original is "to a Judge who is God of all"; this is really the significance; it suggests that He who is the Judge of His people is at the same time their God; that is the order in 10:30; the word is also used of God in Jas. 4:12, RV; (b) of Christ, Acts 10:42; 2 Tim. 4:8; Jas. 5:9; (c) of a ruler in Israel in the times of the Judges, Acts 13:20; (d) of a Roman procurator, Acts 24:10; (e) of those whose conduct provides a standard of "judging," Matt. 12:27; Luke 11:19; (f) in the forensic sense, of one who tries and decides a case, Matt. 5:25 (twice); Luke 12:14 (some mss. have No. 2 here); 12:58 (twice); 18:2; 18:6 (lit., "the judge of unrighteousness," expressing subjectively his character); Acts 18:15; (g) of one who passes, or arrogates to himself, judgment on anything, Jas. 2:4.

2. *dikastes* (1348) denotes "a judge," Acts 7:27, 35.

B. Verbs.

1. **krino** (*2919*) primarily denotes "to separate, select, choose"; hence, "to determine," and so "to judge, pronounce judgment." The uses of this verb in the NT may be analyzed as follows: (a) to assume the office of a judge, Matt. 7:1; John 3:17; (b) to undergo process of trial, John 3:18; 16:11; 18:31; Jas. 2:12; (c) to give sentence, Acts 15:19; 16:4; 21:25; (d) to condemn, John 12:48; Acts 13:27; Rom. 2:27; (e) to execute judgment upon, 2 Thess. 2:12; Acts 7:7; (f) to be involved in a lawsuit, whether as plaintiff, Matt. 5:40; 1 Cor. 6:1; or as defendant, Acts 23:6; (g) to administer affairs, to govern, Matt. 19:28; cf. Judg. 3:10; (h) to form an opinion, Luke 7:43; John 7:24; Acts 4:19; Rom. 14:5; (i) to make a resolve, Acts 3:13; 20:16 1 Cor. 2:2.

2. **anakrino** (*350*), "to examine, investigate, question," is rendered "judged" in 1 Cor. 2:14 (KJV, "are...discerned"), said of the things of the Spirit of God; in v. 15, "judgeth," said of the exercise of a discerning "judgment" of all things as to their true value, by one who is spiritual; in the same verse, "is judged (of no man)," i.e., the merely natural mind cannot estimate the motives of the spiritual; in 4:3, "I should be judged," i.e., as to examining and passing sentence on the fulfillment or nonfulfillment of the apostle's stewardship; so in the same verse, "I judge (not mine own self)," and in v. 4 "(he that) judgeth (me is the Lord)"; in 14:24, "he is judged (of all)," i.e., the light of the heart-searching testimony of the assembly probes the conscience of the unregenerate, sifting him judicially.

3. **diakrino** (*1252*) denotes "to separate throughout" (*dia*, and No. 1), "discriminate, discern," and hence "to decide, to judge" (also "to contend, to hesitate, to doubt"); it is rendered "to judge" in 1 Cor. 6:5, in the sense of arbitrating; in 11:31 (1st part), the RV has "(if we) discerned (ourselves)," KJV "(if we would) judge" (*krino*, No. 1, is used in the 2nd part); so in 14:29, RV, "discern" (KJV, "judge").

JUDGMENT

1. **krisis** (*2920*) primarily denotes "a separating," then, "a decision, judgment," most frequently in a forensic sense, and especially of divine "judgment."

2. **krima** (*2917*) denotes the result of the action signified by the verb **krino**, "to judge"; it is used (a) of a decision passed on the faults of others, Matt. 7:2; (b) of "judgment" by man upon Christ, Luke 24:20; (c) of God's "judgment" upon men, e.g., Rom. 2:2, 3; 3:8; 5:16; 11:33; 13:2; 1 Cor. 11:29; Gal. 5:10; Heb. 6:2; Jas. 3:1; through Christ, e.g., John 9:39; (d) of the right of "judgment," Rev. 20:4; (e) of a lawsuit, 1 Cor. 6:7.

3. **hemera** (*2250*), "a day," is translated "judgment" in 1 Cor. 4:3, where "man's judgment" (lit., "man's day," marg.) is used of the present period in which man's mere "judgment" is exercised, a

period of human rebellion against God, cf. Rev. 1:10, "The Lord's Day," a period of divine judgments.

4. *gnome* (*1106*), primarily "a means of knowing" (akin to *ginosko*, "to know"), came to denote "a mind, understanding"; hence (a) "a purpose," Acts 20:3; (b) "a royal purpose, a decree," Rev. 17:17 (KJV, "will"); (c) "judgment, opinion," 1 Cor. 1:10, "(in the same) judgment"; Rev. 17:13, "mind"; (d) "counsel, advice," 1 Cor. 7:25, "(I give my) judgment"; 7:40, "(after my) judgment"; Philem. 14, "mind."

B. Adjective.

hupodikos (*5267*), "brought to trial, answerable to" (*hupo*, "under," *dike*, "justice"), Rom. 3:19, is translated "under the judgment," RV (KJV, "guilty").

JUDGMENT SEAT

1. *bema* (*968*), primarily, "a step, a pace" (akin to *baino*, "to go"), as in Acts 7:5, translated "to set (his foot) on," lit., "footroom," was used to denote a raised place or platform, where was the place of assembly; from the platform orations were made. The word became used for a tribune, two of which were provided in the law courts of Greece, one for the accuser and one for the defendant; it was applied to the tribunal of a Roman magistrate or ruler, Matt. 27:19; John 19:13; Acts 12:21, translated "throne"; 18:12, 16, 17; 25:6, 10, 17.

In two passages the word is used of the divine tribunal before which all believers are hereafter to stand. In Rom. 14:10 it is called "The judgment seat of God," RV (KJV, "of Christ"), according to the most authentic mss. The same tribunal is called "the judgment seat of Christ," 2 Cor. 5:10, to whom the Father has given all judgment, John 5:22, 27; this is different than the "Great White Throne," Rev. 20:11, at which only "the dead" will appear.

2. *kriterion* (*2922*) primarily "a means of judging" (akin to *krino*, "to judge": Eng., "criterion"), then, a tribunal, law court, or "lawsuit," 1 Cor. 6:2.

JURISDICTION

exousia (*1849*), "power, authority," is used, by metonymy, to denote "jurisdiction," in Luke 23:7.

JUST, JUSTLY

A. Adjectives.

1. *dikaios* (*1342*) was first used of persons observant of *dike*, "custom, rule, right," especially in the fulfillment of duties towards gods and men, and of things that were in accordance with right. The Eng. word "righteous" was formerly spelled "rightwise," i.e., (in a) straight way. In the NT it denotes "righteous," a state of being right, or right conduct, judged whether by the divine stan-

dard, or according to human standards, of what is right. Said of God, it designates the perfect agreement between His nature and His acts (in which He is the standard for all men). It is used (1) in the broad sense, of persons: (a) of God, e.g., John 17:25; Rom. 3:26; 1 John 1:9; 2:29; 3:7; (b) of Christ, e.g., Acts 3:14; 7:52; 22:14; 2 Tim. 4:8; 1 Pet. 3:18; 1 John 2:1; (c) of men, Matt. 1:19; Luke 1:6; Rom. 1:17; 2:13; 5:7. (2) of things; blood (metaphorical), Matt. 23:35; Christ's judgment, John 5:30; any circumstance, fact or deed, Matt. 20:4 (v. 7, in some mss.); Luke 12:57; Acts 4:19; Eph. 6:1; Phil. 1:7; 4:8; Col. 4:1; 2 Thess. 1:6; "the commandment" (the Law), Rom. 7:12; works, 1 John 3:12, the ways of God, Rev. 15:3.

2. *endikos* (*1738*), "just, righteous" (*en*, "in," *dike*, "right"), is said of the condemnation of those who say "Let us do evil, that good may come," Rom. 3:8; of the recompense of reward of transgressions under the Law, Heb. 2:2.

B. Adverb.

dikaios (*1346*), "justly, righteously, in accordance with what is right," is said (a) of God's judgment, 1 Pet. 2:23; (b) of men, Luke 23:41, "justly"; 1 Cor. 15:34, RV, "righteously" (KJV, "to righteousness"); 1 Thess. 2:10, RV, "righteously"; Titus 2:12.

JUSTICE

dike (*1349*), primarily "custom, usage," came to denote "what is right"; then, "a judicial hearing"; hence, "the execution of a sentence," "punishment," 2 Thess. 1:9, RV; Jude 7, (KJV, "vengeance").

JUSTIFICATION, JUSTIFIER, JUSTIFY

A. Nouns.

1. *dikaiosis* (*1347*) denotes the act of pronouncing righteous, justification, acquittal"; its precise meaning is determined by that of the verb *dikaioo*, "to justify" (see B). it is used twice in the Epistle to the Romans, and there alone in the NT, signifying the establishment of a person as just by acquittal from guilt. In Rom. 4:25 the phrase "for our justification," is, lit., "because of our justification," because all that was necessary on God's part for our "justification" had been effected in the death of Christ. On this account He was raised from the dead. In 5:18, "justification of life" means "justification which results in life" (cf. v. 21). That God "justifies" the believing sinner on the ground of Christ's death, involves His free gift of life.

2. *dikaioma* (*1345*) has three distinct meanings, and seems best described comprehensively as "a concrete expression of righteousness"; it is a declaration that a person or thing is righteous, and hence it represents the expression and effect of *dikaiosis* (No. 1). It signifies (a) "an ordinance," Luke 1:6; Rom. 1:32, i.e., what God has declared to be right; Rom. 2:26, righteous requirements enjoined by the Law; so 8:4, "ordinance of the Law," i.e., collectively,

the precepts of the Law, all that it demands as right; in Heb. 9:1, 10, ordinances connected with the tabernacle ritual; (b) "a sentence of acquittal," by which God acquits men of their guilt, on the conditions (1) of His grace in Christ, through His expiatory sacrifice, (2) the acceptance of Christ by faith, Rom. 5:16; (c) "a righteous act," Rom. 5:18, "(through one) act of righteousness," RV.

B. Verb.

dikaioo (1344) primarily "to deem to be right," signifies, in the NT, (a) "to show to be right or righteous"; in the passive voice, to be justified, Matt. 11:19; Luke 7:35; Rom. 3:4; 1 Tim. 3:16; (b) "to declare to be righteous, to pronounce righteous," (1) by man, concerning God, Luke 7:29 (see Rom. 3:4, above); concerning himself, Luke 10:29; 16:15; (2) by God concerning men, who are declared to be righteous before Him on certain conditions laid down by Him.

Ideally the complete fulfillment of the law of God would provide a basis of "justification" in His sight, Rom. 2:13. But no such case has occurred in mere human experience, and therefore no one can be "justified" on this ground, Rom. 3:9-20; Gal. 2:16; 3:10, 11; 5:4. From this negative presentation in Rom. 3, the apostle proceeds to show that He is, through Christ, as "a propitiation...by (*en*, "instrumental") His blood," 3:25, RV, "the Justifier of him that hath faith in Jesus" (v. 26), "justification" being the legal and formal acquittal from guilt by God as Judge, the pronouncement of the sinner as righteous, who believes on the Lord Jesus Christ. In v. 24, "being justified" is in the present continuous tense, indicating the constant process of "justification" in the succession of those who believe and are "justified." In 5:1, "being justified" is in the aorist, or point, tense, indicating the definite time at which each person, upon the exercise of faith, was justified. In 8:1, "justification" is presented as "no condemnation." That "justification" is in view here is confirmed by the preceding chapters and by verse 34.

"Justification" is primarily and gratuitously by faith, subsequently and evidentially by works. In regard to "justification" by works, the so-called contradiction between James and the apostle Paul is only apparent. Paul has in mind Abraham's attitude toward God, his acceptance of God's word, not upon Abraham's character or actions, but upon the contrast between faith and the lack of it, namely, unbelief, cf. Rom. 11:20. James (2:21-26) is occupied with the contrast between faith that is real and faith that is false, a faith barren and dead, which is not faith at all. So with righteousness, or "justification": Paul is occupied with a right relationship with God, James, with right conduct. Paul testifies that the ungodly can be "justified" by faith, James that only the right-doer is "justified."

𝕂

KEEP, KEEPING
Old Testament

A. Verb.

natsach (5329), "to keep, oversee, have charge over." The word appears as "to set forward" in the sense of "to oversee or to lead" in 1 Chron. 23:4, 2 Chron. 34:12, Ezra 3:8, and Ezra 3:9.

B. Participle.

natseach (5329), "overseer; director." *natseach* is found in the Book of Psalms a total of 55 times in the titles of various psalms, Ps. 5, 6, 9, et al. with the meaning, "To the choirmaster" (JB, RSV). Other versions render it "choir director" (NASB); "chief musician" (KJV); and "leader" (NAB). The significance of this title is not clear. Cf. also that the word refers to "overseers" in 2 Chron. 2:18.

C. Adjective.

natsach is used only in Jer. 8:5 in the sense of "enduring."

New Testament

A. Verbs.

1. *tereo* (5083) denotes (a) "to watch over, preserve, keep, watch," e.g., Acts 12:5, 6; 16:23; in 25:21, RV (1st part), "kept" (KJV, "reserved"); the present participle is translated "keepers" in Matt. 28:4, lit. "the keeping (ones)"; it is used of the "keeping" power of God the Father and Christ, exercised over His people, John 17:11, 12, 15; 1 Thess. 5:23, "preserved"; 1 John 5:18, where "He that was begotten of God," RV, is said of Christ as the Keeper ("keepeth him," RV, for KJV, "keepeth himself"); Jude 1, RV, "kept for Jesus Christ" (KJV, "preserved in Jesus Christ"), Rev. 3:10; of their inheritance, 1 Pet. 1:4 ("reserved"); of judicial reservation by God in view of future doom, 2 Pet. 2:4, 9, 17; 3:7; Jude 6, 13; of "keeping" the faith, 2 Tim. 4:7; the unity of the Spirit, Eph. 4:3; oneself, 2 Cor. 11:9; 1 Tim. 5:22; Jas. 1:27; figuratively, one's garments, Rev. 16:15; (b) "to observe, to give heed to," as of keeping commandments, etc., e.g., Matt. 19:17; John 14:15; 15:10; 17:6; Jas. 2:10; 1 John 2:3, 4, 5; 3:22, 24; 5:2 (in some mss.), 3; Rev. 1:3; 2:26; 3:8, 10; 12:17; 14:12; 22:7, 9.

2. *diatereo* (1301), "to keep carefully" (*dia*, intensive, and No. 1), is said of "the mother of Jesus," in keeping His sayings in her

heart, Luke 2:51, and of the command of the apostles and elders in Jerusalem to gentile converts in the churches to "keep" themselves from the evils mentioned in Acts 15:29.

3. *suntereo* (4933) denotes "to preserve, keep safe, keep close" (*sun*, "together with," used intensively, and No. 1), in Luke 2:19, as in v. 51 (see No. 2, above), of the mother of Jesus in regard to the words of the shepherds; in Mark 6:20 it is used of Herod's preservation of John the Baptist from Herodias, RV, "kept (him) safe," KJV, "observed (him)" (marg., "kept"); in Matt. 9:17 (in some mss., Luke 5:38), of the preservation of wineskins.

4. *phulasso* (5442) denotes (a) "to guard, watch, keep watch," e.g., Luke 2:8; in the passive voice, 8:29; (b) "to keep by way of protection," e.g., Luke 11:21; John 12:25; 17:12 (2nd part; No. 1 in 1st part and in v. 11); (c) metaphorically, "to keep a law precept," etc., e.g., Matt. 19:20 and Luke 18:21, "have observed"; Luke 11:28; John 12:47 (in the best mss.); Acts 7:53; 16:4; 21:24; Rom. 2:26; Gal. 6:13; 1 Tim. 5:21 ("observe"); in the middle voice, Mark 10:20 ("have observed"); (d) in the middle voice, "to keep oneself from," Acts 21:25; elsewhere translated by the verb "to beware."

5. *diaphulasso* (1314), an intensive form of No. 4, "to guard thoroughly."

6. *phroureo* (5432), "to keep with a military guard," e.g., Gal. 3:23, RV, "kept in ward."

7. *krateo* (2902), "to be strong, get possession of, hold fast," is used in Mark 9:10, "(and) they kept (the saying)," i.e., they held fast to the Lord's command to refrain from telling what they had seen in the mount of Transfiguration.

B. Noun.

teresis (5084), akin to A, No. 1, denotes (a) "a watching," and hence, "imprisonment, prison," Acts 4:3 and 5:18, "ward," RV (KJV, "hold" and "prison"); (b) "keeping," 1 Cor. 7:19.

TO KEEP, WATCH, GUARD

A. Verb.

natsar (5341), "to watch, to guard, to keep." *natsar* is frequently used to express the idea of "guarding" something, such as a vineyard, Isa. 27:3, or a fortification, Nah. 2:1. "To watch" one's speech is a frequent concern, so advice is given "to watch" one's mouth, Prov. 13:3, the tongue, Ps. 34:13, and the lips, Ps. 141:3. Many references are made to God as the one who "preserves" His people from dangers of all kinds, Deut. 32:10; Ps. 31:23.

shamar (8104), "to keep, tend, watch over, retain." *shamar* means "to keep" in the sense of "tending" and taking care of. So God put Adam "into the garden of Eden to dress it and to keep it," in the sense of taking care of it, as with God and his people, Gen. 2:15; 2 Kings 22:14; Job 2:6; Ps. 121:4.

The word also means "to keep" in the sense of "watching over" or giving attention to, 1 Sam. 26:15; "to watch, observe," 1 Sam. 1:12; "to watch over" in the sense of seeing that one observes the covenant, keeping one to a covenant, Gen. 18:19. *shamar* also signifies fulfilling a responsibility, Judg. 1:24. In a third group of passages this verb means "to keep" in the sense of saving or "retaining," Gen. 41:35.

B. Nouns.

mishmar (4929), "guard; guardpost," a group of soldiers, Gen. 40:3; a place, "guardpost," Neh. 7:3.

mishmeret (4931), "those who guard; obligation," a guard-man, 2 Kings 11:5; a charge or obligation, Gen. 26:5.

KEY

kleis (2807), "a key," is used metaphorically (a) of "the keys of the kingdom of heaven," which the Lord committed to Peter, Matt. 16:19, by which he would open the door of faith, as he did to Jews at Pentecost, and to Gentiles in the person of Cornelius, acting as one commissioned by Christ, through the power of the Holy Spirit; he had precedence over his fellow disciples, not in authority, but in the matter of time, on the ground of his confession of Christ (v. 16); equal authority was committed to them (18:18); (b) of "the key of knowledge," Luke 11:52, i.e., knowledge of the revealed will of God, by which men entered into the life that pleases God; this the religious leaders of the Jews had presumptuously "taken away," so that they neither entered in themselves, nor permitted their hearers to do so; (c) of "the keys of death and of Hades," Rev. 1:18,, indicative of the authority of the Lord over the bodies and souls of men; (d) of "the key of David," Rev. 3:7, a reference to Isa. 22:22, speaking of the deposition of Shebna and the investiture of Eliakim, in terms evidently messianic, the metaphor being that of the right of entrance upon administrative authority; the mention of David is symbolic of complete sovereignty; (e) of "the key of the pit of the abyss," Rev. 9:1; here the symbolism is that of competent authority; the pit represents a shaft or deep entrance into the region, from whence issued smoke, symbolic of blinding delusion; (f) of "the key of the abyss," Rev. 20:1; this is to be distinguished from (e): the symbolism is that of the complete supremacy of God over the region of the lost, in which, by angelic agency, Satan is destined to be confined for a thousand years.

K

KILL

Old Testament

shachat (7819), "to slaughter, kill," i.e., take the life of an animal or human, Gen. 22:10; of animals for food, 1 Sam. 14:32, 34; Isa. 22:13; of killing people, Judg. 12:6; 1 Kings 18:40; 2 Kings 10:7, 14.

Another word with the same above usage, is *harag*, "kill, slay," especially animals, though also great numbers of people Gen. 4:8; also vv. 14-15; Num. 31:7-8.

rashach, "to murder," occurs primarily in the legal material of the Old Testament. This is not a surprise, as God's law included regulations on life and provisions for dealing with the murderer. The Decalogue gives the general principle in a simple statement, which contains the first occurrence of the verb: "Thou shalt not kill [murder]," Exod. 20:13.

The Old Testament recognizes the distinction between premeditated murder and unintentional killing. In order to assure the rights of the manslayer, who unintentionally killed someone, the law provided for three cities of refuge, Num. 35; Deut. 19; Josh. 20; 21. Accidental killing has different, less severe penalties.

The prophets use *rashach* to describe the effect of injustice and lawlessness in Israel, Hos. 4:1-2; cf. Isa. 1:21; Jer. 7:9. The psalmist, too, metaphorically expresses the deprivation of the rights of helpless murder victims, Ps. 94:6.

New Testament

1. *apokteino* (615), "to kill," is used (a) physically, e.g., Matt. 10:28; 14:5, "put...to death," similarly rendered in John 18:31; often of Christ's death; in Rev. 2:13, RV "was killed" (KJV, "was slain"); 9:15, RV, "kill" (KJV, "slay"); 11:13, RV, "were killed" (KJV, "were slain"); so in 19:21; (b) metaphorically, Rom. 7:11, of the power of sin, which is personified, as "finding occasion, through the commandment," and inflicting deception and spiritual death, i.e., separation from God, realized through the presentation of the commandment to conscience, breaking in upon the fancied state of freedom; the argument shows the power of the Law, not to deliver from sin, but to enhance its sinfulness; in 2 Cor. 3:6, "the letter killeth," signifies not the literal meaning of Scripture as contrasted with the spiritual, but the power of the Law to bring home the knowledge of guilt and its punishment; in Eph. 2:16 "having slain the enmity" describes the work of Christ through His death in annulling the enmity, "the Law" (v. 15), between Jew and Gentile, reconciling regenerate Jew and Gentile to God in spiritual unity "in one body."

2. *anaireo* (337) denotes (a) "to take up" (*ana*, "up," *haireo*, "to take"), said of Pharaoh's daughter, in "taking up" Moses, Acts 7:21; (b) "to take away" in the sense of removing, Heb. 10:9, of the legal appointment of sacrifices, to bring in the will of God in the sacrificial offering of the death of Christ; (c) "to kill," used physically only (not metaphorically as in No. 1), e.g., Luke 22:2; in 2 Thess. 2:8, instead of the future tense of this verb, some texts (followed by RV marg.) read the future of *analisko*, "to consume."

3. *thuo* (2380) primarily denotes "to offer firstfruits to a god"; then (a) "to sacrifice by slaying a victim," Acts 14:13, 18, to do sac-

rifice; 1 Cor. 10:20, to sacrifice; 1 Cor. 5:7, "hath been sacrificed," of the death of Christ as our Passover; (b) "to slay, kill," Matt. 22:4; Mark 14:12; Luke 15:23, 27, 30; 22:7; John 10:10; Acts 10:13; 11:7.

KIN, KINSFOLK, KINSMAN, KINSWOMAN

A. Adjective.

sungenes (4773), primarily denoting "congenital, natural, innate" (*sun*, "with," *genos*, "a family, race, offspring"), then, "akin to," is used as a noun, denoting (a) of "family relationship, kin, a kinsman, kinsfolk(s)," Luke 1:58, RV, "kinsfolk" (KJV, "cousins"); 14:12; 21:16; John 18:26; Acts 10:24; (b) of "tribal or racial kinship, fellow nationals," Rom. 9:3; 16:7, 11, 21.

B. Nouns.

1. *sungenis* (4773v), a late feminine form of A (some mss. have *sungenes*), denotes "a kinswoman," Luke 1:36, RV, "kinswoman" (KJV, "cousin").

2. *sungeneus* (4773**), an alternative form of A, is used in Mark 6:4, "kin," and Luke 2:44, "kinsfolk."

KIND (Noun)

1. *genos* (1085), akin to *ginomai*, "to become," denotes (a) "a family," Acts 4:6; 7:13 (KJV, "kindred"); 13:26, "stock"; (b) "an offspring," Acts 17:28; Rev. 22:16; (c) "a nation, a race," Mark 7:26; Acts 4:36, KJV, "of the country (of Cyprus)"; *genos* does not mean "a country"; the word here signifies "parentage"; 7:19, (KJV, "kindred"); 18:2, 24, (KJV, "born"); 2 Cor. 11:26, "countrymen"; Gal. 1:14 (KJV, "nation"); Phil. 3:5, "stock"; 1 Pet. 2:9 (KJV, "generation"); (d) "a kind, sort, class," Matt. 13:47, "kind"; in some mss. in 17:21, KJV, "kind"; Mark 9:29, "kind"; 1 Cor. 12:10, 28, "kinds" (KJV, "diversities"); 14:10 (ditto).

2. *phusis* (5449) among its various meanings denotes "the nature, the natural constitution or power of a person or thing," and is translated "kind" in Jas. 3:7 (twice), "kind" (of beasts, etc.), and "(man)kind," lit., "human kind."

KIND (Adjective), KIND (be), KINDLY, KINDNESS

A. Adjective.

chrestos (5543), "serviceable, good, pleasant" (of things), "good, gracious, kind" (of persons), is translated "kind" in Luke 6:35, of God; in Eph. 4:32, enjoined upon believers.

B. Verb.

chresteuomai (5541), akin to A, "to be kind," is said of love, 1 Cor. 13:4.

C. Nouns.

1. *chrestotes* (*5544*), akin to A, and B, used of "goodness of heart, kindness," is translated "kindness" in 2 Cor. 6:6; Gal. 5:22, RV (KJV, "gentleness"); Eph. 2:7; Col. 3:12; Titus 3:4.

2. *philanthropia* (*5363*), (Eng., "philanthropy"), denotes "kindness," and is so translated in Acts 28:2 and in Titus 3:4, the latter of the "kindness" of God.

D. Adverb.

philanthropos (*5364*), akin to C, No. 2, "humanely, kindly," is translated "kindly" in Acts 27:3 (KJV, "courteously").

KINDLE

1. *hapto* (*681*), properly, "to fasten to," is used in Acts 28:2 (in the most authentic mss., some mss. have No. 3), of "kindling a fire."

2. *periapto* (*4012* and *681*), properly, "to tie about, attach" (*peri*, "around," and No. 1), is used of "lighting" a fire in the midst of a court in Luke 22:55 (some mss. have No. 1).

3. *anapto* (*381*), "to light up" (*ana*, "up," and No. 1), is used (a) literally, in Jas. 3:5, "kindleth"; (b) metaphorically, in the passive voice, in Luke 12:49, of the "kindling" of the fire of hostility.

KING

A. Noun.

basileus (*935*), "a king" (cf. Eng., "Basil"), e.g., Matt. 1:6, is used of the Roman emperor in 1 Pet. 2:13, 17 (a command of general application); of Herod the Tetrarch (used by courtesy), Matt. 14:9; of Christ, as the "King" of the Jews, e.g., Matt. 2:2; 27:11, 29, 37; as the "King" of Israel, Mark 15:32; John 1:49; 12:13; as "King of kings," Rev. 17:14; 19:16; as "the King" in judging nations and men at the establishment of the millennial kingdom, Matt. 25:34, 40; of God, "the great King," Matt. 5:35; "the King eternal, incorruptible, invisible," 1 Tim. 1:17; "King of kings," 1 Tim. 6:15; "King of the ages," Rev. 15:3, RV (KJV, "saints"). Christ's "kingship" was predicted in the OT, e.g., Ps. 2:6, and in the NT, e.g., Luke 1:32, 33; He came as such e.g., Matt. 2:2; John 18:37; was rejected and died as such, Luke 19:14; Matt. 27:37; is now a "King" Priest, after the order of Melchizedek, Heb. 5:6; 7:1, 17; and will reign for ever and ever, Rev. 11:15.

B. Adjectives.

1. *basileios* (*934*), denoting "royal," as in 1 Pet. 2:9, is used in the plural, of the courts or palaces of kings, Luke 7:25, "kings' courts"; a possible meaning is "among royal courtiers or persons."

2. *basilikos* (*937*), "royal, belonging to a king," is used in Acts 12:20 with "country" understood, "their country was fed from the king's," lit., "the royal (country)."

KINGDOM

Old Testament

malkut (4438), "kingdom; reign; rule." The word *malkut* denotes: (1) the territory of the kingdom, Esth. 1:4; (2) the accession to the throne, Esth. 4:14; (3) the year of rule, Esth. 2:16; and (4) anything "royal" or "kingly," Esth. 1:2; royal wine, Esth. 1:7; royal crown, Esth. 1:11; royal word, Esth. 1:19; royal garment, Esth. 6:8, royal palace, Esth. 1:9, royal scepter, Ps. 45:6, and finally, "glory," Ps. 145:11-12.

mamlakah (4467), "kingdom; sovereignty; dominion; reign," is the area and people that constitute a "kingdom." The word refers to non-Israelite nations who are ruled by a *melek*, "king," Isa. 23:17. *mamlikah* is a synonym for *'am*, "people," and *goy*, "nation," Ps. 105:13. The word also denotes Israel as God's "kingdom," Exod. 19:6. The Davidic king was the theocratic agent by whom God ruled over and blessed His people, 2 Sam. 7:16. Nevertheless, the one *mamlakah* after Solomon was divided into two kingdoms which Ezekiel·predicted would be reunited, Ezek. 37:22.

Close to the basic meaning is the usage of *mamlakah* to denote "king," i.e., one who heads the kingdom, 1 Sam. 10:18. The word further has the meaning of the royal "rule," the royal "sovereignty," and the "dominion." The royal "sovereignty" was taken from Saul because of his disobedience, 1 Sam. 28:17. "Royal sovereignty" is also the sense in Jer. 27:1. The Old Testament further defines as expressions of the royal "rule" all things associated with the king: (1) the throne: "And it shall be, when he sitteth upon the throne of his kingdom, that he shall write him a copy of this law in a book out of that which is before the priests the Levites," Deut. 17:18; (2) the pagan sanctuary supported by the throne: "But prophesy not again any more at Beth-el: for it is the king's chapel, and it is the kings court," Amos 7:13; and (3) a royal city, 1 Sam. 27:5.

All human rule is under God's control. Consequently the Old Testament fully recognizes the kingship of God. The Lord ruled as king over His people Israel, 1 Chron. 29:11. He graciously ruled over His people through David and his followers until the Exile, 2 Chron. 13:5.

melek (4428), "king." This word occurs about 2,513 times in the Old Testament. It is found several times in Gen. 14:1: "And it came to pass in the days of Amraphel king of Shinar, Arioch king of El-lasar, Chedorlaomer king of Elam, and Tidal king of nations."

New Testament

basileia (932) is primarily an abstract noun, denoting "sovereignty, royal power, dominion," e.g., Rev. 17:18, translated "(which) reigneth," lit., "hath a kingdom" (RV marg.); then, by metonymy, a concrete noun, denoting the territory or people over whom a king

K

rules, e.g., Matt. 4:8; Mark 3:24. It is used especially of the "kingdom" of God and of Christ.

The Kingdom of God is (a) the sphere of God's rule, Ps. 22:28; 145:13; Dan. 4:25; Luke 1:52; Rom. 13:1, 2. Since, however, this earth is the scene of universal rebellion against God, e.g., Luke 4:5, 6; 1 John 5:19; Rev. 11:15-18, the "kingdom" of God is (b) the sphere in which, at any given time, His rule is acknowledged. God has not relinquished His sovereignty in the face of rebellion, demoniac and human, but has declared His purpose to establish it, Dan. 2:44; 7:14; 1 Cor. 15:24, 25. Meantime, seeking willing obedience, He gave His law to a nation and appointed kings to administer His "kingdom" over it, 1 Chron. 28:5. Israel, however, though declaring still a nominal allegiance shared in the common rebellion, Isa. 1:2-4, and, after they had rejected the Son of God, John 1:11 (cf. Matt. 21:33-43), were "cast away," Rom. 11:15, 20, 25. Henceforth God calls upon men everywhere, without distinction of race or nationality, to submit voluntarily to His rule. Thus the "kingdom" is said to be "in mystery" now, Mark 4:11, that is, it does not come within the range of the natural powers of observation, Luke 17:20, but is spiritually discerned, John 3:3 (cf. 1 Cor. 2:14). When, hereafter, God asserts His rule universally, then the "kingdom" will be in glory, that is, it will be manifest to all; cf. Matt. 25:31-34; Phil. 2:9-11; 2 Tim. 4:1, 18.

The fundamental principle of the Kingdom is declared in the words of the Lord spoken in the midst of a company of Pharisees, "the Kingdom of God is in the midst of you," Luke 17:21 (marg.), where the King is, there is the Kingdom. Thus at the present time and on earth, where the King is and where His rule is acknowledged, is, first, in the heart of the individual believer, Acts 4:19; Eph. 3:17; 1 Pet. 3:15; and then in the churches of God, 1 Cor. 12:3, 5, 11; 14:37; cf. Col. 1:27, where for "in" read "among."

Entrance into the Kingdom of God is by the new birth, Matt. 18:3; John 3:5, for nothing that a man may be by nature, or can attain to by any form of self-culture, avails in the spiritual realm. And as the new nature, received in the new birth, is made evident by obedience, it is further said that only such as do the will of God shall enter into His Kingdom, Matt. 7:21, where, however, the context shows that the reference is to the future, as in 2 Pet. 1:10, 11. Cf. also 1 Cor. 6:9, 10; Gal. 5:21; Eph. 5:5.

The expression "Kingdom of God" occurs four times in Matthew, "Kingdom of the Heavens" usually taking its place. The latter (cf. Dan. 4:26) does not occur elsewhere in NT, but see 2 Tim. 4:18, "His heavenly Kingdom."...This Kingdom is identical with the Kingdom of the Father (cf. Matt. 26:29 with Mark 14:25), and with the Kingdom of the Son (cf. Luke 22:30). Thus there is but one Kingdom, variously described: of the Son of Man, Matt. 13:41; of Jesus, Rev. 1:9; of Christ Jesus, 2 Tim. 4:1; "of Christ and God," Eph. 5:5; "of our

Lord, and of His Christ," Rev. 11:15; "of our God, and the authority of His Christ," 12:10; "of the Son of His love," Col. 1:13.

The Apostle Paul often speaks of the Kingdom of God, not dispensationally but morally, e.g., in Rom. 14:17; 1 Cor. 4:20, but never so of the Kingdom of Heaven. "God" is not the equivalent of "the heavens." He is everywhere and above all dispensations, whereas "the heavens" are distinguished from the earth, until the Kingdom comes in judgment and power and glory (Rev. 11:15, RV) when rule in heaven and on earth will be one.

While, then, the sphere of the Kingdom of God and the Kingdom of Heaven are at times identical, yet the one term cannot be used indiscriminately for the other. In the "Kingdom of Heaven" (32 times in Matt.), heaven is in antithesis to earth, and the phrase is limited to the Kingdom in its earthly aspect for the time being, and is used only dispensationally and in connection with Israel. In the "Kingdom of God," in its broader aspect, God is in antithesis to "man" or "the world," and the term signifies the entire sphere of God's rule and action in relation to the world. It has a moral and spiritual force and is a general term for the Kingdom at any time. The Kingdom of Heaven is always the Kingdom of God, but the Kingdom of God is not limited to the Kingdom of Heaven, until in their final form, they become identical, e.g., Rev. 11:15, RV; John 3:5; Rev. 12:10.

KNEEL

gonupeteo (*1120*) denotes "to bow the knees, kneel," the act of one imploring aid, Matt. 17:14; Mark 1:40; of one expressing reverence and honor, Mark 10:17; in mockery, Matt. 27:29.

KNIT TOGETHER

sumbibazo (*4822*) signifies "to cause to coalesce, to join or knit together," Eph. 4:16, RV, "knit together" (KJV, "compacted)"; Col. 2:2, where some would assign the alternative meaning, "to instruct," as, e.g., in 1 Cor. 2:16; in Col. 2:19, "knit together," it is said of the church, as the body of which Christ is the Head.

KNOW, KNOWN, KNOWLEDGE, UNKNOWN
Old Testament

A. Verbs.

nakar (5234), "to know, regard, recognize, pay attention to, be acquainted with." The basic meaning of the term is a physical apprehension, whether through sight, touch, or hearing. Darkness sometimes makes recognition impossible, Ruth 3:14. People are often "recognized" by their voices, Judg. 18:3. *nakar* sometimes has the meaning "pay attention to," a special kind of recognition. Ruth 2:19. This verb can mean "to be acquainted with," a kind of intellectual awareness, " Job 7:10; cf. Ps. 103:16. The sense of "to distinguish" is seen in Ezra 3:13,

yada' (3045), "to know." Essentially *yada'* means: (1) to know by observing and reflecting (thinking), and (2) to know by experiencing. The first sense appears in Gen. 8:11, where Noah "knew" the waters had abated as a result of seeing the freshly picked olive leaf in the dove's mouth; he "knew" it after observing and thinking about what he had seen. He did not actually see or experience the abatement himself.

In contrast to this knowing through reflection is the knowing which comes through experience with the senses, by investigation and proving, by reflection and consideration (firsthand knowing). Consequently *yada'* is used in synonymous parallelism with "hear," Exod. 3:7, "see," Gen. 18:21, and "perceive, see," Job 28:7.

Thirdly, this verb can represent that kind of knowing which one learns and can give back, Gen. 4:9; 12:11. One can also "know" by being told by a witness, Lev. 5:1. In addition to the essentially cognitive knowing already presented, this verb has a purely experiential side. The "knower" has actual involvement with or in the object of the knowing. So Potiphar was unconcerned about (literally, "did not know about") what was in his house, Gen. 39:6—he had no actual contact with it. In Gen. 4:1 Adam's knowing Eve also refers to direct contact with her—in a sexual relationship. In Gen. 18:19 God says He "knows" Abraham; He cared for him in the sense that He chose him from among other men and saw to it that certain things happened to him. The emphasis is on the fact that God "knew" him intimately and personally.

yada' in the intensive and causative stems is used to express a particular concept of revelation. God did not make Himself known by His name Jehovah to Abraham, Isaac, and Jacob. He did reveal that name to them, that He was the God of the covenant. Nevertheless, the covenant was not fulfilled (they did not possess the Promised Land) until the time of Moses. The statement in Exod. 6:3 implies that now God was going to make Himself known "by His name"; He was going to lead them to possess the land. God makes Himself known through revelatory acts such as bringing judgment on the wicked, Ps. 9:16, and deliverance to His people, Isa. 66:14. He also reveals Himself through the spoken word—for example, by the commands given through Moses, Ezek. 20:11, by promises like those given to David, 2 Sam. 7:21.

B. Noun.

da'at (1847), "knowledge," Gen. 2:9; Exod. 31:3.

New Testament

A. Verbs.

1. *ginosko* (1097) signifies "to be taking in knowledge, to come to

know, recognize, understand," or "to understand completely," e.g., Mark 13:28, 29; John 13:12; 15:18; 21:17; 2 Cor. 8:9; Heb. 10:34; 1 John 2:5; 4:2, 6 (twice), 7, 13; 5:2, 20; in its past tenses it frequently means "to know in the sense of realizing," the aorist or point tense usually indicating definiteness, Matt. 13:11; Mark 7:24; John 7:26; in 10:38 "that ye may know (aorist tense) and understand, (present tense)"; 19:4; Acts 1:7; 17:19; Rom. 1:21; 1 Cor. 2:11 (2nd part), 14; 2 Cor. 2:4; Eph. 3:19; 6:22; Phil. 2:19; 3:10; 1 Thess. 3:5; 2 Tim. 3:1; Jas. 2:20; 1 John 2:13 (twice), 14; 3:6; 4:8; 2 John 1; Rev. 2:24; 3:3, 9. In the passive voice, it often signifies "to become known," e.g., Matt. 10:26; Phil. 4:5. In the sense of complete and ab-solute understanding on God's part, it is used, e.g., in Luke 16:15; John 10:15 (of the Son as well as the Father); 1 Cor. 3:20. In Luke 12:46, KJV, it is rendered "he is...aware."

In the NT *ginosko* frequently indicates a relation between the person "knowing" and the object known; in this respect, what is "known" is of value or importance to the one who knows, and hence the establishment of the relationship, e.g., especially of God's "knowledge," 1 Cor. 8:3, "if any man love God, the same is known of Him"; Gal. 4:9, "to be known of God"; here the "knowing" suggests approval and bears the meaning "to be approved"; so in 2 Tim. 2:19; cf. John 10:14, 27; Gen. 18:19; Nah. 1:7; the relationship implied may involve remedial chastisement, Amos 3:2. The same idea of appreciation as well as "knowledge" underlies several statements concerning the "knowledge" of God and His truth on the part of believers, e.g., John 8:32; 14:20, 31; 17:3; Gal. 4:9 (1st part); 1 John 2:3-13, 14; 4:6, 8, 16; 5:20; such "knowledge" is ob-tained, not by mere intellectual activity, but by operation of the Holy Spirit consequent upon acceptance of Christ. Nor is such "knowledge" marked by finality; see e.g., 2 Pet. 3:18; Hos. 6:3, RV.

The verb is also used to convey the thought of connection or union, as between man and woman, Matt. 1:25; Luke 1:34.

2. *oida* (Perf. of *1492*), from the same root as *eidon*, "to see," is a perfect tense with a present meaning, signifying, primarily, "to have seen or perceived"; hence, "to know, to have knowledge of," whether absolutely, as in divine knowledge, e.g., Matt. 6:8, 32; John 6:6, 64; 8:14; 11:42; 13:11; 18:4; 2 Cor. 11:31; 2 Pet. 2:9; Rev. 2:2, 9, 13, 19; 3:1, 8, 15; or in the case of human "knowledge," to know from observation, e.g., 1 Thess. 1:4, 5; 2:1; 2 Thess. 3:7.

The differences between *ginosko* (No. 1) and *oida* demand con-sideration: (a) *ginosko*, frequently suggests inception or progress in "knowledge," while *oida* suggests fullness of "knowledge," e.g., John 8:55; (b) while *ginosko* frequently implies an active relation between the one who "knows" and the person or thing "known" (see No. 1, above), *oida* expresses the fact that the object has sim-ply come within the scope of the "knower's" perception; thus in Matt. 7:23 "I never knew you" (*ginosko*) suggests "I have never been in approving connection with you," whereas in 25:12, "I know you not" (*oida*) suggests "you stand in no relation to Me."

3. *epiginosko* (*1921*) denotes (a) "to observe, fully perceive, notice attentively, discern, recognize" (*epi*, "upon," and No. 1); it suggests generally a directive, a more special, recognition of the object "known" than does No. 1; it also may suggest advanced "knowledge" or special appreciation; thus, in Rom. 1:32, "knowing the ordinance of God" (*epiginosko*) means "knowing full well," whereas in verse 21 "knowing God" (*ginosko*) simply suggests that they could not avoid the perception.

4. *proginosko* (*4267*), "to know beforehand," is used (a) of the divine "foreknowledge" concerning believers, Rom. 8:29; Israel, 11:2; Christ as the Lamb of God, 1 Pet. 1:20, RV, "foreknown" (KJV, "foreordained"); (b) of human previous "knowledge," of a person, Acts 26:5, RV, "having knowledge of" (KJV, "which knew"); of facts, 2 Pet. 3:17.

5. *sunoida* (*4923*), *sun*, "with," and No. 2, a perfect tense with a present meaning, denotes (a) "to share the knowledge of, be privy to," Acts 5:2; (b) "to be conscious of," especially of guilty consciousness, 1 Cor. 4:4, "I know nothing against (KJV, by) myself." The verb is connected with *suneidon*, found in Acts 12:12; 14:6 (in the best texts).

6. *gnorizo* (*1107*) signifies (a) "to come to know, discover, know," Phil. 1:22, "I wot (not)," i.e., "I know not," "I have not come to know" (the RV, marg. renders it, as under (b), "I do not make known"); (b) "to make known," whether (I) communicating things before "unknown," Luke 2:15, 17; in the latter some mss. have the verb *diagnorizo* (hence the KJV, "made known abroad"); John 15:15, "I have made known"; 17:26; Acts 2:28; 7:13 (1st part); Rom. 9:22, 23; 16:26 (passive voice); 2 Cor. 8:1, "we make known (to you)," RV, KJV, "we do (you) to wit"; Eph. 1:9; 3:3, 5, 10 (all three in the passive voice); 6:19, 21; Col. 1:27; 4:7, 9, "shall make known" (KJV, "shall declare"); 2 Pet. 1:16; or (II), reasserting things already "known," 1 Cor. 12:3, "I give (you) to understand" (the apostle reaffirms what they knew); 15:1, of the gospel; Gal. 1:11 (he reminds them of what they well knew, the ground of his claim to apostleship); Phil. 4:6 (passive voice), of requests to God.

B. Adjectives.

1. *gnostos* (*1110*), a later form of *gnotos* (from No. 1), most frequently denotes "known"; it is used ten times in the Acts, always with that meaning (save in 4:16, where it means "notable"); twice in the Gospel of John, 18:15, 16; in Luke 2:44 and 23:49 it denotes "acquaintance"; elsewhere only in Rom. 1:19, "(that which) may be known (of God)," lit., "the knowable of God," referring to the physical universe, in the creation of which God has made Himself

"knowable," that is, by the exercise of man's natural faculties, without such supernatural revelations as those given to Israel.

2. *phaneros* (*5318*), "visible, manifest," is translated "known" in Matt. 12:16 and Mark 3:12.

C. Nouns.

1. *gnosis* (*1108*), primarily "a seeking to know, an enquiry, investigation" (akin to A, No. 1), denotes, in the NT, "knowledge," especially of spiritual truth; it is used (a) absolutely, in Luke 11:52; Rom. 2:20; 15:14; 1 Cor. 1:5; 8:1 (twice), 7, 10, 11; 13:2, 8; 14:6; 2 Cor. 6:6; 8:7; 11:6; Eph. 3:19; Col. 2:3; 1 Pet. 3:7; 2 Pet. 1:5, 6; (b) with an object: in respect of (1) God, 2 Cor. 2:14; 10:5; (2) the glory of God, 2 Cor. 4:6; (3) Christ Jesus, Phil. 3:8; 2 Pet. 3:18; (4) salvation, Luke 1:77; (c) subjectively, of God's "knowledge," Rom. 11:33; the word of "knowledge," 1 Cor. 12:8; "knowledge" falsely so called, 1 Tim. 6:20.

2. *epignosis* (*1922*), akin to A, No. 3, denotes "exact or full knowledge, discernment, recognition," and is a strengthened form of No. 1, expressing a fuller or a full "knowledge," a greater participation by the "knower" in the object "known," thus more powerfully influencing him. It is not found in the Gospels and Acts. Paul uses it 15 times (16 if Heb. 10:26 is included) out of the 20 occurrences; Peter 4 times, all in his 2nd Epistle. Contrast Rom. 1:28 (*epignosis*) with the simple verb in v. 21. "In all the four Epistles of the first Roman captivity it is an element in the Apostle's opening prayer for his correspondents' well-being, Phil. 1:9; Eph. 1:17; Col. 1:9; Philem. 6" (Lightfoot).

It is used with reference to God in Rom. 1:28; 10:2; Eph. 1:17; Col. 1:10; 2 Pet. 1:3; God and Christ, 2 Pet. 1:2; Christ, Eph. 4:13; 2 Pet. 1:8; 2:20; the will of the Lord, Col. 1:9; every good thing, Philem. 6, RV (KJV, "acknowledging"); the truth, 1 Tim. 2:4; 2 Tim. 2:25, RV; 3:7; Titus 1:1, RV; the mystery of God. Col. 2:2, RV, "(that they) may know" (KJV, "to the acknowledgment of"), lit., "into a full knowledge." It is used without the mention of an object in Phil. 1:9; Col. 3:10, RV, "(renewed) unto knowledge."

K

L

LABORER, FELLOW LABORER

ergates (*2040*), akin to *ergazomai*, "to work," and *ergon*, "work," denotes (a) "a field laborer, a husbandman," Matt. 9:37, 38; 20:1, 2, 8; Luke 10:2 (twice); Jas. 5:4; (b) "a workman, laborer," in a general sense, Matt. 10:10; Luke 10:7; Acts 19:25; 1 Tim. 5:18; it is used (c) of false apostles and evil teachers, 2 Cor. 11:13; Phil. 3:2, (d) of a servant of Christ, 2 Tim. 2:15; (e) of evildoers, Luke 13:27.

LACK, LACKING

A. Noun.

husterema (*5303*) denotes (a) "that which is lacking, deficiency, shortcoming" (akin to *hustereo*, "to be behind, in want"), 1 Cor. 16:17; Phil. 2:30; Col. 1:24.

B. Verb.

hustereo (*5302*), akin to A, "to come or be behind," is used in the sense of "lacking" certain things, Matt. 19:20; Mark 10:21; Luke 22:35; in the sense of being inferior, 1 Cor. 12:24 (middle voice).

LADY

kuria (*2959*) is the person addressed in 2 John 1 and 5. Not improbably it is a proper name, but one who had a special relation with the local church.

LAMB

1. *aren* (*704*), a noun the nominative case of which is found only in early times occurs in Luke 10:3. In normal usage it was replaced by *arnion* (No. 2), of which it is the equivalent.

2. *arnion* (*721*) is a diminutive in form, but the diminutive force is not to be pressed. The general tendency in the vernacular was to use nouns in *-ion* freely, apart from their diminutive significance. It is used only by the apostle John, (a) in the plural, in the Lord's command to Peter, John 21:15, with symbolic reference to young converts; (b) elsewhere, in the singular, in the Apocalypse, some 28 times, of Christ as the "Lamb" of God, the symbolism having reference to His character and His vicarious Sacrifice, as the basis both of redemption and of divine vengeance. He is seen in the position of sovereign glory and honor, e.g., 7:17, which He

shares equally with the Father, 22:1, 3, the center of angelic beings and of the redeemed and the object of their veneration, e.g. 5:6, 8, 12, 13; 15:3, the Leader and Shepherd of His saints, e.g., 7:17; 14:4, the Head of his spiritual bride, e.g., 21:9, the luminary of the heavenly and eternal city, 21:23, the One to whom all judgment is committed, e.g., 6:1, 16; 13:8, the Conqueror of the foes of God and His people, 17:14; the song that celebrates the triumph of those who "gain the victory over the Beast," is the song of Moses...and the song of the Lamb 15:3. His sacrifice, the efficacy of which avails for those who accept the salvation thereby provided, forms the ground of the execution of divine wrath for the rejector, and the defier of God, 14:10; (c) in the description of the second "Beast," Rev. 13:11, seen in the vision "like a lamb," suggestive of his acting in the capacity of a false messiah, a travesty of the true.

3. *amnos* (286), "a lamb," is used figuratively of Christ, in John 1:29, 36, with the article, pointing Him out as the expected One, the One to be well known as the personal fulfillment and embodiment of all that had been indicated in the OT, the One by whose sacrifice deliverance from divine judgment was to be obtained; in Acts 8:32 and 1 Pet. 1:19, the absence of the article stresses the nature and character of His sacrifice as set forth in the symbolism. The reference in each case is to the lamb of God's providing, Gen. 22:8, and the Paschal lamb of God's appointment for sacrifice in Israel, e.g., Ex. 12:5, 14, 27 (cf. 1 Cor. 5:7).

LAMP

1. *lampas* (2985) denotes "a torch" (akin to *lampo*, "to shine"), frequently fed, like a "lamp," with oil from a little vessel used for the purpose (the *angeion* of Matt. 25:4); they held little oil and would frequently need replenishing, as in the parable of the ten virgins, Matt. 25:1, 3, 4, 7, 8; John 18:3, "torches"; Acts 20:8, "lights"; Rev. 4:5; 8:10.

2. *luchnos* (3088) frequently mistranslated "candle," is a portable "lamp" usually set on a stand; the word is used literally, Matt. 5:15; Mark 4:21; Luke 8:16; 11:33, 36; 15:8; Rev. 18:23; 22:5; (b) metaphorically, of Christ as the Lamb, Rev. 21:23, RV, "lamp" (KJV, "light"); of John the Baptist, John 5:35, RV, "the lamp" (KJV, "a... light"); of the eye, Matt. 6:22, and Luke 11:34, RV, "lamp"; of spiritual readiness, Luke 12:35, RV, "lamps"; of "the word of prophecy," 2 Pet. 1:19, RV, "lamp."

LANGUAGE

dialektos (1258), primarily "a conversation, discourse" (akin to *dialegomai*, "to discourse or discuss"), came to denote "the language or dialect of a country or district," in the KJV and RV of Acts 2:6 it is translated "language"; in the following the RV retains "language," for KJV, "tongue," Acts 1:19; 2:8; 21:40; 22:2; 26:14.

LASCIVIOUS, LASCIVIOUSNESS

aselgeia (766) denotes "excess, licentiousness, absence of restraint, indecency, wantonness"; "lasciviousness" in Mark 7:22, one of the evils that proceed from the heart; in 2 Cor. 12:21, one of the evils of which some in the church at Corinth had been guilty; in Gal. 5:19, classed among the works of the flesh; in Eph. 4:19, among the sins of the unregenerate who are "past feeling"; so in 1 Pet. 4:3; in Jude 4, of that into which the grace of God had been turned by ungodly men; it is translated "wantonness" in Rom. 13:13.

LAUGH, LAUGH TO SCORN

1. *gelao* (1070), "to laugh," is found in Luke 6:21, 25. This signifies loud laughter in contrast to demonstrative weeping.

2. *katagelao* (2606) denotes "to laugh scornfully at," more emphatic than No. 1 (*kata*, "down," used intensively, and No. 1), and signifies derisive laughter, Matt. 9:24; Mark 5:40; Luke 8:53.

LAUGHTER

gelos (1071), corresponding to LAUGH, 1, denotes "laughter," Jas. 4:9.

LAW

Old Testament

A. Noun.

torah (8451), "law; direction; instruction," Prov. 13:14; Job 22:22. The "instruction" of the sages of Israel, who were charged with the education of the young, was intended to cultivate in the young a fear of the Lord so that they might live in accordance with God's expectations, Prov. 28:7; cf. 3:1; 4:2; 7:2; also a parent, Prov. 31:26.

The "instruction" given by God to Moses and the Israelites became known as "the law" or "the direction" (*ha-torah*), and quite frequently as "the Law of the Lord," Ps. 119:1; or "the Law of God," Neh. 8:18; or "Law of Moses," Mal. 4:4. The word can refer to the whole of the "law," Ps. 78:5; or to particulars, Deut. 4:44.

God had communicated the "law" that Israel might observe and live, Deut. 4:8. The king was instructed to have a copy of the "law" prepared for him at his coronation, Deut. 17:18. The priests were charged with the study and teaching of, as well as the jurisprudence based upon, the "law," Jer. 18:18. The "law" was retaught in Josiah's day, 2 Chron. 34:15. Jeremiah prophesied concerning God's new dealing with His people in terms of the New Covenant, in which God's law is to be internalized, God's people would willingly obey Him, Jer. 31:33. The last prophet of the Old Testament reminded and challenged God's people to remember the "law," Mal. 4:4.

B. Verb.

yarah (3384), "to throw, cast, direct, teach, instruct." The noun *torah* is derived from this root. The meaning "to cast" appears in Gen. 31:51; "to teach" in 1 Sam. 12:23.

New Testament

A. Noun.

nomos (3551), akin to *nemo*, "to divide out, distribute," primarily meant "that which is assigned"; hence, "usage, custom," and then, "law, law as prescribed by custom, or by statute"; the word *ethos*, "custom," was retained for unwritten "law," while *nomos* became the established name for "law" as decreed by a state and set up as the standard for the administration of justice.

In the NT it is used

(a) of "law" in general, e.g., Rom. 2:12, 13, "a law" (RV), expressing a general principle relating to "law"; v. 14, last part; 3:27, "By what manner of law?" i.e., "by what sort of principle (has the glorying been excluded)?"; 4:15 (last part); 5:13, referring to the period between Adam's trespass and the giving of the Law; 7:1 (1st part, RV marg., "law"); against those graces which constitute the fruit of the Spirit "there is no law," Gal. 5:23.

(b) of a force or influence impelling to action, Rom. 7:21, 23 (1st part), "a different law," RV.

(c) of the Mosaic Law, the "law" of Sinai, (1) with the definite article, e.g., Matt. 5:18; John 1:17; Rom. 2:15, 18, 20, 26, 27; 3:19; 4:15; 7:4, 7, 14, 16, 22; 8:3, 4, 7; Gal. 3:10, 12, 19, 21, 24; 5:3; Eph. 2:15; Phil. 3:6; 1 Tim. 1:8; Heb. 7:19; Jas. 2:9; (2) without the article, thus stressing the Mosaic Law in its quality as "law," e.g., Rom. 2:14 (1st part); 5:20; 7:9, where the stress in the quality lies in this, that "the commandment which was unto (i.e., which he thought would be a means of) life," he found to be "unto (i.e., to have the effect of revealing his actual state of) death"; 10:4; 1 Cor. 9:20; Gal. 2:16, 19, 21; 3:2, 5, 10 (1st part), 11, 18, 23; 4:4, 5, 21 (1st part); 5:4, 18; 6:13; Phil. 3:5, 9; Heb. 7:16; 9:19; Jas. 2:11; (in regard to the statement in Gal. 2:16, that "a man is not justified by the works of the Law."

The following phrases specify "laws" of various kinds; (a) "the law of Christ," Gal. 6:2, i.e., either given by Him (as in the Sermon on the Mount and in John 13:14, 15; 15:4), or the "law" or principle by which Christ Himself lived (Matt. 20:28; John 13:1); these are not actual alternatives, for the "law" imposed by Christ was always that by which He Himself lived in the "days of His flesh." He confirmed the "Law" as being of divine authority (cf. Matt. 5:18); yet He presented a higher standard of life than perfunctory obedience to the current legal rendering of the "Law," a standard which, without annulling the "Law," He embodied in His own character and life (see, e.g., Matt. 5:21-48; this breach with legalism is especially seen in regard to the ritual or ceremonial part of the "Law" in its wide scope); He showed Himself superior to all human interpretations of it; (b) "a law of faith," Rom. 3:27, i.e., a principle which demands only faith on man's part; (c) "the law of my mind," Rom. 7:23, that principle which governs the new nature in virtue of the new birth; (d) "the law of sin," Rom. 7:23, the principle by which sin exerts its influence and power despite the desire to do what is right; "of sin and death," 8:2, death being the effect; (e) "the law of liberty," Jas. 1:25; 2:12, a term comprehensive of all the Scriptures, not a "law" of compulsion enforced from without, but meeting with ready obedience through the desire and delight of the renewed being who is subject to it; into it he looks, and in its teaching he delights; he is "under law (*ennomos*, 'in law,' implying union and subjection) to Christ," 1 Cor. 9:21; cf., e.g., Ps. 119:32, 45, 97; 2 Cor. 3:17; (f) "the royal law," Jas. 2:8, i.e., the "law" of love, royal in the majesty of its power, the "law" upon which all others hang, Matt. 22:34-40; Rom. 13:8; Gal. 5:14; (g) "the law of the Spirit of life," Rom. 8:2, i.e., the animating principle by which the Holy Spirit acts as the imparter of life (cf. John 6:63); (h) "a law of righteousness," Rom. 9:31, i.e., a general principle presenting righteousness as the object and outcome of keeping a "law," particularly the "Law" of Moses (cf. Gal. 3:21); (i) "the law of a carnal commandment," Heb. 7:16, i.e., the "law" respecting the Aaronic priesthood, which appointed men conditioned by the circumstances and limitations of the flesh. In the Epistle to the Hebrews the "Law" is treated of especially in regard to the contrast between the Priesthood of Christ and that established under the "law" of Moses, and in regard to access to God and to worship. In these respects the "Law" "made nothing perfect," 7:19. There was "a disannulling of a foregoing commandment...and a bringing in of a better hope." This is established under the "new Covenant," a covenant instituted on the basis of "better promises," 8:6.

B. Verbs.

1. **nomotheteo** (*3549*), (a) used intransitively, signifies "to make laws"; in the passive voice, "to be furnished with laws," Heb. 7:11, "received the law," lit., "was furnished with (the) law"; (b) used transitively, it signifies "to ordain by law, to enact"; in the passive voice, Heb. 8:6.

2. **paranomeo** (*3891*), "to transgress law" (*para*, "contrary to," and *nomos*), is used in the present participle in Acts 23:3, and translated "contrary to the law," lit., "transgressing the law."

C. Adjectives.

1. **nomikos** (*3544*) denotes "relating to law"; Titus 3:9.

2. *ennomos* (*1772*), (a) "lawful, legal," lit., "in law" (*en*, "in," and *nomos*), or strictly, "what is within the range of law," is translated "lawful" in Acts 19:39, KJV (RV, "regular"), of the legal tribunals in Ephesus; (b) "under law" (RV), in relation to Christ, 1 Cor. 9:21; the word as used by the apostle suggests not merely the condition of being under "law," but the intimacy of a relation established in the loyalty of a will devoted to his Master.

LAWFUL, LAWFULLY

A. Verb.

exesti (*1832*), an impersonal verb, signifying "it is permitted, it is lawful" (or interrogatively, "is it lawful?"), occurs most frequently in the synoptic Gospels and the Acts; elsewhere in John 5:10; 18:31; 1 Cor. 6:12; 10:23; 2 Cor. 12:4; in Acts 2:29, it is rendered "let me (speak)," lit., "it being permitted"; in the KJV of 8:37, "thou mayest," lit., "it is permitted"; 16:21; in 21:37, "may I," lit., "is it permitted?"

B. Adverb.

nomimos (*3545*), "lawfully," is used in 1 Tim. 1:8, "the Law is good, if a man use it lawfully," i.e., agreeably to its design; the meaning here is that, while no one can be justified or obtain eternal life through its instrumentality, the believer is to have it in his heart and to fulfill its requirements; walking "not after the flesh but after the spirit," Rom. 8:4, he will "use it lawfully." In 2 Tim. 2:5 it is used of contending in the games and adhering to the rules.

LAWGIVER

nomothetes (*3550*), "a lawgiver," occurs in Jas. 4:12, as one who gives law.

LAWLESS, LAWLESSNESS

A. Adjective.

anomos (*459*), "without law," also denotes "lawless," and is so rendered in the RV of Acts 2:23, "lawless (men)," marg., "(men) without the law," KJV, "wicked (hands)"; 2 Thess. 2:8, "the lawless one" (KJV, "that wicked"), of the man of sin (v. 4); in 2 Pet. 2:8, of deeds (KJV, "unlawful"), where the thought is not simply that of doing what is unlawful, but of flagrant defiance of the known will of God.

B. Noun.

anomia (*458*), "lawlessness," akin to A, is most frequently translated "iniquity"; in 2 Thess. 2:7, RV, "lawlessness" (KJV, "iniquity"); "the mystery of lawlessness" is not recognized by the world, for it does not consist merely in confusion and disorder (see A); the display of "lawlessness" by the "lawless" one (v. 8) will be the effect of the attempt by the powers of darkness to overthrow the divine government. In 1 John 3:4, the RV adheres to the real meaning of the word, "every one that doeth sin (a practice, not the committal of an act) doeth also lawlessness: and sin is lawlessness." This definition of sin sets forth its essential character as the rejection of the law, or will, of God and the substitution of the will of self.

LAWYER

nomikos (3544), an adjective, "learned in the law" (see Titus 3:9), is used as a noun, "a lawyer," Matt. 22:35; Luke 7:30; 10:25; 11:45, 46, 52 (v. 53 in some mss.); 14:3; Titus 3:13, where Zenas is so named. As there is no evidence that he was one skilled in Roman jurisprudence, the term may be regarded in the usual NT sense as applying to one skilled in the Mosaic Law.

LAYING ON

epithesis (1936), "a laying on" (**epi**, "on," **tithemi**, "to put"), is used in the NT (a) of the "laying" on of hands by the apostles accompanied by the impartation of the Holy Spirit in outward demonstration, in the cases of those in Samaria who had believed, Acts 8:18; such supernatural manifestations were signs especially intended to give witness to Jews as to the facts of Christ and the faith, they were thus temporary; there is no record of their continuance after the time and circumstances narrated in Acts 19 (in v. 6 of which the corresponding verb **epitithemi** is used), nor was the gift delegated by the apostles to others; (b) of the similar act by the elders of a church on occasions when a member of a church was set apart for a particular work, having given evidence of qualifications necessary for it, as in the case of Timothy, 1 Tim. 4:14; of the impartation of a spiritual gift through the laying on of the hands of the apostle Paul, 2 Tim. 1:6, RV, "laying"; KJV, "putting."

The principle underlying the act was that of identification on the part of him who did it with the animal or person upon whom the hands were laid.

LEAN

1. **anakeimai** (345), "to be laid up, to lie," is used of reclining at table, John 13:23, 25, 28.

2. **anapipto** (377), lit., "to fall back," is used of reclining at a repast and translated "leaning back," in John 13:25, RV (the KJV follows the mss. which have **epipipto**, and renders it "lying"); in 21:20, "leaned back."

LEARN, LEARNED (be)

1. **manthano** (3129) denotes (a) "to learn" (akin to **mathetes**, "a

disciple"), "to increase one's knowledge," or "be increased in knowledge," frequently "to learn by inquiry, or observation," e.g., Matt. 9:13; 11:29; 24:32; Mark 13:28; John 7:15; Rom. 16:17; 1 Cor. 4:6; 14:35; Phil. 4:9; 2 Tim. 3:14; Rev. 14:3; said of "learning" Christ, Eph. 4:20, not simply the doctrine of Christ, but Christ Himself, a process not merely of getting to know the person but of so applying the knowledge as to walk differently from the rest of the Gentiles; (b) "to ascertain," Acts 23:27, RV, "learned" (KJV, "understood"); Gal. 3:2, "This only would I learn from you," perhaps with a tinge of irony in the enquiry, the answer to which would settle the question of the validity of the new Judaistic gospel they were receiving; (c) "to learn by use and practice, to acquire the habit of, be accustomed to," e.g., Phil. 4:11; 1 Tim. 5:4, 13; Titus 3:14; Heb. 5:8.

2. *ginosko* (*1097*), "to know by observation and experience," is translated "to learn," in the RV of Mark 15:45; John 12:9.

3. *akriboo* (*198*), "to learn carefully," is so translated in Matt. 2:7, 16, RV (KJV, "diligently enquired").

4. *mueo* (*3453*), "to initiate into mysteries," is translated "I have learned the secret" (passive voice, perfect tense) in Phil. 4:12, RV (KJV, "I am instructed").

LEARNING (Noun)

1. *gramma* (*1121*), "a letter," is used in the plural in Acts 26:24, with the meaning "learning": "(thy much) learning (doth turn thee to madness)," RV, possibly an allusion to the Jewish Scriptures.

2. *didaskalia* (*1319*), "teaching, instruction" (akin to *didasko*, "to teach"), is translated "learning" in Rom. 15:4.

LEAST

1. *elachistos* (*1646*), "least," is a superlative degree formed from the word *elachus*, "little," the place of which was taken by *mikros* (the comparative degree being *elasson*, "less"); it is used of (a) size, Jas. 3:4; (b) amount: of the management of affairs, Luke 16:10 (twice), 19:17, "very little"; (c) importance, 1 Cor. 6:2, "smallest (matters)"; (d) authority: of commandments, Matt. 5:19; (e) estimation, as to persons, Matt. 5:19 (2nd part); 25:40, 45; 1 Cor. 15:9; as to a town, Matt. 2:6; as to activities or operations, Luke 12:26; 1 Cor. 4:3, "a very small thing."

2. *elachistoteros* (*1647*), a comparative degree formed from No. 1, is used in Eph. 3:8, "less than the least."

3. *mikroteros* (*3398*), is used of (a) size, Matt. 13:32, KJV, "the least," RV, "less"; Mark 4:31 [cf. No. 1 (a)]; (b) estimation, Matt. 11:11 and Luke 7:28, KJV, "least," RV, "but little," marg., "lesser" (in the kingdom of heaven), those in the kingdom itself being less than John the Baptist [cf. No. 1 (e)]; Luke 9:48.

LEAVEN (Noun and Verb)

A. Noun.

zume (2219), "leaven, sour dough, in a high state of fermentation," was used in general in making bread. It required time to fulfill the process. Hence, when food was required at short notice, unleavened cakes were used, e.g., Gen. 18:6; 19:3; Exod. 12:8. The Israelites were forbidden to use "leaven" for seven days at the time of Passover, that they might be reminded that the Lord brought them out of Egypt "in haste," Deut. 16:3, with Exod. 12:11; the unleavened bread, insipid in taste, reminding them, too, of their afflictions, and of the need of self-judgment, is called "the bread of affliction." "Leaven" was forbidden in all offerings to the Lord by fire, Lev. 2:11; 6:17. Being bred of corruption and spreading through the mass of that in which it is mixed, and therefore symbolizing the pervasive character of evil, "leaven" was utterly inconsistent in offerings which typified the propitiatory sacrifice of Christ.

In the OT "leaven" is not used in a metaphorical sense. In the NT it is used (a) metaphorically (1) of corrupt doctrine, Matt. 13:33 and Luke 13:21, of error as mixed with the truth (there is no valid reason for regarding the symbol here differently from its application elsewhere in the NT); Matt. 16:6, 11; Mark 8:15 (1st part); Luke 12:1; that the kingdom of heaven is likened to "leaven," does not mean that the kingdom is "leaven." The same statement, as made in other parables, shows that it is the whole parable which constitutes the similitude of the kingdom; the history of Christendom confirms the fact that the pure meal of the doctrine of Christ has been adulterated with error; (2) of corrupt practices, Mark 8:15 (2nd part), the reference to the Herodians being especially applied to their irreligion; 1 Cor. 5:7, 8; (b) literally in Matt. 16:12, and in the general statements in 1 Cor. 5:6 and Gal. 5:9, where the implied applications are to corrupt practice and corrupt doctrine respectively.

B. Verb.

zumoo (2220) signifies "to leaven, to act as leaven," passive voice in Matt. 13:33 and Luke 13:21; active voice in 1 Cor. 5:6 and Gal. 5:9.

LEFT (Adjective)

1. *aristeros* (710), is used (a) of the "left" hand, in Matt. 6:3; in connection with the armor of righteousness, in 2 Cor. 6:7; (b) in the phrase "on the left," Mark 10:37; Luke 23:33.

2. *euonumos* (2176), lit., "of good name," or "omen," a word adopted to avoid the ill-omen attaching to the "left" (omens from the "left" being unlucky), is used euphemistically for No. 1, either (a) simply as an adjective in Rev. 10:2, of the "left" foot; in Acts 21:3,

"on the left"; or (b) with the preposition *ex* (for *ek*), signifying "on the left hand," Matt. 20:21, 23; 25:33, 41; 27:38; Mark 10:40; 15:27.

LEGION

legion (*3003*), otherwise spelled *legeon*, "a legion," occurs in Matt. 26:53, of angels; in Mark 5:9, 15, and Luke 8:30, of demons. Among the Romans a "legion" was primarily a chosen (*lego*, "to choose") body of soldiers divided into ten cohorts, and numbering from 4,200 to 6,000 men.

LEND, LENDER

A. Verb.

daneizo (*1115v*) is translated "to lend" in Luke 6:34, 35.

B. Noun.

danistes or *daneistes* (*1157*) denotes a moneylender (akin to A), translated "lender" in Luke 7:41, RV (KJV, "creditor").

LEPER

lepros (*3015*), an adjective, primarily used of "psoriasis," characterized by an eruption of rough scaly patches; later, "leprous," but chiefly used as a noun, "a leper," Matt. 8:2; 10:8; 11:5; Mark 1:40; Luke 4:27; 7:22; 17:12; especially of Simon. mentioned in Matt. 26:6: Mark 14:3.

LEPROSY

lepra (*3014*), akin to *lepros*, is mentioned in Matt. 8:3; Mark 1:42; Luke 5:12, 13. In the removal of other maladies the verb "to heal" (*iaomai*) is used, but in the removal of "leprosy," the verb "to cleanse" (*katharizo*), except in the statement concerning the Samaritan, Luke 17:15, "when he saw that he was healed." Matt. 10:8 and Luke 4:27 indicate that the disease was common in the nation.

LETTER

gramma (*1121*) primarily denotes "that which is traced or drawn, a picture"; then, "that which is written," (a) "a character, letter of the alphabet," 2 Cor. 3:7; "written," lit., "(in) letters," Gal. 6:11; here the reference is not to the length of the epistle (Paul never uses *gramma*, either in the singular or the plural of his epistles; of these he uses *epistole*, No. 2), but to the size of the characters written by his own hand (probably from this verse to the end, as the use of the past tense, "I have written," is, according to Greek idiom, the equivalent of our "I am writing"). Moreover, the word for "letters" is here in the dative case, *grammasin*, "with (how large) letters"; (b) "a writing, a written document, a bond" (KJV, "bill") Luke 16:6, 7; (c) "a letter, by way of correspondence," Acts 28:21; (d) the Scriptures of the OT, 2 Tim. 3:15; (e) "learning," John 7:15, "letters"; Acts 26:24, "(much) learning" (lit., "many letters"); in the papyri an illiterate person is often spoken of as one who does not know "letters," "which never means anything else than inability to write" (Moulton and Milligan); (f) "the letter," the written commandments of the Word of God, in contrast to the inward operation of the Holy Spirit under the New Covenant, Rom. 2:27, 29; 7:6; 2 Cor. 3:6; (g) "the books of Moses," John 5:47.

LIAR

A. Noun.

pseustes (5583), "a liar," occurs in John 8:44, 55; Rom. 3:4; 1 Tim. 1:10; Titus 1:12; 1 John 1:10; 2:4, 22; 4:20; 5:10.

B. Adjective.

pseudes (5571), "lying, false" (Eng. "pseudo-"), rendered "false" in Acts 6:13 and in the RV of Rev. 2:2 (KJV, "liars"), is used as a noun, "liars," in Rev. 21:8.

LIBERAL, LIBERALITY, LIBERALLY

A. Noun.

1. *haplotes* (572) denotes (a) "simplicity, sincerity, unaffectedness" (from *haplous*, "single, simple," in contrast to *diplous*, "double"), Rom. 12:8, "simplicity"; 2 Cor. 11:3 (in some mss. in 1:12); Eph. 6:5 and Col. 3:22, "singleness"; (b) "simplicity as manifested in generous giving," "liberality," 2 Cor. 8:2; 9:11 (KJV, "bountifulness," RV marg., "singleness"); 9:13 (KJV, "liberal").

B. Adverb.

haplos (574), "liberally, with singleness of heart," is used in Jas. 1:5 of God as the gracious and "liberal" Giver.

LIBERTY

A. Noun.

aphesis (859) "dismissal, release, forgiveness," is rendered "liberty" in the KJV of Luke 4:18, RV, "release."

B. Adjective.

eleutheros (1658) is rendered "at liberty" in 1 Cor. 7:39, KJV (RV "free").

LIE (falsehood: Noun and Verb)

A. Nouns.

1. *pseudos* (5579), "a falsehood, lie." is translated "lie" in John

8:44 (lit., "the lie"); Rom. 1:25, where it stands by metonymy for an idol, as, e.g., in Isa. 44:20; Jer. 10:14; 13:25; Amos 2:4 (plural); 2 Thess. 2:11, with special reference to the lie of v. 4, that man is God (cf. Gen. 3:5); 1 John 2:21, 27; Rev. 21:27; 22:15; in Eph. 4:25, KJV "lying," RV, "falsehood," the practice; in Rev. 14:5, RV, "lie." (some mss. have *dolos*, "guile," KJV); 2 Thess. 2:9, where "lying wonders" is, lit., "wonders of falsehood," i.e., wonders calculated to deceive (cf. Rev. 13:13-15), the purpose being to deceive people into the acknowledgement of the spurious claim to deity on the part of the Man of Sin.

2. *pseusma* (5582), "a falsehood," or "an acted lie," Rom. 3:7, where "my lie" is not idolatry, but either the universal false attitude of man toward God or that with which his detractors charged the apostle; the former seems to be the meaning.

B. Adjectives.

1. *pseudologos* (5573) denotes "speaking falsely" (*pseudes*, "false," *logos*, "a word") in 1 Tim. 4:2, where the adjective is translated "that speak lies," RV (KJV, "speaking lies") and is applied to "demons," the actual utterances being by their human agents.

2. *apseudes* (893) denotes "free from falsehood" (*a*, negative, *pseudes*, "false"), truthful, Titus 1:2, of God, "who cannot lie."

C. Verb.

pseudo (5574), "to deceive by lies" (always in the middle voice in the NT), is used (a) absolutely, in Matt. 5:11, "falsely," lit., "lying" (v, marg.); Rom. 9:1; 2 Cor. 11:31; Gal. 1:20; Col. 3:9 (where the verb is followed by the preposition *eis*, "to"); 1 Tim. 2:7; Heb. 6:18; Jas. 3:14 (where it is followed by the preposition *kata*, "against"); 1 John 1:6; Rev. 3:9; (b) transitively, with a direct object (without a preposition following), Acts 5:3 (with the accusative case) "to lie to (the Holy Ghost)," RV marg., "deceive"; v. 4 (with the dative case) "thou hast (not) lied (unto men, but unto God)."

LIFE, LIVING, LIFETIME, LIFE-GIVING

A. Nouns.

1. *zoe* (2222) (Eng., "zoo," "zoology") is used in the NT "of life as a principle, life in the absolute sense, life as God has it, that which the Father has in Himself, and which He gave to the Incarnate Son to have in Himself, John 5:26, and which the Son manifested in the world, 1 John 1:2. From this life man has become alienated in consequence of the Fall, Eph. 4:18, and of this life men become partakers through faith in the Lord Jesus Christ, John 3:15, who becomes its Author to all such as trust in Him, Acts 3:15, and who is therefore said to be 'the life' of the believer, Col. 3:4, for the life that He gives He maintains, John 6:35, 63. Eternal life is the present actual possession of the believer because of his relation-

ship with Christ, John 5:24; 1 John 3:14, and that it will one day extend its domain to the sphere of the body is assured by the Resurrection of Christ, 2 Cor. 5:4; 2 Tim. 1:10. This life is not merely a principle of power and mobility, however, for it has moral associations which are inseparable from it, as of holiness and righteousness. Death and sin, life and holiness, are frequently contrasted in the Scriptures.

Death came through sin, Rom. 5:12, which is rebellion against God. Sin thus involved the forfeiting of the "life." "The life of the flesh is in the blood," Lev. 17:11. Therefore the impartation of "life" to the sinner must be by a death caused by the shedding of that element which is the life of the flesh. "It is the blood that maketh atonement by reason of the life" (*id.* RV). The separation from God caused by the forfeiting of the "life" could be removed only by a sacrifice in which the victim and the offerer became identified. This which was appointed in the typical offerings in Israel received its full accomplishment in the voluntary sacrifice of Christ. The shedding of the blood in the language of Scripture involves the taking or the giving of the "life." Since Christ had no sins of his own to die for, His death was expiatory and vicarious, John 10:15 with Isa. 53:5, 10, 12; 2 Cor. 5:21. In His sacrifice He endured the divine judgment due to man's sin. By this means the believer becomes identified with Him in His deathless "life," through His resurrection, and enjoys conscious and eternal fellowship with God.

2. *bios* (979) (cf. Eng. words beginning with *bio–*), is used in three respects (a) of "the period or duration of life," e.g., in the KJV of 1 Pet. 4:3, "the time past of our life" (the RV follows the mss. which omit "of our life"); Luke 8:14; 2 Tim. 2:4; (b) of "the manner of life, life in regard to its moral conduct," 1 Tim. 2:2; 1 John 2:16; (c) of "the means of life, livelihood, maintenance, living," Mark 12:44; Luke 8:43; 15:12, 30; 21:4; 1 John 3:17, "goods," RV (KJV, "good").

3. *psuche* (5590), besides its meanings, "heart, mind, soul," denotes "life" in two chief respects, (a) "breath of life, the natural life," e.g., Matt. 2:20; 6:25; Mark 10:45; Luke 12:22; Acts 20:10; Rev. 8:9; 12:11 (cf. Lev. 17:11; Esth. 8:11); (b) "the seat of personality," e.g., Luke 9:24, explained in v. 25 as "own self."

4. *biosis* (981), from *bioo*, "to spend one's life, to live," denotes "a manner of life," Acts 26:4.

B. Adjective.

biotikos (982), "pertaining to life" (*bios*), is translated "of this life," in Luke 21:34, with reference to cares; in 1 Cor. 6:3 "(things) that pertain to this life," and v. 4, "(things) pertaining to this life," i.e., matters of this world, concerning which Christians at Corinth were engaged in public lawsuits one with another; such matters were to be regarded as relatively unimportant in view of the great tribunals to come under the jurisdiction of saints hereafter.

C. Verb.

zoopoieo (2227), "to make alive, cause to live, quicken" (from *zoe*, "life," and *poieo*, "to make"), is used as follows:

(a) of God as the bestower of every kind of life in the universe, 1 Tim. 6:13, and, particularly, of resurrection life, John 5:21; Rom. 4:17; (b) of Christ, who also is the bestower of resurrection life, John 5:21 (2nd part); 1 Cor. 15:45; cf. v. 22; (c) of the resurrection of Christ in "the body of His glory," 1 Pet. 3:18; (d) of the power of reproduction inherent in seed, which presents a certain analogy with resurrection, 1 Cor. 15:36; (e) of the 'changing,' or 'fashioning anew,' of the bodies of the living, which corresponds with, and takes place at the same time as, the resurrection of the dead in Christ, Rom. 8:11; (f) of the impartation of spiritual life, and the communication of spiritual sustenance generally, John 6:63; 2 Cor. 3:6; Gal. 3:2.

LIGHT, Noun, and Verb (bring to, give), LIGHTEN

Old Testament

A. Verb.

'*or* (216), "to become light, become lighted up (of daybreak), give light, cause light to shine." '*or* means "to become light" in Gen. 44:3; "to give light" in Num. 8:2.

B. Nouns.

'*or* (216), "light." "Light" is the opposite of "darkness"; or figurative, Isa. 5:20, 30. In Hebrew various antonyms of '*or* are used in parallel constructions, Isa. 9:2. The basic meaning of '*or* is "daylight," cf. Gen. 1:3. In the Hebrew mind the "day" began at the rising of the sun," 2 Sam. 23:4; of light from heavenly bodies, Isa. 30:26.

In the metaphorical use '*or* signifies life over against death, Ps. 56:13. To walk in the "light" of the face of a superior, Prov. 16:15, or of God, Ps. 89:15, is an expression of a joyful, blessed life in which the quality of life is enhanced.

The noun '*ur* means "shine; light-giving," Isa. 50:11. '*orah* refers to "light," Ps. 139:12. *ma'or* also means "light," Gen. 1:16.

New Testament

A. Noun.

phos (5457), akin to *phao*, "to give light" (from roots *pha*— and *phan*—, expressing "light as seen by the eye," and, metaphorically, as "reaching the mind," whence *phaino*, "to make to appear," *phaneros*, "evident," etc.); cf. Eng., "phosphorus" (lit., "light-bearing"). "Primarily light is a luminous emanation, probably of force, from certain bodies, which enables the eye to discern form and color. Light requires an organ adapted for its reception (Matt. 6:22). Where the eye is absent, or where it has become impaired from any cause, light is useless. Man, naturally, is incapable of receiving spiritual light inasmuch as he lacks the capacity for spiritual things, 1 Cor. 2:14. Hence believers are called 'sons of light,' Luke 16:8, not merely because they have received a revelation from God, but because in the New Birth they have received the spiritual capacity for it.

Apart from natural phenomena, light is used in Scripture of (a) the glory of God's dwelling-place, 1 Tim. 6:16; (b) the nature of God, 1 John 1:5; (c) the impartiality of God, Jas. 1:17; (d) the favor of God, Ps. 4:6; of the King, Prov. 16:15; of an influential man, Job 29:24; (e) God, as the illuminator of His people, Isa. 60:19, 20; (f) the Lord Jesus as the illuminator of men, John 1:4, 5, 9; 3:19; 8:12; 9:5; 12:35, 36, 46; Acts 13:47; (g) the illuminating power of the Scriptures, Ps. 119:105; and of the judgments and commandments of God, Isa. 51:4; Prov. 6:23, cf. Ps. 43:3; (h) the guidance of God, Job 29:3; Ps. 112:4; Isa. 58:10; and, ironically, of the guidance of man, Rom. 2:19; (i) salvation, 1 Pet. 2:9; (j) righteousness, Rom. 13:12; 2 Cor. 11:14, 15; 1 John 2:9, 10; (k) witness for God, Matt. 5:14, 16; John 5:35; (l) prosperity and general well-being, Esth. 8:16; Job 18:18; Isa. 58:8-10.

B. Verb.

photizo (*5461*), used (a) intransitively, signifies "to shine, give light," Rev. 22:5; (b) transitively, (1) "to illumine, to light, enlighten, to be lightened," Luke 11:36; Rev. 21:23; in the passive voice, Rev. 18:1; metaphorically, of spiritual enlightenment, John 1:9; Eph. 1:18; 3:9, "to make...see"; Heb. 6:4; 10:32, "ye were enlightened," RV (KJV, "illuminated"); (2) "to bring to light," 1 Cor. 4:5 (of God's act in the future); 2 Tim. 1:10 (of God's act in the past).

C. Adjective.

photeinos (*5460*), from *phos* (see A), "bright," is rendered "full of light" in Matt. 6:22; Luke 11:34, 36 (twice), figuratively, of the single-mindedness of the eye, which acts as the lamp of the body; in Matt. 17:5, "bright," of a cloud.

LIKE, LIKE (as to, unto), (be) LIKE, (make) LIKE, LIKE (things), LIKEN

A. Adjectives.

1. *homoios* (*3664*), "like, resembling, such as, the same as," is used (a) of appearance or form John 9:9; Rev. 1:13, 15; 2:18; 4:3 (twice), 6, 7; 9:7 (twice), 10, 19; 11:1; 13:2, 11; 14:14; (b) of ability, condition, nature, Matt. 22:39; Acts 17:29; Gal. 5:21, "such like," lit., "and the (things) similar to these"; 1 John 3:2; Rev. 13:4; 18:18; 21:11, 18; (c) of comparison in parables, Matt. 13:31, 33, 44, 45, 47;

20:1; Luke 13:18, 19, 21; (d) of action, thought, etc. Matt. 11:16; 13:52; Luke 6:47, 48, 49; 7:31, 32; 12:36; John 8:55; Jude 7.

2. *paromoios* (3946), "much like" (*para*, "beside," and No. 1), is used in Mark 7:13, in the neuter plural, "(many such) like things."

B. Verbs.

1. *homoioo* (3666), "to make like" (akin to A, No. 1), is used (a) especially in the parables, with the significance of comparing, "likening," or, in the passive voice, "being likened," Matt. 7:24, 26; 11:16; 13:24; 18:23; 22:2 (RV, "likened"); 25:1; Mark 4:30; Luke 7:31; 13:18, RV, "liken" (KJV, "resemble"); v. 20; in several of these instances the point of resemblance is not a specific detail, but the whole circumstances of the parable; (b) of making "like," or, in the passive voice, of being made or becoming "like," Matt. 6:8; Acts 14:11, "in the likeness of (men)," lit., "being made like" (aorist participle, passive); Rom. 9:29; Heb. 2:17, of Christ in being "made like" unto His brethren, i.e., in partaking of human nature, apart from sin (cf. v. 14).

2. *paromoiazo* (3945), "to be like" (from *para*, "by," and a verbal form from *homoios*, A, No. 1), is used in Matt. 23:27 (perhaps with intensive force), in the Lord's comparison of the scribes and Pharisees to whitened sepulchres.

3. *aphomoioo* (871), "to make like" (*apo*, "from," and No. 1), is used in Heb. 7:3, of Melchizedek as "made like" the Son of God, i.e., in the facts related and withheld in the Genesis record.

LIKEMINDED

1. *isopsuchos* (2473), lit., "of equal soul" (*isos*, "equal," *psuche*, "the soul"), is rendered "likeminded" in Phil. 2:20.

2. *homophron* (3675), (*homos*, "the same," *phren*, "the mind"), occurs in 1 Pet. 3:8, RV, "likeminded" (KJV, "of one mind").

LIKENESS, LIKENESS OF (in the)

Old Testament

A. Verb.

damah (1819), "to be like, resemble" and so make a comparison of similar things, Ps. 102:6.

B. Noun.

demut (1823), "likeness; shape; figure; form; pattern." First, the word means "pattern," in the sense of the specifications from which an actual item is made, 2 Kings 16:10. Second, *demut* means "shape" or "form," the thing(s) made after a given pattern, in general, 2 Chron. 4:3; or a particular shape, Ezek. 1:10, 26. Third, *demut* signifies the original after which a thing is patterned, Gen. 1:26.

New Testament

1. **homoioma** (*3667*) denotes "that which is made like something, a resemblance," (a) in the concrete sense, Rev. 9:7, "shapes" (RV, marg., "likenesses"); (b) in the abstract sense, Rom. 1:23, RV, "(for) the likeness (of an image)"; the KJV translates it as a verb, "(into an image) made like to"; the association here of the two words **homoioma** and **eikon** serves to enhance the contrast between the idol and "the glory of the incorruptible God," and is expressive of contempt; in 5:14, "(the) likeness of Adam's transgression" (KJV, "similitude"); in 6:5, "(the) likeness (of His death); in 8:3, "(the) likeness (of sinful flesh); in Phil. 2:7, "the likeness of men." The expression 'likeness of men' does not of itself imply, still less does it exclude or diminish, the reality of the nature which Christ assumed.

2. **homoiosis** (*3669*), "a making like," is translated "likeness" in Jas. 3:9, RV (KJV, "similitude").

3. **homoiotes** (*3665*) is translated "likeness" in Heb. 7:15, RV (KJV, "similitude").

LIVE

Old Testament

A. Verb.

chayah (2421), "to live," in the intensive form, **chayah** means "to preserve alive," Gen. 6:19; or, "to bring to life," Isa. 57:15. "To live" is more than physical existence, Deut. 8:3; 30:16.

B. Noun.

chay (2416), "living thing; life." The use of this word occurs only in the oath formula "as X lives," literally, "by the life of X," Judg. 8:19. This formula summons the power of a superior to sanction the statement asserted, Gen. 42:15; 1 Sam. 1:26. The feminine form of the word, **chayyah**, means "living being," especially animals, Gen. 8:1; even preying, usually wild, animals, Job 37:8. In another nuance the word describes land animals as distinct from birds and fish, Gen. 1:28. Also creatures in a vision are "living animals," Ezek. 1:5. The plural, **chayyim**, is a general word for the state of living as opposed to that of death, Gen. 3:14; 6:17; 27:46; Deut. 30:15.

The "tree of life" is the tree which gives one eternal, everlasting "life," Gen. 2:9. In another nuance this word suggests a special quality of "life," life as a special gift from God (a gift of salvation), Deut. 30:19; or, persons living, Num. 16:48.

C. Adjective.

chay (2416), "alive; living." The word **chay** is used both as an adjective and as a noun. Used adjectivally it modifies men, animals, and God, but never plants, Gen. 2:7. *chay* describes flesh (animal meat or human flesh) under the skin, or "raw flesh," Lev. 13:10; 1 Sam. 2:15.

Applied to liquids, *chay* means "running"; it is used metaphorically describing something that moves, Gen. 26:19. In Jer. 2:13 the NASB translates "living" waters, or waters that give life, cf. Jer. 17:13; Zech. 14:8. The Song of Solomon uses the word in a figure of speech describing one's wife; she is "a well of living waters," 4:15. The emphasis is not on the fact that the water flows but on its freshness; it is not stagnant, and therefore is refreshing and pleasant when consumed.

New Testament

1. *zao* (*2198*), "to live, be alive," is used in the NT of "(a) God, Matt. 16:16; John 6:57; Rom. 14:11; (b) the Son in Incarnation, John 6:57; (c) the Son in Resurrection, John 14:19; Acts 1:3; Rom. 6:10; 2 Cor. 13:4; Heb. 7:8; (d) spiritual life, John 6:57; Rom. 1:17; 8:13b; Gal. 2:19, 20; Heb. 12:9; (e) the present state of departed saints, Luke 20:38; 1 Pet. 4:6; (f) the hope of resurrection, 1 Pet. 1:3; (g) the resurrection of believers, 1 Thess. 5:10; John 5:25; Rev. 20:4, and of unbelievers, v. 5, cf. v. 13; (h) the way of access to God through the Lord Jesus Christ, Heb. 10:20; (i) the manifestation of divine power in support of divine authority, 2 Cor. 13:4b; cf. 12:10, and 1 Cor. 5:5; (j) bread, figurative of the Lord Jesus, John 6:51; (k) a stone, figurative of the Lord Jesus, 1 Pet. 2:4; (l) water, figurative of the Holy Spirit, John 4:10; 7:38; (m) a sacrifice, figurative of the believer, Rom. 12:1; (n) stones, figurative of the believer, 1 Pet. 2:5; (o) the oracles, *logion*, Acts 7:38, and word, *logos*, Heb. 4:12; 1 Pet. 1:23, of God; (p) the physical life of men, 1 Thess. 4:15; Matt. 27:63; Acts 25:24; Rom. 14:9; Phil. 1:21 (in the infinitive mood used as a noun with the article, 'living'), 22; 1 Pet. 4:5; (q) the maintenance of physical life, Matt. 4:4; 1 Cor. 9:14; (r) the duration of physical life, Heb. 2:15; (s) the enjoyment of physical life, 1 Thess. 3:8; (t) the recovery of physical life from the power of disease, Mark 5:23; John 4:50; (u) the recovery of physical life from the power of death, Matt. 9:18; Acts 9:41; Rev. 20:5; (v) the course, conduct, and character of men, (1) good, Acts 26:5; 2 Tim. 3:12; Titus 2:12; (2) evil, Luke 15:13; Rom. 6:2; 8:13a; 2 Cor. 5:15b; Col. 3:7; (3) undefined, Rom. 7:9; 14:7; Gal. 2:14; (w) restoration after alienation, Luke 15:32.

2. *sunzao* (*4800*), "to live together with" (*sun*, "with," and *zao*, "to live"), may be included with *zao* in the above analysis as follows: (g) Rom. 6:8; 2 Tim. 2:11; (s), 2 Cor. 7:3.

3. *anazao* (*326*) *ana*, "again," and *zao*, denotes "to live again," "to revive," Luke 15:24.

4. *zoogoneo* (*2225*) denotes "to preserve alive" (from *zoos*, "alive," and *ginomai*, "to come to be, become, be made"); in Luke 17:33, "shall preserve (it)," i.e., his life, RV marg., "save (it) alive";

cf. the parallels *sozo*, "to save," in Matt. 16:25, and *phulaso*, "to keep," in John 12:25; in Acts 7:19, "live," negatively of the efforts of Pharaoh to destroy the babes in Israel; in 1 Tim. 6:13, according to the best mss. (some have *zoopoieo*, "to cause to live"), "quickeneth" (RV, marg., "preserveth...alive," the preferable rendering).

LIVE LONG

makrochronios (*3118*), an adjective denoting "of long duration, long-lived" (*makros*, "long," *chronos*, "time"), is used in Eph. 6:3, "(that thou mayest) live long," lit., "(that thou mayest be) long-lived."

LOCUST

akris (*200*) occurs in Matt. 3:4 and Mark 1:6, of the animals themselves, as forming part of the diet of John the Baptist; they are used as food; the Arabs stew them with butter, after removing the head, legs and wings; as part of a plague, see Rev. 9:3, 7.

LODGE, LODGING

A. Verb.

xenizo (*3579*), "to receive as a guest" (*xenos*, "a guest, stranger"), "to entertain, lodge," is used in the active voice in Acts 10:23; 28:7, RV, "entertained" (KJV, "lodged"); Heb. 13:2, "have entertained"; in the passive voice, Acts 10:6 (lit., "he is entertained"), 18, 32; 21:16. Its other meaning, "to think strange," is found in 1 Pet. 4:4, 12.

B. Noun.

xenia (*3578*), akin to A, denotes (a) "hospitality, entertainment," Philem. 22; (b) by metonymy, "a place of entertainment, a lodging-place," Acts 28:23 (some put Philem. 22 under this section).

LOINS

osphus (*3751*) is used (a) in the natural sense in Matt. 3:4; Mark 1:6; (b) as "the seat of generative power," Heb. 7:5, 10; metaphorically in Acts 2:30; (c) metaphorically, (1) of girding the "loins" in readiness for active service for the Lord, Luke 12:35; (2) the same, with truth, Eph. 6:14, i.e., bracing up oneself so as to maintain perfect sincerity and reality as the counteractive in Christian character against hypocrisy and falsehood; (3) of girding the "loins" of the mind, 1 Pet. 1:13, RV, "girding," suggestive of the alertness necessary for sobriety and for setting one's hope perfectly on "the grace to be brought...at the revelation of Jesus Christ" (the present participle, "girding," is introductory to the rest of the verse).

LONG (Verb), LONG (after, for), LONGING

A. Verb.

epipotheo (1971), "to long for greatly" (a strengthened form of *potheo*, "to long for," not found in the NT), is translated "I long," in Rom. 1:11; in 2 Cor. 5:2, RV, "longing" (KJV, "earnestly desiring"); in 1 Thess. 3:6 and 2 Tim. 1:4, RV, "longing" (KJV, "desiring greatly"); to long after, in 2 Cor. 9:14; Phil. 1:8; 2:26; to long for, in 1 Pet. 2:2, RV (KJV, "desire"); Jas. 4:5, RV, "long."

B. Adjective.

epipothetos (1973), akin to A, and an intensive form of *pothetos*, "desired. greatly desired," "longed for," is used in Phil. 4:1.

C. Nouns.

1. *epipothia* (1974), "a longing" (akin to A and B), is found in Rom. 15:23, RV "longing" (KJV, "great desire").

2. *epipothesis* (1972), "a longing" (perhaps stressing the process more than No. 1), is found in 2 Cor. 7:7, RV, "longing" (KJV, "earnest desire"); 7:11, RV, "longing" (KJV, "vehement desire").

LONGSUFFERING (Noun and Verb)

A. Noun.

makrothumia (3115), "forbearance, patience, longsuffering" (*makros*, "long," *thumos*, "temper"), is usually rendered "longsuffering," Rom. 2:4; 9:22; 2 Cor. 6:6; Gal. 5:22; Eph. 4:2; Col. 1:11; 3:12; 1 Tim. 1:16; 2 Tim. 3:10; 4:2; 1 Pet. 3:20; 2 Pet. 3:15; "patience" in Heb. 6:12 and Jas. 5:10.

B. Verb.

makrothumeo (3114), akin to A, "to be patient, longsuffering, to bear with," lit., "to be long-tempered," is rendered by the verb "to be longsuffering" in Luke 18:7, RV (KJV, "bear long"); in 1 Thess. 5:14, RV (KJV, "be patient"); so in Jas. 5:7, 8; in 2 Pet. 3:9, KJV and RV, "is longsuffering."

LOOK

Old Testament

nabat (5027), "to look, regard, behold," commonly used of physical "looking," Exod. 3:6; also in a figurative sense to mean a spiritual and inner apprehension, 1 Sam. 16:7. The sense of "consider" (with insight) is expressed in Isa. 51:1-2,12.

New Testament

A. Verbs.

1. *blepo* (991), primarily, "to have sight, to see," then, "observe, discern, perceive," frequently implying special contemplation, is

rendered by the verb "to look" in Luke 9:62, "looking (back)"; John 13:22 "(the disciples) looked (one on another)"; Acts 1:9, RV, "were looking" (KJV, "beheld"); 3:4, "look (on us)"; 27:12, RV, "looking," KJV, "that lieth (towards)," of the haven Phoenix; Eph. 5:15, RV, "look (therefore carefully how ye walk)," KJV, "see (that ye walk circumspectly)"; Rev. 11:9 and 18:9, RV, "look upon" (KJV, "shall see"). There are many cognate words related to this root, which can give different ways, positions, and intensities to the way one "looks."

2. *eidon* (*3708*), used as the aorist tense of *horao*, "to see," in various senses, is translated "to look," in the KJV of John 7:52, RV, "see"; Rev. 4:1 (RV, "I saw"); so in 6:8; 14:1, 14 (as in KJV of v. 6), and 15:5.

3. *epeidon* (*1896*) denotes "to look upon" (*epi*, "upon"), (a) favorably, Luke 1:25 (b) unfavorably, in Acts 4:29.

4. *skopeo* (*4648*), "to look at, consider" (Eng., "scope"), implying mental consideration, is rendered "while we look...at" in 2 Cor. 4:18; "looking to" (KJV, "on") in Phil. 2:4.

5. *episkopeo* (*1983*), lit., "to look upon" (*epi*, and No. 4), is rendered "looking carefully" in Heb. 12:15, RV (KJV, "looking diligently"), *epi* being probably intensive here; in 1 Pet. 5:2, "to exercise the oversight, to visit, care for."

6. *episkeptomai* (*1980*), a later form of No. 5, "to visit," has the meaning of "seeking out," and is rendered "look ye out" in Acts 6:3.

LOOK (for), LOOKING (after, for)

A. Verbs.

1. *prosdokao* (*4328*), "to await, expect" (*pros*, "to" or "towards," *dokeo*, "to think, be of opinion"), is translated "to look for," e.g., in Matt. 11:3; 2 Pet. 3:12, 13, 14; the RV renders it by the verb "to expect, to be in expectation," in some instances, as does the KJV in Luke 3:15; Acts 3:5.

2. *prosdechomai* (*4327*), "to receive favorably," also means "to expect," and is rendered "to look for," e.g., in Luke 2:38; 23:51; Acts 24:15, RV (KJV, "allow"); Titus 2:13; Jude 21.

3. *ekdechomai* (*1551*), primarily "to receive from another," hence, "to expect, to await," is translated "he looked for" in Heb. 11:10; in 1 Cor. 16:11, KJV, "I look for" (RV, "I expect").

B. Nouns.

1. *prosdokia* (*4329*); akin to A, No. 1, is translated "a looking after" in Luke 21:26, KJV ("expectation," as in Acts 12:11, KJV and RV).

2. *ekdoche* (*1561*), akin to A, No. 3, is translated "looking for" in Heb. 10:27, KJV.

LORD, LORDSHIP

Old Testament

'adon (113), or *'adonay* (113), "lord; master; Lord," *'adon* basically describes the one who occupies the position of a "master" or "lord" over a slave or servant, Gen. 24:9. It is used of kings, rulers, and officials, Gen. 45:8; cf. 42:30. *'adon* is often used as a term of polite address, much like "sir," or "madame," Gen. 18:12; 32:18.

When applied to God, *'adon* is used in several senses. It signifies His position as the one who has authority (like a master) over His people to reward the obedient and punish the disobedient, Hos. 12:14. In such contexts God is conceived as a Being who is sovereign ruler and almighty master; or title of respect, Ps. 8:1. In the form *'adonay* the word means "Lord" par excellence or "Lord over all," Josh. 3:11, where He is called the "Lord of all the earth".

Yahweh (3068), "Lord." The four letters of this word (*YHWH*) appear without their own vowels, and the exact pronunciation is uncertain (although Yahweh is most probable). The Hebrew text does insert the vowels for *'adonay*. The meaning of the divine personal name, *YHWH*, relates to the verb "to be." It translates "I am who I am," Exod. 3:14. The meaning of this is debated: one focus is that this God was an eternal, self-existent One with unique being; another focus is that He "will be" present to the people of his covenant promise to Abraham. *YHWH* often has the personal focus of relationship, Gen. 4:26; 12:8; Exod. 3:14-17; 6:2-8.

New Testament

L

A. Nouns.

1. *kurios* (2962), properly an adjective, signifying "having power" (*kuros*) or "authority," is used as a noun, variously translated in the NT, "'Lord,' 'master,' 'Master,' 'owner,' 'Sir,' a title of wide significance, occurring in each book of the NT except Titus and the Epistles of John. It is used (a) of an owner, as in Luke 19:33, cf. Matt. 20:8; Acts 16:16; Gal. 4:1; or of one who has the disposal of anything, as the Sabbath, Matt. 12:8; (b) of a master, i.e., one to whom service is due on any ground, Matt. 6:24; 24:50; Eph. 6:5; (c) of an Emperor or King, Acts 25:26; Rev. 17:14; (d) of idols, ironically, 1 Cor. 8:5, cf. Isa. 26:13; (e) as a title of respect addressed to a father, Matt. 21:30, a husband, 1 Pet. 3:6, a master, Matt. 13:27; Luke 13:8, a ruler, Matt. 27:63, an angel, Acts 10:4; Rev. 7:14; (f) as a title of courtesy addressed to a stranger, John 12:21; 20:15; Acts 16:30; from the outset of His ministry this was a common form of address to the Lord Jesus, alike, by the people, Matt. 8:2; John 4:11, and by His disciples, Matt. 8:25; Luke 5:8; John 6:68; (g) *kurios* is the Sept. and NT representative of Heb. Jehovah ('LORD' in Eng. versions), see Matt. 4:7; Jas. 5:11, e.g., of *'adon*, Lord, Matt. 22:44, and of *'adonay*, Lord, 1:22; it also occurs for *'elohim*, God, 1 Pet. 1:25.

His purpose did not become clear to the disciples until after His resurrection, and the revelation of His Deity consequent thereon. Thomas, when he realized the significance of the presence of a mortal wound in the body of a living man, immediately joined with it the absolute title of Deity, saying, "My Lord and my God," John 20:28. Thereafter, except in Acts 10:4 and Rev. 7:14, there is no record that *kurios* was ever again used by believers in addressing any except God and the Lord Jesus; cf. Acts 2:47 with 4:29, 30.

How soon and how completely the lower meaning had been superseded is seen in Peter's declaration in his first sermon after the resurrection, "God hath made Him—Lord," Acts 2:36, and that in the house of Cornelius, "He is Lord of all," 10:36, cf. Deut. 10:14; Matt. 11:25; Acts 17:24. In his writings the implications of his early teaching are confirmed and developed. Thus Ps. 34:8, "O taste and see that Jehovah is good," is applied to the Lord Jesus, 1 Pet. 2:3, and "Jehovah of Hosts, Him shall ye sanctify," Isa. 8:13, becomes "sanctify in your hearts Christ as Lord," 3:15.

So also James who uses *kurios* alike of God, 1:7 (cf. v. 5); 3:9; 4:15; 5:4, 10, 11, and of the Lord Jesus, 1:1 (where the possibility that *kai* is intended epexegetically, i.e. = even, cf. 1 Thess. 3:11, should not be overlooked); 2:1 (lit., "our Lord Jesus Christ of glory," cf. Ps. 24:7; 29:3; Acts 7:2; 1 Cor. 2:8; 5:7, 8, while the language of 4:10; 5:15, is equally applicable to either.

Jude, v. 4, speaks of "our only—Lord, Jesus Christ," and immediately, v. 5, uses "Lord" of God, as he does later, vv. 9, 14.

Paul ordinarily uses *kurios* of the Lord Jesus, 1 Cor. 1:3, e.g., but also on occasion, of God, in quotations from the OT, 1 Cor. 3:20, e.g., and in his own words, 1 Cor. 3:5, cf. v. 10. It is equally appropriate to either in 1 Cor. 7:25; 2 Cor. 3:16; 8:21; 1 Thess. 4:6, and if 1 Cor. 11:32 is to be interpreted by 10:21, 22, the Lord Jesus is intended, but if by Heb. 12:5-9, then *kurios* here also = God. 1 Tim. 6:15, 16 is probably to be understood of the Lord Jesus, cf. Rev. 17:14.

Though John does not use "Lord" in his Epistles, and though, like the other Evangelists, he ordinarily uses the personal Name in his narrative, yet he occasionally speaks of Him as "the Lord," John 4:1; 6:23; 11:2; 20:20; 21:12.

The full significance of this association of Jesus with God under the one appellation, "Lord," is seen when it is remembered that these men belonged to the only monotheistic race in the world. To associate with the Creator one known to be a creature, however exalted, though possible to Pagan philosophers, was quite impossible to a Jew.

It is not recorded that in the days of His flesh any of His disciples either addressed the Lord, or spoke of Him, by His personal Name. Where Paul has occasion to refer to the facts of the gospel history he speaks of what the Lord Jesus said, Acts 20:35, and did, 1 Cor. 11:23, and suffered, 1 Thess. 2:15; 5:9, 10. It is our Lord Jesus who is coming, 1 Thess. 2:19, etc. In prayer also the title is given, 3:11; Eph. 1:3; the sinner is invited to believe on the Lord Jesus, Acts 16:31; 20:21, and the saint to look to the Lord Jesus for deliverance, Rom. 7:24, 25, and in the few exceptional cases in which the personal Name stands alone a reason is always discernible in the immediate context.

2. *despotes* (1203), "a master, lord, one who possesses supreme authority," is used in personal address to God in Luke 2:29; Acts 4:24; Rev. 6:10; with reference to Christ, 2 Pet. 2:1; Jude 4; elsewhere it is translated "master," "masters," 1 Tim. 6:1, 2; 2 Tim. 2:21 (of Christ); Titus 2:9; 1 Pet. 2:18.

B. Verbs.

1. *kurieuo* (2961) denotes "to be lord of, to exercise lordship over," Luke 22:25; Rom. 6:9, 14; 7:1; 14:9; 2 Cor. 1:24; 1 Tim. 6:15.

2. *katakurieuo* (2634), a strengthened form of No. 1, is rendered "lording it" in 1 Pet. 5:3.

C. Adjective.

kuriakos (2960), from *kurios* (A, No. 1), signifies "pertaining to a lord or master"; "lordly" is not a legitimate rendering for its use in the NT, where it is used only of Christ; in 1 Cor. 11:20, of the Lord's Supper, or the Supper of the Lord; in Rev. 1:10, of the Day of the Lord.

LOSE, (suffer) LOSS, LOST

1. *apollumi* (622) signifies (I) In the active voice, (a) "to destroy, destroy utterly, kill," e.g., Matt. 10:28; Mark 1:24; 9:22; (b) "to lose utterly," e.g., Matt. 10:42, of "losing" a reward; Luke 15:4 (1st part), of "losing" a sheep; Luke 9:25, of "losing" oneself (of the "loss" of well-being hereafter); metaphorically, John 6:39, of failing to save; 18:9, of Christ's not "losing" His own; (II), in the middle voice (a) "to perish," of things, e.g., John 6:12 "(that nothing) be lost"; of persons, e.g., Matt. 8:25, "we perish"; of the "loss" of eternal life, usually (always in the RV) translated to perish, John 3:16; 17:12, KJV, "is lost," RV, "perished"; 2 Cor. 4:3, "are perishing," KJV, "are lost"; (b) "to be lost," e.g., Luke 15:4 (2nd part), "which is lost"; metaphorically, from the relation between shepherd and flock, of spiritual destitution and alienation from God, Matt. 10:6, "(the) lost (sheep)" of the house of Israel; Luke 19:10 (the perfect tense translated "lost" is here intransitive).

2. *zemioo* (2210), "to damage" (akin to *zemia*, "damage," e.g., Acts 27:10, 21), is used in the NT, in the passive voice, signifying "to suffer loss, forfeit, lose," Matt. 16:26; Mark 8:36, of losing one's soul or life; Luke 9:25, RV, "forfeit (his own self)," KJV, "be cast away"

(for the preceding verb see No. 1); 1 Cor. 3:15, "he shall suffer loss," i.e., at the Judgment-Seat of Christ (see v. 13 with 2 Cor. 5:10); 2 Cor. 7:9, "(that) ye might suffer loss," RV (KJV, "might receive damage"); though the apostle did regret the necessity of making them sorry by his letter, he rejoiced that they were made sorry after a godly sort, and that they thus suffered no spiritual loss, which they would have done had their sorrow been otherwise than after a godly manner; in Phil. 3:8, "I suffered the loss (of all things)," RV, i.e., of all things which he formerly counted gain (especially those in verses 5 and 6, to which the article before "all things" points).

LOSS

zemia (2209), akin to No. 2, above, is used in Acts 27:10, RV, "loss" (KJV, "damage"); v. 21, KJV and RV, "loss," of ship and cargo; in Phil. 3:7, 8 of the apostle's estimate of the things which he formerly valued, and of all things on account of "the excellency of the knowledge of Christ Jesus."

LOT, LOTS

Old Testament

goral (1486), "lot," i.e., a pebble, stick, or stone, with special markings, which was thrown to discover God's decisions, Lev. 16:8, usually with a "yes," or "no," Josh. 15:1. In an extended use the word *goral* represents the idea "fate" or "destiny," Isa. 17:14. Since God is viewed as controlling all things absolutely, the result of the casting of the "lot" is divinely controlled, Prov. 16:33. Thus, providence (divine control of history) is frequently figured as one's "lot."

New Testament

A. Noun.

kleros (2819) denotes (a) an object used in casting or drawing lots, which consisted of bits, or small tablets, of wood or stone (the probable derivation is from *klao*, "to break"); these were sometimes inscribed with the names of persons, and were put into a receptacle or a garment ("a lap," Prov. 16:33), from which they were cast, after being shaken together; he whose "lot" first fell out was the one chosen. The method was employed in a variety of circumstances, e.g., of dividing or assigning property, Matt. 27:35; Mark 15:24; Luke 23:34; John 19:24 (cf., e.g., Num. 26:55); of appointing to office, Acts 1:26 (cf., e.g., 1 Sam. 10:20); for other occurrences in the OT, see, e.g., Josh. 7:14 (the earliest instance in Scripture), Lev. 16:7-10; Esth. 3:7; 9:24; (b) "what is obtained by lot, an allotted portion," e.g., of the ministry allotted to the apostles, Acts 1:17; of those the spiritual care of, and charge over, whom is assigned to elders, 1 Pet. 5:3.

B. Verb.

lanchano (2975) denotes (a) "to draw lots," John 19:24; (b) "to obtain by lot, to obtain," Luke 1:9, "his lot was," lit., "he received by lot," i.e., by divine appointment; Acts 1:17, of the portion "allotted" by the Lord to His apostles in their ministry (cf. A, above); 2 Pet. 1:1, "that have obtained (a like precious faith)," i.e., by its being "allotted" to them, not by acquiring it for themselves, but by divine grace (an act independent of human control, as in the casting of "lots").

LOVE (Noun and Verb)
Old Testament

A. Verb.

'ahab (157), or *'aheb* (157), "to love; like," i.e., a strong emotional attachment to and desire either to possess or to be in the presence of the object; familial, romantic, or friendship, Gen. 22:2; 24:67; Gen. 34:3; Ruth 4:15. In a very few instances *'ahab* (or *'aheb*) may signify sexual lust, cf. 2 Sam. 13:1. Making love usually is represented by *yada'*, "to know," or by *shakab*, "to lie with." Though *'ahab* can also mean this, 1 Kings 11:1; cf. Jer. 2:25; Zech. 13:6.

'ahab (or *'aheb*) sometimes depicts a special strong attachment a servant may have toward a master under whose dominance he wishes to remain, Exod. 21:5. Perhaps there is an overtone here of family love; he "loves" his master as a son "loves" his father, cf. Deut. 15:16; 1 Sam. 16:21; 18:16.

B. Noun.

'ahabah (160), "love," (see Verb. above) has the same range of meanings as the verb. It can refer to family, friend, romantic, or sexual "love," as a state of being, or actions of strong affection and commitment, Gen. 29:20; Deut. 7:8; 1 Sam. 18:3; In Hos. 3:1.

C. Participle.

'ahab (157), "friend," Prov. 14:20.

New Testament

A. Verbs.

1. *agapao* (25) and the corresponding noun *agape* are used in the NT (a) to describe the attitude of God toward His Son, John 17:26; the human race, generally, John 3:16; Rom. 5:8, and to such as believe on the Lord Jesus Christ particularly John 14:21; (b) to convey His will to His children concerning their attitude one toward another, John 13:34, and toward all men, 1 Thess. 3:12; 1 Cor. 16:14; 2 Pet. 1:7; (c) to express the essential nature of God, 1 John 4:8.

Love can be known only from the actions it prompts. God's love is seen in the gift of His Son, 1 John 4:9, 10. But obviously this is not the love of complacency, or affection, that is, it was not drawn out by any excellency in its objects, Rom. 5:8. It was an exercise of the divine will in deliberate choice, made without assignable cause save that which lies in the nature of God Himself, cf. Deut. 7:7, 8.

Love had its perfect expression among men in the Lord Jesus Christ, 2 Cor. 5:14; Eph. 2:4; 3:19; 5:2; Christian love is the fruit of His Spirit in the Christian, Gal. 5:22. Christian love has God for its primary object, and expresses itself first of all in implicit obedience to His commandments, John 14:15, 21, 23; 15:10; 1 John 2:5; 5:3; 2 John 6. Self-will, that is, self-pleasing, is the negation of love to God.

Christian love, whether exercised toward the brethren, or toward men generally, is not an impulse from the feelings, it does not always run with the natural inclinations, nor does it spend itself only upon those for whom some affinity is discovered. Love seeks the welfare of all, Rom. 15:2, and works no ill to any, 13:8-10; love seeks opportunity to do good to "all men, and especially toward them that are of the household of the faith," Gal. 6:10. See further 1 Cor. 13 and Col. 3:12-14.

2. *phileo* (5368) is to be distinguished from *agapao* in this, that *phileo* more nearly represents "tender affection." The two words are used for the "love" of the Father for the Son, John 3:35 (No. 1), and 5:20 (No. 2); for the believer, 14:21 (No. 1) and 16:27 (No. 2); both, of Christ's "love" for a certain disciple, 13:23 (No. 1), and 20:2 (No. 2). Yet the distinction between the two verbs remains, and they are never used indiscriminately in the same passage; if each is used with reference to the same objects, as just mentioned, each word retains its distinctive and essential character.

phileo is never used in a command to men to "love" God; it is, however, used as a warning in 1 Cor. 16:22; *agapao* is used instead, e.g., Matt. 22:37; Luke 10:27; Rom. 8:28; 1 Cor. 8:3; 1 Pet. 1:8; 1 John 4:21. The distinction between the two verbs finds a conspicuous instance in the narrative of John 21:15-17.

B. Nouns.

1. *agape* (26), the significance of which has been pointed out in connection with A, No. 1, is always rendered "love" in the RV where the KJV has "charity," a rendering nowhere used in the RV; in Rom. 14:15, where the KJV has "charitably," the RV, adhering to the translation of the noun, has "in love."

2. *philanthropia* (5363) denotes, lit., "love for man" (*phileo* and *anthropos*, "man"); hence, "kindness," Acts 28:2, in Titus 3:4, "(His) love toward man."

LOVE FEASTS

agape (26) is used in the plural in Jude 12, 2 Pet. 2:13; this refers to the common meals of the early churches (cf. 1 Cor. 11:21).

LOVER

This is combined with other words, forming compound adjectives as follows:

1. *philotheos* (5377), "a lover of God," 2 Tim. 3:4.
2. *philoxenos* (5382), "loving strangers" (*xenia*, "hospitality"), translated "a lover of hospitality" in Titus 1:8, KJV (RV, "given to h."); elsewhere, in 1 Tim. 3:2; 1 Pet. 4:9.
3. *philagathos* (5358), "loving that which is good" (*agathos*), Titus 1:8, "a lover of good," RV.
4. *philarguros* (5366), "loving money" (*arguros*, "silver"), translated "lovers of money" in Luke 16:14; 2 Tim. 3:2, RV (KJV, "covetous").
5. *philautos* (5367), "loving oneself," 2 Tim. 3:2, RV.
6. *philedonos* (5369), "loving pleasure" (*hedone*, "pleasure"), 2 Tim. 3:4, "lovers of pleasure."

LOVING-KINDNESS

A. Noun.

chesed (2617), "loving-kindness; steadfast love; grace; mercy; faithfulness; goodness; devotion." The word refers primarily to mutual and reciprocal rights (always grounded in truth) and obligations between the parties of a relationship (especially Yahweh and Israel), 1 Kings 8:23. But *chesed* is not only a matter of obligation; it is also of generosity. It is not only a matter of loyalty, but also of mercy. The weaker party seeks the protection and blessing of the patron and protector, but he may not lay absolute claim to it. The stronger party remains committed to his promise, but retains his freedom, especially with regard to the manner in which he will implement those promises. *chesed* implies personal involvement and commitment in a relationship beyond the rule of law.

Marital love is often related to *chesed*. Marriage certainly is a legal matter, and there are legal sanctions for infractions. Yet the relationship, if sound, far transcends mere legalities. The prophet Hosea applies the analogy to Yahweh's *chesed* to Israel within the covenant (e.g., 2:21). Hence, "devotion" is sometimes the single English word best capable of capturing the nuance of the original. The RSV attempts to bring this out by its translation, "steadfast love." Hebrew writers often underscored the element of steadfastness (or strength) by pairing *chesed* with *'emet* ("truth," reliability") and *'emunah* ("faithfulness").

Man exercises *chesed* toward various units within the community—toward family and relatives, but also to friends, guests, masters, and servants. *chesed* toward the lowly and needy is often specified. The Bible prominently uses the term *chesed* to summarize and characterize a life of sanctification within, and in response to, the covenant. Thus, Hos. 6:6 states that God desires "mercy [RSV, "steadfast love"] and not sacrifice" (i.e., faithful living in addition to worship). Similarly, Mic. 6:8 features *chesed* in the prophets' summary of biblical ethics.

Behind all these uses with man as subject, however, stand the repeated references to God's *chesed*. It is one of His most central characteristics. God's loving-kindness is offered to His people, who need redemption from sin, enemies, and troubles. A recurrent refrain describing God's nature is "abounding/plenteous in *chesed*," Exod. 34:6; Neh. 9:17; Ps. 103:8; Jonah 4:2. The entire history of Yahweh's covenantal relationship with Israel can be summarized in terms of *chesed*. It is the one permanent element in the flux of covenantal history. Even the Creation is the result of God's *chesed*, Ps. 136:5-9. His love lasts for a "thousand generations," Deut. 7:9; cf. Deut. 5:10 and Exod. 20:6, indeed "forever" (especially in the refrains of certain psalms, such as Ps. 136).

The association of *chesed* with "covenant" keeps it from being misunderstood as mere providence or love for all creatures; it applies primarily to God's particular love for His chosen and covenanted people. "Covenant" also stresses the reciprocity of the relationship; but since God's *chesed* is ultimately beyond the covenant, it will not ultimately be abandoned, even when the human partner is unfaithful and must be disciplined, Isa. 54:8, 10. Since its final triumph and implementation is eschatological, *chesed* can imply the goal and end of all salvation-history, Ps. 85:7, 10; 130:7; Mic. 7:20.

B. Adjective.

chasid (2623), "pious; devout; faithful; godly." The adjective *chasid*, derived from *chesed*, is often used to describe the faithful Israelite. God's *chesed* provides the pattern, model, and strength by which the life of the *chasid* is to be directed. One reference to the "godly" man appears in Ps. 12:1.

LOW (to bring, to make), LOW (estate, degree)

A. Verb.

tapeinoo (5013), "to bring low, to humble," is translated "shall be brought low" in Luke 3:5.

B. Adjective.

tapeinos (5011) denotes "of low degree or estate," Rom. 12:16 "things that are lowly," RV (KJV, "men of low estate").

C. Noun.

tapeinosis (5014), "abasement, humiliation, low estate," is translated "low estate" in Luke 1:48; in Jas. 1:10, "that he is made low," lit., "in his abasement."

LOWER (Adjective, and Verb, to make), LOWEST

A. Adjectives.

1. *katoteros* (2737), the comparative degree of *kato*, "beneath," is used in Eph. 4:9, of Christ's descent into "the lower parts of the earth"; two of the various interpretations of this phrase are (1) that the earth is in view in contrast to heaven, (2) that the region is that of hades, the Sheol of the OT. Inasmuch as the passage is describing the effects not merely of the Incarnation but of the death and resurrection of Christ, the second interpretation is to be accepted.

2. *eschatos* (2078), "last, utmost, lowest," is rendered "lowest" in Luke 14:9, 10, of the "lowest" place at a meal.

B. Verb.

elattoo (1642) denotes "to make less" (*elatton*, "less"), and is used in the active voice in Heb. 2:7, and in the passive in v. 9, "was made... lower," and John 3:30, lit., "be made less."

LOWLINESS, LOWLY

tapeinophrosune (5012), "lowliness of mind, humbleness," is translated "lowliness" or "lowliness of mind" in Acts 20:19, RV; Eph. 4:2; Phil. 2:3.

LUCRE (filthy)

A. Noun.

kerdos (2771), "gain," Phil. 1:21 and 3:7; "lucre" in Titus 1:11 (preceded by *aischros*, "filthy").

B. Adjectives.

1. *aischrokerdes* (146) denotes "greedy of base gains" (*aischros*, and A, as above), 1 Tim. 3:8, "greedy of filthy lucre"; so the RV in Titus 1:7, KJV, "given to filthy lucre." In some mss. 1 Tim. 3:3.

2. *aischrokerdos* (147) denotes "from eagerness for base gain," 1 Pet. 5:2, "for filthy lucre."

LUKEWARM

chliaros (5513), "tepid, warm" (akin to *chlio*, "to become warm," not found in the NT or Sept.), is used metaphorically in Rev. 3:16, of the state of the Laodicean church, which afforded no refreshment to the Lord.

LUST (Noun and Verb)

A. Noun.

epithumia (1939) denotes "strong desire" of any kind, the various kinds being frequently specified by some adjective. The word is used of a good desire in Luke 22:15; Phil. 1:23, and 1 Thess. 2:17 only. Everywhere else it has a bad sense. In Rom. 6:12 the injunction against letting sin reign in our mortal body to obey the "lust" thereof, refers to those evil desires which are ready to express themselves in bodily activity. They are equally the "lusts" of the flesh, Rom. 13:14; Gal. 5:16, 24; Eph. 2:3; 2 Pet. 2:18; 1 John 2:16, a phrase which describes the emotions of the soul, the natural tendency towards things evil. Such "lusts" are not necessarily base and immoral, they may be refined in character, but are evil if inconsistent with the will of God.

Other descriptions besides those already mentioned are:—"of the mind," Eph. 2:3; "evil (desire)," Col. 3:5; "the passion of," 1 Thess. 4:5, RV; "foolish and hurtful," 1 Tim. 6:9; "youthful," 2 Tim. 2:22; "divers," 2 Tim. 3:6 and Titus 3:3; "their own," 2 Tim. 4:3; 2 Pet. 3:3; Jude 16; "worldly," Titus 2:12; "his own," Jas. 1:14; "your former," 1 Pet. 1:14, RV; "fleshly," 2:11; "of men," 4:2; "of defilement," 2 Pet. 2:10; "of the eyes," 1 John 2:16; of the world ("thereof"), v. 17; "their own ungodly," Jude 18. In Rev. 18:14 "(the fruits) which thy soul lusted after" is, lit., "of thy soul's lust."

B. Verb.

epithumeo (1937), akin to A, has the same twofold meaning as the noun, namely (a) "to desire," used of the Holy Spirit against the flesh, Gal. 5:17; of the Lord Jesus, Luke 22:15, "I have desired"; of the holy angels, 1 Pet. 1:12; of good men, for good things, Matt. 13:17; 1 Tim. 3:1; Heb. 6:11; of men, for things without moral quality, Luke 15:16; 16:21; 17:22; Rev. 9:6; (b) of "evil desires," in respect of which it is translated "to lust" in Matt. 5:28; 1 Cor. 10:6; Gal. 5:17; Jas. 4:2; to covet, Acts 20:23; Rom. 7:7; 13:9.

M

MAD, MADNESS

A. Verbs.

1. *mainomai* (*3105*), "to rage, be mad," is translated by the verb "to be mad" in John 10:20; Acts 12:15; 26:24, 25; 1 Cor. 14:23.

2. *emmainomai* (*1693*), an intensive form of No. 1, prefixed by *en*, "in," implying "fierce rage, to be furious against"; it is rendered "being exceedingly mad" in Acts 26:11 (cf. 9:1).

B. Nouns.

1. *mania* (*3130*), akin to A, and transliterated into English, denotes "frenzy, madness," Acts 26:24 "(thy much learning doth turn thee to) madness," RV; KJV, "(doth make thee) mad."

2. *anoia* (*454*), lit., "without understanding" (*a*, negative, *nous*, "mind, understanding"), denotes "folly," 2 Tim. 3:9, and this finding its expression in violent rage, Luke 6:11.

3. *paraphronia* (*3913*), "madness" (from *para*, "contrary to," and *phren*, "the mind"), is used in 2 Pet. 2:16.

MAGISTRATE

1. *strategos* (*4755*), besides its application to "the captain of the Temple," denotes "a magistrate or governor," Acts 16:20, 22, 35, 36, 38. These were, in Latin terminology, the *duumviri* or *praetores*, so called in towns which were Roman colonies. They were attended by lictors or "sergeants," who executed their orders. In the circumstances of Acts 16 they exceeded their powers, in giving orders for Roman citizens to be scourged; hence they became suppliants.

MAGNIFICENCE

megaleiotes (*3168*) denotes "splendor, magnificence" (from *megaleios*, "magnificent," mighty," Acts 2:11, *megas*, "great"), translated "magnificence" in Acts 19:27, of the splendor of the goddess Diana. In Luke 9:43, RV (KJV, "mighty power"); in 2 Pet. 1:16, "majesty."

MAGNIFY

Old Testament

A. Verb.

gadal (1431), "to become strong, grow up, be great or wealthy, evidence oneself as great (magnified), be powerful, significant, or valuable." This verb can signify the increasing of size and age as with the maturing process of human life, Gen. 21:8; or animals, 2 Sam. 12:3; and plants, Isa. 44:14; anything that can grow, Dan. 8:9. *gadal* can represent the status of "being great or wealthy," Gen. 24:35. In the intensive stem the verb sets forth a fact, "I will make great," Gen. 12:2.

This word is sometimes used with the meaning "to be great, to evidence oneself as great," Num. 14:17. This meaning of "great," is to have high status and honor in the esteem of others, 2 Sam. 7:22. Another emphasis of *gadal* is "to be great, powerful, important, or valuable." This nuance arises when the word is applied to kings, as when Pharaoh said to Joseph, Gen. 41:40. The nuance "to be valuable" appears in 1 Sam. 26:24. In the reflexive stem *gadal* may signify "to magnify oneself." When God is the subject this is proper, Ezek. 38:23. When spoken of a proud person though it is improper pride and boasting, Isa. 10:15; Job 19:5.

B. Nouns.

gedullah (1420), "greatness; great things." It means "greatness," as a state or condition, Ps. 71:21; or an object or event, 2 Sam. 7:21.

godel (1433), "greatness." *godel* means "greatness" in terms of spatial size, Ezek. 31:7; of divine power, Ps. 79:11; of divine dignity, Deut. 32:3; of divine majesty, Deut. 3:24; of divine mercy, Num. 14:19; or insolence, Isa. 9:9.

migdal (4026), "strong place," Gen. 11:4-5; "wooden podium," Neh. 8:4.

C. Adjective.

gadol (1419), "great." *gadol* is used of extended dimension, Gen. 1:21, of number, Gen. 12:2, of power, Deut. 4:37, of punishment, Gen. 4:13, and of value or importance, Gen. 39:9. "Great," is used in such a variety of ways, that it is best to summarize that it is used with quantities, states of being, numbers of collections or masses, or spatial sizes, even to denote intensity.

New Testament

megaluno (3170), "to make great" (*megas*), is translated "to magnify" in Luke 1:46; in v. 58, RV, "had magnified (His mercy)," KJV, "had shewed great (mercy)"; Acts 5:13; 10:46; 19:17; 2 Cor. 10:15, RV (KJV, "we shall be enlarged"), i.e., by their faith in its practical effect he will be so assisted as to enlarge the scope of his gospel ministry and carry its message to regions beyond them.

MAID, MAIDEN, MAIDSERVANT

Old Testament

betulah (1330), "maiden, virgin." This word can mean "virgin," as a female who has not yet had sexual intercourse, Deut. 22:17, 19, 21. In several passages this word merely means a grown-up girl or a "maiden," who may or may not have known a man, Jer. 31:4, 21. The other nations are also called *betuloth*: Isa. 23:12—Sidon; Isa. 47:1—Babylon; Jer. 46:11—Egypt. These nations are hardly being commended for their purity!

New Testament

paidiske (3814), translated "maid," "maids," in the KJV and RV in Mark 14:66, 69; Luke 22:56, in the RV (KJV, "damsel"), in Matt. 26:69; John 18:17; Acts 12:13; 16:16; in Luke 12:45, "maidservants" (KJV "maidens"); in Gal. 4:22, 23, 30, 31, RV, "handmaid" (KJV, "bondmaid" or "bondwoman").

MAJESTY

megalosune (3172), from *megas*, "great," denotes "greatness, majesty"; it is used of God the Father, signifying His greatness and dignity, in Heb. 1:3, "the Majesty (on high)," and 8:1, "the Majesty (in the Heavens)"; and in an ascription of praise acknowledging the attributes of God in Jude 25.

TO MAKE (CUT) A COVENANT

M

A. Verb.

karat (3772), "to cut off, cut down, fell, cut or make (a covenant or agreement)." Basically *karat* means "to sever" something from something else by cutting it with a blade. The nuance depends upon the thing being cut off. In the case of a branch, one "cuts it down," Num. 13:23, and one "[swings] the axe to cut down the tree," Deut. 19:5. The word is also used of "chopping down" wooden idols, Exod. 34:13. *karat* can signify "chopping off" a man's head and feet, 1 Sam. 5:4.

"To cut off" can mean "to exterminate or destroy," Gen. 9:11. *karat* can be used of spiritual and social extermination. A person "cut off" in this manner is not necessarily killed but may be driven out of the family and removed from the blessings of the covenant, Gen. 17:14.

One of the best known uses of this verb is "to make" a covenant. The process by which God made a covenant with Abraham is called "cutting," Gen. 15:18. Animals were literally severed into two parts. Later, "cutting" a covenant did not necessarily include this act of literal "cutting," but seems to be an allusion to the Abrahamic covenantal process, cf. Jer. 34:18. In such a covenant the one passing through the pieces pledged his faithfulness to the covenant, Neh. 9:38.

B. Noun.

keritut (3748), refers to a "bill of divorcement." This word implies the cutting off of a marriage by means of a "bill of divorcement," Deut. 24:1.

MAKER

demiourgos (1217), lit., "one who works for the people" (from *demos*, "people," *ergon*, "work"; an ancient inscription speaks of the magistrates of Tarsus as *demiourgoi*: the word was formerly used thus regarding several towns in Greece; it is also found used of an artist), came to denote, in general usage, a builder or "maker," and is used of God as the "Maker" of the heavenly city, Heb. 11:10.

MALEFACTOR

1. *kakourgos* (2557), an adjective, lit., "evil-working" (*kakos*, "evil," *ergon*, "work"), is used as a noun, translated "malefactor(s)" in Luke 23:32, 33, 39, and in the RV in 2 Tim. 2:9 (KJV, "evil doer").

2. *kakopoios* (2555), an adjective, lit., "doing evil," is used in 1 Pet. 2:12, 14; 3:16 (in some mss.); 4:15.

MALICE, MALICIOUSNESS, MALICIOUS

kakia (2549), "badness in quality" (the opposite of *arete*, "excellence"), "the vicious character generally" (Lightfoot), is translated "malice" in 1 Cor. 5:8; 14:20; Eph. 4:31; Col. 3:8; Titus 3:3; 1 Pet. 2:1.

MAMMON

mamonas (3126), a common Aramaic word for "riches," akin to a Hebrew word signifying "to be firm, steadfast" (whence "Amen"), hence, "that which is to be trusted"; Gesenius regards it as derived from a Heb. word signifying "treasure," Gen. 43:23; it is personified in Matt. 6:24; Luke 16:9, 11, 13.

MAN (See also MEN)

Old Testament

Nouns.

'adam (120) is translated "person, human," which means a single human being of either sex, Psa. 49:20.

'adam is translated "humankind, mankind," meaning a class of beings created by God without regard to sex, with a focus as a

class of creature, distinct from animals, plants, or even spiritual beings, Gen. 1:26. Similarly, *'adam* also refers to the first human who was directly created by God, in his image, from the (red?) dust of the ground, Gen. 2:20. Note that one has to carefully distinguish each of the above meanings to *'adam*, according to context, especially in the first chapters of Genesis.

ben 'adam are two Hebrew words, translated "son of man" and means low class person, i.e., a person of low social status, implying poverty, Prov. 49:2

ben 'adam is also translated "son of man" and has the far more common meaning in the Bible of a person who is in the class of humanity, as contrasted to other classes of supernatural beings, Ezek 2:1.

The Fall greatly affected the nature of "man," but he did not cease to be in God's image, Gen. 9:6. Fallen "man" occupies a new and lower position before God, Gen. 6:5; cf. 8:21. No longer does "man" have perfect communion with the Creator; he is now under the curse of sin and death.

geber (1397), "man." The root meaning "to be strong" is no longer obvious in the usage of *geber*, since it is often indistinguishable from *'ish*, Jer. 22:30. Other synonyms to *geber* are *zakar*, "male," Jer. 30:6; *'enosh*, "man," Job 4:17; and *'adam*, "man," Job 14:10. A *geber* denotes a "male," as an antonym of a "woman," Deut. 22:5.

'ish (376) can be translated "man," with the meaning of a male or female human as a class or kind in contrast to other classes of created beings, Exod. 19:13. More specifically, *'ish* can be translated "man," with the meaning of a mature, adult male of a created species (usually a human), Gen. 2:24; 7:2. Even more particularly, *'ish* can be translated "husband," with the meaning of a male spouse in a marriage, Gen. 16:3.

'ish can be translated "each, every," with the meaning of one or every one of a totality, with a focus on the individual parts of a whole group, collections of things, of a mass of things, Gen. 40:5. *'ish* also can be translated "anyone, whoever, someone, a certain one," with a reference to whom or what is spoken about which is not explicit, Lev. 15:5. With the Hebrew word *lo* (not) translates as "none, not anyone," with the meaning of a negative reference to an entity, event, or state, a kind of opposite to the first pronouns, Gen. 23:6.

'ish can also be a kind of helper word to change a Hebrew noun of an idea or concept into a noun about an individual person related to that abstract idea. For example, *'ish mashchit*, "destroyer," is translated in form as "man of destruction," Prov. 28:24. Or another example is *'ish matsut*, "enemy," but is in form translated "man of strife," Isa. 41:12. Space would not allow all the samples, for they are many.

M

Another meaning of *'ish* in combination with other words is **zera *'ish***, translated " offspring," formally translated "seed of man," with the meaning of a child of a parent, 1 Sam. 1:11.

Yet another meaning of *'ish* in combination with other words is **'ish shem**, translated "well-known person," with the meaning of a person known in the community, with a generally favorable view, and so has high status and community standing, Num. 16:2.

So also another meaning of *'ish* in combination with other words is **'ish el 'ach**, translated, "to each other, to one another, among yourselves," with a formal translation, "each (or *man*) to his brother," and so this phrase has the meaning of a reciprocal reference of two or more associating with one another in some way, Gen. 37:19; 42:21,28; Exod. 16:15; 25:20; 37:9; Num. 14:4; 2 Kin. 7:6; Jer. 13:14; 23:35; 25:26; Ezek. 24:23

Lastly a meaning of *'ish* in combination with other words is **'ish 'elohim**, translated "prophet," with a formal translation of "man of God," with the meaning of one who speaks words that a deity gives by vision, words, or other forms of revelation, Deut. 33:1; 1 Sam. 9:6; 1 Kin. 13:1-31.

'enosh (582), "man." *'enosh* has the meaning of man as a class of being, with a focus on the frailty and mortality of mankind, Ps. 103:15.

New Testament

1. **anthropos** (444) is used (a) generally, of "a human being, male or female," without reference to sex or nationality, e.g., Matt. 4:4; 12:35; John 2:25; (b) in distinction from God, e.g., Matt. 19:6; John 10:33; Gal. 1:11; Col. 3:23; (c) in distinction from animals, etc., e.g., Luke 5:10; (d) sometimes, in the plural, of "men and women," people, e.g., Matt. 5:13, 16; in Mark 11:2 and 1 Tim. 6:16, lit., "no one of men"; (e) in some instances with a suggestion of human frailty and imperfection e.g., 1 Cor. 2:5; Acts 14:15 (2nd part); (f) in the phrase translated "after man," "after the manner of men," "as a man" (KJV), lit. "according to (**kata**) man," is used only by the apostle Paul, of (1) the practices of fallen humanity 1 Cor. 3:3; (2) anything of human origin, Gal. 1:11; (3) the laws that govern the administration of justice among men, Rom. 3:5; (4) the standard generally accepted among men, Gal. 3:15; (5) an illustration not drawn from Scripture, 1 Cor. 9:8; (6) probably equals "to use a figurative expression,," i.e., to speak evil of men with whom he had contended at Ephesus as "beasts" (cf. 1 Cor. 4:6), 1 Cor. 15:32.

(g) in the phrase "the inward man," the regenerate person's spiritual nature personified, the inner self of the believer, Rom. 7:22, as approving of the law of God; in Eph. 3:16, as the sphere of the renewing power of the Holy Spirit; in 2 Cor. 4:16 (where **anthropos** is not repeated), in contrast to "the outward man," the physical frame, the "man" as cognizable by the senses; the "inward" man is identical with "the hidden man of the heart," 1 Pet. 3:4.

(h) in the expressions "the old man," "the new man," which are confined to Paul's epistles, the former standing for the unregenerate nature personified as the former self of a believer, which, having been crucified with Christ, Rom. 6:6, is to be apprehended practically as such, and to be "put off," Eph. 4:22; Col. 3:9, being the source and seat of sin; the latter, "the new man," standing for the new nature personified as the believer's regenerate self, a nature "created in righteousness and holiness of truth," Eph. 4:24, and having been "put on" at regeneration, Col. 3:10; being "renewed after the image of Him that created him," it is to be "put on" in practical apprehension of these facts.

2. *aner* (435) is never used of the female sex; it stands (a) in distinction from a woman, Acts 8:12; 1 Tim. 2:12; as a husband, Matt. 1:16; John 4:16; Rom. 7:2; Titus 1:6; (b) as distinct from a boy or infant, 1 Cor. 13:11; metaphorically in Eph. 4:13; (c) in conjunction with an adjective or noun, e.g., Luke 5:8, lit., "a man, a sinner"; 24:19, lit., "a man, a prophet."

MAN'S, OF MAN, MANKIND (see also MEN)

anthropinos (442), "human, belonging to man," is used (a) of man's wisdom, in 1 Cor. 2:13 (some mss. have it in v. 4, where indeed it is implied; see, however, the RV); (b) of "man's judgment," 1 Cor. 4:3; (c) of "mankind," Jas. 3:7, lit., "the human nature," RV marg. (KJV marg., "nature of man"); (d) of human ordinance, 1 Pet. 2:13.

MANGER

phatne (5336), "a manger," Luke 2:7, 12, 16, also denotes "a stall," 13:15.

MANIFEST (Adjective and Verb)

A. Adjectives.

1. *emphanes* (1717), manifest (akin to *emphaino*, "to show in, to exhibit"; *en*, "in," *phaino*, "to cause to shine"), is used (a) literally in Acts 10:40, RV "(gave Him to be made) manifest"; (b) metaphorically in Rom. 10:20, "(I was made) manifest."

2. *phaneros* (5318), "open to sight, visible, manifest" (the root *phan*—, signifying "shining," exists also in No. 1), is translated "manifest" in Luke 8:17; Acts 4:16; 7:13, RV (KJV, "known"); Rom. 1:19; 1 Cor. 3:13; 11:19; 14:25; Gal. 5:19; Phil. 1:13; 1 Tim. 4:15 (KJV "appear"); 1 John 3:10.

3. *aphanes* (852) denotes "unseen, hidden," Heb. 4:13, "not manifest" (*a*, negative and *phaino*).

B. Verbs.

1. *phaneroo* (*5319*), "to make visible, clear, manifest, known" (akin to A, No. 2), is used especially in the writings of the apostles John and Paul, occurring 9 times in the Gospel, 9 times in 1 John, 2 in Rev.; in the Pauline Epistles (including Heb.) 24 times; in the other Gospels, only in Mark, 3 times; elsewhere in 1 Pet. 1:20; 5:4.

The true meaning is "to uncover, lay bare, reveal." The following are variations in the rendering, which should be noted: Mark 16:12, 14 (RV, "was manifested," KJV, "appeared"); John 21:1 (RV, "manifested," KJV, "shewed"; cf. v. 14); Rom. 1:19 (RV, "manifested," KJV, "hath shewed"); 2 Cor. 3:3 (RV, "being made manifest," KJV, "are manifestly declared"); 2 Cor. 5:10; 7:12 and Rev. 3:18 (RV, "be made manifest," KJV, "appear"); 2 Cor. 11:6 (RV, "we have made it manifest," KJV, "we have been thoroughly made manifest"); Col. 1:26 (RV "hath it been manifested," KJV, "is made manifest"); 3:4 (RV, "be manifested," KJV, "appear"; so 1 Pet. 5:4); 1 Tim. 3:16 (RV, "was manifested," KJV, "was manifest"); 2 Tim. 1:10 (RV, "hath...been manifested," KJV, "is...made manifest"; cf. Rom. 16:26, 2 Cor. 4:10, 11; 1 Pet. 1:20); Heb. 9:26 (RV, "hath He been manifested," KJV, "hath He appeared"); 1 John 2:28; 3:2 (RV, "is...made manifest," KJV, "doth appear").

2. *emphanizo* (*1718*), akin to A, No. 1, is translated "to manifest, make manifest," in John 14:21, 22; Heb. 11:14.

MANIFESTATION

phanerosis (*5321*), "a manifestation," occurs in 1 Cor. 12:7 and 2 Cor. 4:2.

MANNA

manna (*3131*), the supernaturally provided food for Israel during their wilderness journey, for details see Exod. 16 and Num. 11; cf. John 6:31-35. The "hidden manna" is promised as one of the rewards of the overcomer, Rev. 2:17. None of the natural substances called "manna" is to be identified with that which God provided for Israel.

MANNER

A. Nouns.

1. *ethos* (*1485*), "a habit, custom" (akin to the verb *etho*, "to be accustomed"), is always translated "custom" in the RV ("manner" in the KJV of John 19:40; Acts 15:1; 25:16; Heb. 10:25).

2. *ethos* (*2239*), primarily "a haunt, abode," then, "a custom, manner," occurs in the plural in 1 Cor. 15:33, i.e., ethical conduct, morals.

3. *tropos* (*5158*), "a turning, fashion, manner, character, way of life," is translated "manner" in Acts 1:11, with reference to the

Lord's ascension and return, in Jude 7, of the similarity of the evil of those mentioned in vv. 6 and 7.

B. Adverb.

homoios (3668), akin to the adjective *homoios*, "like," signifies in "like manner, equally"; in the following the RV has "in like manner" for KJV, "likewise"; Matt. 27:41; Mark 4:16; Luke 10:32; 13:3; 16:25; John 5:19; (Heb. 9:21); Jas. 2:25; 1 Pet. 3:1, 7; Rev. 8:12; in Rev. 2:15 the KJV "which thing I hate" translates a variant reading (*ho miso*).

C. Verb.

tropophoreo (5159), "to bear another's manners," is translated "suffered He (their) manners" in Acts 13:18.

MANSERVANT

pais (3816), "a child, boy, youth," also means "a servant, attendant," Luke 12:45.

MANSIONS

mone (3438), primarily "a staying abiding" (akin to *meno*, "to abide"), denotes an "abode" (Eng., "manor," "manse," etc.), translated "mansions" in John 14:2; "abode" in v. 23. There is nothing in the word to indicate separate compartments in heaven; neither does it suggest temporary resting places on the road.

MANSLAYERS

androphonos (409), from *aner*, "a man," and *phoneus*, "a murderer," occurs in the plural in 1 Tim. 5:9.

MARAN-ATHA

maran-atha (3134), an expression used in 1 Cor. 16:22, is the Greek spelling for two Aramaic words, likely meaning the "Our Lord, come," or "O Lord, come." The character of the context, however, indicates that the apostle is making a statement rather than expressing a desire or uttering a prayer. As to the reason why it was used, most probably it was a current phrase of joy among early Christians, as embodying the consummation of their desires.

MARK (Noun)

1. *charagma* (5480) denotes "a stamp, impress," translated "mark" in Rev. 13:16, 17, etc.

2. *stigma* (4742) denotes "a tattooed mark" or "a mark burnt in, a brand" (akin to *stizo*, "to prick"), translated "marks" in Gal. 6:17. It is probable that the apostle refers to the physical sufferings he had endured since he began to proclaim Jesus as Messiah and

Lord [e.g., at Lystra and Philippi]. It is probable, too, that this reference to his scars was intended to set off the insistence of the Judaizers upon a body-mark which cost them nothing. Over against the circumcision they demanded as a proof of obedience to the law he set the indelible tokens, sustained in his own body, of his loyalty to the Lord Jesus. As to the origin of the figure, it was indeed customary for a master to brand his slaves, but this language does not suggest that the apostle had been branded by His Master.

MARKET, MARKETPLACE

agora (*58*), primarily "an assembly," or, in general, "an open space in a town." In the NT it denotes "a place of assembly, a public place or forum, a marketplace." A variety of circumstances, connected with it as a public gathering place, is mentioned, e.g., business dealings such as the hiring of laborers, Matt. 20:3; the buying and selling of goods, Mark 7:4 (involving risk of pollution); the games of children, Matt. 11:16; Luke 7:32; exchange of greetings, Matt. 23:7; Mark 12:38; Luke 11:43; 20:46; the holding of trials, Acts 16:19; public discussions, Acts 17:17. Mark 6:56 records the bringing of the sick there. The word always carries with it the idea of publicity, in contrast to private circumstances.

MARRIAGE (give in), MARRY

A. Noun.

gamos (*1062*), "a marriage, wedding," or "wedding feast," is used to denote (a) the ceremony and its proceedings, including the "marriage feast," John 2:1, 2; of the "marriage ceremony" only, figuratively, Rev. 19:7, as distinct from the "marriage feast" (v. 9); (b) "the marriage feast," RV in Matt. 22:2-4, 9; in v. 8, 10, "wedding"; in 25:10, RV "marriage feast"; so Luke 12:36; 14:8; in Matt. 22:11, 12, the "wedding garment" is, lit., "a garment of a wedding." In Rev. 19, where, under the figure of a "marriage," the union of Christ, as the Lamb of God, with His heavenly bride is so described, the marriage itself takes place in heaven during the Parousia, v. 7 (the aorist or point tense indicating an accomplished fact; the bride is called "His wife"); the "marriage feast" or supper is to take place on earth, after the Second Advent, v. 9. That Christ is spoken of as the Lamb points to His atoning sacrifice as the ground upon which the spiritual union takes place. The background of the phraseology lies in the OT description of the relation of God to Israel, e.g., Isa. 54:4,ff.; Ezek. 16:7,ff.; Hos. 2:19; (c) "marriage" in general, including the "married" state, which is to be "had in honor," Heb. 13:4, RV.

B. Verbs.

1. *gameo* (*1060*), "to marry" (akin to A), is used (a) of "the man,"

Matt. 5:32; 19:9, 10; 22:25 (RV; KJV, "married a wife"); v. 30; 24:38; Mark 6:17; 10:11; 12:25; Luke 14:20; 16:18; 17:27, RV, "married" (AV, "married wives"); 20:34, 35; 1 Cor. 7:28 (1st part); v. 33; (b) of "the woman," in the active voice, Mark 10:12; 1 Cor. 7:28 (last part); ver. 34; 1 Tim. 5:11, 14; in the passive voice, 1 Cor. 7:39; (c) of "both sexes," 1 Cor. 7:9, 10, 36; 1 Tim. 4:3.

2. *gamizo* (*1061v*), "to give in marriage," is used in the passive voice in Matt. 22:30 (2nd clause); Mark 12:25; Luke 17:27; 20:35 (last word), passive; in the active voice, Matt. 24:38; further, of giving a daughter in "marriage," 1 Cor. 7:38 (twice), which, on the whole, may be taken as the meaning. In this part of the Epistle, the apostle was answering a number of questions on matters about which the church at Corinth had written to him, and in this particular matter the formal transition from "marriage" in general to the subject of giving a daughter in "marriage," is simple. Eastern customs naturally would involve the inclusion of the latter in the inquiry and the reply.

MARVEL (Noun and Verb), MARVELLOUS

Old Testament

A. Verb.

pala' (6381), "to be marvelous, be extraordinary, be beyond one's power to do, do wonderful acts." *pala'* is used primarily with God as its subject, expressing actions that are beyond the bounds of human powers or expectations, Ps. 118:23. Deliverance from Egypt was the result of God's wondrous acts, Exod. 3:20. Praise is constantly due God for all His wonderful deeds, Ps. 9:1. At the same time, God does not require anything of His people that is too hard for them, Deut. 30:11.

M

B. Noun.

pele' (6382), "wonder; marvel." This noun frequently expresses the "wonder," the extraordinary aspects, of God's dealings with His people, Exod. 15:11; Ps. 77:11; Isa. 9:6; 29:14.

New Testament

A. Noun.

thauma (2295), "a wonder" (akin to *theaomai*, "to gaze in wonder"), is found in the most authentic mss. in 2 Cor. 11:14 (some mss. have the adjective *thaumastos:* see C, below), "(no) marvel"; in Rev. 17:6, RV, "wonder" (KJV, "admiration"), said of John's astonishment at the vision of the woman described as Babylon the Great.

B. Verbs.

1. *thaumazo* (2296) signifies "to wonder at, marvel" (akin to A);

the following are RV differences from the KJV: Luke 2:33, "were marveling" for "marveled"; Luke 8:25 and 11:14, "marveled" for "wondered"; 9:43, "were marveling" for "wondered"; 2 Thess. 1:10, "marveled at" for "admired" (of the person of Christ at the time of the shining forth of His Parousia, at the Second Advent).

2. *ekthaumazo* (*1537*) and (*2296*), a strengthened form of No. 1 (*ek*, intensive), is found in the best mss. in Mark 12:17, RV, "wondered greatly" (some mss. have No. 1).

C. Adjective.

thaumastos (*2298*), "marvellous" (akin to A and B), is said (a) of the Lord's doing in making the rejected Stone the Head of the corner, Matt. 21:42; Mark 12:11; (b) of the erstwhile blind man's astonishment that the Pharisees knew not from whence Christ had come, and yet He had given him sight, John 9:30, RV, "the marvel," KJV, "a marvellous thing"; (c) of the spiritual light into which believers are brought, 1 Pet. 2:9; (d) of the vision of the seven angels having the seven last plagues, Rev. 15:1; (e) of the works of God, 15:3.

MASTER (Noun and Verb)

A. Nouns.

1. *didaskalos* (*1320*), "a teacher" (from *didasko*, "to teach"), is frequently rendered "Master" in the four Gospels, as a title of address to Christ, e.g., Matt. 8:19; Mark 4:38 (there are more instances in Luke than in the other Gospels); John 1:38, where it interprets "Rabbi"; 20:16, where it interprets "Rabboni." It is used by Christ of Himself in Matt. 23:8 and John 13:13-14; by others concerning Him, Matt. 17:24; 26:18; Mark 5:35; 14:14; Luke 8:49; 22:11; John 11:28. In John 3:10, the Lord uses it in addressing Nicodemus, RV, "the teacher" (KJV, "a master"), where the article does not specify a particular "teacher," but designates the member of a class; for the class see Luke 2:46, "the doctors" (RV, marg., "teachers"). It is used of the relation of a disciple to his "master," in Matt. 10:24, 25; Luke 6:40. It is not translated "masters" in the rest of the NT, save in the KJV of Jas. 3:1 "(be not many) masters," where obviously the RV "teachers" is the meaning.

2. *kurios* (*2962*), "a lord, one who exercises power," is translated "masters" in Matt. 6:24; 15:27; Mark 13:35; Luke 16:13; Acts 16:16, 19; Rom. 14:4, KJV (RV, "lord"); Eph. 6:5, 9 (twice), the 2nd time of Christ; so in Col. 3:22; 4:1.

3. *despotes* (*1203*), one who has "absolute ownership and uncontrolled power," is translated "masters" in 1 Tim. 6:1, 2; Titus 2:9; 1 Pet. 2:18; of Christ, 2 Tim. 2:21; 2 Pet. 2:1, RV (for KJV, Lord); in Jude 4, RV, it is applied to Christ "(our only) Master (and Lord, Jesus Christ)," KJV "(the only) Lord (God)"; in Rev. 6:10, RV, in an

address to God, "O Master" (KJV, "O Lord"). It is rendered "Lord" in Luke 2:29 and Acts 4:24.

4. *rabbei* (*4461*) was an Aramaic word signifying "my master," a title of respectful address to Jewish teachers, Matt. 26:25. In the following the RV has "Rabbi" for KJV "Master"; Matt. 26:25, 49; Mark 9:5; 11:21; 14:45; John 4:31; 9:2; 11:8. In other passages the KJV has "Rabbi," Matt 23:7-8; John 1:38, 49; 3:2, 26; 6:25.

5. *epistates* (*1988*) denotes "a chief, a commander, overseer master." It is used by the disciples in addressing the Lord, in recognition of His authority rather than His instruction; it occurs only in Luke 5:5; 8:24, 45; 9:33, 49; 17:13.

B. Verb.

katakurieuo (*2634*), "to exercise lordship" (*kata*, "down upon," *kurios*, "a lord"), is translated "mastered" in Acts 19:16, RV, of the action of the evil spirit on the sons of Sceva (KJV, "overcame").

MASTERBUILDER

architekton (*753*), from *arche*, "rule, beginning " and *tekton*, "an artificer" (whence Eng., "architect"), "a principal artificer," is used figuratively by the apostle in 1 Cor. 3:10, of his work in laying the foundation of the local church in Corinth, inasmuch as the inception of the spiritual work there devolved upon him.

MEASURE (Noun and Verb)
Old Testament

A. Verb.

madad (*4058*), "to measure, measure off, extend." The basic meaning of the verb is to measure a volume, or length against a normal standard, the way we use feet and pounds to "measure things, Exod. 16:18; Deut. 21:2; Num. 35:5. *madad* can express the idea of extending, stretching, 1 Kings 17:21.

B. Noun.

middah (*4060*), "measure; measurement; extent; size; stature; section; area." This noun refers to the act of "measurement," Lev. 19:35; Ezek. 41:17. Second, *middah* means the thing measured, or the "size." Exod. 26:2; Ps. 39:4; 1 Chron. 11:23. Third, *middah* sometimes represents a "measured portion" of a thing, Neh. 3:11.

New Testament

A. Nouns.

metron (*3358*) denotes (I) "that which is used for measuring, a measure," (a) of "a vessel," figuratively, Matt. 23:32; Luke 6:38 (twice); in John 3:34, with the preposition *ek*, "(He giveth not the Spirit) by measure," RV (which is a necessary correction; the italicized words "*unto him*," KJV, detract from the meaning). Not only had Christ the Holy Spirit without "measure," but God so gives the Spirit through Him to others. It is the ascended Christ who gives the Spirit to those who receive His testimony and set their seal to this, that God is true. The Holy Spirit is imparted neither by degrees, nor in portions, as if He were merely an influence; He is bestowed personally upon each believer, at the time of the New Birth; (b) of "a graduated rod or rule for measuring," figuratively, Matt. 7:2; Mark 4:24; literally, Rev. 21:15 (in the best mss.; see the RV); v. 17; (II) "that which is measured, a determined extent, a portion measured off," Rom. 12:3; 2 Cor. 10:13 (twice); Eph. 4:7, "(according to the) measure (of the gift of Christ)"; the gift of grace is "measured" and given according to the will of Christ; whatever the endowment, His is the bestowment and the adjustment; v. 13, "the measure (of the stature of the fullness of Christ)," the standard of spiritual stature being the fullness which is essentially Christ's; v. 16, "(according to the working in due) measure (of each several part)," i.e., according to the effectual working of the ministration rendered in due "measure" by every part.

B. Adjective.

ametros (*280*), "without measure" (*a*, negative, and A), is used in the neuter plural in an adverbial phrase in 2 Cor. 10:13, 15, *eis ta ametra*, lit., "unto the (things) without measure," RV, "(we will not glory) beyond our measure," KJV, "(we will not boast) of things without measure," referring to the sphere divinely appointed for the apostle as to his gospel ministry; this had reached to Corinth, and by the increase of the faith of the church there, would extend to regions beyond. His opponents had no scruples about intruding into the spheres of other men's work.

C. Verbs.

1. *metreo* (*3354*), "to measure" (akin to A), is used (a) of space, number, value, etc., Rev. 11:1, 2; 21:15, 16, 17; metaphorically, 2 Cor. 10:12; (b) in the sense of "measuring" out, giving by "measure," Matt. 7:2, "ye mete" (some mss. have No. 2); Mark 4:24; in some mss. in Luke 6:38.

2. *antimetreo* (*488*), "to measure in return" (*anti*, "back, in return" and No. 1), is used in the passive voice, and found in some mss. in Matt. 7:2 (the most authentic have No. 1); in Luke 6:38 the most authentic have this verb.

MEDIATOR

mesites (*3316*), lit., "a go-between" (from *mesos*, "middle," and *eimi*, "to go"), is used in two ways in the NT, (a) "one who mediates" between two parties with a view to producing peace, as in 1 Tim. 2:5, though more than mere "mediatorship" is in view, for the salvation of men necessitated that the Mediator should Himself possess the nature and attributes of Him towards whom He acts, and should likewise participate in the nature of those for whom He acts (sin apart); only by being possessed both of deity and humanity could He comprehend the claims of the one and the needs of the other; further, the claims and the needs could be met only by One who, Himself being proved sinless. would offer Himself an expiatory sacrifice on behalf of men; (b) "one who acts as a guarantee" so as to secure something which otherwise would not be obtained. Thus in Heb. 8:6; 9:15; 12:24 Christ is the Surety of "the better covenant," "the new covenant," guaranteeing its terms for His people.

In Gal. 3:19 Moses is spoken of as a "mediator," and the statement is made that "a mediator is not a mediator of one," v. 20, that is, of one party. Here the contrast is between the promise given to Abraham and the giving of the Law. The Law was a covenant enacted between God and the Jewish people, requiring fulfillment by both parties. But with the promise to Abraham, all the obligations were assumed by God, which is implied in the statement, "but God is one."

MEDITATE

Old Testament

hagah (1897), "to meditate, moan, growl, utter, speak." This word means to think about something in earnest, often with the focus on thinking about future plans and contingencies, possibly speaking to God or oneself in low tones. It seems to be an onomatopoetic term, reflecting the sighing and low sounds one may make while musing, at least as the ancients practiced it, Josh. 1:8; Ps. 1:2. *hagah* also expresses the "growl" of lions, Isa. 31:4; "coo" of doves, Isa. 38:14.

New Testament

1. *meletao* (3191), primarily, "to care for" (akin to *melete*, "care"; cf. *melei*, "it is a care"), denotes (a) "to attend to, practice," 1 Tim. 4:15, RV, "be diligent in" (KJV, "meditate upon"); to practice is the prevalent sense of the word, and the context is not against this significance in the RV rendering; some mss. have it in Mark 13:11; (b) "to ponder, imagine," Acts 4:25.

2. *promeletao* (4304), "to premeditate," is used in Luke 21:14.

MEEK, MEEKNESS

A. Adjective.

praus or *praos* (4239) denotes "gentle, mild, meek"; for its significance see the corresponding noun, below, B. Christ uses it of His own disposition, Matt. 11:29; He gives it in the third of His

Beatitudes, 5:5; it is said of Him as the King Messiah, 21:5, from Zech. 9:9; it is an adornment of the Christian profession, 1 Pet. 3:4.

B. Nouns.

1. *prautes*, or *praotes*, an earlier form, (*4240*) denotes "meekness." In its use in Scripture, in which it has a fuller, deeper significance than in non-scriptural Greek writings, it consists not in a person's outward behavior only; nor yet in his relations to his fellow-men; as little in his mere natural disposition. Rather it is an inwrought grace of the soul, and the exercises of it are first and chiefly towards God. It is that temper of spirit in which we accept His dealings with us as good, and therefore without disputing or resisting; it is closely linked with the word *tapeinophrosune* [humility], and follows directly upon it, Eph. 4:2; Col. 3:12; cf. the adjectives in the Sept. of Zeph. 3:12, "meek and lowly."

The meaning of *prautes* is not readily expressed in English, for the terms meekness, mildness, commonly used, suggest weakness and pusillanimity to a greater or less extent, whereas *prautes* does nothing of the kind. Nevertheless, it is difficult to find a rendering less open to objection than "meekness"; "gentleness" has been suggested, but as *prautes* describes a condition of mind and heart, and as "gentleness" is appropriate rather to actions, this word is no better than that used in both English Versions. It must be clearly understood, therefore, that the meekness manifested by the Lord and commended to the believer is the fruit of power. The common assumption is that when a man is meek it is because he cannot help himself; but the Lord was "meek" because he had the infinite resources of God at His command. Described negatively, meekness is the opposite to self-assertiveness and self-interest; it is equanimity of spirit that is neither elated nor cast down, simply because it is not occupied with self at all.

2. *praupathia*, "a meek disposition, meekness" (*praus*, "meek," *pascho*, "to suffer"), is found in the best texts in 1 Tim. 6:11.

MEMBER

melos (*3196*), "a limb of the body," is used (a) literally, Matt. 5:29-30; Rom. 6:13 (twice), 19 (twice); 7:5, 23 (twice); 12:4 (twice); 1 Cor. 12:12 (twice), 14, 18-20, 22, 25-26 (twice); Jas. 3:5, 6; 4:1; in Col. 3:5, "mortify therefore your members which are upon the earth", since our bodies and their "members" belong to the earth, and are the instruments of sin, they are referred to as such (cf. Matt. 5:29-30; Rom. 7:5, 23, mentioned above); the putting to death is not physical, but ethical; as the physical "members" have distinct individualities, so those evils, of which the physical "members" are agents, are by analogy regarded as examples of the way in which the "members" work if not put to death; this is not precisely the same as "the old man," v. 9, i.e., the old nature, though there is a connection; (b) metaphorically, "of believers as members of Christ," 1 Cor. 6:15 (1st part); of one another, Rom. 12:5 (as with the natural illustration, so with the spiritual analogy, there is not only vital unity, and harmony in operation, but diversity, all being essential to effectivity; the unity is not due to external organization but to common and vital union in Christ); there is stress in v. 5 upon "many" and "in Christ" and "members"; 1 Cor. 12:27 (of the "members" of a local church as a body); Eph. 4:25 (of the "members" of the whole Church as the mystical body of Christ); in 1 Cor. 6:15 (2nd part), of one who practices fornication.

MEMORIAL

mnemosunon (3422) denotes "a memorial," that which keeps alive the memory of someone or something (from *mnemon*, "mindful"), Matt. 26:13; Mark 14:9; Acts 10:4.

MEN-PLEASERS

anthropareskos (441), an adjective signifying "studying to please men" (*anthropos*, "man," *aresko*, "to please"), designates, "not simply one who is pleasing to men..., but one who endeavors to please men and not God" (Cremer). It is used in Eph. 6:6 and Col. 3:22.

MEN-STEALERS

andrapodistes (405), "a slave dealer, kidnapper," from *andrapodon*. The verb *andrapodizo* supplied the noun "with the like odious meaning," which appears in 1 Tim. 1:10.

M

MEND

katartizo (2675), from *kata*, "down," intensive and *artios*, "fit," has three meanings, (a) "to mend, repair," Matt. 4:21; Mark 1:19, of nets; (b) "to complete, furnish completely, equip, prepare," Luke 6:40; Rom. 9:22; Heb. 11:3 and in the middle voice, Matt. 21:16; Heb. 10:5; (c) "ethically, to prepare, perfect," Gal. 6:1; 1 Thess. 3:10; 1 Pet. 5:10; Heb. 13:21; and in the passive voice, 1 Cor. 1:10; 2 Cor. 13:11.

MENTION (Noun and Verb)

A. Noun.

mneia (3417), "remembrance, mention" (akin to *mimnesko*, "to remind, remember"), is always used in connection with prayer, and translated "mention" in Rom. 1:9; Eph. 1:16; 1 Thess. 1:2; Philem. 4, in each of which it is preceded by the verb to make; "remembrance" in Phil. 1:3; 1 Thess. 3:6; 2 Tim. 1:3. Some mss. have it in Rom. 12·13, instead of *chreiais*, necessities.

B. Verb.

mnemoneuo (*3421*), which most usually means "to call to mind, remember," signifies "to make mention of," in Heb. 11:22.

MERCHANDISE (Noun, and Verb, to make)

A. Nouns.

1. *emporia* (*1711*) denotes "commerce, business, trade" [akin to No. 2, and to *emporos*, "one on a journey," "a merchant"], occurs in Matt. 22:5.

2. *emporion* (*1712*) denotes "a trading place, exchange" (Eng., "emporium"), John 2:16, "(a house) of merchandise."

B. Verb.

emporeuomai (*1710*) primarily signifies "to travel," especially for business; then, "to traffic, trade," Jas. 4:13; then, "to make a gain of, make merchandise of," 2 Pet. 2:3.

MERCIFUL (Adjective, and Verb, to be), MERCY (Noun, and Verb, to have, etc.)

A. Nouns.

1. *eleos* (*1656*) "is the outward manifestation of pity; it assumes need on the part of him who receives it, and resources adequate to meet the need on the part of him who shows it. It is used (a) of God, who is rich in mercy, Eph. 2:4, and who has provided salvation for all men, Titus 3:5, for Jews, Luke 1:72, and Gentiles, Rom. 15:9. He is merciful to those who fear him, Luke 1:50, for they also are compassed with infirmity, and He alone can succor them. Hence they are to pray boldly for mercy, Heb. 4:16, and if for themselves, it is seemly that they should ask for mercy for one another, Gal. 6:16; 1 Tim. 1:2. When God brings His salvation to its issue at the Coming of Christ, His people will obtain His mercy, 2 Tim. 1:16; Jude 21; (b) of men; for since God is merciful to them, He would have them show mercy to one another, Matt. 9:13; 12:7; 23:23; Luke 10:37; Jas. 2:13.

2. *oiktirmos* (*3628*), "pity, compassion for the ills of others," is used (a) of God, Who is "the Father of mercies," 2 Cor. 1:3; His "mercies" are the ground upon which believers are to present their bodies a living sacrifice, holy, acceptable to God, as their reasonable service, Rom. 12:1; under the Law he who set it at nought died without compassion, Heb. 10:28; (b) of men; believers are to feel and exhibit compassions one toward another, Phil. 2:1, RV "compassions," and Col. 3:12, RV "(a heart) of compassion"; in these two places the word is preceded by No. 3, rendered "tender mercies" in the former, and "a heart" in the latter, RV.

3. *splanchnon* (*4698*), "affections, the heart," always in the plural

in the NT, has reference to "feelings of kindness, goodwill, pity," Phil. 2:1, RV, "tender mercies."

B. Verbs.

1. *eleeo* (1653), akin to A, No. 1, signifies, in general, "to feel sympathy with the misery of another," and especially sympathy manifested in act, (a) in the active voice, "to have pity or mercy on, to show mercy" to, e.g., Matt. 9:27; 15:22; 17:15; 18:33; 20:30, 31 (three times in Mark, four in Luke); Rom. 9:15, 16, 18; 11:32; 12:8; Phil. 2:27; Jude 22, 23; (b) in the passive voice, "to have pity or mercy shown one to obtain mercy," Matt. 5:7; Rom. 11:30, 31; 1 Cor. 7:25; 2 Cor. 4:1; 1 Tim. 1:13, 16; 1 Pet. 2:10.

2. *oikteiro* (3627), akin to A, No. 2, "to have pity on" (from *oiktos*, "pity": *oi*, an exclamation, = oh!), occurs in Rom. 9:15 (twice), where it follows No. 1 (twice); the point established there and in Exod. 33:19, from the Sept. of which it is quoted, is that the "mercy" and compassion shown by God are determined by nothing external to His attributes. Speaking generally *oikteiro* is a stronger term than *eleeo*.

3. *hilaskomai* (2433) in profane Greek meant "to conciliate, appease, propitiate, cause the gods to be reconciled"; their goodwill was not regarded as their natural condition, but as something to be earned. The heathen believed their gods to be naturally alienated in feeling from man. In the NT the word never means to conciliate God; it signifies (a) "to be propitious, merciful," Luke 18:13, in the prayer of the publican; (b) "to expiate, make propitiation for," Heb. 2:17, "make propitiation."

That God is not of Himself already alienated from man, see John 3:16. His attitude toward the sinner does not need to be changed by his efforts. With regard to his sin, an expiation is necessary, consistently with God's holiness and for His righteousness' sake, and that expiation His grace and love have provided in the atoning sacrifice of His Son; man, himself a sinner, justly exposed to God's wrath (John 3:36), could never find an expiation. As Lightfoot says, "when the NT writers speak at length on the subject of Divine wrath, the hostility is represented, not as on the part of God, but of men." Through that which God has accomplished in Christ, by His death, man, on becoming regenerate, escapes the merited wrath of God. The making of this expiation [(b) above], with its effect in the mercy of God (a) is what is expressed in *hilaskomai*.

M

C. Adjectives.

1. *eleemon* (1655), "merciful," akin to A, No. 1, not simply possessed of pity but actively compassionate, is used of Christ as a High Priest, Heb. 2:17, and of those who are like God, Matt. 5:7 (cf.

Luke 6:35, 36, where the RV, "sons" is to be read, as representing characteristics resembling those of their Father."

2. *oiktirmon* (3629) pitiful, compassionate for the ills of others," a stronger term than No. 1 (akin to A, No. 2), is used twice in Luke 6:36, "merciful" (of the character of God, to be expressed in His people); Jas. 5:11, RV, "merciful," KJV, "of tender mercy."

3. *hileos* (2436), "propitious, merciful" (akin to B, No. 3), was used in profane Greek just as in the case of the verb (which see). There is nothing of this in the use of the word in Scripture. The quality expressed by it there essentially appertains to God, though man is undeserving of it. It is used only of God, Heb. 8:12; in Matt. 16:22, "Be it far from Thee" (Peter's word to Christ) may have the meaning given in the RV marg., "(God) have mercy on Thee," lit., "propitious to Thee" (KJV marg., "Pity Thyself").

4. *aneleos* or *anileos* (448), "unmerciful, merciless," occurs in Jas. 2:13, said of judgment on him who shows no mercy.

MERCY SEAT

hilasterion (2435), "the lid or cover of the ark of the covenant," signifies the Propitiatory, so called on account of the expiation made once a year on the great Day of Atonement, Heb. 9:5. For the formation see Exod. 25:17-21.

MERRY (to be, to make)

euphraino (2165), in the active voice, "to cheer, make glad," 2 Cor. 2:2, is used everywhere else in the passive voice, signifying, "to be happy, rejoice, make merry," and translated "to be merry" in Luke 12:19; 15:23, 24, 29, 32; in 16:19, "fared (sumptuously)"; in Rev. 11:10, make merry.

MESSAGE

1. *angelia* (31), akin to *angello*, "to bring a message, proclaim," denotes a "message, proclamation, news," 1 John 1:5 [some mss. have *epangelia*]; 1 John 3:11, where the word is more precisely defined (by being followed by the conjunction "that," expressing the purpose that we should love one another) as being virtually equivalent to an order.

2. *kerugma* (2782), "that which is proclaimed by a herald, a proclamation, preaching," is translated "the message" in Titus 1:3, RV (KJV, preaching).

MESSENGER

1. *angelos* (32), "a messenger, an angel, one sent," is translated "messenger," of John the Baptist, Matt. 11:10; Mark 1:2; Luke 7:27; in the plural, of John's "messengers," 7:24; of those whom Christ sent before Him when on His journey to Jerusalem, 9:52; of Paul's

"thorn in the flesh," "a messenger of Satan," 2 Cor. 12:7; of the spies as received by Rahab, Jas. 2:25.

2. *apostolos* (*652*), "an apostle," is translated "messengers" in 2 Cor. 8:23 regarding Titus and "the other brethren," whom Paul describes to the church at Corinth as "messengers of the churches," in respect of offerings from those in Macedonia for the needy in Judea; in Phil. 2:25, of Epaphroditus as the "messenger" of the church at Philippi to the apostle in ministering to his need; RV marg. in each case, "apostle."

MESSIAH (See also CHRIST)

A. Nouns.

mashiach (4899), "anointed one; Messiah." First, *mashiach* refers to one who is anointed with oil, symbolizing the reception of the Holy Spirit, enabling him to do an assigned task. Kings, 1 Sam. 24:6, high priests, and some prophets, 1 Kings 19:16, were so anointed, Lev. 4:3. In the case of Cyrus, he was anointed with God's Spirit only and commissioned an "anointed deliverer" of Israel, Isa. 45:1. The patriarchs, too, are called "anointed ones," Ps. 105:15. Second, the word is sometimes transliterated "Messiah." After the promise to David, 2 Sam. 7:13, *mashiach* refers immediately to the Davidic dynasty, but ultimately it points to the "Messiah," Jesus the Christ, Ps. 2:2; Dan. 9:25; cf. John 1:41.

B. Verb.

mashach (4886), "to smear with oil or paint, anoint." The objects of this verb are people, sacrificial victims, and objects of worship. Aaron and his sons are the objects of this verb in Exod. 30:30.

M

MIGHT (Noun), MIGHTY, MIGHTILY, MIGHTIER

Old Testament

geburah (1369), "might." The primary meaning of *geburah* is "power" or "physical strength." Certain animals are known for their "strength," such as horses, Ps. 147:10, and crocodiles, Job 41:4. Man also demonstrates "might" in heroic acts, Judg. 8:21, and in war, Isa. 3:25. David's powerful regime is expressed as a "kingship of *geburah*," 1 Chron. 29:30. Since both physical strength and wisdom were necessary for leadership, these two qualities are joined together, Prov. 8:14. God is of course the ultimate example of combining might and wisdom, Ps. 54:1; 65:6

New Testament

A. Nouns.

1. *dunamis* (*1411*), "power," (a) used relatively, denotes "inherent ability, capability, ability to perform anything," e.g., Matt. 25:15, "ability"; Acts 3:12, "power"; 2 Thess. 1:7, RV, "(angels) of His

power" (KJV, "mighty"); Heb. 11:11, RV, "power" (KJV, "strength"); (b) used absolutely, denotes (1) "power to work, to carry something into effect," e.g., Luke 24:49; (2) "power in action," e.g., Rom. 1:16; 1 Cor. 1:18; it is translated "might" in the KJV of Eph. 1:21 (RV, "power"); so 3:16; Col. 1:11 (1st clause); 2 Pet. 2:11; in Rom. 15:19, KJV, this noun is rendered "mighty"; RV, "(in the) power of signs."

2. *ischus* (2479) denotes "might, strength, power," (a) inherent and in action as used of God, Eph. 1:19, RV, "(the strength, *kratos*, of His) might," KJV, "(His mighty) power," i.e., power (over external things) exercised by strength; Eph. 6:10, "of His might"; 2 Thess. 1:9, RV, "(from the glory of His might" (KJV "power"); Rev. 5:12, RV, "might" (KJV, "strength"); 7:12, "might"; (b) as an endowment, said (1) of angels, 2 Pet. 2:11; here the order is No. 2 and No. 1, RV, "might and power," which better expresses the distinction than the KJV, "power and might"; in some mss. in Rev. 18:2 it is said of the voice of an angel; the most authentic mss. have the adjective *ischuros*, "mighty"; (2) of men, Mark 12:30, 33; Luke 10:27.

B. Adjectives.

1. *dunatos* (1415), "powerful, mighty" (akin to A, No. 1), is used, with that significance, (1) of God, Luke 1:49, "mighty"; Rom. 9:22, "power" (here the neuter of the adjective is used with the article, as a noun, equivalent to *dunamis*); frequently with the meaning "able"; (2) of Christ, regarded as a prophet, Luke 24:19 ("in deed and word"); (3) of men: Moses, Acts 7:22 ("in his words and works"); Apollos, 18:24, "in the Scriptures"; of those possessed of natural power, 1 Cor. 1:26; of those possessed of spiritual power, 2 Cor. 10:4. For the shades of meaning in the translation "strong," see Rom. 15:1; 2 Cor. 12:10; 13:9.

2. *ischuros* (2478), "strong, mighty" (akin to A, No. 2, and with corresponding adjectival significance), is usually translated "strong"; "mighty" in Luke 15:14 (of a famine); Rev. 19:6 (of thunders); 19:18 (of men): in the following, where the KJV has "mighty," the RV substitutes "strong," 1 Cor. 1:27; Rev. 6:15 (KJV, "mighty men"); 18:10, 21; Heb. 11:34, RV, "(waxed) mighty" (KJV, "valiant").

3. *ischuroteros* (2478*), "stronger, mightier," the comparative degree of No. 2, is translated "mightier" in Matt. 3:11; Mark 1:7; Luke 3:16; "stronger" in Luke 11:22; 1 Cor. 1:25; 10:22.

4. *biaios* (972), "violent" (from *bia*, "force, violence, strength," found in Acts 5:26; 21:35; 24:7; 27:41), occurs in Acts 2:2, of wind.

C. Verb.

dunateo (1414), "to be powerful" (akin to A, No. 1 and B, No. 1), is found in the most authentic mss. in Rom. 14:4 (some have *dunatos*, B, No. 1), RV "(the Lord) hath power," KJV, "(God) is able"; similarly, as regard mss., in 2 Cor. 9:8, where the RV and KJV have "(God) is able"; in 2 Cor. 13:3, KJV, "is mighty," RV, "is powerful" (according to the general significance of **dunamis**).

MILLSTONE

A. Noun.

mulos (*3458*) denotes "a handmill," consisting of two circular stones, one above the other, the lower being fixed. From the center of the lower a wooden pin passes through a hole in the upper, into which the grain is thrown, escaping as flour between the stones and falling on a prepared material below them. The handle is inserted into the upper stone near the circumference. Small stones could be turned by one woman (millgrinding was a work deemed fit only for women and slaves; cf. Judg. 16:21); larger ones were turned by two or more.

Still larger ones were turned by an ass (**onikos**), Matt. 18:6, RV, "a great millstone" (marg., "a millstone turned by an ass"), indicating the immediate and overwhelming drowning of one who causes one young believer to stumble; Mark 9:42 (where some mss. have **lithos mulikos**, "a stone of a mill," as in Luke 17:2).

B. Adjectives.

1. **mulikos** (*3457*), "of a mill," occurs in Luke 17:2.

2. **mulinos** (*3458(v)*), "made of millstone," is used with **lithos**, "a stone"; and with the adjective **megas**, "great," in the best mss. in Rev. 18:21 (some have the word **mulos**.

MIND (Noun and Verb)

A. Nouns.

1. **nous** (*3563*), "mind," denotes, speaking generally, the seat of reflective consciousness, comprising the faculties of perception and understanding, and those of feeling, judging and determining.

Its use in the NT may be analyzed as follows: it denotes (a) the faculty of knowing, the seat of the understanding, Luke 24:45; Rom. 1:28; 14:5; 1 Cor. 14:15, 19; Eph. 4:17; Phil. 4:7; Col. 2:18; 1 Tim. 6:5; 2 Tim. 3:8; Titus 1:15; Rev. 13:18; 17:9; (b) counsels, purpose, Rom. 11:34 (of the "mind" of God); 12:2; 1 Cor. 1:10; 2:16, twice (1) of the thoughts and counsels of God, (2) of Christ, a testimony to His Godhood; Eph. 4:23; (c) the new nature, which belongs to the believer by reason of the new birth, Rom. 7:23, 25, where it is contrasted with "the flesh," the principle of evil which dominates fallen man. Under (b) may come 2 Thess. 2:2, where it stands for the determination to be steadfast amidst afflictions, through the confident expectation of the day of rest and recompense mentioned in the first chapter.

2. **dianoia** (*1271*), lit. "a thinking through, or over, a meditation,

reflecting," signifies (a) like No. 1, "the faculty of knowing, under-standing, or moral reflection," (1) with an evil significance, a consciousness characterized by a perverted moral impulse, Eph. 2:3 (plural); 4:18; (2) with a good significance, the faculty renewed by the Holy Spirit, Matt. 22:37; Mark 12:30; Luke 10:27; Heb. 8:10; 10:16; 1 Pet. 1:13; 1 John 5:20; (b) "sentiment, disposition" (not as a function but as a product); (1) in an evil sense, Luke 1:51, "imagination"; Col. 1:21; (2) in a good sense, 2 Pet. 3:1.

3. *ennoia* (*1771*), "an idea, notion, intent," is rendered "mind" in 1 Pet. 4:1.

4. *noema* (*3540*), "thought, design," is rendered "minds" in 2 Cor 3:14; 4:4; 11:3; Phil. 4:7.

5. *phronema* (*5427*) denotes "what one has in the mind, the thought" (the content of the process expressed in *phroneo*, "to have in mind, to think"); or "an object of thought"; in Rom. 8:6 (KJV, "to be carnally minded" and "to be spiritually minded"), the RV, adhering to the use of the noun, renders by "the mind of the flesh," in vv. 6 and 7, and "the mind of the spirit," in v. 6. In v. 27 the word is used of the "mind" of the Holy Spirit.

B. Verbs.

1. *phroneo* (*5426*) signifies (a) "to think, to be minded in a certain way"; (b) "to think of, be mindful of." It implies moral interest or reflection, not mere unreasoning opinion. Under (a) it is rendered by the verb "to mind" in the following: Rom. 8:5, "(they that are after the flesh) do mind (the things of the flesh)"; 12:16, "be of (the same) mind," lit., "minding the same," and "set (not) your mind on," RV, KJV, "mind (not)"; 15:5, "to be of (the same) mind," RV, (KJV, "to be like-minded"); so the RV in 2 Cor. 13:11, KJV, "be of (one) mind"; Gal. 5:10, "ye will be (none otherwise) minded"; Phil. 1:7, RV, "to be (thus) minded," KJV, "to think (this)"; 2:2, RV, "be of (the same) mind," KJV, "be likeminded," and "being...of (one) mind," lit., "minding (the one thing)"; 2:5, RV, "have (this) mind," KJV, "let (this) mind be," lit., "mind this"; 3:15, "let us...be (thus) minded," and "(if...)ye are (otherwise) minded" (some mss. have the verb in v. 16); 3:19, "(who) mind (earthly things)"; 4:2, "be of (the same) mind"; Col. 3:2, RV and KJV marg., "set your mind," lit., "mind (the things above)," KJV, "set your affection."

2. *sophroneo* (*4993*) signifies (a) "to be of sound mind," or "in one's right mind, sober-minded" (*sozo*, "to save," *phren*, "the mind"), Mark 5:15 and Luke 8:35, "in his right mind"; 2 Cor. 5:13, RV, "we are of sober mind" (KJV, "we be sober"); (b) "to be temperate, self-controlled," Titus 2:6, "to be sober-minded"; 1 Pet. 4:7, RV, "be ye...of sound mind" (KJV, "be ye sober").

C. Adjective.

homophron (3675), "agreeing, of one mind" (*homos*, "same," *phren*, "the mind"), is used in 1 Pet. 3:8.

MINDED

1. *boulomai* (1014), "to wish, will, desire, purpose" (akin to *boule*, "counsel, purpose"), is translated "was minded" in Matt. 1:19; Acts 15:37, RV (KJV, "determined"); 18:27, RV (KJV, "was disposed"); 19:30, RV (KJV, "would have"); 5:33, RV, "were minded" (KJV, "took counsel"); 18:15, RV, "I am (not) minded (to be)," KJV, "I will (be no)"; Heb. 6:17, "being minded," RV (KJV, "willing"), said of God.

2. *bouleuo* (1011), "to take counsel," is translated "to be minded" in Acts 27:39; 2 Cor. 1:17, middle voice in each case.

MINDFUL OF (to be)

1. *mimnesko* (5403), the tenses of which are from the older verb *mnaomai*, signifies "to remind"; but in the middle voice, "to remember, to be mindful of," in the sense of caring for, e.g., Heb. 2:6, "Thou art mindful"; in 13:3, "remember"; in 2 Tim. 1:4, RV, "remembering" (KJV, "being mindful of"); so in 2 Pet. 3:2.

2. *mnemoneuo* (3421), "to call to mind, remember," is rendered "they had been mindful" in Heb. 11:15.

MINGLE

kerannumi (2767), "to mix, to mingle," chiefly of the diluting of wine, implies "a mixing of two things, so that they are blended and form a compound, as in wine and water. It is used in Rev. 18:6.

M

MINISTER (Noun and Verb)
Old Testament

A. Verb.

sharat (8334), "to minister, serve, officiate." As a term for serving or ministering, *sharat* is to be distinguished from the term for more menial serving, *'abad*, from which the word meaning "slave" or "servant" is derived. *sharat* is characteristically used of "serving" done by royal household workers, 2 Sam. 13:17; 1 Kings 10:5. In the manner of the modern "public servant" idea, the word is used in reference to court officials and royal servants, 1 Chron. 27:1; 28:1; Esth. 1:10. This term is used most frequently as the special term for service in worship to the Lord, Deut. 10:8; Num. 16:9; Ezek. 44:11-14.

B. Noun.

sharat (8334), "minister; servant." The noun form of the verb appears several times meaning "minister" or "servant." As humans, Exod. 24:13; or angels, Ps. 103:21; cf. Ps. 104:4.

New Testament

A. Nouns.

1. *diakonos* (1249), "a servant, attendant, minister, deacon," is translated "minister" in Mark 10:43; Rom. 13:4 (twice); 15:8; 1 Cor. 3:5; 2 Cor. 3:6; 6:4; 11:15 (twice); Gal. 2:17; Eph. 6:21; Col. 1:7, 23, 25; 4:7; 1 Thess. 3:2; 1 Tim. 4:6.

2. *leitourgos* (3011) denoted among the Greeks, firstly, "one who discharged a public office at his own expense," then, in general, "a public servant, minister." In the NT it is used (a) of Christ, as a "Minister of the sanctuary" (in the Heavens), Heb. 8:2; (b) of angels, Heb. 1:7 (Ps. 104:4); (c) of the apostle Paul, in his evangelical ministry, fulfilling it as a serving priest, Rom. 15:16; that he used it figuratively and not in an ecclesiastical sense, is obvious from the context; (d) of Epaphroditus, as ministering to Paul's needs on behalf of the church at Philippi, Phil. 2:25; here, representative service is in view; (e) of earthly rulers, who though they do not all act consciously as servants of God, yet discharge functions which are the ordinance of God, Rom. 13:6.

B. Verbs.

1. *diakoneo* (1247), akin to A, No. 1, signifies "to be a servant, attendant, to serve, wait upon, minister." In the following it is translated "to minister," except where "to serve" is mentioned: it is used (a) with a general significance, e.g., Matt. 4:11; 20:28; Mark 1:13; 10:45; John 12:26 ("serve," twice); Acts 19:22; Philem. 13; (b) of waiting at table, "ministering" to the guests, Matt. 8:15; Luke 4:39; 8:3; 12:37; 17:8, "serve"; 22:26, "serve," v. 27, "serveth," twice; the 2nd instance, concerning the Lord, may come under (a); so of women preparing food, etc., Mark 1:31; Luke 10:40, "serve"; John 12:2, "served"; (c) of relieving one's necessities, supplying the necessaries of life, Matt. 25:44; 27:55; Mark 15:41; Acts 6:2, "serve"; Rom. 15:25; Heb. 6:10; more definitely in connection with such service in a local church, 1 Tim. 3:10, 13 [there is nothing in the original representing the word "office"; RV, "let them serve as deacons," "they that have served (well) as deacons"]; (d) of attending, in a more general way, to anything that may serve another's interests, as of the work of an amanuensis, 2 Cor. 3:3 (metaphorical): of the conveyance of material gifts for assisting the needy, 2 Cor. 8:19, 20, RV, "is ministered" (KJV, "is administered"); of a variety of forms of service, 2 Tim. 1:18; of the testimony of the OT prophets, 1 Pet. 1:12; of the ministry of believers one to another in various ways, 1 Pet. 4:10, 11 (not here of discharging ecclesiastical functions).

2. *leitourgeo* (3008), (akin to A, No. 2), in classical Greek, signified at Athens "to supply public offices at one's own cost, to render public service to the State"; hence, generally, "to do service,"

said, e.g., of service to the gods. In the NT it is used (a) of the prophets and teachers in the church at Antioch, who "ministered to the Lord," Acts 13:2; (b) of the duty of churches of the Gentiles to "minister" in "carnal things" to the poor Jewish saints at Jerusalem, in view of the fact that the former had "been made partakers" of the "spiritual things" of the latter, Rom. 15:27; (c) of the official service of priests and Levites under the Law, Heb. 10:11.

MINISTERING, MINISTRATION, MINISTRY

A. Nouns.

1. *diakonia* (1248), "the office and work of a *diakonos*," "service, ministry," is used (a) of domestic duties, Luke 10:40; (b) of religious and spiritual "ministration," (1) of apostolic "ministry" e.g., Acts 1:17, 25; 6:4; 12:25; 21:19; Rom. 11:13, RV (KJV, "office"); (2) of the service of believers, e.g., Acts 6:1; Rom. 12:7; 1 Cor. 12:5, RV, "ministrations" (KJV, "administrations"); 1 Cor. 16:15; 2 Cor. 8:4; 9:1, 12, RV, "ministration"; v. 13; Eph. 4:12, RV, "ministering" (KJV, "the ministry," not in the sense of an ecclesiastical function); 2 Tim. 4:11, RV, "(for) ministering"; collectively of a local church, Acts 11:29, "relief" (RV marg. "for ministry"); Rev. 2:19, RV, "ministry" (KJV, "service"); of Paul's service on behalf of poor saints, Rom. 15:31; (3) of the "ministry" of the Holy Spirit in the gospel, 2 Cor. 3:8; (4) of the "ministry" of angels, Heb. 1:14, RV, "to do service" (KJV, "to minister"); (5) of the work of the gospel, in general, e.g., 2 Cor. 3:9, "of righteousness"; 5:18, "of reconciliation"; (6) of the general "ministry" of a servant of the Lord in preaching and teaching, Acts 20:24; 2 Cor. 4:1; 6:3; 11:8; 1 Tim. 1:12, RV, "(to His) service"; 2 Tim. 4:5; undefined in Col. 4:17; (7) of the Law, as a "ministration" of death, 2 Cor. 3:7; of condemnation, 3:9.

2. *leitourgia* (3009), akin to *leitourgos*, to which the meanings of *leitourgia* correspond, is used in the NT of "sacred ministrations," (a) priestly, Luke 1:23; Heb. 8:6; 9:21; (b) figuratively, of the practical faith of the members of the church at Philippi regarded as priestly sacrifice, upon which the apostle's lifeblood might be poured out as a libation, Phil. 2:17; (c) of the "ministration" of believers one to another, regarded as priestly service, 2 Cor. 9:12; Phil. 2:30.

B. Adjective.

leitourgikos (3010), "of or pertaining to service, ministering," is used in Heb. 1:14, of angels as "ministering spirits."

MIRACLE

1. *dunamis* (1411), "power, inherent ability," is used of works of a supernatural origin and character, such as could not be produced by natural agents and means. It is translated "miracles" in the RV

and KJV in Acts 8:13 (where variant readings give the words in different order); 19:11; 1 Cor. 12:10, 28, 29; Gal. 3:5; KJV only, in Acts 2:22 (RV, "mighty works"); Heb. 2:4 (RV, "powers"). In Gal. 3:5, the word may be taken in its widest sense, to include "miracles" both physical and moral.

2. *semeion* (4592), "a sign, mark, token" (akin to *semaino*, "to give a sign"; *sema*, "a sign"), is used of "miracles" and wonders as signs of divine authority; it is translated "miracles" in the RV and KJV of Luke 23:8; Acts 4:16, 22; most usually it is given its more appropriate meaning "sign," "signs," e.g., Matt. 12:38, 39, and in every occurrence in the Synoptists, except Luke 23:8; in the following passages in John's Gospel the RV substitutes "sign" or "signs" for the KJV "miracle or miracles"; 2:11, 23; 3:2; 4:54; 6:2, 14, 26; 7:31; 9:16; 10:41; 11:47; 12:18, 37; the KJV also has "signs" elsewhere in this Gospel; in Acts, RV, "signs," KJV, "miracles," in 6:8; 8:6; 15:12; elsewhere only in Rev. 13:14; 16:14; 19:20.

MISERABLE, MISERABLY, MISERY

A. Adjectives.

1. *eleeinos* (1652), "pitiable, miserable" (from *eleos*, "mercy, pity"), is used in Rev. 3:17, in the Lord's description of the church at Laodicea; here the idea is probably that of a combination of "misery" and pitiableness.

2. *kakos* (2556), "bad, evil," is translated "miserable" in Matt. 21:41, RV (KJV, "wicked").

B. Adverb.

kakos (2560), "badly, ill," is translated "miserably" in Matt. 21:41 (see A, No. 2). Adhering to the meaning "evil," and giving the designed stress, the sentence may be rendered, "evil (as they are) he will evilly destroy them."

C. Noun.

talaiporia (5004), "hardship, suffering, distress" (akin to *talaiporos*, "wretched," Rom. 7:24; Rev. 3:17, and to *talaiporeo*, in the middle voice, "to afflict oneself," in Jas. 4:9, "be afflicted"), is used as an abstract noun, "misery," in Rom. 3:16; as a concrete noun, "miseries," in Jas. 5:1.

MIST

1. *achlus* (887), "a mist," especially a dimness of the eyes, is used in Acts 13:11.

2. *homichle* (3658a), "a mist" (not so thick as *nephos* and *nephele*, "a cloud"), occurs in 2 Pet. 2:17 (1st part), RV, "mists"; some mss. have *nephelai*, "clouds" (KJV)."

3. *zophos* (2217) is rendered "mist" in the KJV of 2 Pet. 2:17 (2nd part), RV, "blackness"; "murkiness" would be a suitable rendering.

MOCK, MOCKER, MOCKING

A. Verbs.

1. *empaizo* (*1702*), a compound of *paizo*, "to play like a child" (*pais*), "to sport, jest," prefixed by *en*, "in" or "at," is used only in the Synoptics, and, in every instance, of the "mockery" of Christ, except in Matt. 2:16 (there in the sense of deluding, or deceiving, of Herod by the wise men) and in Luke 14:29, of ridicule cast upon the one who after laying a foundation of a tower is unable to finish it. The word is used (a) prophetically by the Lord, of His impending sufferings, Matt. 20:19; Mark 10:34; Luke 18:32; (b) of the actual insults inflicted upon Him by the men who had taken Him from Gethsemane, Luke 22:63; by Herod and his soldiers, Luke 23:11; by the soldiers of the governor, Matt. 27:29, 31; Mark 15:20; Luke 23:36; by the chief priests, Matt. 27:41; Mark 15:31.

2. *mukterizo* (*3456*), from *mukter*, "the nose," hence, "to turn up the nose at, sneer at, treat with contempt," is used in the passive voice in Gal. 6:7, where the statement "God is not mocked" does not mean that men do not mock Him; the apostle vividly contrasts the essential difference between God and man. It is impossible to impose upon Him who discerns the thoughts and intents of the heart.

3. *chleuazo* (*5512*), "to jest, mock, jeer at" (from *chleue*, "a jest"), is said of the ridicule of some of the Athenian philosophers at the apostle's testimony concerning the resurrection of the dead, Acts 17:32.

4. *diachleuazo*, an intensive form of No. 3, "to scoff at," whether by gesture or word, is said of those who jeered at the testimony given on the Day of Pentecost, Acts 2:13 (some mss. have No. 3).

M

B. Nouns.

1. *empaiktes* (*1703*), "a mocker" (akin to A, No. 1), is used in 2 Pet. 3:3, RV, "mockers," (KJV, "scoffers"); Jude 18, RV and KJV, "mockers."

2. *empaigmos* (*1701*), the act of the *empaiktes*, "a mocking," is used in Heb. 11:36, "mockings."

3. *empaigmone* (*1702d*), an abstract noun, "mockery," is used in 2 Pet. 3:3 (some mss. omit it, as in KJV): (see also No. 1, above).

MODEST

kosmios (*2887*), "orderly, well-arranged, decent, modest" (akin to *kosmos*, in its primary sense as "harmonious arrangement adornment"; cf. *kosmikos*, of the world, which is related to *kosmos* in its secondary sense as the world), is used in 1 Tim. 2:9 of the apparel with which Christian women are to adorn themselves; in 3:2 (RV, "orderly"; KJV, "of good behavior"), of one of the qualifications essential for a bishop or overseer.

MOMENT

1. **atomos** (*823*) lit. means "indivisible" (from *a*, negative, and **temno**, "to cut"; Eng., "atom"); hence it denotes "a moment," 1 Cor. 15:52.

2. **stigme** (*4743*), "a prick, a point" (akin to **stizo**, "to prick"), is used metaphorically in Luke 4:5, of a "moment," with **chronos**, "a moment (of time)."

MONEY

1. **argurion** (*694*), properly, "a piece of silver," denotes (a) "silver," e.g., Acts 3:6; (b) a "silver coin," often in the plural, "pieces of silver," e.g., Matt. 26:15; so 28:12, where the meaning is "many, (**hikanos**) pieces of silver"; (c) "money"; it has this meaning in Matt. 25:18, 27; 28:15; Mark 14:11; Luke 9:3; 19:15, 23; 22:5; Acts 8:20 (here the RV has "silver").

2. **chrema** (*5536*), lit., "a thing that one uses" (akin to **chraomai** "to use"), hence, (a) "wealth, riches," Mark 10:23, 24; Luke 18:24; (b) "money," Acts 4:37, singular number, "a sum of money"; plural in 8:18, 20; 24:26.

3. **chalkos** (*5475*), "copper," is used, by metonymy, of "copper coin," translated "money," in Mark 6:8; 12:41.

4. **kerma** (*2772*), primarily "a slice" (akin to **keiro**, "to cut short"), hence, "a small coin, change," is used in the plural in John 2:15, "the changers' money," probably considerable heaps of small coins.

5. **nomisma** (*3546*), primarily "that which is established by custom" (**nomos**, "a custom, law"), hence, "the current coin of a state, currency," is found in Matt. 22:19, "(tribute) money."

MONEY (love of)

philarguria (*5365*), from **phileo**, "to love," and **arguros**, "silver," occurs in 1 Tim. 6:10 (cf. **philarguros**, "covetous, avaricious"). Trench contrasts this with **pleonexia**, "covetousness."

MONTH, MONTHS

1. **men** (*3376*), connected with **mene**, "the moon," akin to a Sanskrit root *ma*—, "to measure" (the Sanskrit *masa* denotes both moon and month, cf., e.g., Lat. *mensis*, Engs., "moon" and "month," the moon being in early times the measure of the "month"). The interval between the 17th day of the second "month" (Gen. 7:11) and the 17th day of the seventh "month," is said to be 150 days (8:3, 4), i.e., five months of 30 days each; hence the year would be 360 days (cf. Dan. 7:25; 9:27; 12:7 with Rev. 11:2-3; 12:6, 14; 13:5; whence we conclude that 3 1/2 years or 42 months = 1260 days, i.e., one year = 60 days); this was the length of the old Egyptian year; later, five days were added to correspond to the solar year. The Hebrew

year was as nearly solar as was compatible with its commencement, coinciding with the new moon, or first day of the "month." This was a regular feast day, Num. 10:10; 28:11-14; the Passover coincided with the full moon (the 14th of the month Abib).

Except in Gal. 4:10; Jas. 5:17; Rev. 9:5, 10, 15; 11:2; 13:5; 22:2, the word is found only in Luke's writings, Luke 1:24, 26, 36, 56; 4:25; Acts 7:20; 18:11; 19:8; 20:3; 28:11, examples of Luke's care as to accuracy of detail.

MOON

1. *selene* (4582), from *selas*, "brightness" (the Heb. words are *yareach*, "wandering," and *lebanah*, "white"), occurs in Matt. 24:29; Mark 13:24; Luke 21:25; Acts 2:20; 1 Cor. 15:41; Rev. 6:12; 8:12; 12:1; 21:23. In Rev. 12:1, "the moon under her feet" is suggestive of derived authority, just as her being clothed with the sun is suggestive of supreme authority; everything in the symbolism of the passage centers in Israel. In 6:12 the similar symbolism of the sun and "moon" is suggestive of the supreme authority over the world, and of derived authority, at the time of the execution of divine judgments upon nations at the close of the present age.

2. *neomenia* (3561), or *noumeniua*, denoting "a new moon" (*neos*, "new," *men*, "a month,") is used in Col. 2:16, of a Jewish festival. Judaistic tradition added special features in the liturgy of the synagogue in connection with the observance of the first day of the month, the new "moon" time.

MORTAL, MORTALITY

thnetos (2349), "subject or liable to death, mortal" (akin to *thnesko*, "to die"), occurs in Rom. 6:12, of the body, where it is called "mortal," not simply because it is liable to death, but because it is the organ in and through which death carries on its death-producing activities; in 8:11, the stress is on the liability to death, and the quickening is not reinvigoration but the impartation of life at the time of the Rapture, as in 1 Cor. 15:53, 54 and 2 Cor. 5:4 (RV, "what is mortal"; KJV, "mortality"); in 2 Cor. 4:11, it is applied to the flesh, which stands, not simply for the body, but the body as that which consists of the element of decay, and is thereby death-doomed. Christ's followers are in this life delivered unto death, that His life may be manifested in that which naturally is the seat of decay and death. That which is subject to suffering is that in which the power of Him who suffered here is most manifested.

MORTIFY

1. *thanatoo* (2289), "to put to death" (from *thanatos*, "death," akin to *thnetos*, "mortal," see above), is translated "mortify" in Rom. 8:13 (Amer. RV, "put to death"); in 7:4, "ye were made dead" (pas-

sive voice), betokens the act of God on the believer, through the death of Christ; here in 8:13 it is the act of the believer himself, as being responsible to answer to God's act, and to put to death "the deeds of the body."

2. *nekroo* (*3499*), "to make dead" (from *nekros*), is used figuratively in Col. 3:5 and translated "mortify" (Amer. RV, "put to death").

MOTE

karphos (*2595*), "a small, dry stalk, a twig, a bit of dried stick," is used metaphorically of a minor fault, Matt. 7:3, 4, 5; Luke 6:41, 42.

MOTH

ses (*4597*) denotes "a clothes moth," Matt. 6:19, 20; Luke 12:33.

MOTHER

Old Testament

'em (517), "mother, grandmother, caregiver, source." *'em* is translated "mother," with the meaning of biological or adoptive female parent of any creature, Gen. 2:24; Exod. 22:30. *'em* is also translated "grandmother," with the meaning of the mother of one's parents, 1 Kin. 15:10,13; 2 Chron. 15:16. *'em* is translated "care giver, provider," (lit. "mother") with the meaning of one who cares, helps, and protects an object as a figurative extension of a biological mother who cares for a child, Judg. 5:7; 2 Sam. 20:19. *'em* is translated "fork of the road," with the meaning of an intersecting point in two different paths, as a particular place on a path or road, Ezek. 21:21.

'em is also used in combination with other Hebrew words, *min beten 'em*, translated "birth," with a literal translation of "from womb of mother," with the meaning of the time of one's coming into the world from the womb, Judg. 16:17; Job 31:18; cf. also "loins of the mother," Isa. 49:1.

New Testament

1. *meter* (*3384*) is used (a) of the natural relationship, e.g., Matt. 1:18; 2 Tim. 1:5; (b) figuratively, (1) of "one who takes the place of a mother," Matt. 12:49, 50; Mark 3:34, 35; John 19:27; Rom. 16:13; 1 Tim. 5:2; (2) of "the heavenly and spiritual Jerusalem," Gal. 4:26. (3) symbolically, of "Babylon," Rev. 17:5, as the source from which has proceeded the religious harlotry.

2. *ametor* (*282*), "without a mother" (*a*, negative, and No. 1), is used in Heb. 7:3, of the Genesis record of Melchizedek, certain details concerning him being purposely omitted, in order to conform the description to facts about Christ as the Son of God. The

word has been found in this sense in the writings of Euripides the dramatist and Herodotus the historian.

MOUNT, MOUNTAIN

Old Testament

har (2022), "mountain range; mountainous region; mount." *har* has the normal meaning of an elevated geographical area, translated "hill," or "mountain," either general or named specifically; this can also refer to a series of mountains, as a mountain-range, Gen. 8:4; Gen. 31:21; Josh. 21:11.

In the poetical literature of the Old Testament, the view of the world held by men of that era finds its reflection. One can speak of the foundations of the mountains as rooted in the underworld, Deut. 32:22, serving to support the earth as the "bars" of the earth, Jonah 2:6. Mountain peaks may be said to reach into the heavens where God dwells, Isa. 24:21; in Gen. 11:4, the men who built the tower at Babel erroneously thought they were going to reach God's dwelling place. "Mountains" often serve as a symbol of strength, Zech. 4:7, inasmuch as they carried mythological significance since many people thought of them as sacred areas, Jer. 3:22-23, and they were the locations of strong fortresses, Josh. 10:6. Even the "mountains" tremble before the Lord; He is mightier than they are, Job 14:18.

New Testament

oros (3735) is used (a) without specification, e.g., Luke 3:5 (distinct from *bounos*, "a hill"); John 4:20; (b) of "the Mount of Transfiguration," Matt. 17:1, 9; Mark 9:2, 9; Luke 9:28, 37 (KJV, "hill"); 2 Pet. 1:18; (c) of "Zion," Heb. 12:22; Rev. 14:1; (d) of "Sinai," Acts 7:30, 38; Gal. 4:24, 25; Heb. 8:5; 12:20; (e) of "the Mount of Olives," Matt. 21:1; 24:3; Mark 11:1; 13:3; Luke 19:29, 37; 22:39; John 8:1; Acts 1:12; (f) of "the hill districts as distinct from the lowlands," especially of the hills above the Sea of Galilee, e.g., Matt. 5:1; 8:1; 18:12; Mark 5:5; (g) of "the mountains on the east of Jordan" and "those in the land of Ammon" and "the region of Petra," etc., Matt. 24:16; Mark 13:14; Luke 21:21; (h) proverbially, "of overcoming difficulties, or accomplishing great things," 1 Cor. 13:2; cf. Matt. 17:20; 21:21; Mark 11:23; (i) symbolically, of "a series of the imperial potentates of the Roman dominion, past and future," Rev. 17:9.

MOURN, MOURNING

Old Testament

'abal (56), "to mourn, lament." When *'abal* is used of mourning for the dead in a literal sense, the word is found in prose sections and in the reflexive form, indicating action back on the subject, Gen. 37:34. When used in the figurative sense, *'abal* expresses

"mourning" by gates, Isa. 3:26, by the land, Isa. 24:4, and by pastures, Amos 1:2. In addition to mourning for the dead, "mourning" may be over Jerusalem, Isa. 66:10, over sin, Ezra 10:6, or over God's judgment, Exod. 33:4. One may pretend to be a mourner, 2 Sam. 14:2, simply by putting on mourning clothes.

New Testament

A. Verbs.

1. **kopto** (*2875*), to cut or beat, used in the middle voice of "beating the breast or head in mourning" (cf. Luke 23:27), is translated "shall mourn" in Matt. 24:30.

2. **pentheo** (*3996*), "to mourn for, lament," is used (a) of mourning in general, Matt. 5:4; 9:15; Luke 6:25; (b) of sorrow for the death of a loved one, Mark 16:10; (c) of "mourning" for the overthrow of Babylon and the Babylonish system, Rev. 18:11, 15, RV, "mourning" (KJV, "wailing"); v. 19 (ditto); (d) of sorrow for sin or for condoning it, Jas. 4:9; 1 Cor. 5:2; (e) of grief for those in a local church who show no repentance for evil committed, 2 Cor. 12:21, RV, "mourn" (KJV, "bewail").

3. **threneo** (*2354*), "to lament, wail" (akin to **threnos**, "a lamentation, a dirge"), is used (a) in a general sense, of the disciples during the absence of the Lord, John 16:20, "lament"; (b) of those who sorrowed for the sufferings and the impending crucifixion of the Lord, Luke 23:27, "lamented"; the preceding word is **kopto** (No. 1); (c) of "mourning" as for the dead, Matt. 11:17, RV, "wailed" (KJV, "have mourned"); Luke 7:32 (ditto).

B. Nouns.

1. **odurmos** (*3602*), "lamentation, mourning," is translated "mourning" in Matt. 2:18 and 2 Cor. 7:7.

2. **penthos** (*3997*), akin to A, No. 2, "mourning," is used in Jas. 4:9; Rev. 18:7 (twice), RV, "mourning" (KJV, "sorrow"); v. 8, "mourning"; 21:4, RV, "mourning" (KJV, "sorrow").

MOUTH

Old Testament

peh (*6310*) "mouth; edge; opening; entrance; collar; utterance; order; command; evidence." **peh** can be translated "mouth," meaning of the entrance orifice of the body on the face, for ingestion, breathing, and communication, Gen. 8:11; Num. 22:28; 1 Sam. 14:27. It should be noted that the mouth may include the area of the mouth, including lips and tongue. Other renderings related to the mouth include "taste," meaning of a desire for tasting a certain food, Gen. 25:28, and the related state of "hunger," with the meaning of the physical desire for food, Prov. 16:26; and "communication, speech," meaning the speaking function of the mouth that gives information, exhortation, or commands, Gen. 41:40.

peh can be translated more generally, "opening," meaning the entrance area to a space, making that space accessible, like a door or gate "opening," or more limited space as a "collar," on a piece of clothing, Gen. 29:2; Exod. 28:32; Psa. 133:2. *peh* can be translated "edge," the sharp, thin shape of a sword or knife, Gen. 34:26. This can also mean "double-edged," as the shape of a sword or knife, Judg. 3:16. So also *peh* can be translated "part, number, portion," a single unit of something which can be numbered, Gen. 47:12; Deut. 21:17; 2 Kin. 2:9. Then *peh* can be translated "end, border, extremity," the outer geographical limits of the boundaries of a space, 2 Kin. 10:21; 21:16.

Finally, *peh* can also be used in a combination of Hebrew words. One of the more common phrases is *peh el peh*, translated "face to face," (lit. "mouth to mouth") with the meaning of a position of persons across from each other, Num. 12:8, and in some contexts it has a focus on personal relationship, Jer. 32:4; 34:3. The phrase *pi shenayim* (literally, "two mouths") has two different meanings. In Deut. 21:17 it means "double portion" (two parts). This same phrase, however, also means "two thirds," Zech. 13:8.

New Testament

stoma (4750), akin to *stomachos* (which originally meant "a throat, gullet"), is used (a) of "the mouth" of man, e.g., Matt. 15:11; of animals, e.g., Matt. 17:27; 2 Tim. 4:17 (figurative); Heb. 11:33; Jas. 3:3; Rev. 13:2 (2nd occurrence); (b) figuratively of "inanimate things," of the "edge" of a sword, Luke 21:24; Heb. 11:34; of the earth, Rev. 12:16; (c) figuratively, of the "mouth," as the organ of speech, (1) of Christ's words, e.g., Matt. 13:35; Luke 11:54; Acts 8:32; 22:14; 1 Pet. 2:22; (2) of human, e.g., Matt. 18:16; 21:16; Luke 1:64; Rev. 14:5; as emanating from the heart, Matt. 12:34; Rom. 10:8, 9; of prophetic ministry through the Holy Spirit, Luke 1:70; Acts 1:16; 3:18; 4:25; of the destructive policy of two world potentates at the end of this age, Rev. 13:2, 5, 6; 16:13 (twice); of shameful speaking, Eph. 4:29 and Col. 3:8; (3) of the Devil speaking as a dragon or serpent, Rev. 12:15, 16; 16:13; (d) figuratively, in the phrase "face to face" (lit., "mouth to mouth"), 2 John 12; 3 John 14; (e) metaphorically, of "the utterances of the Lord, in judgment," 2 Thess. 2:8; Rev. 1:16; 2:16; 19:15, 21; of His judgment upon a local church for its lukewarmness, Rev. 3:16; (f) by metonymy, for "speech," Matt. 18:16; Luke 19:22; 21:15; 2 Cor. 13:1.

MULTIPLY

Old Testament

A. Verb.

rabah (7235), "to multiply, become numerous, become great." Basically this word connotes numerical increase, either of things or of a length of time, Gen. 1:22; cf. Job 29:18. *rabah* sometimes refers to increasing in wealth, although in such cases the material is clearly specified, cf. Deut. 8:13. In a special nuance this verb signifies the process of growing up, Job 39:4. *rabah* can also be used of the end product, Ezek. 16:7. A somewhat different nuance occurs in Ezek. 19:2, where the verb speaks of a parent's care for an offspring.

B. Nouns.

marbeh, which appears once means "abundance," Isa. 33:23. *marbit*, which is found 5 times, refers to a "greater number," 1 Sam. 2:33, or the "greater half," 2 Chron. 9:6. *tarbut* has a single appearance to mean " increase," Num. 32:14. *tarbit*, which occurs 6 times, can mean "interest, increment, usury," Lev. 25:36.

New Testament

1. *plethuno* (*4129*), used (a) transitively, denotes "to cause to increase, to multiply," 2 Cor. 9:10; Heb. 6:14 (twice); in the passive voice, "to be multiplied," Matt. 24:12, RV, "(iniquity) shall be multiplied" (KJV, "shall abound"); Acts 6:7; 7:17; 9:31; 12:24; 1 Pet. 1:2; 2 Pet. 1:2; Jude 2; (b) intransitively it denotes "to be multiplying," Acts 6:1, RV, "was multiplying" (KJV, "was multiplied").

2. *pleonazo* (*4121*), used intransitively, "to abound," is translated "being multiplied" in the RV of 2 Cor. 4:15 (KJV, "abundant"); the active voice, aorist tense, here would be more accurately rendered "having superabounded" or "superabounding" or "multiplying."

MULTITUDE

Old Testament

A. Noun.

hamon (1995), "multitude; lively commotion; agitation; tumult; uproar; commotion; turmoil; noise; crowd; abundance." The word represents a "lively commotion or agitation," Isa. 63:15; the stirring or agitation of a crowd of people, 2 Sam. 18:29. In Isa. 17:12 the word is synonymously parallel to *sha'on*, "rumbling."

hamon sometimes means a "multitude or crowd" from which a tumult may arise. Frequently the word represents a large army, Judg. 4:7; cf. 1 Sam. 14:16. Elsewhere *hamon* represents a whole people, 2 Sam. 6:19. Finally, any great throng, or a great number of people, Gen. 17:4; or of things, 1 Chron. 29:16; Ps. 37:16; cf. Eccl. 5:10. Finally, *hamon* refers to a group of people organized around a king, specifically, his courtiers, Ezek. 31:2.

B. Verb.

hamah (1993), "to make a noise, be tumultuous, roar, groan, bark, sound, moan," Psalm 83:2.

New Testament

ochlos (3793) is used frequently in the four Gospels and the Acts; elsewhere only in Rev. 7:9; 17:15; 19:1, 6; it denotes (a) "a crowd or multitude of persons, a throng," e.g., Matt. 14:14, 15; 15:33; often in the plural, e.g., Matt. 4:25; 5:1; with *polus*, "much" or "great," it signifies "a great multitude," e.g., Matt. 20:29, or "the common people," Mark 12:37, perhaps preferably "the mass of the people." Field supports the meaning in the text, but either rendering is suitable. The mass of the people was attracted to Him (for the statement "heard Him gladly" cf. what is said in Mark 6:20 of Herod Antipas concerning John the Baptist); in John 12:9, "the common people," RV, stands in contrast with their leaders (v. 10); Acts 24:12, RV, "crowd"; (b) "the populace, an unorganized multitude," in contrast to *demos*, "the people as a body politic," e.g., Matt. 14:5; 21:26; John 7:12 (2nd part); (c) in a more general sense, "a multitude or company" e.g., Luke 6:17, RV, "a (great) multitude (of His disciples)," KJV, "the company"; Acts 1:15, "a multitude (of persons)," RV, KJV, "the number (of names)"; Acts 24:18, RV, "crowd" (KJV, "multitude").

MURDER

phonos (5408) is used (a) of a special act, Mark 15:7; Luke 23:19, 25; (b) in the plural, of "murders" in general, Matt. 15:19; Mark 7:21 (Gal. 5:21, in some inferior mss.); Rev. 9:21; in the singular, Rom. 1:29; (c) in the sense of "slaughter," Heb. 11:37, "they were slain with the sword," lit., "(they died by) slaughter (of the sword)"; in Acts 9:1, "slaughter."

MURDERER

M

1. *phoneus* (5406), akin to *phoneuo* and *phonos*, is used (a) in a general sense, in the singular, 1 Pet. 4:15; in the plural, Rev. 21:8; 22:15; (b) of those guilty of particular acts, Matt. 22:7; Acts 3:14, lit. "a man (*aner*), a murderer"; 7:52; 28:4.

2. *anthropoktonos* (443), an adjective lit., "manslaying" used as a noun, "a manslayer, murderer" (*anthropos*, "a man," *kteino*, "to slay"), is used of Satan, John 8:44; of one who hates his brother, and who, being a "murderer," has not eternal life, 1 John 3:15 (twice).

3. *patroloas* (or *patral*—) (3964) "a murderer of one's father," occurs in 1 Tim. 1:9.

MURMUR, MURMURING

A. Verbs.

1. *gonguzo* (1111), "to mutter, murmur, grumble, say anything in a low tone" (Eng., "gong"), an onomatopoeic word, representing the significance by the sound of the word, as in the word "mur-

mur' itself, is used of the laborers in the parable of the house-holder, Matt. 20:11; of the scribes and Pharisees, against Christ, Luke 5:30; of the Jews, John 6:41, 43, of the disciples, 6:61; of the people, 7:32 (of debating secretly); of the Israelites, 1 Cor. 10:10 (twice).

2. *diagonguzo* (*1234*), lit., "to murmur through" (*dia*, i.e., "through a whole crowd," or "among themselves"), is always used of indignant complaining, Luke 15:2; 19:7.

B. Noun.

gongusmos (*1112*), "a murmuring, muttering" (akin to A, No. 1), is used (a) in the sense of secret debate among people, John 7:12 (as with the verb in v. 32); (b) of displeasure or complaining (more privately than in public), said of Grecian Jewish converts against Hebrews, Acts 6:1; in general admonitions, Phil. 2:14; 1 Pet. 4:9, RV, "murmuring" (KJV "grudging").

MURMURER

gongustes (*1113*), "a murmurer" (akin to A, No. 1, and B, above), "one who complains," is used in Jude 16, especially perhaps of ut-terances against God (see v. 15).

MYRRH

A. Noun.

smurna (*4666*), whence the name "Smyrna," a word of Semitic origin, Heb., *mor*, from a root meaning "bitter," is a gum resin from a shrubby tree, which grows in Yemen and neighboring re-gions of Africa; the fruit is smooth and somewhat larger than a pea. The color of myrrh varies from pale reddish-yellow to red-dish-brown or red. The taste is bitter, and the substance astrin-gent, acting as an antiseptic and a stimulant. It was used as a per-fume, Ps. 45:8, where the language is symbolic of the graces of the Messiah; Prov. 7:17; Song of Sol. 1:13; 5:5; it was one of the ingre-dients of the "holy anointing oil" for the priests, Ex. 30:23 (RV, "flowing myrrh"); it was used also for the purification of women, Esth. 2:12; for embalming, John 19:39; as an anodyne see B), it was one of the gifts of the Magi, Matt. 2:11.

B. Verb.

smurnizo (*4669*) is used transitively in the NT, with the meaning "to mingle or drug with myrrh," Mark 15:23; the mixture was doubtless offered to deaden the pain (Matthew's word "gall" sug-gests that "myrrh" was not the only ingredient). Christ refused to partake of any such means of alleviation; He would retain all His mental power for the complete fulfillment of the Father's will.

MYSTERY

musterion (*3466*), primarily that which is known to the *mustes*, "the initiated" (from *mueo*, "to initiate into the mysteries"; cf. Phil. 4:12, *mueomai*, "I have learned the secret," RV). In the NT it denotes, not the mysterious (as with the Eng. word), but that which, being outside the range of unassisted natural apprehension, can be made known only by divine revelation, and is made known in a manner and at a time appointed by God, and to those only who are illumined by His Spirit. In the ordinary sense a "mystery" implies knowledge withheld; its Scriptural significance is truth revealed. Hence the terms especially associated with the subject are "made known," "manifested," "revealed," "preached," "understand," "dispensation." The definition given above may be best illustrated by the following passage: "the mystery which hath been hid from all ages and generations: but now hath it been manifested to His saints" (Col. 1:26, RV). It is used of:

(a) spiritual truth generally, as revealed in the gospel, 1 Cor. 13:2; 14:2 [cf. 1 Tim. 3:9]. Among the ancient Greeks "the mysteries" were religious rites and ceremonies practiced by secret societies into which any one who so desired might be received. Those who were initiated into these "mysteries" became possessors of certain knowledge, which was not imparted to the uninitiated, and were called "the perfected," cf. 1 Cor. 2:6-16 where the Apostle has these "mysteries" in mind and presents the gospel in contrast thereto; here "the perfected" are, of course the believers, who alone can perceive the things revealed; (b) Christ, who is God Himself revealed under the conditions of human life, Col. 2:2; 4:3, and submitting even to death, 1 Cor. 2:1 [in some mss., for *marturion*, testimony], 7, but raised from among the dead, 1 Tim. 3:16, that the will of God to coordinate the universe in Him, and subject it to Him, might in due time be accomplished, Eph. 1:9 (cf. Rev. 10:7), as is declared in the gospel Rom. 16:25; Eph. 6:19; (c) the Church, which is Christ's Body, i.e., the union of redeemed men with God in Christ, Eph. 5:32 [cf. Col. 1:27]; (d) the rapture into the presence of Christ of those members of the Church which is His Body who shall be alive on the earth at His Parousia, 1 Cor. 15:51; (e) the operation of those hidden forces that either retard or accelerate the Kingdom of Heaven (i.e., of God), Matt. 13:11; Mark 4:11; (f) the cause of the present condition of Israel, Rom. 11:25; (g) the spirit of disobedience to God, 2 Thess. 2:7; Rev. 17:5, 7, cf. Eph. 2:2.

To these may be added (h) the seven local churches, and their angels, seen in symbolism, Rev. 1:20; (i) the ways of God in grace, Eph. 3:9. The word is used in a comprehensive way in 1 Cor. 4:1.

M

N

NAIL (Noun and Verb)

A. Noun.

helos (2247) A device to fasten an object to another object, made of tempered metal such as iron, and pounded into a sharpened point on one end, and a blunt end on the other, Used in the Crucifixion by nailing through the hole in the wrist bones (so, considered the upper part of the hand), and just above the ankle bones, John 20:25.

B. Verb.

proseloo (4338), "to nail to" (*pros*, "to," and a verbal form of A), is used in Col. 2:14, in which the figure of a bond (ordinances of the Law) is first described as cancelled, and then removed; the idea in the verb itself is not that of the cancellation, to which the taking out of the way was subsequent, but of nailing up the removed thing in triumph to the cross. The death of Christ not only rendered the Law useless as a means of salvation, but gave public demonstration that it was so.

NAKED (Adjective and Verb), NAKEDNESS
Old Testament

A. Nouns.

'erwah (6172), "nakedness; indecent thing." This word represents male or female sexual organs. In its first biblical appearance *'erwah* implies shameful exposure, Gen. 9:22-23; symbolical of shame, Lam. 1:8; euphemism for cohabitation, Lev. 18:6. The phrase "indecent thing" represents any uncleanness. In Deut. 24:1 *'erwah* appears to bear this emphasis on any violation of the laws of purity—if a groom is dissatisfied with his bride, Deut. 22:13ff. The "undefended parts" or "nakedness" of a land is represented by *'erwah* in Gen. 42:9.

ma'ar, which refers to "sexual nakedness," appears in a figurative sense in Nah. 3:5. *'Erom* appears as a noun abstract in several instances, Ezek. 16:7, 39.

Two nouns, *ta'ar* and *morah*, have a different significance. *ta'ar*, which occurs 13 times, means "razor," Num. 6:5, or a "knife" to sharpen scribal pens, Jer. 36:23. The word's meaning of a "sword sheath," 1 Sam. 17:51, has a cognate in Ugaritic. ***morah*** also means "razor,"1 Sam. 1:11.

B. Adjectives.

'arom (6174), "naked," Gen. 2:25. Another adjective, is ***'eryah***, with the same meaning is found in Ezek. 16:22.

C. Verb.

'arah (6168), "to pour out," Isa. 32:15; "make bare," Lev. 20:19; "destroy," Isa. 3:17; "spread oneself out," Ps. 37:35.

New Testament

A. Adjective.

gumnos (*1131*) signifies (a) "unclothed," Mark 14:52; in v. 51 it is used as a noun ("*his*" and "*body*" being italicized); (b) "scantily or poorly clad," Matt. 25:36, 38, 43, 44; Acts 19:16 (with torn garments); Jas. 2:15; (c) "clad in the undergarment only" (the outer being laid aside), John 21:7; (d) metaphorically, (1) of "a bare seed," 1 Cor. 15:37; (2) of "the soul without the body," 2 Cor. 5:3; (3) of "things exposed to the all-seeing eye of God," Heb. 4:13; (4) of "the carnal condition of a local church," Rev. 3:17; (5) of "the similar state of an individual," 16:15; (6) of "the desolation of religious Babylon," 17:16.

B. Verb.

gumniteuo (*1130*), "to be naked or scantily clad" (akin to A), is used in 1 Cor. 4:11. In the *Koine* writings it is used of being light-armed.

C. Noun.

gumnotes (*1132*), "nakedness" (akin to A), is used (a) of "want of sufficient clothing," Rom. 8:35; 2 Cor. 11:27; (b) metaphorically, of "the nakedness of the body," said of the condition of a local church, Rev. 3:18.

NAME

Old Testament

shem (8034), "name; reputation; memory; renown." Sometimes this word is used in the sense of a name as an identification appears in Gen. 2:19, though not always. ***shem*** can be a synonym for "reputation" or "fame," Gen. 11:4. To "give a name for one" is to make him famous, 2 Sam. 7:23. If a name goes forth for one, his "reputation" of fame is made known, Ezek. 16:14. Fame may include power, 2 Sam. 23:18.

This word is sometimes a synonym for "memory," 2 Sam. 14:7. In this respect "name" may include property, or an inheritance, Num. 27:4. ***shem*** can connote "renown" and "continuance" (in those remaining after one), Num. 16:2. This significance is in the phrase "to raise up his name after him," cf. Deut. 9:14; 25:6; Ruth 4:5.

New Testament

A. Noun.

onoma (3686) is used (I) in general of the "name" by which a person or thing is called, e.g., Mark 3:16, 17, "(He) surnamed," lit., "(He added) the name"; 14:32, lit., "(of which) the name (was)"; Luke 1:63; John 18:10, sometimes translated "named," e.g., Luke 8:5, "named (Zacharias)," lit., "by name"; in the same verse, "named (Elizabeth)," lit., "the name of her," an elliptical phrase, with "was" understood; Acts 8:9, RV, "by name," 10:1; the "name" is put for the reality in Rev. 3:1; in Phil. 2:9, the "Name" represents "the title and dignity" of the Lord, as in Eph. 1:21 and Heb. 1:4;

(II) for all that a "name" implies, of authority, character, rank, majesty, power, excellence, etc., of everything that the "name" covers: (a) of the "Name" of God as expressing His attributes, etc., e.g., Matt. 6:9; Luke 1:49; John 12:28; 17:6, 26; Rom. 15:9; 1 Tim. 6:1; Heb. 13:15; Rev. 13:6; (b) of the "Name" of Christ, e.g., Matt. 10:22; 19:29; John 1:12; 2:23; 3:18; Acts 26:9; Rom. 1:5; Jas. 2:7; 1 John 3:23; 3 John 7; Rev. 2:13; 3:8; also the phrases rendered "in the name"; these may be analyzed as follows: (1) representing the authority of Christ, e.g., Matt. 18:5 (with *epi*, "on the ground of My authority"); so Matt. 24:5 (falsely) and parallel passages; as substantiated by the Father, John 14:26; 16:23 (last clause), RV; (2) in the power of (with *en*, "in"), e.g., Mark 16:17; Luke 10:17; Acts 3:6; 4:10; 16:18; Jas. 5:14; (3) in acknowledgement or confession of, e.g., Acts 4:12; 8:16; 9:27, 28; (4) in recognition of the authority of (sometimes combined with the thought of relying or resting on), Matt. 18:20; cf. 28:19; Acts 8:16; 9:2 (*eis*, "into"); John 14:13; 15:16; Eph. 5:20; Col. 3:17; (5) owing to the fact that one is called by Christ's "Name" or is identified with Him, e.g. 1 Pet. 4:14 (with *en*, "in"); with *heneken*, "for the sake of," e.g., Matt. 19:29; with *dia*, "on account of," Matt. 10:22; 24:9; Mark 13:13; Luke 21:17; John 15:21; 1 John 2:12; Rev. 2:3.

(III) as standing, by metonymy, for "persons," Acts 1:15; Rev. 3:4; 11:13 (RV, "persons").

B. Verbs.

1. *onomazo* (3687) denotes (a) "to name," "mention," or "address by name," Acts 19:13, RV, "to name" (KJV, "to call"); in the passive voice, Rom. 15:20; Eph. 1:21; 5:3; to make mention of the "Name" of the Lord in praise and worship, 2 Tim. 2:19; (b) "to name, call, give a name to," Luke 6:13, 14; passive voice, 1 Cor. 5:11, RV, "is named" (KJV, "is called"); Eph. 3:15 (some mss. have the verb in this sense in Mark 3:14 and 1 Cor. 5:1).

2. *eponomazo* (2028), "to call by a name, surname" (*epi*, "on," and

No. 1), is used in Rom. 2:17, passive voice, RV, "bearest the name of" (KJV, "art called").

3. *prosagoreuo* (4316) primarily denotes "to address, greet, salute"; hence, "to call by name," Heb. 5:10, RV, "named (of God, a High Priest)" (KJV, "called"), expressing the formal ascription of the title to Him whose it is; "called" does not adequately express the significance.

4. *kaleo* (2564), "to call," is translated "named" in Acts 7:58, RV (KJV, "whose name was").

NARRATIVE

diegesis (1335), translated "a declaration" in the KJV of Luke 1:1, denotes a "narrative," RV (akin to *diegeomai*, "to set out in detail, recount, describe").

NARROW

A. Adjective.

stenos (4728), from a root *sten*-, seen in *stenazo*, "to groan," *stenagmos*, "groaning" (Eng., "stenography," lit., "narrow writing"), is used figuratively in Matt. 7:13, 14, of the gate which provides the entrance to eternal life; "narrow" because it runs counter to natural inclinations, and "the way" is similarly characterized; so in Luke 13:24 (where the more intensive word *agonizomai*, "strive," is used); RV, "narrow" (KJV, "strait") in each place.

B. Verb.

thlibo (2346), "to press," is translated "narrow" in Matt. 7:14, KJV, lit., "narrowed" (RV, "straitened"; the verb is in the perfect participle, passive voice), i.e., hemmed in, like a mountain gorge; the way is rendered "narrow" by the divine conditions, which make it impossible for any to enter who think the entrance depends upon self-merit, or who still incline towards sin, or desire to continue in evil.

NATION

Old Testament

goy (1471), "nation; people; heathen." *goy* refers to a "people or nation," usually with overtones of territorial or governmental unity/identity, Gen. 12:2; cf. Num. 14:12. So *goy* represents a group of individuals who are considered as a unit with respect to origin, language, land, jurisprudence, and government, Gen. 10:5; Deut. 4:32ff. The word *'am*, "people, nation," suggests subjective personal interrelationships based on common familial ancestry and/or a covenantal union, while *goy* suggests a political entity with a land of its own, Exod. 33:13. *goy* may be used of a people, however, apart from its territorial identity, Exod. 19:6.

goy is sometimes almost a derogatory name for non-Israelite groups, or the "heathen," Lev. 26:33. This negative connotation is not always present, however, when the word is used of the heathen, Num. 23:9.

New Testament

1. *ethnos* (*1484*), originally "a multitude," denotes (a) "a nation" or "people," e.g., Matt. 24:7; Acts 10:35; the Jewish people, e.g., Luke 7:5; 23:2; John 11:48, 50-52; Acts 10:22; 24:2, 10, 17; in Matt. 21:43, the reference is to Israel in its restored condition, (b) in the plural "the nations" as distinct from Israel.

2. *genos* (*1085*), "a race," Philip. 3:5.

3. *allophulos* (*246*), "foreign, of another race" (*allos*, "another," *phulon*, "a tribe"), is used in Acts 10:28, "one of another nation."

NATURAL, NATURALLY

A. Adjectives.

1. *phusikos* (*5446*) originally signifying "produced by nature, inborn," from *phusis*, "nature," cf. Eng., "physical," "physics," etc., denotes (a) "according to nature," Rom. 1:26, 27; (b) "governed by mere natural instincts," 2 Pet. 2:12, RV, "(born) mere animals," KJV and RV marg., "natural (brute beasts)."

2. *psuchikos* (*5591*), "belonging to the *psuche*, soul" (as the lower part of the immaterial in man), "natural, physical," describes the man in Adam and what pertains to him (set in contrast to *pneumatikos* "spiritual"), 1 Cor. 2:14; 15:44 (twice), 46 (in the latter used as a noun); Jas. 3:15, "sensual" (RV marg., "natural" or "animal"), here relating perhaps more especially to the mind, a wisdom in accordance with, or springing from, the corrupt desires and affections; so in Jude 19.

B. Noun.

genesis (*1078*), "birth," is used in Jas. 1:23, of the "natural face," lit., "the face of his birth," "what God made him to be" (Hort).

C. Adverb.

phusikos (*5447*), "naturally, by nature" (akin to A, No. 1), is used in Jude 10.

NATURE

1. *phusis* (*5449*), from *phuo*, "to bring forth, produce," signifies (a) "the nature" (i.e., the natural powers or constitution) of a person or thing, Eph. 2:3; Jas. 3:7 ("kind"); 2 Pet. 1:4; (b) "origin, birth," Rom. 2:27, one who by birth is a Gentile, uncircumcised, in contrast to one who, though circumcised, has become spiritually uncircumcised by his iniquity; Gal. 2:15; (c) "the regular law or order of nature," Rom. 1:26, against "nature" (*para*, "against"); 2:14, ad-

verbially, "by nature"; 1 Cor. 11:14; Gal. 4:8, "by nature (are no gods)," here "nature" is the emphatic word, and the phrase includes demons, men regarded as deified, and idols; these are gods only in name (the negative, *me*, denies not simply that they were gods, but the possibility that they could be).

2. *genesis* (1078) is used in the phrase in Jas. 3:6, "the wheel of nature," or "course of life," with a focus on the constant changes in life.

NEED, NEEDS, NEEDFUL

Old Testament

A. Noun.

'ebyon (34), "needy (person)." This noun refers, first, to someone who is poor in a material sense. Such a one may have lost the land of his inheritance, Exod. 23:11. He has come into difficult financial straits, Job 30:25, and perhaps lacks clothing, Job 31:19, or food, Ps. 132:15. Secondly, *'ebyon* may refer to the lack of social standing which causes a need for protection, Exod. 23:6; Job 29:16; cf. Prov. 31:9; Rom. 3:14-15. Divine provisions are encased in the Mosaic stipulations such as the seventh-year reversion of ancestral hereditary lands, Exod. 23:11, cancellation of loans, Deut. 15:4, and special extension of loans, Deut. 15:7, 9, 11. Thirdly, this noun sometimes describes one's spiritual condition before God, Amos 2:6. In this verse *'ebyon* is in synonymous parallelism to "righteous," which means that it describes a moral quality.

B. Verb.

'abah (14), "to accede, accept, consent." This verb means "to consent to" in Deut. 13:8.

New Testament

A. Nouns.

1. *chreia* (5532) denotes "a need," in such expressions as "there is a need"; or "to have need of" something, e.g., Matt. 3:14; 6:8; 9:12. In Luke 10:42 it is translated "needful," where the "one thing" is surely not one dish, or one person, but is to be explained according to Matt. 6:33 and 16:26. In Eph. 4:29, for the KJV, "(to the use (of edifying)," the RV more accurately has "(for edifying) as the need may be," marg., "the building up of the need," i.e., "to supply that which (is) needed in each case"; so Westcott, who adds "The need represents a gap in the life which the wise word 'builds up,' fills up solidly and surely." In Phil. 4:19 the RV has "every need of yours" (KJV, "all your need"); in 1 Thess. 4:12, RV, "need" (KJV, "lack"); in Acts 28:10, RV, "(such things) as we needed" (KJV, "as were necessary"), lit., "the things for the needs (plural)."

2. *ananke* (318), "a necessity, need," is translated "it must needs

be" in Matt. 18:7, with the verb "to be" understood (according to the best mss.); in Luke 14:18, "I must needs" translates the verb *echo*, "to have," with this noun as the object, lit., "I have need"; in Rom. 13:5 "(ye) must needs," lit., "(it is) necessary (to be subject)."

B. Verbs.

1. *chrezo* (5535), "to need, to have need of" (akin to *chre*, "it is necessary, fitting"), is used in Matt. 6:32; Luke 11:8; 12:30; Rom. 16:2, RV, "may have need" (KJV, "hath need"); 2 Cor. 3:1.

2. *dei* (1163), an impersonal verb, signifying "it is necessary," is rendered "must needs" in Mark 13:7; John 4:4; Acts 1:16, KJV (RV, "it was needful"); 17:3, KJV (RV, "it behooved"); (in some mss. in Acts 21:22); 2 Cor. 11:30; 12:1; in Acts 15:5, "it was needful."

3. *deon* (1163**), the neuter of the present participle of No. 2, is used as a noun, signifying "that which is needful, due, proper," in 1 Pet. 1:6, with the meaning "need," "(if) need (be)," with the verb to be understood.

4. *prosdeomai* (4326), "to want besides, to need in addition" (*pros*, "besides," *deomai*, "to want"), is used in Acts 17:25, "(as though) He needed (anything)"; the literal sense of *pros* is not to be stressed.

5. *opheilo* (3784), "to owe, be bound, obliged to do something," is translated "must ye needs," in 1 Cor. 5:10; in 7:36 it is used impersonally, signifying "it is due," and followed by the infinitive mood of *ginomai*, "to become, to occur, come about," lit. "it is due to become," translated "(if) need (so) require."

C. Adjectives.

1. *anankaioteros* (316*), the comparative degree of *anankaios*, "necessary," is translated "more needful" in Phil. 1:24.

2. *epitedeios* (2006), primarily, "suitable, convenient," then, "useful, necessary," is translated "needful" in Jas. 2:16, neuter plural, "necessaries."

NEEDLE

1. *rhaphis* (4476), from *rhapto*, "to sew," occurs in Matt. 19:24; Mark 10:25.

2. *belone* (956), akin to *belos*, "a dart," denotes a sharp point, hence, "a needle," Luke 18:25 (some mss. have No. 1).

Note: The idea of applying "the needle's eye" to small gates seems to be a modern one; there is no ancient trace of it. The Lord's object in the statement is to express human impossibility and there is no need to endeavor to soften the difficulty by taking the needle to mean anything more than the ordinary instrument. An attempt is sometimes made to explain the words as a reference to the small door, a little over 2 feet square, in the large heavy gate of a walled city. This mars the figure and receives no justification from the language and traditions of Palestine.

NEGLECT, NEGLIGENT

1. *ameleo* (272) denotes (a) "to be careless, not to care" (*a*, negative, *melei*, "it is a care"; from *melo*, "to care, to be a care"), Matt. 22:5, "made light of"; (b) "to be careless of, neglect," 1 Tim. 4:14; Heb. 2:3; 8:9, "I regarded (them) not."

2. *paratheoreo* (3865), primarily, "to examine side by side, compare" (*para*, "beside," *theoreo*, "to look at"), hence, "to overlook, to neglect," is used in Acts 6:1, of the "neglect" of widows in the daily ministration in Jerusalem.

NEIGHBOR

1. *geiton* (1069), lit., "one living in the same land," denotes "a neighbor," always plural in the NT, Luke 14:12; 15:6, 9; John 9:5.

2. *perioikos* (4040), an adjective, lit., "dwelling around" (*peri*, "around," *oikos*, "a dwelling"), is used as a noun in Luke 1:58, "neighbors".

3. *plesion* (4139), the neuter of the adjective *plesios* (from *pelas*, "near"), is used as an adverb accompanied by the article, lit., "the (one) near"; hence, one's "neighbor."

This and Nos. 1 and 2 have a wider range of meaning than that of the Eng. word "neighbor." There were no farmhouses scattered over the agricultural areas of Palestine; the populations, gathered in villages, went to and fro to their toil. Hence domestic life was touched at every point by a wide circle of neighborhood. The terms for neighbor were therefore of a very comprehensive scope. This may be seen from the chief characteristics of the privileges and duties of neighborhood as set forth in Scripture, (a) its helpfulness, e.g., Prov. 27:10; Luke 10:36; (b) its intimacy, e.g., Luke 15:6, 9; Heb. 8:11; (c) its sincerity and sanctity, e.g., Ex. 22:7, 10; Prov. 3:29; 14:21; Rom. 13:10; 15:2; Eph. 4:25; Jas. 4:12. The NT quotes and expands the command in Lev. 19:18, "to love one's neighbor as oneself"; see, e.g., Matt. 5:43; 19:19; 22:39; Mark 12:31, 33; Luke 10:27; Gal. 5:14; Jas. 2:8.

NEW; NEW MOON

Old Testament

A. Verb.

chadash (2318), "to renew," i.e., to reaffirm a relationship and have a prior state or condition exist once again, 1 Sam. 11:14.

B. Noun.

chodesh (2320), "new moon; month." The word refers to the day on which the crescent of the moon reappears, 1 Sam. 20:24; so a feast day occurs at this time, Isa. 1:14.

chodesh can refer to a "month," or the period from one new moon to another, Gen. 38:24; Exod. 13:4.

C. Adjective.

chadash (2319), "new; renewed." *chadash* means "new" both in the sense of recent or fresh (as the opposite of old) and in the sense of something not previously existing, a king, Exod. 1:8; new song (not existing before), Isa. 42:10; new contrasted to the former, Isa. 42:9; Jer. 31:31-34; cf. Ezek. 11:19; 18:31.

New Testament

1. *kainos* (2537) denotes "new," of that which is unaccustomed or unused, not "new" in time, recent, but "new" as to form or quality, of different nature from what is contrasted as old. "The new tongues," *kainos*, of Mark 16:17 are the "other tongues," *heteros*, of Acts 2:4. These languages, however, were "new" and "different," not in the sense that they had never been heard before, or that they were new to the hearers, for it is plain from v. 8 that this is not the case; they were new languages to the speakers, different from those in which they were accustomed to speak.

The new things that the Gospel brings for present obedience and realization are: a new covenant, Matt. 26:28 in some texts; a new commandment, John 13:34; a new creative act, Gal. 6:15; a new creation, 2 Cor. 5:17; a new man, i.e., a new character of manhood, spiritual and moral, after the pattern of Christ, Eph. 4:24; a new man, i.e., "the Church which is His (Christ's) body," Eph. 2:15.

The new things that are to be received and enjoyed hereafter are: a new name, the believer's, Rev. 2:17; a new name, the Lord's, Rev. 3:12; a new song, Rev. 5:9; a new Heaven and a new Earth, Rev. 21:1; the new Jerusalem, Rev. 3:12; 21:2; "And He that sitteth on the Throne said, Behold, I make all things new," Rev. 21:5.

kainos is translated "fresh" in the RV of Matt. 9:17; Mark 2:22 (in the best texts) and Luke 5:38, of wineskins.

2. *neos* (3501) signifies "new" in respect of time, that which is recent; it is used of the young, and so translated, especially the comparative degree "younger"; accordingly what is *neos* may be a reproduction of the old in quality or character. *neos* and *kainos* are sometimes used of the same thing, but there is a difference, as already indicated. Thus the "new man" in Eph. 2:15 (*kainos*) is "new" in differing in character; so in 4:24; but the "new man" in Col. 3:10 (*neos*) stresses the fact of the believer's "new" experience, recently begun, and still proceeding. "The old man in him...dates as far back as Adam; a new man has been born, who therefore is fitly so called" [i.e., *neos*], Trench, *Syn*. Sec. lx. The "New" Covenant in Heb. 12:24 is "new" (*neos*) compared with the Mosaic, nearly fifteen hundred years before; it is "new" (*kainos*) compared with the Mosaic, which is old in character, ineffective, 8:8, 13; 9:15.

3. **prosphatos** (4732), originally signifying "freshly slain," acquired the general sense of "new," as applied to flowers, oil, misfortune, etc. It is used in Heb. 10:20 of the "living way" which Christ "dedicated for us... through the veil...His flesh" (which stands for His expiatory death by the offering of His body, v. 10).

NEWNESS

kainotes (2538), akin to **kainos**, is used in the phrases (a) "newness of life," Rom. 6:4, i.e., life of a new quality; the believer, being a new creation (2 Cor. 5:17), is to behave himself consistently with this in contrast to his former manner of life; (b) "newness of the spirit," RV, Rom. 7:6, said of the believer's manner of serving the Lord. While the phrase stands for the new life of the quickened spirit of the believer, it is impossible to dissociate this (in an objective sense) from the operation of the Holy Spirit, by whose power the service is rendered.

NOBLE

Old Testament

A. Nouns.

'addir (117), "noble; principal; stately one." As a noun, *'addir* is paralleled to "mighty" in Judg. 5:13. The word also occurs in Jer. 14:3 and Jer. 30:21. In 2 Chron. 23:20 *'addir* is paralleled to "captains and governors." The word is applied to the Messiah; the Messiah is none other than God Himself, Isa. 33:21.

Two less frequently occurring nouns are *'adderet* and *'eder*. *'adderet* may mean "luxurious outer garment, mantle, cloak" Gen. 25:25; *'eder* may refer to a "luxurious outer garment" Mic. 2:8.

N

B. Adjectives.

'addir (117), "mighty; majestic." In its first appearance the adjective *'addir* describes God's superior (majestic) holiness which was demonstrated by His delivering Israel from Egyptian bondage, Exod. 15:11. The idea of superior power is also suggested here, cf. Exod. 15:6; 1 Sam. 4:8. It is God's eternal and sovereign might which overcame His enemies, Ps. 136:18—He was/is mightier than mighty kings. Hence, His name (His person) is lauded as sovereign in power and majesty, Ps. 8:1; Ps. 93:4.

Two other adjectives are related to this word. *'adderet* used as an adjective and a noun appears 12 times. In Ezek. 17:8 the word implies "noble or majestic": "It was planted in a good soil by great waters...that it might be a goodly [*'adderet*] vine." *'eder* occurs once as an adjective, Zech. 11:13; there it modifies the value of an amount of money.

C. Verb.

'adar (142), "to be majestic," Isa. 42:21.

New Testament

1. *eugenes* (2104), an adjective, lit., "well born" (*eu*, "well," and *genos*, "a family, race"), (a) signifies "noble," 1 Cor. 1:26; (b) is used with *anthropos*, "a man," i.e., "a nobleman," in Luke 19:12.

2. *eugenesteros* (2104*), the comparative degree of No. 1, occurs in Acts 17:11, "more noble," i.e., "more noble-minded."

3. *kratistos* (2903) is translated "most noble" in the KJV of Acts 24:3 and 26:25 (RV, most excellent).

NOBLEMAN

basilikos (937), an adjective, "royal, belonging to a king" (*basileus*), is used of the command, "thou shalt love thy neighbor as thyself," "the royal law," Jas. 2:8; this may mean a law which covers or governs other laws and therefore has a specially regal character (as Hort suggests), or because it is made by a King (a meaning which Deissmann assigns) with whom there is no respect of persons; it is used with the pronoun *tis*, "a certain one," in John 4:46, 49, of a courtier, one in the service of a king, "a nobleman" (some mss. have the noun *basiliskos*, "a petty king," in these two verses). It is used of a country in Acts 12:20, "the king's (country)," and of royal apparel in v. 21.

NOISE

A. Adverb.

rhoizedon (4500), from *rhoizos*, "the whistling of an arrow," signifies "with rushing sound," as of roaring flames, and is used in 2 Pet. 3:10, of the future passing away of the heavens.

B. Verbs.

1. *akouo* (191), "to hear," is translated "it was noised" in Mark 2:1 (passive voice), of the rapid spread of the information that Christ was "in the house" in Capernaum.

2. *dialaleo* (1255), lit., "to speak through," is rendered "were noised abroad" in Luke 1:65.

NOSE

A. Noun.

'ap (639) is translated by many different words, with their corresponding meanings:

'ap usually means parts of the body; and can be translated "nostril," meaning the breathing passage of the nose, as a particular part of the nose, Gen. 2:7; or "nose," meaning any part of the nose, internal cartilage or external protuberance of any creature, Gen.

3:19; 24:47; Pr 11:22; "face," meaning the entire front of the head, including eyes, nose, mouth, chin, etc., Gen. 19:1; or translated "breath," meaning the vapor and air which comes out of the lungs through the mouth, Song. 7:8.

'ap is also used figuratively, translated "anger, wrath, resentment," and so meaning to have a strong feeling of displeasure over a person or a situation, as a figurative extension of the nose as an area that can change color when blood rushes to it when one is angry, Gen. 27:45; and in phrases Gen. 30:2 it can mean "quick-tempered, hot-tempered," so pertaining to being angry with relatively little provocation, Prov. 14:17. "Long of nose" is "patient, slow to anger, tolerant, enduring," meaning not being easily angered in a potentially hostile situation, as a figurative extension of a nose not changing color (getting "hot") when one is angry, Prov. 16:32.

'ap can also be translated "before," lit., "face," meaning a spatial position in front of another object, 1 Sam. 25:23. 'ap is also translated "double portion," meaning an amount which is a multiple of twice as much, as a figurative extension of a pair of nostrils, 1 Sam. 1:5. 'ap lastly, is translated "pride, arrogance," meaning an improper haughtiness and self-confidence, as a moral failure, as a figurative extension of having one's nose high in the air, Psa. 10:4.

B. Verb.

'anap (599), "to be angry," Isa. 12:1.

NOTABLE, OF NOTE

1. **gnostos** (1110), an adjective, signifying "known" (from **ginosko**, "to know"), is used (a) as an adjective, most usually translated "known," whether of facts, e.g., Acts 1:19; 2:14; 4:10; or persons, John 18:15-16; it denotes "notable" in Acts 4:16, of a miracle; (b) as a noun, "acquaintance," Luke 2:44 and 23:49.

2. **episemos** (1978), primarily meant "bearing a mark," e.g., of money "stamped, coined," (from **epi**, "upon," and **sema**, "a mark, a sign"; cf. **semaino**, "to give a sign, signify, indicate," and **semeioo**, "to note"); it is used in the NT, metaphorically, (a) in a good sense, Rom. 16:7, "of note, illustrious," said of Andronicus and Junias; (b) in a bad sense, Matt. 27:16, "notable," of the prisoner Barabbas.

3. **epiphanes** (2016), "illustrious, renowned, notable" (akin to **epiphaino**, "to show forth, appear"; Eng., "epiphany"), is translated "notable" in Acts 2:20, of the great Day of the Lord. The appropriateness of this word (compared with Nos. 1 and 2) to that future occasion is obvious.

NOTE (Verb)

semeioo (4593), from **semeion**, "a sign, token," signifies "to mark, to note," in the middle voice, "to note for oneself," and is so used in 2 Thess. 3:14, in an injunction to take cautionary note of one who refuses obedience to the apostle's word by the Epistle.

NOUGHT (for, bring to, come to, set at)

A. Pronoun.

ouden (*3762*), "nothing" (the neuter of *oudeis*, no one), is translated "nought" in Acts 5:36.

B. Adverb.

dorean (*1432*), "freely, as a gift," is translated "for nought" in Gal. 2:21, RV (KJV, "in vain"); in 2 Thess. 3:8, in a denial by the apostle that he lived on the hospitality of others at Thessalonica.

C. Verbs.

1. *katargeo* (*2673*) is used in 1 Cor. 1:28, "(that) He might bring to nought"; 1 Cor. 2:6 (passive voice in the original); 1 Cor. 6:13, RV, "will bring to nought" (KJV "will destroy"); so 2 Thess. 2:8 and Heb. 2:14.

2. *exoutheneo* (*1848*), "to set at nought, treat with utter contempt, despise," is translated "set at nought" in Luke 18:9, RV (KJV, "despised"); in 23:11, "set (Him) at nought"; "was set at nought" in Acts 4:11; in Rom. 14:3, RV, "set at nought" (KJV, "despise"); v. 10, "set at nought."

3. *exoudeneo* or *exoudenoo* (*1847*) has the same meaning as No. 2, and is virtually the same word (*outhen* being another form of *ouden*, "nothing"), i.e., "to treat as nothing" (*ex*, intensive), and is translated "be set at nought" in Mark 9:12.

4. *ekpipto* (*1601*), "to fall out," is used in Rom. 9:6 in the sense of falling from its place, failing, of the word of God, RV, "hath come to nought" (KJV, "hath taken none effect").

5. *atheteo* (*114*), "to set aside, reject," is translated "set at nought" in Heb. 10:28, RV (KJV, "despised"); so Jude 8.

NOURISH, NOURISHMENT

1. *trepho* (*5142*), "to rear, feed, nourish," is translated by the verb "to nourish" in Jas. 5:5 (of luxurious living); Rev. 12:14 (of God's care for Israel against its enemies); so v. 6, RV (KJV, feed); in Acts 12:20, RV, "was fed" (KJV, "was nourished").

2. *anatrepho* (*397*), "to nurse, bring up" (*ana*, "up," and No. 1), is translated "nourished" in Acts 7:20 (KJV, "nourished up"); in 21, "nourished," KJV and RV.

3. *ektrepho* (*1625*), *ek*, "from, out of," and No. 1, primarily used of children, "to nurture, rear," is translated "nurture" of the care of one's own flesh, Eph. 5:29, and in Eph. 6:4, RV (KJV, "bring...up").

4. *entrepho* (*1789*), "to train up, nurture," is used metaphorical-

ly, in the passive voice, in 1 Tim. 4:6, of being "nourished" in the faith.

NOVICE

neophutos (3504), an adjective, lit., "newly-planted" (from *neos*, "new," and *phuo*, "to bring forth, produce"), denotes "a new convert, neophyte, novice," 1 Tim. 3:6, of one who by inexperience is unfit to act as a bishop or overseer in a church.

TO NUMBER, VISIT, PUNISH

A. Verb.

paqad (6485), "to number, visit, be concerned with, look after, make a search for, punish." The verb is used in an expression which is unique to Hebrew and which shows great intensity of meaning. Such an occurrence appears in Exod. 3:16ff., in which it is used twice in two different grammatical forms to portray the intensity of the action; the text reads (literally): "Looking after, I have looked after" (KJV, "I have surely visited"). The usage refers to God's intervention in His saving the children of Israel from their bondage in Egypt. The same verb in a similar expression can also be used for divine intervention for punishment: "Shall I not *visit* them for these things?," Jer. 9:9, which means literally: "Shall I not *punish* them for these things?"

However, the most common usage of the verb in the whole of the Old Testament is in the sense of "drawing up, mustering, or numbering," i.e., count and add up collections of objects or persons; as of troops for marching or battle, Exod. 30:12; or take a census, Num. 14:29.

B. Noun.

paqid (6496), "one who looks after." This noun, possibly means "one who draws up troops," hence "officer," 2 Chron. 24:11; Jer. 20:1.

NURSE

trophos (5162), translated "nurse" in 1 Thess. 2:7, there denotes a "nursing" mother, as is clear from the statement "cherisheth her own children"; this is also confirmed by the word *epios*, "gentle" (in the same verse), which was commonly used of the kindness of parents towards children.

OATH

1. *horkos* (3727) is primarily equivalent to *herkos*, "a fence, an enclosure, that which restrains a person"; hence, "an oath." The Lord's command in Matt. 5:33 was a condemnation of the minute and arbitrary restrictions imposed by the scribes and Pharisees in the matter of adjurations, by which God's Name was profaned. The injunction is repeated in Jas. 5:12. The language of the apostle Paul, e.g., in Gal. 1:20 and 1 Thess. 5:27 was not inconsistent with Christ's prohibition, read in the light of its context. Contrast the "oaths" mentioned in Matt. 14:7, 9; 26:72; Mark 6:26.

Heb. 6:16 refers to the confirmation of a compact among men, guaranteeing the discharge of liabilities; in their disputes "the oath is final for confirmation." This is referred to in order to illustrate the greater subject of God's "oath" to Abraham, confirming His promise; cf. Luke 1:73; Acts 2:30.

2. *horkomosia* (3728) denotes "an affirmation on oath" (from No. 1 and *omnumi*, "to swear"). This is used in Heb. 7:20-21 (twice), 28, of the establishment of the Priesthood of Christ, the Son of God, appointed a Priest after the order of Melchizedek, and "perfected for evermore."

OBEDIENCE, OBEDIENT, OBEY

A. Nouns.

1. *hupakoe* (5218), "obedience" (*hupo*, "under," *akouo*, "to hear"), is used (a) in general, Rom. 6:16 (1st part), RV, "(unto) obedience," KJV, "(to) obey"; here "obedience" is not personified, as in the next part of the verse, "servants...of obedience [see (c)], but is simply shown to be the effect of the presentation mentioned; (b) of the fulfillment of apostolic counsels, 2 Cor. 7:15; 10:6; Philem. 21; (c) of the fulfillment of God's claims or commands, Rom. 1:5 and 16:26, "obedience of faith," which grammatically might be objective, to the faith (marg.), or subjective, as in the text. Since faith is one of the main subjects of the Epistle, and is the initial act of obedience in the new life, as well as an essential characteristic thereof, the text rendering is to be preferred; Rom. 6:16 (2nd part); 15:18, RV "(for) the obedience," KJV, "(to make) obedient"; 16:19; 1 Pet. 1:2, 14, RV, "(children of) obedience," i.e., characterized by "obedience," KJV, "obedient (children)"; v. 22, RV, "obedience (to the

truth)," KJV, "obeying (the truth)"; (d) of "obedience" to Christ (objective), 2 Cor. 10:5; (e) of Christ's "obedience," Rom. 5:19 (referring to His death; cf. Phil. 2:8); Heb. 5:8, which refers to His delighted experience in constant "obedience" to the Father's will (not to be understood in the sense that He learned to obey).

2. *hupotage* (5292), subjection (*hupo*, "under," *tasso*, "to order"), is translated "obedience" in 2 Cor. 9:13, RV (KJV, "subjection").

B. Verbs.

1. *hupakouo* (5219), "to listen, attend" (as in Acts 12:13), and so, "to submit, to obey," is used of "obedience" (a) to God, Heb. 5:9; 11:8; (b) to Christ, by natural elements, Matt. 8:27; Mark 1:27; 4:41; Luke 8:25; (c) to disciples of Christ, Luke 17:6; (d) to the faith, Acts 6:7; the gospel, Rom. 10:16; 2 Thess. 1:8; Christian doctrine, Rom. 6:17 (as to a form or mold of teaching); (e) to apostolic injunctions, Phil. 2:12; 2 Thess. 3:14; (f) to Abraham by Sarah, 1 Pet. 3:6; (g) to parents by children, Eph. 6:1; Col. 3:20; (h) to masters by servants, Eph. 6:5; Col. 3:22; (i) to sin, Rom. 6:12; (j) in general, Rom. 6:16.

2. *peitho* (3982), "to persuade, to win over," in the passive and middle voices, "to be persuaded, to listen to, to obey," is so used with this meaning, in the middle voice, e.g., in Acts 5:36-37 (in v. 40, passive voice, "they agreed"); Rom. 2:8; Gal. 5:7; Heb. 13:17; Jas. 3:3. The "obedience" suggested is not by submission to authority, but resulting from persuasion.

peitho and *pisteuo*, "to trust," are closely related etymologically; the difference in meaning is that the former implies the obedience that is produced by the latter, cf. Heb. 3:18-19, where the disobedience of the Israelites is said to be the evidence of their unbelief. Faith is of the heart, invisible to men; obedience is of the conduct and may be observed. When a man obeys God he gives the only possible evidence that in his heart he believes God. Of course it is persuasion of the truth that results in faith (we believe because we are persuaded that the thing is true, a thing does not become true because it is believed), but *peitho*, in NT suggests an actual and outward result of the inward persuasion and consequent faith.

3. *peitharcheo* (3980), "to obey one in authority" (No. 2, and *arche*, "rule"), is translated "obey" in Acts 5:29, 32; "to be obedient," Titus 3:1, RV (KJV, "to obey magistrates"); in Acts 27:21, "hearkened."

4. *apeitheo* (544), "to disobey, be disobedient" (*a*, negative, and No. 2), is translated "obey not" in Rom. 2:8; 1 Pet. 3:1; 4:17.

C. Adjective.

hupekoos (5255), "obedient" (akin to A, No. 1), "giving ear, subject," occurs in Acts 7:39, RV, "(would not be) obedient," KJV,

"(would not) obey"; 2 Cor. 2:9; Phil. 2:8, where the RV "*even*" is useful as making clear that the "obedience" was not to death but to
the Father.

OBSERVATION, OBSERVE

A. Noun.

parateresis (3907), "attentive watching" (akin to *paratereo*, "to
observe"), is used in Luke 17:20, of the manner in which the kingdom of God (i.e., the operation of the spiritual kingdom in the
hearts of men) does not come, "in such a manner that it can be
watched with the eyes" (Grimm-Thayer), or, as KJV marg., "with
outward show."

B. Verb.

paratereo (3906), "to watch closely, observe narrowly," is translated "ye observe" in Gal. 4:10, where the middle voice suggests
that their religious observance of days, etc. was not from disinter-
ested motives, but with a view to their own advantage.

ODOR

osme (3744), "a smell, an odor" (akin to *ozo*, "to smell"), is translated "odor" in John 12:3; it is used metaphorically in Eph. 5:2, RV,
"an odor (of a sweet smell)," KJV, "(a sweet smelling) savor," of the
effects Godward of the sacrifice of Christ; in Phil. 4:18 of the effect
of sacrifice, on the part of those in the church at Philippi, who sent
material assistance to the apostle in his imprisonment. The word
is translated "savor" in 2 Cor. 2:14, 16 (twice).

OFFENCE (OFFENSE)

A. Nouns.

1. *skandalon* (4625) originally was "the name of the part of a trap
to which the bait is attached, hence, the trap or snare itself, as in
Rom. 11:9, RV, "stumblingblock," quoted from Psa. 69:22, and in
Rev. 2:14, for Balaam's device was rather a trap for Israel than a
stumblingblock to them, and in Matt. 16:23, for in Peter's words
the Lord perceived a snare laid for Him by Satan.

In NT *skandalon* is always used metaphorically, and ordinarily
of anything that arouses prejudice, or becomes a hindrance to
others, or causes them to fall by the way. Sometimes the hindrance is in itself good, and those stumbled by it are the wicked.

Thus it is used (a) of Christ in Rom. 9:33, "(a rock) of offense"; so
1 Pet. 2:8; 1 Cor. 1:23 (KJV and RV, "stumblingblock"), and of His
cross, Gal. 5:11 (RV, ditto); of the "table" provided by God for Israel, Rom. 11:9; (b) of that which is evil, e.g., Matt. 13:41, RV, "things
that cause stumbling" (KJV, "things that offend"), lit., "all stum-
blingblocks"; 18:7, RV, "occasions of stumbling" and "occasion";

Luke 17:1 (ditto); Rom. 14:13, RV, "an occasion of falling" (KJV, "an occasion to fall"), said of such a use of Christian liberty as proves a hindrance to another; 16:17, RV, "occasions of stumbling," said of the teaching of things contrary to sound doctrine; 1 John 2:10, "occasion of stumbling," of the absence of this in the case of one who loves his brother and thereby abides in the light. Love, then, is the best safeguard against the woes pronounced by the Lord upon those who cause others to stumble.

2. *proskomma* (*4348*), "an obstacle against which one may dash his foot" (akin to *proskopto*, "to stumble" or "cause to stumble"; *pros*, "to or against," *kopto*, "to strike"), is translated "offense" in Rom. 14:20, in v. 13, "a stumblingblock," of the spiritual hindrance to another by a selfish use of liberty (cf. No. 1 in the same verse); so in 1 Cor. 8:9. It is used of Christ, in Rom. 9:32-33, RV, "(a stone) of stumbling," and 1 Pet. 2:8, where the KJV also has this rendering.

3. *proskope* (*4349*), like No. 2, and formed from the same combination, occurs in 2 Cor. 6:3, RV, "occasion of stumbling" (KJV, "offense"), something which leads others into error or sin.

B. Adjective.

aproskopos (*677*), akin to A, No. 3, with *a*, negative, prefixed, is used (a) in the active sense, "not causing to stumble," in 1 Cor. 10:32, metaphorically of "refraining from doing anything to lead astray" either Jews or Greeks or the church of God (i.e., the local church), RV, "no occasion of stumbling" (KJV, "none offense"); (b) in the passive sense, "blameless, without stumbling," Acts 24:16, "(a conscience) void of offense"; Phil. 1:10, "void of (KJV, without) offense." The adjective is found occasionally in the papyri writings.

OFFEND

skandalizo (*4624*), signifies "to put a snare or stumblingblock in the way," always metaphorically in the NT, in the same ways as the noun, which see. It is used 14 times in Matthew, 8 in Mark, twice in Luke, twice in John; elsewhere in 1 Cor. 8:13 (twice) and 2 Cor. 11:29. It is absent in the most authentic mss. in Rom. 14:21. The RV renders it by the verb "to stumble," or "cause to stumble," in every place save the following, where it uses the verb "to offend," Matt. 13:57; 15:12; 26:31, 33; Mark 6:3; 14:27, 29.

OFFENDER

opheiletes (*3781*), "a debtor," is translated "offenders" in Luke 13:4, RV (RV and KJV marg., "debtors"; KJV, "sinners").

OFFER, OFFERING
Old Testament

A. Verb.

qarab (7126), "to offer, come near, approach"; i.e., to approach spatially, apart from any sense of intimacy, Gen. 12:11; Exod. 32:19; Num. 9:6. This verb also is used of temporal "nearness," in the sense that something is to occur, like a special occasion, or any occasion, even presenting sacrifice or meeting God, Deut. 15:9; Exod. 16:9. The word is also used of the imminence of foreboding events, Gen. 27:41. *qarab* is used also in the sense of relationship which is not spatial, Ps. 27:2, 3; in sexual relations, Gen. 20:4; cf. Deut. 22:14; Isa. 8:3.

B. Nouns.

qorban (7133), "offering; oblation," i.e., valuable products of the land and flock presented to the Lord, Lev. 1:2. Some other related nouns appear less frequently: *qarob*, "neighbor," Exod. 32:27; *qirbah* occurs twice with the meaning of drawing near to worship God and offer sacrifice, Ps. 73:28; Isa. 58:2.

minchah (4503), "grain offering; offering; tribute; present; gift; sacrifice; oblation." *minchah* is used many times in the Old Testament to designate a "gift" or "present" which is given by one person to another, Gen. 32:13-15; 43:11; 1 Kings 10:25. Frequently *minchah* is used in the sense of "tribute" paid to a king or overlord, so a gift which is more or less required, Judg. 3:15-23; 2 Sam. 8:2; Ps. 72:10. *minchah* is often used to refer to any "offering" or "gift" made to God, the produce of flock or the ground, Gen. 4:3-5; or later sacrifices in the Torah, Lev. 2:14; 14:10, 21; 23:13; Num. 7:13. Note that the KJV translators regularly use "meat" instead of "grain" to translate this word.

minchah provides an interesting symbolism for the prophet when he refers to the restoration of the Jews, Isa. 66:20. In his vision of the universal worship of God, even in Gentile lands, Malachi saw the *minchah* given as "a pure offering" to God by believers everywhere, Mal. 1:11.

terumah (8641), "heave offering; offering; oblation." In more than a third of its occurrences in the text, the KJV translates *terumah* as "heave offering," all of these instances being found in Exodus, Leviticus, Numbers (where the majority are found), and Deuteronomy. This translation apparently is derived from the fact that the word is based on the common Semitic root, "to be high, exalted." The inference seems to be that such "offerings" were raised high by the priest in some sort of motion as it was placed on the altar. This is clearly illustrated in Num. 15:20. *terumah* often is used to designate those gifts or contributions to God, but which were set apart specifically for the priests, Num. 5:9. Such "offerings" were to go to the priests because of a special covenant God had made, Num. 18:19, RSV. Such offerings, or contributions, sometimes were of grain or grain products, Lev. 7:13-14. Part of the animal sacrifices was also designated as a *terumah* for the priests, Lev. 7:32; cf. Lev. 10:14-15; Num. 6:20. This portion was for the sustenance of the priest, Deut. 14:28-29.

In order to provide for the materials necessary for the construction of the wilderness tabernacle, Moses was instructed to receive a voluntary "offering" or *terumah*, Exod. 25:3-9; 35:5, 6-8. The *terumah* sometimes was an "offering" which had the meaning of a tax, an obligatory assessment which was made against every Israelite male who was twenty years old or older, to be paid for the support of the tabernacle and later, the temple, Exod. 30:11-16; or as a ransom to God, 2 Sam. 24:1; or for a king's taxes, 1 Kings 12.

A very different use of *terumah* is found in Ezek. 45:1; 48:9, 20-21, where it refers to an "oblation" which was that portion of land on which the post-exilic temple was to be built, as well as accommodations for the priests and Levites. This tract of land is referred to as "the holy oblation," Ezek. 48:20; RSV, "holy portion," since it belongs to God just as much as the *terumah* which was given to Him as a sacrifice.

qorban (7133), "offering; oblation; sacrifice." *qorban* may be translated as "that which one brings near to God or the altar." It is not surprising, then, that the word is used as a general term for all sacrifices, whether animal or vegetable. The very first reference to "sacrifice" in Leviticus is to the *qorban* as a burnt "offering," Lev. 1:2-3; cf. Lev. 1:10; 3:2, 6; 4:23; or any offering of precious metals or other valuable materials, Num. 7:1-89.

qurban (7133), "wood offering." *qurban* is closely related to *qorban*, and it is found in Neh. 10:34; 13:31. Here it refers to the "wood offering" which was to be provided for the burning of the sacrifices in the Second Temple. Lots were to be cast among the people, priests, and Levites to determine who would bring in the "wood offering" or fuel at the scheduled times throughout the year.

'olah (5930), "whole burnt offering," *'olah*, is similar in meaning to the above words of sacrifice and offering to God. The special feature of this word is that it is an animal given as a sin offering and presented whole (and skinned) to God. The offering was then wholly consumed by fire on the altar, Gen. 8:20; Lev. 1:3-15. The animal skin was given to the priest as his portion, Lev. 7:8. The *'olah* was the most common sacrifice, given daily and also at special times, Exod. 29:38-42; Num. 28:11-29. The central significance of *'olah* as the "whole burnt offering" was the total surrender of the heart and life of the offerer to God. Sin offerings could accompany them when the offerer was especially concerned with a cover-

ing or expiation for sin, 2 Chron. 29:27. When peace offerings accompanied "burnt offerings," the offerer's concern focused on fellowship with God, 2 Chron. 29:31-35. Before the Mosaic legislation, it appears, the "whole burnt offering" served the full range of meanings expressed in all the various Mosaic sacrifices.

'ishsheh (801), "fire offering." All legitimate sacrifices had to be presented before God at His altar, and all of them involved burning to some degree. Thus they may all be called fire offerings. The word *'ishsheh* first occurs in Exod. 29:18: "And thou shalt burn the whole ram upon the altar: it is a burnt offering unto the Lord: it is a sweet savor, an offering made by fire unto the Lord."

'asham (817), "guilt offering; offense; guilt; gift of restitution; gift of atonement." The most frequent meaning of the word is "guilt offering," Lev. 5:6. This specialized kind of sin offering, Lev. 5:7, was to be offered when someone had been denied what was due to him. The valued amount defrauded was to be repaid plus 20 percent, Lev. 5:16; 6:5. Ritual infractions and periods of leprosy and defilement took from God a commodity or service rightfully belonging to Him and required repayment plus restitution. Every violation of property rights required paying full reparation and the restitution *price* (20 percent) to the one violated as well as presenting the guilt offering to God as the Lord of all (i.e., as a feudal lord over all). If the offended party was dead, reparation and restitution were made to God (i.e., given to the priests; Num. 5:5-10), usually a ram was offered, Lev. 14:14. In some passages, *'asham* is used of an offense against God and the guilt incurred by it, Gen. 26:10. In two verses, Num. 5:7-8, *'asham* represents the repayment made to one who has been wronged. This basic idea is extended so that the word comes to mean a gift made to God to remove guilt, 1 Sam. 6:3, or atone for sin, Isa. 53:10, other than the specified offerings to be presented at the altar.

C. Adjectives.

qarob (7138), "near," can represent nearness in space, Gen. 19:20; Ezek. 6:12; and an epistemological nearness, Deut. 30:14.

The adjective *qareb* parallels *qarob* in meaning. It represents intimate proximity (usually in a cultic context referring to cultic activity), Ezek. 45:4.

New Testament

A. Verbs.

1. *prosphero* (4374), primarily, "to bring to" (*pros*, "to," *phero*, "to bring"), also denotes "to offer," (a) of the sacrifice of Christ Himself, Heb. 8:3; of Christ in virtue of his High Priesthood (RV, "this *high priest*"; KJV, "this man"); 9:14, 25 (negative), 28; 10:12; (b) of offerings under, or according to, the Law, e.g., Matt. 8:4; Mark 1:44; Acts 7:42; 21:26; Heb. 5:1, 3; 8:3; 9:7, 9; 10:1-2, 8, 11; (c) of "offerings"

previous to the Law, Heb. 11:4, 17 (of Isaac by Abraham); (d) of gifts "offered" to Christ, Matt. 2:11, RV, "offered" (KJV, "presented unto"); (e) of prayers "offered" by Christ, Heb. 5:7; (f) of the vinegar "offered" to Him in mockery by the soldiers at the cross, Luke 23:36; (g) of the slaughter of disciples by persecutors, who think they are "offering" service to God, John 16:2, RV (KJV, "doeth"); (h) of money "offered" by Simon the sorcerer, Acts 8:18.

2. *anaphero* (399), primarily, "to lead" or "carry up" (*ana*), also denotes "to offer," (a) of Christ's sacrifice, Heb. 7:27; (b) of sacrifices under the Law, Heb. 7:27; (c) of such previous to the Law, Jas. 2:21 (of Isaac by Abraham); (d) of praise, Heb. 13:15; (e) of spiritual sacrifices in general, 1 Pet. 2:5.

3. *spendo* (4689), "to pour out as a drink offering, make a libation," is used figuratively in the passive voice in Phil. 2:17, "offered" (RV marg., "poured out as a drink offering"; KJV marg. "poured forth"). In 2 Tim. 4:6, "I am already being offered," RV (marg., "poured out as a drink-offering"), the apostle is referring to his approaching death, upon the sacrifice of his ministry. This use of the word is exemplified in the papyri writings.

B. Nouns.

1. *prosphora* (4376), lit., "a bringing to" (akin to A, No. 1), hence an "offering," in the NT a sacrificial "offering " (a) of Christ s sacrifice, Eph. 5:2; Heb. 10:10 (of His body); 10:14; negatively, of there being no repetition, 10:18; (b) of "offerings" under, or according to, the Law, Acts 21:26; Heb. 10:5, 8; (c) of gifts in kind conveyed to needy Jews, Acts 24:17; (d) of the presentation of believers themselves (saved from among the Gentiles) to God, Rom. 15:16.

2. *holokautoma* (3646), "a burnt offering," see *'olah* in Old Testament section

3. *anathema* (334) denotes "a gift set up in a temple a votive offering" (*ana*, "up," *tithemi*, "to place"), Luke 21:5, RV "offerings" (KJV, "gifts").

OFFICE

A. Nouns.

1. *praxis* (4234), "a doing, deed" (akin to *prasso*, "to do or practice"), also denotes "an acting" or "function," translated "office" in Rom. 12:4.

2. *hieroteia* (2405), or *hieratia*, denotes "a priest's office," Luke 1:9; Heb. 7:5, RV, "priest's office" (KJV "office of the priesthood").

B. Verb.

hierateuo (2407), "to officiate as a priest" (akin to A, No. 2) is translated "he executed the priest's office" in Luke 1:8. The word is frequent in inscriptions.

OFFICER

1. **huperetes** (5257), is translated "officer," with the following applications, (a) to a magistrate's attendant, Matt. 5:25; (b) to officers of the synagogue, or officers or bailiffs of the Sanhedrin, Matt. 26:58; Mark 14:54, 65; John 7:32, 45-46; 18:3, 12, 18, 22; 19:6; Acts 5:22, 26.

2. **praktor** (4233), lit., "one who does," or "accomplishes" (akin to **prasso**, "to do"), was used in Athens of one who exacts payment, a collector (the word is frequently used in the papyri of a public accountant); hence, in general, a court "officer," an attendant in a court of justice (so Deissmann); the word is used in Luke 12:58 (twice).

OFFSCOURING

peripsema (4067), "that which is wiped off"; in NT it means, "refuse, rubbish," i.e., "scum."

OFFSPRING

1. **gennema** (1081), akin to **gennao**, "to beget," denotes "the offspring of men and animals," Matt. 3:7; 12:34; 23:33; Luke 3:7, RV, "offspring" (KJV, "generation").

2. **genos** (1085), "a race, family," denotes "an offspring," Acts 17:28, 29; Rev. 22:16.

OIL

Old Testament

A. Noun.

shemen (8081), "(olive) oil; olive; perfume; olivewood." **shemen** means olive "oil," i.e., the viscous plant-oil that is derived by crushing and draining the liquid out of the olive fruit, Gen. 28:18; Exod. 25:6; 2 Kings 9:6. Olive oil was used in a wide variety of ceremonies, 2 Sam. 14:2; Ps. 23:5; cf. Lev. 14:17. **shemen** is used as a preservative on shield-leather, 2 Sam. 1:21, and in baking, Exod. 29:2, and as a medication, Ezek. 16:9, or lamp oil, Exod. 25:6. Its many uses made olive oil a valuable trade item, Ezek. 27:17, and of course food, Isa. 25:6. **shemen** is "a kind of perfume," or olive oil mixed with certain sweet-smelling herbs and ground-up barks as a perfume, Song of Sol. 1:3.

B. Verb.

The verb **saman**, means "to grow or be fat," Neh. 9:25; Jer. 5:28.

C. Adjective.

The adjective **shaman**, translated "fat," Ezek. 34:16; "rich" in the sense of fattening, Gen. 49:20; "fertile," Num. 13:20; "robust or muscular," Judg. 3:29; and "large," Hab. 1:16.

New Testament

elaion (*1637*), "olive oil"; in the NT the uses mentioned were (a) for lamps, in which the "oil" is a symbol of the Holy Spirit, Matt. 25:3-4, 8; (b) as a medicinal agent, for healing, Luke 10:34; (c) for anointing at feasts, Luke 7:46; (d) on festive occasions, Heb. 1:9, where the reference is probably to the consecration of kings; (e) as an accompaniment of miraculous power, Mark 6:13, or of the prayer of faith, Jas. 5:14. For its general use in commerce, see Luke 16:6; Rev. 6:6; 18:13.

OINTMENT

muron (*3464*), a word derived by the ancients from *muro*, "to flow," or from *murra*, "myrrh-oil" (it is probably of foreign origin). The "ointment" is mentioned in the NT in connection with the anointing of the Lord on the occasions recorded in Matt. 26:7, 9, 12; Mark 14:3-4; Luke 7:37-38, 46; John 11:2; 12:3 (twice), 5. The alabaster cruse mentioned in the passages in Matthew, Mark and Luke was the best of its kind, and the spikenard was one of the costliest of perfumes. "Ointments" were used in preparing a body for burial, Luke 23:56 ("ointments"). Of the act of the woman mentioned in Matt. 26:6-13, the Lord said, "she did it to prepare Me for burial"; her devotion led her to antedate the customary ritual after death, by showing both her affection and her understanding of what was impending. For the use of the various kinds of "ointments" as articles of commerce, see Rev. 18:13.

OLD

A. Adjectives.

1. *archaios* (*744*), "original, ancient" (from *arche*, "a beginning": Eng., "archaic," "archaeology," etc.), is used (a) of persons belonging to a former age," (to) them of old time," Matt. 5:21, 33, RV; in some mss. v. 27; the RV rendering is right; not ancient teachers are in view; what was said to them of old time was "to be both recognized in its significance and estimated in its temporary limitations, Christ intending His words to be regarded not as an abrogation, but a deepening and fulfilling" (Cremer); of prophets, Luke 9:8, 19; (b) of time long gone by, Acts 15:21; (c) of days gone by in a person's experience, Acts 15:7, "a good while ago," lit., "from old (days)," i.e., from the first days onward in the sense of originality, not age; (d) of Mnason, "an early disciple," Acts 21:16, RV, not referring to age, but to his being one of the first who had accepted the gospel from the beginning of its proclamation; (e) of things which are "old" in relation to the new, earlier things in contrast to things present, 2 Cor. 5:17, i.e., of what characterized and conditioned the time previous to conversion in a believer's experience, RV, "they are become new," i.e., they have taken on a new com-

O

plexion and are viewed in an entirely different way; (f) of the world (i.e., the inhabitants of the world) just previous to the Flood, 2 Pet. 2:5; (g) of the Devil, as "that old serpent," Rev. 12:9; 20:2, "old," not in age, but as characterized for a long period by the evils indicated.

2. *palaios* (3820), akin to Eng., "paleontology," etc., "of what is of long duration, old in years," etc., a garment, wine (in contrast to new), Matt. 9:16-17; Mark 2:21-22 (twice); Luke 5:36-37, 39 (twice); of the treasures of divine truth, Matt. 13:52 (compared with new); of what belongs to the past, e.g., the believer's former self before his conversion, his "old man"; "old" because it has been superseded by that which is new, Rom. 6:6; Eph. 4:22 (in contrast to *kainos*); Col. 3:9 (in contrast to *neos*); of the covenant in connection with the Law, 2 Cor. 3:14; of leaven, metaphorical of moral evil, 1 Cor. 5:7, 8 (in contrast to *neos*); of that which was given long ago and remains in force, an "old" commandment, 1 John 2:7 (twice), that which was familiar and well known in contrast to that which is fresh (*kainos*).

3. *presbuteros* (4245), "older, elder," is used in the plural, as a noun, in Acts 2:17, "old men."

B. Nouns.

1. *geron* (1088) denotes "an old man" (from the same root comes Eng., "gray"), John 3:4.

2. *presbutes* (4246), "an old man," Luke 1:18, is translated "aged" in Titus 2:2; Philem. 9.

3. *geras* (1094), "old age," occurs in Luke 1:36.

C. Adverbs.

1. *palai* (3819) denotes "long ago, of old," Heb. 1:1, RV, "of old time" (KJV, "in time past"); in Jude 4, "of old"; it is used as an adjective in 2 Pet. 1:9, "(his) old (sins)," lit., "his sins of old."

2. *ekpalai* (1597), "from of old, for a long time" (*ek*, "from," and No. 1), occurs in 2 Pet. 2:3, RV, "from of old" (KJV, "of a long time"); 3:5.

Note: In 1 Pet. 3:5, KJV, the particle *pote*, "once, formerly, ever, sometime," is translated "in the old time" (RV, "aforetime"); in 2 Pet. 1:21, "in old time" (RV, "ever"), KJV marg., "at any time."

D. Verbs.

1. *palaioo* (3822), akin to A, No. 2, denotes, in the active voice, "to make or declare old," Heb. 8:13 (1st part); in the passive voice, "to become old," of things worn out by time and use, Luke 12:33; Heb. 1:11, "shall wax old," lit., "shall be made old," i.e., worn out; in 8:13 (2nd part), RV, "is becoming old" (KJV "decayeth"); here and in the 1st part of the verse, the verb may have the meaning "to abrogate."

2. *gerasko* (1095), from *geras*, "old age" (akin to B, No. 1), "to

grow old," is translated "thou shalt be old," in John 21:18; "waxeth aged," Heb. 8:13, RV (KJV, "waxeth old").

OLDNESS

palaiotes (*3821*), from *palaios*, occurs in Rom. 7:6, of "the letter," i.e., "the law," with its rules of conduct, mere outward conformity to which has yielded place in the believer's service to a response to the inward operation of the Holy Spirit. The word is contrasted with *kainotes*, "newness."

OLD WIVES'

graodes (*1126*), an adjective, signifying "old-womanish" (from *graus*, "an old woman"), is said of fables, in 1 Tim. 4:7.

ONCE (at; for all)

1. *hapax* (*530*) denotes (a) "once, one time," 2 Cor. 11:25; Heb. 9:7, 26-27; 12:26-27; in the phrase "once and again," lit., "once and twice," Phil. 4:16; 1 Thess. 2:18; (b) "once for all," of what is of perpetual validity, not requiring repetition, Heb. 6:4; 9:28; 10:2; 1 Pet. 3:18; Jude 3, RV, "once for all" (KJV, "once"); v. 5 (ditto); in some mss. 1 Pet. 3:20 (so the KJV).

2. *ephapax* (*2178*), a strengthened form of No. 1 (*epi*, "upon"), signifies (a) "once for all," Rom. 6:10; Heb. 7:27, RV (KJV, "once"); 9:12 (ditto); 10:10; (b) "at once," 1 Cor. 15:6.

3. *pote* (*4218*) denotes "once upon a time, formerly, sometime," e.g., Rom. 7:9; Gal. 1:23, 1st part, RV, "once" (KJV, "in times past"); 2nd part, KJV and RV, "once"; Gal. 2:6, RV marg., "what they once were" (to be preferred to the text, "whatsoever they were"), the reference probably being to the association of the twelve apostles with the Lord during His ministry on earth; upon this their partisans based their claim for the exclusive authority of these apostles, which Paul vigorously repudiated; in Eph. 5:8, RV, "once" (KJV, "sometimes").

O

ONE ANOTHER or ONE... ANOTHER, ONE...THE OTHER

This translates a number of words and phrases in Greek, and one of the meanings of "one another" in English has the basic idea of reciprocity, i.e., the state or condition in which one has a relationship with another person, and in which one person does similar acts and words. The word in itself can have a negative or positive associative meaning. Here is an edited list of the "one-anothers" in the New Testament representing the Greek word *allelon* or *allelous*, which has the idea of mutuality and reciprocity. It is a beautiful and edifying concept pertaining to Christian interpersonal relationships. Jesus commands that Christians are to love one another, John 13:34-35; 15:12, 17. The NT writers give the Church varied exhortations to promote a rich church life, see Rom. 12:10, 16; 13:8; 14:13, 19; 15:5,7, 14; 16:16; 1 Cor.11:33; 12:25; Gal. 5:13, 15, 26; 6:2; Eph. 4:2,25, 32; 5:21; Phil. 2:3; Col. 3:9, 13; 1 Thess. 3:12; 4:9, 18; 5:11,15; Heb. 10:24; James 4:11; 5:9, 16; 1 Pet. 1:22; 4:9; 5:5; 1 John.3:11.

ONLY

1. **monos** (3441), "alone, solitary," is translated "only," e.g., in Matt. 4:10; 12:4; 17:8; 1 Cor. 9:6; 14:36; Phil. 4:15; Col. 4:11; 2 John 1; it is used as an attribute of God in John 5:44; 17:3; Rom. 16:27; 1 Tim. 1:17; 1 Tim. 6:15-16; Jude 4, 25; Rev. 15:4.

2. **monogenes** (3439), "only begotten" (No. 1 and **genos**, "off-spring"), has the meaning "only," of human offspring, in Luke 7:12; 8:42; 9:38; the term is one of endearment, or status, as well as of singleness in some contexts.

ONLY BEGOTTEN

monogenes (3439) is used five times, all in the writings of the apostle John, of Christ as the Son of God; it is translated "only be-gotten" in Heb. 11:17 of the relationship of Isaac to Abraham.

With reference to Christ, the phrase "the only begotten from the Father," John 1:14 indicates that as the Son of God He was the sole representative of the Being and character of the One who sent Him. In the original the definite article is omitted both before "only begotten" and before "Father," and its absence in each case serves to lay stress upon the characteristics referred to in the terms used. The apostle's object is to demonstrate what sort of glory it was that he and his fellow apostles had seen. That he is not merely making a comparison with earthly relationships is indicated by **para**, "from." The glory was that of a unique relationship and the word "begotten" does not imply a beginning of His Son-ship. It suggests relationship indeed, but must be distinguished from generation as applied to man.

We can only rightly understand the term "the only begotten" when used of the Son, in the sense of unoriginated relationship. "The begetting is not an event of time, however remote, but a fact irrespective of time. The Christ did not *become*, but necessarily and eternally *is* the Son. He, a Person, possesses every attribute of pure Godhood. This necessitates eternity, absolute being; in this respect He is not 'after' the Father" (Moule). The expression also suggests the thought of the deepest affection, as in the case of the OT word **yachid**, variously rendered, "only one," Gen. 22:2, 12; "only son," Jer. 6:26; Amos 8:10; Zech. 12:10; "only beloved," Prov. 4:3, and "darling," Ps. 22:20; 35:17.

In John 1:18 the clause "the only begotten son, which is in the bosom of the Father," expresses both His eternal union with the

Father in the Godhead and the ineffable intimacy and love between them, the Son sharing all the Father's counsels and enjoying all His affections. Another reading is *monogenes theos*, "God only-begotten." In John 3:16 the statement, "God so loved the world that He gave His only begotten son," must not be taken to mean that Christ became the only begotten son by incarnation. The value and the greatness of the gift lay in the Sonship of Him who was given. His Sonship was not the effect of His being given. In John 3:18 the phrase "the name of the only begotten son of God" lays stress upon the full revelation of God's character and will, His love and grace, as conveyed in the name of One who, being in a unique relationship to Him, was provided by Him as the object of faith. In 1 John 4:9 the statement "God hath sent His only begotten son into the world" does not mean that God sent out into the world one who at His birth in Bethlehem had become His Son.

OPEN, OPENING

A. Verbs.

1. *anoigo* (455) is used (1) transitively, (a) literally, of "a door or gate," e.g., Acts 5:19; graves, Matt. 27:52; a sepulchre, Rom. 3:13; a book, e.g., Luke 4:17; Rev. 5:2-5; 10:8; the seals of a roll, e.g., Rev. 5:9; 6:1; the eyes, Acts 9:40; the mouth of a fish, Matt. 17:27; "the pit of the abyss," Rev. 9:2, RV; heaven and the heavens, Matt. 3:16; Luke 3:21; Acts 10:11; Rev. 19:11; "the temple of the tabernacle of the testimony in heaven," Rev. 15:5; by metonymy, for that which contained treasures, Matt. 2:11; (b) metaphorically, e.g., Matt. 7:7-8; 25:11; Rev. 3:7; Hebraistically, "to open the mouth," of beginning to speak, e.g., Matt. 5:2; 13:35; Acts 8:32, 35; 10:34; 18:14; Rev. 13:6 (cf., e.g., Num. 22:28; Job. 3:1; Isa. 50:5), and of recovering speech, Luke 1:64; of the earth "opening," Rev. 12:16; of the "opening" of the eyes, Acts 26:18; the ears, Mark 7:35 (in the best mss.; some have No. 2); (2) intransitively (perfect tense, active, in the Greek), (a) literally, of "the heaven," John 1:51, RV, "opened"; (b) metaphorically, of "speaking freely," 2 Cor. 6:11.

2. *dianoigo* (1272), "to open up completely" (*dia*, "through," intensive, and No. 1), is used (a) literally, Luke 2:23; Acts 7:56, in the best mss.; (b) metaphorically, of the eyes, Mark 7:34; Luke 24:31; of the Scriptures, v. 32 and Acts 17:3; of the mind, Luke 24:45, RV (KJV, "understanding"); of the heart, Acts 16:14.

B. Nouns.

1. *anoixis* (457), "an opening" (akin to A, No. 1), is used in Eph. 6:19, metaphorically of the "opening" of the mouth as in A, No. 1 (2), (b).

2. *ope* (3692), "an opening, a hole," is used in Jas. 3:11, of the opening of a fountain.

OPENLY

parrhesia (*3954*), "freedom of speech, boldness," is used adverbially in the dative case and translated "openly" in Mark 8:32, of a saying of Christ; in John 7:13, of a public statement; in 11:54, of Christ's public appearance; in 7:26 and 18:20, of His public testimony; preceded by the preposition ***en***, "in," John 7:4, lit., "in boldness" (cf. v. 10, RV, "publicly").

OPPORTUNITY

A. Nouns.

1. ***kairos*** (*2540*), primarily, "a due measure," is used of "a fixed and definite period, a time, season," and is translated "opportunity" in Gal. 6:10 and Heb. 11:15.

2. ***eukairia*** (*2120*), "a fitting time, opportunity" (***eu***, "well," and No. 1), occurs in Matt. 26:16 and Luke 22:6.

B. Verb.

eukaireo (*2119*), "to have time or leisure" (akin to A, No. 2), is translated "he shall have opportunity" in 1 Cor. 16:12, RV (KJV, "convenient time").

OPPOSE

1. ***antitasso*** (*498*) is used in the middle voice in the sense of setting oneself against (***anti***, "against," ***tasso***, "to order, set"), "opposing oneself to," Acts 18:6; elsewhere rendered by the verb "to resist," Rom. 13:2; Jas. 4:6; 5:6; 1 Pet. 5:5.

2. ***antidiatithemi*** (*475*) signifies "to place oneself in opposition, oppose" (***anti***, "against," ***dia***, "through," intensive, ***tithemi***, "to place"), 2 Tim. 2:25.

OPPOSITIONS

antithesis (*477*), "a contrary position" (***anti***, "against," ***tithemi***, "to place"; Eng., "antithesis"), occurs in 1 Tim. 6:20.

OPPRESS

katadunasteuo (*2616*), "to exercise power over" (***kata***, "down," ***dunastes***, "a potentate": ***dunamai*** "to have power"), "oppress," is used, in the passive voice, in Acts 10:38; in the active, in Jas. 2:6.

ORACLE

logion (*3051*), a diminutive of ***logos***, "a word, narrative, statement," denotes "a divine response or utterance, an oracle"; it is used of (a) the contents of the Mosaic Law, Acts 7:38; (b) all the written utterances of God through OT writers, Rom. 3:2; (c) the substance of Christian doctrine, Heb. 5:12; (d) the utterances of God through Christian teachers, 1 Pet. 4:11.

ORATION

demegoreo (*1215*), from *demos*, "the people" and *agoreuo*, "to speak in the public assembly, to deliver an oration," occurs in Acts 12:21.

ORATOR

rhetor (*4489*), from an obsolete present tense, *rheo*, "to say" (cf. Eng., "rhetoric"), denotes "a public speaker, an orator," Acts 24:1, of Tertullus. Such a person, distinct from the professional lawyer, was hired, as a professional speaker, to make a skillful presentation of a case in court. His training was not legal but rhetorical.

ORDAIN

1. *kathistemi* (*2525*), from *kata*, "down," or "over against," and *histemi*, "to cause to stand, to set," is translated "to ordain" in the KJV of Titus 1:5; Heb. 5:1; 8:3.

2. *tasso* (*5021*) is translated "to ordain," in Acts 13:48 and Rom. 13:1.

3. *diatasso* (*1299*) is translated "to ordain" in 1 Cor. 7:17; 9:14; Gal. 3:19, the last in the sense of "administered."

4. *horizo* (*3724*) is twice used of Christ as divinely "ordained" to be the Judge of men, Acts 10:42; 17:31.

5. *krino* (*2919*), "to divide, separate, decide, judge," is translated "ordained" in Acts 16:4, of the decrees by the apostles and elders in Jerusalem.

ORDER (Noun and Verb)

A. Nouns.

1. *taxis* (*5010*), "an arranging, arrangement, order" (akin to *tasso*, "to arrange, draw up in order"), is used in Luke 1:8 of the fixed succession of the course of the priests; of due "order," in contrast to confusion, in the gatherings of a local church, 1 Cor. 14:40; of the general condition of such, Col. 2:5 (some give it a military significance here); of the divinely appointed character or nature of a priesthood, of Melchizedek, as foreshadowing that of Christ, Heb. 5:6, 10; 6:20; 7:11 (where also the character of the Aaronic priesthood is set in contrast); 7:17 (in some mss., v. 21).

2. *tagma* (*5001*), a more concrete form of No. 1, signifying "that which has been arranged in order," was especially a military term, denoting "a company"; it is used metaphorically in 1 Cor. 15:23 of the various classes of those who have part in the first resurrection.

B. Verbs.

1. *anatassomai* (*392*), "to arrange in order" (*ana*, "up," and the middle voice of *tasso*, "to arrange"), is used in Luke 1:1, KJV, "to

set forth in order" (RV, "to draw up"); the probable meaning is to bring together and so arrange details in "order."

2. *diatasso* (*1299*), "to appoint, arrange, charge, give orders to," is used, in the middle voice, in Acts 24:23, "gave order" (RV); 1 Cor. 11:34, "will I set in order"; in the active voice, in 1 Cor. 16:1, "I gave order" (RV).

3. *epidiorthoo* (*1930*), "to set in order" (*epi* "upon," *dia*, "through, intensive," and *orthos*, "straight"), is used in Titus 1:5, in the sense of setting right again what was defective, a commission to Titus, not to add to what the apostle himself had done, but to restore what had fallen into disorder since the apostle had labored in Crete; this is suggested by the *epi*.

C. Adverb.

kathexes (*2517*) is translated "in order" in Luke 1:3; Acts 11:4, RV (KJV, "by order"); Acts 18:23.

ORDERLY

kosmios (*2887*), an adjective signifying "decent, modest, orderly" (akin to *kosmos*, "order, adornment"), is translated "modest" in 1 Tim. 2:9; "orderly" in 3:2, RV (KJV, "of good behavior").

ORDINANCE

A. Nouns.

1. *diatage* (*1296*) is translated "ordinances," in Rom. 13:2.

2. *dogma* (*1378*) is translated "ordinances" in Eph. 2:15 and Col. 2:14.

3. *ktisis* (*2937*), "a creation, creature," is translated "ordinance" in 1 Pet. 2:13.

B. Verb.

dogmatizo (*1379*), akin to A, No. 2, "to decree," signifies, in the middle voice, "to subject oneself to an ordinance," Col. 2:20.

OVERCOME

1. *nikao* (*3528*), is used (a) of God, Rom. 3:4 (a law term), RV, "mightest prevail"; (b) of Christ, John 16:33; Rev. 3:21; 5:5; 17:14; (c) of His followers, Rom. 12:21 (2nd part); 1 John 2:13-14; 4:4; 5:4-5; Rev. 2:7, 11, 17, 26; 3:5, 12, 21; 12:11; 15:2; 21:7; (d) of faith, 1 John 5:4; (e) of evil (passive voice), Rom. 12:21; (f) of predicted human potentates, Rev. 6:2; 11:7; 13:7.

2. *hettaomai* (*2274*), "to be made inferior, be enslaved," is rendered "is (are) overcome," in 2 Pet. 2:19-20.

3. *katakurieuo* (*2634*) is translated "overcome" in Acts 19:16.

OVERFLOW, OVERFLOWING

A. Verbs.

1. *huperperisseuo* (*5248*), "to abound more exceedingly," Rom. 5:20, is used in the middle voice in 2 Cor. 7:4, RV, "I overflow (with joy)," KJV, "I am exceeding (joyful)."

2. *katakluzo* (*2626*), "to inundate, deluge," is used in the passive voice in 2 Pet. 3:6, of the Flood.

B. Noun.

perisseia (*4050*) is translated "overflowing" in Jas. 1:21, RV.

OVERLOOK

hupereidon (*5237*), "to overlook" (an aorist form), is used in Acts 17:30, RV (KJV, "winked at"), i.e., God bore with them without interposing by way of punishment, though the debasing tendencies of idolatry necessarily developed themselves.

OVERSHADOW

1. *episkiazo* (*1982*), "to throw a shadow upon" (*epi*, "over," *skia*, "a shadow"), "to overshadow," is used (a) of the bright cloud at the Transfiguration, Matt. 17:5; Mark 9:7; Luke 9:34; (b) metaphorically of the power of "the Most High" upon the Virgin Mary, Luke 1:35; (c) of the apostle Peter's shadow upon the sick, Acts 5:15.

2. *kataskiazo* (*2683*), lit., "to shadow down," is used of the "overshadowing" (RV) of the cherubim of glory above the mercy seat, Heb. 9:5 (KJV, "shadowing").

OVERSIGHT (exercise, take)

episkopeo (*1983*), lit., "to look upon" (*epi*, "upon," *skopeo*, "to look at, contemplate"), is found in 1 Pet. 5:2 (some ancient authorities omit it), "exercising the oversight," RV (KJV, "taking..."); "exercising" is the right rendering; the word does not imply the entrance upon such responsibility, but the fulfillment of it. It is not a matter of assuming a position, but of the discharge of the duties. The word is found elsewhere in Heb. 12:15, "looking carefully," RV.

OVERTAKE

1. *katalambano* (*2638*), "to lay hold of," has the significance of "overtaking," metaphorically, in John 12:35 (RV, "overtake," KJV, "come upon") and 1 Thess. 5:4.

2. *prolambano* (*4301*), "to anticipate" (*pro*, "before," *lambano*, "to take"), is used of the act of Mary, in Mark 14:8; of forestalling the less favored at a social meal, 1 Cor. 11:21; of being "overtaken" in any trespass, Gal. 6:1, where the meaning is not that of detecting a person in the act, but of his being caught by the trespass, through his being off his guard (see 5:21 and contrast the pre-

meditated practice of evil in 5:26). The modern Greek version is "even if a man, through lack of circumspection, should fall into any sin."

OWE

A. Verbs.

1. *opheilo* (3784), "to owe, to be a debtor" (in the passive voice, "to be owed, to be due"), is translated by the verb "to owe" in Matt. 18:28 (twice); Luke 7:41; 16:5, 7; Rom. 13:8; in 15:27, RV, "they (gentile converts) owe it" (KJV, "it is their duty"); Philem. 18.

2. *prosopheilo* (4359), "to owe besides" (*pros*, "in addition," and No. 1), is used in Philem. 19, "thou owest (to me even thine own self) besides," i.e., "thou owest me already as much as Onesimus," debt, and in addition "even thyself" (not "thou owest me much more").

B. Noun.

opheiletes (3781), "a debtor" (akin to A, No. 1), is translated "which owed" in Matt. 18:24, lit., "a debtor (of ten thousand talents)."

OWN (Adjective)

1. *gnesios*, primarily, "lawfully begotten," and hence "true, genuine," is translated "own" in the KJV of 1 Tim. 1:2 and Titus 1:4 (RV, "true").

2. In Acts 5:4, "was it not thine own?" is, lit., "did it not remain (*meno*) to thee?"

3. In Jude 6 (1st part), KJV, *heauton*, "of themselves," "their own" (RV), is rendered "their"; in the 2nd part, RV, *idios*, one's own, is translated "their proper" (KJV, "their own").

4. In Gal. 1:14, RV, *sunelikiotes*, is rendered "of mine own age" (KJV, "my equals"; marg., "equals in years").

OWNER

1. *kurios* (2962), "one having power" (*kuros*) or "authority, a lord, master," signifies "an owner" in Luke 19:33.

2. *naukleros* (3490), "a ship owner" (*naus*, "a ship," *kleros*, "a lot"), "a shipmaster," occurs in Acts 27:11, "(the) owner of the ship."

P

PAIN (Noun and Verb)

A. Nouns.

1. *ponos* (*4192*) is translated "pain" in Rev. 16:10; 21:4; "pains" in 16:11.

2. *odin* (*5604*), "a birth pang, travail pain," is rendered "travail" metaphorically, in Matt. 24:8 and Mark 13:8, RV (KJV, "sorrows"); by way of comparison, in 1 Thess. 5:3; translated "pains (of death)," Acts 2:24 (RV, "pangs").

B. Verb.

bosanizo (*928*) primarily signifies "to rub on the touchstone, to put to the test" (from *basanos*, "a touchstone," a dark stone used in testing metals); hence, "to examine by torture," and, in general, "to distress"; in Rev. 12:2, "in pain," RV (KJV, "pained"), in connection with parturition.

PALACE

praitorion (*4232*) signified originally "a general's (praetor's) tent." Then it was applied to "the council of army officers"; then to "the official residence of the governor of a province"; finally, to "the imperial bodyguard." In the KJV the word appears only once, Mark 15:16, "the hall, called Praetorium" (RV, "within the court which is the Praetorium," marg., "palace"); in the Greek of the NT it also occurs in Matt. 27:27, KJV, "the common hall," marg., "the governor's house"; RV, "palace," see marg.; John 18:28 (twice), KJV, "the hall of judgment"; and "judgment hall," marg., "Pilate's house," RV, "palace"; 18:33 and 19:9, KJV, "judgment hall," RV, "palace," see marg.; so in Acts 23:35; in Phil. 1:13, KJV, "in all the palace," marg., "Caesar's court," RV, "throughout the whole praetorian guard," marg., "in the whole Praetorium."

In the Gospels the term denotes the official residence in Jerusalem of the Roman governor, and the various translations of it in our versions arose from a desire either to indicate the special purpose for which that residence was used on the occasion in question, or to explain what particular building was intended. But whatever building the governor occupied was the Praetorium. It is most probable that in Jerusalem he resided in the well-known palace of Herod. Pilate's residence has been identified with the castle of Antonia, which was occupied by the regular garrison. The probability is that it was the same as Herod's palace. Herod's palace in Caesarea was used as the Praetorium there, and the expression in Acts 23:35, marg., "Herod's praetorium," is abbreviated from "the praetorium of Herod's palace."

In Phil. 1:13, marg., "the whole Praetorium" has been variously explained. It has been spoken of as "the palace," in connection with 4:22, where allusion is made to believers who belong to Caesar's household. Others have understood it of the barracks of the "praetorian" guard, but Lightfoot shows that this use of the word cannot be established, neither can it be regarded as referring to the barracks of the "palace" guard. The phrase "and to all the rest" in 1:13 indicates that persons are meant. Mommsen, followed by Ramsay (*St. Paul the Traveller*, p. 357) regards it as improbable that the apostle was committed to the "praetorian" guard and holds the view that Julius the centurion, who brought Paul to Rome, belonged to a corps drafted from legions in the provinces, whose duty it was to supervise the corn supply and perform police service, and that Julius probably delivered his prisoners to the commander of his corps. Eventually Paul's case came before the praetorian council, which is the "praetorium" alluded to by the apostle, and the phrase "to all the rest" refers to the audience of the trial.

PALM (of the hand)

Old Testament

kap (3709), "palm (of hand)." *kap* is often translated "hand," with the meaning of a body part on the end of arms (including the fingers), very important for manipulation and ability to do things, 2 Sam. 18:14. Also it is translated "palm of the hand," meaning the padded part of the hand, when face up can make a shallow pool to hold liquid in the hand, Lev. 14:15. Sometimes translated "sole of the foot, paw" meaning the padded, very bottom part of the foot, that makes contact with the ground (of any footed creature), Deut. 58:56; Lev. 11:27. *kap* can also be translated "control," meaning to be under the power of another, Judg. 6:13.

kap can also be different useful objects. It can be translated "handle," meaning a part of a door lock and bolt assembly that you grab to lock, close, or open, Song. Sol. 5:5. Also it can be translated "pocket of a sling," meaning the part of a sling that holds the stone before release, 1 Sam. 25:29. Another translation is "socket, joint" meaning the opening or hollow place of a joint to connect the parts, Gen. 32:33. Lastly for objects, it can be translated "dish, shallow pan," meaning a metal container, shallow (as an extension of the shallow part of the hand), Num. 7:14-80. Note: in context this pan refers to an incense burning container.

kap can also be used in combination with other Hebrew words; *kap* is translated "handful," meaning an amount that can be held in the hand, as a general measure of volume Lev. 9:17; 1 Kin. 17:12. Note: it is not clear if the hand is clenched or open in the measure. *sim nephesh be kap*, can be translated "live in danger," (lit. take life in palm), meaning to take a great risk, that might even endanger one's life, 1 Sam. 19:5.

PAPER

chartes (5489), "a sheet of paper made of strips of papyrus," 2 John 12. The pith of the stem of the plant was cut into thin strips, placed side by side to form a sheet. Another layer was laid upon this at right angles to it. The two layers were united by moisture and pressure with the natural sap of the plant. The sheets, after being dried and polished, were ready for use. Normally, the writing is on that side of the papyrus on which the fibers lie horizontally, parallel to the length of the roll, but where the material was scarce the writer used the other side also (cf. Rev. 5:1).

PARABLE

1. *parabole* (3850) lit. denotes "a placing beside" (akin to *paraballo*, "to throw" or "lay beside, to compare"). It signifies "a placing of one thing beside another" with a view to comparison (some consider that the thought of comparison is not necessarily contained in the word). In the NT it is found outside the gospels, only in Heb. 9:9 and 11:19. It is generally used of a somewhat lengthy utterance or narrative drawn from nature or human circumstances, the object of which is to set forth a spiritual lesson, e.g., those in Matt. 13 and Synoptic parallels; sometimes it is used of a short saying or proverb, e.g., Matt. 15:15; Mark 3:23; 7:17; Luke 4:23; 5:36; 6:39. It is the lesson that is of value; the hearer must catch the analogy if he is to be instructed (this is true also of a proverb). Such a narrative or saying, dealing with earthly things with a spiritual meaning, is distinct from a fable, which attributes to things what does not belong to them in nature.

2. *paroimia* (3942) denotes "a wayside saying" (from *paroimos*, "by the way"), "a byword," "maxim," or "problem," 2 Pet. 2:22. The word is sometimes spoken of as a "parable," John 10:6, i.e., a figurative discourse (RV marg., "proverb"); see also 16:25, 29, where the word is rendered "proverbs" (marg. "parables") and "proverb."

PARADISE

paradeisos (3857) is an Oriental word, first used by the historian Xenophon, denoting "the parks of Persian kings and nobles." It is of Persian origin (Old Pers. *pairidaeza*, akin to Gk. *peri*, "around," and *teichos*, "a wall") whence it passed into Greek.

In Luke 23:43, the promise of the Lord to the repentant robber was fulfilled the same day; Christ, at His death, having committed His spirit to the Father, went in spirit immediately into Heaven itself, the dwelling place of God (the Lord's mention of the place as "paradise" must have been a great comfort to the malefactor; to the oriental mind it expressed the sum total of blessedness). Thither the apostle Paul was caught up, 2 Cor. 12:4, spoken of as "the third heaven" (v. 3 does not introduce a different vision), beyond the heavens of the natural creation (see Heb. 4:14, RV, with reference to the Ascension). The same region is mentioned in Rev. 2:7, where the "tree of life," the figurative antitype of that in Eden, held out to the overcomer, is spoken of as being in "the Paradise of God" (RV), marg., "garden," as in Gen. 2:8.

PARCHMENT

membrana (*3200*) is a Latin word, properly an adjective, from *membrum*, "a limb," but denoting "skin, parchment." The word *membrana* is found in 2 Tim. 4:13, where Timothy is asked to bring to the apostle "the books, especially the parchments." The writing material was prepared from the skin of the sheep or goat. The skins were first soaked in lime for the purpose of removing the hair, and then shaved, washed, dried, stretched and ground or smoothed with fine chalk or lime and pumice stone. The finest kind is called "vellum," and is made from the skins of calves or kids.

PARENTS

goneus (*1118*), "a begetter, a father" (akin to *ginomai*, "to come into being, become"), is used in the plural in the NT, Matt. 10:21; Mark 13:12; six times in Luke (in Luke 2:43, RV, "His parents," KJV, "Joseph and His mother"); six in John; elsewhere, Rom. 1:30; 2 Cor. 12:14 (twice); Eph. 6:1; Col. 3:20; 2 Tim. 3:2.

PARTAKE, PARTAKER

A. Nouns.

1. *koinonos* (*2844*), an adjective, signifying "having in common" (*koinos*, "common"), is used as a noun, denoting "a companion, partner, partaker," translated "partakers" in Matt. 23:30; 1 Cor. 10:18, KJV; 2 Cor. 1:7; Heb. 10:33, RV; 2 Pet. 1:4; "partaker" in 1 Pet. 5:1.

2. *sunkoinonos* (*4791*) denotes "partaking jointly with" (*sun*, and No. 1), Rom. 11:17, RV, "(didst become) partaker with them" (KJV, "partakest"); 1 Cor. 9:23, RV, "a joint partaker," i.e., with the gospel, as cooperating in its activity; the KJV misplaces the "with" by attaching it to the superfluous italicized pronoun "*you*"; Phil. 1:7, "partakers with (me of grace)," RV, and KJV marg.; not as KJV

text, "partakers (of my grace)"; Rev. 1:9, "partaker with (you in the tribulation, etc.)," KJV, "companion."

B. Verbs.

1. *koinoneo* (2841), "to have a share of, to share with, take part in" (akin to A, No. 1), is translated "to be partaker of" in 1 Tim. 5:22; Heb. 2:14 (1st part), KJV, "are partakers of," RV, "are sharers in"; 1 Pet. 4:13; 2 John 11, RV, "partaketh in" (KJV, "is partaker of"); in the passive voice in Rom. 15:27.

2. *metecho* (3348), "to partake of, share in" (*meta*, "with," *echo*, "to have"), is translated "of partaking" in 1 Cor. 9:10, RV (KJV, "be partaker of"); "partake of" in 9:12, RV (KJV, "be partakers of"); so in 10:17, 21: in v. 30 "partake"; in Heb. 2:14, the KJV "took part of" is awkward; Christ "partook of" flesh and blood, RV; cf. No. 1 in this verse; in Heb. 5:13, metaphorically, of receiving elementary spiritual teaching, RV, "partaketh of (milk)," KJV, "useth"; in Heb. 7:13, it is said of Christ (the antitype of Melchizedek) as "belonging to" (so RV) or "partaking of" (RV marg.) another tribe than that of Levi (KJV, "pertaineth to").

3. *antilambano* (482), "to take hold of, to lay hold of" something before one, has the meaning "to partake of" in 1 Tim. 6:2, RV, "partake of," marg., "lay hold of," KJV, "are...partakers of" (*anti*, "in return for," *lambano*, "to take or receive"); the benefit mentioned as "partaken" of by the masters would seem to be the improved quality of the service rendered; the benefit of redemption is not in view here.

4. *metalambano* (3335), "to have, or get, a share of," is translated "to be partaker (or partakers) of" in 2 Tim. 2:6 and Heb. 12:10.

5. *summerizo* (4829), primarily, "to distribute in shares" (*sun*, "with," *meros*, "a part"), in the middle voice, "to have a share in," is used in 1 Cor. 9:13, KJV, "are partakers with (the altar)," RV, "have their portion with," i.e., they feed with others on that which, having been sacrificed, has been placed upon an altar; so the believer feeds upon Christ (who is the altar in Heb. 13:10).

PARTIAL, PARTIALITY

A. Verb.

diakrino (1252), "to separate, distinguish, discern, judge, decide," Jas. 2:4.

B. Noun.

prosklisis (4346) denotes "inclination" (*pros*, "towards," *klino*, "to lean"); it is used with *kata* in 1 Tim. 5:21, lit., "according to partiality."

C. Adjective.

adiakritos (87) primarily signifies "not to be parted," hence, "without uncertainty," or "indecision," Jas. 3:17, KJV, "without partiality" (marg. "wrangling"), RV, "without variance" (marg., "Or, doubtfulness Or, partiality"). In the Sept., Prov. 25:1.

PARTITION

phragmos (*5418*), primarily "a fencing" in (akin to *phrasso*, "to fence in, stop, close"), is used metaphorically in Eph. 2:14, of "the middle wall of partition"; "the partition" is epexegetic of "the middle wall," namely, the "partition" between Jew and Gentile. J. A. Robinson suggests that Paul had in mind the barrier between the outer and inner courts of the Temple, notices fixed to which warned Gentiles not to proceed further on pain of death.

PARTNER

1. *koinonos* (*2844*), an adjective, signifying "having in common" (*koinos*), is used as a noun, "partners" in Luke 5:10, "partner" in 2 Cor. 8:23; Philem. 17 (in spiritual life and business).

2. *metochos* (*3353*), an adjective, signifying "having with, sharing," is used as a noun, "partners" in Luke 5:7.

PASS, PASS BY, COME TO PASS

1. *parerchomai* (*3928*), from *para*, "by," *erchomai*, "to come" or "go," denotes (I), literally, "to pass, pass by," (a) of persons, Matt. 8:28; Mark 6:48; Luke 18:37; Acts 16:8; (b) of things, Matt. 26:39, 42; of time, Matt. 14:15; Mark 14:35; Acts 27:9, KJV, "past" (RV, "gone by"); 1 Pet. 4:3; (II), metaphorically, (a) "to pass away, to perish," Matt. 5:18; 24:34, 35; Mark 13:30, 31; Luke 16:17; 21:32, 33; 2 Cor. 5:17; Jas. 1:10; 2 Pet. 3:10; (b) "to pass by, disregard, neglect, pass over," Luke 11:42; 15:29, "transgressed."

2. *dierchomai* (*1330*), denotes "to pass through or over," (a) of persons, e.g., Matt. 12:43, RV, "passeth (KJV, walketh) through", Mark 4:35, KJV, "pass (RV, go) over"; Luke 19:1, 4; Heb. 4:14, RV, "passed through" (KJV "into"); Christ "passed through" the created heavens to the throne of God; (b) of things, e.g., Matt. 19:24, "to go through"; Luke 2:35, "shall pierce through" (metaphorically of a sword).

3. *aperchomai* (*565*), "to go away," is rendered "to pass" in Rev. 9:12; 11:14; "passed away" in Rev. 21:4.

PASSION

A. Noun.

pathema (*3804*), "a suffering" or "a passive emotion," is translated "passions" in Rom. 7:5, RV, "(sinful) passions," KJV, "motions," and Gal. 5:24, RV.

B. Verb.

pascho (*3958*), "to suffer," is used as a noun, in the aorist infinitive with the article, and translated "passion" in Acts 1:3, of the suffering of Christ at Calvary.

C. Adjective.

homoiopathes (*3663*), "of like feelings or affections," is rendered "of like passions" in Acts 14:15 (RV marg., "nature"); in Jas. 5:17, RV, ditto (KJV, "subject to like passions").

PASSOVER

pascha (*3957*), the Greek spelling of the Aramaic word for the Passover, from the Hebrew *pasach*, "to pass over, to spare," a feast instituted by God in commemoration of the deliverance of Israel from Egypt, and anticipatory of the expiatory sacrifice of Christ. The word signifies (I) "the Passover Feast," e.g., Matt. 26:2; John 2:13, 23; 6:4; 11:55; 12:1; 13:1; 18:39; 19:14; Acts 12:4; Heb. 11:28; (II), by metonymy, (a) "the Paschal Supper," Matt. 26:18, 19; Mark 14:16; Luke 22:8, 13; (b) "the Paschal lamb," e.g., Mark 14:12, cf. Exod. 12:21; Luke 22:7; (c) "Christ Himself," 1 Cor. 5:7.

PASTURE

nome (*3542*) denotes (a) "pasture, pasturage," figuratively in John 10:9; (b) "grazing, feeding," figuratively in 2 Tim. 2:17, of the doctrines of false teachers, lit., "their word will have feeding as a gangrene."

PATIENCE, PATIENT, PATIENTLY

A. Nouns.

1. *hupomone* (*5281*), lit., "an abiding under" (*hupo*, "under," *meno*, "to abide"), is almost invariably rendered "patience." "Patience, which grows only in trial"; Jas. 1:3 may be passive, i.e., = "endurance," as, (a) in trials, generally, Luke 21:19 (which is to be understood by Matt. 24:13), cf. Rom. 12:12; Jas. 1:12; (b) in trials incident to service in the gospel, 2 Cor. 6:4; 12:12; 2 Tim. 3:10; (c) under chastisement, which is trial viewed as coming from the hand of God our Father, Heb. 12:7; (d) under undeserved affliction, 1 Pet. 2:20; or active, i.e. = "persistence, perseverance," as (e) in well doing, Rom. 2:7 (KJV, "patient continuance"); (f) in fruit bearing, Luke 8:15; (g) in running the appointed race, Heb. 12:1.

2. *makrothumia* (*3115*), "longsuffering," is rendered "patience" in Heb. 6:12; Jas. 5:10.

B. Verbs.

1. *hupomeno* (*5278*), akin to A, No. 1, (a) used intransitively, means "to tarry behind, still abide," Luke 2:43; Acts 17:14; (b) tran-

sitively, "to wait for," Rom. 8:24 (in some mss.), "to bear patiently, endure," translated "patient" (present participle) in Rom. 12:12; "ye take it patiently," 1 Pet. 2:20 (twice).

2. *makrothumeo* (*3114*), akin to A, No. 2, "to be long-tempered," is translated "to have patience," or "to be patient," in Matt. 18:26, 29; 1 Thess. 5:14, KJV (RV, "be longsuffering"); Jas. 5:7 (1st part, "be patient"; 2nd part, RV, "being patient," KJV, "hath long patience"); in Heb. 6:15, RV, "having (KJV, after he had) patiently endured."

PATRIARCH

patriarches (*3966*), from *patria*, "a family," and *archo*, "to rule," is found in Acts 2:29; 7:8, 9; Heb. 7:4.

PATTERN

A. Nouns.

1. *tupos* (*5179*) is translated "pattern" in Titus 2:7, KJV; Heb. 8:5 (KJV and RV).

2. *hupotuposis* (*5296*) is translated "pattern" in 1 Tim. 1:16, KJV; 2 Tim. 1:13, RV.

B. Adjective.

antitupos (*499*) is translated "like in pattern" in Heb. 9:24, RV.

PAVEMENT

lithostrotos (*3038*), an adjective, denoting "paved with stones" (*lithos*, "a stone," and *stronnuo*, "to spread"), especially of tessellated work, is used as a noun in John 19:13, of a place near the Praetorium in Jerusalem, called Gabbatha, a Greek transliteration of an Aramaic word.

PAY (Verb), PAYMENT

1. *apodidomi* (*591*), "to give back, to render what is due, to pay," used of various obligations in this respect, is translated "to pay, to make payment," in Matt. 5:26; 18:25 (twice), 26, 28, 29, 30, 34; 20:8, RV (KJV, "give").

2. *teleo* (*5055*), "to bring to an end, complete, fulfill," has the meaning "to pay" in Matt. 17:24 and Rom. 13:6.

PEACE, PEACEABLE, PEACEABLY

Old Testament

A. Nouns.

shalom (*7965*), "peace; completeness; welfare; health." The use of *shalom* is frequent (237 times) and varied in its semantic range. The first two occurrences in Genesis already indicate the changes in meaning, "at ease," Gen. 15:15; and "unharmed," Gen. 26:29.

Yet, both uses are essentially the same, as they express the root meaning of "to be whole," Ps. 41:9; cf. Jer. 20:10. The relationship is one of harmony and wholeness, which is the opposite of the state of strife and war, Ps. 120:7. *shalom* as a harmonious state of the soul and mind encourages the development of the faculties and powers. The state of being at ease is experienced both externally and internally. In Hebrew it finds expression in the phrase *beshalom* ("in peace"): "I will both lay me down in peace |*beshalom*|, and sleep: for thou, Lord, only makest me dwell in safety," Ps. 4:8.

Closely associated to the above is the meaning "welfare," specifically personal "welfare" or "health," 2 Sam. 20:9. *shalom* also signifies "peace," indicative of a prosperous relationship between two or more parties. *shalom* in this sense finds expression in speech, Jer. 9:8; in diplomacy, Judg. 4:17; in warfare, Deut. 20:11.

Isaiah prophesied concerning the "prince of peace," Isa. 9:6, whose kingdom was to introduce a government of "peace," Isa. 9:7. Ezekiel spoke about the new covenant as one of "peace," Ezek. 37:26. Psalm 122 is one of those great psalms in celebration of and in prayer for the "peace of Jerusalem."

Another related noun is *shelem*, "peace offering," Exod. 24:5.

B. Verbs.

shalem (7999), "to be complete, be sound," 1 Kings 9:25. Another verb, *shalam*, means "to make peace," Prov. 16:7.

C. Adjective.

shalem (8003), "complete; perfect," Gen. 15:16; the word means "perfect" in Deut. 25:15.

New Testament

A. Noun.

eirene (1515) occurs in each of the books of the NT, save 1 John and except in Acts 7:26 |'(at) one again'| it is translated "peace" in the RV. It describes (a) harmonious relationships between men, Matt. 10:34; Rom. 14:19; (b) between nations, Luke 14:32; Acts 12:20; Rev. 6:4; (c) friendliness, Acts 15:33; 1 Cor. 16:11; Heb. 11:31; (d) freedom from molestation, Luke 11:21; 19:42; Acts 9:31 (RV, 'peace,' KJV, 'rest'); 16:36; (e) order, in the State, Acts 24:2 (RV, 'peace,' KJV, 'quietness'); in the churches, 1 Cor. 14:33; (f) the harmonized relationships between God and man, accomplished through the gospel, Acts 10:36; Eph. 2:17; (g) the sense of rest and contentment consequent thereon, Matt. 10:13; Mark 5:34; Luke 1:79; 2:29; John 14:27; Rom. 1:7; 3:17; 8:6; in certain passages this idea is not distinguishable from the last, Rom. 5:1.

"The God of peace" is a title used in Rom. 15:33; 16:20; Phil. 4:9; 1 Thess. 5:23; Heb. 13:20; cf. 1 Cor. 14:33; 2 Cor. 13:11. The corresponding Heb. word *shalom* primarily signifies "wholeness": see its use in Josh. 8:31, "unhewn"; Ruth 2:12, "full"; Neh. 6:15, "finished"; Isa. 42:19, marg., "made perfect." Hence there is a close connection between the title in 1 Thess. 5:23 and the word *holokleros*, "entire," in that verse.

B. Verb.

eireneuo (*1514*), primarily, "to bring to peace, reconcile," denotes in the NT, "to keep peace or to be at peace": in Mark 9:50, RV, the Lord bids the disciples "be at peace" with one another, gently rebuking their ambitious desires; in Rom. 12:18 (RV, "be at peace," KJV, "live peaceably") the limitation "if it be possible, as much as in you liveth," seems due to the phrase "with all men," but is not intended to excuse any evasion of the obligation imposed by the command; in 2 Cor. 13:11 it is rendered "live in peace," a general exhortation to believers; in 1 Thess. 5:13, "be at peace (among yourselves)."

C. Adjective.

eirenikos (*1516*), akin to A, denotes "peaceful." It is used (a) of the fruit of righteousness, Heb. 12:11, "peaceable" (or "peaceful") because it is produced in communion with God the Father, through His chastening; (b) of "the wisdom that is from above," Jas. 3:17.

PEACE (hold one's)

sigao (*4601*) signifies (a), used intransitively, "to be silent" (from *sige*, "silence"), translated "to hold one's peace," in Luke 9:36; 18:39; 20:26; Acts 12:17; 15:13 (in v. 12, "kept silence"; similarly rendered in 1 Cor. 14:28, 30, KJV, "hold his peace," 34); (b) used transitively, "to keep secret"; in the passive voice, "to be kept secret," Rom. 16:25, RV, "hath been kept in silence."

PEACEMAKER

eirenopoios (*1518*), an adjective signifying peace making (*eirene*, and *poieo*, "to make"), is used in Matt. 5:9, "peacemakers."

PENTECOST

pentekostos (*4005*), an adjective denoting "fiftieth," is used as a noun, with "day" understood, i.e., the "fiftieth" day after the Passover, counting from the second day of the Feast, Acts 2:1; 20:16; 1 Cor. 16:8. For the divine instructions to Israel see Exod. 23:16; 34:22; Lev. 23:15-21; Num. 28:26-31; Deut. 16:9-11.

PEOPLE

Old Testament

'*am* (5971), "people; relative." The word bears subjective and personal overtones. First, '*am* represents a familial relationship. In Ruth 3:11 the word means "male kinsmen." In the plural the word refers to all the individuals who are related to a person through his father, Lev. 21:4. Second, '*am* may signify those relatives (including women and children) who are grouped together locally whether or not they permanently inhabit a given location, Gen. 32:7. Third, this word may refer to the whole of a nation formed and united primarily by their descent from a common ancestor, Gen. 11:6. '*am* may also include those who enter by religious adoption and marriage, Exod. 1:9. Later the basic unity in a common covenant relationship with God becomes the unifying factor underlying '*am*. When they left Egypt, the people of Israel were joined by many others, Exod. 12:38.

'*am* can mean all those physical ancestors who lived previously and are now dead, Gen. 25:8. There might be covenantal overtones here in the sense that Abraham was gathered to all those who were true believers. Jesus argued that such texts taught the reality of life after death, Matt. 22:32.

'*am* can represent the individuals who together form a familial (and covenantal) group within a larger group, Judg. 5:18 There is no distinction between the concepts "militia" and "kinsmen," Josh. 8:1, 5. '*am* may signify the inhabitants of a city regardless of their familial or covenantal relationship; it is a territorial or political term, Ruth 4:9.

Finally, sometimes '*am* used of an entire nation has political and territorial overtones. As such it may be paralleled to the Hebrew word with such overtones (*goy*), Deut. 14:2; cf. Exod. 19:5-6.

New Testament

1. *laos* (2992) is used of (a) "the people at large," especially of people assembled, e.g., Matt. 27:25; Luke 1:21; 3:15; Acts 4:27; (b) "a people of the same race and language," e.g., Rev. 5:9; in the plural, e.g., Luke 2:31; Rom. 15:11; Rev. 7:9; 11:9; especially of Israel, e.g., Matt. 2:6; 4:23; John 11:50; Acts 4:8; Heb. 2:17; in distinction from their rulers and priests, e.g., Matt. 26:5; Luke 20:19; Heb. 5:3; in distinction from Gentiles, e.g., Acts 26:17, 23; Rom. 15:10; (c) of Christians as the people of God, e.g., Acts 15:14; Titus 2:14; Heb. 4:9; 1 Pet. 2:9.

2. *demos* (1218), "the common people, the people generally" (Eng., "demagogue," "democracy," etc.), especially the mass of the "people" assembled in a public place, Acts 12:22; 17:5; 19:30, 33.

3. *ethnos* (1484) denotes (a) "a nation," e.g., Matt. 24:7; Acts 10:35; "the Jewish people," e.g., Luke 7:5; Acts 10:22; 28:19; (b) in the plur-

al, "the rest of mankind" in distinction from Israel or the Jews, e.g., Matt. 4:15; Acts 28:28; (c) "the people of a city," Acts 8:9; (d) gentile Christians, e.g., Rom. 10:19; 11:13; 15:27; Gal. 2:14.

PERCEIVE

1. *ginosko* (1097), "to know by experience and observation," is translated "to perceive" in Matt. 12:15, RV (KJV, "knew"); 16:8; 21:45; 22:18; 26:10, RV, (KJV, "understood"); Mark 8:17; 12:12 and 15:10, RV (KJV, "knew"); so Luke 9:11; 18:34; in Luke 7:39, RV (KJV, "known"); 20:19; John 6:15; 8:27, RV (KJV, "understood"); 16:19, RV (KJV, "knew"); Acts 23:6; Gal. 2:9; in 1 John 3:16, KJV, "perceive" (RV, "know," perfect tense, lit., "we have perceived," and therefore "know").

2. *epiginosko* (1921), a strengthened form of No. 1, "to gain a full knowledge of, to become fully acquainted with," is translated "to perceive" in Mark 5:30, RV (KJV, "knowing"); Luke 1:22; 5:22; Acts 19:34, RV (KJV, knew).

PERFECT (Adjective and Verb), PERFECTLY

Old Testament

A. Adjective.

tamim (8549), "perfect; blameless; sincerity; entire; whole; complete; full." *tamim* means "complete," in the sense of the entire or whole thing, Lev. 3:9; a "whole" time period, Josh. 10:13; Lev. 23:15; a "full" year, Lev. 25:30. This word may also mean "intact," or not cut up into pieces, Ezek. 15:5. *tamim* may mean incontestable or free from objection, so "perfect," Deut. 18:13; 32:4; meets all the requirements of God's law, cf. Ps. 18:23.

In certain contexts the word has a wider background. When one is described by it, there is nothing in his outward activities or internal disposition that is odious to God, Gen. 6:9. This word describes his entire relationship to God. In Judg. 9:16, where *tamim* describes a relationship between men it is clear that more than mere external activity is meant, Gen. 17:1; with Rom. 4 where Paul argues that Abraham fulfilled God's condition but that he did so only through faith.

B. Noun.

tom (8537), "completeness," Job 21:23; innocency or simplicity, 2 Sam. 15:11; integrity, Gen. 20:5.

C. Verb.

tamam (8552), "to be complete, be finished, be consumed, be without blame," Gen. 47:18.

New Testament

A. Adjectives.

1. *teleios* (5049) signifies "having reached its end" (*telos*), "finished, complete perfect." It is used (I) of persons, (a) primarily of physical development, then, with ethical import, "fully grown, mature," 1 Cor. 2:6; 14:20 ("men"; marg., "of full age"); Eph. 4:13; Phil. 3:15; Col. 1:28; 4:12; in Heb. 5:14, RV, "fullgrown" (marg., "perfect"), KJV, "of full age" (marg., "perfect"); (b) "complete," conveying the idea of goodness without necessary reference to maturity or what is expressed under (a) Matt. 5:48; 19:21; Jas. 1:4 (2nd part); 3:2. It is used thus of God in Matt. 5:48; (II), of "things, complete, perfect," Rom. 12:2; 1 Cor. 13:10 (referring to the complete revelation of God's will and ways, whether in the completed Scriptures or in the hereafter); Jas. 1:4 (of the work of patience); v. 25; 1 John 4:18.

2. *teleioteros* (5046*), the comparative degree of No. 1, is used in Heb. 9:11, of the very presence of God.

B. Verbs.

1. *teleioo* (5048), "to bring to an end by completing or perfecting," is used (I) of "accomplishing"; (II), of "bringing to completeness," (a) of persons: of Christ's assured completion of His earthly course, in the accomplishment of the Father's will, the successive stages culminating in His death, Luke 13:32; Heb. 2:10, to make Him "perfect," legally and officially, for all that He would be to His people on the ground of His sacrifice; cf. 5:9; 7:28, RV, "perfected" (KJV, "consecrated"); of His saints, John 17:23, RV, "perfected" (KJV, "made perfect"); Phil. 3:12; Heb. 10:14; 11:40 (of resurrection glory); 12:23 (of the departed saints); 1 John 4:18, of former priests (negatively), Heb. 9:9; similarly of Israelites under the Aaronic priesthood, 10:1; (b) of things, Heb. 7:19 (of the ineffectiveness of the Law); Jas. 2:22 (of faith made "perfect" by works); 1 John 2:5, of the love of God operating through him who keeps His word; 4:12, of the love of God in the case of those who love one another; 4:17, of the love of God as "made perfect with" (RV) those who abide in God, giving them to be possessed of the very character of God, by reason of which "as He is, even so are they in this world."

2. *epiteleo* (2005), "to bring through to the end" (*epi*, intensive, in the sense of "fully," and *teleo*, "to complete"), is used in the middle voice in Gal. 3:3, "are ye (now) perfected," continuous present tense, indicating a process, lit., "are ye now perfecting yourselves"; in 2 Cor. 7:1, "perfecting (holiness)"; in Phil. 1:6, RV, "will perfect (it)," KJV, "will perform."

3. *katartizo* (2675), "to render fit, complete," is used of mending nets, Matt. 4:21; Mark 1:19, and is translated "restore" in Gal. 6:1. It does not necessarily imply, however, that that to which it is applied has been damaged, though it may do so, as in these pas-

P

sages; it signifies, rather, right ordering and arrangement, Heb. 11:3, "framed"; it points out the path of progress, as in Matt. 21:16; Luke 6:40; cf. 2 Cor. 13:9; Eph. 4:12, where corresponding nouns occur. It indicates the close relationship between character and destiny, Rom. 9:22, "fitted." It expresses the pastor's desire for the flock, in prayer, Heb. 13:21, and in exhortation, 1 Cor. 1:10, RV, "perfected" (KJV, "perfectly joined"); 2 Cor. 13:11, as well as his conviction of God's purpose for them, 1 Pet. 5:10. It is used of the Incarnation of the Word in Heb. 10:5, "prepare," quoted from Ps. 40:6 (Sept.), where it is apparently intended to describe the unique creative act involved in the Virgin Birth, Luke 1:35. In 1 Thess. 3:10 it means to supply what is necessary, as the succeeding words show."*

C. Adverbs.

1. *akribos* (199), accurately, is translated "perfectly" in 1 Thess. 5:2, where it suggests that Paul and his companions were careful ministers of the Word.

2. *akribesteron* (197), the comparative degree of No. 1, Acts 18:26; 23:15.

3. *teleios* (5049), "perfectly," is so translated in 1 Pet. 1:13, RV (KJV, "to the end"), of setting one's hope on coming grace.

PERFECTION, PERFECTING (noun), PERFECTNESS

A. Nouns.

1. *katartisis* (2676), "a making fit," is used figuratively in an ethical sense in 2 Cor. 13:9, RV, "perfecting" (KJV, "perfection"), implying a process leading to consummation (akin to *katartizo*).

2. *katartismos* (2677) denotes, in much the same way as No. 1, "a fitting or preparing fully," Eph. 4:12.

3. *teleiosis* (5050) denotes "a fulfillment, completion, perfection, an end accomplished as the effect of a process," Heb. 7:11; in Luke 1:45, RV, "fulfillment" (KJV, "performance").

4. *teleiotes* (5047) denotes much the same as No. 3, but stressing perhaps the actual accomplishment of the end in view, Col. 3:14, "perfectness"; Heb. 6:1, "perfection."

B. Verb.

telesphoreo (5052), "to bring to a completion" or "an end in view" (*telos*, "an end," *phero*, "to bear"), is said of plants, Luke 8:14.

PERFORM, PERFORMANCE

1. *teleo* (5055), "to finish," is translated "performed" in Luke 2:39, KJV.

2. *apoteleo* (658), "to bring to an end, accomplish," is translated

"I perform" in Luke 13:32, RV (KJV, "I do"); some mss. have No. 3; in Jas. 1:15, it is used of sin, "fullgrown" RV (KJV, "finished").

3. *epiteleo* (*2005*), Rom. 15:28, KJV, "performed" (RV, "accomplished"); 2 Cor. 8:11, KJV, "perform" (RV, "complete"); Phil. 1:6, KJV, "perform" (RV, "perfect").

4. *poieo* (*4160*), "to do," is translated "to perform" in Rom. 4:21; in Luke 1:72, KJV (RV, "to show").

5. *apodidomi* (*591*), "to give back, or in full," is translated "thou...shalt perform" in Matt. 5:33.

PERISH

Old Testament

A. Verb.

'abad (6), "to perish, die, be lost, go astray, go to ruin, succumb, be carried off, fail." Basically *'abad* represents the disappearance of someone or something. In its strongest sense the word means "to die or to cease to exist," Lev. 26:38; or "utterly destroy," Num. 33:52. A somewhat different emphasis of *'abad* is "to go to ruin" or "to be ruined," Exod. 10:7; Num. 21:29-30. Closely related to the immediately preceding emphasis is that of "to succumb." This use of *'abad* focuses on the process rather than the conclusion, Num. 17:12-13; 18:5.

'abad can also speak of being carried off to death or destruction by some means, Num. 16:33. This same nuance appears when God says the people will "perish" from off the land if they do not keep the covenant, Deut. 4:26. The verb may mean to disappear but not be destroyed, in other words "to be lost," Deut. 22:3; so, "lost sheep," Jer. 50:6. Another nuance of the verb is "to go astray" in the sense of wandering, Deut. 26:5.

Finally, *'abad* can be applied to human qualities which are lessening or have lessened, Deut. 32:28. The word can also be used of the failure of human wisdom as in Ps. 146:4: as for men "his breath goeth forth, he returneth to his earth; in that very day his thoughts perish."

B. Nouns.

There are three nouns related to the verb. *'abedah*, which is found 4 times, refers to a "thing which has been lost," Exod. 22:9. The noun *'abaddon* occurs 6 times and means "the place of destruction," Job 26:6. *'abdan* occurs once with the meaning "destruction," Esth. 9:5.

New Testament

1. *apollumi* (*622*), "to destroy," signifies, in the middle voice, "to perish," and is thus used (a) of things, e.g., Matt. 5:29, 30; Luke 5:37; Acts 27:34, RV, "perish" (in some texts *pipto*, "to fall," as KJV); Heb. 1:11; 2 Pet. 3:6; Rev. 18:14 (2nd part), RV, "perished" (in some texts

aperchomai, "to depart," as KJV); (b) of persons, e.g., Matt. 8:25; John 3:(15), 16; 10:28; 17:12, RV, "perished" (KJV, "is lost"); Rom. 2:12; 1 Cor. 1:18, lit., "the perishing," where the perfective force of the verb implies the completion of the process of destruction; 8:11; 15:18; 2 Pet. 3:9; Jude 11.

2. *sunapollumi* (4881), in the middle voice, denotes "to perish together" (*sun*, "with," and No. 1), Heb. 11:31.

3. *aphanizo* (853), "to make unseen" (*a*, negative, *phaino*, "to cause to appear"), in the passive voice, is translated "perish" in Acts 13:41 (RV, marg., "vanish away").

4. *diaphtheiro* (1311), "to corrupt," is rendered "perish" in 2 Cor. 4:16, KJV (RV, "is decaying").

PERMISSION

sungnome (4774), lit., "a joint opinion, mind or understanding," "a fellow feeling," hence, "a concession, allowance," is translated "permission," in contrast to "commandment," in 1 Cor. 7:6.

PERMIT

epitrepo (2010), lit., "to turn to," "to entrust," signifies "to permit," Acts 26:1; 1 Cor. 14:34; 1 Cor. 16:7; 1 Tim. 2:12, RV "permit" (KJV,"suffer"); Heb. 6:3.

PERPLEX, PERPLEXITY

A. Verbs

1. *aporeo* (639) is rendered "perplexed" in 2 Cor. 4:8, and in the most authentic mss. in Luke 24:4.

2. *diaporeo* (1280), "was much perplexed" in Luke 9:7.

B. Noun.

aporia (640), akin to A, No. 1, is translated "perplexity" in Luke 21:25 (lit., "at a loss for a way," *a*, negative, *poros*, "a way, resource"), of the distress of nations, finding no solution to their embarrassments; papyri illustrations are in the sense of being at one's wit's end, at a loss how to proceed, without resources.

PERSECUTE, PERSECUTION

A. Verbs.

1. *dioko* (1377) has the meanings (a) "to put to flight, drive away," (b) "to pursue," whence the meaning "to persecute," Matt. 5:10-12, 44; 10:23; 23:34; Luke 11:49 (No. 2 in some mss.); 21:12; John 5:16; 15:20 (twice); Acts 7:52; 9:4, 5, and similar passages; Rom. 12:14; 1 Cor. 4:12; 15:9; 2 Cor. 4:9, KJV (RV, "pursued"); Gal. 1:13, 23; 4:29; Gal. 5:11, RV, "am...persecuted" (KJV, "suffer persecution"); so 6:12; Phil. 3:6; 2 Tim. 3:12, "shall suffer persecution"; Rev. 12:13.

2. *ekdioko* (*1559*), *ek*, "out," and No. 1, is used in 1 Thess. 2:15, KJV, "persecuted" (RV, "drove out").

B. Noun.

diogmos (*1375*), akin to A, No. 1 occurs in Matt. 13:21; Mark 4:17; 10:30; Acts 8:1; 13:50; Rom. 8:35; 2 Cor. 12:10; 2 Thess. 1:4; 2 Tim. 3:11, twice.

PERSECUTOR

dioktes (*1376*), akin to *dioko*, 1 Tim. 1:13.

PERSEVERANCE

proskarteresis (*4343*) occurs in Eph. 6:18.

PERSON

1. *prosopon* (*4383*), is translated "person" or "persons" in Matt. 22:16; Mark 12:14; Luke 20:21; 2 Cor. 1:11; 2 Cor. 2:10; Gal. 2:6; Jude 16, lit., "(admiring, or showing respect of, RV) persons."
2. *anthropos* (*444*), a generic name for man, is translated "persons" in Rev. 11:13, RV (KJV, "men").

PERSONS (respect of)

A. Nouns.

1. *prosopolemptes* (*4381*) denotes "a respecter of persons" (*prosopon*, "a face" or "person," *lambano*, "to lay hold of"), Acts 10:34.
2. *prosopolempsia* (in inferior texts without the letter m) (*4382*) denotes "respect of persons, partiality" (akin to No. 1), the fault of one who, when responsible to give judgment, has respect to the position, rank, popularity, or circumstances of men, instead of their intrinsic conditions, preferring the rich and powerful to those who are not so, Rom. 2:11; Eph. 6:9; Col. 3:25; Jas. 2:1.

B. Verb.

prosopolempteo (*4380*), "to have respect of persons," Jas. 2:9.

C. Adverb.

aprosopolemptos (*678*), "without respect of persons, impartially" (*a*, negative), occurs in 1 Pet. 1:17.

PERSUADE

1. *peitho* (*3982*) in the active voice, signifies "to apply persuasion, to prevail upon or win over, to persuade," bringing about a change of mind by the influence of reason or moral considerations, e.g., in Matt. 27:20; 28:14; Acts 13:43; 19:8; in the passive voice, "to be persuaded, believe," e.g., Luke 16:31; 20:6; Acts 17:4,

RV (KJV, "believed"); 21:14; 26:26; Rom. 8:38; 14:14; 15:14; 2 Tim. 1:5, 12; Heb. 6:9; 11:13, in some mss.; 13:18, RV (KJV, "trust").

2. *anapeitho* (*374*), "to persuade, induce," in an evil sense (*ana*, "back," and No. 1), is used in Acts 18:13.

PERSUASIVE, PERSUASIVENESS

A. Adjective.

peithos (*3981*), an adjective (akin to *peitho*), not found elsewhere, is translated "persuasive" in 1 Cor. 2:4, RV (KJV, "enticing").

B. Noun.

pithanologia (*4086*), "persuasiveness of speech," is used in Col. 2:4, RV.

PERSUASION

peismone (*3988*), akin to *peitho*, is used in Gal. 5:8, where the meaning is "this influence that has won you over, or that seems likely to do so"; the use of *peitho*, in the sense of "to obey," in v. 7, suggests a play upon words here.

PERTAIN TO

metecho (*3348*), in Heb. 7:13, means "belong to."

PERVERSE, PERVERT

1. *apostrepho* (*654*), "to turn away" (*apo*, "from," *strepho*, "to turn"), is used metaphorically in the sense of "perverting" in Luke 23:14 (cf. No. 2 in v. 2).

2. *diastrepho* (*1294*), "to distort, twist" (*dia*, "through," and *strepho*), is translated "to pervert" in Luke 23:2 (cf. No. 1 in v. 14); Acts 13:10 [in v. 8, "to turn aside" (KJV, "away")]; in the perfect participle, passive voice, it is translated "perverse," lit., "turned aside, corrupted," in Matt. 17:17; Luke 9:41; Acts 20:30; Phil. 2:15.

3. *metastrepho* (*3344*), "to transform into something of an opposite character" (*meta*, signifying "a change," and *strepho*,) as the Judaizers sought to "pervert the gospel of Christ," Gal. 1:7; cf. "the sun shall be turned into darkness," Acts 2:20; laughter into mourning and joy to heaviness, Jas. 4:9.

4. *ekstrepho* (*1612*), "to turn inside out" (*ek*, "out"), "to change entirely," is used metaphorically in Titus 3:11, RV, "is perverted" (KJV, "is subverted").

PESTILENCE, PESTILENT FELLOW

Old Testament

deber (*1698*), "pestilence." The meaning of *deber* is best denoted by the English word "pestilence" or "plague," cf. 2 Sam. 24:13ff.

The nature of the "plague" (bubonic or other) is often difficult to determine from the contexts, as the details of medical interest are not given or are scanty. In the prophetical writings, the "plague" occurs with other disasters: famine, flood, and the sword, Jer. 14:12.

New Testament

loimos (3061), "a pestilence, any deadly infectious malady," is used in the plural in Luke 21:11 (in some mss., Matt. 24:7); in Acts 24:5, metaphorically, "a pestilent fellow."

PETITION

aitema (155), from *aiteo*, "to ask" is rendered "petitions" in 1 John 5:15.

PHARISEES

pharisaios (5330), from an Aramaic word *peras* (found in Dan. 5:28), signifying "to separate," owing to a different manner of life from that of the general public. The "Pharisees" and Sadducees appear as distinct parties in the latter half of the 2nd cent. B.C., though they represent tendencies traceable much earlier in Jewish history, tendencies which became pronounced after the return from Babylon (537 B.C.). The immediate progenitors of the two parties were, respectively, the Hasidaeans and the Hellenizers; the latter, the antecedents of the Sadducees, aimed at removing Judaism from its narrowness and sharing in the advantages of Greek life and culture. The Hasidaeans, a transcription of the Hebrew *chasidim*, i.e., "pious ones," were a society of men zealous for religion, who acted under the guidance of the scribes, in opposition to the godless Hellenizing party; they scrupled to oppose the legitimate high priest even when he was on the Greek side. Thus the Hellenizers were a political sect, while the Hasidaeans, whose fundamental principle was complete separation from non-Jewish elements, were the strictly legal party among the Jews, and were ultimately the more popular and influential party. In their zeal for the Law they almost deified it and their attitude became merely external, formal, and mechanical. They laid stress, not upon the righteousness of an action, but upon its formal correctness. Consequently their opposition to Christ was inevitable; His manner of life and teaching was essentially a condemnation of theirs; hence His denunciation of them, e.g., Matt. 6:2, 5, 16; 15:7 and chapter 23.

While the Jews continued to be divided into these two parties, the spread of the testimony of the gospel must have produced what in the public eye seemed to be a new sect, and in the extensive development which took place at Antioch, Acts 11:19-26, the name "Christians" seems to have become a popular term applied to the disciples as a sect, the primary cause, however, being their witness to Christ. The opposition of both "Pharisees" and Sadducees (still mutually antagonistic, Acts 23:6-10) against the new "sect" continued unabated during apostolic times.

PHILOSOPHER

philosophos (5386), lit., "loving wisdom" (*philos*, "loving," *sophia*, "wisdom"), occurs in Acts 17:18.

PHILOSOPHY

philosophia (5385) denotes "the love and pursuit of wisdom," hence, "philosophy," the investigation of truth and nature; in Col. 2:8, the so-called "philosophy" of false teachers.

PHYLACTERY

phulakterion (5440), primarily "an outpost," or "fortification" (*phulax*, "a guard"), then, "any kind of safeguard," became used especially to denote "an amulet." In the NT it denotes a prayer fillet, "a phylactery," a small strip of parchment, with portions of the Law written on it; it was fastened by a leather strap either to the forehead or to the left arm over against the heart, to remind the wearer of the duty of keeping the commandments of God in the head and in the heart; cf. Ex. 13:16; Deut. 6:8; 11:18. It was supposed to have potency as a charm against evils and demons. The Pharisees broadened their "phylacteries" to render conspicuous their superior eagerness to be mindful of God's Law, Matt. 23:5.

PIERCE

1. *diikneomai* (1338), "to go through, penetrate" (*dia*, "through," *ikneomai*, "to go"), is used of the power of the Word of God, in Heb. 4:12, "piercing."

2. *dierchomai* (1330), "to go through," is translated "shall pierce through" in Luke 2:35.

3. *ekkenteo* (1574), primarily "to prick out" (*ek*, "out," *kenteo*, "to prick"), signifies "to pierce," John 19:37; Rev. 1:7.

4. *nusso* (3572), "to pierce" or "pierce through," often of inflicting severe or deadly wounds, is used of the piercing of the side of Christ, John 19:34 (in some mss., Matt. 27:49).

5. *peripeiro* (4044), "to put on a spit," hence, "to pierce," is used metaphorically in 1 Tim. 6:10, of torturing one's soul with many sorrows, "have pierced (themselves) through."

PIETY (to shew)

eusebeo (2151), "to reverence, to show piety" towards any to whom dutiful regard is due (akin to *eusebes*, "pious, godly, devout"), is used in 1 Tim. 5:4 of the obligation on the part of children and grandchildren (RV) to express in a practical way their dutifulness "towards their own family"; in Acts 17:23 of worshiping God.

PILGRIM

parepidemos (3927), an adjective signifying "sojourning in a strange place, away from one's own people" (*para*, "from," expressing a contrary condition, and *epidemeo*, "to sojourn"; *demos*, "a people"), is used of OT saints, Heb. 11:13, "pilgrims" (coupled with *xenos*, "a foreigner"); of Christians, 1 Pet. 1:1, "sojourners (of the Dispersion)," RV; 2:11, "pilgrims" (coupled with *paroikos*, "an alien, sojourner"); the word is thus used metaphorically of those to whom Heaven is their own country, and who are sojourners on earth.

PILLAR

Old Testament

'ayil (352), "pillar, post," meaning a vertical piece of finished wood used in construction, 1 Kings 6:31.

mashshebah (4676), "pillar; monument; sacred stone," This word refers to a "pillar" as a personal memorial in 2 Sam. 18:18. In Gen. 28:18 the "monument" is a memorial of the Lord's appearance. *mashshebah* is used in connection with the altar built by Moses in Exod. 24:4, and it refers to "sacred stones or pillars."

New Testament

stulos (4769), "a column supporting the weight of a building," is used (a) metaphorically, of those who bear responsibility in the churches, as of the elders in the church at Jerusalem, Gal. 2:9; of a local church as to its responsibility, in a collective capacity, to maintain the doctrines of the faith by teaching and practice, 1 Tim. 3:15; some would attach this and the next words to the statement in v. 16; the connection in the Eng. versions seems preferable; (b) figuratively in Rev. 3:12, indicating a firm and permanent position in the spiritual, heavenly and eternal Temple of God; (c) illustratively, of the feet of the angel in the vision in Rev. 10:1, seen as flames rising like columns of fire indicative of holiness and consuming power, and thus reflecting the glory of Christ as depicted in 1:15; cf. Ezek. 1:7.

PINNACLE

pterugion (4419) denotes (a) "a little wing" (diminutive of *pterux*, "a wing"); (b) "anything like a wing, a turret, battlement," of the temple in Jerusalem, Matt. 4:5 and Luke 4:9 (of the *hieron*, "the entire precincts," or parts of the main building, as distinct from the *naos*, "the sanctuary"). This "wing" has been regarded (1) as the apex of the sanctuary, (2) the top of Solomon's porch, (3) the top of the Royal Portico, which Josephus describes as of tremendous height.

PIOUS

chacid (2623), "one who is pious, godly." Basically, *chasid* means one who practices "loving-kindness," so translated the "pious" or "godly one."

PIPE (Noun and Verb)

A. Noun.

aulos (836), "a wind instrument," e.g., "a flute" (connected with *aemi*, "to blow"), occurs in 1 Cor. 14:7.

B. Verb.

auleo (832), "to play on an *aulos*," is used in Matt. 11:17; Luke 7:32; 1 Cor. 14:7 (2nd part).

PIT

Old Testament

be'er (875), "pit; well." *be'er* means a "well" in which there may be water. Such a "well" may have a narrow enough mouth that it can be blocked with a stone which a single, strong man could move, Gen. 29:2, 10. In the desert country of the ancient Near East a "well" was an important place and its water the source of deep satisfaction for the thirsty. This concept pictures the role of a wife for a faithful husband, Prov. 5:15.

A "pit" may contain something other than water, like slimepits, Gen. 14:10. A "pit" may contain nothing as does the "pit" which becomes one's grave, Ps. 55:23. In some passages the word was to represent more than a depository for the body but a place where one exists after death, Ps. 69:15.

New Testament

1. *phrear* (5421), "a well, dug for water" (distinct from *pege*, "a fountain"), denotes "a pit" in Rev. 9:1, 2, RV, "the pit (of the abyss)," "the pit," i.e., the shaft leading down to the abyss, KJV, "(bottomless) pit"; in Luke 14:5, RV, well (KJV, "pit"); in John 4:11, 12, "well."

2. *bothunos* (999) is rendered "pit" in Matt. 12:11.

PITIABLE (most)

eleeinoeros (1652*), the comparative degree of *eleeinos*, "miserable, pitiable" (*eleos*, "pity"), is used in 1 Cor. 15:19, "most pitiable" (RV), lit., "more pitiable than all men."

PITIFUL, PITY

1. *polusplanchnos* (*4184*) denotes "very pitiful" or "full of pity" (*polus*, "much," *splanchnon*, "the heart"; in the plural, "the affections"), occurs in Jas. 5:11, RV, "full of pity."

2. *eusplanchnos* (*2155*), "compassionate, tenderhearted," lit., "of good heartedness" (*eu*, "well," and *splanchnon*), is translated "pitiful" in 1 Pet. 3:8, KJV, RV, "tenderhearted," as in Eph. 4:32.

PLAGUE

1. *mastix* (*3148*), "a whip, scourge," Acts 22:24, "by scourging"; Heb. 11:36, "scourgings," is used metaphorically of "disease" or "suffering," Mark 3:10; 5:29, 34; Luke 7:21.

2. *plege* (*4127*), "a stripe, wound" (akin to *plesso*, "to smite"), is used metaphorically of a calamity, "a plague," Rev. 9:20; 11:6; 15:1, 6, 8; 16:9, 21 (twice); 18:4, 8; 21:9; 22:18.

PLAY

paizo (*3815*), properly, "to play as a child" (*pais*), hence denotes "to play" as in dancing and making merry, 1 Cor. 10:7.

PLEAD

Old Testament

A. Verb.

rib (*7378*), "to plead, strive, conduct a legal case, make a charge." The prophets use *rib* frequently to indicate that God has an indictment, a legal case, against Israel, Amos 7:4. Micah 6 is a classic example of such a legal case against Judah, calling on the people "to plead" their case (6:1) and progressively showing how only God has a valid case (6:8).

B. Noun.

rib (*7379*), "strife; dispute," Mic. 6:2.

New Testament

entunchano (*1793*), "to make petition," is used of the "pleading" of Elijah against Israel, Rom. 11:2, RV, "pleadeth with" (KJV, "maketh intercession to").

PLEASE, PLEASING (Noun), WELL-PLEASING, PLEASURE

A. Verbs.

1. *aresko* (*700*) signifies (a) "to be pleasing to, be acceptable to," Matt. 14:6; Mark 6:22; Acts 6:5; Rom. 8:8; 15:2; 1 Cor. 7:32-34; Gal. 1:10; 1 Thess. 2:15; 4:1 (where the preceding *kai*, "and," is epexegetical, "even," explaining the "walking," i.e., Christian manner

P

of life as "pleasing" God; in Gen. 5:22, where the Hebrew has "Enoch walked with God," the Sept. has "Enoch pleased God"; cf. Mic. 6:8; Heb. 11:5); 2 Tim. 2:4; (b) "to endeavor to please," and so "to render service," doing so evilly in one's own interests, Rom 15:1, which Christ did not, v. 3; or unselfishly, 1 Cor. 10:33; 1 Thess 2:4.

2. *euaresteo* (2100) signifies "to be well-pleasing" (*eu*, "well," and a form akin to No. 1); in the active voice, Heb. 11:5, RV, "he had been "well-pleasing" (unto God)," KJV, "he pleased"; so v. 6; in the passive voice, Heb. 13:16.

3. *eudokeo* (2106) signifies (a) "to be well pleased, to think it good" [*eu*, "well," and *dokeo*], not merely an understanding of what is right and good as in *dokeo*, but stressing the willingness and freedom of an intention or resolve regarding what is good, e.g., Luke 12:32, "it is (your Father's) good pleasure"; so Rom. 15:26, 27, RV; 1 Cor. 1:21; Gal. 1:15; Col. 1:19; 1 Thess. 2:8, RV, "we were well pleased" (KJV, "we were willing"); this meaning is frequently found in the papyri in legal documents; (b) "to be well pleased with," or "take pleasure in," e.g., Matt. 3:17; 12:18; 17:5; 1 Cor. 10:5; 2 Cor. 12:10; 2 Thess. 2:12; Heb. 10:6, 8, 38; 2 Pet. 1:17.

4. *thelo* (2309), "to will, wish, desire," is translated "it pleased (Him)" in 1 Cor. 12:18; 15:38, RV.

5. *spatalao* (4684), "to live riotously," is translated "giveth herself to pleasure" in 1 Tim. 5:6, RV (KJV, "liveth in pleasure"); "taken your pleasure" in Jas. 5:5, KJV, "been wanton."

B. Adjectives.

1. *arestos* (701) denotes "pleasing, agreeable," John 8:29, RV, "(the things that are) pleasing," KJV, "(those things that) please," KJV and RV in 1 John 3:22; in Acts 6:2, "fit" (RV marg., "pleasing"), 12:3, "it pleased," lit., "it was pleasing."

C. Noun.

areskeia (or -*ia*) (699), a "pleasing," a giving pleasure, Col. 1:10, of the purpose Godward of a walk worthy of the Lord (cf. 1 Thess. 4:1).

PLEASURE
Old Testament

A. Noun.

chepets (2656), "pleasure; delight; desire; request; affair; thing." This word often means "pleasure" or "delight," 1 Sam. 15:22; acceptable words, Eccl. 12:10, i.e., words that were both true and aesthetically pleasing; "willingly" [in delight], Prov. 31:13. *chepets* can mean not simply what one takes pleasure in or what gives someone delight but one's wish or desire, 2 Sam. 23:5; "to grant a request," 1 Kings 5:8; precious stones, Isa. 54:12. Third, *chepets* sometimes represents *one's affairs* as that *in which one takes de light*, Eccl. 3:1. In Isa. 58:13 the first occurrence of this word means "pleasure" or "delight." Finally, in one passage this word means "affair" in the sense of a "thing" or "situation," Eccl. 5:8.

B. Verb.

chapets (2654), "to take pleasure in, take care of, desire, delight in, have delight in," 2 Sam. 15:26.

C. Adjective.

chapets (2655), "delighting in, having pleasure in," Ps. 35:27.

New Testament

A. Nouns.

1. *hedone* (2237), "pleasure," is used of the gratification of the natural desire or sinful desires (akin to *hedormai*, "to be glad," and *hedeos*, "gladly"), Luke 8:14; Titus 3:3; Jas. 4:1, 3, RV, "pleasures" (KJV, "lusts"); in the singular, 2 Pet. 2:13.

2. *eudokia* (2107), "good pleasure," Eph. 1:5, 9; Phil. 2:13; 2 Thess. 1:11.

3. *apolausis* (619), "enjoyment," is used with *echo*, "to have," and rendered "enjoy the pleasures" (lit., "pleasure") in Heb. 11:25.

B. Adjective.

philedonos (5369), "loving pleasure" (*philos*, "loving," and A, No. 1), occurs in 2 Tim. 3:4, RV, "lovers of pleasure" (KJV, "...pleasures").

PLENTEOUS

polus (4183), "much," is rendered "plenteous" in Matt. 9:37, of a harvest of souls, and Luke 10:2, RV (KJV, "great").

PLOT

epiboule (1917), lit., "a plan against" (*epi*, "against," *boule*, "a counsel, plan"), is translated "plot" in the RV (KJV, "laying await" and "lying in wait") in Acts 9:24; 20:3, 19; 23:30.

P

PLUCK (out)

1. *tillo* (5089) is used of "plucking off ears of corn," Matt. 12:1; Mark 2:23; Luke 6:1.

2. *harpazo* (726), "to seize, snatch," is rendered "pluck" in John 10:28, 29, KJV, RV, "snatch."

3. *exaireo* (1807), "to take out" (*ex* for *ek*, "out," haireo, "to take"), is translated "pluck out," of the eye as the occasion of sin, in Matt. 5:29; 18:9, indicating that, with determination and promptitude, we are to strike at the root of unholy inclinations, ridding ourselves of whatever would stimulate them.

4. **exorusso** (*846*), "to dig out or up," is rendered "ye would have plucked out (your eyes)" in Gal. 4:15, an indication of their feelings of gratitude to, and love for, the apostle. The metaphor affords no real ground for the supposition of a reference to some weakness of his sight, and certainly not to the result of his temporary blindness at his conversion, the recovery from which must have been as complete as the infliction. There would be some reason for such an inference had the pronoun "ye" been stressed; but the stress is on the word "eyes"; their devotion prompted a readiness to part with their most treasured possession on his behalf.

5. **ekrizoo** (*1610*), "to pluck up by the roots" (**ek**, "out," **rhiza**, "a root"), is so translated in Jude 12 (figuratively), and in the KJV in Luke 17:6, RV, "rooted up"; "root up," Matt. 13:29; "shall be rooted up," 15:13.

POINT, POINTS

A. Noun.

kephalaion (*2774*), the neuter of the adjective **kephalaios**, "of the head," is used as a noun, signifying (a) "a sum, amount, of money," Acts 22:28; (b) "a chief point," Heb. 8:1, not the summing up of the subject, as the KJV suggests, for the subject was far from being finished in the Epistle; on the contrary, in all that was being set forth by the writer "the chief point" consisted in the fact that believers have "a High Priest" of the character already described.

B. Verb.

deloo (*1213*), "to make plain" (**delos**, "evident"), is translated "did point unto" in 1 Pet. 1:11, RV (KJV, "did signify"), of the operation of "the Spirit of Christ" in the prophets of the Old Testament in "pointing" on to the time and its characteristics, of the sufferings of Christ and subsequent glories.

POLLUTE, POLLUTION

Old Testament

chalal (*2490*), "to pollute, defile, profane, begin." The most frequent use of this Hebrew root is in the sense of "to pollute, defile." This may be a ritual defilement, such as that resulting from contact with a dead body, Lev. 21:4; ceremonial profaning of the sacred altar by the use of tools in order to shape the stones, Exod. 20:25. In more than 50 instances, this root is used in the sense of "to begin," Gen. 4:26.

New Testament

alisgema (*234*), akin to a late verb **alisgeo**, "to pollute," denotes "a pollution, contamination," Acts 15:20; "pollutions of idols," i.e., all the contaminating associations connected with idolatry including meats from sacrifices offered to idols.

POMP

phantasia (5325), as a philosophic term, denoted "an imagination"; then, "an appearance," like *phantasma*, "an apparition"; later, "a show, display, pomp" (Eng., "phantasy"), Acts 25:23. In the Sept., Hab. 2:18; 3:10; Zech. 10:1.

PONDER

sumballo (4820), "to throw together, confer," etc., has the meaning "to ponder," i.e., "to put one thing with another in considering circumstances," in Luke 2:19.

POOR

Old Testament

A. Nouns.

'ani (6041), "poor; weak; afflicted; humble." This noun is frequently used in synonymous parallelism with *'ebyon* ("needy") and/or *dal* ("poor"). It differs from both in emphasizing some kind of disability or distress. A hired servant as one who is in a lower (oppressive) social and material condition is described both as an *'ebyon* and *'ani*, Deut. 24:14-15. An *'ani* can call on God for defense. Financially, the *'ani* lives from day to day and is socially defenseless, being subject to oppression, Exod. 22:25. The godly protect and deliver the "afflicted," Isa. 10:2; Ezek. 18:17, while the ungodly take advantage of them, increasing their oppressed condition, Isa. 58:7. The king is especially charged to protect the *'ani*: "Open thy mouth, judge righteously, and plead the cause of the poor and needy," Prov. 31:9.

'ani can refer to one who is physically oppressed, Isa. 51:21. Physical oppression is sometimes related to spiritual oppression as in Ps. 22:24; 25:16; 68:10. In such cases spiritual poverty and want are clearly in view. Sometimes the word means "humble" or "lowly," as it does in Zech. 9:9; cf. Ps. 18:27; Prov. 3:34; Isa. 66:2.

dal (1800), "one who is low, poor, reduced, helpless, weak." *dal* is related to, but differs from, *'ani* (which suggests affliction of some kind), *'ebyon* (which emphasizes need), and *rash* (which suggests destitution). The *dallim* constituted the middle class of Israel—those who were physically deprived (in the ancient world the majority of people were poor). For example, the *dallim* may be viewed as the opposite of the rich, Exod. 30:15; cf. Ruth 3:10; Prov. 10:15.

In addition, the word may connote social poverty or lowliness. As such, *dal* describes those who are the counterparts of the great, Lev. 19:15; cf. Amos 2:7; of low status, or weak, Judg. 6:15; cf.

2 Sam. 3:1. God commands that society protect the poor, the lowly, and the weak, Exod. 23:2-3; cf. Lev. 14:21; Isa. 10:2. He also warns that if men fail to provide justice, He will do so, Isa. 11:4. A fourth emphasis appears in Gen. 41:19 (the first biblical appearance of the word), where *dal* is contrasted to "healthy" or "fat," 2 Sam. 13:4.

B. Verbs.

dalal (1809), "to be low, hang down," Ps. 79:8.

'anah (6031), "to afflict, oppress, humble," Gen. 15:13.

C. Adjective.

'anaw (6035), "humble; poor; meek." *'anaw* depicts the objective condition as well as the subjective stance of Moses. He was entirely dependent on God and saw that he was, Num. 12:3.

New Testament

A. Adjectives.

1. *ptochos* (4434), has the broad sense of "poor," (a) literally, e.g., Matt. 11:5; 26:9, 11; Luke 21:3 (with stress on the word, "a conspicuously poor widow"); John 12:5, 6, 8; 13:29; Jas. 2:2, 3, 6; the "poor" are constantly the subjects of injunctions to assist them, Matt. 19:21; Mark 10:21; Luke 14:13, 21; 18:22; Rom. 15:26; Gal. 2:10; (b) metaphorically, Matt. 5:3; Luke 6:20; Rev. 3:17.

2. *penichros* (3998), akin to B, "needy, poor," is used of the widow in Luke 21:2 (cf. No. 1, of the same woman, in v. 3); it is used frequently in the papyri.

B. Noun.

penes (3993), "a laborer" (akin to *penomai*, "to work for one's daily bread"), is translated "poor" in 2 Cor. 9:9.

PORCH

1. *stoa* (4745), "a portico," is used (a) of the "porches" at the pool of Bethesda, John 5:2; (b) of the covered colonnade in the Temple, called Solomon's "porch," John 10:23; Acts 3:11; 5:12 a portico on the eastern side of the temple; this and the other "porches" existent in the time of Christ were almost certainly due to Herod's restoration.

2. *pulon* (440), akin to *pule*, "a gate" (Eng., "pylon"), is used of "a doorway, porch or vestibule" of a house or palace, Matt. 26:71. In the parallel passage Mark 14:68, No. 3 is used, and *pulon* doubtless stands in Matt. 26 for *proaulion*.

3. *proaulion* (4259), "the exterior court" or "vestibule," between the door and the street, in the houses of well-to-do folk, Mark 14:68, "porch" (RV marg., "forecourt").

PORTION

A. Nouns.

1. *meros* (*3313*), "a part," is translated "portion" in Matt. 24:51; Luke 12:46; 15:12.

2. *kleros* (*2819*), "a lot," is translated "portion" in Acts 1:17, RV.

3. *meris* (*3310*), "a part," is translated "portion" in 2 Cor. 6:15, RV.

B. Verb.

summerizo (*4829*), "to have a part with" (akin to A, No. 3), is translated "have their portion with" in 1 Cor. 9:13. RV.

C. Adverb

polumeros (*4181*) signifies "in many parts" or "portions" (*polus*, "many," and A, No. 1), Heb. 1:1, RV (KJV, "at sundry times").

POSSIBLE

A. Adjective.

dunatos (*1415*), "strong, mighty, powerful, able (to do)," in its neuter form signifies "possible," Matt. 19:26; 24:24; 26:39; Mark 9:23; 10:27; 13:22; 14:35, 36; Luke 18:27; Acts 2:24; 20:16 (27:39, in some mss; *dunamai*, "to be able," in the most authentic, RV, "they could"); Rom. 12:18; Gal. 4:15.

B. Verb.

eimi (*1510*), "to be," is used in the third person singular, impersonally, with the meaning "it is possible," negatively in 1 Cor. 11:20, RV, (KJV, "it is not"), and Heb. 9:5, "we cannot," lit., "it is not possible."

POVERTY

ptocheia (*4432*), "destitution," is used of the "poverty" which Christ voluntarily experienced on our behalf, 2 Cor. 8:9; of the destitute condition of saints in Judea, v. 2; of the condition of the church in Smyrna, Rev. 2:9, where the word is used in a general sense.

POWER (Noun, and Verb, to have, bring under)
Old Testament

koach (*3581*), "strength; power; force; ability." The basic meaning of *koach* is an ability to do something. Samson's "strength" lay in his hair, Judg. 16:5, and we must keep in mind that his "strength" had been demonstrated against the Philistines. Nations and kings exert their "powers," Josh. 17:17; Dan. 8:24. In the Old Testament it is recognized that by eating one gains "strength," 1 Sam. 28:22, whereas one loses one's "abilities" in fasting, 1 Sam. 28:20. A special sense of *koach* is the meaning "property," Ezra 2:69. A proverb warns against adultery, because one's "strength," or one's wealth, may be taken by others, Prov. 5:10.

In the Old Testament, God had demonstrated His "strength" to Israel. The language of God's "strength" is highly metaphorical. God's right hand gloriously manifests His "power," Exod. 15:6; loud, Ps. 29:4; power, Exod. 32:11.

New Testament

A. Nouns.

1. *dunamis* (1411), is sometimes used, by metonymy, of persons and things, e.g., (a) of God, Matt. 26:64; Mark 14:62; (b) of angels, e.g., perhaps in Eph. 1:21, RV, "power," KJV, "might" (cf. Rom. 8:38; 1 Pet. 3:22); (c) of that which manifests God's "power": Christ, 1 Cor. 1:24; the gospel, Rom. 1:16; (d) of mighty works (RV, marg., "power" or "powers"), e.g., Mark 6:5, "mighty work"; so 9:39, RV (KJV, "miracle"); Acts 2:22 (ditto); 8:13, "miracles"; 2 Cor. 12:12, RV, "mighty works" (KJV, "mighty deeds").

2. *exousia* (1849) denotes "freedom of action, right to act"; used of God, it is absolute, unrestricted, e.g., Luke 12:5 (RV marg., "authority"); in Acts 1:7 "right of disposal" is what is indicated; used of men, authority is delegated. Angelic beings are called "powers" in Eph. 3:10 (cf. 1:21); 6:12; Col. 1:16; 2:15 (cf. 2:10).

3. *ischus* (2479), "ability, force, strength," is nowhere translated "power" in the RV (KJV in 2 Thess. 1:9).

4. *kratos* (2904) is translated "power" in the RV and KJV in 1 Tim. 6:16; Heb. 2:14; in Eph. 1:19 (last part); 6:10, KJV, "power" (RV, "strength").

B. Verb.

exousiazo (1850), "to exercise authority" (akin to A, No. 2), is used (a) in the active voice, Luke 22:25, RV, "have authority" (KJV, "exercise authority"), of the "power" of rulers; 1 Cor. 7:4 (twice), of marital relations and conditions; (b) in the passive voice, 1 Cor. 6:12, to be brought under the "power" of a thing; here, this verb and the preceding one connected with it, *exesti*, present a *paronomasia*, which Lightfoot brings out as follows: "All are within my power; but I will not put myself under the power of any one of all things."

POWERFUL, POWERFULLY

Adjective.

ischuros (2478), "strong, mighty," akin to *ischus*, is translated "powerful" in 2 Cor. 10:10, KJV (RV, "strong).

B. Adverb.

eutonos (2159) signifies "vigorously, vehemently" (*eu*, "well," *teino*, "to stretch"), Luke 23:10, "vehemently," of the accusation of the chief priests and scribes against Christ; Acts 18:28, RV, "powerfully" (KJV, "mightily"), of Apollos in confuting Jews. In the Sept., Josh. 6:8.

PRAISE

Old Testament

A. Verbs.

halal (1984), "to praise, celebrate, glory, sing (praise), boast." While *halal* is often used simply to indicate "praise" of people, including the king, 2 Chron. 23:12, or the beauty of Absalom, 2 Sam. 14:25, the word is usually used in reference to the "praise" of God. Indeed, not only all living things but all created things, including the sun and moon, are called upon "to praise" God, Ps. 148:2-5, 13; 150:1. Typically, such "praise" is called for and expressed in the sanctuary, especially in times of special festivals, Isa. 62:9. The Book of Psalms contains more than half the occurrences of *halal* in its various forms.

The word *halal* is the source of "Hallelujah," a Hebrew expression of "praise" to God which has been taken over into virtually every language of mankind. The Hebrew *Hallelujah* is generally translated *"Praise the Lord!"* The Hebrew term is more technically translated *"Let us praise Yah,"* the term "Yah" being a shortened form of "Yahweh," Ps. 68:4; cf. Rev. 19:1, 3-4, 6.

yadah (3034), "to give thanks, laud, praise." As is to be expected, this word is found most frequently in the Book of Psalms (some 70 times). As an expression of thanks or praise, it is a natural part of ritual or public worship as well as personal praise to God, Ps. 30:9, 12; 35:18.

B. Nouns.

tehillah (8416), "glory; praise; song of praise; praiseworthy deeds." *tehillah* denotes a quality or attribute of some person or thing, "glory or praiseworthiness," Deut. 10:21. Israel is God's "glory" when she exists in a divinely exalted and blessed state, Isa. 62:7; cf. Jer. 13:11. Second, in some cases *tehillah* represents the words or song by which God is publicly lauded, or by which His "glory" is publicly declared, Ps. 22:22, 25. In a third nuance *tehillah* is a technical-musical term for a song (*shir*) which exalts or praises God: "David's psalm of praise" (heading for Ps. 145; v. 1 in the Hebrew). Finally, *tehillah* may represent deeds which are worthy of "praise," or deeds for which the doer deserves "praise and glory," Exod. 15:11.

todah (8426), "thanksgiving." *todah* is used to indicate "thanksgiving" in songs of worship, Ps. 26:7; 42:4. Sometimes the word is used to refer to the thanksgiving choir or procession, Neh. 12:31,

38. One of the peace offerings was designated the thanksgiving offering, Lev. 7:12.

New Testament

A. Nouns.

1. *ainos* (*136*), primarily "a tale, narration," came to denote "praise"; in the NT only of praise to God, Matt. 21:16; Luke 18:43.

2. *epainos* (*1868*), a strengthened form of No. 1 (*epi* upon), denotes "approbation, commendation, praise"; it is used (a) of those on account of, and by reason of, whom as God's heritage, "praise" is to be ascribed to God, in respect of His glory (the exhibition of His character and operations), Eph. 1:12 in v. 14, of the whole company, the church, viewed as "*God's* own possession" (RV); in v. 6, with particular reference to the glory of His grace towards them; in Phil. 1:11, as the result of "the fruits of righteousness" manifested in them through the power of Christ; (b) of "praise" bestowed by God, upon the Jew spiritually (Judah = "praise"), Rom. 2:29; bestowed upon believers hereafter at the judgment seat of Christ, 1 Cor. 4:5 (where the definite article indicates that the "praise" will be exactly in accordance with each person's actions); as the issue of present trials, "at the revelation of Jesus Christ," 1 Pet. 1:7; (c) of whatsoever is "praiseworthy," Phil. 4:8; (d) of the approbation by churches of those who labor faithfully in the ministry of the gospel, 2 Cor. 8:18; (e) of the approbation of well-doers by human rulers, Rom. 13:3; 1 Pet. 2:14.

3. *ainesis* (*133*), "praise" (akin to No. 1), is found in Heb. 13:15, where it is metaphorically represented as a sacrificial offering.

B. Verbs

1. *aineo* (*134*), "to speak in praise of, to praise" (akin to A, No. 1), is always used of "praise" to God, (a) by angels, Luke 2:13; (b) by men, Luke 2:13; 19:37; 24:53; Acts 2:20, 47; 3:8, 9; Rom. 15:11 (No. 2 in some texts); Rev. 19:5.

2. *epaineo* (*1867*), akin to A, No. 2, is rendered "praise," 1 Cor. 11:2, 17, 22.

3. *humneo* (*5214*) denotes (a) transitively, "to sing, to laud, sing to the praise of" (Eng., "hymn"), Acts 16:25, KJV, "sang praises" (RV, "singing hymns"); Heb. 2:12, RV, "will I sing (Thy) praise," KJV, "will I sing praise (unto Thee)," lit., "I will hymn Thee"; (b) intransitively, "to sing," Matt. 26:30; Mark 14:26, in both places of the singing of the paschal hymns (Ps. 113-118, and 136), called by Jews the Great Hallel.

4. *psallo* (*5567*), primarily, "to twitch" or "twang" (as a bowstring, etc.), then, "to play" (a stringed instrument with the fingers), in the NT, to sing a hymn, sing "praise"; in Jas. 5:13, RV, "sing praise" (KJV, "sing psalms").

PRATE

phluareo (5396) signifies "to talk nonsense" (from *phluo*, "to babble"; cf. the adjective *phluaros*, "babbling, garrulous, tattlers," 1 Tim. 5:13), "to raise false accusations," 3 John 10.

PRAY, PRAYER

Old Testament

A. Verb.

palal (6419), "to pray, intervene, mediate, judge." In the intensive form *palal* expresses the idea of "to mediate, to come between two parties," always between human beings, 1 Sam. 2:25; "to mediate" requires "making a judgment," as in Ezek. 16:52.

The first occurrence of *palal* in the Old Testament is in Gen. 20:7, where the reflexive or reciprocal form of the verb expresses the idea of "interceding for, prayer in behalf of." Samuel "intercedes" continually for Israel, 1 Sam. 12:23. Prayer is directed not only toward Yahweh but toward pagan idols as well, Isa. 44:17. Sometimes prayer is made to Yahweh that He would act against an enemy, 2 Kings 19:20.

B. Noun.

tepillah (8605), "prayer." This word means to "make a request," which when referring to asking God is translated "prayer," 1 Kings 8:28; or as a title in scripture, psalm title in 5 psalms; Hab. 3:1, related to music in some way.

New Testament

A. Verbs.

1. *euchomai* (2172), "to pray (to God)," is used with this meaning in 2 Cor. 13:7; v. 9, RV, "pray" (KJV, "wish"); Jas. 5:16; 3 John 2, RV, "pray" (KJV, wish). Even when the RV and KJV translate by "I would," Acts 26:29, or "wished for," Acts 27:29 (RV, marg., "prayed"), or "could wish," Rom. 9:3 (RV, marg., "could pray"), the indication is that "prayer" is involved.

2. *proseuchomai* (4336), "to pray," is always used of "prayer" to God, and is the most frequent word in this respect, especially in the Synoptists and Acts, once in Romans, 8:26; in Ephesians, 6:18; in Philippians, 1:9; in 1 Timothy, 2:8; in Hebrews, 13:18; in Jude, v. 20. For the injunction in 1 Thess. 5:17.

P

B. Nouns.

1. *euche* (2171), akin to A, No. 1, denotes "a prayer," Jas. 5:15; "a vow," Acts 18:18 and 21:23.

2. *proseuche* (4335), akin to A, No. 2, denotes (a) "prayer" (to God), the most frequent term, e.g., Matt. 21:22; Luke 6:12, where the phrase is not to be taken literally as if it meant, "the prayer of

God" (subjective genitive), but objectively, "prayer to God." In Jas. 5:17, "He prayed fervently," RV, is, lit., "he prayed with prayer" (a Hebraistic form): Eph. 6:18; Phil. 4:6; 1 Tim. 2:1; 5:5; (b) "a place of prayer," Acts 16:13, 16, a place outside the city wall, RV.

3. *deesis* (*1162*), primarily "a wanting, a need," then, "an asking, entreaty, supplication," in the NT is always addressed to God and always rendered "supplication" or "supplications" in the RV; in the KJV "prayer," or "prayers," in Luke 1:13; 2:37; 5:33; Rom. 10:1; 2 Cor. 1:11; 9:14; Phil. 1:4 (in the 2nd part, "request"); 1:19; 2 Tim. 1:3; Heb. 5:7; Jas. 5:16; 1 Pet. 3:12.

PREACH, PREACHING

A. Verbs.

1. *euangelizo* (*2097*) is almost always used of "the good news" concerning the Son of God as proclaimed in the gospel (exceptions are e.g., Luke 1:19; 1 Thess. 3:6, in which the phrase "to bring (or show) good (or glad) tidings" does not refer to the gospel; Gal. 1:8 (2nd part). With reference to the gospel the phrase "to bring, or declare, good, or glad, tidings" is used in Acts 13:32; Rom. 10:15; Heb. 4:2.

In Luke 4:18 the RV "to preach good tidings" gives the correct quotation from Isaiah, rather than the KJV "to preach the Gospel."

2. *kerusso* (*2784*) signifies (a) "to be a herald," or, in general, "to proclaim," e.g., Matt. 3:1; Mark 1:45, "publish"; in Luke 4:18, RV, "to proclaim," KJV, "to preach"; so verse 19; Luke 12:3; Acts 10:37; Rom. 2:21; Rev. 5:2. In 1 Pet. 3:19 the probable reference is, not to glad tidings (which there is no real evidence that Noah preached, nor is there evidence that the spirits of antediluvian people are actually "in prison"), but to the act of Christ after His resurrection in proclaiming His victory to fallen angelic spirits; (b) "to preach the gospel as a herald," e.g., Matt. 24:14; Mark 13:10, RV, "be preached" (KJV, "be published"); 14:9; 16:15, 20; Luke 8:1; 9:2; 24:47; Acts 8:5; 19:13; 28:31; Rom. 10:14, present participle, lit., "(one) preaching," "a preacher"; 10:15 (1st part); 1 Cor. 1:23; 15:11, 12; 2 Cor. 1:19; 4:5; 11:4; Gal. 2:2; Phil. 1:15; Col. 1:23; 1 Thess. 2:9; 1 Tim. 3:16; (c) "to preach the word," 2 Tim. 4:2 (of the ministry of the Scriptures, with special reference to the gospel).

3. *prokerusso* (*4296*), lit., "to proclaim as a herald" (*pro*, before, and No. 2), is used in Acts 13:24, "had first preached." Some mss. have the verb in Acts 3:20.

B. Nouns.

kerugma (*2782*), "a proclamation by a herald" (akin to A, No. 2), denotes "a message, a preaching" (the substance of what is "preached" as distinct from the act of "preaching"), Matt. 12:41;

Luke 11:32; Rom. 16:25; 1 Cor. 1:21; 2:4; 15:14; in 2 Tim. 4:17 and Titus 1:3, RV, "message," marg., "proclamation," KJV, "preaching."

PREACHER

kerux (2783), "a herald" (akin to A, No. 2 and B, above), is used (a) of the "preacher" of the gospel, 1 Tim. 2:7; 2 Tim. 1:11; (b) of Noah, as a "preacher" of righteousness, 2 Pet. 2:5.

PRECEDE

phthano (5348), "to anticipate, to come sooner," is translated "shall (in no wise) precede" in 1 Thess. 4:15, RV (KJV, "prevent"), i.e., "shall in no wise obtain any advantage over" (the verb does not convey the thought of a mere succession of one event after another); the apostle, in reassuring the bereaved concerning their departed fellow believers, declares that, as to any advantage, the dead in Christ will "rise first."

PRECEPT

1. *entole* (1785), "a commandment," is translated "precept" in Mark 10:5 (RV, "commandment"); so Heb. 9:19.

2. *entalma* (1778) is always translated "precepts" in the RV, Matt. 15:9.

PRECIOUS, PRECIOUSNESS

Old Testament

A. Adjective.

yaqar (3368), "precious; rare; excellent; weighty; noble." First, *yaqar* means "precious" in the sense of being rare and valuable, 2 Sam. 12:30; or, "rare," 1 Sam. 3:1. Second, the word can focus on the value of a thing, Ps. 36:7. Third, this word means "weighty," Eccl. 10:1; or "noble," Lam. 4:2.

B. Verb.

yaqar (3365), "to be difficult, be valued from, be valued or honored, be precious," 1 Sam. 26:21.

C. Noun.

yeqar (3366), "precious thing; value; price; splendor; honor." The word signifies "value or price," Zech. 11:13; "splendor," Esth. 1:4; "honor," Esth. 8:16.

New Testament

1. *timios* (5093), translated "precious," e.g., in Jas. 5:7; 1 Pet. 1:19; 2 Pet. 1:4; in 1 Cor. 3:12, KJV (RV, "costly").

2. *entimos* (1784), "precious," 1 Pet. 2:4, 6.

3. *poluteles* (*4185*), "very expensive," translated "very precious" in Mark 14:3, KJV (RV, "very costly").

4. *polutimos* (*4186*), "of great value"; comparative degree in 1 Pet. 1:7.

5. *barutimos* (*927*), "of great value, exceeding precious" (*barus*, "weighty," *time*, value), is used in Matt. 26:7.

PREDESTINATE

proorizo (*4309*): "to make a choice," the full theological implications are much debated, Acts 4:28; Rom. 8:29, 30; 1 Cor. 2:7; Eph 1:5, 11.

PREEMINENCE (to have the)

1. *proteuo* (*4409*), "to be first" (*protos*), "to be preeminent," is used of Christ in relation to the Church, Col. 1:18.

2. *philoproteuo* (*5383*), lit., "to love to be preeminent" (*philos*, "loving"), "to strive to be first," is said of Diotrephes, 3 John 9.

PREFER, PREFERRING

proegeomai (*4285*), "to go before and lead," is used in Rom. 12:10, in the sense of taking the lead in showing deference one to another, "(in honor) preferring one another."

PREJUDICE

prokrima (*4299*) denotes "prejudging" (akin to *prokrino*, "to judge beforehand"), 1 Tim. 5:21, RV, "prejudice" (marg., "preference"), preferring one person, another being put aside, by unfavorable judgment due to partiality.

PRESENCE

Noun.

parousia (*3952*): lit. "coming," so meaning the being present in a place, with a focus on the return of the person, Matt. 24:37. This can refer to the presence of any person, but Christians look forward to the return of Christ.

PRESENT (to be)

Verbs.

1. *pareimi* (*3918*) signifies (a) "to be by, at hand or present," of persons, e.g., Luke 13:1; Acts 10:33; 24:19; 1 Cor. 5:3; 2 Cor. 10:2, 11; Gal. 4:18, 20; of things, John 7:6, of a particular season in the Lord's life on earth, "is (not yet) come," or "is not yet at hand"; Heb. 12:11, of chastening "(for the) present" (the neuter of the present participle, used as a noun); in 13:5 "such things as ye have" is, lit., "the things that are present"; 2 Pet. 1:12, of the truth "(which) is with

(you)" (not as KJV, "the present truth," as if of special doctrines applicable to a particular time); in v. 9 "he that lacketh" is lit., "to whom are not present"; (b) "to have arrived or come," Matt. 26:50, "thou art come," RV; John 11:28; Acts 10:21; Col. 1:6.

2. *enistemi* (*1764*), "to set in," or, in the middle voice and perfect tense of the active voice, "to stand in, be present," is used of the present in contrast with the past, Heb. 9:9, where the RV correctly has "(for the time) *now* present" (for the incorrect KJV, "then present"); in contrast to the future, Rom. 8:38; 1 Cor. 3:22; Gal. 1:4, "present"; 1 Cor. 7:26, where "the present distress" is set in contrast to both the past and the future; 2 Thess. 2:2, where the RV, the *now* present" gives the correct meaning (KJV, incorrectly, "is at hand"); the saints at Thessalonica, owing to their heavy afflictions were possessed of the idea that "the day of the Lord," RV (not as KJV, "the day of Christ"), had begun; this mistake the apostle corrects; 2 Tim. 3:1, "shall come."

B. Adverb.

nun (*3568*), "now," is translated "present," with reference to this age or period ("world"), in Rom. 8:18; 11:5; 2 Tim. 4:10; Titus 2:12.

PRESENT (Verb)

paristemi (*3936*) denotes, when used transitively, "to place beside" (*para*, "by," *histemi*, "to set"), "to present," e.g., Luke 2:22; Acts 1:3, "He shewed (Himself)"; 9:41; 23:33; Rom. 6:13 (2nd part), RV, "present," KJV "yield"; so 6:19 (twice); 12:1; 2 Cor. 4:14; 11:2; Eph. 5:27; Col. 1:22, 28; 2 Tim. 2:15, RV (KJV, "shew").

PRESERVE

1. *tereo* (*5083*) is translated "to preserve" in 1 Thess. 5:23, where the verb is in the singular number, as the threefold subject, "spirit and soul and body," is regarded as the unit, constituting the person. The aorist or "point" tense regards the continuous "preservation" of the believer as a single, complete act, without reference to the time occupied in its accomplishment; in Jude 1, KJV (RV, "kept").

2. *phulasso* (*5442*), "to guard, protect, preserve," is translated "preserved" in 2 Pet. 2:5, RV (KJV, "saved").

PREVAIL

1. *ischuo* (*2480*), "to be strong, powerful," is translated "to prevail" in Acts 19:16, 20; Rev. 12:8.

2. *katischuo* (*2729*), "to be strong against" (*kata*, "against," and No. 1), is used in Matt. 16:18, negatively of the gates of Hades; positively in Luke 21:36.

3. *nikao* (*3528*), "to conquer, prevail," is used as a law term in Rom. 3:4, "(that) Thou...mightest prevail [KJV, 'overcome'] (when

Thou comest into judgment)"; that the righteousness of the judge's verdict compels an acknowledgement on the part of the accused, is inevitable where God is the judge. God's promises to Israel provided no guarantee that an unrepentant Jew would escape doom. In Rev. 5:5, KJV, "hath prevailed" (RV, "hath overcome").

PRICE

A. Noun.

time (5092) denotes "a valuing," hence, objectively, (a) "price paid or received," Matt. 27:6, 9; Acts 4:34 (plural); 5:2, 3; 7:16, RV, "price (in silver)," KJV, "sum (of money)"; 19:19 (plural); 1 Cor. 6:20; 7:23; (b) "value, honor, preciousness."

B. Verb.

timao (5091), "to fix the value, to price," is translated "was priced" and "did price" in the RV of Matt. 27:9 (KJV, "was valued" and "did value").

C. Adjectives

1. *poluteles* (4185), "of great price," 1 Pet. 3:4.
2. *polutimos* (4186), "of great price," Matt. 13:46.

PRIDE

A. Nouns.

1. *alazonia* (or —*eia*) (212) is translated "pride" in 1 John 2:16, KJV.

2. *huperephania* (5243), "pride," Mark 7:22.

B. Verb.

tuphoo (5187), "lifted up with pride," 1 Tim. 3:6, KJV (RV, "puffed up").

PRIEST

Old Testament

A. Noun.

kohen (3548), "priest." This word means a person specially authorized by position or heritage, who is a worker or servant of a deity, with a special focus on worship and liturgical duties, and must be "clean" ceremonially in the god's eyes: Egyptian "priests," Gen. 41:50; 46:20; 47:26; Philistine, 1 Sam. 6:2; of Dagon, 1 Sam. 5:5; of Baal, 2 Kings 10:19; of Chemosh, Jer. 48:7; and (the most common use), of the Lord, the true God, Num. 16:5-7.

The Priesthood of Aaron is the most common in the OT, Exod. 28:1, 41; 29:9, 29-30. However, not all individuals born in the family of Aaron could serve as "priest." Certain physical deformities excluded a man from that perfection of holiness which a "priest" should manifest before Yahweh, Lev. 21:17-23.

A priest of Yahweh must go through rigorous ceremonies to keep "clean" and so presentable to work in a consecrated area, and wear special clothing, Exod. 29:1-37 and Lev. 8. The duties of the priesthood were very clearly defined by the Mosaic law. These duties were assumed on the eighth day of the service of consecration, Lev. 9:1. Another function of the priests was to act as teachers of the Law, Lev. 10:10-11; Deut. 33:10; 2 Chron. 5:3; 17:7-9; Ezek. 44:23; Mal. 2:6-9; medical diagnosis, Lev. 13-14; be sentencing judges, and other civil matters, Deut. 21:5; 2 Chron. 19:8-11.

B. Verb.

kahan (3547), "to act as a priest." This verb, which appears 23 times in biblical Hebrew, is derived from the noun *kohen.* The verb appears only in the intensive stem, Exod. 28:1.

New Testament

1. *hiereus* (2409), "one who offers sacrifice and has the charge of things pertaining thereto," is used (a) of a "priest" of the pagan god Zeus, Acts 14:13; (b) of Jewish "priests," e.g., Matt. 8:4; 12:4, 5; Luke 1:5, where allusion is made to the 24 courses of "priests" appointed for service in the Temple, cf. 1 Chron. 24:4ff.; John 1:19; Heb. 8:4; (c) of believers, Rev. 1:6; 5:10; 20:6. Israel was primarily designed as a nation to be a kingdom of "priests," offering service to God, e.g., Ex. 19:6, the Israelites having renounced their obligations, Ex. 20:19, the Aaronic priesthood was selected for the purpose, till Christ came to fulfill His ministry in offering up Himself; since then the Jewish priesthood has been abrogated, to be resumed nationally, on behalf of Gentiles, in the millennial kingdom, Is. 61:6; 66:21. Meanwhile all believers, from Jews and Gentiles, are constituted "a kingdom of priests," Rev. 1:6, "a holy priesthood," 1 Pet. 2:5, and "royal," v. 9. The NT knows nothing of a sacerdotal class in contrast to the laity; all believers are commanded to offer the sacrifices mentioned in Rom. 12:1; Phil. 2:17; 4:18; Heb. 13:15, 16; 1 Pet. 2:5; (d) of Christ, Heb. 5:6; 7:11, 15, 17, 21; 8:4 (negatively); (e) of Melchizedek, as the foreshadower of Christ, Heb. 7:1, 3.

2. *archiereus* (749) designates (a) "the high priests" of the Levitical order, frequently called "chief priests" in the NT, including "ex-high priests" and members of "high priestly" families, e.g., Matt. 2:4; 16:21; 20:18; 21:15; in the singular, a "high priest," e.g., Abiathar, Mark 2:26; Annas and Caiaphas, Luke 3:2, where the RV rightly has "in the high priesthood of A. and C." (cf. Acts 4:6). As to the combination of the two in this respect, Annas was the "high priest" from A.D. 7-14, and, by the time referred to, had been deposed for some years; his son-in-law, Caiaphas, the fourth "high

priest" since his deposition, was appointed about A.D. 24. That Annas was still called the "high priest" is explained by the facts (1) that by the Mosaic law the high priesthood was held for life, Num. 35:25; his deposition was the capricious act of the Roman procurator, but he would still be regarded legally and religiously as "high priest" by the Jews; (2) that he probably still held the office of deputy-president of the Sanhedrin, cf. 2 Kings 25:18; (3) that he was a man whose age, wealth and family connections gave him a preponderant influence, by which he held the real sacerdotal power; indeed at this time the high priesthood was in the hands of a clique of some half dozen families; the language of the writers of the gospels is in accordance with this, in attributing the high priesthood rather to a caste than a person; (4) the "high priests" were at that period mere puppets of Roman authorities who deposed them at will, with the result that the title was used more loosely than in former days.

The divine institution of the priesthood culminated in the "high priest," it being his duty to represent the whole people, e.g., Lev. 4:15, 16; ch. 16. The characteristics of the Aaronic "high priests" are enumerated in Heb. 5:1-4; 8:3; 9:7, 25; in some mss., 10:11 (RV, marg.); 13:11.

(b) Christ is set forth in this respect in the Ep. to the Hebrews, where He is spoken of as "a high priest," 4:15; 5:5, 10; 6:20; 7:26; 8:1, 3 (RV); 9:11; "a great high priest," 4:14; "a great priest," 10:21; "a merciful and faithful high priest," 2:17; "the Apostle and high priest of our confession," 3:1, RV; "a high priest after the order of Melchizedek," 5:10. One of the great objects of this Epistle is to set forth the superiority of Christ's High Priesthood as being of an order different from and higher than the Aaronic, in that He is the Son of God (see especially 7:28), with a priesthood of the Melchizedek order. Seven outstanding features of His priesthood are stressed, (1) its character, 5:6, 10; (2) His commission, 5:4, 5; (3) His preparation, 2:17; 10:5; (4) His sacrifice, 8:3; 9:12, 14, 27, 28; 10:4-12; (5) His sanctuary, 4:14; 8:2; 9:11, 12, 24; 10:12, 19; (6) His ministry, 2:18; 4:15; 7:25; 8:6; 9:15, 24; (7) its effects, 2:15; 4:16; 6:19, 20; 7:16, 25; 9:14, 28; 10:14-17, 22, 39; 12:1; 13:13-17.

PRIESTHOOD, PRIEST'S OFFICE

Nouns.

1. *hierateuma* (2406) denotes "a priesthood" (akin to *hierateuo*), "a body of priests," consisting of all believers, the whole church (not a special order from among them), called "a holy priesthood," 1 Pet. 2:5; "a royal priesthood," v. 9; the former term is associated with offering spiritual sacrifices, the latter with the royal dignity of showing forth the Lord's excellencies (RV).

2. *hierosune* (2420), "a priesthood," signifies the office, quality,

rank and ministry of "a priest," Heb. 7:11, 12, 24, where the contrasts between the Levitical "priesthood" and that of Christ are set forth.

3. *hierateia* (2405), "a priesthood," denotes the priest's office, Luke 1:9; Heb. 7:5, RV, "priest's office."

PRINCE

Old Testament

nashi' (5387), "prince; chief; leader." This noun is clearly associated with leadership, both Israelite and non-Israelite, sometimes called a "prince," and so be a leader by one's heritage or position in the clan, Gen. 17:20; cf. 25:16; or "ruler," Exod. 16:22; or "leader," Exod. 34:31; cf. Josh. 22:30.

New Testament

1. *archegos* (747), primarily an adjective signifying "originating, beginning," is used as a noun, denoting "a founder, author, prince or leader," Acts 3:15, "Prince" (marg., "Author"); 5:31.

2. *archon* (758), aside from human rulers, (a) of Christ, as "the Ruler (KJV, Prince) of the kings of the earth," Rev. 1:5; (b) of the Devil, as "prince" of this world, John 12:31; 14:30; 16:11; of the power of the air, Eph. 2:2, "the air" being that sphere in which the inhabitants of the world live and which, through the rebellious and godless condition of humanity, constitutes the seat of his authority; (c) of Beelzebub, the "prince" of the demons, Matt. 9:24; 12:24; Mark 3:22; Luke 11:15.

PRINCIPAL

protos (4413), "first," is translated "principal men" in the RV of Luke 19:47 and Acts 25:2.

PRINCIPALITY

arche (746), "beginning, government, rule," is used of supramundane beings who exercise rule, called "principalities"; (a) of holy angels, Eph. 3:10, the church in its formation being to them the great expression of "the manifold (or "much-varied") wisdom of God"; Col. 1:16; (b) of evil angels, Rom. 8:38; Col. 2:15.

PRINCIPLES

1. *arche* (746), "beginning," is used in Heb. 6:1, in its relative significance, of the beginning of the thing spoken of; here "the first principles of Christ," lit., "the account (or word) of the beginning of Christ," denotes the teaching relating to the elementary facts concerning Christ.

2. *stoicheion* (4747) is translated "principles" in Heb. 5:12.

PRISON, PRISON-HOUSE

phulake (*5438*), denotes a "prison," e.g., Matt. 14:10; Mark 6:17; Acts 5:19; 2 Cor. 11:23; in 2 Cor. 6:5 and Heb. 11:36 it stands for the condition of imprisonment; in Rev. 2:10; 18:2, "hold" (twice, RV, marg., "prison"; in the 2nd case, KJV, "cage"); 20:7.

PRISONER

1. *desmios* (*1198*), an adjective, primarily denotes "binding, bound," then, as a noun, "the person bound, a captive, prisoner" (akin to *deo*, "to bind"), Matt. 27:15, 16; Mark 15:6; Acts 16:25, 27; 23:18; 25:14, RV (KJV, "in bonds"), 27; 28:16, 17; Eph. 3:1; 4:1; 2 Tim. 1:8; Philem. 1, 9; in Heb. 10:34 and 13:3, "in bonds."

2. *desmotes* (*1202*), akin to No. 1, occurs in Acts 27:1, 42.

3. *sunaichmalotos* (*4869*), "a fellow prisoner," primarily "one of fellow captives in war" (from *aichme*, "a spear," and *haliskomai*, "to be taken"), is used by Paul of Andronicus and Junias, Rom. 16:7; of Epaphras, Philem. 23; of Aristarchus, Col. 4:10.

PRIVATE, PRIVATELY

A. Adjective.

idios (*2398*), one's own, is translated "private" in 2 Pet. 1:20.

B. Adverbial Phrase.

kat 'idian is translated "privately" in Matt. 24:3; Mark 4:34, RV (KJV, "when they were alone"); 6:32 (KJV only); 7:33, RV; 9:28; 13:3; Luke 10:23; Acts 23:19; Gal. 2:2. Contrast 2:14.

PRIZE

1. *brabeion* (*1017*), "a prize bestowed in connection with the games" (akin to *brabeus*, "an umpire," and *brabeuo*, "to decide, arbitrate," "rule," Col. 3:15), 1 Cor. 9:24, is used metaphorically of "the reward" to be obtained hereafter by the faithful believer, Phil. 3:14; the preposition *eis*, "unto," indicates the position of the goal. The "prize" is not "the high calling," but will be bestowed in virtue of, and relation to, it, the heavenly calling, Heb. 3:1, which belongs to all believers and directs their minds and aspirations heavenward; for the "prize" see especially 2 Tim. 4:7, 8.

2. *harpagmos* (*725*), akin to *harpazo*, "to seize, carry off by force," is found in Phil. 2:6, "(counted it not) a prize," RV (marg., "a thing to be grasped"), KJV, "(thought it not) robbery"; it may have two meanings, (a) in the active sense, "the act of seizing, robbery," a meaning in accordance with a rule connected with its formation, (b) in the passive sense, "a thing held as a prize."

PROCLAIM

1. **kerusso** (*2784*) is translated "to proclaim" in the RV, for KJV, "to preach," in Matt. 10:27; Luke 4:19; Acts 8:5; 9:20.

2. **katangello** (*2605*), "to declare, proclaim," is translated "to proclaim" in the RV, for KJV, to "show," in Acts 16:17; 26:23; 1 Cor. 11:26, where the verb makes clear that the partaking of the elements at the Lord's Supper is a "proclamation" (an evangel) of the Lord's death; in Rom. 1:8, for KJV, "spoken of"; in 1 Cor. 2:1, for KJV, "declaring."

PROCONSUL

anthupatos (*446*), from **anti**, "instead of," and **hupatos**, "supreme," denotes "a consul, one acting in place of a consul, a proconsul, the governor of a senatorial province" (i.e., one which had no standing army). The "proconsuls" were of two classes, (a) exconsuls, the rulers of the provinces of Asia and Africa, who were therefore "proconsuls" (b) those who were ex-praetors or "proconsuls" of other senatorial provinces (a praetor being virtually the same as a consul). To the former belonged the "proconsuls" at Ephesus, Acts 19:38 (KJV, "deputies"); to the latter, Sergius Paulus in Cyprus, Acts 13:7, 8, 12, and Gallio at Corinth, 18:12. In the NT times Egypt was governed by a prefect. Provinces in which a standing army was kept were governed by an imperial legate (e.g., Quirinius in Syria, Luke 2:2).

PROFANE (Adjective and Verb)

A. Adjective.

bebelos (*952*), primarily, "permitted to be trodden, accessible" (from **baino**, "to go," whence **belos**, "a threshold," hence, "unhallowed, profane" (opposite to **hieros**, "sacred"), is used of (a) persons, 1 Tim. 1:9; Heb. 12:16; (b) things, 1 Tim. 4:7; 6:20; 2 Tim. 2:16.

B. Verb.

bebeloo (*953*), primarily, "to cross the threshold," hence, "to profane, pollute," occurs in Matt. 12:5 and Acts 24:6 (the latter as in 21:28, 29.

PROFESS, PROFESSION

A. Verbs.

1. **epangello** (*1861*), "to announce, proclaim, profess," is rendered "to profess" in 1 Tim. 2:10, of godliness, and 6:21, of "the knowledge...falsely so called."

2. **homologeo** (*3670*) is translated "to profess" in Matt. 7:23 and Titus 1:16; in 1 Tim. 6:12, KJV (RV, "confess").

3. **phasko** (*5335*), "to affirm, assert."

B. Noun.

homologia (*3671*), akin to A, No. 2, "confession," is translated "profession" and "professed" in the KJV only.

PROFIT (Noun and Verb), PROFITABLE, PROFITING

A. Nouns.

1. *opheleia* (*5622*) primarily denotes "assistance"; then, "advantage, benefit, profit," in Rom. 3:1.

2. *ophelos* (*3786*), "profit" in Jas. 2:14, 16.

3. *sumpheron* (*4851d*), the neuter form of the present participle of *sumphero*, is used as a noun with the article in Heb. 12:10, "(for our) profit"; in some mss. in 1 Cor. 7:35 and 10:33; in 1 Cor. 12:7, preceded by *pros*, "with a view to, towards," translated "to profit withal," lit., "towards the profiting."

4. *sumphoros* (*4851d*), akin to No. 3, an adjective, signifying "profitable, useful, expedient," is used as a noun, and found in the best texts, with the article, in 1 Cor. 7:35 and 10:33 (1st part), the word being understood in the 2nd part.

B. Verbs.

1. *sumphero* (*4851*), "to be profitable," Matt. 5:29, 30; Acts 20:20.

2. *opheleo* (*5623*), akin to A, No. 1, is translated "to profit" in Matt. 15:5; 16:26; Mark 7:11; 8:36; Luke 9:25, RV; John 6:63; Rom. 2:25; 1 Cor. 13:3; 14:6; Gal. 5:2; Heb. 4:2; 13:9.

C. Adjectives.

1. *chresimos* (*5539*), "useful" (akin to *chraomai*, "to use"), is translated as a noun in 2 Tim. 2:14, "to (no) profit," lit., "to (nothing) profitable.

2. *euchrestos* (*2173*), "useful, serviceable" (*eu*, "well," *chrestos*, "serviceable," akin to *chraomai*, see No. 1), is used in Philem. 11, "profitable," in contrast to *achrestos*, "unprofitable" (*a*, negative), with a delightful play upon the name "Onesimus," signifying "profitable" (from *onesis*, "profit"), a common name among slaves. Perhaps the prefix *eu* should have been brought out by some rendering like "very profitable," "very serviceable," the suggestion being that whereas the runaway slave had done great disservice to Philemon, now after his conversion, in devotedly serving the apostle in his confinement, he had thereby already become particularly serviceable to Philemon himself, considering that the latter would have most willingly rendered service to Paul, had it been possible.

3. *ophelimos* (*5624*), "useful, profitable" (akin to B, No. 2), is translated "profitable" in 1 Tim. 4:8, both times in the RV (KJV, "profiteth" in the 1st part), of physical exercise, and of godliness;

355 Vine's Dictionary **PROMISE**

in 2 Tim. 3:16 of the God-breathed Scriptures; in Titus 3:8, of maintaining good works.

PROLONG

parateino (*3905*), "to stretch out along" (*para*, "along," *teino*, "to stretch"), is translated "prolonged" in Acts 20:7.

PROMISE (Noun and Verb)

A. Noun.

1. *epangelia* (*1860*), primarily a law term, denoting "a summons" (*epi*, "upon," *angello*, "to proclaim, announce"), also meant "an undertaking to do or give something, a promise." Except in Acts 23:21 it is used only of the "promises" of God. It frequently stands for the thing "promised," and so signifies a gift graciously bestowed, not a pledge secured by negotiation; thus, in Gal. 3:14, "the promise of the Spirit" denotes "the promised Spirit": cf. Luke 24:49; Acts 2:33 and Eph. 1:13; so in Heb. 9:15, "the promise of the eternal inheritance" is "the promised eternal inheritance." On the other hand, in Acts 1:4, "the promise of the Father," is the "promise" made by the Father.

In Gal. 3:16, the plural "promises" is used because the one "promise" to Abraham was variously repeated, Gen. 12:1-3; 13:14-17; 15:18; 17:1-14; 22:15-18, and because it contained the germ of all subsequent "promises"; cf. Rom. 9:4; Heb. 6:12; 7:6; 8:6; 11:17; Gal. 3 is occupied with showing that the "promise" was conditional upon faith and not upon the fulfillment of the Law. The Law was later than, and inferior to, the "promise," and did not annul it, v. 21; cf. 4:23, 28. Again, in Eph. 2:12, "the covenants of the promise" does not indicate different covenants, but a covenant often renewed, all centering in Christ as the "promised" Messiah-Redeemer, and comprising the blessings to be bestowed through Him.

In 2 Cor. 1:20 the plural is used of every "promise" made by God: cf. Heb. 11:33; in 7:6, of special "promises" mentioned. For other applications of the word, see, e.g., Eph. 6:2; 1 Tim. 4:8; 2 Tim. 1:1; Heb. 4:1; 2 Pet. 3:4, 9; in 1 John 1:5 some mss. have this word, instead of *angelia*, "message."

The occurrences of the word in relation to Christ and what centers in Him, may be arranged under the headings (1) the contents of the "promise," e.g., Acts 26:6; Rom. 4:20; 1 John 2:25; (2) the heirs, e.g., Rom. 9:8; 15:8; Gal. 3:29; Heb. 11:9; (3) the conditions, e.g., Rom. 4:13, 14; Gal. 3:14-22; Heb. 10:36.

B. Verbs.

1. *epangello* (*1861*), "to announce, proclaim," has in the NT the two meanings "to profess" and "to promise," each used in the middle voice; "to promise" (a) of "promises" of God, Acts 7:5; Rom.

4:21; in Gal. 3:19, passive voice; Titus 1:2; Heb. 6:13; 10:23; 11:11; 12:26; Jas. 1:12; 2:5; 1 John 2:25; (b) made by men, Mark 14:11; 2 Pet. 2:19.

2. *proepangello* (4279), in the middle voice, "to promise before" *pro*, and No. 1), occurs in Rom. 1:2; 2 Cor. 9:5.

PRONOUNCE

lego (3004), "to say, declare," is rendered "pronounceth (blessing)" in Rom. 4:6, RV, which necessarily repeats the verb in v. 9 (it is absent from the original), for KJV, "*cometh*" (italicized).

PROOF

dokimion (1383), "a test, a proof," is rendered "proof" in Jas. 1:3, RV (KJV, "trying"); it is regarded by some as equivalent to *dokimeion*, "a crucible, a test"; it is the neuter form of the adjective *dokimios*, used as a noun, which has been taken to denote the means by which a man is tested and "proved" (Mayor), in the same sense as *dokime* in 2 Cor. 8:2; the same phrase is used in 1 Pet. 1:7.

PROPER

asteios (791) is translated "proper" in Heb. 11:23, RV, "goodly."

PROPHECY, PROPHESY, PROPHESYING

Old Testament

A. Verb.

naba' (5012), "to prophesy." This word means to speak God's message to the people, under the influence of the divine spirit, 1 Kings 22:8; Jer. 29:27; Ezek. 37:10; by compulsion, Amos 3:8; cf. Jer. 20:7; possibly in an ecstatic experience, 1 Sam. 10:6, 11; 19:20. Music is sometimes spoken of as a means of prophesying, as in 1 Chron. 25:1-3. The false prophets, although not empowered by the divine spirit, are spoken of as prophesying, Jer. 23:21. The false prophet is roundly condemned because he speaks a non-authentic word, Ezek. 13:2-3.

"To prophesy" is much more than the prediction of future events. Indeed, the first concern of the prophet is to speak God's word to the people of his own time, calling them to covenant faithfulness. The prophet's message is conditional, dependent upon the response of the people. Thus, by their response to this word, the people determine in large part what the future holds, as is well illustrated by the response of the Ninevites to Jonah's preaching. Of course, prediction does enter the picture at times, such as in Nahum's prediction of the fall of Nineveh, Nah. 2:13, and in the various messianic passages, Isa. 9:1-6; 11:1-9; 52:13-53:12)

B. Noun.

nabi' (5030), "prophet." *nabi'* represents "prophet," whether a true or false prophet, male or female, cf. Deut. 13:1-5; Isa. 8:3. True prophets were mouthpieces of the true God, Exod. 7:1; 1 Chron. 29:29. This basic meaning of *nabi'* is supported by other passages, Deut. 18:14-22. A prophet was held to a very high standard, Deut. 18:19, 20.

In the plural *nabi'* is used of some who do not function as God's mouthpieces. In the time of Samuel there were men who followed him. They went about praising God (frequently with song) and trying to stir the people to return to God, 1 Sam. 10:5, 10; 19:20. The word is also used of "heathen prophets," 1 Kings 18:19.

New Testament

A. Noun.

propheteia (4394) signifies "the speaking forth of the mind and counsel of God" (*pro*, "forth," *phemi*, "to speak"; in the NT it is used (a) of the gift, e.g., Rom. 12:6; 1 Cor. 12:10; 13:2; (b) either of the exercise of the gift or of that which is "prophesied," e.g., Matt. 13:14; 1 Cor. 13:8; 14:6, 22 and 1 Thess. 5:20, "prophesying (s)"; 1 Tim. 1:18; 4:14; 2 Pet. 1:20, 21; Rev. 1:3; 11:6; 19:10; 22:7, 10, 18, 19.

In such passages as 1 Cor. 12:28; Eph. 2:20, the "prophets" are placed after the "Apostles," since not the prophets of Israel are intended, but the "gifts" of the ascended Lord, Eph. 4:8, 11; cf. Acts 13:1; the purpose of their ministry was to edify, to comfort, and to encourage the believers, 1 Cor. 14:3, while its effect upon unbelievers was to show that the secrets of a man's heart are known to God, to convict of sin, and to constrain to worship, vv. 24, 25.

B. Adjective.

prophetikos (4397), "of or relating to prophecy," or "proceeding from a prophet, prophetic," is used of the OT Scriptures, Rom. 16:26, "of the prophets," lit., "(by) prophetic (Scriptures)"; 2 Pet. 1:19, "the word of prophecy (*made* more sure)," i.e., confirmed by the person and work of Christ (KJV, "a more sure, etc."), lit., "the prophetic word."

C. Verb.

propheteuo (4395), "to be a prophet, to prophesy," is used (a) with the primary meaning of telling forth the divine counsels, e.g., Matt. 7:22; 26:68; 1 Cor. 11:4, 5; 13:9; 14:1, 3-5, 24, 31, 39; Rev. 11:3; (b) of foretelling the future, e.g., Matt. 15:7; John 11:51; 1 Pet. 1:10; Jude 14.

PROPHET

1. *prophetes* (4396), "one who speaks forth or openly," "a proclaimer of a divine message," denoted among the Greeks an interpreter of the oracles of the gods.

In the NT the word is used (a) of "the OT prophets," e.g., Matt. 5:12; Mark 6:15; Luke 4:27; John 8:52; Rom. 11:3; (b) of "prophets in general," e.g., Matt. 10:41; 21:46; Mark 6:4; (c) of "John the Baptist," Matt. 21:26; Luke 1:76; (d) of "prophets in the churches," e.g., Acts 13:1; 15:32; 21:10; 1 Cor. 12:28, 29; 14:29, 32, 37; Eph. 2:20; 3:5; 4:11; (e) of "Christ, as the aforepromised Prophet," e.g., John 1:21; 6:14; 7:40; Acts 3:22; 7:37, or, without the article, and, without reference to the Old Testament, Mark 6:15; Luke 7:16; in Luke 24:19 it is used with *aner*, "a man"; John 4:19; 9:17; (f) of "two witnesses" yet to be raised up for special purposes, Rev. 11:10, 18; (g) of "the Cretan poet Epimenides," Titus 1:12; (h) by metonymy, of "the writings of prophets," e.g., Luke 24:27; Acts 8:28.

2. *pseudoprophetes* (5578), "a false prophet," is used of such (a) in OT times, Luke 6:26; 2 Pet. 2:1; (b) in the present period since Pentecost, Matt. 7:15; 24:11, 24; Mark 13:22; Acts 13:6; 1 John 4:1; (c) with reference to a false "prophet" destined to arise as the supporter of the "Beast" at the close of this age, Rev. 16:13; 19:20; 20:10 (himself described as "another beast," 13:11).

PROPHETESS

prophetis (4398), the feminine of *prophetes* (see above), is used of Anna, Luke 2:36; of the self-assumed title of "the woman Jezebel" in Rev. 2:20.

PROPITIATION

A. Verb.

hilaskomai (2433) was used amongst the Greeks with the significance "to make the gods propitious, to appease, propitiate," inasmuch as their good will was not conceived as their natural attitude, but something to be earned first. This use of the word is foreign to the Greek Bible, with respect to God whether in the Sept. or in the NT. It is never used of any act whereby man brings God into a favorable attitude or gracious disposition. It is God who is "propitiated" by the vindication of His holy and righteous character, whereby through the provision He has made in the vicarious and expiatory sacrifice of Christ, He has so dealt with sin that He can show mercy to the believing sinner in the removal of his guilt and the remission of his sins.

Thus in Luke 18:13 it signifies "to be propitious" or "merciful to" (with the person as the object of the verb), and in Heb. 2:17 "to expiate, to make propitiation for" (the object of the verb being sins); here the RV, "to make propitiation" is an important correction of the KJV "to make reconciliation." Through the "propitiatory" sacrifice of Christ, he who believes upon Him is by God's own act delivered from justly deserved wrath, and comes under the covenant of grace. Never is God said to be reconciled, a fact itself indicative that the enmity exists on man's part alone, and that it is man who needs to be reconciled to God, and not God to man. God is always the same and, since He is Himself immutable, His relative attitude does change towards those who change. He can act differently towards those who come to Him by faith, and solely on the ground of the "propitiatory" sacrifice of Christ, not because He has changed, but because He ever acts according to His unchanging righteousness.

The expiatory work of the Cross is therefore the means whereby the barrier which sin interposes between God and man is broken down. By the giving up of His sinless life sacrificially, Christ annuls the power of sin to separate between God and the believer.

In the OT the Hebrew verb **kaphar** is connected with **kopher**, "a covering," and is used in connection with the burnt offering, e.g., Lev. 1:4; 14:20; 16:24, the guilt offering, e.g., Lev. 5:16, 18, the sin offering, e.g., Lev. 4:20, 26, 31, 35, the sin offering and burnt offering together, e.g., Lev. 5:10; 9:7, the meal offering and peace offering e.g., Ezek. 45:15, 17, as well as in other respects. It is used of the ram offered at the consecration of the high priest, Ex. 29:33, and of the blood which God gave upon the altar to make "propitiation" for the souls of the people, and that because "the life of the flesh is in the blood," Lev. 17:11, and "it is the blood that maketh atonement by reason of the life" (RV). Man has forfeited his life on account of sin and God has provided the one and only way whereby eternal life could be bestowed, namely, by the voluntary laying down of His life by His Son, under divine retribution. Of this the former sacrifices appointed by God were foreshadowings.

B. Nouns.

1. *hilasterion* (2435), akin to A, is regarded as the neuter of an adjective signifying "propitiatory." In the Sept. it is used adjectivally in connection with *epithema*, "a cover," in Exod. 25:17 and 37:6, of the lid of the ark, but it is used as a noun (without *epithema*), of locality, in Exod. 25:18, 19, 20, 21, 22; 31:7; 35:12; 37:7, 8, 9; Lev. 16:2, 13, 14, 15; Num. 7:89, and this is its use in Heb. 9:5.

Elsewhere in the NT it occurs in Rom. 3:25, where it is used of Christ Himself; the RV text and punctuation in this verse are important: "whom God set forth to be a propitiation, through faith, by His blood." The phrase "by His blood" is to be taken in immediate connection with "propitiation." Christ, through His expiatory death, is the personal means by whom God shows the mercy of His justifying grace to the sinner who believes. His "blood" stands for the voluntary giving up of His life, by the shedding of His blood in expiatory sacrifice under divine judgment righteously due to us as sinners, faith being the sole condition on man's part.

2. *hilasmos* (2434), akin to *hileos* ("merciful, propitious"), signifies "an expiation, a means whereby sin is covered and remitted."

It is used in the NT of Christ Himself as "the propitiation," in 1 John 2:2 and 4:10, signifying that He Himself, through the expiatory sacrifice of His death, is the personal means by whom God shows mercy to the sinner who believes on Christ as the One thus provided. In the former passage He is described as "the propitiation for our sins; and not for ours only, but also for the whole world." The italicized addition in the KJV, "the sins of," gives a wrong interpretation. What is indicated is that provision is made for the whole world, so that no one is, by divine predetermination, excluded from the scope of God's mercy; the efficacy of the "propitiation," however, is made actual for those who believe. In 4:10, the fact that God "sent His Son to be the propitiation for our sins," is shown to be the great expression of God's love toward man, and the reason why Christians should love one another.

PROPORTION

analogia (356), Cf. Eng., "analogy," signified in classical Greek "the right relation, the coincidence or agreement existing or demanded according to the standard of the several relations, not agreement as equality" (Cremer). It is used in Rom. 12:6, where "let us prophesy according to the proportion of our faith," RV, recalls v. 3. It is a warning against going beyond what God has given and faith receives.

PROSELYTE

proselutos (4339), akin to *proserchomai*, "to come to," primarily signifies "one who has arrived, a stranger"; in the NT it is used of converts to Judaism, or foreign converts to the Jewish religion, Matt. 23:15; Acts 2:10; 6:5; 13:43. There seems to be no connection necessarily with Palestine, for in Acts 2:10 and 13:43 it is used of those who lived abroad.

PROSPER

Old Testament

tsaleach (6743), "to succeed, prosper." This word generally expresses the idea of a successful venture, as contrasted with failure. The source of such success is God, 2 Chron. 26:5

New Testament

euodoo (2137), "to help on one's way" (*eu*, "well," *hodos*, "a way or journey"), is used in the passive voice signifying "to have a prosperous journey," Rom. 1:10; metaphorically, "to prosper, be prospered," 1 Cor. 16:2, RV, "(as) he may prosper," KJV, "(as God) hath prospered (him)," lit., "in whatever he may be prospered," i.e., in material things; the continuous tense suggests the successive circumstances of varying prosperity as week follows week; in 3 John 2, of the "prosperity" of physical and spiritual health.

PROUD

huperephanos (5244) signifies "showing oneself above others, preeminent" (**huper**, "above," **phainomai**, "to appear, be manifest"); it is always used in Scripture in the bad sense of "arrogant, disdainful, proud," Luke 1:51; Rom. 1:30; 2 Tim. 3:2; Jas. 4:6; 1 Pet. 5:5.

PROVE

A. Verbs.

1. **dokimazo** (1381), "to test, prove," with the expectation of approving, is translated "to prove" in Luke 14:19; Rom. 12:2; 1 Cor. 3:13, RV (KJV, "shall try"); 11:28, RV (KJV, "examine"); 2 Cor. 8:8, 22; 13:5; Gal. 6:4; Eph. 5:10; 1 Thess. 2:4 (2nd part), RV (KJV, "trieth"); 5:21; 1 Tim. 3:10; in some mss., Heb. 3:9 (the most authentic have the noun **dokimasia**, "a proving"); 1 Pet. 1:7, RV (KJV, "tried"); 1 John 4:1, RV (KJV, "try").

2. **peirazo** (3985), "to try," either in the sense of attempting, e.g., Acts 16:7, or of testing, is rendered "to prove" in John 6:6.

B. Noun.

peirasmos (3986), (a) "a trying, testing," (b) "a temptation," is used in sense (a) in 1 Pet. 4:12, with the preposition **pros**, "towards" or "with a view to," RV, "to prove" (KJV, "to try"), lit., "for a testing."

PROVIDE, PROVIDENCE, PROVISION

A. Verbs.

1. **hetoimazo** (2090), "to prepare," is translated "hast provided" in Luke 12:20, KJV.

2. **ktaomai** (2932), "to get, to gain," is rendered •provide" in Matt. 10:9.

3. **paristemi** (3936), "to present," signifies "to provide" in Acts 23:24.

4. **problepo** (4265), "to foresee," is translated "having provided" in Heb. 11:40.

5. **pronoeo** (4306), "to take thought for, provide," is translated "provide... for" in 1 Tim. 5:8; in Rom. 12:17 and 2 Cor. 8:21, RV, to take thought for (KJV, "to provide").

B. Noun.

pronoia (4307), "forethought" (**pro**, "before," **noeo**, "to think"), is translated "providence" in Acts 24:2; "provision" in Rom. 13:14.

PROVINCE

1. *eparcheia*, or —*ia* (*1885*) was a technical term for the administrative divisions of the Roman Empire. The original meaning was the district within which a magistrate, whether consul or praetor, exercised supreme authority. The word *provincia* acquired its later meaning when Sardinia and Sicily were added to the Roman territories, 227 B.C. On the establishment of the empire the proconsular power over all "provinces" was vested in the emperor. Two "provinces," Asia and Africa, were consular, i.e., held by ex-consuls; the rest were praetorian. Certain small "provinces," e.g. Judea and Cappadocia, were governed by procurators. They were usually districts recently added to the empire and not thoroughly Romanized. Judea was so governed in the intervals between the rule of native kings; ultimately it was incorporated in the "province" of Syria. The "province" mentioned in Acts 23:34 and 25:1 was assigned to the jurisdiction of an *eparchos*, "a prefect or governor."

2. *kanon* (*2583*) originally denoted "a straight rod," used as a ruler or measuring instrument, or, in rare instances, "the beam of a balance," the secondary notion being either (a) of keeping anything straight, as of a rod used in weaving, or (b) of testing straightness, as a carpenter's rule; hence its metaphorical use to express what serves "to measure or determine" anything. By a common transition in the meaning of words, "that which measures," was used for "what was measured." In general the word thus came to serve for anything regulating the actions of men, as a standard or principle. In Gal. 6:16, those who "walk by this rule (*kanon*)" are those who make what is stated in vv. 14 and 15 their guiding line in the matter of salvation through faith in Christ alone, apart from works, whether following the principle themselves or teaching it to others. In 2 Cor. 10:13, 15, 16, it is translated "province," RV (KJV, "rule" and "line of things"; marg., "line"; RV marg., "limit" or "measuring rod.") Here it signifies the limits of the responsibility in gospel service as measured and appointed by God.

PROVOCATION, PROVOKE

Old Testament

ka'as (*3707*), "to provoke, vex, make angry." This word means to be intensely displeased with another, often implying that an action venting the anger will occur, Deut. 4:25; 2 Kings 23:19.

New Testament

A. Nouns.

1. *parapikrasmos* (*3894*), from *para*, "amiss" or "from," used in-

tensively, and *pikraino*, "to make bitter" (*pikros*, "sharp, bitter"), "provocation," occurs in Heb. 3:8, 15.

2. *paroxusmos* (*3948*) denotes "a stimulation" (Eng., "paroxysm"), (cf. B, No. 2): in Heb. 10:24, "to provoke," lit., "unto a stimulation (of love)."

B. Verbs.

1. *parapikraino* (*3893*), "to embitter, provoke" (akin to A, No. 1), occurs in Heb. 3:16.

2. *paroxuno* (*3947*), primarily, "to sharpen" (akin to A, No. 2), is used metaphorically, signifying "to rouse to anger, to provoke," in the passive voice, in Acts 17:16, RV, "was provoked" (KJV, "was stirred"); in 1 Cor. 13:5, RV, "is not provoked" (the word "easily" in KJV, represents no word in the original).

3. *parorgizo* (*3949*), "to provoke to wrath."

4. *parazeloo* (*3863*), "to provoke to jealousy."

PRUDENCE, PRUDENT

A. Nouns.

1. *phronesis* (*5428*), akin to *phroneo*, "to have understanding" (*phren*, "the mind"), denotes "practical wisdom, prudence in the management of affairs." It is translated "wisdom" in Luke 1:17; "prudence" in Eph. 1:8.

2. *sunesis* (*4907*), "understanding," is rendered "prudence" in 1 Cor. 1:19, RV (KJV, "understanding"); it suggests quickness of apprehension, the penetrating consideration which precedes action.

B. Adjective.

sunetos (*4908*) signifies "intelligent, sagacious, understanding" (akin to *suniemi*, "to perceive"), translated "prudent" in Matt. 11:25, KJV (RV, "understanding"); Luke 10:21 (ditto); Acts 13:7, RV, "(a man) of understanding"; in 1 Cor. 1:19, "prudent," RV and KJV.

PSALM

psalmos (*5568*) primarily denoted "a striking or twitching with the fingers (on musical strings)"; then, "a sacred song, sung to musical accompaniment, a psalm." It is used (a) of the OT book of "Psalms," Luke 20:42; 24:44; Acts 1:20; (b) of a particular "psalm," Acts 13:33 (cf. v. 35); (c) of "psalms" in general, 1 Cor. 14:26; Eph. 5:19; Col. 3:16.

PUBLIC

demosios (*1219*), "belonging to the people" (*demos*, "the people"), is translated "public" in Acts 5:18, RV, "public (ward)," KJV, "common (prison)."

PUBLICAN

telones (5057) primarily denoted "a farmer of the tax" (from *telos*, "toll, custom, tax"), then, as in the NT, a subsequent subordinate of such, who collected taxes in some district, "a tax gatherer"; such were naturally hated intensely by the people; they are classed with "sinners," Matt. 9:10, 11; 11:9; Mark 2:15, 16; Luke 5:30; 7:34; 15:1; with harlots, Matt. 21:31, 32; with "the Gentile," Matt. 18:17; some mss. have it in Matt. 5:47, the best have *ethnikoi*, "Gentiles." See also Matt. 5:46; 10:3; Luke 3:12; 5:27, 29; 7:29; 18:10, 11, 13.

PUBLISH

1. *kerusso* (2784), "to be a herald, to proclaim, preach," is translated "to publish" in Mark 1:45; 5:20; 7:36; 13:10, KJV (RV, "preached"); Luke 8:39.

2. *diaphero* (1308), "to bear through," is translated "was published" in Acts 13:49, KJV (RV, "was spread abroad").

3. *ginomai* (1096), "to become, come to be," is translated "was published" in Acts 10:37, lit., "came to be."

4. *diangello* (1229), "to publish abroad," is so translated in Luke 9:60, RV (KJV, "preach"), and Rom. 9:17.

PUFF (up)

1. *phusioo* (5448), "to puff up, blow up, inflate" (from *phusa*, "bellows"), is used metaphorically in the NT, in the sense of being "puffed" up with pride, 1 Cor. 4:6, 18, 19; 5:2; 8:1; 13:4; Col. 2:18.

2. *tuphoo* (5187) is always rendered "to puff up" in the RV.

PUNISH

1. *kolazo* (2849) primarily denotes "to curtail, prune, dock" (from *kolos*, "docked"); then, "to check, restrain, punish"; it is used in the middle voice in Acts 4:21; passive voice in 2 Pet. 2:9, KJV, "to be punished" (RV, "under punishment," lit., "being punished"), a futurative present tense.

2. *timoreo* (5097), primarily, "to help," then, "to avenge" (from *time*, "value, honor," and *ouros*, "a guardian"), i.e., "to help" by redressing injuries, is used in the active voice in Acts 26:11, RV, "punishing" (KJV, "I punished"); passive voice in 22:5, lit., "(that) they may be punished."

PUNISHMENT

1. *ekdikesis* (1557): for 1 Pet. 2:14, KJV, "punishment" (RV, "vengeance").

2. *epitimia* (2009) in the NT denotes "penalty, punishment," 2 Cor. 2:6. Originally it signified the enjoyment of the rights and privileges of citizenship; then it became used of the estimate

(*time*) fixed by a judge on the infringement of such rights, and hence, in general, a "penalty."

3. *kolasis* (2851), akin to *kolazo*, "punishment," is used in Matt. 25:46, "(eternal) punishment," and 1 John 4:18, "(fear hath) punishment," RV (KJV, "torment"), which there describes a process, not merely an effect; this kind of fear is expelled by perfect love; where God's love is being perfected in us, it gives no room for the fear of meeting with His reprobation; the "punishment" referred to is the immediate consequence of the sense of sin, not a holy awe but a slavish fear, the negation of the enjoyment of love.

4. *dike* (1349), "justice," or "the execution of a sentence," is translated "punishment" in Jude 7, RV (KJV, "vengeance").

PURCHASE

1. *peripoieo* (4046) signifies "to gain" or "get for oneself, purchase"; middle voice in Acts 20:28 and 1 Tim. 3:13 (RV "gain"); see GAIN.

2. *agorazo* (59) is rendered "to purchase" in the RV of Rev. 5:9; 14:3, 4.

PURE, PURENESS, PURITY

A. Adjectives.

1. *hagnos* (53), "pure from defilement, not contaminated" (from the same root as *hagios*, "holy"), is rendered "pure" in Phil. 4:8; 1 Tim. 5:22; Jas. 3:17; 1 John 3:3.

2. *katharos* (2513), "pure," as being cleansed, e.g., Matt. 5:8; 1 Tim. 1:5; 3:9; 2 Tim. 1:3; 2:22; Titus 1:15; Heb. 10:22; Jas. 1:27; 1 Pet. 1:22; Rev. 15:6; 21:18; 22:1 (in some mss.).

3. *eilikrines* (1506) signifies "unalloyed, pure", (a) it was used of unmixed substances; (b) in the NT it is used of moral and ethical "purity," Phil. 1:10, "sincere"; so the RV in 2 Pet. 3:1 (KJV, "pure"). Some regard the etymological meaning as "tested by the sunlight" (Cremer).

B. Nouns.

1. *hagnotes* (54), the state of being *hagnos* (A, No. 1), occurs in 2 Cor. 6:6, "pureness"; 11:3, in the best mss., "(and the) purity," RV.

2. *hagneia* (47), synonymous with No. 1, "purity," occurs in 1 Tim. 4:12; 5:2, where it denotes the chastity which excludes all impurity of spirit, manner, or act.

PURGE (to cleanse)

1. *kathairo* (2508), akin to *katharos*, "to cleanse," is used of pruning, John 15:2, KJV, "purgeth" (RV, "cleanseth").

2. *ekkathairo* (1571), "to cleanse out, cleanse thoroughly," is said

of "purging" out leaven, 1 Cor. 5:7; in 2 Tim. 2:21, of "purging" oneself from those who utter "profane babblings," vv. 16-18.

3. *diakathairo* (*1223* and *2508*), "to cleanse thoroughly," is translated "will thoroughly purge" in Luke 3:17.

4. *kathakizo* (*2511*), "to cleanse, make clean," is translated "purging (all meats)," in Mark 7:19, KJV, RV, "making (all meats) clean"; Heb. 9:14, KJV, "purge" (RV, "cleanse"); so 9:22 (for v. 23, see PURIFY) and 10:2.

5. *diakatharizo* (*1245*), "to cleanse thoroughly," is translated "will thoroughly purge" in Matt. 3:12, KJV.

PURIFICATION, PURIFY, PURIFYING

A. Nouns.

1. *katharismos* (*2512*) is rendered "a cleansing," Mark 1:44; Luke 5:14; in Heb. 1:3, RV, "purification."

2. *katharotes* (*2514*), "cleansing," Heb. 9:13.

3. *hagnismos* (*49*) denotes "a ceremonial purification," Acts 21:26, for the circumstances of which with reference to the vow of a Nazirite (RV), see Num. 6:9-13.

B. Verbs.

1. *hagnizo* (*48*), akin to *hagnos*, "pure," "to purify, cleanse from defilement," is used of "purifying" (a) ceremonially, John 11:55; Acts 21:24, 26 (cf. No. 3 above); 24:18; (b) morally, the heart, Jas. 4:8; the soul, 1 Pet. 1:22; oneself, 1 John 3:3.

2. *katharizo* (*2511*), "to cleanse, make free from admixture," is translated "to purify" in Acts 15:9, KJV (RV, "cleansing"); Titus 2:14; Heb. 9:23, KJV (RV, "cleansed").

PURPLE

A. Noun.

porphura (*4209*) originally denoted the "purple-fish," then, "purple dye" (extracted from certain shell fish): hence, "a purple garment," Mark 15:17, 20; Luke 16:19; Rev. 18:12.

B. Adjective.

porphureos (*4210*), "purple, a reddish purple," a color extracted from certain shell fish, is used of the robe put in mockery on Christ, John 19:2, 5; Rev. 18:16, as a noun (with *himation*, "a garment," understood).

PURPOSE (Noun and Verb)

A. Nouns.

1. *boulema* (*1013*), "a purpose or will" (akin to *boulomai*, "to will, wish, purpose"), "a deliberate intention," occurs in Acts 27:43,

"purpose"; Rom. 9:19, "will"; 1 Pet. 4:3, in the best mss. (some have *thelema*), KJV, "will," RV, "desire."

2. *prothesis* (*4286*), "a setting forth" (used of the "showbread"), "a purpose" (akin to B, No. 2), is used (a) of the "purposes of God," Rom. 8:28; 9:11; Eph. 1:11; 3:11; 2 Tim. 1:9; (b) of "human purposes," as to things material, Acts 27:13; spiritual, Acts 11:23; 2 Tim. 3:10.

3. *gnome* (*1106*), "an opinion, purpose, judgment," is used in the genitive case with *ginomai*, "to come to be," in Acts 20:3, "he purposed," KJV (RV, "he determined"), lit., "he came to be of purpose."

B. Verbs.

1. *bouleuo* (*1011*), "to take counsel, resolve," always in the middle voice in the NT, "to take counsel with oneself," to determine with oneself, is translated "I purpose" in 2 Cor. 1:17 (twice).

2. *protithemi* (*4388*), "to set before, set forth" (*pro*, "before," and No. 2, akin to A, No. 2), is used in Rom. 3:25, "set forth," RV marg., "purposed," KJV marg., "foreordained," middle voice, which lays stress upon the personal interest which God had in so doing; either meaning, "to set forth" or "to purpose," would convey a scriptural view, but the context bears out the former as being intended here; in Rom. 1:13, "I purposed"; Eph. 1:9, "He purposed (in Him)," RV.

P

Q

QUATERNION

tetradion (*5069*), "a group of four" (*tetra—*,"four"), occurs in Acts 12:4. A "quaternion" was a set of four men occupied in the work of a guard, two soldiers being chained to the prisoner and two keeping watch; alternatively one of the four watched while the other three slept. The night was divided into four watches of three hours each; there would be one "quaternion" for each watch by day and by night.

QUENCH, UNQUENCHABLE

A. Verb.

sbennumi (*4570*) is used (a) of "quenching" fire or things on fire, Matt. 12:20, quoted from Isa. 42:3, figurative of the condition of the feeble; Heb. 11:34; in the passive voice, Matt. 25:8, of torches, RV, "are going out," lit., "are being quenched"; of the retributive doom hereafter of sin unrepented of and unremitted in this life, Mark 9:48 (in some mss. in vv. 44, 46); (b) metaphorically, of "quenching" the fire-tipped darts of the evil one, Eph. 6:16; of "quenching" the Spirit, by hindering His operations in oral testimony in the church gatherings of believers, 1 Thess. 5:19. The peace, order, and edification of the saints were evidence of the ministry of the Spirit among them, 1 Cor. 14:26, 32, 33, 40, but if, through ignorance of His ways, or through failure to recognize, or refusal to submit to, them, or through impatience with the ignorance or self-will of others, the Spirit was quenched, these happy results would be absent.

B. Adjective.

asbestos (*762*), "not quenched" (*a*, negative, and A), is used of the doom of persons described figuratively as "chaff," Matt. 3:12 and Luke 3:17, "unquenchable"; of the fire of Gehenna, Mark 9:43, RV, "unquenchable fire" (in some mss. v. 45).

QUESTION (Noun and Verb), QUESTIONING

A. Nouns.

1. *zetesis* (*2214*), primarily "a seeking, search" (*zeteo*, "to seek"), is used in John 3:25; Acts 25:20, RV, "(being perplexed) how to inquire (concerning these things)," KJV "(because I doubted of such manner) of questions," lit., "being perplexed as to the inquiry (or

discussion) concerning these things"; in 1 Tim. 1:4 (in some mss.); 6:4; 2 Tim. 2:23; Titus 3:9.

2. *zetema* (*2213*), synonymous with No. 1, but, generally speaking, suggesting in a more concrete form the subject of an inquiry, occurs in Acts 15:2; 18:15; 23:29; 25:19; 26:3.

B. Verbs.

1. *suzeteo* (*4802*) or *sunzeteo*, "to search together," "to discuss, dispute," is translated "to question" (or "question with or together") in Mark 1:27; 8:11; 9:10, 14, 16; 12:28, RV (KJV, "reasoning together"); Luke 22:23, RV (KJV, "inquire"); 24:15, RV (KJV, "reasoned").

2. *eperotao* (*1905*), "to ask," is translated "asked...a question," in Matt. 22:35, 41; in Luke 2:46, "asking...questions"; "questioned" in Luke 23:9.

QUICKEN

suzoopoieo (*4806*) or *sunzoopoieo*, "to quicken together with, make alive with," is used in Eph. 2:5; Col. 2:13, of the spiritual life with Christ, imparted to believers at their conversion.

QUIET, QUIETNESS

A. Adjectives.

1. *eremos* (*2263*), "quiet, tranquil," occurs in 1 Tim. 2:2, RV, "tranquil" (KJV, "quiet"); it indicates tranquillity arising from without.

2. *hesuchios* (*2272*) has much the same meaning as No. 1, but indicates "tranquillity arising from within," causing no disturbance to others. It is translated "quiet" in 1 Tim. 2:2, RV (KJV, "peaceable"); "quiet" in 1 Pet. 3:4, where it is associated with "meek," and is to characterize the spirit or disposition.

B. Verbs

hesuchazo (*2270*), akin to A, No. 2, "to be still, to live quietly."

C. Nouns.

1. *eirene* (*1515*), "peace," is translated "quietness" in Acts 24:2, KJV (RV, "peace").

2. *hesuchia* (*2271*), akin to A, No. 2, and B. No. 1, denotes "quietness," 2 Thess. 3:12; it is so translated in the RV of 1 Tim. 2:11, 12 (KJV, "silence"); in Acts 22:2, RV, "(they were the more) quiet," KJV, "(they kept the more) silence," lit., "they kept quietness the more."

QUIT

1. *apallasso* (*525*), "to free from," is used in the passive voice in Luke 12:58, RV, "to be quit" (KJV, "to be delivered").

2. *andrizo* (*407*) signifies "to make a man of" (*aner*, "a man"); in the middle voice, in 1 Cor. 16:13, "to play the man," "quit you like men."

R

RABBI

rabbei or *rabbi* (*4461*), from a word *rab*, primarily denoting "master" in contrast to a slave; this with the added pronominal suffix signified "my master" and was a title of respect by which teachers were addressed. The suffix soon lost its specific force, and in the NT the word is used as courteous title of address. It is applied to Christ in Matt. 26:25, 49; Mark 9:5; 11:21; 14:45; John 1:38 (where it is interpreted as *didaskalos*, "master," marg., "teacher"; v. 49; 3:2; 4:31; 6:25; 9:2; 11:8; to John the Baptist in John 3:26. In Matt. 23:7, 8 Christ forbids his disciples to covet or use it. In the latter verse it is again explained as *didaskalos*, "master."

RABBONI

rabbounei or *rabboni* (*4462*), formed in a similar way to the above, was an Aramaic form of a title even more respectful than Rabbi, and signified "My great master"; in its use in the NT the pronominal force of the suffix is apparently retained (contrast Rabbi above); it is found in Mark 10:51 in the best texts, RV, "Rabboni" (KJV, "Lord"), addressed to Christ by blind Bartimaeus, and in John 20:16 by Mary Magdalene.

RACA

raka (*4469*) is an Aramaic word akin to the Heb. *req*, "empty," the first *a* being due to a Galilean change. In the KJV of 1611 it was spelled *racha*; in the edition of 1638, *raca*. It was a word of utter contempt, signifying "empty," intellectually rather than morally, "empty-headed," like Abimelech's hirelings, Judg. 9:4, and the "vain" man of Jas. 2:20; condemned by Christ, Matt. 5:22.

RACE (contest)

agon (*73*) is translated "race" in Heb. 12:1, one of the modes of athletic contest, this being the secondary meaning of the word.

RAGE, RAGING

phruasso (*5433*) was primarily used of "the snorting, neighing and prancing of horses"; hence, metaphorically, of "the haughtiness and insolence of men," Acts 4:25.

RAIL

blasphemeo (*987*), a verb, "to blaspheme, rail, revile," is translated "to rail at, or on," in Matt. 27:39, RV (KJV, "reviled"); Mark 15:29; Luke 23:39; 2 Pet. 2:10, RV (KJV, "to speak evil of"); 2:12, RV (KJV, "speak evil of").

RAINBOW

iris (*2463*), whence Eng., "iris," the flower, describes the "rainbow" seen in the heavenly vision, "round about the throne, like an emerald to look upon," Rev. 4:3; emblematic of the fact that, in the exercise of God's absolute sovereignty and perfect counsels, He will remember His covenant concerning the earth, Gen. 9:9-17.

RAISE (up)

1. **egeiro** (*1453*), for the various meanings of which, is used (a) of "raising" the dead, active and passive voices, e.g. of the resurrection of Christ, Matt. 16:21; 17:23; 20:19, RV; 26:32, RV, "(after) I am raised up" (KJV, "...risen again"); Luke 9:22; 20:37; John 2:19; Acts 3:15; 4:10 [not 5:30, see (c) below]; 10:40 [not 13:23 in the best texts, see (c) below]; 13:30, 37; Rom. 4:24, 25; 6:4, 9; 7:4; 8:11 (twice); 8:34, RV; 10:9; 1 Cor. 6:14 (1st part); 15:13, 14, RV; 15:15 (twice), 16, 17; 15:20, RV; 2 Cor. 4:14; Gal. 1:1; Eph. 1:20; Col. 2:12; 1 Thess. 1:10; 1 Pet. 1:21; in 2 Tim. 2:8, RV, "risen"; (b) of the resurrection of human beings, Matt. 10:8; 11:5; Matt. 27:52, RV (KJV, "arose"); Mark 12:26, RV; Luke 7:22; John 5:21; 12:1, 9, 17; Acts 26:8; 1 Cor. 15:29 and 32, RV; 15:35, 42, 43 (twice), 44, 52; 2 Cor. 1:9; 4:14; Heb. 11:19; (c) of "raising" up a person to occupy a place in the midst of a people, said of Christ, Acts 5:30; in 13:23, KJV only (the best texts have **ago**, to bring RV, "hath...brought"); of David, Acts 13:22 (for v. 33 see No. 2); (d) metaphorically, of a horn of salvation, Luke 1:69; (e) of children, from stones, by creative power, Luke 3:8; (f) of the Temple, as the Jews thought, John 2:20, RV, "wilt Thou raise (it) Up" (KJV, "rear"); (g) of "lifting" up a person, from physical infirmity, Mark 1:31, RV, "raised...up" (KJV, "lifted"); so 9:27; Acts 3:7; 10:26, RV (KJV, "took"); Jas. 5:15, "shall raise...up"; (h) metaphorically, of "raising" up affliction, Phil. 1:17, RV (in the best texts; the KJV, v. 16, following those which have **epiphero**, has "to add").

2. **anistemi** (*450*), translated "to raise or raise up," (a) of the resurrection of the dead by Christ, John 6:39, 40, 44, 54; (b) of the resurrection of Christ from the dead, Acts 2:24 (for v. 30 see RV, **kathizo**, "to set," as in the best texts); 2:32; 13:34, see (c) below; Acts 17:31; (c) of "raising" up a person to occupy a place in the midst of a nation, said of Christ, Acts 3:26; 7:37; 13:33, RV, "raised up Jesus," not here by resurrection from the dead, as the superfluous "again" of the KJV would suggest; this is confirmed by the latter part of the verse, which explains the "raising" up as being by way

R

of His incarnation, and by the contrast in v. 34, where stress is laid upon His being "raised" from the dead, the same verb being used: (d) of "raising" up seed, Matt. 22:24; (e) of being "raised" from natural sleep, Matt. 1:24, KJV.

RANSOM

lutron (*3383*), lit., "a means of loosing" (from *luo*, "to loose"), occurs frequently in the Sept., where it is always used to signify "equivalence." Thus it is used of the "ransom" for a life, e.g., Exod. 21:30, of the redemption price of a slave, e.g., Lev. 19:20, of land, 25:24, of the price of a captive, Isa. 45:13. In the NT it occurs in Matt. 20:28 and Mark 10:45, where it is used of Christ's gift of Himself as "a ransom for many."

RAVENING

harpax (*727*), an adjective signifying "rapacious," is translated "ravening" (of wolves) in Matt. 7:15.

READ, READING

anaginosko (*314*), primarily, "to know certainly, to know again, recognize" (*ana*, "again," *ginosko*, "to know"), is used of "reading" written characters, e.g., Matt. 12:3, 5; 21:16; 24:15; of the private "reading" of Scripture, Acts 8:28, 30, 32; of the public "reading" of Scripture, Luke 4:16; Acts 13:27; 15:21; 2 Cor. 3:15; Col. 4:16 (thrice); 1 Thess. 5:27; Rev. 1:3.

READINESS

1. *prothumia* (*4288*), "eagerness, willingness, readiness" (*pro*, "forward," *thumos*, "mind, disposition"), akin to *prothumos*, is translated "readiness of mind" in Acts 17:11, "readiness" in 2 Cor. 8:11; in v. 12, RV (KJV, "a willing mind"); in v. 19, RV "(our) readiness," KJV, "(your) ready mind"; in 9:2, RV, "readiness."

2. *hetoimos* (*2092*), an adjective, is used with *echo*, "to have," and *en*, "in," idiomatically, as a noun in 2 Cor. 10:6, RV, "being in readiness" (KJV, "having in readiness"), of the apostle's aim for the church to be obedient to Christ.

READY

hetoimos (*2092*), "prepared, ready" (akin to *hetoimasia*, "preparation"), is used (a) of persons, Matt. 24:44; 25:10; Luke 12:40; 22:33; Acts 23:15, 21 (for 2 Cor. 10:6, see above); Titus 3:1; 1 Pet. 3:15; (b) of things, Matt. 22:4 (2nd part), 8; Mark 14:15, RV, "ready" (KJV, "prepared"); Luke 14:17; John 7:6; 2 Cor. 9:5; 10:16, RV, "things ready" (KJV, "things made ready"); 1 Pet. 1:5.

REAP

therizo (2325), "to reap" (akin to ***theros***, "summer, harvest"), is used (a) literally, Matt. 6:26; 25:24, 26; Luke 12:24; 19:21, 22; Jas. 5:4 (2nd part), KJV, "have reaped"; (b) figuratively or in proverbial expressions, John 4:36 (twice), 37, 38, with immediate reference to bringing Samaritans into the kingdom of God, in regard to which the disciples would enjoy the fruits of what Christ Himself had been doing in Samaria; the Lord's words are, however, of a general application in respect of such service; in 1 Cor. 9:11, with reference to the right of the apostle and his fellow missionaries to receive material assistance from the church, a right which he forbore to exercise; in 2 Cor. 9:6 (twice), with reference to rendering material help to the needy, either "sparingly" or "bountifully," the "reaping" being proportionate to the sowing; in Gal. 6:7, 8 (twice), of "reaping" corruption, with special reference, according to the context, to that which is naturally shortlived transient (though the statement applies to every form of sowing to the flesh), and of "reaping" eternal life (characteristics and moral qualities being in view), as a result of sowing "to the Spirit," the reference probably being to the new nature of the believer, which is, however, under the controlling power of the Holy Spirit, v. 9, the "reaping" (the effect of well doing) being accomplished, to a limited extent, in this life, but in complete fulfillment at and beyond the judgment seat of Christ; diligence or laxity here will then produce proportionate results; in Rev. 14:15 (twice), 16, figurative of the discriminating judgment divinely to be fulfilled at the close of this age, when the wheat will be separated from the tares (see Matt. 13:30).

REASON (Noun)

logos (3056), "a word," etc., has also the significance of "the inward thought itself, a reckoning, a regard, a reason," translated "reason" in Acts 18:14, in the phrase "reason would," ***kata logon***, lit., "according to reason (I would bear with you)"; in 1 Pet. 3:15, "a reason (concerning the hope that is in you)."

REASON (Verb)

1. ***dialogizomai*** (1260), "to bring together different reasons and reckon them up, to reason," is used in the NT (a) chiefly of thoughts and considerations which are more or less objectionable, e.g., of the disciples who "reasoned" together, through a mistaken view of Christ's teaching regarding leaven, Matt. 16:7, 8 and Mark 8:16, 17; of their "reasoning" as to who was the greatest among them, Mark 9:33, RV, "were ye reasoning," KJV, "ye disputed"; of the scribes and Pharisees in criticizing Christ's claim to forgive sins, Mark 2:6, 8 (twice) and Luke 5:21, 22; of the chief

priests and elders in considering how to answer Christ's question regarding John's baptism, Matt. 21:25; Mark 11:31.

2. *sullogizomai* (*4817*), "to compute" (*sun*, "with," and *logizomai*, cf. Eng., "syllogism"), also denotes "to reason," and is so rendered in Luke 20:5.

REASONABLE

logikos (*3050*), pertaining to "the reasoning faculty, reasonable, rational," is used in Rom. 12:1, of the service (*latreia*) to be rendered by believers in presenting their bodies "a living sacrifice, holy, acceptable to God." The sacrifice is to be intelligent, in contrast to those offered by ritual and compulsion; the presentation is to be in accordance with the spiritual intelligence of those who are new creatures in Christ and are mindful of "the mercies of God."

TO REBEL

A. Verb.

marah (4784), "to rebel, be contentious." *marah* signifies an opposition to someone motivated by pride, Deut. 21:18; cf. Isa. 3:8 (NASB). More particularly, the word generally connotes a rebellious attitude against God, Deut. 9:7; Jer. 4:17. The primary meaning of *marah* is "to disobey," 1 Kings 13:21; cf. 13:26. The Old Testament sometimes specifically states that someone "rebelled" against the Lord; at other times it may refer to a rebelling against the word of the Lord, Ps. 105:28; 107:11, or against the mouth of God, Num. 20:24; Deut. 1:26, 43; 9:23; 1 Sam. 12:14-15. The intent of the Hebrew is to signify the act of defying the command of God, Lam. 1:18. An individual, Deut. 21:18, 20, a nation, Num. 20:24, and a city, Zeph. 3:1, may be described as "being rebellious." Zephaniah gave a vivid image of the nature of the rebellious spirit, Zeph. 3:1-2, RSV.

B. Nouns.

meri (4805), "rebellion," Deut. 31:27; cf. Prov. 17:11. The noun *meratayim* means "double rebellion." This reference to Babylon, Jer. 50:21, is generally made a proper name, "Merathaim."

C. Adjective.

meri (4805), "rebellious," Ezek. 2:8.

REBUKE (Verb and Noun)

A. Verbs.

1. *epitimao* (*2008*), primarily, "to put honor upon," then, "to adjudge," hence signifies "to rebuke." Except for 2 Tim. 4:2 and Jude 9, it is confined in the NT to the Synoptic Gospels, where it is frequently used of the Lord's rebukes to (a) evil spirits, e.g., Matt. 17:18; Mark 1:25; 9:25; Luke 4:35, 41; 9:42; (b) winds, Matt. 8:26;

Mark 4:39; Luke 8:24; (c) fever, Luke 4:39; (d) disciples, Mark 8:33; Luke 9:55; contrast Luke 19:39. For rebukes by others see Matt. 16:22; 19:13; 20:31; Mark 8:32; 10:13; 10:48, RV, "rebuked" (KJV, "charged"); Luke 17:3; 18:15, 39; 23:40.

2. *elencho* (1651), "to convict, refute, reprove," is translated "to rebuke" in the KJV of the following (the RV always has the verb "to reprove"): 1 Tim. 5:20; Titus 1:13; 2:15; Heb. 12:5; Rev. 3:19.

3. *epiplesso* (1969), "to strike at" (*epi*, "upon" or "at," *plesso*, "to strike, smite"), hence, "to rebuke," is used in the injunction against "rebuking" an elder, 1 Tim. 5:1.

B. Noun.

elenxis (1649), akin to A, No. 2, denotes "rebuke"; in 2 Pet. 2:16, it is used with *echo*, "to have," and translated "he was rebuked," lit., "he had rebuke."

RECKON, RECKONING
Old Testament
A. Verb.

yachas (3187), "to reckon (according to race or family)," 1 Chron. 5:17; cf. 1 Chron. 7:5 and Ezra 2:62.

B. Noun.

yachas (3188), "genealogy." This word appears in the infinitive form as a noun to indicate a register or table of genealogy, 1 Chron. 7:40; cf. 2 Chron. 31:18.

New Testament

logizomai (3049) is properly used (a) of "numerical calculation," e.g., Luke 22:37; (b) metaphorically, "by a reckoning of characteristics or reasons, to take into account," Rom. 2:26, "shall...be reckoned," RV (KJV, "counted"), of "reckoning" uncircumcision for circumcision by God's estimate in contrast to that of the Jew regarding his own condition (v. 3); in 4:3, 5, 6, 9, 11, 22, 23, 24, of "reckoning" faith for righteousness, or "reckoning" righteousness to persons, in all of which the RV uses the verb "to reckon" instead of the KJV "to count or to impute"; in v. 4 the subject is treated by way of contrast between grace and debt, which latter involves the "reckoning" of a reward for works; what is owed as a debt cannot be "reckoned" as a favor, but the faith of Abraham and his spiritual children sets them outside the category of those who seek to be justified by self-effort, and, *vice versa*, the latter are excluded from the grace of righteousness bestowed on the sole condition of faith; so in Gal. 3:6 (RV, "was reckoned," KJV, "was accounted"); since Abraham, like all the natural descendants of Adam, was a sinner, he was destitute of righteousness in the sight of God; if, then, his relationship with God was to be rectified (i.e., if he was to be justified before

R

God), the rectification could not be brought about by works of merit on his part; in Jas. 2:23, RV, "reckoned," the subject is viewed from a different standpoint.

RECOMPENCE, RECOMPENSE

Old Testament

shalam (7999), "to recompense, reward, be whole, be complete, sound." In its first occurrence in the Old Testament, the word has the sense of "repaying" or "restoring": "Why have you returned evil for good?" Gen. 44:4, RSV. Sometimes it means "to complete or finish," 1 Kings 9:25. In Lev. 24:18, *shalam* describes compensation for injury.

New Testament

A. Nouns.

1. *antapodoma* (*468*), akin to *antapodidomi*, "to recompense" (see below), lit., "a giving back in return" (*anti*, "in return," *apo*, back, *didomi*, "to give"), a requital, recompense, is used (a) in a favorable sense, Luke 14:12; (b) in an unfavorable sense, Rom. 11:9, indicating that the present condition of the Jewish nation is the retributive effect of their transgressions, on account of which that which was designed as a blessing ("their table") has become a means of judgment.

2. *antapodosis* (*469*), derived, like No. 1, from *antapodidomi*, is rendered "recompense" in Col. 3:24, RV (KJV, "reward").

B. Verb.

antapodidomi (*467*), akin to A, No. 1 and No. 2, "to give back as an equivalent, to requite, recompense" (the *anti* expressing the idea of a complete return), is translated "render" in 1 Thess. 3:9, here only in the NT of thanksgiving to God; elsewhere it is used of "recompense," whether between men (but in that case only of good, not of evil, see No. 2 in 1 Thess. 5:15), Luke 14:14 *a*, cf. the corresponding noun in v. 12; or between God and evil-doers, Rom. 12:19, RV (KJV, "repay"); Heb. 10:30, cf. the noun in Rom. 11:9; or between God and those who do well, Luke 14:14 *b*; Rom. 11:35, cf. the noun in Col. 3:24; in 2 Thess. 1:6 both reward and retribution are in view.

RECONCILE

katallasso (*2644*) properly denotes "to change, exchange" (especially of money); hence, of persons, "to change from enmity to friendship, to reconcile." With regard to the relationship between God and man, the use of this and connected words shows that primarily "reconciliation" is what God accomplishes, exercising His grace towards sinful man on the ground of the death of Christ in propitiatory sacrifice under the judgment due to sin, 2 Cor. 5:19, where both the verb and the noun are used. By reason of this men in their sinful condition and alienation from God are invited to be "reconciled" to Him; that is to say, to change their attitude, and accept the provision God has made, whereby their sins can be remitted and they themselves be justified in His sight in Christ.

The removal of God's wrath does not contravene His immutability. He always acts according to His unchanging righteousness and lovingkindness, and it is because He changes not that His relative attitude does change towards those who change. All His acts show that He is Light and Love. Anger, where there is no personal element, is a sign of moral health if, and if only, it is accompanied by grief. There can be truest love along with righteous indignation, Mark 3:5, but love and enmity cannot exist together. It is important to distinguish "wrath" and "hostility." The change in God's relative attitude toward those who receive the "reconciliation" only proves His real unchangeableness. Not once is God said to be "reconciled." The enmity is alone on our part. It was we who needed to be "reconciled" to God, not God to us, and it is propitiation, which His righteousness and mercy have provided, that makes the "reconciliation" possible to those who receive it.

The subject finds its great unfolding in 2 Cor. 5:18-20, which states that God "reconciled us (believers) to Himself through Christ," and that "the ministry of reconciliation" consists in this, "that God was in Christ reconciling the world unto Himself." The insertion of a comma in the KJV after the word "Christ" is misleading; the doctrine stated here is not that God was in Christ (the unity of the Godhead is not here in view), but that what God has done in the matter of reconciliation He has done in Christ, and this is based upon the fact that "Him who knew no sin He made to be sin on our behalf; that we might become the righteousness of God in Him." On this ground the command to men is "be ye reconciled to God."

RECOVER

sozo (4982), "to save," is sometimes used of "healing" or "restoration to health," the latter in John 11:12, RV, "he will recover," marg., "be saved" (KJV, "he shall do well").

REDEEM, REDEMPTION
Old Testament

A. Verbs.

ga'al (1350), "to redeem, deliver, avenge, act as a kinsman." This word's basic use had to do with the deliverance of persons or property that had been sold for debt, as in Lev. 25:25-47. A poor man may sell himself to a fellow Israelite, Lev. 25:39, or to an alien living in Israel, Lev. 25:47. The responsibility "to redeem" belonged to the nearest relative—brother, uncle, uncle's son, or a blood relative from his family, Lev. 25:25, 48-49. The person (kinsman) who "redeemed" the one in financial difficulties was known as a kinsman-redeemer, as the NIV translates the word in Ruth 2:20. In Deut. 19:6 the redeemer is called the "avenger of blood" whose duty it was to execute the murderer of his relative. The verb occurs in this sense 12 times and is translated "revenger" in KJV, Num. 35:19, 21, 24, 27, or "avenger," Num. 35:12; always so in NASB and NIV. The Book of Ruth is a beautiful account of the kinsman-redeemer. The greater usage of this word group is of God who promised to redeem, Exod. 6:6; cf. Ps. 77:15; Exod. 15:13; Ps. 78:35.

The Book of Isaiah evidences the word "Redeemer" used of God 13 times, all in chapters 41—63, and *ga'al* is used 9 times of God, first in 43:1. Israel's "Redeemer" is "the Holy One of Israel," 41:14, "the creator of Israel, your King," 43:14-15.

padah (6299), "to redeem, ransom." *padah* indicates that some intervening or substitutionary action effects a release from an undesirable condition; save from death, 1 Sam. 14:45; from slavery, Exod. 21:8; Lev. 19:20. The word is connected with the laws of the firstborn, Exod. 13:15. God accepted the separation of the tribe of Levi for liturgical service in lieu of all Israelite firstborn, Num. 3:40ff. However, the Israelite males still had to be "redeemed" (*padah*) from this service by payment of specified "redemption money," Num. 3:44-51.

When God is the subject of *padah*, the word emphasizes His complete, sovereign freedom to liberate human beings. Sometimes God is said to "redeem" individuals, Abraham, Isa. 29:22; David, 1 Kings 1:29; and often in the Psalter, e.g., 26:11; 21:5; 71:23; but usually Israel, the elect people, is the beneficiary.

kapar (3722), "to ransom, atone, expiate, propitiate." On its most basic level of meaning, *kapar* denotes a material transaction or "ransom." Sometimes man is the subject of *kapar*, 2 Sam. 21:3. Moses ascends the mountain yet a third time in an effort to "make an atonement" for the people's sin (apparently merely by intercession, although this is not explicitly stated). God is often the subject of *kapar* in this general sense, too. In 2 Chron. 30:18, Hezekiah prays for God to "pardon" those who were not ritually prepared for the Passover. At the conclusion of the Song of Moses, Yahweh is praised because He "will atone for His land and His people," Deut. 32:43, NASB. Similar general uses of the word appear in Ps. 65:3; 78:38; and Dan. 9:24. Jeremiah once uses *kapar* to pray bitterly that Yahweh not "forgive" the iniquity of those plotting to slay him, Jer. 18:23, and in Ps. 79:9 the word means "to purge" sin. Most often *kapar* is used in connection with specific rites, and the immediate subject is a priest. All types of ritual sacrifice are explained in terms of *kapar*. We find the priests' smearing of blood on the altar during the "sin offering" (*chatta't*) described as "atonement," Exod. 29: 36-37; Lev. 4:20, 31; 10:17; Num. 28:22; 29:5; Neh. 10:33.

Most English versions prefer to render **kapar** with the more neutral term "atone" or even "ransom." But various translations often have "expiate" or "propitiate" as well. The terms are partly synonymous. In any sacrifice, the action is directed both toward God (*propitiation*) and toward the offense (*expiation*).

B. Noun.

ge'ullah (1353), "(right of) redemption." This word is used in regard to deliverance of persons or property that had been sold for debt. The law required that the "right of redemption" of land and of persons be protected, Lev. 25:24, 48. The redemption price was determined by the number of years remaining until the release of debts in the year of jubilee, Lev. 25:27-28.

pedut: "ransom or redemption," Ps. 111:9.

New Testament

Verbs.

1. *exagorazo* (*1805*), a strengthened form of *agorazo*, "to buy," denotes "to buy out" (*ex* for *ek*), especially of purchasing a slave with a view to his freedom. It is used metaphorically in Gal. 3:13 and 4:5, of the deliverance by Christ of Christian Jews from the Law and its curse.

2. *lutroo* (3084), "to release on receipt of ransom" (akin to *lutron*, "a ransom"), is used in the middle voice, signifying "to release by paying a ransom price, to redeem" (a) in the natural sense of delivering, Luke 24:21, of setting Israel free from the Roman yoke; (b) in a spiritual sense, Titus 2:14, of the work of Christ in "redeeming" men "from all iniquity" (*anomia*, "lawlessness," the bondage of self-will which rejects the will of God); 1 Pet. 1:18 (passive voice), "ye were redeemed," from a vain manner of life, i.e., from bondage to tradition. In both instances the death of Christ is stated as the means of "redemption."

B. Noun.

apolutrosis (629), a strengthened form of No. 1, lit., "a releasing, for (i.e., on payment of) a ransom." It is used of (a) "deliverance" from physical torture, Heb. 11:35; (b) the deliverance of the people of God at the coming of Christ with His glorified saints, "in a cloud with power and great glory," Luke 21:28, a "redemption" to be accomplished at the "outshining of His Parousia," 2 Thess. 2:8, i.e., at His second advent; (c) forgiveness and justification, "redemption" as the result of expiation, deliverance from the guilt of sins, Rom. 3:24, "through the redemption that is in Christ Jesus"; Eph. 1:7, defined as "the forgiveness of our trespasses," RV; so Col. 1:14, "the forgiveness of our sins," indicating both the liberation from the

R

guilt and doom of sin and the introduction into a life of liberty, "newness of life" (Rom. 6:4,; Heb. 9:15), "for the redemption of the transgressions that were under the first covenant," RV, here "redemption of" is equivalent to "redemption from," the genitive case being used of the object from which the "redemption" is effected, not from the consequence of the transgressions, but from the transgressions themselves; (d) the deliverance of the believer from the presence and power of sin, and of his body from bondage to corruption, at the coming (the Parousia in its inception) of the Lord Jesus, Rom. 8:23; 1 Cor. 1:30; Eph. 1:4; 4:30.

REFRAIN

pauo (3973), "to stop," is used in the active voice in the sense of "making to cease, restraining" in 1 Pet. 3:10, of causing the tongue to refrain from evil; elsewhere in the middle voice.

REFRESH, REFRESHING

A. Verbs.

1. *anapauo* (373), "to give intermission from labor, to give rest, refresh" (*ana*, "back," *pauo*, "to cause to cease"), is translated "to refresh" in 1 Cor. 16:18; 2 Cor. 7:13; Philem. 7, 20.

2. *sunanapauomai* (4875), "to lie down, to rest with" (*sun*, "with," and No. 1 in the middle voice), is used metaphorically of being "refreshed" in spirit with others, in Rom. 15:32, KJV, "may with (you) be refreshed" (RV, "...find rest").

B. Noun.

anapsuxis (403), "a refreshing," occurs in Acts 3:19.

REFUSE (Verb)

1. *arneomai* (720), "to deny, renounce, reject," in late Greek came to signify "to refuse to acknowledge, to disown," and is translated "to refuse" in Acts 7:35; Heb. 11:24.

2. *paraiteomai* (3868), denotes "to refuse" in Acts 25:11; 1 Tim. 4:7; 5:11; 2 Tim. 2:23, RV (KJV, "avoid"); Titus 3:10, RV (marg., "avoid"; KJV, "reject"); Heb. 12:25 (twice), perhaps in the sense of "begging off."

REGARD

1. *phroneo* (5426), "to think, set the mind on," implying moral interest and reflection, is translated "to regard" in Rom. 14:6 (twice); the second part in the KJV represents an interpolation and is not part of the original.

2. *oligoreo* (3643) denotes "to think little of" (*oligos*, "little," *ora*, "care"), "to regard lightly," Heb. 12:5, RV (KJV, "despise").

3. *prosecho* (4337), "to take or give heed," is translated "they had regard" in Acts 8:11, KJV (RV, "they gave heed").

REGENERATION

palingenesia (3824), "new birth" (*palin*, "again," *genesis*, "birth"), is used of "spiritual regeneration," Titus 3:5, involving the communication of a new life, the two operating powers to produce which are "the word of truth," Jas. 1:18; 1 Pet. 1:23, and the Holy Spirit, John 3:5, 6; the *loutron*, "the laver, the washing," is explained in Eph. 5:26, "having cleansed it by the washing (*loutron*) of water with the word."

The new birth and "regeneration" do not represent successive stages in spiritual experience, they refer to the same event but view it in different aspects. The new birth stresses the communication of spiritual life in contrast to antecedent spiritual death; "regeneration" stresses the inception of a new state of things in contrast with the old; hence the connection of the use of the word with its application to Israel, in Matt. 19:28. Some regard the *kai* in Titus 3:5 as epexegetic, "even"; but, as Scripture marks two distinct yet associated operating powers, there is not sufficient ground for this interpretation.

REGRET

metamelomai (3338), a verb, "to regret, to repent one," is translated "to regret" in 2 Cor. 7:8, RV (twice), KJV, "repent."

REIGN (Verb and Noun)

Old Testament

malak (4427), "to reign, be king (or queen)." Basically the word means to fill the functions of ruler over someone. To hold such a position was to function as the commander-in-chief of the army, the chief executive of the group, and to be an important, if not central, religious figure. The king was the head of his people and, therefore, in battle was the king to be killed, his army would disperse until a new king could be chosen, Gen. 36:31; Ps. 2:6; cf. 2 Kings 11:3.

New Testament

1. *basileuo* (936), "to reign," is used (I) literally, (a) of God, Rev. 11:17; 19:6, in each of which the aorist tense (in the latter, translated "reigneth") is "ingressive," stressing the point of entrance; (b) of Christ, Luke 1:33; 1 Cor. 15:25; Rev. 11:15; as rejected by the Jews, Luke 19:14, 27; (c) of the saints, hereafter, 1 Cor. 4:8 (2nd part), where the apostle, casting a reflection upon the untimely exercise of authority on the part of the church at Corinth, anticipates the due time for it in the future (see No. 2); Rev. 5:10; 20:4,

R

where the aorist tense is not simply of a "point" character, but "constative," that is, regarding a whole action as having occurred, without distinguishing any steps in its progress (in this instance the aspect is future); v. 6; 22:5; (d) of earthly potentates, Matt. 2:22; 1 Tim. 6:15, where "kings" is, lit., "them that reign"; (II), metaphorically, (a) of believers, Rom. 5:17, where "shall reign in life" indicates the activity of life in fellowship with Christ in His sovereign power, reaching its fullness hereafter; 1 Cor. 4:8 (1st part), of the carnal pride that laid claim to a power not to be exercised until hereafter; (b) of divine grace, Rom. 5:21; (c) of sin, Rom. 5:21; 6:12; (d) of death, Rom. 5:14, 17.

2. *sunbasileuo* (*4821*), "to reign together with" (*sun*, "with," and No. 1), is used of the future "reign" of believers together and with Christ in the kingdom of God in manifestation, 1 Cor. 4:8 (3rd part); of those who endure, 2 Tim. 2:12. cf. Rev. 20:6.

REINS

nephros (*3510*), "a kidney" (Eng., "nephritis," etc.), usually in the plural, is used metaphorically of "the will and the affections," Rev. 2:23, "reins" (cf. Ps. 7:9; Jer. 11:20; 17:10; 20:12). The feelings and emotions were regarded as having their seat in the "kidneys."

REJECT

A. Verbs.

1. *apodokimazo* (*593*), "to reject" as the result of examination and disapproval (*apo*, "away from," *dokimazo*, "to approve"), is used (a) of the "rejection" of Christ by the elders and chief priests of the Jews, Matt. 21:42; Mark 8:31; 12:10; Luke 9:22; 20:17; 1 Pet. 2:4, 7 (KJV, "disallowed"); by the Jewish people, Luke 17:25; (b) of the "rejection" of Esau from inheriting "the blessing," Heb. 12:17.

2. *atheteo* (*114*), properly, "to do away" with what has been laid down, to make *atheton* (i.e., "without place," *a*, negative, *tithemi*, "to place"), hence, besides its meanings "to set aside, make void, nullify, disannul," signifies "to reject"; in Mark 6:26, regarding Herod's pledge to Salome, it almost certainly has the meaning "to break faith with." In Mark 7:9 "ye reject (the commandment)" means "ye set aside"; in Luke 7:30, "ye reject" may have the meaning of "nullifying or making void the counsel of God"; in Luke 10:16 (four times), "rejecteth," RV (KJV, "despiseth"); "rejecteth" in John 12:48; "reject" in 1 Cor. 1:19 (KJV, "bring to nothing"); 1 Thess. 4:8, "to despise," where the reference is to the charges in v. 2; in 1 Tim. 5:12 RV, "have rejected" (KJV, "have cast off").

3. *ekptuo* (*1609*), "to spit out" (*ek*, "out," and *ptuo*, "to spit"), i.e., "to abominate, loathe," is used in Gal. 4:14, "rejected" (marg., "spat out"), where the sentence is elliptical: "although my disease repelled you, you did not refuse to hear my message."

B. Adjective.

1. *adokimos* (*96*), "not standing the test," is translated "rejected" in 1 Cor. 9:27, RV; Heb. 6:8, KJV and RV.

REJOICE

Old Testament

A. Verb.

samach (8055), "to rejoice, be joyful." *samach* usually refers to a spontaneous emotion or extreme happiness which is expressed in some visible and/or external manner. It does not normally represent an abiding state of well-being or feeling. This emotion arises at festivals, circumcision feasts, wedding feasts, harvest feasts, the overthrow of one's enemies, and such other events. The men of Jabesh broke out joyously when they were told that they would be delivered from the Philistines, 1 Sam. 11:9. The verb *samach* suggests three elements: (1) a spontaneous, unsustained feeling of jubilance, 1 Sam. 18:6; (2) a feeling so strong that it finds expression in some external act, Exod. 4:27; (3) a feeling prompted by some external and unsustained stimulus, Exod. 4:14.

B. Noun.

simchah (8057), "joy." *simchah* is both a technical term for the external expression of "joy," Gen. 31:27; and (usually) a representation of the abstract feeling or concept "joy," Deut. 28:47.

C. Adjective.

sameach (8056), "joyful; glad," Deut. 16:15.

New Testament

1. *chairo* (*5463*), "to rejoice," is most frequently so translated. As to this verb, the following are grounds and occasions for "rejoicing," on the part of believers: in the Lord, Phil. 3:1; 4:4; His incarnation, Luke 1:14; His power Luke 13:17· His presence with the Father, John 14:28; His presence with them John 16:22; 20:20; His ultimate triumph, 8:56; hearing the gospel, Acts 13:48; their salvation, Acts 8:39; receiving the Lord, Luke 19:6; their enrollment in Heaven, Luke 10:20; their liberty in Christ, Acts 15:31; their hope, Rom. 12:12 (cf. Rom. 5:2; Rev. 19:7); their prospect of reward, Matt. 5:12; the obedience and godly conduct of fellow believers, Rom. 16:19, RV, "I rejoice" (KJV, "I am glad"); 2 Cor. 7:7, 9; 13:9; Col. 2:5· 1 Thess. 3:9; 2 John 4; 3 John 3; the proclamation of Christ, Phil. 1:18; the gospel harvest, John 4:36; suffering with Christ, Acts 5:41; 1 Pet. 4:13; suffering in the cause of the gospel, 2 Cor. 13:9 (1st part); Phil. 2:17 (1st part); Col. 1:24; in persecutions, trials and afflictions, Matt. 5:12; Luke 6:23; 2 Cor. 6:10; the manifestation of grace, Acts 11:23; meeting with fellow believers, 1 Cor. 16:17, RV, "I

R

rejoice"; Phil. 2:28; receiving tokens of love and fellowship, Phil. 4:10; the "rejoicing" of others, Rom. 12:15; 2 Cor. 7:13; learning of the well-being of others, 2 Cor. 7:16.

2. *agalliao* (*21*), "to rejoice greatly, to exult," is used, (I) in the active voice, of "rejoicing" in God, Luke 1:47; in faith in Christ, 1 Pet. 1:8, RV (middle voice in some mss.), "ye rejoice greatly"; in the event of the marriage of the Lamb, Rev. 19:7, "be exceeding glad," RV; (II), in the middle voice, (a) of "rejoicing" in persecutions, Matt. 5:12 (2nd part); in the light of testimony for God, John 5:35; in salvation received through the gospel, Acts 16:34, "he rejoiced greatly," RV; in salvation ready to be revealed, 1 Pet. 1:6; at the revelation of His glory, 1 Pet. 4:13, "with exceeding joy," lit., "ye may rejoice, exulting"; (b) of Christ's "rejoicing" (greatly) "in the Holy Spirit," Luke 10:21, RV; said of His praise, as foretold in Ps. 16:9, quoted in Acts 2:26; (c) of Abraham's "rejoicing," by faith, to see Christ's day, John 8:56. 4. *euphraino* (*2165*), in the active voice, "to cheer, gladden" (*eu*, "well," *phren*, "the mind"), signifies in the passive voice "to rejoice, make merry"; it is translated "to rejoice" in Acts 2:26, RV, "was glad," KJV, "did... rejoice," of the heart of Christ as foretold in Ps. 16:9 [cf. No. 3, 11 (b)]; in Acts 7:41, of Israel's idolatry; in Rom. 15:10 with the Jews in their future deliverance by Christ from all their foes, at the establishment of the messianic kingdom) the apostle applies it to the effects of the gospel.

RELEASE

apoluo (*630*), "to loose from," is translated "to release" in Matt. 18:27, RV (KJV, "loosed"); 27:15, 17, 21, 26; Mark 15:6, 9, 11, 15; Luke 6:37 (twice), RV (KJV, "forgive" and "ye shall be forgiven"); 23:16 (v. 17, in some mss.), 18, 20, 25; 23:22, RV (KJV, "let...go"); John 18:39 (twice); 19:10; in 19:12, in the 1st part, KJV and RV; in the 2nd part, RV, "release" (KJV, "let...go"); so in Acts 3:13.

RELIEF

anesis (*425*), "a loosening, relaxation" (akin to *aniemi*, "to send away, let go, loosen"), is translated "relief" in 2 Cor. 2:13 and 7:5 (KJV, "rest").

RELIEVE

eparkeo (*1884*) signifies "to be strong enough for," and so either "to ward off," or "to aid, to relieve" (a strengthened form of *arkeo*, which has the same three meanings, *epi* being intensive); it is used in 1 Tim. 5:10, 16 (twice).

RELIGION

threskeia (*2356*) signifies "religion" in its external aspect (akin to *threskos*, see below), "religious worship," especially the ceremonial service of "religion"; it is used of the "religion" of the Jews, Acts 26:5; of the "worshiping" of angels, Col. 2:18, which they themselves repudiate (Rev. 22:8, 9); "there was an officious parade of humility in selecting these lower beings as intercessors rather than appealing directly to the Throne of Grace" (Lightfoot); in Jas. 1:26, 27 the writer purposely uses the word to set in contrast that which is unreal and deceptive, and the "pure religion" which consists in visiting "the fatherless and widows in their affliction," and in keeping oneself "unspotted from the world." He is "not herein affirming...these offices to be the sum total, nor yet the great essentials, of true religion, but declares them to be the body, the *threskeia*, of which godliness, or the love of God, is the informing soul" (Trench). Cf. also *threskos* (2357), "religious, careful of the externals of divine service," Jas. 1:26.

REMAINDER; REMNANT

A. Nouns.

yether (3499), "remainder; remnant." The more general meaning of *yether* is "whatever remains" from the whole of a single unit of something: prey, Num. 31:32; or a collection: giants, Deut. 3:11; the kingdom, Josh. 13:27; and the people, Judg. 7:6. The prophets used *she'erit* as a technical term for "the remnant of Israel," Hag. 2:2-3; cf. Mic. 5:3.

B. Verb.

yathar (3498), "to be superfluous," Dan. 10:13.

REMEMBER, REMEMBRANCE, REMINDED
Old Testament

A. Verb.

zakar (2142), "to remember, think of, mention." This word basically means to "recall information," but usually has the added focus that a response to a need or situation will also occur, implying that there is a relationship, or a renewal of an old relationship, Gen. 8:1; 18:17-33; 19:29; Exod. 6:5-6; Lev. 26:40-45; Psa. 98:3; 105:8, 42; 106:45; Jer. 31:34. Men also "remember." Joseph said to Pharaoh's butler: "But think on me..., and make mention of me unto Pharaoh..." Gen. 40:14.; cf. Ps. 20:7. The covenant commanded Israel to "remember this day, in which ye came out from Egypt..." Exod. 13:3; to "remember the sabbath day..." Exod. 20:8.

B. Nouns.

zeker (2143), "remembrance; memorial," Exod. 3:15; cf. Ps. 30:4; 135:13. Moses was told to write an account of the war with Amalek, Exod. 17:14.

The noun *zikkaron* has similar meanings. God gave the bronze

R

plates covering the altar, Num. 16:40, and the heap of stones at the Jordan, Josh. 4:7, 20-24, as perpetual "memorials" for the sons of Israel. The names of the twelve tribes of Israel were engraved on two stones that were attached to the ephod as "stones of memorial unto the children of Israel: and Aaron shall bear their names before the Lord," Exod. 28:12; cf. v. 29.

New Testament

A. Verbs.

1. *mimnesko* (3403), from the older form *mnaomai*, in the active voice signifies "to remind"; in the middle voice, "to remind oneself of," hence, "to remember, to be mindful of"; the later form is found only in the present tense, in Heb. 2:6, "are mindful of," and 13:3, "remember"; the perfect tense in 1 Cor. 11:2 and in 2 Tim. 1:4 (RV, "remembering," KJV, "being mindful of"), is used with a present meaning. RV variations from the KJV are, in Luke 1:54, RV, "that He might remember" (KJV, "in remembrance of"); 2 Pet. 3:2, "remember" (KJV, "be mindful of"); Rev. 16:19 (passive voice), "was remembered" (KJV, "came in remembrance"). The passive voice is used also in Acts 10:31, KJV and RV, "are had in remembrance."

2. *mnemoneuo* (3421) signifies "to call to mind, remember"; it is used absolutely in Mark 8:18; everywhere else it has an object, (a) persons, Luke 17:32; Gal. 2:10; 2 Tim. 2:8, where the RV rightly has "remember Jesus Christ, risen from the dead"; Paul was not reminding Timothy (nor did he need to) that Christ was raised from the dead (KJV), what was needful for him was to "remember" (to keep in mind) the One who rose, the Source and Supplier of all his requirements; (b) things, e.g., Matt. 16:9; John 15:20; 16:21; Acts 20:35; Col. 4:18; 1 Thess. 1:3; 2:9; Heb. 11:15, "had been mindful of"; 13:7; Rev. 18:5; (c) a clause, representing a circumstance, etc., John 16:4; Acts 20:31; Eph. 2:11; 2 Thess. 2:5; Rev. 2:5; 3:3; in Heb. 11:22 it signifies "to make mention of."

3. *anamimnesko* (363), *ana*, "back," and No. 1, signifies in the active voice "to remind, call to one's mind," 1 Cor. 4:17, "put (KJV, bring)...into remembrance"; so 2 Tim. 1:6; in the passive voice, "to remember, call to (one's own) mind," Mark 11:21, "calling to remembrance"; 14:72, "called to mind"; 2 Cor. 7:15, "remembereth"; Heb. 10:32, "call to remembrance."

4. *hupomimnesko* (5279) signifies "to cause one to remember, put one in mind of" (*hupo*, "under," often implying suggestion, and No. 1), John 14:26, "shall... bring...to (your) remembrance"; 2 Tim. 2:14, "put...in remembrance"; Titus 3:1, "put...in mind"; 3 John 10, RV, "I will bring to remembrance" (KJV, "I will remember"); Jude 5, "to put...in remembrance." In Luke 22:61 it is used in the passive voice, "(Peter) remembered," lit., "was put in mind."

B. Nouns.

1. *anamnesis* (*364*), "a remembrance" (*ana*, "up," or "again," and A, No. 1), is used (a) in Christ's command in the institution of the Lord's Supper, Luke 22:19; 1 Cor. 11:24, 25, not "in memory of" but in an affectionate calling of the Person Himself to mind; (b) of the "remembrance" of sins, Heb. 10:3, RV, "a remembrance" (KJV, "a remembrance again"; but the prefix *ana* does not here signify "again"); what is indicated, in regard to the sacrifices under the Law, is not simply an external bringing to "remembrance," but an awakening of mind.

2. *hupomnesis* (*5280*) denotes "a reminding, a reminder"; in 2 Tim. 1:5 it is used with *lambano*, "to receive," lit., "having received a reminder," RV, "having been reminded" (KJV, "when I call to remembrance"); in 2 Pet. 1:13 and 3:1, "remembrance."

3. *mneia* (*3417*) denotes "a remembrance," or "a mention."

4. *mneme* (*3420*) denotes "a memory" (akin to *mnaomai*, A, No. 1), "remembrance, mention," 2 Pet. 1:15, "remembrance."

REMISSION, REMIT

A. Nouns.

1. *aphesis* (*859*), "a dismissal, release" (from *aphiemi*, B), is used of the forgiveness of sins and translated "remission" in Matt. 26:28; Mark 1:4; Luke 1:77; 3:3; 24:47; Acts 2:38; 5:31 (KJV, "forgiveness"); 10:43; 13:38, RV (KJV, "forgiveness"); 26:18 (ditto); Heb. 9:22; 10:18.

2. *paresis* (*3929*), "a passing by of debt or sin," Rom. 3:25, KJV, "remission" (RV and KJV marg., "passing over").

B. Verb.

aphiemi (*863*), "to send away" (akin to A, No. 1), is translated "to remit" in John 20:23 (twice), KJV (RV, "to forgive"). Scripture makes clear that the Lord's words could not have been intended to bestow the exercise of absolution, which Scripture declares is the prerogative of God alone.

REMNANT

Old Testament

A. Nouns.

she'erit (*7611*), "rest; remnant; residue." The idea of the "remnant" plays a prominent part in the divine economy of salvation throughout the Old Testament. The "remnant" concept is applied especially to the Israelites who survived such calamities as war, pestilence, and famine—people whom the Lord in His mercy spared to be His chosen people, 2 Kings 19:31; cf. Ezra 9:14. The Israelites repeatedly suffered major catastrophes that brought them to the brink of extinction. So they often prayed as in Jer.

R

42:2. Isaiah used the word *she'erit* 5 times to denote those who would be left after the Assyrian invasions, Isa. 37:32. Micah also announced the regathering of the Jewish people after the Exile, Mic. 2:12; 4:7; 5:7-8; 7:18. Jeremiah discussed the plight of the Jews who fled to Egypt after Jerusalem's capture by Nebuchadnezzar, Jer. 40:11, 15. Zephaniah, a seventh-century prophet, identified the "remnant" with the poor and humble, 2:3, 7; 3:12-13. Zechariah announced that a "remnant" would be present at the time of the coming of the Messiah's kingdom, 12:10-13:1; 13:8-9.

she'ar (7605), "rest; remnant; residue," Isa. 10:20.

B. Verb.

sha'ar (7604), "to remain, be left over." In the pre-exilic period, this remnant idea is stressed by Isaiah. Isaiah tells of the judgment on the earth from which a remnant will "remain," Isa. 24:6. In the writing prophets, the idea of the "remnant" acquired a growing significance. Yet the idea may be found as early as the Pentateuch. The idea of "those being left" or "having escaped," especially a portion of the Israelite people, may be traced back to Deut. 4:27: "And the Lord shall scatter you among the nations, and ye shall be left few in number among the heathen, whither the Lord shall lead you," cf. Deut. 28:62. In these passages, Moses warns that if Israel failed to live up to the stipulations of the Mosaic covenant, the Lord would scatter them among the nations, and then He would regather a "remnant."

New Testament

1. *loipos* (3062), an adjective (akin to *leipo*, "to leave") signifying "remaining," is used as a noun and translated "the rest" in the RV, where the KJV has "the remnant," Matt. 22:6; Rev. 11:13; 12:17; 19:21.

2. *leimma* (3005), "that which is left" (akin to *leipo*, "to leave"), "a remnant," is used in Rom. 11:5, "there is a remnant," more lit., "there has come to be a remnant," i.e., there is a spiritual "remnant" saved by the gospel from the midst of apostate Israel. While in one sense there has been and is a considerable number, yet, compared with the whole nation, past and present, the "remnant" is small, and as such is an evidence of God's electing grace (see v. 4).

3. *hupoleimma* (5259, and 3005), *hupo*, "under," signifying "diminution," and No. 2, is used in Rom. 9:27; cf. Isa. 10:22, 23 and Hosea 1:10.

RENDER

1. *apodidomi* (591), "to give up or back," is translated "to render," (a) of righteous acts, (1) human, Matt. 21:41; 22:21; Mark 12:17; Luke 16:2, RV (KJV, "give"); Luke 20:25; Rom. 13:7, 1 Cor. 7:3; (2) di-

vine, Matt. 16:27, RV, "shall render" (KJV, "shall reward"), an important RV change; Rom. 2:6; 2 Tim. 4:14, RV (KJV, "reward"); Rev. 18:6 (ditto); 22:12, RV (KJV, "give"); (b) of unrighteous acts, Rom. 12:17, RV (KJV, "recompense"); 1 Thess. 5:15; 1 Pet. 3:9.

2. *antapodidomi* (*467*), to give in return for," is translated "render" in 1 Thess. 3:9.

RENEW, RENEWING (Verb and Noun)

A. Verbs.

1. *anakainoo* (*341*), "to make new" (*ana*, "back" or "again," *kainos*, "new," not recent but different), "to renew," is used in the passive voice in 2 Cor. 4:16, of the daily renewal of "the inward man" (in contrast to the physical frame), i.e., of the "renewal" of spiritual power; in Col. 3:10, of "the new man" (in contrast to the old unregenerate nature), which "is being renewed unto knowledge," RV (cf. No. 3 in Eph. 4:23), i.e., the true knowledge in Christ, as opposed to heretical teachings.

2. *anakainizo* (*340*) is a variant form of No. 1, used in Heb. 6:6, of the impossibility of "renewing" to repentance those Jews who professedly adhered to the Christian faith, if, after their experiences of it (not actual possession of its regenerating effects), they apostatized into their former Judaism.

3. *ananeoo* (*365*), "to renew, make young" (*ana*, as in No. 1, and *neos*, "recent," not different), is used in Eph. 4:23, "be renewed (in the spirit of your mind)." The "renewal" here mentioned is not that of the mind itself in its natural powers of memory, judgment and perception, but "the spirit of the mind," which, under the controlling power of the indwelling Holy Spirit, directs its bent and energies Godward in the enjoyment of "fellowship with the Father and with His Son, Jesus Christ," and of the fulfillment of the will of God. The word is frequent in inscriptions and in the papyri.

B. Noun.

anakainosis (*342*), akin to A, No. 1, "a renewal," is used in Rom. 12:2, "the renewing (of your mind)," i.e., the adjustment of the moral and spiritual vision and thinking to the mind of God, which is designed to have a transforming effect upon the life; in Titus 3:5, where "the renewing of the Holy Spirit" is not a fresh bestowment of the Spirit, but a revival of His power, developing the Christian life; this passage stresses the continual operation of the indwelling Spirit of God; the Romans passage stresses the willing response on the part of the believer.

RENOUNCE

1. *apeipon* (*550*), lit., "to tell from" (*apo*, "from," *eipon*, an aorist form used to supply parts of *lego*, "to say"), signifies "to renounce,"

2 Cor. 4:2 (middle voice), of disowning "the hidden things of shame."

2. *apotasso* (657), "to set apart, to appoint," in NT meaning "taking leave of," Acts 18:18; Luke 14:33.

REPAY

1. *antapodidomi* (467), "to give in return for," is translated "I will repay" in Rom. 12:19, KJV (RV, "I will recompense").

2. *apotino* or *apotio* (661), signifying "to pay off" (*apo*, "off," *tino*, "to pay a fine"), is used in Philem. 19, of Paul's promise to "repay."

REPENT, REPENTANCE

Old Testament

nacham (5162), "to repent, comfort." *nacham* apparently translates "to repent" about 40 times and "to comfort" about 65 times in the Old Testament. Most uses of the term in the Old Testament are connected with God's repentance, which means choose a particular course of action (often as a response to a change in a person's attitude or change in a situation), as a figurative way of saying to "change his mind," Jer. 18:8, 10; Joel 2:13 God usually changed His mind and "repented" of His actions because of man's intercession and repentance of his evil deeds. Moses pleaded with God as the intercessor for Israel, Exod. 32:12, 14; Jonah 3:10. In such instances, God "repented," or changed His mind, to bring about a change of plan. Again, however, God remained faithful to His absolutes of righteousness in His relation to and with man.

When referring to a human, it means to turn away from wickedness, and so have change from an apostate state to a state of belief and acceptance in a relationship, Jer. 8:6; 31:19, 20.

nacham may also mean "to comfort," i.e., bring acts of kindness and favor, and encouraging words to another, Ezek. 14:23; the connection between "comfort" and "repent" here resulted from the calamity God brought upon Jerusalem as a testimony to the truth of His Word. David "comforted" Bathsheba after the death of her child born in sin, 2 Sam. 12:24; this probably indicates his repentance of what had happened in their indiscretion.

New Testament

A. Verbs.

1. *metanoeo* (3340), lit., "to perceive afterwards" (*meta*, "after," implying "change," *noeo*, "to perceive"; *nous*, "the mind, the seat of moral reflection"), in contrast to *pronoeo*, "to perceive beforehand," hence signifies "to change one's mind or purpose," always, in the NT, involving a change for the better, an amendment, and always, except in Luke 17:3, 4, of "repentance" from sin. The word

is found in the Synoptic Gospels (in Luke, nine times), in Acts five times, in the Apocalypse twelve times, eight in the messages to the churches, 2:5 (twice), 16, 21 (twice), RV, "she willeth not to repent" (2nd part); 3:3, 19 (the only churches in those chapters which contain no exhortation in this respect are those at Smyrna and Philadelphia); elsewhere only in 2 Cor. 12:21.

2. *metamelomai* (3338), *meta*, as in No. 1, and *melo*, "to care for," is used in the passive voice with middle voice sense, signifying "to regret, to repent oneself," Matt. 21:29, RV, "repented himself"; v. 32, RV, "ye did (not) repent yourselves" (KJV, "ye repented not"); 27:3, "repented himself"; 2 Cor. 7:8 (twice), RV, "regret" in each case; Heb. 7:21, where alone in the NT it is said (negatively) of God.

B. Adjective.

ametameletos (278), "not repented of, unregretted" (*a*, negative, and a verbal adjective of A, No. 2), signifies "without change of purpose"; it is said (a) of God in regard to his "gifts and calling," Rom. 11:29; (b) of man, 2 Cor. 7:10.

C. Noun.

metanoia (3341), "afterthought, change of mind, repentance," corresponds in meaning to A, No. 1, and is used of "repentance" from sin or evil, except in Heb. 12:17, where the word "repentance" seems to mean, not simply a change of Isaac's mind, but such a change as would reverse the effects of his own previous state of mind. Esau's birthright-bargain could not be recalled; it involved an irretrievable loss.

As regards "repentance" from sin, (a) the requirement by God on man's part is set forth, e.g., in Matt. 3:8; Luke 3:8; Acts 20:21; 26:20; (b) the mercy of God in giving "repentance" or leading men to it is set forth, e.g., in Acts 5:31; 11:18; Rom. 2:4; 2 Tim. 2:25. The most authentic mss. omit the word in Matt. 9:13 and Mark 2:17, as in the RV.

In the NT the subject chiefly has reference to "repentance" from sin, and this change of mind involves both a turning from sin and a turning to God. The parable of the Prodigal Son is an outstanding illustration of this. Christ began His ministry with a call to "repentance," Matt. 4:17, but the call is addressed, not as in the OT to the nation, but to the individual. In the Gospel of John, as distinct from the Synoptic Gospels, referred to above, "repentance" is not mentioned, even in connection with John the Baptist's preaching; in John's gospel and 1st epistle the effects are stressed, e.g., in the new birth, and, generally, in the active turning from sin to God by the exercise of faith (John 3:3; 9:38; 1 John 1:9), as in the NT in general.

R

REPETITIONS (use vain)

battalogeo or *battologeo* (945), "to repeat idly," is used in Matt. 6:7, "use (not) vain repetitions"; the meaning "to stammer" is scarcely to be associated with this word. The word is probably from an Aramaic phrase and onomatopoeic in character, "repetitive babbling."

REPORT (Noun and Verb)

A. Nouns.

1. *euphemia* (2162), "a good report, good reputation" (*eu*, "well," *pheme* "a saying or report"), is used in 2 Cor. 6:8.

2. *dusphemia* (1426), "evil-speaking, defamation" (*dus-*, an inseparable prefix, the opposite to *eu*, "well"), is used in 2 Cor. 6:8.

B. Adjective.

euphemos (2613), akin to A, No. 1, primarily, "uttering words or sounds of good omen," then, "avoiding ill-omened words," and hence "fair-sounding," "of good report," is so rendered in Phil. 4:8.

C. Verbs.

1. *apangello* (518), "to report" (*apo*, "from," *angello*, "to give a message"), "announce, declare" (by a messenger, speaker, or writer), is translated "reported" in Acts 4:23; 16:36, RV (KJV, "told"); v. 38 (some mss. have No. 2; KJV, "told"); "report" in 1 Cor. 14:25, KJV (RV, "declaring"); 1 Thess. 1:9, RV, "report" (KJV, "shew"); so Acts 28:21.

2. *anangello* (312), "to bring back word," in later Greek came to have the same meaning as No. 1, "to announce, declare"; it is translated "are reported" in 1 Pet. 1:12, KJV (RV, "have been announced").

REPROACH (Noun and Verb), REPROACHFULLY

Old Testament

A. Noun.

cherpah (2781), "reproach." "Reproach" has a twofold usage. On the one hand, the word denotes the state in which one finds himself. The unmarried woman, Isa. 4:1, or the woman without children, Gen. 30:23, carried a sense of disgrace in a society where marriage and fertility were highly spoken of. The destruction of Jerusalem and the Exile brought Judah to the state of "reproach," Dan. 9:16.

Whatever the occasion of the disgrace was, whether defeat in battle, exile, or enmity, the psalmist prayed for deliverance from the "reproach," Ps. 119:22—see context; cf. Ps. 109:25; cf. also the prophets use, Jer. 29:18; cf. Ezek. 5:14. However, the Lord graciously promised to remove the "reproach" at the accomplishment of His purpose, Isa. 25:8.

B. Verb.

charap (2778), "to say sharp things, reproach," Ps. 42:10.

New Testament

A. Nouns.

1. *oneidismos* (3680), "a reproach, defamation," is used in Rom. 15:3; 1 Tim. 3:7; Heb. 10:33; 11:26; 13:13.

2. *oneidos* (3681), akin to No. 1, is used in Luke 1:25 in the concrete sense of "a matter of reproach, a disgrace." To have no children was, in the Jewish mind, more than a misfortune, it might carry the implication that this was a divine punishment for some secret sin.

3. *atimia* (819), "dishonor," is translated "reproach" in 2 Cor. 11:21, KJV (RV, "disparagement).

B. Verbs.

1. *oneidizo* (3679), akin to A, Nos. 1 and 2, signifies (a), in the active voice, "to reproach, upbraid," Matt. 5:11, RV, "shall reproach" (KJV, "shall revile"); 11:20, "to upbraid"; 27:44, RV, "cast...reproach" [KJV, "cast...in (His) teeth"]; Mark 15:32 RV, "reproached" (KJV, "reviled"); 16:14 "upbraided"; Luke 6:22 "shall reproach," Rom. 15:3; Jas. 1:5, "upbraideth"; (b) in the passive voice, "to suffer reproach, be reproached," 1 Tim. 4:10 (in some mss. in the 2nd part); 1 Pet. 4:14.

2. *hubrizo* (5195), akin to *hubris*, used transitively, denotes "to outrage, insult, treat insolently"; it is translated "Thou reproachest" in Luke 11:45. The word is much stronger than "to reproach"; the significance is "Thou insultest (even us)," i.e., who are superior to ordinary Pharisees.

REPROBATE

adokimos (96), signifying "not standing the test, rejected" (*a*, negative, *dokimos*, "approved"), was primarily applied to metals, cf. Isa. 1:22; it is used always in the NT in a passive sense, (a) of things, Heb. 6:8, "rejected," of land that bears thorns and thistles; (b) of persons, Rom. 1:28, of a "reprobate mind," a mind of which God cannot approve, and which must be rejected by Him, the effect of refusing "to have God in their knowledge"; in 1 Cor. 9:27; 2 Cor. 13:5, 6, 7, where the RV rightly translates the adjective "reprobate" (KJV, "reprobates"), here the reference is to the great test as to whether Christ is in a person; in 2 Tim. 3:8 of those "reprobate concerning the faith," i.e., men whose moral sense is perverted and whose minds are beclouded with their own speculations; in Titus 1:16, of the defiled, who are "unto every good work reprobate," i.e., if they are put to the test in regard to any good work (in contrast to their profession), they can only be rejected.

REPROOF, REPROVE

Old Testament

yakach (3198), "to decide, prove, convince, judge." It is evident in most of the uses of *yakach* that there is a value judgment involved, as in Job 5:17; Ps. 50:21; Prov. 3:12, RSV.

New Testament

A. Noun.

elegmos (1650), "a reproof" (akin to B), is found in the best texts in 2 Tim. 3:16 (some mss. have *elenchos*, which denotes "a proof, proving, test," as in Heb. 11:1, "proving," RV marg., "test").

B. Verb.

elencho (1651), "to convict, rebuke, reprove," is translated "to reprove" in Luke 3:19; John 3:20, RV marg., "convicted"; the real meaning here is "exposed" (KJV marg., "discovered"); Eph. 5:11, 13, where "to expose" is again the significance; in John 16:8, KJV, "will reprove" (RV, "will convict"); in 1 Cor. 14:24, RV, "reproved" (KJV, "convinced"); in the following the RV has "to reprove," for KJV, "to rebuke," 1 Tim. 5:20; Titus 2:15; Heb. 12:5; Rev. 3:19.

REPUTATION, REPUTE

dokeo (1380) signifies (a) "to be of opinion" (akin to *doxa*, "an opinion"), "to suppose," e.g., Luke 12:51; 13:2; (b) "to seem, to be reputed"; in Gal. 2:2, RV, "who were of repute" (KJV, "which were of reputation"); in 2:6 (twice), and 9, RV, "were reputed" and "were of repute" (KJV, "seemed"); in each case the present participle of the verb with the article is used, lit., "(well) thought of" by them, persons held in consideration; in v. 6, RV, "(those) who were reputed to be somewhat" (KJV "who seemed to be somewhat"): so v. 9. where there is no irony [cf. the rendering "are accounted" in Mark 10:42 (i.e., not rulers nominally)], Paul recognized that James, Cephas, and John were, as they were "reputed" by the church at Jerusalem, its responsible guides; (c) impersonally, "to think, to seem good."

REQUEST (Noun and Verb)

A. Nouns.

1. *aitema* (155) denotes "that which has been asked for" (akin to *aiteo*, "to ask"); in Luke 23:24, RV, "what they asked for" (KJV, "as they required"), lit., "their request (should be done, *ginomai*)"; in Phil. 4:6, "requests"; in 1 John 5:15, "petitions."

2. *deesis* (*1162*), "an asking, entreaty, supplication," is translated "request" in Phil. 1:4, KJV (RV, supplication).

B. Verbs.

1. *deomai* (*1189*), akin to A, No. 2, "to beseech, pray, request," in Rom. 1:10.

2. *aiteo* (*154*), "to ask," is translated "to make request" in Col. 1:9, RV (KJV, "to desire").

3. *erotao* (*2065*), "to ask," is translated "to make request" in 1 John 5:16.

REQUIRE

1. *zeteo* (*2212*), "to seek, seek after," also signifies "to require, demand," "shall be required," Luke 12:48; in 1 Cor. 4:2, "it is required (in stewards)."

2. *ekzeteo* (*1567*), "to seek out" (*ek*, "out," and No. 1), also denotes "to demand, require," Luke 11:50, 51, of executing vengeance for the slaughter of the prophets, cf. 2 Sam. 4:11; Ezek. 3:18.

3. *apaiteo* (*523*), "to ask back, demand back" (*apo*, "from," or "back," *aiteo*, "to ask"), is translated "shall be required" in Luke 12:20, lit. "do they require," in the impersonal sense; elsewhere, Luke 6:30, "to ask again." It is used in the papyri frequently in the sense of "demanding, making demands."

RESCUE

exaireo (*1807*), "to take out" (*ek*, "from," *haireo*, "to take"), is used of "delivering" from persons and circumstances, and translated "rescued" in Acts 23:27.

RESERVE

tereo (*5083*), "to guard, keep, preserve, give heed to," is translated "to reserve," (a) with a happy issue, 1 Pet. 1:4; (b) with a retributive issue, 2 Pet. 2:4; v. 9, KJV (RV, "keep"); 2:17; 3:7; Jude 6, KJV (RV, "hath kept"); v. 13; (c) with the possibility either of deliverance or execution, Acts 25:21, KJV (RV, kept).

RESIST

1. *anthistemi* (*436*), "to set against" (*anti*, "against," *histemi*, "to cause to stand"), used in the middle (or passive) voice and in the intransitive 2nd aorist and perfect active, signifying "to withstand oppose, resist," is translated "to resist" in Matt. 5:39; Acts 6:10, KJV (RV, withstand); Rom. 9:19, KJV (RV, "withstandeth"); 13:2 (2nd and 3rd parts; for 1st part, see No. 3), KJV (RV, "withstandeth" and "withstand"); Gal. 2:11, RV (KJV, "withstood"); 2 Tim. 3:8 (2nd part), KJV (RV, "withstand"); Jas. 4:7; 1 Pet. 5:9, KJV (RV, "withstand"); "to withstand" in Acts 13:8; Eph. 6:13; 2 Tim. 3:8 (1st part); 4:15.

R

2. **antikathistemi** (*478*), "to stand firm against" (*anti*, "against," **kathistemi**, "to set down," *kata*), is translated "ye have (not) resisted" in Heb. 12:4.

3. **antitasso** (*498*), *anti*, "against," **tasso**, "to arrange," originally a military term, "to range in battle against," and frequently so found in the papyri, is used in the middle voice signifying "to set oneself against, resist," (a) of men, Acts 18:6, "opposed themselves"; elsewhere "to resist," of resisting human potentates, Rom. 13:2; (b) of God, Jas. 4:6; 5:6, negatively, of leaving persistent evildoers to pursue their self-determined course, with eventual retribution, 1 Pet. 5:5.

4. **antipipto** (*496*), lit., and primarily, "to fall against or upon" (*anti*, "against," **pipto**, "to fall"), then, "to strive against, resist," is used in Acts 7:51 of "resisting" the Holy Spirit.

RESPECT (Noun and Verb)

A. Noun.

meros (*3313*), "a part," has occasionally the meaning of "a class" or "category," and, used in the dative case with *en*, "in," signifies "in respect of," 2 Cor. 3:10, "in (this) respect"; 9:3, RV, KJV, "in (this) behalf"; Col. 2:16, "in respect of (a feast day)."

B. Verbs.

1. **apoblepo** (*578*), "to look away from all else at one object" (*apo*, "from"), hence, "to look steadfastly," is translated "he had respect" in Heb. 11:26, KJV (RV, "looked").

2. **epiblepo** (*1914*), "to look upon" (*epi*), is translated "have respect" in Jas. 2:3 (RV "regard").

REST (Noun and Verb)

Old Testament

nuach (5117), "to rest, remain, be quiet." **nuach** sometimes indicates a complete envelopment and thus permeation, as in the spirit of Elijah "resting" on Elisha, 2 Kings 2:15, the hand of God "resting" on the mountain, Isa. 25:10, and when Wisdom "resteth in the heart of him that hath understanding," Prov. 14:33. Frequently **nuach** means "to be quiet" or "to rest" after hard work, Exod. 20:11, from onslaught of one's enemies, Esth. 9:16, from trouble, Job 3:26, and in death, Job 3:17.

It should be noted that while **nuach** is used sometimes as a synonym for **shabat**, "to cease, to rest," Exod. 20:11, **shabat** really is basically "to cease" from work which may imply rest, but not necessarily so. The writer of Gen. 2:3 is not stressing rest from work but rather God ceasing from His creative work since it was complete.

New Testament

A. Nouns.

1. *anapausis* (372), "cessation, refreshment, rest" (*ana*, "up," *pauo*, "to make to cease"), the constant word in the Sept. for the Sabbath "rest," is used in Matt. 11:29; here the contrast seems to be to the burdens imposed by the Pharisees. Christ's "rest" is not a "rest" from work, but in work, "not the rest of inactivity but of the harmonious working of all the faculties and affections—of will, heart, imagination, conscience—because each has found in God the ideal sphere for its satisfaction and development" (J. Patrick, in *Hastings' Bib. Dic.*); it occurs also in Matt. 12:43; Luke 11:24; Rev. 4:8, RV, "(they have no) rest" [KJV, "(they) rest (not)"], where the noun is the object of the verb *echo*, "to have"; so in 14:11.

2. *katapausis* (2663), in classical Greek, denotes "a causing to cease" or "putting to rest"; in the NT, "rest, repose"; it is used (a) of God's "rest," Acts 7:49; Heb. 3:11, 18; 4:1, 3 (twice), RV (1st part), "that rest" (the KJV, "rest," is ambiguous), 5, 11; (b) in a general statement, applicable to God and man, 4:10.

3. *anesis* (425), translated "rest" in 2 Cor. 2:13, KJV (RV, "relief"); 7:5 (ditto); in 2 Thess. 1:7, the subject is not the "rest" to be granted to the saints, but the divine retribution on their persecutors; hence the phrase "and to you that are afflicted rest with us," is an incidental extension of the idea of recompense, and is to be read parenthetically. The time is not that at which the saints will be relieved of persecution, as in 1 Thess. 4:15-17, when the Parousia of Christ begins, but that at which the persecutors will be punished, namely, at the epiphany (or out-shining) of His Parousia (2 Thess. 2:8). For similar parentheses characteristic of epistolary writings see v. 10; 1 Thess. 1:6, 2:15, 16.

4. *sabbatismos* (4520), "a Sabbath-keeping," is used in Heb. 4:9, RV, "a sabbath rest," KJV marg., "a keeping of a sabbath" (akin to *sabbatizo*, "to keep the Sabbath," used, e.g., in Exod. 16:30, not in the NT); here the sabbath-keeping is the perpetual sabbath "rest" to be enjoyed uninterruptedly by believers in their fellowship with the Father and the Son, in contrast to the weekly Sabbath under the Law. Because this sabbath "rest" is the "rest" of God Himself, 4:10, its full fruition is yet future, though believers now enter into it. In whatever way they enter into divine "rest," that which they enjoy is involved in an indissoluble relation with God.

5. *koimesis* (2838), "a resting, reclining" (akin to *keimai*, "to lie"), is used in John 11:13, of natural sleep, translated "taking rest," RV.

B. Verbs.

1. *anapauo* (373), akin to A, No. 1, in the active voice, signifies "to give intermission from labor, to give rest, to refresh," Matt. 11:28; 1 Cor. 16:18, "have refreshed"; Philem. 20, "refresh"; passive voice,

"to be rested, refreshed," 2 Cor. 7:13, "was refreshed"; Philem. 7, "are refreshed"; in the middle voice, "to take or enjoy rest," Matt. 26:45; Mark 6:31; 14:41; Luke 12:19, "take thine ease"; 1 Pet. 4:14; Rev. 6:11; 14:13. In the papyri it is found as an agricultural term, e.g., of giving land "rest" by sowing light crops upon it. In inscriptions it is found on gravestones of Christians, followed by the date of death (Moulton and Milligan).

2. *katapauo* (*2664*), akin to A, No. 2, used transitively, signifies "to cause to cease, restrain," Acts 14:18; "to cause to rest," Heb. 4:8; intransitively, "to rest," Heb. 4:4, 10.

3. *episkenoo* (*1981*), "to spread a tabernacle over" (*epi*, "upon," *skene*, "a tent"), is used metaphorically in 2 Cor. 12:9, "may rest upon (me)," RV, marg., "cover," "spread a tabernacle over."

4. *kataskenoo* (*2681*), "to pitch one's tent, lodge," is translated "shall rest," in Acts 2:26, KJV (RV, "shall dwell").

5. *hesuchazo* (*2270*), "to be still, to rest from labor," is translated "they rested" in Luke 23:56.

6. *epanapauo* (*1879*), "to cause to rest," is used in the middle voice, metaphorically, signifying "to rest upon" (*epi*, "upon," and No. 1), in Luke 10:6 and Rom. 2:17.

REST (the)

1. *loipos* (*3062*), "remaining," is frequently used to mean "the rest," and is generally so translated in the RV (KJV, "others" in Luke 8:10; Acts 28:9; Eph. 2:3; 1 Thess. 4:13; 5:6; 1 Tim. 5:20; KJV, "other" in Luke 18:11; Acts 17:9; Rom. 1:13; 2 Cor. 12:13; 13:2; Gal. 2:13; Phil. 1:13; 4:3); the neut. plur., lit., "remaining things," is used in Luke 12:26; 1 Cor. 11:34.

2. *epiloipos* (*1954*), signifying "still left, left over" (*epi*, "over," and No. 1), is used in the neuter with the article in 1 Pet. 4:2, "the rest (of your time)."

RESTLESS

akatastatos (*182*), "unsettled, unstable, disorderly" (*a*, negative, *kathistemi*, "to set in order"), is translated "unstable" in Jas. 1:8; "restless" in 3:8, RV [in the latter, the KJV "unruly" represents the word *akataschetos*, signifying "that cannot be restrained" (*a*, negative, *katecho*, "to hold down, restrain").

RESTORATION

apokatastasis (*605*), from *apo*, "back, again," *kathistemi*, "to set in order," is used in Acts 3:21, RV, "restoration" (KJV, "restitution"). In the papyri it is used of a temple cell of a goddess, a "repair" of a public way, the "restoration" of estates to rightful owners, a "balancing" of accounts. Apart from papyri illustrations the word is found in an Egyptian reference to a consummating agreement of the world's cyclical periods, an idea somewhat similar to that in the Acts passage (Moulton and Milligan).

RESTORE

1. *apodidomi* (591), "to give back," is translated "I restore" in Luke 19:8.

2. *apokathistemi* or the alternative form *apokathistano* (600) is used (a) of "restoration" to a former condition of health, Matt. 12:13; Mark 3:5; 8:25; Luke 6:10; (b) of the divine "restoration" of Israel and conditions affected by it, including the renewal of the covenant broken by them, Matt. 17:11; Mark 9:12; Acts 1:6; (c) of "giving" or "bringing" a person back, Heb. 13:19. In the papyri it is used of financial restitution, of making good the breaking of a stone by a workman by his substituting another, of the reclamation of land, etc. (Moulton and Milligan).

3. *katartizo* (2675), "to mend, to furnish completely," is translated "restore" in Gal. 6:1, metaphorically, of the "restoration," by those who are spiritual, of one overtaken in a trespass, such a one being as a dislocated member of the spiritual body.

RESTRAIN

katecho (2722), "to hold fast or down," is translated "restraineth" in 2 Thess. 2:6 and 7. In v. 6 lawlessness is spoken of as being "restrained" in its development: in v. 7 "one that restraineth" is, lit., "the restrainer" (the article with the present participle, "the restraining one"); this may refer to an individual, as in the similar construction in 1 Thess. 3:5, "the tempter" (cf. 1:10, lit., "the Deliverer"); or to a number of persons presenting the same characteristics, just as "the believer" stands for all believers, e.g., Rom. 9:33; 1 John 5:10. V. 6 speaks of a principle, v. 7 of the principle as embodied in a person or series of persons; cf. what is said of "the power" in Rom. 13:3, 4, a phrase representing all such rulers. Probably such powers, i.e., "constituted governments," are the "restraining" influence here intimated (specifications being designedly withheld).

RESURRECTION

1. *anastasis* (386) denotes (I) "a raising up," or "rising" (*ana*, "up," and *histemi*, "to cause to stand"), Luke 2:34, "the rising up"; the KJV "again" obscures the meaning; the Child would be like a stone against which many in Israel would stumble while many others would find in its strength and firmness a means of their salvation and spiritual life; (II), of "resurrection" from the dead, (a) of Christ, Acts 1:22; 2:31; 4:33; Rom. 1:4; 6:5; Phil. 3:10; 1 Pet. 1:3; 3:21; by metonymy, of Christ as the Author of "resurrection," John 11:25; (b) of those who are Christ's at His Parousia, Luke 14:14, "the resurrection of the just"; Luke 20:33, 35, 36; John 5:29 (1st part),

R

"the resurrection of life"; 11:24; Acts 23:6; 24:15 (1st part); 1 Cor. 15:21, 42; 2 Tim. 2:18; Heb. 11:35 (2nd part); Rev. 20:5, "the first resurrection"; hence the insertion of "is" stands for the completion of this "resurrection," of which Christ was "the firstfruits"; 20:6; (c) of "the rest of the dead," after the Millennium (cf. Rev. 20:5); John 5:29 (2nd part), "the resurrection of judgment"; Acts 24:15 (2nd part), "of the unjust"; (d) of those who were raised in more immediate connection with Christ's "resurrection," and thus had part already in the first "resurrection," Acts 26:23 and Rom. 1:4 (in each of which "dead" is plural; see Matt. 27:52); (e) of the "resurrection" spoken of in general terms, Matt. 22:23; Mark 12:18; Luke 20:27; Acts 4:2; 17:18; 23:8; 24:21; 1 Cor. 15:12, 13; Heb. 6:2; (f) of those who were raised in OT times, to die again, Heb. 11:35 (1st part), lit., "out of resurrection."

2. *exanastasis* (*1815*), *ek*, "from" or "out of," and No. 1, Phil. 3:11, followed by *ek*, lit., "the out-resurrection from among the dead."

3. *egersis* (*1454*), "a rousing" (akin to *egeiro*, "to arouse, to raise"), is used of the "resurrection" of Christ, in Matt. 27:53.

REVEAL

1. *apokalupto* (*601*) signifies "to uncover, unveil" (*apo*, "from," *kalupto*, "to cover"); both verbs are used in Matt. 10:26; in Luke 12:2, *apokalupto* is set in contrast to *sunkalupto*, "to cover up, cover completely." "The NT occurrences of this word fall under two heads, subjective and objective. The subjective use is that in which something is presented to the mind directly, as, (a) the meaning of the acts of God, Matt. 11:25; Luke 10:21; (b) the secret of the Person of the Lord Jesus, Matt. 16:17; John 12:38; (c) the character of God as Father, Matt. 11:27; Luke 10:22; (d) the will of God for the conduct of His children, Phil. 3:15; (e) the mind of God to the prophets of Israel, 1 Pet. 1:12, and of the Church, 1 Cor. 14:30; Eph. 3:5.

The objective use is that in which something is presented to the senses, sight or hearing, as, referring to the past, (f) the truth declared to men in the gospel, Rom. 1:17; 1 Cor. 2:10; Gal. 3:23; (g) the Person of Christ to Paul on the way to Damascus, Gal. 1:16; (h) thoughts before hidden in the heart, Luke 2:35; referring to the future, (i) the coming in glory of the Lord Jesus, Luke 17:30; (j) the salvation and glory that await the believer, Rom. 8:18; 1 Pet. 1:5; 5:1; (k) the true value of service, 1 Cor. 3:13; (l) the wrath of God (at the Cross, against sin, and, at the revelation of the Lord Jesus, against the sinner), Rom. 1:18; (m) the Lawless One, 2 Thess. 2:3, 6, 8.

2. *chrematizo* (*5537*), "to give divine admonition, instruction, revelation," is translated "it had been revealed," in Luke 2:26.

REVELATION

apokalupsis (*602*), "an uncovering" (akin to *apokalupto*; see above), is used in the NT of (a) the drawing away by Christ of the veil of darkness covering the Gentiles, Luke 2:32; cf. Isa. 25:7; (b) 'the mystery,' the purpose of God in this age, Rom. 16:25; Eph. 3:3; (c) the communication of the knowledge of God to the soul, Eph. 1:17; (d) an expression of the mind of God for the instruction of the church, 1 Cor. 14:6, 26, for the instruction of the Apostle Paul, 2 Cor. 12:1, 7; Gal. 1:12, and for his guidance, Gal. 2:2; (e) the Lord Jesus Christ, to the saints at His Parousia, 1 Cor. 1:7, RV (KJV, 'coming'); 1 Pet. 1:7, RV (KJV, 'appearing'), 13; 4:13; (f) the Lord Jesus Christ when He comes to dispense the judgments of God, 2 Thess. 1:7; cf. Rom. 2:5; (g) the saints, to the creation, in association with Christ in His glorious reign, Rom. 8:19, RV, 'revealing' (KJV, 'manifestation'); (h) the symbolic forecast of the final judgments of God, Rev. 1:1 (hence the Greek title of the book, transliterated 'Apocalypse' and translated 'Revelation').

REVEL, REVELING

1. *truphe* (*5172*), "luxuriousness, daintiness, reveling," is translated freely by the verb "to revel" in 2 Pet. 2:13, RV (KJV, "to riot"), lit., "counting reveling in the daytime a pleasure." In Luke 7:25 it is used with *en*, "in," and translated "delicately."

2. *komos* (*2970*), "a revel, carousal," the concomitant and consequence of drunkenness, is used in the plural, Rom. 13:13, translated by the singular, RV, "reveling" (KJV, "rioting"); Gal. 5:21 and 1 Pet. 4:3, "revelings."

REVERENCE (Noun and Verb)

A. Verbs.

1. *entrepo* (*1788*), lit., "to turn in" (i.e., upon oneself), "to put to shame," denotes, when used in the passive voice, "to feel respect for, to show deference to, to reverence," Matt. 21:37; Mark 12:6; Luke 20:13; Heb. 12:9.

2. *phobeo* (*5399*), "to fear," is used in the passive voice in the NT; in Eph. 5:33 of reverential fear on the part of a wife for a husband, KJV, "reverence" (RV, "fear").

B. Noun

eulabeia (*2124*), "caution, reverence," is translated "reverence" in Heb. 12:28 (1st part in the best mss; some have *aidos*).

REVERENT

hieroprepes (*2412*), "suited to a sacred character, reverend" (*hieros*, "sacred," *prepo*, "to be fitting"), is translated "reverent" in Titus 2:3, RV (KJV, "as becometh holiness").

R

REVILE, REVILING, REVILER

A. Verbs.

1. *loidoreo* (*3058*) denotes "to abuse, revile," John 9:28; Acts 23:4; 1 Cor. 4:12; 1 Pet. 2:23 (1st clause).

2. *oneidizo* (*3679*), "to reproach, upbraid," is translated "to revile" in Matt. 5:11, KJV, and Mark 15:32 (RV, "reproach").

3. *blasphemeo* (*987*), "to speak profanely, rail at," is translated "reviled" in Matt. 27:39, KJV (RV, "railed on"); Luke 22:65, RV, "reviling" (KJV, "blasphemously").

4. *antiloidoreo* (*486*), "to revile back or again" (*anti*, and No. 1), is found in 1 Pet. 2:23 (2nd clause).

B. Adjective.

loidoros (*3060*), akin to A, No. 1, "abusive, railing, reviling," is used as a noun, 1 Cor. 5:11, RV, "a reviler" (KJV "a railer"); 6:10, "revilers."

C. Noun.

loidoria (*3059*), akin to A, No. 1, and B, "abuse, railing," is used in 1 Tim. 5:14, RV, "for (*charin*, 'for the sake of') reviling" (KJV, "to speak reproachfully"—a paraphrase); 1 Pet. 3:9 (twice), RV, "reviling" (KJV, "railing").

REVIVE

1. *anathallo* (*330*), "to flourish anew" (*ana*, "again, anew," *thallo*, "to flourish or blossom"), hence, "to revive," is used metaphorically in Phil. 4:10, RV, "ye have revived (your thought for me)," KJV, "(your care of me) hath flourished again."

2. *anazao* (*326*), "to live again" (*ana*, "and" *zao*, "to live"), "to regain life," is used of moral "revival," Luke 15:24, "is alive again"; (b) of sin, Rom. 7:9, "revived," lit., "lived again" i.e., it sprang into activity, manifesting the evil inherent in it; here sin is personified, by way of contrast to the man himself. Some mss. have it in Rom. 14:9, for *zao*, as in the RV, which italicizes "*again*."

REWARD (Noun and Verb)

A. Noun.

misthos (*3408*), primarily "wages, hire," and then, generally, "reward," (a) received in this life, Matt. 5:46; 6:2, 5, 16; Rom. 4:4; 1 Cor. 9:17, 18; of evil "rewards," Acts 1:18; (b) to be received hereafter, Matt. 5:12; 10:41 (twice), 42; Mark 9:41; Luke 6:23, 35; 1 Cor. 3:8, 14; 2 John 8; Rev. 11:18; 22:12.

B. Verb.

apodidomi (*591*), "to give back," is nowhere translated "to reward" in the RV; KJV, Matt. 6:4, 6, 18; Matt. 16:27; 2 Tim. 4:14; Rev. 18:6.

REWARDER

misthapodotes (*3406*), "one who pays wages" (*misthos*, "wages," *apo*, "back," *didomi*, "to give"), is used by metonymy in Heb. 11:6, of God, as the "Rewarder" of those who "seek after Him" (RV).

RICH, RICHES, RICHLY, RICH MAN

A. Adjective.

plousios (*4145*), akin to B, C, No. 1, "rich, wealthy," is used (I) literally, (a) adjectivally (with a noun expressed separately) in Matt. 27:57; Luke 12:16; 14:12; 16:1, 19; (without a noun), 18:23; 19:2; (b) as a noun, singular, a "rich" man (the noun not being expressed), Matt. 19:23, 24; Mark 10:25; 12:41; Luke 16:21, 22; 18:25; Jas. 1:10, 11, "the rich," "the rich (man)"; plural, Mark 12:41, lit., "rich (ones)"; Luke 6:24 (ditto); 21:1; 1 Tim. 6:17, "(them that are) rich," lit., "(the) rich"; Jas. 2:6, RV, "the rich"; 5:1, RV, "ye rich"; Rev. 6:15 and 13:16, RV, "the rich"; (II), metaphorically, of God, Eph. 2:4 ("in mercy"); of Christ, 2 Cor. 8:9; of believers, Jas. 2:5, RV, "(*to be*) rich (in faith)"; Rev. 2:9, of spiritual "enrichment" generally; 3:17, of a false sense of "enrichment."

B. Verbs.

1. *plouteo* (*4147*), "to be rich," in the aorist or point tense, "to become rich," is used (a) literally, Luke 1:53, "the rich," present participle, lit., "(ones or those) being rich"; 1 Tim. 6:9, 18; Rev. 18:3, 15, 19 (all three in the aorist tense); (b) metaphorically, of Christ, Rom. 10:12 (the passage stresses the fact that Christ is Lord; see v. 9, and the RV); of the "enrichment" of believers through His poverty, 2 Cor. 8:9 (the aorist tense expressing completeness, with permanent results); so in Rev. 3:18, where the spiritual "enrichment" is conditional upon righteousness of life and conduct; of a false sense of "enrichment," 1 Cor. 4:8 (aorist), RV, "ye are become rich" (KJV, "ye are rich"); Rev. 3:17 (perfect tense, RV, "I...have gotten riches," KJV, "I am... increased with goods"); of not being "rich" toward God, Luke 12:21.

2. *ploutizo* (*4148*), "to make rich, enrich," is rendered "making (many) rich" in 2 Cor. 6:10 (metaphorical of "enriching" spiritually).

R

C. Nouns

1. *ploutos* (*4149*) is used in the singular (I) of material "riches," used evilly, Matt. 13:22; Mark 4:19; Luke 8:14; 1 Tim. 6:17; Jas. 5:2; Rev. 18:17; (II) of spiritual and moral "riches," (a) possessed by God and exercised towards men, Rom. 2:4, "of His goodness and forbearance and longsuffering"; 9:23 and Eph. 3:16, "of His glory" (i.e.,

of its manifestation in grace towards believers); Rom. 11:33, of His wisdom and knowledge; Eph. 1:7 and 2:7, "of His grace"; 1:18, "of the glory of His inheritance in the saints"; 3:8, "of Christ"; Phil. 4:19, "in glory in Christ Jesus," RV; Col. 1:27, "of the glory of this mystery...Christ in you, the hope of glory"; (b) to be ascribed to Christ, Rev. 5:12; (c) of the effects of the gospel upon the Gentiles, Rom. 11:12 (twice); (d) of the full assurance of understanding in regard to the mystery of God, even Christ, Col. 2:2, RV; (e) of the liberality of the churches of Macedonia, 2 Cor. 8:2 (where "the riches" stands for the spiritual and moral value of their liberality); (f) of "the reproach of Christ" in contrast to this world's treasures, Heb. 11:26.

2. *chrema* (*5536*), "what one uses or needs" (*chraomai*, "to use"), "a matter, business," hence denotes "riches," Mark 10:23, 24; Luke 18:24.

D. Adverb.

plousios (*4146*), "richly, abundantly," akin to A, is used in Col. 3:16; 1 Tim. 6:17; Titus 3:6, RV, "richly" (KJV, "abundantly"); 2 Pet. 1:11 (ditto).

RIGHT (opp. to left), RIGHT HAND, RIGHT SIDE

Old Testament

yamin (*3225*), "right hand." This word has cognates attested in Ugaritic, Arabic, Syriac, Aramaic, and Ethiopic. It appears about 137 times and in all periods of biblical Hebrew.

First, the word represents the bodily part called the "right hand," simply as opposed to the left hand, Gen. 48:13; with the associative meaning of strength and authority or high status, Exod. 15:6; 20:4; Deut. 4:15-19; Ps. 77:10. Second, *yamin* represents the direction, to the "right," which means "south," in our language, since the orientation is to stand in the direction of the sunrise, Gen. 13:9; or in some contexts, "the right side," with no reference to a compass direction, Exod. 14:29. Third, *yamin* can be used of bodily parts other than the right hand, Judg. 3:16.

New Testament

dexios (*1188*), an adjective, used (a) of "the right" as opposite to the left, e.g., Matt. 5:29, 30; Rev. 10:5, RV, "right hand"; in connection with armor (figuratively), 2 Cor. 6:7; with *en*, followed by the dative plural, Mark 16:5; with *ek*, and the genitive plural, e.g., Matt. 25:33, 34; Luke 1:11; (b) of giving the "right hand" of fellowship, Gal. 2:9, betokening the public expression of approval by leaders at Jerusalem of the course pursued by Paul and Barnabas among the Gentiles; the act was often the sign of a pledge, e.g., 2 Kings 10:15; 1 Chron. 29:24, marg.; Ezra 10:19; Ezek. 17:18; figuratively, Lam. 5:6; it is often so used in the papyri; (c) metaphorically of "power" or "authority," Acts 2:33; with *ek*, signifying "on," followed by the genitive plural, Matt. 26:64; Mark 14:62; Heb. 1:13; (d) similarly of "a place of honor in the messianic kingdom," Matt. 20:21; Mark 10:37.

RIGHT (not wrong—Noun and Adjective), RIGHTLY

A. Noun.

exousia (*1849*), "authority, power," is translated "right" in the RV, for KJV, "power," in John 1:12; Rom. 9:21; 1 Cor. 9:4, 5, 6, 12 (twice), 18; 2 Thess. 3:9, where the "right" is that of being maintained by those among whom the ministers of the gospel had labored, a "right" possessed in virtue of the "authority" given them by Christ, Heb. 13:10; Rev. 22:14.

exousia first denotes "freedom to act" and then "authority for the action." This is first true of God, Acts 1:7. It was exercised by the Son of God, as from, and in conjunction with, the Father when the Lord was upon earth, in the days of His flesh, Matt. 9:6; John 10:18, as well as in resurrection, Matt. 28:18; John 17:2. All others hold their freedom to act from God (though some of them have abused it), whether angels, Eph. 1:21, or human potentates, Rom. 13:1. Satan offered to delegate his authority over earthly kingdoms to Christ, Luke 4:6, who, though conscious of His "right" to it, refused, awaiting the divinely appointed time.

B. Adjectives.

1. *dikaios* (*1342*), "just, righteous, that which is in accordance with" *dike*, "rule, right, justice," is translated "right" in Matt. 20:4; v. 7, KJV only (RV omits, according to the most authentic mss., the clause having been inserted from v. 4, to the detriment of the narrative); Luke 12:57; Acts 4:19; Eph. 6:1; Phil. 1:7, RV (KJV, "meet"); 2 Pet. 1:13 (KJV, "meet").

2. *euthus* (*2117*), "straight," hence, metaphorically, "right," is so rendered in Acts 8:21, of the heart; 13:10, of the ways of the Lord; 2 Pet. 2:15.

RIGHTEOUS, RIGHTEOUSLY
Old Testament

R

A. Verb.

tsadaq (*6663*), "to be righteous, be in the right, be justified, be just." The basic meaning of *tsadaq* is "to be righteous." It is a legal term which involves the whole process of justice. God "is righteous" in all of His relations, and in comparison with Him man is not righteous: "Shall mortal man be more just [righteous] than God?" Job 4:17. In a derived sense, the case presented may be characterized as a just cause in that all facts indicate that the person is to be cleared of all charges. Isaiah called upon the nations to produce witnesses who might testify that their case was right, 43:9. Job was concerned about his case and defended it before his friends, 9:15. *tsadaq* may also be used to signify the outcome of the verdict, when a man is pronounced "just" and is judicially cleared of all charges. Job believed that the Lord would ultimately vindicate him against his opponents, Job 13:18.

In its causative pattern, the meaning of the verb brings out more clearly the sense of a judicial pronouncement of innocence "If there be a controversy between men, and they come unto judgment, that the judges may judge them; then they shall justify [*tsadaq*] the righteous [*tsaddiq*], and condemn the wicked," Deut. 25:1. The Israelites were charged with upholding righteousness in all areas of life. When the court system failed became of corruption, the wicked were falsely "justified" and the poor were robbed of justice because of trumped-up charges. Absalom, thus, gained a large following by promising justice to the landowner, 2 Sam. 15:4. God, however, assured Israel that justice would be done in the end: "Thou shalt not wrest the judgment of thy poor in his cause. Keep thee far from a false matter; and the innocent and righteous slay thou not: for I will not justify the wicked," Exod. 23:6-7. The righteous person followed God's example. The psalmist exhorts his people to change their judicial system, Ps. 82:3.

B. Nouns.

tsedeq (6664); *tsedaqah* (6666), "righteousness." Exegetes have spilled much ink in an attempt to understand contextually the words *tsedeq* and *tsedaqah.* The conclusions of the researchers indicate a twofold significance. On the one hand, the relationships among people and of a man to his God can be described as *tsedeq*, supposing the parties are faithful to each other's expectations. It is a relational word. In Jacob's proposal to Laban, Jacob used the word *tsedaqah* to indicate the relationship. The KJV gives the following translation of *tsedaqah:* "So shall my righteousness answer for me in time to come, when it shall come for my hire before thy face..." Gen. 30:33. The NASB gives the word "righteousness" in a marginal note, but prefers the word "honesty" in the text itself. The NEB reads "fair offer" instead. Finally, the NIV has: "And my honesty [*tsedaqah*] will testify for me in the future, whenever you check on the wages you have paid me." On the other hand, "righteousness" as an abstract or as the legal status of a relationship is also present in the Old Testament. The *locus classicus* is Gen. 15:6: "...And he [the Lord] counted it to him [Abraham] for righteousness."

tsedeq and *tsedaqah* are legal terms signifying justice in conformity with the Law, Deut. 16:20; the judicial process, Jer. 22:3, the justice of the king as judge, 1 Kings 10:9; Ps. 119:121; Prov. 8:15, and also the source of justice, God Himself: "Judge me, O Lord my God, according to thy righteousness; and let them not rejoice over me....And my tongue shall speak of thy righteousness and of thy praise all the day long," Ps. 35:24, 28.

The word "righteousness" also embodies all that God expects of His people. The verbs associated with "righteousness" indicate the practicality of this concept. One judges, deals, sacrifices, and speaks righteously; and one learns, teaches, and pursues after righteousness. Based upon a special relationship with God, the Old Testament saint asked God to deal righteously with him: "Give the king thy judgments, O God, and thy righteousness unto the king's son," Ps. 72:1.

C. Adjective.

tsaddiq (6662), "righteous; just," of God, Exod. 9:27; of a nation, Gen. 20:4.

New Testament

A. Adjective.

dikaios (1342) signifies "just," without prejudice or partiality, e.g., of the judgment of God, 2 Thess. 1:5, 6; of His judgments, Rev. 16:7; 19:2; of His character as Judge, 2 Tim. 4:8; Rev. 16:5; of His ways and doings, Rev. 15:3.

In the following the RV substitutes "righteous" for the KJV "just"; Matt. 1:19; 13:49; 27:19, 24; Mark 6:20; Luke 2:25; 15:7; 20:20; 23:50; John 5:30; Acts 3:14; 7:52; 10:22; 22:14; Rom. 1:17; 7:12; Gal. 3:11; Heb. 10:38; Jas. 5:6; 1 Pet. 3:18; 2 Pet. 2:7; 1 John 1:9; Rev. 15:3.

B. Adverb.

dikaios (1346) is translated "righteously" in 1 Cor. 15:34, RV "(awake up) righteously," KJV, "(awake to) righteousness"; 1 Thess. 2:10, RV (KJV, "justly"); Titus 2:12; 1 Pet. 2:23.

RIGHTEOUSNESS

dikaiosune (1343) is "the character or quality of being right or just"; it was formerly spelled "rightwiseness," which clearly expresses the meaning. It is used to denote an attribute of God, e.g., Rom. 3:5, the context of which shows that "the righteousness of God" means essentially the same as His faithfulness, or truthfulness, that which is consistent with His own nature and promises; Rom. 3:25, 26 speaks of His "righteousness" as exhibited in the death of Christ, which is sufficient to show men that God is neither indifferent to sin nor regards it lightly. On the contrary, it demonstrates that quality of holiness in Him which must find expression in His condemnation of sin.

R

dikaiosune is found in the sayings of the Lord Jesus, (a) of whatever is right or just in itself, whatever conforms to the revealed will of God, Matt. 5:6, 10, 20; John 16:8, 10; (b) whatever has been appointed by God to be acknowledged and obeyed by man, Matt. 3:15; 21:32; (c) the sum total of the requirements of God, Matt. 6:33; (d) religious duties, Matt. 6:1 (distinguished as almsgiving, man's duty to his neighbor, vv. 2-4, prayer, his duty to God, vv. 5-15, fasting, the duty of self-control, vv. 16-18).

In the preaching of the apostles recorded in Acts the word has the same general meaning. So also in Jas. 1:20, 3:18, in both Epp. of Peter, 1st John and the Revelation. In 2 Pet. 1:1, "the righteousness of our God and Savior Jesus Christ," is the righteous dealing of God with sin and with sinners on the ground of the death of Christ. "Word of righteousness," Heb. 5:13, is probably the gospel, and the Scriptures as containing the gospel, wherein is declared the righteousness of God in all its aspects.

This meaning of *dikaiosune*, right action, is frequent also in Paul's writings, as in all five of its occurrences in Rom. 6; Eph. 6:14, etc. But for the most part he uses it of that gracious gift of God to men whereby all who believe on the Lord Jesus Christ are brought into right relationship with God. This righteousness is unattainable by obedience to any law, or by any merit of man's own, or any other condition than that of faith in Christ....The man who trusts in Christ becomes "the righteousness of God in Him," 2 Cor. 5:21, i.e., becomes in Christ all that God requires a man to be, all that he could never be in himself. Because Abraham accepted the Word of God, making it his own by that act of the mind and spirit which is called faith, and, as the sequel showed, submitting himself to its control, therefore God accepted him as one who fulfilled the whole of His requirements, Rom. 4:3.

Righteousness is not said to be imputed to the believer save in the sense that faith is imputed ("reckoned" is the better word) for righteousness. It is clear that in Rom. 4:6, 11, "righteousness reckoned" must be understood in the light of the context, "faith reckoned for righteousness," vv. 3, 5, 9, 22. "For" in these places is *eis*, which does not mean "instead of," but "with a view to." The faith thus exercised brings the soul into vital union with God in Christ, and inevitably produces righteousness of life, that is, conformity to the will of God.

RIOT, RIOTING, RIOTOUS, RIOTOUSLY

A. Noun.

asotia (810), "prodigality, a wastefulness, profligacy" (*a*, negative, *sozo*, "to save"), is rendered "riot" in Eph. 5:18, RV (KJV, "excess"); Titus 1:6 and 1 Pet. 4:4 (KJV and RV, "riot"). The corresponding verb is found in a papyrus writing, telling of "riotous living."

B. Adverb.

asotos (*811*), "wastefully" (akin to A), is translated "with riotous living" in Luke 15:13; though the word does not necessarily signify "dissolutely," the parable narrative makes clear that this is the meaning here.

ROAR, ROARING

A. Verbs.

1. *mukaomai* (*3455*), properly of oxen, "to low, bellow," is used of a lion, Rev. 10:3.

2. *oruomai* (*5612*), "to howl" or "roar," is used of a lion, 1 Pet. 5:8, as a simile of Satan.

B. Noun.

echos (*2279*), "a noise" or "sound" (Eng., "echo"), is used of the "roaring" of the sea in Luke 21:25, in the best mss., "for the roaring (of the sea and the billows), RV; some mss. have the present participle of *echeo*, "to sound," KJV "(the sea and the waves) roaring."

ROB

1. *sulao* (*4813*), "to plunder, spoil," is translated "I robbed" in 2 Cor. 11:8.

2. *katabrabeuo* (*2603*), "to give judgment against, to condemn" (*kata*, "against," and *brabeus*, "an umpire"; cf. *brabeion*, "a prize in the games," 1 Cor. 9:24; Phil. 3:14, and *brabeuo*, "to act as an umpire, arbitrate," Col. 3:15), occurs in Col. 2:18, RV, "let (no man) rob (you) of your prize" (KJV, "...beguile...of your reward"), said of false teachers who would frustrate the faithful adherence of the believers to the truth, causing them to lose their reward. Another rendering closer to the proper meaning of the word, as given above, is "let no man decide for or against you" (i.e., without any notion of a prize); this suitably follows the word "judge" in v. 16, i.e., "do not give yourselves up to the judgment and decision of any man" (KJV, marg., "judge against").

ROBBER

1. *lestes* (*3027*), "a robber, brigand" (akin to *leia*, "booty"), "one who plunders openly and by violence" (in contrast to *kleptes*, "a thief," see below), is always translated "robber" or "robbers" in the RV, as the KJV in John 10:1, 8, 18:40; 2 Cor. 11:26; the KJV has "thief" or "thieves" in Matt. 21:13, and parallel passages; 26:55, and parallel passages; 27:38, 44 and Mark 15:27; Luke 10:30, 36; but "thief" is the meaning of *kleptes*.

2. *hierosulos* (*2417*), an adjective signifying "robbing temples" (*hieron*, "a temple," and *sulao*, "to rob"), is found in Acts 19:37.

ROCK

Old Testament

tsur (*6697*), "rock; rocky wall; cliff; rocky hill; mountain; rocky surface; boulder." This can mean the material that the earth (hard and often very heavy) is made up of, from the size of a huge rock wall or cliff (which is often high up and so hard to get to, making a natural "fortress"), Exod. 17:6; of mountains, Isa. 2:10, 19; or boulders, Num. 23:9; or a flat rock, 2 Sam. 21:10; cf. Prov. 30:19.

"Rock" is frequently used to picture God's support and defense of His people, Deut. 32:15. In some cases this noun is an epithet, or meaningful name, of God, Deut. 32:4, or of heathen gods: "For their rock [god] is not as our Rock [God]..." Deut. 32:31.

New Testament

1. *petra* (*4073*) denotes "a mass of rock," as distinct from *petros*, "a detached stone or boulder," or a stone that might be thrown or easily moved. For the nature of *petra*, see Matt. 7:24, 25; 27:51, 60; Mark 15:46; Luke 6:48 (twice), a type of a sure foundation (here the true reading is as in the RV, "because it had been well builded"); Rev. 6:15, 16, cf. Isa. 2:19ff.; Hos. 10:8; Luke 8:6, 13, used illustratively; 1 Cor. 10:4 (twice), figuratively, of Christ; in Rom. 9:33 and 1 Pet. 2:8, metaphorically, of Christ; in Matt. 16:18, metaphorically, of Christ and the testimony concerning Him; here the distinction between *petra*, concerning the Lord Himself, and *petros*, the apostle, is clear.

2. *spilas* (*4694*), "a rock or reef," over which the sea dashes, is used in Jude 12, "hidden rocks," RV, metaphorical of men whose conduct is a danger to others. A late meaning ascribed to it is that of "spots," (KJV), but that rendering seems to have been influenced by the parallel passage in 2 Pet. 2:13, where *spiloi*, "spots," occurs.

ROCKY

petrodes (*4075*), "rock-like" (*petra*, "a rock," *eidos*, "a form, appearance"), is used of "rock" underlying shallow soil, Matt. 13:5, 20, RV, "the rocky places" (KJV, "stony places"); Mark 4:5, RV, "the rocky ground" (KJV, "stony ground"); v. 16, RV, "rocky places" (KJV, "stony ground").

ROD

A. Noun.

rhabdos (*4464*), "a staff, rod, scepter," is used (a) of Aaron's "rod," Heb. 9:4; (b) a staff used on a journey, Matt. 10:10, RV, "staff" (KJV, "staves"); so Luke 9:3; Mark 6:8, "staff"; Heb. 11:21, "staff"; (c) a ruler's staff, a "scepter," Heb. 1:8 (twice); elsewhere a "rod," Rev. 2:27; 12:5; 19:15; (d) a "rod" for chastisement (figuratively), 1 Cor. 4:21; (e) a measuring rod, Rev. 11:1.

B. Verb.

rhabdizo (4463), "to beat with a rod," is used in Acts 16:22, RV, "to beat...with rods"; 2 Cor. 11:25. The "rods" were those of the Roman lictors or "sergeants" (*rhabdouchoi*, lit., "rodbearers"); the Roman beating with "rods" is distinct from the Jewish infliction of stripes.

ROLL (Noun and Verb)

A. Verb.

heilisso, or *helisso* (1507), "to roll," or "roll up," is used (a) of the "rolling" up of a mantle, illustratively of the heavens, Heb. 1:12, RV; (b) of the "rolling" up of a scroll, Rev. 6:14, illustratively of the removing of the heaven.

B. Noun.

kephalis (2777), lit., "a little head" (a diminutive of *kephale*, "a head"; Lat., *capitulum*, a diminutive of *caput*), hence, "a capital of a column," then, "a roll" (of a book), occurs in Heb. 10:7, RV, "in the roll" (KJV, "in the volume"), lit., "in the heading of the scroll" (from Ps. 40:7).

ROUSE

exupnos (1853), "roused out of sleep" (*ek*, "out of," *hupnos*, "sleep"), occurs in Acts 16:27.

ROYAL

1. *basileios* (934), from *basileus*, "a king," is used in 1 Pet. 2:9 of the priesthood consisting of all believers.

2. *basilikos* (937), "belonging to a king," is translated "royal" in Acts 12:21; Jas. 2:8.

RUDIMENTS

stoicheion (4747), "one of a row or series," is translated "rudiments" in the RV of Gal. 4:3, 9; Heb. 5:12, and the KJV and RV of Col. 2:8, 20.

R

RUIN

1. *rhegma* (4485), akin to *rhegnumi*, "to break," denotes "a cleavage, fracture," in NT by metonymy, that which is broken, "a ruin," Luke 6:49.

2. *katestrammena* (2690**), the neuter plural, perfect participle,

passive, of *katastrepho*, "to overturn," is translated "ruins" in Acts 15:16.

RULE (Noun and Verb)

Old Testament

mashal (4910), "to rule, reign, have dominion." *mashal* is used most frequently in the text to express the "ruling or dominion" of one person over another, Gen. 3:16; 24:2. Cain is advised "to rule over" or "master" sin, Gen. 4:7. Joseph's brothers respond to his dreams with the angry question: "Shalt thou indeed reign over us?" Gen. 37:8.

As Creator and Sovereign over His world, God "ruleth by his power for ever," Ps. 66:7. When God allowed Israel to have a king, it was with the condition that God was still the ultimate King and that first loyalty belonged to Him, Deut. 17:14-20. This theocratic ideal is perhaps best expressed by Gideon: "I will not rule over you, neither shall my son rule over you: the Lord shall rule over you," Judg. 8:23.

New Testament

A. Nouns.

1. *arche* (746), "a beginning," etc., denotes "rule," Luke 20:20, RV, "rule" (KJV, "power"); 1 Cor. 15:24; Eph. 1:21, RV, "rule" (KJV, "principality").

2. *kanon* (2583) is translated "rule" in the KJV of 2 Cor. 10:13, 15; in Gal. 6:16, KJV and RV; in Phil. 3:16, KJV (RV, in italics).

B. Verbs.

1. *oikodespoteo* (3616), from *oikos*, "a house," and *despotes*, "a master," signifies "to rule the household"; so the RV in 1 Tim. 5:14 (KJV, "guide the house").

2. *hegeomai* (2233), "to lead," is translated "to rule" in Heb. 13:7, 17, 24 (KJV marg., in the first two, "are the guides" and "guide."

3. *poimaino* (4165), "to act as a shepherd, tend flocks," is translated "to rule" in Rev. 2:27; 12:5; 19:15, all indicating that the governing power exercised by the Shepherd is to be of a firm character; in Matt. 2:6, KJV, "shall rule" (RV, "shall be shepherd of").

RULER

1. *archon* (758), "a ruler, chief, prince," is translated "rulers," e.g., in 1 Cor. 2:6, 8, RV (KJV, "princes"); "ruler," Rev. 1:5 (KJV, prince).

2. *kosmokrator* (2888) denotes "a ruler of this world" (contrast *pantokrator*, "almighty"). In Greek literature, in Orphic hymns, etc., and in rabbinic writings, it signifies a "ruler" of the whole world, a world lord. In the NT it is used in Eph. 6:12, "the world

rulers (of this darkness)," RV, KJV, "the rulers (of the darkness) of this world."

RUMOR

1. *akoe* (*189*), "a hearing," is translated "rumor" in Matt. 24:6; Mark 13:7.

2. *echos* (*2279*), "a noise, sound," is translated "rumor" in Luke 4:37, RV (KJV, "fame").

R

S

SABACHTHANI

sabachthani (4518), an Aramaic word signifying "Thou hast forsaken Me," is recorded as part of the utterance of Christ on the cross, Matt. 27:46; Mark 15:34, a quotation from Ps. 22:1. Recently proposed renderings which differ from those of the KJV and RV have not been sufficiently established to require acceptance.

SABAOTH

sabaoth (4519) is the transliteration of a Hebrew word which denotes "hosts" or "armies," Rom. 9:29; Jas. 5:4. While the word "hosts" probably had special reference to angels, the title "the LORD of hosts" became used to designate Him as the One who is supreme over all the innumerable hosts of spiritual agencies, or of what are described as "the armies of heaven." Eventually it was used as equivalent to "the LORD all-sovereign."

SABBATH

sabbaton (4521) The observation of the seventh day of the week, enjoined upon Israel, was a sign between God and His earthly people, based upon the fact that after the six days of creative operations He rested, Exod. 31:16, 17, with 20:8-11. The OT regulations were developed and systematized to such an extent that they became a burden upon the people (who otherwise rejoiced in the rest provided) and a byword for absurd extravagance. Two treatises of the Mishna (the *Shabbath* and *Erubin*) are entirely occupied with regulations for the observance; so with the discussions in the Gemara, on rabbinical opinions. The effect upon current opinion explains the antagonism roused by the Lord's cures wrought on the "Sabbath," e.g., Matt. 12:9-13; John 5:5-16, and explains the fact that on a "Sabbath" the sick were brought to be healed after sunset, e.g., Mark 1:32. According to rabbinical ideas, the disciples, by plucking ears of corn (Matt. 12:1; Mark 2:23), and rubbing them (Luke 6:1), broke the "sabbath" in two respects; for to pluck was to reap, and to rub was to thresh. The Lord's attitude towards the "sabbath" was by way of freeing it from these vexatious traditional accretions by which it was made an end in itself, instead of a means to an end (Mark 2:27).

In the Epistles the only direct mentions are in Col. 2:16, "a sabbath day," RV (which rightly has the singular, see 1st parag., above), where it is listed among things that were "a shadow of the things to come" (i.e., of the age introduced at Pentecost), and in Heb. 4:4-11, where the perpetual *sabbatismos* is appointed for believers; inferential references are in Rom. 14:5 and Gal. 4:9-11. For the first three centuries of the Christian era the first day of the week was never confounded with the "sabbath"; the confusion of the Jewish and Christian institutions was due to declension from apostolic teaching.

SACRED

hieros (2413) denotes "consecrated to God," e.g., the Scriptures, 2 Tim. 3:15, RV, "sacred" (KJV "holy"); it is used as a noun in the neuter plural in 1 Cor. 9:13, RV, "sacred things" (KJV, "holy things"). The neuter singular, *hieron*, denotes "a temple."

SACRIFICE (Noun and Verb)

Old Testament

zebach (2077), "sacrifice." The basic meaning of *zebach* is "sacrifice." When a "sacrifice" had been slaughtered by the priest, he then offered it to God. The purpose was not just to create communion between God and man; rather, the "sacrifice" represented the principle that, without the shedding of blood, there is no forgiveness of sins, Lev. 17:11; cf. Heb. 9:22. In the act of "sacrifice" the faithful Israelite submitted himself to the priest, who, in keeping with the various detailed regulations (see Leviticus), offered the "sacrifice" in accordance with God's expectations. The "sacrifices" are the Passover "sacrifice," Exod. 12:27, "sacrifice" of the peace offering, Lev. 3:1ff., "sacrifice" of thanksgiving, Lev. 7:12, and "sacrifice" of the priest's offering, *qarban*; Lev. 7:16. The *zebach* was not like the burnt offering (*'olah*), which was completely burnt on the altar; and it was unlike the sin offering (*chatta't*), where the meat was given to the priest, for most of the meat of the *zebach* was returned to the person who made the "sacrifice." The fat was burned on the altar, Lev. 3:4-5, and the blood was poured out around the altar, 3:2. The person who made the *zebach* had to share the meat with the officiating priest, Exod. 29:28; Lev. 7:31-35; Deut. 18:3.

The prophets looked with condemnation on apostate Israel's "sacrifices": "To what purpose is the multitude of your sacrifices unto me? saith the Lord: I am full of the burnt offerings of rams, and the fat of fed beasts; and I delight not in the blood of bullocks, or of lambs, or of he goats," Isa. 1:11. Hosea spoke about the necessity of Israel's love for God, Hos. 6:6. Samuel the prophet rebuked Saul with familiar words, 1 Sam. 15:22. David knew the proper response to God when he had sinned, Ps. 51:16-17.

New Testament

A. Noun.

thusia (*2378*) primarily denotes "the act of offering"; then, objectively, "that which is offered" (a) of idolatrous "sacrifice," Acts 7:41; (b) of animal or other "sacrifices," as offered under the Law, Matt. 9:13; 12:7; Mark 9:49; 12:33; Luke 2:24; 13:1; Acts 7:42; 1 Cor. 10:18; Heb. 5:1; 7:27 (RV, plural); 8:3; 9:9; 10:1, 5, 8 (RV, plural), 11; 11:4; (c) of Christ, in His "sacrifice" on the cross, Eph. 5:2; Heb. 9:23, where the plural antitypically comprehends the various forms of Levitical "sacrifices" in their typical character; 9:26; 10:12, 26; (d) metaphorically, (1) of the body of the believer, presented to God as a living "sacrifice," Rom. 12:1; (2) of faith, Phil. 2:17; (3) of material assistance rendered to servants of God, Phil. 4:18; (4) of praise, Heb. 13:15; (5) of doing good to others and communicating with their needs, Heb. 13:16; (6) of spiritual "sacrifices" in general, offered by believers as a holy priesthood, 1 Pet. 2:5.

B. Verb.

thuo (*2380*) is used of "sacrificing by slaying a victim," (a) of the "sacrifice" of Christ, 1 Cor. 5:7, RV, "hath been sacrificed" (KJV, "is sacrificed"); (b) of the Passover "sacrifice," Mark 14:12, RV, "they sacrificed" (KJV, "they killed"); Luke 22:7, RV, "(must) be sacrificed," KJV, "(must) be killed"; (c) of idolatrous "sacrifices," Acts 14:13, 18; 1 Cor. 10:20 (twice).

SAFE, SAFELY, SAFETY

A. Nouns.

1. *asphaleia* (*803*), "certainty, safety," is translated "safety" in Acts 5:23; 1 Thess. 5:3.

2. *soteria* (*4991*), "salvation," is translated "safety" in Acts 27:34, RV (KJV, "health").

B. Verbs.

1. *diasozo* (*1295*), "to bring safely through danger," and, in the passive voice, "to come safe through" (*dia*, "through," *sozo*, "to save"), is translated "bring safe" in Acts 23:24; "escaped safe" in 27:44.

2. *hugiaino* (*5198*), "to be sound, healthy" (Eng., "hygiene," etc.), is translated "safe and sound" in Luke 15:27, lit., "being healthy."

SAINT(S)

hagios (*40*), used as a noun in the singular in Phil. 4:21, where *pas*, "every," is used with it. In the plural, as used of believers, it designates all such and is not applied merely to persons of exceptional holiness, or to those who, having died, were characterized by exceptional acts of "saintliness." See especially 2 Thess.

1:10, where "His saints" are also described as "them that believed," i.e., the whole number of the redeemed.

SALT (Noun, Adjective and Verb), SALTNESS

A. Noun.

halas (*251*), a late form of *hals* (found in some mss. in Mark 9:49), is used (a) literally in Matt. 5:13 (2nd part); Mark 9:50 (1st part, twice); Luke 14:34 (twice); (b) metaphorically, of "believers," Matt. 5:13 (1st part); of their "character and condition," Mark 9:50 (2nd part); of "wisdom" exhibited in their speech, Col. 4:6.

Being possessed of purifying, perpetuating and antiseptic qualities, "salt" became emblematic of fidelity and friendship among eastern nations. To eat of a person's "salt" and so to share his hospitality is still regarded thus among the Arabs. So in Scripture, it is an emblem of the covenant between God and His people, Num. 18:19; 2 Chron. 13:5; so again when the Lord says "Have salt in yourselves, and be at peace one with another" (Mark 9:50). In the Lord's teaching it is also symbolic of that spiritual health and vigor essential to Christian virtue and counteractive of the corruption that is in the world, e.g., Matt. 5:13, see (b) above. Food is seasoned with "salt" (see B); every meal offering was to contain it, and it was to be offered with all offerings presented by Israelites, as emblematic of the holiness of Christ, and as betokening the reconciliation provided for man by God on the ground of the death of Christ, Lev. 2:13. To refuse God's provision in Christ and the efficacy of His expiatory sacrifice is to expose oneself to the doom of being "salted with fire," Mark 9:49.

B. Verb.

halizo (*233*), akin to A, signifies "to sprinkle" or "to season with salt," Matt. 5:13; Mark 9:49.

C. Adjectives.

1. *halukos* (*252*) occurs in Jas. 3:12, "salt (water)."

2. *analos* (*358*) denotes "saltless" (*a*, negative, *n*, euphonic, and A), insipid, Mark 9:50, "have lost its saltness," lit., "have become (*ginomai*) saltless (*analos*)."

SALVATION

A. Nouns.

1. *soteria* (*4991*) denotes "deliverance, preservation, salvation." "Salvation" is used in the NT (a) of material and temporal deliverance from danger and apprehension, (1) national, Luke 1:69, 71; Acts 7:25, RV marg., "salvation" (text, "deliverance"); (2) personal, as from the sea, Acts 27:34; RV, "safety" (KJV, "health"); prison, Phil. 1:19; the flood, Heb. 11:7; (b) of the spiritual and eternal de-

S

liverance granted immediately by God to those who accept His conditions of repentance and faith in the Lord Jesus, in whom alone it is to be obtained, Acts 4:12, and upon confession of Him as Lord, Rom. 10:10; for this purpose the gospel is the saving instrument, Rom. 1:16; Eph. 1:13; (c) of the present experience of God's power to deliver from the bondage of sin, e.g., Phil. 2:12, where the special, though not the entire, reference is to the maintenance of peace and harmony; 1 Pet. 1:9; this present experience on the part of believers is virtually equivalent to sanctification; for this purpose, God is able to make them wise, 2 Tim. 3:15; they are not to neglect it, Heb. 2:3; (d) of the future deliverance of believers at the Parousia of Christ for His saints, a salvation which is the object of their confident hope, e.g., Rom. 13:11; 1 Thess. 5:8, and v. 9, where "salvation" is assured to them, as being deliverance from the wrath of God destined to be executed upon the ungodly at the end of this age (see 1 Thess. 1:10; 2 Thess. 2:13; Heb. 1:14; 9:28; 1 Pet. 1:5; 2 Pet. 3:15; (e) of the deliverance of the nation of Israel at the second advent of Christ at the time of "the epiphany (or shining forth) of His Parousia" (2 Thess. 2:8); Luke 1:71; Rev. 12:10; (f) inclusively, to sum up all the blessings bestowed by God on men in Christ through the Holy Spirit, e.g., 2 Cor. 6:2; Heb. 5:9; 1 Pet. 1:9, 10; Jude 3; (g) occasionally, as standing virtually for the Savior, e.g., Luke 19:9; cf. John 4:22; (h) in ascriptions of praise to God, Rev. 7:10, and as that which it is His prerogative to bestow, 19:1 (RV).

2. *soterion* (*4992*), the neuter of the adjective, is used as a noun in Luke 2:30; 3:6, in each of which it virtually stands for the Savior, as in No. 1 (g); in Acts 28:28, as in No. 1 (b); in Eph. 6:17, where the hope of "salvation" [see No. 1 (d)] is metaphorically described as "a helmet."

B. Adjective.

soterios (*4992***), "saving, bringing salvation," describes the grace of God, in Titus 2:11.

SANCTIFICATION, SANCTIFY
Old Testament

A. Verb.

qadash (*6942*), "to sanctify, be holy." In the primary stem the verb signifies an act whereby, or a state wherein, people or things are set aside for worship of God: they are consecrated or "made sacred." By this act and in this state the thing or person consecrated is to be withheld from workaday use (or profane use) and to be treated with special care as a possession of God, Exod. 29:21. There are also overtones of ethical-moral (spiritual) holiness here since the atoning blood was applied to the people involved. The state appears to be emphasized when the word is used in Exod. 29:37. In some cases "set aside for God," means destruction, 2 Sam. 6:6ff., while in others it means such things are to be used only by those who are ritualistically pure, Num. 4:15; 1 Sam. 21:6.

In the passive stem the verb means "to prove oneself holy," Num. 20:13. This proving refers not to an act of judgment against sin (an ethical-moral holiness) but a miraculous act of deliverance. Another emphasis is "to be treated as holy, Isa. 5:16; Deut. 6:3, 5ff.

qadash can mean "to declare something holy" or to declare it to be said exclusively for celebrating God's glory, Exod. 20:8; or a pagan god, 2 Kings 10:20. The word comes to mean "to declare" and "to make proper preparations for war, Jer. 6:4; cf. Mic. 3:5; Jer. 51:27. This stem may also be used of putting something or someone into a state reserved exclusively for God's use, Exod. 13:2, 12-13; 1 Sam. 1:24.

qadash may also be used in the sense of making something or someone cultically pure and meeting all God's requirements for purity in persons or things used in the formal worship of Him. This act appears in Exod. 19:10. Although the primary emphasis here is ritualistic, there are ethical-moral overtones. Thus, God directed Moses to have the artisans make special clothing for Aaron, Exod. 28:4.

qadash is also applied to the consecration of things by placing them into a state of ritualistic or cultic purity and dedicating them solely to God's use, cultic use; cf. Exod. 29:36; Lev. 16:19. In some cases consecrating something to God requires no act upon the object, but leaving it entirely alone. Moses acknowledges to God that "the people cannot come up to mount Sinai: for thou chargedst us, saying, Set bounds about the mount, and sanctify it," Exod. 19:23. In the causative stem the word means "to give for God's use," Exod. 28:38. The act whereby someone gives things to God is also described by the word *qadash*. The priests performed the actual consecration ceremony while an individual decided that something he owned was to be given to God, 2 Sam. 8:11.

God's consecrating something or someone may also mean that He accepts that person or thing as in His service, 1 Kings 9:3; Jer. 1:5; cf. 12:3. This verb also means "to prepare to approach God," Zeph. 1:7.

B. Nouns.

qodesh (6944), "holy thing." First, *qodesh* is used of things or people belonging to God. All Israel is holy, Exod. 30:31, separated to God's service, and therefore should keep itself separated to that service by observing the distinction between things holy (allowed by God) and things unclean, Lev. 10:10.

qodesh can also be used of what God makes a person, place, or thing to be. He designates a place to be His (Exod. 3:5—the first biblical appearance of the word), that is, separate and unique. Even more, God designates His sanctuary a holy place, Exod. 36:1. The outer part of the sanctuary is *the* holy place, the inner part the holy of holies, Exod. 26:33, and the altar a most holy place. This means that to varying degrees these places are identified with the holy God, 2 Sam. 6:10-11, the God who is separate from and hates all that is death and/or associated with death and idolatry, Ezek. 39:25.

The noun *miqdash*, represents a "sacred place" or "sanctuary," a place set aside by men upon God's direction and acceptance as the place where He meets them and they worship Him, Exod. 15:17.

C. Adjective.

qadosh (6918), "holy." The adjective *qados* occurs about 116 times in biblical Hebrew and in all periods. This adjective is more focused in emphasis than the noun *qodesh. qadosh* can refer (infrequently) to cultic holiness, or ritualistic ceremonial holiness, Num. 5:17. Its most frequent use, however, represents God's majestic, 1 Sam. 2:2, moral, Lev. 11:44, and dynamistic holiness; holiness as power; 1 Sam. 6:20.

New Testament

A. Noun.

hagiasmos (38), "sanctification," is used of (a) separation to God, 1 Cor. 1:30; 2 Thess. 2:13; 1 Pet. 1:2; (b) the course of life befitting those so separated, 1 Thess. 4:3, 4, 7; Rom. 6:19, 22; 1 Tim. 2:15; Heb. 12:14. Sanctification is that relationship with God into which men enter by faith in Christ, Acts 26:18; 1 Cor. 6:11, and to which their sole title is the death of Christ, Eph. 5:25, 26; Col. 1:22; Heb. 10:10, 29; 13:12.

Sanctification is also used in NT of the separation of the believer from evil things and ways. This sanctification is God's will for the believer, 1 Thess. 4:3, and His purpose in calling him by the gospel, v. 7; it must be learned from God, v. 4, as He teaches it by His Word, John 17:17, 19, cf. Ps. 17:4; 119:9, and it must be pursued by the believer, earnestly and undeviatingly, 1 Tim. 2:15; Heb. 12:14. For the holy character, *hagiosune*, 1 Thess. 3:13, is not vicarious, i.e., it cannot be transferred or imputed, it is an individual possession, built up, little by little, as the result of obedience to the Word of God, and of following the example of Christ, Matt. 11:29; John 13:15; Eph. 4:20; Phil. 2:5, in the power of the Holy Spirit, Rom. 8:13; Eph. 3:16.

B. Verb.

hagiazo (37), "to sanctify," "is used of (a) the gold adorning the

Temple and of the gift laid on the altar, Matt. 23:17, 19; (b) food, 1 Tim. 4:5; (c) the unbelieving spouse of a believer, 1 Cor. 7:14; (d) the ceremonial cleansing of the Israelites, Heb. 9:13; (e) the Father's Name, Luke 11:2; (f) the consecration of the Son by the Father, John 10:36; (g) the Lord Jesus devoting Himself to the redemption of His people, John 17:19; the setting apart of the believer for God, Acts 20:32; cf. Rom. 15:16; (i) the effect on the believer of the Death of Christ, Heb. 10:10, said of God, and 2:11; 13:12, said of the Lord Jesus; (j) the separation of the believer from the world in his behavior—by the Father through the Word, John 17:17, 19; (k) the believer who turns away from such things as dishonor God and His gospel, 2 Tim. 2:21; (l) the acknowledgment of the Lordship of Christ, 1 Pet. 3:15.

SANCTUARY

1. *hagion* (39), the neuter of the adjective *hagios*, "holy," is used of those structures which are set apart to God, (a) of "the tabernacle" in the wilderness, Heb. 9:1, RV, "its sanctuary, a *sanctuary* of this world" (KJV, "a worldly sanctuary"); in v. 2 the outer part is called "the Holy place," RV (KJV, "the sanctuary"); here the neuter plural *hagia* is used, as in v. 3.

2. *naos* (3485) is used of the inner part of the Temple in Jerusalem, in Matt. 23:35, RV, "sanctuary."

SAPPHIRE

sappheiros (4552) is mentioned in Rev. 21:19 (RV, marg., "*lapis lazuli*") as the second of the foundations of the wall of the heavenly Jerusalem (cf. Isa. 54:11). It was one of the stones in the high priest's breastplate, Exod. 28:18; 39:11; as an intimation of its value see Job 28:16; Ezek. 28:13. See also Exod. 24:10; Ezek. 1:26; 10:1. The sapphire has various shades of blue and ranks next in hardness to the diamond.

SATAN

Old Testament

satan (7854), "adversary; Satan." This word has two clear references: (a) an evil being who is the opponent of the true God, Job 1:6-12; 2:1-7; (b) a human being who is an opponent to God or another human. Ps. 38:20; 71:13; Ps. 109:4; cf. also 2 Sam. 16:5ff. God can also be the "adversary." When Balaam went to curse the sons of Israel, God warned him not to do so. When the prophet persisted, God disciplined him, Num. 22:22; with Solomon, 1 Kings 11:14. One must carefully read in some contexts to decide who the "satan," or "Satan" is. But in the New Testament, it nearly always refers to the person of Satan.

New Testament

satanas (*4567*), a Greek form derived from the Aramaic (Heb., **satan**), "an adversary," is used (a) of an angel of Jehovah in Num. 22:22 (the first occurrence of the Word in the OT); (b) of men, e.g., 1 Sam. 29:4; Ps. 38:20; 71:13; four in Ps. 109; (c) of "Satan," the Devil, some seventeen or eighteen times in the OT; in Zech. 3:1, where the name receives its interpretation, "to be (his) adversary," RV (see marg.; KJV, "to resist him").

In the NT the word is always used of "Satan," the adversary (a) of God and Christ, e.g., Matt. 4:10; 12:26; Mark 1:13; 3:23, 26; 4:15; Luke 4:8 (in some mss.); 11:18; 22:3; John 13:27; (b) of His people, e.g., Luke 22:31; Acts 5:3; Rom. 16:20; 1 Cor. 5:5; 7:5; 2 Cor. 2:11; 11:14; 12:7; 1 Thess. 2:18; 1 Tim. 1:20; 5:15; Rev. 2:9, 13 (twice), 24; 3:9; (c) of mankind, Luke 13:16; Acts 26:18; 2 Thess. 2:9; Rev. 12:9; 20:7.

His doom, sealed at the Cross, is foretold in its stages in Luke 10:18; Rev. 20:2, 10. Believers are assured of victory over him, Rom. 16:20.

The appellation was given by the Lord to Peter, as a "Satan-like" man, on the occasion when he endeavored to dissuade Him from death, Matt. 16:23; Mark 8:33.

"Satan" is not simply the personification of evil influences in the heart, for he tempted Christ, in whose heart no evil thought could ever have arisen (John 14:30; 2 Cor. 5:21; Heb. 4:15); moreover his personality is asserted in both the OT and the NT, and especially in the latter, whereas if the OT language was intended to be figurative, the NT would have made this evident.

SATISFY

Old Testament

saba' (*7646*), "to be satisfied, sated, surfeited." *saba'* expresses the idea of "being filled, sated," Exod. 16:8; often in reference to eating, Jer. 50:19. *saba'* sometimes expresses "being surfeited with," as in Prov. 25:16; Isa. 1:11. *saba'* often indicates God "satisfying, supplying," man with his material needs, Ps. 103:5. But even when God "fed them to the full," Israel was not satisfied and went after strange gods, Jer. 5:7.

New Testament

1. *chortazo* (*5526*), "to fill or satisfy with food," is translated "satisfy" in Mark 8:4, KJV (RV, "to fill").

2. *empiplemi* or *empletho* (*1705*), "to fill up, fill full, satisfy" (*en*, "in," *pimplemi* or *pletho*, "to fill"), is used metaphorically in Rom. 15:24, of taking one's fill of the company of others, RV, "I shall have been satisfied" (KJV, "I be...filled").

SAVE, SAVING

Old Testament

A. Verb.

yasha' (3467), "to help, deliver, save." *yasha'* signifies to remove someone from a burden or job, Josh. 10:6. *yasha'* is used in other situations as when Jephthah tells the Ephraimites that they had been summoned to the war at a crucial time but did not respond, Judg. 12:2. Militarily the word can also be used of "helping," emphasizing the union of forces so as to forge a single and stronger fighting unit. This is no last-ditch stand for the unit being helped, 2 Sam. 10:11-19.

In the realm of justice and civil law *yasha'* represents an obligation on the part of anyone who hears an outcry of one being mistreated, Deut. 22:27; cf. 28:29. Therefore, one may appeal especially to the king as the one obligated to help maintain one's rights, 2 Sam. 14:4; cf. 2 Kings 6:26. The king also "delivered" his people from subjection to their enemies, 1 Sam. 10:27; Hos. 13:10. The word appears in many prayer petitions: "Arise, O Lord; save me, O my God…" Ps. 3:7; 20:9; 72:4.

B. Nouns.

yesu'ah (3444), "salvation." This word refers primarily to God's acts of help which have already occurred and been experienced. In Gen. 49:18 (the first biblical occurrence), the word includes the idea of "salvation" through divinely appointed means and from inequity. In 1 Sam. 14:45 *yeshu'ah* is used of a human act, Isa. 12:3. The noun *teshu'ah* also means "salvation," 1 Sam. 11:13; rendered "deliverance," Judg. 15:18; or "victory," 2 Sam. 19:2.

The noun *yesha'* signifies that which God will do in man's behalf, 2 Sam. 22:3, or that which has been done by Him for man, 2 Sam. 22:36.

New Testament

1. *sozo* (4982), a verb, "to save," is used (as with the noun *soteria*, "salvation") (a) of material and temporal deliverance from danger, suffering, etc., e.g., Matt. 8:25; Mark 13:20; Luke 23:35; John 12:27; 1 Tim. 2:15; 2 Tim. 4:18 (KJV, "preserve"); Jude 5; from sickness, Matt. 9:22, "made…whole" (RV, marg., "saved"); so Mark 5:34; Luke 8:48; Jas. 5:15; (b) of the spiritual and eternal salvation granted immediately by God to those who believe on the Lord Jesus Christ, e.g., Acts 2:47, RV "(those that) were being saved"; 16:31; Rom. 8:24, RV, "were we saved"; Eph. 2:5, 8; 1 Tim. 2:4; 2 Tim. 1:9; Titus 3:5; of human agency in this, Rom. 11:14; 1 Cor. 7:16; 9:22; (c) of the present experiences of God's power to deliver from the bondage of sin, e.g., Matt. 1:21, Rom. 5:10; 1 Cor. 15:2; Heb. 7:25; Jas. 1:21; 1 Pet. 3:21; of human agency in this, 1 Tim. 4:16; (d) of the future

deliverance of believers at the second coming of Christ for His saints, being deliverance from the wrath of God to be executed upon the ungodly at the close of this age and from eternal doom, e.g., Rom. 5:9; (e) of the deliverance of the nation of Israel at the second advent of Christ, e.g., Rom. 11:26; (f) inclusively for all the blessings bestowed by God on men in Christ, e.g., Luke 19:10; John 10:9; 1 Cor. 10:33; 1 Tim. 1:15; (g) of those who endure to the end of the time of the Great Tribulation, Matt. 10:22; Mark 13:13; (h) of the individual believer, who, though losing his regard at the judgment seat of Christ hereafter, will not lose his salvation, 1 Cor. 3:15; 5:5; (i) of the deliverance of the nations at the Millennium, Rev. 21:24 (in some mss.).

2. *diasozo* (*1295*), "to bring safely through" (*dia*, "through," and No. 1), is used (a) of the healing of the sick by the Lord, Matt. 14:36, RV, "were made whole" (KJV adds "perfectly"); Luke 7:3; (b) of bringing "safe" to a destination, Acts 23:24; (c) of keeping a person "safe," 27:43; (d) of escaping through the perils of shipwreck, 27:44; 28:1, 4, passive voice; (e) through the Flood, 1 Pet. 3:20.

SAVIOR

soter (*4990*), "a savior, deliverer, preserver," is used (a) of God, Luke 1:47; 1 Tim. 1:1; 2:3; 4:10 (in the sense of "preserver," since He gives "to all life and breath and all things"); Titus 1:3; 2:10; 3:4; Jude 25; (b) of Christ, Luke 2:11; John 4:42; Acts 5:31; 13:23 (of Israel); Eph. 5:23 (the sustainer and preserver of the church, His "body"); Phil. 3:20 (at His return to receive the Church to Himself); 2 Tim. 1:10 (with reference to His incarnation, "the days of His flesh"); Titus 1:4 (a title shared, in the context, with God the Father); 2:13, RV, "our great God and Savior Jesus Christ," the pronoun "our," at the beginning of the whole clause, includes all the titles; Titus 3:6; 2 Pet. 1:1, "our God and Savior Jesus Christ; RV, where the pronoun "our," coming immediately in connection with "God," involves the inclusion of both titles as referring to Christ, just as in the parallel in v. 11, "our Lord and Savior Jesus Christ" (KJV and RV); these passages are therefore a testimony to His deity; 2 Pet. 2:20; 3:2, 18; 1 John 4:14.

SAY

1. *lego* (*3004*), primarily to pick out, gather," chiefly denotes "to say, speak, affirm," whether of actual speech, e.g., Matt. 11:17, or of unspoken thought, e.g., Matt. 3:9, or of a message in writing, e.g., 2 Cor. 8:8. The 2nd aorist form *eipon* is used to supply that tense, which is lacking in *lego*.

2. *phemi* (*5346*), "to declare, say," (a) is frequently used in quoting the words of another, e.g., Matt. 13:29; 26:61; (b) is interjected into the recorded words, e.g., Acts 23:35; (c) is used impersonally, 2 Cor. 10:10.

SCATTER

Old Testament

puts (6327), "to scatter, disperse, be scattered." *puts*, in the sense of "scattering," often has an almost violent connotation to it, 1 Sam. 11:11. Such "scattering" of forces seems to have been a common thing after defeats in battle, 1 Kings 22:17; 2 Kings 25:5. Many references are made to Israel as a people and nation "being scattered" among the nations, especially in the imagery of a scattered flock of sheep, Ezek. 34:5-6; Zech. 13:7.

In a figurative sense, this word is used to refer to lightning as arrows which God "scatters," 2 Sam. 22:15. According to Job, "the clouds scatter his lightning," Job 37:11, RSV. No harvest is possible unless first the seeds "are scattered" in rows, Isa. 28:25.

New Testament

A. Verbs.

1. *skorpizo* (4650) is used in Matt. 12:30; Luke 11:23; John 10:12; 16:32; 2 Cor. 9:9, RV.

2. *diaskorpizo* (1287), "to scatter abroad," is rendered "to scatter" in Matt. 25:24, 26, RV (KJV, "strawed"); 26:31; Mark 14:27; Luke 1:51; John 11:52; Acts 5:37, RV.

3. *diaspeiro* (1289), "to scatter abroad" (*dia*, "throughout," *speiro*, "to sow seed"), is used in Acts 8:1, 4; 11:19, all of the church in Jerusalem "scattered" through persecution; the word in general is suggestive of the effects of the "scattering" in the sowing of the spiritual seed of the Word of life.

B. Noun.

diaspora (1290), "a dispersion," is rendered "scattered abroad" in Jas. 1:1, KJV; "scattered" in 1 Pet. 1:1, KJV.

SCHISM

schisma (4978), "a rent, division," is translated "schism" in 1 Cor. 12:25, metaphorically of the contrary condition to that which God has designed for a local church in "tempering the body together" (v. 24), the members having "the same care one for another" ("the same" being emphatic).

SCHOOL

schole (4981) (whence Eng., "school") primarily denotes "leisure," then, "that for which leisure was employed, a disputation, lecture"; hence, by metonymy, "the place where lectures are delivered, a school," Acts 19:9.

S

SCIENCE

gnosis (1108) is translated "science" in the KJV of 1 Tim. 6:20; the word simply means "knowledge" (RV), where the reference is to the teaching of the Gnostics (lit., "the knowers") "falsely called knowledge." Science in the modern sense of the word, viz., the investigation, discovery, and classification of secondary laws, is unknown in Scripture.

SCOFF

ekmukterizo (1592), "to hold up the nose in derision at" (*ek*, "from," used intensively, *mukterizo*, "to mock"; from *mukter*, "the nose"), is translated "scoffed at" in Luke 16:14, RV (KJV, "derided"), of the Pharisees in their derision of Christ on account of His teaching; in 23:35 (ditto), of the mockery of Christ on the cross by the rulers of the people.

SCOURGE (Noun and Verb)

A. Noun.

phragellion (5416), "a whip" (from Latin, *flagellum*), is used of the "scourge" of small cords which the Lord made and employed before cleansing the Temple, John 2:15. However He actually used it, the whip was in itself a sign of authority and judgment.

B. Verbs.

1. *phragelloo* (5417) (akin to A: Latin, *flagello*; Eng., "flagellate"), is the word used in Matt. 27:26, and Mark 15:15, of the "scourging" endured by Christ and administered by the order of Pilate. Under the Roman method of "scourging," the person was stripped and tied in a bending posture to a pillar, or stretched on a frame. The "scourge" was made of leather thongs, weighted with sharp pieces of bone or lead, which tore the flesh of both the back and the breast (cf. Ps. 22:17). Eusebius (*Chron.*) records his having witnessed the suffering of martyrs who died under this treatment.

2. *mastigoo* (3146), akin to *mastix* (see below), is used (a) as mentioned under No. 1; (b) of Jewish "scourgings," Matt. 10:17 and 23:34; (c) metaphorically, in Heb. 12:6, of the "chastening" by the Lord administered in love to His spiritual sons.

3. *mastizo* (3147), akin to No. 2, occurs in Acts 22:25 (see No. 1, above).

SCOURGING (-S)

mastix (3148), "a whip, scourge," is used (a) with the meaning "scourging," in Acts 22:24, of the Roman method, (b) in Heb. 11:36, of the "sufferings" of saints in the OT times. Among the Hebrews the usual mode, legal and domestic, was that of beating with a rod (see 2 Cor. 11:25); (c) metaphorically, of "disease" or "suffering."

SCRIBE (-S)

grammateus (*1122*), from *gramma*, "a writing," denotes "a scribe, a man of letters, a teacher of the law"; the "scribes" are mentioned frequently in the Synoptists, especially in connection with the Pharisees, with whom they virtually formed one party (see Luke 5:21), sometimes with the chief priests, e.g., Matt. 2:4; Mark 8:31; 10:33; 11:18, 27; Luke 9:22. They are mentioned only once in John's gospel, 8:3, three times in the Acts, 4:5; 6:12; 23:9; elsewhere only in 1 Cor. 1:20, in the singular. They were considered naturally qualified to teach in the synagogues, Mark 1:22. They were ambitious of honor, e.g., Matt. 23:5-11, which they demanded especially from their pupils, and which was readily granted them, as well as by the people generally. Like Ezra, Ezra 7:12, the "scribes" were found originally among the priests and Levites. The priests being the official interpreters of the Law, the "scribes" ere long became an independent company; though they never held political power, they became leaders of the people.

SCRIPTURE

graphe (*1124*), akin to *grapho*, "to write" (Eng., "graph," "graphic," etc.), primarily denotes "a drawing, painting"; then "a writing," (a) of the OT Scriptures, (1) in the plural, the whole, e.g., Matt. 21:42; 22:29; John 5:39; Acts 17:11; 18:24; Rom. 1:2, where "the prophets" comprises the OT writers in general; 15:4; 16:26, lit., "prophetic writings," expressing the character of all the Scriptures; (2) in the singular in reference to a particular passage, e.g., Mark 12:10; Luke 4:21; John 2:22; 10:35 (though applicable to all); 19:24, 28, 36, 37; 20:9; Acts 1:16; 8:32, 35; Rom. 4:3; 9:17; 10:11; 11:2; Gal. 3:8, 22; 4:30; 1 Tim. 5:18, where the 2nd quotation is from Luke 10:7, from which it may be inferred that the apostle included Luke's gospel as "Scripture" alike with Deuteronomy, from which the first quotation is taken; in reference to the whole, e.g. Jas. 4:5 (see RV, a separate rhetorical question from the one which follows); in 2 Pet. 1:20, "no prophecy of Scripture," a description of all, with special application to the OT in the next verse; (b) of the OT Scriptures (those accepted by the Jews as canonical) and all those of the NT which were to be accepted by Christians as authoritative, 2 Tim. 3:16; these latter were to be discriminated from the many forged epistles and other religious "writings" already produced and circulated in Timothy's time. Such discrimination would be directed by the fact that "every Scripture," characterized by inspiration of God, would be profitable for the purposes mentioned; so the RV. The KJV states truth concerning the completed canon of Scripture, but that was not complete when the apostle wrote to Timothy.

The Scriptures are frequently personified by the NT writers (as

S

by the Jews, John 7:42), (a) as speaking with divine authority, e.g., John 19:37; Rom. 4:3; 9:17, where the Scripture is said to speak to Pharaoh, giving the message actually sent previously by God to him through Moses; Jas. 4:5 (see above); (b) as possessed of the sentient quality of foresight, and the active power of preaching, Gal. 3:8, where the Scripture mentioned was written more than four centuries after the words were spoken. The Scripture, in such a case, stands for its divine Author with an intimation that it remains perpetually characterized as the living voice of God. This divine agency is again illustrated in Gal. 3:22 (cf. v. 10 and Matt. 11:13).

SEA

Old Testament

yam (3220), "sea; ocean." This word refers to the body of water as distinct from the land bodies (continents and islands) and the sky (heavens), Exod. 20:11. Used in this sense *yam* means "ocean," Gen. 1:10; or fresh water body, Num. 34:11. *yam* is used of the "great basin" or "bath," as a small body of water, 1 Kings 7:23; Jer. 27:19. *yam* is also used of mighty rivers such as the Nile, Isa. 19:5; Ezek. 32:2. The word is sometimes used of the direction "west" or "westward," Gen. 13:14; Ezek. 42:19. Exod. 10:19 uses *yam* as an adjective modifying "wind."

In some instances the word *yam* may represent the Canaanite god *Yamm*, Job 9:8. If understood as a statement about Yamm, this passage would read: "and tramples upon the back of Yamm."

New Testament

1. *thalassa* (2281) is used (a) chiefly literally, e.g., "the Red Sea," Acts 7:36; 1 Cor. 10:1; Heb. 11:29; the "sea" of Galilee or Tiberias, Matt. 4:18; 15:29; Mark 6:48, 49, where the acts of Christ testified to His deity; John 6:1; 21:1; in general, e.g., Luke 17:2; Acts 4:24; Rom. 9:27; Rev. 16:3; 18:17; 20:8, 13; 21:1; in combination with No. 2, Matt. 18:6; (b) metaphorically, of "the ungodly men" described in Jude 13 (cf. Isa. 57:20); (c) symbolically, in the apocalyptic vision of "a glassy sea like unto crystal," Rev. 4:6, emblematic of the fixed purity and holiness of all that appertains to the authority and judicial dealings of God; in 15:2, the same, "mingled with fire," and, standing by it (RV) or on it (KJV and RV marg.), those who had "come victorious from the beast" (ch. 13); of the wild and restless condition of nations, Rev. 13:1 (see 17:1, 15), where "he stood" (RV) refers to the dragon, not John (KJV); from the midst of this state arises the beast, symbolic of the final gentile power dominating the federated nations of the Roman world (see Dan., chs. 2, 7, etc.).

2. *pelagos* (989), "the deep sea, the deep," is translated "the depth" in Matt. 18:6, and is used of the "Sea of Cilicia" in Acts 27:5.

pelagos signifies "the vast expanse of open water"; *thalassa*, "the sea as contrasted with the land."

SEAL (Noun and Verb)

A. Noun.

sphragis (4973) denotes (a) "a seal" or "signet," Rev. 7:2, "the seal of the living God," an emblem of ownership and security, here combined with that of destination (as in Ezek. 9:4), the persons to be "sealed" being secured from destruction and marked for reward; (b) "the impression" of a "seal" or signet, (1) literal, a "seal" on a book or roll, combining with the ideas of security and destination those of secrecy and postponement of disclosures, Rev. 5:1, 2, 5, 9; 6:1, 3, 5, 7, 9, 12; 8:1; (2) metaphorical, Rom. 4:11, said of "circumcision," as an authentication of the righteousness of Abraham's faith, and an external attestation of the covenant made with him by God; the rabbis called circumcision "the seal of Abraham"; in 1 Cor. 9:2, of converts as a "seal" or authentication of Paul's apostleship; in 2 Tim. 2:19, "the firm foundation of God standeth, having this seal, The Lord knoweth them that are His," RV, indicating ownership, authentication, security and destination, "and, Let every one that nameth the Name of the Lord depart from unrighteousness," indicating a ratification on the part of the believer of the determining counsel of God concerning him; Rev. 9:4 distinguishes those who will be found without the "seal" of God on their foreheads [see (a) above and B].

B. Verb.

sphragizo (4972), "to seal" (akin to A), is used to indicate (a) security and permanency (attempted but impossible), Matt. 27:66; on the contrary, of the doom of Satan, fixed and certain, Rev. 20:3, RV, "sealed it over"; (b) in Rom. 15:28, "when...I have... sealed to them this fruit," the formal ratification of the ministry of the churches of the Gentiles in Greece and Galatia to needy saints in Judea, by Paul's faithful delivery of the gifts to them; this material help was the fruit of his spiritual ministry to the Gentiles, who on their part were bringing forth the fruit of their having shared with them in spiritual things; the metaphor stresses the sacred formalities of the transaction (Deissmann illustrates this from the papyri of Fayyum, in which the "sealing" of sacks guarantees the full complement of the contents); (c) secrecy and security and the postponement of disclosure, Rev. 10:4; in a negative command 22:10; (d) ownership and security, together with destination, Rev. 7:3, 4, 5 (as with the noun in v. 2; see A); the same three indications are conveyed in Eph. 1:13, in the metaphor of the "sealing" of believers by the gift of the Holy Spirit, upon believing (i.e., at the time of their regeneration, not after a lapse of time in their spiritual life, "having also believed"—not as KJV, "after that

S

ye believed"; the aorist participle marks the definiteness and completeness of the act of faith); the idea of destination is stressed by the phrase "the Holy Spirit of promise" (see also v. 14); so 4:30, "ye were sealed unto the day of redemption"; so in 2 Cor. 1:22, where the middle voice intimates the special interest of the Sealer in His act; (e) authentication by the believer (by receiving the witness of the Son) of the fact that "God is true," John 3:33; authentication by God in sealing the Son as the Giver of eternal life (with perhaps a figurative allusion to the impress of a mark upon loaves), 6:27.

SEARCH

1. *eraunao* or *ereunao*, an earlier form, (2045), "to search, examine," is used (a) of God, as "searching" the heart, Rom. 8:27; (b) of Christ, similarly, Rev. 2:23; (c) of the Holy Spirit, as "searching" all things, 1 Cor. 2:10, acting in the spirit of the believer; (d) of the OT prophets, as "searching" their own writings concerning matters foretold of Christ, testified by the Spirit of Christ in them, 1 Pet. 1:11 (cf. No. 2); (e) of the Jews, as commanded by the Lord to "search" the Scriptures, John 5:39, KJV, and RV marg., "search," RV text, "ye search," either is possible grammatically; (f) of Nicodemus as commanded similarly by the chief priests and Pharisees, John 7:52.

2. *exeraunao* (1830), a strengthened form of No. 1 (*ek*, or *ex*, "out"), "to search out," is used in 1 Pet. 1:10, "searched diligently"; cf. No. 1 (d).

3. *exetazo* (1833), "to examine closely, inquire carefully" (from *etazo*, "to examine"), occurs in Matt. 2:8, RV, "search out."

SEASON (Noun)

A. Nouns.

1. *kairos* (2540), primarily, "due measure, fitness, proportion," is used in the NT to signify "a season, a time, a period" possessed of certain characteristics, frequently rendered "time" or "times"; in the following the RV substitutes "season" for the KJV "time," thus distinguishing the meaning from *chronos* (see No. 2): Matt. 11:25; 12:1; 14:1; 21:34; Mark 11:13; Acts 3:19; 7:20; 17:26; Rom. 3:26; 5:6; 9:9; 13:11; 1 Cor. 7:5; Gal. 4:10; 1 Thess. 2:17, lit., "for a season (of an hour)," 2 Thess. 2:6; in Eph. 6:18, "at all seasons" (KJV, "always"); in Titus 1:3, "His own seasons" (marg., "its"; KJV, "in due times"); in the preceding clause *chronos* is used.

2. *chronos* (5550), whence Eng. words beginning with "chron"—,denotes "a space of time," whether long or short: (a) it implies duration, whether longer, e.g., Acts 1:21, "(all the) time"; Acts 13:18; 20:18, RV, "(all the) time" (KJV, "at all seasons"); or shorter, e.g.,

Luke 4:5; (b) it sometimes refers to the date of an occurrence, whether past, e.g., Matt. 2:7, or future, e.g., Acts 3:21; 7:17.

chronos marks quantity, *kairos*, quality. Sometimes the distinction between the two words is not sharply defined as, e.g., in 2 Tim. 4:6, though even here the apostle's "departure" signalizes the time (*kairos*). In Rev. 10:6 *chronos* has the meaning "delay" (RV, marg.), an important rendering for the understanding of the passage (the word being akin to *chronizo*, "to take time, to linger, delay," Matt. 24:48; Luke 12:45).

3. *hora* (*5610*), "an hour," is translated "season" in John 5:35; 2 Cor. 7:8; Philem. 15.

B. Adverbs.

1. *akairos* (*171*) denotes "out of season, unseasonably" (akin to *akairos*, "unseasonable," *a*, negative, and A, No. 1), 2 Tim. 4:2.

2. *eukairos* (*2122*), "in season" (*eu*, "well"), 2 Tim. 4:2; it occurs also in Mark 14:11, "conveniently."

SEASON (Verb)

artuo (*741*), "to arrange, make ready" (cf. *artios*, "fitted"), is used of "seasoning," Mark 9:50; Luke 14:34; Col. 4:6.

SECRET, SECRETLY

Old Testament

sod (5475), "secret or confidential plan(s); secret or confidential talk; secret; council; gathering; circle." *sod* means, first, "confidential talk," Ps. 64:2. In Prov. 15:22 the word refers to plans which one makes on one's own and before they are shared by others, Prov. 25:9. Second, the word represents a group of intimates with whom one shares confidential matters, Gen. 49:6; Jer. 6:11; Ps. 55:14.

New Testament

1. *kruptos* (2927), adj., "secret, hidden" (akin to *krupto*, "to hide"), Eng., "crypt," "cryptic," etc., is used as an adjective and rendered "secret" in Luke 8:17, KJV (RV, "hid"); in the neuter, with *en*, "in," as an adverbial phrase, "in secret," with the article, Matt. 6:4, 6 (twice in each v.), without the article, John 7:4, 10; 18:20; in the neuter plural, with the article, "the secrets (of men)," Rom. 2:16; of the heart, 1 Cor. 14:25; in Luke 11:33, KJV, "a secret place" (RV, "cellar").

2. *apokruphos* (614) (whence "Apocrypha"), "hidden " is translated "kept secret" in Mark 4:22, KJV (RV, "made secret"); "secret" in Luke 8:17, RV (KJV, "hid").

3. *kruphaios* (2928d) occurs in the best mss. in Matt. 6:18 (twice; some have No. 1).

S

B. Verb.

krupto (2928), "to hide," is translated "secretly" in John 19:38 [perfect participle, passive voice, lit., "(but) having been hidden"], referring to Nicodemus as having been a "secret" disciple of Christ; in Matt. 13:35, KJV, it is translated "kept secret" (RV, "hidden").

SECURE (Verb)

perikrates (4031), an adjective, signifies "having full command of" (*peri*, "around, about," *krateo*, "to be strong, to rule"); it is used with *ginomai*, "to become," in Acts 27:16, RV, "to secure (the boat)," KJV, "to come by."

SECURITY

Old Testament

A. Nouns.

mibtach (4009), "the act of confiding; the object of confidence; the state of confidence or security." The word refers to "the act of confiding" in Prov. 21:22, *mibtach* means the "object of confidence" in Job 8:14 and the "state of confidence or security" in Prov. 14:26.

betach is a noun meaning "security, trust." One occurrence is in Isa. 32:17.

B. Verb.

batach (982), "to be reliant, trust, be unsuspecting," Deut. 28:52.

C. Adjective.

betach (983), "secure," Judg. 8:11; cf. Isa. 32:17.

D. Adverb.

betach (983), "securely." In its first occurrence *betach* emphasizes the status of a city which was certain of not being attacked, Gen. 34:25. Thus the city was unsuspecting regarding the impending attack.

New Testament

hikanos (2425), "sufficient," is used in its neuter form with the article, as a noun, in Acts 17:9, "(when they had taken) security," i.e., satisfaction, lit., "the sufficient," 1 Thess. 2:18.

SEDITION

A. Nouns.

1. *stasis* (4714), "a dissension, an insurrection," is translated "sedition" in Acts 24:5, KJV.

2. *dichostasia* (1370), lit., "a standing apart" (*dicha*, "asunder,

apart," *stasis*, "a standing"), hence "a dissension, division," is translated "seditions" in Gal. 5:20, KJV.

B. Verb.

anastatoo (*387*), "to excite, unsettle," or "to stir up to sedition," is so translated in Acts 21:38, RV (KJV, "madest an uproar"); in 17:6, "have turned (the world) upside down," i.e., "causing tumults"; in Gal. 5:12, RV, "unsettle" (KJV, "trouble"), i.e., by false teaching (here in the continuous present tense, lit., "those who are unsettling you"). The word was supposed not to have been used in profane authors. It has been found, however, in several of the papyri writings.

SEDUCE, SEDUCING

A. Verbs.

1. *planao* (*4105*), "to cause to wander, lead astray," is translated "to seduce" in 1 John 2:26, KJV (RV, "lead...astray"); in Rev. 2:20, "to seduce."

2. *apoplanao* (*635*) is translated "seduce" in Mark 13:22 (RV, "lead astray").

B. Adjective.

planos (*4108*), akin to A, lit., "wandering," then, "deceiving," is translated "seducing" in 1 Tim. 4:1.

SEE, SEEING
Old Testament

A. Verb.

ra'ah (*7200*), "to see, observe, perceive, get acquainted with, gain understanding, examine, look after (see to), choose, discover." Basically *ra'ah* connotes seeing with one's eyes, Gen. 27:1. The second primary meaning is "to perceive," or to be consciously aware of—so idols "neither see, nor hear," Deut. 4:28. Third, *ra'ah* can represent perception in the sense of hearing something, Gen. 2:19. In Isa. 44:16 the verb means "to enjoy."

This verb has several further extended meanings. For example, *ra'ah* can refer to "perceiving or ascertaining" something apart from seeing it with one's eyes, as when Hagar saw that she had conceived, Gen. 16:4. It can represent mentally recognizing that something is true, Gen. 26:28. Seeing and hearing together can mean "to gain understanding," Isa. 52:15; "to distinguish," Mal. 3:18.

In addition to these uses of *ra'ah* referring to intellectual seeing, there is seeing used in the sense of living. "To see the light" is to live life, Job 3:16; cf. 33:28. It can mean "experience" in the sense of what one is aware of as he lives, Job 4:8.

A fourth idea of seeing is "to examine," Gen. 39:23. Used in this sense **ra'ah** can imply looking upon with joy or pain. Hagar asked that she not be allowed to look on the death of Ishmael, Gen. 21:16. This verb may be used of attending to or visiting, 2 Sam. 13:5.

B. Nouns.

ro'eh (7203), "seer; vision." **ro'eh**, which occurs 11 times, refers to a "prophet," emphasizing the means by which revelation was received; 1 Sam. 9:9; and to "vision," Isa. 28:7.

mar'ah means "visionary appearance" or "(prophetic) vision," Gen. 46:2 and "looking glasses," Exod. 38:8.

New Testament

1. **blepo** (991), "to have sight," is used of bodily vision, e.g., Matt. 11:4; and mental, e.g. Matt. 13:13, 14; it is said of God the Father in Matt. 6:4, 6, 18; of Christ as "seeing" what the Father doeth, John 5:19. It especially stresses the thought of the person who "sees."

2. **horao** (3708), with the form **eidon**, serving for its aorist tense, and **opsomai**, for its future tense (middle voice), denotes "to see," of bodily vision, e.g., John 6:36; and mental, e.g., Matt. 8:4; it is said of Christ as "seeing" the Father, John 6:46, and of what He had "seen" with the Father, 8:38. It especially indicates the direction of the thought to the object "seen."

3. **aphorao** (872), with **apeidon** serving as the aorist tense, "to look away from one thing so as to see another" (**apo**, "from," and No. 2), as in Heb. 12:2, simply means "to see" in Phil. 2:23.

4. **kathorao** (2529), lit., "to look down" (**kata**, and No. 2), denotes "to discern clearly," Rom. 1:20, "are clearly seen."

5. **diablepo** (1227), "to see clearly" (**dia**, "through," and No. 1), is used in Matt. 7:5; Luke 6:42; in Mark 8:25, RV, "he looked steadfastly" (No. 6 is used in the next clause; No. 1 in v. 24, and No. 2 in the last part).

6. **emblepo** (1689), "to look at" (**en**, "in," and No. 1), used of earnestly looking, is translated "saw" in Mark 8:25 (last part); "could (not) see" in Acts 22:11.

7. **anablepo** (308), "to look up," is translated "see," of the blind, in Luke 7:22, KJV (RV, "receive their sight").

SEED

1. **sperma** (4690), akin to **speiro**, "to sow" (Eng., "sperm," "spermatic," etc.), has the following usages, (a) agricultural and botanical, e.g., Matt. 13:24, 27, 32 (for the KJV of vv. 19, 20, 22, 23, as in the RV); 1 Cor. 15:38; 2 Cor. 9:10; (b) physiological, Heb. 11:11; (c) metaphorical and by metonymy for "offspring, posterity," (1) of natural offspring, e.g., Matt. 22:24, 25, RV, "seed" (KJV, "issue"); John 7:42; 8:33, 37; Acts 3:25; Rom. 1:3; 4:13, 16, 18; 9:7 (twice), 8, 29;

11:1; 2 Cor. 11:22; Heb. 2:16; 11:18; Rev. 12:17; Gal. 3:16, 19, 29; in the 16th v., "He saith not, And to seeds, as of many; but as of one, And to thy seed, which is Christ," quoted from the Sept. of Gen. 13:15 and 17:7, 8, there is especial stress on the word "seed," as referring to an individual (here, Christ) in fulfillment of the promises to Abraham—a unique use of the singular. While the plural form "seeds," neither in Hebrew nor in Greek, would have been natural any more than in English (it is not so used in Scripture of human offspring; its plural occurrence is in 1 Sam. 8:15, of crops), yet if the divine intention had been to refer to Abraham's natural descendants, another word could have been chosen in the plural, such as "children"; all such words were, however, set aside, "seed" being selected as one that could be used in the singular, with the purpose of showing that the "seed" was Messiah. Some of the rabbis had even regarded "seed," e.g., in Gen. 4:25 and Isa. 53:10, as referring to the Coming One. Descendants were given to Abraham by other than natural means, so that through him Messiah might come, and the point of the apostle's argument is that since the fulfillment of the promises of God is secured alone by Christ, they only who are "in Christ" can receive them; (2) of spiritual offspring, Rom. 4:16, 18; 9:8; here "the children of the promise are reckoned for a seed" points, firstly, to Isaac's birth as being not according to the ordinary course of nature but by divine promise, and, secondly, by analogy, to the fact that all believers are children of God by spiritual birth, Gal. 3:29.

As to 1 John 3:9, "his seed abideth in him," it is possible to understand this as meaning that children of God (His "seed") abide in Him, and do not go on doing (practicing) sin (the verb "to commit" does not represent the original in this passage). Alternatively, the "seed" signifies the principle of spiritual life as imparted to the believer, which abides in him without possibility of removal or extinction; the child of God remains eternally related to Christ, he who lives in sin has never become so related, he has not the principle of life in him. This meaning suits the context and the general tenor of the Epistle.

2. *sporos* (4703), akin to No. 1, properly "a sowing," denotes "seed sown," (a) natural, Mark 4:26, 27; Luke 8:5, 11 (the natural being figuratively applied to the Word of God); 2 Cor. 9:10 (1st part); (b) metaphorically of material help to the needy, 2 Cor. 9:10 (2nd part), RV, "(your) seed for sowing" (KJV, "seed sown").

3. *spora* (4701), akin to No. 1, and like No. 2, "a sowing, seedtime," denotes "seed sown," 1 Pet. 1:23, of human offspring.

SEEK

Old Testament

A. Verbs.

baqash (1245), "to seek, search, consult." *baqash* means "to seek" to find something that is lost or missing, or, at least, whose location is unknown, Gen. 37:15; 1 Sam. 13:14; 1 Kings 10:24. The sense "seek to secure" emphasizes the pursuit of a wish or the accomplishing of a plan. Moses asked the Levites who rebelled against the unique position of Aaron and his sons, Num. 16:10. This word may have an emotional coloring, such as, "to aim at, devote oneself to, and be concerned about," Ps. 4:2. Cultically one may "seek" to secure God's favor or help, 2 Chron. 20:4.

This sense of "seeking to secure" may also be used of seeking one's life (*nepesh*). God told Moses to "go, return into Egypt: for all the men are dead which sought thy life," Exod. 2:15; 4:19.

Theologically, this verb can be used not only "to seek" a location before the Lord (to stand before Him in the temple and seek to secure His blessing), but it may also be used of a state of mind, Deut. 4:29. In instances such as this where the verb is used in synonymous parallelism with *darash*, the two verbs have the same meaning.

darash (1875), "to seek, inquire, consult, ask, require, frequent." One of the most frequent uses of this word is in the expression "to inquire of God," which sometimes indicates a private seeking of God in prayer for direction, Gen. 25:22, and often it refers to the contacting of a prophet who would be the instrument of God's revelation, 1 Sam. 9:9; 1 Kings 22:8; or seek pagan gods or demons, Deut. 18:10-11; cf. 1 Sam. 28:3ff. This word is often used to describe the "seeking of" the Lord in the sense of entering into covenantal relationship with Him. The prophets often used *darash* as they called on the people to make an about-face in living and instead "seek ye the Lord while he may be found..." Isa. 55:6.

B. Noun.

midrash can mean "study; commentary; story," 2 Chron. 13:22; 2 Chron. 24:27.

New Testament

1. *zeteo* (2212) signifies (a) "to seek, to seek for," e.g., Matt. 7:7, 8; 13:45; Luke 24:5; John 6:24; of plotting against a person's life, Matt. 2:20; Acts 21:31; Rom. 11:3; metaphorically, to "seek" by thinking, to "seek" how to do something, or what to obtain, e.g., Mark 11:18; Luke 12:29; to "seek" to ascertain a meaning, John 16:19, "do ye inquire"; to "seek" God, Acts 17:27, RV; (b) "to seek or strive after, endeavor, to desire," e.g., Matt. 12:46, 47, RV, "seeking" (KJV, "desiring"); Luke 9:9, RV, "sought" (KJV, "desired"); John 7:19,

RV, "seek ye" (KJV. "go ye about"); so v. 20; Rom. 10:3, RV, "seeking" (AV, "going about"); of "seeking" the kingdom of God and His righteousness, in the sense of coveting earnestly, striving after, Matt. 6:33; "the things that are above," Col. 3:1; peace, 1 Pet. 3:11; (c) "to require or demand," e.g., Mark 8:12; Luke 11:29 (some mss. have No. 4); 1 Cor. 4:2, "it is required"; 2 Cor. 13:3, "ye seek."

2. *anazeteo* (327), "to seek carefully" (*ana*, "up," used intensively, and No. 1), is used of searching for human beings, difficulty in the effort being implied, Luke 2:44, 45 (some mss. have No. 1 in the latter v.), Acts 11:25; numerous illustrations of this particular meaning in the papyri are given by Moulton and Milligan.

3. *ekzeteo* (1567) signifies (a) "to seek out (*ek*) or after, to search for"; e.g., God, Rom. 3:11; the Lord, Acts 15:17; in Heb. 11:6, RV, "seek after" (KJV, "diligently seek"); 12:17, RV, "sought diligently" (KJV, "sought carefully"); 1 Pet. 1:10, RV, "sought" (KJV, "have inquired"), followed by *exeraunao*, "to search diligently," (b) "to require or demand," Luke 11:50, 51.

4. *epizeteo* (1934), "to seek after" (directive, *epi*, "towards") is always rendered in the RV, by some form of the verb "to seek," Acts 13:7, "sought" (KJV, "desired"); 19:39, "seek" (KJV, "inquire"); Phil. 4:17, "seek for" (KJV, "desire"), twice; elsewhere, Matt. 6:32; 12:39; 16:4; Mark 8:12 (in some texts); Luke 12:30; Acts 12:19; Rom. 11:7; Heb. 11:14; 13:14.

SEEM

dokeo (1380) denotes (a) "to be of opinion" (akin to *doxa*, "opinion"), e.g., Luke 8:18, RV, "thinketh" (KJV, "seemeth"); so 1 Cor. 3:18; to think, suppose, Jas. 1:26, RV, "thinketh himself (KJV, "seem"); (b) "to seem, to be reputed," e.g., Acts 17:18; 1 Cor. 11:16; 12:22; 2 Cor. 10:9; Heb. 4:1; 12:11; for Gal. 2:2, 6, 9; (c) impersonally (1) to think, (2) to "seem" good, Luke 1:3; Acts 15:22, RV, "it seemed good" (KJV, "it pleased"); 15:25, 28 (v. 34 in some mss.); in Heb. 12:10, the neuter of the present participle is used with the article, lit., "the (thing) seeming good," RV, "(as) seemed good," KJV, "after (their own) pleasure."

SELF-WILLED

authades (829), "self-pleasing" (*autos*, "self," *hedomai*, "to please"), denotes one who, dominated by self-interest, and inconsiderate of others, arrogantly asserts his own will, "self-willed," Titus 1:7; 2 Pet. 2:10 (the opposite of *epieikes*, "gentle," e.g., 1 Tim. 3:3), "one so far overvaluing any determination at which he has himself once arrived that he will not be removed from it."

S

SELL

Old Testament

makar (4376), "to sell," i.e., an exchange of money, services, or other bartered good, as a way to do business, Gen. 25:31. Anything tangible may be "sold": land, Gen. 47:20; houses, Lev. 25:29; Exod. 21:35; Gen. 37:27-28.

makar is often used in the figurative sense to express various actions. Nineveh is accused of "selling" or "betraying" other nations, Nah. 3:4. Frequently it is said that God "sold" Israel into the power of her enemies, meaning that He gave them over entirely into their hands, Judg. 2:14. Similarly, it was said that "the Lord shall sell Sisera into the hand of a woman," Judg. 4:9. "To be sold" sometimes means to be given over to death, Esth. 7:4.

New Testament

1. *poleo* (4453), "to exchange or barter, to sell," is used in the latter sense in the NT, six times in Matthew, three in Mark, six in Luke; in John only in connection with the cleansing of the Temple by the Lord, 2:14, 16; in Acts only in connection with the disposing of property for distribution among the community of believers, 4:34, 37; 5:1; elsewhere, 1 Cor. 10:25; Rev. 13:17.

2. *piprasko* (4097), from an earlier form, *perao*, "to carry across the sea for the purpose of selling or to export," is used (a) literally, Matt. 13:46; 18:25; 26:9; Mark 14:5; John 12:5; Acts 2:45; 4:34; 5:4; (b) metaphorically, Rom. 7:14, "sold under sin," i.e., as fully under the domination of sin as a slave is under his master.

SENSES

aistheterion (145), "sense, the faculty of perception, the organ of sense" (akin to *aisthanomai*, "to perceive"), is used in Heb. 5:14, "senses," the capacities for spiritual apprehension.

SENTENCE

A. Nouns.

1. *krima* (2917), "a judgment," a decision passed on the faults of others, is used especially of God's judgment upon men, and translated "sentence" in 2 Pet. 2:3, RV (KJV, judgment).

2. *katadike* (2613), "a judicial sentence, condemnation," is translated "sentence" in Acts 25:15, RV (KJV, "judgment"); some mss. have *dike*.

B. Verbs.

1. *krino* (2919), "to judge, to adjudge," is translated "(my) sentence is" in Acts 15:19, KJV, RV, "(my) judgment is," lit., "I (*ego*, emphatic) judge," introducing the substance or draft of a resolution.

2. *epikrino* (1948), "to give sentence," is used in Luke 23:24.

SEPARATE
Old Testament

A. Verbs.

parad (6504), "to divide, separate." This word often expresses separation of people from each other, sometimes with hostility, Gen. 13:9. A reciprocal separation seems to be implied in the birth of Jacob and Esau, Gen. 25:23. Sometimes economic status brings about separation, Prov. 19:4.

nazar (5144), "to separate, be separated." "To separate" and "to consecrate" are not distinguished from one another in the early Old Testament books. For example, the earliest use of *nazar* in the Pentateuch is in Lev. 15:31.

In prophetic literature, the verb *nazar* indicates Israel's deliberate separation from Jehovah to dedication of foreign gods or idols. In Hos. 9:10, the various versions differ in their rendering of *nazar*. The prophet Ezekiel employed *nazar*, Ezek. 14:7.

B. Noun.

nazir (5139), "one who is separated; Nazirite." There are 16 occurrences of the word in the Old Testament. The earliest use of *nazir* is found in Gen. 49:26; cf. Deut. 33:16. Most frequently in Old Testament usage, *nazir* is an appellation for one who vowed to refrain from certain things for a period of time, Num. 6:13. According to Num. 6, a lay person of either sex could take a special vow of consecration to God's service for a certain period of time. A "Nazirite" usually made a vow voluntarily; however, in the case of Samson, Judg. 13:5, 7, his parents dedicated him for life. Whether or not this idea of separation to God was distinctive alone to Israel has been debated. Num. 6:1-23 laid down regulatory laws pertaining to Naziritism. There were two kinds of "Nazirites": the temporary and the perpetual. The first class was much more common than the latter kind. From the Bible we have knowledge only of Samson, Samuel, and John the Baptist as persons who were lifelong "Nazirites." During the time of his vow, a "Nazirite" was required to abstain from wine and every kind of intoxicating drink. He was also forbidden to cut the hair of his head or to approach a dead body, even that of his nearest relative. If a "Nazirite" accidentally defiled himself, he had to undergo certain rites of purification and then had to begin the full period of consecration over again. The "Nazirite" was "holy unto the Lord," and he wore upon his head a diadem of his consecration.

New Testament

A. Verbs.

1. *aphorizo* (873), "to mark off by bounds" (*apo*, "from," *horizo*, "to determine"; *horos*, "a limit"), "to separate," is used of (a) the

Divine action in setting men apart for the work of the gospel, Rom. 1:1; Gal. 1:15; (b) the Divine judgment upon men, Matt. 13:49; 25:32; (c) the separation of Christians from unbelievers, Acts 19:9; 2 Cor. 6:17; (d) the separation of believers by unbelievers, Luke 6:22; (e) the withdrawal of Christians from their brethren, Gal. 2:12. In (c) is described what the Christian must do, in (d) what he must be prepared to suffer, and in (e) what he must avoid.

2. *chorizo* (5563), "to put asunder, separate," is translated "to separate" in Rom. 8:35, 39; in the middle voice, "to separate oneself, depart"; in the passive voice in Heb. 7:26, RV, "separated" (KJV, "separate"), the verb here relates to the resurrection of Christ, not, as KJV indicates, to the fact of His holiness in the days of His flesh; the list is progressive in this respect that the first three qualities apply to His sinlessness, the next to His resurrection, the last to His ascension.

3. *apodiorizo* (592), "to mark off" (*apo*, "from," *dia*, "asunder," *horizo*, "to limit"), hence denotes metaphorically to make "separations," Jude 19, RV (KJV, "separate themselves"), of persons who make divisions (in contrast with v. 20); there is no pronoun in the original representing "themselves."

B. Preposition.

choris (5565), "apart from, without" (cf. *aneu*, "without," a rarer word than this), is translated "separate from" in Eph. 2:12 (KJV, without).

SERGEANT (-S)

rhabdouchos (4465), "a rod bearer," one who carries a staff of office, was, firstly, an umpire or judge, later, a Roman lictor, Acts 16:35, 38. The duty of these officials was to attend Roman magistrates to execute their orders, especially administering punishment by scourging or beheading.

SERPENT

ophis (3789): the characteristics of the "serpent" as alluded to in Scripture are mostly evil (though Matt. 10:16 refers to its caution in avoiding danger); its treachery, Gen. 49:17; 2 Cor. 11:3; its venom, Ps. 58:4; 1 Cor. 10:9; Rev. 9:19; its skulking, Job 26:13; its murderous proclivities, e.g., Ps. 58:4; Prov. 23:32; Eccl. 10:8, 11; Amos 5:19; Mark 16:18; Luke 10:19; the Lord used the word metaphorically of the scribes and Pharisees, Matt. 23:33 (cf. Matt. 3:7; 12:34). The general aspects of its evil character are intimated in the Lord's rhetorical question in Matt. 7:10 and Luke 11:11. Its characteristics are concentrated in the arch-adversary of God and man, the Devil, metaphorically described as the serpent, 2 Cor. 11:3; Rev. 12:9, 14, 15; 20:2.

SERVANT

A. Nouns.

1. **doulos** (*1401*), an adjective, signifying "in bondage," Rom. 6:19 (neuter plural, agreeing with **mele**, "members"), is used as a noun, and as the most common and general word for "servant," frequently indicating subjection without the idea of bondage; it is used (a) of natural conditions, e.g., Matt. 8:9; 1 Cor. 7:21, 22 (1st part); Eph. 6:5; Col. 4:1; 1 Tim. 6:1; frequently in the four Gospels; (b) metaphorically of spiritual, moral and ethical conditions: "servants" (1) of God, e.g., Acts 16:17; Titus 1:1; 1 Pet. 2:16; Rev. 7:3; 15:3; the perfect example being Christ Himself, Phil. 2:7; (2) of Christ, e.g., Rom. 1:1; 1 Cor. 7:22 (2nd part); Gal. 1:10; Eph. 6:6; Phil. 1:1; Col. 4:12; Jas. 1:1; 2 Pet. 1:1; Jude 1; (3) of sin, John 8:34 (RV, "bondservants"); Rom. 6:17, 20; (4) of corruption, 2 Pet. 2:19 (RV, "bondservants"); cf. the verb **douloo** (see B).

2. **diakonos** (*1249*), translated "servant" or "servants" in Matt. 22:13 (RV marg., "ministers"); 23:11 (RV marg., ditto); Mark 9:35, KJV (RV, "minister"); John 2:5, 9; 12:26; Rom. 16:1.

3. **pais** (*3816*), denotes "an attendant"; it is translated "servant" (a) of natural conditions, in Matt. 8:6, 8, 13; 14:2; Luke 7:7 ("menservants" in 12:45); 15:26; (b) of spiritual relation to God, (1) of Israel, Luke 1:54; (2) of David, Luke 1:69; Acts 4:25; (3) of Christ, so declared by God the Father, Matt. 12:18; spoken of in prayer, Acts 4:27, 30, RV (KJV, "child"); Acts 4; Matt. 12.

4. **oiketes** (*3610*), "a house servant" (**oikeo**, "to dwell," **oikos**, "a house"), is translated "servant" in Luke 16:13 (RV marg., "household servant"); so Rom. 14:4 and 1 Pet. 2:18; in Acts 10:7, KJV and RV, "household servants."

B. Verb.

douloo (*1402*), "to enslave, to bring into bondage" (akin to A, No. 1), e.g., 1 Cor. 9:19, RV, "I brought (myself) under bondage (to all)," KJV, "I made myself servant," denotes in the passive voice, "to be brought into bondage, to become a slave or servant," rendered "ye became servants (of righteousness)" in Rom. 6:18; "being...become servants (to God)," v. 22.

SERVE

Old Testament

A. Verbs.

sharat (*8334*), "to serve, minister." **sharat** often denotes "service" rendered in connection with Israel's worship, 1 Sam. 2:11; 3:1. This kind of "service" was to honor only the Lord, for Israel was not to be "as the heathen, as the families of the countries; to serve wood and stone," Ezek. 20:32.

S

In a number of situations, the word is used to denote "service" rendered to a fellow human being. Though the person "served" usually is of a higher rank or station in life, this word never describes a slave's servitude to his master, Num. 3:6; cf. 8:26. Elisha "ministered" to Elijah, 1 Kings 19:21. Abishag is said to have "ministered" unto David, 1 Kings 1:15. Various kinds of officials "ministered" to David, 1 Chron. 28:1. David's son, Amnon had a "servant that ministered unto him," 2 Sam. 13:17.

'abad (5647), "to serve, cultivate, enslave, work." *'abad* is often used toward God: "...Ye shall serve God upon this mountain," Exod. 3:12, meaning "to worship," Deut. 6:13, or "...hearken diligently unto my commandments which I command you this day, to love the Lord your God, and to serve him..." Deut. 11:13; Ps. 100:2.

B. Nouns.

'abodah (5656), "work; labors; service." The more general meaning of *'abodah* is close to our English word for "work," field work, 1 Chron. 27:26; daily "work," Ps. 104:23; linen industry, 1 Chron. 4:21. The more limited meaning of the word is "service." Israel was in the "service" of the Lord, Josh. 22:27. Whenever God's people were not fully dependent on Him, they had to choose to serve the Lord God or human kings with their requirements of forced "labor" and tribute, 2 Chron. 12:8. Further specialization of the usage is in association with the tabernacle and the temple. The priests were chosen for the "service" of the Lord, Num. 3:7. The Levites also had many important functions in and around the temple; they sang, played musical instruments, and were secretaries, scribes, and doorkeepers, 2 Chron. 34:13; cf. 8:14. Thus anything, people and objects, 1 Chron. 28:13, associated with the temple was considered to be in the "service" of the Lord.

'ebed (5650), "servant." This words represents a person usually an indentured servant, possibly to pay off a debt, Exod. 21:2; hired, 1 Kings 5:6; yet they can also be slaves bought and sold, Lev 25:44. *'ebed* was used as a mark of humility and courtesy, as in Gen. 18:3. The "servant" was not a free man. He was subject to the will and command of his master. But one might willingly and lovingly submit to his master, Exod. 21:5, remaining in his service when he was not obliged to do so. Hence it is a very fitting description of the relationship of man to God.

Of prime significance is the use of "my servant" for the Messiah in Isaiah, 42:1-7; 49:1-7; 50:4-10; 52:13-53:12. Israel was a blind and deaf "servant," Isa. 42:18-22. So the Lord called "my righteous servant," Isa. 53:11; cf. 42:6 "[to bear] the sin of many," Isa. 53:12, "that thou mayest be my salvation unto the end of the earth," Isa. 49:6.

sharat (8334), "servant; minister." This word is most regularly translated "minister," Josh. 1:1; Ezek. 46:24. The privilege of serving the Lord is not restricted to human beings, Ps. 103:21. Fire and wind, conceived poetically as persons, are also God's "ministers," Ps. 104:3-4.

New Testament

1. *diakoneo* (1247), "to minister" (akin to *diakonos*, "to render any kind of service"), is translated "to serve," e.g., in Luke 10:40; 12:37; 17:8; 22:26, 27 (twice).

2. *douleuo* (1398), "to serve as a *doulos*" (No. 1, above), is used (a) of serving God (and the impossibility of serving mammon also), Matt. 6:24 and Luke 16:13; Rom. 7:6; in the gospel, Phil. 2:22; (b) Christ, Acts 20:19; Rom. 12:11; 14:18; 16:18; Eph. 6:7; Col. 3:24; (c) the law of God, Rom. 7:25; (d) one another, Gal. 5:13, RV, "be servants to" (KJV, "serve"); (e) a father, Luke 15:29 (with a suggestion of acting as a slave); (f) earthly masters, Matt. 6:24; Luke 16:13; 1 Tim. 6:2, RV, "serve"; (g) the younger by the elder, Rom. 9:12; (h) of being in bondage to a nation, Acts 7:7; Gal. 4:25, to the Romans, actually, though also spiritually to Judaizers; (i) to idols, Gal. 4:8, RV, "were in bondage" (KJV, "did service"); (j) to "the weak and beggarly rudiments," v. 9 (RV), "to be in bondage" (aorist tense in the best texts, suggesting "to enter into bondage"), i.e., to the religion of the Gentiles ("rudiments" being used in v. 3 of the religion of the Jews); (k) sin, Rom. 6:6, RV, "be in bondage" (KJV, "serve"); (l) "divers lusts and pleasures," Titus 3:3; (m) negatively, to any man—a proud and thoughtless denial by the Jews, John 8:33.

3. *latreuo* (3000), primarily "to work for hire" (akin to *latris*, "a hired servant"), signifies (1) to worship, (2) to "serve"; in the latter sense it is used of service (a) to God, Matt. 4:10; Luke 1:74 ("without fear"); 4:8; Acts 7:7; 24:14, RV, "serve" (KJV, "worship"); 26:7 27:23; Rom. 1:9 ("with my spirit"); 2 Tim. 1:3; Heb. 9:14; 12:28, KJV, "we may serve," RV, "we may offer service"; Rev. 7:15; (b) to God and Christ ("the Lamb"), Rev. 22:3; (c) in the tabernacle, Heb. 8:5, RV; 13:10; (d) to "the host of heaven," Acts 7:42, RV, "to serve" (KJV, "to worship"); (e) to "the creature," instead of the Creator, Rom. 1:25.

4. *hupereteo* (5256), translated "to serve" in Acts 13:36; there is a contrast intimated between the service of David, lasting for only a generation, and the eternal character of Christ's ministry as the One who not having seen corruption was raised from the dead.

SERVICE, SERVING

1. *diakonia* (1248) is rendered "service" in Rom. 15:31, KJV; "serving" in Luke 10:40.

2. *leitourgia* (3009) is rendered "service" in 2 Cor. 9:12; Phil. 2:17, 30.

3. *latreia* (2999), akin to *latreuo* (see No. 3, above), primarily "hired service," is used (a) of the "service" of God in connection with the tabernacle, Rom. 9:4; Heb. 9:1, "divine service"; v. 6, plur-

S

al, RV, "services" (KJV, "service," and, in italics, "of God"); (b) of the intelligent "service" of believers in presenting their bodies to God, a living sacrifice, Rom. 12:1, RV marg., "worship"; (c) of imagined "service" to God by persecutors of Christ's followers, John 16:2.

SEVEN

hepta (*2033*), whence Eng. words beginning with "hept"—corresponds to the Heb. *sheba'* (which is akin to *saba'*, signifying "to be full, abundant"), sometimes used as an expression of fullness, e.g., Ruth 4:15: it generally expresses completeness, and is used most frequently in the Apocalypse; it is not found in the Gospel of John, nor between the Acts and the Apocalypse, except in Heb. 11:30 (in Rom. 11:4 the numeral is *heptakischilioi*, "seven thousand"); in Matt. 22:26 it is translated "seventh" (marg., "seven").

SEVEN TIMES

heptakis (*2034*) occurs in Matt. 18:21, 22; Luke 17:4 (twice).

SEVENTY

hebdomekonta (*1440*) occurs in Luke 10:1, 17; in Acts 7:14 it precedes *pente*, "five," lit., "seventy-five," rendered "threescore and fifteen."

SEVENTY TIMES

hebdomekontakis (*1441*) occurs in Matt. 18:22, where it is followed by *hepta*, "seven," "seventy times seven"; RV marg. has "seventy times and seven," which many have regarded as the meaning; cf. Gen. 4:24; whether this is literal or figurative or a greater number is debated among the sources,

The Lord's reply "until seventy times seven" was indicative of completeness, the absence of any limit, and was designed to turn away Peter's mind from a merely numerical standard. God's forgiveness is limitless; so should man's be.

SEVERITY

1. *apotomia* (*663*), "steepness, sharpness" (*apo*, "off," *temno*, "to cut"; *tome*, "a cutting"), is used metaphorically in Rom. 11:22 (twice) of "the severity of God," which lies in His temporary retributive dealings with Israel. In the papyri it is used of exacting to the full the provisions of a statute.

2. *apheidia* (*857*), primarily "extravagance" (*a*, negative, *pheidomai*, "to spare"), hence, "unsparing treatment, severity," is used in Col. 2:23, RV, "severity (to the body)," KJV, "neglecting of" (marg., "punishing, not sparing"); here it refers to ascetic discipline; it was often used among the Greeks of courageous exposure to hardship and danger.

SHADOW (Noun)

1. *skia* (*4639*) is used (a) of "a shadow," caused by the interception of light, Mark 4:32; Acts 5:15; metaphorically of the darkness and spiritual death of ignorance, Matt. 4:16; Luke 1:79; (b) of "the image" or "outline" cast by an object, Col. 2:17, of ceremonies under the Law; of the tabernacle and its appurtenances and of ferings, Heb. 8:5; of these as appointed under the Law, Heb. 10:1.

2. *aposkiasma* (*644*), "a shadow," is rendered "shadow that is cast" in Jas. 1:17, RV; the KJV makes no distinction between this and No. 1. The probable significance of this word is "overshadowing" or "shadowing-over" (which *apo* may indicate), and this with the genitive case of *trope*, "turning," yields the meaning "shadowing-over of mutability" implying an alternation of "shadow" and light; of this there are two alternative explanations, namely, "overshadowing" (1) not caused by mutability in God, or (2) caused by change in others, i.e., "no changes in this lower world can cast a shadow on the unchanging Fount of light."

SHAMBLES

makellon (*3111*), a term of late Greek borrowed from the Latin *macellum*, denotes a "meat market," translated "shambles" in 1 Cor. 10:25.

SHAME (Noun, and Verb)

Old Testament

A. Verb.

bosh (*954*), "to be ashamed, feel ashamed." The word has overtones of being or feeling worthless. *bosh* means "to be ashamed" in Isa. 1:29.

B. Noun.

boshet (*1322*), "shame; shameful thing." This word means a "shameful thing" as a reference to Baal, Jer. 3:24; cf. Jer. 11:13; Hos. 9:10. This substitution also occurs in proper names: Ish-bo-sheth, 2 Sam. 2:8, the "man of shame," was originally Esh-baal, cf. 1 Chron. 8:33.

This word means both "shame and worthlessness, 1 Sam. 20:30; 2 Chron. 32:21.

New Testament

A. Nouns.

1. *atimia* (*819*) signifies (a) "shame, disgrace," Rom. 1:26, "vile (passions)," RV, lit., "(passions) of shame"; 1 Cor. 11:14; (b) "dishonor," e.g., 2 Tim. 2:20, where the idea of disgrace or "shame" does not attach to the use of the word; the meaning is that while in a

great house some vessels are designed for purposes of honor, others have no particular honor (*time*) attached to their use (the prefix *a* simply negatives the idea of honor).

2. *entrope* (*1791*), 1 Cor. 6:5 and 15:34.

3. *aschemosune* (*808*) denotes (a) "unseemliness," Rom. 1:27, RV (AV, "that which is unseemly"); (b) "shame, nakedness," Rev. 16:15.

B. Adjective.

aischros (*150*), "base, shameful" (akin to *aischos*, "shame"), of that which is opposed to modesty or purity, is translated as a noun in 1 Cor. 11:6; 14:35, KJV (RV, "shameful"); Eph. 5:12; in Titus 1:11, "filthy (lucre)," lit., "shameful (gain)."

C. Verbs.

1. *atimazo* (*818*), "to dishonor, put to shame (akin to A, No. 1).

2. *entrepo* (*1788*), lit., "to turn in upon, to put to shame" (akin to A, No. 2), is translated "to shame (you)" in 1 Cor. 4:14.

3. *kataischuno* (*2617*), "to put to shame" (*kata*, perhaps signifying "utterly"), is translated "ye...shame (them)" in 1 Cor. 11:22, KJV, RV, "ye...put (them) to shame."

SHAMEFASTNESS (KJV, SHAMEFACEDNESS)

aidos (*127*), "a sense of shame, modesty," is used regarding the demeanor of women in the church, 1 Tim. 2:9 (some mss. have it in Heb. 12:28 for *deos*, "awe": here only in NT). Shamefastness is that modesty which is "fast" or rooted in the character...The change to "shamefacedness" is the more to be regretted because shamefacedness...has come rather to describe an awkward diffidence, such as we sometimes call sheepishness.

SHAPE

1. *eidos* (*1491*), rendered "shape" in the KJV of Luke 3:22 and John 5:37.

2. *homoioma* (*3667*), rendered "shapes" in Rev. 9:7.

SHARP, SHARPER, SHARPLY, SHARPNESS

A. Adjectives.

1. *oxus* (*3691*) denotes (a) of a sword, Rev. 1:16 (b) of motion, "swift," Rom. 3:15.

2. *tomos* (*5114**), akin to *temno*, "to cut" [Eng., "(ana)tomy," etc.], is used metaphorically in the comparative degree, *tomoteros*, in Heb. 4:12, of the Word of God.

B. Adverb.

apotomos (*664*) signifies "abruptly, curtly," lit., "in a manner that cuts" (*apo*, "from," *temno*, "to cut"), hence "sharply, severely," 2 Cor. 13:10, RV, "(that I may not... deal) sharply," KJV, "(use) sharpness"; the pronoun "you" is to be understood, i.e., "that I may not use (or deal with)...sharply"; Titus 1:13, of rebuking.

SHEAR, SHEARER, SHORN

keiro (2751) is used (a) of "shearing sheep," Acts 8:32, "shearer," lit., "the (one) shearing": (b) in the middle voice, "to have one's hair cut off, be shorn," Acts 18:18; 1 Cor. 11:6 (twice; cf. *xurao*, "to shave").

SHED

1. *ekcheo* (1632), "to pour out," is translated "to shed" or "to shed forth" in Acts 2:33; Titus 3:6, KJV; of "shedding" blood in murder, Rom. 3:15.

2. *ekchuno*, or *ekchunno* (1632), a later form of No. 1, is used of the voluntary giving up of His life by Christ through the "shedding" of His blood in crucifixion as an atoning sacrifice, Matt. 26:28; Mark 14:24; Luke 22:20, KJV, "is shed," RV, "is poured out"; these passages do not refer to the effect of the piercing of His side (which took place after His death); of the murder of servants of God, Matt. 23:35; Luke 11:50; Acts 22:20 (in the best texts; others have No. 1); of the love of God in the hearts of believers through the Holy Spirit, Rom. 5:5. For the "pouring out" of the Holy Spirit, Acts 10:45. (The form in the last two passages might equally well come from No. 1, above.)

SHEEP

1. *probaton* (4263), from *probaino*, "to go forward," i.e., of the movement of quadrupeds, was used among the Greeks of small cattle, sheep and goats; in the NT, of "sheep" only (a) naturally, e.g., Matt. 12:11, 12; (b) metaphorically, of those who belong to the Lord, the lost ones of the house of Israel, Matt. 10:6; of those who are under the care of the Good Shepherd, e.g., Matt. 26:31; John 10:1, lit., "the fold of the sheep," and vv. 2-27; 21:16, 17 in some texts; Heb. 13:20; of those who in a future day, at the introduction of the millennial kingdom, have shown kindness to His persecuted earthly people in their great tribulation, Matt. 25:33; of the clothing of false shepherds, Matt. 7:15; (c) figuratively, by way of simile, of Christ, Acts 8:32; of the disciples, e.g., Matt. 10:16; of true followers of Christ in general, Rom. 8:36; of the former wayward condition of those who had come under His Shepherd care, 1 Pet. 2:25; of the multitudes who sought the help of Christ in the days of His flesh, Matt. 9:36; Mark 6:34.

2. *probation* (4263*), a diminutive of No. 1, "a little sheep," is found in the best texts in John 21:16, 17 (some have No. 1); distinct from *arnia*, "lambs" (v. 15), but used as a term of endearment.

SHEET

othone (*3607*) primarily denoted "fine linen," later, "a sheet," Acts 10:11; 11:5.

SHEOL

she'ol (*7585*), "Sheol." First, the word means the state of death," Ps. 6:5; cf. 18:5. It is the final resting place of all men, Job 21:13. "Sheol" is parallel to Hebrew words for "pit" or "hell," Job 26:6, "corruption" or "decay," Ps. 16:10, and "destruction," Prov. 15:11. Second, "Sheol" is used of a place of conscious existence after death, Gen. 37:35. All men go to "Sheol," Ps. 16:10. The wicked receive punishment there, Num. 16:30; Deut. 32:22; Ps. 9:17. They are put to shame and silenced in "Sheol," Ps. 31:17. Jesus alluded to Isaiah's use of *she'ol*, 14:13-15, in pronouncing judgment on Capernaum, Matt. 11:23, translating "Sheol" as "Hades" or "Hell," meaning the place of conscious existence and judgment.

SHEPHERD

Old Testament

A. Verb.

ra'ah (*7462*), "to pasture, shepherd." *ra'ah* represents what a shepherd allows domestic animals to do when they feed on grasses in the fields, Gen. 29:7. *ra'ah* can also represent the entire job of a shepherd, Gen. 37:2. Used metaphorically this verb represents a leader's or a ruler's relationship to his people, 2 Sam. 5:2; fig. to provide nourishment or "to enliven," Prov. 10:21.

ra'ah is used intransitively describing what cattle do when they feed on the grass of the field, Gen. 41:2. This usage is applied metaphorically to men in Isa. 14:30.

B. Nouns.

ro'eh (*7462*), "shepherd." This noun occurs about 62 times in the Old Testament. It is applied to God, the Great Shepherd, who pastures or feeds His sheep, Ps. 23:1-4; cf. John 10:11. This concept of God, the Great Shepherd, is very old, having first appeared in the Bible on Jacob's lips in Gen. 49:24: "From thence is the shepherd, the stone of Israel."

New Testament

poimen (*4166*) is used (a) in its natural significance, Matt. 9:36; 25:32; Mark 6:34; Luke 2:8, 15, 18, 20; John 10:2, 12; (b) metaphorically of Christ, Matt. 26:31; Mark 14:27; John 10:11, 14, 16; Heb. 13:20; 1 Pet. 2:25; (c) metaphorically of those who act as pastors in the churches, Eph. 4:11.

SHEW (SHOW)

1. *deiknumi*, or *deiknuo*, (*1166*) denotes (a) "to show, exhibit," e.g., Matt. 4:8; 8:4; John 5:20; 20:20; 1 Tim. 6:15; (b) "to show by making known," Matt. 16:21; Luke 24:40; John 14:8, 9; Acts 10:28; 1 Cor. 12:31; Rev. 1:1; 4:1; 22:6; (c) "to show by way of proving," Jas. 2:18; 3:13.

2. *anadeiknumi* (*322*) signifies (a) "to lift up and show, show forth, declare" (*ana*, "up," and No. 1), Acts 1:24; (b) to "appoint," Luke 10:1.

3. *endeiknumi* (*1731*) signifies (1) "to show forth, prove" (middle voice), said (a) of God as to His power, Rom. 9:17; His wrath, 9:22; the exceeding riches of His grace, Eph. 2:7; (b) of Christ, as to His longsuffering, 1 Tim. 1:16; (c) of Gentiles, as to "the work of the Law written in their hearts," Rom. 2:15; (d) of believers, as to the proof of their love, 2 Cor. 8:24; all good fidelity, Titus 2:10; meekness, 3:2; love toward God's Name, Heb. 6:10; diligence in ministering to the saints, v. 11; (2) "to manifest by evil acts," 2 Tim. 4:14, "did (me much evil)," marg., "showed."

4. *epideiknumi* (*1925*), *epi*, "upon," intensive, and No. 1, signifies (a) "to exhibit, display," Matt. 16:1; 22:19; 24:1; Luke 17:14 (in some mss. 24:40; No. 1 in the best texts); in the middle voice, "to display," with a special interest in one's own action, Acts 9:39; (b) "to point out, prove, demonstrate," Acts 18:28; Heb. 6:17.

5. *hupodeiknumi* (*5263*), primarily, "to show secretly (*hupo*, 'under'), or by tracing out," hence, "to make known, warn," is translated "to show" in Luke 6:47; Acts 9:16; in 20:35, KJV (RV, "I gave...an example").

SHEWBREAD

The phrase rendered "the shewbread" is formed by the combination of the nouns *prothesis*, "a setting forth" (*pro*, "before," *tithemi*, "to place") and *artos*, "a loaf" (in the plural), each with the article, Matt. 12:4; Mark 2:26 and Luke 6:4, lit., "the loaves of the setting forth"; in Heb. 9:2, lit., "the setting forth of the loaves." The corresponding OT phrases are lit., "bread of the face," Exod. 25:30, i.e., the presence, referring to the Presence of God (cf. Isa. 63:9 with Exod. 33:14, 15); "the bread of ordering," 1 Chron. 9:32, marg. In Num. 4:7 it is called "the continual bread"; in 1 Sam. 21:4, 6, "holy bread" (KJV, "hallowed"). In the Sept. of 1 Kings 7:48, it is called "the bread of the offering" (*prosphora*, "a bearing towards"). The twelve loaves, representing the tribes of Israel, were set in order every Sabbath day before the Lord, "on the behalf of the children," Lev. 24:8, RV (marg., and KJV, "from"), "an everlasting covenant." The loaves symbolized the fact that on the basis of the sacrificial atonement of the Cross, believers are accepted before God, and nourished by Him in the person of Christ. The

S

showbread was partaken of by the priests, as representatives of the nation. Priesthood now being coextensive with all who belong to Christ, 1 Pet. 2:5, 9, He, the Living Bread, is the nourishment of all, and where He is, there, representatively, they are.

SHEWING

anadeixis (323), "a shewing forth" (*ana*, "up or forth," and *deiknumi*, "to show"), is translated "showing" in Luke 1:80.

SHINE, SHINING

A. Verbs.

1. *phaino* (5316), "to cause to appear," denotes, in the active voice, "to give light, shine," John 1:5; 5:35; in Matt. 24:27, passive voice; so Phil. 2:15, RV, "ye are seen" (for KJV, "ye shine"); 2 Pet. 1:19 (active); so 1 John 2:8, Rev. 1:16; in 8:12 and 18:23 (passive); 21:23 (active).

2. *epiphaino* (2014), "to shine upon" (*epi*, "upon," and No. 1), is so translated in Luke 1:79, RV (KJV, "to give light").

3. *lampo* (2989), "to shine as a torch," occurs in Matt. 5:15, 16, 17:2; Luke 17:24; Acts 12:7; 2 Cor. 4:6 (twice).

4. *eklampo* (1584), "to shine forth" (*ek*, "out" and No. 3), is used in Matt. 13:43, of the future shining "forth" of the righteous "in the Kingdom of their Father."

5. *perilampo* (4034), "to shine around" (*peri*, "around," and No. 3), is used in Luke 2:9, "shone round about," of the glory of the Lord; so in Acts 26:13, of the light from Heaven upon Saul of Tarsus.

B. Noun.

astrape (796), denotes (a) "lightning," (b) "bright shining," of a lamp, Luke 11:36.

SHOUT (Noun and Verb)

A. Noun.

keleusma (2752), "a call, summons, shout of command," John 5:28.

B. Verb.

epiphoneo (2019), "to call out" (*epi*, "upon," *phoneo*, "to utter a sound"), is translated "shouted" in Acts 12:22, RV (KJV, "gave a shout").

SHOW (make a)

deigmatizo (1165), "to make a show of, expose," is used in Col. 2:15 of Christ's act regarding the principalities and powers, displaying them "as a victor displays his captives or trophies in a triumphal procession" (Lightfoot). Some regard the meaning as being that He showed the angelic beings in their true inferiority. For its other occurrence, Matt. 1:19.

SHRINE

naos (3485), "the inmost part of a temple, a shrine," is used in the plural in Acts 19:24, of the silver models of the pagan "shrine" in which the image of Diana (Greek Artemis) was preserved. The models were large or small, and were signs of wealth and devotion on the part of purchasers. The variety of forms connected with the embellishment of the image provided "no little business" for the silversmiths.

SHUT, SHUT UP

Old Testament

cagar (5462), "to shut, close, shut up or imprison." The obvious use of this verb is to express the "shutting" of doors and gates, and it is used in this way many times in the text, Gen. 19:10; Josh. 2:7. More specialized uses are: fat closing over the blade of a sword, Judg. 3:22, and closing up a breach in city walls, 1 Kings 11:27. Figuratively, men may "close their hearts to pity," Ps. 17:10. In the books of Samuel, *cagar* is used in the special sense of "to deliver up," implying that all avenues of escape "are closed," 1 Sam. 17:46; cf. 1 Sam. 24:18; 26:8; 2 Sam. 18:28. In Lev. 13-14, in which the priest functions as a medical inspector of contagious diseases, *cagar* is used a number of times in the sense of "to isolate," Lev. 13:5, 11, 21, 26.

New Testament

1. *kleio* (2808) is used (a) of things material, Matt. 6:6; 25:10; Luke 11:7; John 20:19, 26; Acts 5:23; 21:30; Rev. 20:3; figuratively, 21:25; (b) metaphorically, of the kingdom of heaven, Matt. 23:13; of heaven, with consequences of famine, Luke 4:25; Rev. 11:6; of compassion, 1 John 3:17.

2. *apokleio* (608), to shut fast (*apo*, away from, and No. 1), is used in Luke 13:25, expressing the impossibility of entrance after the closing.

3. *katakleio* (2623), lit., to shut down" (the *kata* has, however, an intensive use), signifies "to shut up in confinement," Luke 3:20; Acts 26:10.

SICK, SICKLY, SICKNESS

Old Testament

A. Verb.

chalah (2470), "to be sick, weak." A meaning of *chalah* is physical weakness, Judg. 16:7; or being in a wounded state, 2 Kings 8:29;

S

or not top-quality livestock, Mal. 1:8. This word is sometimes used in the figurative sense of overexerting oneself, thus becoming "weak," Jer. 12:13; or even "love-sick," Song of Sol. 2:5.

B. Noun.

choli (2483), "sickness." The use of this word in the description of the Suffering Servant in Isa. 53:3-4 has resulted in various translations. The RSV, KJV, and NASB render it "grief." It is "sufferings" in the NEB, JB, TEV and "infirmity" in the NAB. The meaning of "sickness" occurs in Deut. 7:15.

New Testament

A. Verb.

astheneo (770), lit., "to be weak, feeble" (*a*, negative, *sthenos*, "strength"), is translated "to be sick," e.g., in Matt. 10:8, "(the) sick"; 25:36; v. 39 in the best texts (some have B); Mark 6:56; Luke 4:40; 7:10 (RV omits the word); 9:2; John 4:46; 5:3, RV (KJV, "impotent folk"); v. 7; 6:2, RV (KJV, "were diseased"); 11:1-3, 6; Acts 9:37; 19:12; Phil. 2:26, 27; 2 Tim. 4:20; Jas. 5:14.

B. Adjective.

asthenes (772), lit., "without strength," hence, "feeble, weak," is used of "bodily debility," Matt. 25:43 (for v. 39, see A, No. 1), 44; some texts have it in Luke 9:2 (the best omit it, the meaning being "to heal" in general); 10:9; Acts 5:15, 16; in 4:9 it is rendered "impotent."

C. Noun.

astheneia (769), "weakness, sickness" (akin to A and B), is translated "sickness" in John 11:4.

SIGH

1. *stenazo* (4727), "to groan," is translated "He sighed" in Mark 7:34.

2. *anastenazo* (389), "to sigh deeply" (*ana*, "up," suggesting "deep drawn," and No. 1), occurs in Mark 8:12.

SIGHT (verb)

anablepo (308), "to look up," also denotes "to receive or recover sight" (akin to A, No. 5), e.g., Matt. 11:5; 20:34; Mark 10:51, 52; Luke 18:41-43; John 9:11, 15, 18 (twice); Acts 9:12, 17, 18; 22:13.

SIGN

Old Testament

'ot (226), "sign; mark." This word represents something by which a person or group is characteristically marked, i.e., a symbol or signal that has meaning, without necessarily using verbal words,

Gen. 4:15; Exod. 8:23; Num. 2:2; Josh. 2:12, 18. The word also means "sign" as a reminder of one's duty, Gen. 9:12. In passages such as Exod. 4:8 *'ot* represents a miraculous "sign," as an act of power signaling God's deliverance, cf. Deut. 13:1-5. Several passages use *'ot* of omens and/or indications of future events, 1 Sam. 14:10; or "warning sign," Num. 16:38.

New Testament

semeion (4592), "a sign, mark, indication, token," is used (a) of that which distinguished a person or thing from others, e.g., Matt. 26:48; Luke 2:12; Rom. 4:11; 2 Cor. 12:12 (1st part); 2 Thess. 3:17, "token," i.e., his autograph attesting the authenticity of his letters; (b) of a "sign" as a warning or admonition, e.g., Matt. 12:39, "the sign of (i.e., consisting of) the prophet Jonas"; 16:4; Luke 2:34; 11:29, 30; (c) of miraculous acts (1) as tokens of divine authority and power, e.g., Matt. 12:38, 39 (1st part); John 2:11, RV, "signs"; 3:2 (ditto); 4:54, "(the second) sign," RV; 10:41 (ditto); 20:30; in 1 Cor. 1:22, "the Jews ask for signs," RV, indicates that the Apostles were met with the same demand <u>from Jews as Christ</u> had been: "signs were vouchsafed in plenty, signs of God's power and love, but these were not the signs which they sought....They wanted signs of an outward Messianic Kingdom, of temporal triumph, of material greatness for the chosen people.... With such cravings the Gospel of a 'crucified Messiah' was to them a stumblingblock indeed" (Lightfoot); 1 Cor. 14:22; (2) by demons, Rev. 16:14; (3) by false teachers or prophets, indications of assumed authority, e.g., Matt. 24:24; Mark 13:22; (4) by Satan through his special agents, 2 Thess. 2:9; Rev. 13:13, 14; 19:20; (d) of tokens portending future events, e. g., Matt. 24:3, where "the sign of the Son of Man" signifies, subjectively, that the Son of Man is Himself the "sign" of what He is about to do; Mark 13:4; Luke 21:7, 11, 25; Acts 2:19; Rev. 12:1, RV; 12:3, RV; 15:1.

SIGNS (to make)

enneuo (1770), "to nod to" (*en*, "in," *neuo*, "to nod"), denotes "to make a sign to" in Luke 1:62.

SIGNIFY

semaino (4591), "to give a sign, indicate," "to signify," is so translated in John 12:33; 18:32; 21:19; Acts 11:28; 25:27; Rev. 1:1, where perhaps the suggestion is that of expressing by signs.

SILENCE

A. Noun.

sige (4602) occurs in Acts 21:40; Rev. 8:1, where the "silence" is introductory to the judgments following the opening of the seventh seal.

B. Verb.

phimoo (5392), "to muzzle," is rendered "to put to silence" in Matt. 22:34; 1 Pet. 2:15.

SILVER

A. Noun.

keseph (3701), "silver; money; price; property." This refers to the precious metal which comes from the earth. It can mean unprocessed "metal ore silver," Prov. 25:4; cf. Job 28:1; or refined silver from ore, in jewelry, bars, lumps, etc., as a form of wealth and exchange, Gen. 24:53; 1 Kings 10:21; Lev. 25:50. *keseph* sometimes represents the color "silver," Ps. 68:13.

SIN (Noun and Verb)

Old Testament

A. Nouns.

'awen (205), "iniquity; vanity; sorrow." *'awen* may be a general term for a crime or offense, Micah 2:1. In some passages, the word refers to falsehood or deception, Ps. 36:3; Zech. 10:2.

'asham (817), "sin; guilt; guilt offering; trespass; trespass offering." *'asham* implies the condition of "guilt" incurred through some wrongdoing, Gen. 26:10. The word may also refer to the offense itself which entails the guilt, Jer. 51:5; Ps. 68:21.

Most occurrences of *'asham* refer to the compensation given to satisfy someone who has been injured, or to the "trespass offering" or "guilt offering" presented on the altar by the repentant offender after paying a compensation of six-fifths of the damage inflicted, Num. 5:7-8. The "trespass offering" was the blood sacrifice of a ram, Lev. 5:18; cf. Lev. 7:5, 7; 14:12-13.

'amal (5999), "evil; trouble; misfortune; mischief; grievance; wickedness; labor." In general, *'amal* refers either to the trouble and suffering which sin causes the sinner or to the trouble that he inflicts upon others. Jer. 20:18 depicts self-inflicted sorrow, cf. also Deut. 26:7.

'awon (5771), "iniquity." *'awon* portrays sin as a perversion of life (a twisting out of the right way), a perversion of truth (a twisting into error), or a perversion of intent (a bending of rectitude into willful disobedience). The word "iniquity" is the best single-word equivalent, although the Latin root *iniquitas* really means "injustice; unfairness; hostile; adverse." *'awon* occurs frequently throughout the Old Testament in parallelism with other words related to sin, such as *chatta't* ("sin") and *pesha'* ("transgression"). Some examples are 1 Sam. 20:1: "And David...said before Jona-

than, what have I done? what is mine iniquity [*'awon*]? and what is my sin [*chatta't*] before thy father, that he seeketh my life?" cf. Isa. 43:24; Jer. 5:25. Also note Job 14:17: "My transgression [*pesha'*] is sealed up in a bag, and thou sewest up mine iniquity [*'awon*]," cf. Ps. 107:17; Isa. 50:1.

The penitent wrongdoer recognized his "iniquity," Isa. 59:12; cf. 1 Sam. 3:13. "Iniquity" is something to be confessed, Lev. 16:21; Neh. 9:2; cf. Ps. 38:18. The grace of God may remove or forgive "iniquity": "And unto him he said, Behold, I have caused thine iniquity to pass from thee..." Zech. 3:4; cf. 2 Sam. 24:10. His atonement may cover over "iniquity": "By mercy and truth iniquity is purged; and by the fear of the Lord men depart from evil," Prov. 16:6; cf. Ps. 78:38.

rasha' (7563), "wicked; criminal; guilty." *rasha'* generally connotes a turbulence and restlessness, cf. Isa. 57:21, or something disjointed or ill-regulated. In some instances, *rasha'* carries the sense of being "guilty of crime": "Thou shalt not raise a false report: put not thine hand with the wicked to be an unrighteous witness," Exod. 23:1; "Take away the wicked from before the king, and his throne shall be established in righteousness," Prov. 25:5. "An ungodly witness scorneth judgment: and the mouth of the *wicked* [plural form] devoureth iniquity," Prov. 19:28; cf. Prov. 20:26 The *rasha'* is guilty of hostility to God and His people, Ps. 7:9; 17:13; Isa. 13:11; Hab. 1:13.

chatta't (2403), "sin; sin-guilt; sin-purification; sin offering." The basic nuance of this word is "sin" conceived as missing the road or mark (155 times). *chatta't* can refer to an offense against a man, Gen. 31:36. It is such passages which prove that *chatta't* is not simply a general word for "sin"; since Jacob used two different words, he probably intended two different nuances. In addition, a full word study shows basic differences between *chatta't* and other words rendered "sin." For the most part this word represents a sin against God, Lev. 4:14. Men are to return from "sin," which is a path, a life-style, or act deviating from that which God has marked out, 1 Kings 8:35. They should depart from "sin," 2 Kings 10:31, be concerned about it, Ps. 38:18, and confess it, Num. 5:7. The noun first appears in Gen. 4:7, where Cain is warned that "sin lieth at the door."

chatta't means "sin offering.". The law of the "sin offering" is recorded in Lev. 4-5:13; 6:24-30. This was an offering for some specific "sin" committed unwittingly, without intending to do it and perhaps even without knowing it at the time (Lev. 4:2; 5:15).

chet', means "sin" in the sense of missing the mark or the path. This may be sin against either a man, Gen. 41:9; or God, Deut. 9:18. Second, it connotes the "guilt" of such an act, Num. 27:3.

S

B. Adjectives.

rasha' (7563), "wicked; guilty," Deut. 25:2, this word refers to a person "guilty of a crime," Jer. 5:26. *rasha'* is used specifically of murderers in 2 Sam. 4:11.

ra' (7451), "bad; evil; wicked; sore." *ra'* refers to that which is "bad" or "evil," in a wide variety of applications. A greater number of the word's occurrences signify something morally evil or hurtful, often referring to man or men: "Then answered all the wicked men and men of Belial, of those that went with David..." 1 Sam. 30:22; Esth. 7:6; Job 35:12; cf. Ps. 10:15. *ra'* is also used to denote evil words, Prov. 15:26, evil thoughts, Gen. 6:5, or evil actions, Deut. 17:5, Neh. 13:17. Ezek. 6:11 depicts grim consequences for Israel as a result of its actions.

In less frequent uses, *ra'* implies severity, Ezek. 14:21; cf. Deut. 6:22; unpleasantness, Deut. 7:15; cf. Deut. 28:59; deadliness, Ezek. 5:16; cf. "hurtful sword," Ps. 144:10; or sadness, Neh. 2:2. The word may also refer to something of poor or inferior quality, such as "bad" land, Num. 13:19, "naughty" figs, Jer. 24:2, "ill-favored" cattle, Gen. 41:3, 19, or a "bad" sacrificial animal, Lev. 27:10, 12, 14.

C. Verbs.

'abar (5674), "to transgress, cross over, pass over." This word occurs as a verb only when it refers to sin. *'abar* often carries the sense of "transgressing" a covenant or commandment—i.e., the offender "passes beyond" the limits set by God's law and falls into transgression and guilt. This meaning appears in Num. 14:41: "And Moses said, wherefore now do ye transgress the commandment of the Lord? but it shall not prosper." Another example is in Judg. 2:20: "And the anger of the Lord was hot against Israel; and he said, Because that this people hath transgressed my covenant which I commanded their fathers, and have not hearkened unto my voice," cf. 1 Sam. 15:24; Hos. 8:1.

Most frequently, *'abar* illustrates the motion of "crossing over" or "passing over." (The Latin *transgredior*, from which we get our English word *transgress*, has the similar meaning of "go beyond" or "cross over.") This word refers to crossing a stream or boundage, "pass through," Num. 21:22, invading a country, "passed over," Judg. 11:32, crossing a boundary as a hostile army, "go over," 1 Sam. 14:4, marching over, "go over," Isa. 51:23, overflowing the banks of a river or other natural barriers, "pass through," Isa. 23:10, passing a razor over one's head, "come upon," Num. 6:5, and the passing of time "went over," 1 Chron. 29:30.

chata' (2398), "to miss, sin, be guilty, forfeit, purify." The basic meaning of this verb "to miss aim," is illustrated in Judg. 20:16.

From this basic meaning comes the word's chief usage to indicate moral failure toward both God and men, and certain results of such wrongs. The first occurrence of the verb is in Gen. 20:6,

God's word to Abimelech after he had taken Sarah: "Yes, I know that in the integrity of your heart you have done this, and also I have kept you from sinning against Me," NASB; cf. Gen. 39:9.

Sin against God is defined in Josh. 7:11· "Israel hath sinned, and they have also transgressed my covenant which I commanded them...." Also note Lev. 4:27: "And if any one of the common people sin through ignorance, while he doeth somewhat against any of the commandments of the Lord concerning things which ought not to be done, and be guilty." The verb may also refer to the result of wrongdoing, as in Gen. 43:9: "then let me bear the blame for ever." Deut. 24:1-4, after forbidding adulterous marriage practices, concludes: "for that is abomination before the Lord: and thou shalt not cause the land to sin..." (KJV); the RSV renders this passage: "You shall not bring guilt upon the land." Similarly, those who pervert justice are described as "those who by a word make a man out to be guilty," Isa. 29:21, NIV. This leads to the meaning in Lev. 9:15: "And he...took the goat... and slew it, and offered it for sin." The effect of the offerings for sin is described in Ps. 51:7: "Purge me with hyssop, and I shall be clean"; cf. Num. 19:1-13.

New Testament

A. Noun.

hamartia (*266*) is, lit., "a missing of the mark," but this etymological meaning is largely lost sight of in the NT. It is the most comprehensive term for moral obliquity. It is used of "sin" as (a) a principle or source of action, or an inward element producing acts, e.g., Rom. 3:9; 5:12, 13, 20; 6:1, 2; 7:7 (abstract for concrete); 7:8 (twice), 9, 11, 13, "sin, that it might be shown to be sin," i.e., "sin became death to me, that it might be exposed in its heinous character": in the last clause, "sin might become exceeding sinful," i.e., through the holiness of the Law, the true nature of sin was designed to be manifested to the conscience;

(b) a governing principle or power, e.g., Rom. 6:6, "(the body) of sin," here "sin" is spoken of as an organized power, acting through the members of the body, though the seat of "sin" is in the will (the body is the organic instrument); in the next clause, and in other passages, as follows, this governing principle is personified, e.g., Rom. 5:21; 6:12, 14, 17; 7:11, 14, 17, 20, 23, 25; 8:2; 1 Cor. 15:56; Heb. 3:13; 11:25; 12:4; Jas. 1:15 (2nd part);

(c) a generic term (distinct from specific terms such as No. 2 yet sometimes inclusive of concrete wrong doing, e.g., John 8:21, 34, 46; 9:41; 15:22, 24; 19:11); in Rom. 8:3, "God, sending His own Son in the likeness of sinful flesh," lit., "flesh of sin," the flesh stands for the body, the instrument of indwelling "sin" [Christ, pre-existently the Son of God, assumed human flesh, "of the substance of the Virgin Mary"; the reality of incarnation was His, without taint of sin, and *as an offering* for sin," i.e., "a sin offering," "condemned

S

sin in the flesh," i.e., Christ, having taken human nature, "sin" apart (Heb. 4:15), and having lived a sinless life, died under the condemnation and judgment due to our "sin"; for the generic sense see further, e.g., Heb. 9:26; 10:6, 8, 18; 13:11; 1 John 1:7, 8; 3:4 (1st part; in the 2nd part, "sin" is defined as "lawlessness," RV), 8, 9; in these verses the KJV use of the verb to commit is misleading; not the committal of an act is in view, but a continuous course of "sin," as indicated by the RV, "doeth." The apostle's use of the present tense of *poieo*, "to do," virtually expresses the meaning of *prasso*, "to practice," which John does not use (it is not infrequent in this sense in Paul's Epp., e.g., Rom. 1:32, RV; 2:1; Gal. 5:21; Phil. 4:9); 1 Pet. 4:1 (singular in the best texts), lit., "has been made to cease from sin," i.e., as a result of suffering in the flesh, the mortifying of our members, and of obedience to a Savior who suffered in flesh. Such no longer lives in the flesh, "to the lusts of men, but to the will of God"; sometimes the word is used as virtually equivalent to a condition of "sin," e.g., John 1:29, "the sin (not sins) of the world"; 1 Cor. 15:17; or a course of "sin," characterized by continuous acts, e.g., 1 Thess. 2:16; in 1 John 5:16 (2nd part) the RV marg., is probably to be preferred, "there is sin unto death," not a special act of "sin," but the state or condition producing acts; in v. 17, "all unrighteousness is sin" is not a definition of "sin" (as in 3:4), it gives a specification of the term in its generic sense;

(d) a sinful deed, an act of "sin," e.g., Matt. 12:31; Acts 7:60; Jas. 1:15 (1st part); 2:9; 4:17; 5:15, 20; 1 John 5:16 (1st part).

B. Verb.

hamartano (264), lit., "to miss the mark," is used in the NT (a) of "sinning" against God, (1) by angels, 2 Pet. 2:4; (2) by man, Matt. 27:4; Luke 15:18, 21 (heaven standing, by metonymy, for God); John 5:14; 8:11; 9:2, 3; Rom. 2:12 (twice); 3:23; 5:12, 14, 16; 6:15; 1 Cor. 7:28 (twice), 36; 15:34; Eph. 4:26; 1 Tim. 5:20; Titus 3:11; Heb. 3:17; 10:26; 1 John 1:10; in 2:1 (twice), the aorist tense in each place, referring to an act of "sin"; on the contrary, in 3:6 (twice), 8, 9, the present tense indicates, not the committal of an act, but the continuous practice of "sin"; in 5:16 (twice) the present tense indicates the condition resulting from an act, "unto death" signifying "tending towards death"; (b) against Christ, 1 Cor. 8:12; (c) against man, (1) a brother, Matt. 18:15, RV, "sin" (KJV, "trespass"); v. 21; Luke 17:3, 4, RV, "sin" (KJV, "trespass"); 1 Cor. 8:12; (2) in Luke 15:18, 21, against the father by the Prodigal Son, "in thy sight" being suggestive of befitting reverence; (d) against Jewish law, the Temple, and Caesar, Acts 25:8, RV, "sinned" (KJV, "offended"); (e) against one's own body, by fornication, 1 Cor. 6:18; (f) against earthly masters by servants, 1 Pet. 2:20, RV, "(when) ye sin (and are buffeted for it)," KJV, "(when) ye be buffeted) for your faults," lit., "having sinned."

SINCERE, SINCERELY, SINCERITY

A. Adjectives.

1. *adolos* (*97*), "guileless, pure," is translated "sincere" in 1 Pet. 2:2, KJV, "without guile," RV.

2. *gnesios* (*1103*), "true, genuine, sincere," is used in the neuter, as a noun, with the article, signifying "sincerity," 2 Cor. 8:8 (of love).

B. Adverb.

hagnos (*55*) denotes "with pure motives," is rendered "sincerely" in Phil. 1:17, RV (v. 16, KJV).

C. Noun.

eilikrinia (or —*eia*) (*1505*), denotes "sincerity, purity"; it is described metaphorically in 1 Cor. 5:8 as "unleavened (bread)"; in 2 Cor. 1:12, "sincerity (of God)," RV, KJV, "(godly) sincerity," it describes a quality possessed by God, as that which is to characterize the conduct of believers; in 2 Cor. 2:17 it is used of the rightful ministry of the Scriptures.

SINFUL

hamartolos (*268*), an adjective, akin to *hamartano*, "to sin," is used as an adjective, "sinful" in Mark 8:38; Luke 5:8; 19:7; 24:7; John 9:16, 24; Rom. 7:13.

SING, SINGING

Old Testament

A. Verbs.

ranan (*7442*), "to sing, shout, cry out." *ranan* is often used to express joy, exultation, which seems to demand loud singing, especially when it is praise to God, Isa. 12:6); cries aloud, Prov. 8:3; shout for joy, Ps. 32:11.

shir (*7891*), "to sing." Over one quarter of the instances of *shir* are found in the Book of Psalms, often in the imperative form, calling the people to express their praise to God in singing, Ps. 96:1. Frequently *shir* is found in parallelism with *zamar*, "to sing," Ps. 68:4, 32.

B. Participle.

shir (*7891*), "singers"; Levitical "singers," 1 Chron. 15:16; female singers, 2 Sam. 19:35; 2 Chron. 35:25; Eccl. 2:8.

C. Noun.

shir (*7892*), "song." *shir* is used of a joyous, triumphal, religious, "song" in Gen. 31:27; Judg. 5:12; Neh. 12:46. The book that is com-

S

monly designated "The Song of Solomon" actually has the title "The Song of Songs" in Hebrew.

New Testament

ado (*103*) is used always of "praise to God," (a) intransitively, Eph. 5:19; Col. 3:16; (b) transitively, Rev. 5:9; 14:3; 15:3.

SINGLE

haplous (*573*), "simple, single," is used in a moral sense in Matt. 6:22 and Luke 11:34, said of the eye; "singleness" of purpose keeps us from the snare of having a double treasure and consequently a divided heart.

SINGLENESS

aphelotes (*858*) denotes "simplicity," Acts 2:46; the idea here is that of an unalloyed benevolence expressed in act.

SINNER

hamartolos (*268*), lit., "one who misses the mark" (a meaning not to be pressed), is an adjective, most frequently used as a noun; it is the most usual term to describe the fallen condition of men; it is applicable to all men, Rom. 5:8, 19. In the Synoptic Gospels the word is used not infrequently, by the Pharisees, of publicans (tax collectors) and women of ill repute, e.g., "a woman which was in the city, a sinner," Luke 7:37; "a man that is a sinner," 19:7. In Gal. 2:15, in the clause "not sinners of the Gentiles," the apostle is taking the Judaizers on their own ground, ironically reminding them of their claim to moral superiority over Gentiles; he proceeds to show that the Jews are equally sinners with Gentiles.

SISTER

Old Testament

'achot (*269*), "sister." *'achot* can mean a female sibling, Gen. 4:22; or one's half-sister, Gen. 20:12; or aunt on the father's side, Lev. 18:12; 20:19; or on the mother's side, Lev. 18:13; 20:19. The use of *'achot* more generally denotes female relatives, Gen. 24:60. This meaning lies behind the metaphorical use, where two divisions of a nation, i.e., Judah and Israel; Jer. 3:7, and two cities, i.e., Sodom and Samaria; Ezek. 16:46, are portrayed as sisters—Hebrew names of geographical entities are feminine. The more specialized meaning "beloved" is found only in Song of Sol. 4:9.

New Testament

adelphe (*79*) is used (a) of natural relationship, e.g., Matt. 19:29; of the "sisters" of Christ, the children of Joseph and Mary after the virgin birth of Christ, e.g., Matt. 13:56; (b) of "spiritual kinship" with Christ, an affinity marked by the fulfillment of the will of the

Father, Matt. 12:50; Mark 3:35; of spiritual relationship based upon faith in Christ, Rom. 16:1; 1 Cor. 7:15; 9:5, KJV and RV marg.; Jas. 2:15; Philem. 2, RV.

SLACK (Verb), SLACKNESS

A. Verb.

braduno (*1019*), used intransitively signifies "to be slow, to tarry" (*bradus*, "slow"), said negatively of God, 2 Pet. 3:9, "is (not) slack"; in 1 Tim. 3:15, translated "(if) I tarry."

B. Noun.

bradutes (*1022*), "slowness" (akin to A), is rendered "slackness" in 2 Pet. 3:9.

SLANDERER

diabolos (*1228*), an adjective, "slanderous, accusing falsely," 1 Tim. 3:11; 2 Tim. 3:3; Titus 2:3.

SLAUGHTER

Old Testament

A. Verb.

zabach (*2076*), "to slaughter, sacrifice." This word often means to kill an animal, for the use of making a sacrifice to God, Exod. 20:24. While there were grain and incense offerings prescribed as part of the Mosaic laws dealing with sacrifice, see Lev. 2, the primary kind of sacrifice was the blood offering which required the slaughter of an animal, cf. Deut. 17:1; 1 Chron. 15:26. *zabach* is also used as a term for "slaughter for eating," 1 Kings 19:21.

B. Nouns.

zebach (*2077*), "sacrifice." This noun occurs more than 160 times in biblical Hebrew. The "sacrifice" which was part of a covenant ritual involved the sprinkling of the blood on the people and upon the altar, which presumably symbolized God as the covenant partner, see Exod. 24:6-8. Another special "sacrifice" was "the sacrifice of the feast of the Passover," Exod. 34:25. In this case the sacrificial lamb provided the main food for the Passover meal, and its blood was sprinkled on the doorposts of the Israelite homes as a sign to the death angel.

The "sacrifice" of animals was in no way unique to Israelite religion, for sacrificial rituals generally are part of all ancient religious cults. Indeed, the mechanics of the ritual were quite similar, especially between Israelite and Canaanite religions. However, the differences are very clear in the meanings which the rituals had as they were performed either to capricious Canaanite gods or for the one true God who kept His covenant with Israel. The

S

noun *zebach* is used of "sacrifices" to the one true God in Gen. 46:1, cf. Exod. 10:25; Neh. 12:43. The noun refers to "sacrifices" to other deities in Exod. 34:15. cf. Num. 25:2; 2 Kings 10:19. The idea of "sacrifice" certainly is taken over into the New Testament, for Christ became "the Lamb of God, who takes away the sin of the world," John 1:29, RSV. The writer of Hebrews makes much of the fact that with the "sacrifice" of Christ, no more sacrifices are necessary, Heb. 9.

mizbeach (4196), "altar." Frequent use is obviously another direct evidence of the centrality of the sacrificial system in Israel. The first appearance of *mizbeach* is in Gen. 8:20, where Noah built an "altar" after the Flood. Countless "altars" are referred to as the story of Israel progresses on the pages of the Old Testament: that of Noah, Gen. 8:20; of Abram at Sichem, Gen. 12:7, at Beth-el, Gen. 12:8, and at Moriah, Gen. 22:9; of Isaac at Beersheba, Gen. 26:25; of Jacob at Shechem, Gen. 33:20; of Moses at Horeb, Exod. 24:4, of Samuel at Ramah, 1 Sam. 7:17; of the temple in Jerusalem, 1 Kings 6:20; 8:64; and of the two "altars" planned by Ezekiel for the restored temple, Ezek. 41:22; 43:13-17.

New Testament

sphage (4967) is used in two quotations from the Sept., Acts 8:32 from Isa. 53:7, and Rom. 8:36 from Ps. 44:22; in the latter the quotation is set in a strain of triumph, the passage quoted being an utterance of sorrow. In Jas. 5:5 there is an allusion to Jer. 12:3, the luxurious rich, getting wealth by injustice, spending it on their pleasures, are "fattening themselves like sheep unconscious of their doom."

SLAVE

soma (4983), "a body," is translated "slaves" in Rev. 18:13 (RV and KJV marg., "bodies"), an intimation of the unrighteous control over the bodily activities of "slaves"; the next word "souls" stands for the whole being.

SLAY, SLAIN, SLEW

1. *apokteino* (615), the usual word for "to kill," is so translated in the RV wherever possible (e.g., for KJV, "to slay," in Luke 11:49; Acts 7:52; Rev. 2:13; 9:15; 11:13; 19:21); in the following the verb "to kill" would not be appropriate, Rom. 7:11, "slew," metaphorically of sin, as using the commandment; Eph. 2:16, "having slain," said metaphorically of the enmity between Jew and Gentile.

2. *anaireo* (337), "to take away, destroy, kill," is rendered "to slay" in Matt. 2:16; Acts 2:23; 5:33, 36; 9:29, KJV (RV, "to kill"); 10:39; 13:28; 22:20; 23:15, RV; in 2 Thess. 2:8 the best texts have this verb (for *analisko*, "to consume," KJV and RV marg.); hence the RV, "shall slay," of the destruction of the man of sin.

3. *sphazo* or *sphatto* (*4969*), "to slay," especially of victims for sacrifice, is used (a) of taking human life, 1 John 3:12 (twice); Rev. 6:4, RV, "slay" (KJV, "kill"), in 13:3, probably of assassination, RV, "smitten (unto death)," KJV, "wounded (to death)," RV marg., "slain"; 18:24; (b) of Christ, as the Lamb of sacrifice, Rev. 5:6, 9, 12; 6:9; 13:8.

4. *katasphazo* (*2695v*), "to kill off" (*kata*, used intensively, and No. 3), is used in Luke 19:27.

SLEIGHT

kubia (or —*eia*) (*2940*) denotes "dice playing"; hence, metaphorically, "trickery, sleight," Eph. 4:14. The Eng. word is connected with "sly" ("not with slight").

SLOTHFUL

1. *nothros* (*3576*), "indolent, sluggish," is rendered "slothful" in Heb. 6:12, KJV.

2. *okneros* (*3636*), "shrinking, irksome," is translated "slothful" in Matt. 25:26, and Rom. 12:11, where "in diligence not slothful," RV, might be rendered "not flagging in zeal."

SLOW

bradus (*1021*) is used twice in Jas. 1:19, in an exhortation to "be slow to speak" and "slow to wrath"; in Luke 24:25, metaphorically of the understanding.

SLUGGISH

nothros (*3576*), translated "sluggish" in Heb. 6:12, RV; here it is set in contrast to confident and constant hope; in 5:11 ("dull") to vigorous growth in knowledge.

SLUMBER (Verb)

nustazo (*3573*) denotes "to nod in sleep" (akin to *neuo*, "to nod"), "fall asleep," and is used (a) of natural slumber, Matt. 25:5; (b) metaphorically in 2 Pet. 2:3, negatively, of the destruction awaiting false teachers.

SMITE

1. *patasso* (*3960*), "to strike, smite," is used (I) literally, of giving a blow with the hand, or fist or a weapon, Matt. 26:51, RV, "smote" (KJV, "struck"); Luke 22:49, 50; Acts 7:24; 12:7; (II) metaphorically, (a) of judgment meted out to Christ, Matt. 26:31; Mark 14:27; (b) of the infliction of disease, by an angel, Acts 12:23; of plagues to be inflicted upon men by two divinely appointed witnesses, Rev. 11:6; (c) of judgment to be executed by Christ upon the nations, Rev. 19:15, the instrument being His Word, described as a sword.

S

2. *tupto* (*5180*), "to strike, smite, beat," is rendered "to smite" in Matt. 24:49, KJV (RV, "beat"); 27:30; Mark 15:19; Luke 6:29; 18:13; in some texts in 22:64 (1st part: RV omits; for the 2nd part see No. 3); 23:48; Acts 23:2, 3 (twice).

3. *paio* (*3817*) signifies "to strike or smite" (a) with the hand or fist, Matt. 26:68; Luke 22:64 (see No. 2); (b) with a sword, Mark 14:47; John 18:10, KJV (RV, "struck"); (c) with a sting, Rev. 9:5, "striketh."

4. *dero* (*1194*), "to flay, to beat," akin to *derma*, "skin," is translated "to smite" in Luke 22:63, KJV (RV, "beat"); John 18:23; 2 Cor. 11:20.

6. *rhapizo* (*4474*), primarily "to strike with a rod" (*rhapis*, "a rod"), then, "to strike the face with the palm of the hand or the clenched fist," is used in Matt. 5:39; 26:67, where the marg. of KJV and RV has "with rods."

7. *sphazo* (*4969*), "to slay," is translated "smitten unto death" in Rev. 13:3.

SMOOTH

leois (*3006*), "smooth," occurs in Luke 3:5, figurative of the change in Israel from self-righteousness, pride and other forms of evil, to repentance, humility and submission.

SNARE

1. *pagis* (*3803*), "a trap, a snare" (akin to *pegnumi*, "to fix," and *pagideuo*, "to ensnare," which see), is used metaphorically of (a) the allurements to evil by which the Devil "ensnares" one, 1 Tim. 3:7; 2 Tim. 2:26; (b) seductions to evil, which "ensnare" those who "desire to be rich," 1 Tim. 6:9; (c) the evil brought by Israel upon themselves by which the special privileges divinely granted them and centering in Christ, became a "snare" to them, their rejection of Christ and the Gospel being the retributive effect of their apostasy, Rom. 11:9; (d) of the sudden judgments of God to come upon those whose hearts are "overcharged with surfeiting, and drunkenness, and cares of this life," Luke 21:34 (v. 35 in KJV).

2. *brochos* (*1029*), "a noose, slipknot, halter," is used metaphorically in 1 Cor. 7:35, "a snare" (RV, marg., "constraint," "noose").

SOBER, SOBERLY, SOBERMINDED

A. Adjective.

sophron (*4998*) denotes "of sound mind" (*sozo*, "to save," *phren*, "the mind"); hence, "self-controlled, soberminded," always rendered "sober-minded" in the RV; in 1 Tim. 3:2 and Titus 1:8, KJV, "sober"; in Titus 2:2, KJV, "temperate"; in 2:5, KJV, "discreet."

B. Verbs.

1. *nepho* (*3525*) signifies "to be free from the influence of intoxi-

cants"; in the NT, metaphorically, it does not in itself imply watchfulness, but is used in association with it, 1 Thess. 5:6, 8; 2 Tim. 4:5; 1 Pet. 1:13; 4:7, RV (KJV, "watch"); 5:8.

2. *sophroneo* (*4993*), akin to A, is rendered "to think soberly," Rom. 12:3; "to be sober," 2 Cor. 5:13; "to be soberminded," Titus 2:6; in 1 Pet. 4:7, KJV "be ye sober" (RV, "of sound mind").

3. *sophronizo* (*4994*) denotes "to cause to be of sound mind, to recall to one's senses"; in Titus 2:4, RV, it is rendered "they may train" (KJV, "they may teach...to be sober," marg., "wise"); "train" expresses the meaning more adequately; the training would involve the cultivation of sound judgment and prudence.

SOBERNESS, SOBRIETY

sophrosune (*4997*) denotes "soundness of mind," Acts 26:25, "soberness"; 1 Tim. 2:9, 15, "sobriety."

SOJOURN, SOJOURNER, SOJOURNING

Old Testament

A. Verb.

gur (*1481*), "to dwell as a client, sojourn." This verb means "to dwell in a land as a client." The first occurrence of the word is in Gen. 12:10, where it is reported that Abram journeyed to Egypt and dwelt there as a client, Gen. 21:23.

B. Nouns.

ger (*1616*), "client; stranger." A "client" was not simply a foreigner (*nakri*) or a stranger (*zar*). He was a permanent resident, once a citizen of another land, who had moved into his new residence. Frequently he left his homeland under some distress, as when Moses fled to Midian, Exod. 2:22. Whether the reason for his journey was to escape some difficulty or merely to seek a new place to dwell, he was one who sought acceptance and refuge. Consequently he might also call himself a *toshab*, a settler. Neither the settler nor the "client" could possess land. In the land of Canaan the possession of land was limited to members or descendants of the original tribal members. Only they were full citizens who enjoyed all the rights of citizenry, which meant sharing fully in the inheritance of the gods and forefathers—the feudal privileges and responsibilities, cf. Ezek. 47:22.

In Israel a *ger*, like a priest, could possess no land and enjoyed the special privileges of the third tithe. Every third year the tithe of the harvest was to be deposited at the city gate with the elders and distributed among those in need, Deut. 14:29. In the eschaton such "clients" were to be treated as full citizens. Ezek. 47:22. Under the Mosaic law aliens were not slaves but were usually in the service of some Israelite whose protection they enjoyed, Deut.

S

24:14. This, however, was not always the case. Sometimes a "client" was rich and an Israelite would be in his service, Lev. 25:47.

The *ger* was to be treated (except for feudal privileges and responsibilities) as an Israelite, being responsible to and protected by the law, Deut. 1:16; Lev. 18:26; Lev. 24:22. The *ger* also enjoyed the Sabbath rest, Lev. 25:6, and divine protection, Deut. 10:18. God commanded Israel to love the "client" as himself, Lev. 19:34.

New Testament

A. Verb.

paroikeo (3939) denotes "to dwell beside, among or by" (*para*, "beside," *oikeo*, "to dwell"); then, "to dwell in a place as a *paroikos*, a stranger," Luke 24:18, RV, "Dost thou (alone) sojourn...?" [marg., "Dost thou sojourn (alone)" is preferable], KJV, "art thou (only) a stranger?" (*monos*, "alone," is an adjective, not an adverb); in Heb. 11:9, RV, "he became a sojourner" (KJV, "he sojourned"), the RV gives the force of the aorist tense.

B. Adjective.

paroikos (3941), an adjective, akin to A, No. 1, lit., "dwelling near" (see above), then, "foreign, alien" (found with this meaning in inscriptions), hence, as a noun, "a sojourner," is used with *eimi*, "to be," in Acts 7:6, "should sojourn," lit., "should be a sojourner"; in 7:29, RV, "sojourner" (KJV, "stranger"); in Eph. 2:19, RV, "sojourners" (KJV, "foreigners"), the preceding word rendered "strangers" is *xenos*; in 1 Pet. 2:11, RV, ditto (KJV, "strangers").

C. Noun.

paroikia (3940), "a sojourning" (akin to A and B), occurs in Acts 13:17, rendered "they sojourned," RV, KJV, "dwelt as strangers," lit., "in the sojourning"; in 1 Pet. 1:17, "sojourning."

SOLID

stereos (4731), meaning "solid" in Heb. 5:12, 14, of food.

SON

huios (5207) primarily signifies the relation of offspring to parent (see John 9:18-20; Gal. 4:30). It is often used metaphorically of prominent moral characteristics (see below). "It is used in the NT of (a) male offspring, Gal. 4:30; (b) legitimate, as opposed to illegitimate offspring, Heb. 12:8; (c) descendants, without reference to sex, Rom. 9:27; (d) friends attending a wedding, Matt. 9:15; (e) those who enjoy certain privileges, Acts 3:25; (f) those who act in a certain way, whether evil, Matt. 23:31, or good, Gal. 3:7; (g) those who manifest a certain character, whether evil, Acts 13:10; Eph. 2:2, or good, Luke 6:35; Acts 4:36; Rom. 8:14; (h) the destiny that corresponds with the character, whether evil, Matt. 23:15; John 17:12; 2 Thess. 2:3, or good, Luke 20:36; (i) the dignity of the relationship with God whereunto men are brought by the Holy Spirit when they believe on the Lord Jesus Christ, Rom. 8:19; Gal. 3:26....

The Apostle John does not use *huios*, "son," of the believer, he reserves that title for the Lord; but he does use *teknon*, "child," as in his Gospel, 1:12; 1 John 3:1, 2; Rev. 21:7 (*huios*) is a quotation from 2 Sam. 7:14. The Lord Jesus used *huios* in a very significant way, as in Matt. 5:9, "Blessed are the peacemakers, for they shall be called the sons of God," and vv. 44, 45, "Love your enemies, and pray for them that persecute you; that ye may be (become) sons of your Father which is in heaven." The disciples were to do these things, not in order that they might become children of God, but that, being children (note "your Father" throughout), they might make the fact manifest in their character, might "become sons." See also 2 Cor. 6:17, 18.

As to moral characteristics, the following phrases are used: (a) sons of God, Matt. 5:9, 45; Luke 6:35; (b) sons of the light, Luke 16:8; John 12:36; (c) sons of the day, 1 Thess. 5:5; (d) sons of peace, Luke 10:6; (e) sons of this world, Luke 16:8; (f) sons of disobedience, Eph. 2:2; (g) sons of the evil one, Matt. 13:38, cf. "of the Devil," Acts 13:10; (h) son of perdition, John 17:12; 2 Thess. 2:3. It is also used to describe characteristics other than moral, as: (i) sons of the resurrection, Luke 20:36; (j) sons of the Kingdom, Matt. 8:12; 13:38; (k) sons of the bridechamber, Mark 2:19; (l) sons of exhortation, Acts 4:36; (m) sons of thunder, Boanerges, Mark 3:17.

The Son of God

In this title the word "Son" is used sometimes (a) of relationship, sometimes (b) of the expression of character. Thus, e.g., when the disciples so addressed Him, Matt. 14:33; 16:16; John 1:49, when the centurion so spoke of Him, Matt. 27:54, they probably meant that (b) He was a manifestation of God in human form. But in such passages as Luke 1:32, 35; Acts 13:33, which refer to the humanity of the Lord Jesus,...the word is used in sense (a).

The Lord Jesus Himself used the full title on occasion, John 5:25; 9:35 [some mss. have "the Son of Man"; see RV marg.]; 11:4, and on the more frequent occasions on which He spoke of Himself as "the Son," the words are to be understood as an abbreviation of "the Son of God," not of "The Son of Man"; this latter He always expressed in full; see Luke 10:22; John 5:19, etc.

John uses both the longer and shorter forms of the title in his Gospel, see 3:16-18; 20:31, e.g., and in his Epistles; cf. Rev. 2:18. So does the writer of Hebrews, 1:2; 4:14; 6:6, etc. An eternal relation subsisting between the Son and the Father in the Godhead is to be understood. That is to say, the Son of God, in His eternal relationship with the Father, is not so entitled because He at any time began to derive His being from the Father (in which case He could not be co-eternal with the Father), but because He is and ever has been the expression of what the Father is; cf. John 14:9, "he that hath seen Me hath seen the Father." The words of Heb. 1:3, "Who being the effulgence of His (God's) glory, and the very image of His (God's) substance" are a definition of what is meant by "Son of God." Thus absolute Godhead, not Godhead in a secondary or derived sense, is intended in the title.

Other titles of Christ as the "Son of God" are: "His Son," 1 Thess. 1:10 (in Acts 13:13, 26, RV, *pais* is rendered "servant"); "His own Son," Rom. 8:32; "My beloved Son," Matt. 3:17; "His Only Begotten Son," John 3:16; "the Son of His love," Col. 1:13.

In addressing the Father in His prayer in John 17 He says, "Thou lovedst Me before the foundation of the world." Accordingly in the timeless past the Father and the "Son" existed in that relationship, a relationship of love, as well as of absolute Deity. In this passage the "Son" gives evidence that there was no more powerful plea in the Father's estimation than that co-eternal love existing between the Father and Himself.

The declaration "Thou art My Son, this day have I begotten Thee," Ps. 2:7, quoted in Acts 13:33; Heb. 1:5; 5:5, refers to the birth of Christ, not to His resurrection. In Acts 13:33 the verb "raise up" is used of the raising up of a person to occupy a special position in the nation, as of David in verse 22 (so of Christ as a Prophet in 3:22 and 7:37). The word "again" in the KJV in v. 33 represents nothing in the original. The RV rightly omits it. In v. 34 the statement as to the resurrection of Christ receives the greater stress in this respect through the emphatic contrast to that in v. 33 as to His being raised up in the nation, a stress imparted by the added words "from the dead." Accordingly v. 33 speaks of His incarnation, v. 34 of His resurrection.

Son of Man

In the NT this is a designation of Christ, almost entirely confined to the Gospels. Elsewhere it is found in Acts 7:56, the only occasion where a disciple applied it to the Lord and in Rev. 1:13; 14:14 (see below).

"Son of Man" is the title Christ used of Himself; John 12:34 is not an exception, for the quotation by the multitude was from His own statement. The title is found especially in the Synoptic Gospels. The occurrences in John's gospel, 1:51; 3:13, 14; 5:27; 6:27, 53, 62; 8:28 (9:35 in some texts); 12:23, 34 (twice); 13:31, are not parallel to those in the Synoptic Gospels. In the latter the use of the title falls into two groups, (a) those in which it refers to Christ's humanity, His earthly work, sufferings and death, e.g., Matt. 8:20; 11:19; 12:40; 26:2, 24; (b) those which refer to His glory in resurrection and to that of His future advent, e.g., Matt. 10:23; 13:41; 16:27, 28; 17:9; 24:27, 30 (twice), 37, 39, 44.

While it is a messianic title it is evident that the Lord applied it to Himself in a distinctive way, for it indicates more than Messiahship, even universal headship on the part of One who is Man. It therefore stresses His manhood, manhood of a unique order in comparison with all other men, for He is declared to be of heaven, 1 Cor. 15:47, and even while here below, was "the Son of Man, which is in Heaven," John 3:13. As the "Son of Man" He must be appropriated spiritually as a condition of possessing eternal life, John 6:53. In His death, as in His life, the glory of His Manhood was displayed in the absolute obedience and submission to the will of the Father (12:23; 13:31), and, in view of this, all judgment has been committed to Him, who will judge in full understanding experimentally of human conditions, sin apart, and will exercise the judgment as sharing the nature of those judged, John 5:22, 27. Not only is He man, but He is "Son of Man," not by human generation but, according to the Semitic usage of the expression, partaking of the characteristics (sin apart) of manhood belonging to the category of mankind. Twice in the Apocalypse, 1:13 and 14:14, He is described as "One like unto a Son of man," RV (KJV, "...the Son of Man"), cf. Dan. 7:13. He who was thus seen was indeed the "Son of Man," but the absence of the article in the original serves to stress what morally characterizes Him as such. Accordingly in these passages He is revealed, not as the Person known by the title, but as the One who is qualified to act as the Judge of all men. He is the same Person as in the days of His flesh, still continuing His humanity with His Deity. The phrase "like unto" serves to distinguish Him as there seen in His glory and majesty in contrast to the days of His humiliation.

SOOTHSAYING

manteuomai (*3132*), "to divine, practice divination" (from *mantis*, "a seer, diviner"), occurs in Acts 16:16. The word is allied to *mainomai*, "to rave," and *mania*, "fury" displayed by those who were possessed by the evil spirit (represented by the pagan god or goddess) while delivering their oracular messages. Trench draws a distinction between this verb and *propheteuo*, not only as to their meanings, but as to the fact of the single occurrence of *manteuomai* in the NT, contrasted with the frequency of *propheteuo*, exemplifying the avoidance by NT writers of words the employment of which "would tend to break down the distinction between heathenism and revealed religion."

SOP

psomion (*5596*), a diminutive of *psomos*, "a morsel," denotes "a fragment, a sop," John 13:26 (twice), 27, 30. It had no connection with the modern meaning of "sop," something given to pacify (as in the classical expression "a sop to Cerberus").

SORCERER

1. *magos* (*3097*), (a) "one of a Median caste, a magician"; (b) "a wizard, sorcerer, a pretender to magic powers, a professor of the arts of witchcraft," Acts 13:6, 8, where Bar-Jesus was the Jewish name, Elymas, an Arabic word meaning "wise." Hence the name Magus, "the magician," originally applied to Persian priests.

2. *pharmakos* (*5333*), an adjective signifying "devoted to magical arts," is used as a noun, "a sorcerer," especially one who uses drugs, potions, spells, enchantments, Rev. 21:8, in the best texts (some have *pharmakeus*), and 22:15.

SORCERY

A. Nouns.

1. *pharmakia* (or —*eia*) (*5331*) (Eng., "pharmacy," etc.) primarily signified "the use of medicine, drugs, spells"; then, "poisoning"; then, "sorcery," Gal. 5:20, RV, "sorcery" (KJV, "witchcraft"), mentioned as one of "the works of the flesh." See also Rev. 9:21; 18:23.

2. *magia* (or —*eia*) (*3095*), "the magic art," is used in the plural in Acts 8:11.

B. Verb.

mageuo (*3096*), akin to A, No. 2, "to practice magic," Acts 8:9, "used sorcery," is used as in A, No. 2, of Simon Magnus.

SORE (Noun, Verb)

A. Noun.

helkos (*1668*), "a sore" or "ulcer" (primarily a wound), occurs in Luke 16:21; Rev. 16:2, 11.

B. Verb.

helkoo (*1669*), "to wound, to ulcerate," is used in the passive voice, signifying "to suffer from sores," to be "full of sores," Luke 16:20 (perfect participle).

SORROW (Noun and Verb), SORROWFUL

A. Nouns.

1. *lupe* (*3077*), "grief, sorrow," is translated "sorrow" in Luke 22:45; John 16:6, 20-22; Rom. 9:2, RV (KJV, "heaviness"); 2 Cor. 2:1, RV; 2:3, 7; 7:10 (twice); Phil. 2:27 (twice).

2. *odune* (*3601*), "pain, consuming grief, distress," whether of body or mind, is used of the latter, Rom. 9:2, RV, "pain"; 1 Tim. 6:10.

3. *odin* (*5604*), "a birth-pang, travail, pain," "sorrows," Matt. 24:8; Mark 13:8.

4. *penthos* (3997), "mourning," "sorrow," Rev. 18:7 (twice); 21:4.

B. Verb.

odunao (3600), "to cause pain" (akin to A, No. 2), is used in the middle voice in Luke 2:48; Acts 20:38.

C. Adjective.

perilupos (4036), "very sad, deeply grieved" (*peri*, intensive), is used in Matt. 26:38 and Mark 14:34, "exceeding sorrowful"; Mark 6:26; Luke 18:23 (v. 24 in some mss.).

SORRY

A. Verb.

lupeo (3076) is rendered "to be sorry" (passive voice) in Matt. 14:9, KJV (RV, "grieved"); 17:23; 18:31; 2 Cor. 2:2 [1st part, active voice, "make sorry" (as in 7:8, twice); 2nd part, passive]; 2:4, RV, "made sorry"; 9:9 and 11, RV, "ye were made sorry."

B. Adjective.

perilupos (4036) is translated "exceeding sorry" in Mark 6:26.

SOUL

Old Testament

A. Noun.

nephesh (5315), "soul; self; life; person; heart." The Hebrew contrasts two other concepts which are not found in the Greek and Latin tradition: "the inner self" and "the outer appearance" or, as viewed in a different context, "what one is to oneself" as opposed to "what one appears to be to one's observers." The inner person is *nephesh*, while the outer person, or reputation, is *shem*, most commonly translated "name." In narrative or historical passages of the Old Testament, *nephesh* can be translated as "life" or "self," as in Lev. 17:11. It is often translated as the common pronoun "I" or "me, my," Ps 16:10, often with a focus on the animate life of the person. The soul can have physical cravings and desires, Psa 109:7; seat of emotions, Psa. 10:3. See the New Testament section for the unique perspectives of the eternal aspects of the soul.

B. Verb.

naphash means "to breathe; respire; be refreshed," Exod. 23:12; 31:17; 2 Sam. 16:14.

New Testament

psuche (5590) denotes "the breath, the breath of life," then "the soul," in its various meanings. The NT uses may be analyzed approximately as follows:

(a) the natural life of the body, Matt. 2:20; Luke 12:22; Acts 20:10;

S

Rev. 8:9; 12:11; cf. Lev. 17:11; 2 Sam. 14:7; Esth. 8:11; (b) the immaterial, invisible part of man, Matt. 10:28; Acts 2:27; cf. 1 Kings 17:21;
(c) the disembodied (or "unclothed" or "naked," 2 Cor. 5:3, 4) man,
Rev. 6:9; (d) the seat of personality, Luke 9:24, explained as = "own
self," v. 25; Heb. 6:19; 10:39; cf. Isa. 53:10 with 1 Tim. 2:6; (e) the seat
of the sentient element in man, that by which he perceives, reflects, feels, desires, Matt. 11:29; Luke 1:46; 2:35; Acts 14:2, 22; cf.
Ps. 84:2; 139:14; Isa. 26:9; (f) the seat of will and purpose, Matt.
22:37; Acts 4:32; Eph. 6:6; Phil. 1:27; Heb. 12:3; cf. Num. 21:4; Deut.
11:13; (g) the seat of appetite, Rev. 18:14; cf. Ps. 107:9; Prov. 6:30; Isa.
5:14 ("desire"); 29:8; (h) persons, individuals, Acts 2:41, 43; Rom.
2:9; Jas. 5:20; 1 Pet. 3:20; 2 Pet. 2:14; cf. Gen. 12:5; 14:21 ("persons");
Lev. 4:2 ('any one'); Ezek. 27:13; of dead bodies, Num. 6:6, lit., "dead
soul"; and of animals, Lev. 24:18, lit., "soul for soul"; (i) the equivalent of the personal pronoun, used for emphasis and effect:—1st
person, John 10:24 ("us"); Heb. 10:38; cf. Gen. 12:13; Num. 23:10;
Judg. 16:30; Ps. 120:2 ("me"); 2nd person, 2 Cor. 12:15; Heb. 13:17;
Jas. 1:21; 1 Pet. 1:9; 2:25; cf. Lev. 17:11; 26:15; 1 Sam. 1:26; 3rd person, 1 Pet. 4:19; 2 Pet. 2:8; (j) an animate creature, human or other,
1 Cor. 15:45; Rev. 16:3; cf. Gen. 1:24; 2:7, 19; (k) "the inward man,"
the seat of the new life, Luke 21:19 (cf. Matt. 10:39); 1 Pet. 2:11;
3 John 2.

Body and soul are the constituents of the man according to
Matt. 6:25; 10:28; Luke 12:20; Acts 20:10; body and spirit according
to Luke 8:55; 1 Cor. 5:3; 7:34; Jas. 2:26. In Matt. 26:38 the emotions
are associated with the soul, in John 13:21 with the spirit; cf. also
Ps. 42:11 with 1 Kings 21:5. In Ps. 35:9 the soul rejoices in God, in
Luke 1:47 the spirit. Apparently, then, the relationships may be
thus summed up; *soma*, body, and *pneuma*, spirit, may be separated, *pneuma* and *psuche*, soul, can only be distinguished.

SOUND (Noun and Verb)

A. Noun.

phone (5456), most frequently "a voice," is translated "sound" in
Matt. 24:31 (KJV marg., "voice"); John 3:8, KJV (RV, "voice"); so
1 Cor. 14:7 (1st part), 8; Rev. 1:15; 18:22 (2nd part, RV, "voice"); KJV
and RV in 9:9 (twice); in Acts 2:6, RV, "(this) sound (was heard),"
KJV, "(this) was noised abroad."

B. Verbs.

1. *echeo* (2278), akin to A, No. 2, occurs in 1 Cor. 13:1, "sounding
(brass)"; in some mss., Luke 21:25.

2. *execheo* (1837), "to sound forth as a trumpet" or "thunder" (*ex*,
"out," and No. 1), is used in 1 Thess. 1:8, "sounded forth," passive
voice, lit., "has been sounded out." In the Sept., Joel 3:14.

SOUND (Health), BE SOUND

A. Adjective.

hugies (*199*), "whole, healthy," is used metaphorically of "sound speech," Titus 2:8.

B. Verb.

hugiaino (*5198*), "to be healthy, sound in health" (Eng., "hygiene," etc.), translated "safe and sound" in Luke 15:27, is used metaphorically of doctrine, 1 Tim. 1:10; 2 Tim. 4:3; Titus 1:9; 2:1; of words, 1 Tim. 6:3, RV (KJV, "wholesome," RV marg., "healthful"); 2 Tim. 1:13; "in the faith," Titus 1:13 (RV marg., "healthy"); "in faith," Titus 2:2 (RV marg., ditto).

SOUNDNESS

holokleria (*3647*), "completeness, soundness," Acts 3:16.

SOW (Verb), SOWER

Old Testament

A. Verb.

zara' (2232), "to sow, scatter seed, make pregnant." In an agricultural society such as ancient Israel, *zara'* would be most important and very commonly used, especially to describe the annual sowing of crops, Judg. 6:3; Gen. 26:12. Used in the figurative sense, it is said that Yahweh "will sow" Israel in the land, Hos. 2:23; Jer. 31:27; Ps. 126:5. "Sow seed" means "conceive [*zara*] seed [*zera'*]," Num. 5:28.

B. Noun.

zera' (2233), "seed; sowing; seedtime; harvest; offspring; descendant(s); posterity." *zera'* frequently means "seed," i.e., that which propagates a new generation of plants, shrubs, or trees, Gen. 47:19; some seed may be eaten, cf. Lev. 27:30.

zera' sometimes means "semen," or a man's "seed," Lev. 15:16. *zera'* often means "offspring." Only rarely is this nuance applied to animals, Gen. 3:15. This verse uses the word in several senses. The first appearance means both the descendants of the snake and those of the spiritual being who used the snake (evil men). The second appearance of the word refers to all the descendants of the woman and ultimately to a particular descendant (Christ). In Gen. 4:25 *zera'* appears not as a collective noun but refers to a particular and immediate "offspring"; upon the birth of Seth, Eve said: "God...hath appointed me another seed [offspring]...." Gen. 46:6 uses the word (in the singular) of one's entire family including children and grandchildren, cf. Gen. 17:12. One's larger family, including all immediate relatives, is included in the word in

S

passages such as 1 Kings 11:14. The word is used of an entire nation of people in Esth. 10:3.

New Testament

speiro (4687), "to sow seed," is used (1) literally, especially in the Synoptic Gospels; elsewhere, 1 Cor. 15:36, 37; 2 Cor. 9:10, "the sower," (2) metaphorically, (a) in proverbial sayings, e.g., Matt. 13:3, 4; Luke 19:21, 22; John 4:37; 2 Cor. 9:6; (b) in the interpretation of parables, e.g., Matt. 13:19-23 (in these vv., RV, "was sown," for KJV, "received seed"); (c) otherwise as follows: of "sowing" spiritual things in preaching and teaching, 1 Cor. 9:11; of the interment of the bodies of deceased believers, 1 Cor. 15:42-44; of ministering to the necessities of others in things temporal (the harvest being proportionate to the "sowing"), 2 Cor. 9:6, 10 (see above); of "sowing" to the flesh, Gal. 6:7, 8 ("that" in v. 7 is emphatic, "that and that only," what was actually "sown"); in v. 8, *eis*, "unto," signifies "in the interests of"; of the "fruit of righteousness" by peacemakers, Jas. 3:18.

SPARE, SPARINGLY

A. Verb.

pheidomai (5339), "to spare," i.e., "to forego" the infliction of that evil or retribution which was designed, is used with a negative in Acts 20:29; Rom. 8:32; 11:21 (twice); 2 Cor. 13:2; 2 Pet. 2:4, 5; positively, in 1 Cor. 7:28; 2 Cor. 1:3; rendered "forbear" in 2 Cor. 12:6.

B. Adverb.

pheidomenos (5340), akin to A, "sparingly," occurs in 2 Cor. 9:6 (twice), of sowing and reaping.

SPARROW

strouthion (4765), a diminutive of *strouthos*, "a sparrow," occurs in Matt. 10:29, 31; Luke 12:6, 7.

SPEAK

Old Testament

A. Verb.

dabar (1696), "to speak, say." This verb focuses not only on the content of spoken verbal communication but also and especially on the time and circumstances of what is said. Unlike *'amar*, "to say," *dabar* often appears without any specification of what was communicated. Those who "speak" are primarily persons (God or men) or organs of speech. In Gen. 8:15 (the first occurrence of this verb) God "spoke" to Noah, while in Gen. 18:5 one of the three men "spoke" to Abraham.

B. Nouns.

dabar (1697), "word, matter; something." The noun *dabar* refers, first, to what is said, to the actual "word" itself, Gen. 11:1. This noun can also be used of the content of speaking. When God "did according to the word of Moses," Exod. 8:13, He granted his request. The noun can connote "matter" or "affair," as in Gen. 12:17, where it is reported that God struck Pharaoh's household with plagues because of the "matter of Sarah" (KJV, "because of Sarai"). *dabar* can be used as a more general term in the sense of "something"—so in Gen. 24:66 the "everything" (KJV, "all things") is literally "all of something(s)"; it is an indefinite generalized concept rather than a reference to everything in particular.

As a biblical phrase "the word of the Lord" is quite important; it occurs about 242 times. Against the background just presented it is important to note that "word" here may focus on the content (meaning) of what was said, but it also carries overtones of the actual "words" themselves. It was the "word of the Lord" that came to Abram in a vision after his victory over the kings who had captured Lot, Gen. 15:1.

The "word" of God indicates God's thoughts and will. This should be contrasted with His name, which indicates His person and presence. Therefore, God's "word" is called "holy" only once, cf. Ps. 105:42, while His name is frequently called "holy."

There is much discussion regarding the "word" as a hypostatization of divine reality and attributes as seen, for example, in John 1:1: "In the beginning was the Word." This theme is rooted in such Old Testament passages as Isa. 9:8: "The Lord sent a word into Jacob..." cf. 55:10-11; Ps. 107:20; 147:15. Some scholars argue that this is no more than the poetical device of personification and does not foreshadow John's usage. Their evidence is that human attributes are frequently separated from a man and objectivized as if they had a separate existence, cf. Ps. 85:11-12.

New Testament

1. *laleo* (2980), is used several times in 1 Cor. 14; the command prohibiting women from speaking in a church gathering, vv. 34, 35, is regarded by some as an injunction against chattering, a meaning which is absent from the use of the verb everywhere else in the NT; it is to be understood in the same sense as in vv. 2, 3-6, 9, 11, 13, 18, 19, 21, 23, 27-29, 39.

2. *proslaleo* (4354), "to speak to or with" (*pros*, "to," and No. 2), is used in Acts 13:43 and 28:20.

3. *phthengomai* (5350), "to utter a sound or voice," is translated "to speak" in Acts 4:18; 2 Pet. 2:16; in 2:18, KJV, "speak" (RV, "utter").

4. *apophthengomai* (669), "to speak forth" (*apo*, "forth," and No.

S

4), is so rendered in Acts 2:14, RV (KJV, "said"), and 26:25; in 2:2 it denotes to give utterance.

5. *sullaleo* (4814), "to speak together" (*sun*, "with," and No. 2), is rendered "spake together" in Luke 4:36, RV.

SPEAKER (chief)

In Acts 14:12 the verb *hegeomai*, "to lead the way, be the chief," is used in the present participle with the article (together equivalent to a noun), followed by the genitive case of *logos*, "speech," with the article, the phrase being rendered "the chief speaker," lit., "the leader of the discourse."

SPEAKING (evil, much)

pololugia (4180), "loquacity," "much speaking" (*polus*, "much," *logos*, "speech"), is used in Matt. 6:7. In the Sept., Prov. 10:19.

SPECIAL

tuchon, the 2nd aorist participle of *tunchano*, "to happen, meet with, chance," is used with a negative signifying "not common or ordinary, special," Acts 19:11; so in 28:2.

SPECTACLE

theatron (2302), akin to *theaomai*, "to behold," denotes (a) "a theater" (used also as a place of assembly), Acts 19:29, 31; (b) "a spectacle, a show," metaphorically in 1 Cor. 4:9.

SPEECH

1. *logos* (3056), rendered "word," signifies "speech," as follows: (a) "discourse," e.g., Luke 20:20, RV, "speech" (KJV, "words"); Acts 14:12; 20:7; 1 Cor. 2:1, 4; 4:19, KJV (RV, "word"); 2 Cor. 10:10; (b) "the faculty of speech," e.g., 2 Cor. 11:6; (c) "the manner of speech," e.g., Matt. 5:37, RV, "speech" (KJV, "communication"); Col. 4:6; (d) "manner of instruction," Titus 2:8; 1 Cor. 14:9, RV (KJV, "words"); Eph. 4:29, RV (KJV, "communication").

2. *lalia* (2981), akin to *laleo*, denotes "talk, speech," (a) of "a dialect," Matt. 26:73; Mark 14:70; (b) "utterances," John 4:42, RV, "speaking" (KJV, "saying"); 8:43.

3. *eulogia* (2129) has the meaning "fair speaking, flattering speech" in Rom. 16:18, RV, "fair speech" (KJV, "fair speeches"); cf. also Rom. 16:18.

SPEECHLESS

1. *eneos* (or *enneos*) (1769), "dumb, speechless," occurs in Acts 9:7.

2. *kophos*, which means either "deaf" or "dumb," is translated "speechless" in Luke 1:22.

SPEND, SPENT

1. *dapanao* (*1159*) denotes (a) "to expend, spend," Mark 5:26; 2 Cor. 12:15 (1st part: for "be spent," see No. 2); (b) "to consume, squander," Luke 15:14; Jas. 4:3.

2. *ekdapanao* (*1550*), lit., "to spend out" (*ek*), an intensive form of No. 1, "to spend entirely," is used in 2 Cor. 12:15, in the passive voice, with reflexive significance, "to spend oneself out (for others)," RV marg., "spent out" (see No. 1).

3. *prosdapanao* (*4325*), "to spend besides" (*pros*, and No. 1), is used in Luke 10:35, "thou spendest more."

4. *prosanalisko* (*4321*), "to spend besides," a strengthened form of *analisko*, "to expend, consume," occurs in most texts in Luke 8:43.

SPEW (KJV, SPUE)

emeo (*1692*), "to vomit" (cf. Eng., "emetic"), is used in Rev. 3:16, figuratively of the Lord's utter abhorrence of the condition of the church at Laodicea.

SPIKENARD

nardos (*3487*), is derived, through the Semitic languages (Heb. *nerd*, Syriac *nardin*), from the Sanskrit *nalada*, "a fragrant oil," procured from the stem of an Indian plant. The Arabs call it the "Indian spike." The adjective *pistikos* is attached to it in the NT, Mark 14:3; John 12:3; *pistikos*, if taken as an ordinary Greek word, would signify "genuine." There is evidence, however, that it was regarded as a technical term. It has been suggested that the original reading was *pistakes*, i.e., the *Pistacia Terebinthus*, which grows in Cyprus, Syria, Palestine, etc., and yields a resin of very fragrant odor, and in such inconsiderable quantities as to be very costly. Nard was frequently mixed with aromatic ingredients...so when scented with the fragrant resin of the *pistake* it would quite well be called *nardos pistakes*.

SPIRIT

Old Testament

ruach (*7307*), "breath; air; strength; wind; breeze; spirit; courage; temper; Spirit." First, this word means "breath," air for breathing, air that is being breathed, Jer. 14:6; catching the breath is to revive, Judg. 15:19; overwhelmed is breathless, 1 Kings 10:4-5; one must pass air over the vocal cords to speak, Ps. 33:6; cf. Exod. 15:8; Job 4:9; 19:17. Second, this word can be used with emphasis on the invisible, intangible, fleeting quality of "air": "O remember that my life is wind: mine eyes shall no more see good," Job 7:7. There may be a suggestion of purposelessness, uselessness, or even vanity (emptiness), Jer. 5:13; "empty knowledge," Job 15:2; cf. Eccl.

1:14, 17; "nothing," Prov. 11:29. Third, *ruach* can mean "wind," Gen. 3:8; Exod. 10:13, 19; Jer. 4:11; Amos 4:13. Fourth, the wind represents direction, as a compass direction, Jer. 49:36.

Fifth, *ruach* frequently represents the element of life in a man, his natural "spirit," Gen. 7:21-22; of animals, cf. Ps. 104:29. On the other hand, in Prov. 16:2 the word appears to mean more than just the element of life; it seems to mean "soul." Sixth, *ruach* is often used of a man's mind-set, disposition, or "temper," Ps. 32:2; Ezek. 13:3. *ruach* can represent particular dispositions, Josh. 2:11; cf. Josh. 5:1; Job 15:13. Another disposition represented by this word is "temper," Eccl. 10:4. David prayed that God would "restore unto me the joy of thy salvation; and uphold me with thy free Spirit," Ps. 51:12.

Seventh, the Bible often speaks of God's "Spirit," the third person of the Trinity. This is the use of the word in its first biblical occurrence: "And the earth was without form, and void; and darkness was upon the face of the deep. And the Spirit of God moved upon the face of the waters," Gen. 1:2. Isa. 63:10-11 and Ps. 51:12 specifically speak of the "holy or free Spirit." Eighth, the non-material beings (angels) in heaven are sometimes called "spirits": "And there came forth a spirit, and stood before the Lord, and said, I will persuade him," 1 Kings 22:21; cf. 1 Sam. 16:14.

New Testament

pneuma (4151) primarily denotes "the wind" (akin to *pneo*, "to breathe, blow"); also "breath"; then, especially "the spirit," which, like the wind, is invisible, immaterial and powerful. The NT uses of the word may be analyzed approximately as follows:

(a) the wind, John 3:8 (where marg. is, perhaps, to be preferred); Heb. 1:7; (b) the breath, 2 Thess. 2:8; Rev. 11:11; 13:15; (c) the immaterial, invisible part of man, Luke 8:55; Acts 7:59; 1 Cor. 5:5; Jas. 2:26; (d) the disembodied (or 'unclothed,' or 'naked,' 2 Cor. 5:3, 4) man, Luke 24:37, 39; Heb. 12:23; 1 Pet. 4:6; (e) the resurrection body, 1 Cor. 15:45; 1 Tim. 3:16; 1 Pet. 3:18; (f) the sentient element in man, that by which he perceives, reflects, feels, desires, Matt. 5:3; 26:41; Mark 2:8; Luke 1:47, 80; Acts 17:16; 20:22; 1 Cor. 2:11; 5:3, 4; 14:4, 15; 2 Cor. 7:1; cf. Gen. 26:35; Isa. 26:9; Ezek. 13:3; Dan. 7:15; (g) purpose, aim, 2 Cor. 12:18; Phil. 1:27; Eph. 4:23; Rev. 19:10; cf. Ezra 1:5; Ps. 78:8; Dan. 5:12; (h) the equivalent of the personal pronoun, used for emphasis and effect: 1st person, 1 Cor. 16:18; cf. Gen. 6:3; 2nd person, 2 Tim. 4:22; Philem. 25; cf. Ps. 139:7; 3rd person, 2 Cor. 7:13; cf. Isa. 40:13; (i) character, Luke 1:17; Rom. 1:4; cf. Num. 14:24; (j) moral qualities and activities: bad, as of bondage, as of a slave, Rom. 8:15; cf. Isa. 61:3; stupor, Rom. 11:8; cf. Isa. 29:10; timidity, 2 Tim. 1:7; cf. Josh. 5:1; good, as of adoption, i.e., liberty as of a son, Rom. 8:15; cf. Ps. 51:12; meekness, 1 Cor. 4:21; cf. Prov. 16:19; faith, 2 Cor. 4:13; quietness, 1 Pet. 3:4; cf. Prov. 14:29; (k) the

Holy Spirit, e.g., Matt. 4:1 (see below); Luke 4:18; (l) 'the inward man' (an expression used only of the believer, Rom. 7:22; 2 Cor. 4:16; Eph. 3:16); the new life, Rom. 8:4-6, 10, 16; Heb. 12:9; cf. Ps. 51:10; (m) unclean spirits, demons, Matt. 8:16; Luke 4:33; 1 Pet. 3:19; cf. 1 Sam. 18:10; (n) angels, Heb. 1:14; cf. Acts 12:15; (o) divine gift for service, 1 Cor. 14:12, 32; (p) by metonymy, those who claim to be depositories of these gifts, 2 Thess. 2:2; 1 John 4:1-3; (q) the significance, as contrasted with the form, of words, or of a rite, John 6:63; Rom. 2:29; 7:6; 2 Cor. 3:6; (r) a vision, Rev. 1:10; 4:2; 17:3; 21:10.

The Holy Spirit

The "Holy Spirit" is spoken of under various titles in the NT ("Spirit" and "Ghost" are renderings of the same word, **pneuma**; the advantage of the rendering "Spirit" is that it can always be used, whereas "Ghost" always requires the word "Holy" prefixed.) In the following list the omission of the definite article marks its omission in the original (concerning this see below): "Spirit, Matt. 22:43; Eternal Spirit, Heb. 9:14; the Spirit, Matt. 4:1; Holy Spirit Matt. 1:18; the Holy Spirit, Matt. 28:19; the Spirit, the Holy Matt. 12:32; the Spirit of promise, the Holy, Eph. 1:13; Spirit of God, Rom. 8:9; Spirit of (the) living God, 2 Cor. 3:3; the Spirit of God 1 Cor. 2:11; the Spirit of our God, 1 Cor. 6:11; the Spirit of God, the Holy Eph. 4:30; the Spirit of glory and of God, 1 Pet. 4:14; the Spirit of Him that raised up Jesus from the dead (i.e., God), Rom. 8:11; the Spirit of your Father, Matt. 10:20; the Spirit of His Son, Gal. 4:6; Spirit of (the) Lord, Acts 8:39; the Spirit of (the) Lord, Acts 5:9; (the) Lord, (the) Spirit, 2 Cor. 3:18; the Spirit of Jesus, Acts 16:7; Spirit of Christ, Rom. 8:9; the Spirit of Jesus Christ, Phil. 1:19; Spirit of adoption, Rom. 8:15; the Spirit of truth, John 14:17; the Spirit of life, Rom. 8:2; the Spirit of grace, Heb. 10:29.

The use or absence of the article in the original where the "Holy Spirit" is spoken of cannot always be decided by grammatical rules, nor can the presence or absence of the article alone determine whether the reference is to the "Holy Spirit." Examples where the Person is meant when the article is absent are Matt. 22:43 (the article is used in Mark 12:36); Acts 4:25, RV (absent in some texts); 19:2, 6; Rom. 14:17; 1 Cor. 2:4; Gal. 5:25 (twice); 1 Pet. 1:2. Sometimes the absence is to be accounted for by the fact that **pneuma** (like **theos**) is substantially a proper name, e.g., in John 7:39. As a general rule the article is present where the subject of the teaching is the Personality of the Holy Spirit, e.g., John 14:26, where He is spoken of in distinction from the Father and the Son. See also 15:26 and cf. Luke 3:22.

In Gal. 3:3, in the phrase "having begun in the Spirit," it is difficult to say whether the reference is to the "Holy Spirit" or to the quickened spirit of the believer; that it possibly refers to the lat-

S

ter is not to be determined by the absence of the article, but by the contrast with "the flesh"; on the other hand, the contrast may be between the "Holy Spirit" who in the believer sets His seal on the perfect work of Christ, and the flesh which seeks to better itself by works of its own. There is no preposition before either noun, and if the reference is to the quickened spirit it cannot be dissociated from the operation of the "Holy Spirit." In Gal. 4:29 the phrase "after the Spirit" signifies "by supernatural power," in contrast to "after the flesh," i.e., "by natural power," and the reference must be to the "Holy Spirit"; so in 5:17.

The full title with the article before both **pneuma** and **hagios** (the "resumptive" use of the article), lit., "the Spirit the Holy," stresses the character of the Person, e.g., Matt. 12:32; Mark 3:29; 12:36; 13:11; Luke 2:26; 10:21 (RV); John 14:26; Acts 1:16; 5:3; 7:51; 10:44, 47; 13:2; 15:28; 19:6; 20:23, 28; 21:11; 28:25; Eph. 4:30; Heb. 3:7; 9:8; 10:15.

The Personality of the Spirit is emphasized at the expense of strict grammatical procedure in John 14:26; 15:26; 16:8, 13, 14, where the emphatic pronoun **ekeinos**, "He," is used of Him in the masculine, whereas the noun **pneuma** is neuter in Greek, while the corresponding word in Aramaic, the language in which our Lord probably spoke, is feminine (**rucha**, cf. Heb. **ruach**). The rendering "itself" in Rom. 8:16, 26, due to the Greek gender, is corrected to "Himself" in the RV.

SPIRIT (OF THE DEAD), NECROMANCER

'ob (178), "spirit (of the dead); necromancer; pit." The word usually represents the troubled spirit (or spirits) of the dead, Isa. 29:4. Its second meaning, "necromancer," refers to a professional who claims to summon forth such spirits when requested (or hired) to do so, Lev. 19:31—first occurrence; 1 Sam. 28:8.

God forbade Israel to seek information by this means, which was so common among the pagans, Lev. 19:31; Deut. 18:11. Perhaps the pagan belief in manipulating one's basic relationship to a god (or gods) explains the relative silence of the Old Testament regarding life after death. Yet God's people believed in life after death, from early times, e.g., Gen. 37:35; Isa. 14:15ff. Necromancy was so contrary to God's commands that its practitioners were under the death penalty, Deut. 13. Necromancers' unusual experiences do not prove that they truly had power to summon the dead. For example, the medium of Endor could not snatch Samuel out of God's hands against His wishes. But in this particular incident, it seems that God rebuked Saul's apostasy, either through a revived Samuel or through a vision of Samuel. Mediums do not have power to summon the spirits of the dead, since this is reprehensible to God and contrary to His will.

SPIRITUAL

A. Adjective.

pneumatikos (4152) always connotes the ideas of invisibility and of power; it is in fact an after-Pentecost word. In the NT it is used as follows: (a) the angelic hosts, lower than God but higher in the scale of being than man in his natural state, are "spiritual hosts" Eph. 6:12; (b) things that have their origin with God, and which therefore, are in harmony with His character, as His law is, are "spiritual," Rom. 7:14; (c) "spiritual" is prefixed to the material type in order to indicate that what the type sets forth, not the type itself, is intended, 1 Cor. 10:3, 4; (d) the purposes of God revealed in the gospel by the Holy Spirit, 1 Cor. 2:13a, and the words in which that revelation is expressed, are "spiritual," 13b, matching. or combining, spiritual things with spiritual words [or, alternatively, "interpreting spiritual things to spiritual men," see (e) below]; "spiritual songs" are songs of which the burden is the things revealed by the Spirit, Eph. 5:19; Col. 3:16; "spiritual wisdom and understanding" is wisdom in, and understanding of those things, Col. 1:9; (e) men in Christ who walk so as to please God are "spiritual," Gal. 6:1; 1 Cor. 2:13b, 15; 3:1; 14:37; (f) the whole company of those who believe in Christ is a "spiritual house," 1 Pet. 2:5a; (g) the blessings that accrue to regenerate men at this present time are called "spiritualities," Rom. 15:27; 1 Cor. 9:11; "spiritual blessings," Eph. 1:3; "spiritual gifts," Rom. 1:11; (h) the activities Godward of regenerate men are "spiritual sacrifices," 1 Pet. 2:5b; their appointed activities in the churches are also called "spiritual gifts," lit., "spiritualities," 1 Cor. 12:1; 14:1; (i) the resurrection body of the dead in Christ is "spiritual," i.e., such as is suited to the heavenly environment, 1 Cor. 15:44; (j) all that is produced and maintained among men by the operations of the Spirit of God is "spiritual," 1 Cor. 15:46.

B. Adverb.

pneumatikos (4153), "spiritually," occurs in 1 Cor. 2:14, with the meaning as (j) above, and Rev. 11:8, with the meaning as in (c). Some mss. have it in 1 Cor. 2:13.

SPITEFULLY (ENTREAT)

hubrizo (5195), used transitively, denotes "to outrage, treat insolently"; "to entreat shamefully" in Matt. 22:6, RV (KJV, "spitefully"); so in Luke 18:32, RV; in Acts 14:5 (KJV, "use despitefully"); in 1 Thess. 2:2, KJV and RV; in Luke 11:45, "reproachest."

SPLENDOR

hod (1935), "splendor; majesty; authority." The basic significance of "splendor and majesty" with overtones of superior power and position is attested in the application of this word to kings, Jer. 22:18; of weather, Job 37:22. In many cases *hod* focuses on "dignity and splendor" with overtones of superior power and position but not to the degree seen in oriental kings: "And thou shalt put some of thine honor upon him, that all the congregation of the children of Israel may be obedient," Num. 27:20—the first occurrence of the word. When used of the olive tree, Hos. 14:6, *hod* focuses on its "splendor and dignity" as the most desired and desirable of the trees, cf. Judg. 9:9-15.

SPOIL (Noun and Verb), SPOILING

A. Nouns.

1. *skulon* (4661), used in the plural, denotes "arms stripped from a foe"; "spoils" in Luke 11:22.

2. *akrothinion* (205), primarily "the top of a heap" (*akros*, "highest, top," and *this*, "a heap"), hence "firstfruit offerings," and in war "the choicest spoils, Heb. 7:4.

3. *harpage* (724), "pillage," is rendered "spoiling" in Heb. 10:34.

B. Verbs.

1. *diarpazo* (1283), "to plunder," is found in Matt. 12:29, 2nd part (the 1st has *harpazo*, in the best texts), lit., "(then) he will completely (*dia*, intensive) spoil (his house)"; Mark 3:27 (twice).

2. *harpazo* (726), "to seize, snatch away," is rendered "spoil" in Matt. 12:29a (see No. 1).

3. *sulagogeo* (4812), "to carry off as spoil, lead captive" (*sule*, "spoil," *ago*, "to lead"), is rendered "maketh spoil of" in Col. 2:8, RV (KJV, "spoil"), rather "carry you off as spoil." The false teacher, through his "philosophy and vain deceit," would carry them off as so much booty.

4. *apekduo* (554), in the middle voice is translated "having spoiled" in Col. 2:15, KJV, RV, "having put off from Himself (the principalities and the powers)." These are regarded by some as the unsinning angels, because they are mentioned twice before in the Epistle (1:16; 2:10).

SPOT (Noun and Verb)

A. Nouns.

1. *spilos* (4696), "a spot or stain," is used metaphorically (a) of moral blemish, Eph. 5:27; (b) of lascivious and riotous persons, 2 Pet. 2:13.

2. *spilas* (4694) is rendered "spots" in Jude 12, KJV.

B. Verb.

spiloo (4695), akin to A, No. 1, is used in Jude 23, in the clause "hating even the garment spotted by the flesh," the garment representing that which, being brought into contact with the polluting element of the flesh, becomes defiled.

C. Adjective.

aspilos (784), "unspotted, unstained" (*a*, negative, and A), is used of a lamb, 1 Pet. 1:19; metaphorically, of keeping a commandment without alteration and in the fulfillment of it, 1 Tim. 6:14; of the believer in regard to the world, Jas. 1:27, and free from all defilement in the sight of God, 2 Pet. 3:14.

SPRINKLE, SPRINKLING

Old Testament

zaraq (2236), "to throw; sprinkle; strew; toss; scatter abundantly." This word expresses the "throwing" or "sprinkling" of blood against the sacrificial altar or on the people. Thus, it appears very often in Leviticus, 1:5, 11; 3:2, 8, 13 et al. Ezekiel's version of "the New Covenant" includes the "sprinkling" of the water of purification, Ezek. 36:25. In the first use of *zaraq* in the Old Testament, it describes the "throwing" a handful of dust into the air which would settle down on the Egyptians and cause boils, Exod. 9:8, 10.

New Testament

A. Verb.

rhantizo (4472), "to sprinkle" (a later form of *rhaino*), is used in the active voice in Heb. 9:13, of "sprinkling" with blood the unclean, a token of the efficacy of the expiatory sacrifice of Christ, His blood signifying the giving up of His life in the shedding of His blood (cf. 9:22) under divine judgment upon sin (the voluntary act to be distinguished from that which took place after His death in the piercing of His side); so again in vv. 19, 21 (see B); in Heb. 10:22, passive voice, of the purging (on the ground of the same efficacy) of the hearts of believers from an evil conscience.

B. Nouns.

1. *rhantismos* (4473), "sprinkling," akin to A, is used of the "sprinkling" of the blood of Christ, in Heb. 12:24 and 1 Pet. 1:2, an allusion to the use of the blood of sacrifices, appointed for Israel, typical of the sacrifice of Christ (see under A).

2. *proschusis* (4378), "a pouring or sprinkling upon," occurs in Heb. 11:28, of the "sprinkling" of the blood of the Passover lamb.

SPY (Noun and Verb)

A. Nouns.

1. *enkathetos* (1455), an adjective denoting "suborned to lie in wait" (*en*, "in," *kathiemi*, "to send down"), is used as a noun in Luke 20:20, "spies."

2. *kataskopos* (*2685*) denotes "a spy" (*kata*, "down," signifying "closely," and *skopeo*, "to view"), Heb. 11:31.

B. Verb.

kataskopeo (*2684*), "to view closely" (akin to A, No. 2), "spy out, search out" with a view to overthrowing, is used in Gal. 2:4.

STAR

1. *aster* (*792*), "a star," Matt. 2:2-10; 24:29; Mark 13:25; 1 Cor. 15:41; Rev. 6:13; 8:10-12; 9:1; 12·1, 4, is used metaphorically, (a) of Christ, as "the morning star," figurative of the approach of the day when He will appear as the "sun of righteousness," to govern the earth in peace, an event to be preceded by the rapture of the Church, Rev. 2:28; 22:16, the promise of the former to the overcomer being suggestive of some special personal interest in Himself and His authority; (b) of the angels of the seven churches, Rev. 1:16, 20; 2:1· 3:1; (c) of certain false teachers, described as "wandering stars," Jude 13, as if the "stars," intended for light and guidance, became the means of deceit by irregular movements.

2. *astron* (*798*), practically the same as No. 1, is used (a) in the sing. in Acts 7:43, "the star of the god Rephan," RV, the symbol or "figure," probably of Saturn, worshiped as a god, apparently the same as Chiun in Amos 5:26 (Rephan being the Egyptian deity corresponding to Saturn, Chiun the Assyrian); (b) in the plur., Luke 21:25; Acts 27:20; Heb. 11:12.

STATUE

tselem (*6754*), "statue; image; copy." This word signifies an "image or copy" of something in the sense of a replica, 1 Sam. 6:5; Ezek. 23:14. The word also means "image" in the sense of essential nature, Gen. 5:3. Human nature in its internal and external characteristics is what is meant here rather than an exact duplicate So, too, God made man in His own "image," reflecting some of His own perfections: perfect in knowledge, righteousness, and holiness, and with dominion over the creatures, Gen. 1:26. Being created in God's "image" meant being created male and female, in a loving unity of more than one person, Gen. 1:27. It is noteworthy that in Gen. 1:26 (the first occurrence of the word) the "image" of God is represented by two Hebrew words (*tselem* and *demut*); by *tselem* alone in Gen. 1:27 and 9:6; and by *demut* alone in Gen. 5:1. This plus the fact that in other contexts the words are used exactly the same leads to the conclusion that the use of both in passages such as Gen. 1:26 is for literary effect.

STATUTE, ORDINANCE

A. Nouns.

choq (2706), "statute; prescription; rule; law; regulation." The word *choq* also signifies "law," or "statute." In a general sense it refers to the "laws" of nature like rain, Job 28:26; cf. Jer. 5:22; and the celestial bodies, Ps. 148:6; Jer. 31:35-36. Moreover, the word *choq* denotes a "law" promulgated in a country, Gen. 47:26.

Finally, and most important, the "law" given by God is also referred to as a *choq*: "When they have a matter, they come unto me; and I judge between one and another, and I do make them know the statutes [*choq*] of God, and his laws [*torah*]," Exod. 18:16. The word's synonyms are *mitswah*, "commandment"; *mishpat*, "judgment"; *berit*, "covenant"; *torah*, "law"; and *'edut*, "testimony." It is not easy to distinguish between these synonyms, as they are often found in conjunction with each other: "Ye shall diligently keep the commandments [*mitswah*] of the Lord your God, and his testimonies [*'edah*], and his statutes [*choq*], which he hath commanded thee," Deut. 6:17.

chuqqah (2708), "statute; regulation; prescription; term," is found for the first time in God's words of commendation about Abraham to Isaac: "Because that Abraham obeyed my voice, and kept my charge, my commandments [*mitswah*], my statutes [*chuqqah*], and my laws [*torah*]" (Gen. 26:5), together with its synonyms *mishmeret*, *mitswah*, and *torah*. In non-religious usage, the word *chuqqah* refers to the customs of the nations, Lev. 18:3; cf. 20:23. The reason for the requirement to abstain from the pagan practices is that they were considered to be degenerate, Lev. 18:30.

The most significant usage of *chuqqah* is God's "law." It is more specific in meaning than *choq*. Whereas *choq* is a general word for "law," *chuqqah* denotes the "law" of a particular festival or ritual. There is the "law" of the Passover, Exod. 12:14, Unleavened Bread, Exod. 12:17, Feast of Tabernacles, Lev. 23:41, the Day of Atonement, Lev. 16:29ff., the priesthood, Exod. 29:9, and the blood and fat, Lev. 3:17.

The word *chuqqah* has many synonyms. At times it forms a part of a series of three: "Beware that thou forget not the Lord thy God, in not keeping his commandments [*mitswah*], and his judgments [*mishpat*], and his statutes [*chuqqah*], which I command thee this day" (Deut. 8:11), and at other times of a series of four: "Therefore thou shalt love the Lord thy God, and keep his charge [*mishmeret*], and his statutes [*chuqqah*] and his judgments [*mishpat*], and his commandments [*mitswah*], always," Deut. 11:1; cf. Gen. 26:5 with *torah* instead of *mishpat*.

The "statutes" of people are to be understood as the practices contrary to God's expectations, Mic. 6:16; Ezek. 5:6; 33:15.

S

B. Verb.

chaqaq (2710), "to cut in, determine, decree." *chaqaq* is used in Isa. 22:16 with the meaning "to cut in."

STEAL

klepto (2813), "to steal," akin to *kleptes*, "a thief" (cf. Eng., "kleptomania"), occurs in Matt. 6:19, 20; 19:18; 27:64; 28:13; Mark 10:19; Luke 18:20; John 10:10; Rom. 2:21 (twice); 13:9; Eph. 4:28 (twice).

STEDFAST, STEDFASTNESS

A. Adjectives.

1. *bebaios* (949), "firm, secure" (akin to *baino*, "to go"), is translated "steadfast" in 2 Cor. 1:7; Heb. 2:2; 3:14, KJV (RV, "firm"); 6:19.

2. *hedraios* (1476) primarily denotes "seated" (*hedra*, "a seat"); hence, "steadfast," metaphorical of moral fixity, 1 Cor. 7:37; 15:58; Col. 1:23, RV (KJV, "settled").

3. *stereos* (4731), firm, is rendered "steadfast" in 1 Pet. 5:9.

B. Nouns.

1. *stereoma* (4733), primarily "a support, foundation," denotes "strength, steadfastness," Col. 2:5.

2. *sterigmos* (4740), "a setting firmly, supporting," then "fixedness, steadfastness" (akin to *sterizo*, "to establish"), is used in 2 Pet. 3:17.

STEEP

kremnos (2911), "a steep bank," occurs in Matt. 8:32; Mark 5:13; Luke 8:33, RV, "the steep" (KJV, "a steep place").

STEWARD, STEWARDSHIP

A. Nouns.

1. *oikonomos* (3623) primarily denoted "the manager of a household or estate" (*oikos*, "a house," *nemo*, "to arrange"), "a steward" (such were usually slaves or freedmen), Luke 12:42; 16:1, 3, 8; 1 Cor. 4:2; Gal. 4:2, RV (KJV, "governors"); in Rom. 16:23, the "treasurer" (RV) of a city; it is used metaphorically, in the wider sense, of a "steward" in general, (a) of preachers of the gospel and teachers of the Word of God, 1 Cor. 4:1; (b) of elders or bishops in churches, Titus 1:7; (c) of believers generally, 1 Pet. 4:10.

2. *oikonomia* (3622) is rendered "stewardship" in Luke 16:2, 3, 4, and in the RV in 1 Cor. 9:17.

B. Verb.

oikonomeo (3621), akin to A, signifies "to be a house steward," Luke 16:2.

STIFF-NECKED

sklerotrachelos (4644), from *skleros*, "harsh, hard," *trachelos*, "a neck," is used metaphorically in Acts 7:51.

STIR, STIR UP (Noun and Verb)

A. Noun.

tarachos (5017), akin to *tarache*, "trouble," and *tarasso*, "to trouble," is rendered "stir" in Acts 12:18; 19:23.

B. Verbs.

1. *anazopureo* (329) denotes "to kindle afresh," or "keep in full flame" (*ana*, "up," or "again," *zoos*, "alive," *pur*, "fire"), and is used metaphorically in 2 Tim. 1:6, where "the gift of God" is regarded as a fire capable of dying out through neglect. The verb was in common use in the vernacular of the time.

2. *seio* (4579), "to move to and fro," is rendered "was stirred" in Matt. 21:10, RV (KJV, "was moved").

3. *anaseio* (383) primarily denotes "to shake back or out, move to and fro"; then, "to stir up," used metaphorically in Mark 15:11, RV, "stirred...up" (KJV, "moved"), and Luke 3:14; 23:5.

4. *saleuo* (4531), "stirred up" in Acts 17:13.

5. *erethizo* (2042), "hath stirred" in 2 Cor. 9:2, RV.

6. *anastatoo* (387), "to excite, unsettle" (akin to *anistemi*, "to raise up," and *anastasis*, "a raising"), is used (a) of "stirring up" to sedition, and tumult, Acts 17:6, "turned...upside down"; 21:38, RV, "stirred up to sedition," KJV, "madest an uproar"; (b) "to upset" by false teaching, Gal. 5:12, RV, "unsettle" (KJV, "trouble").

STONE (Noun, Verb, and Adjective)

Old Testament

'eben (68), "stone." Beyond their use as a construction material, stones served as covers for wells, Gen. 29:3ff., storage containers, Exod. 7:19, weights, Deut. 25:13; Prov. 11:1, and slingstones, 1 Sam. 17:49. Plumblines were suspended stones, Isa. 34:11; pavement was sometimes made of "stone," 2 Kings 16:17; and the Bible speaks of hailstones, Josh. 10:11; Ezek. 13:11ff. The Israelite custom of cave burials presumes stone tombs, Isa. 14:19; on 3 occasions when bodies were not interred, they were heaped with "stones," Josh. 7:26; 8:29; 2 Sam. 18:17; an instrument for capital punishment, Lev. 24:23; Num. 15:35-36; Deut. 22:21, 24; carving into idols, Lev. 26:1.

Precious "stones" such as onyx, Gen. 2:12, and sapphire, Ezek. 1:26, are mentioned frequently in the Bible, especially with regard to the high priest's ephod and breastplate, Exod. 39:6ff. The expensiveness of the high priest's garments corresponded to the special workmanship of the most holy place where Aaron served.

S

In certain texts, *'eben* has been given theological interpretations. God is called the "stone of Israel" in Gen. 49:24. And several occurrences of *'eben* in the Old Testament have been viewed as messianic, as evidenced by the Greek Old Testament, rabbinic writings, and the New Testament, among them: Gen. 28:18; Ps. 118:22; Isa. 8:14; 28:16; Dan. 2:34; Zech. 4:7.

New Testament

A. Nouns.

1. *lithos* (3037) is used (1) literally, of (a) the "stones" of the ground, e.g., Matt. 4:3, 6; 7:9; (b) "tombstones," e.g., Matt. 27:60, 66; (c) "building stones," e.g., Matt. 21:42; (d) "a millstone," Luke 17:2; cf. Rev. 18:21; (e) the "tables (or tablets)" of the Law, 2 Cor. 3:7; (f) "idol images," Acts 17:29; (g) the "treasures" of commercial Babylon, Rev. 18:12, 16; (II), metaphorically, of (a) Christ, Rom. 9:33; 1 Pet. 2:4, 6, 8; (b) believers, 1 Pet. 2:5; (c) spiritual edification by scriptural teaching, 1 Cor. 3:12; (d) the adornment of the foundations of the wall of the spiritual and heavenly Jerusalem, Rev. 21:19; (e) the adornment of the seven angels in Rev. 15:6, RV (so the best texts; some have *linon*, "linen," KJV); (f) the adornment of religious Babylon, Rev. 17:4; (III) figuratively, of Christ, Rev. 4:3; 21:11, where "light" stands for "Light-giver" (*phoster*).

2. *psephos* (5586), "a smooth stone, a pebble," worn smooth as by water, or polished (akin to *psao*, "to rub"), denotes (a) by metonymy, a vote (from the use of "pebbles" for this purpose; cf. *psephizo*, "to count"), Acts 26:10, RV (KJV, "voice"); (b) a (white) "stone" to be given to the overcomer in the church at Pergamum, Rev. 2:17 (twice); a white "stone" was often used in the social life and judicial customs of the ancients; festal days were noted by a white "stone," days of calamity by a black; in the courts a white "stone" indicated acquittal, a black condemnation. A host's appreciation of a special guest was indicated by a white "stone" with the name or a message written on it; this is probably the allusion here.

B. Verbs.

1. *lithoboleo* (3036), "to pelt with stones" (A, No. 1, and *ballo*, "to throw"), "to stone to death," occurs in Matt. 21:35; 23:37; Luke 13:34 (John 8:5 in some mss.: see No. 2); Acts 7:58, 59; 14:5; Heb. 12:20.

2. *lithazo* (3034), "to stone," virtually equivalent to No. 1, but not stressing the casting, occurs in John 8:5 (in the most authentic mss.); 10:31-33; 11:8; Acts 5:26; 14:19; 2 Cor. 11:25; Heb. 11:37.

STOP

phrasso (5420), "to fence in" (akin to *phragmos*, "a fence"), "close, stop," is used (a) metaphorically, in Rom. 3:19, of "preventing" all excuse from Jew and Gentile, as sinners; in 2 Cor. 11:10, lit., "this boasting shall not be stopped to me"; passive voice in both; (b) physically, of the mouths of lions, Heb. 11:33 (active voice).

STORE (Verb)

1. *thesaurizo* (2343), "to lay up, store up," is rendered "in store" (lit., "storing"), with a view to help a special case of need, 1 Cor. 16:2; said of the heavens and earth in 2 Pet. 3:7, RV, "have been stored up (for fire)," marg., "stored (with fire)," KJV, "kept in store (reserved unto fire)."

2. *apothesaurizo* (597), "to treasure up, store away" (*apo*), is used in 1 Tim. 6:19, of "laying up in store" a good foundation for the hereafter by being rich in good works.

STORY

tristegos (5152), an adjective denoting "of three stories," occurs in Acts 20:9 (with *oikema*, "a dwelling," understood), RV, "the third story" (KJV, "the third loft").

STRAIN OUT

diulizo (1368), primarily denotes "to strain thoroughly" (*dia*, "through," intensive, *hulizo*, "to strain"), then, "to strain out," as through a sieve or strainer, as in the case of wine, so as to remove the unclean midge, Matt. 23:24, RV (KJV, "strain at").

STRANGE

A. Adjectives.

1. *xenos* (3581) denotes (a) "foreign, alien," Acts 17:18, of gods; Heb. 13:9, of doctrines; (b) "unusual," 1 Pet. 4:12, 2nd part, of the fiery trial of persecution (for 1st part, see B).

2. *allotrios* (245) denotes (a) "belonging to another" (*allos*); (b) "alien, foreign, strange," Acts 7:6; Heb. 11:9, KJV, RV, "(a land) not his own."

3. *paradoxos* (3861), "contrary to received opinion" (*para*, "beside," *doxa*, "opinion"; Eng. "paradoxical"), is rendered "strange things" in Luke 5:26.

4. *exo* (1845), outside, is rendered "strange" in Acts 26:11, KJV.

B. Verb.

xenizo (3579) denotes "to think something strange," 1 Pet. 4:4, 12, passive voice, i.e., "they are surprised," and "be (not) surprised"; in Acts 17:20, the present participle, active, is rendered "strange," i.e., "surprising."

STRANGER

A. Adjectives (used as nouns).

1. *xenos* (3581), "strange" (see No. 1 above), denotes "a stranger,

foreigner," Matt. 25:35, 38, 43, 44; 27:7; Acts 17:21; Eph. 2:12, 19; Heb. 11:13; 3 John 5.

2. *allotrios* (245), "strangers," Matt. 17:25, 26; John 10:5 (twice): see No. 2, above.

3. *allogenes* (241) (*allos*, "another," *genos*, "a race") occurs in Luke 17:18.

B. Verb.

xenodocheo (3580), "to receive strangers" (*xenos*, No. 1, above, and *dechomai*, "to receive"), occurs in 1 Tim. 5:10, RV, "(if) she hath used hospitality to strangers," KJV, "(if) she have lodged strangers."

C. Noun.

philoxenia (5381), "love of strangers," occurs in Rom. 12:13, "hospitality," and Heb. 13:2, RV, "to show love unto strangers," KJV, "to entertain strangers."

STRANGLED

pniktos (4156), from *pnigo*, "to choke," i.e., kill but not let the blood, Acts 15:20, 29; 21:25; cf. Lev. 17:13, 14.

STRENGTH, STRENGTHEN

Old Testament

chayil (2458), "strength; power; wealth; property; capable; valiant; army; troops; influential; upper-class people (courtiers)." First, this word signifies a faculty or "power," the ability to effect or produce something. The word is used of physical "strength" in the sense of power that can be exerted, Eccl. 10:10. Quite often this word appears in a military context. Here it is the physical strength, power, and ability to perform in battle that is in view, 1 Sam. 2:4; cf. Ps. 18:32, 39. Ps. 33:17 applies the word to a war horse. An interesting use of *chayil* appears in Num. 24:17-18, where Balaam prophesied the destruction of Moab and Edom at the hands of Israel. Second, *chayil* means "wealth, property," Gen. 34:29; cf. Deut. 8:18; Ruth 4:11. Third, several passages use the word in the sense of "able," i.e., have the capacity or potency to actualize an event, Gen. 47:6; Ruth 3:11; Prov. 12:4. When used in some contexts, the word may be translated "valiant," 1 Sam. 14:52; cf. Num. 24:18; 1 Sam. 14:48. Fourth, this word sometimes means "army," Exod. 14:4. The word can also refer to the army as troops in the sense of a combination of a lot of individuals. Under such an idea the word can represent the members of an army distributed to perform certain functions, 2 Chron. 17:2. Fifth, *chayil* sometimes represents the "upper class," who, as in all feudal systems, were at once soldiers, wealthy, and influential; Sanballat "spake before his brethren and the army of Samaria," i.e., in the royal court, Neh. 4:2. The Queen of Sheba was accompanied by a large escort of upper-class people from her homeland: "And she came to Jerusalem with a very great train," 1 Kings 10:2.

New Testament

A. Nouns.

1. *dunamis* (*1411*) is rendered "strength" in the RV and KJV of Rev. 1:16; elsewhere the RV gives the word its more appropriate meaning "power," for KJV, "strength," 1 Cor. 15:56; 2 Cor. 1:8; 12:9; Heb. 11:11; Rev. 3:8; 12:10.

2. *ischus* (*2479*), "ability, strength," is rendered "strength" in Mark 12:30, 33; Luke 10:27; in Rev. 5:12, KJV (RV, "might").

3. *kratos* (*2904*), "force, might," is rendered "strength" in Luke 1:51, RV and KJV; RV, "strength" (KJV, "power") in Eph. 1:19 and 6:10.

B. Verbs.

1. *dunamoo* (*1412*), "to strengthen," occurs in Col. 1:11, and in the best texts in Heb. 11:34, "were made strong" (some have No. 2); some have it in Eph. 6:10 (the best have No. 2).

2. *endunamoo* (*1743*), "to make strong," is rendered "increased...in strength" in Acts 9:22; "to strengthen" in Phil. 4:13; 2 Tim. 2:1, RV, "be strengthened"; 4:17.

3. *ischuo* (*2480*), akin to A, No. 2, "to have strength," is so rendered in Mark 5:4, RV (KJV, "could"); in Luke 16:3, RV, "I have not strength to" (KJV, "I cannot").

4. *enischuo* (*1765*), akin to A, No. 2, a strengthened form of No. 3, is used in Luke 22:43 and Acts 9:19.

5. *krataioo* (*2901*), "to strengthen," is rendered "to be strengthened" in Eph. 3:16.

6. *sthenoo* (*4599*), from *sthenos*, "strength," occurs in 1 Pet. 5:10, in a series of future tenses, according to the best texts, thus constituting divine promises.

STRICKEN (in years)

probaino (*4260*), "to go forward," is used metaphorically of age, in Luke 1:7, 18, with the phrases "in their (her) days," translated "well stricken in years" (see marg.); in 2:36, "of a great age" (marg., "advanced in many days").

STRIFE

Old Testament

S

A. Verb.

rib (*7378*), "to strive, contend," i.e., struggle or strife: physical, Exod. 21:18; verbal, Judg. 6:32.

B. Nouns.

rib (7379), "strife; quarrel; dispute; case; contentions; cause." The noun *rib* is used of conflicts outside the realm of law cases and courts, Gen. 13:7-8. *rib* sometimes represents a "dispute" between two parties. This "dispute" is set in the context of a mutual law structure binding both parties and a court which is empowered to decide and execute justice. This may involve "contention" between two unequal parties (an individual and a group), as when all Israel quarreled with Moses, asserting that he had not kept his end of the bargain by adequately providing for them. Moses appealed to the Judge, who vindicated him by sending water from a rock (cliff?) smitten by Moses: "And he called the name of the place Massah, and Meribah, because of the chiding [quarrel] of the children of Israel..." Exod. 17:7. God decided who was the guilty party, Moses or Israel. The "contention" may be between two individuals as in Deut. 25:1, where the two disputants go to court (having a "case or dispute" does not mean one is a wrongdoer): "If there be a controversy between men, and they come unto judgment, that the judges may judge them; then they shall justify the righteous, and condemn the wicked." So in Isa. 1:23 the unjust judge accepts a bribe and does not allow the widow's just "cause" (NASB, "widow's plea") to come before him. Prov. 25:8-9 admonishes the wise to "debate thy cause with thy neighbor" when that neighbor has "put thee to shame."

New Testament

1. *eris* (2054), "strife, contention," is the expression of "enmity," Rom. 1:29, RV, "strife" (KJV, "debate"); 13:13; 1 Cor. 1:11, "contentions" (RV and KJV); 3:3; 2 Cor. 12:20, RV, "strife" (KJV, "debates"); Gal. 5:20, RV, "strife" (KJV, "variance"); Phil. 1:15; 1 Tim. 6:4; Titus 3:9, RV, "strifes" (KJV, "contentions").

2. *erithia* (or —*eia*) (2052), 2 Cor. 12:20.

STRIKER

plektes (4131), "a striker, a brawler" (akin to *plesso*, "to strike," smite), occurs in 1 Tim. 3:3; Titus 1:7.

STRIVE

1. *agonizomai* (75), "to contend" (Eng., "agonize"), is rendered "to strive" in Luke 13:24; 1 Cor. 9:25; Col. 1:29; 4:12, RV (KJV, "laboring fervently").

2. *machomai* (3164), "to fight, to quarrel, dispute," is rendered "to strive" in John 6:52; Acts 7:26; 2 Tim. 2:24.

3. *diamachomai* (1264), "to struggle against" (*dia*, intensive, and No. 2), is used of "contending" in an argument, Acts 23:9, "strove."

4. *erizo* (2051), "to wrangle, strive" (*eris*, "strife"), is used in Matt. 12:19.

5. *logomacheo* (3054), "to strive about words" (*logos*, "a word," and No. 2), is used in 2 Tim. 2:14.

6. *antagonizomai* (464), "to struggle against" (*anti*), is used in Heb. 12:4, "striving against."

7. *sunagonizomai* (4865), "to strive together with" (*sun*), is used in Rom. 15:30.

8. *sunathleo* (4866), "to strive together," Phil. 1:27.

STRONG, STRONGER

Old Testament

A. Verb.

chazaq (2388), "to be strong, strengthen, harden, take hold of." In the sense of personal strength *chazaq* is first used in Deut. 11:8 in the context of the covenant, Deut. 3:28. The covenant promise accompanies the injunction to "be strong and of a good courage," Deut. 31:6. The same encouragement was given to the returned captives as they renewed the work of rebuilding the temple, Zech. 8:9, 13; cf. Hag. 2:4.

chazaq, can mean pure physical strength: as in a building up, of a city, Judg. 1:28; 2 Kings 12:6; 2 Chron. 26:9. In battle *chazaq* means: "So David prevailed over the Philistine..." 1 Sam. 17:50.

In summary, this word group describes the physical and moral strength of man and society. God communicates strength to men, even to the enemies of His people as chastisement for His own. Men may turn their strength into stubbornness against God.

B. Adjective.

chazaq (2389), "strong; mighty; heavy; severe; firm; hard." First, the word means "firm" or "hard" in the sense that something is impenetrable, like rock, Ezek. 3:8-9; or metals, Job 37:18. Second, this word means "strong." In its basic meaning it refers to physical strength, cf. Deut. 4:15, 19; able to effect, Num. 13:18; have healthy animals, Ezekiel 34:16. Third, *chazaq* means "heavy." When applied to a battle or war, it describes the event(s) as severe, 1 Sam. 14:52. The word is also used to indicate a severe sickness, 1 Kings 17:17, and famine, 1 Kings 18:2.

New Testament

A. Adjectives.

1. *dunatos* (1415), "powerful, mighty," is translated "strong," in Rom. 15:1, where the "strong" are those referred to in ch. 14, in contrast to "the weak in faith," those who have scruples in regard to eating meat and the observance of days; 2 Cor. 12:10, where the strength lies in bearing sufferings in the realization that the endurance is for Christ's sake; 2 Cor. 13:9, where "ye are strong" implies the good spiritual condition which the apostle desires for

S

the church at Corinth in having nothing requiring his exercise of discipline (contrast No. 2 in 1 Cor. 4:10).

2. *ischuros* (*2478*), "strong, mighty," is used of (a) persons: (1) God, Rev. 18:8; (2) angels, Rev. 5:2; 10:1; 18:21; (3) men, Matt. 12:29 (twice) and parallel passages; Heb. 11:34, KJV, "valiant" (RV, "mighty"); Rev. 6:15 (in the best texts; some have No. 1); 19:18, "mighty"; metaphorically, (4) the church at Corinth, 1 Cor. 4:10, where the apostle reproaches them ironically with their unspiritual and self-complacent condition; (5) of young men in Christ spiritually strong, through the Word of God, to overcome the evil one, 1 John 2:14; of (b) things: (1) wind, Matt. 14:30 (in some mss.), "boisterous"; (2) famine, Luke 15:14; (3) things in the mere human estimate, 1 Cor. 1:27; (4) Paul's letters, 2 Cor. 10:10; (5) the Lord's crying and tears, Heb. 5:7; (6) consolation, 6:18; (7) the voice of an angel, Rev. 18:2 (in the best texts; some have *megas*, "great"); (8) Babylon, Rev. 18:10; (9) thunderings, Rev. 19:6.

B. Verbs.

1. *endunamoo* (*1743*), "to make strong" (*en*, "in," *dunamis*, "power"), "to strengthen," is rendered "waxed strong" in Rom. 4:20, RV (KJV, "was strong"); "be strong," Eph. 6:10; "were made strong," Heb. 11:34.

2. *krataioo* (*2901*), "to strengthen" (akin to *kratos*, "strength"), is rendered (a) "to wax strong," Luke 1:80; 2:40; "be strong," 1 Cor. 16:13, lit., "be strengthened"; "to be strengthened," Eph. 3:16 (passive voice in each place).

STRONGHOLDS

ochuroma (*3794*), "a stronghold, fortress" (akin to *ochuroo*, "to make firm"), is used metaphorically in 2 Cor. 10:4, of those things in which mere human confidence is imposed.

STUMBLE

Old Testament

kashal (*3782*), "to stumble, stagger, totter, be thrown down." Other than literal stumbling, Lev. 26:37, this word is often used figuratively to describe the consequences of divine judgment on sin, Jer. 6:21; cf. also Jer. 50:32.

New Testament

1. *proskopto* (*4350*), "to strike against," is used of "stumbling," (a) physically, John 11:9, 10; (b) metaphorically, (1) of Israel in regard to Christ, whose Person, teaching, and atoning death, and the gospel relating thereto, were contrary to all their ideas as to the means of righteousness before God, Rom. 9:32; 1 Pet. 2:8; (2) of a brother in the Lord in acting against the dictates of his conscience, Rom. 14:21.

2. *ptaio* (4417), "to cause to stumble," signifies, intransitively, "to stumble," used metaphorically in Rom. 11:11, in the sense (b) (1) in No. 1; with moral significance in Jas. 2:10 and 3:2 (twice), RV, "stumble" (KJV, "offend"); in 2 Pet. 1:10, RV, "stumble" (KJV, "fall").

STUPID FELLOW

kesil (3684), "stupid fellow; dull person; fool." The *kesil* is "insolent" in religion and "stupid or dull" in wise living Ps. 92:6, 7; Prov. Prov. 1:22.

STUPOR

katanuxis (2659), "a pricking" (akin to *katanusso*, "to strike" or "prick violently," Acts 2:37), is used in Rom. 11:8, RV, "stupor" (KJV, "slumber").

SUBDUE

katagonizomai (2610), primarily, "to struggle against" (*kata*, "against," *agon*, "a contest"), came to signify "to conquer," Heb. 11:33, "subdued."

SUBJECT (Verb)

hupotasso (5293), primarily a military term, "to rank under" (*hupo*, "under," *tasso*, "to arrange"), denotes (a) "to put in subjection, to subject," Rom. 8:20 (twice); in the following, the RV, has to subject for KJV, "to put under," 1 Cor. 15:27 (thrice), 28 (3rd clause); Eph. 1:22; Heb. 2:8 (4th clause); in 1 Cor. 15:28 (1st clause), for KJV "be subdued"; in Phil. 3:21, for KJV, "subdue"; in Heb. 2:5, KJV, "hath...put in subjection"; (b) in the middle or passive voice, to subject oneself, to obey, be subject to, Luke 2:51; 10:17, 20; Rom. 8:7; 10:3, RV, "did (not) subject themselves" [KJV, "have (not) submitted themselves"]; 13:1, 5; 1 Cor. 14:34, RV, "be in subjection" (KJV, "be under obedience"); 15:28 (2nd clause); 16:16 RV, "be in subjection" (KJV, "submit, etc."); so Col. 3:18; Eph. 5:21, RV, "subjecting yourselves" (KJV, "submitting, etc."); v. 22, RV in italics, according to the best texts; v. 24, "is subject"; Titus 2:5, 9, RV, "be in subjection" (KJV, "be obedient"); 3:1, RV, "to be in subjection" (KJV, "to be subject"); Heb. 12:9, "be in subjection"; Jas. 4:7, RV, "be subject" (KJV, "submit yourselves"); so 1 Pet. 2:13; v. 18, RV, "be in subjection"; so 3:1, KJV and RV; v. 5, similarly; 3:22, "being made subject"; 5:5, RV, "be subject" (KJV, "submit yourselves"); in some texts in the 2nd part, as KJV.

SUBMIT

hupeiko (5226), "to retire, withdraw" (*hupo*, under, *eiko*, "to yield"), hence, "to yield, submit," is used metaphorically in Heb. 13:17, of "submitting" to spiritual guides in the churches.

S

SUBORN

hupoballo (*5260*), "to throw or put under, to subject," denoted "to suggest, whisper, prompt"; hence, "to instigate," translated "suborned" in Acts 6:11. To "suborn" in the legal sense is to procure a person who will take a false oath. The idea of making suggestions is probably present in this use of the word.

SUBSTANCE

1. **ouisia** (*3776*), derived from a present participial form of **eimi**, "to be," denotes "substance, property," Luke 15:12, 13, RV, "substance," KJV, "goods" and "substance."

2. **huparchonta** (*5224*), the neuter plural of the present participle of **huparcho**, "to be in existence," is used as a noun with the article, signifying one's "goods," and translated "substance" in Luke 8:3.

3. **huparxis** (*5223*), existence (akin to No. 2), possession.

4. **hupostasis** (*5287*), is translated "substance" (a) in Heb. 1:3, of Christ as "the very image" of God's "substance"; here the word has the meaning of the real nature of that to which reference is made in contrast to the outward manifestation (see the preceding clause); it speaks of the divine essence of God existent and expressed in the revelation of His Son. The KJV, "person" is an anachronism; the word was not so rendered till the 4th cent. Most of the earlier Eng. versions have "substance"; (b) in Heb. 11:1 it has the meaning of "confidence, assurance" (RV), marg., "the giving substance to," KJV, "substance," something that could not equally be expressed by **elpis**, "hope."

SUBTLY

katasophizomai (*2686*), "to deal subtly," Acts 7:19.

SUBVERT, SUBVERTING

A. Verb.

anaskeuazo (*384*), primarily, "to pack up baggage" (**ana**, "up," **skeuos**, "a vessel"), hence, from a military point of view, "to dismantle a town, to plunder," is used metaphorically in Acts 15:24, of unsettling or "subverting" the souls of believers. In the papyri it is used of going bankrupt.

B. Noun.

katastrophe (*2692*), "an overthrow," 2 Pet. 2:6 (Eng. "catastrophe"), is rendered "subverting" in 2 Tim. 2:14.

SUCCORER

prostatis (*4368*), a feminine form of **prostates**, denotes "a protectress, patroness"; it is used metaphorically of Phoebe in Rom. 16:2.

SUCK (GIVE SUCK), SUCKLING

thelazo (*2337*), from *thele*, "a breast," is used (a) of the mother, "to suckle," Matt. 24:19; Mark 13:17; Luke 21:23; in some texts in 23:29 (the best have *trepho*); (b) of the young, "to suck," Matt. 21:16, "sucklings"; Luke 11:27.

SUFFER

(a) *to permit*

1. **eao** (*1439*), "to let, permit," is translated "to suffer" in Matt. 24:43; Luke 4:41; 22:51; Acts 14:16; 16:7; 19:30; 28:4; 1 Cor. 10:13.

2. **proseao** (*4330*), "to permit further" (*pros*, and No. 1), occurs in Acts 27:7.

3. **epitrepo** (*2010*), rendered "to suffer" in KJV and RV in Matt. 8:21; Mark 10:4; Luke 9:59; Acts 28:16; RV only, Luke 9:61 (KJV, "let"); KJV only, Acts 21:39; in some texts, Matt. 8:31, KJV only.

4. **aphiemi** (*863*), "to send away," signifies "to permit, suffer," in Matt. 3:15 (twice); Matt. 19:14; 23:13; Mark 1:34; 5:19, 37; 10:14; 11:16; Luke 8:51; 12:39, KJV (RV, "left"); 18:16; John 12:7, RV, KJV and RV marg., "let (her) alone"; Rev. 11:9.

(b) *to endure suffering*

1. **anecho** (*430*), in the middle voice, "to bear with," is rendered "to suffer" in Matt. 17:17 and parallel passages; KJV only, 1 Cor. 4:12 (RV, "endure"); 2 Cor. 11:19, 20 and Heb. 13:22 (RV, bear with).

2. **pascho** (*3958*), "to suffer," is used (I) of the "sufferings" of Christ (a) at the hands of men, e.g., Matt. 16:21; 17:12; 1 Pet. 2:23; (b) in His expiatory and vicarious sacrifice for sin, Heb. 9:26; 13:12; 1 Pet. 2:21; 3:18; 4:1; (c) including both (a) and (b), Luke 22:15; 24:26, 46; Acts 1:3, "passion"; 3:18; 17:3; Heb. 5:8; (d) by the antagonism of the evil one, Heb. 2:18; (II), of human "suffering" (a) of followers of Christ, Acts 9:16; 2 Cor. 1:6; Gal. 3:4; Phil. 1:29; 1 Thess. 2:14; 2 Thess. 1:5; 2 Tim. 1:12; 1 Pet. 3:14, 17; 5:10; Rev. 2:10; in identification with Christ in His crucifixion, as the spiritual ideal to be realized, 1 Pet. 4:1; in a wrong way, 4:15; (b) of others, physically, as the result of demoniacal power, Matt. 17:15, RV, "suffereth (grievously)," KJV, "is (sore) vexed"; cf. Mark 5:26; in a dream, Matt. 27:19; through maltreatment, Luke 13:2; 1 Pet. 2:19, 20; by a serpent (negatively), Acts 28:5, RV, "took"; (c) of the effect upon the whole body through the "suffering" of one member, 1 Cor. 12:26, with application to a church.

3. **propascho** (*4310*), "to suffer before" (*pro*, and No. 2), occurs in 1 Thess. 2:2.

4. **sumpascho** (*4841*), "to suffer with" (*sun*, and No. 2), is used in Rom. 8:17 of "suffering" with Christ; in 1 Cor. 12:26 of joint "suffering" in the members of the body.

S

5. **hupecho** (5254), "to hold under" (**hupo**, "under," **echo**, "to have or hold"), is used metaphorically in Jude 7 of "suffering" punishment.

6. **kakoucheo** (2558), "to ill-treat" (**kakos**, "evil," and **echo**, "to have"), is used in the passive voice in Heb. 11:37, RV, "evil entreated" (KJV, "tormented"); in 13:3, RV, "are evil entreated" (KJV, "suffer adversity").

7. **sunkakoucheomai** (4778), "to endure adversity with," is used in Heb. 11:25 (**sun**, "with," and No. 6), RV, "to be evil entreated with," KJV, "to suffer affliction with."

8. **makrothumeo** (3114) is rendered "suffereth long" in 1 Cor. 13:4.

9. **adikeo** (91), "to do wrong, injustice" (**a**, negative, **dike**, "right"), is used in the passive voice in 2 Pet. 2:13, RV, "suffering wrong" (some texts have **komizo**, "to receive," KJV); there is a play upon words here which may be brought out thus, "being defrauded (of the wages of fraud)," a use of the verb illustrated in the papyri.

SUFFERING

pathema (3804) is rendered "sufferings" in the RV (KJV, "afflictions") in 2 Tim. 3:11; Heb. 10:32; 1 Pet. 5:9; in Gal. 5:24, "passions" (KJV, "affections").

SUFFICE, SUFFICIENT

A. Verbs.

1. **arkeo** (714), "to suffice," is rendered "is sufficient" in John 6:7; 2 Cor. 12:9; "it sufficeth" in John 14:8.

2. **hikanoo** (2427), "to make sufficient, render fit," is translated "made (us) sufficient" in 2 Cor. 3:6, RV (KJV, "hath made... able").

B. Adjectives.

1. **hikanos** (2425), akin to A, No. 2, "enough, sufficient, fit," etc. is translated "sufficient" in 2 Cor. 2:6, 16; 3:5.

2. **arketos** (713), akin to A, No. 1, used with **eimi**, "to be," is translated "may suffice" in 1 Pet. 4:3.

SUFFICIENCY

Old Testament

day (1767), "sufficiency; the required; enough." Often used with the meaning of that which is enough or an amount which is sufficient for a need or standard, Exod. 36:7; Jer. 49:9. There are many special uses of **day** where the basic meaning is in the background and the context dictates a different nuance. In Job 39:25 the word preceded by the preposition **be** may be rendered "as often as": "As often as the trumpet sounds he says, Aha!" (NASB). When preceded by the preposition **ke**, "as," the word usually means "according to": "...The judge shall cause him to lie down, and to be beaten before his face, according to his fault, by a certain number," Deut. 25:2. Preceded by *min*, "from," the word sometimes means "regarding the need," 1 Sam. 7:16.

New Testament

1. *autarkeia* (*841*) (*autos*, "self," *arkeo*, see A, above; Eng., "autarchy"), "contentment," 1 Tim. 6:6, is rendered "sufficiency" in 2 Cor. 9:5.

2. *hikanotes* (*2426*) is rendered "sufficiency" in 2 Cor. 3:5.

SUM (Noun), SUM UP

anakephalaioo (*346*), "to sum up, gather up" (*ana*, "up," *kephale*, "a head"), "to present as a whole," is used in the passive voice in Rom. 13:9, RV, "summed up" (KJV, "briefly comprehended"), i.e., the one commandment expresses all that the Law enjoins, and to obey this one is to fulfill the Law (cf. Gal. 5:14); middle voice in Eph. 1:10, RV, "sum up" (KJV, "gather together"), of God's purpose to "sum up" all things in the heavens and on the earth in Christ, a consummation extending beyond the limits of the church, though the latter is to be a factor in its realization.

SUMPTUOUS, SUMPTUOUSLY

A. Adjective.

lampros (*2986*), "bright," is rendered "sumptuous" in Rev. 18:14, RV.

B. Adverb.

lampros (*2988*), the corresponding adverb, is used in Luke 16:19, "sumptuously."

SUPERFLUOUS

perissos (*4053*), "abundant, more than sufficient," is translated "superfluous" in 2 Cor. 9:1.

SUPERSCRIPTION

epigraphe (*1923*), lit., "an overwriting" (*epi*, "over," *grapho*, "to write") (the meaning of the anglicized Latin word "superscription"), denotes "an inscription, a title." On Roman coins the emperor's name was inscribed, Matt. 22:20; Mark 12:16; Luke 20:24. In the Roman Empire, in the case of a criminal on his way to execution, a board on which was inscribed the cause of his condemnation, was carried before him or hung round his neck; the inscription was termed a "title" (*titlos*). The four Evangelists state that at the crucifixion of Christ the title was affixed to the cross, Mark (15:26), and Luke (23:38), call it a "superscription"; Mark says it was "written over" (*epigrapho*, the corresponding verb). Matthew

S

calls it "His accusation"; John calls it "a title" (a technical term). The wording varies: the essential words are the same, and the variation serves to authenticate the narratives, showing that there was no consultation leading to an agreement as to the details.

SUPERSTITIOUS

deisidaimon (*1175*), "reverent to the deity" (*deido*, "to fear"; *daimon*, "a demon," or "pagan god"), occurs in Acts 17:22 in the comparative degree, rendered "somewhat superstitious," RV (KJV, "too superstitious"), a meaning which the word sometimes has; others, according to its comparative form, advocate the meaning "more religious (than others)," "quite religious" (cf. the noun in 25:19).

SUPPLICATION

1. *deesis* (*1162*) is always translated "supplication," or the plural, in the RV.

2. *hiketeria* (*2428*) is the feminine form of the adjective *hiketerios*, denoting "of a suppliant," and used as a noun, formerly "an olive branch" carried by a suppliant (*hiketes*), then later, "a supplication," used with No. 1 in Heb. 5:7.

SUPPLY (Noun and Verb)

A. Verbs.

1. *choregeo* (*5524*) primarily, among the Greeks, signified "to lead a stage chorus or dance" (*choros*, and *hegeomai*, "to lead"), then, "to defray the expenses of a chorus"; hence, later, metaphorically, "to supply," 2 Cor. 9:10 (2nd part; see also No. 2), RV, "supply" (KJV "minister"); 1 Pet. 4:11, RV, "supplieth" (KJV, "giveth").

2. *epichoregeo* (*2023*), "to supply fully, abundantly" (a strengthened form of No. 1), is rendered "to supply" in the RV of 2 Cor. 9:10 (1st part) and Gal. 3:5 (for KJV, "to minister"), where the present continuous tense speaks of the work of the Holy Spirit in all His ministrations to believers individually and collectively; in Col. 2:19, RV, "being supplied" (KJV, "having nourishment ministered"), of the work of Christ as the Head of the church His body, in 2 Pet. 1:5, "supply" (KJV, "add"); in v. 11, "shall be...supplied" (KJV, "shall be ministered"), of the reward hereafter which those are to receive, in regard to positions in the kingdom of God, for their fulfillment here of the conditions mentioned.

3. *anapleroo* (*378*), "to fill up, fulfill," is rendered "to supply" in 1 Cor. 16:17 and Phil. 2:30.

4. *prosanapleroo* (*4322*), "to fill up by adding to, to supply fully" (*pros*, "to," and No. 3), is translated "supplieth" in 2 Cor. 9:12, KJV (RV, "filleth up the measure of"); in 11:9, RV and KJV, "supplied."

B. Noun.

epichoregia (*2024*), "a full supply," occurs in Eph. 4:16, "supplieth," lit., "by the supply of every joint," metaphorically of the members of the church, the body of which Christ is the Head, and Phil. 1:19, "the supply (of the Spirit of Jesus Christ)," i.e., "the bountiful supply"; here "of the Spirit" may be taken either in the subjective sense, the Giver, or the objective, the Gift.

SUPPOSE

1. *nomizo* (*3543*), "to consider, suppose, think," is rendered "to suppose" in Matt. 20:10; Luke 2:34; 3:23; Acts 7:25; 14:19; 16:27; 21:29; 1 Tim. 6:5; in 1 Cor. 7:26, KJV, "I think"); in Acts 16:13, the RV adheres to the meaning "to suppose," "(where) we supposed (there was a place of prayer)"; this word also signifies "to practice a custom" (*nomos*) and is commonly so used by Greek writers. Hence the KJV, "was wont (to be made)"; it is rendered "to think" in Matt. 5:17; 10:34; Acts 8:20; 17:29; 1 Cor. 7:36.

2. *dokeo* (*1380*), "to be of opinion," is translated "to suppose" in Mark 6:49; Luke 24:37; John 20:15; Acts 27:13; in the following, KJV "suppose," RV, "think," Luke 12:51; 13:2; Heb. 10:29. It is most frequently rendered "to think," always in Matthew; always in John, except 11:31, "supposing," RV [where the best texts have this verb (for *lego*, KJV, "saying")], and 20:15 (see above).

3. *hupolambano* (*5274*), when used of mental action, signifies "to suppose," Luke 7:43, and Acts 2:15.

4. *huponoeo* (*5282*), "to suspect, to conjecture," is translated "suppose ye" in Acts 13:25, RV (KJV, "think ye"); "I supposed" in 25:18.

SUPREME

huperecho (*5242*), "to be superior, to excel," is translated "supreme" in 1 Pet. 2:13.

SURE

A. Adjectives.

1. *asphales* (*804*), "safe," is translated "sure" in Heb. 6:19.

2. *bebaios* (*949*), "firm, steadfast," is used of (a) God's promise to Abraham, Rom. 4:16; (b) the believer's hope, Heb. 6:19, "steadfast"; (c) the hope of spiritual leaders regarding the welfare of converts, 2 Cor. 1:7, "steadfast"; (d) the glorying of the hope, Heb. 3:6, "firm"; (e) the beginning of our confidence, 3:14, RV, "firm" (KJV, "steadfast"); (f) the Law given at Sinai, Heb. 2:2, "steadfast"; (g) the testament (or covenant) fulfilled after a death, 9:17, "of force"; (h) the calling and election of believers, 2 Pet. 1:10, to be made "sure" by the fulfillment of the injunctions in vv. 5-7; (i) the word of prophecy, "*made* more sure," 2 Pet. 1:19, RV, KJV, "a more sure (word of

prophecy)"; what is meant is not a comparison between the prophecies of the OT and NT, but that the former have been confirmed in the person of Christ (vv. 16-18).

B. Verb.

asphalizo (*805*), "to make safe or sure" (akin to A, No. 1), is rendered "to make sure" in Matt. 27:64, 65, 66, of the sepulchre of Christ; elsewhere, Acts 16:24, of making feet fast in the stocks.

SURETY (Noun)

enguos (*1450*) primarily signifies "bail," the bail who personally answers for anyone, whether with his life or his property (to be distinguished from *mesites*, "a mediator"); it is used in Heb. 7:22, "(by so much also hath Jesus become) the Surety (of a better covenant)," referring to the abiding and unchanging character of His Melchizedek priesthood, by reason of which His suretyship is established by God's oath (vv. 20, 21). As the Surety, He is the personal guarantee of the terms of the new and better covenant, secured on the ground of His perfect sacrifice (v. 27).

SURFEITING

kraipale (*2897*) signifies "the giddiness and headache resulting from excessive wine-bibbing, a drunken nausea," "surfeiting," Luke 21:34. Trench distinguishes this and the synonymous words, *methe*, "drunkenness," *oinophlugia*, "wine-bibbing" (KJV, "excess of wine," 1 Pet. 4:3), *komos*, "revelling."

SURNAME

epikaleo (*1941*), "to put a name upon" (*epi*, "upon," *kaleo*, "to call"), "to surname," is used in this sense in the passive voice, in some texts in Matt. 10:3 (it is absent in the best); in Luke 22:3, in some texts (the best have *kaleo*, "to call"); Acts 1:23; 4:36; 10:5, 18, 32; 11:13; 12:12, 25; in some texts, 15:22 (the best have *kaleo*).

SWADDLING CLOTHES

sparganoo (*4683*), "to swathe" (from *sparganon*, "a swathing band"), signifies "to wrap in swaddling clothes" in Luke 2:7, 12. The idea that the word means "rags" is without foundation.

SWEAR, SWORN

Old Testament

shaba' (7650), "to swear; take an oath." Often "to swear or to take an oath" is to strongly affirm a promise, with sanctions for not following through, often divine sanctions, Josh. 6:22. David and Jonathan strongly affirmed their love for each other with an oath,

1 Sam. 20:17. Allegiance to God is pledged by an oath, Isa. 19:18. Zephaniah condemns the idolatrous priests "that worship and that swear by the Lord, and that swear by Malcham [the Ammonite god]," Zeph. 1:5.

New Testament

omnumi or *omnuo* (*3660*) is used of "affirming or denying by an oath," e.g., Matt. 26:74; Mark 6:23; Luke 1:73; Heb. 3:11, 18; 4:3; 7:21; accompanied by that by which one swears, e.g., Matt. 5:34, 36; 23:16; Heb. 6:13, 16; Jas. 5:12; Rev. 10:6.

SWEET

glukus (*1099*) (cf. Eng., "glycerin," "glucose"), occurs in Jas. 3:11, 12 (KJV, "fresh" in this verse); Rev. 10:9, 10.

SWERVE

astocheo (*795*), "to miss the mark," is translated "having swerved" in 1 Tim. 1:6. Moulton and Milligan illustrate the use of the verb from the papyri, e.g., of a man in extravagant terms bewailing the loss of a pet fighting cock, "(I am distraught, for my cock) has failed (me)."

SWORD

Old Testament

A. Noun.

chereb (2719), "sword; dagger; flint knife; chisel." Usually *chereb* represents an implement that can be or is being used in war, such as a "sword," Gen. 34:26. It can also refer to a shorter sword, a "dagger," Judg. 3:16; or any knife, Josh. 5:2; or hewing instrument, Exod. 20:25.

This two-edged "sword" can be compared to a tongue; words can be sharp and cut, and wound and kill, Ps. 57:4. This usage tells us not only about the shape of the "sword" but that such a tongue is a violent, merciless, attacking weapon. In Gen. 27:40 "sword" is symbolic of violence: "And by thy sword shalt thou live...." Prov. 5:4 uses *chereb* (of a long two-edged "sword") to depict the grievous result of dealing with an adulteress; it is certain death: "But her end is bitter as wormwood, sharp as a two-edged sword."

The "sword" is frequently depicted as an agent of God. It is not only used to safeguard the garden of Eden, but figures the judgment of God executed upon His enemies: "For my sword shall be bathed in heaven: behold, it shall come down upon Idumea..." (Isa. 34:5; cf. Deut. 28:22).

S

B. Verb.

charab means "to smite down, slaughter." This verb, which appears 3 times in biblical Hebrew, has cognates in Arabic. The word appears in 2 Kings 3:23: "This is blood: the kings are surely slain."

New Testament

1. *machaira* (3162), "a short sword or dagger" (distinct from No. 2), e.g., Matt. 26:47, 51, 52 and parallel passages; Luke 21:24; 22:38, possibly "a knife"; Heb. 4:12; metaphorically and by metonymy, (a) for ordinary violence, or dissensions, that destroy peace, Matt. 10:34; (b) as the instrument of a magistrate or judge, e.g., Rom. 13:4; (c) of the Word of God, "the sword of the Spirit," probing the conscience, subduing the impulses to sin, Eph. 6:17.

2. *rhomphaia* (4501), a word of somewhat doubtful origin, denoted "a Thracian weapon of large size," whether a sword or spear is not certain, but usually longer than No. 1; it occurs (a) literally in Rev. 6:8; (b) metaphorically, as the instrument of anguish, Luke 2:35; of judgment, Rev. 1:16; 2:12, 16; 19:15, 21, probably figurative of the Lord's judicial utterances.

SYNAGOGUE

sunagoge (4864), properly "a bringing together" (*sun*, "together," *ago*, "to bring"), denoted (a) "a gathering of things, a collection," then, of "persons, an assembling, of Jewish religious gatherings," e.g., Acts 9:2; an assembly of Christian Jews, Jas. 2:2, RV, "synagogue" (KJV, marg.; text, "assembly"); a company dominated by the power and activity of Satan, Rev. 29; 39; (b) by metonymy, "the building" in which the gathering is held, e.g. Matt. 6:2; Mark 1:21. The origin of the Jewish "synagogue" is probably to be assigned to the time of the Babylonian exile. Having no temple, the Jews assembled on the Sabbath to hear the Law read, and the practice continued in various buildings after the return.

SYNAGOGUE (put out of the)

aposunagogos (656), an adjective denoting "expelled from the congregation, excommunicated," is used (a) with *ginomai*, "to become, be made," John 9:22; 12:42; (b) with *poieo*, "to make," John 16:2. This excommunication involved prohibition not only from attendance at the "synagogue," but from all fellowship with Israelites.

SYNAGOGUE (ruler of the)

archisunagogos (752) denotes "the administrative official," with the duty of preserving order and inviting persons to read or speak in the assembly, Mark 5:22, 35, 36, 38; Luke 8:49; 13:14; Acts 13:15; "chief ruler" (KJV) in Acts 18:8, 17.

T

TABERNACLE
Old Testament

A. Noun.

mishkan (4908), "dwelling place; tabernacle; shrine." This was a construction made of leather and goat hair, which was moveable. This construction was used as a holy place to worship the Lord, Exod. 25:9; Lev. 15:31; cf. Num. 19:13. The Tabernacle was built in the time of Moses and remained the holy place of Israel until the Temple was built, 2 Sam. 7:6; Ps. 132:4-5. The meaning of *mishkan* was also extended to include the whole area surrounding the temple, including as much as the city Jerusalem, Ps. 46:4; 87:2.

The defilement of the city and the temple area was sufficient reason for God to leave the temple, Ezek. 10, and to permit the destruction of His "dwelling place" by the brutish Babylonians, Ps. 74:7. In the Lord's providence He had planned to restore His people and the temple so as to assure them of His continued presence, Ezek. 37:27-28. John comments that Jesus Christ was God's "tabernacle": "And the Word was made flesh, and dwelt among us, (and we beheld his glory, the glory as of the only begotten of the Father,) full of grace and truth," John 1:14, and Jesus later referred to Himself as the temple: "But He spake of the temple of his body," John 2:21.

B. Verb.

shakan (7934), "to dwell, inhabit," Ps. 37:27.

New Testament

1. *skene* (4633), "a tent, booth, tabernacle," is used of (a) tents as dwellings, Matt. 17:4; Mark 9:5; Luke 9:33; Heb. 11:9, KJV, "tabernacles" (RV, "tents"); (b) the Mosaic tabernacle, Acts 7:44; Heb. 8:5; 9:1 (in some mss.); 9:8, 21, termed "the tent of meeting," RV (i.e., where the people were called to meet God), a preferable description to "the tabernacle of the congregation," as in the KJV in the OT; the outer part 9:2, 6; the inner sanctuary, 9:3; (c) the heavenly prototype, Heb. 8:2; 9:11; Rev. 13:6; 15:5; 21:3 (of its future descent); (d) the eternal abodes of the saints, Luke 16:9, RV, "tabernacles" (KJV, "habitations"); (e) the Temple in Jerusalem, as continuing the service of the tabernacle, Heb. 13:10; (f) the house of David, i.e.,

metaphorically of his people, Acts 15:16; (g) the portable shrine of the god Moloch, Acts 7:43.

2. *skenos* (*4636*), the equivalent of No. 1, is used metaphorically of the body as the "tabernacle" of the soul, 2 Cor. 5:1, 4.

3. *skenoma* (*4638*) occurs in Acts 7:46; 2 Pet. 1:13, 14.

4. *skenopegia* (*4634*), properly "the setting up of tents or dwellings" (No. 1, and *pegnumi*, "to fix"), represents the word "tabernacles" in "the feast of tabernacles," John 7:2. This feast, one of the three Pilgrimage Feasts in Israel, is called "the feast of ingathering" in Exod. 23:16; 34:22; it took place at the end of the year, and all males were to attend at the "tabernacle" with their offerings. In Lev. 23:34; Deut. 16:13; 31:10; 2 Chron. 8:13; Ezra 3:4 (cf. Neh. 8:14-18), it is called "the feast of tabernacles" (or "booths," *sukkoth*), and was appointed for seven days at Jerusalem from the 15th to the 22nd Tishri (approximately October), to remind the people that their fathers dwelt in these in the wilderness journeys. Cf. Num. 29:15-38, especially v. 35-38, for the regulations of the eighth or "last day, the great day of the feast" (John 7:37).

TABLE

1. *trapeza* (*5132*) is used of (a) "a dining table," Matt. 15:27; Mark 7:28; Luke 16:21; 22:21, 30; (b) "the table of shewbread," Heb. 9:2; (c) by metonymy, of "what is provided on the table" (the word being used of that with which it is associated), Acts 16:34; Rom. 11:9 (figurative of the special privileges granted to Israel and centering in Christ); 1 Cor. 10:21 (twice), "the Lord's table," denoting all that is provided for believers in Christ on the ground of His death (and thus expressing something more comprehensive than the Lord's Supper); "the table of demons," denoting all that is partaken of by idolaters as the result of the influence of demons in connection with their sacrifices; (d) "a moneychanger's table," Matt. 21:12; Mark 11:15; John 2:15; (e) "a bank," Luke 19:23; (f) by metonymy for "the distribution of money," Acts 6:2.

2. *plax* (*4109*) primarily denotes "anything flat and broad," hence, "a flat stone, a tablet," 2 Cor. 3:3 (twice); Heb. 9:4.

TALK (Noun and Verb)

A. Noun.

leros (*3026*) denotes "foolish talk, nonsense," Luke 24:11, RV, "idle talk" (KJV, "idle tales").

B. Verbs.

1. *laleo* (*2980*), "to speak, say," is always translated "to speak" in the RV, where the KJV renders it by "to talk," Matt. 12:46; Mark 6:50; Luke 24:32; John 4:27 (twice); 9:37; 14:30; Acts 26:31; Rev. 4:1; 17:1; 21:9, 15. The RV rendering is preferable; the idea of "chat" or

"chatter" is entirely foreign to the NT, and should never be regarded as the meaning in 1 Cor. 14:34, 35.

2. *sullaleo* (*4814*), "to speak with" (*sun*), is translated "to talk with," Matt. 17:3; Mark 9:4; Luke 9:30.

3. *homileo* (*3656*), "to be in company with, consort with" (*homilos*, "a throng"; *homilia*, "company"), hence, "to converse with," is rendered "to talk with," Acts 20:11.

4. *sunomileo* (*4926*), "to converse, talk with," occurs in Acts 10:27.

TALKERS (vain)

mataiologos (*3151*), an adjective denoting "talking idly" (*mataios*, "vain, idle," *lego*, "to speak"), is used as a noun (plural) in Titus 1:10.

TALKING (vain, foolish)

1. *mataiologia* (*3150*), a noun corresponding to the above, is used in 1 Tim. 1:6, RV, "vain talking" (KJV, "vain jangling").

2. *morologia* (*3473*), from *moros*, "foolish, dull, stupid," and *lego*, is used in Eph. 5:4; it denotes more than mere idle "talk." Trench describes it as "that 'talk of fools' which is foolishness and sin together."

TAME

damazo (*1150*), "to subdue, tame," is used (a) naturally in Mark 5:4 and Jas. 3:7 (twice); (b) metaphorically, of the tongue, in Jas. 3:8.

TANNER

burseus (*1038*), "a tanner" (from *bursa*, "a hide"), occurs in Acts 9:43; 10:6, 32.

TARES

zizanion (*2215*) is a kind of darnel, the commonest of the four species, being the bearded, growing in the grain fields, as tall as wheat and barley, and resembling wheat in appearance. It was credited among the Jews with being degenerate wheat. The rabbis called it "bastard." The seeds are poisonous to man and herbivorous animals, producing sleepiness, nausea, convulsions and even death (they are harmless to poultry). The plants can be separated out, but the custom, as in the parable, is to leave the cleaning out till near the time of harvest, Matt. 13:25-27, 29, 30, 36, 38, 40. The Lord describes the tares as "the sons of the evil *one*"; false teachings are not distinguishable from their propagandists.

TARRY

1. *meno* (*3306*), "to abide," is translated by the verb "to abide," in

the RV, for KJV, "to tarry," in Matt. 26:38; Mark 14:34; Luke 24:29; John 4:40; Acts 9:43; 18:20; the RV retains the verb "to tarry" in John 21:22, 23; in Acts 20:5, KJV, "tarried" (RV, "were waiting"). Some mss. have it in Acts 20:15 (KJV, "tarried").

2. *epimeno* (*1961*), to abide, continue, a strengthened form of No. 1, is translated "to tarry" in Acts 10:48; 21:4, 10; 28:12, 14; 1 Cor. 16:7, 8; Gal. 1:18, RV (KJV, "abode").

3. *hupomeno* (*5278*), "to endure," is rendered "tarried behind" in Luke 2:43.

4. *prosmeno* (*4357*), "to abide still, continue," is translated "tarried" in Acts 18:18, suggesting patience and steadfastness in remaining after the circumstances which preceded; in 1 Tim. 1:3, RV, "to tarry" (KJV, "to abide still").

5. *diatribo* (*1304*), is invariably rendered "to tarry," in the RV; KJV, twice, John 3:22; Acts 25:6; "continued" in John 11:54; Acts 15:35; "abode," Acts 12:19; 14:3, 28; 20:6; "abiding," 16:12, "had been," 25:14.

6. *chronizo* (*5549*), "to spend or while away time"; "to tarry," Matt. 25:5; Luke 1:21; Heb. 10:37.

7. *braduno* (*1019*), "to be slow," is rendered "I tarry long," 1 Tim. 3:15; "is...slack," 2 Pet. 3:9.

8. *kathizo* (*2523*), "to make to sit down," or, intransitively, "to sit down," is translated "tarry ye" in Luke 24:49.

9. *mello* (*3195*), "to be about to," is rendered "(why) tarriest thou?" in Acts 22:16.

10. *ekdechomai* (*1551*), "to expect, await" (*ek*, "from," *dechomai*, "to receive"), is translated "tarry" in 1 Cor. 11:33, KJV (RV, "wait").

TASTE

geuo (*1089*), "to make to taste," is used in the middle voice, signifying "to taste" (a) naturally, Matt. 27:34; Luke 14:24; John 2:9; Col. 2:21; (b) metaphorically, of Christ's "tasting" death, implying His personal experience in voluntarily undergoing death, Heb. 2:9; of believers (negatively) as to "tasting" of death, Matt. 16:28; Mark 9:1; Luke 9:27; John 8:52; of "tasting" the heavenly gift (different from receiving it), Heb. 6:4; "the good word of God, and the powers of the age to come," 6:5; "that the Lord is gracious," 1 Pet. 2:3.

TATTLER

phluaros (*5397*), "babbling, garrulous" (from *phluo*, "to babble": cf. *phluareo*, "to prate against"), is translated "tattlers" in 1 Tim. 5:13.

TAUGHT (Adjective)

1. *didaktos* (*1318*), primarily "what can be taught," then, "taught," is used (a) of persons, John 6:45; (b) of things, 1 Cor. 2:13

(twice), "(not in words which man's wisdom) teacheth, (but which the Spirit) teacheth," lit., "(not in words) taught (of man's wisdom, but) taught (of the Spirit)."

2. *theodidaktos* (2312), "God-taught" (*theos*, "God," and No. 1), occurs in 1 Thess. 4:9, lit., "God-taught (persons)"; while the missionaries had "taught" the converts to love one another, God had Himself been their Teacher. Cf. John 6:45 (see No. 1).

TEACH

Old Testament

A. Verbs.

lamad (3925), "to teach, learn, cause to learn." In its simple, active form, this verb has the meaning "to learn," but it is also found in a form giving the causative sense, "to teach," Deut. 4:1. In Deut. 5:1 *lamad* is used of learning God's laws, cf. Ps. 119:7.

yarah (3384), "throw, teach, shoot, point out." The basic idea of "to throw" is easily extended to mean the shooting of arrows, 1 Sam. 20:36-37. "To throw" seems to be further extended to mean "to point," by which fingers are thrown in a certain direction, Gen. 46:28; Prov. 6:13. From this meaning it is only a short step to the concept of teaching as the "pointing out" of fact and truth. Thus, Bezalel was inspired by God "to teach" others his craftsmanship, Exod. 35:34; the false prophets "teach" lies, Isa. 9:15; and the father "taught" his son, Prov. 4:4.

B. Noun.

torah (8451), "direction; instruction; guideline." *torah* is much more than law or a set of rules. *torah* is not restriction or hindrance, but instead the means whereby one can reach a goal or ideal. In the truest sense, *torah* was given to Israel to enable her to truly become and remain God's special people. One might say that in keeping *torah*, Israel was kept. Unfortunately, Israel fell into the trap of keeping *torah* as something imposed, and for itself, rather than as a means of becoming what God intended for her. The means became the end. Instead of seeing *torah* as a guideline, it became an external body of rules, and thus a weight rather than a freeing and guiding power. This burden, plus the legalism of Roman law, forms the background of the New Testament tradition of law, especially as Paul struggles with it in his Letter to the church at Rome.

C. Adjective.

limmud means "taught." This adjective forms an exact equivalent to the New Testament idea of "disciple, one who is taught," Isa. 8:16; 54:13.

T

New Testament

A. Verbs.

1. *didasko* (*1321*) is used (a) absolutely, "to give instruction," e.g., Matt. 4:23; 9:35; Rom. 12:7; 1 Cor. 4:17; 1 Tim. 2:12; 4:11; (b) transitively, with an object, whether persons, e.g., Matt. 5:2; 7:29, and frequently in the Gospels and Acts, or things "taught," e.g., Matt. 15:9; 22:16; Acts 15:35; 18:11; both persons and things, e.g., John 14:26; Rev. 2:14, 20.

2. *katecheo* (*2727*), rendered "to teach" in 1 Cor. 14:19, KJV (RV, "instruct").

3. *heterodidaskaleo* (*2085*), "to teach a different doctrine" (*heteros*, "different," to be distinguished from *allos*, "another of the same kind," is used in 1 Tim. 1:3; 6:3, RV, KJV, "teach (no) other doctrine" and "teach otherwise," of what is contrary to the faith.

B. Adjective.

didaktikos (*1317*), "skilled in teaching" (akin to No. 1 above: Eng., "didactic"), is translated "apt to teach" in 1 Tim. 3:2; 2 Tim. 2:24.

TEACHER, FALSE TEACHERS

1. *didaskalos* (*1320*) is rendered "teacher" or "teachers" in Matt. 23:8, by Christ, of Himself; in John 3:2 of Christ; of Nicodemus in Israel, 3:10, RV; of "teachers" of the truth in the churches, Acts 13:1; 1 Cor. 12:28, 29; Eph. 4:11; Heb. 5:12; Jas. 3:1, RV; by Paul of his work among the churches, 1 Tim. 2:7; 2 Tim. 1:11; of "teachers," wrongfully chosen by those who have "itching ears," 2 Tim. 4:3.

2. *kalodidaskalos* (*2567*) denotes "a teacher of what is good" (*kalos*), Titus 2:3.

3. *pseudodidaskalos* (*5572*), "a false teacher," occurs in the plural in 2 Pet. 2:1.

TEARS

dakruon or *dakru* (*1144*), akin to *dakruo*, "to weep," is used in the plural, Mark 9:24; Luke 7:38, 44 (with the sense of washing therewith the Lord's feet); Acts 20:19, 31; 2 Cor. 2:4; 2 Tim. 1:4; Heb. 5:7; 12:17; Rev. 7:17; 21:4.

TEDIOUS (to be)

enkopto (*1465*), "to hinder," is rendered "to be tedious" in Acts 24:4, of detaining a person unnecessarily.

TELL

Old Testament

A. Verb.

nagad (*5046*), "to tell, explain, inform." The first emphasis of the word is "to tell," i.e., speak verbal information to another, often reporting an event, Gen. 9:22; or giving an important message, Gen. 14:13; finally, *nagad* means "to explain or reveal" something one does not otherwise know, Gen. 3:11. 1 Sam. 27:11; Isa. 58:1.

B. Noun.

nagid (5057), "chief leader." In 1 Sam. 9:16 the word is used as a "chief leader" that is equivalent to a king, 1 Chron. 9:11, 20.

C. Preposition.

neged (5048), "before; in the presence of; in the sight of; in front of; in one's estimation; straight ahead." Basically the word indicates that its object is immediately "before" something or someone. It is used in Gen. 2:18, where God said He would make Adam "a help meet for him," or someone to correspond to him, just as the males and females of the animals corresponded to (matched) one another. To be immediately "before" the sun is to be fully in the sunlight, Num. 25:4. In Exod. 10:10 Pharaoh told Moses that evil was immediately "before" his face, or was in his mind. *neged* signifies "in front of," Exod. 19:2, "before" in the sense of "in one's estimation," Isa. 40:17, and "straight ahead (before)," Josh. 6:5.

D. Adverb.

neged (5048), "opposite; over against," Gen. 21:16.

New Testament

1. *lego* (*3004*) and the 2nd aorist form *eipon*, used to supply this tense in *lego*, are frequently translated "to tell," e.g., Matt. 2:13, RV, "I tell," KJV, "I bring (thee) word"; 10:27.

2. *laleo* (*2980*), rendered "to speak," in the RV (for KJV, "to tell"), e.g., Matt. 26:13; Luke 1:45; 2:17, 18, 20; Acts 11:14; 27:25; but RV and KJV, "to tell" in John 8:40; Acts 9:6; 22:10.

3. *apangello* (*518*), "to announce, declare, report" (usually as a messenger), is frequently rendered "to tell," e.g., Matt. 8:33; 14:12.

4. *anangello* (*312*), "to bring back word, announce," is sometimes rendered "to tell," e.g., John 5:15; 2 Cor. 7:7.

TEMPERANCE, TEMPERATE

A. Noun.

enkrateia (*1466*), from *kratos*, "strength," occurs in Acts 24:25; Gal. 5:23; 2 Pet. 1:6 (twice), in all of which it is rendered "temperance"; the RV marg., "self-control" is the preferable rendering, as "temperance" is now limited to one form of self-control; the various powers bestowed by God upon man are capable of abuse; the right use demands the controlling power of the will under the operation of the Spirit of God; in Acts 24:25 the word follows "righteousness," which represents God's claims, self-control being

T

man's response thereto; in 2 Pet. 1:6, it follows "knowledge," suggesting that what is learned requires to be put into practice.

B. Adjectives.

1. *enkrates* (1468), akin to A, denotes "exercising self-control," rendered "temperate" in Titus 1:8.

2. *nephalios* (3524), translated "temperate" in 1 Tim. 3:2, RV (KJV, "vigilant"); in 3:11 and Titus 2:2, RV (KJV, "sober").

C. Verb.

enkrateuomai (1467), akin to A and B, No. 1, rendered "is temperate" in 1 Cor. 9:25, is used figuratively of the rigid self-control practiced by athletes with a view to gaining the prize.

TEMPEST

1. *thuella* (2366), "a hurricane, cyclone, whirlwind" (akin to *thuo*, "to slay," and *thumos*, "wrath"), is used in Heb. 12:18.

2. *seismos* (4578), "a shaking" (Eng., "seismic," etc.), is used of a "tempest" in Matt. 8:24.

3. *cheimon* (5494), "winter, a winter storm," hence, in general, "a tempest," is so rendered in Acts 27:20.

4. *lailaps* (2978), "a tempest," 2 Pet. 2:17, KJV.

TEMPESTUOUS

tuphonikos (5189), from *tuphon*, "a hurricane, typhoon," is translated "tempestuous" in Acts 27:14.

TEMPLE

Old Testament

hekal (1964), "palace; temple." This is a construction, often very beautiful and ornate, as the dwelling place of a king or a god (or the true God), 1 Sam. 1:9. The word "palace" in English versions is a residence for a king, 1 Kings 21:1; of the king of Babylon, 2 Kings 20:18; of Nineveh, Nah. 2:6. *hekal* with the meaning "temple" is generally clarified in the context by two markers that follow. The first marker is the addition "of the Lord," Ezra 3:10; it was a holy place, Ps. 79:1. Sometimes the definite article suffices to identify the "temple in Jerusalem," Isa. 6:1; Ezekiel's temple, Ezek. 41.

The Old Testament also speaks about the heavenly *hekal*, the *hekal* of God. It is difficult to decide on a translation, whether "palace" or "temple." Most versions opt in favor of the "temple" idea: "Hear, all ye people; hearken, O earth, and all that therein is: and let the Lord God be witness against you, the Lord from his holy temple," Mic. 1:2; cf. Ps. 5:7; 11:4; Hab. 2:20.

New Testament

1. *hieron* (2411), the neuter of the adjective *hieros*, "sacred," is

used as a noun denoting "a sacred place, a temple," that of Artemis (Diana), Acts 19:27; that in Jerusalem, Mark 11:11, signifying the entire building with its precincts, or some part thereof, as distinct from the *naos*, "the inner sanctuary" (see No. 2); apart from the Gospels and Acts, it is mentioned only in 1 Cor. 9:13. Christ taught in one of the courts, to which all the people had access. *hieron* is never used figuratively. The Temple mentioned in the Gospels and Acts was begun by Herod in 20 B.C., and destroyed by the Romans in A.D. 70.

2. *naos* (*3485*), "a shrine or sanctuary," was used (a) among the heathen, to denote the shrine containing the idol, Acts 17:24; 19:24 (in the latter, miniatures); (b) among the Jews, the sanctuary in the "Temple," into which only the priests could lawfully enter, e.g., Luke 1:9, 21, 22; Christ, as being of the tribe of Judah, and thus not being a priest while upon the earth (Heb. 7:13, 14; 8:4), did not enter the *naos*; for 2 Thess. 2:4; (c) by Christ metaphorically, of His own physical body, John 2:19, 21; (d) in apostolic teaching, metaphorically, (1) of the church, the mystical body of Christ, Eph. 2:21; (2) of a local church, 1 Cor. 3:16, 17; 2 Cor. 6:16; (3) of the present body of the individual believer, 1 Cor. 6:19; (4) of the "Temple" seen in visions in the Apocalypse, 3:12; 7:15; 11:19; 14:15, 17; 15:5, 6, 8; 16:1, 17; (5) of the Lord God Almighty and the Lamb, as the "Temple" of the new and heavenly Jerusalem, Rev. 21:22.

TEMPORAL

proskairos (*4340*), "for a season" (*pros*, "for," *kairos*, "a season"), is rendered "temporal" in 2 Cor. 4:18.

TEMPT

A. Verbs.

1. *peirazo* (*3985*) signifies (1) "to try, attempt, assay"; (2) "to test, try, prove," in a good sense, said of Christ and of believers, Heb. 2:18, where the context shows that the temptation was the cause of suffering to Him, and only suffering, not a drawing away to sin, so that believers have the sympathy of Christ as their High Priest in the suffering which sin occasions to those who are in the enjoyment of communion with God; so in the similar passage in 4:15; in all the temptations which Christ endured, there was nothing within Him that answered to sin. There was no sinful infirmity in Him. While He was truly man, and His divine nature was not in any way inconsistent with His Manhood, there was nothing in Him such as is produced in us by the sinful nature which belongs to us; in Heb. 11:37, of the testing of OT saints; in 1 Cor. 10:13, where the meaning has a wide scope, the verb is used of "testing" as permitted by God, and of the believer as one who should be in the realization of his own helplessness and his dependence upon God; in

T

a bad sense, "to tempt" (a) of attempts to ensnare Christ in His speech, e.g., Matt. 16:1; 19:3; 22:18, 35, and parallel passages; John 8:6; (b) of temptations to sin, e.g., Gal. 6:1, where one who would restore an erring brother is not to act as his judge, but as being one with him in liability to sin, with the possibility of finding himself in similar circumstances, Jas. 1:13, 14; of temptations mentioned as coming from the Devil, Matt. 4:1; and parallel passages; 1 Cor. 7:5; 1 Thess. 3:5; (c) of trying or challenging God, Acts 15:10; 1 Cor. 10:9 (2nd part); Heb. 3:9; the Holy Spirit, Acts 5:9: cf. No. 2.

2. *ekpeirazo* (*1598*), an intensive form of the foregoing, is used in much the same way as No. 1 (2) (c), in Christ's quotation from Deut. 6:16, in reply to the Devil, Matt. 4:7; Luke 4:12; so in 1 Cor. 10:9, RV, "the Lord" (KJV, "Christ"); of the lawyer who "tempted" Christ, Luke 10:25.

B. Adjective.

apeirastos (*551*), "untempted, untried" (*a*, negative, and A, No. 1), occurs in Jas. 1:13, with *eimi*, "to be," "cannot be tempted," "untemptable" (Mayor).

TEMPTATION

peirasmos (*3986*), akin to A, above, is used of (1) "trials" with a beneficial purpose and effect, (a) of "trials" or "temptations," divinely permitted or sent, Luke 22:28; Acts 20:19; Jas. 1:2; 1 Pet. 1:6; 4:12, RV, "to prove," KJV, "to try"; 2 Pet. 2:9 (singular); Rev. 3:10, RV, "trial" (KJV, "temptation"); in Jas. 1:12, "temptation" apparently has meanings (1) and (2) combined, and is used in the widest sense; (b) with a good or neutral significance, Gal. 4:14, of Paul's physical infirmity, "a temptation" to the Galatian converts, of such a kind as to arouse feelings of natural repugnance; (c) of "trials" of a varied character, Matt. 6:13 and Luke 11:4, where believers are commanded to pray not to be led into such by forces beyond their own control; Matt. 26:41; Mark 14:38; Luke 22:40, 46, where they are commanded to watch and pray against entering into "temptations" by their own carelessness or disobedience; in all such cases God provides "the way of escape," 1 Cor. 10:13 (where *peirasmos* occurs twice). (2) Of "trial" definitely designed to lead to wrong doing, "temptation," Luke 4:13; 8:13; 1 Tim. 6:9; (3) of "trying" or challenging God, by men, Heb. 3:8.

TEMPTER

The present participle of *peirazo*, "to tempt," preceded by the article, lit., "the (one) tempting," is used as a noun, describing the Devil in this character, Matt. 4:3; 1 Thess. 3:5. See TEMPT 1, above.

TENDER

hapalos (527), "soft, tender," is used of the branch of a tree, Matt. 24:32; Mark 13:28.

TENTMAKERS

skenopoios (4635), an adjective, "tentmaking," is used as a noun in Acts 18:3.

TERM (appointed)

prothesmios (4287), an adjective denoting "appointed beforehand," is used as a noun, *prothesmia* (grammatically feminine, with *hemera*, "a day," understood), as in Greek law, "a day appointed before," Gal. 4:2, RV, "the term appointed," i.e., "a stipulated date" (KJV, "the time appointed").

TERRESTRIAL

epigeios (1919), "on earth, earthly" (*epi*, "on," *ge*, "the earth") is rendered "terrestrial" in 1 Cor. 15:40 (twice), in contrast to *epouranios*, "heavenly."

TERRIFY

A. Verbs.

1. *ptoeo* (4422), "to terrify," is used in the passive voice, Luke 21:9; 24:37.

2. *ekphobeo* (1629), "to frighten away" (*ek*, "out," *phobos*, "fear"), occurs in 2 Cor. 10:9.

3. *pturo* (4426), "to scare," Phil. 1:28.

B. Adjective.

emphobos (1719), "terrified," is so rendered in the RV of Acts 24:25.

TERROR

1. *phobos* (5401), "fear," is rendered "terror" in Rom. 13:3; in 2 Cor. 5:11 and 1 Pet. 3:14, KJV (RV, "fear").

2. *phobetron* (5400), "that which causes fright. a terror," is translated "terrors" in Luke 21:11, RV (KJV, "fearful sights").

TO TEST

A. Verb.

tsarap (6884), "to refine, try, smelt, test." *tsarap* has the meaning "to refine" in rabbinic and modern Hebrew, but lost the primary significance of "to smelt," and then also a meaning, "test, try." Jeremiah describes the process of smelting and refining, Jer. 6:30; Isa. 40:19; 41:7. *tsarap* is also used metaphorically with the sense "to refine by means of suffering," Ps. 66:10-12; Isa. 1:25. Those who were thus purified are those who call on the name of the Lord and receive the gracious benefits of the covenant, Zech. 13:9. The coming of the messenger of the covenant (Jesus Christ) is compared to the work of a smith, Mal. 3:2-3. The believer can take comfort in the Word of God which alone on earth is tried and purified and by which we can be purified: "Thy promise is well tried, and thy servant loves it," Ps. 119:140, RSV; cf. Ps. 18:30; Prov. 30:5.

B. Nouns.

Two nouns derived from the verb *tsarap* occur rarely. *tsorpi* occurs once to mean "goldsmith," Neh. 3:31. *matsrep* occurs twice and refers to a "crucible," Prov. 17:3; cf. Prov. 27:21.

TESTATOR

diatithemi (1303), "to arrange, dispose," is used only in the middle voice in the NT; in Heb. 9:16, 17. "There can be little doubt that the word (*diatheke*) must be invariably taken in this sense of 'covenant' in the NT, and especially in a book...so impregnated with the language of the Sept. as the Epistle to the Hebrews" (Hatch). We may render somewhat literally thus: For where a covenant (is), a death (is) necessary to be brought in of the one covenanting; for a covenant over dead ones (victims) is sure, since never has it force when the one covenanting lives [Christ being especially in view]. The writer is speaking from a Jewish point of view, not from that of the Greeks. "To adduce the fact that in the case of wills the death of the testator is the condition of validity, is, of course, no proof at all that a death is necessary to make a covenant valid...To support his argument, proving the necessity of Christ's death, the writer adduces the general law that he who makes a covenant does so at the expense of life" (Marcus Dods). This refers not to the making of a will (a testator), but the making of a covenant.

TESTIFY

1. *martureo* (3140), rendered "to bear witness, to witness," in the RV, where KJV renders it "to testify," John 2:25; 3:11, 32; 5:39; 15:26; 21:24; 1 Cor. 15:15; Heb. 7:17; 11:4; 1 John 4:14; 5:9; 3 John 3. In the following, however, the RV, like the KJV, has the rendering "to testify," John 4:39, 44; 7:7; 13:21; Acts 26:5; Rev. 22:16, 18, 20.

2. *epimartureo* (1957), "to bear witness to" (a strengthened form of No. 1), is rendered "testifying" in 1 Pet. 5:12.

3. *marturomai* (3143), primarily, "to summon as witness," then, "to bear witness" (sometimes with the suggestion of solemn protestation), is rendered "to testify" in Acts 20:26, RV (KJV, "I take...to record"); 26:22, in the best texts (some have No. 1), RV; Gal. 5:3; Eph. 4:17; 1 Thess. 2:11, in the best texts (some have No. 1), RV, "testifying" (KJV, "charged").

4. *diamarturomai* (*1263*), "to testify or protest solemnly," an intensive form of No. 3, is translated "to testify" in Luke 16:28; Acts 2:40; 8:25; 10:42; 18:5; 20:21, 23, 24; 23:11; 28:23; 1 Thess. 4:6; Heb. 2:6; "to charge" in 1 Tim. 5:21; 2 Tim. 2:14; 4:8.

5. *promarturomai* (*4303*), "to testify beforehand," occurs in 1 Pet. 1:11, where the pronoun "it" should be "He" (the "it" being due to the grammatically neuter form of *pneuma*; the personality of the Holy Spirit requires the masculine pronoun).

TESTIMONY
Old Testament

'edut (*5715*), "testimony; ordinance." This word refers to the Ten Commandments as a solemn divine charge or duty. In particular, it represents those commandments as written on the tablets and existing as a reminder and "testimony" of Israel's relationship and responsibility to God, Exod. 31:18. Elsewhere these tablets are called simply "the testimony," Exod. 25:16. Since they were kept in the ark, it became known as the "ark of the testimony," Exod. 25:22, or simply "the testimony": "As the Lord commanded Moses, so Aaron laid it up before the Testimony, to be kept," Exod. 16:34. The word sometimes refers to the entire law of God, Ps. 19:7. Here *'edut* is synonymously parallel to "law," making it a synonym to that larger concept. Special or particular laws are sometimes called "testimonies," 1 Kings 2:3.

New Testament

1. *marturion* (*3142*), "a testimony, witness," is almost entirely translated "testimony" in both KJV and RV. The only place where both have "witness" is Acts 4:33. In Acts 7:44 and Jas. 5:3, the RV has "testimony" (KJV, "witness").

In 2 Thess. 1:10, "our testimony unto you," RV, refers to the fact that the missionaries, besides proclaiming the truths of the gospel, had borne witness to the power of these truths. *kerugma*, "the thing preached, the message," is objective, having especially to do with the effect on the hearers; *marturion* is mainly subjective, having to do especially with the preacher's personal experience.

2. *marturia* (*3141*), "witness, evidence, testimony," is almost always rendered "witness" in the RV (for KJV, "testimony" in John 3:32, 33; 5:34; 8:17; 21:24, and always for KJV, "record," e.g., 1 John 5:10, 11), except in Acts 22:18 and in the Apocalypse, where both, with one exception, have "testimony," 1:2, 9; 6:9; 11:7; 12:11, 17; 19:10 (twice); 20:4 (KJV, "witness"). In 19:10, "the testimony of Jesus" is objective, the "testimony" or witness given to Him (cf. 1:2, 9; as to those who will bear it, see Rev. 12:17, RV). The statement "the testimony of Jesus is the spirit of prophecy," is to be understood in the light, e.g., of the "testimony" concerning Christ and

T

Israel in the Psalms, which will be used by the godly Jewish remnant in the coming time of "Jacob's Trouble." All such "testimony" centers in and points to Christ.

TETRARCH

A. Noun.

tetraarches or *tetrarches* (5076) denotes "one of four rulers" (*tetra*, "four," *arche*, "rule"), properly, "the governor of the fourth part of a region"; hence, "a dependent princeling," or "any petty ruler" subordinate to kings or ethnarchs; in the NT, Herod Antipas, Matt. 14:1; Luke 3:19; 9:7; Acts 13:1.

B. Verb.

tetraarcheo or *tetrarcheo* (5075), "to be a tetrarch," occurs in Luke 3:1 (thrice), of Herod Antipas, his brother Philip and Lysanias. Antipas and Philip each inherited a fourth part of his father's dominions. Inscriptions bear witness to the accuracy of Luke's details.

THANK, THANKS (Noun and Verb), THANKFUL, THANKFULNESS, THANKSGIVING, THANKWORTHY

A. Nouns.

1. *charis* (5485), rendered "thank" in Luke 6:32, 33, 34; in 17:9, "doth he thank" is lit., "hath he thanks to"; it is rendered "thanks (be to God)" in Rom. 6:17, RV (KJV, "God be thanked"); "thanks" in 1 Cor. 15:57; in 1 Tim. 1:12 and 2 Tim. 1:3, "I thank" is, lit., "I have thanks"; "thankworthy," 1 Pet. 2:19, KJV (RV, "acceptable").

2. *eucharistia* (2169), *eu*, "well," *charizomai*, "to give freely" (Eng., "eucharist"), denotes (a) "gratitude," "thankfulness," Acts 24:3; (b) "giving of thanks, thanksgiving," 1 Cor. 14:16; 2 Cor. 4:15; 9:11, 12 (plur.); Eph. 5:4; Phil. 4:6; Col. 2:7; 4:2; 1 Thess. 3:9 ("thanks"); 1 Tim. 2:1 (plur.); 4:3, 4; Rev. 4:9, "thanks"; 7:12.

B. Verbs.

1. *eucharisteo* (2168), akin to A, No. 2, "to give thanks," (a) is said of Christ, Matt. 15:36; 26:27; Mark 8:6; 14:23; Luke 22:17, 19; John 6:11, 23; 11:41; 1 Cor. 11:24; (b) of the Pharisee in Luke 18:11 in his self-complacent prayer; (c) is used by Paul at the beginning of all his epistles, except 2 Cor. (see, however, *eulogetos* in 1:3), Gal., 1 Tim., 2 Tim. (see, however, *charin echo*, 1:3), and Titus, (1) for his readers, Rom. 1:8; Eph. 1:16; Col. 1:3; 1 Thess. 1:2; 2 Thess. 1:3 (cf. 2:13); virtually so in Philem. 4; (2) for fellowship shown, Phil. 1:3; (3) for God's gifts to them, 1 Cor. 1:4; (d) is recorded (1) of Paul elsewhere, Acts 27:35; 28:15; Rom. 7:25; 1 Cor. 1:14; 14:18; (2) of Paul and others, Rom. 16:4; 1 Thess. 2:13; of himself, representatively,

as a practice, 1 Cor. 10:30; (3) of others, Luke 17:16; Rom. 14:6 (twice); 1 Cor. 14:17; Rev. 11:17; (e) is used in admonitions to the saints, the Name of the Lord Jesus suggesting His character and example, Eph. 5:20; Col. 1:12; 3:17; 1 Thess. 5:18; (f) as the expression of a purpose, 2 Cor. 1:11, RV; (g) negatively of the ungodly, Rom. 1:21. "Thanksgiving" is the expression of joy Godward, and is therefore the fruit of the Spirit (Gal. 5:22); believers are encouraged to abound in it (e.g., Col. 2:7, and see C, below).

2. *exomologeo* (*1843*), in the middle voice, signifies "to make acknowledgment," whether of sins (to confess), or in the honor of a person, as in Rom. 14:11; 15:9 (in some mss. in Rev. 3:5); this is the significance in the Lord's address to the Father, "I thank (Thee)," in Matt. 11:25 and Luke 10:21, the meaning being "I make thankful confession" or "I make acknowledgment with praise."

3. *anthomologeomai* (*437*), "to acknowledge fully, to celebrate fully (*anti*) in praise with thanksgiving," is used of Anna in Luke 2:35.

C. Adjective.

eucharistos (*2170*), primarily, "gracious, agreeable" (as in the Sept., Prov. 11:16, of a wife, who brings glory to her husband), then "grateful, thankful," is so used in Col. 3:15.

THEATER

theatron (*2302*), "a theater," was used also as "a place of assembly," Acts 19:29, 31; in 1 Cor. 4:9 it is used of "a show" or "spectacle."

THEFT

1. *klope* (*2829*), akin to *klepto*, "to steal," is used in the plural in Matt. 15:19; Mark 7:22.

2. *klemma* (*2809*), "a thing stolen," and so, "a theft," is used in the plural in Rev. 9:21.

THIEF, THIEVES

1. *kleptes* (*2812*) is used (a) literally, Matt. 6:19, 20; 24:43; Luke 12:33, 39; John 10:1, 10; 12:6; 1 Cor. 6:10; 1 Pet. 4:15; (b) metaphorically of "false teachers," John 10:8; (c) figuratively, (1) of the personal coming of Christ, in a warning to a local church, with most of its members possessed of mere outward profession and defiled by the world, Rev. 3:3; in retributive intervention to overthrow the foes of God, 16:15; (2) of the Day of the Lord, in divine judgment upon the world, 2 Pet. 3:10 and 1 Thess. 5:2, 4.

2. *lestes* (*3027*) is frequently rendered "thieves" in the KJV, e.g., Matt. 21:13.

T

THINK

Old Testament

A. Verb.

chashab (2803), "to think, devise, purpose, esteem, count, imagine, impute." *chashab* can be translated as "devise" in association with the sense of "to think and reckon." A gifted person of God "devises" excellent works in gold and other choice objects, Exod. 35:35. The word may deal with evil, as when Haman "devised" an evil plot against the Jewish people, Esth. 8:3. The word may mean "think." Some "thought" to do away with David by sending him against the Philistines, 1 Sam. 18:25; Judah "thought" Tamar to be a harlot, Gen. 38:15; and Eli "thought" Hannah was drunk, 1 Sam. 1:13. God repented of the evil concerning the judgment he "thought" to bring upon Israel, Jer. 18:8. Those who fear the Lord may also "think" upon His name, Mal. 3:16. *chashab* may be rendered "to purpose" or "esteem," Job 41:27. A classic usage of "esteem" appears in Isa. 53:3-4.

Translated as "count," the word is used in a number of ways. It had a commercial connotation, as when land was being redeemed and the price was established, based on the value of crops until the next year of Jubilee, Lev. 25:27; Num. 18:30.

Other unique translations of *chashab* occur. In order to approach God, Asaph had to remember and "consider" the days of old, Ps. 77:5. God had a controversy with Nebuchadnezzar, king of Babylon, because he "conceived" a plan against Him and His people, Jer. 49:30. The prophet Amos cites people who "invent" instruments of music and enjoy it, Amos 6:5. Huram of Tyre sent a man to help Solomon in the building of the temple, who knew how to "find out" all the works of art—i.e., he could work in various metals and fabrics to design a work of beauty, 2 Chron. 2:14. Joseph had to remind his brethren that he did not seek to do them harm because they had sold him into slavery, since God "meant" it for the good of the preservation of Jacob's sons, Gen. 50:20.

B. Adjective.

chashab (2803), "cunning," Exod. 38:23. This meaning of *chashab* as "cunning" appears 11 times in Exodus. But this skill was more than human invention—it indicated how the Spirit of God imparts wisdom, understanding, and knowledge, cf. Exod. 36:8; 39:3.

New Testament

1. *dokeo* (1380), "to suppose, to think, to form an opinion," which may be either right or wrong, is sometimes rendered "to think," e.g., Matt. 3:9; 6:7.

2. *hegeomai* (2233), rendered "to think" in Acts 26:2; 2 Cor. 9:5, "I thought"; Phil. 2:6, KJV (RV, "counted"); 2 Pet. 1:13.

3. *noeo* (*3539*), "to perceive, understand, apprehend," is rendered "think" in Eph. 3:20.

4. *huponoeo* (*5282*), "to suppose, surmise" (*hupo*, "under," and No. 3), is rendered "to think" in Acts 13:25, KJV (RV, "suppose).

5. *logizomai* (*3049*), "to reckon," is rendered "to think," in Rom. 2:3, KJV (RV, "reckonest"); 1 Cor. 13:5, KJV, RV, "taketh (not) account of," i.e., love does not reckon up or calculatingly consider the evil done to it (something more than refraining from imputing motives); 13:11, "I thought"; in the following, for the KJV, "to think," in 2 Cor. 3:5, RV, "to account"; 10:2 (twice), "count"; 10:7, "consider"; 10:11, "reckon"; 12:6, "account." In Phil. 4:8, "think on (these things)," it signifies "make those things the subjects of your thoughtful consideration," or "carefully reflect on them" (RV marg., "take account of").

6. *phroneo* (*5426*), "to be minded in a certain way" (*phren*, "the mind"), is rendered "to think," in Rom. 12:3 (2nd and 3rd occurrences).

7. *axioo* (*515*), "to regard as worthy" (*axios*), "to deem it suitable," is rendered "thought (not) good" in Acts 15:38.

8. *enthumeomai* (*1760*), "to reflect on, ponder," is used in Matt. 1:20; 9:4.

9. *huperphroneo* (*5252*), "to be overproud, high-minded," occurs in Rom. 12:3, rendered "to think of himself more highly."

10. *dienthumeomai* (*1223*) and *1760*), "to consider deeply" (*dia*, intensive), is used of Peter in Acts 10:19, in the best texts.

THIRST (Noun and Verb), THIRSTY (to be), ATHIRST

A. Noun.

dipsos (*1373*), "thirst" (cf. Eng., "dipsomania"), occurs in 2 Cor. 11:27.

B. Verb.

dipsao (*1372*) is used (a) in the natural sense, e.g., Matt. 25:35, 37, 42; in v. 44, "athirst" (lit., "thirsting"); John 4:13, 15; 19:28; Rom. 12:20; 1 Cor. 4:11; Rev. 7:16; (b) figuratively, of spiritual "thirst," Matt. 5:6; John 4:14; 6:35; 7:37; in Rev. 21:6 and 22:17, "that is athirst."

THOUGHT (Noun)

1. *epinoia* (*1963*), "a thought by way of a design" (akin to *epinoeo*, "to contrive," *epi*, intensive, *noeo*, "to consider"), is used in Acts 8:22.

2. *noema* (*3540*), "a purpose, device of the mind," is rendered "thought" in 2 Cor. 10:5, "thoughts" in Phil. 4:7.

T

3. *dianoema* (*1270*), "a thought," occurs in Luke 11:17, where the sense is that of "machinations."

4. *enthumesis* (*1761*), is translated "thoughts" in Matt. 9:4; 12:25; Heb. 4:12.

THOUGHT (to take)

1. *merimnao* (*3309*) denotes "to be anxious, careful." For the KJV, "to take thought," the RV substitutes "to be anxious" in Matt. 6:25, 27, 28, 31, 34; 10:19; Luke 12:11, 22, 25, 26.

2. *promerimnao* (*4305*), "to be anxious beforehand," occurs in Mark 13:11.

3. *phroneo* (*5426*): for Phil. 4:10, RV, "ye did take thought."

4. *pronoeo* (*4306*), "to provide," is rendered "to take thought" in Rom. 12:17 and 2 Cor. 8:21.

THREATEN

1. *apeileo* (*546*) is used of Christ, negatively, in 1 Pet. 2:23; in the middle voice, Acts 4:17, where some texts have the noun *apeile* in addition, hence the KJV, "let us straitly threaten," lit., "let us threaten...with threatening."

2. *prosapeileo* (*4324*), "to threaten further" (*pros*, and No. 1), occurs in the middle voice in Acts 4:21.

THREATENING

apeile (*547*), akin to *apeileo* (see above), occurs in Acts 4:29 (in some mss. v. 17); 9:1; Eph. 6:9.

THRONE

Old Testament

kisse' (*3678*), "throne; seat." In the Old Testament the basic meaning of *kisse'* is "seat" or "chair." Visitors were seated on a chair, 1 Kings 2:19, as well as guests, 2 Kings 4:10, and older men, 1 Sam. 1:9. When the king or elders assembled to administer justice, they sat on the throne of justice, Prov. 20:8; cf. Ps. 9:4. In these contexts *kisse'* is associated with honor. However, in the case of the prostitute, Prov. 9:14, and soldiers who set up their chairs, Jer. 1:15—*kisse'* may mean "throne" here; cf. KJV, NASB, NIV), *kisse'* signifies a place and nothing more. The more frequent sense of *kisse'* is "throne" or "seat of honor," also known as the "royal seat": "And it shall be, when he sitteth upon the throne of his kingdom, that he shall write him a copy of this law in a book out of that which is before the priests the Levites," Deut. 17:18; cf. 1 Kings 1:46. Since the Davidic dynasty received the blessing of God, the Old Testament has a number of references to "the throne of David," 2 Sam. 3:10; Jer. 22:2, 30; 36:30; Isa. 9:7.

The word *kisse'* was also used to represent "kingship" and the succession to the throne. David had sworn that Solomon would sit on his "throne," 1 Kings 1:13; cf. 2 Kings 10:3. Above all human kingship and "thrones" was the God of Israel, Ps. 47:8; Isa. 6:1; Jer. 3:17.

New Testament

1. *thronos* (2362), "a throne, a seat of authority," is used of the "throne" (a) of God, e.g., Heb. 4:16, "the throne of grace," i.e., from which grace proceeds; 8:1; 12:2; Rev. 1:4; 3:21 (2nd part); 4:2 (twice); 5:1; frequently in Rev.; in 20:12, in the best texts, "the throne" (some have *theos*, "God," KJV); cf. 21:3; Matt. 5:34; 23:22; Acts 7:49; (b) of Christ, e.g. Heb. 1:8; Rev. 3:21 (1st part); 22:3; His seat of authority in the Millennium, Matt. 19:28 (1st part); (c) by metonymy for angelic powers, Col. 1:16; (d) of the Apostles in millennial authority, Matt. 19:28 (2nd part); Luke 22:30; (e) of the elders in the heavenly vision, Rev. 4:4 (2nd and 3rd parts), RV, "thrones" (KJV, "seats"); so 11:16; (f) of David, Luke 1:32; Acts 2:30; (g) of Satan, Rev. 2:13, RV, "throne" (KJV, "seat"); (h) of "the beast," the final and federal head of the revived Roman Empire, Rev. 13:2; 16:10.

2. *bema* (968), used of the throne or tribunal of Herod, Acts 12:21.

THUNDER, THUNDERING

bronte (1027): aside from the lit. meaning, used fig. in Mark 3:17 "sons of thunder" is the interpretation of Boanerges, the name applied by the Lord to James and John; their fiery disposition is seen in 9:38 and Luke 9:54.

TIDINGS (give)

A. Noun.

phasis (5334), akin to *phemi*, "to speak," denotes "information," especially against fraud or other delinquency, and is rendered "tidings" in Acts 21:31.

B. Verbs.

1. *euangelizo* (2097) is used of any message designed to cheer those who receive it; it is rendered "to bring, declare, preach," or "show good or glad tidings," e.g., Luke 1:19; 2:10; 3:18, RV; 4:43, RV; 7:22, RV; 8:1; Acts 8:12 and 10:36, RV; 14:15, RV; in 1 Thess. 3:6, "brought us glad (KJV, good) tidings"; in Heb. 4:2, RV, "we have had good tidings preached."

TIE

1. *deo* (1210), "to bind," is rendered "to tie" in Matt. 21:2; Mark 11:2, 4; Luke 19:30.

2. *proteino* (4385), "to stretch out or forth," is used of preparations for scourging, Acts 22:25, RV, "had tied (him) up" (KJV, "bound").

T

TIME

Old Testament

A. Noun.

'et (6256), "time; period of time; appointed time; proper time; season." Basically this noun connotes "time" conceived as an opportunity or season. First, the word signifies an appointed, fixed, and set time or period, Esth. 1:13. God alone, however, knows and reveals such "appointed times," Jer. 8:12. This noun also is used of the concept "proper or appropriate time," Eccl. 7:17. It is used of the "appropriate or suitable time" for a given activity in life, Eccl. 3:11; cf. Ps. 104:27. Finally, the "appropriate time" for divine judgment is represented by *'et*, Ps. 119:126. A third use connotes "season," or a regular fixed period of time such as springtime, Gen. 18:10; or rainy season, Ezra 10:13. This noun also is applied to differing "extensions of time," as when the sun is setting, Gen. 8:11; or a special occasion, Mic. 5:3; or other periods of time, Exod. 18:22; Dan. 12:11.

B. Verb.

'anah means "to be exercised." The noun *'et* may be derived from this verb which occurs only 3 times in Hebrew poetry (cf. Eccl. 1:13). In later Hebrew this root means "to worry."

New Testament

1. *chronos* (5550), a noun, denotes "a space of time," whether short, e.g., Matt. 2:7; Luke 4:5, or long, e.g., Luke 8:27; 20:9; or a succession of "times," shorter, e.g., Acts 20:18, or longer, e.g., Rom. 16:25, RV, "times eternal"; or duration of "time," e.g., Mark 2:19, 2nd part, RV, "while" (KJV, "as long as"), lit., "for whatever time."

2. *kairos* (2540), primarily "due measure, due proportion," when used of "time," signified "a fixed or definite period, a season," sometimes an opportune or seasonable "time," e.g., Rom. 5:6, RV, "season"; Gal. 6:10, "opportunity." In Mark 10:30 and Luke 18:30, "this time" (*kairos*), i.e., "in this lifetime," is contrasted with "the coming age." In 1 Thess. 5:1, "the times and the seasons," "times" (*chronos*) refers to the duration of the interval previous to the Parousia of Christ and the length of "time" it will occupy, as well as other periods; "seasons" refers to the characteristics of these periods.

3. *hora* (5610), primarily, "any time or period fixed by nature," is translated "time" in Matt. 14:15; Luke 14:17; Rom. 13:11, "high time"; in the following the RV renders it "hour," for KJV, "time," Matt. 18:1; Luke 1:10; John 16:2, 4, 25; 1 John 2:18 (twice); Rev. 14:15; in Mark 6:35, RV, "day"; in 1 Thess. 2:17, RV, "a short (season)," lit., "(the season, KJV, 'time') of an hour."

TITHE (Verb)

1. **dekatoo** (*1183*), from **dekatos**, "tenth," in the active voice denotes "to take tithes of," Heb. 7:6, RV, "hath taken (KJV, received) tithes"; in the passive, "to pay tithes," 7:9, RV, "hath paid (KJV, 'payed') tithes."

2. **apodekatoo** (*586*) denotes (a) "to tithe" (**apo**, "from," **dekatos**, "tenth"), Matt. 23:23 (KJV, "pay tithe of"); Luke 11:42; in Luke 18:12 (where the best texts have the alternative form **apodekateuo**), "I give tithes"; (b) "to exact tithes" from Heb. 7:5.

3. **apodekateuo** (*586v*), "to give tithes," in Luke 18:12 (some texts have No. 2).

TITLE

titlos (*5102*), from Latin **titulus**, is used of the inscription above the cross of Christ, John 19:19, 20.

TITTLE

keraia or **kerea** (*2762*), "a little horn" (**keras**, "a horn"), was used to denote the small stroke distinguishing one Hebrew letter from another. The rabbis attached great importance to these; hence the significance of the Lord's statements in Matt. 5:18 and Luke 16:17, charging the Pharisees with hypocrisy, because, while professing the most scrupulous reverence to the Law, they violated its spirit.

TOIL (Verb and Noun)

A. Verbs.

1. **kopiao** (*2872*), "to be weary, to labor," is rendered "to toil" in Matt. 6:28; Luke 5:5 (12:27 in some mss.); in 1 Cor. 4:12, RV (KJV, "we labor").

2. **basanizo** (*928*), primarily, "to rub on the touchstone, to put to the test," then, "to examine by torture" (**basanos**, "touchstone, torment"), hence denotes "to torture, torment, distress"; in the passive voice it is rendered "toiling" in Mark 6:48, KJV (RV, "distressed").

B. Noun.

kopos (*2873*), "labor, trouble," is rendered "toil" in Rev. 2:2, RV (KJV, "labor").

TOKEN

1. **semeion** (*4592*), "a sign, token or indication," is translated "token" in 2 Thess. 3:17, of writing of the closing salutations, the apostle using the pen himself instead of his amanuensis, his autograph attesting the authenticity of his Epistles.

2. *sussemon* (*4953*), "a fixed sign or signal, agreed upon with others" (*sun*, "with"), is used in Mark 14:44, "a token."

3. *endeigma* (*1730*), "a plain token, a proof" (akin to *endeiknumi*, "to point out, prove"), is used in 2 Thess. 1:5 "a manifest token," said of the patient endurance and faith of the persecuted saints at Thessalonica, affording proof to themselves of their new life, and a guarantee of the vindication by God of both Himself and them.

4. *endeixis* (*1732*), "a pointing out, showing forth," is rendered "evident token" in Phil. 1:28.

TOLERABLE

anektos (*414*) (akin to *anecho*, in the middle voice, "to endure"), is used in its comparative form, *anektoteros*, in Matt. 10:15; 11:22, 24; Luke 10:12, 14; some texts have it in Mark 6:11.

TOMB

1. *mnemeion* (*3419*) is almost invariably rendered "tomb" or "tombs" in the RV, never "grave," sometimes "sepulchre"; in the KJV, "tomb" in Matt. 8:28; 27:60; Mark 5:2; 6:29.

2. *mnema* (*3418*), rendered "tombs" in Mark 5:3, 5; Luke 8:27.

3. *taphos* (*5028*), akin to *thapto*, "to bury," is translated "tombs" in Matt. 23:29; elsewhere "sepulchre."

TOMORROW

Old Testament

A. Noun.

machar (4279), "tomorrow," i.e., "the day following the present day," Exod. 16:23; as noun, Prov. 27:1.

B. Adverbs.

machar (4279), "tomorrow," i.e., pertaining to a time of the next day, Exod. 19:10; meaning "later," in some passages, Gen. 30:33.

machorat (4283), "the next day," related to the noun *machar*, *machorat* is joined to the preposition *min* to mean "on the next day," Gen. 19:34; cf. also 1 Sam. 30:17.

C. Verb.

'achar means "to be behind, tarry, defer," i.e., to extend a period of time, Judg. 5:28.

New Testament

aurion (*839*) is used either without the article, e.g., Matt. 6:30; 1 Cor. 15:32; Jas. 4:13; or with the article in the feminine form, to agree with *hemera*, "day," e.g., Matt. 6:34; Acts 4:3, RV, "the morrow" (KJV, "next day"); Jas. 4:14; preceded by *epi*, "on," e.g., Luke 10:35; Acts 4:5.

TONGUE (-S)

Old Testament

lashon (3956), "tongue; language; speech." The basic meaning of *lashon* is "tongue," which as an organ of the body refers to humans, Lam. 4:4, and animals, Exod. 11:7; Job 41:1. The extended meaning of the word as an organ of speech occurs more frequently. A person may be "heavy" or "slow" of tongue or have a stammering "tongue," Exod. 4:10; or he may be fluent and clear, Isa. 32:4. "Tongue" with the meaning "speech" has as a synonym *peh*, "mouth," Ps. 66:17, and more rarely *sapah*, "lip," Job 27:4.

A further extension of meaning is "language." In Hebrew both *sapah* and *lashon* denote a foreign "language": "For with stammering lips and another tongue will he speak to this people," Isa. 28:11. The foreigners to the "language" are well described in these words, Isa. 33:19.

lashon also refers to objects that are shaped in the form of a tongue. Most important is the "tongue of fire," which even takes the character of "eating" or "devouring," Isa. 5:24. The association in Isaiah of God's appearance in judgment with smoke and fire gave rise to a fine literary description of the Lord's anger: "Behold, the name of the Lord cometh from far, burning with his anger, and the burden thereof is heavy: his lips are full of indignation, and his tongue as a devouring fire," Isa. 30:27. Notice the words "lips" and "tongue" here with the meaning of "flames of fire," even though the language evokes the representation of a tongue (as an organ of the body) together with a tongue (of fire). Also a bar of gold, Josh. 7:21, and a bay of the sea, Isa. 11:15, shaped in the form of a tongue were called *lashon*.

New Testament

A. Nouns.

1. *glossa* (1100) is used of (1) the "tongues...like as of fire" which appeared at Pentecost; (2) "the tongue," as an organ of speech, e.g., Mark 7:33; Rom. 3:13; 14:11; 1 Cor. 14:9; Phil. 2:11; Jas. 1:26; 3:5, 6, 8; 1 Pet. 3:10; 1 John 3:18; Rev. 16:10; (3) (a) "a language," coupled with *phule*, "a tribe," *laos*, "a people," *ethnos*, "a nation," seven times in the Apocalypse, 5:9; 7:9; 10:11; 11:9; 13:7; 14:6; 17:15; (b) "the supernatural gift of speaking in another language without its having been learnt"; in Acts 2:4-13 the circumstances are recorded from the viewpoint of the hearers; to those in whose language the utterances were made it appeared as a supernatural phenomenon; to others, the stammering of drunkards; what was uttered was not addressed primarily to the audience but consisted in recounting "the mighty works of God"; cf. 2:46; in 1 Cor., chapters 12 and 14, the use of the gift of "tongues" is mentioned as exercised in the gatherings of local churches; 12:10 speaks of the gift

in general terms, and couples with it that of "the interpretation of tongues"; chapt. 14 gives instruction concerning the use of the gift, the paramount object being the edification of the church; unless the "tongue" was interpreted the speaker would speak "not unto men, but unto God," v. 2; he would edify himself alone, v. 4, unless he interpreted, v. 5, in which case his interpretation would be of the same value as the superior gift of prophesying, as he would edify the church, vv. 4-6; he must pray that he may interpret, v. 13; if there were no interpreter, he must keep silence, v. 28, for all things were to be done "unto edifying," v. 26. "If I come... speaking with tongues, what shall I profit you," says the apostle (expressing the great object in all oral ministry), "unless I speak to you either by way of revelation, or of knowledge, or of prophesying, or of teaching?" (v. 6). "Tongues" were for a sign, not to believers, but to unbelievers, v. 22, and especially to unbelieving Jews (see v. 21): cf. the passages in the Acts.

There is no evidence of the continuance of this gift after apostolic times nor indeed in the later times of the apostles themselves; this provides confirmation of the fulfillment in this way of 1 Cor. 13:8, that this gift would cease in the churches, just as would "prophecies" and "knowledge" in the sense of knowledge received by immediate supernatural power (cf. 14:6). The completion of the Holy Scriptures has provided the churches with all that is necessary for individual and collective guidance, instruction, and edification.

2. *dialektos* (*1258*), "language" (Eng., "dialect"), is rendered "tongue" in the KJV of Acts 1:19; 2:6, 8; 21:40; 22:2; 26:14.

B. Adjective.

heteroglossos (*2804*) is rendered "strange tongues" in 1 Cor. 14:21, RV (*heteros*, "another of a different sort").

C. Adverb.

hebraisti (or *ebraisti*, Westcott and Hort) (*1447*) denotes (a) "in Hebrew," Rev. 9:11, RV (AV, "in the Hebrew tongue"); so 16:16; (b) in the Aramaic vernacular of Palestine, John 5:2, KJV, "in the Hebrew tongue" (RV, "in Hebrew"); in 19:13, 17, KJV, "in the Hebrew" (RV, "in Hebrew"); in v. 20, KJV and RV, "in Hebrew"; in 20:16, RV only, "in Hebrew (Rabboni)."

TORMENT (Noun and Verb)

A. Nouns.

1. *basanismos* (*929*), akin to *basanizo*, used of divine judgments in Rev. 9:5; 14:11; 18:7, 10, 15.

2. *basanos* (*931*), primarily "a touchstone," employed in testing metals, hence, "torment," is used (a) of physical diseases, Matt. 4:24: (b) of a condition of retribution in Hades, Luke 16:23, 28.

B. Verbs.

1. *basanizo* (928), translated "to torment," (a) of sickness, Matt. 8:6; (b) of the doom of evil spirits, Mark 5:7; Luke 8:28; (c) of retributive judgments upon impenitent mankind at the close of this age, Rev. 9:5; 11:10; (d) upon those who worship the Beast and his image and receive the mark of his name, 14:10; (e) of the doom of Satan and his agents, 20:10.

2. *kakoucheo* (2558), "to treat evilly" in the passive voice is translated "tormented" in Heb. 11:37, KJV (RV, "evil entreated").

3. *odunao* (3600), rendered, "I am (thou art) tormented" in Luke 16:24, 25, KJV.

TORMENTOR

basanistes (930), properly, "a torturer," "one who elicits information by torture," is used of jailers, Matt. 18:34.

TORTURE (Verb)

tumpanizo (5178) primarily denotes "to beat a drum" (*tumpanon*, "a kettledrum," Eng., "tympanal," "tympanitis," "tympanum"), hence, "to torture by beating, to beat to death," Heb. 11:35.

TOUCH (Verb)

Old Testament

A. Verb.

naga' (5060), "to touch, strike, reach, smite." Meaning physical touch, this word is used involving various kinds of objects, Gen. 32:25, 32; Exod. 19:12; Lev. 5:2-3. Sometimes *naga'* is used figuratively in the sense of emotional involvement, 1 Sam. 10:26; NEB; or sexual contact, Gen. 20:6; or divine chastisement, Job 19:21.

B. Noun.

nega' (5061), "plague: stroke; wound." This noun formed from *naga'* occurs about 76 times in the Old Testament. The word refers to a "plague" most frequently, Gen. 12:17; Exod. 11:1. *nega'* can also mean "stroke," Deut. 17:8; 21:5, or "wound," Prov. 6:33. Each meaning carries with it the sense of a person "being stricken or smitten in some way."

New Testament

1. *hapto* (681), primarily, "to fasten to," hence, of fire, "to kindle," denotes, in the middle voice (a) "to touch," e.g., Matt. 8:3, 15; 9:20, 21, 29; (b) "to cling to, lay hold of," John 20:17; here the Lord's prohibition as to clinging to Him was indicative of the fact that communion with Him would, after His ascension, be by faith, through the Spirit; (c) "to have carnal intercourse with a woman," 1 Cor.

7:1; (d) "to have fellowship and association with unbelievers," 2 Cor. 6:17; (e) (negatively) "to adhere to certain Levitical and ceremonial ordinances," in order to avoid contracting external defilement, or to practice rigorous asceticism, all such abstentions being of "no value against the indulgence of the flesh," Col. 2:21, KJV (RV, "handle"); (f) "to assault," in order to sever the vital union between Christ and the believer, said of the attack of the Evil One, 1 John 5:18.

2. *thingano* (2345), "to touch," a lighter term than No. 1, though Heb. 11:28 approximates to it, in expressing the action of the Destroyer of the Egyptian firstborn; in Heb. 12:20 it signifies "to touch," and is not to be interpreted by Ps. 104:32, "He toucheth the hills and they smoke"; in Col. 2:21, RV (KJV, handle).

3. *prospsauo* (4379), "to touch upon, to touch slightly," occurs in Luke 11:46.

4. *pselaphao* (5584), "to feel, to handle," is rendered "that might be touched" in Heb. 12:18.

5. *katago* (2609), to bring down, is used of bringing a ship to land in Acts 27:3.

6. *sumpatheo* (4834), rendered "be touched with" in Heb. 4:15.

7. *paraballo* (3846), rendered "touched at" in Acts 20:15, RV.

TOWN

1. *komopolis* (2969), denotes a country town," Mark 1:38, "a large village" usually without walls.

2. *kome* (2968), "a village," or "country town without walls." The RV always renders this "village" or "villages," KJV, "town" or "towns," Matt. 10:11; Mark 8:23, 26 (twice), 27; Luke 5:17; 9:6, 12; John 7:42; 11:1, 30.

TOWN CLERK

grammateus (1122), "a writer, scribe," is used in Acts 19:35 of a state "clerk," an important official, variously designated, according to inscriptions found in Graeco-Asiatic cities. He was responsible for the form of decrees first approved by the Senate, then sent for approval in the popular assembly, in which he often presided. The decrees having been passed, he sealed them with the public seal in the presence of witnesses. Such an assembly frequently met in the theater. The Roman administration viewed any irregular or unruly assembly as a grave and even capital offense, as tending to strengthen among the people the consciousness of their power and the desire to exercise it. In the circumstances at Ephesus the town clerk feared that he might himself be held responsible for the irregular gathering.

TRACE

A. Verb.

parakoloutheo (3877), "to follow up," is used of investigating or "tracing" a course of events, Luke 1:3, where the writer, humbly differentiating himself from those who possessed an essential apostolic qualification, declares that he "traced the course of all things" (RV) about which he was writing (KJV, "having had...understanding, etc.").

B. Adjective.

anexichniastos (421) signifies "that cannot be traced out" (*a*, negative, *ex*, for *ek*, "out," *ichnos*, "a track"), is rendered "past tracing out" in Rom. 11:33, RV (KJV, "past finding out"); in Eph. 3:8, "unsearchable."

TRADE (Noun and Verb)

A. Verbs.

1. *ergazomai* (2038), "to work," is rendered "traded" in Matt. 25:16; in Rev. 18:17, KJV, "trade," RV, "gain their living."

2. *pragmateuomai* (4231) is rendered "trade ye" in Luke 19:13.

3. *diapragmateuomai* (1281), "to accomplish by traffic, to gain by trading," occurs in Luke 19:15.

4. *emporeuomai* (1710) is rendered "trade" in Jas. 4:13.

B. Nouns.

1. *techne* (5078), "an art" (Eng., "technique," "technical"), is used in Acts 18:3 (2nd part) of a "trade," RV (KJV, "occupation").

2. *meros* (3313), "a portion," is used of "a trade" in Acts 19:27.

TRADITION

paradosis (3862), "a handing down or on" (akin to *paradidomi*, "to hand over, deliver"), denotes "a tradition," and hence, by metonymy, (a) "the teachings of the rabbis," interpretations of the Law, which was thereby made void in practice, Matt. 15:2, 3, 6; Mark 7:3, 5, 8, 9, 13; Gal. 1:14; Col. 2:8; (b) of "apostolic teaching," 1 Cor. 11:2, RV, "traditions" (KJV, "ordinances"), of instructions concerning the gatherings of believers (instructions of wider scope than ordinances in the limited sense); in 2 Thess. 2:15, of Christian doctrine in general, where the apostle's use of the word constitutes a denial that what he preached originated with himself, and a claim for its divine authority (cf. *paralambano*, "to receive," 1 Cor. 11:23; 15:3); in 2 Thess. 3:6, it is used of instructions concerning everyday conduct.

TRAITOR

prodotes (4273) denotes "a betrayer, traitor"; the latter term is assigned to Judas, virtually as a title, in Luke 6:16; in 2 Tim. 3:4 it occurs in a list of evil characters, foretold as abounding in the last days.

TRAMPLE

katapateo (2662), "to tread down, trample under foot," is rendered "trample in Matt. 7:6.

TRANCE

ekstasis (1611), denotes "a trance" in Acts 10:10; 11:5; 22:17, a condition in which ordinary consciousness and the perception of natural circumstances were withheld, and the soul was susceptible only to the vision imparted by God.

TRANSFIGURE

metamorphoo (3339), "to change into another form" (*meta*, implying change, and *morphe*, "form:" is used in the passive voice (a) of Christ's "transfiguration," Matt. 17:2; Mark 9:2; Luke (in 9:29) avoids this term, which might have suggested to gentile readers the metamorphoses of heathen gods, and uses the phrase *egeneto heteron*, "was altered," lit., "became (*ginomai*) different (*heteros*)"; (b) of believers, Rom. 12:2, "be ye transformed," the obligation being to undergo a complete change which, under the power of God, will find expression in character and conduct; *morphe* lays stress on the inward change, *schema* lays stress on the outward; the present continuous tenses indicate a process; 2 Cor. 3:18 describes believers as being "transformed (RV) into the same image" (i.e., of Christ in all His moral excellencies), the change being effected by the Holy Spirit.

TRANSFORM

1. *metamorphoo* (3339) is rendered "transformed" in Rom. 12:2.
2. *metaschematizo* (3345) in the passive voice is rendered "to be transformed" in the KJV of 2 Cor. 11:13, 14, 15.

TRANSGRESS, TRANSGRESSION
Old Testament
A. Verb.

pasha' (6586), "to transgress, rebel." The basic sense of *pasha'* is "to rebel." There are two stages of rebellion. First, the whole process of rebellion has independence in view, 2 Kings 1:1. Second, the final result of the rebellion is the state of independence, 2 Kings 8:20, NASB. A more radical meaning is the state of rebellion in which there is no end of the rebellion in view, 1 Kings 12:19. Thus far, the usage has a king or a nation as the object of the revolt. Translations generally give the rendering "transgress" for *pasha'* when the act is committed against the Lord, Hos. 7:13. This meaning also appears in Isa. 66:24.

B. Noun.

pesha' (6588), "transgression; guilt; punishment; offering." A cognate of this word appears in Ugaritic. *pesha'* appears 93 times and in all periods of biblical Hebrew.

Basically, this noun signifies willful deviation from, and therefore rebellion against, the path of godly living. This emphasis is especially prominent in Amos 2:4: "For three transgressions of Judah, and for four, I will not turn away the punishment thereof; because they have despised the law of the Lord, and have not kept his commandments, and their lies caused them to err, after the which their fathers have walked." Such a willful rebellion from a prescribed or agreed-upon path may be perpetrated against another man, "Jacob answered and said to Laban, What is my trespass? What is my sin, that thou hast so hotly pursued after me?"; Gen. 31:36—the first occurrence of the word. Jacob is asking what he has done by way of violating or not keeping his responsibility (contract) with Laban. A nation can sin in this sense against another nation: "For three transgressions of Damascus, and for four...because they have threshed Gilead with threshing instruments of iron," Amos 1:3.

This word sometimes represents the guilt of such a transgression: "I am clean, without [guilt of] transgression, I am innocent; neither is there iniquity in me," Job 33:9.

pesha' can signify the punishment for transgression: "And a host was given him against the daily sacrifice by reason of transgression," Dan. 8:12; "How long shall be the vision concerning the daily sacrifice, and [punishment for] the transgression of desolation, to give both the sanctuary and the host to be trodden under foot?"; Dan. 8:13.

Finally, in Mic. 6:7 *pesha'* signifies an offering for "transgression": "Shall I give my first-born for my transgression [NASB, "for my rebellious acts"]?"

New Testament

A. Verbs.

1. *parabaino* (3845), lit., "to go aside" (*para*), hence "to go beyond," is chiefly used metaphorically of "transgressing" the tradition of the elders, Matt. 15:2; the commandment of God, 15:3; in Acts 1:25, of Judas, KJV, "by transgression fell" (RV, "fell away"); in 2 John 9 some texts have this verb (KJV, "transgresseth"), the best have *proago*.

2. *huperbaino* (5233), lit., "to go over" (*huper*), used metaphorically and rendered "transgress" in 1 Thess. 4:6 (KJV, "go beyond"),

i.e., of "overstepping" the limits separating chastity from licen-tiousness, sanctification from sin.

3. *parerchomai* (*3928*), "to come by" (*para*, "by," *erchomai*, "to come"), "pass over," and hence, metaphorically, "to transgress," is so used in Luke 15:29.

B. Nouns.

1. *parabasis* (*3847*), akin to A, No. 1, primarily "a going aside," then, "an overstepping," is used metaphorically to denote "trans-gression" (always of a breach of law): (a) of Adam, Rom. 5:14; (b) of Eve, 1 Tim. 2:14; (c) negatively, where there is no law, since "trans-gression" implies the violation of law, none having been enacted between Adam's "transgression" and those under the Law, Rom. 4:15; (d) of "transgressions" of the Law, Gal. 3:19, where the state-ment "it was added because of transgressions" is best understood according to Rom. 4:15; 5:13 and 5:20; the Law does not make men sinners, but makes them "transgressors"; hence sin becomes "ex-ceeding sinful," Rom. 7:7, 13. Conscience thus had a standard ex-ternal to itself; by the Law men are taught their inability to yield complete obedience to God, that thereby they may become con-vinced of their need of a Savior; in Rom. 2:23, RV, "transgression (of the Law)," KJV, "breaking (the Law)"; Heb. 2:2; 9:15.

2. *paranomia* (*3892*), "law-breaking" (*para*, "contrary to," *nomos*, "law"), is rendered "transgression" in 2 Pet. 2:16, RV (KJV, "iniqui-ty").

TRANSGRESSOR

1. *parabates* (*3848*), lit. and primarily, "one who stands beside," then, "one who oversteps the prescribed limit, a transgressor"; so Rom. 2:25, RV (KJV, "a breaker"); v. 27, RV, "a transgressor" (KJV, "dost transgress"); Gal. 2:18; Jas. 2:9, 11.

2. *anomos* (*459*), "without law" (*a*-, negative), is translated "trans-gressors" in Luke 22:37 (in some texts, Mark 15:28), in a quotation from Isa. 53:12.

TRANSLATE, TRANSLATION

A. Verbs.

1. *methistemi* or *methistano* (*3179*), "to change, remove" (*meta*, implying "change," *histemi*, "to cause to stand"), is rendered "hath translated" in Col. 1:13.

2. *metatithemi* (*3346*), "to transfer to another place" (*meta*, "change," *tithemi*, "to put"), is rendered "to translate" in Heb. 11:5 (twice).

B. Noun.

metathesis (*3331*), "a change of position" (akin to A, No. 2), is rendered "translation" in Heb. 11:5.

TRAVAIL (Noun and Verb)

A. Nouns.

1. *mochthos* (3449), "labor, involving painful effort," is rendered "travail" in 2 Cor. 11:27, RV (KJV, "painfulness"); in 1 Thess. 2:9 and 2 Thess. 3:8 it stresses the toil involved in the work.

2. *odin* (5604), a birth pang, "travail pain," is used illustratively in 1 Thess. 5:3 of the calamities which are to come upon men at the beginning of the Day of the Lord; the figure used suggests the inevitableness of the catastrophe.

B. Verbs.

1. *odino* (5605), akin to A, No. 2, is used negatively in Gal. 4:27, "(thou) that travailest (not)," quoted from Isa. 54:1; the apostle applies the circumstances of Sarah and Hagar (which doubtless Isaiah was recalling) to show that, whereas the promise by grace had temporarily been replaced by the works of the Law (see Gal. 3:17), this was now reversed, and, in the fulfillment of the promise to Abraham, the number of those saved by the gospel would far exceed those who owned allegiance to the Law. Isa. 54 has primary reference to the future prosperity of Israel restored to God's favor, but frequently the principles underlying events recorded in the OT extend beyond their immediate application.

In 4:19 the apostle uses it metaphorically of a second travailing on his part regarding the churches of Galatia; his first was for their deliverance from idolatry (v. 8), now it was for their deliverance from bondage to Judaism. There is no suggestion here of a second regeneration necessitated by defection. There is a hint of reproach, as if he was enquiring whether they had ever heard of a mother experiencing second birth pangs for her children.

In Rev. 12:2 the woman is figurative of Israel; the circumstances of her birth pangs are mentioned in Isa. 66:7 (see also Micah 5:2, 3). Historically the natural order is reversed. The Manchild, Christ, was brought forth at His first advent; the travail is destined to take place in "the time of Jacob's trouble," the "great tribulation," Matt. 24:21; Rev. 7:14. The object in 12:2 in referring to the birth of Christ is to connect Him with His earthly people Israel in their future time of trouble, from which the godly remnant, the nucleus of the restored nation, is to be delivered, Jer. 30:7.

2. *sunodino* (4944), "to be in travail together," is used metaphorically in Rom. 8:22, of the whole creation.

3. *tikto* (5088), "to beget," is rendered "travail" in John 16:21.

TREASURE (Noun and Verb)

A. Nouns.

1. *thesauros* (2344) denotes (1) "a place of safe keeping" (possibly akin to *tithemi*, "to put"), (a) "a casket," Matt. 2:11; (b) "a store-

house," Matt. 13:52; used metaphorically of the heart, Matt. 12:35, twice (RV, "out of his treasure"); Luke 6:45; (2) "a treasure," Matt. 6:19, 20, 21; 13:44; Luke 12:33, 34; Heb. 11:26; "treasure" (in heaven or the heavens), Matt. 19:21; Mark 10:21; Luke 18:22; in these expressions (which are virtually equivalent to that in Matt. 6:1, "with your Father which is in Heaven") the promise does not simply refer to the present life, but looks likewise to the hereafter; in 2 Cor. 4:7 it is used of "the light of the knowledge of the glory of God in the face of Jesus Christ," descriptive of the gospel, as deposited in the earthen vessels of the persons who proclaim it (cf. v. 4); in Col. 2:3, of the wisdom and knowledge hidden in Christ.

2. *gaza* (*1047*), a Persian word, signifying "royal treasure," occurs in Acts 8:27.

B. Verb.

thesaurizo (*2343*), akin to A, No. 1, is used metaphorically in Rom. 2:5 of "treasuring up wrath."

TREASURY

1. *gazophulakion* (*1049*), from *gaza*, "a treasure," *phulake*, "a guard," is used by Josephus for a special room in the women's court in the Temple in which gold and silver bullion was kept. This seems to be referred to in John 8:20; in Mark 12:41 (twice), 43 and Luke 21:1 it is used of the trumpet-shaped or ram's-horn-shaped chests, into which the temple offerings of the people were cast. There were 13 chests, six for such gifts in general, seven for distinct purposes.

2. *korbanas* (*2878*), signifying "the place of gifts," denoted the Temple "treasury," Matt. 27:6.

TREATISE

logos (*3056*), "a word," denotes "a treatise or written narrative" in Acts 1:1.

TREE

Old Testament

'ets (*6086*), "tree; wood; timber; stick; stalk." This word may signify a single "tree," as it does in Gen. 2:9; or genus of tree, Isa. 41:19. *'ets* can mean "wood as a material from which things are constructed, as a raw material to be carved, Exod. 31:5. Large unprocessed pieces of "wood or timber" are also signified by *'ets*, Hag. 1:8. The end product of wood already processed and fashioned into something may be indicated by *'ets*, Lev. 11:32. This word means "stick" or "piece of wood" in Ezek. 37:16. This may also refer to a "pole" or "gallows," Gen. 40:19. *'ets* one time means "stalk," Josh. 2:6.

'ayil (352), "large, mighty tree." This does not mean a particular genus or species of tree but merely a large, mighty tree, Isa. 1:29.

'elon (436), "large tree." This noun is probably related to *'ayil*, "large tree," Judg. 9:37.

New Testament

1. ***dendron*** (1186), "a living, growing tree" (cf. Eng., "rhododendron," lit., "rose tree"), known by the fruit it produces, Matt. 12:33; Luke 6:44; certain qualities are mentioned in the NT; "a good tree," Matt. 7:17, 18; 12:33; Luke 6:43; "a corrupt tree" (ditto); in Jude 12, metaphorically, of evil teachers, "autumn trees (KJV, 'trees whose fruit withereth') without fruit, twice dead, plucked up by the roots," RV; in Luke 13:19 in some texts, "a great tree," KJV (RV, "a tree"); for this and Matt. 13:32; in Luke 21:29 "the fig tree" is illustrative of Israel, "all the trees" indicating gentile nations.

2. ***xulon*** (3586), "wood, a piece of wood, anything made of wood," is used, with the rendering "tree," (a) in Luke 23:31, where "the green tree" refers either to Christ, figuratively of all His living power and excellencies, or to the life of the Jewish people while still inhabiting their land, in contrast to "the dry," a figure fulfilled in the horrors of the Roman massacre and devastation in A.D. 70 (cf. the Lord's parable in Luke 13:6-9; see Ezek. 20:47, and cf. 21:3); (b) of "the cross," the tree being the ***stauros***, the upright pale or stake to which Romans nailed those who were thus to be executed, Acts 5:30; 10:39; 13:29; Gal. 3:13; 1 Pet. 2:24; (c) of "the tree of life," Rev. 2:7; 22:2 (twice), 14, 19, RV, KJV, "book."

TREMBLE, TREMBLING

A. Verbs.

1. ***tremo*** (5141), "to tremble, especially with fear," is used in Mark 5:33; Luke 8:47 (Acts 9:6, in some mss.); 2 Pet. 2:10, RV, "they tremble (not)," KJV, "they are (not) afraid."

2. ***seio*** (4579), "to move to and fro, shake," is rendered "will I make to tremble" in Heb. 12:26, RV (KJV, "I shake").

B. Noun.

tromos (5156), "a trembling" (akin to A, No. 1), occurs in Mark 16:8, RV, "trembling (...had come upon them)"; 1 Cor. 2:3; 2 Cor. 7:15; Eph. 6:5; Phil. 2:12.

TRESPASS (Noun and Verb)

Old Testament

A. Verb.

ma'al (4603), "to trespass, act unfaithfully." *ma'al* has basically the meaning "to sin," Lev. 5:15. Second, the meaning of *ma'al* is

T

further expressed by a verb indicating the intent of being unfaithful to one's neighbor for personal profit, Lev. 6:2. The offense is against God, even when one acts unfaithfully against one's neighbor, 2 Chron. 29:6. Dan. 9:7. In view of the additional significance of "treachery," many versions translate the verb "to act unfaithfully" or "to act treacherously" instead of "to transgress" or "to commit a trespass." Both the verb and the noun have strongly negative overtones, which the translator must convey in English, Ezek. 14:13.

ma'al generally expresses man's unfaithfulness to God, Lev. 26:40; Deut. 32:51; 2 Chron. 12:2; Ezra 10:2; Ezek. 14:13. The word further signifies man's unfaithfulness to his fellow man; particularly it is illustrative of unfaithfulness in marriage, Num. 5:12-13; Lev. 6:2.

B. Noun.

ma'al (4604), "trespass; unfaithful, treacherous act." In addition to the primary sense of "trespass," given in KJV, there may be an indication of the motivation through which the sin was committed. Most of the usages support the idea of "faithlessness, treachery," Josh. 7:1. Joshua challenged Israel not to follow the example of Achan, and so be faithless, Josh. 22:20. In 2 Chron. 29:19 the "faithlessness" was committed against God.

New Testament

A. Noun.

paraptoma (3900), primarily "a false step, a blunder" (akin to *parapipto*, "to fall away," Heb. 6:6), lit., "a fall beside," used ethically, denotes "a trespass," a deviation, from uprightness and truth, Matt. 6:14, 15 (twice); 18:35, in some mss.; Mark 11:25, 26; in Romans the RV substitutes "trespass" and "trespasses" for KJV, "offense" and "offenses," 4:25, "for (i.e., because of) our trespasses"; 5:15 (twice), where the trespass is that of Adam (in contrast to the free gift of righteousness, v. 17, a contrast in the nature and the effects); 5:16, where "of many trespasses" expresses a contrast of quantity; the condemnation resulted from one "trespass," the free gift is "of (*ek*, expressing the origin, and throwing stress upon God's justifying grace in Christ) many trespasses"; v. 17, introducing a contrast between legal effects and those of divine grace; v. 18, where the RV, "through one trespass," is contrasted with "one act of righteousness"; this is important, the difference is not between one man's "trespass" and Christ's righteousness (as KJV), but between two acts, that of Adam's "trespass" and the vicarious death of Christ; v. 20; in 2 Cor. 5:19, KJV and RV, "trespasses"; in Eph. 1:7, RV, "trespasses" (KJV, "sins"); in 2:1, RV, "(dead through your) trespasses," KJV, "(dead in) trespasses"; 2:5, RV, "(dead through our) trespasses," KJV, "(dead in) sins"; so Col. 2:13

(1st part); in the 2nd part, KJV and RV, "trespasses."

In Gal. 6:1, RV, "(in any) trespass" (KJV, "fault"), the reference is to "the works of the flesh" (5:19), and the thought is that of the believer's being found off his guard, the "trespass" taking advantage of him; in Jas. 5:16, KJV, "faults" (RV, "sins" translates the word *hamartias*, which is found in the best texts), auricular confession to a priest is not in view here or anywhere else in Scripture; the command is comprehensive, and speaks either of the acknowledgment of sin where one has wronged another, or of the unburdening of a troubled conscience to a godly brother whose prayers will be efficacious, or of open confession before the church.

In Rom. 11:11, 12, the word is used of Israel's "fall," i.e., their deviation from obedience to God and from the fulfillment of His will (to be distinguished from the verb *ptaio*, "fall," in the 1st part of v. 11, which indicates the impossibility of recovery).

B. Verb.

hamartano (*264*), "to sin," is translated "to trespass," in the KJV of Matt. 18:15, and Luke 17:3, 4 (RV, "to sin").

TRIAL

1. *dokime* (*1382*), rendered "trial" in 2 Cor. 8:2, KJV (RV, "proof").

2. *peira* (*3984*), "a making trial, an experiment," is used with *lambano*, "to receive or take," in Heb. 11:29, rendered "assaying," and v. 36, in the sense of "having experience of" (akin to *peirao*, "to assay, to try"), "had trial."

3. *peirasmos* (*3986*), akin to No. 2, is rendered "trials" in Acts 20:19, RV.

4. *purosis* (*4451*), akin to *puroo*, "to set on fire," signifies (a) "a burning"; (b) "a refining," metaphorically in 1 Pet. 4:12, "fiery trial," or rather "trial by fire," referring to the refining of gold (1:7).

TRIBE (-S)

Old Testament

A. Nouns.

matteh (4294), "staff; rod; shaft; branch; tribe." The basic meaning of *matteh* is "staff." The use of the "staff" was in shepherding. Judah was a shepherd and gave his "staff" to his daughter-in-law Tamar, as a pledge of sending her a kid of the flock, Gen 38:17-18, cf. also Exod. 4:2ff.; Exod. 17:9. The "staff" was also a token of authority. The Egyptian magicians had "staffs" as symbols of their authority over the magical realm by which they duplicated several miracles, Exod. 7:12; even the authority of a nation, Isa. 9:4· 10:5-6; or authority of God, Ps. 110:2. A derived sense of *matteh* is "tribe," which means one of the major subdivisions of a national unit, comprising thousands of persons, Josh. 14:1.

shebet (7626), "tribe; rod." The "rod" as a tool is used by the shepherd, Lev. 27:32, and the teacher, 2 Sam. 7:14. It is a symbol of authority in the hands of a ruler, whether it is the scepter, Amos 1:5, 8, or an instrument of warfare and oppression, Ps. 2:9; cf. Zech. 10:11. The symbolic element comes to expression in a description of the messianic rule, Isa. 11:4. The word *shebet* is most frequently used to denote a "tribe," a division in a nation, Gen. 49:16; Exod. 28:21. Jeremiah referred to all of Israel as the "tribe," 51:19.

B. Verb.

natah (5186), "to stretch out, spread out, extend," Exod. 9:22.

New Testament

1. *phule* (5443), "a company of people united by kinship or habitation, a clan, tribe," is used (a) of the peoples of the earth, Matt. 24:30; in the following the RV has "tribe(-s)" for KJV, "kindred(-s)," Rev. 1:7; 5:9; 7:9; 11:9; 13:7; 14:6; (b) of the "tribes" of Israel, Matt. 19:28; Luke 2:36; 22:30; Acts 13:21; Rom. 11:1; Phil. 3:5; Heb. 7:13, 14; Jas. 1:1; Rev. 5:5; 7:4-8; 21:12.

2. *dodekaphulos* (1429), an adjective signifying "of twelve tribes" (*dodeka*, "twelve," and No. 1), used as a noun in the neuter, occurs in Acts 26:7.

TRIBULATION

thlipsis (2347), is translated "tribulation" in the RV (for KJV, "affliction") in Mark 4:17; 13:19; plural in 2 Thess. 1:4, KJV, "tribulations," RV, "afflictions"; in Acts 14:22 "many tribulations" (KJV, "much tribulation"); in Matt. 24:9, "unto tribulation" (KJV, "to be afflicted"); in 2 Cor. 1:4; 7:4; 2 Thess. 1:6, KJV, "tribulation" for RV, "affliction"; RV and KJV, "tribulation(-s)," e.g., in Rom. 2:9; 5:3 (twice); 8:35; 12:12; Eph. 3:13; Rev. 1:9; 2:9, 10, 22.

In Rev. 7:14, "the great tribulation," RV, lit., "the tribulation, the great one" (not as KJV, without the article), is not that in which all saints share; it indicates a definite period spoken of by the Lord in Matt. 24:21, 29; Mark 13:19, 24, where the time is mentioned as preceding His second advent, and as a period in which the Jewish nation, restored to Palestine in unbelief by gentile instrumentality, will suffer an unprecedented outburst of fury on the part of the antichristian powers confederate under the Man of Sin (2 Thess. 2:10-12; cf. Rev. 12:13-17); in this tribulation gentile witnesses for God will share (Rev. 7:9), but it will be distinctly "the time of Jacob's trouble," Jer. 30:7; its beginning is signalized by the setting up of the "abomination of desolation" (Matt. 24:15; Mark 13:14, with Dan. 11:31; 12:11).

TRIBUTE

1. *phoros* (*5411*), akin to *phero*, "to bring," denotes "tribute" paid by a subjugated nation, Luke 20:22; 23:2; Rom. 13:6, 7.

2. *kensos* (*2778*), Lat. and Eng., "census," denotes "a poll tax," Matt. 17:25; 22:17, 19; Mark 12:14.

3. *didrachmon* (*1323*), "the half-shekel," is rendered "tribute" in Matt. 17:24 (twice).

TRIUMPH

thriambeuo (*2358*) denotes (a) "to lead in triumph," used of a conqueror with reference to the vanquished, 2 Cor. 2:14. Theodoret paraphrases it, "He leads us about here and there and displays us to all the world." This is in agreement with evidences from various sources. Those who are led are not captives exposed to humiliation, but are displayed as the glory and devoted subjects of Him who leads (see the context). This is so even if there is a reference to a Roman "triumph." On such occasions the general's sons, with various officers, rode behind his chariot (Livy, xlv. 40). But there is no necessary reference here to a Roman "triumph."

In Col. 2:15 the circumstances and subjects are quite different, and relate to Christ's victory over spiritual foes at the time of His death; accordingly the reference may be to the triumphant display of the defeated.

TROUBLE (Noun and Verb)

A. Noun.

thlipsis (*2347*), rendered "trouble" in the KJV of 1 Cor. 7:28 (RV, "tribulation"); 2 Cor. 1:4 (2nd clause), 8 (RV, "affliction").

B. Verbs.

1. *tarasso* (*5015*), akin to *tarache*, is used (1) in a physical sense, John 5:7 (in some mss. v. 4), (2) metaphorically, (a) of the soul and spirit of the Lord, John 11:33, where the true rendering is "He troubled Himself"; (b) of the hearts of disciples, 14:1, 27; (c) of the minds of those in fear or perplexity, Matt. 2:3; 14:26; Mark 6:50; Luke 1:12; 24:38; 1 Pet. 3:14; (d) of subverting the souls of believers, by evil doctrine, Acts 15:24; Gal. 1:7; 5:10; (e) of stirring up a crowd, Acts 17:8; v. 13 in the best texts, "troubling (the multitudes)," RV.

2. *diatarasso* (*1298*), "to agitate greatly" (*dia*, "throughout," and No. 1), is used of the Virgin Mary, Luke 1:29.

3. *ektarasso* (*1613*), "to throw into great trouble, agitate," is used in Acts 16:20, "do exceedingly trouble (our city)."

4. *thlibo* (*2346*), "to afflict," is rendered "to trouble" in the KJV, e.g., 2 Cor. 4:8 (RV, "pressed"); 7:5.

5. *enochleo* (*1776*), from *en*, "in," *ochlos*, "a throng, crowd," is

T

used in Heb. 12:15 of a root of bitterness; in Luke 6:18 (in the best texts; some have *ochleo*), RV, "were troubled" (KJV, "were vexed").

6. *parenochleo* (*3926*), "to annoy concerning anything" (*para*, and No. 5), occurs in Acts 15:19, "we trouble (not them)."

7. *skullo* (*4660*), primarily "to flay," hence, "to vex, annoy" ("there was a time when the Greek, in thus speaking, compared his trouble to the pains of flaying alive," Moulton, *Proleg.*, p. 89), is used in the active voice in Mark 5:35; Luke 8:49; in the passive voice, Matt. 9:36, in the best texts, RV, "they were distressed" (some have *ekluo*, KJV, "they fainted"); in the middle voice, Luke 7:6, "trouble (not thyself)." The word is frequent in the papyri.

8. *anastatoo* (*387*) is rendered "trouble" in Gal. 5:12, KJV.

9. *thorubeo* (*2350*), akin to *thorubos*, "a tumult," in the middle voice, "to make an uproar," is rendered "trouble not yourselves" in Acts 20:10, KJV.

10. *throeo* (*2360*), "to make an outcry" (*throos*, "a tumult"), is used in the passive voice, Matt. 24:6; Mark 13:7; Luke 24:37; 2 Thess. 2:2.

11. *thorubazo* (*2351*), "to disturb, to trouble" (akin to No. 9), is used in Luke 10:41, in the best texts (in some, *turbazo*, with the same meaning).

12. *ademoneo* (*85*), "to be much troubled, distressed" (perhaps from *a*, negative, and *demon*, "knowing," the compound therefore originally suggesting bewilderment), is translated "sore troubled" in Matt. 26:37 and Mark 14:33, RV (KJV, "very heavy"); so the RV in Phil. 2:26 (KJV, "full of heaviness"); Lightfoot renders it "distressed," a meaning borne out in the papyri.

13. *diaponeo* (*1278*) denotes "to work out with toil," hence, "to be sore troubled"; so the RV in Acts 4:2 and 16:18 (KJV, "grieved"); Mark 14:4 in some texts.

TRUE, TRULY, TRUTH

A. Adjectives.

1. *alethes* (*227*), primarily, "unconcealed, manifest" (*a*, negative, *letho*, "to forget," = *lanthano*, "to escape notice"), hence, actual, "true to fact," is used (a) of persons, "truthful," Matt. 22:16; Mark 12:14; John 3:33; 7:18; 8:26; Rom. 3:4; 2 Cor. 6:8; (b) of things, "true," conforming to reality, John 4:18, "truly," lit., "true"; 5:31, 32; in the best texts, 6:55 (twice), "indeed"; 8:13, 14 (v. 16 in some texts: see No. 2), 17; 10:41; 19:35; 21:24; Acts 12:9; Phil. 4:8; Titus 1:13; 1 Pet. 5:12; 2 Pet. 2:22; 1 John 2:8, 27; 3 John 1:2.

2. *alethinos* (*228*), akin to No. 1, denotes "true" in the sense of real, ideal, genuine; it is used (a) of God, John 7:28 (cf. No. 1 in 7:18, above); 17:3; 1 Thess. 1:9; Rev. 6:10; these declare that God fulfills the meaning of His Name; He is "very God," in distinction from all other gods, false gods (*alethes*, see John 3:33 in No. 1, signifies that

He is veracious, "true" to His utterances, He cannot lie); (b) of Christ, John 1:9; 6:32; 15:1; 1 John 2:8; 5:20 (thrice); Rev. 3:7, 14; 19:11; His judgment, John 8:16 (in the best texts, instead of No. 1); (c) God's words, John 4:37; Rev. 19:9, 21:5; 22:6; the last three are equivalent to No. 1; (d) His ways, Rev. 15:3; (e) His judgments, Rev. 16:7; 19:2; (f) His riches, Luke 16:11; (g) His worshipers, John 4:23; (h) their hearts, Heb. 10:22; (i) the witness of the apostle John, John 19:35; (j) the spiritual, antitypical tabernacle, Heb. 8:2; 9:24, not that the wilderness tabernacle was false, but that it was a weak and earthly copy of the heavenly.

3. *gnesios* (*1103*), primarily "lawfully begotten" (akin to *ginomai*, "to become"), hence, "true, genuine, sincere," is used in the apostle's exhortation to his "true yoke-fellow" in Phil. 4:3.

B. Verb.

aletheuo (*226*) signifies "to deal faithfully or truly with anyone" (cf. Gen. 42:16, Sept., "whether ye deal truly or no"), Eph. 4:15, "speaking the truth"; Gal. 3:16, "I tell (you) the truth," where probably the apostle is referring to the contents of his epistle.

C. Noun.

aletheia (*225*), "truth," is used (a) objectively, signifying "the reality lying at the basis of an appearance; the manifested, veritable essence of a matter" (Cremer), e.g., Rom. 9:1; 2 Cor. 11:10; especially of Christian doctrine, e.g., Gal. 2:5, where "the truth of the Gospel" denotes the "true" teaching of the Gospel, in contrast to perversions of it; Rom. 1:25, where "the truth of God" may be "the truth concerning God" or "God whose existence is a verity"; but in Rom. 15:8 "the truth of God" is indicative of His faithfulness in the fulfillment of His promises as exhibited in Christ; the word has an absolute force in John 14:6; 17:17; 18:37, 38; in Eph. 4:21, where the RV, "even as truth is in Jesus," gives the correct rendering, the meaning is not merely ethical "truth," but "truth" in all its fullness and scope, as embodied in Him; He was the perfect expression of the truth; this is virtually equivalent to His statement in John 14:6; (b) subjectively, "truthfulness," "truth," not merely verbal, but sincerity and integrity of character, John 8:44; 3 John 3, RV; (C) in phrases, e.g., "in truth" (*epi*, "on the basis of"), Mark 12:14; Luke 20:21; with *en*, "in," 2 Cor. 6:7; Col. 1:6; 1 Tim. 2:7, RV (KJV, "in...verity"), 1 John 3:18; 2 John 1, 3, 4.

D. Adverbs.

1. *alethos* (*230*), "truly, surely," is rendered "of a truth" in Matt. 14:33; 26:73 and Mark 14:70, RV, (KJV, "surely"); Luke 9:27; 12:44; 21:3; John 6:14; 7:40; 17:8, RV, "of a truth (KJV, surely); Acts 12:11, RV (KJV, "of a surety"); "in truth," 1 Thess. 2:13; "truly," Matt. 27:54; Mark 15:39.

T

2. *gnēsios* (*1104*), "sincerely, honorably" (akin to A, No. 3), is rendered "truly" (marg., "genuinely") in Phil. 2:20 (KJV, "naturally").

TRUMP, TRUMPET

A. Noun.

salpinx (*4536*) is used (1) of the natural instrument, 1 Cor. 14:8; (2) of the supernatural accompaniment of divine interpositions, (a) at Sinai, Heb. 12:19; (b) of the acts of angels at the second advent of Christ, Matt. 24:31; (c) of their acts in the period of divine judgments preceding this, Rev. 8:2, 6, 13; 9:14; (d) of a summons to John to the presence of God, Rev. 1:10; 4:1; (e) of the act of the Lord in raising from the dead the saints who have fallen asleep and changing the bodies of those who are living, at the Rapture of all to meet Him in the air, 1 Cor. 15:52, where "the last trump" is a military allusion, familiar to Greek readers, and has no connection with the series in Rev. 8:6 to 11:15; there is a possible allusion to Num. 10:2-6, with reference to the same event, 1 Thess. 4:16, "the (lit., a) trump of God" (the absence of the article suggests the meaning "a trumpet such as is used in God's service").

B. Verb.

salpizo (*4537*), "to sound a trumpet," Matt. 6:2; as in (2) (c) above, Rev. 8:6, 7 8, 10, 12, 13; 9:1, 13; 10:7; 11:15; as in (2) (e) 1 Cor. 15:52.

TRUMPETER

salpistes (*4538*) occurs in Rev. 18:22.

TRUST (Noun and Verb)

A. Noun.

pepoithesis (*4006*) is rendered "trust" in 2 Cor. 3:4, KJV.

B. Verbs.

1. *peitho* (*3982*), intransitively, in the perfect and pluperfect active, "to have confidence, trust," is rendered "to trust" in Matt. 27:43; Mark 10:24; Luke 11:22; 18:9; 2 Cor. 1:9; 10:7; Phil, 2:24; 3:4, KJV (RV, "to have confidence"); Heb. 2:13; in the present middle, Heb. 13:18, KJV (RV, "are persuaded").

2. *pisteuo* (*4100*), "to entrust," or, in the passive voice, "to be entrusted with," is rendered "to commit to one's trust," in Luke 16:11; 1 Tim. 1:11; "to be put in trust with," 1 Thess. 2:4, KJV (RV, "to be intrusted").

TRY, TRIED

1. *dokimazo* (*1381*) is rendered "to try" in the KJV in 1 Cor. 3:13; 1 Thess. 2:4; 1 Pet. 1:7; 1 John 4:1.

2. *peirazo* (*3985*) is rendered "to try" in Heb. 11:17; Rev. 2:2, 10;

3:10. In Acts 16:7 it is rendered "assayed"; in 24:6, RV, "assayed" (KJV, "hath gone about").

TUMULT

1. *akatastasia* (*181*) is rendered "tumults" in Luke 21:9, RV; 2 Cor. 6:5; 12:20.

2. *thorubos* (*2351*), "a noise, uproar, tumult," is rendered "tumult" in Matt. 27:24 and Mark 5:38; in Matt. 26:5, RV (KJV, "uproar"), so in Mark 14:2; in Acts 20:1, "uproar," KJV and RV; in 24:18, "tumult"; in 21:34, KJV, "tumult" (RV, "uproar").

TWINKLING

rhipe (*4493*), akin to *rhipto*, "to hurl," was used of any rapid movement, e.g., the throw of a javelin, the rush of wind or flame; in 1 Cor. 15:52 of the "twinkling" of an eye.

T

U

UNBELIEF

1. *apistia* (570), "unbelief," Matt. 13:58; Mark 9:24; Rom. 3:3.

2. *apeitheta* (543) is always rendered "disobedience" in the RV; Rom. 11:30, 32; Heb. 4:6, 11.

UNBELIEVER

apistos (571), an adjective, is used as a noun, rendered "unbeliever" in 2 Cor. 6:15 and 1 Tim. 5:8, RV; plural in 1 Cor. 6:6 and 2 Cor. 6:14; KJV only, Luke 12:46 (RV, "unfaithful").

UNBELIEVING

A. Adjective.

apistos (571), "unbelieving," Matt. 17:17.

B. Verb.

apeitheo (544), "refuse to believe," John 3:36.

UNBLAMEABLE, UNBLAMEABLY

A. Adjective.

amemptos (273), "unblameable" (from *a*, negative, and *memphomai*, "to find fault"), is so rendered in 1 Thess. 3:13, i.e., "free from all valid charge."

B. Adverb.

amemptos (274) is used in 1 Thess. 2:10, "unblameably," signifying that no charge could be maintained, whatever charges might be made.

UNCERTAIN, UNCERTAINLY, UNCERTAINTY

A. Adjective.

adelos (82) denotes (a) "unseen"; with the article, translated "which appear not" (*a*, negative, *delos*, "evident"), Luke 11:44; (b) "uncertain, indistinct," 1 Cor. 14:8.

B. Adverb.

adelos (84), "uncertainly" (akin to A), occurs in 1 Cor. 9:26.

C. Noun.

adelotes (*83*), "uncertainty" (akin to A and B), occurs in 1 Tim. 6:17, "(the) uncertainty (of riches)," RV (the KJV translates it as an adjective, "uncertain"), i.e., riches the special character of which is their "uncertainty"; the Greek phrase is a rhetorical way of stressing the noun "riches"; when a genitive (here "of riches") precedes the governing noun (here "uncertainty") the genitive receives emphasis.

UNCHANGEABLE

aparabatos (*531*) is used of the priesthood of Christ, in Heb. 7:24.

UNCLEAN

Old Testament

A. Verb.

tame' (2930), "to be unclean," usually with the meaning of ceremonial uncleanness, Lev. 11:26. *tame'* is the opposite of *taher*, "to be pure."

B. Noun.

tum'ah (2932), "uncleanness." This noun is means ceremonial uncleanness, Num. 5:19; ethical and religious uncleanness, Lev 16:16.

C. Adjective.

tame' (2931), "unclean." This adjective occurs usually in Leviticus, with the meaning of ceremonial or ritual cleanness, so as to be pure to the Lord, Lev. 5:2. The usage of *tame'* in the Old Testament resembles that of *tahor*, "pure." First, uncleanness is a state of being. The leper was compelled to announce his uncleanness wherever he went, Lev. 13:45; however, even here there is a religious overtone, in that his uncleanness was ritual. Hence, it is more appropriate to recognize that the second usage is most basic. *tame'* in the religio-cultic sense is a technical term denoting a state of being ceremonially unfit, Num. 19:22; even from genital issues, Lev. 15:2, 25.

New Testament

A. Adjectives.

1. *akathartos* (*169*), "unclean, impure" (*a*, negative, *kathairo*, "to purify"), is used (a) of "unclean" spirits, frequently in the Synoptists, not in John's gospel; in Acts 5:16; 8:7; Rev. 16:13; 18:2a (in the 2nd clause the birds are apparently figurative of destructive satanic agencies); (b) ceremonially, Acts 10:14, 28; 11:8; 1 Cor. 7:14; (c) morally, 2 Cor. 6:17, including (b), RV; "no unclean thing"; Eph. 5:5;

U

Rev. 17:4, RV, "the unclean things" (KJV follows the text which have the noun *akathartes*, "the filthiness").

2. *koinos* (*2839*), "common," is translated "unclean" in Rom. 14:14 (thrice).

B. Verb.

koinoo (*2840*), to make *koinos*, "to defile," is translated "unclean" in Heb. 9:13, KJV, where the perfect participle, passive, is used with the article, hence the RV, "them that have been defiled."

C. Noun.

akatharsia (*167*), akin to A, No. 1, denotes "uncleanness," (a) physical, Matt. 23:27 (instances in the papyri speak of tenants keeping houses in good condition); (b) moral, Rom. 1:24; 6:19; 2 Cor. 12:21; Gal. 5:19; Eph. 4:19; 5:3; Col. 3:5; 1 Thess. 2:3 (suggestive of the fact that sensuality and evil doctrine are frequently associated); 4:7.

UNCONDEMNED

akatakritos (*178*), rendered "uncondemned" in Acts 16:37; 22:25, properly means "without trial, not yet tried."

UNCOVER

apostegazo (*648*) signifies "to unroof" (*apo*, from, *stege*, "a roof"), Mark 2:4.

UNDEFILED

amiantos (*283*), "undefiled, free from contamination" (*a*, negative, *miaino*, "to defile"), is used (a) of Christ, Heb. 7:26; (b) of pure religion, Jas. 1:27; (c) of the eternal inheritance of believers, 1 Pet. 1:4; (d) of the marriage bed as requiring to be free from unlawful sexual intercourse, Heb. 13:4.

UNDERSTAND, UNDERSTOOD
Old Testament

A. Verbs.

sakal (*7919*), "to be prudent, act wisely, give attention to, ponder, prosper." The basic meaning of *sakal* seems to be "to look at, to give attention to," as illustrated in this parallelism: "That they may see, and know, and consider, and understand…" Isa. 41:20. From this develops the connotation of insight, intellectual comprehension, Jer. 9:23-24. As here, it is frequently used along with and in parallelism to the Hebrew *yada'*, "to know" (primarily experientially). As is true of *chakam*, "to be wise," *sakal* never concerns abstract prudence, but acting prudently, Amos 5:13; Ps. 36:3.

bin (*995*), "to understand, be able, deal wisely, consider, pay attention to, regard, notice, discern, perceive, inquire." *bin* appears in Jer. 9:12 with the meaning "to understand"; Job 6:30, "to discern"; and in Deut. 32:7 it means "to consider."

B. Nouns.

binah (998), "understanding." This noun represents the "act of understanding," Dan. 1:20. Elsewhere *binah* signifies the faculty "understanding," Job 20:3. In other passages the object of knowledge, in the sense of what one desires to know, is indicated by *binah*, Deut. 4:6; cf. 1 Chron. 22:12.

tebunah (8394), "understanding." This word, which occurs 42 times, is also a wisdom term. Like *binah*, it represents the act, Job 26:12, faculty, Exod. 31:3, object, Prov. 2:3.

maskil (4905), "didactic psalm(?)." This noun form, derived from *sakal*, is found in the title of 13 psalms and also in Ps. 47:7. Scholars are not agreed on the significance of this term, but on the basis of the general meaning of *sakal*, such psalms must have been considered didactic or teaching psalms.

New Testament

A. Verbs.

1. *suniemi* (4920), primarily, "to bring or set together," is used metaphorically of "perceiving, understanding, uniting" (*sun*), so to speak, the perception with what is perceived, e.g., Matt. 13:13-15, 19, 23, 51; 15:10; 16:12; 17:13, and similar passages in Mark and Luke; Acts 7:25 (twice); 28:26, 27; in Rom. 3:11, the present participle, with the article, is used as a noun, lit., "there is not the understanding (one)," in a moral and spiritual sense; Rom. 15:21; 2 Cor. 10:12, RV, "are (without) understanding," KJV, "are (not) wise"; Eph. 5:17, RV, "understand."

2. *noeo* (3539), "to perceive with the mind," as distinct from perception by feeling, is so used in Matt. 15:17, KJV, "understand," RV, "perceive"; 16:9, 11; 24:15 (here rather perhaps in the sense of considering) and parallels in Mark (not in Luke); John 12:40; Rom. 1:20; 1 Tim. 1:7; Heb. 11:3; in Eph. 3:4, KJV, "may understand" (RV, "can perceive"); 3:20, "think"; 2 Tim. 2:7, "consider."

3. *ginosko* (1097), "to know, to come to know," is translated "to understand" in the KJV in Matt. 26:10 and John 8:27 (RV, "to perceive"); KJV and RV in John 8:43; 10:6; in 10:38, RV (in some texts *pisteuo*, KJV, "believe"); KJV and RV in 12:16; 13:7 RV, KJV, "know"; Acts 8:30; in Phil. 1:12, KJV, RV, "know" (in some texts, Acts 24:11, KJV).

B. Adjectives.

1. *eusemos* (2154), primarily denotes "conspicuous" or "glorious" (as in Ps. 81:3, Sept.; RV, "solemn"), then, "distinct, clear to under-

U

standing," 1 Cor. 14:9, "easy to be understood" (KJV, marg., "significant").

2. *dusnoetos* (*1425*), "hard to be understood," occurs in 2 Pet. 3:16.

UNDERSTANDING

A. Nouns.

1. *nous* (*3563*), translated "understanding" in Luke 24:45, KJV (RV, "mind"); 1 Cor. 14:14, 15 (twice), 19; Phil. 4:7; Rev. 13:18.

2. *sunesis* (*4907*), akin to *suniemi*, "to set together, to understand," denotes (a) "the understanding, the mind or intelligence," Mark 12:33; (b) "understanding, reflective thought," Luke 2:47; 1 Cor. 1:19, RV, "prudence," Eph. 3:4, RV (AV, "knowledge"); Col. 1:9; 2:2; 2 Tim. 2:7.

3. *dianoia* (*1271*), rendered "understanding" in Eph. 4:18; 1 John 5:20.

B. Adjective.

asunetos (*801*), "without understanding or discernment" (*a*, negative, *sunetos*, "intelligent, understanding"), is translated "without understanding" in Matt. 15:16; Mark 7:18; Rom. 1:31; 10:19, RV, "void of understanding" (KJV, "foolish"); in Rom. 1:21, RV, "senseless" (KJV, "foolish").

UNFAITHFUL

apistos (*571*), "unbelieving, faithless," is translated "unfaithful" in Luke 12:46, RV (KJV, "unbelievers").

UNGODLINESS, UNGODLY

A. Noun.

asebeia (*763*), "impiety, ungodliness," is used of (a) general impiety, Rom. 1:18; 11:26; 2 Tim. 2:16; Titus 2:12; (b) "ungodly" deeds, Jude 15, RV, "works of ungodliness"; (c) of lusts or desires after evil things, Jude 18. It is the opposite of *eusebeia*, "godliness."

B. Adjective.

asebes (*765*), "impious, ungodly" (akin to A), "without reverence for God," not merely irreligious, but acting in contravention of God's demands, Rom. 4:5; 5:6; 1 Tim. 1:9; 1 Pet. 4:18; 2 Pet. 2:5 (v. 6 in some mss.); 3:7; Jude 4, 15 (twice).

C. Verb.

asebeo (*764*), akin to A and B, signifies (a) "to be or live ungodly," 2 Pet. 2:6; (b) "to commit ungodly deeds," Jude 15.

UNHOLY

1. *anosios* (462), "unholy, profane," occurs in 1 Tim. 1:9; 2 Tim. 3:2.

2. *koinon* (2839), the neut. of *koinos*, "common," is translated "an unholy thing" in Heb. 10:29.

UNITY

henotes (1775), from *hen*, the neuter of *heis*, "one." is used in Eph. 4:3, 13.

UNJUST

adikos (94), "not in conformity with *dike*, "right," is rendered "unjust" in the KJV and RV in Matt. 5:45; Luke 18:11; Acts 24:15; elsewhere for the KJV "unjust" the RV has "unrighteous.

UNLAWFUL

athemitos (111), a late form for *athemistos* (*themis*, "custom, right"; in classical Greek "divine law"), "contrary to what is right," is rendered "an unlawful thing" (neuter) in Acts 10:28; in 1 Pet. 4:3, "abominable."

UNLEARNED

1. *agrammatos* (62), lit., "unlettered" (*grammata*, "letters": *grapho*, "to write") Acts 4:13, means either; "unversed in the learning of the Jewish schools"; or "one who cannot write."

2. *amathes* (261), "unlearned" (*manthano*, "to learn"), is translated "unlearned" in 2 Pet. 3:16, KJV (RV, "ignorant").

3. *apaideutos* (521), "uninstructed" (*paideuo*, "to train, teach"), is translated "unlearned" in 2 Tim. 2:23, KJV (RV, "ignorant").

UNLOOSE

luo (3089), "to loose," is rendered "to unloose" in Mark 1:7; Luke 3:16; John 1:27; in Acts 13:25, RV.

UNMARRIED

agamos (22), *a*, negative, *gameo*, "to marry," occurs in 1 Cor. 7:8, 11, 32, 34.

UNMERCIFUL

aneleemon (415), "without mercy" (*a*, negative, *n*, euphonic, *eleemon*, "merciful"), occurs in Rom. 1:31.

UNPREPARED

aparaskeuastos (532), "unprepared," occurs in 2 Cor. 9:4.

U

UNPROFITABLE, UNPROFITABLENESS

A. Adjectives.

1. *achreios* (*888*), "useless" (*chreia*, "use"), "unprofitable," occurs in Matt. 25:30 and Luke 17:10.

2. *achrestos* (*890*), "unprofitable, unserviceable" (*chrestos*, "serviceable"), is said of Onesimus, Philem. 11, antithetically to *euchrestos*, "profitable," with a play on the name of the converted slave (from *onesis*, "profit").

3. *alusiteles* (*255*), "not advantageous, not making good the expense involved" (*lusiteles*, "useful") occurs in Heb. 13:17.

4. *anopheles* (*512*), "not beneficial or serviceable" (*a*, negative, *n*, euphonic, *opheleo*, "to do good, to benefit"), is rendered "unprofitable" in Titus 3:9; in the neuter, used as a noun, "unprofitableness," Heb. 7:18, said of the Law as not accomplishing that which the "better hope" could alone bring.

B. Verb.

achreoo, or *achreioo* (*889*), akin to A, No. 1, "to make useless," occurs in Rom. 3:12, in the passive voice, rendered "they have...become unprofitable."

UNREASONABLE

alogos (*249*), "without reason, irrational," is rendered "unreasonable" in Acts 25:27.

UNRIGHTEOUS

adikos (*94*), not conforming to *dike*, "right," is translated "unrighteous" in Luke 16:10 (twice), RV, 11; Rom. 3:5; 1 Cor. 6:1, RV; 6:9; Heb. 6:10; 1 Pet. 3:18, RV; 2 Pet. 2:9, RV.

UNRIGHTEOUSNESS

A. Noun.

adikia (*93*) denotes (a) "injustice," Luke 18:6, lit., "the judge of injustice"; Rom. 9:14; (b) "unrighteousness, iniquity," e.g., Luke 16:8, lit., "the steward of unrighteousness," RV marg., i.e., characterized by "unrighteousness"; Rom. 1:18, 29; 2:8; 3:5; 6:13; 1 Cor. 13:6, RV, "unrighteousness"; 2 Thess. 2:10, "[with all (lit., 'in every) deceit'] of unrighteousness," i.e., deceit such as "unrighteousness" uses, and that in every variety; Antichrist and his ministers will not be restrained by any scruple from words or deeds calculated to deceive; 2 Thess. 2:12, of those who have pleasure in it, not an intellectual but a moral evil; distaste for truth is the precursor of the rejection of it; 2 Tim. 2:19, RV; 1 John 1:9, which includes (c); (c) "a deed or deeds violating law and justice" (virtually the same as *adikema*, "an unrighteous act"), e.g., Luke 13:27, "iniquity"; 2 Cor.

12:13, "wrong," the wrong of depriving another of what is his own, here ironically of a favor; Heb. 8:12, 1st clause, "iniquities," lit., "unrighteousnesses" (plural, not as KJV); 2 Pet. 2:13, 15, RV, "wrongdoing," KJV, "unrighteousness"; 1 John 5:17.

B. Verb.

adikeo (91), "to do wrong," is rendered in Rev. 22:11, RV, firstly, "he that is unrighteous," lit., "the doer of unrighteousness" (present participle of the verb, with the article), secondly, "let him do unrighteousness (still)," the retributive and permanent effect of a persistent course of unrighteous-doing (KJV, "he that is unjust, let him be unjust").

UNRULY

1. *anupotaktos* (506), "not subject to rule" (*a*, negative, *n*, euphonic, *hupotasso*, "to put in subjection"), is used (a) of things, Heb. 2:8, RV, "not subject" (KJV, "not put under"); (b) of persons, "unruly," 1 Tim. 1:9, RV (KJV, "disobedient"); Titus 1:6, 10.

2. *ataktos* (814) is rendered "unruly" in 1 Thess. 5:14, KJV (marg. and RV, "disorderly).

UNSEARCHABLE

1. *anexeraunetos*, or *anexereunetos* (419), (*a*, negative, *n*, euphonic, *ex* [ek], "out," *eraunao*, "to search, examine"), is used in Rom. 11:33, of the judgments of God.

2. *anexichniastos* (421), with the same prefixes as in No. 1 and an adjectival form akin to *ichneuo*, "to trace out" (*ichnos*, "a footprint, a track"), is translated "unsearchable" in Eph. 3:8, of the riches of Christ; in Rom. 11:33, "past tracing out," of the ways of the Lord (cf. No. 1, in the same verse). The ways of God are the outworkings of His judgment. Of the two questions in v. 34, the first seems to have reference to No. 1, the second to No. 2.

UNSEEMLINESS, UNSEEMLY

aschemosune (808), from *aschemon*, "unseemly," is rendered "unseemliness" in Rom. 1:27, RV.

UNSPEAKABLE

1. *anekdiegetos* (411) denotes "inexpressible" (*a*, negative, *n*, euphonic, *ekdiegeomai*, "to declare, relate"), 2 Cor. 9:15, "unspeakable" (of the gift of God); regarding the various explanations of the gift, it seems most suitable to view it as the gift of His Son.

2. *aneklaletos* (412) denotes "unable to be told out" (*eklaleo*, "to speak out"), 1 Pet. 1:8, of the believer joy.

3. *arrhetos* (731), primarily, "unspoken" (*a*, negative, *rhetos*, "spoken"), denotes "unspeakable," 2 Cor. 12:4, of the words heard by Paul when caught up into paradise. The word is common in sa-

U

cred inscriptions especially in connection with the Greek Mysteries; hence Moulton and Milligan suggest the meaning "words too sacred to be uttered."

UNSTABLE, UNSTEADFAST

1. *asteriktos* (*793*), (*a*, negative, *sterizo*, "to fix"), is used in 2 Pet. 2:14; 3:16, KJV, "unstable," RV, "unsteadfast."

2. *akatastatos* (*182*), from *kathistemi*, "to set in order," is rendered "unstable" in Jas. 1:8.

UNTHANKFUL

acharistos (*884*) denotes "ungrateful, thankless" (*charis*, "thanks"), Luke 6:35; 2 Tim. 3:2.

UNVEILED

akatakaluptos (*177*), "uncovered" (*a*, negative, *katakalupto*, "to cover"), is used in 1 Cor. 11:5, 13, RV, "unveiled," with reference to the injunction forbidding women to be "unveiled" in a church gathering. Whatever the character of the covering, it is to be on her head as "a sign of authority" (v. 10), RV, the meaning of which is indicated in v. 3 in the matter of headships, and the reasons for which are given in vv. 7-9, and in the phrase "because of the angels," intimating their witness of, and interest in, that which betokens the headship of Christ.

UNWASHED

aniptos (*449*), "unwashed" (*a*, negative, *nipto*, "to wash"), occurs in Matt. 15:20; Mark 7:2 (v. 5 in some mss.).

UNWISE

1. *anoetos* (*453*) is translated "unwise" in Rom. 1:14, KJV.

2. *aphron* (*878*) is translated "unwise" in Eph. 5:17, KJV.

3. *asophos* (*781*), rendered "unwise" in Eph. 5:15, RV (KJV, "fools.)"

UNWORTHILY, UNWORTHY

A. Adverb.

anaxios (*371*) is used in 1 Cor. 11:27, of partaking of the Lord's Supper "unworthily," i.e., treating it as a common meal, the bread and cup as common things, not apprehending their solemn symbolic import.

B. Adjective.

anaxios (*370*) is used in 1 Cor. 6:2. In modern Greek it signifies "incapable."

UPRIGHT, UPRIGHTNESS
Old Testament

A. Adjective.

yashar (3477), "upright; right; righteous; just." The basic meaning is the root meaning "to be straight" in the sense of "to be level." The legs of the creatures in Ezekiel's vision were straight, Ezek. 1:7. The Israelites designated an easy road for traveling as a "level road." It had few inclines and declines compared to the mountain roads, cf. Jer. 31:9.

yashar with the meaning "right" pertains to things and to abstracts. Samuel promised himself to instruct God's people in "the good and the right way," 1 Sam. 12:23. Nehemiah thanked God for having given just ordinances, Neh. 9:13. Based on His revelation God expected His people to please Him in being obedient to Him, Deut. 6:18.

When *yashar* pertains to people, it is best translated "just" or "upright." God is the standard of uprightness for His people, Ps. 25:8. His word, Ps. 33:4, judgments, Ps. 19:9, and ways, Hos. 14:9, reveal His uprightness and are a blessing to His people. The believer follows Him in being "upright" in heart, Ps. 32:11; cf. 7:10; 11:2.

B. Verb.

yashar (3474), "to be straight, be smooth, be right." One occurrence of the verb is in 1 Chron. 13:4: "And all the congregation said that they would do so: for the thing was right in the eyes of all the people." In this usage *yashar* has the sense of being pleasing or agreeable. In Hab. 2:4 the word implies an ethical uprightness.

C. Nouns.

yosher (3476), "straightness," Prov. 2:13. Other nouns occur less frequently. *yishrah* means "uprightness" and occurs once, 1 Kings 3:6. The noun *yeshurun* is an honorific title for Israel, Deut. 32:15; 33:5. *mishor* means "level place, uprightness." In 1 Kings 20:23 *mishor* refers to "level country"; in Isa. 11:4 the word refers to "uprightness."

New Testament

euthutes (2118), from *euthus*, "straight," is rendered "uprightness" in Heb. 1:8, RV, KJV, "righteousness," marg., "rightness," or, "straightness."

UPROAR (Verbs)

thorubeo (2350), used in the middle voice, denotes "to make a noise or uproar," or, transitively, in the active voice, "to trouble, throw into confusion," Acts 17:5.

U

URGE

(1) In Acts 13:50, KJV, *parotruno*, "to urge on" (RV), is rendered "stirred up." (2) In Acts 13:43, *peitho*, "to persuade," is rendered "urged," RV (KJV, "persuaded"). (3) *enecho* is rendered "to urge" in Luke 11:53.

USURY

Note: The RV, "interest," Matt. 25:27; Luke 19:23, is the preferable rendering of *tokos* here.

UTTER

1. *laleo* (*2980*), "to speak," is rendered "to utter" in 2 Cor. 12:4 and Rev. 10:3, 4 (twice).

2. *ereugomai* (*2044*), primarily, "to spit or spue out," or, of oxen, "to bellow, roar," hence, "to speak aloud, utter," occurs in Matt. 13:35.

3. *aphiemi* (*863*), "to send forth," is used of "uttering" a cry, Mark 15:37, of Christ's final "utterance" on the cross, RV, "uttered" (KJV, "cried").

UTTERANCE

logos (*3056*), "a word," is translated "utterance" in 1 Cor. 1:5; 2 Cor. 8:7; Eph. 6:19.

V

VAIN, IN VAIN, VAINLY

A. Adjectives.

1. *kenos* (2756), "empty," with special reference to quality, is translated "vain" (as an adjective) in Acts 4:25; 1 Cor. 15:10, 14 (twice); Eph. 5:6; Col. 2:8; Jas. 2:20.

2. *mataios* (3152), "void of result," is used of (a) idolatrous practices, Acts 14:15, RV, "vain things" (KJV, "vanities"); (b) the thoughts of the wise, 1 Cor. 3:20; (c) faith, if Christ is not risen, 1 Cor. 15:17; (d) questionings, strifes, etc., Titus 3:9; (e) religion, with an unbridled tongue, Jas. 1:26; (f) manner of life, 1 Pet. 1:18.

B. Verbs.

1. *mataioo* (3154), "to make vain, or foolish," corresponding in meaning to A, No. 2, occurs in Rom. 1:21, "became vain."

2. *kenoo* (2758), "to empty," corresponding to A, No. 1, is translated "should be in vain" in 2 Cor. 9:3, KJV.

C. Adverbs.

1. *maten* (3155), properly the accusative case of *mate*, "a fault, a folly," signifies "in vain, to no purpose," Matt. 15:9; Mark 7:7.

2. *dorean* (1432), the accusative of *dorea*, "a gift," is used adverbially, denoting (a) "freely" (see FREE, D); (b) "uselessly," "in vain," Gal. 2:21, KJV (RV, "for nought").

3. *eike* (1500) denotes (a) "without cause," "vainly," Col. 2:18; (b) "to no purpose," "in vain," Rom. 13:4; Gal. 3:4 (twice); 4:11.

VAINGLORY, VAINGLORIOUS

A. Nouns.

1. *kenodoxia* (2754), from *kenos*, "vain, empty," *doxa*, "glory," is used in Phil. 2:3.

2. *alazoneia*, or -*ia* (212) denotes "boastfulness, vaunting," translated "vainglory" in 1 John 2:16, RV (KJV, "pride"); in Jas. 4:16, RV, "vauntings" (KJV, "boastings").

B. Adjective.

kenodoxos (2755), akin to A, No. 1, is rendered "vainglorious" in Gal. 5:26, RV (KJV, "desirous of vain glory").

VALUE

A. Verb.

diaphero (*1308*), used intransitively, means "to differ, to excel," hence "to be of more value," Matt. 6:26, RV, "are (not) ye of (much) more value" (KJV, "better"); 12:12 and Luke 12:24, ditto; Matt. 10:31; Luke 12:7.

B. Noun.

time (*5092*) denotes "a valuing, a price, honor"; in Col. 2:23, RV, "(not of any) value (against the indulgence of the flesh)" [KJV, "(not in any) honor..."], i.e., the ordinances enjoined by human tradition are not of any value to prevent (*pros*, "against"; cf. Acts 26:14) indulgence of the flesh.

VANISH, VANISHING

A. Verb.

aphanizo (*853*), "to render unseen," is translated "vanisheth away" in Jas. 4:14 (passive voice, lit., "is made to disappear").

B. Noun.

aphanismos (*854*), (*a*, negative, *phaino*, "to cause to appear" akin to A), occurs in Heb. 8:13, RV, "(nigh unto) vanishing away"; the word is suggestive of abolition.

VANITY

mataiotes (*3153*), "emptiness as to results," akin to *mataios*, is used (a) of the creation, Rom. 8:20, as failing of the results designed, owing to sin; (b) of the mind which governs the manner of life of the Gentiles, Eph. 4:17; (c) of the "great swelling *words*" of false teachers, 2 Pet. 2:18.

VAPOR

atmis (*822*) is used of "smoke," Acts 2:19; figuratively of human life, Jas. 4:14.

VARIABLENESS, VARIATION

parallage (*3883*) denotes, in general, "a change" (Eng., "parallax," the difference between the directions of a body as seen from two different points), "a transmission" from one condition to another; it occurs in Jas. 1:17, RV, "variation" (KJV, "variableness"); the reference may be to the sun, which "varies" its position in the sky.

VARIANCE

dichazo (*1369*), "to cut apart, divide in two," is used metaphorically in Matt. 10:35, "to set at variance."

VAUNT (ONESELF)

perpereuomai (*4068*), "to boast or vaunt oneself" (from *perperos*, "vainglorious, braggart," not in the NT), is used in 1 Cor. 13:4, negatively of love.

VEHEMENTLY

1. *deinos* (*1171*), is rendered "vehemently" in Luke 11:53.

2. *eutonos* (*2159*), vigorously, is translated "vehemently" in Luke 23:10, of accusations against Christ.

3. *ekperissos* (*1537* and *4053*), formed from *ek*, "out of," and the adverb *perissos*, "exceedingly, the more," is found in Mark 14:31, in the best texts (some have *ek perissou*, the genitive case of the adjective *perissos*, "more"), RV, "exceeding vehemently" (KJV, "the more vehemently"), of Peter's protestation of loyalty; the RV gives the better rendering.

VEIL

1. *katapetasma* (*2665*), lit., "that which is spread out" (*petannumi*) "before" (*kata*), hence, "a veil," is used (a) of the inner "veil" of the tabernacle, Heb. 6:19; 9:3; (b) of the corresponding "veil" in the Temple, Matt. 27:51; Mark 15:38; Luke 23:45; (c) metaphorically of the "flesh" of Christ, Heb. 10:20, i.e., His body which He gave up to be crucified, thus by His expiatory death providing a means of the spiritual access of believers, the "new and living way," into the presence of God.

2. *kalumma* (*2571*), "a covering," is used (a) of the "veil" which Moses put over his face when descending Mount Sinai, thus preventing Israel from beholding the glory, 2 Cor. 3:13; (b) metaphorically of the spiritually darkened vision suffered retributively by Israel, until the conversion of the nation to their Messiah takes place, vv. 14, 15, 16.

3. *peribolaion* (*4018*), rendered "a veil" in the KJV marg. of 1 Cor. 11:15.

VENGEANCE

ekdikesis (*1557*), lit., ("that which proceeds) out of justice," not, as often with human "vengeance," out of a sense of injury or merely out of a feeling of indignation. The word is most frequently used of divine "vengeance," e.g., Rom. 12:19; Heb. 10:30. The judgments of God are holy and right (Rev. 16:7), and free from any element of self-gratification or vindictiveness.

VERILY

1. *alethos* (230), "truly" (akin to *aletheia*, "truth"), is translated "verily" in 1 John 2:5.

2. *amen* (281), the transliteration of a Heb. word = "truth," is usually translated "verily" in the four Gospels; in John's gospel the Lord introduces a solemn pronouncement by the repeated word "verily, verily" twenty-five times.

VESSEL

Old Testament

keli (3627), "vessel," can mean an utensil or container of many different kinds and made of many different materials. It is similar to the way we use "thing," as a descriptor, as in "hand me that *thing*." Context will best demand what the meaning of the *thing* is: receptacle; stuff; clothing; utensil; tool; instrument; ornament or jewelry; armor or weapon, Gen. 31:37; Lev. 6:28; 1 Sam. 17:22 the word is used of baggage; or cargo, Jon. 1:5. Ships are called "receptacles," presumably because they can hold people, Isa. 18:2.

This word may be used of various "implements or tools": "Simeon and Levi are brethren instruments of cruelty are in their habitations," Gen. 49:5. In Jer. 22:7 the word represents "tools" with which trees may be cut down: "And I will prepare destroyers against thee, every one with his weapons: and they shall cut down thy choice cedars, and cast them into the fire." Isaac told Esau to take his gear, his quiver, and his bow, "and go out to the field, and take me some venison," Gen. 27:3.

Weapons for war are called "implements": "And they [the Israelites] went after them unto Jordan: and, lo, all the way was full of garments and vessels, which the Syrians had cast away in their haste," 2 Kings 7:15. A bearer of implements is an armor-bearer, Judg. 9:54. A house of arms or an armory is referred to in 2 Kings 20:13.

In Amos 6:5 and such passages, 2 Chron. 5:13; 7:6; 23:13; cf. Ps. 71:22, "musical instruments" are called *kelim:* "That chant to the sound of the viol, and invent to themselves instruments of music...."

New Testament

skeuos (4632) is used (a) of "a vessel or implement" of various kinds, Mark 11:16; Luke 8:16; John 19:29; Acts 10:11, 16; 11:5; 27:17 (a sail); Rom. 9:21; 2 Tim. 2:20; Heb. 9:21; Rev. 2:27; 18:12; (b) of "goods or household stuff," Matt. 12:29 and Mark 3:27, "goods"; Luke 17:31, RV, "goods" (KJV, "stuff"); (c) of "persons," (1) for the service of God, Acts 9:15, "a (chosen) vessel"; 2 Tim. 2:21, "a vessel (unto honor)"; (2) the "subjects" of divine wrath, Rom. 9:22; (3) the "subjects" of divine mercy, Rom. 9:23; (4) the human frame, 2 Cor.

4:7; perhaps 1 Thess. 4:4; (5) a husband and wife, 1 Pet. 3:7; of the
wife, probably, 1 Thess. 4:4; while the exhortation to each one "to
possess himself of his own vessel in sanctification and honor" is
regarded by some as referring to the believer's body, the view that
the "vessel" signifies the wife, and that the reference is to the
sanctified maintenance of the married state, is supported by the
facts that in 1 Pet. 3:7 the same word *time*, "honor," is used with
regard to the wife, again in Heb. 13:4, *timios*, "honorable" (RV, "in
honor") is used in regard to marriage; further, the preceding command in 1 Thess. 4 is against fornication, and the succeeding one
(v. 6) is against adultery.

VEX

1. *ochleo* (3791), "to disturb, trouble," is used in the passive voice,
of being "troubled" by evil spirits, Acts 5:16.
2. *basanizo* (928), "to torment," is translated "vexed" in 2 Pet. 2:8.

VICTORY, VICTORIOUS

A. Nouns.

1. *nike* (3529), "victory," is used in 1 John 5:4.
2. *nikos* (3534), a later form of No. 1, is used in Matt. 12:20; 1 Cor.
15:54, 55, 57.

B. Verb.

nikao (3528), "to conquer, overcome," is translated "(them) that
come victorious (from)" in Rev. 15:2, RV (KJV, "that had gotten the
victory").

VILE

A. Noun.

atimia (819), "dishonor," is translated "vile" in Rom. 1:26, RV,
marg., "(passions) of dishonor."

B. Adjectives.

1. *rhuparos* (4508), "filthy dirty," is used (a) literally, of old shabby clothing, Jas. 2:2, "vile"; (b) metaphorically, of moral defilement, Rev. 22:11 (in the best texts).
2. *poneros* (4190), "evil," is translated "vile" in Acts 17:5, RV (KJV,
"lewd").

VILLAGE

kome (2968), "a village," or "country town," primarily as distinct
from a walled town, occurs in the Gospels; elsewhere only in Acts
8:25. The difference between *polis*, "a city," and *kome*, is maintained in the NT, as in Josephus. Among the Greeks the point of
the distinction was not that of size or fortification, but of constitu-

tion and land. In the OT the city and the village are regularly distinguished. The Mishna makes the three distinctions, a large city, a city, and a village.

The RV always substitutes "village(-s)" for KJV, "town(-s)," Matt. 10:11; Mark 8:23, 26, 27; Luke 5:17; 9:6, 12; John 7:42; 11:1, 30.

VILLANY

1. *rhadiourgia* (*4468*) lit. and primarily denotes "ease in working" (*rhadios*, "easy," *ergon*, "work"), "easiness, laziness"; hence "recklessness, wickedness," Acts 13:10, RV, "villany," KJV, "mischief." In the papyri it is used of "theft."

2. *rhadiourgema* (*4467*), "a reckless act" (akin to No. 1), occurs in Acts 18:14, RV, "villany" (KJV, "lewdness").

VINEGAR

oxos (*3690*), akin to *oxus*, "sharp," denotes "sour wine," the ordinary drink of laborers and common soldiers; it is used in the four Gospels of the "vinegar" offered to the Lord at His crucifixion. In Matt. 27:34 the best texts have *oinos*, "wine" (RV). Some have *oxos* (KJV, "vinegar"), but Mark 15:23 (KJV and RV) confirms the RV in the passage in Matthew. This, which the soldiers offered before crucifying, was refused by Him, as it was designed to alleviate His sufferings; the "vinegar" is mentioned in Mark 15:36; so Luke 23:36, and John 19:29, 30.

VINEYARD

kerem (3754), "vineyard." Isaiah gives a vivid description of the work involved in the preparation, planting, and cultivation of a "vineyard," Isa. 5:1-7. The "vineyard" was located on the slopes of a hill, Isa. 5:1. The soil was cleared of stones before the tender vines were planted, Isa. 5:2. A watchtower provided visibility over the "vineyard," Isa. 5:2; and a winevat and place for crushing the grapes were hewn out of the rock, Isa. 5:2. When all the preparations were finished, the "vineyard" was ready and in a few years it was expected to produce crops. In the meantime the *kerem* required regular pruning, Lev. 25:3-4. The time between planting and the first crop was of sufficient import as to free the owner from military duty, Deut. 20:6.

The words "vineyard" and "olive grove," (*zayit*) are often found together in the biblical text. These furnished the two major permanent agricultural activities in ancient Israel, as both required much work and time before the crops came in. God promised that the ownership of the "vineyards" and orchards of the Canaanites was to go to His people as a blessing from Him, Deut. 6:11-12. The "vineyards" were located mainly in the hill country and in the low-lying hill country. The Bible mentions the "vineyard" at Timnath,

Judg. 14:5, Jezreel, 1 Kings 21:1, the hill country of Samaria, Jer. 31:5, and even at En-gedi, Song of Sol. 1:14.

The metaphorical use of *kerem* allows the prophet Isaiah to draw an analogy between the "vineyard" and Israel, Isa. 5:7. It has also been suggested that the "vineyard" in the Song of Solomon is better understood metaphorically as "person," cf. Song of Sol. 1:6.

VIOLENCE, VIOLENT, VIOLENTLY

Old Testament

A. Noun.

chamas (2555), "violence; wrong; maliciousness." Basically *chamas* connotes the disruption of the divinely established order of things. It has a wide range of nuances within this legal sphere. The expression "a witness in the case of violent wrongdoing" means someone who bears witness in a case having to do with such an offense, cf. Deut. 19:16. In this context the truthfulness of the witness is not established except upon further investigation, Deut. 19:18. Once he was established as a false witness, the penalty for the crime concerning which he bore false witness was to be executed against the liar, cf. Deut. 19:19.

chamas perhaps connotes a "violent wrongdoing" which has not been righted, the guilt of which lies on an entire area (its inhabitants) disrupting their relationship with God and thereby interfering with His blessings, Gen. 6:11; 16:5.

B. Verb.

chamas (2554) means "to treat violently," Jer. 22:3.

New Testament

A. Nouns.

1. *bia* (*970*) denotes "force, violence," said of men, Acts 5:26; 21:35; 24:7; of waves, 27:41.

2. *biastes* (*973*), "a forceful or violent man," is used in Matt. 11:12.

B. Verbs.

1. *diaseio* (*1286*), "to shake violently," is used in Luke 3:14, "do violence," including intimidation.

2. *biazo* (*971*), in the passive voice, is rendered "suffereth violence" in Matt. 11:12;

VIPER

echidna (*2191*) is probably a generic term for "poisonous snakes." It is rendered "viper" in the NT, (a) of the actual creature, Acts 28:3; (b) metaphorically in Matt. 3:7; 12:34; 23:33; Luke 3:7.

VIRGIN

Old Testament

'almah (5959), "virgin; maiden." That *'almah* can mean "virgin" is quite clear in Song of Sol. 6:8. The word *'almah* represents those who are eligible for marriage but are neither wives (queens) nor concubines. These "maidens" all loved the king and longed to be chosen to be with him (to be his bride), even as did the Shulamite who became his bride, 1:3-4. In Gen. 24:43 the word describes Rebekah, of whom it is said in Gen. 24:16 that she was a "maiden" with whom no man had had relations. Thus *'almah* appears to be used more of the concept "virgin" than that of "maiden," yet always of a woman who had not borne a child. This makes it the ideal word to be used in Isa. 7:14, since the word *betulah* emphasizes virility more than virginity. The reader of Isa. 7:14 in the days preceding the birth of Jesus would read that a "virgin who is a maiden" would conceive a child. This was a possible, but irregular, use of the word since the word can refer merely to the unmarried status of the one so described. The child immediately in view was the son of the prophet and his wife (cf. Isa. 8:3) who served as a sign to Ahaz that his enemies would be defeated by God. On the other hand, the reader of that day must have been extremely uncomfortable with this use of the word, since its primary connotation is "virgin" rather than "maiden." Thus the clear translation of the Greek in Matt. 1:23 whereby this word is rendered "virgin" satisfies its fullest implication. Therefore, there was no embarrassment to Isaiah when his wife conceived a son by him, since the word *'almah* allowed for this. Neither is there any embarrassment in Matthew's understanding of the word.

New Testament

parthenos (3933) is used (a) of "the Virgin Mary," Matt. 1:23; Luke 1:27 [cf. "virginity," Luke 2:36]; (b) of the ten "virgins" in the parable, Matt. 25:1, 7, 11; (c) of the "daughters" of Philip the evangelist, Acts 21:9; (d) those concerning whom the apostle Paul gives instructions regarding marriage, 1 Cor. 7:25, 28, 34; in vv. 36, 37, 38, the subject passes to that of "virgin *daughters*" (RV), which almost certainly formed one of the subjects upon which the church at Corinth sent for instructions from the apostle; one difficulty was relative to the discredit which might be brought upon a father (or guardian), if he allowed his daughter or ward to grow old unmarried. The interpretation that this passage refers to a man and woman already in some kind of relation by way of a spiritual marriage and living together in a vow of virginity and celibacy, is untenable if only in view of the phraseology of the passage; (e) figuratively, of "a local church" in its relation to Christ, 2 Cor. 11:2; (f) metaphorically, of "chaste persons," Rev. 14:4.

VIRGINITY

parthenia (*3932*), akin to the above, occurs in Luke 2:36.

VIRTUE

arete (*703*) properly denotes whatever procures preeminent estimation for a person or thing; hence, "intrinsic eminence, moral goodness, virtue," (a) of God, 1 Pet. 2:9, "excellencies" (KJV, "praises"); here the original and general sense seems to be blended with the impression made on others, i.e., renown, excellence or praise (Hort); in 2 Pet. 1:3, "(by His own glory and) virtue," RV (instrumental dative), i.e., the manifestation of His divine power; this significance is frequently illustrated in the papyri and was evidently common in current Greek speech; (b) of any particular moral excellence, Phil. 4:8; 2 Pet. 1:5 (twice), where virtue is enjoined as an essential quality in the exercise of faith, RV, "(in your faith supply) virtue."

VISION

Old Testament

A. Nouns.

chazon (*2377*), "vision," i.e., a means of divine revelation. First, it refers to the means itself, to a prophetic "vision" by which divine messages are communicated, Ezek. 12:22. Second, this word represents the message received by prophetic "vision," Prov. 29:18. Finally, *chazon* can represent the entirety of a prophetic or prophet's message as it is written down, Isa. 1:1. Thus the word inseparably related to the content of a divine communication focuses on the means by which that message is received, Isa. 29:7.

chizzayon (*2384*), "vision." This noun, which occurs 9 times, refers to a prophetic "vision" in Joel 2:28: "And it shall come to pass afterward, that I will pour out my spirit upon all flesh; and your sons and your daughters shall prophesy, your old men shall dream dreams, your young men shall see visions. *chizzayon* refers to divine communication in 2 Sam. 7:17 (the first biblical occurrence) and to an ordinary dream in Job 4:13.

B. Verb.

chazah (*2372*), "to see, behold, select for oneself." It means "to see or behold" in general, Prov. 22:29, "to see" in a prophetic vision, Num. 24:4, and "to select for oneself," Exod. 18:21. In Lam. 2:14 the word means "to see" in relation to prophets' vision.

New Testament

1. *horama* (*3705*), "that which is seen" (*horao*), denotes (a) "a spectacle, sight," Matt. 17:9; Acts 7:31 ("sight"); (b) "an appearance,

vision," Acts 9:10 (v. 12 in some mss.): 10:3, 17, 19; 11:5; 12:9; 16:9, 10; 18:9.

2. *horasis* (*3706*), "sense of sight," is rendered "visions" in Acts 2:17; Rev. 9:17.

3. *optasia* (*3701*) (a late form of *opsis*, "the act of seeing"), from *optano*, "to see, a coming into view," denotes a "vision" in Luke 1:22; 24:23; Acts 26:19; 2 Cor. 12:1.

VISIT

episkeptomai (*1980*), primarily, "to inspect" (a late form of *episkopeo*, "to look upon, care for, exercise oversight"), signifies (a) "to visit" with help, of the act of God, Luke 1:68, 78; 7:16; Acts 15:14; Heb. 2:6; (b) "to visit" the sick and afflicted, Matt. 25:36, 43; Jas. 1:27; (c) "to go and see," "pay a visit to," Acts 7:23; 15:36; (d) "to look out" certain men for a purpose, Acts 6:3.

2. *historeo* (*2477*), from *histor*, "one learned in anything," denotes "to visit" in order to become acquainted with, Gal. 1:18, RV, "visit" (KJV, "see"), RV marg., "become acquainted with."

3. *epiphero* (*2018*), for which see BRING, No. 6, is rendered "visiteth (with wrath)" in Rom. 3:5, RV, KJV, "taketh (vengeance)."

VISITATION

episkope (*1984*), denotes "a visitation," whether in mercy, Luke 19:44, or in judgment, 1 Pet. 2:12.

VOID

1. *kenoo* (*2758*), "to empty, make of no effect," is rendered "to make void," in Rom. 4:14; 1 Cor. 1:17, RV; 9:15; 2 Cor. 9:3, RV.

2. *atheteo* (*114*), rendered "to make void" in Gal. 2:21, RV (KJV, "frustrate"); 3:15, RV.

3. *akuroo* (*208*), "to make void" in Matt. 15:6; Mark 7:13, RV.

VOLUNTARY

In Col. 2:18, *thelo* is rendered "(in a) voluntary (humility)," present participle, i.e., "being a voluntary (in humility)," KJV marg., RV marg., "of his own mere will (by humility)," *en*, "in," being rendered as instrumental; what was of one's own mere will, with the speciousness of humility, would mean his being robbed of his prize.

VOW

Old Testament

A. Verb.

nadar (*5087*), "to vow," i.e., to make a promise to another, with sanctions for not completing the promise. Numbers 30 deals with the law concerning vows.

B. Noun.

neder (5088), "vow; votive offering." The vow has two basic forms, the unconditional and the conditional. The unconditional is an "oath" where someone binds himself without expecting anything in return, Ps. 116:14. The conditional "vow" generally had a preceding clause before the oath giving the conditions which had to come to pass before the "vow" became valid, Gen. 28:20-22.

"Vows" usually occurred in serious situations. Jacob needed the assurance of God's presence before setting out for Padan-aram, Gen. 28:20-22; Jephthah made a rash "vow" before battle, Judg. 11:30; cf. Num. 21:1-3; Hannah greatly desired a child, 1 Sam. 1:11, when she made a "vow." Once a vow was made, it must be kept. One cannot annul the "vow." However, the Old Testament allows for "redeeming" the "vow"; by payment of an equal amount in silver, a person, a field, or a house dedicated by "vow" to the Lord could be redeemed, Lev. 27:1-25. This practice, however, declined in Jesus' time, and therefore the Talmud frowns upon the practice of "vowing" and refers to those who vow as "sinners."

neder signifies a kind of offering, Deut. 12:6. In particular the word represents a kind of peace or "votive offering," Ezra 7:16. It also is a kind of thank offering, Nah. 1:15. Here even Gentiles expressed their thanks to God presumably with a gift promised upon condition of deliverance, cf. Num. 21:1-3.

New Testament

euche (2171) denotes also "a vow," Acts 18:18; 21:23; Jas. 5:15, "prayer."

WAGES

1. *opsonion* (*3800*), denotes (a) "soldier's pay," Luke 3:14; 1 Cor. 9:7 ("charges"); (b) in general, "hire, wages of any sort," used metaphorically, Rom. 6:23, of sin; 2 Cor. 11:8, of material support which Paul received from some of the churches which he had established and to which he ministered in spiritual things; their support partly maintained him at Corinth, where he forebore to receive such assistance (vv. 9, 10).

2. *misthos* (*3408*), "hire," is rendered "wages" in John 4:36; in 2 Pet. 2:15, KJV (RV, hire).

WAIL, WAILING

(1) *alalazo* is rendered "to wail" in Mark 5:38. (2) *kopto* is rendered "to wail" in Rev. 1:7, KJV (RV, "shall mourn") and 18:9, RV, "wail" (KJV, "lament"). (3) *pentheo* is rendered "to wail" in Rev. 18:15, 19, KJV. (4) *klauthmos* is rendered "wailing" in Matt. 13:42, 50, KJV. (5) In Matt. 11:17 and Luke 7:32, KJV, *threneo*, "to wail" (RV), is rendered to mourn.

WAIT

1. *ekdechomai* (*1551*), rendered "to wait" in John 5:3, KJV; Acts 17:16; 1 Cor. 11:33, RV.

2. *apekdechomai* (*553*), "to await or expect eagerly," is rendered "to wait for" in Rom. 8:19, 23, 25; 1 Cor. 1:7; Gal. 5:5; Phil. 3:20, RV (KJV, "look for"); Heb. 9:28, RV (KJV, "look for"), here "them that wait" represents believers in general, not a section of them; 1 Pet. 3:20 (in the best texts; some have No. 1).

3. *prosdechomai* (*4327*), "to look for" with a view to favorable reception, is rendered "to wait for" in Mark 15:43; Luke 2:25; 12:36; 23:51.

4. *prosdokao* (*4328*), "to await," is rendered "to wait for" in Luke 1:21; 8:40; Acts 10:24; in 27:33, RV "ye wait" (KJV, "have tarried")

5. *anameno* (*362*), "to wait for," is used in 1 Thess. 1:10, of "waiting" for the Son of God from heaven; the word carries with it the suggestion of "waiting" with patience and confident expectancy.

6. *perimeno* (*4037*), "to await an event," is used in Acts 1:4, of "waiting" for the Holy Spirit, "the promise of the Father."

7. *proskartereo* (4342), to continue steadfastly, is rendered "to wait on," in Mark 3:9 and Acts 10:7.

WAKE

gregoreo (1127), translated "wake" in 1 Thess. 5:10, is rendered "watch" in the RV marg., as in the text in v. 6, and the RV in the twenty-one other places in which it occurs in the NT (save 1 Pet. 5:8, "be watchful"). It is not used in the metaphorical sense of "to be alive"; here it is set in contrast with *katheudo*, "to sleep," which is never used by the apostle with the meaning "to be dead" (it has this meaning only in the case of Jairus' daughter). Accordingly the meaning here is that of vigilance and expectancy as contrasted with laxity and indifference. All believers will live together with Christ from the time of the Rapture described in ch. 4; for all have spiritual life now, though their spiritual condition and attainment vary considerably. Those who are lax and fail to be watchful will suffer loss (1 Cor. 3:15; 9:27; 2 Cor. 5:10, e.g.), but the apostle is not here dealing with that aspect of the subject. What he does make clear is that the Rapture of believers at the second coming of Christ will depend solely on the death of Christ for them, and not upon their spiritual condition. The Rapture is not a matter of reward, but of salvation.

WALK

Old Testament

A. Verb.

halak (1980), "to go, walk, behave." Essentially, this root refers to linear movement without any suggestion of direction, or elevation change: of man, Gen. 9:23; of beasts, Gen. 3:14; or inanimate objects Gen. 2:14. This root is used in various other special ways. It may be used to emphasize that a certain thing occurred; Jacob "went" and got the kid his mother requested, in other words, he actually did the action, Gen. 27:14. In Gen. 8:3 the waters of the flood steadily receded from the surface of the earth. Sometimes this verb implies movement away from, as in Gen. 18:33, when the Lord "departed" from Abraham.

God is said to "walk" or "go" in three senses. First, there are certain cases where He assumed some kind of physical form. For example, Adam and Eve heard the sound of God "walking" to and fro in the garden of Eden, Gen. 3:8. He "walks" on the clouds, Ps. 104:3, or in the heavens, Job 22:14; these are probably anthropomorphisms (God is spoken of as if He had bodily parts). Even more often God is said to accompany His people, Exod. 33:14, to go to redeem (deliver) them from Egypt, 2 Sam. 7:23, and to come to save them, Ps. 80:2. Men may also "walk...after the imagination of their evil heart," or act stubbornly, Jer. 3:17. The pious followed or practiced God's commands; they "walked" in righteousness, Isa. 33:15, in humility, Mic. 6:8, and in integrity, Ps. 15:2.

B. Nouns.

halikah (1979), "course; doings; traveling company; caravan; procession." This noun occurs 6 times in the Old Testament.

This word conveys several nuances. In Nah. 2:5 *halikah* refers to a "course," Prov. 31:27; "traveling-company" or "caravan," Job 6:19; "procession," Ps. 68:24.

Several other related nouns occur infrequently. *mahalak*, which appears 5 times, means "passage," Ezek. 42:4; "journey," Neh. 2:6. *helek* occurs twice and means a "visitor," 2 Sam. 12:4.

New Testament

1. *peripateo* (4043) is used (a) physically, in the Synoptic Gospels (except Mark 7:5); always in the Acts except in 21:21; never in the Pauline Epistles, nor in those of John; (b) figuratively, signifying the whole round of the activities of the individual life, whether of the unregenerate, Eph. 4:17, or of the believer, 1 Cor. 7:17; Col. 2:6. It is applied to the observance of religious ordinances, Acts 21:21; Heb. 13:9, marg., as well as to moral conduct. The Christian is to walk in newness of life, Rom. 6:4, after the spirit, 8:4, in honesty, 13:13, by faith, 2 Cor. 5:7, in good works, Eph. 2:10, in love, 5:2, in wisdom, Col. 4:5, in truth, 2 John 4, after the commandments of the Lord, v. 6. And, negatively, not after the flesh, Rom. 8:4; not after the manner of men, 1 Cor. 3:3; not in craftiness, 2 Cor. 4:2; not by sight, 5:7; not in the vanity of the mind, Eph. 4:17; not disorderly, 2 Thess. 3:6.

2. *poreuo* (4198), used in the middle voice and rendered "to walk" in Luke 1:6, of the general activities of life; so in Luke 13:33, KJV, "walk" (RV, "go on My way"); Acts 9:31; 14:16; 1 Pet. 4:3; 2 Pet. 2:10; Jude 16, 18.

3. *stoicheo* (4748), from *stoichos*, "a row," signifies "to walk in line," and is used metaphorically of "walking" in relation to others (No. 1 is used more especially of the individual walk); in Acts 21:24, it is translated "walkest orderly"; in Rom. 4:12, "walk (in... steps)"; in Gal. 5:25 it is used of walking "by the Spirit," RV, in an exhortation to keep step with one another in submission of heart to the Holy Spirit, and therefore of keeping step with Christ, the great means of unity and harmony in a church (contrast No. 1 in v. 16; v. 25 begins a new section which extends to 6:10); in 6:16 it is used of walking by the rule expressed in vv. 14, 15; in Phil. 3:16 the reference is to the course pursued by the believer who makes "the prize of the high calling" the object of his ambition.

4. *orthopodeo* (3716), "to walk in a straight path" (*orthos*, "straight," *pous*, "a foot"), is used metaphorically in Gal. 2:14, sig-

nifying a "course of conduct" by which one leaves a straight track for others to follow ("walked...uprightly").

WALLET

pera (4082), "a traveler's leather bag or pouch for holding provisions," is translated "wallet" in the RV (KJV, "scrip"), Matt. 10:10; Mark 6:8; Luke 9:3; 10:4; 22:35, 36.

WALLOW (Verb and Noun)

A. Verb.

kulio (2947) in the active voice denotes "to roll, roll along"; in the middle voice in Mark 9:20, rendered "wallowed."

B. Noun.

kulismos (2946**), "a rolling, wallowing," akin to A (some texts have *kulisma*), is used in 2 Pet. 2:22, of the proverbial sow that had been washed.

WANT (Noun and Verb)

A. Nouns.

1. *husteresis* (5304), akin to B, No. 1 (below), occurs in Mark 12:14 and Phil. 4:11.

2. *husterema* (5305) denotes (more concretely than No. 1) (a) "that which is lacking"; (b) "need, poverty, want," rendered "want" in Luke 21:4 (KJV, "penury"); 2 Cor. 8:14 (twice); 9:12; 11:9 (2nd occurrence), RV, "want" (KJV, "that which was lacking").

3. *chreia* (5532) is rendered "want" in Phil. 2:25, KJV (RV, need).

B. Verbs.

1. *hustereo* (5302) signifies "to be in want," Luke 15:14; 2 Cor. 11:9 (1st occurrence); Phil. 4:12, RV (KJV "to suffer need"); in John 2:3, KJV, "wanted" (RV, "failed").

2. *leipo* (3007), "to leave," is rendered "to be wanting" in Titus 1:5 and 3:13, and in the KJV in Jas. 1:4.

WANTONNESS, WANTON, WANTONLY

A. Nouns.

1. *aselgeia* (766), "lasciviousness, licentiousness," is rendered "wantonness" in 2 Pet. 2:18, KJV.

2. *strenos* (4764), "insolent luxury," is rendered "wantonness" in Rev. 18:3, RV (marg., "luxury"; KJV, "delicacies," not a sufficiently strong rendering).

B. Verbs.

1. *streniao* (4763), akin to A, No. 2, "to run riot," is rendered

"waxed wanton" in Rev. 18:7, RV, and "lived wantonly" in v. 8. The root of the verb is seen in the Latin *strenuus*.

2. *katastreniao* (*2691*), an intensive form of No. 1, "to wax wanton against," occurs in 1 Tim. 5:11.

WAR (Verb and Noun)

Old Testament

A. Noun.

milchamah (4421), "war; battle; skirmish; combat." This word means "war," the over-all confrontation of two forces, Gen. 14:2. It can refer to the engagement in hostilities considered as a whole, the "battle," Gen. 14:8. *milchamah* sometimes represents the art of soldiering, or "combat," Exod. 15:3.

There are several principles which were supposed to govern "war" in the Old Testament. Unjust violence was prohibited, but "war" as a part of ancient life was led, Judg. 4:13, and used by God, Num. 21:14. If it was preceded by sacrifices recognizing His leadership and sovereignty, 1 Sam. 7:9, and if He was consulted and obeyed, Judg. 20:23, Israel was promised divine protection, Deut. 20:1-4. Not one life would be lost, Josh. 10:11. At the beginning Israel's army consisted of every man over twenty and under fifty, Num. 1:2-3. Sometimes only certain segments of this potential citizens' army were summoned, Num. 31:3-6. There were several circumstances which could exempt one from "war," Num. 1:48-49; Deut. 20:5-8. Under David and Solomon there grew a professional army. It was especially prominent under Solomon, whose army was renowned for its chariotry. Cities outside Palestine were to be offered terms of surrender before being attacked. Compliance meant subjugation to slavery, Deut. 20:10-11. Cities and peoples within the Promised Land were to be utterly wiped out. They were under the ban, Deut. 2:34; 3:6; 20:16-18.

B. Verb.

lacham (3898), "to engage in battle, fight, wage war," Exod. 1:10.

New Testament

A. Verbs.

1. *polemeo* (*4170*) (Eng., "polemics"), "to fight, to make war," is used (a) literally, Rev. 12:7 (twice), RV; 13:4; 17:14; 19:11; (b) metaphorically, Rev. 2:16, RV; (C) hyperbolically, Jas. 4:2.

2. *strateuo* (*4754*), used in the middle voice, "to make war" (from *stratos*, "an encamped army"), is translated "to war" in 2 Cor. 10:3; metaphorically, of spiritual "conflict," 1 Tim. 1:18; 2 Tim. 2:3, KJV; Jas. 4:1; 1 Pet. 2:11.

3. *antistrateuomai* (*497*), "to make war against," (*anti*), Rom. 7:23.

B. Noun.

polemos (4171), "war" (akin to A, No. 1), is so translated in the RV, for KJV, "battle," 1 Cor. 14:8; Rev. 9:7, 9; 16:14; 20:8; for KJV, "fight," Heb. 11:34; KJV and RV in Jas. 4:1, hyperbolically of private "quarrels"; elsewhere, literally, e.g., Matt. 24:6; Rev. 11:7.

WARD

1. *phulake* (5438), "a guard," is used of the place where persons are kept under guard (akin to *phulax*, "a keeper"), and translated "ward" in Acts 12:10.

2. *teresis* (5084) primarily denotes "a watching" (*tereo*, "to watch"); hence "imprisonment, ward," Acts 4:3 (KJV, "hold"); 5:18, RV, "(public) ward" [KJV, "(common) prison"].

WARE OF

phulasso (5442) denotes "to guard, watch"; in 2 Tim. 4:15.

WARFARE

strateia, or *-tia* (4756), primarily "a host or army," came to denote "a warfare," and is used of spiritual "conflict" in 2 Cor. 10:4; 1 Tim. 1:15.

WARN

1. *noutheteo* (3560), "to put in mind, warn," is translated "to warn" in the KJV; the RV always translates this word by the verb "to admonish."

2. *hupodeiknumi* (5263), primarily, "to show secretly" (*hupo*, "under," *deiknumi*, "to show"), hence, generally, "to teach, make known," is translated "to warn" in Matt. 3:7; Luke 3:7; 12:5, RV (KJV, "forewarn").

3. *chrematizo* (5537), translated "to warn" in Matt. 2:12, 22; Acts 10:22; Heb. 8:5, RV (KJV, "admonished"); 11:7; 12:25, RV (KJV, "spake").

WASH

Old Testament

rachas (7364), "to wash, bathe." When the word is used figuratively to express vengeance, the imagery is a bit more gruesome, Ps. 58:10. Pilate's action in Matt. 27:24 is reminiscent of the psalmist's statement, "I will wash mine hands in innocency," Ps. 26:6. Literally, used to describe cleansing meat, Exod. 29:17. *rachas* is frequently used in the sense of "bathing," Exod. 2:5; 2 Sam. 11:2.

kabas (3526), "to wash." The word is used in the Old Testament primarily in the sense of "washing" clothes, both for ordinary cleansing, 2 Sam. 19:24, and for ritual cleansing, Exod. 19:10, 14; Lev. 11:25.

New Testament

1. *nipto* (3538) is chiefly used of "washing part of the body," John 13:5-6, 8 (twice, figuratively in 2nd clause), 12, 14 (twice); in 1 Tim. 5:10, including the figurative sense; in the middle voice, to wash oneself, Matt. 6:17; 15:2; Mark 7:3; John 9:7, 11, 15; 13:10.

2. *louo* (3068) signifies "to bathe, to wash the body," (a) active voice, Acts 9:37; 16:33; (b) passive voice, John 13:10, RV, "bathed" (KJV, "washed"); Heb. 10:22, lit., "having been washed as to the body," metaphorical of the effect of the Word of God upon the activities of the believer; (c) middle voice, 2 Pet. 2:22. Some inferior mss. have it instead of *luo*, "to loose," in Rev. 1:5 (see RV).

3. *apolouo* (628), "to wash off or away," is used in the middle voice, metaphorically, "to wash oneself," in Acts 22:16, where the command to Saul of Tarsus to "wash away" his sins indicates that by his public confession, he would testify to the removal of his sins, and to the complete change from his past life; this "washing away" was not in itself the actual remission of his sins, which had taken place at his conversion; the middle voice implies his own particular interest in the act (as with the preceding verb "baptize," lit., "baptize thyself," i.e., "get thyself baptized"); the aorist tenses mark the decisiveness of the acts; in 1 Cor. 6:11, lit., "ye washed yourselves clean"; here the middle voice (rendered in the passive in KJV and RV, which do not distinguish between this and the next two passives; see RV marg.) again indicates that the converts at Corinth, by their obedience to the faith, voluntarily gave testimony to the complete spiritual change divinely wrought in them.

4. *baptizo* (907) is rendered "washed" in Luke 11:38.

WASHING

1. *baptismos* (909) denotes "the act of washing, ablution," with special reference to purification, Mark 7:4 (in some texts, v. 8); Heb. 6:2, "baptisms"; 9:10, "washings."

2. *loutron* (3067), "a bath, a laver" (akin to *louo*, see above), is used metaphorically of the Word of God, as the instrument of spiritual cleansing, Eph. 5:26; in Titus 3:5.

WASTE (Noun and Verb)

A. Noun.

apoleia (684), "destruction," is translated "waste" in Matt. 26:8; Mark 14:4.

B. Verbs.

1. *diaskorpizo* (*1287*), "to scatter abroad," is used metaphorically of "squandering property," Luke 15:13; 16:1.

2. *portheo* (*4199*), "to ravage," is rendered "wasted" in Gal. 1:13, KJV.

3. *lumaino* (*3075*), "to outrage, maltreat," is used in the middle voice in Acts 8:3, of Saul's treatment of the church, RV, "laid waste" (KJV, "made havoc of").

WATCH (Noun and Verb), WATCHERS, WATCHFUL, WATCHINGS
Old Testament

A. Nouns.

mishmeret (*4931*); *mishmar* (*4929*), "watch; guard; post; confinement; prison; custody; division." The noun *mishmar* means a "military watch over a city," Neh. 4:9. *mishmar* can also represent a "place of confinement," such as a jail, Gen. 40:3; 42:17. *mishmar* sometimes represents a group of attendants, especially in the temple. In this nuance the word may represent the temple guard-units, 1 Chron. 26:16. However, in Neh. 12:24 the service rendered is the Levitical service in general, therefore, "division corresponding to division." All these Levitical "divisions" constituted the full services of the temple, Neh. 13:14.

mishmeret often is used to represent a more abstract idea than *mishmar*, whereas *mishmar* means the units of Levites who served the Lord (perhaps with the exception of Neh. 13:30, where *mishmeret* may mean "service-unit"). *mishmeret* refers to the priestly or Levitical service itself, Lev. 8:35; Num. 3:25 .This word often refers to divine obligation or service in general, a non-cultic obligation, Gen. 26:5; cf. Deut. 11:1.

B. Verb.

shamar (*8104*), "to keep, watch," Job 14:16.

New Testament

A. Nouns.

1. *phulake* (*5438*) is used (a) with the meaning "a watch," actively, "a guarding," Luke 2:8, lit., "(keeping, *phulasso*) watches"; (b) of "the time during which guard was kept by night, a watch of the night," Matt. 14:25; 24:43; Mark 6:48; Luke 12:38.

2. *koustodia* (*2892*), from Lat., *custodia* (cf. Eng., "custody"), is rendered "watch" in Matt. 27:65, 66 and 28:11, KJV.

3. *agrupnia* (*70*), "sleeplessness" (akin to B, No. 3), is rendered "watchings" in 2 Cor. 6:5; 11:27.

B. Verbs.

1. *gregoreo* (*1127*), "to watch," is used (a) of "keeping awake," e.g., Matt. 24:43; 26:38, 40, 41; (b) of "spiritual alertness," e.g., Acts 20:31; 1 Cor. 16:13; Col. 4:2; 1 Thess. 5:6, 10; 1 Pet. 5:8, RV, "be watchful" (KJV, "be vigilant"); Rev. 3:2, 3; 16:15.

2. *paratereo* (*3906*), "to observe," especially with sinister intent, is rendered "to watch" in Mark 3:2; Luke 6:7; 14:1; 20:20; Acts 9:24.

3. *agrupneo* (*69*), "to be sleepless" (from *agreuo*, "to chase," and *hupnos*, "sleep"), is used metaphorically, "to be watchful," in Mark 13:33; Luke 21:36; Eph. 6:18; Heb. 13:17. The word expresses not mere wakefulness, but the "watchfulness" of those who are intent upon a thing.

WATER (Noun and Verb), WATERING, WATERLESS

Old Testament

mayim (*4325*), "water; flood." First, "water" is one of the original basic substances, which in moderation and proper amounts gives and sustains life. This is water of any kind, fresh, stale, salt, sweet, from a well or cistern, or from a river or spring, Gen. 1:2; 26:19; Jer. 8:14. The phrase, *me raglayim* ("water of one's feet") is urine, 2 Kings 18:27; cf. Isa. 25:10.

This word is used figuratively in many senses. *mayim* symbolizes danger or distress: "He sent from above, he took me; he drew me out of many waters," 2 Sam. 22:17. Outbursting force is represented by *mayim* in 2 Sam. 5:20. Thus the word is used to picture something impetuous, violent, and overwhelming, Job 27:20. In other passages "water" is used to represent timidity, Josh. 7:5. Related to this nuance is the connotation "transitory," Job 11:16. In Isa. 32:2 "water" represents that which is refreshing. Outpoured "water" represents bloodshed, Deut. 12:16, wrath, Hos. 5:10, justice, Amos 5:24; KJV, "judgment," and strong feelings, Job 3:24.

tehom (*8415*), "deep water; ocean; water table; waters; flood of waters." The word represents the "deep water" whose surface freezes when cold, Job 38:30. In Ps. 135:6 *tehom* is used of the "ocean" in contrast to the seas. The word has special reference to the deep floods or sources of water. Sailors in the midst of a violent storm "mount up to the heaven, they go down again to the depths," Ps. 107:26. *tehom* can represent an inexhaustible source of water or, by way of poetic comparison, of blessings: "with blessings of heaven above, blessings of the deep that lieth under," Gen. 49:25. In such contexts the word represents the "water table" always available below the surface of the earth—what was tapped by digging wells, out of which flowed springs, and what was one with the waters beneath the surface of oceans, lakes, seas, and rivers.

New Testament

A. Noun.

hudor (5204), whence Eng. prefix, "hydro-," is used (a) of the natural element, Jas. 3:12 (b) The word "water" is used symbolically in John 3:5, either (1) of the Word of God, as in 1 Pet. 1:23 (cf. the symbolic use in Eph. 5:26), or, in view of the preposition *ek*, "out of," (2) of the truth conveyed by baptism, this being the expression, not the medium, the symbol, not the cause, of the believer s identification with Christ in His death, burial and resurrection. So the New Birth is, in one sense, the setting aside of all that the believer was according to the flesh, for it is evident that there must be an entirely new beginning. Some regard the *kai*, "and," in John 3:5, as epexegetic, = "even," in which case the "water" would be emblematic of the Spirit, as in John 7:38 (cf. 4:10, 14), but not in 1 John 5:8. where the Spirit and the "water" are distinguished. "The water of life," Rev. 21:6 and 22:1, 17, is emblematic of the maintenance of spiritual life in perpetuity. In Rev. 17:1 "the waters" are symbolic of nations, peoples, etc.

B. Verb.

potizo (4222), "to give to drink," is used (a) naturally in Luke 13:15, "watering," with reference to animals; (b) figuratively, with reference to spiritual ministry to converts, 1 Cor. 3:6-8.

WAY

Old Testament

A. Nouns.

derek (1870), "way (path, road, highway); distance; journey; manner, conduct; condition; destiny." This word refers to a path, a road, or a highway, Gen. 3:24; or a distance between two points, Gen. 30:36. In other passages *derek* refers to the action or process of "taking a journey," Gen. 45:23. In an extended nuance *derek* means "undertaking," Isa. 58:13; cf. Gen. 24:21; Deut. 28:29. In another emphasis this word connotes how and what one does, a "manner, custom, behavior, mode of life," Gen. 19:31. In 1 Kings 2:4 *derek* is applied to an activity that controls one, one's life-style. In 1 Kings 16:26 *derek* is used of Jeroboam's attitude. *derek* also refers to a "condition" in the sense of what has happened to someone. This is clear by the parallelism of Isa. 40:27. In one passage *derek* signifies the overall course and fixed path of one's life, or his "destiny," Jer. 10:23.

'orach (734), "way; path; course; conduct; manner." In meaning this word parallels Hebrew *derek*, Gen. 49:17; Judg. 5:6; Ps. 19:5; Prov. 9:15. *'orach* signifies the ground itself as the path upon which one treads, Isa. 41:3. In Job 30:12 the word seems to represent an obstruction or dam. The word can refer to a recurring life

event typical of an individual or a group. In its first biblical occurrence, Gen. 18:11, it is used of "the manner of women" (menstruation). Job 16:22 mentions the "way whence I shall not return," or death, while other passages speak of life actions, Job 34:11; literally, "conduct," or life-style, Prov. 15:10.

B. Verb.

'arach means "to go, wander," Job 34:7-8.

New Testament

hodos (*3598*) denotes (a) "a natural path, road, way," frequent in the Synoptic Gospels; elsewhere, e.g., Acts 8:26; 1 Thess. 3:11; Jas. 2:25; Rev. 16:12; (b) "a traveler's way"; (C) metaphorically, of "a course of conduct," or "way of thinking," e.g., of righteousness, Matt. 21:32; 2 Pet. 2:21; of God, Matt. 22:16, and parallels, i.e., the "way" instructed and approved by God; so Acts 18:26 and Heb. 3:10, "My ways" (cf. Rev. 15:3); of the Lord, Acts 18:25; "that leadeth to destruction," Matt. 7:13; "…unto life," 7:14; of peace, Luke 1:79; Rom. 3:17; of Paul's "ways" in Christ, 1 Cor. 4:17 (plural); "more excellent" (of love), 1 Cor. 12:31; of truth, 2 Pet. 2:2; of the right "way," 2:15; of Balaam (*ibid.*), of Cain, Jude 11; of a "way" consisting in what is from God, e.g., of life, Acts 2:28 (plural); of salvation, Acts 16:17; personified, of Christ as the means of access to the Father, John 14:6; of the course followed and characterized by the followers of Christ, Acts 9:2; 19:9, 23; 24:22.

2. *parodos* (*938*), "a passing or passage," is used with *en*, "in," 1 Cor. 16:7, "by the way" (lit., "in passing").

3. *tropos* (*5158*), "a turning, a manner," is translated "way" in Rom. 3:2, "(every) way"; Phil. 1:18, "(in every) way."

WEAK, WEAKENED, WEAKER, WEAKNESS

A. Adjectives.

1. *asthenes* (*772*), lit., "strengthless," is translated "weak," (a) of physical "weakness," Matt. 26:41; Mark 14:38; 1 Cor. 1:27; 4:10; 11:30 (a judgment upon spiritual laxity in a church); 2 Cor. 10:10; 1 Pet. 3:7 (comparative degree); (b) in the spiritual sense, said of the rudiments of Jewish religion, in their inability to justify anyone, Gal. 4:9; of the Law, Heb. 7:18; in Rom. 5:6, RV, "weak" (KJV, "without strength"), of the inability of man to accomplish his salvation; (c) morally or ethically, 1 Cor. 8:7, 10; 9:22; (d) rhetorically, of God's actions according to the human estimate, 1 Cor. 1:25, "weakness," lit., "the weak things of God."

2. *adunatos* (*102*), lit., "not powerful," is translated "weak" in Rom. 15:1, of the infirmities of those whose scruples arise through lack of faith (see 14:22, 23), in the same sense as No. 1 (c); the change in the adjective (cf. 14:1) is due to the contrast with *duna-*

toi, the "strong," who have not been specifically mentioned as such in ch. 14.

B. Verb.

astheneo (770), "to lack strength," is used in much the same way as A, No. 1, and translated "being...weak" in Rom. 4:19, KJV (RV, "being weakened"); 8:3; 14:1, 2 (in some texts, 1 Cor. 8:9); 2 Cor. 11:21, 29 (twice); 12:10; 13:3, 4, 9.

C. Noun.

astheneia (769), rendered "weakness," of the body, 1 Cor. 2:3; 15:43; 2 Cor. 11:30, RV; 12:5 (plural, RV), 9, 10, RV; Heb. 11:34; in 2 Cor. 13:4, "He was crucified through weakness" is said in respect of the physical sufferings to which Christ voluntarily submitted in giving Himself up to the death of the cross.

WEAKER ONE, LITTLE ONE

tap (2945), "weaker one; child; little one." Basically this word signifies those members of a nomadic tribe who are not able to march or who can only march to a limited extent. The word implies the "weaker ones." Thus we read of the men and the *tapim*, or the men and those who were unable to move quickly over long stretches, Gen. 43:8; 50:7-8. In several passages *tap* represents only the children and old ones, Gen. 34:26, 29.

WEALTH

Old Testament

hon (1952), "wealth; substance; riches; possessions; enough." *hon* usually refers to movable goods considered as "wealth," Prov. 6:31; cf. Ezek. 27:12. "Wealth" can be good and a sign of blessing, Ps. 112:3. The creation is God's wealth, Ps. 119:14. In the Proverbs "wealth" is usually an indication of ungodliness, Prov. 10:15. Finally, *hon* means "enough," only in Prov. 30:15-16.

New Testament

euporia (2142), primarily "facility" (*eu*, "well," *poros*, "a passage"), hence "plenty, wealth," occurs in Acts 19:25.

WEAR, WEARING

A. Verbs.

1. *phoreo* (5409), a frequentative form of *phero*, "to bear," and denoting "repeated or habitual action," is chiefly used of clothing, weapons, etc., of soft raiment, Matt. 11:8; fine clothing, Jas. 2:3; the crown of thorns, John 19:5.

2. *endidusko* (1737), "to put on," is used in the active voice in Mark 15:17 (in good mss.; some have No. 3); in Luke 8:27 (middle voice), in some texts; the best have No. 3.

3. *enduo* (*1746*) is rendered "to wear" in Luke 8:27 (middle voice; see No. 2).

4. *klino* (*2827*), "to bend, decline," is used of a day, "wearing" away, Luke 9:12 (in 24:29, is far spent).

5. *hupopiazo* (*5299*) is translated "wear (me) out" in Luke 18:5, RV (KJV, "weary").

B. Noun.

perithesis (*4025*), "a putting around or on" (*peri*, "around," *tithemi*, "to put"), is used in 1 Pet. 3:3 of "wearing" jewels of gold (RV).

WEARY

1. *kopiao* (*2872*), "to grow weary, be beaten out" (*kopos*, "a beating, toil"), is used of the Lord in John 4:6 (used in His own word "labor" in Matt. 11:28), in Rev. 2:3, RV.

2. *kamno* (*2577*), "to be weary," is rendered "to wax weary" in Heb. 12:3, RV.

3. *ekkakeo* or *enkakeo* (*1573*), rendered "to be weary" in Gal. 6:9; 2 Thess. 3:13.

WEEP, WEEPING

A. Verbs.

1. *klaio* (*2799*) is used of "any loud expression of grief," especially in mourning for the dead, Matt. 2:18; Mark 5:38, 39; 16:10; Luke 7:13; 8:52 (twice); John 11:31, 33 (twice); 20:11 (twice), 13, 15; Acts 9:39; otherwise, e.g., in exhortations, Luke 23:28; Rom. 12:15; Jas. 4:9; 5:1; negatively, "weep not," Luke 7:13; 8:52; 23:28; Rev. 5:5 (cf. Acts 21:13); in 18:9, RV, "shall weep" (KJV, "bewail").

2. *dakruo* (*1145*), "to shed tears" (*dakruon*, "a tear"), is used only of the Lord Jesus, John 18:35.

B. Noun.

klauthmos (*2805*), akin to A, No. 1, denotes "weeping, crying," Matt. 2:18; 8:12; 13:42, 50, RV (KJV, "wailing"); 22:13; 24:51; 25:30; Luke 13:28; Acts 20:37.

WELCOME

1. *apodechomai* (*588*), "to receive gladly," is rendered "to welcome" in the RV of Luke 8:40; 9:11.

2. *hupolambano* (*5274*), "to take up, to entertain," is rendered "to welcome" in 3 John 8, RV, of a hearty "welcome" to servants of God.

WELL PLEASED

A. Noun.

eudokia (*2107*), "good pleasure," occurs in the genitive case in

Luke 2:14, lit., "(men) of good pleasure" (so RV marg.), RV, "(men) in whom He is well pleased" (the genitive is objective); the KJV, "good will (toward men)," follows the inferior texts which have the nominative.

W

B. Verb.

eudokeo (*2106*), "to be well pleased."

WELL-PLEASING

A. Adjective.

euarestos (*2101*) is used in Rom. 12:1, 2, translated "acceptable (RV marg., "well-pleasing"); in the following the RV has "well-pleasing," Rom. 14:18; 2 Cor. 5:9; Eph. 5:10; in Phil. 4:18 and Col. 3:20 (RV and KJV); in Titus 2:9, RV, "well-pleasing" (KJV, "please...well"); in Heb. 13:21, RV and KJV.

B. Verb.

euaresteo (*2100*), akin to A, is rendered "to be well-pleasing" in Heb. 11:5, 6, RV (KJV, "please"); in Heb. 13:16, "is well pleased."

C. Noun.

eudokia (*2107*), lit., "good pleasure," is rendered "well-pleasing" in Matt. 11:26 and Luke 10:21.

WHALE

ketos (*2785*) means "a huge fish, a sea monster," Matt. 12:40.

WHISPERER, WHISPERING

1. *psithuristes* (*5588*), "a whisperer," occurs in an evil sense in Rom. 1:29.

2. *psithurismos* (*5587*), "a whispering," is used of "secret slander" in 2 Cor. 12:20.

WICKED

Old Testament

A. Nouns.

rasha' (*7563*), "wicked; ungodly; guilty." The narrow meaning of *rasha'* lies in the concept of "wrongdoing" or "being in the wrong." It is a legal term. The person who has sinned against the law is guilty, " Prov. 28:4. *rasha'* also denotes the category of people who have done wrong, are still living in sin, and are intent on continuing with wrongdoing, the "wicked," Ps. 10:4; he challenges God, Ps. 10:13. In his way of life the "wicked" loves violence, Ps. 11:5, oppresses the righteous, Ps. 17:9, does not repay his debts, Ps. 37:21, and lays a snare to trap the righteous, Ps. 119:110.

Two other related nouns occur in the Old Testament. *resha'*, means "wickedness," Deut. 9:27. *rish'ah*, refers to "wickedness" or "guilt," Deut. 9:4.

B. Adjective.

rasha' (7563), "wicked; guilty," Deut. 25:2. The characteristics of a "wicked" person qualify him as a godless, impious man, 2 Sam. 4:11; cf. Ezek. 3:18-19.

C. Verb.

rasha' (7561), "to be wicked, act wickedly," 2 Chron. 6:37.

New Testament

poneros (4190), translated "wicked" in the KJV and RV in Matt. 13:49; 18:32; 25:26; Luke 19:22; Acts 18:14; 1 Cor. 5:13; in the following the RV substitutes "evil" for KJV, "wicked": Matt. 12:45 (twice); 13:19; 16:4; Luke 11:26; Col. 1:21; 2 Thess. 3:2; and in the following, where Satan is mentioned as "the (or that) evil one": Matt. 13:38; Eph. 6:16; 1 John 2:13, 14; 3:12 (1st part); 5:18; in v. 19 for AV, "wickedness"; he is so called also in KJV and RV in John 17:15; 2 Thess. 3:3; KJV only in Luke 11:4; in 3 John 10, KJV, the word is translated "malicious," RV, "wicked."

WICKEDNESS

Old Testament

beliya'al (1100), "wickedness; wicked; destruction." The basic meaning of this word appears in a passage such as Judg. 20:13, where the sons of *beliya'al* are perpetrators of wickedness (they raped and murdered a man's concubine). The psalmist uses *beliya'al* as a synonym of death, Ps. 18:4, NASB.

New Testament

1. *poneria* (4189), akin to *poneros*, is always rendered "wickedness" save in Acts 3:26.

2. *kakia* (2549), "evil," is rendered "wickedness" in Acts 8:22; RV in Jas. 1:21, KJV, "naughtiness."

WIDOW

Old Testament

'almanah (490), "widow." The word represents a woman who, because of the death of her husband, has lost her social and economic position. The gravity of her situation was increased if she had no children. In such a circumstance she returned to her father's home and was subjected to the Levirate rule whereby a close male relative surviving her husband was to produce a child through her in her husband's behalf, Gen. 38:11. Even if children had been born before her husband's death, a widow's lot was not a happy one, 2 Sam. 14:5. Israel was admonished to treat "widows"

and other socially disadvantaged people with justice, God Himself standing as their protector, Exod. 22:21-24.

Wives whose husbands shut them away from themselves are sometimes called "widows," 2 Sam. 20:3. Destroyed, plundered Jerusalem is called a "widow," Lam. 1:1.

New Testament

chera (5503), Matt. 28:13 (in some texts); Mark 12:40, 42, 43; Luke 2:37; 4:25, 26, lit., "a woman a widow"; 7:12; 18:3, 5; 20:47; 21:2, 3; Acts 6:1; 9:39, 41; 1 Tim. 5:3 (twice), 4, 5, 11, 16 (twice); Jas. 1:27; 1 Tim. 5:9 refers to elderly "widows" (not an ecclesiastical "order"), recognized, for relief or maintenance by the church (cf. vv. 3, 16), as those who had fulfilled the conditions mentioned; where relief could be ministered by those who had relatives that were "widows" (a likely circumstance in large families), the church was not to be responsible; there is an intimation of the tendency to shelve individual responsibility at the expense of church funds. In Rev. 18:7, it is used figuratively of a city forsaken.

WIFE, WIVES

1. *gune* (1135) denotes (1) "a woman, married or unmarried"; (2) "a wife," e.g., Matt. 1:20; 1 Cor. 7:3, 4; in 1 Tim. 3:11, RV, "women," the reference may be to the "wives" of deacons, as the KJV takes it.

2. *gunaikeios* (1134), an adjective denoting "womanly, female," is used as a noun in 1 Pet. 3:7, KJV, "wife," RV, "woman."

WIFE'S MOTHER

penthera (3994) denotes "a mother-in-law," Matt. 8:14; 10:35; Mark 1:30; Luke 4:38; 12:53 (twice).

WILDERNESS

1. *eremia* (2047), "an uninhabited place," is translated "wilderness" in the KJV of Matt. 15:33 and Mark 8:4 (RV, "a desert place"); RV and KJV, "wilderness" in 2 Cor. 11:26.

2. *eremos* (2048), an adjective signifying "desolate, deserted, lonely," is used as a noun, and rendered "wilderness" 32 times in the KJV; in Matt. 24:26 and John 6:31, RV, "wilderness" (KJV, "desert"). For the RV, "deserts" in Luke 5:16 and 8:29.

WILES

methodia, or —*eia* (3180) denotes "craft, deceit" (*meta*, "after," *hodos*, "a way"), "a cunning device, a wile," and is translated "wiles (of error)" in Eph. 4:14, RV [AV paraphrases it, "they lie in wait (to deceive)"], lit., "(with a view to) the craft (singular) of deceit"; in 6:11, "the wiles (plural) (of the Devil.)"

WILL, WOULD

Old Testament

'abah (14), "to will, be willing, consent," Gen. 24:5. It is to be noted that in all but 2 instances of its use in the Old Testament (Job 39:9; Isa. 1:19), the word is used with a negation, to indicate lack of willingness or consent. Even in these two positive uses, there seems to be a negative aspect or expectation implied.

New Testament

A. Nouns.

1. *thelema* (2307) signifies (a) objectively, "that which is willed, of the will of God," e.g., Matt. 18:14; Mark 3:35, the fulfilling being a sign of spiritual relationship to the Lord, John 4:34; 5:30; 6:39, 40; Acts 13:22, plural, "my desires"; Rom. 2:18; 12:2, lit., "the will of God, the good and perfect and acceptable"; here the repeated article is probably resumptive, the adjectives describing the will, as in the Eng. versions; Gal. 1:4; Eph. 1:9; 5:17, "of the Lord"; Col. 1:9; 4:12; 1 Thess. 4:3; 5:18, where it means "the gracious design," rather than "the determined resolve"; 2 Tim. 2:26, which should read "which have been taken captive by him" [(*autou*), i.e., by the Devil; the RV, "by the Lord's servant" is an interpretation; it does not correspond to the Greek] unto His (*ekeinou*) will" (i.e., "God's will"; the different pronoun refers back to the subject of the sentence, viz., God); Heb. 10:10; Rev. 4:11, RV, "because of Thy will"; of human will, e.g., 1 Cor. 7:37; (b) subjectively, the "will" being spoken of as the emotion of being desirous, rather than as the thing "willed"; of the "will" of God, e.g., Rom. 1:10; 1 Cor. 1:1; 2 Cor. 1:1; 8:5; Eph. 1:1, 5, 11; Col. 1:1; 1 Tim. 1:1; Heb. 10:7, 9, 36; 1 John 2:17; 5:14; of human "will," e.g., John 1:13; Eph. 2:3, "the desires of the flesh"; 1 Pet. 4:3 (in some texts); 2 Pet. 1:21.

2. *thelesis* (2308) denotes "a willing, a wishing" [similar to No. 1 (b)], Heb. 2:4.

3. *boulema* (1013), "a deliberate design, that which is purposed," Rom. 9:19; 1 Pet. 4:3 (in the best texts).

4. *eudokia* (2107) (*eu*, "well," *dokeo*, "to think") is rendered "good will" in Luke 2:14; Phil. 1:15.

B. Adjective.

hekon (1635), "of free will, willingly," occurs in Rom. 8:20, RV, "of its own will" (KJV, "willingly"); 1 Cor. 9:17, RV, "of my own will" (KJV, "willingly").

C. Verbs.

When "will" is not part of the translation of the future tense of verbs, it represents one of the following:

1. *thelo* (2309), expresses "desire" or "design"; it is most fre-

quently translated by "will" or "would"; see especially Rom. 7:15, 16, 18-21. In 1 Tim. 2:4, RV, "willeth" signifies the gracious "desire" of God for all men to be saved; not all are "willing" to accept His condition, depriving themselves either by the self-established criterion of their perverted reason, or because of their self-indulgent preference for sin. In John 6:21, the KJV renders the verb "willingly" (RV, "they were willing"); in 2 Pet. 3:5, KJV, the present participle is translated "willingly" (RV, "wilfully").

The following are RV renderings for the KJV, "will": Matt. 16:24, 25, "would"; "wouldest," 19:21 and 20:21; "would," 20:26, 27; Mark 8:34, 35; 10:43, 44; "would fain," Luke 13:31; "would," John 6:67; "willeth," 7:17; in 8:44, "it is your will (to do)"; "wouldest," Rom. 13:3; "would," 1 Cor. 14:35 and 1 Pet. 3:10.

2. *boulomai* (*1014*), expresses the deliberate exercise of volition more strongly than No. 1, and is rendered as follows in the RV, where the KJV has "will": Matt. 11:27 and Luke 10:22, "willeth"; Jas. 4:4, "would"; in Jas. 3:4, RV, "willeth" (KJV, "listeth"). In Jas. 1:18 the perfect participle is translated "of His own will," lit. "having willed."

WINE

Old Testament

yayin (3196), "wine." This is the usual Hebrew word for naturally fermented grape, capable of intoxicating if overused. It is usually rendered "wine," Gen. 14:18; cf. 27:25. Passages such as Ezek. 27:18 inform us that "wine" was an article of commerce. Proverbs recommends that kings avoid "wine" and beer but that it be given to those troubled with problems that they might drink and forget their problems, Prov. 31:4-7. "Wine" was used to make merry, to make one feel good without being intoxicated, 2 Sam. 13:28. Second, "wine" was used in rejoicing before the Lord. Once a year all Israel is to gather in Jerusalem. The money realized from the sale of a tithe of all their harvest was to be spent, Deut. 14:26. "Wine" was offered to God at His command as part of the prescribed ritual, Exod. 29:40. In Gen. 9:24 *yayin* means drunkenness.

tirosh is distinguished from *yayin* by referring only to new wine not fully fermented; *yayin* includes "wine" at any stage. In Gen. 27:28 (the first biblical occurrence of the word) Jacob's blessing includes the divine bestowal of an abundance of new wine. In 1 Sam. 1:15 *yayin* parallels *shekar*, "grain or fruit drink." *shekar* in early times included wine, Num. 28:7, but meant strong drink made from any fruit or grain, Num. 6:3. People in special states of holiness were forbidden to drink "wine," such as the Nazirites, Num. 6:3, Samson's mother, Judg. 13:4, and priests approaching God, Lev. 10:9.

New Testament

1. *oinos* (*3631*) is the general word for "wine." The mention of the bursting of the wineskins, Matt. 9:17; Mark 2:22; Luke 5:37, implies fermentation.

The drinking of "wine" could be a stumbling block and the apostle enjoins abstinence in this respect, as in others, so as to avoid giving an occasion of stumbling to a brother, Rom. 14:21. Contrast 1 Tim. 5:23, which has an entirely different connection. The word is used metaphorically (a) of the evils ministered to the nations by religious Babylon, 14:8; 17:2; 18:3; (b) of the contents of the cup of divine wrath upon the nations and Babylon, Rev. 14:10; 16:19; 19:15.

2. *gleukos* (*1098*) denotes sweet "new wine," or "must," Acts 2:13, where the accusation shows that it was intoxicant and must have been undergoing fermentation some time.

WINEBIBBER

oinopotes (*3630*), "a wine drinker" (*oinos*, and *potes*, "a drinker"), is used in Matt. 11:19; Luke 7:34.

WINEPRESS, WINE-VAT

lenos (*3025*) denotes "a trough or vat," used especially for the treading of grapes, Matt. 21:33. Not infrequently they were dug out in the soil or excavated in a rock, as in the rock vats in Palestine today. In Rev. 14:19, 20 (twice) and 19:15 (where *oinos* is added, lit.. "the winepress of the wine") the word is used metaphorically with reference to the execution of divine judgment upon the gathered foes of the Jews at the close of this age preliminary to the establishment of the millennial kingdom.

WISDOM

1. *sophia* (*4678*) is used with reference to (a) God, Rom. 11:33; 1 Cor. 1:21, 24; 2:7; Eph. 3:10; Rev. 7:12; (b) Christ, Matt. 13:54; Mark 6:2; Luke 2:40, 52; 1 Cor. 1:30; Col. 2:3; Rev. 5:12; (c) "wisdom" personified, Matt. 11:19; Luke 7:35; 11:49; (d) human "wisdom" (1) in spiritual things, Luke 21:15; Acts 6:3, 10; 7:10; 1 Cor. 2:6 (1st part); 12:8; Eph. 1:8, 17; Col. 1:9, RV, "(spiritual) wisdom," 28; 3:16; 4:5; Jas. 1:5; 3:13, 17; 2 Pet. 3:15; Rev. 13:18; 17:9; (2) in the natural sphere, Matt. 12:42; Luke 11:31; Acts 7:22; 1 Cor. 1:17, 19, 20, 21 (twice), 22; 2:1, 4, 5, 6 (2nd part), 13; 3:19; 2 Cor. 1:12; Col. 2:23; (3) in its most debased form, Jas. 3:15, "earthly, sensual, devilish" (marg., "demoniacal").

2. *phronesis* (*5428*), "understanding, prudence," i.e., a right use of *phren*, "the mind," is translated "wisdom" in Luke 1:17.

WISE, WISER, WISELY
Old Testament

A. Adjective.

chakam (2450), "wise; skillful; practical." The *chakam* in secular usage signified a man who was a "skillful" craftsman. The manufacturers of the objects belonging to the tabernacle were known to be wise, or experienced in their crafts, Exod. 36:4. Even the man who was skillful in making idols was recognized as a craftsman, Isa. 40:20; cf. Jer. 10:9.

Based on the characterization of wisdom as a skill, a class of counselors known as "wise men" arose. They were to be found in Egypt, Gen. 41:8, in Babylon, Jer. 50:35, in Tyre, Ezek. 27:9, in Edom, Obad. 8, and in Israel. In pagan cultures the "wise" man practiced magic and divination, Exod. 7:11; Isa. 44:25.

The religious sense of *chakam* excludes delusion, craftiness, shrewdness, and magic. God is the source of wisdom, as He is "wise," Isa. 31:2. The man or woman who, fearing God, lives in accordance with what God expects and what is expected of him in a God-fearing society is viewed as an integrated person. He is "wise" in that his manner of life projects the fear of God and the blessing of God rests upon him. Even as the craftsman is said to be skillful in his trade, the Old Testament *chakam* was learning and applying wisdom to every situation in life, and the degree in which he succeeded was a barometer of his progress on the road of wisdom.

B. Nouns.

chokmah (2451), "wisdom; experience; shrewdness." *chokmah* is the knowledge and the ability to make the right choices at the opportune time. The consistency of making the right choice is an indication of maturity and development. The prerequisite for "wisdom" is the fear of the Lord: "The fear of the Lord is the beginning of knowledge: but fools despise wisdom and instruction," Prov. 1:7. "Wisdom" is viewed as crying out for disciples who will do everything to pursue her, Prov. 1:20. The person who seeks *chokmah* diligently will receive understanding, Prov. 2:6; he will benefit in his life by walking with God, Prov. 2:20. The advantages of "wisdom" are many, Prov. 3:2-4. The prerequisite is a desire to follow and imitate God as He has revealed Himself in Jesus Christ, without self-reliance and especially *not* in a spirit of pride, Prov. 1:5-7. The fruits of *chokmah* are many, and the Book of Proverbs describes the characters of the *chakam* and *chokmah*.

The importance of "wisdom" explains why books were written about it. Songs were composed in celebration of "wisdom," Job 28. Even "wisdom" is personified in Proverbs. *chokmah* as a person stands for that divine perfection of "wisdom" which is manifest in

God's creative acts. As a divine perfection it is visible in God's creative acts, Prov. 8:1, 12, 22, 30, 32.

C. Verb.

chakam (2449), "to be wise, act wisely, make wise, show oneself wise," Prov. 23:15; cf. Ps. 119:98 where *chakam* means "to make wise."

New Testament

A. Adjectives.

1. *sophos* (4680) is used of (a) God, Rom. 16:27; in 1 Tim. 1:17 and Jude 25 *sophos* is absent, in the best mss. (see the RV), the comparative degree, *sophoteros*, occurs in 1 Cor. 1:25, where "foolishness" is simply in the human estimate; (b) spiritual teachers in Israel, Matt. 23:34; (c) believers endowed with spiritual and practical wisdom, Rom. 16:19; 1 Cor. 3:10; 6:5; Eph. 5:15; Jas. 3:13; (d) Jewish teachers in the time of Christ, Matt. 11:25; Luke 10:21; (e) the naturally learned, Rom. 1:14, 22; 1 Cor. 1:19, 20, 26, 27; 3:15-20.

2. *phronimos* (5429), "prudent, sensible, practically wise," Matt. 7:24; 10:16; 24:45; 25:2, 4, 8, 9; Luke 12:42; 16:8 (comparative degree, *phronimoteros*); 1 Cor. 10:15; in an evil sense, "wise (in your own conceits)," lit., "wise (in yourselves)," i.e., "judged by the standard of your self-complacency," Rom. 11:25; 12:16; ironically, 1 Cor. 4:10; 2 Cor. 11:19.

B. Noun.

magos (3097) denotes "a Magian," one of a sacred caste, originally Median, Matt. 2:1, 7, 16.

C. Verbs.

1. *sophizo* (4679) is rendered "to make wise" in 2 Tim. 3:15.

2. *suniemi* or *sunio* (4920), "to perceive, understand," is used negatively in 2 Cor. 10:12, KJV, "are not wise" (RV, "are without understanding").

D. Adverb.

phronimos (5430), "wisely" (akin to A, No. 2), occurs in Luke 16:8.

WISH

1. *euchomai* (2172) is rendered "to wish" in Acts 27:29 (RV marg., "prayed"); so Rom. 9:3; in 2 Cor. 13:9 and 3 John 2, RV, "pray."

2. *boulomai* (1014), in Mark 15:15, RV, is translated "wishing" (KJV, "willing"); so 2 Pet. 3:9; in Acts 25:22, RV, "could wish" (KJV, "would").

3. *thelo* (2309), in 1 Cor. 16:7, RV, is translated "wish" (KJV, "will"); Gal. 4:20, "I could wish" (KJV, "I desire").

WITNESS (Noun and Verb)
Old Testament

A. Noun.

'ed (5707), "witness." This word has to do with the legal or judicial sphere. First, in the area of civil affairs the word can mean someone who is present at a legal transaction and can confirm it if necessary. Such people worked as notaries, e.g., for an oral transfer of property, Ruth 4:7, 9. At a later time the "witnesses" not only acted to attest the transaction and to confirm it orally, but they signed a document or deed of purchase. Thus "witness" takes on the new nuance of those able and willing to affirm the truth of a transaction by affixing their signatures, Jer. 32:12. An object or animal(s) can signify the truthfulness of an act or agreement. Its very existence or the acceptance of it by both parties (in the case of the animals given to Abimelech in Gen. 21:30) bears witness, Gen. 31:44; or stone pillar or heap as a further "witness," Gen. 31:48.

In Mosaic criminal law the accused has the right to be faced by his/her accuser and to give evidence of his/her innocence. In the case of a newly married woman charged by her own husband, his testimony is sufficient to prove her guilty of adultery unless her parents have clear evidence proving her virginity before her marriage, Deut. 22:14ff. Usually the accused is faced with someone who either saw or heard of his guilt, Lev. 5:1. Heavy penalties fell on anyone who lied to a court. The ninth commandment may well have immediate reference to such a concrete court situation, Exod. 20:16. If so, it serves to sanction proper judicial procedure, to safeguard individuals from secret accusation and condemnation and giving them the right and privilege of self-defense. In the exchange between Jacob and Laban mentioned above, Jacob also cites God as a "witness," Gen. 31:50, between them, the one who will see violations; God, however, is also the Judge. Although human courts are (as a rule) to keep judge and "witness" separate, the "witnesses" do participate in executing the penalty upon the guilty party, Deut. 17:7, even as God does.

B. Verb.

'ud (5749), "to take as witness, bear witness, repeat, admonish, warn, assure protection, relieve." In 1 Kings 21:10 *'ud* means "to bear witness"; "to warn" in Jer. 6:10.

New Testament

A. Nouns.

1. *martus* or *martur* (*3144*) (whence Eng., "martyr," one who bears "witness" by his death) denotes "one who can or does aver what he has seen or heard or knows"; it is used (a) of God, Rom.

1:9; 2 Cor. 1:23; Phil. 1:8; 1 Thess. 2:5, 10 (2nd part); (b) of Christ, Rev. 1:5; 3:14; (c) of those who "witness" for Christ by their death, Acts 22:20; Rev. 2:13; Rev. 17:6; (d) of the interpreters of God's counsels, yet to "witness" in Jerusalem in the times of the Antichrist, Rev. 11:3; (e) in a forensic sense, Matt. 18:16; 26:65; Mark 14:63; Acts 6:13; 7:58; 2 Cor. 13:1; 1 Tim. 5:19; Heb. 10:28; (f) in a historical sense, Luke 11:48; 24:48; Acts 1:8, 22; 2:32; 3:15; 5:32; 10:39, 41; 13:31; 22:15; 26:16; 1 Thess. 2:10 (1st part); 1 Tim. 6:12; 2 Tim. 2:2; Heb. 12:1, "(a cloud) of witnesses," here of those mentioned in ch. 11, those whose lives and actions testified to the worth and effect of faith, and whose faith received "witness" in Scripture, 1 Pet. 5:1.

2. *marturia* (3141), "testimony, a bearing witness," is translated "witness" in Mark 14:55, 56, 59; Luke 22:71; John 1:7, 19 (RV); 3:11, 32 and 33 (RV); 5:31, 32, 34 (RV), 36; RV in 8:13, 14, 17; 19:35; 21:24; KJV in Titus 1:13; KJV and RV in 1 John 5:9 (thrice), 10a; RV in 10b, 11; 3 John 12.

3. *marturion* (3142), "testimony or witness as borne, a declaration of facts," is translated "witness" in Matt. 24:14, KJV; Acts 4:33; 7:44 (KJV); Jas. 5:3 (KJV).

4. *pseudomartus* or *-tur* (5571) and 3144) denotes "a false witness," Matt. 26:60; 1 Cor. 15:15.

5. *pseudomarturia* (5577), "false witness," occurs in Matt. 15:19; 26:59.

B. Verbs.

1. *martureo* (3140) denotes (I) "to be a *martus*" (see A, No. 1), or "to bear witness to," sometimes rendered "to testify"; it is used of the witness (a) of God the Father to Christ, John 5:32, 37; 8:18 (2nd part); 1 John 5:9, 10; to others, Acts 13:22; 15:8; Heb. 11:2, 4 (twice), 5, 39; (b) of Christ, John 3:11, 32; 4:44; 5:31; 7:7; 8:13, 14, 18 (1st part); 13:21; 18:37; Acts 14:3; 1 Tim. 6:13; Rev. 22:18, 20; of the Holy Spirit, to Christ, John 15:26; Heb. 10:15; 1 John 5:7, 8, RV, which rightly omits the latter part of v. 7; it finds no support in Scripture; (c) of the Scriptures, to Christ, John 5:39; Heb. 7:8, 17; (d) of the works of Christ, to Himself, and of the circumstances connected with His death, John 5:36; 10:25; 1 John 5:8; (e) of prophets and apostles, to the righteousness of God, Rom. 3:21; to Christ, John 1:7, 8, 15, 32, 34; 3:26; 5:33, RV; 15:27; 19:35; 21:24; Acts 10:43; 23:11; 1 Cor. 15:15; 1 John 1:2; 4:14; Rev. 1:2; to doctrine, Acts 26:22 (in some texts, so KJV; see No. 2); to the Word of God, Rev. 1:2; (f) of others, concerning Christ, Luke 4:22; John 4:39; 12:17; (g) of believers to one another, John 3:28; 2 Cor. 8:3; Gal. 4:15; Col. 4:13; 1 Thess. 2:11 (in some texts: see No. 2); 3 John 3, 6, 12 (2nd part); (h) of the apostle Paul concerning Israel, Rom. 10:2; (i) of an angel, to the churches, Rev. 22:16; (j) of unbelievers, concerning themselves, Matt. 23:31; concerning Christ, John 18:23; concerning others, John 2:25; Acts 22:5; 26:5; (II), "to give a good report, to approve of," Acts 6:3; 10:22;

16:2; 22:12; 1 Tim. 5:10; 3 John 12 (1st part); some would put Luke 4:22 here.

2. *marturomai* (*3143*), strictly meaning "to summon as a witness," signifies "to affirm solemnly, adjure," and is used in the middle voice only, rendered "to testify" in Acts 20:26, RV (KJV, "I take...to record"); 26:22, RV, in the best texts [see No. 1 (e)]; Gal. 5:3; Eph. 4:17; 1 Thess. 2:11, in the best texts [see No. 1 (g)].

3. *summartureo* (*4828*) denotes "to bear witness with" (*sun*), Rom. 2:15; 8:16; 9:1.

4. *sunepimartureo* (*4901*) denotes "to join in bearing witness with others," Heb. 2:4.

5. *katamartureo* (*2649*) denotes "to witness against" (*kata*), Matt. 26:62; 27:13; Mark 14:60 (in some mss., 15:4, for *kategoreo*, "to accuse," RV).

6. *pseudomartureo* (*5576*), "to bear false witness" (*pseudes*, "false"), occurs in Matt. 19:18; Mark 10:19; 14:56, 57; Luke 18:20; in some texts, Rom. 13:9.

C. Adjective.

amarturos (*267*) denotes "without witness" (*a*, negative, and *martus*), Acts 14:17.

WOE

ouai (*3759*), an interjection, is used (a) in denunciation, Matt. 11:21; 18:7 (twice); eight times in ch. 23; 24:19; 26:24; Mark 13:17; 14:21; Luke 6:24, 25 (twice), 26; 10:13; six times in ch. 11; 17:1; 21:23; 22:22; 1 Cor. 9:16; Jude 11; Rev. 8:13 (thrice); 12:12; as a noun, Rev. 9:12 (twice); 11:14 (twice); (b) in grief, "alas," Rev. 18:10, 16, 19 (twice in each).

WOMAN

Old Testament

'ishshah (*802*), "woman; wife; betrothed one; bride; each." This noun connotes one who is a female human being regardless of her age or virginity. Therefore, it appears in correlation to "man" (*ish*), Gen. 2:22, 23. The stress on the family role of a "wife" appears in passages such as Gen. 8:16. In Lam. 2:20 *'ishshah* is a synonym for "mother," Gen. 29:21 (cf. Deut. 22:24. This word can also be used figuratively describing foreign warriors and/or heroes as "women," in other words as weak, unmanly, and cowardly," Isa. 19:16. In a few passages *'ishshah* means "each" or "every," Exod. 3:22; cf. Amos 4:3.

New Testament

1. *gune* (*1135*), "woman" unmarried or married, e.g., Matt. 11:11; 14:21; Luke 4:26, of a "widow"; Rom. 7:2; in the vocative case, used in addressing a "woman," it is a term not of reproof or severity, but

of endearment or respect, Matt. 15:28; John 2:4, where the Lord's words to His mother at the wedding in Cana, are neither rebuff nor rebuke. The question is, lit., "What to Me and to thee?" and the word "woman," the term of endearment, follows this. The meaning is "There is no obligation on Me or you, but love will supply the need." She confides in Him, He responds to her faith. There was lovingkindness in both hearts. His next words about "His hour" suit this; they were not unfamiliar to her. Cana is in the path to Calvary; Calvary was not yet, but it made the beginning of signs possible. See also 4:21; 19:26.

2. *gunaikarion* (*1133*), a diminutive of No. 1, a "little woman," is used contemptuously in 2 Tim. 3:6, "a silly woman."

3. *presbuteros* (*4245*), "elder, older," in the feminine plural, denotes "elder women" in 1 Tim. 5:2.

4. *presbutis* (*4247*), the feminine of *presbutes*, "aged," is used in the plural and translated "aged women" in Titus 2:3.

5. *theleia* (*2338***), the feminine of the adjective *thelus*, denotes "female," and is used as a noun, Rom. 1:26, 27.

WOMB

1. *koilia* (*2836*) denotes "the womb," Matt. 19:12; Luke 1:15, 41, 42, 44; 2:21; 11:27; 23:29; John 3:4; Acts 3:2; 14:8; Gal. 1:15.

2. *gaster* (*1064*), is rendered "womb" in Luke 1:31.

3. *metra* (*3388*), the matrix (akin to meter "a mother"), occurs in Luke 2:23; Rom. 4:19.

WONDER (Noun and Verb)

Old Testament

mopet (*4159*), "wonder; sign; portent." First, this word signifies a divine act or a special display of divine power, Exod. 4:21. Second, the word can represent a "sign" from God or a token of a future event, 1 Kings 13:3; Zech. 3:8.

New Testament

1. *teras* (*5059*), a noun, "something strange," causing the beholder to marvel, is always used in the plural, always rendered "wonders," and generally follows *semeia*, "signs"; the opposite order occurs in Acts 2:22, 43; 6:8, RV; 7:36; in Acts 2:19 "wonders" occurs alone. A sign is intended to appeal to the understanding, a "wonder" appeals to the imagination, a power (*dunamis*) indicates its source as supernatural. "Wonders" are manifested as divine operations in thirteen occurrences (9 times in Acts); three times they are ascribed to the work of Satan through human agents, Matt. 24:24; Mark 13:22 and 2 Thess. 2:9.

2. *thambos* (*2285*), "amazement," is rendered "wonder" in Acts 3:10.

WONDERFUL (THING, WORK)

(1) In Matt. 7:22, KJV, *dunamis* (in the plural) is rendered "wonderful works" (RV, "mighty works," marg., "powers"). (2) In Acts 2:11, KJV, the adjective *megaleios*, "magnificent," in the neuter plural with the article, is rendered "the wonderful works" (RV, "the mighty works"). (3) In Matt. 21:15, the neuter plural of the adjective *thaumasios*, "wonderful," is used as a noun, "wonderful things," lit., "wonders."

WONT

etho (*1486*), "to be accustomed," is used in the pluperfect tense (with imperfect meaning), *eiotha*, rendered "was wont" in Matt. 27:15; Mark 10:1.

WORD

1. *logos* (*3056*) denotes (I) "the expression of thought"—not the mere name of an object—(a) as embodying a conception or idea, e.g., Luke 7:7; 1 Cor. 14:9, 19; (b) a saying or statement, (1) by God, e.g., John 15:25; Rom. 9:9; 9:28, RV, "word" (KJV, "work"); Gal. 5:14; Heb. 4:12; (2) by Christ, e.g., Matt. 24:35 (plur.); John 2:22; 4:41; 14:23 (plur.); 15:20. In connection with (1) and (2) the phrase "the word of the Lord," i.e., the revealed will of God (very frequent in the OT), is used of a direct revelation given by Christ, 1 Thess. 4:15; of the gospel, Acts 8:25; 13:49; 15:35, 36; 16:32; 19:10; 1 Thess. 1:8; 2 Thess. 3:1; in this respect it is the message from the Lord, delivered with His authority and made effective by His power (cf. Acts 10:36); for other instances relating to the gospel see Acts 13:26; 14:3; 15:7; 1 Cor. 1:18, RV; 2 Cor. 2:17; 4:2; 5:19; 6:7; Gal. 6:6; Eph. 1:13; Phil. 2:16; Col. 1:5; Heb. 5:13; sometimes it is used as the sum of God's utterances, e.g., Mark 7:13; John 10:35; Rev. 1:2, 9; (c) discourse, speech, of instruction, etc., e.g., Acts 2:40; 1 Cor. 2:13; 12:8; 2 Cor. 1:18; 1 Thess. 1:5; 2 Thess. 2:15; Heb. 6:1, RV, marg.; doctrine, e.g., Matt. 13:20; Col. 3:16; 1 Tim. 4:6; 2 Tim. 1:13; Titus 1:9; 1 John 2:7;

(II) "The Personal Word," a title of the Son of God; this identification is substantiated by the statements of doctrine in John 1:1-18, declaring in verses 1 and 2 (1) His distinct and superfinite Personality, (2) His relation in the Godhead (*pros*, "with," not mere company, but the most intimate communion), (3) His deity; in v. 3 His creative power; in v. 14 His incarnation ("became flesh," expressing His voluntary act; not as KJV, "was made," the reality and totality of His human nature, and His glory "as of the only begotten from the Father," RV (marg., "an only begotten from a father"), the absence of the article in each place lending stress to the nature and character of the relationship; His was the *shekinah* glory in open manifestation; v. 18 consummates the identification: "the only-begotten Son (RV marg., many ancient authorities read "God only begotten,"), which is in the bosom of the Father, He hath declared Him," thus fulfilling the significance of the title "*Logos*," the "Word," the personal manifestation, not of a part of the divine nature, but of the whole deity.

The title is used also in 1 John 1, "the Word of life" combining the two declarations in John 1:1 and 4 and Rev. 19:13.

2. *rhema* (*4487*) denotes "that which is spoken, what is uttered in speech or writing"; in the singular, "a word," e.g., Matt. 12:36; 27:14; 2 Cor. 12:4; 13:1; Heb. 12:19; in the plural, speech, discourse, e.g., John 3:34; 8:20; Acts 2:14; 6:11, 13; 11:14; 13:42; 26:25; Rom. 10:18; 2 Pet. 3:2; Jude 17; it is used of the gospel in Rom. 10:8 (twice), 17, RV, "the word of Christ" (i.e., the "word" which preaches Christ); 10:18; 1 Pet. 1:25 (twice); of a statement, command, instruction, e.g., Matt. 26:75; Luke 1:37, RV, "(no) word (from God shall be void of power)," v. 38; Acts 11:16; Heb. 11:3.

WORK (Noun and Verb), WROUGHT

Old Testament

A. Verbs.

pa'al (*6466*), "to do, work." It is used primarily as a poetic synonym for the much more common verb *'ashah*, "to do, to make, Exod. 15:17; Ps. 15:2.

'ashah (*6213*), "to make, do, create." In its primary sense this verb represents the production of various objects. This includes making images and idols, Exod. 20:4; Isa. 44:17. In Gen. 12:5 *'ashah* means "to acquire." Used in association with "Sabbath" or the name of other holy days, this word signifies "keeping" or "celebrating": "All the congregation of Israel shall keep it [the Passover]," Exod. 12:47. In a related sense the word means "to spend" a day, Eccl. 6:12.

'ashah may represent the relationship of an individual to another in his action or behavior, in the sense of what one does, Gen. 12:18. With the particle *le* the verb signifies inflicting upon another some act or behavior, Gen. 20:9. With the particle *'im* the word may mean "to show," or "to practice" something toward someone, Gen. 24:12. In Gen. 26:29 *'ashah* appears twice in the sense "to practice toward." Used of plants this verb signifies "bringing forth." In Gen. 1:11 it means "to bear fruit," Hos. 8:7; or branches, Ezek. 17:8.

This verb is also applied specifically to all aspects of divine acts and actions. In the general sense of His actions toward His people Israel, the word first occurs in Gen. 12:2, where God promises "to make" Abram a great nation. *'ashah* is also the most general Old Testament expression for divine creating. Every aspect of this activity is described by this word, Exod. 20:11. This word is used of God's acts effecting the entire created world and individual men,

Exod. 20:6. God's acts and words perfectly correspond, so that what He says He does, and what He does is what He has said, Gen. 21:1; Ps. 115:3.

B. Noun.

ma'aseh (4639), "work; deed; labor; behavior." The basic meaning of *ma'aseh* is "work." Lamech used the word to signify agricultural labor, Gen. 5:29. The Israelites were commanded to celebrate the Festival of the Firstfruits, as it signified the blessing of God upon their "labors," Exod. 23:16. It is not to be limited to this. As the word is the most general word for "work," it may be used to refer to the "work" of a skillful craftsman, Exod. 26:1, a weaver, 26:36, a jeweler, 28:11, and a perfumer, 30:25.

The phrase "work of one's hands" signifies the worthlessness of the idols fashioned by human hands, Hos. 14:3. However, the prayer of the psalmist includes the request that the "works" of God's people might be established, Ps. 90:17. Since the righteous work out God's work and are a cause of God's rejoicing, Ps. 104:31. In addition to "work," *ma'aseh* also denotes "deed," "practice," or "behavior," Gen. 44:15. The Israelites were strongly commanded not to imitate the grossly immoral behavior of the Canaanites and the surrounding nations, Lev. 18:3; cf. Exod. 23:24.

Thus far, we have dealt with *ma'aseh* from man's perspective. The word may have a positive connotation ("work, deed") as well as a negative ("corrupt practice"). The Old Testament also calls us to celebrate the "work" of God. The psalmist was overwhelmed with the majesty of the Lord, as he looked at God's "work" of creation, Ps. 8:3; cf. 19:1; 102:25. The God of Israel demonstrated His love by His mighty acts of deliverance on behalf of Israel, Josh. 24:31; cf. versions. All of God's "works" are characterized by faithfulness to His promises and covenant, Ps. 33:4.

New Testament

A. Nouns.

1. *ergon* (*2041*) denotes (I) "work, employment, task," e.g., Mark 13:34; John 4:34; 17:4; Acts 13:2; Phil. 2:30; 1 Thess. 5:13; in Acts 5:38 with the idea of enterprise; (II), "a deed, act," (a) of God, e.g., John 6:28, 29; 9:3; 10:37; 14:10; Acts 13:41; Rom. 1:10; 2:7; 3:9; 4:3, 4, 10; Rev. 15:3; (b) of Christ, e.g., Matt. 11:2; especially in John, 5:36; 7:3, 21; 10:25, 32, 33, 38; 14:11, 12; 15:24; Rev. 2:26; (c) of believers, e.g., Matt. 5:16; Mark 14:6; Acts 9:36; Rom. 13:3; Col. 1:10; 1 Thess. 1:3; "work of faith," here the initial act of faith at conversion (turning to God, v. 9); in 2 Thess. 1:11, "*every* work of faith," RV, denotes every activity undertaken for Christ's sake; 2:17; 1 Tim. 2:10; 5:10; 6:18; 2 Tim. 2:21; 3:17; Titus 2:7, 14; 3:1, 8, 14; Heb. 10:24; 13:21; frequent in James, as the effect of faith [in 1:25, KJV, "(a doer) of the work," RV, "(a doer) that worketh"]; 1 Pet. 2:12; Rev. 2:2

and in several other places in chs. 2 and 3; 14:13; (d) of unbelievers, e.g., Matt. 23:3, 5; John 7:7; Acts 7:41 (for idols); Rom. 13:12; Eph. 5:11; Col. 1:21; Titus 1:16 (1st part); 1 John 3:12; Jude 15, RV; Rev. 2:6, RV; of those who seek justification by works, e.g., Rom. 9:32; Gal. 3:10; Eph. 2:9; described as the works of the law, e.g., Gal. 2:16; 3:2, 5; dead works, Heb. 6:1; 9:14; (e) of Babylon, Rev. 18:6; (f) of the Devil, John 8:41; 1 John 3:8.

2. *ergasia* (*2039*) denotes "a work" or "business," also "a working, performance," Eph. 4:19, where preceded by *eis*, "to," it is rendered "to work" (marg., "to make a trade of").

B. Verbs.

1. *ergazomai* (*2038*) is used (I) intransitively, e.g., Matt. 21:28; John 5:17; 9:4 (2nd part); Rom. 4:4, 5; 1 Cor. 4:12; 9:6; 1 Thess. 2:9; 4:11; 2 Thess. 3:8, 10–12; (II) transitively, (a) "to work something, produce, perform," e.g., Matt. 26:10, "she hath wrought"; John 6:28, 30; 9:4 (1st part); Acts 10:35; 13:41; Rom. 2:10; 13:10; 1 Cor. 16:10; 2 Cor. 7:10a, in the best texts, some have No. 2; Gal. 6:10, RV, "let us work"; Eph. 4:28; Heb. 11:33; 2 John 8; (b) "to earn by working, work for," John 6:27, RV, "work" (KJV, "labor").

2. *katergazomai* (*2716*), an emphatic form of No. 1, signifies "to work out, achieve, effect by toil," rendered "to work" (past tense, "wrought") in Rom. 1:27; 2:9, RV; 4:15 (the Law brings men under condemnation and so renders them subject to divine wrath); 5:3; 7:8, 13; 15:18; 2 Cor. 4:17; 5:5; 7:10 (see No. 1), 11; 12:12; Phil. 2:12, where "your own salvation" refers especially to freedom from strife and vainglory; Jas. 1:3, 20; 1 Pet. 4:3.

3. *energeo* (*1754*), lit., "to work in" (*en*, and A, No. 1), "to be active, operative," is used of (a) God, 1 Cor. 12:6; Gal. 2:8; 3:5; Eph. 1:11, 20; 3:20; Phil. 2:13a; Col. 1:29; (b) the Holy Spirit, 1 Cor, 12:11; (c) the Word of God, 1 Thess. 2:13 (middle voice; KJV, 'effectually worketh'); (d) supernatural power, undefined, Matt. 14:2; Mark 6:14; (e) faith, as the energizer of love, Gal. 5:6; (f) the example of patience in suffering, 2 Cor. 1:6; (g) death (physical) and life (spiritual), 2 Cor. 4:12; (h) sinful passions, Rom. 7:5; (i) the spirit of the Evil One, Eph. 2:2; (j) the mystery of iniquity, 2 Thess. 2:7. (k) the active response of believers to the inworking of God, Phil. 2:13b, RV, "to work (for)," KJV, "to do (of)"; (l) the supplication of the righteous, Jas. 5:16, RV, "in its working" (KJV, "effectual fervent").

4. *poieo* (*4160*), "to do," is rendered "to work" in Matt. 20:12, KJV (RV, "spent"); Acts 15:12, "had wrought"; 19:11; 21:19; Heb. 13:21; Rev. 16:14; 19:20; 21:27, KJV (RV, "maketh"; marg., "doeth").

5. *sunergeo* (*4903*), "to work with or together" (*sun*), occurs in Mark 16:20; Rom. 8:28, "work together"; 1 Cor. 16:16, "helpeth with"; 2 Cor. 6:1, "workers together," present participle, "working together"; the "*with Him*" represents nothing in the Greek; Jas. 2:22, "wrought with."

6. *ginomai* (*1096*), "to become, take place," is rendered "wrought" in Mark 6:2; Acts 5:12, "were...wrought."

WORKER, WORKFELLOW, FELLOW WORKERS, WORKMAN

1. *ergates* (*2040*) is translated "workers" in Luke 13:27 ("of iniquity"); 2 Cor. 11:13 ("deceitful"); Phil. 3:2 ("evil"); "workman," Matt. 10:10, KJV (RV, "laborer"); "workman," 2 Tim. 2:15; "workmen," Acts 19:25.

2. *sunergos* (*4904*) denotes "a worker with," and is rendered "workfellow" in Rom. 16:21, KJV, RV, "fellow worker"; in Col. 4:11, "fellow workers" (see RV). See the RV, "God's fellow workers," in 1 Cor. 3:9.

WORKING

1. *energeia* (*1753*) (Eng., "energy") is used (1) of the "power" of God, (a) in the resurrection of Christ, Eph. 1:19; Col. 2:12, RV, "working" (KJV, "operation"); (b) in the call and enduement of Paul, Eph. 3:7; Col. 1:29; (c) in His retributive dealings in sending "a working of error" (KJV, "strong delusion") upon those under the rule of the Man of Sin who receive not the love of the truth, but have pleasure in unrighteousness, 2 Thess. 2:11; (2) of the "power" of Christ (a) generally, Phil. 3:21; (b) in the church, individually, Eph. 4:16; (3) of the power of Satan in energizing the Man of Sin in his "parousia," 2 Thess. 2:9, "coming."

2. *energema* (*1755*), "what is wrought," the effect produced by No. 1, occurs in 1 Cor. 12:6, RV, "workings" (KJV, "operations"); v. 10.

WORLD

1. *kosmos* (*2889*), primarily "order, arrangement, ornament, adornment" (1 Pet. 3:3), is used to denote (a) the "earth," e.g., Matt. 13:35; John 21:25; Acts 17:24; Rom. 1:20 (probably here the universe: it had this meaning among the Greeks, owing to the order observable in it); 1 Tim. 6:7; Heb. 4:3; 9:26; (b) the "earth" in contrast with Heaven, 1 John 3:17 (perhaps also Rom. 4:13); (c) by metonymy, the "human race, mankind," e.g., Matt. 5:14; John 1:9 [here "that cometh (RV, 'coming') into the world" is said of Christ, not of "every man"; by His coming into the world He was the light for all men]; v. 10; 3:16, 17 (thrice), 19; 4:42, and frequently in Rom., 1 Cor. and 1 John; (d) "Gentiles" as distinguished from Jews, e.g., Rom. 11:12, 15, where the meaning is that all who will may be reconciled (cf. 2 Cor. 5:19); (e) the "present condition of human affairs," in alienation from and opposition to God, e.g., John 7:7; 8:23; 14:30; 1 Cor. 2:12; Gal. 4:3; 6:14; Col. 2:8; Jas. 1:27; 1 John 4:5 (thrice); 5:19; (f) the "sum of temporal possessions," Matt. 16:26;

1 Cor. 7:31 (1st part); (g) metaphorically, of the "tongue" as "a world (of iniquity)," Jas. 3:6, expressive of magnitude and variety.

2. *aion* (165), "an age, a period of time," marked in the NT usage by spiritual or moral characteristics, is sometimes translated "world"; the RV marg. always has "age." The following are details concerning the world in this respect; its cares, Matt. 13:22; its sons, Luke 16:8; 20:34; its rulers, 1 Cor. 2:6, 8; its wisdom, 1 Cor. 1:20; 2:6; 3:18; its fashion, Rom. 12:2; its character, Gal. 1:4; its god, 2 Cor. 4:4. The phrase "the end of the world" should be rendered "the end of the age," in most places; in 1 Cor. 10:11, KJV, "the ends (*tele*) of the world," RV, "the ends of the ages," probably signifies the fulfillment of the divine purposes concerning the ages in regard to the church. In Heb. 11:3 [lit., "the ages (have been prepared)"] the word indicates all that the successive periods contain; cf. 1:2.

3. *oikoumene* (3625), "the inhabited earth," is used (a) of the whole inhabited world, Matt. 24:14; Luke 4:5; 21:26; Rom. 10:18; Heb. 1:6; Rev. 3:10; 16:14; by metonymy, of its inhabitants, Acts 17:31; Rev. 12:9; (b) of the Roman Empire, the world as viewed by the writer or speaker, Luke 2:1; Acts 11:28; 24:5; by metonymy, of its inhabitants, Acts 17:6; 19:27; (c) the inhabited world in a coming age, Heb. 2:5.

WORLDLY

kosmikos (2886), "pertaining to this world," is used (a) in Heb. 9:1, of the tabernacle, KJV, "worldly," RV, "of this world" (i.e., made of mundane materials, adapted to this visible world, local and transitory); (b) in Titus 2:12, ethically, of "worldly lusts," or desires.

WORMWOOD

apsinthos (894) (Eng., "absinthe"), a plant both bitter and deleterious, and growing in desolate places, figuratively suggestive of "calamity" (Lam. 3:15) and injustice (Amos 5:7), is used in Rev. 8:11 (twice; in the 1st part as a proper name).

WORSE

A. Adjectives.

1. *cheiron* (5501), used as the comparative degree of *kakos*, "evil," describes (a) the condition of certain men, Matt. 12:45; Luke 11:26; 2 Pet. 2:20; (b) evil men themselves and seducers, 2 Tim. 3:13; (c) indolent men who refuse to provide for their own households, and are worse than unbelievers, 1 Tim. 5:8, RV; (d) a rent in a garment, Matt. 9:16; Mark 2:21; (e) an error, Matt. 27:64; (f) a person suffering from a malady, Mark 5:26; (g) a possible physical affliction, John 5:14; (h) a punishment, Heb. 10:29, "sorer."

2. *elasson* or *elatton* (1640) is said of wine in John 2:10.

3. *hesson* or *hetton* (2276), "less, inferior," used in the neuter, after *epi*, "for," is translated "worse" in 1 Cor. 11:17; in 2 Cor. 12:15 the neuter, used adverbially, is translated "the less."

B. Verbs.

1. *hustereo* (5302) is rendered "are we the worse" in 1 Cor. 8:8.

2. *proecho* (4281), "to hold before, promote," is rendered "are we better" in Rom. 3:9, KJV (passive voice); RV, "are we in worse case."

WORSHIP (Verb and Noun), WORSHIPING

Old Testament

shachah (7812), "to worship, prostrate oneself, bow down." The act of bowing down in homage is generally done before a superior or a ruler. Thus, David "bowed" himself before Saul, 1 Sam. 24:8. Sometimes it is a social or economic superior to whom one bows, as when Ruth "bowed" to the ground before Boaz, Ruth 2:10. In a dream, Joseph saw the sheaves of his brothers "bowing down" before his sheaf, Gen. 37:5, 9-10. *shachah* is used as the common term for coming before God in worship, as in 1 Sam. 15:25 and Jer. 7:2.

New Testament

A. Verbs.

1. *proskuneo* (4352), "to make obeisance, do reverence to" (from *pros*, "towards," and *kuneo*, "to kiss"), is the most frequent word rendered "to worship." It is used of an act of homage or reverence (a) to God, e.g., Matt. 4:10; John 4:21-24; 1 Cor. 14:25; Rev. 4:10; 5:14; 7:11; 11:16; 19:10 (2nd part) and 22:9; (b) to Christ, e.g., Matt. 2:2, 8, 11; 8:2; 9:18; 14:33; 15:25; 20:20; 28:9, 17; John 9:38; Heb. 1:6, in a quotation from the Sept. of Deut. 32:43, referring to Christ's second advent; (c) to a man, Matt. 18:26; (d) to the Dragon, by men, Rev. 13:4; (e) to the Beast, his human instrument, Rev. 13:4, 8, 12; 14:9, 11; (f) the image of the Beast, 13:15; 14:11; 16:2; (g) to demons, Rev. 9:20; (h) to idols, Acts 7:43.

2. *sebomai* (4576), "to revere," stressing the feeling of awe or devotion, is used of "worship" (a) to God, Matt. 15:9; Mark 7:7; Acts 16:14; 18:7, 13; (b) to a goddess, Acts 19:27.

3. *sebazomai* (4573), akin to No. 2, "to honor religiously," is used in Rom. 1:25.

4. *latreuo* (3000), "to serve, to render religious service or homage," is translated "to worship" in Phil. 3:3, "(who) worship (by the Spirit of God)," RV, KJV, "(which) worship (God in the spirit)"; the RV renders it "to serve" (for KJV, "to worship") in Acts 7:42; 24:14; KJV and RV, "(the) worshipers" in Heb. 10:2, present participle, lit., "(the ones) worshiping."

5. *eusebeo* (*2151*), "to act piously towards," is translated "ye worship" in Acts 17:23.

B. Nouns.

1. *sebasma* (*4574*) denotes "an object of worship" (akin to A, No. 3); Acts 17:23; in 2 Thess. 2:4, "that is worshiped"; every object of "worship," whether the true God or pagan idols, will come under the ban of the Man of Sin.

2. *ethelothreskeia* (or *-ia*) (*1479*), "will-worship" (*ethelo*, "to will," *threskeia*, "worship"), occurs in Col. 2:23, voluntarily adopted "worship," whether unbidden or forbidden, not that which is imposed by others, but which one affects.

3. *threskeia* (*2356*), translated "worshiping" in Col. 2:18.

WORSHIPER

1. *proskunetes* (*4353*), akin to *proskuneo*, occurs in John 4:23.

2. *neokoros* (*3511*) is translated "worshiper" in Acts 19:35 KJV.

3. *theosebes* (*2318*) denotes "reverencing God" (*theos*, "God," *sebomai*, "to revere"), and is rendered "a worshiper of God" in John 9:35.

WORTHY, WORTHILY

A. Adjectives.

1. *axios* (*514*), "of weight, worth, worthy," is said of persons and their deeds: (a) in a good sense, e.g., Matt. 10:10, 11, 13 (twice), 37 (twice), 38; 22:8; Luke 7:4; 10:7; 15:19, 21; John 1:27; Acts 13:25; 1 Tim. 5:18; 6:1; Heb. 11:38; Rev. 3:4; 4:11; 5:2, 4, 9, 12; (b) in a bad sense, Luke 12:48; 23:15; Acts 23:29; 25:11, 25; 26:31; Rom. 1:32; Rev. 16:6.

2. *hikanos* (*2425*), "sufficient," is translated "worthy" in this sense in Matt. 3:11 (marg., "sufficient"); so 8:8; Mark 1:7; Luke 3:16; 7:6.

3. *enochos* (*1777*), "held in, bound by," is translated "worthy (of death)" in Matt. 26:66 and Mark 14:64, RV (marg., "liable to"; KJV, "guilty").

B. Verbs.

1. *axioo* (*515*), "to think or count worthy," is used (1) of the estimation formed by God (a) favorably, 2 Thess. 1:11, "may count (you) worthy (of your calling)," suggestive of grace (it does not say "may make you worthy"); Heb. 3:3, "of more glory," of Christ in comparison with Moses; (b) unfavorably, 10:29, "of how much sorer punishment"; (2) by a centurion (negatively) concerning himself, Luke 7:7; (3) by a church, regarding its elders, 1 Tim. 5:17, where "honor" stands probably for "honorarium," i.e., "material support."

2. *kataxioo* (*2661*), a strengthened form of No. 1, occurs in Luke 20:35; 21:36, in some texts; Acts 5:41; 2 Thess. 1:5.

C. Adverb.

axios (516), "worthily," so translated in the RV [with one exception, see (c)], for KJV, "worthy" and other renderings, (a) "worthily of God," 1 Thess. 2:12, of the Christian walk as it should be; 3 John 6, RV, of assisting servants of God in a way which reflects God's character and thoughts; (b) "worthily of the Lord," Col. 1:10; of the calling of believers, Eph. 4:1, in regard to their "walk" or manner of life; (c) "worthy of the gospel of Christ," Phil. 1:27, of a manner of life in accordance with what the gospel declares; (d) "worthily of the saints," RV, of receiving a fellow believer, Rom. 16:2, in such a manner as befits those who bear the name of "saints."

WOT

1. *oida*, "to know," in Acts 3:17; 7:40; Rom. 11:2.
2. *gnorizo*, "to come to know," in Phil. 1:22.

WOUND (Noun and Verb)

A. Noun.

trauma (5134), "a wound," occurs in Luke 10:34.

B. Verb.

traumaizo (5135), "to wound" (from A), occurs in Luke 20:12 and Acts 19:16.

WRANGLINGS

diaparatribe (3859v), found in 1 Tim. 6:5, denotes "constant strife," "obstinate contests" (Ellicott), "mutual irritations" (Field), KJV, "perverse disputings" (marg., "gallings one of another"), RV "wranglings." Some texts have *paradiatribe*. The preposition *dia-* is used intensively, indicating thoroughness, completeness. The simple word *paratribe* (not found in the NT), denotes "hostility, enmity."

WRATH

Old Testament

A. Noun.

chemah (2534), "wrath; heat; rage; anger." The word indicates a state of anger. Most of the usage involves God's "anger." His "wrath" is expressed against Israel's sin in the wilderness, Deut. 9:19. The psalmist prayed for God's mercy in the hour of God's "anger," Ps. 6:1.

chemah also denotes man's reaction to everyday circumstances. Man's "rage" is a dangerous expression of his emotional state, as it inflames everybody who comes close to the person in rage. "Wrath" may arise for many reasons. Proverbs speaks strongly against *chemah*, as jealousy, 6:34; cf. "Wrath is cruel, and anger is outrageous; but who is able to stand before envy?" Prov. 27:4; cf. Ezek. 16:38. The man in rage may be culpable of crime and be condemned, Job 19:29. The wise response to "rage" is a soft answer, Prov. 15:1.

chemah is associated with *qin'ah*, "jealousy," and also with *naqam*, "vengeance," as the angered person intends to save his name or avenge himself on the person who provoked him. In God's dealing with Israel He was jealous of His Holy name, for which reason He had to deal justly with idolatrous Israel by avenging Himself, Ezek. 24:8; but He also avenges His people against their enemies, Nah. 1:2.

There are two special meanings of *chemah*. One is "heat," Ezek. 3:14; the other is "poison," or "venom," Deut. 32:33.

B. Verb.

yacham (3179), "to be fiery, be hot." This verb, which occurs only 10 times in biblical Hebrew, is the root of the noun *chemah*.

In Deut. 19:6 *yacham* means "to be hot": "Lest the avenger of the blood pursue the slayer, while his heart is hot, and overtake him...."

New Testament

1. *thumos* (2372), "hot anger, passion," translated "wrath" in Luke 4:28; Acts 19:28; Rom. 2:8, RV; Gal. 5:20; Eph. 4:31; Col. 3:8; Heb. 11:27; Rev. 12:12; 14:8, 10, 19; 15:1, 7; 16:1; 18:3; "wraths" in 2 Cor. 12:20; "fierceness" in Rev. 16:19; 19:15 (followed by No. 1).

2. *parorgismos* (3950) occurs in Eph. 4:26.

WRESTLE, WRESTLING

pale (3823), "a wrestling" (akin to *pallo*, "to sway, vibrate"), is used figuratively in Eph. 6:12, of the spiritual conflict engaged in by believers, RV, "(our) wrestling," KJV, "(we) wrestle."

WRETCHED

talaiporos (5005), "distressed, miserable, wretched," is used in Rom. 7:24 and Rev. 3:17.

WRITE, WROTE, WRITTEN

Old Testament

A. Verb.

katab (3789), "to write, inscribe, describe, take dictation, engrave." Basically, this verb represents writing down a message. The judgment (ban) of God against the Amalekites was to be recorded in the book, Exod. 17:14. One may "write" upon a stone or "write" a message upon it, Deut. 27:2-3. This use of the word implies something more than keeping a record of something so that it will be remembered. This is obvious in the first passage because the memory of Amalek is "to be recorded" and also blotted out. In such passages "to be recorded," therefore, refers to the un-changeableness and binding nature of the Word of God. God has said it, it is fixed, and it will occur. An extended implication in the case of divine commands is that man must obey what God "has recorded," Deut. 27:2-3.

Sometimes *katab* appears to mean "to inscribe" and "to cover with inscription," Exod. 31:18. The verb means not only to write in a book but "to write a book," not just to record something in a few lines on a scroll but to complete the writing, Exod. 32:32. Here "book" probably refers to a scroll rather than a codex-book in the present-day sense.

Among the special uses of *katab* is the meaning "to record a survey," Josh. 18:4. A second extended nuance of *katab* is "to re-ceive dictation," Jer. 36:4. The word can also be used of signing one's signature, Neh. 9:38.

B. Nouns.

ketab (3791), "something written; register; scripture." In 1 Chron. 28:19 *ketab* is used to mean "something written," such as an "edict." The word also refers to a "register," Ezra 2:62, and to "scripture," Dan. 10:21.

Two other related nouns are *ketobet* and *miktab*. *ketobet* oc-curs once to mean something inscribed, specifically a "tatooing" (Lev. 19:28). *miktab* appears about 9 times and means "something written, a writing" (Exod. 32:16; Isa. 38:9).

New Testament

A. Verbs.

1. *grapho* (1125) is used (a) of "forming letters" on a surface or writing material, John 8:6; Gal. 6:11, where the apostle speaks of his having "written" with large letters in his own hand, which not improbably means that at this point he took the pen from his amanuensis and finished the epistle himself; this is not negatived by the fact that the verb is in the aorist or past definite tense, lit., "I wrote," for in Greek idiom the writer of a letter put himself be-side the reader and spoke of it as having been "written" in the past; in Eng. we should say "I am writing," taking our point of view from the time at which we are doing it; cf. Philem. 19 (this Ep. is undoubtedly a holograph), where again the equivalent English translation is in the present tense (see also Acts 15:23; Rom. 15:15); possibly the apostle, in Galatians, was referring to his having "written" the body of the epistle but the former alternative seems the more likely; in 2 Thess. 3:17 he says that the closing salutation is written by his own hand and speaks of it as "the token in every

epistle" which some understand as a purpose for the future rather than a custom; see, however, 1 Cor. 16:21 and Col. 4:18. The absence of the token from the other epistles of Paul can be explained differently, their authenticity not being dependent upon this; (b) "to commit to writing, to record," e.g., Luke 1:63; John 19:21, 22; it is used of Scripture as a standing authority, "it is written," e.g., Mark 1:2; Rom. 1:17 (cf. 2 Cor. 4:13); (c) of "writing directions or giving information," e.g., Rom. 10:5, "(Moses) writeth," RV (KJV, "describeth"); 15:15; 2 Cor. 7:12; (d) of "that which contained a record or message," e.g., Mark 10:4, 5; John 19:19; 21:25; Acts 23:25.

2. *epistello* (1989) denotes "to send a message by letter, to write word" (*stello*, "to send"; Eng., "epistle"), Acts 15:20; 21:25 (some mss. have *apostello*, "to send"); Heb. 13:22.

3. *prographo* (4270) denotes "to write before," Rom. 15:4 (in the best texts; some have *grapho*), Eph. 3:3.

4. *engrapho* (1449) denotes "to write in," Luke 10:20; 2 Cor. 3:2, 3.

5. *epigrapho* (1924) is rendered "to write over or upon" (*epi*) in Mark 15:26; figuratively, on the heart, Heb. 8:10; 10:16; on the gates of the heavenly Jerusalem, Rev. 21:12.

B. Adjective.

graptos (1123), from A, No. 1, "written," occurs in Rom. 2:15.

WRONG (Noun and Verb), WRONGDOER, WRONGDOING

A. Nouns.

1. *adikia* (93), *a*, negative, *dike*, "right," is translated "wrong" in 2 Pet. 2:13 (2nd part), 15, RV, "wrongdoing" (KJV, unrighteousness); in 2 Cor. 12:13, it is used ironically.

2. *adikema* (92) denotes "a misdeed, injury," in the concrete sense (in contrast to No. 1), Acts 18:14, "a matter of wrong"; 24:20, RV, "wrongdoing" (KJV, "evil doing").

B. Verb.

adikeo (91), "to do wrong," is used (a) intransitively, to act unrighteously, Acts 25:11, RV, "I am a wrongdoer" (KJV, "...an offender"); 1 Cor. 6:8; 2 Cor. 7:12 (1st part); Col. 3:25 (1st part); cf. Rev. 22:11; (b) transitively, "to wrong," Matt. 20:13; Acts 7:24 (passive voice), 26, 27; 25:10; 2 Cor. 7:2, v. 12 (2nd part; passive voice); Gal. 4:12, "ye did (me no) wrong," anticipating a possible suggestion that his vigorous language was due to some personal grievance; the occasion referred to was that of his first visit; Col. 3:25 (2nd part), lit., "what he did wrong," which brings consequences both in this life and at the judgment seat of Christ; Philem. 18; 2 Pet. 2:13 (1st part); in the middle or passive voice, "to take or suffer wrong, to suffer (oneself) to be wronged," 1 Cor. 6:7.

WRONGFULLY

adikos (95), akin to the above, occurs in 1 Pet. 2:19.

WROTH (be)

W

Old Testament

A. Verb.

qatsap (7107), "to be wroth, angry." The general meaning of *qatsap* is a strong emotional outburst of anger, especially when man is the subject of the reaction, Gen. 40:2-3; cf. 41:10; Exod. 16:20. In these examples an exalted person demonstrated his anger in radical measures against his people, Esth. 2:21.

The noun derived from *qatsap* particularly refers to God's anger. The object of the anger is often indicated by the preposition *'al* ("against"), Deut. 9:19. The Lord's anger expresses itself against disobedience, Lev. 10:6, and sin, Eccl. 5:5ff. However, people themselves can be the cause for God's anger, Ps. 106:32.

B. Noun.

qetsep (7110), "wrath." One occurrence of God's "wrath" is in 2 Chron. 29:8; man's wrath, Esth. 1:18.

New Testament

1. *orgizo* (3710), always in the middle or passive voice in the NT, is rendered "was (were) wroth" in Matt. 18:34; 22:7; Rev. 11:18, RV, (KJV, were angry); 12:17, RV, "waxed wroth."

2. *thumoo* (2373) signifies "to be very angry" (from *thumos*, "wrath, hot anger"), "to be stirred into passion," Matt. 2:16, of Herod (passive voice).

3. *cholao* (5520), primarily, "to be melancholy" (*chole*, "gall"), signifies "to be angry," John 7:23, RV, "are ye wroth" (KJV, "...angry").

YEAR

Old Testament

shanah (8141), "year." There are several ways of determining what a "year" is. First, the "year" may be based on the relationship between the seasons and the sun, the solar year or agricultural year. Second, it can be based on a correlation of the seasons and the moon (lunar year). Third, the "year" may be decided on the basis of the correlation between the movement of the earth and the stars (stellar year). At many points the people of the Old Testament period set the seasons according to climatic or agricultural events, such as harvest, Exod. 23:16.

The Gezer calendar shows that by the time it was written (about the tenth century B.C.) some in Palestine were using the lunar calendar, since it exhibits an attempt to correlate the agricultural and lunar systems. The lunar calendar began in the spring (the month Nisan, March-April) and had twelve lunations, or periods between new moons. It was necessary periodically to add a thirteenth month in order to synchronize the lunar calendar and the number of days in a solar year. The lunar calendar also seems to have underlain Israel's religious system with a special rite to celebrate the first day of each lunar month, Num. 28:11-15. The major feasts, however, seem to be based on the agricultural cycle, and the date on which they were celebrated varied from year to year according to work in the fields, e.g., Deut. 16:9-12. This solar-agricultural year beginning in the spring is similar to (if not derived from) the Babylonian calendar.

New Testament

A. Nouns.

1. *etos* (2094) is used (a) to mark a point of time at or from which events take place, e.g., Luke 3:1 (dates were frequently reckoned from the time when a monarch began to reign); in Gal. 3:17 the time of the giving of the Law is stated as 430 "years" after the covenant of promise given to Abraham; there is no real discrepancy between this and Ex. 12:40; the apostle is not concerned with the exact duration of the interval, it certainly was not less than 430 "years"; the point of the argument is that the period was very considerable; Gal. 1:18 and 2:1 mark events in Paul's life; as to the for-

mer the point is that three "years" elapsed before he saw any of the apostles; in 2:1 the 14 "years" may date either from his conversion or from his visit to Peter mentioned in 1:18; the latter seems the more natural. (b) to mark a space of time, e.g., Matt. 9:20; Luke 12:19; 13:11; John 2:20; Acts 7:6, where the 400 "years" mark not merely the time that Israel was in bondage in Egypt, but the time that they sojourned or were strangers there, Heb. 3:17; Rev. 20:2-7; (c) to date an event from one's birth, e.g., Mark 5:42; Luke 2:42; 3:23; John 8:57; Acts 4:22; 1 Tim. 5:9; (d) to mark recurring events, Luke 2:41 (with *kata*, used distributively); 13:7; (e) of an unlimited number, Heb. 1:12.

2. *eniautos* (1763), originally "a cycle of time," is used (a) of a particular time marked by an event, e.g., Luke 4:19; John 11:49, 51; 18:13; Gal. 4:10; Rev. 9:15; (b) to mark a space of time, Acts 11:26; 18:11; Jas. 4:13; 5:17; (c) of that which takes place every year, Heb. 9:7.

3. *dietia* (1333) denotes "a space of two years" (*dis*, "twice," and No. 1), Acts 24:27; 25:30.

4. *trietia* (5148) denotes "a space of three years" (*treis*, "three," and No. 1) Acts 20:31.

B. Adjectives.

1. *dietes* (1332), akin to A, No. 3, denotes "lasting two years, two years old," Matt. 2:16.

2. *hekatontaetes* (1541) denotes "a hundred years old," Rom. 4:19.

C. Adverb.

perusi (4070), "last year, a year ago" (from *pera*, "beyond"), is used with *apo*, "from" 2 Cor. 8:10; 9:2.

YOKE, YOKED

A. Nouns.

1. *zugos* (2218), "a yoke," serving to couple two things together, is used (1) metaphorically, (a) of submission to authority, Matt. 11:29, 30, of Christ's "yoke," not simply imparted by Him but shared with Him; (b) of bondage, Acts 15:10 and Gal. 5:1, of bondage to the Law as a supposed means of salvation; (c) of bond service to masters, 1 Tim. 6:1; (2) to denote "a balance," Rev. 6:5.

2. *zeugos* (2201), "a pair of animals," Luke 14:19.

B. Verb.

heterozugeo (2086), "to be unequally yoked," is used metaphorically in 2 Cor. 6:14.

YOKEFELLOW

sunzugos or **suzugos** (*4805*), Phil. 4:3, "a yokefellow, fellow laborer"; probably here it is a proper name, "Synzygus."

YOUNG, YOUNG (children, daughter, man, men, woman, women)

1. **neoteros** (*3501*), the comparative degree of **neos**, "new, youthful," is translated "young" in John 21:18; in the plural, Acts 5:6, "young men" (marg., "younger"); Titus 2:6, KJV, RV, "younger men."

2. **neos** (*3501*), in the feminine plural, denotes "young women," Titus 2:4.

3. **neanias** (*3494*), "a young man," occurs in Acts 7:58; 20:9; 23:17, 18 (in some texts).

4. **neaniskos** (*3495*), a diminutive of No. 3, "a youth, a young man," occurs in Matt. 19:20, 22; Mark 14:51 (1st part; RV omits in 2nd part); 16:5; Luke 7:14; Acts 2:17; 5:10 (i.e., attendants); 23:18 (in the best texts), 22; 1 John 2:13, 14, of the second branch of the spiritual family.

5. **nossos** or **neossos** (*3502*), "a young bird" (akin to No. 2), is translated "young" in Luke 2:24; cf. also 13:34, and Matt. 23:37.

YOUNGER

1. **neoteros** (*3501*), occurs in Luke 15:12, 13; 22:26; 1 Tim. 5:1 ("younger men"); 5:2, feminine; v. 11, "younger (widows)"; v. 14, "younger (widows), 1 Pet. 5:5.

2. **elasson** (*1640*) is rendered "younger" in Rom. 9:12.

YOUTH

Old Testament

na'ar (*5288*), "youth; lad; young man." The basic meaning of **na'ar** is "youth," over against an older man. At times it may signify a very young child, Isa. 7:16. Generally **na'ar** denotes a "young man" who is of marriageable age but is still a bachelor. We must keep in mind the opposition of youth and old age, so that we can better understand that Jeremiah, while claiming to be only a "youth," was not necessarily a youngster, Jer. 1:6; cf. also Absalom, 2 Sam. 18:5.

Another meaning of **na'ar** is "servant," usually with a focus on the servant as a youth, 1 Sam. 14:1. The **na'ar** ("servant") addressed his employer as "master," Judg. 19:11. Kings and officials had "attendants" who were referred to by the title **na'ar**, Esth. 2:2. When a **na'ar** is commissioned to carry messages, he is a "messenger." Thus, we see that the meaning of the word **na'ar** as "servant" does not denote a "slave" or a performer of low duties. He carried important documents, was trained in the art of warfare, and even gave counsel to the king.

New Testament

neotes (*3503*), from *neos*, "new," occurs in Mark 10:20; Luke 18:21; Acts 26:4; 1 Tim. 4:12.

Y

YOUTHFUL

neoterikos (*3512*), from *neoteros*, "new," is used especially of qualities, of lusts, 2 Tim. 2:22.

Z

ZEAL

zelos (2205) denotes "zeal" in the following passages: John 2:17, with objective genitive, i.e., "zeal for Thine house"; so in Rom. 10:2, "a zeal for God"; in 2 Cor. 7:7, RV, "(your) zeal (for me)," KJV, "(your) fervent mind (toward me)"; used absolutely in 7:11; 9:2; Phil. 3:6 (in Col. 4:13 in some texts; the best have **ponos**, labor, RV).

ZEALOUS

A. Noun.

zelotes (2207) is used adjectivally, of "being zealous" (a) "of the Law," Acts 21:20; (b) "toward God," lit., "of God," 22:3, RV, "for God"; (c) "of spiritual gifts," 1 Cor. 14:12, i.e., for exercise of spiritual gifts (lit., "of spirits," but not to be interpreted literally); (d) "for (KJV, 'of') the traditions of my fathers," Gal. 1:14, of Paul's loyalty to Judaism before his conversion; (e) "of good works," Titus 2:14.

The word is, lit., "a zealot," i.e., "an uncompromising partisan." The "Zealots" was a name applied to an extreme section of the Pharisees, bitterly antagonistic to the Romans. Josephus (*Antiq.* xviii. 1. 1, 6; *B.J.* ii. 8. 1) refers to them as the "fourth sect of Jewish philosophy" (i.e., in addition to the Pharisees, Sadducees, and Essenes), founded by Judas of Galilee (cf. Acts 5:37). After his rebellion in A.D. 6, the Zealots nursed the fires of revolt, which, bursting out afresh in A.D. 66, led to the destruction of Jerusalem in 70. To this sect Simon, one of the apostles, had belonged, Luke 6:15; Acts 1:13. The equivalent Hebrew and Aramaic term was "Cananaean" (Matt. 10:4); this is not connected with Canaan, as the KJV "Canaanite" would suggest, but is derived from Heb. **qanna**, "jealous."

B. Verbs.

1. *zeloo* (2206), "to be jealous," also signifies "to seek or desire eagerly"; in Gal. 4:17, RV, "they zealously seek (you)," in the sense of taking a very warm interest in, so in v. 18, passive voice, "to be zealously sought" (KJV, "to be zealously affected"), i.e., to be the object of warm interest on the part of others; some texts have this verb in Rev. 3:19 (see No. 2).

2. *zeleuo*, a late and rare form of No. 1, is found in the best texts in Rev. 3:19, "be zealous."

ADDITIONAL NOTES

ON THE PARTICLE *KAI* (2532)

(a) The particle *kai*, "and," chiefly used for connecting words, clauses and sentences (the copulative or connective use), not infrequently signifies "also." This is the *adjunctive*, or *amplificatory*, use, and it is to be distinguished from the purely copulative significance "and." A good illustration is provided in Matt. 8:9, in the words of the centurion, "I also am a man under authority." Other instances are Matt. 5:39, 40; 8:9; 10:18; 18:33; 20:4; Luke 11:49; 12:41, 54, 57; 20:3; John 5:26, "the Son also," RV; 7:3; 12:10; 14:1, 3, 7, 19; 15:9, 27; 17:24; Acts 11:17; Rom. 1:13; 6:11; 1 Cor. 7:3; 11:25; 15:30; Gal. 6:1; Phil. 4:12, "I know also," RV, 1 Thess. 3:12. In 1 Cor. 2:13 the *kai* phrase signifies "which are the very things we speak, with the like power of the Holy Spirit."

This use includes the meanings "so," or "just so," by way of comparison, as in Matt. 6:10, and "so also," e.g., John 13:33; cf. Rom. 11:16. In Heb. 7:26 the most authentic mss. have *kai* in the first sentence, which may be rendered "for such a High Priest also became us." Here it virtually has the meaning "precisely."

(b) Occasionally *kai* tends towards an *adversative* meaning, expressing a contrast, "yet," almost the equivalent of *alla*, "but"; see, e.g., Mark 12:12, "yet they feared"; Luke 20:19; John 18:28, "yet they themselves entered not." Some take it in this sense in Rom. 1:13, where, however, it may be simply parenthetic. Sometimes in the English versions the "yet" has been added in italics, as in 2 Cor. 6:8, 9, 10.

(c) In some passages *kai* has the meaning "and yet," e.g., Matt. 3:14, "and yet comest Thou to me?"; 6:26, "and yet (RV 'and,' KJV, 'yet') your Heavenly Father feedeth them"; Luke 18:7, "and yet He is longsuffering"; John 3:19, "and yet men loved the darkness"; 4:20, "and yet we say"; 6:49, "and yet they died"; 1 Cor. 5:2, "and yet ye are puffed up"; 1 John 2:9, "and yet hateth his brother."

(d) In some passages it has a *temporal* significance, "then." In Luke 7:12 the *kai*, which is untranslated in the English versions, provides the meaning "then, behold, there was carried out"; so Acts 1:10, "then, behold, two men stood."

(e) There is also the *inferential* use before a question, e.g., Mark 10:26, "then who can be saved?" RV. This is commonly expressed by the English "and," as in Luke 10:29; John 9:36.

(f) Occasionally it has almost the sense of *hoti*, "that," e.g., Matt. 26:15 (first part); Mark 14:40 (last part); Luke 5:12, 17, where, if the *kai* had been translated, the clause might be rendered "that, behold, a man...," lit., " and behold..."; so v. 17; see also 9:51, where *kai*, "that," comes before "He steadfastly set"; in 12:15, "take heed that ye keep."

(g) Sometimes it has the consecutive meaning of "and so": e.g., Matt. 5:15, "and so it shineth"; Phil. 4:7, "and so the peace..."; Heb. 3:19, "and so we see."

(h) The *epexegetic* or *explanatory* use. This may be represented by the expressions "namely," "again," "and indeed," "that is to say"; it is usually translated by "and." In such cases not merely an addition is in view. In Matt. 21:5, "and upon a colt" means "that is to say, upon a colt." In John 1:16 the clause "and grace for grace" is explanatory of the "fullness." In John 12:48, "and receiveth not My sayings," is not simply an addition to "that rejecteth Me," it explains what the rejection involves, as the preceding verse shows. In Mark 14:1, "and the unleavened bread" is perhaps an instance, since the Passover feast is so defined in Luke 22:1. In Acts 23:6 the meaning is "the hope, namely, the resurrection of the dead." In Rom. 1:5 "grace and apostleship" may signify "grace expressed in apostleship." In Eph. 1:1 "and the faithful" does not mark a distinct class of believers, it defines "the saints"; but in this case it goes a little further than what is merely epexegetical, it adds a more distinctive epithet than the preceding and may be taken as meaning "yes indeed."

In regard to Titus 3:5, "the renewing of the Holy Ghost" is coordinate with "the washing of regeneration," and some would regard it as precisely explanatory of that phrase, taking the *kai* as signifying "namely." Certainly the "renewing" is not an additional and separate impartation of the Holy Spirit; but the scope of the renewal is surely not limited to regeneration; the second clause goes further than what is merely epexegetic of the first. Just so in Rom. 12:2, "the renewing of your mind" is not a single act, accomplished once and for all, as in regeneration. The Holy Ghost, as having been "shed on us," continues to act in renewing us, in order to maintain by His power the enjoyment of the relationship into which He has brought us.

(i) The *ascensive* use. This is somewhat similar to the epexegetic significance. It represents, however, an advance in thought upon what precedes and has the meaning "even." The context alone can determine the occurrences of this use. The following are some instances. In Matt. 5:46, 47, the phrases "even the publicans" and "even the Gentiles" represent an extension of thought in regard to the manner of reciprocity exhibited by those referred to, in comparison with those who, like the Pharisees, were considered superior to them. In Mark 1:27, "even the unclean spirits" represents an advance in the minds of the people concerning Christ's miraculous power, in comparison with the authority exercised by the Lord in less remarkable ways. So in Luke 10:17. In Acts 10:45, the *kai*, rendered "also," in the phrase "on the Gentiles also," seems necessary to be regarded in the same way, in view of the amazement manifested by those of the circumcision, and thus the rendering will be "even on the Gentiles was poured out the gift"; cf. 11:1.

In Rom. 13:5, the clause "but also for conscience sake" should probably be taken in this sense. In Gal. 2:13, the phrase "even Barnabas" represents an advance of thought in comparison with the waywardness of others; as much as to say, "the Apostle's closest associate, from whom something different might be expected, was surprisingly carried away." In Phil. 4:16 there are three occurrences of *kai*, the first ascensive, "even"; the second (untranslated) meaning "both," before the word "once"; the third meaning "and." In 1 Thess. 1:5, in the clause "and in the Holy Ghost," the *kai* rendered "and," is ascensive, conveying an extension of thought beyond "power"; that is to say, "power indeed, but the power of the Holy Spirit." In 1 Pet. 4:14 "the Spirit of God" is "the Spirit of glory." Here there is an advance in idea from the abstract to the personal.

ON THE PARTICLE *DE* (1161)

The particle *de* has two chief uses, (a) *continuative* or *copulative*, signifying "and," or "in the next place," (b) *adversative*, signifying "but," or "on the other hand." The first of these, (a), is well illustrated in the genealogy in Matt. 1:2-16, the line being simply reckoned from Abraham to Christ. So in 2 Cor. 6:15, 16, where the *de* anticipates a negative more precisely than would be the case if *kai* had been used. In 1 Cor. 15:35; Heb. 12:6, e.g., the *de* "and (scourgeth)" is purely copulative.

(b) The adversative use distinguishes a word or clause from that which precedes. This is exemplified, for instance, in Matt. 5:22, 28, 32, 34, 39, 44, in each of which the *ego*, "I," stands out with pronounced stress by way of contrast. This use is very common. In Matt. 23:4 the first *de* is copulative, "Yea, they bind heavy burdens" (RV), the second is adversative, "but they themselves will not..."

In Rom. 3:22, in the clause "even the righteousness," the *de* serves to annex not only an explanation, defining "a righteousness of God" (v. 21, RV), but an extension of the thought; so in 9:30, "even the righteousness which is of faith."

In 1 Cor. 2:6, in the clause "yet a wisdom," an exception (not an addition) is made to what precedes; some would regard this as belonging to (a) it seems, however, clearly adversative. In 4:7 the first *de* is copulative, "and what hast thou...?"; the second is adversative, "but if thou didst receive..."

In 1 Thess. 5:21 "many ancient authorities insert 'but'" (see RV marg.), so translating *de*, between the two injunctions "despise not prophesyings" and "prove all things," and this is almost certainly the correct reading. In any case the injunctions are probably thus contrastingly to be connected.

In 2 Pet. 1:5-7, after the first *de*, which has the meaning "yea," the six which follow, in the phrases giving virtues to be supplied, suggest the thought "but there is something further to be done." These are not merely connective, as expressed by the English "and," but adversative, as indicating a contrast to the possible idea that to add virtue to our faith is sufficient for the moral purpose in view.

ON THE PREPOSITIONS *ANTI* (473) AND *HUPER* (5228)

The basic idea of *anti* is "facing." This may be a matter of opposition, unfriendliness or antagonism, or of agreement. These meanings are exemplified in compounds of the preposition with verbs, and in nouns. The following are instances: *antiparerchomai* in Luke 10:31, 32, where the verb is rendered "passed by on the other side," i.e., of the road, but facing the wounded man; *antiballo* in Luke 24:17, where the *anti* suggests that the two disciples, in exchanging words (see RV marg.), turned to face one another, indicating the earnest nature of their conversation. The idea of antagonism is seen in *antidikos*, "an adversary," Matt. 5:25, *antichristos*, "antichrist," 1 John 4:3, etc.

There is no instance of the uncompounded preposition signifying "against." Arising from the basic significance, however, there are several other meanings attaching to the separate use of the preposition. In the majority of the occurrences in the NT, the idea is that of "in the place of," "instead of," or of exchange; e.g., Matt. 5:38, "an eye for (*anti*) an eye"; Rom. 12:17, "evil for evil"; so 1 Thess. 5:15; 1 Pet. 3:9, and, in the same verse, "reviling for reviling." The ideas of substitution and exchange are combined, e.g., in Luke 11:11, "for a fish...a serpent"; Heb. 12:16, "for one mess of meat.. his own birthright." So in Matt. 17:27, "a shekel (*stater*)...for thee and Me," where the phrase is condensed; that is to say, the exchange is that of the coin for the tax demanded from Christ and Peter, rather than for the persons themselves. So in 1 Cor. 11:15, where the hair is a substitute for the covering.

Of special doctrinal importance are Matt. 20:28; Mark 10:45, "to give His life a ransom (*lutron*) for (*anti*) many." Here the substitutionary significance, "instead of," is clear, as also with the compound *antilutron* in 1 Tim. 2:6, "who gave Himself a ransom (*antitutron*) for (*huper*) all"; here the use of *huper*, "on behalf of," is noticeable. Christ gave Himself as a ransom (of a substitutionary character), not instead of all men, but on behalf of *all*. The actual substitution, as in the passages in Matthew and Mark, is expressed by the *anti*, instead of, "*many.*" The unrepentant man should not be told that Christ was his substitute, for in that case the exchange would hold good for him and though unregenerate he would not be in the place of death, a condition in which, however, he exists while unconverted. Accordingly the "many" are those who, through faith, are delivered from that condition. The substitutionary meaning is exemplified in Jas. 4:15, where the KJV and RV render the *anti* "for that" (RV, marg., "instead of").

In Heb. 12:2, "for (*anti*) the joy that was set before Him endured the cross," neither the thought of exchange nor that of substitution is conveyed; here the basic idea of facing is present. The cross and the joy faced each other in the mind of Christ and He chose the one with the other in view.

In John 1:16 the phrase "grace for grace" is used. The idea of "following upon" has been suggested, as wave follows wave. Is not the meaning that the grace we receive corresponds to the grace inherent in Christ, out of whose fullness we receive it?

The primary meaning of *huper* is "over," "above." Hence, metaphorically, with the accusative case, it is used of superiority, e.g., Matt. 10:24, "above his master" (or teacher); or of measure in excess, in the sense of beyond, e.g., 1 Cor. 4:6, "beyond the things that are written"; or "than," after a comparative, e.g., Luke 16:8; Heb. 4:12; or "more than," after a verb, e.g., Matt. 10:37. With the genitive it means "on behalf of, in the interests of," e.g., of prayer, Matt. 5:44; of giving up one's life, and especially of Christ's so doing for man's redemption, e.g. John 10:15; 1 Tim. 2:6, "on behalf of all" (see under *anti*); 2 Thess. 2:1, "in the interest of (i.e., 'with a view to correcting your thoughts about') the Coming."

In some passages *huper* may be used in the substitutionary sense, e.g., John 10:11, 15; Rom. 8:32.

ON THE PREPOSITIONS *APO* (575) AND *EK* (1537).

The primary meaning of *apo* is "off"; this is illustrated in such compounds as *apokalupto*, "to take the veil off, to reveal"; *apokopto*, "to cut off"; hence there are different shades of meaning, the chief of which is "from" or "away from," e.g., Matt. 5:29, 30; 9:22; Luke 24:31, lit., "He became invisible from them"; Rom. 9:3.

The primary meaning of *ek* is "out of," e.g., Matt. 3:17, "a voice out of the heavens" (RV); 2 Cor. 9:7, lit., "out of necessity." Omitting such significances of *ek* as "origin, source, cause, occasion," etc., our consideration will here be confined to a certain similarity between *apo* and *ek*. Since *apo* and *ek* are both frequently to be translated by "from" they often approximate closely in meaning. The distinction is largely seen in this, that *apo* suggests a starting point from without, *ek* from within; this meaning is often involved in *apo*, but *apo* does not give prominence to the "within-ness," as *ek* usually does. For instance, *apo* is used in Matt. 3:16, where the RV rightly reads "Jesus...went up straightway from the water"; in Mark 1:10 *ek* is used, "coming up out of the water"; *ek* (which stands in contrast to *eis* in v. 9) stresses more emphatically than *apo* the fact of His having been baptized in the water.

The literal meaning "out of" cannot be attached to *ek* in a considerable number of passages. In several instances *ek* obviously has the significance of "away from"; and where either meaning seems possible, the context, or some other passage, affords guidance. The following are examples in which *ek* does not mean "out of the midst of" or "out from within," but has much the same significance as *apo*: John 17:15, "that Thou shouldest keep them from the evil one"; 1 Cor. 9:19, "though I was free from all men"; 2 Cor. 1:10, "who delivered us from so great a death" (KJV); 2 Pet. 2:21, "to turn back from the holy commandment"; Rev. 15:2, "them that had come victorious from the beast, and from his image, and from the number of his name" (*ek* in each case).

Concerning the use of *ek*, in 1 Thess. 1:10, "Jesus, which delivereth (the present tense, as in the RV, is important) us from the wrath to come" [or, more closely to the original, "our Deliverer (cf. the same phrase in Rom. 11:26) from the coming wrath"], the passage makes clear that the wrath signifies the calamities to be visited by God upon men when the present period of grace is closed.

ON THE PREPOSITION *EN* (1772)

en, "in," is the most common preposition. It has several meanings, e.g., "of place" (e.g., Heb. 1:3, lit., "on the right hand," i.e., in that position), and time, e.g., in 1 Thess. 2:19; 3:13; 1 John 2:28, in each of which the phrase "at His coming" (inadequately so rendered, and lit., "in His Parousia") combines place and time; the noun, while denoting a period, also signifies a presence involving accompanying circumstances, e.g., 1 Thess. 4:15.

Further consideration must here be confined to the instrumental use, often rendered "with" (though *en* in itself does not mean "with"), e.g., Matt. 5:13, "wherewith" (lit., 'in what,' i.e., by what means) shall it be salted"; 7:2, "with what measure ye mete." Sometimes the instrumental is associated with the locative significance (which indeed attaches to most of its uses), e.g., Luke 22:49, "shall we smite with the sword?" the smiting being viewed as located in the sword; so in Matt. 26:52, "shall perish with the sword"; cf. Rev. 2:16; 6:8; 13:10. In Matt. 12:24, "by (marg., 'in') Beelzebub," indicates that the casting out is located in Beelzebub. Cf. Luke 1:51, "with His arm." In Heb. 11:37, the statement "they were slain with the sword" is lit., "they died by (*en*) slaughter of the sword." There is a noticeable change in Rom. 12:21, from *hupo*, "by," to *en*, "with," in this instrumental and locative sense; the lit. rendering is "be not overcome by (*hupo*) evil, but overcome evil with (*en*) good," *en* expressing both means and circumstances. A very important instance of the instrumental *en* is in Rom. 3:25, where the RV, "faith, by His blood," corrects the KJV, "faith in His blood," and the commas which the RV inserts are necessary. Thus the statement reads "whom God set forth to be a propitiation, through faith, by His blood."